Le Corbusier
Le Grand

This book is dedicated to the memory of Jean-Louis Cohen
Conceived and edited by Phaidon editors
with an introduction by Jean-Louis Cohen
and chapter introductions by Tim Benton

LE CORBUSIER LE GRAND

Φ

The Man with a Hundred Faces
by Jean-Louis Cohen
.6

Childhood and Early Travels (1887–1917)
.18

Becoming Le Corbusier (1917–1926)
.84

Urban Visions and Purist Villas (1922–1935)
.120

In Search of the Big Commission (1926–1942)
.222

Paris, Vichy, and the War (1937–1943)
.308

Grand Projects on a Human Scale (1942–1952)
.362

Passage to India (1950–1962)
.436

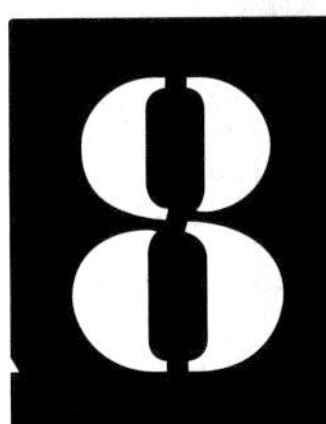
The Sacred and the Sublime (1950–1959)
.554

Mediterranean Days (1950–1959)
.642

10
Retrospection (1954–1965)
.684

Documents
Notes
Chronology
Selected Bibliography
Index
.756

The Man with a Hundred Faces
by Jean-Louis Cohen

By the 1930s, the physical image of Le Corbusier had become so identified with that of the modern architect that advertisements intended to appeal to members of the profession would show architects wearing circular, black-rimmed glasses and a bow tie, in imitation of the original. By this time Le Corbusier was a real media star: for almost six decades he never stopped mobilizing the press, radio, and film in support of his ideas and schemes. At first under his original identity—the name he was given at birth, Charles-Edouard Jeanneret—and then, from 1920, using his assumed name of Le Corbusier, he wrote thirty-four books containing some seven thousand pages of text, plus hundreds of articles and lectures that he presented in every continent except Australia. His dominant presence in the public sphere, combined with his fascination for technology and its objects, made him into a sort of total architect, deeply committed to the process of modernization. The contrivance of a striking physical and sartorial image was clearly part of his effort to seize public attention, as is suggested by Fernand Léger's recollection of his first meeting with him. The artist speaks of having seen him approach "bolt upright, an extraordinary mobile object in a bowler hat, with glasses and a black overcoat. The object was riding a bicycle, scrupulously obeying the laws of perspective."[1]

The nearly geometric rigidity of this figure in his corporeal and sartorial frame was evidently an artificial construct, a deliberately prepared camouflage. His private correspondence, together with the innumerable professional communications issued in the course of his architect's life, reveals the intensity of his personal relationships with his mentors, associates, and friends. These intimate messages constitute the inseparable flip side of the speeches flung in the face of the public. They also tell us a great deal about his personality, which was at the very least double, as he could hardly have stated more clearly in a letter of 1926 to Josef Červ: "Le Corbusier is a pseudonym. Le Corbusier practices architecture, exclusively. He pursues unbiased ideas. He has no right to entangle himself in betrayals, in compromises. He is an entity freed from the weight of the flesh. . . . Ch. Edouard Jeanneret is the man of flesh and blood, who has had all the radiant or heartbreaking adventures of a pretty eventful life. Jeanneret Ch. E. paints; for, not being a painter, he has retained his enthusiasm for painting and he has always painted—as a Sunday painter."[2]

Le Corbusier's productivity was impressive. Between the Villa Fallet, built in the architect's Swiss hometown of La Chaux-de-Fonds in 1907, and the numerous commissions still being considered at the time of his death in 1965, he was responsible for the creation of seventy-eight buildings in twelve countries, though this was a fraction of the roughly three hundred five projects that he had designed, sometimes in great detail. His professional activity was truly protean, and the range of disciplines that he practiced with varying degrees of satisfaction remains bewildering, and in fact unique among his contemporaries. The number of buildings planned and completed by Frank Lloyd Wright is certainly much larger, and the extent of his production as a writer is almost comparable, but the American left barely any works of plastic art. The architecture of Mies van der Rohe, like that of Le Corbusier, succeeded in establishing new spatial principles, but the literary output of the German is almost negligible. The variety and scope of disciplines practiced by Le Corbusier is therefore unique in his generation. Intrigued by the prospect of becoming an architect, he became one fully once he abandoned the idea of being an engraver of watchcases, the path his father intended he should follow (such was the dominance of clock- and watchmaking in his hometown). It was as an architect that he approached the most characteristic projects of his long professional life, as an architect that he applied himself to observing the world.

The Visionary

By 1911, when Jeanneret set up his modest office as a "consulting architect for all questions of decoration,"[3] having returned to his hometown after four years of itinerant training, he had already committed to his notebooks thousands of observations drawn and written during his travels across Europe, while also photo-

Opposite. Le Corbusier in his rue Nungesser-et-Coli apartment, late 1940s

graphing and sketching numerous sites and monuments. He always retained this practice of visual notation, and the little sketchbooks tucked into his pockets would accompany him on his wanderings, becoming the principal support for his memory. Together with press clippings, photographs collected here or there, postcards, and the books in his library, they laid the foundations for a body of documentation that Le Corbusier would never cease to consult and that would help him, whatever the circumstances, to elicit his memories.

By looking at the world, Le Corbusier expanded his horizons, with his focus pivoting to encompass a larger world: his attentive observation of the buildings of Florence continued in Germany and Central Europe, with further revelations in Istanbul and Athens. His interest in the metropolis, which he developed a taste for during the years before World War I, when he lived in Berlin and then in Paris for several months, broadened to include the rugged landscapes that he saw during his travels in Europe, an appreciation that was reinforced when he visited South America in 1929. But he continually changed his way of looking at urban scenes. His initial observations, made at ground level and written in letters and sketchbooks, were attuned to the picturesque: he sought out unusual shapes, contrasts, dissonances. When he started traveling by automobile, by boat, or by aircraft, the scale of his observations grew larger and, like so many others of his generation, he discovered the great urban patterns, the huge expanses of land, and the vast oceans, responding now to the sublime, as defined by Edmund Burke in the eighteenth century. His admiration for objects that embodied the achievements of modern technology, such as dams, canal locks, and skyscrapers, is another aspect of this.

Posing as a clairvoyant, Le Corbusier also became, on occasion, a voyeur, having begun to haunt Montmartre and Montparnasse by night. During his first years in Paris he succumbed to the lure of the cabaret and sometimes to that of more secret forms of entertainment, including the erotic play among women in brothels, which he sketched in his notebooks. His drawings might be categorized using the Hollywood studios' codes: category A, the first-rank projects, which Le Corbusier included (with varying degrees of emphasis) in his own publications; category B, considered less significant or forming part of a series; and finally, category X, these drawings of women, in pairs or alone, intended for Le Corbusier's own pleasure or that of his closest friends.

The Builder

Having been shaped in no small part by the industrial environment of La Chaux-de-Fonds, Le Corbusier was driven to transform the physical world. His observations and notes are not those of an aesthete seeking knowledge or visual pleasure, but those of someone interested in construction. From his immersion in the world of clock- and watchmaking to his work in concrete with the engineer Max Du Bois, by way of experience gained with the Perret brothers in Paris and his research into German industrial art, Jeanneret came to know modern production methods. This in turn alerted him to the advent of Taylorism, the most radical reconfiguration of labor processes since the Industrial Revolution, based on principles shaped by American engineer Frederick W. Taylor.

Adherence to modern technologies was not, in this case, abstract. It led Le Corbusier to open the "eyes that do not see"[4] of his contemporaries to the new technological objects—ocean liners, airplanes, automobiles—but, above all, to draw their attention to the *retardataire* character of contemporary building sites. Jeanneret set himself the challenge of reforming how buildings were constructed, devising the "Domino" principle, the name of which—derived from the first syllables of the Latin word *domus* (house) and the French word *innovation*—itself suggested a program. Between this first exploration of using concrete for orthogonal grid structures and subsequent research on slender shells in the same material (the Monol houses), on steel structures (the Clarté apartment block), and then, after 1945, on structures using cables (the Philips Pavilion and the cultural center in Firminy-Vert), the thread of innovation would remain unbroken.

Nonetheless, it would be wrong to see Le Corbusier as no more than an apologist for technological invention and a fetishist of novelty. Vernacular building styles fascinated him as much as the experiments of the engineers. A long series of projects using brick, rubble stones, or wood developed in parallel with his other work, revealing another facet of Le Corbusier as an architect: one committed to an economy of means. Conceived during the German Occupation of France, the Constructions Murondins—another neologism, combining the French words *murs* (walls) and *rondins* (logs)[5]—cannot be disassociated from the war-related scarcity of building materials. But the Catalan vaults of the Maisons Jaoul's brick-ceilinged interiors are one of Le Corbusier's most conscious allusions to Mediterranean building traditions; his own *cabanon* (shack) in Roquebrune-

Cap-Martin on France's Riviera provides an even more populist interpretation, alluding as it does to the rickety shanties on the outskirts of Marseille.

Le Corbusier did, from time to time, delegate certain technical tasks to colleagues, such as his cousin Pierre Jeanneret, who between 1922 and 1940 was the heart and soul of the architectural studio, and after 1945, to Vladimir Bodiansky's Atelier des Bâtisseurs, a multidisciplinary organization of architects, engineers, and technicians, known by its abbreviation ATBAT. Nonetheless, Le Corbusier possessed a keen sense of the practice of building. He liked to be photographed surrounded by wooden scaffolding and metal armatures, but his presence in the mud and apparent disorder of a building site was not just for show. Many of the architectonic solutions he came up with emerged not from a preliminary drawing but from his response to problems of execution or from his consideration of mistakes that occurred during construction. This reactivity and this capitalizing on chance opportunities are lacking in the projects completed after Le Corbusier's death, which are often too polished and appear as if frozen in scrupulous respect for the original drawing.

A Man of Geometry

The matrix through which Le Corbusier's observation of the world led to its transformation, and in which the work of the painter or sculptor was made to resonate with the work of the architect, was geometry. It was an element of the very identity of the young Charles-Edouard: when he attended a Montessori kindergarten, he was taught using the methods of the German pedagogue Friedrich Wilhelm Froebel, based on the well-known building blocks and other materials—the same method by which Paul Klee, Piet Mondrian, and Georges Braque were taught. The young Frank Lloyd Wright also discovered it, thanks to his mother, who gave him a set of Froebel's wooden blocks. In his kindergarten classes at La Chaux-de-Fonds, Jeanneret employed the graphic component of the system, which consisted of drawing vegetal or animal shapes using little squares. The idea that every shape, organic or mechanical, can ultimately be simplified into a geometric structure would remain fundamental for him throughout his life.

Aware of the importance of geometry from that point on, Jeanneret endeavored, during the travels of his youth, to measure the dimensions of buildings as well as of urban compositions, and he discovered the writings of German historians and architects on harmonic proportion. His enthusiasm for these was such that he incorporated this research into his book *Vers une architecture* (*Toward an Architecture*), in which he presented his theories on "regulating lines."[6] He demonstrated the presence of these proportional grids in historical buildings such as the cathedral of Notre-Dame in Paris or the Petit Trianon in Versailles, and he used them in his own work as an architect—above all, in drafting the facades of the Atelier Ozenfant, of the Villa La Roche–Jeanneret, and of all the Parisian villas that followed.

Though harshly criticized in 1928 by the Russian architect El Lissitzky, and then by the Czech critic Karel Teige, because of his perceived fetish for the golden section and the harmonic proportions employed in his Mundanéum project, Le Corbusier was not to be deterred. He pursued these ideas in collaboration with artists and mathematicians and, in 1945, succeeded in devising a complete system of proportions linking the principle of modularity and the golden section. Devising yet another linguistic invention, he gave the name Modulor to this system, which was based on the statistical height of the average man: 1.75 meters (5 feet 9 inches). From that point on, the measuring scale of the Modulor enabled Le Corbusier to establish the dimensions of all the elements in any one of his buildings, which would thus be considered automatically adjusted to "the measure of man"—and thus harmoniously coordinated with one another.[7]

The City Planner

Le Corbusier was born in a town with a regularized street grid: La Chaux-de-Fonds had been rebuilt, after destruction by fire in 1794, to the strictly modular and orthogonal plan of Charles-Henri Junod. Le Corbusier harbored a desire to reform the structure of large cities. Beyond his recommendation that the traditional scales based on the pedestrian and the horse be replaced by a larger scale set by the automobile, he was also interested in the radical restructuring of the metropolis according to new criteria. Echoing the propositions of the Frenchman Eugène Hénard and of the American Harvey Wiley Corbett, Le Corbusier imagined an elevated "city on *pilotis*" (stilts), allowing for the radical separation of vehicles from pedestrians.

In this, as in so many other areas, Le Corbusier appropriated numerous propositions formulated by his contemporaries or simply condensed ideas that were in the air at the time. So it was with the principle of zoning by function, which he took as the starting point for his ideas on urban planning. For example, he supplied his own, somewhat extremist, version of the conclusion of the Congrès Internationaux d'Architecture Moderne (CIAM), held in Greece in 1933, and published in 1943 as *La charte d'Athènes* (The Athens Charter). The text proposed establishing a new catechism, that the city should be rethought around the four functions of dwelling, working, recreation, and circulation. This issue was not new, for since the nineteenth century German city planners had been dividing the city into zones differentiated by the regulations applied to each. In Le Corbusier's account, however, this issue assumes a new magnitude and a new architectural language: no more blocks (even open ones), no more streets (even wide ones), but an urban landscape composed of large traffic arteries and isolated buildings.

Though reverberating through his published writings, from *Urbanisme* (*The City of Tomorrow*) to *Trois établissements humains* (*The Three Human Establishments*), by way of *La ville radieuse* (*The Radiant City*), Le Corbusier's views on city planning had almost no built applications in his own work. He realized only a tiny fraction of the forty or so important city planning projects for which he made extensive drawings and plans, projects that ranged from the development of a small railroad station plaza at La Chaux-de-Fonds to the plan for a residential and cultural complex in the French town of Firminy-Vert. The only city that he succeeded in conceiving in its totality was Chandigarh, India, the new capital of the Punjab, for which Jawaharlal Nehru gave him the commission in 1950; and even there Le Corbusier's plan was based in part on an earlier project proposed by American architect Albert Mayer.

It is easy to understand Le Corbusier's bitterness, as he grew old, at those colleagues who sometimes plagiarized his work. The most noteworthy of his projects, such as his Plan Voisin for Paris, the Obus project for Algiers, and the plan for the reconstruction of Saint-Dié, France, remained on paper, even though he endeavored to reduce them to fragments that were buildable. They nonetheless generated countless derivations that have generally proved to be more faithful to the letter than to the spirit and that have tended to discredit their origins through the poverty of their execution. Le Corbusier quickly became a scapegoat for those keen to denounce the urban ventures accompanying the modernization of the world after 1945, but his rare realized projects possess a distinct sense of space and an inimitable poetic quality.

The Writer

Among Le Corbusier's daily occupations, writing was unquestionably just as important to him as drawing. As a writer, he worked in a variety of registers, including private notes for his own use, articles for publications and texts for lectures, and books articulating his ideas, as well as an extensive correspondence. And the literary forms of this intense written output were no less diverse. More than any other architect of the twentieth century—with the exception of Frank Lloyd Wright—Le Corbusier was able to assemble, sometimes within one and the same text, erudite allusion, autobiographical reminiscence, a public harangue, and a critique of his contemporaries. Playing masterfully with the French language, he combined several kinds of linguistic discourse with a sure sense of parody, moving from a scholarly vocabulary to the most common slang, using technological terminology as readily as he evoked the classics of Western culture.

His voluminous published output addressed to the public comprises dozens of articles (often gathered into books); many pieces conceived and written at a single sitting; and the often revised versions of hundreds of lectures. The books that Le Corbusier published during his lifetime belong to several categories, demonstrating the breadth of his interests. He succeeded in publishing, in 1912, his *Etude sur le mouvement d'art décoratif en Allemagne* (Study of the Decorative Art Movement in Germany), but two ambitious projects of his youth remained unpublished: "La construction des villes" (The Construction of Cities), devoted to the question of plotting urban outlines and applying his ideas to La Chaux-de-Fonds, and "France ou Allemagne?" (France or Germany?), a Perret-inspired reaction to the "anti-Boche" propaganda of World War I. The articles written during his long tour of the Balkans in 1911 were not published in book form until 1966, when *Le voyage d'Orient* (*Journey to the East*) appeared posthumously.

The manifestos published by Le Corbusier in the early 1920s were perhaps more effective in asserting his stature within the European architectural scene than were his first executed architectural projects for Paris. With *Vers une architecture*, *Urbanisme*, and *L'art décoratif d'aujourd'hui* (*The Decorative Art of Today*) in the "L'Esprit Nouveau" collection, he established the pillars of his theoretical discourse and put forward his interpretation of the modern world. Then, in 1930, with the first volume of his *Oeuvre complète* (Complete Works), he inaugurated a series of books devoted to his work as an architect, not editing these himself but nonetheless becoming very closely involved in their production. Under his own imprint he collected, in *La ville radieuse*, the articles that he had published in the journal *Plans* together with his city planning schemes, and twenty years later he provided a chronicle of his views in *Plans de Paris* (Plans of Paris), while sporadically publishing works addressing issues of current concern such as *Des canons, des munitions? Merci! Des logis . . . S.V.P.* (Guns, Ammunition? Thanks! Housing . . . Please)—or devoted to a particular project.

The small manuals entitled *Les trois établissements humains* and *Le Modulor* belong to a different category, prescribing a method of regional planning and one of design, respectively, but they, too, are rarely lacking in personal reminiscence. In fact, Le Corbusier often wrote in the first person, notably in a striking series of books recording professional setbacks and sometimes serving as a way to take revenge for those defeats and disappointments. With *Une maison, un palais* (A House, a Palace), he tries to convince the public of the injustice of his having lost the competition to design the League of Nations headquarters. Then, in *Quand les cathédrales étaient blanches* (*When the Cathedrals Were White*), he voices bittersweet reflections on an America that denied him the honor of architectural commissions. In *Poésie sur Alger* (Poetry on Algiers), he recalled his twelve years of fruitless efforts to build in North Africa. Some books that he intended for revenge did not get beyond a first draft. This was the case with "Réponse à Moscou" (Response to Moscow), in which he intended to give an account of his experiences in the USSR, and with a book on the United Nations, in his own words "an unlooked for sequel" to *Une maison, un palais*, conceived in 1947 to express his bitterness at having been marginalized in the design process for the UN building in New York.[8]

Le Corbusier always concerned himself with the material form of his books. He focused methodically on improving their typography, and he mastered every aspect of what Gérard Genette has defined as the "paratext," playfully combining titles, epigraphs, notes, captions, sidebars, and quotations. On their pages he exploited all the resources of iconography, assembling photographs, geometrical drawings, diagrams, sketches, and press clippings to serve his argument. Every book has its own script, unfolding in a dramatic narrative punctuated by new turns and marked by thought-provoking visual oppositions on facing pages—and intentionally evoking the frame-to-frame progression of a film. When necessary, he knew how to bend to the demands of literary publishers, such as Plon or Gallimard. But in the 1950s he commissioned Jean Petit to make a series of books under the imprint Forces Vives, some of them almost pure works of art, such as the *Poème électronique* (Electronic Poem)—a transcription of the text set to music by Edgard Varèse for performance in the Philips Pavilion at the 1958 world's fair in Brussels.

The Painter and Sculptor

From the first exhibition of his paintings at the Galerie Thomas in Paris, in 1918, Le Corbusier never ceased throughout his life to insist on being recognized as an artist. He declared that painting, which he did every morning, was the "secret laboratory" in which he worked out many of the forms for his architectural projects, but he endeavored to make it an autonomous activity, and until 1930 he even signed his canvases with his original name rather than his assumed one. In purely quantitative terms, his output as an artist was substantial. He made more than four hundred paintings, eight thousand drawings, twenty-seven cartoons for tapestries, and forty-four sculptures. He also created engraved compositions on various materials and worked in enamel.

Le Corbusier's works explored several distinct realms, all suggesting poetic interpretations. In his Purist still lifes, which he painted in tandem with those by his friend Amédée Ozenfant, depicting groups of *objets-types*—carafes, bistro glasses, guitars, soda siphons—he restored a visual order that Cubism had overturned. Then, in the late 1920s, he combined human figures with plant forms, rocks, and shells in an almost Surrealist vein. These unexpected encounters between "objects of poetic reaction" had an impact on his work as an architect, just as the accumulation of vertical shapes in the Purist pictures found an echo in the assembly of dividing walls and staircases of his Parisian villas. Soon after settling permanently in Paris, Le Corbusier became friends with the naive painter André Bauchant as well as with Cubist painter Fernand Léger, and he was well aware of every contemporary current in painting. Alert to the advances made by Léger and by Pablo Picasso, he painted female bodies during the 1930s before throwing himself, during the 1950s, into creating a bestiary dominated by the figure of the bull. To the director of the Solomon R. Guggenheim Museum in New York, James Sweeney, who had missed his exhibition at the Pierre Matisse Gallery in 1957 and who appeared reluctant to include any of his works in the museum's collection, Le Corbusier insisted: "I am a painter, in all seriousness."[9]

Le Corbusier was rather less directly engaged in sculpture. He built a sculpture studio for Jacques Lipchitz in Boulogne-sur-Seine and installed one of his own sculptural works in the garden of the Villa de Mandrot in Le Pradet, on the French Riviera, although he failed to get one included next to the Centrosoyuz building in Moscow. Two decades later, he embarked on his work as a sculptor by drawing sketches that the Breton cabinetmaker Joseph Savina would then execute in wood, with Le Corbusier subsequently resolving the texture and coloring of the surfaces through instructions relayed either from a distance or on the spot. After 1945 he turned to the theme of the "synthesis of the arts," a slogan to be understood in various ways. On the one hand, painters, sculptors, tapestry makers, and other artists were invited to cooperate with architects, on the condition that they remain quietly in their place. On the other, and with regard to his own work, Le Corbusier emphasized the "unicity" of the sculptural approach, a term he used from the time of his writings in the 1920s to convey the sculptural effects of architecture. In one of his most frequently repeated declarations, he insisted: "There are no sculptors only, painters only, architects only. The sculptural idea is in One Form—in the service of poetry."[10] Only a few of his works fully measured up to this ambition: the Philips Pavilion, in which the music of Edgard Varèse and the images chosen by Le Corbusier to be projected on its walls occupied a surprising new type of container, and perhaps the lithographic plates of *Le poème de l'angle droit* (Poem of the Right Angle), in which literary myths, drawings of city planning schemes, architectural forms, and pictorial figures each find their place.

The Historian

In 1907 Le Corbusier read Friedrich Nietzsche's *Thus Spake Zarathustra* (given to him by his art-school teacher, Charles L'Eplattenier). Then only nineteen, he saw himself as one who might stand up to the conservatives and be someone who "breaks their tablets of values, the breaker, the law-breaker," that is to say, "the creator."[11] He would also read Nietzsche's *The Gay Science* and would later repeatedly "pilfer" (to use his own term) such reading matter from his youth. However, even though he never ceased to oppose the "crows of the academy," whom he met at the Ecole des Beaux-Arts in Paris, in Stalin's Russia, and in right-thinking America, Le Corbusier was by no means an absolute iconoclast. Very much to the contrary: he knew at every juncture in his work how to mobilize an awareness of history. His unfinished manuscript "France ou Allemagne?" (France or Germany?) is nothing less than a detailed historical investigation into the parallel development of architecture and the decorative arts in those two countries. Le Corbusier thus explored the events that he would still have in mind when he was designing the Museum of Western Art in Tokyo and envisioned (though in vain) a "room of the nineteenth century,"[12] which would have charted and elucidated the transformations brought about by the Industrial Revolution.

During the 1920s, history was a constant presence both in Le Corbusier's writings—for example, the "lesson of Rome,"[13] in *Vers une architecture,* was for him that of the great works of antiquity and of Michelangelo, rather than that of the Baroque—and in his own architectural projects. His inclusion of en suite rooms in his Parisian villas derived from a knowledge of the *hôtels particuliers* (aristocratic mansions) of eighteenth-century Paris, and his composition for the Mundanéum echoes that of Babylonian complexes published in art history textbooks.

Ideas that Le Corbusier arrived at during the last two decades of his life often led him to break with his older work—as at the chapel at Ronchamp, which surprised all his followers by its sculptural form and curvilinear language. But he frequently maintained continuity with his earlier thinking, reviving the idea of the "free plan," which was rendered possible because the load-bearing walls were replaced by isolated posts. He also discovered other historical buildings, which he analyzed and drew, such as the Romanesque cloister of Le Thoronet, reinterpreted in his own monastery of La Tourette, and the Mogul astronomical observatories, which inspired some of the forms at Chandigarh. For his design of a hospital in Venice (a scheme that remained on paper), based on analyses made in 1935, he realized that "if one cannot copy [the] skin" of the city, "one must respect its physiology."[14]

From the Intimate to the Public

The fields in which Le Corbusier directed his emotional energy ranged from those with a very narrow focus to those encompassing a broad spectrum of ideas and applications. And no undertaking was exclusively intimate or totally public for him, but a fusion of the two: he knew how to make people close to him witnesses to the successes and the mishaps in his professional life, just as he frequently described episodes of his personal life in his public lectures and in his writings. The enormous diversity of his involvement in such a variety of fields is apparent if we read his notebooks and his diaries, in which one can perceive the intensity of a daily routine made up of multiple concerns.

In the topography of Le Corbusier, one might say that his architectural projects occupied two different networks. In the first were places of retreat, sometimes hermitages, such as the houses he designed for his parents, his *cabanon* at Roquebrune-Cap-Martin, and some of the houses he created for friends. In the second were projects in which Le Corbusier was to some extent playing a more public role in the company of industrialists, men of politics, and the artists who were indispensable to his professional activities. But his energy flowed constantly between the two networks, as is clear in the six thousand letters written to his closest friends, relatives, and colleagues, in which one can read, both directly and between the lines, about the trials and tribulations of the public figure.

His Mother's Son

Between setting off for his first journey to Tuscany, in 1907, and the death of his mother, Marie-Charlotte-Amélie Jeanneret, in 1960, in her one-hundredth year, Le Corbusier wrote to her at least once a week, telling her in detail of his meetings and his projects and his current undertakings and making no mystery of all his investigations. These touching messages, often written in the third person and signed "your Edouard," suggest that the Jeannerets' younger son still felt the need to claim his place in the family. In this small circle, much taken with music but scarcely at all by the visual arts, the hopes of success rested on the elder son, Albert, a composer. The architect, on the other hand, was regarded as a failure in the making. Having internalized this secondary status, Le Corbusier constantly exaggerated what he had achieved, perhaps so that his mother would finally love him as much as he wanted.

Le Corbusier's professional misfortunes proved costly to those close to him. The financial burden of what was known as the Maison Blanche, which he built for his parents in 1912 at La Chaux-de-Fonds and which resonated with architectural memories of his travels in Italy and Turkey, became overwhelming, and they had to sell it. The failure of the building-materials business established by Jeanneret during World War I must also have been a drain on the resources of his father (an enameler of watch faces by trade), and his parents withdrew to the Petite Maison, which their son built for them at Corseaux, on the shores of Lake Geneva. This descent from the "high country" of the Jura to the lakeshore gave Le Corbusier the opportunity to create a remarkable house for them, capturing in its long horizontal window the reflections of the lake's surface and the surrounding mountains.

More than simply justifying himself to his mother, Le Corbusier also confided in her. It was to Marie-Charlotte-Amélie that he described the triumph of the opening of the housing development of Pessac in 1926, describing a film in which her "great, awkward boy of an architect [was] portrayed in all his aspects."[15] It was also to her, two years later, that he confessed his anxieties at the time of his first journey to Moscow, when he fought to obtain the commission for the Centrosoyuz building. During the 1950s his meetings with the Catholics of Ronchamp and of La Tourette revived, in this Protestant, the dread of the power of Rome that he constantly shared with his mother.

Two Couples

Le Corbusier seems to have first come to fully appreciate the intimacy between himself and his mother when, in 1922, he met Yvonne Gallis, whom he married in 1930. He congratulated himself, in his letters to his mother, on his relationship with this "honest girl,"[16] as he called her, who "is taking on the generous task of being the companion of a man who has fads." With Yvonne, Le Corbusier's life changed. The fast-living bachelor finally settled down. In 1934 the couple moved into the top-floor apartment of a building designed and constructed by Le Corbusier on rue Nungesser-et-Coli on the western edge of Paris, where they would receive friends and visitors from afar.

However, Le Corbusier's monogamy had its limits. There is no proof that he had an affair with the singer and dancer Josephine Baker, whom he drew in the nude on a voyage across the South Atlantic on board the ship *Lutétia* in 1929; but his long 1935 stay in the United States was due in great part to his liaison with Marguerite Tjader Harris. After the trials of World War II united Charles-Edouard and Yvonne, they rediscovered their old intimacy every summer at Roquebrune-Cap-Martin, sharing the simple joys of life in the open air. The touching little wooden *cabanon* built there by Le Corbusier evoked the barrel of Diogenes, whose asceticism the architect had praised in *L'art décoratif d'aujourd'hui*.

In 1922 Le Corbusier joined forces with his cousin, Pierre Jeanneret, also an architect, thus forming another couple, a professional one. Using stationery with a unique letterhead that gave no first names—Le Corbusier being forbidden at that point to run a company after the failure of his building-materials business—they would remain partners until 1940. Pierre, in this role, was absolutely essential to his cousin's professional development, as is made clear in the titles of the three volumes of the *Oeuvre complète de Le Corbusier et Pierre Jeanneret*, published between 1930 and 1938.

It was Pierre who organized the day-to-day work of the studio, recruited draftsmen, and kept the accounts; but it was also he who urged Le Corbusier to take on certain projects and calmed impatient clients when, following the example of Charles de Beistegui, they protested vehemently while Le Corbusier was traveling. Along with the young designer Charlotte Perriand, Pierre was also deeply involved in conceiving the remarkable ensemble of modern furniture presented at the Salon d'Automne of 1929. An openly leftist activist, he also exerted a big influence on the studio's young draftsmen at the time of the Popular Front (1936); during the war, he took active part in the French Resistance against the Nazis and temporarily broke with Le Corbusier over political differences. The relationship between the cousins was revived during the 1950s, when Pierre settled in India to become the site manager for Chandigarh, the new capital city of Punjab, designing most of the residential buildings in accordance with Le Corbusier's overall scheme.

The Friends

Each significant episode in Le Corbusier's life coincided with an intense phase in his friendships. In his youth, with his friends Léon Perrin and August Klipstein, he discovered the landscapes of Europe, also getting to know the Swiss writer William Ritter, with whom he would correspond for decades. The benevolent tutelage of Auguste Perret—who taught him to ride a bicycle—and the epistolary dialogue with him shaped Jeanneret's vision of the world until 1918. It was then supplanted by his friendship with Amédée Ozenfant, who led Le Corbusier to their joint formulation of Purism, to the creation of the journal *L'Esprit Nouveau*, and to the construction of one of Le Corbusier's first buildings in Paris. His quarrel with Perret in 1922 and that with Ozenfant in 1925 were all the more irreparable because his friendship with each of them had been so deep and fundamental.

Le Corbusier maintained links with Swiss friends living in Paris, among them the publisher Daniel Niestlé. He socialized with Fernand Léger, whose American contacts he used when he sold the Palace of Soviets model to the Museum of Modern Art in the late 1930s. He struck up a friendship with the publisher Christian Zervos and his wife, Yvonne, with whom Le Corbusier spent some of the Occupation, until alienating them with his imprudent comments on their activities in the Resistance. At Vézelay, France, there was Jean Badovici, whose journal *L'Architecture Vivante* had published between 1927 and 1936 the first systematic presentation of Le Corbusier's work. In the house that Eileen Gray had built for Badovici at Roquebrune-Cap-Martin, Le Corbusier made a present to his friend of mural paintings in 1938–39, but their bold patterns disturbed the elegant serenity of the seaside setting. Le Corbusier's friends also included the factory worker turned writer Hyacinthe Dubreuil, an observer of American and European Fordism, and the industrialist André Jaoul, whom he had met during an ocean crossing and for whom he would build two houses in Neuilly-sur-Seine, near Paris, in 1955.

In New York after World War II, Le Corbusier came to know the Italian sculptor Costantino Nivola, whom he visited often in New York. Among his clients, he became close to Eugène Claudius-Petit, a parliamentary deputy whose role as minister for reconstruction was to prove decisive in allowing Le Corbusier to design and build the Marseille Unité d'Habitation—which would involve the largest construction site for any of Le Corbusier's buildings to date in France. To those of his correspondents who were deeply involved in CIAM, such as Sigfried Giedion and Walter Gropius, Le Corbusier wrote bluntly about the ingratitude of the young. With age, the casual relationships of his earlier years became more formal and established, at precisely the moment when Le Corbusier's fame at last gave him access to those with a real voice in world affairs.

The Globe-trotting Expert

Like British city planner Raymond Unwin, American architect Daniel H. Burnham, and Parisian landscape designer Jean Claude Nicolas Forestier, Le Corbusier gained recognition as an expert on the modernization of large cities, thanks to the publication of his books and to some of his more widely known completed architectural projects. Invited to lecture, he would rapidly deliver an uncompromising diagnosis of the problems of the city then welcoming him, which would result in his devising a plan for radically transforming it. This pattern recurred throughout his travels during the years between the two world wars. He drew up his plan for Moscow two years after his trip there in 1928, and it became the basis of his Ville Radieuse. During his trip to South America in 1929, he made sketches for his urban plans for Buenos Aires and for Rio de Janeiro on the spot and then immediately presented them to the audiences attending his lectures.

In collaboration with the organizations or authorities that acted as forces of change in each of these cities—whether private individuals, associations, or public bodies—he would thoroughly assimilate what each city asked for and become its spokesman. Invited by the Friends of Algiers to draw up a plan for that city, he devised one that would act like a projectile into the future and sent it to Mayor Charles Brunel with the name Plan Obus. His plans for the development of the industrial valleys of Zlín, Czechoslovakia, and Hellocourt, France, barely relate to his commissions from the shoe manufacturer Bat'a, for whom they were intended; instead, they are unprompted initiatives that Le Corbusier came up with to seduce the directors of this Czech multinational company. His schematic plan for Addis Ababa, the capital of Ethiopia, worked out in indirect collaboration with Giuseppe Bottai, leader of the modernizing wing of the Italian Fascist Party, belongs to the same category.

After 1945 Le Corbusier became more cautious about the commissions he accepted. After his experience at Chandigarh, for example, he refused to take on the plan for the reconstruction of Agadir, on the Moroccan coast, which had been destroyed by an earthquake in 1960. Nonetheless, from time to time he continued to go one better than his clients. Not content, for example, to devise a simple Museum of Western Art, as requested by the Japanese in 1954, he instead argued for the construction of a "modern cultural center" in Tokyo.[17] During this phase of his life, his urban projects became increasingly complex and above all more collaborative, as with the plan for the redevelopment of Bogotá, designed between 1949 and 1951, which he produced with Germán Samper, Rogelio Salmona, and Reinaldo Valencia, in consultation with José Luis Sert and Paul Lester Wiener. But his illusions about his prospects for obtaining big commissions on his own did not altogether vanish, as evident in his efforts to win the urban planning competition held by the West German and West Berlin governments in 1958 for restructuring Berlin's entire city center. Le Corbusier brought pressure to bear on Gropius, who was to participate in the jury's discussion, and tried to circumvent the requirement that all the entrants remain anonymous, so convinced was he that his plan would be the irresistible choice if his identity as its creator were known.

The Public Figure

A man of the century that was transformed by the diffusion of the automobile and the conquest of the air, among other technological advances, Le Corbusier was especially quick to seize on the potential of the media: photography, the illustrated press, radio, and film. He initiated some of his projects less with the goal of building them or seeing his ideas materialize than of having an impact on public opinion: by creating a sensation, he knew that in due course he would be able to obtain commissions for more realistic projects. His Plan Voisin for Paris, for example, which was first publicly presented at the *Exposition internationale des arts décoratifs et industriels modernes* of 1925 and was widely reported and discussed in the French press, ultimately had the effect of making Le Corbusier known to potential Parisian clients, just as the publication of his book *Vers une architecture* had prompted Henri Frugès to give him his first commissions for workers' housing. He tried to achieve something of the same effect when he made his long anticipated trip to New York in 1935. Annoyed at not having been greeted by photographers when he disembarked, he made some startling pronouncements, which were reported in the *New York Herald Tribune* under the headline "Skyscrapers Not Big Enough, Says LeCorbusier at First Sight,"[18] before he presented his project for a "cellular reconstruction" of the city.

When Le Corbusier gave lectures, he turned them into veritable spectacles, uniting gesture, the spoken word, and the projection of drawings that he made right there in the lecture hall, giving the audience the impression that they were attending the unveiling of previously concealed truths and the birth, in quasi-real time, of new and amazing projects. He used photography as a fundamental vehicle for communicating his ideas, whether through images from the distant or recent past to suggest historical precedents (where necessary, heavily retouching commercially obtained photographs) or to present his own built works. With an acute awareness of photographers, he took control of the pictures they took of his buildings and often recropped their images for publication. Our visual awareness of Le Corbusier's work is facilitated but also governed by the close connection he maintained (from 1949 to the end of his career) with Lucien Hervé, whose high-contrast photographs have imposed an image of rugged concrete and strong oppositions between light and shade.

Le Corbusier also found a role for himself in film. In *Architectures d'aujourd'hui* (1931; Architectures of Today), Pierre Chenal filmed him in two different scenes: first, arriving proudly in his automobile, an Avions Voisins C12, in front of the Villa Stein–de Monzie; then standing in front of a model of his Plan Voisin and pointing out its main features, including a startling close-up shot of the hand of the demiurge poised above the model of the Paris of the future. When the Popular Front was in power, Jean Epstein, a former contributor to *L'Esprit Nouveau*, made Le Corbusier and Auguste Perret the heroes of his film *Les bâtisseurs* (1938; Builders), which was commissioned by CGT, the leftist trade union, to promote a modern image of the building industry. But it should also be said that the presence of Le Corbusier in the public life of postwar Europe was at its strongest when it came without any images at all. The interviews broadcast on French radio, such as those of him speaking with Robert Mallet, Georges Charensol, and Georges Charbonnier, provide the most moving documentation of his hopes and frustrations. The autobiographical insights they contain are often "embellished," but they do give a good account of how Le Corbusier wanted his experiences to be understood.

The Political Animal

It is all too easy to caricature Le Corbusier's relationship to politics and to focus only on the eighteen or so months that he spent, during the Occupation, currying favor with the Vichy regime. His political behavior was inconstant throughout his life, and in fact underwent violent swings from time to time. In a period of several months, Le Corbusier first offered his services to the Fascist government in Italy, then to the Socialist prime minister of France, Léon Blum; and in 1944, barely a few months passed between his last overtures to Vichy and the Liberation of Paris by the Allies, after which he tried to appear as if he had taken part in the Resistance. Meanwhile, in early 1944, he had inspired a biography (*Le Corbusier ou l'architecture au service de l'homme* [Le Corbusier or Architecture in the Service of Mankind]), by Maximilien Gauthier, who presented Le Corbusier as the creator "of a world seeking to be born, of a world that is going to be born"[19]—in short, as a revolutionary.

A supporter of the Union Sacrée (Sacred Union) against Germany in World War I, Le Corbusier told William Ritter at the time that he had stopped being "socio" (socialist) in order to become "national."[20] For about fifteen years after his own frustrating experiences as a small businessman, he identified with employers' circles, in particular "Redressement Français" (French Recovery), for which he published a brochure praising Taylorism. After the setback he suffered in Russia in 1932, he became reconciled with the "non-conformists," reformers of an anti-democratic tendency, with whom he published the journal *Plans*. It advocated a regionalist corporatism that would have been all the more palatable to Vichy because some of the editors of the journal had already allied themselves with the regime. Under pressure from his entourage—Pierre Jeanneret, Charlotte Perriand, and the young people at the studio—Le Corbusier made a sharp swing to the left in the mid-1930s and upheld the cause of Republican Spain, as revealed in his painting *The Fall of Barcelona* (1939).

In his old age, Le Corbusier kept a certain distance from political confrontation. This reserve was the result of an unshakeable lassitude during that period, but his fame was such that he still had access to political and business leaders off-camera and without the intermediary of political networks or pressure groups such as CIAM. After his painful experience with the United Nations in 1947, he became definitively anti-American. In the game of French politics, it was a period of recuperation and realignment, and the political parties couldn't resist trying to benefit from his aura. The Communists, who offered him no help in realizing his reconstruction project for Saint-Dié in 1945, celebrated him just three years later as "the man who wants to build radiant cities."[21] Under the Fifth Republic, General de Gaulle's Minister of Culture, André Malraux, whom Le Corbusier had known in the 1930s at the Maison de la Culture, was an attentive intermediary; but the only official commission he received for a large public building in Paris, the Musée du XXème Siècle (Museum of the Twentieth Century), envisaged for La Défense, came too late for him to respond before his death in August 1965.

Reminiscences

During the last years of his life, Le Corbusier became more and more interested, both through his reading and through his own writing and drawing, in the symbolic and mythic dimensions of art and architecture.

He returned also to the experiences of his youth, initiating an edition of his 1911 *Voyage d'Orient* and agreeing to let his great books of the 1920s be reprinted. It is true that these reprints are very much of their moment in terms of Le Corbusier's aesthetic values. The 1958 reprint of *Vers une architecture* conforms to the original edition, but it has a new acetate jacket that features a bull, a characteristic subject in postwar painting. Elsewhere there is evidence of fundamental rethinking, as in his project, fortunately not pursued, to restore the Villa Savoye with elements of *béton brut* (rough concrete) similar to those used at La Tourette.

Well aware of his historical stature, Le Corbusier entrusted the task of organizing his archives to the editor and publisher Jean Petit, who in 1968 compiled excerpts from them into a one-volume chronological account of his life and career, *Le Corbusier lui-même* (Le Corbusier Himself). This book marked the start of a new cycle of posthumous analyses, liberated from the injunctions and myth-making of the architect and based on the historical documents conserved after his death by the Fondation Le Corbusier, which had been established according to his principles. Opening these holdings to the public has permitted the meticulous study of the architect's ideas, writings, and projects, and of the buildings themselves, spanning six decades of one of the twentieth century's most intensely creative lives. By no means has this reduced the perceived significance of Le Corbusier's work. Rather, it has contributed to a better understanding of its internal dynamics and of how it is rooted in the conflicts of the series of historical eras through which he lived. From the most naive to the most critical, this research has supported the assessment by an architect writing in the Russian press in 1928, who saw in Le Corbusier, whose glory was then still in its early stages, "the very figure of the new man."[22]

1 Childhood and Early Travels (1887–1917)

Brought up a Lutheran in La Chaux-de-Fonds, Switzerland, Charles-Edouard Jeanneret did not believe in predestination, as so many of his Calvinist compatriots did, but from a young age he did have a strong sense of personal destiny—which was not matched by his early achievements. At the local art school, Edouard (as he was called by his family and friends) came under the spell of the charismatic teacher Charles L'Eplattenier. The master's ideal, evident in Jeanneret's early work, was to create an Arts and Crafts decorative style that would reflect the character of the surrounding Jura mountain landscape. Encouraged by L'Eplattenier, in September 1907 Jeanneret began a ten-year cycle of travels across Europe and the Middle East. During these trips he veered dramatically in his interests and taste, almost always under the influence of a new friend and mentor.

Near Florence he visited the Carthusian monastery at Val d'Ema, which provided a prototype he never forgot. "I would like to live my whole life in what they call their cells. This is the solution of the archetypal single house or, better, heaven on earth." Soon afterward he was in Paris, where he began a period of hero worship of the architect Auguste Perret, working in his office from June 1908 to the end of 1909. Under his influence, Jeanneret abruptly abandoned the Arts and Crafts principles for a strict structural rationalism based on the use of reinforced concrete. He spent his afternoons in the Paris museums and the Bibliothèque Nationale, developing his art historical knowledge. He later said that the trouble with most architects was that they lacked a sense of art history and knowledge of the great rules of art.

In 1910 Jeanneret was in Germany, where he worked for Peter Behrens for seven months. From him, Jeanneret learned some of the discipline of designing in a rigorous classical style. The young man suffered from a severe lack of confidence, writing to his parents: "Each day a great chasm opens up beneath my feet. Each time I begin something where I think myself not to be an idiot, it turns out that I am one, to a revolting and unacceptably unjust degree."

Yet another strong influence on Jeanneret was the German novelist and poet William Ritter, with whom he struck up an intense friendship. Ritter ignited his interest in the exoticism of the Middle East and Balkans and also helped Jeanneret to refine his writing style. It was with all these enthusiasms competing for his attention that he set off for his great adventure, a journey of seven months hitch-hiking through the Balkans, Istanbul, Athens, and Italy. The Parthenon made a profound impact on him, and he would include his sketches of the buildings on the Acropolis in many of his later books and lectures. Returning through Italy, he spent a memorable time in Pompeii, where some of his first really analytical architectural sketches were made, and in Rome, visiting Hadrian's Villa at Tivoli and exploring the works of Michelangelo—in particular, St. Peter's.

The young Jeanneret's architectural career had already begun back home, with the help of a local builder. He designed three houses for professors at his art school in 1907 and 1908. In 1912 he designed both a house for his parents, the Maison Blanche, and the elegant Villa Favre-Jacot for an industrialist in the neighboring town of Le Locle. Three years later Jeanneret designed the Villa Schwob for one of the wealthy Jewish families for whom he had already carried out a number of interior decoration schemes. This was the only building from his years in La Chaux-de-Fonds that he was later to include among his published works.

Opposite. The young Charles-Edouard Jeanneret, Paris, 1910s

Registre des naissances A. Folio 331

N° 660
Jeanneret-Gris
Charles-Edouard

Le Six Octobre mil huit cent quatre-vingt-sept à neuf heures – minutes du soir est né à la Chaux de Fonds rue de la Serre N° 38 Jeanneret-Gris Charles-Edouard fils légitime de Jeanneret-Gris Georges Edouard Profession : Emailleur fils de Edouard & de Lise née Rauss de Locle domicilié à la Chaux de Fonds et de Marie-Charlotte Amélie née Perret fille de Frédéric Louis Marie & de Amélie née Pingeon de la Sagne.

Inscrit au présent registre le sept Octobre mil huit cent quatre-vingt-sept sur la déclaration de son père Edouard Jeanneret.

Confirmé après lecture faite :

E Jeanneret Perret

L'officier de l'état civil :

Alb. Dufemmun

Communiqué au Locle le 10 Octobre 1887

ÉGLISE RÉFORMÉE ÉVANGÉLIQUE
DU CANTON DE NEUCHATEL

CERTIFICAT DE BAPTÊME

Paroisse de La Chaux-de-Fonds

Le 17 juin 1888
a été baptisé Charles-Edouard JEANNERET-GRIS dit LE CORBUSIER
né le 6 octobre 1887
fils de Georges-Edouard JEANNERET-GRIS
de Le Locle et La Chaux-de-Fonds (Neuchâtel)
domicilié à La Chaux-de-Fonds
et de Marie-Charlotte-Amélie née Jeanneret
Parrain -----
Marraine -----

A La Chaux-de-Fonds, le 17 octobre 1957

Pour extrait conforme :
Registre de l'Eglise Evangélique indépendante

Pour *Le Pasteur de la Paroisse :*

SECRETARIAT PAROISSIAL
DE L'ÉGLISE RÉF. EV.
LA CHAUX-DE-FONDS, CURE 9
J. Grebere

Le présent certificat n'est pas un acte de l'état civil et ne peut tenir lieu d'acte de naissance.

Early years in La Chaux-de-Fonds, Switzerland

Charles-Edouard Jeanneret (1887–1965) was born in La Chaux-de-Fonds, a town in northwestern Switzerland, near the Jura mountain range, that was known as a Swiss watchmaking center. His parents—Georges-Edouard Jeanneret-Gris and Marie-Charlotte-Amélie Perret—were descendants of local craftsmen and merchants, respectively.

Destroyed by a fire in 1794, La Chaux-de-Fonds was rebuilt along a rigid grid, which gave the town a reputation for an absence of charm but may also have inspired Jeanneret's later visions of a new urban landscape.

Opposite, top. Charles-Edouard Jeanneret-Gris's Register of Birth, 6 October 1887, filed on 7 October

Opposite, bottom. Charles-Edouard's Certificate of Baptism, 17 June 1888, reissued in 1957 for his trip to Baghdad

Right. Charles-Edouard, on pedestal, with his brother, Albert, and their mother and father, Georges-Edouard and Marie-Charlotte-Amélie Jeanneret, 1889

Far right. Georges-Edouard and Marie-Charlotte-Amélie Jeanneret, 1908

Below. Charles-Edouard (second from right) and Albert (right), with two unidentified children in a studio portrait, 1890

Left. Jeanneret's birthplace and childhood home at 38 rue de la Serre, La Chaux-de-Fonds, Switzerland

Below. Postcard of La Chaux-de-Fonds and the wooded hills beyond, c. 1912

Opposite, top. Watercolor of the Jura countryside, painted by Jeanneret on 15 October 1902, when he was fifteen years old

Opposite, bottom. Postcard of a farm in the Jura mountains, c. 1912

"La Chaux-de-Fonds is a leprous blot on the landscape... but with a remarkable wind of idealism blowing through it that gives us real hope. The art tradition here ended with the old farms of the seventeenth century; but these splendid old houses are the yardstick of what we can do if we try."

—Letter to William Ritter, 6 September 1910

His education begins: Charles L'Eplattenier and the Ecole d'Art, La Chaux-de-Fonds, 1900–1906

At age thirteen Jeanneret began his studies at the local art school, which had been established to train skilled watch engravers. There he met his first mentor, Charles L'Eplattenier, an instructor who emphasized aesthetics over mechanics and encouraged an appreciation for nature as a source of creative inspiration.

"Mr. L'Eplattenier instilled in me some indefinable sense of the sacred, the great—but above all of the abstract and impalpable: a thirst for art, and a potent critical faculty I consider as healthy as a young man of my age can hope for." —Letter to his parents, 2 June 1908

Opposite, top. Charles L'Eplattenier, an instructor at the Ecole d'Art, La Chaux-de-Fonds, and Jeanneret's mentor

Opposite, bottom. Jeanneret (back row, far left) and classmates at the Ecole d'Art, c. 1903

Top. Furniture designs by Charles L'Eplattenier

Above. Watchcase designed and engraved by Jeanneret in 1906 at the Ecole d'Art

Right. Mythologie figurée de la Grèce (Illustrated Mythology of Greece), 1903, one of the books Jeanneret owned while attending art school

Left. Landscape study with pine trees, 1906

Below. Jeanneret (back row, second from right,) and classmates sketching in La Chaux-de-Fonds, c. 1906

Opposite. Watercolor study of pine trees, c. 1906.

"My master, an excellent teacher who eschewed all routine, a thoroughgoing man of the woods, made us men of the woods… My master had said, 'The only inspiration is nature: she alone is true and can underpin human striving. But do not work at nature as the landscapers do, under a single aspect: inquire into its underlying cause, its form, its vital development and, by introducing ornamentation, achieve the all-embracing picture.'"

—"La famille," Le Corbusier lui-même

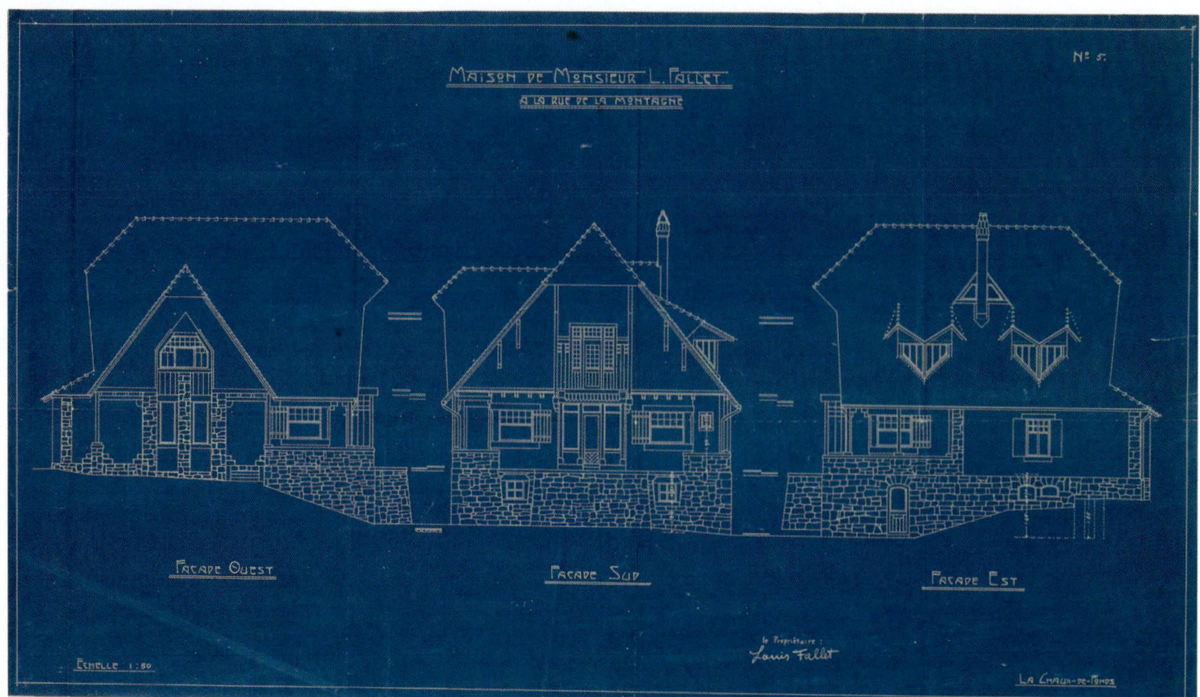

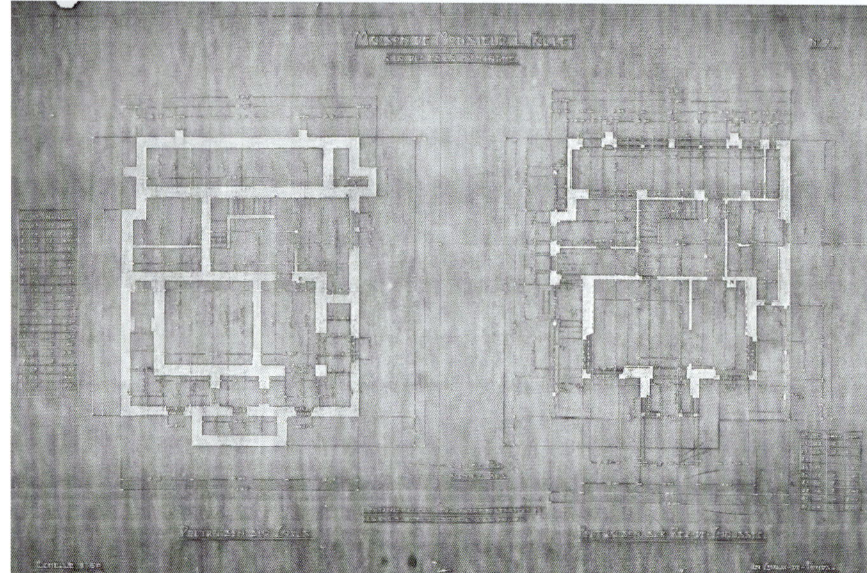

Young Jeanneret's first commission: Villa Fallet, La Chaux-de-Fonds, 1905–7

In 1905 Louis Fallet, one of Jeanneret's professors, gave him his first architectural commission. The Villa Fallet's design was greatly influenced by Charles L'Eplattenier, who envisioned an artistic style expressive of the Jura landscape. Situated on the edge of La Chaux-de-Fonds, the villa bore considerable resemblance to the chalets found throughout the region. However, it was distinguished by decorative motifs derived from pinecones and other natural forms in the surrounding landscape.

"At the age of seventeen I had the good luck to meet a man without prejudices who entrusted me with the building of his house. Between eighteen and nineteen, I built this house with enormous care and plenty of details... moving! This house is probably dreadfully ugly, but there is nothing routine about its architecture. I understood, then, that a house is built with materials and by workmen, and that success or failure hinges on plan and section. This gave me a horror of official teachings, formulas, and divinely ordained preconceptions, and I became convinced, during this period of uncertainty, of the need to rely on my own judgment." —"1905," Le Corbusier lui-même

Opposite, top. West, south, and east facades, Villa Fallet, La Chaux-de-Fonds, 1905–7

Opposite, middle. Basement and ground-floor plans

Opposite, bottom. View from southwest

Top. Sketches exploring the pine tree as a decorative architectural element, c. 1907

Above. Postcard of winter landscape with pine trees, La Chaux-de-Fonds

Right. Wrought-iron balcony railing incorporating pine-tree motif

Left. Jeanneret executing his sgraffito designs on the facade of Villa Fallet, La Chaux-de-Fonds, 1907

Below. Detail of facade ornamentation

Opposite. Jeanneret (middle) with his friends Octave Matthey (left) and Louis Houriet (right) during construction of Villa Fallet, 1907

Friends and family, La Chaux-de-Fonds

Even though Jeanneret yearned for the opportunity to escape provincial La Chaux-de-Fonds, he maintained a deep, lifelong connection to his roots through his relationships with his father, mother, and brother, Albert. The Jeanneret household was characterized by hard work and love of music and literature. Father Georges earned his living applying decorative enameling to watchcases, mother Marie-Charlotte-Amélie taught piano, and Albert grew up to become a professional musician and composer.

Below left. Jeanneret (far right), friend Léon Perrin (far left), and unidentified companions, c. 1906. The hand-written note reads: "Thank you for having developed my photos When will you send them to me?"

Below right. Jeanneret (left) and friends boating near La Chaux-de-Fonds, c. 1906

Bottom left. Jeanneret (seated on floor) with his father, brother, and mother, c. 1906

Bottom right. Jeanneret with his family at La Chaux-de-Fonds, 1910

Opposite. Jeannere in Italy, 30 August 1907

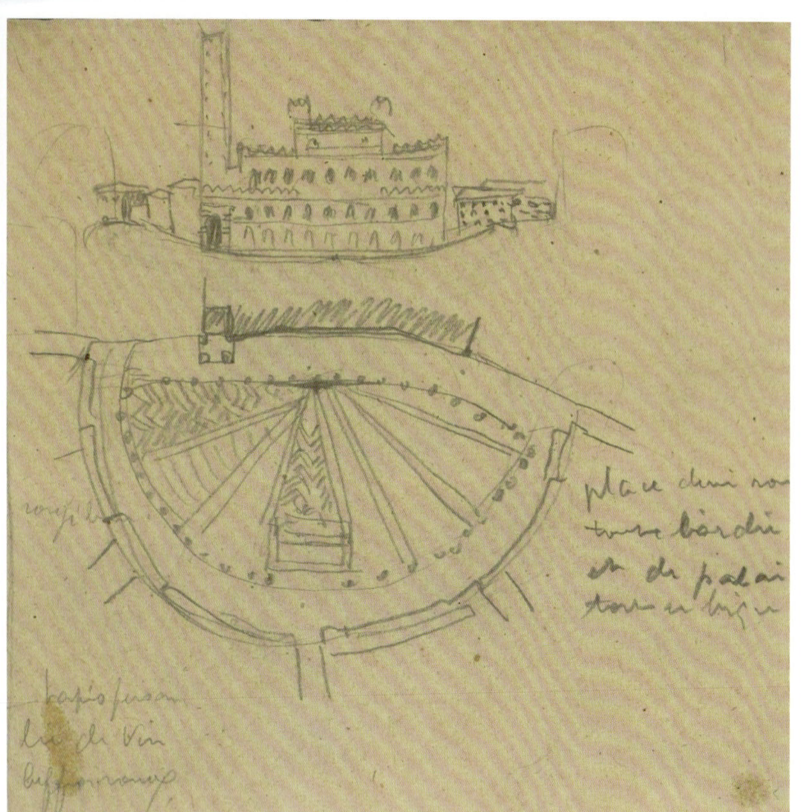

First trip to Italy, 1907

With his fee for the Villa Fallet in hand, Jeanneret set out for a two-month tour of Italy. He went first to Milan, then continued to Florence, where he met up with Léon Perrin, a friend from art school. Together they visited sixteen northern Italian cities and towns, including Venice, Bologna, Siena, Ravenna, Padua, and Pisa. Their sojourn ended with a brief stop in Budapest and an extended stay in Vienna.

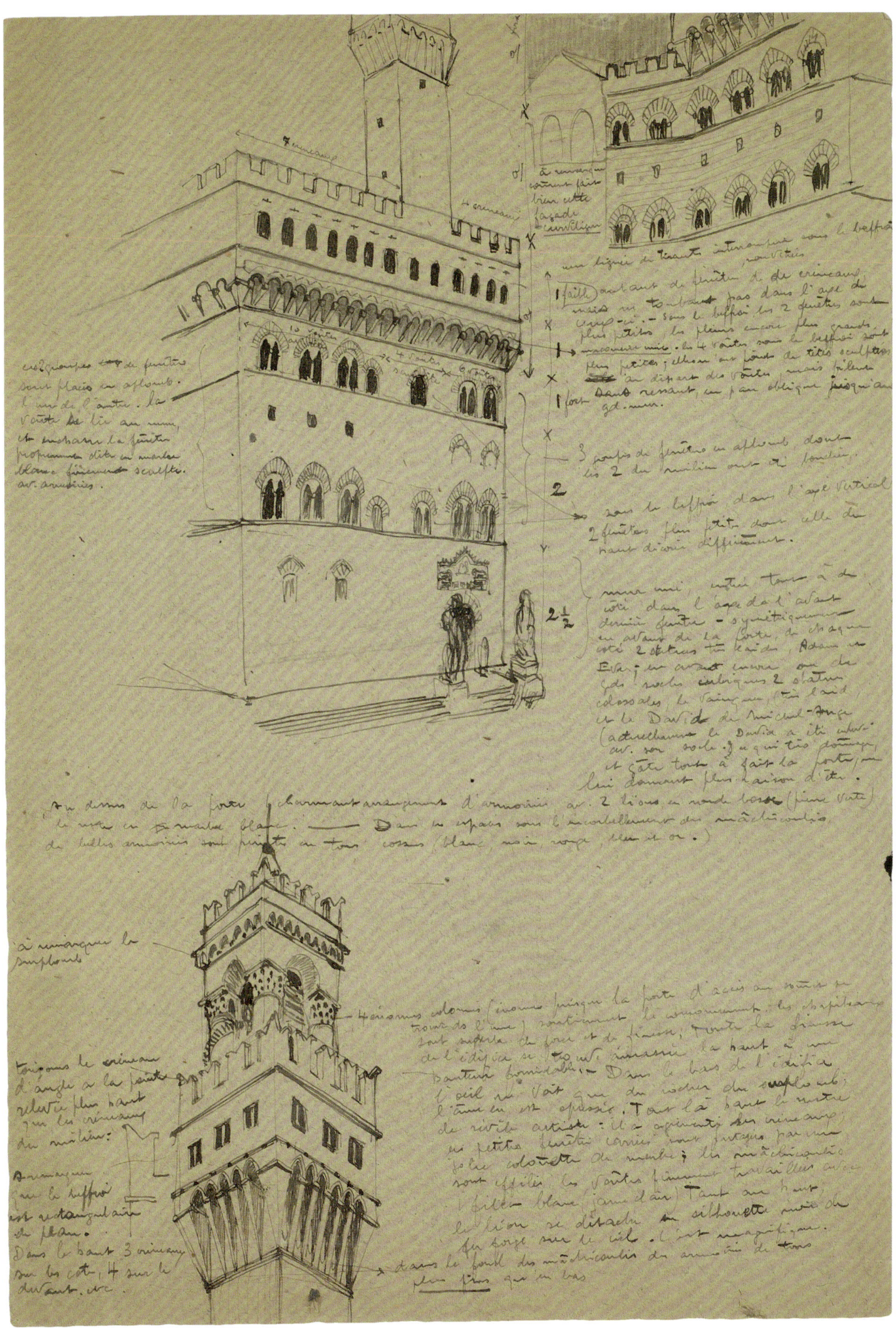

Opposite, top left. Sketch of the Piazza del Campo, Siena, 1907

Opposite, top right. Postcard of Pisa, c. 1900

Opposite, bottom. Sketches of facade and details, Baptistry of St. John, Siena, 1907

Above. Sketches of Palazzo Vecchio, Florence, 1907. Jeanneret annotated the page with detailed descriptions of the facade, windows, crenellations, sculptural elements, and materials, commenting: "At the very top the lion stands out as a black wrought iron silhouette against the sky. It's magnificent."

Florence and the monastery at Val d'Ema, 1907

In Florence, Jeanneret explored beyond the city's major artistic monuments. Of all the sites he visited and sketched in and around the city, the one that most deeply affected him was the fourteenth-century Carthusian monastery Certosa del Galluzzo, in nearby Val d'Ema. Its communal arrangement of small double-height cells, each with a private garden, became an archetype that would influence the designs for many of his most significant buildings, including the Villa Schwob, Maison Citrohan, Immeubles-Villas, Cité de Refuge, and Unité d'Habitation.

Opposite. Rendering of a Donatello statue on the facade of Orsanmichele, Florence, 1 October 1907. Le Corbusier's note reads "Florence, 1413. Niche of Donatello at Or San Michele. White marble inlaid with black marble."

Right. Jeanneret's sketches of the plan and cross section of the monastery

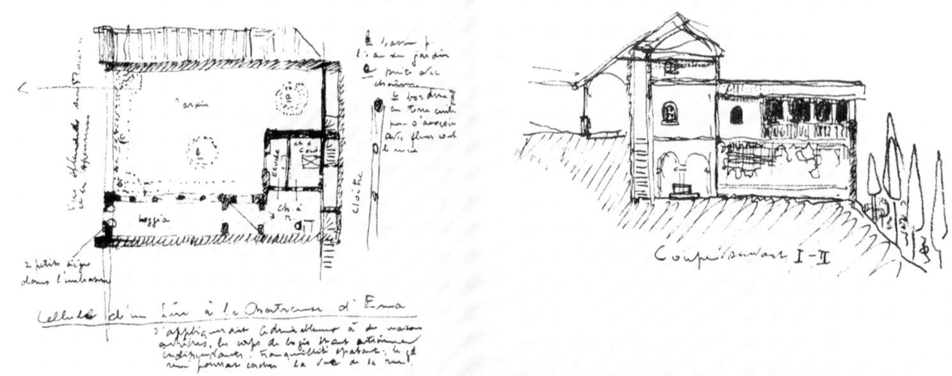

Above and below. Views of Certosa del Galluzzo, the fourteenth-century Carthusian monastery in Val d'Ema, outside Florence, c. 1938

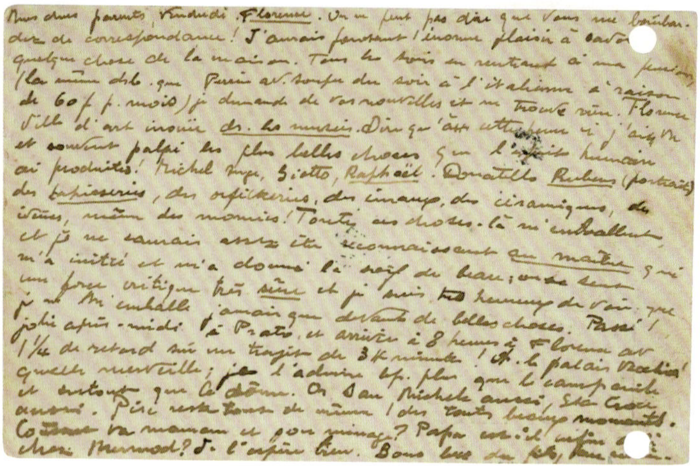

Above. Charles-Edouard Jeanneret to his parents, from Italy, 9 October 1907, commenting that he has seen the most beautiful things the human spirit has produced, including work by Michelangelo, Giotto, and Raphael

Below. Sketches of the interior of the Basilica of Santa Croce, Florence, 1907

Above. Rendering of Romanesque arches and tombs, Church of Santa Maria Novella, Florence, 8 October 1907. Jeanneret annotated the drawing at bottom right: "Florence. Tombeaux Sta M. Novella. Oct 1907."

VI siècle
Ravenne. St Vitale
oct. 1907. Ch.-E. Jeanneret.

Byzantine beauty in Ravenna, 1907

Jeanneret and his friend Léon Perrin headed north from Florence, staying in a series of northern towns, including Bologna and Ravenna, for a few days each before moving on to Venice. Jeanneret was particularly impressed by the intricate mosaics in the sixth-century Byzantine churches of San Vitale and Sant'Apollinare Nuovo, in Ravenna.

Opposite. Detail of interior columns and capitals, Basilica of San Vitale, Ravenna, 15 October 1907

Above. Rendering of mosaic depicting, as Jeanneret notes, "procession of 21 virgins," Basilica of Sant'Apollinare Nuovo, 15 October 1907

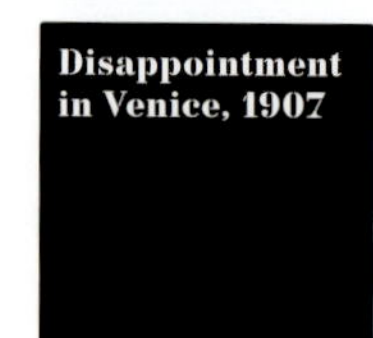

Jeanneret's visit to Venice was "plagued by bad weather and flagging interest." He made only two known drawings there, but took several photographs of the city's monuments.

"All the same, two or three brief sunny spells let us see Venice in its true beauty, and the other evening we were even granted a veritable apotheosis: a dramatic sky overlaid with black clouds drowning in the yellow mist, with the sun breaking vividly through beside the dome of Santa Maria della Salute; the sea, the sky, and the houses were all one immense, blazing torch seen through tears."

—Letter to Charles L'Eplattenier, 1 November 1907

Jeanneret's photographs of Venice:

Top left. Piazza San Marco, Venice, 1907

Left. Doge's Palace, Venice, 1907

Above. Basilica of San Marco, Venice, 1907

Opposite, top. Sketches of Piazza San Marco, Venice, 1907

Opposite, bottom. Sketches of exterior details, Doge's Palace, Venice, 1907

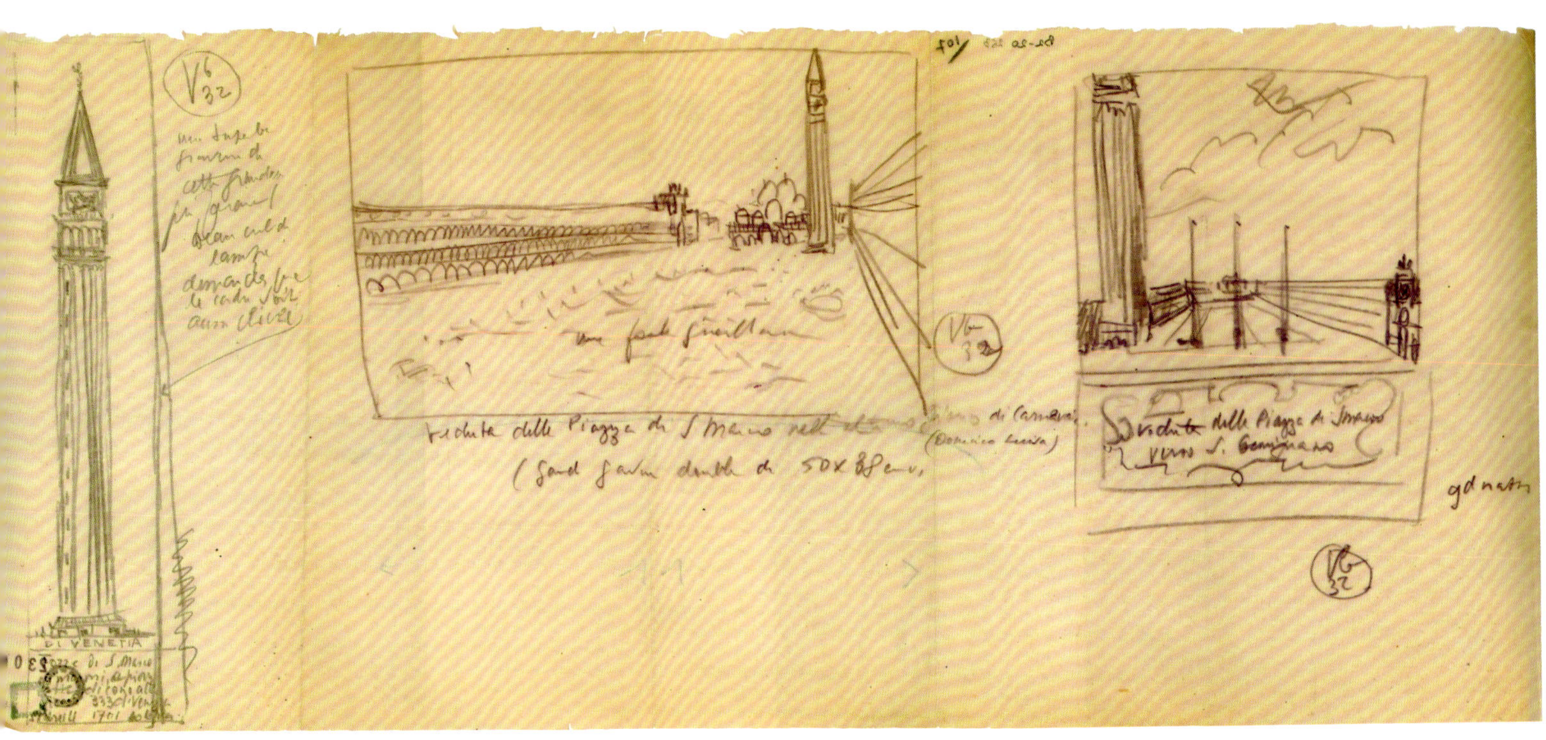

Sous toutes les vides des trèfles ne comptent pas de la construction. Ils n'affaiblissent aucunement, mais au contraire préviennent les écrasements où l'appareillage B donne toujours, à la longue, aux points c. Le souvenir des murs pleins du Parthénon qui ont pris un singulier aspect. Le souvenir de ce procédé quand un gd poids doit reposer sur des assemblages pareils.

A

B

Le gros boudin a domine et suit toutes les phases de la courbe, l'enveloppe générale de la moulure est à double chanfrein; bien le remarquer et ne pas croire que cette moulure soit creusée. Elle obtient ainsi une grande force de volume et beaucoup de moelleux

Les fenêtres sont en retrait de la façade, seul 1 léger cordon très engrisaillé par les entailles sertit la fenêtre.

Depression in Vienna, 1907

Jeanneret had looked forward to an extended stay in Vienna, which had a reputation as a mecca for modern architecture and design. However, he was disappointed by what he identified as the Viennese passion for all things fashionable rather than the truly beautiful. This disappointment extended to the emerging modernist masters Otto Wagner, Josef Hoffmann, and Adolf Loos. Depressed and increasingly desperate for employment, Jeanneret arrived unannounced at the offices of Wagner and Hoffmann. Though he later claimed that Hoffmann had offered him a job, at the time Jeanneret wrote to his former teacher Charles L'Eplattenier that Hoffmann was out of the office and the two never met. At an impasse, Jeanneret decided to head to Paris.

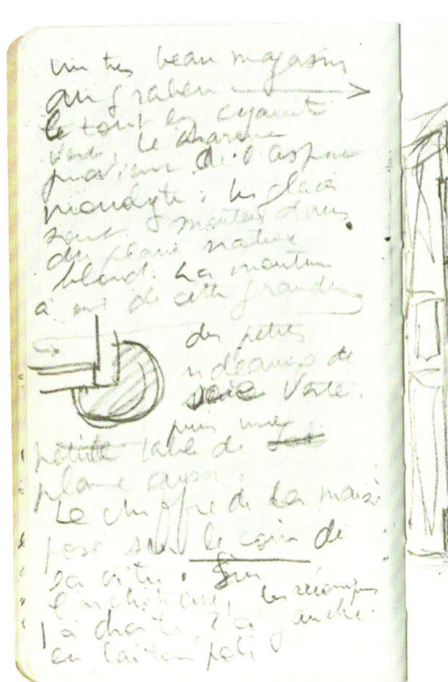

Opposite, top left. Charles-Edouard Jeanneret to his parents, from Vienna, 3 November 1907, discussing Budapest ("people not very nice") and Vienna ("first impression excellent")

Opposite, top right. Charles-Edouard Jeanneret to his parents, from Vienna, 17 November 1907. He writes, "Your son's losing his grip, getting bad-tempered."

Opposite, middle and bottom left. Envelopes from the Vienna letters

Opposite, middle right. Postcard of the Vienna Secession building, designed by Joseph Maria Olbrich, 1898

Above. Notes and facade sketch, c. 1910, Knize department store, Vienna, designed by Adolf Loos in 1909–10

Above right. Sketch of the view from Jeanneret's hotel in Vienna, 1907

Below. Plans and sections, Café Fledermaus, Vienna, 1907. The building was designed and furnished by Josef Hoffmann.

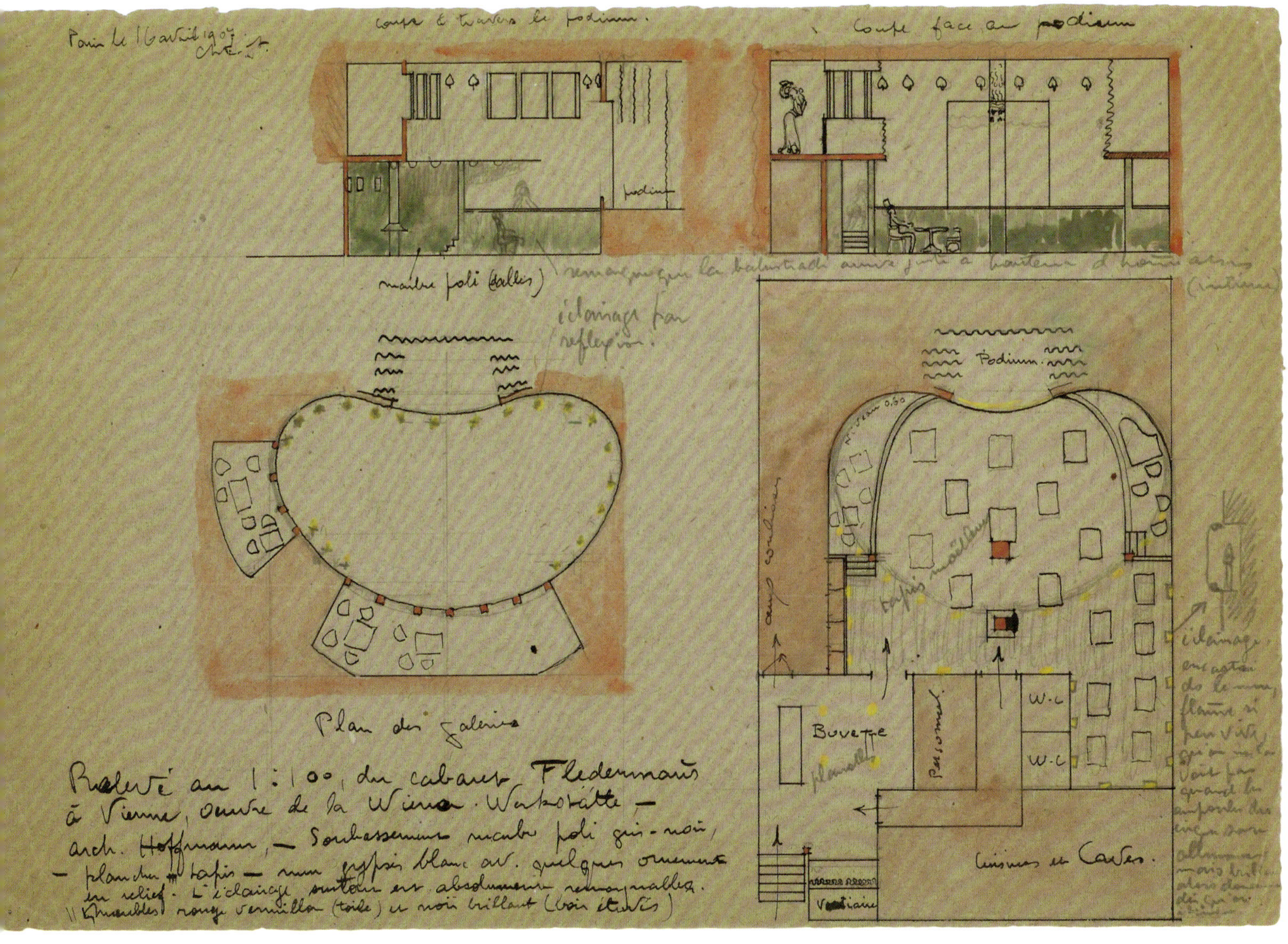

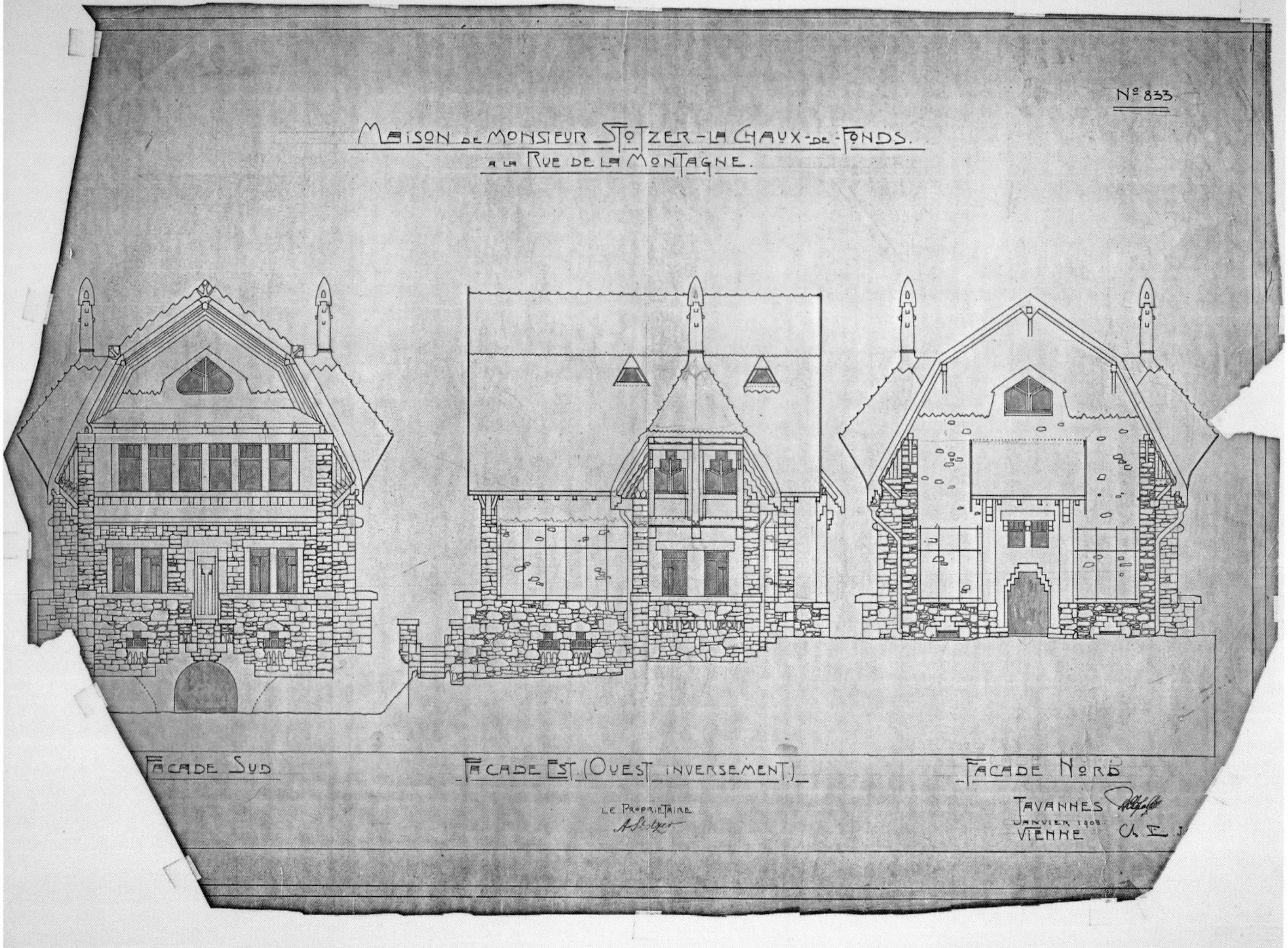

N° 833.

MAISON DE MONSIEUR STOTZER – LA CHAUX-DE-FONDS.

À LA RUE DE LA MONTAGNE.

FAÇADE SUD

FAÇADE EST. (OUEST INVERSEMENT.)

FAÇADE NORD

LE PROPRIÉTAIRE

TAVANNES

JANVIER 1908.

VIENNE

maison du Prof. A. Stotzer.
La Chaux-de-Fonds.
1907-1908. Ch. E. Jt.

Two hometown commissions: Villa Stotzer and Villa Jacquemet, La Chaux-de-Fonds, 1907–8

Jeanneret designed the Villa Stotzer and the Villa Jacquemet while living in Vienna in 1907–8. He mailed his drawings and models to René Chapallaz, who completed the drawings and oversaw the houses' construction. Both clients were relatives of Louis Fallet, Jeanneret's first client, and had similarly progressive attitudes and artistic interests.

The houses combine elements of a Jura farmhouse, rusticated Gothic stonework, plain stucco walls, and pine-tree motifs (in the eaves and windows), with a structure of reinforced concrete—which was becoming increasingly common in residential buildings in the region at that time.

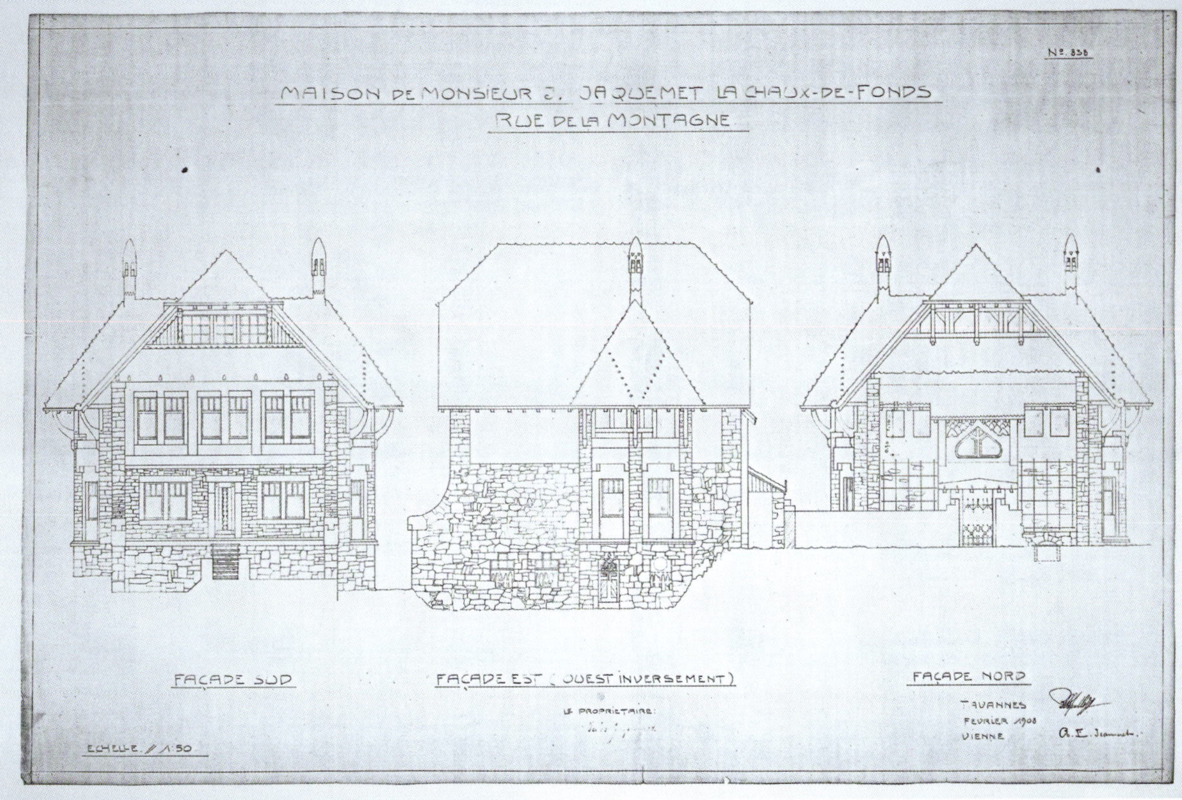

Opposite, top. South, east, and north facades, Villa Stotzer, La Chaux-de-Fonds, 1907–8

Opposite, bottom. View from southeast, Villa Stotzer

Top. South, east, and north facades, Villa Jacquemet, La Chaux-de-Fonds, 1907–8

Above left. Clay model of Villa Jacquemet sculpted and photographed by Jeanneret, December 1907

Above right. View from southwest, Villa Jacquemet

Right. View from southeast, Villa Jacquemet

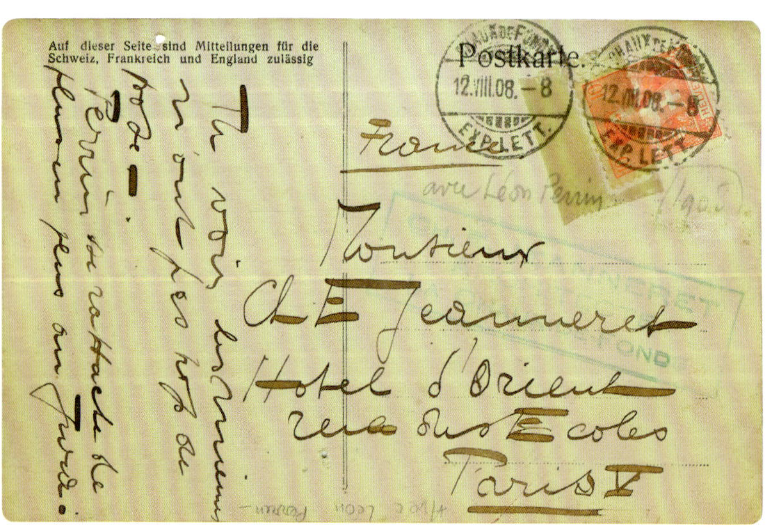

"I have Viollet-le-Duc and, as a laboratory-bench, so to speak, I have Notre-Dame. In this marvelous building I check the pronouncements of Viollet-le-Duc and make my little personal observations. It's there too that I do my drawings 'from the antique' (!) and I can tell you, these drawing sessions are not the merriest moments of the day."

—Letter to Charles L'Eplattenier, 3 July 1908

Visits Paris and lands a job at the Atelier Perret, 1908–9

Shortly after his arrival in Paris, Jeanneret made two decisive moves that would color the rest of his career: he rejected the traditional academy and he sought advice from the architect Eugène Grasset, one of his heroes. Grasset told him about the work being done by Auguste and Gustave Perret in a revolutionary material called reinforced concrete. Unlike his disappointment in Vienna, Jeanneret's introduction to the world of the Perret brothers was exhilarating. Here, finally, were two masters dedicated to the expression of a structure's function through a rational selection of technology and materials rather than the latest decorative trend.

Jeanneret worked in the Perrets' studio for the next fourteen months, during which time his projects included various private house commissions, a hotel in Rio de Janeiro, and a cathedral in Algeria, for which the Perrets served as engineers.

Opposite, top left. Watercolor of Notre-Dame cathedral, 1908

Opposite, top right. Paris rooftops, painted from Jeanneret's room at the Hotel d'Orient, 9 rue des Ecoles, July 1908

Opposite, bottom. Postcard to Jeanneret in Paris from an unidentified correspondent in La-Chaux-de-Fonds, 1908. The message concludes: "Perrin is more and more attached to the Jura."

Right. Jeanneret (front) and his brother, Albert, Paris, 1908

Below. Jeanneret in his attic room, Paris,

CH-E. JEANNERET
ARCHITECTE

ÉTUDE SUR LE MOUVEMENT D'ART DÉCORATIF EN ALLEMAGNE

1 9 1 2

Travels around Germany, 1910

During a brief return to La Chaux-de-Fonds, Jeanneret worked on designs (unbuilt) for a center for the newly organized group of local artists known as the Ateliers d'Art Réunis. He then took a trip through Germany to research the latest developments in architecture and engineering. Determined to work for architect Peter Behrens, he traveled to Berlin, but was unable even to secure an interview. This triggered a depression even deeper than the one he had experienced in Vienna, but his persistence with Behrens eventually paid off.

Munich le 29 juin 1910

LC ms 56

Mes bien chers parents

Me voici dans mon bercail depuis dimanche. Mon voyage "de plaisir" est terminé. Et vous allez me qualifier de veinard, de flemmard, vous penserez que je sais me tailler la part facile. Or notez bien que le régime de plaisir que je mène, spécialement celui de ces 20 jours de voyage a fait de ma figure ce que l'image ci à côté vous montre. Jamais je n'ai fait 1 vie aussi éreintante et voici 2 jours que je ne puis travailler sérieusement. J'ai vu et étudié tant de choses, en général toutes concernant directement mon métier, que les heures furent souvent pénibles. Seulement comme je sentais que ce que je voyais je ne le reverrais plus, il fallait se secouer, et parfois 1 peu fatiguer la machine... les 6 derniers jours à travers 10 à 12 villes achevèrent de m'amortir et je vous assure bien que j'étais heureux de retrouver mon Stammlokal.

Je pensais reprendre et terminer ce prochain 15 mon travail, mais j'ai bien l'intention d'y renoncer et de venir le finir aux Eplatures, ds 1 mois. Mon étudiant av. lequel j'avais commencé 1 échange journalier de conversation s'en est retourné ds son patelin de sorte que j'en ai repêché 1 autre bcp plus intéressant, qui s'occupe d'histoire de l'Art et a énormément voyagé. Il quitte Munich le 21 juillet, et il se pourrait qu'alors plus rien ne me retienne, à moins..... du contraire.

Il est évidemment très juste que vous sachiez à quoi j'ai occupé ces 2 mois passés à Munich. Ce n'est point à 1 "colossal travail" comme dit papa, mais tout simplement à 1 étude sur l'art de bâtir les villes. Cette étude se terminera par 1 critique vigoureuse des moyens employés à La Chaux-de-Fonds et a pour but de la faire transformer du tout au tout. Cette étude sera publiée en 1 brochure, dont l'importance dépasse mes prévisions. Ce fut pour moi 1 passionnante question et j'espère bcp en ses résultats directs. Elle sera signée de L'Ep. et de moi. et aura 1 intérêt pas exclusivement local.

La documentation fut longue, me coûta passa:

Opposite, top left. Cover of Jeanneret's *Etude sur le mouvement d'art décoratif en Allemagne* (A Study of the Decorative Arts Movement in Germany), which he researched throughout Germany and published in 1912

Opposite, top right and middle right. Postcards from Munich, 1910, showing the Frauenkirch and Villa Stuck

Opposite, bottom. Charles-Edouard Jeanneret to his parents, from Munich, 29 June 1910. He writes that he is working on "a study on the art of building cities."

Above. Watercolor of Schloss Sanssouci, Potsdam, 1910. Jeanneret's notation reads, in part: "This watercolor was done on 5 November 1910 at 3 pm in Potsdam... at the moment when Wilhelm II and the tsar of Russia were about to go by."

Below. Sketches of Schloss Sanssouci, c. October 1910. In his notation on the sketch at bottom left, Jeanneret refers to the "handsome and commanding" dome.

Works for Peter Behrens in Berlin, 1910–11

Within two months of his arrival in Berlin in 1910, Jeanneret had secured a position in Behrens's office, where Walter Gropius and Mies van der Rohe had worked earlier that year. It was Behrens's reputation for pursuing a radical functionalism free of traditional architectural motifs that attracted such remarkable young talent. However, Jeanneret soon found himself oppressed by Behrens's severity as well as disheartened by what he came to view as the studio's superficial approach to design. It was this discontentment that made Jeanneret decide to head off yet again, this time for the East.

Above. Jeanneret (far left), with his brother Albert, and friends in Hellerau, the garden city district of Dresden, October 1910

Opposite, top. Jeanneret in the room he rented at 81 bei Riedel, Berlin, April 1911

Opposite, bottom. Peter Behrens, AEG Turbine Factory Assembly Hall, Berlin, 1908–9

"I'm living in one of those garden cities that surround Berlin and have found an enormous room with balcony, heating and lunch for 28 marks. 4 young people from Behrens's studio live here too, and I eat with them at one o'clock in one of their rooms. Ma Wirthin serves dinner for 1 mark; today it was ample and good. This also means I have to speak German, which is perfect." —Letter to his parents, 28 October 1910

Journey to the East, 1911: Turkey

In the spring of 1911, having left Behrens's office, Jeanneret embarked with his friend August Klipstein on a six-month journey through the Balkans to Turkey, Greece, and Italy. Encountering structures ranging from vernacular architecture in Romania to the great Süleyman Mosque in Istanbul, Jeanneret recorded his impressions in the many sketches he completed during the trip, establishing a lifelong method of investigation.

Left. Süleyman Mosque, Istanbul, photographed by Jeanneret, summer 1911

Below. Jeanneret (right, in costume) and August Klipstein in Pera, the then-European area of northern Istanbul

Opposite, top. The Seraglio as seen from the Bosporus, Istanbul, summer 1911

Opposite, bottom lef Süleyman Mosque Istanbul, summer 1911

Opposite, bottom right. View into the Caravansary, Edirne, northwestern Turkey, June 1911. In his note at top right, Jeanneret describe the symmetrical staircases as the "solution of stairways."

"The night is yellow and trickles with gold. All the marble statuary of all the palaces of Byzantium is there, as well as all the treasures of the sultans and all the gems of the Seraglios!" —Journey to the East, 1911

Journey to the East, 1911: Greece

Late in the summer of 1911, Jeanneret moved on through Thrace to Mount Athos, where he was profoundly inspired by a series of dramatically sited monasteries, and then to Athens,

where he visited the Parthenon every day for three weeks.

Above. The Parthenon and Acropolis, Athens, September 1911

Below. Jeanneret at the Acropolis, next to a fallen column from the Parthenon, September 1911

Opposite. Jeanneret at the Acropolis, 15 September 1911

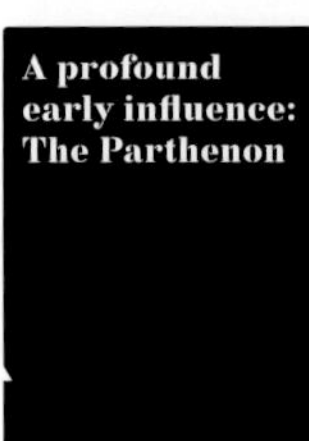

A profound early influence: The Parthenon

While in Athens, Jeanneret produced pages of sketches and drawings of the Parthenon. The ancient Doric temple remained a source of inspiration for him throughout his career; as Le Corbusier, he dedicated an entire chapter to the Parthenon in his book, *Vers une architecture* (*Toward an Architecture*). In the chapter titled "Architecture: Pure Creation of the Mind," Le Corbusier wrote: "For two thousand years, those who have seen the Parthenon have felt: this was a decisive moment for architecture."

Below and opposite. Sketches and plans of the Parthenon, Athens, 1911. On the pen-and-ink drawing below, he concludes his notation: "Everywhere a disconcerting asymmetry prevails."

"The uniformly red landscape is reflected by the temples. Their marbles have the luster of new bronze against the azure sky. Close-up, they really seem as reddish brown as terra-cotta. Never in my life have I experienced the subtleties of such monochromy. The body, the mind, the heart gasp, suddenly overpowered." —Journey to the East, 1911

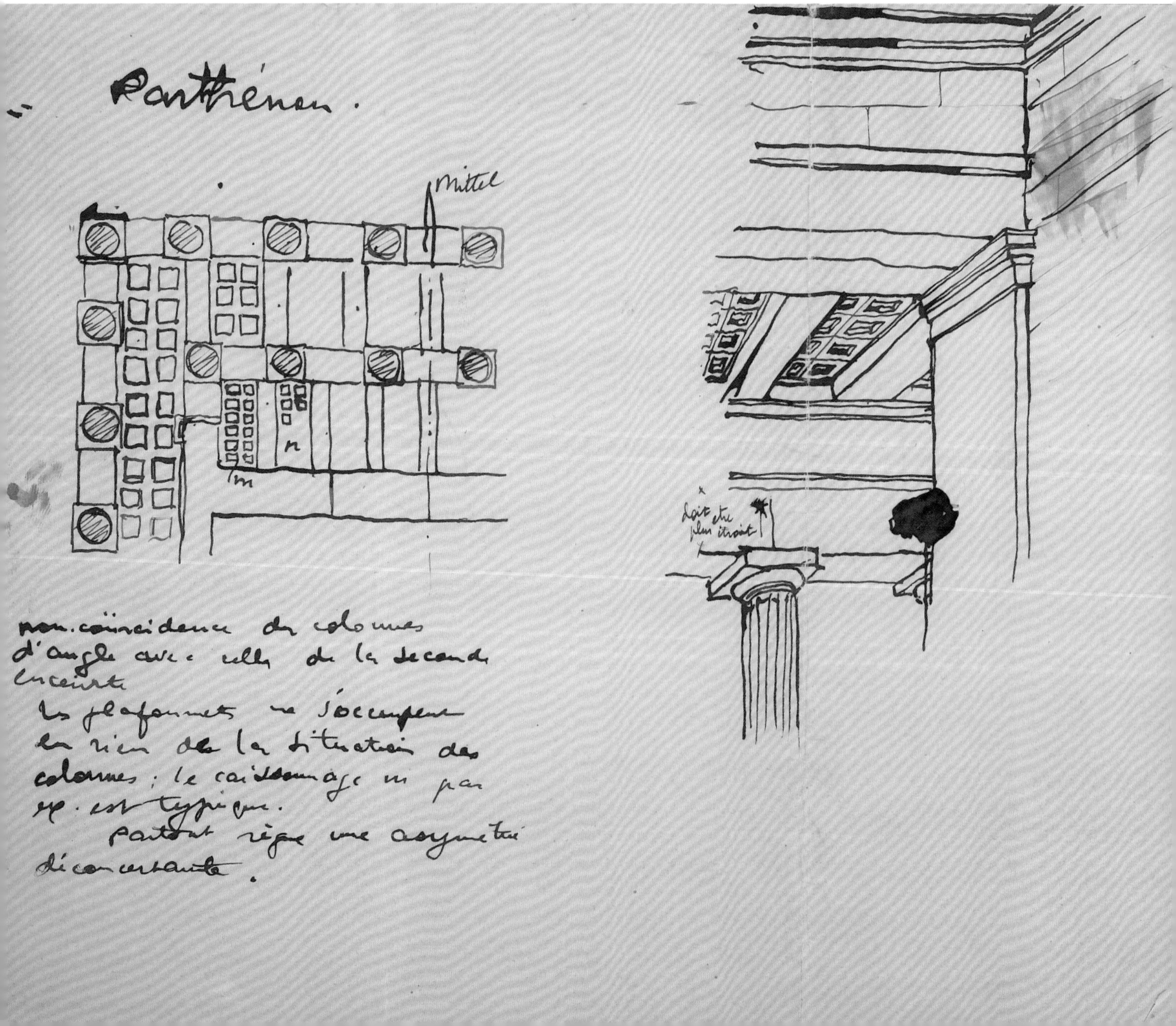

casa di diomede
terrasse
mur de clôture
plan du jardin
65
40
pavillon

Return to the West: Pompeii, 1911

Once in Italy, Jeanneret made careful studies of the ancient domestic building typologies at Pompeii, such as the House of the Tragic Poet and the House of the Silver Wedding, as well as of Pompeii's Forum.

Opposite. Sketches and plans of houses in Pompeii, 13–28 September 1911.

Top to bottom: Salluste House; House of the Labyrinth; and plan of the House of the Silver Wedding, one of the largest patrician dwellings in Pompeii.

Above. Two views of the Forum, Pompeii, photographed by Jeanneret, September 1911

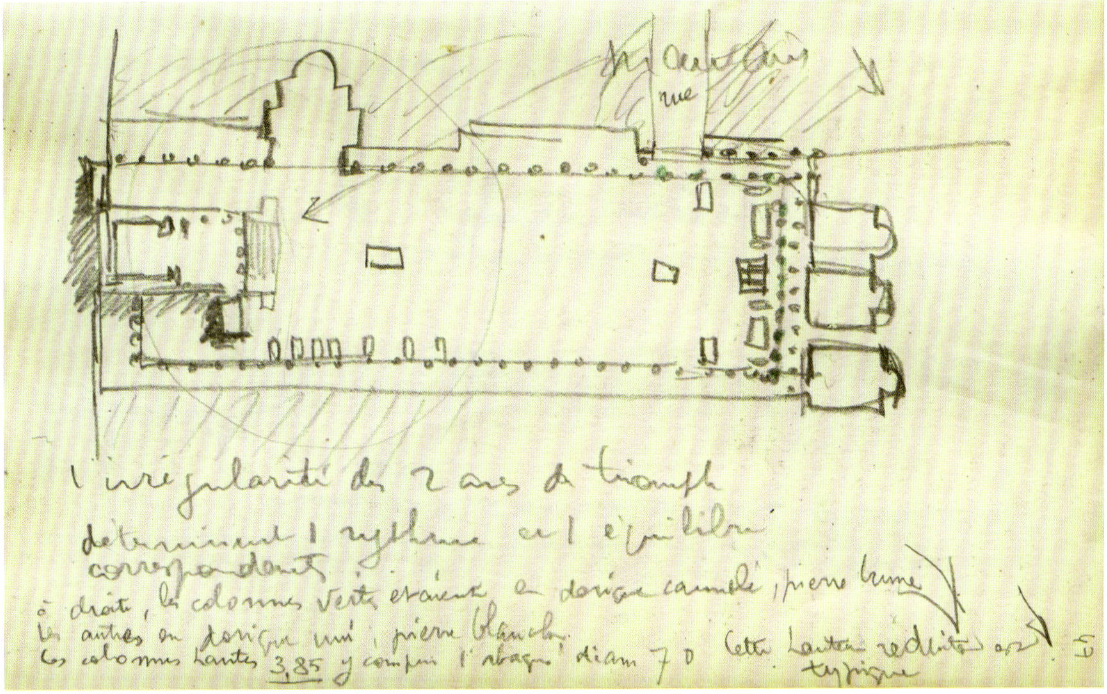

Right, and below right. Plan and sketch of the Forum, Pompeii, September 1911

Rome and Tuscany, 1911

Jeanneret spent his time in Rome at the Colosseum, the Pantheon, and the ruins of the ancient baths. He was also deeply impressed by the work of Michelangelo at St. Peter's Basilica.

Significantly, Jeanneret also made a return visit to the Carthusian monastery at Val d'Ema, the Certosa del Galluzzo.

Left. Giotto's bell tower in the Piazza del Duomo, Florence, 1911

Above. Arcetri and the Torre del Gallo as seen from the Boboli Gardens, Florence, 1911

Below. Piazza dei Miracoli, Pisa, 1911, including the Baptistery, Duomo, and Camposanto

Bottom left. Gateway in Fiesole, outside Florence, 1911. Jeanneret's note reads, "It is truly an entrance!"

Bottom right. The Leaning Tower and Duomo, Pisa, 1911

Opposite, top. Jeanneret sitting in the Piazza San Pietro, Rome, 1911

Opposite, bottom left and right. The Roman Forum and the dome of the Pantheon, photographed by Jeanneret, 1911

Starts his career in La Chaux-de-Fonds, 1911–13

After his Journey to the East, Jeanneret returned to La Chaux-de-Fonds. Here he headed a new section of the Ecole d'Art started by Charles L'Eplattenier, and opened his own design firm, closely allied to the Ateliers d'Art Réunis.

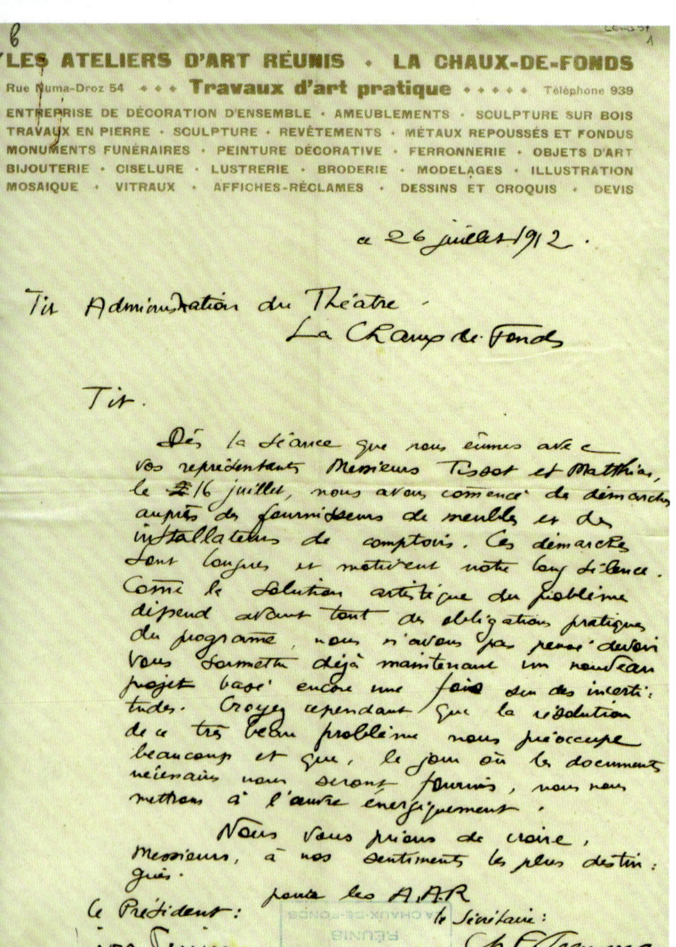

LES ATELIERS D'ART RÉUNIS • LA CHAUX-DE-FONDS

Rue Numa-Droz 54 • • • Travaux d'art pratique • • • • • Téléphone 939

ENTREPRISE DE DÉCORATION D'ENSEMBLE • AMEUBLEMENTS • SCULPTURE SUR BOIS
TRAVAUX EN PIERRE • SCULPTURE • REVÊTEMENTS • MÉTAUX REPOUSSÉS ET FONDUS
MONUMENTS FUNÉRAIRES • PEINTURE DÉCORATIVE • FERRONNERIE • OBJETS D'ART
BIJOUTERIE • CISELURE • LUSTRERIE • BRODERIE • MODELAGES • ILLUSTRATION
MOSAIQUE • VITRAUX • AFFICHES-RÉCLAMES • DESSINS ET CROQUIS • DEVIS

le 26 juillet 1912.

Tit. Administration du Théâtre
La Chaux de Fonds

Tit.

Dès la séance que nous eûmes avec vos représentants Messieurs Tissot et Matthias, le 16 juillet, nous avons commencé des démarches auprès des fournisseurs de meubles et des installateurs de comptoirs. Ces démarches sont longues et motivent notre long silence. Comme la solution artistique du problème dépend avant tout des obligations pratiques du programme, nous n'avons pas pensé devoir vous soumettre déjà maintenant un nouveau projet basé encore une fois sur des incertitudes. Croyez cependant que la résolution de ce très beau problème nous préoccupe beaucoup et que, le jour où les documents nécessaires nous seront fournis, nous nous mettrons à l'œuvre énergiquement.

Nous vous prions de croire, Messieurs, à nos sentiments les plus distingués.

pour les A.A.R

le Président: Léon Perrin
le Secrétaire: Ch E Jeanneret

CH.-E. JEANNERET :: ARCHITECTE
ARCHITECTE DES ATELIERS D'ART RÉUNIS

CONSTRUCTION DE VILLAS, DE MAISONS DE CAMPAGNE, D'IMMEUBLES LOCATIFS — CONSTRUCTIONS INDUSTRIELLES (SPÉCIALITÉ DE BETON ARMÉ) — TRANSFORMATIONS ET RÉPARATIONS — INSTALLATIONS DE MAGASINS — ARCHITECTURE D'INTÉRIEUR — ARCHITECTURE DE JARDINS

LA CHAUX-DE-FONDS, 54 RUE NUMA-DROZ 2 aout 1912 TÉLÉPHONE 939

Above. Charles-Edouard Jeanneret and Léon Perrin to the La Chaux-de-Fonds theater, 26 July 1912, regarding their interior-design project for the theater

Above right. Letterhead for Jeanneret and his firm, La Chaux-de-Fonds, 1912

Below. Membership card for the Cercle du Sapin, a regional group (*sapin* is the French word for "pine tree"), 1914

Right. Page from Jeanneret's notebook, Carnet A1, c. 1914, with sketches of an insignia design incorporating his intitials, "ChE"

Opposite. Portrait of Jeanneret

Par devoir

CERCLE DU SAPIN

Monsieur Albert Kocher
Serre 39
EN VILLE

est convoqué à la séance du ~~Comité~~ Match au Billard
du vendredi 13 mars 1914
à 8 heures du soir.

Le Secrétaire.

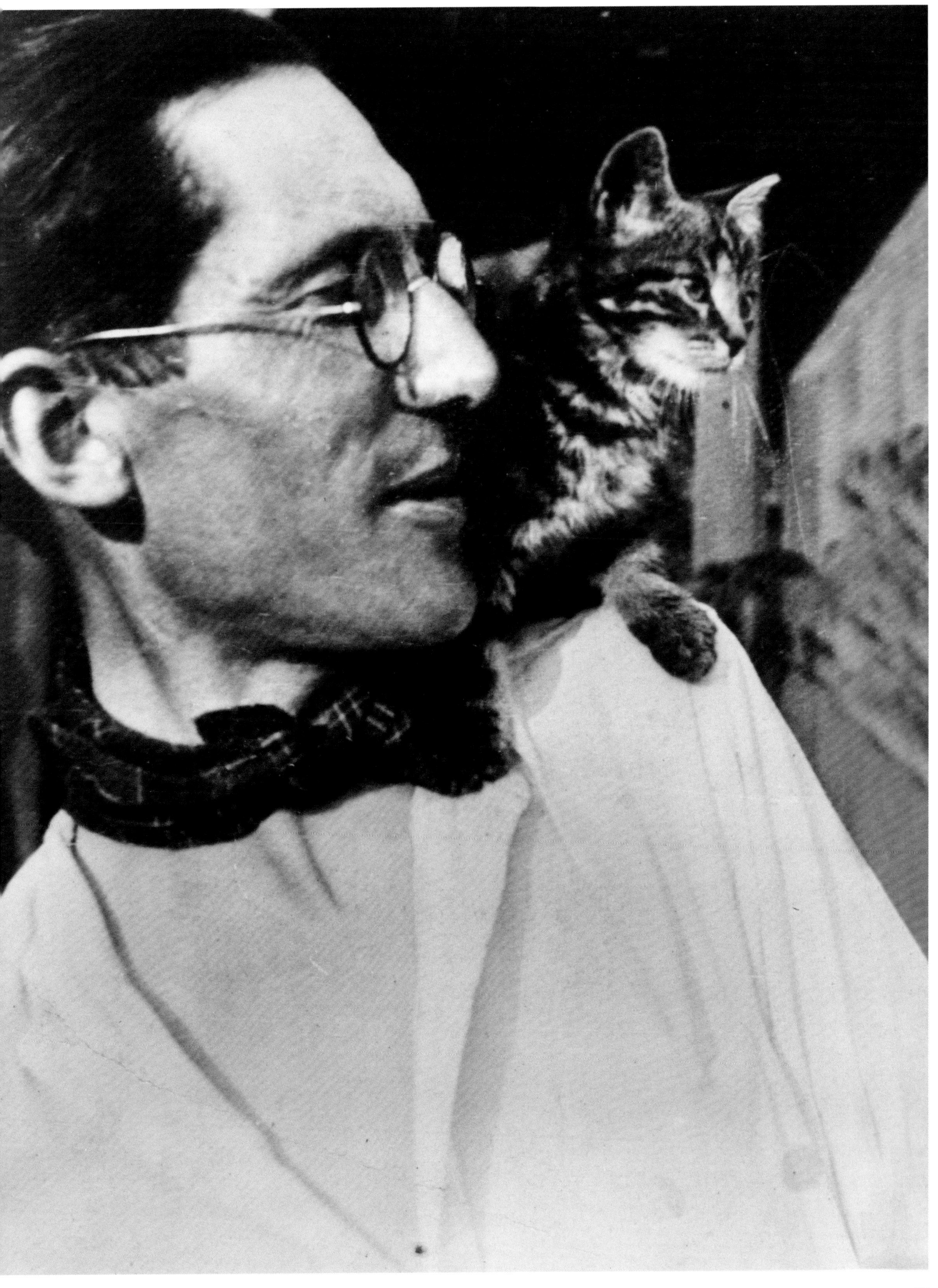

Left and below. Sketches of geometric and pine-tree motifs, August 1905 (left), and c. 1911 (below). The drawing below may have been made in connection with Jeanneret's teaching.

Opposite. Sapin en hiver (Pine Tree in Winter), 1911

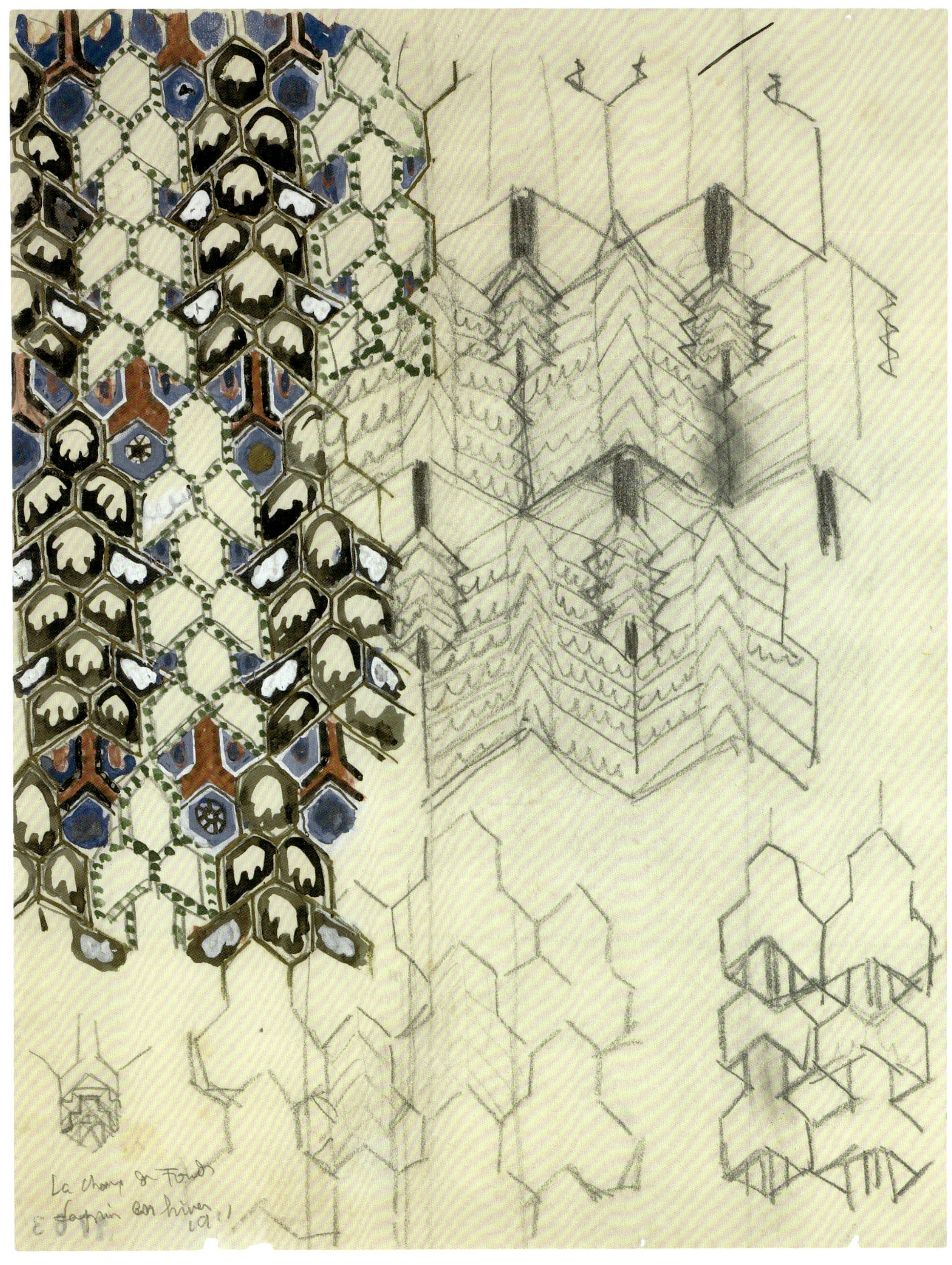

“Our childhood was made of Ruskin’s exhortations. A rich, complex, contradictory, paradoxical apostle. The times were unbearable, and the situation could not last, with its crushing, mindless middle-classness drowning in materialism and wreathed in idiotic, utterly mechanical ornamentation.” —Le Corbusier, *L’art décoratif d’aujourd’hui*, 1925

His first modernist mansion: Villa Favre-Jacot, Le Locle, Switzerland, 1912

Wealthy watch manufacturer Georges Favre-Jacot commissioned Jeanneret to design a state-of-the-art house that would be visually integrated into the landscape of Le Locle, between La Chaux-de-Fonds and the French border. Jeanneret's design depended heavily on lessons he had learned from the work of Peter Behrens and Josef Hoffmann.

Opposite, top. South facade, Villa Favre-Jacot, Le Locle, Switzerland, 1912

Opposite, bottom. Bird's-eye perspective, March 1912

Right. West facade

Below. Jeanneret on the patio at the southwest corner of Villa Favre-Jacot, 1912

An ambitious house for his parents: Villa Jeanneret-Perret, La Chaux-de-Fonds, 1912

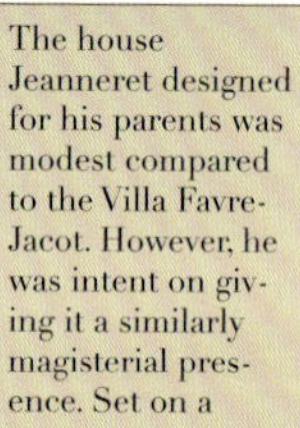

The house Jeanneret designed for his parents was modest compared to the Villa Favre-Jacot. However, he was intent on giving it a similarly magisterial presence. Set on a plinth surrounded by a colonnaded garden, the Villa Jeanneret-Perret—or Maison Blanche, as it came to be known locally—has a strongly geometric, and formal, profile.

One enters through a garden gate and continues up and around the plinth, in a procession reminiscent of the Parthenon.

Clockwise from top:

Perspective from south-east, Villa Jeanneret-Perret, La Chaux-de-Fonds, March–April 1912

Ground-floor plan, 1912

West facade, c. 1912–14

Garden terrace

Above. View from southwest, c. 1912

Left. Door handle in salamander motif, c. 1912

Right. Cloakroom with circular window, upper floor, c. 1912

Below. Jeanneret (left) in his bedroom with his brother, Albert. Jeanneret also had an adjoining study, equipped with electric lighting behind frosted glass to provide indirect light.

25 Ozenfant -
Albert Jeanneret
Charles-Edouard J.
26 Albert et Charles Edouard

Pages from Jeanneret's photo album with images of the Villa Jeanneret-Perret, La Chaux-de-Fonds:

Opposite, top. Left to right: Amédée Ozenfant, Albert, and Charles-Edouard in the latter's studio, August 1919

Opposite, bottom. The Jeanneret family photographed from the pergola, looking toward rear entrance to the house, c. 1912. Jeanneret's parents are in the foreground, Albert and Charles-Edouard behind them.

Top. Charles-Edouard and his father at the stairway leading to the terrace garden

Above left. Jeanneret's parents in their bedroom

Above right. Walkway to the Villa Jeanneret-Perret

Projects, furniture, and interiors, La Chaux-de-Fonds, 1911–15

Jeanneret relied on commissions for furniture design, decorating, and even trading in antiques to augment his income as an architect. Many of his projects during this period came from his social circle. He designed a house (unbuilt) for August Klipstein, his traveling companion on their recent journey to the East. He also developed a scheme for an electricity plant with engineering graduate and businessman Max Du Bois. Though never constructed, the project was the first of Jeanneret's many interactions with Du Bois, which would eventually prove fruitful.

"I hate this city. And by extension the people too. I can do nothing here... but abase myself. And there's not much work, either. No major works are carried out in this city. I've had nothing to do this year. And will continue to have nothing... My ambition, my Vanity and my pride drive me toward great things." —Letter to William Ritter, 9 May 1915

Opposite. Jeanneret in the cabbage patch in front of Le Couvent, an old farmhouse on the outskirts of La Chaux-de-Fonds, 1911–12. Jeanneret rented a small space in the farmhouse for nearly a year.

Above. Study for Paul Ditisheim Store and Warehouse in La Chaux-de-Fonds, 1913 (unbuilt). Ditisheim was a local watch manufacturer.

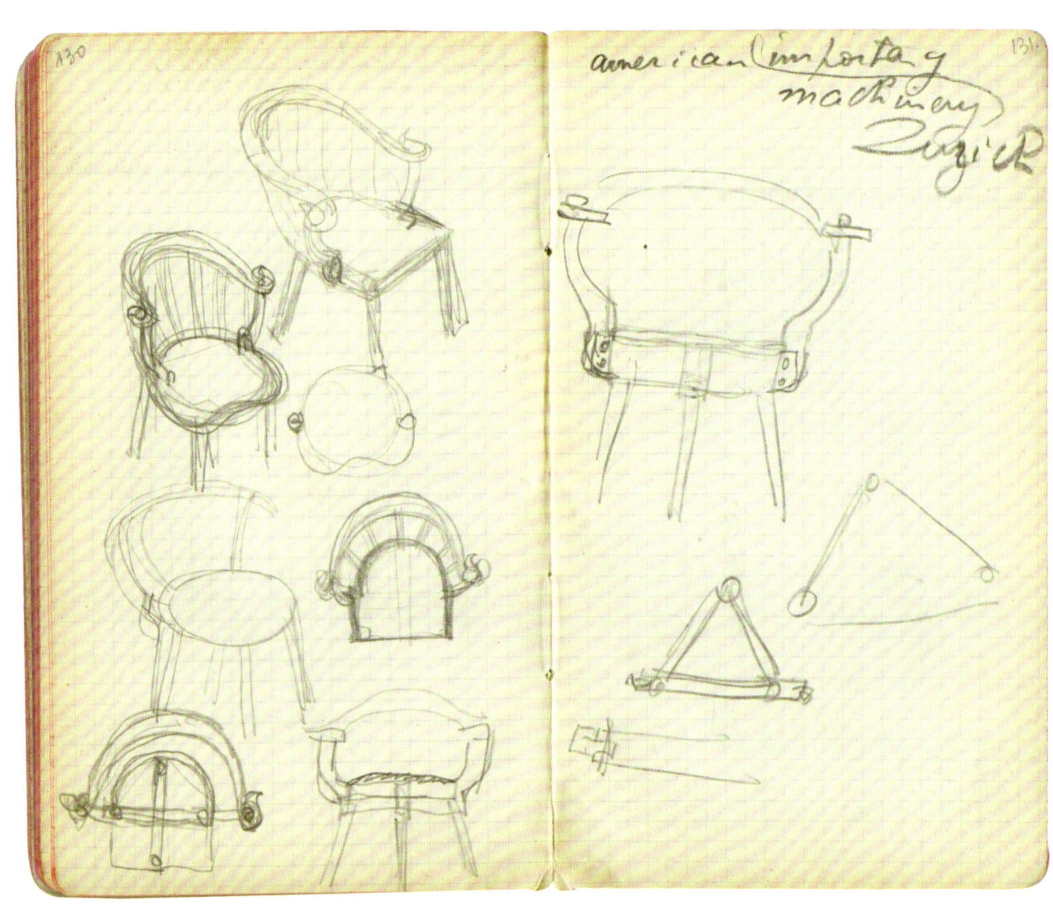

Right. Chair sketches in the travel notebooks that Jeanneret kept during his journey to the East and his return to La Chaux-de-Fonds, 1911. His note reads, "American machinery importing, Zurich."

Above. Watercolor study of terrace for a house in Le Moulinet, France, 1916 (unbuilt)

Left. Sketch of a desk that Jeanneret designed for his mother for the Villa Jeanneret-Perret, 1915

Opposite, top. Smoking room in Hermann Ditisheim's apartment, La Chaux-de-Fonds, 1915. The interior, fireplace, and furniture were designed by Jeanneret.

Opposite, bottom. Desk designed by Jeanneret, c. 1916–19

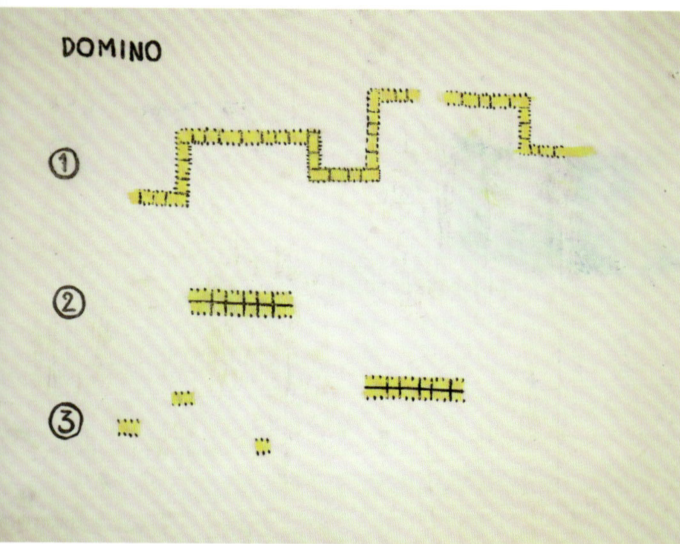
DOMINO
①
②
③
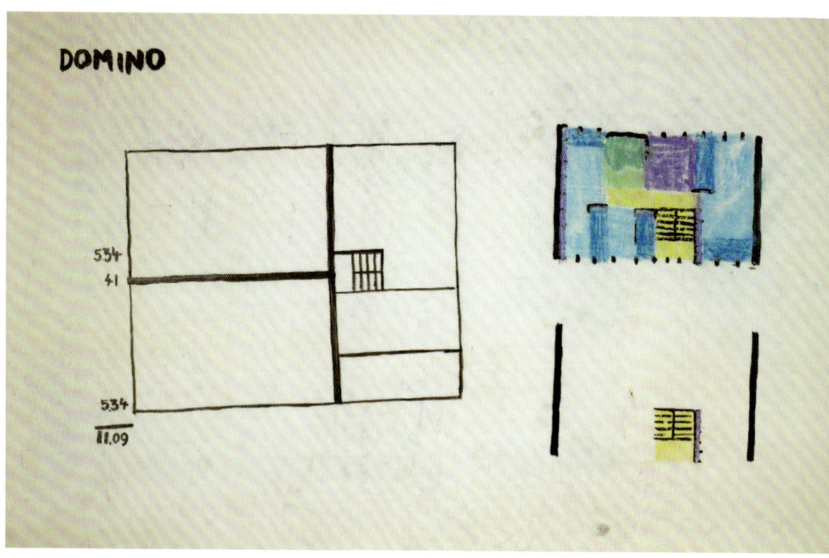
DOMINO
534
41
534
11.09
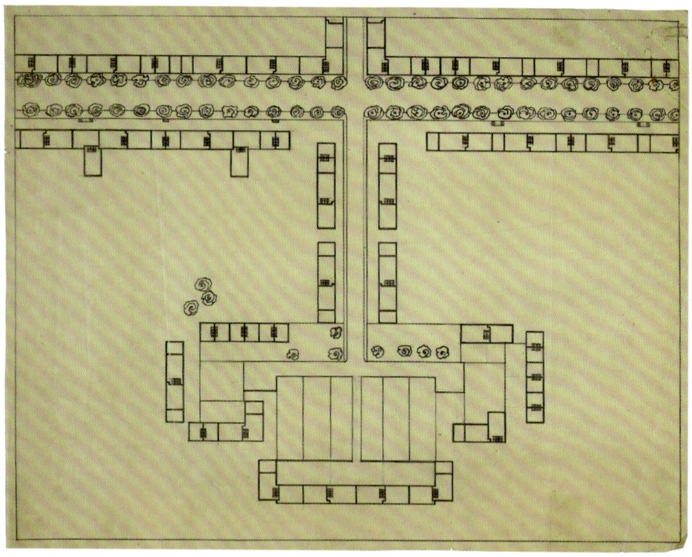
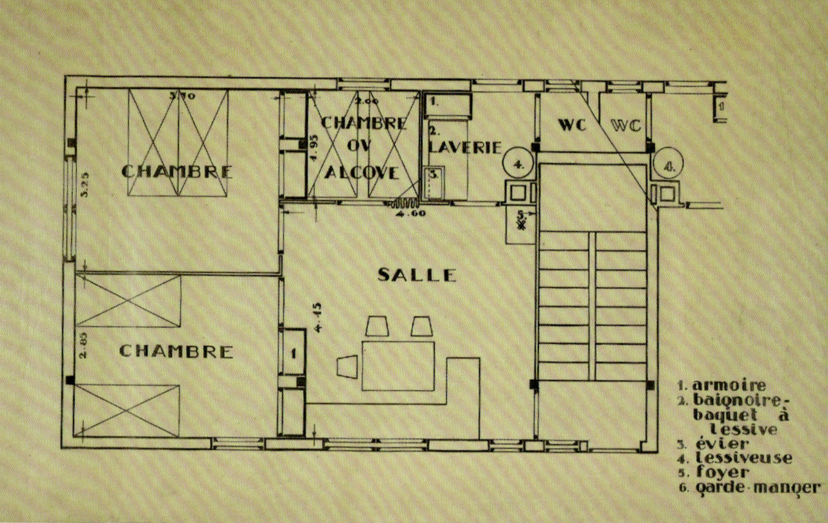
CHAMBRE
CHAMBRE OU ALCOVE
LAVERIE
WC
WC
SALLE
CHAMBRE
1. armoire
2. baignoire-baquet à lessive
3. évier
4. lessiveuse
5. foyer
6. garde-manger

PLACE

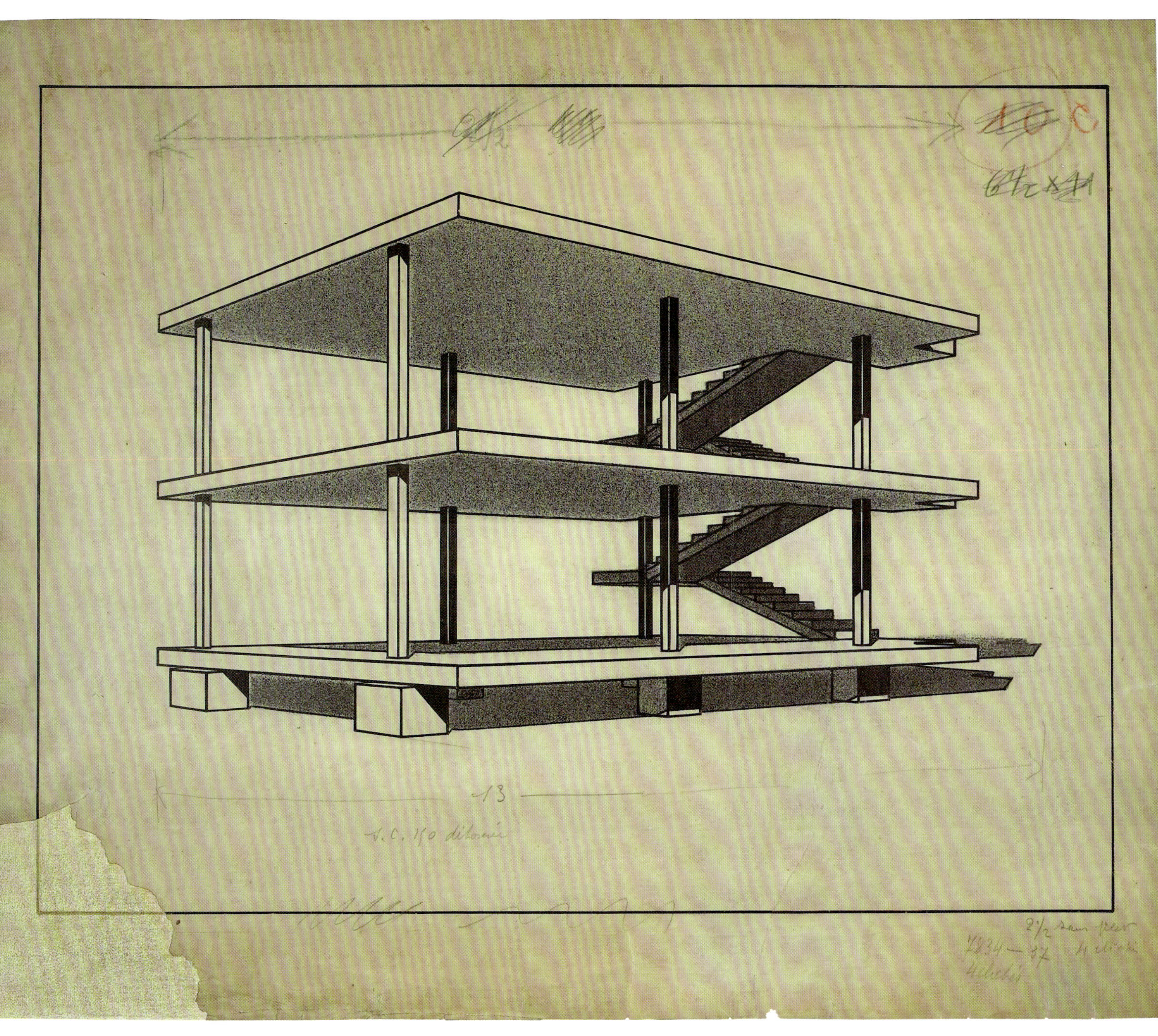

Invents the Dom-ino system, 1914–15

Developed as a response to the destruction at the beginning of World War I, the Dom-ino system exploited standardized components for its structural skeleton, infill walls composed of rubble, and mass-produced fixtures and finishes. Jeanneret named the system Dom-ino in reference to the Latin *domus* (house) plus *innovation*, as well as the resemblance of the system in plan to a set of dominoes. The system's skeleton proved to be a turning point in Jeanneret's creative development: comprising three horizontal slabs on six thin supports, the structural system would be the basis for Le Corbusier's revolutionary "Five Points of a New Architecture" and ultimately for the modernist International Style.

Opposite, top left. Early Dom-ino study, 1914

Opposite, top right. Plan and sketch of a Dom-ino house, 1914

Opposite, middle left. Diagrammatic plan for Dom-ino housing, 1914

Opposite, middle right. Ground-floor plan, Maison Dom-ino, 1914

Opposite, bottom. Perspective and plan showing how linked Dom-ino modules could be used for apartment buildings, 1915 or 1916

Above. Dom-ino skeleton, 1914–15. The structural elements function solely to support the roof slabs and stairs.

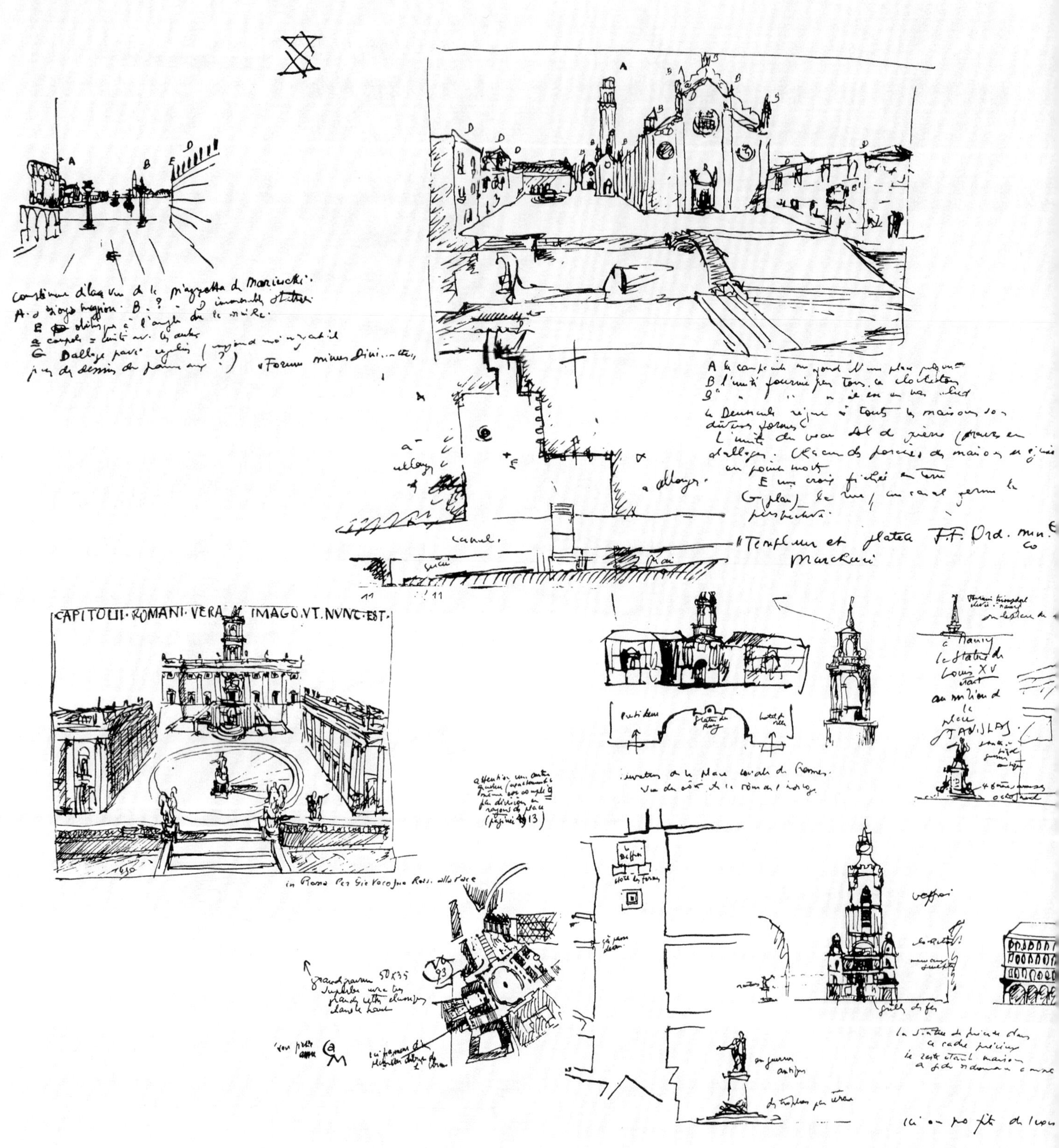

Venise — Rome — France

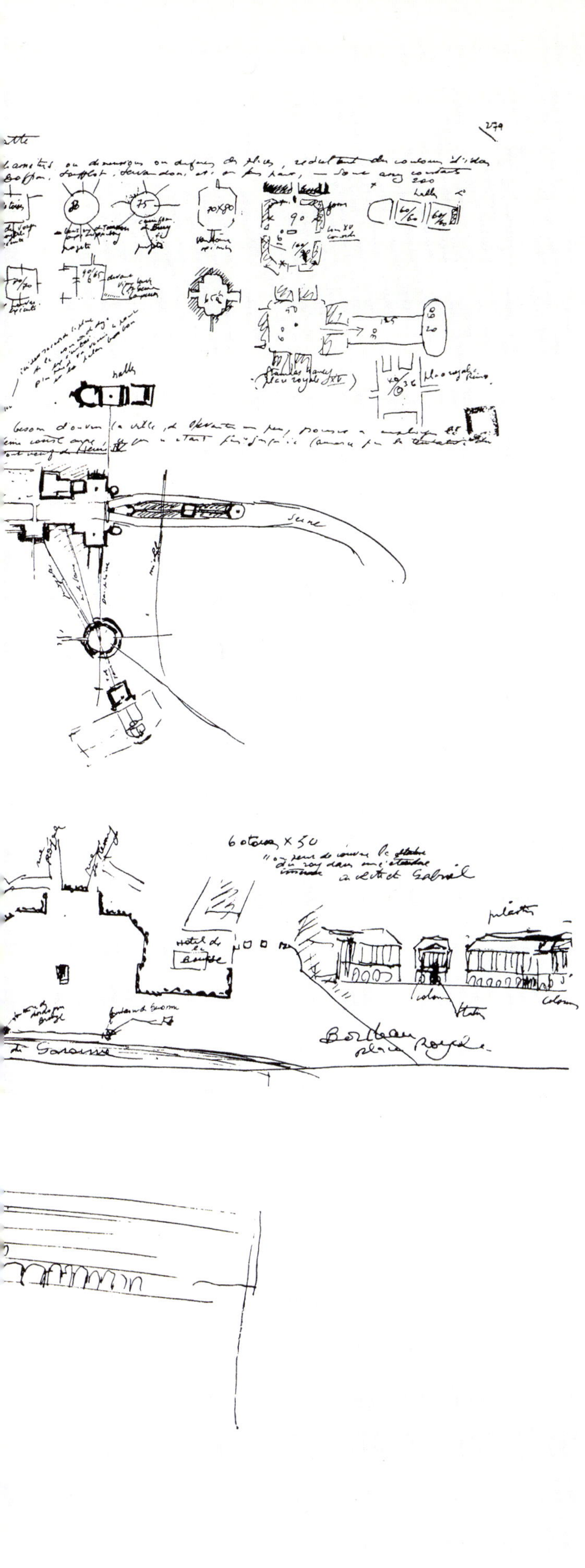

Left. Page from *Oeuvre complète: Volume 1, 1910–29*, reproducing sketches Jeanneret made on his trips to Venice, Rome, and France

Above. Notes by Jeanneret about various family members and friends in his life, including Léon Perrin; William Ritter and Janko Csadra; Albert Jeanneret; Auguste Perret; Charles Auguste Humbert; and Rose Vildra, 30 April 1917

The young architect looks back, 1915

Jeanneret visited Paris several times between July and September 1915 to study books and prints at the Bibliothèque Nationale in preparation for the book he was planning to write, "La construction des villes" (never completed). While there, he made many sketches of the buildings and monuments he had seen on his trips to Venice and Rome, plus several in France. He later assembled these for a page in his *Oeuvre complète: Volume 1, 1910–29*, shown here.

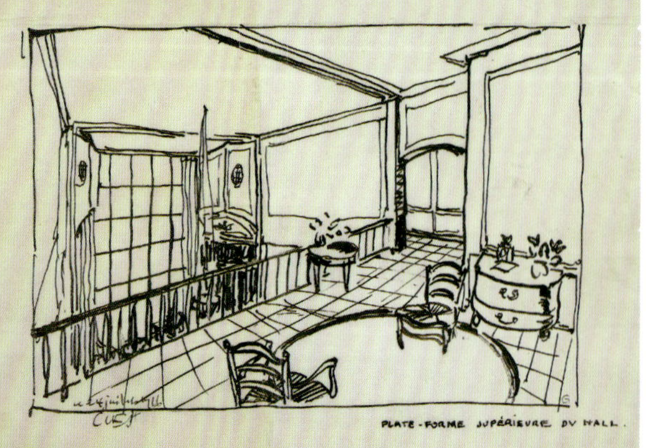

The last hometown commission: Villa Schwob, La Chaux-de-Fonds, 1916–17

The Schwobs were another wealthy watch-making family, who commissioned Jeanneret to design a distinguished showplace. He took this as an opportunity to synthesize the lessons of classicism gleaned from his travels, the industrial aesthetic of the German Werkbund, and his own investigations into concrete construction and the Dom-ino system.

Though awkward in certain respects, the composition represents the initial combination of motifs that would be present in Le Corbusier's work for decades to come, including double-height living spaces with an upper gallery, and the complex progression through spaces that would be known as the *promenade architecturale*.

7
CUISINE
OFFICE
VESTIAIRE
PREAU COUVERT
SALLE A MANGER
LIVING ROOM
SALLE DE JEUX
COIN DE FEU
BIBLIOTHEQUE
LE PROPRIÉTAIRE:
L'ARCHITECTE:
LA CHAUX-DE-FONDS 8. SEPT. 1916.
VILLA DE Mr ANATOLE SCHWOB - RUE DU DOUBS 167 PLAN DU REZ-DE-CHAUSSEE ECHELLE 1:50

VUE DE LA COUR CROISÉE
1917

VUE INTÉRIEURE DU PAVILLON
3 mars
1917

SALLE DE BAINS

PLATE-FORME SUPÉRIEURE DU HALL

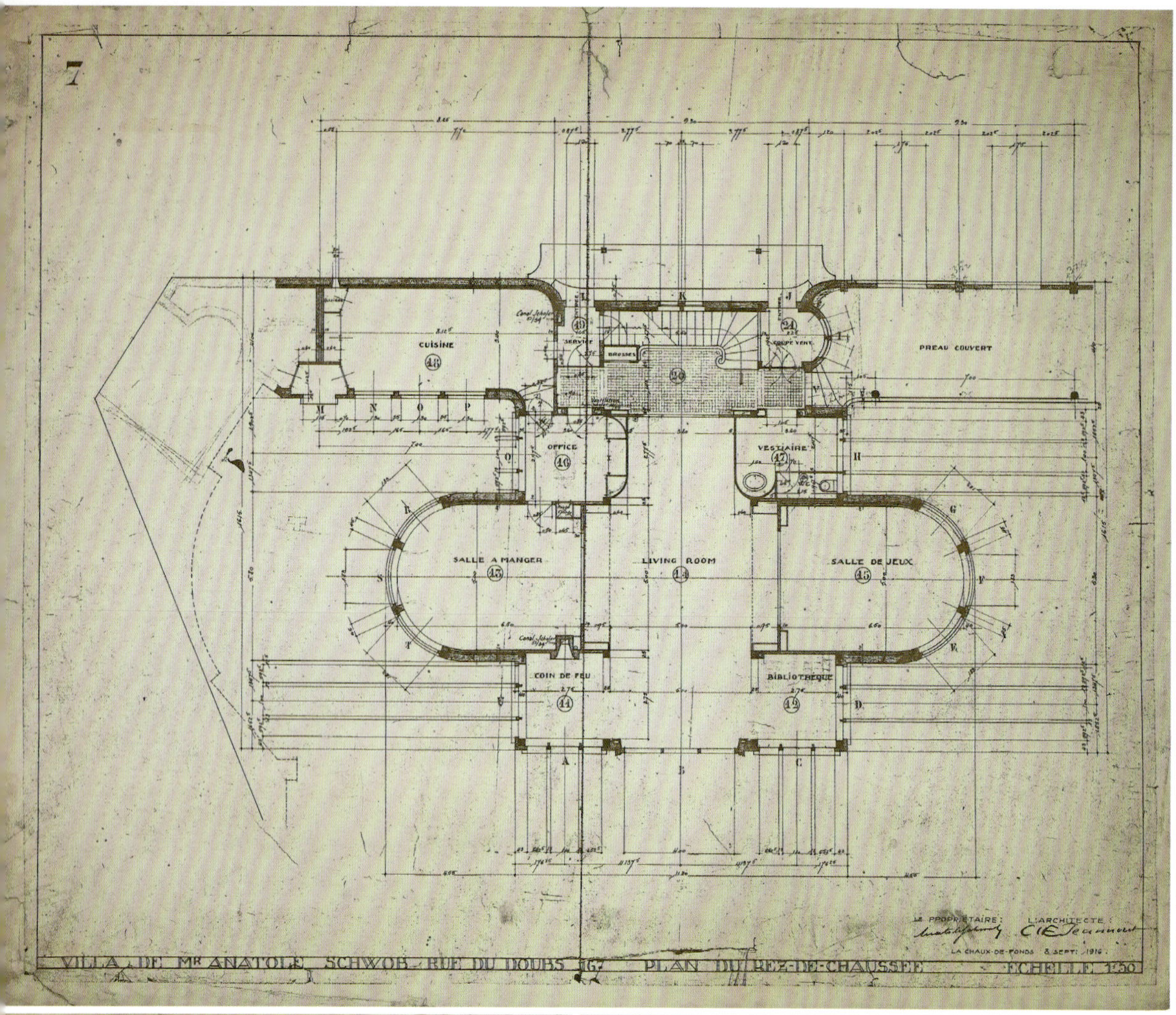

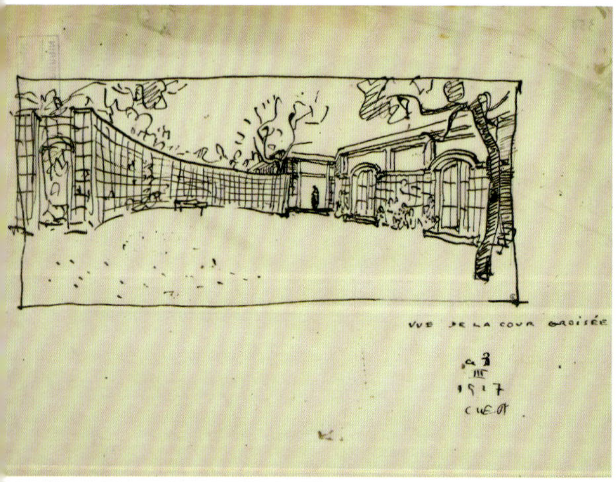

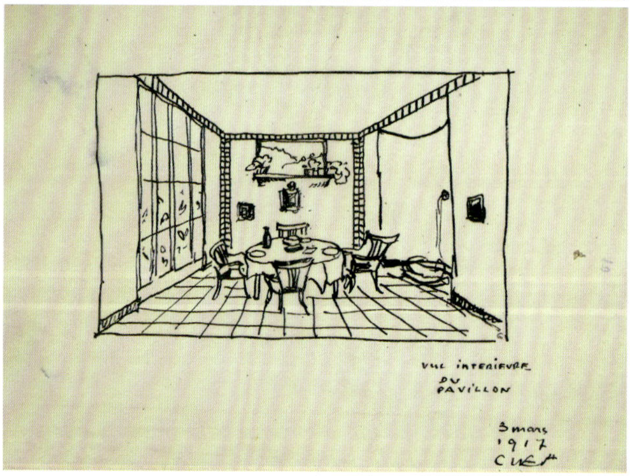

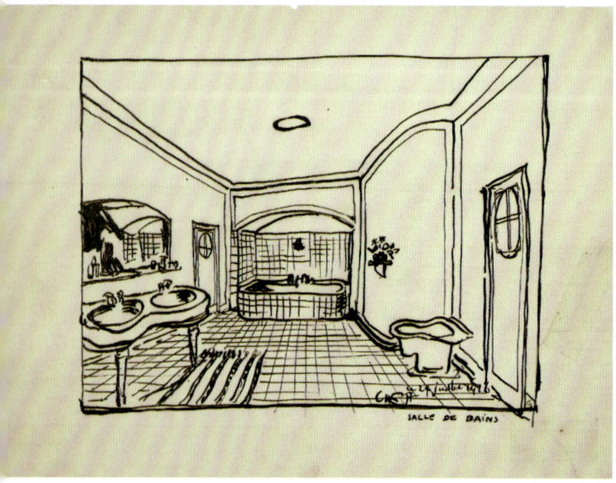

Opposite, top. Ground-floor plan, 1916, Villa Schwob, La Chaux-de-Fonds, 1916–17

Opposite, bottom. Clockwise from top left:

Renderings of courtyard, dining pavilion interior, hall on upper landing, bathroom, all 1917

Right. Attic solarium, west facade

Below left. View from southwest

Below right. View from northwest

Bottom. View from southeast

Opposite.
Le Corbusier, Paris, c. 1920

2 Becoming Le Corbusier (1917–1926)

When Jeanneret relocated to Paris in 1917, he had two quite different careers in mind. The first was to establish himself as an avant-garde painter in association with Amédée Ozenfant, to whom he was introduced by Auguste Perret in December 1917. Ozenfant had already founded an art and fashion journal, *L'Elan*, and managed a fashion boutique. This career was moderately successful for Jeanneret. Ozenfant taught him how to paint in his Purist style, and they wrote two books together, *Après le cubisme* (1918; *After Cubism*) and *La peinture moderne* (1925; *Modern Painting*). These, plus their articles and exhibitions, created a small stir in the Parisian avant-garde scene. By 1918 Jeanneret had moved into an attic apartment on the rue Jacob, close to the fashionable Left Bank cafés on the boulevard Saint-Germain.

The more ambitious project was to become an industrial architect and to make a quick fortune as a manufacturer and entrepreneur. For three years Jeanneret made designs for industrial buildings in reinforced concrete, most of which were never built. He also took on the directorship of a small factory in the Paris suburb of Alfortville, making bricks and tiles from the waste product of a power plant. Both enterprises, as well as a number of other harebrained schemes, were total failures, and by 1923 Jeanneret was certified bankrupt, heavily in debt to several of his friends and to his father.

Despite all his financial troubles, in the summer of 1920 he founded the magazine *L'Esprit Nouveau* with Ozenfant and Paul Dermée (an experienced journalist and poet). To his parents, who could not understand his industrial aspirations, he wrote: "Business is becoming critical, the vise is tightening. I don't know whether I'm going to survive… My time is therefore pitiless and the Review takes me late into the night." He writes about his hard life, "I have withdrawn into myself, I no longer take any interest in details and have lost any sociability… You have no idea what the struggle in Paris is like. You have to have staked your claim to find this out. And this in the world of ideas."

This period of great anxiety and grueling hard work was also the period in which Le Corbusier's architectural theory was formed and published, and his reputation established. By 1924 he was able to look back on his early years with Nietzschean detachment: "Morally, I have become a free man, happy and joyous. And I can say without stupid pride that every one of my actions now leads toward something that is of public utility; having acquired an elevated moral status, what I do serves to teach others."

"Le Corbusier" was born as the nom de plume for a series of articles that Jeanneret wrote for *L'Esprit Nouveau*. Derived from an ancestor—Lecorbésier—his adopted name takes a form that had particular resonance in France, recalling artists such as Charles Le Brun or even Le Douanier Rousseau. *L'Esprit Nouveau*, which ran for five years, established Le Corbusier all over the world as a leading thinker in modern architecture and design. The books and exhibitions with which he publicized his ideas, and the houses he began to design in Paris and elsewhere in 1922, launched his architectural career, and by 1925 he was at least solvent. The first of four books to be published from *L'Esprit Nouveau* articles was *Vers une architecture* (1923; *Toward an Architecture*), which, in its slightly altered second edition in 1925, became one of the most reprinted books on architecture of the twentieth century. His *Urbanisme* (1925; *The City of Tomorrow*) was also very influential, and both books were translated quickly into multiple languages, including German and English.

arts a new life Paris, 1917

Jeanneret was in line at the passport office in Neuchâtel, Switzerland, planning to get the papers needed so that he could work on various municipal projects in Germany, when he impulsively requested that he be allowed entry into France instead. With the help of his old friend Max Du Bois, he found employment in Paris and was introduced to Swiss expatriate and French business circles. He soon moved into the apartment that he would inhabit for the following seventeen years, at 20 rue Jacob, in St. Germain-des-Prés. Amenities in the sixteenth-century town house were few, but its charm and the vitality of the bohemian neighborhood comforted and invigorated Jeanneret.

Jeanneret in his apartment, 20 rue Jacob, Paris, c. 1920, with drafting tools (opposite), reclining in bed (right), and at his writing desk (below). The photographs document his emerging identities as an architect, artist, and writer.

d'une destinée autre, la mienne, la dure et véhémente, la solitaire et violente et infatigable.
Cette ville est belle, et la vie s'y développe bonne!
Mes pensées d'art s'élèvent vers la plastique, une forme, une ligne toujours plus ésotérique. Mes essais sont difformes, décevants. Toute mon imagination travaille. Je veux une clarté, un poli, une netteté qui ne tiennent que par crayon, discipline de rythme, et modulation de couleur. Et je peins des ordures. Mes femmes sont d'une lascivité bestiale, grossières, en rut. Et je m'arrête de toucher une femme nue, tant son dos, ses seins, sa bouche sont d'une adorable matière, sont comme un rêve surgi sur de mes doigts rudes je gâterais. Mes esprits de sens restent presque en dehors de la réalité et j'ai une plus intime joie douloureuse à enfoncer ma langue dans une grande rose fraîche, une de ces roses de ces jours où il y en a plein mes chambres, si grandes, si rouges, si denses, si profondes, et dont le parfum est une salive d'autant plus rafraîchissante!
Je perds ces temps de trop de temps de bon, et mon courage s'effondre devant l'idée d'un tableau d'art à commencer.
Jetés en vingt minutes pressées, son [illegible] sur un papier, à violentes [illegible] d'ocre rouge et de bleu, c'était l'enivrante promesse d'un talent possible qui ne demanderait que le temps de s'exprimer. Mais j'envisage peut-être chaque semaine un bon jour entier pour

~~peindre seulement~~, c'est l'angoisse ~~de toute~~ une vocation qui se présente. Peindre avec sérieux? Halte-là, c'est donc devenir peintre. Je recule devant cet engrenage vers lequel ma main se dirige.
Et au dedans de moi, l'élection déjà s'est faite. D'instinct je rentre chez moi pour fuir les camaraderies futiles. Ou si je vais vers l'attirance des boulevards où sont les femmes, c'est pour trouver une expression de la plus idéale mathématique à ce rêve de beauté que mes pinceaux s'ingénient à vouloir créer.
Des rencontres brusques: hier un mot d'une conversation sur le tombeau des Médicis, et c'est toute cette journée de dimanche, Michel Ange et Léonard qui me hantent. Les femmes de Titien et de Giorgione. L'Italie toujours! Et toujours plus une peinture formelle, écrite, une clarté égyptienne.
J'ai toujours plus foi dans la peinture moderne, plus foi dans ceux si nombreux qui comme moi rêvent, mais qui mieux doués réalisent.
Comme un homme est seul au monde!
J'ai reçu de maman une longue lettre toute en dehors de la question. D'abord ce canon, ces gothas, qui n'existent plus et n'ont jamais plus l'emmerdé qu'un taon qui vous pique dans une belle course au milieu des champs. Puis surtout une

QUITTANCE DE LOYER

N°
Maison Rue d'Astorg
N° 29
Locataire
Mr Jeanneret
Loyer annuel 6500

Timbre		7 10
Loyer	3250	
Portes et Fenêtres		
Éclairage		
Eau		
Enregistrement		
Droit proportionnel	162 50	
Tapis		
Ascenseur		
Téléphone		
Balayage		
Ramonage		
Taxe municipale		
Total	3419 50	

Je soussigné reconnais avoir reçu de Monsieur Jeanneret la somme de Trois mille deux cent cinquante Fr. pour son loyer des lieux qu'il occupe dans une maison sise Rue d'Astorg 29 & dont je suis Propriétaire.
Les 2 termes d'avance suivant bail 1 avril 1919
Dont quittance sans préjudice du terme courant et sous la réserve de tous mes droits.

Douze juin mil neuf cent dix neuf
Forest
15 R. de Marignan

12-6-19
12-6-19

Paris, le 6 octobre

Police des Habitants de la commune de La Chaux-de-Fonds.

MMS.
Ayant quitté définitivement La Chaux-de-Fonds pour me vouer complètement à mon bureau de Paris, je vous serai obligé de m'indiquer ce que je dois faire pour régulariser ma situation.
Je suis porteur d'un passeport. Mon acte d'origine a été retenu à la Chancellerie d'État.
Concernant le paiement de mes impôts, je vous dirai avoir reconnu au Département cantonal des finances.
Veuillez agréer, MMS, mes salutations distinguées
Ch E Jeanneret
architecte
20 rue Jacob, Paris

Paris le 17 fev. 1918.

Mes bien chers.

Je vous ai sérieusement boudé! Depuis novembre 1917, vous n'aviez pas trouvé le temps de m'écrire; trois mois! Il a fallu les gothas et leurs bombes. J'avais décidé de ne pas rompre le premier cet incroyable silence. Si vous pensez tous les jours à moi comme je pense si fréquemment à vous, il n'en reste pas moins que cela demeure dans l'impalpable. Or un témoignage de temps à autre indispensable, étant donné que nos sens sont organisés pour percevoir objectivement. Vous ne me verrez jamais en retard de correspondance si vous ne m'y incitez pas. Voilà qui est dit.

Or donc les gothas auraient pu me supprimer tout aussi bien que la foule qui le sort fatal avait tiré le mauvais numéro. Il est tombé une bombe tout près de mon bureau et aussi tout près de mon domicile. J'étais alors à mi-chemin, et j'ai passé le temps de l'alerte sur le Pont des Arts d'où le spectacle était saisissant et l'audition complète ..... mais dans le roulement du canon et les coups violents des bombes, je n'ai rien discerné, et c'est le lendemain seulement que j'ai su qu'enfin cette fois, les gothas étaient arrivés sur Paris et y avaient craché leur mitraille. Voici la lune qui revient; avec elle les Boches reviendront. En ce moment, par la nuit glaciale, on entend le vrombissement des avions de garde. C'est une sécurité morale qu'on offre aux Parisiens.

Cette nuit glaciale me vaut des soucis plus impératifs. J'ai à Alfortville, pour plus de 1500 f de marchandise fabriquée ces trois derniers jours et le gel peut, demain avoir tout anéanti. De quoi déranger les calculs humains: Alfortville me prend un temps considérable. Cette entreprise

deviendra intéressante et fructueuse, si les "si" demeurent des "si" ou ne se réalisent point trop méchamment. Depuis mes dernières aventures, je me suis carré d'un scepticisme salutaire qui n'entame du reste point mon courage et mon entrain. Je suis plus que jamais disposé à toutes les tentatives, et muni pour résister aux coups du sort. Il aurait pu se produire que cette lettre fût triomphante. J'ai fait un énorme effort ces deux derniers mois. La symphonie Jackson [?] tendait vers un tutti éblouissant .... Panne. Incident .... peut-être accident! Hélas, malgré ma volonté de réagir, mon coeur est encore faible et souffre.

J'ai assez de vanité pour vouloir sur ces travaux qui fument encore, - de mon aventure là-bas champ-de-tonnerre, - souffler quelques fanfares qui soient comme un pet à leur nez et comme des oriflammes que je brandirais au-dessus d'eux. Tant que cette satisfaction que je poursuis ne m'est pas accordée, mon bagage demeurera obscur comme ce que je vous écris ici. J'attends, je suscite le fait qui me permette cette vengeance d'amour-propre.

A part cela, de ma vie, dont vous désirez des détails, rien, ou peu de choses. En tous cas, et pour n'en plus parler, sachez bien que ni Montparnasse ni Montmartre, selon certaines craintes que vous émites, ne me voient jamais. Tout est de ma vie, entre l'Opéra et St Augustin, le coeur des affaires. Et ma vie n'est que d'affaires, intensément et surtout pour le jour à d'heures ouvrables. Ce serait écoeurant si je n'y découvrais des plaisirs, si je ne me prenais à trouver dans l'intense vie des affaires, bien des secrets de l'esprit humain, des grands du moins des grandeurs.

II

Aussi mon logis demeure-t-il désert, voire même qu'il est certains soirs hostile quand depuis une semaine presque, je n'ai pas déplacé une chaise, si tant est que la mort se manifeste jusque dans ces objets inanimés: une tasse, un rideau, un pot de fleurs, qu'une étagère [main] de femme de ménage a placés selon un rythme qui n'est plus le mien.

Il est vrai que mon bureau est agréable, et dans une situation que j'apprécie tous les jours davantage. Mes débuts à Paris, rue de Belzunce avaient été sinistres.

Quelques soirs pourtant, il fait bon et je peins. Tout cela s'enfouit dans un album dont chaque feuillet recueille une sensation. De plus en plus je me confirme dans ce sentiment que l'homme travaille pour lui seul, pour assouvir ces étranges passions qui sont nées avec lui et dont il est esclave. Et pourtant la possibilité de vivre, - je ne le point condamne, exige que cet effort soit connu, discuté, haï ou aimé, des autres; il faut se mêler aux hommes.

Nous avons découvert avec Ozenfant que nous sommes voisins, lui rue de Penthièvre, moi rue d'Astorg, à 100 mètres l'un de l'autre. Nous dînons souvent ensemble, et sa compagnie m'est des plus précieuses. Il est de cent coudées au-dessus de moi; sa peinture est d'un sérieux qui permet toutes espérances dans le nouveau courant d'idées qui renie le relâché et veut s'harmoniser à la splendeur de la science; son esprit est tout de belle philosophie, de culture positive étayant le rêve le plus hardi.

Il a sa vie comme chef d'une des plus délicates maisons de couture, de pair avec la soeur de Poiret - qui est brouillée avec son frère -.

Mais aussi, chez Ozenfant, dans son bureau, le sort imbécile fait des siennes, et dans le terrain du reste. Les novateurs ne peuvent échapper à leur destinée et celle-ci ne leur fait pas faux bond.

Eh oui, cher papa, ta lettre était un peu "j'm'en fous", ce qui n'est pas du tout une louange. Dire ou écrire « Est-ce donc que l'homme est redevenu une bête pour ...; a-t-il perdu toute noblesse? ... etc. » Tu sais bien que non. C'est de la viande creuse pour contourner le vrai problème. L'homme des tranchées n'est pas une bête et il est de la plus sublime noblesse; et ils sont des millions dans tous les pays comme ça. La guerre a au contraire surélevé l'homme. La question est bien plutôt de savoir pourquoi et pour qui on se bat, en vertu de quelle ignoble fausse idole, fausse croyance, criminel faux-idéal. Il faut au contraire envisager le problème vers des solutions car il y en a. Et les pires révolutions de l'esprit ou des usages ne seront jamais rien au regard des horreurs de ces temps. Cher papa, ton avant dernière lettre était magnifique de style et d'idées. Pour ta prochaine, secoue-toi! Mille pardons mais c'est parce que je sais que tu le peux; c'est parce que, avec tes si belles qualités, je suis navré de penser que tu ne nous en laisses pas assez de souvenirs palpables. Je te l'ai déjà dit cent fois: à ton infect métier, car tu avais le plus beau remède. Il en est temps encore. Tu devrais écrire le journal

Opposite, top. Pages from Jeanneret's journal, 12 May 1918, expressing anxiety over his "entire career that is beginning to take shape."

Opposite, bottom left. Rent receipt signed by Jeanneret's landlord, 12 June 1919, for his office at 29 rue d'Astorg

Opposite, bottom right. Jeanneret to officials in La Chaux-de-Fonds, 6 October 1921. Responding to an inquiry about outstanding taxes, Jeanneret explains, from Paris, that he has established permanent residence in France.

Above. Jeanneret to his parents, 17 February 1918, writing about the war—bombs are falling near his office and apartment in Paris—and questioning "why and for what we're fighting?" He describes his friendship with Amédée Ozenfant as "crucial."

Watercolor drawings, 1917, based on Jeanneret's visits to Parisian brothels

Clockwise from top left:

Groupe de trois nus féminins (Group of Three Nude Women)

Couple enlacé (Embracing Couple)

Nu féminin agenouillé (Female Nude Kneeling)

Nu féminin agenouillé (Female Nude Reclining)

Couple de femmes en positions érotique (Female Couple in Erotic Positions)

Opposite. Self-portrait, 1917

"My thoughts on art rise toward ever the plastic, all a form, a line more esoteric. My attempts are formless, disappointing. My entire imagination is at work. I want a clarity, a sheen, a sharpness that tolerate only pure pencil, discipline and rhythm, and moderation of color. And I paint filth. My women are bestially lascivious, prurient, in heat." —Notebook, 12 May 1918

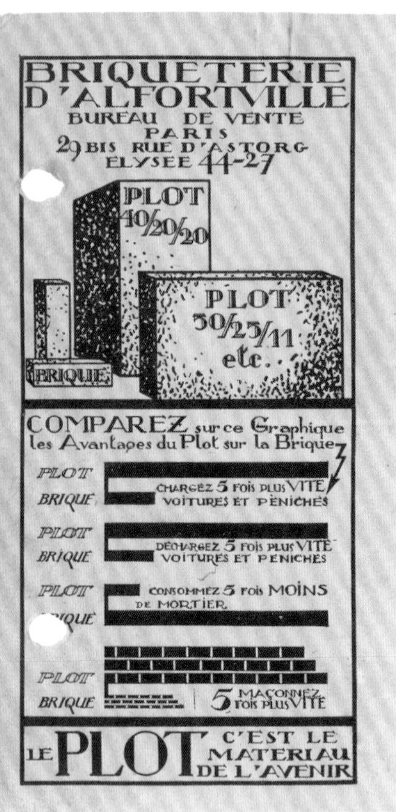

Industrial projects and failed schemes, 1917–18

Shortly after his thirtieth birthday, Jeanneret, with backing from Max Du Bois, opened a factory for making concrete bricks. Although it remained operational until 1921, the factory posed constant financial problems and, following extensive flooding from the Seine, it was finally closed.

Around this time, Jeanneret also designed a number of industrial projects, including slaughterhouses, a hydroelectric plant, an arsenal, and workers' housing. The only one to be realized during his first year in Paris was a water tower Podensac, in soutl western France, which featured an enclosed viewing platform with an interior suggestin the ambience of a library or club room.

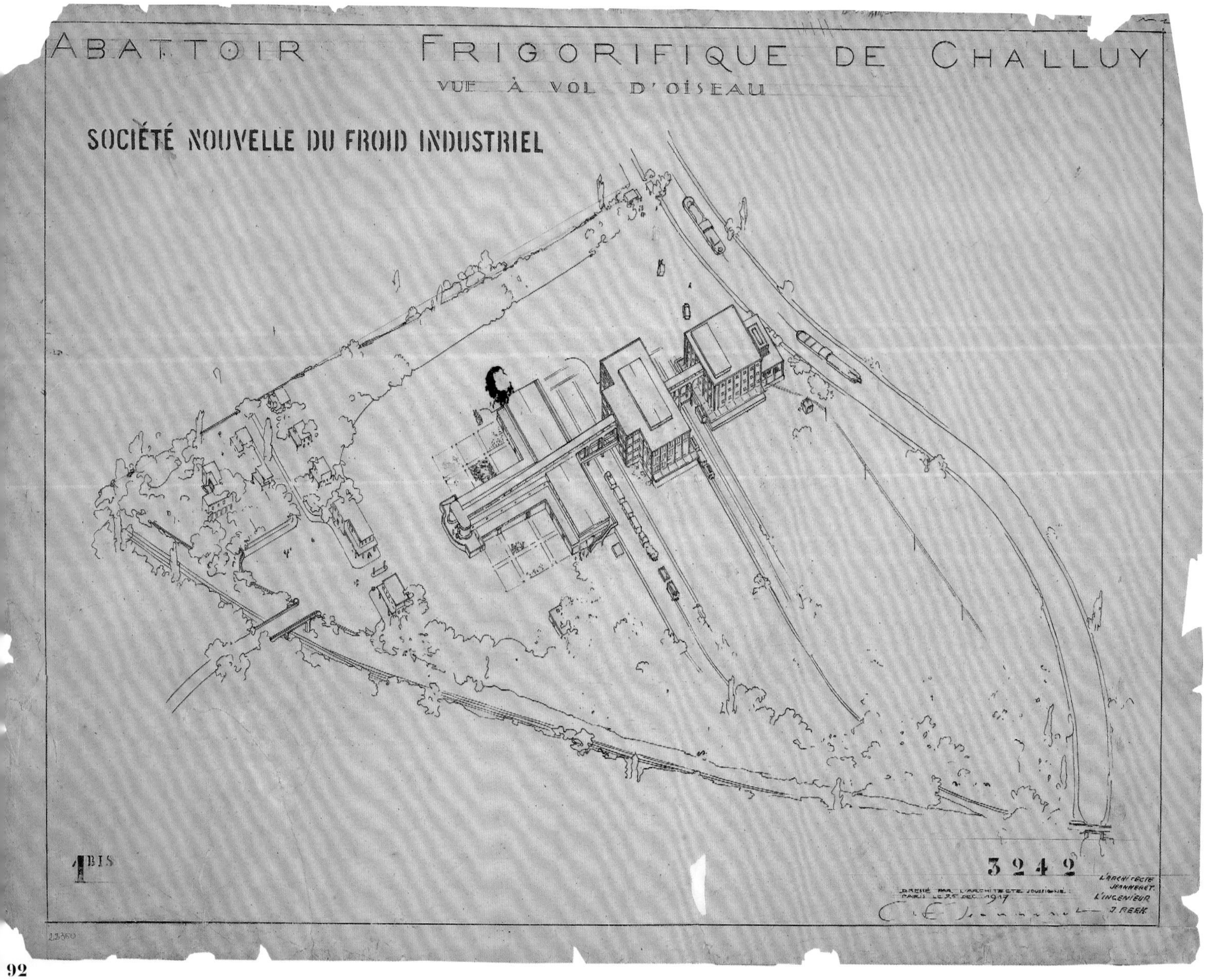

ABATTOIR FRIGORIFIQUE DE CHALLUY

VUE À VOL D'OISEAU

SOCIÉTÉ NOUVELLE DU FROID INDUSTRIEL

1 BIS

3242

DRESSÉ PAR L'ARCHITECTE SOUSSIGNÉ PARIS LE 25 DEC 1917

L'ARCHITECTE JEANNERET. L'INGENIEUR J. REEK.

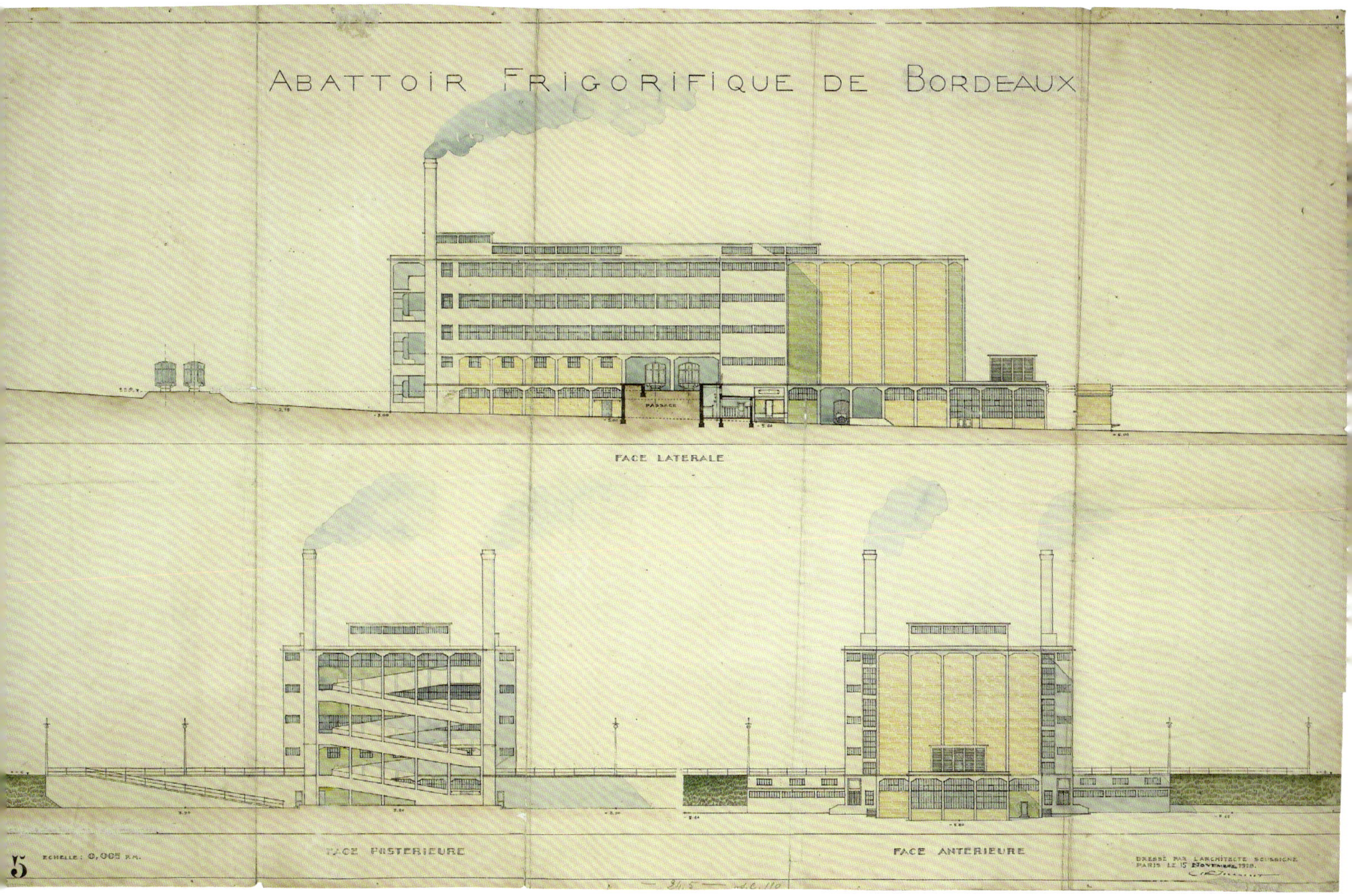

ABATTOIR FRIGORIFIQUE DE BORDEAUX

FACE LATERALE

FACE POSTERIEURE

FACE ANTERIEURE

5 ECHELLE : 0,005 P.M.

DRESSÉ PAR L'ARCHITECTE SOUSSIGNÉ PARIS LE 15 NOVEMBRE 1918.

Opposite, top left. Advertisement for Jeanneret's brick factory in Alfortville, France, near Paris, printed in *L'Esprit Nouveau*, 1920–21

Opposite, top right. Brick factory in Alfortville, 1919

Opposite, bottom. Bird's-eye view, 25 December 1917, refrigerated slaughterhouse at Challuy, France. Jeanneret worked with the Société Nouvelle du Froid Industriel, a group of investors.

Above. Elevations, 15 November 1918, refrigerated slaughterhouse at Garchizy, France

Below. Perspective, hydroelectric plant and dam at L'Isle-Jourdain, western France, 1917

Left. Perspective of interior *gloriette* (viewing room), water tower at Podensac, southwestern France, 1917

Below. Section, elevation, and plan

Opposite, left. Letter of agreement from the Société d'Applications du Béton Armé (SABA) to Jeanneret, confirming terms of his appointment as a consultant

Opposite, right. Water tower at Podensac

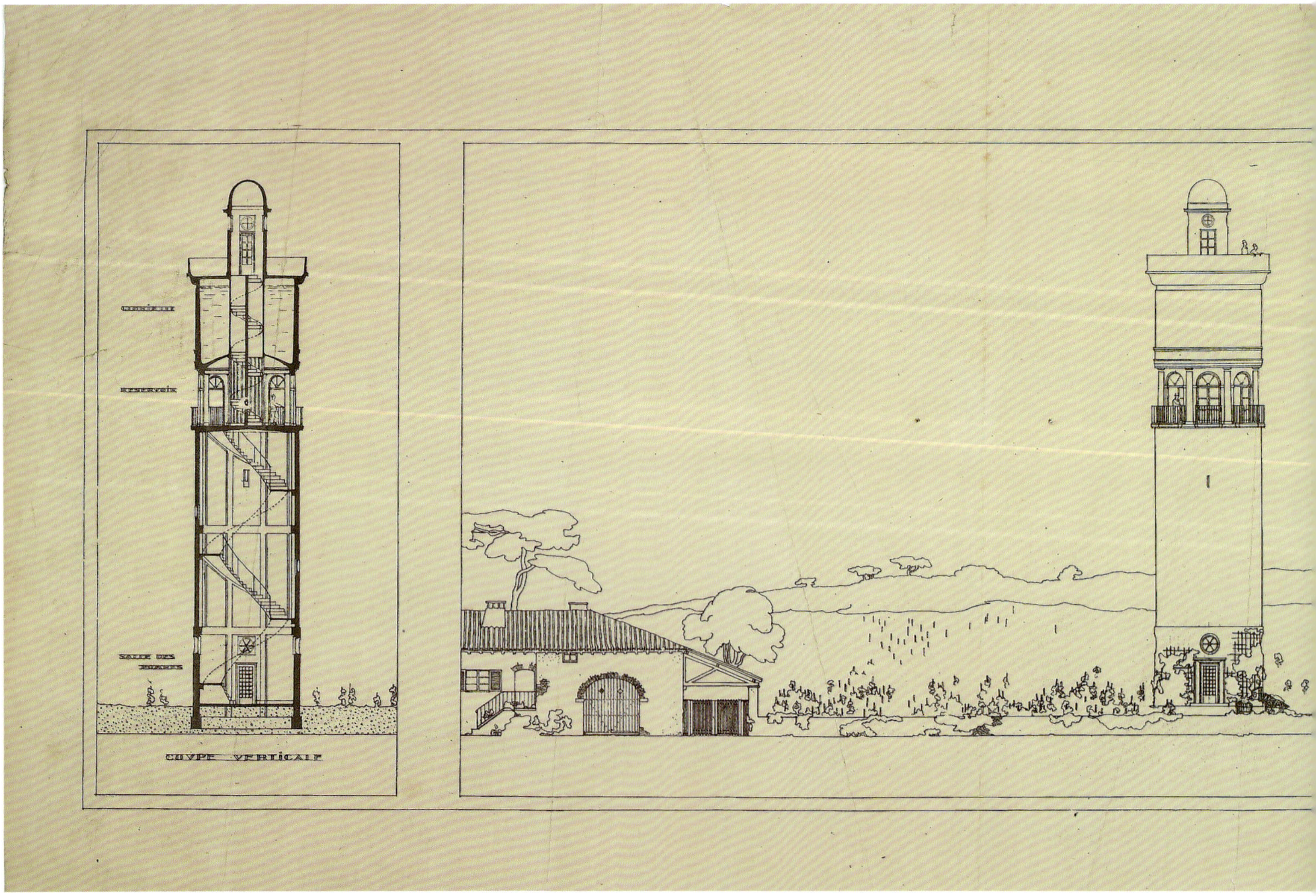

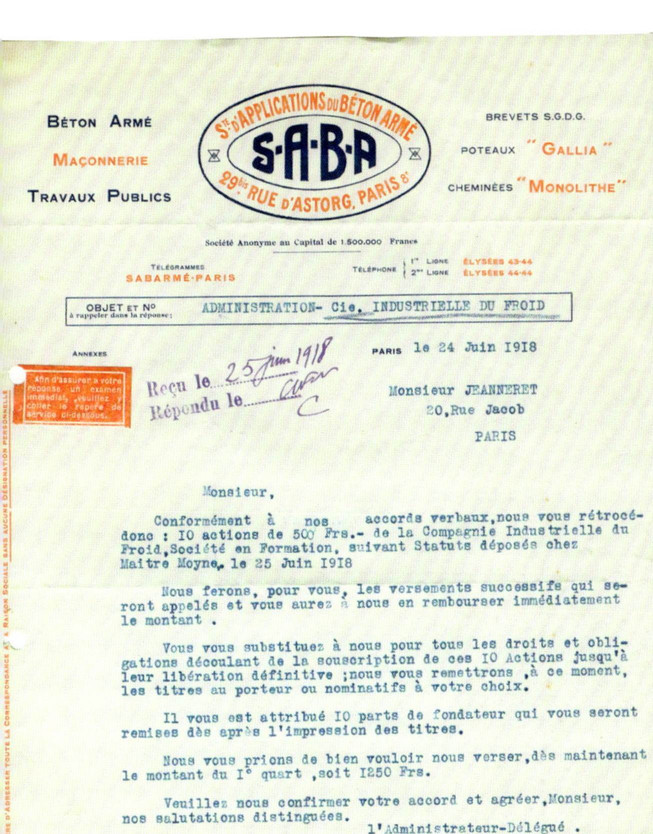

BÉTON ARMÉ

MAÇONNERIE

TRAVAUX PUBLICS

Sté D'APPLICATIONS DU BÉTON ARMÉ

S·A·B·A

29bis RUE D'ASTORG, PARIS 8e

BREVETS S.G.D.G.

POTEAUX "GALLIA"

CHEMINÉES "MONOLITHE"

Société Anonyme au Capital de 1.500.000 Francs

TÉLÉGRAMMES SABARMÉ-PARIS

TÉLÉPHONE 1re LIGNE ÉLYSÉES 43-44
2me LIGNE ÉLYSÉES 44-44

OBJET ET No à rappeler dans la réponse : ADMINISTRATION- Cie. INDUSTRIELLE DU FROID

ANNEXES

PARIS le 24 Juin 1918

Reçu le 25 juin 1918
Répondu le

Monsieur JEANNERET
20, Rue Jacob
PARIS

Monsieur,

Conformément à nos accords verbaux, nous vous rétrocédons : 10 actions de 500 Frs.- de la Compagnie Industrielle du Froid, Société en Formation, suivant Statuts déposés chez Maitre Moyne, le 25 Juin 1918

Nous ferons, pour vous, les versements successifs qui seront appelés et vous aurez à nous en rembourser immédiatement le montant .

Vous vous substituez à nous pour tous les droits et obligations découlant de la souscription de ces 10 Actions jusqu'à leur libération définitive ; nous vous remettrons , à ce moment, les titres au porteur ou nominatifs à votre choix.

Il vous est attribué 10 parts de fondateur qui vous seront remises dès après l'impression des titres.

Nous vous prions de bien vouloir nous verser, dès maintenant le montant du 1° quart , soit 1250 Frs.

Veuillez nous confirmer votre accord et agréer, Monsieur, nos salutations distinguées.

l'Administrateur-Délégué .

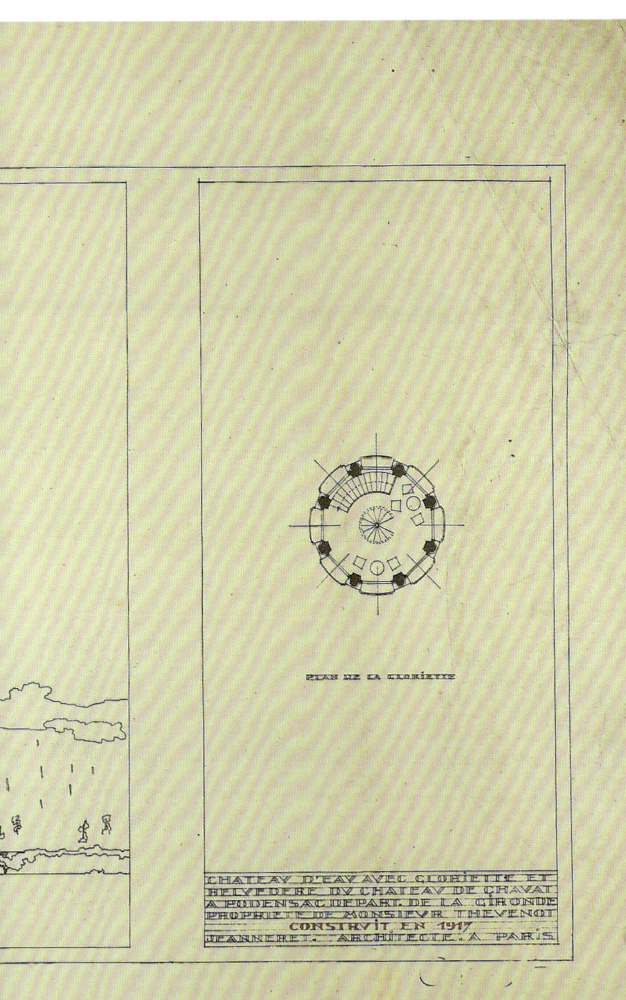

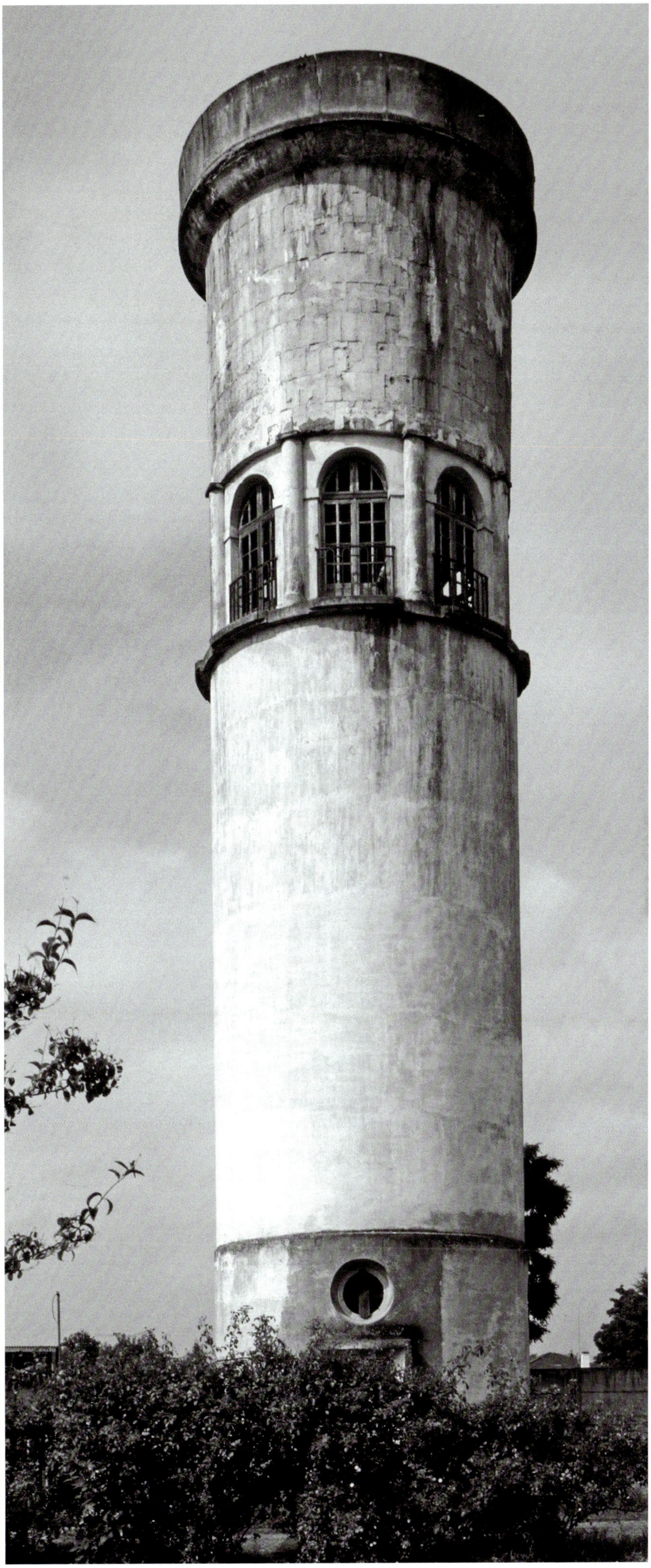

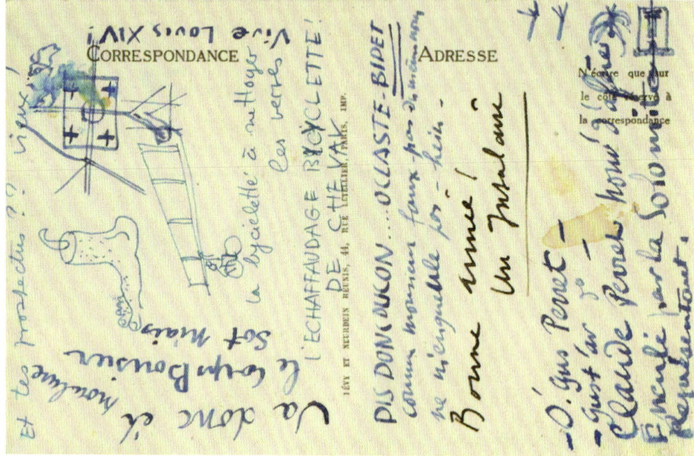

A life-changing friendship: Amédée Ozenfant

In 1916 Auguste Perret founded a group of artists called Art et Liberté. One of the members was Amédée Ozenfant, the son of one of Perret's clients. Ozenfant was a socialite and part-time couturier as well as a painter.

At a meeting of this group, Perret introduced Jeanneret to Ozenfant, and the two quickly embarked on an intense friendship that would last for a decade.

TÉLÉPHONES
ÉLYSÉES 40-87 / 40-88 / 44-27

29bis RUE D'ASTORG
PARIS (8e)

14 juin 1921

Mon cher Jeanneret.

posite, top left. nneret's portrait Amédée enfant, 1918

posite, top right. nt and back of stcard of Paris h doodles by nneret, and the name "Le Corbousier" written on the front, c. 1923

Opposite, bottom. Amédée Ozenfant to Charles-Edouard Jeanneret, 14 June 1921, expressing his concern that Jeanneret has "seemed very unhappy and very much at sea" the last few months. Ozenfant offers advice and reassures him that they remain close friends.

Right and bottom right. Ozenfant (left) and Jeanneret in Rome, 1921

Below. Ozenfant in Rome, 1921

Bottom left. Ozenfant (left) and Jeanneret in a studio portrait, Paris, c. 1923

Jeanneret becomes a Purist

Ozenfant coined the term Purism in *L'Elan*, his avant-garde journal. He defined it as a "cleansing" of form—an idea that immediately appealed to Jeanneret.

The Purist aesth[e]... became the great[est]... creative bond between the Parisian artist an[d]... the Swiss archite[ct]...

Left. Vue sur les toits de Paris (View of Paris Rooftops), c. 1917. One of Jeanneret's earliest oil paintings shows the view from his rue Jacob apartment.

Bottom left. La Cheminée (The Mantelpiece), 1918. Le Corbusier later wrote in *New World of Space* (1948) that this was his first painting, though the existence of earlier paintings disprov[es] the claim.

Bottom right. Natu[re] morte à l'oeuf (Sti[ll] Life with an Egg) 1919

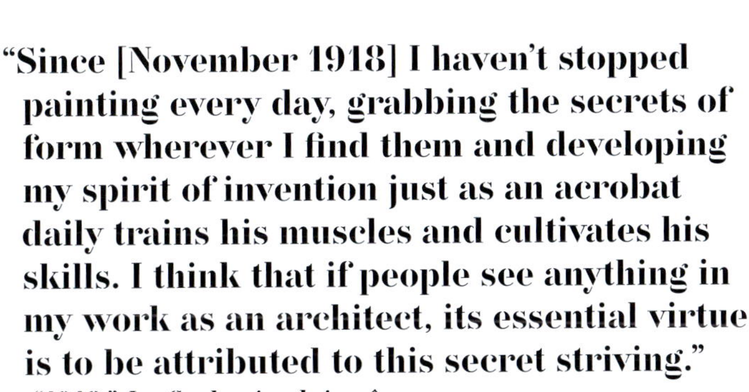

"Since [November 1918] I haven't stopped painting every day, grabbing the secrets of form wherever I find them and developing my spirit of invention just as an acrobat daily trains his muscles and cultivates his skills. I think that if people see anything in my work as an architect, its essential virtue is to be attributed to this secret striving."
—"1918," Le Corbusier lui-même

Clockwise from top left:

Amédée Ozenfant, *Flacon, guitare, verre et bouteilles à la table verte* (Flask, Guitar, Glass, and Bottles on a Green Table), 1920. The work shares formal and compositional similarities with Jeanneret's paintings of the time (see *Composition à la lanterne et à la guitare*, top right). Their works followed a geometric grid, and both artists reduced objects to minimal – even architectural – forms.

Composition à la lanterne et à la guitare (Composition with Lantern and Guitar), 1920

La bouteille de vin rouge (Bottle of Red Wine), 1922

Nature morte à la pile d'assiettes et au livre (Still life with Stack of Plates and Book), 1920

Nature morte à la cruche blanche sur fond bleu (Still Life with White Pitcher on Blue Background), 1920

commentaires
sur l'art et la vie moderne

Ier VOLUME — PRIX DE CE VOLUME ~~4 fr. 50~~ 5 fr.

OZENFANT ET JEANNERET

APRÈS LE CUBISME

DEUXIÈME ÉDITION

MDCCCCXVIII

PARIS
Édition des Commentaires
5, rue de Penthièvre, 5

TABLE DES MATIÈRES

			Pages
INTRODUCTION			1
CHAPITRE I — OÙ EN EST LA PEINTURE	AVANT LE CUBISME		12
	LE CUBISME	Le Cubisme et l'Opinion (*l'Opposition*)	14
		La Non-Représentation	14
		L'Obscurité	15
		L'Impropriété des Titres	16
		La quatrième Dimension	16
		Critique du Cubisme	17
		Le Cubisme et l'Opinion (*le Triomphe*)	19
CHAPITRE II — OÙ EN EST LA VIE MODERNE	L'ESPRIT MODERNE		26
	LES INCERTITUDES DE L'ART ACTUEL		29
	VERS UN ART CONSCIENT		32
CHAPITRE III — LES LOIS	LES LOIS	La Recherche des Invariants	40
		Qu'est-ce qu'une Loi?	41
		Recherche des Lois	41
		Parallèle entre les Méthodes d'analyse de la Science et celles de l'Art	42
		But de l'Analyse	43
		Mécanisme de l'Émotion	43
		Les Lois et leurs rapports avec l'Art plastique. Le Choix. Anthropocentrisme, Anthropomorphisme	45
CHAPITRE IV — APRÈS LE CUBISME	LE TABLEAU	Les Lois naturelles au point de vue plastique	53
		Le Choix	54
		Forme, Couleur	55
		Les Proportions	55
		Conception	55
		Les Déformations	57
		L' « Effet »	58
	LE PURISME		59

THOMAS
TABLEAUX
5, RUE DE PENTHIÈVRE 5, PARIS
(PRÈS LA RUE DE LA BOÉTIE)

DU 22 DÉCEMBRE AU 11 JANVIER 1919

EXPOSITION
OZENFANT & JEANNERET

Ouverte la semaine
de 2 h. 1/2 à 6 heures.

INVITATION
pour deux personnes.

GALERIE "L'EFFORT MODERNE"
Léonce Rosenberg
19, Rue de La Baume - Paris (VIIIe)

... ET DU CUBISME VERS UNE RENAISSANCE PLASTIQUE

ŒUVRES PAR:

Georges BRAQUE, J. CSAKY, Albert GLEIZES, Juan GRIS, Henri HAYDEN, Auguste HERBIN, JEANNERET, Henri LAURENS, Fernand LÉGER, MARCOUSSIS, Jean METZINGER, OZENFANT, Pablo PICASSO, Jacques VILLON, Georges VALMIER

INVITATION
VALABLE POUR DEUX PERSONNES

Exposées du 25 Mars au 25 Avril 1922 inclus
de 10 à 12 heures et de 14 à 17 heures
(Dimanches et Fêtes exceptés)

Top. Cover and table of contents, *Après le cubisme*, by Ozenfant and Jeanneret, Paris, 1918. The publication was the first volume in a new series, "Commentaires sur l'art et la vie moderne," published by Edition des Commentaires.

Above left. Invitation to Jeanneret and Ozenfant's exhibition at Galerie Thomas, Paris, 22 December 1918–11 January 1919

Above right. Invitation to... *et du cubisme vers une renaissance plastique*, exhibition of paintings at Léonce Rosenberg's Galerie de "L'Effort Moderne," Paris, 25 March–25 April 1922. Ozenfant and Jeanneret each had one painting in the show.

Opposite, top. Cover and interior pages, *Bulletin Thomas*, no. 1, 15 November 1918. Catalog for the exhibition at Galerie Thomas

Opposite, bottom. Jeanneret in front of Galerie Thomas

The first exhibitions and *Après le cubisme*, 1918

Ozenfant encouraged Jeanneret to paint, and in 1918 the two mounted a joint exhibition of their work at Galerie Thomas in Paris. The related volume that they produced together, *Après le cubisme* (*After Cubism*), was a sort of Purist manifesto, which expressed with great clarity the principles of what Jeanneret and Ozenfant considered to be a revolutionary move away from Cubism to a more ordered, logical, even classical visual expression.

BULLETIN THOMAS

N° 1

15 NOVEMBRE 1918.

PRIX 1 fr. 50

chez THOMAS

5, RUE DE PENTHIÈVRE

(près la Rue la Boëtie)

PARIS

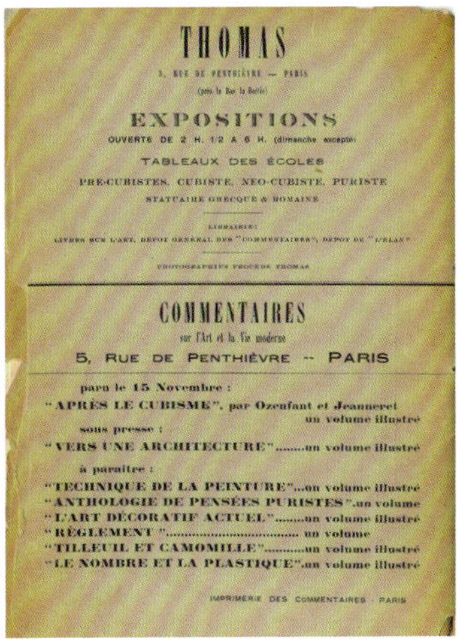

THOMAS

5, RUE DE PENTHIÈVRE — PARIS

(près la Rue la Boëtie)

EXPOSITIONS

OUVERTS DE 2 H. 1/2 A 6 H. (dimanche excepté)

TABLEAUX DES ÉCOLES

PRE-CUBISTES, CUBISTE, NEO-CUBISTE, PURISTE

STATUAIRE GRECQUE & ROMAINE

LIBRAIRIE:

LIVRES SUR L'ART, DÉPOT GÉNÉRAL DES "COMMENTAIRES", DÉPOT DE "L'ÉLAN"

PHOTOGRAPHIES PROCÉDÉ THOMAS

COMMENTAIRES

sur l'Art et la Vie moderne

5, RUE DE PENTHIÈVRE -- PARIS

paru le 15 Novembre :

"APRÈS LE CUBISME", par Ozenfant et Jeanneret ... un volume illustré

sous presse :

"VERS UNE ARCHITECTURE" .... un volume illustré

à paraître :

"TECHNIQUE DE LA PEINTURE" ... un volume illustré

"ANTHOLOGIE DE PENSÉES PURISTES" . un volume

"L'ART DÉCORATIF ACTUEL" .... un volume illustré

"RÈGLEMENT" .... un volume

"TILLEUIL ET CAMOMILLE" .... un volume illustré

"LE NOMBRE ET LA PLASTIQUE" . un volume illustré

IMPRIMERIE DES COMMENTAIRES · PARIS

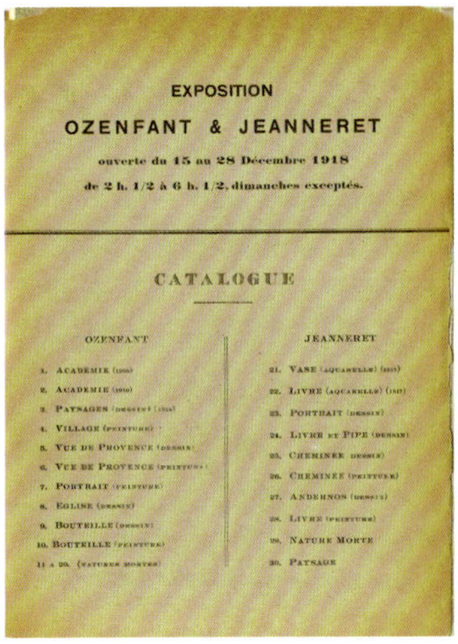

EXPOSITION

OZENFANT & JEANNERET

ouverte du 15 au 28 Décembre 1918

de 2 h. 1/2 à 6 h. 1/2, dimanches exceptés.

CATALOGUE

OZENFANT	JEANNERET
1. ACADÉMIE	21. VASE (AQUARELLE)
2. ACADÉMIE (1910)	22. LIVRE (AQUARELLE)
3. PAYSAGES (DESSINS)	23. PORTRAIT (DESSIN)
4. VILLAGE (PEINTURE)	24. LIVRE ET PIPE (DESSIN)
5. VUE DE PROVENCE (DESSIN)	25. CHEMINÉE (DESSIN)
6. VUE DE PROVENCE (PEINTURE)	26. CHEMINÉE (PEINTURE)
7. PORTRAIT (PEINTURE)	27. ANDERNOS (DESSIN)
8. EGLISE (DESSIN)	28. LIVRE (PEINTURE)
9. BOUTEILLE (DESSIN)	29. NATURE MORTE
10. BOUTEILLE (PEINTURE)	30. PAYSAGE
11 A 20. (NATURES MORTES)	

An important early patron: Raoul La Roche

One of the Swiss expatriates to whom Max Du Bois introduced Jeanneret was the banker and art collector Raoul La Roche, who was to become one of Jeanneret's most important clients in the 1920s. Following completion of the Villa La Roche (current home of the Fondation Le Corbusier) in 1925, Le Corbusier gave his generous client an album of watercolor, pastel, and pencil landscapes and still lifes that is now known as the Album La Roche.

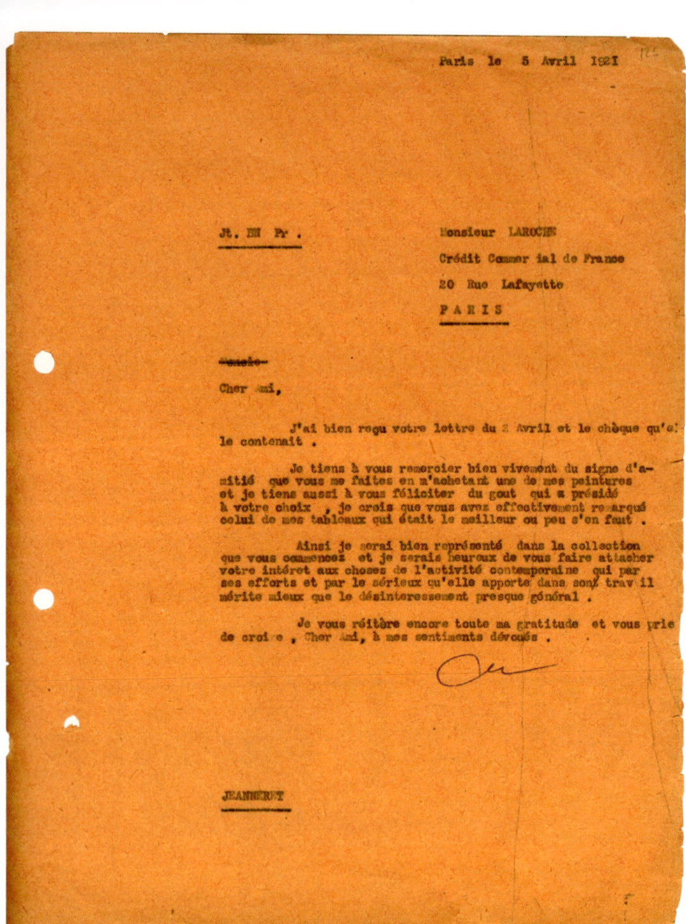

Paris le 5 Avril 1921

Jt. BN Fr.

Monsieur LAROCHE
Crédit Commer ial de France
20 Rue Lafayette
PARIS

~~Cher Ami~~

Cher Ami,

J'ai bien reçu votre lettre du 2 Avril et le chèque qu'elle contenait.

Je tiens à vous remercier bien vivement du signe d'amitié que vous me faites en m'achetant une de mes peintures et je tiens aussi à vous féliciter du gout qui a présidé à votre choix, je crois que vous avez effectivement remarqué celui de mes tableaux qui était le meilleur ou peu s'en faut.

Ainsi je serai bien représenté dans la collection que vous commencez et je serais heureux de vous faire attacher votre intéret aux choses de l'activité contemporaine qui par ses efforts et par le sérieux qu'elle apporte dans son travail mérite mieux que le désinteressement presque général.

Je vous réitère encore toute ma gratitude et vous prie de croire, Cher Ami, à mes sentiments dévoués.

JEANNERET

Opposite, top. Charles-Edouard Jeanneret to Raoul La Roche, 5 April 1921, thanking him for buying one of his paintings and congratulating La Roche on his good taste.

Opposite, bottom. Page from Album La Roche, 1922, depicting the islands of San Giorgio Maggiore and Giudecca, and the Zitelle, seen from Zattere

Above. Pages from Album La Roche, showing views of Lac Léman, Switzerland; and in Venice, the Grand Canal, Giudecca island, and San Giorgio Maggiore

Le Corbu lui-même

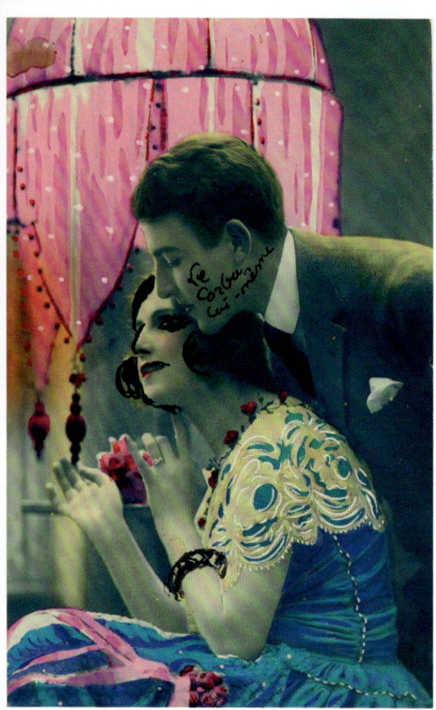

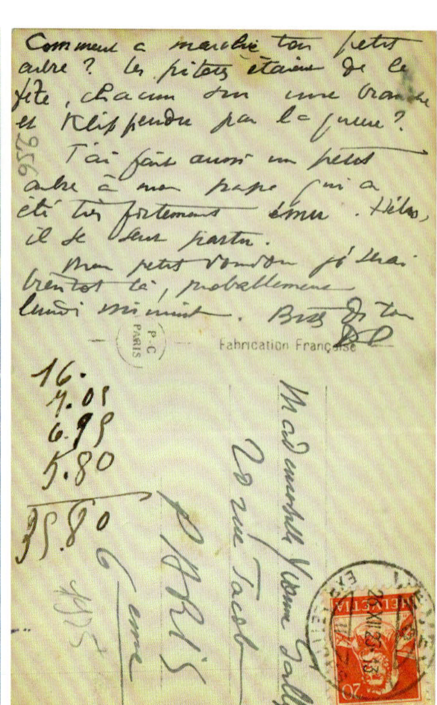

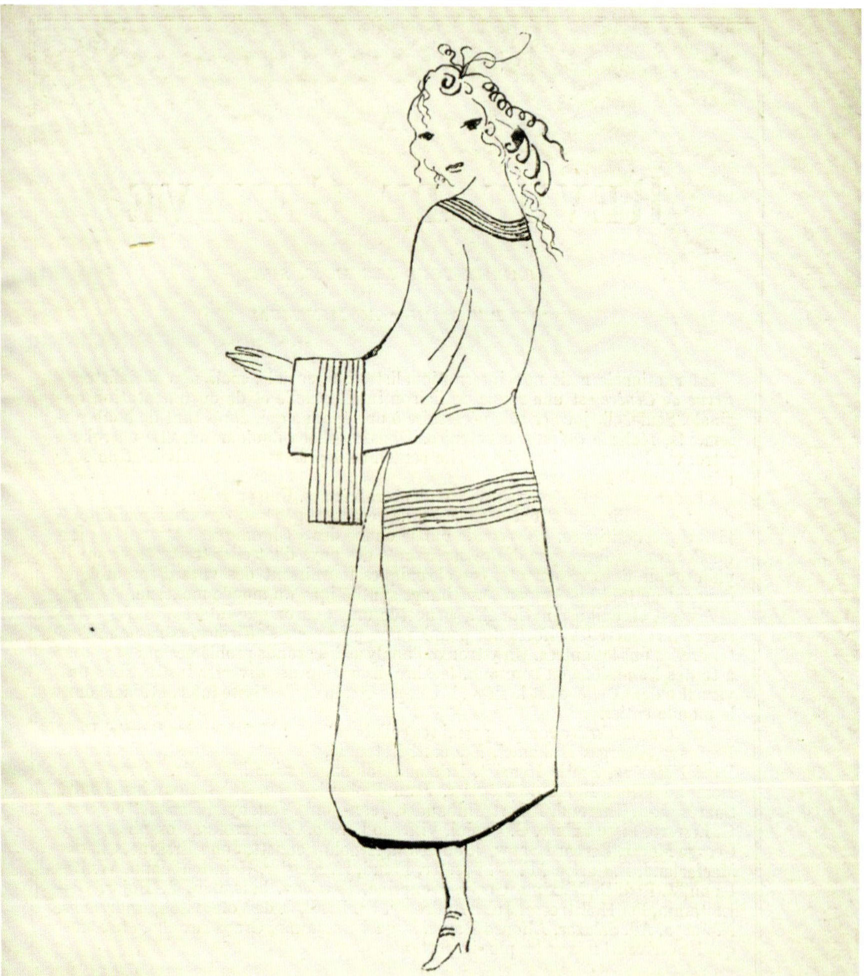

Comment a marché ton petit arbre? Les petits étaient de la fête, chacun son une branche et Klipp pendu par la queue?

J'ai fait aussi un petit arbre à mon papa qui a été très fortement ému. Hélas, il se sent partir.

Mon petit vondon je serai bientôt là, probablement lundi minuit. Bises de ton

Fabrication Française

16.
7.05
6.95
5.80
35.80

Mademoiselle Yvonne Gallis
20 rue Jacob
PARIS
6eme

Meets his future wife: Yvonne Gallis

The relationship between Jeanneret/Le Corbusier and Yvonne Gallis was a private affair; she rarely made an appearance at public functions related to her husband's architectural projects. Born in Monaco, Gallis was a thirty-year-old dressmaker and model when she met Jeanneret in 1922. Her fun-loving personality and irreverent sense of humor countered Jeanneret's cerebral nature.

Dessin de Marie Laurencin
une robe de
Jove
couturier
5, RUE DE PENTHIÈVRE
PARIS

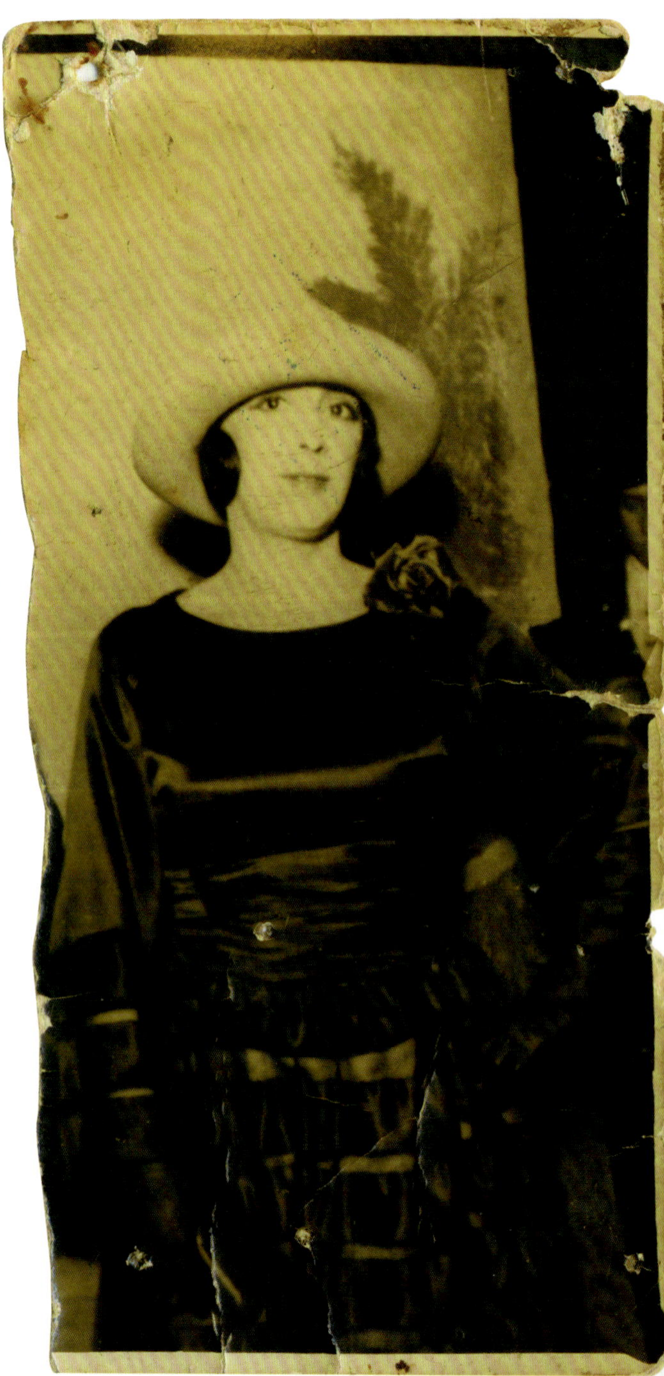

posite, top. Front d back of post- d from Le rbusier, in itzerland, to onne Gallis, in ris, 26 December 25. "My little nvon I'll soon be re..."

Opposite, bottom left. Advertisement, c. 1921, for the couture house Jove, Paris, where Yvonne Gallis worked as a model and salesgirl

Opposite, bottom right. Yvonne Gallis

Above. Le Corbusier (far right), Yvonne Gallis (second from left), and Pierre Jeanneret (third from left) in a studio photograph, Paris, c. 1925

Below, left and right. Le Corbusier, Amédée Ozenfant, Yvonne Gallis, and Pierre Jeanneret in costume

"Every evening, when I had finished running all over town and was alone in my room, I sought in my eyes the visage of Vonvon, and her photo would have consoled me. When I'm home again I'll have something better than the photo, I'll have you. And I'm counting the days."

—Letter to Yvonne Gallis, from Vicenza, Italy, 21 September 1922

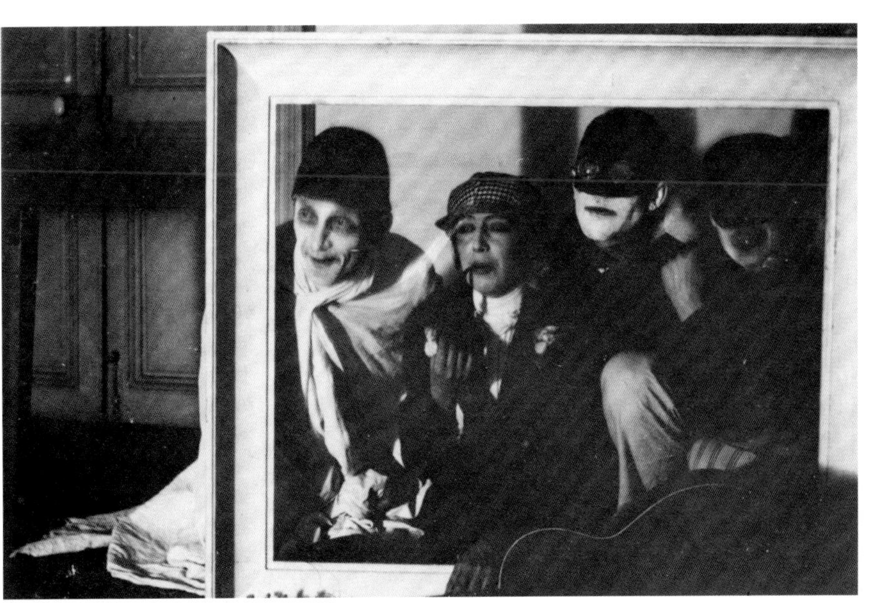

"Fernand Léger recounted as follows his first meeting with Le Corbusier at the Rotonde café in Montparnasse: 'I saw him coming toward me, very stiff, an extra-ordinary object in motion, a kind of cut-out figure topped with a bowler hat and wearing glasses and a clergyman's coat. The object advanced slowly on a bicycle, sticking scrupulously to the rules of perspective.'" —"1920," *Le Corbusier lui-même*

A fellow painter, bohemian, and cyclist: Fernand Léger

One of the most notable of Jeanneret's acquaintances during this period was painter Fernand Léger. Having found common ground in machine-age aesthetics, the two soon formed an enduring friendship.

They shared many evenings together in cafés on the boulevard Montparnasse and routinely indulged in their shared hobby of cycling.

Opposite. André Lhote, poster for gala costume ball and artists' benefit in Montparnasse, Paris, 30 June 1922. Numerous artists, including Léger and Jeanneret, are listed as sponsors of the event, which featured attractions such as clowns, gymnasts, "Hindus," sports, and "miracles."

Above. Left to right: Fernand Léger, Pierre Jeanneret, and Le Corbusier, Spain, 1930

Below. Left to right: Yvonne Gallis, Le Corbusier, Nadia Khodassiévitch, Léger, and unidentified man, 1925

ANDRÉ BAUCHANT Auzouer
ARTISTE PEINTRE le 10 Août
AUZOUER (I.-&-L.) 1924

Monsieur Jeanneret

Bien reçu votre lettre et je finirai votre portrait chez vous n'étant davantage de votre patience
A mon regret je ne puis accepter le chèque de 365.25 pour le [illegible] ce qui n'est pour ainsi que le prix de la matière sans compter mon temps ou jusqu'à ce jour j'ai fait des sacrifices de temps – et dans ce cas je serais formellement disposé à le reprendre – ou le faire mettre en dépôt dans Paris
En janvier vous m'avez parlé de 500 frs je vous faisais [illegible] que je voulais un peu plus et en Mars dernier [illegible]
et autres travaux accessoires – que je désirais davantage ou vous m'avez dit que vous feriez le nécessaire auprès de la personne
J'ai bien trouvé à le vendre comme je vous l'ai annoncé à un prix convenable je n'ai voulu [illegible] que je vous avais donné parole –
Ma dernière lettre qui [illegible] de l'envoi annonce bien que je retoucherai les portraits lors de mon passage chez vous ne vous ayant sous les yeux est ce [illegible] mon intention
Si le chèque pour le [illegible] est de 365.25 ne l'envoyez pas je reprendrai ce tableau ou attendez votre [illegible]
Je vous présente Monsieur l'expression de meilleurs sentiments

A Bauchant

Le char d'Apollon [illegible] par ce qu'il a été [illegible] sur une bonne toile de lin forte et serrée
A vous lire

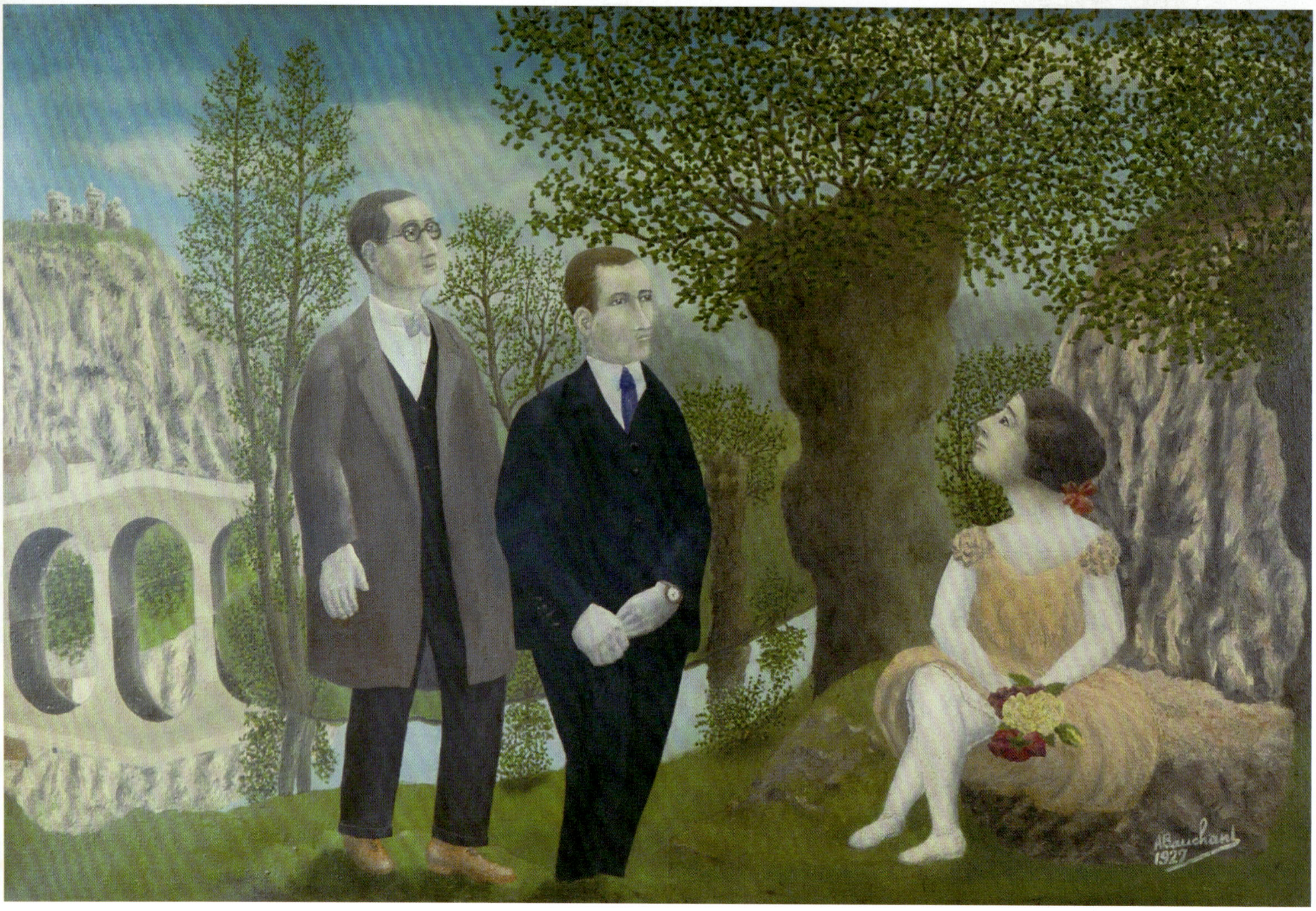

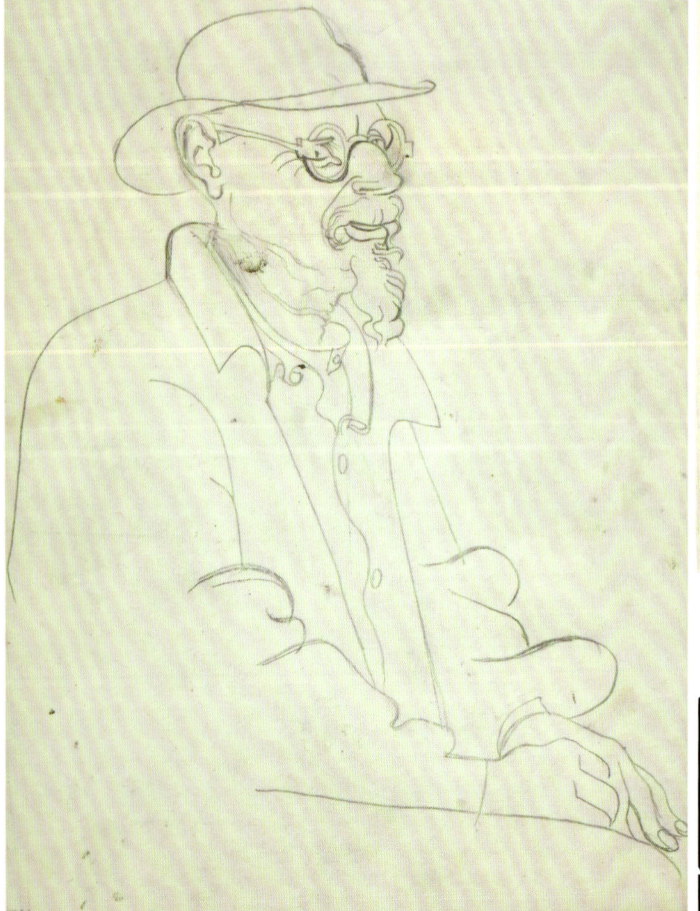

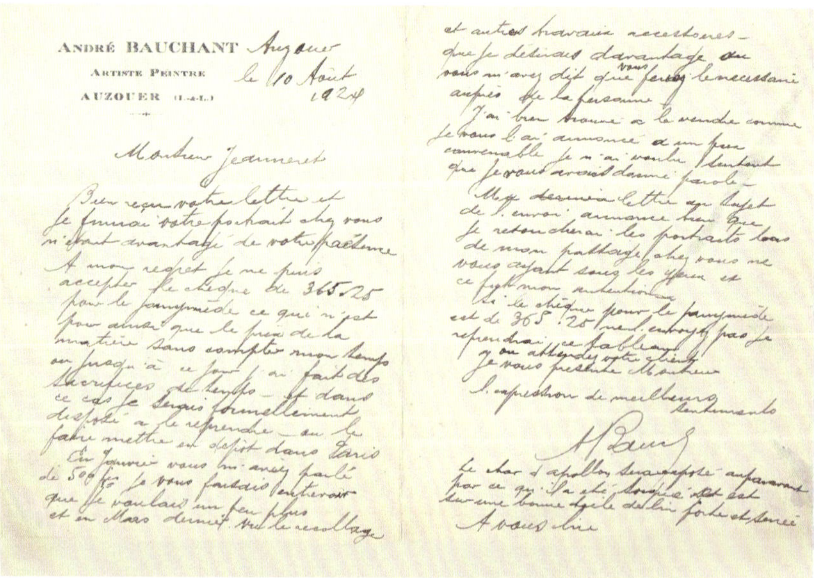

Another painter joins Jeanneret's circle: André Bauchant

Jeanneret became captivated by the work of a painter from the French provinces named André Bauchant. Like Yvonne Gallis, Bauchant had a frank and candid nature that, together with the naive style of his painting, made him popular in Jeanneret and Ozenfant's circle of acquaintances. Jeanneret would help support Bauchant for the following few years – in part by commissioning a portait of himself and Yvonne.

Opposite, top. André Bauchant, *Pierre, Édouard et Yvonne*, 1927. Depicted are Le Corbusier (left), Pierre Jeanneret, and Yvonne Gallis.

Opposite, bottom left. Le Corbusier, portrait of André Bauchant

Opposite, bottom right. André Bauchant to "Monsieur Jeanneret," 10 August 1924, regarding what Bauchant considers to be inadequate payment for a painting and his refusal to accept Jeanneret's check

Top. Left to right: Pierre Jeanneret, Bauchant, Gallis, and Le Corbusier with Bauchant's painting *Pierre, Édouard et Yvonne*, 1935

Above left. Bauchant in his studio in Auzouer, France, 1935

Above right. Left to right: Pierre Jeanneret, Bauchant, and Le Corbusier in Auzouer, France, 1935

An elegant interior in Paris, and early housing projects, 1920–23

During the early 1920s Jeanneret kept his morale and his bank account buoyant through various interior design and industrial housing projects. Among the former, the Villa Berque, an elegant neoclassical town house, was notable for Jeanneret's adaptation of motifs that he had earlier developed in La Chaux-de-Fonds.

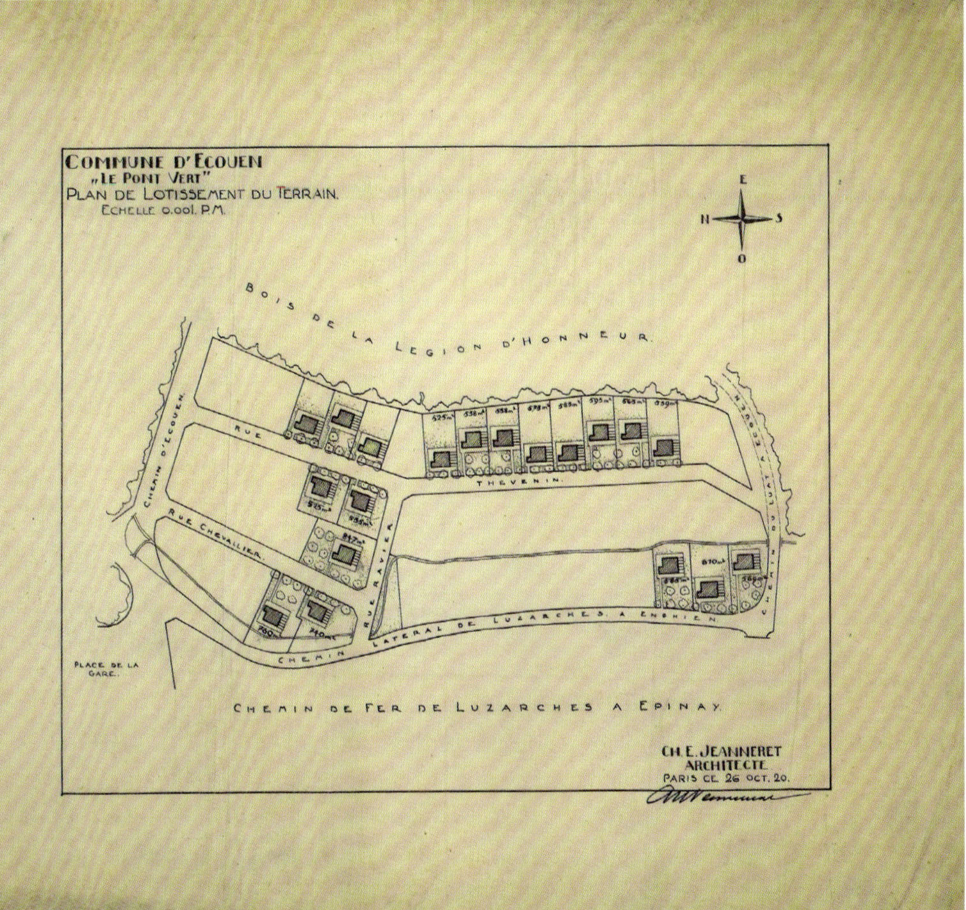

Opposite, top. Rendering of ground-floor living room, Villa Berque, Paris-Auteuil, France, 1921–22

Opposite, bottom. Three views of the concrete terrace added by Le Corbusier, Villa Berque

Top. Study for student housing, Cité Audincourt, France, 1925

Above. Perspective, 30 October 1920, "Le Pont Vert" workers' housing, Ecouen, France, 1923

Right. Site plan, 26 October 1920, "Le Pont Vert"

Jeanneret becomes Le Corbusier: *L'Esprit Nouveau*, 1920–25

In 1920 Jeanneret and Amédée Ozenfant founded the magazine *L'Esprit Nouveau*, which during its five-year life span would publish articles by such avant-garde luminaries as Jean Cocteau, Adolf Loos, and Theo van Doesburg. The magazine also functioned as a platform for its founders, who championed the virtues of Purism in its pages, writing under various pseudonyms. One of those was "Le Corbusier," which Jeanneret and Ozenfant derived from an ancestral name in Jeanneret's family; the latter would use "Le Corbusier" for his architectural projects starting around 1920, but signed his paintings "Charles-Edouard Jeanneret" until 1930.

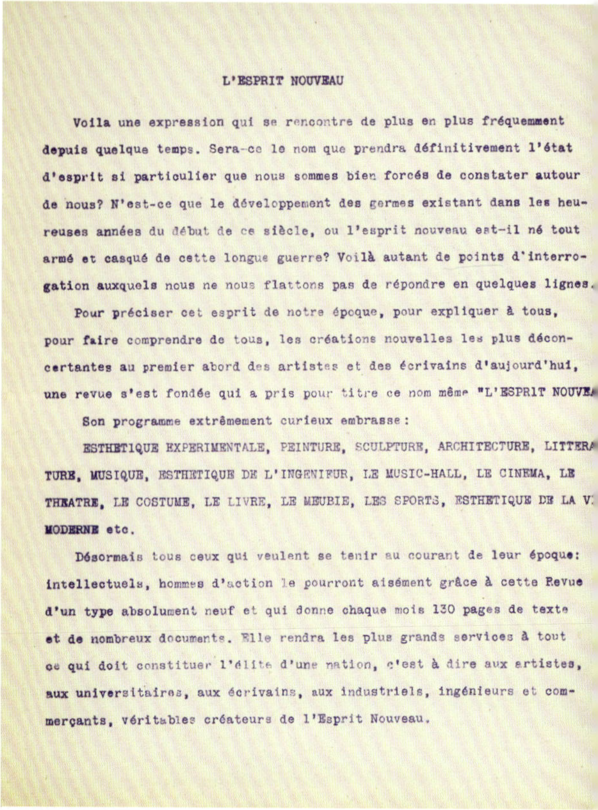

L'ESPRIT NOUVEAU

Voila une expression qui se rencontre de plus en plus fréquemment depuis quelque temps. Sera-ce le nom que prendra définitivement l'état d'esprit si particulier que nous sommes bien forcés de constater autour de nous? N'est-ce que le développement des germes existant dans les heureuses années du début de ce siècle, ou l'esprit nouveau est-il né tout armé et casqué de cette longue guerre? Voilà autant de points d'interrogation auxquels nous ne nous flattons pas de répondre en quelques lignes.

Pour préciser cet esprit de notre époque, pour expliquer à tous, pour faire comprendre de tous, les créations nouvelles les plus déconcertantes au premier abord des artistes et des écrivains d'aujourd'hui, une revue s'est fondée qui a pris pour titre ce nom même "L'ESPRIT NOUVEA

Son programme extrêmement curieux embrasse :

ESTHETIQUE EXPERIMENTALE, PEINTURE, SCULPTURE, ARCHITECTURE, LITTERATURE, MUSIQUE, ESTHETIQUE DE L'INGENIEUR, LE MUSIC-HALL, LE CINEMA, LE THEATRE, LE COSTUME, LE LIVRE, LE MEUBLE, LES SPORTS, ESTHETIQUE DE LA V[illegible] MODERNE etc.

Désormais tous ceux qui veulent se tenir au courant de leur époque: intellectuels, hommes d'action le pourront aisément grâce à cette Revue d'un type absolument neuf et qui donne chaque mois 130 pages de texte et de nombreux documents. Elle rendra les plus grands services à tout ce qui doit constituer l'élite d'une nation, c'est à dire aux artistes, aux universitaires, aux écrivains, aux industriels, ingénieurs et commerçants, véritables créateurs de l'Esprit Nouveau.

"There is a new spirit abroad: a spirit of re-construction and unification, guided by a clear notion of things. A great epoch has begun."—Charles-Edouard Jeanneret and Amédée Ozenfant in the first issue of *L'Esprit Nouveau*

Above left. Jeanneret's I.D. card for *L'Esprit Nouveau*, 1921. The word *editor* is crossed out, replaced by the word *director*.

Above right. Mimeograph handbill announcing *L'Esprit Nouveau*, c. 1920

Below. Jeanneret (far right) with his brother, Albert (next to him), and Amédée Ozenfant (with guitar) in the offices of *L'Esprit Nouveau*, Paris, 1921

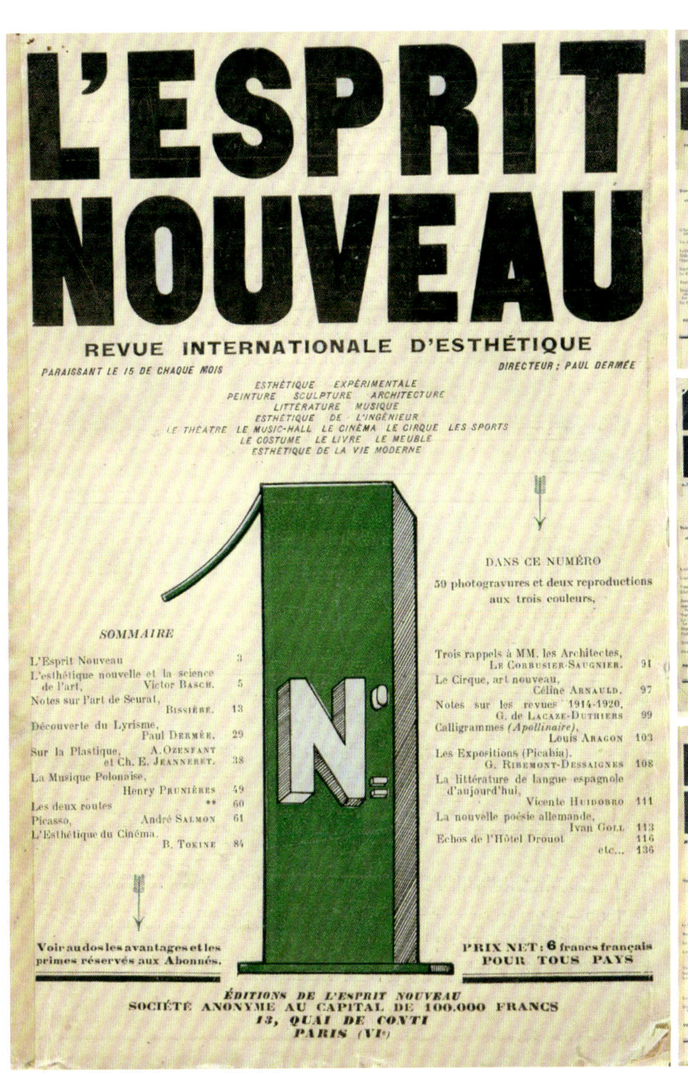

L'ESPRIT NOUVEAU

REVUE INTERNATIONALE D'ESTHÉTIQUE

PARAISSANT LE 15 DE CHAQUE MOIS

DIRECTEUR : PAUL DERMÉE

ESTHÉTIQUE EXPÉRIMENTALE
PEINTURE SCULPTURE ARCHITECTURE
LITTÉRATURE MUSIQUE
ESTHÉTIQUE DE L'INGÉNIEUR
LE THÉATRE LE MUSIC-HALL LE CINÉMA LE CIRQUE LES SPORTS
LE COSTUME LE LIVRE LE MEUBLE
ESTHÉTIQUE DE LA VIE MODERNE

N° 1

SOMMAIRE

L'Esprit Nouveau	3
L'esthétique nouvelle et la science de l'art, Victor BASCH.	5
Notes sur l'art de Seurat, BISSIÈRE.	13
Découverte du Lyrisme, Paul DERMÉE.	29
Sur la Plastique, A. OZENFANT et Ch. E. JEANNERET.	38
La Musique Polonaise, Henry PRUNIÈRES	49
Les deux routes **	60
Picasso, André SALMON	61
L'Esthétique du Cinéma, B. TOKINE	84
Trois rappels à MM. les Architectes, LE CORBUSIER-SAUGNIER.	91
Le Cirque, art nouveau, Céline ARNAULD.	97
Notes sur les revues 1914-1920, G. de LACAZE-DUTHIERS	99
Calligrammes (Apollinaire), Louis ARAGON	103
Les Expositions (Picabia), G. RIBEMONT-DESSAIGNES	108
La littérature de langue espagnole d'aujourd'hui, Vicente HUIDOBRO	111
La nouvelle poésie allemande, Ivan GOLL	113
Echos de l'Hôtel Drouot	116
etc...	136

DANS CE NUMÉRO
50 photogravures et deux reproductions aux trois couleurs,

Voir au dos les avantages et les primes réservés aux Abonnés.

PRIX NET : 6 francs français POUR TOUS PAYS

ÉDITIONS DE L'ESPRIT NOUVEAU
SOCIÉTÉ ANONYME AU CAPITAL DE 100.000 FRANCS
13, QUAI DE CONTI
PARIS (VIe)

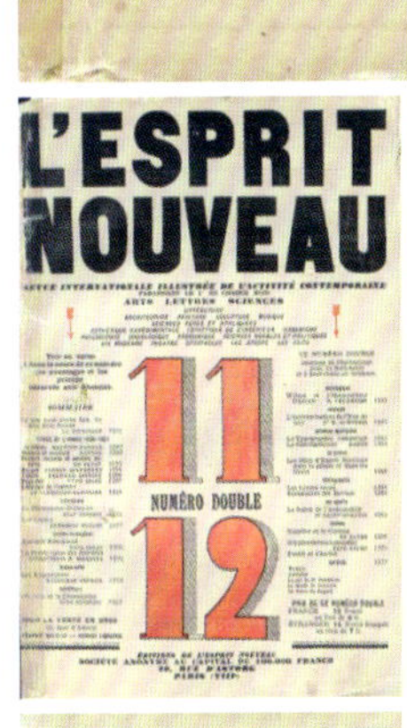

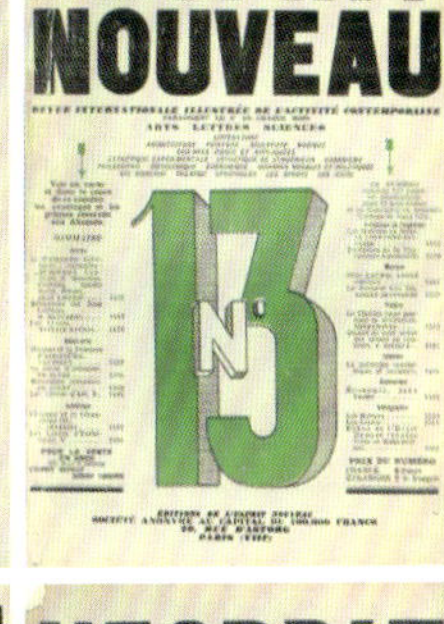

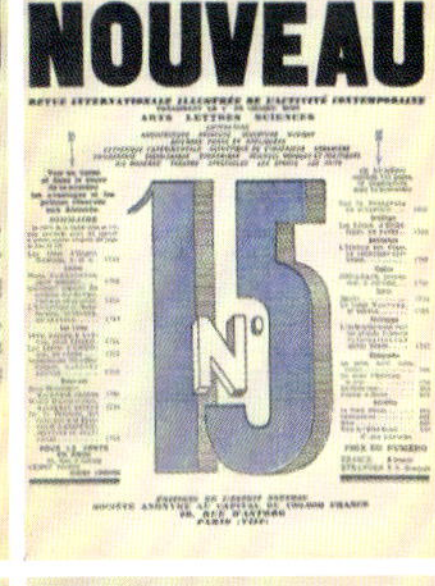

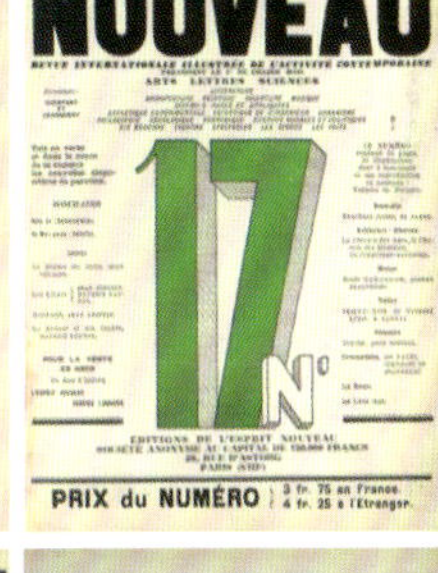

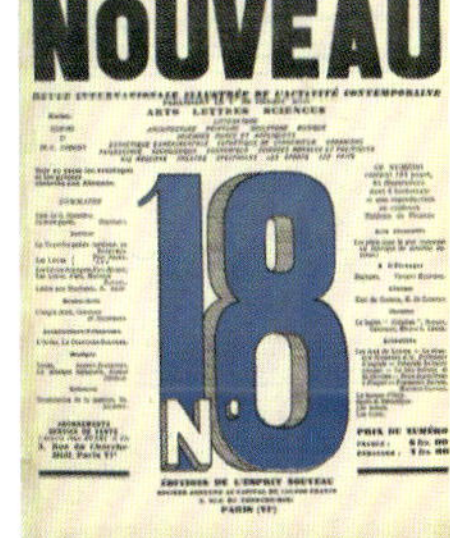
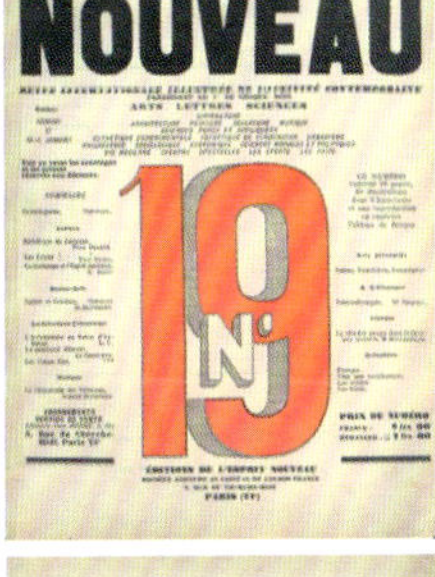
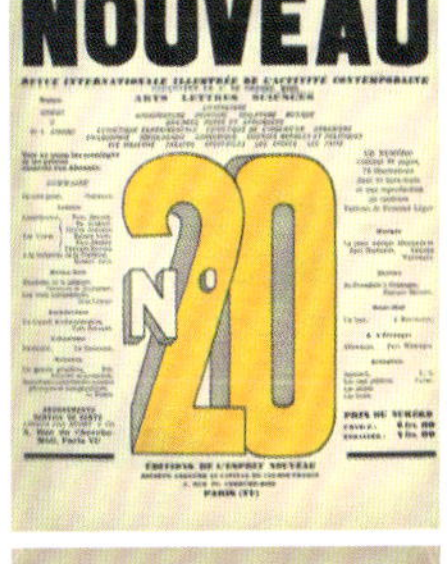
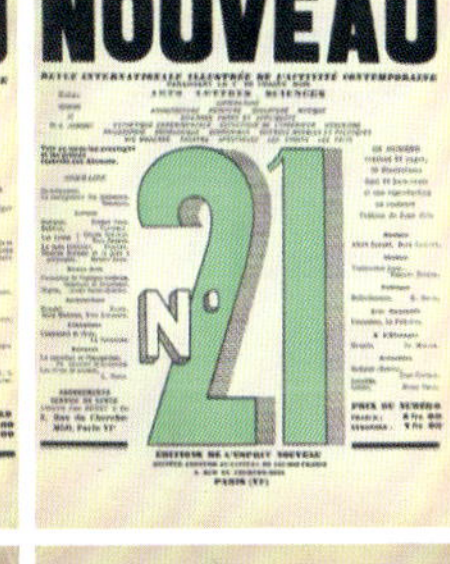
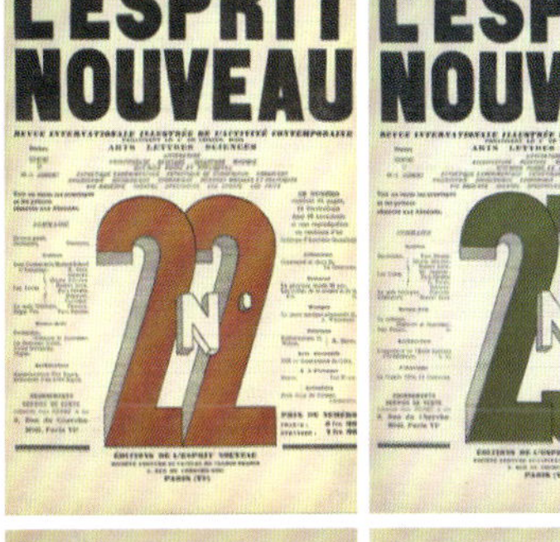
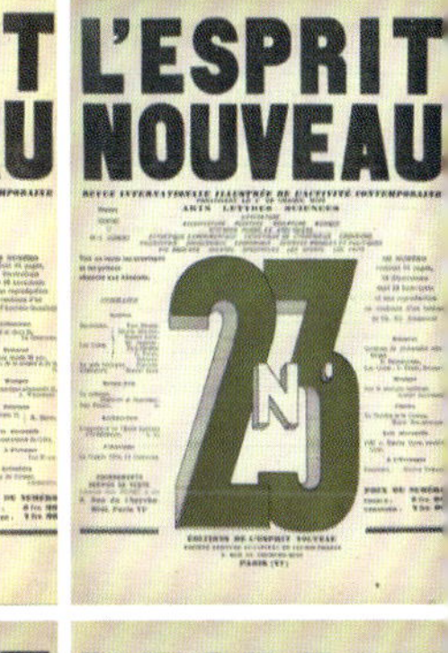
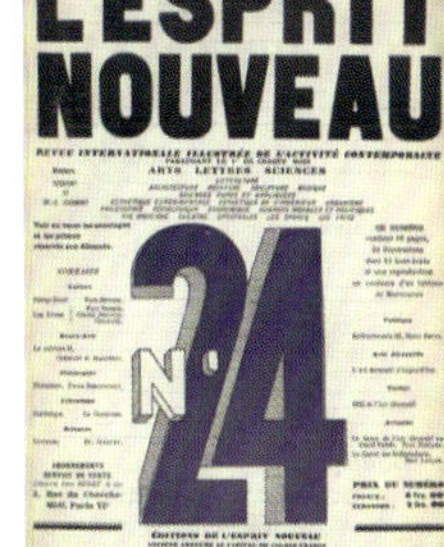
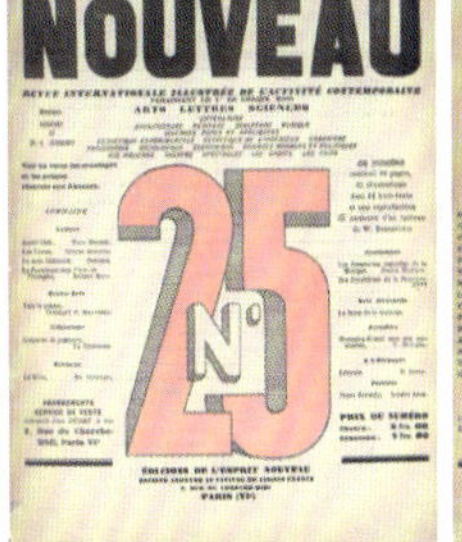
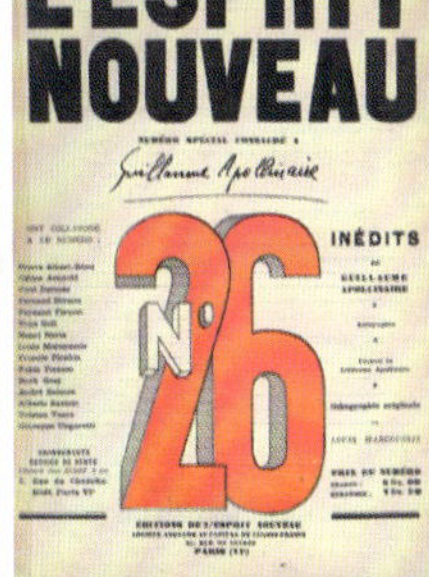

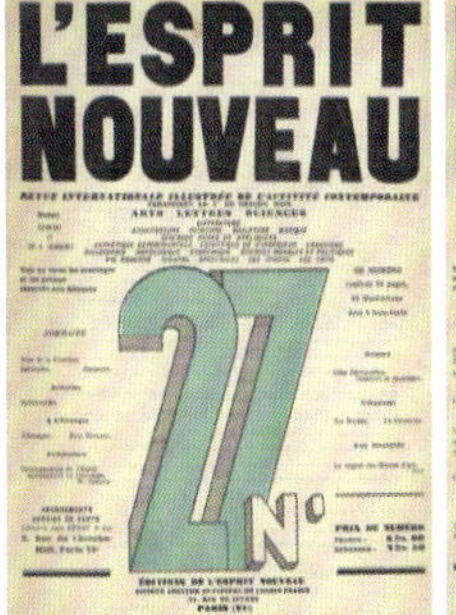
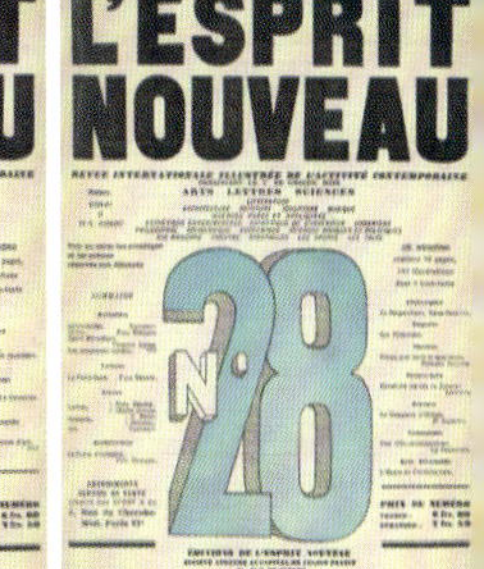

Covers of all twenty-eight issues of *L'Esprit Nouveau*, 1920–25. In the first issue, dated 15 October 1920, Jeanneret signed his articles using two forms of his name, "Ch. E. Jeanneret" and "Le Corbusier-Saugnier."

“ L'ESPRIT NOUVEAU ”

Il y a un esprit nouveau : c'est un esprit de construction et de synthèse guidé par une conception claire.

Quoi qu'on en pense, il anime, aujourd'hui, la plus grande partie de l'activité humaine.

Né dans quelques fortes individualités au XIXe siècle — époque de préparation, donc époque de trouble — l'esprit nouveau mène, à l'heure présente, toutes les élites : les élites des arts et des lettres, aussi bien que les élites des sciences et de l'industrie. La société, elle-même, tend enfin, à s'organiser selon l'esprit nouveau.

Ainsi que le montre l'histoire, les forces libérées en des siècles de bouillonnement et de désordre, se conjuguent un beau jour et s'orientent pour un effort commun. Et nous voyons alors surgir les grandes époques.

Une grande époque vient de commencer, car toutes les formes de l'activité humaine s'organisent enfin selon le même principe.

L'esprit de construction et de synthèse, d'ordre et de volonté consciente qui se manifeste de nouveau, n'est pas moins indispensable, qu'on le sache, aux arts et aux lettres, qu'aux sciences pures ou appliquées ou qu'à la philosophie.

Que serait un génie sans esprit constructif ? Il ne pourrait rien réaliser de ses inspirations ! Il ne laisserait point de chefs-d'œuvre comme témoignages. Il passerait sans laisser de traces.

Nous voulons, au contraire, affirmer avec force que l'esprit constructif est aussi nécessaire pour créer un tableau ou un poème que pour bâtir un pont.

Bien mieux : nous affirmons la nécessité des systèmes esthétiques pour les créateurs.

L'art, comme la science, comme la philosophie, c'est l'ordre mis par l'homme dans ses représentations. Il n'y a pas d'œuvre d'art sans système esthétique plus ou moins conscient, plus ou

1

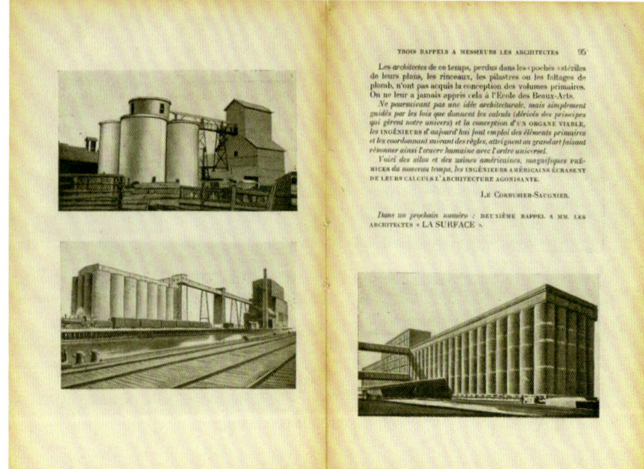

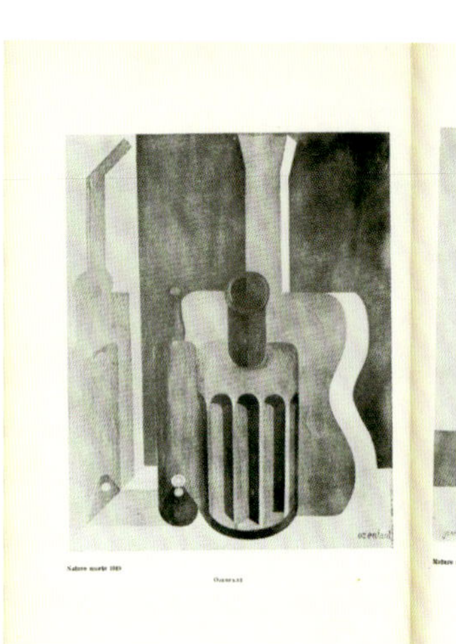

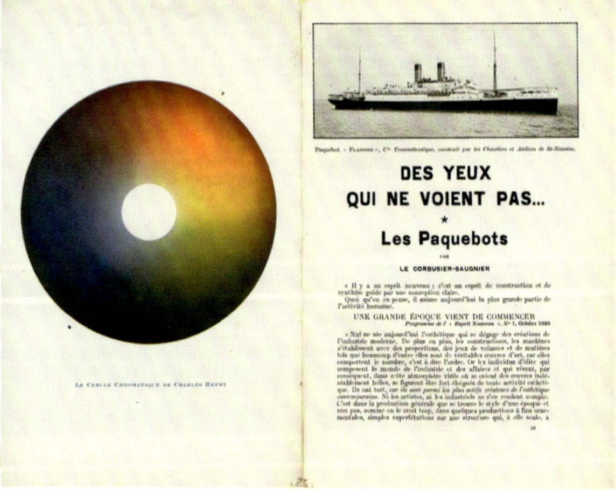

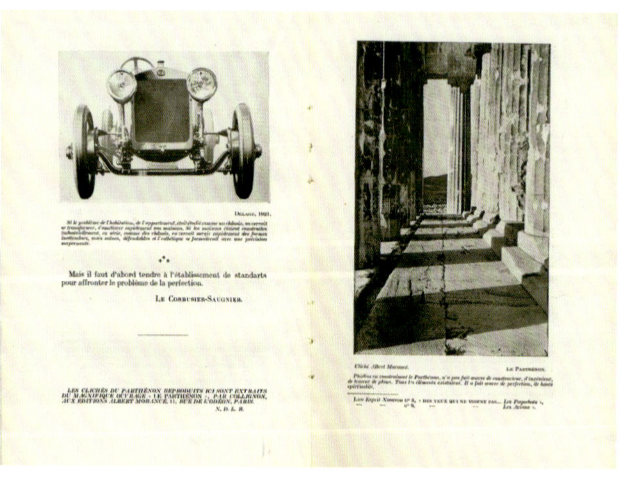

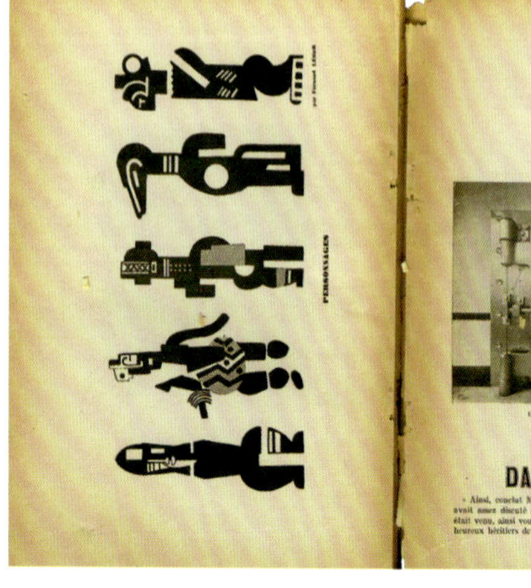

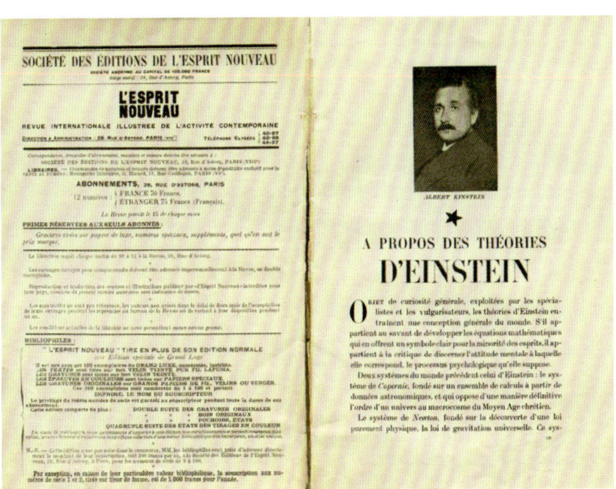

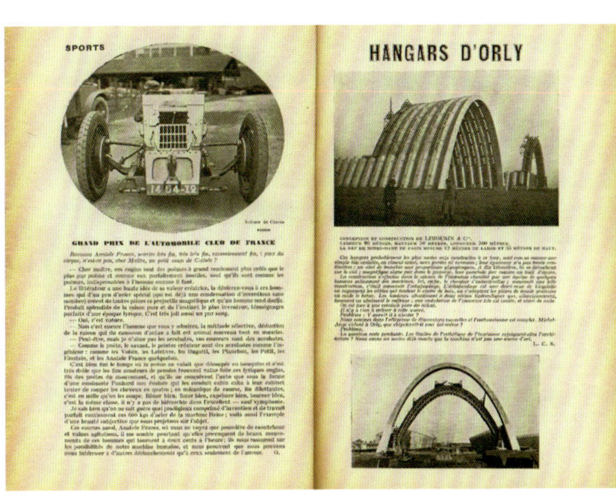

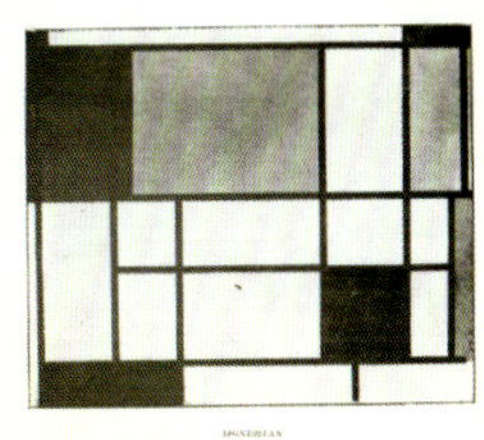

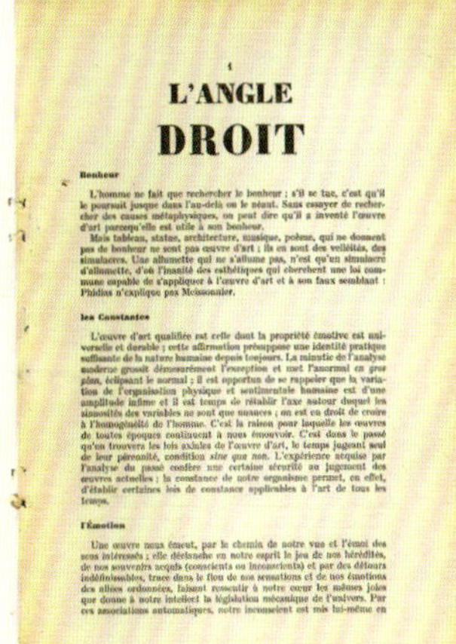

1925
EXPO. ARTS. DÉCO.

CONSÉQUENCES DE CRISE

Opposite and above. Spreads from selected issues of *L'Esprit Nouveau*, 1920–25. Le Corbusier reprinted most of the articles that appeared in *L'Esprit Nouveau* in books he published from 1923 to 1926

"The mock-ups of my (then collected) articles created amazement and indignation at Arrault's – our printers – in Tours: of me they were saying, 'He's crazy.' Already! And regarding typesetting and the typesetter's trade, Vers une architecture (1920–21) reveals an orderly mind."—"1925," *Le Corbusier lui-même*

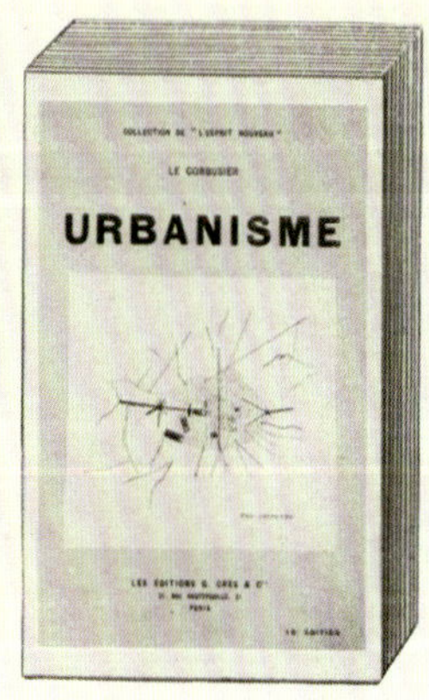

Le Corbusier's first important book: *Vers une architecture*, 1923

Le Corbusier contributed a number of articles on architecture to the pages of *L'Esprit Nouveau*. These were later collected in a book, *Vers une architecture* (*Toward an Architecture*), which established Le Corbusier's reputation among the international avant-garde and is widely regarded as one of the most influential architecture texts of the twentieth century.

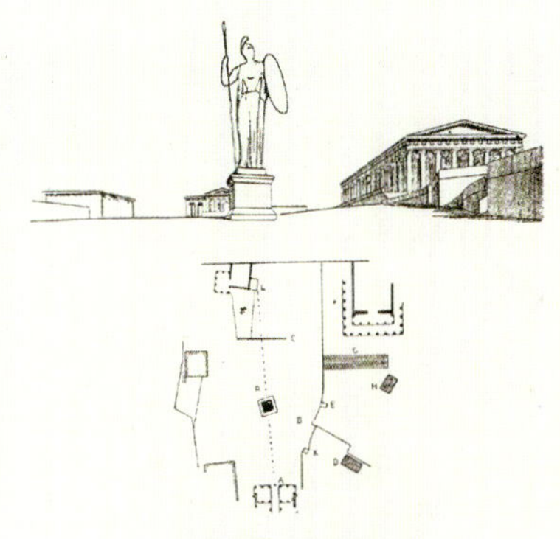

TROIS RAPPELS
A MESSIEURS LES ARCHITECTES

III

LE PLAN

ACROPOLE D'ATHÈNES. Coup d'œil sur le Parthénon, l'Erechtéion, l'Athéna-Parthénos depuis les Proplyées. Il ne faut pas oublier que le sol de l'Acropole est très mouvementé, avec des différences de niveaux considérables qui ont été employées pour constituer des socles imposants aux édifices. Les fausses équerres ont fourni des vues riches et d'un effet subtil; les masses asymétriques des édifices créent un rythme intense. Le spectacle est massif, élastique, nerveux, écrasant d'acuité, dominateur.

PORTE SAINT-DENIS (Blondel).

LES TRACÉS RÉGULATEURS

Cliché Dræger.

DES YEUX QUI NE VOIENT PAS...

II

LES AVIONS

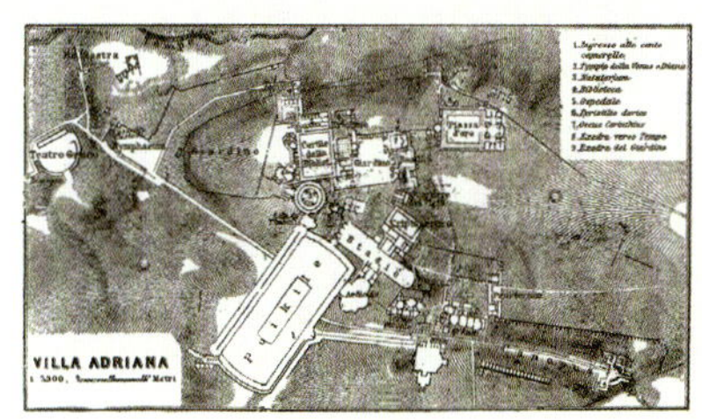

LA VILLA ADRIANA, près Tivoli, an 130 après J.-C.

ARCHITECTURE

I

LA LEÇON DE ROME

Cliché Hostache.

MAISONS EN SÉRIE

Centrale électrique de Gennevilliers. Turbine de 40,000 kw.

ARCHITECTURE
OU RÉVOLUTION

23

Opposite, top. Cover sketch, maquette, and actual cover of *Vers une architecture* (*Toward an Architecture*), Paris, Crès, 1923

Opposite, bottom. Covers of six books by Le Corbusier published in the series "Collection de l'Esprit Nouveau," as reproduced in Le Corbusier, *Oeuvre complète*, vol.1 (Complete Works). The series began with *Vers une architecture*.

Above. Selected pages from *Vers une architecture*

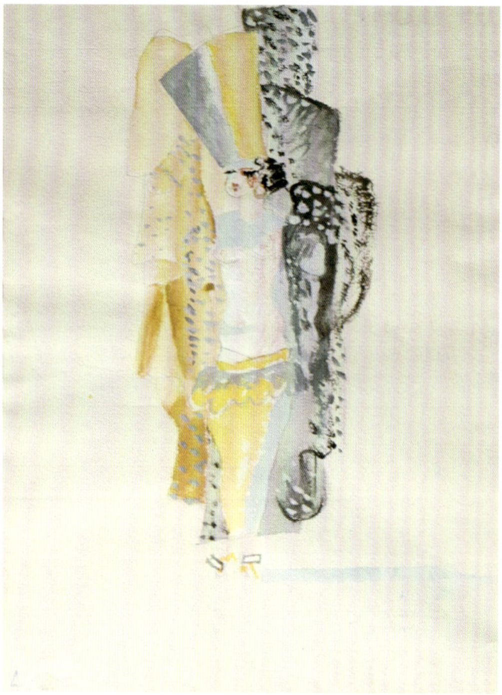

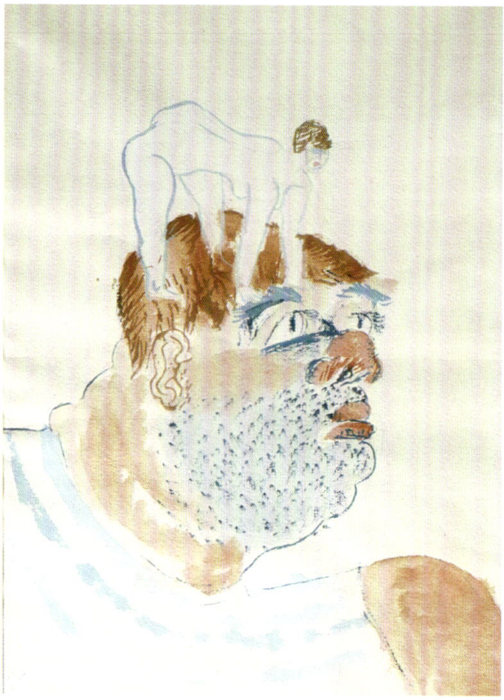

This page and opposite. Selection of plates from *50 aquarelles de Music-Hall* (50 Music-Hall Watercolors), 1926

Paris by night: The Music-Hall Watercolors, 1926

Swiss watch manufacturer Marcel Levaillant, one of Le Corbusier's childhood friends, commissioned the architect to produce a series of paintings on the theme of the music hall.

The result was a collection of fifty watercolors captu ing the joie de viv of Paris.

3
4
5
6

Opposite. Le Corbusier, Paris, c. 1925

Urban Visions and Purist Villas (1922–1935)

In 1922 Le Corbusier made a significant public impact in Paris, beyond the narrow circle of the *L'Esprit Nouveau* readership, with an exhibition stand at the Salon d'Automne. There he presented a large white plaster model of his Maison Citrohan, a standard concrete house type, and more spectacularly, a large diorama showing a modern city for three million people, featuring a business district filled with cruciform glass skyscrapers. Furthermore, he indicated in a caption and in a sketch plan how Paris might be transformed in a similar way. Now began the love/hate relationship of Le Corbusier with the general public: newspaper journalists and even newsreel cameras flocked to the stand to sneer or admire.

Le Corbusier's architectural career began to prosper only after he established a partnership in 1922 with his cousin Pierre Jeanneret, who had received professional architectural training in Geneva and in the office of the Perret brothers. In 1923 they set up a studio in the corridor of a monastery on the rue de Sèvres, near the Bon Marché department store.

During the next five years Le Corbusier and Pierre Jeanneret designed houses for his artist friends, including Amédée Ozenfant, Jacques Lipchitz, and Oscar Miestchaninoff, as well as for the wealthy art lovers Raoul La Roche, Michael and Sarah Stein, William Cook, and Henry Church. This became the corpus of Purist villas that, reproduced around the world in carefully staged photographs, would anchor Le Corbusier's reputation as a leading modernist architect. In 1925, in Paris, his Pavillon de l'Esprit Nouveau became a beacon of radicalism at the *Exposition international des arts décoratifs et industriels modernes*. Tucked away out of sight behind the Grand Palais, this little temporary building was a full-size reconstruction of one of the prototype housing cells he proposed for construction in blocks of apartments.

Two years later, Le Corbusier and Pierre were invited to design and build two full-size permanent houses at the Weissenhof-Siedlung housing exhibition, in Stuttgart, Germany. It was there Le Corbusier became aware that all the leading German and Dutch designers were creating radical furniture designs in tubular steel. Having resisted designing furniture in the modern style until then, he took on the gifted young Art Deco designer Charlotte Perriand to help him produce his own modern interiors, and the three tubular steel chairs they created have become modernist icons.

Less successful were Le Corbusier and Pierre's attempts to design mass housing. They were commissioned by the industrialist Henri Frugès to design a modest group of 150 workers' houses at Pessac, near Bordeaux, of which fifty-one were built. This was an ambitious attempt to take standardization to new heights, using industrial steel windows and doors, sewage-treatment cylinders, hot-air heating, and an incredibly expensive American system of sprayed concrete. As Le Corbusier admitted in an article in 1925, the project was a failure, and the houses they actually managed to build were constructed by hand. In 1928 Le Corbusier and Pierre developed a system of prefabricated steel houses. Not one of these houses was ever built, but the principles were used in the design of a number of their projects in the 1930s.

By 1929, and especially after his visits to Moscow and to South America that year, Le Corbusier's devotion to Purist geometry came to an end. He rediscovered his dormant fascination with vernacular architecture and the use of natural materials. At the same time, his paintings loosened up in style and content, turning from still life to outdoor scenes featuring sensuous nudes and organic forms.

Partnership with Pierre Jeanneret begins, 1922

In 1922 Le Corbusier entered into a partnership with his second cousin Pierre Jeanneret. This arrangement would endure despite disruptions for the rest of Le Corbusier's life. Although they named their firm Le Corbusier–Pierre Jeanneret, Le Corbusier always maintained creative authority. Pierre, however, proved to be an invaluable collaborator and manager of the firm that would invariably be referred to by the public as the "atelier Le Corbusier."

"Since 1 October Pierre and I have been working until one in the morning without easing up a single day... Pierre has been admirably hardworking and reliable. Without him I could do nothing and he's displayed enthusiasm and ability of the first order."—Letter to his parents, 2 November 1922

Opposite, top. Le Corbusier's brother, Albert Jeanneret, and his wife, Lotti Raaf (both seated), on their wedding day, 26 June 1923. Standing, from left to right: Pastor Huguenin, Amédée Ozenfant, Le Corbusier, and Pierre Jeanneret

Opposite, bottom left. Left to right: N. Colley, Yvonne Gallis, Le Corbusier, and Pierre Jeanneret at Le Corbusier's rue Jacob apartment, Paris

Opposite, bottom right. A light moment at the first CIAM conference, La Sarraz, Switzerland, July 1928. Le Corbusier is at center, with José Luis Sert (center front), Pierre Jeanneret (far right), Gabriel Guévrékian (far left), and André Lurçat (second from left)

Above. Le Corbusier on the beach at Le Piquey, in southwestern France, with Pierre Jeanneret, 1933

Two influential housing schemes: Maison Citrohan and Immeubles-Villas (both unbuilt), 1920–22

Around the time the partnership with Pierre Jeanneret was established, Le Corbusier developed two schemes that would inform his designs throughout the 1920s. Both the Maison Citrohan (so called to conjure an image of the Citroën automobile) and the apartment block he called the Immeubles-Villas (part of his Ville Contemporaine urban planning project exhibited at the 1922 Salon d'Automne) demonstrated the lessons Le Corbusier had learned at the Val d'Ema monastery—notably, the idea of beginning a sequence with a closed facade, followed by the gradual expansion of spaces culminating in a rear garden.

7

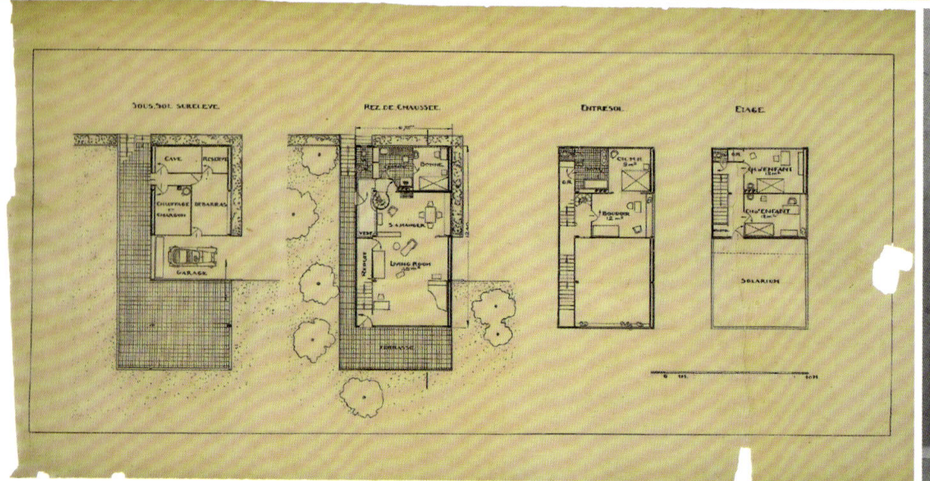

posite, top.
etch of a Maison
rohan villa by
sea

posite, middle.
ghboring
ison Citrohan
as

posite, bottom left.
ns, Maison
rohan

posite,
om right.
ster model
he Maison
rohan displayed
he Salon

d'Automne, Paris, 1922

Right. Renderings of the Immeubles-Villas for Paris reproduced in a journal. The drawing at top shows a building for 120 villas, and the one at bottom shows the glass facade and individual apartments. The accompanying text begins, "To build homes for the great cities, we must reconsider the cell, the apartment."

Below. Perspective sketch, block of Immeubles-Villas in Geneva for the client Edmond Wanner, 18 March 1928

POUR CONSTRUIRE LES MAISONS DE LA GRANDE VILLE IL FAUT FAIRE LA REVISION DE LA CELLULE, DE L'APPARTEMENT. ON N'ATTEINT AU TYPE PUR, QUE PAR LES EXPÉRIENCES MULTIPLIÉES. DANS LE PASSÉ, IL Y FALLAIT LES SIÈCLES; AUJOURD'HUI, LA MACHINE IMPOSE LE TRAVAIL EN SÉRIE. LE TRAVAIL EN SÉRIE REMPLACE LE SIÈCLE PAR LA DÉCADE. IL FAUT DONC CONSTRUIRE EN SÉRIE POUR ÉTABLIR LE TYPE ET ATTEINDRE LA PERFECTION.

A paraître, en avril 1923, aux Éditions Georges CRÈS & Cie, 21, rue Hautefeuille, à Paris.
***VERS UNE ARCHITECTURE**. par Le Corbusier. — Un volume in-8° raisin d'environ 300 pages, avec nombreuses illustrations.*

1060

24,5

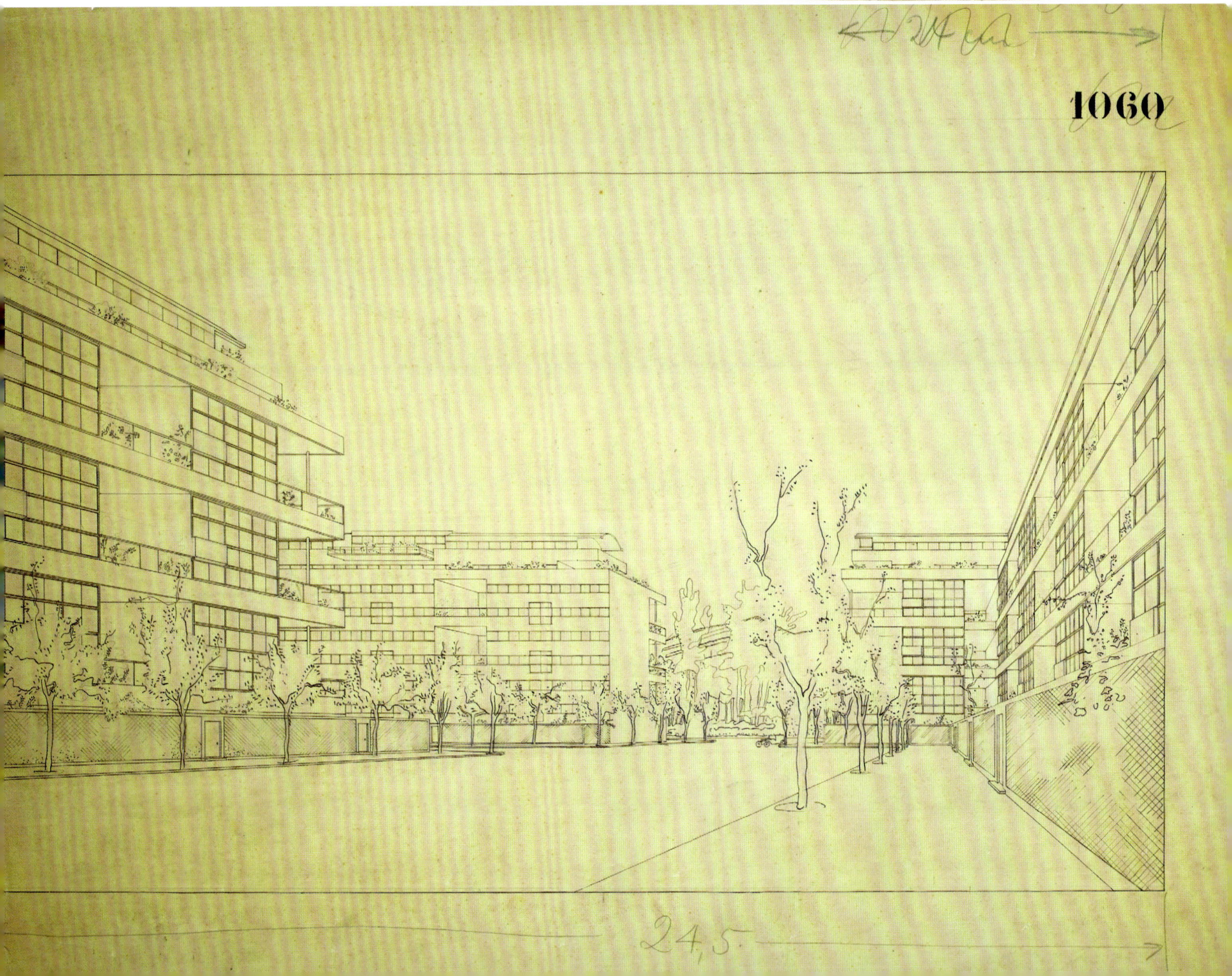

1022

"The Immeubles-Villas... sprang from an after-lunch memory that cropped up of an Italian Carthusian monastery in Ema (serene happiness), and which I scribbled on the back of a menu. The key to urbanism is a man who can be horrified by the disorganization of the urban phenomenon or delighted and overwhelmed by the attention given to specifically human needs."

—"1922," *Le Corbusier lui-même*

Facade study for Immeubles-Villas, 13 February 1928. Each apartment was owned individually, but facilities such as kitchens and gymnasiums were communal.

Trying out the machine aesthetic: Villa Vaucresson, Vaucresson, France, 1922

Georges Besnus commissioned Le Corbusier to build a house for him in Vaucresson, France, after seeing a model of the Maison Citrohan at the 1922 Salon d'Automne. Here Le Corbusier finally saw an opportunity to realize a built version of the Maison Citrohan, which would be his touchstone throughout the 1920s. However, responding to a complex site and a highly traditional context, he ultimately created a scheme that mediates between the classicism of the Villa Schwob and the machine aesthetic of the Maison Citrohan.

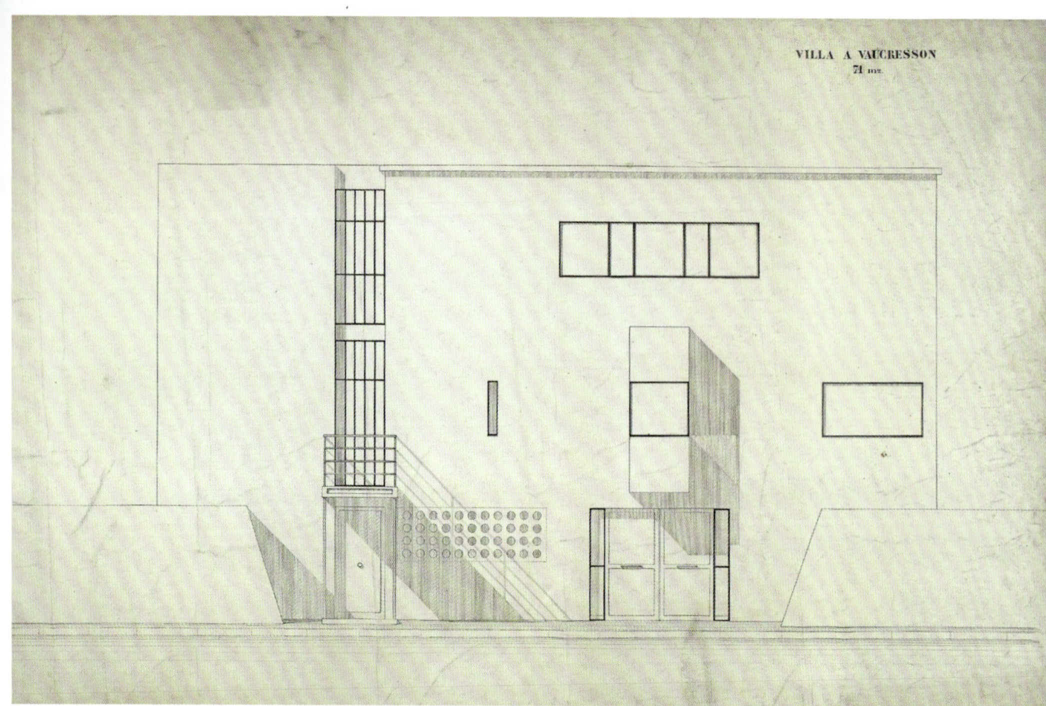

Above. Principal elevation, Villa Vaucresson, 1922

Left. Interior sket

Below left. Principal facade

Below right. Entrance and staircase

cination h cars and nes

identification ne Maison ohan with the mobile as well ith the ramps bridges that ld soon take pe in projects the Villa La he reflects Le Corbusier's preoccupation with forms of modern mobility. This preoccupation also found expression in Le Corbusier's writing (including *L'Esprit Nouveau* and *Vers une architecture*), as well as in later projects such as the Villa Savoye and the houses for the Weissenhof-Siedlung housing exhibition.

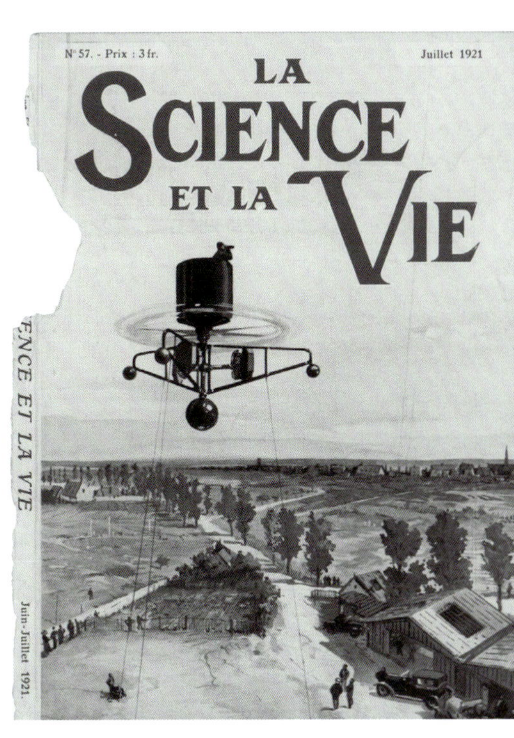

ft. Photograph lanes, from Le busier's ection

right. Cover of journal *Science vie*, June July 1, depicting a ng machine

Below. Images of automobiles and ships from *Vers une architecture* (*Toward an Architecture*) by Le Corbusier, 1923

Bottom. Le Corbusier standing in front of a Voisin automobile

"In the name of the liner, the airplane, and the automobile, we demanded logic, boldness, harmony, perfection." —***Toward an Architecture*, 1923**

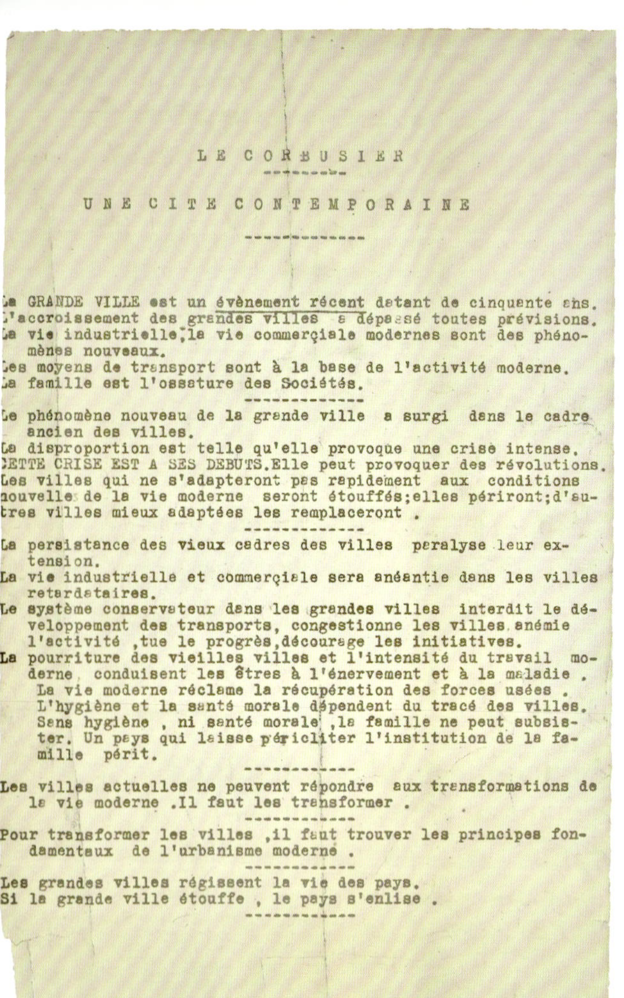

LE CORBUSIER

UNE CITE CONTEMPORAINE

La GRANDE VILLE est un évènement récent datant de cinquante ans.
L'accroissement des grandes villes a dépassé toutes prévisions.
La vie industrielle, la vie commerçiale modernes sont des phénomènes nouveaux.
Les moyens de transport sont à la base de l'activité moderne.
La famille est l'ossature des Sociétés.

Le phénomène nouveau de la grande ville a surgi dans le cadre ancien des villes.
La disproportion est telle qu'elle provoque une crise intense.
CETTE CRISE EST A SES DEBUTS. Elle peut provoquer des révolutions.
Les villes qui ne s'adapteront pas rapidement aux conditions nouvelle de la vie moderne seront étouffés; elles périront; d'autres villes mieux adaptées les remplaceront .

La persistance des vieux cadres des villes paralyse leur extension.
La vie industrielle et commerçiale sera anéantie dans les villes retardataires.
Le système conservateur dans les grandes villes interdit le développement des transports, congestionne les villes anémie l'activité ,tue le progrès, décourage les initiatives.
La pourriture des vieilles villes et l'intensité du travail moderne conduisent les êtres à l'énervement et à la maladie .
La vie moderne réclame la récupération des forces usées .
L'hygiène et la santé morale dépendent du tracé des villes.
Sans hygiène , ni santé morale ,la famille ne peut subsister. Un pays qui laisse péricliter l'institution de la famille périt.

Les villes actuelles ne peuvent répondre aux transformations de la vie moderne .Il faut les transformer .

Pour transformer les villes ,il faut trouver les principes fondamentaux de l'urbanisme moderne .

Les grandes villes régissent la vie des pays.
Si la grande ville étouffe , le pays s'enlise .

A city for three million inhabitants: Ville Contemporaine, 1922

Exhibited at the 1922 Salon d'Automne, the Ville Contemporaine—or, as Le Corbusier preferred to call it, "A City of Three Million Inhabitants"—addressed the various planning demands of a new industrial city. Functions such as manufacturing, business, recreation, and habitation each occupied its own zone. Variations between tall towers and large-scale parks would allow residents access to open green space without sacrificing urban density. While the Ville Contemporaine operated as a critique of nineteenth-century planning principles, later critics attacked its relentless uniformity.

"The new techniques bring about freedoms... Instead of having views onto other houses, building houses that are tall allows a liberation of grounds that can be counted in acres. Multiply the experience and you get a city that is green through your windows."

—Interview, 1962, *The Oral History of Architecture*

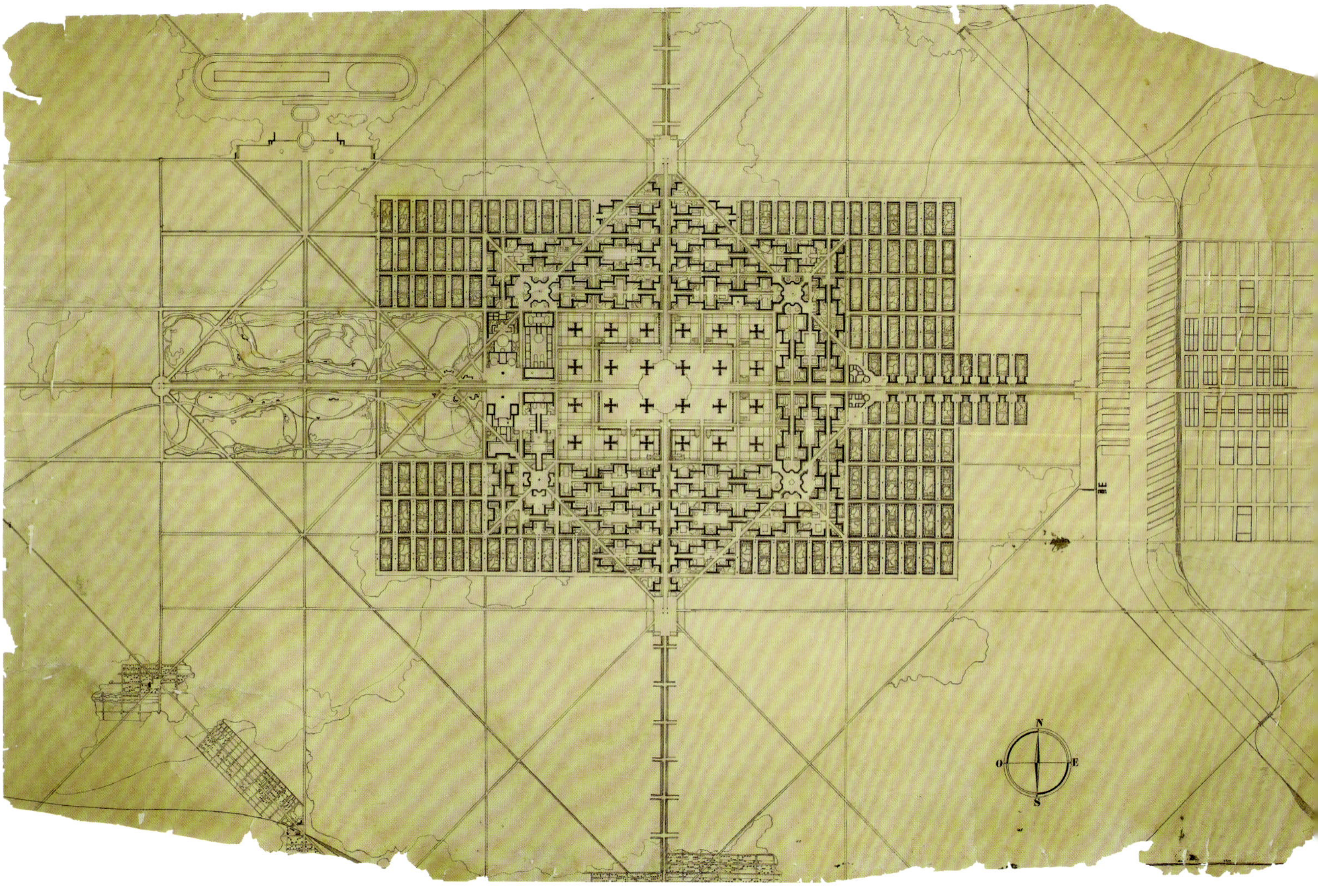

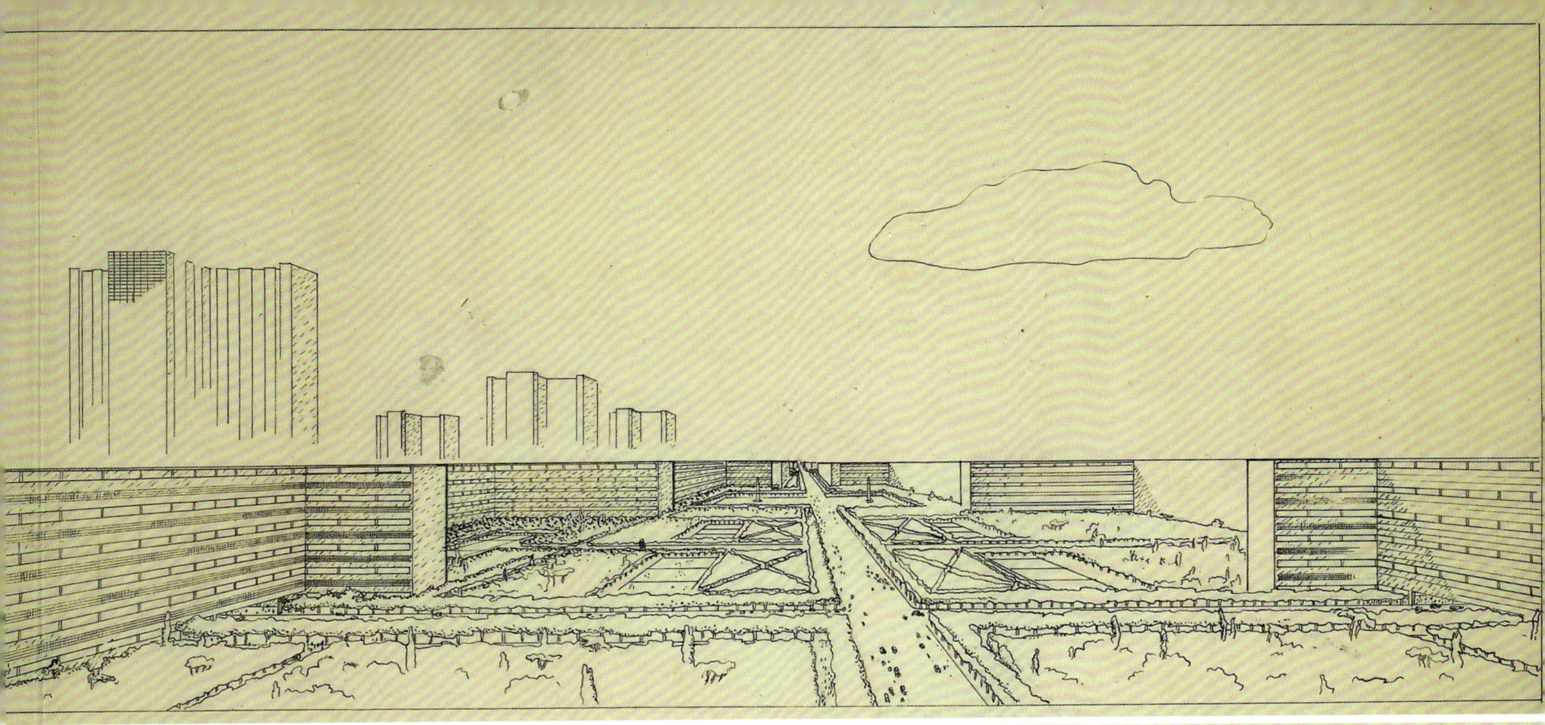

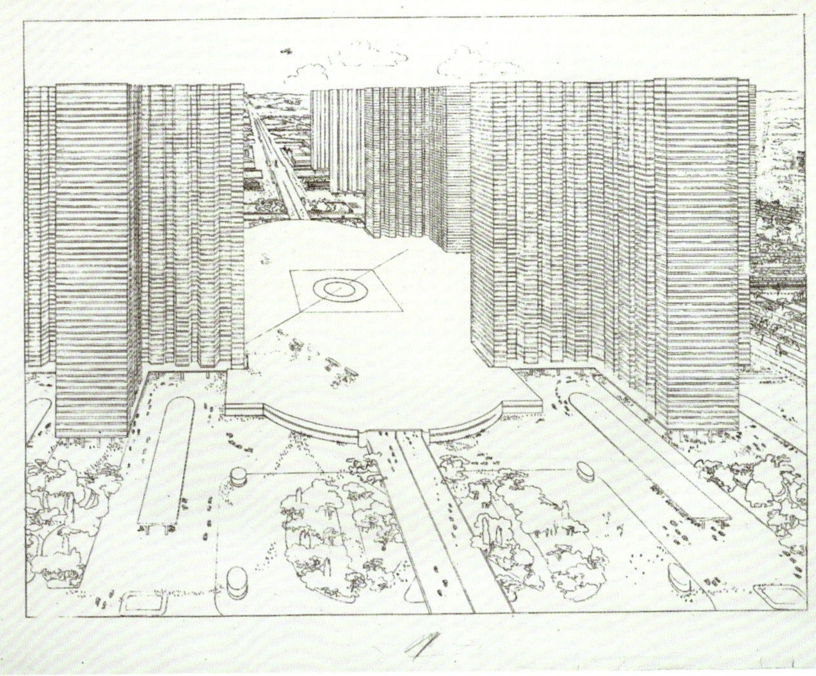

pposite, top. ypescript by Le orbusier, "Une cité ontemporaine" contemporary ty)

Opposite, bottom. Plan, Ville Contemporaine, 1922

Top. Perspective of the Ville Contemporaine

Above. Rendering of the Ville Contemporaine

Right. Perspective of the later Plan Voisin, 1925, showing a central transportation hub (with airplanes on the roof), flanked by cruciform skyscrapers that recall those used in the Ville Contemporaine

Right. Two perspective drawings of the Ville Contemporaine

Below. Bird's-eye perspective of the Ville Contemporaine

Opposite. Plans comparing population density in Paris in previous centuries (left) and Le Corbusier's recommended schemes for two different densities in modern cities.

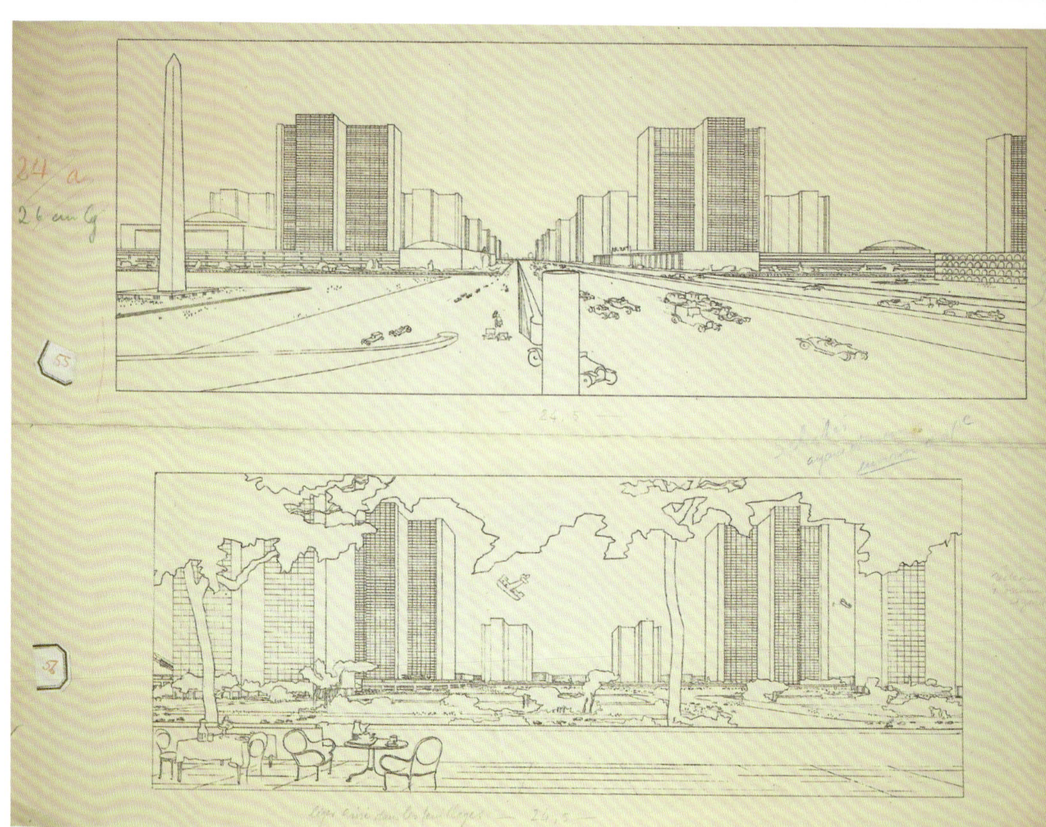

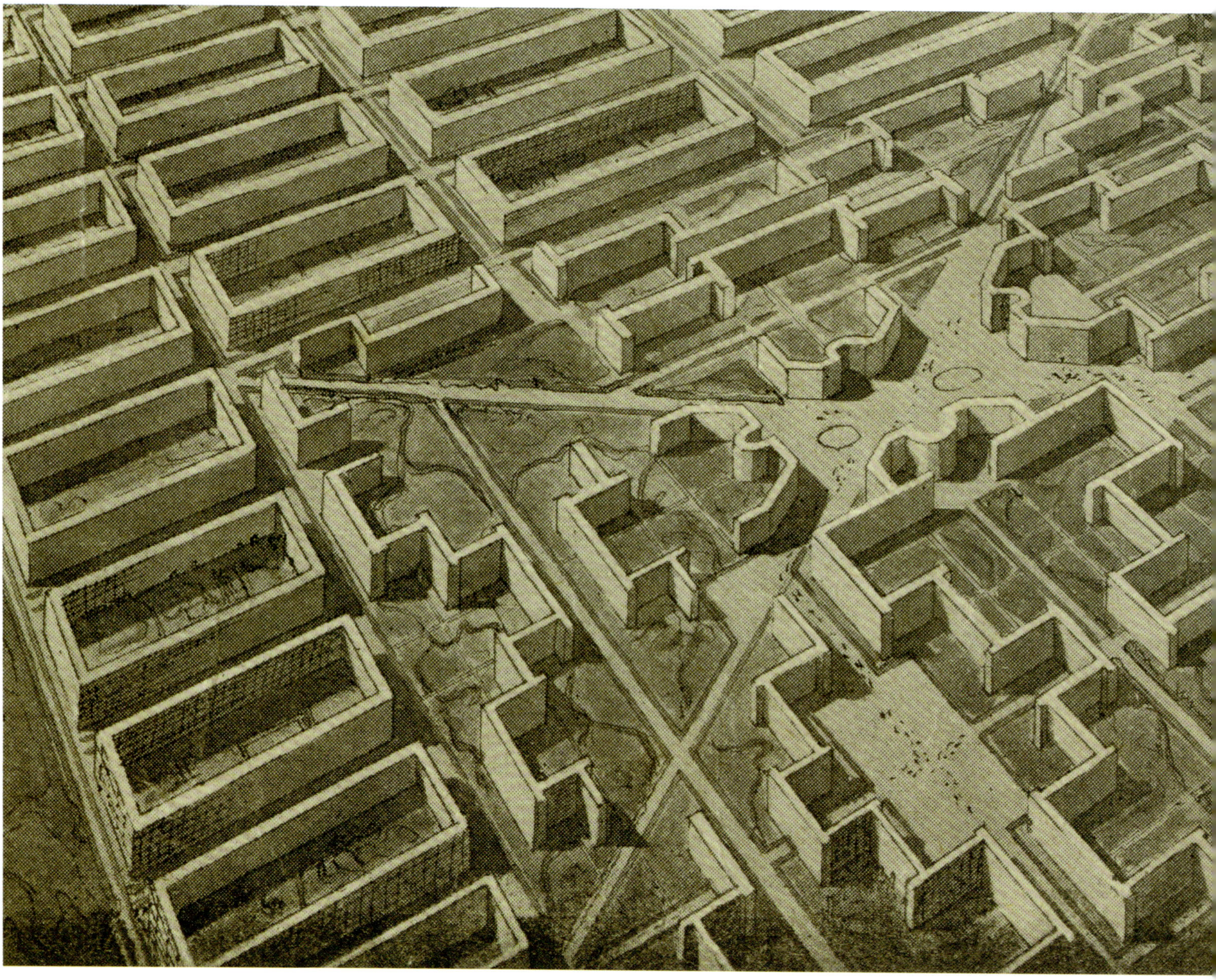

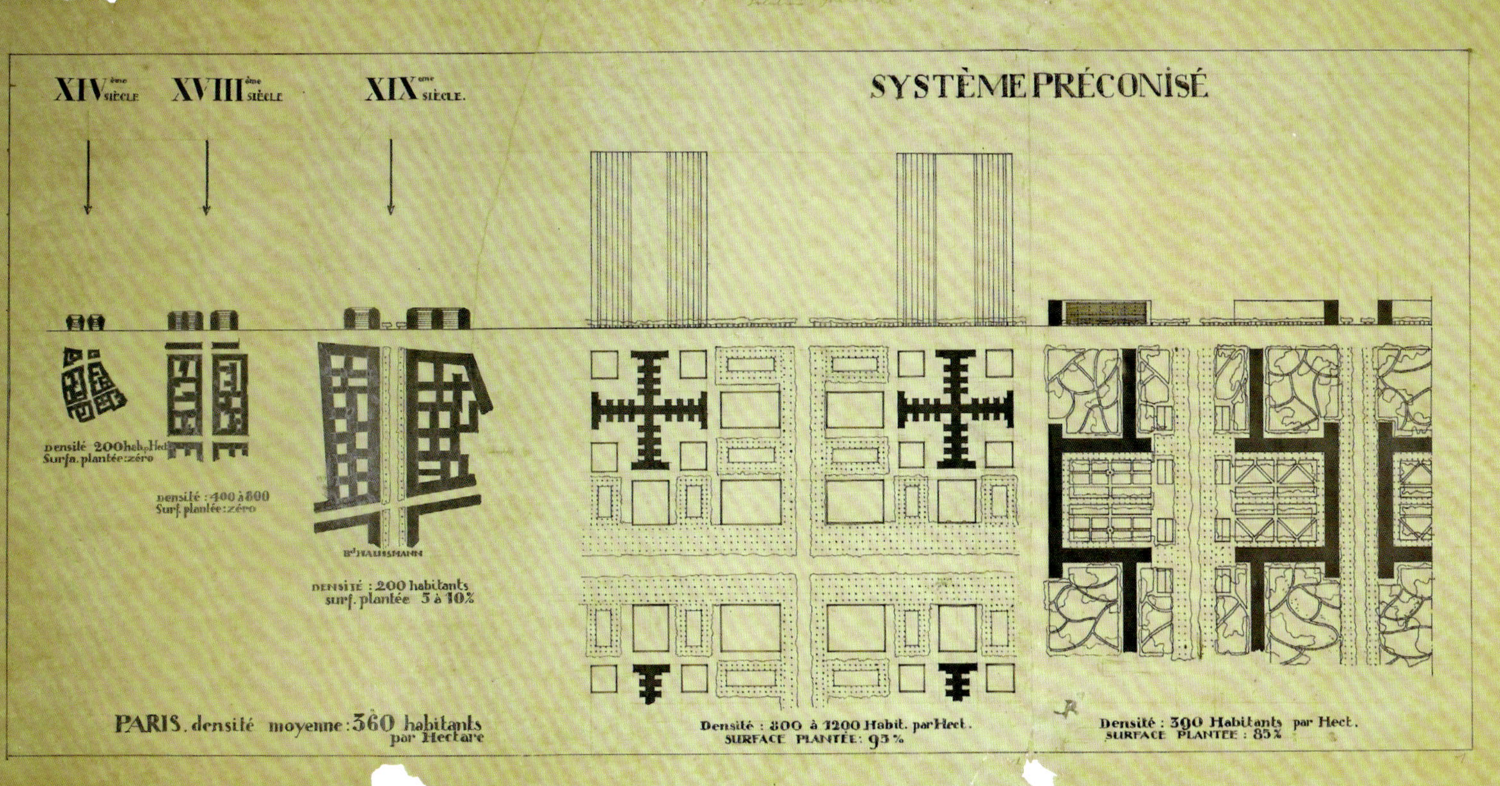
XIVème SIÈCLE
XVIIIème SIÈCLE
XIXème SIÈCLE
SYSTÈME PRÉCONISÉ
Densité 200 hab./Hect.
Surfa. plantée: zéro
densité: 400 à 800
Surf. plantée: zéro
Bd HAUSSMANN
densité: 200 habitants
surf. plantée 5 à 10%
PARIS. densité moyenne: 360 habitants par Hectare
Densité: 800 à 1200 Habit. par Hect.
SURFACE PLANTÉE: 95%
Densité: 300 Habitants par Hect.
SURFACE PLANTÉE: 85%

A TOUS, MERCI !

Ceux qui ont aidé, 35 rue de Sèvres . . . «Nous avons travaillé dans l'amitié, la conviction et la confiance.» La nomenclature ne fut établie qu'à partir du 28 février 1925. La numérotation des dessins partant de 501 et arrivant à 5635 au 19 novembre 1959.

Le Corbusier – Pierre Jeanneret – Emery – François Faure – 1925 – Roth – 1929 – Weismann – Frey – Mayekawa – Sert – Burhan – Sokol – Tsuchihashi – Rice – Wettstein – Busztin – Colley – 1930 – Beathy – Geiser – Saporta – Ducret – Size – Mme Perriand – Safranek – MacIver – Erlich – Renner – Michaelides – Komter – Weber – Vànec – Chavardes – Brechbühler – 1931 – Bossu – Alazard – Delporte – Senn – von Tobel – Oreste Maltos – Orazèm – Sedlak – André – MacCellan – Altherr – Wanner – Bosshardt – Jansen – Sakakura – Sammer – Poursain – David – Gruson – Stephenson – Kepes – 1932 – Joss – West – Waldkirch – Oswald – Davilla – White – Streiff – Streb – Adam – Castrillo – Feiniger – Cronstedt – 1933 – Diehl – Burckhardt – Neidhardt – Kropf – Verrier – Sever – Salomonson – Gomez Gavazzo – Reiner – Miquel – Berhamnc – 1934 – Barkaï – Boyer – Rentsch – 1935 – Pollak – Fawcett – Dupré – Hornstra – Schneider – 1936 – Braem – Mercier – Pantovic – Benes – 1937 – Christen – Dubois – 1938 – Krunic – Renard – Burri – 1939 – Tépina – Almairac – Ravnikar – Willem H. G. de Moor – Epio Borg – Wogenscky – Nielsen Tage – Hanning – 1940 – Welti – Zupo – Pfister – Zupencic – Bollinger – de Graaf – 1944 – Aujame – de Looze – 1945 – Soltan – 1946 – Bodiansky – Danielle Janin – Candilis – Gardien – Zalewsky – Dubois – 1947 – Nadir Afonso – Michaud – Andréini – 1948 – Gonzales de Léon – Masson – Salmona – Weismann – Pirko Hirvela – 1949 – Bruaux – *Kennedy* – *Provelenghios* – Vaculic – Woods – Hoesli – Olek Kujawski – Xénakis – Clémot – Samper – Serralta – Solomita – Wurster – Takamasa Yosizaka – Walter – Valencia – Mme Heilbuth – 1951 – Maisonnier – Mazet – Doshi – Pérez – 1952 – Michel – Lemarchand – Mériot – Duhart – Kim Chun Up – Melle Gabillard – 1953 – Véret – Tobito – Sachinidis – 1954 – Talati – 1959 – Jullian – Tavés – Oubrerie.

Xénakis, Maisonnier, Tobito qui ont quitté l'Atelier en 1959, ont demandé à être désignés: architectes chefs d'études.

5 Ceux qui ont aidé

Opens rue de Sèvres office, Paris, 1925

Le Corbusier and Pierre Jeanneret moved their practice into a corridor in a former monastery at 35 rue de Sèvres. This peculiar space sheltered a row of drawing tables that would serve as the training ground for three generations of architects from around the globe.

Above left. Published list of the office staff at 35 rue de Sèvres from 1925 to 1959

Left. Portrait of Pierre Jeanneret by Le Corbusier

Opposite. Cover and selected pages of the *Livre noir* (black book), ledger of drawings made for the office of Le Corbusier and Pierre Jeanneret, beginning in 1925

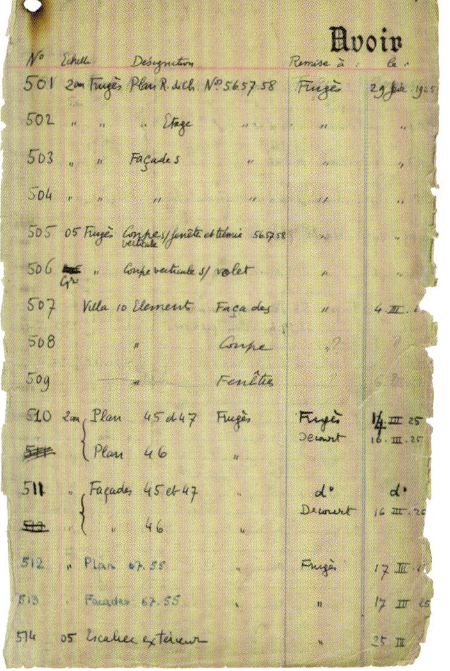
Avoir

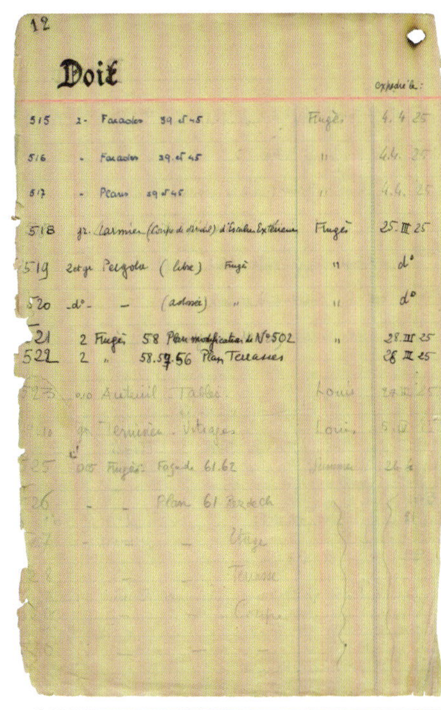
Doit

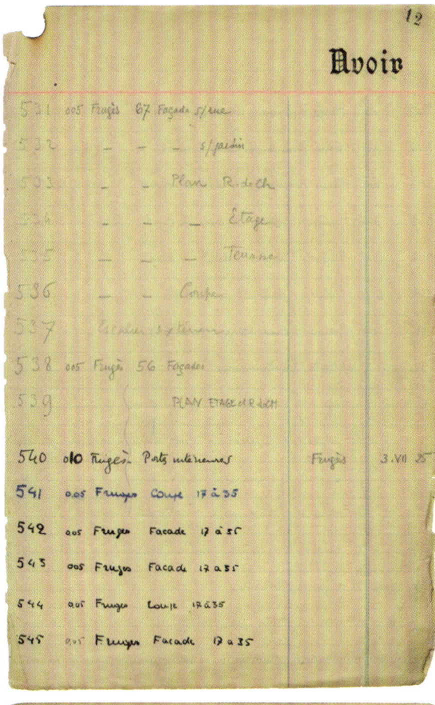
Avoir

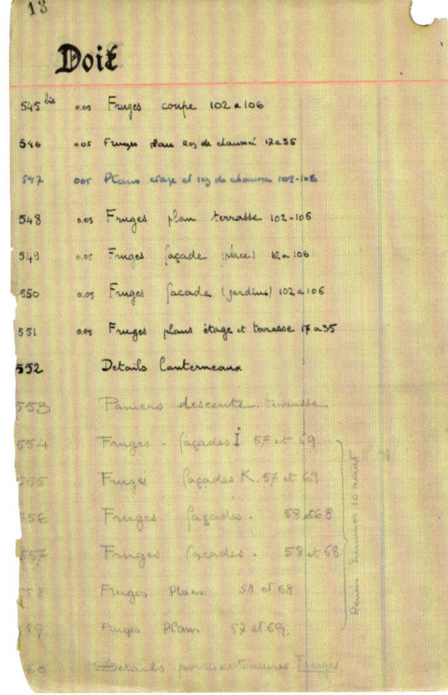
Doit

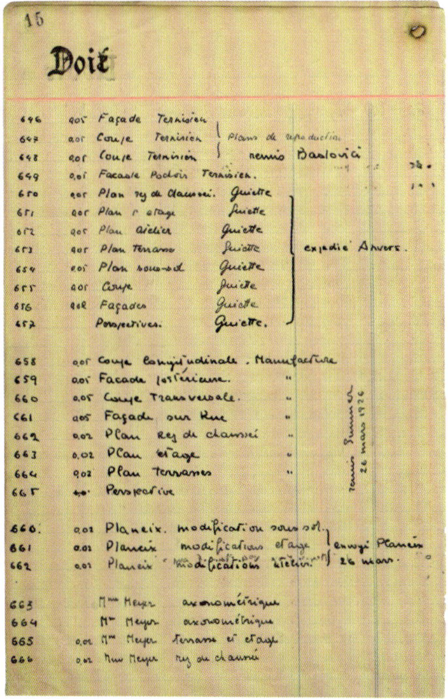
Doit

“In art, as in science and industry, reason dominates and orders the work. Sensibility, which is an uncontrollable subconscious attached to the individual personality, determines the work’s emotion.

The simultaneous effort of reason and sensibility realizes the *conception*.”

—Charles-Edouard Jeanneret and Amédée Ozenfant, *After Cubism*, 1918

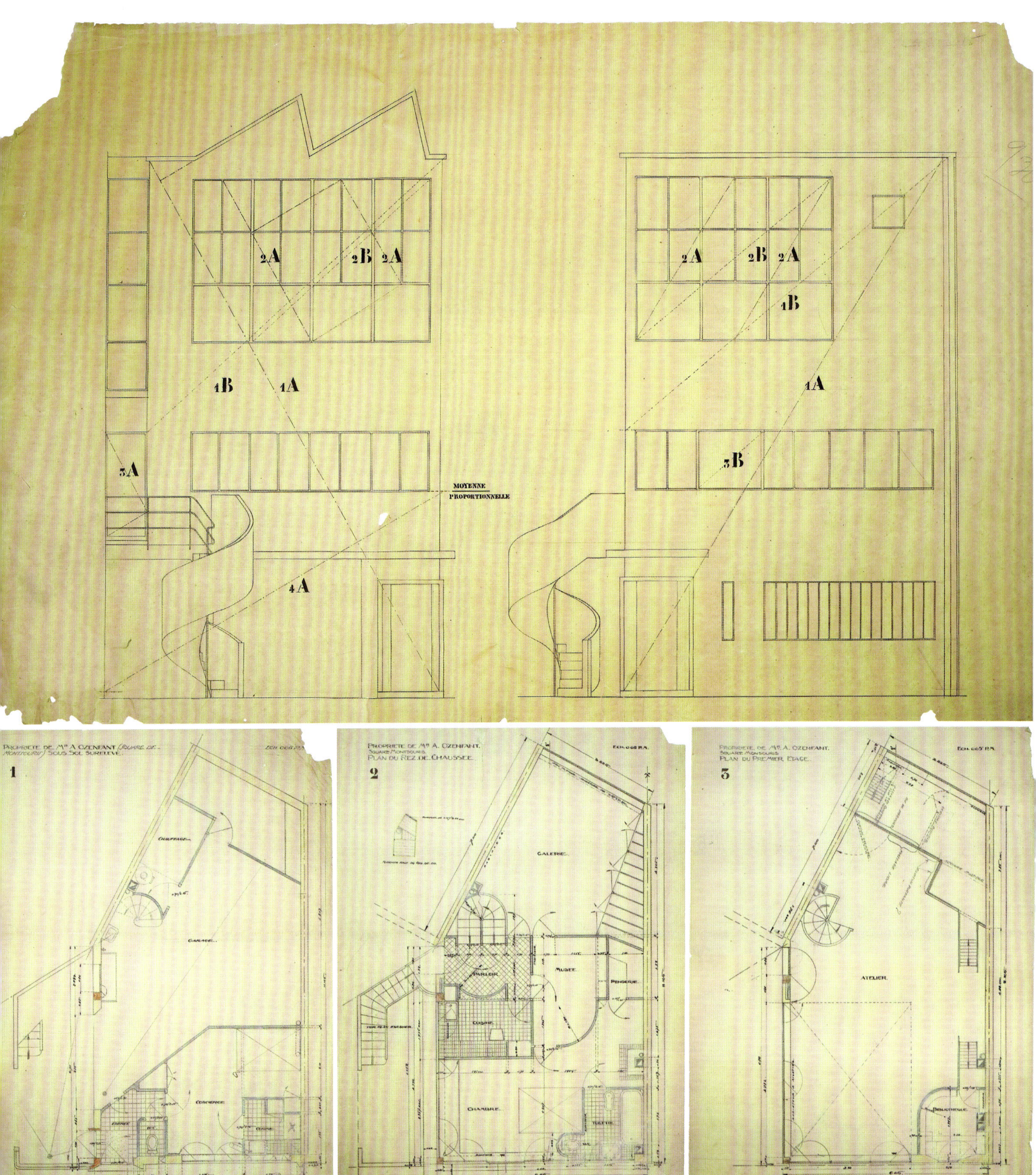

Inventing a functional space for a friend: House and studio for Amédée Ozenfant, Paris, 1922–24

Le Corbusier built a combined house and studio for Amédée Ozenfant on a wedge-shaped corner site in the fourteenth arrondissement. With its pristine white concrete walls, double-height factory windows, roof composed of serrated skylights, and spiral staircase with a ribbon-like balustrade, the structure had a strikingly inventive profile. Interior spaces were compartmentalized and functional, dominated by the two-story skylit studio at the top. There was also a compact study, positioned like a floating monk's cell at the top of a narrow stair with double risers. For all its industrial materials, the Ozenfant studio was also remarkable for its engagement with its natural surroundings.

Opposite. Sketches for the house and studio for Amédée Ozenfant, Paris, 1922–24

Top. Elevations with regulating lines

Above. Left to right: Basement, ground-floor, and first-floor plans

AVENUE
REILLE

Opposite. View of the Ozenfant house and studio from the corner of avenue Reille, showing later alterations, including removal of the garage and the serrated skylight

Left. The studio in its original configuration

Below and bottom. Two interior views of the double-height studio

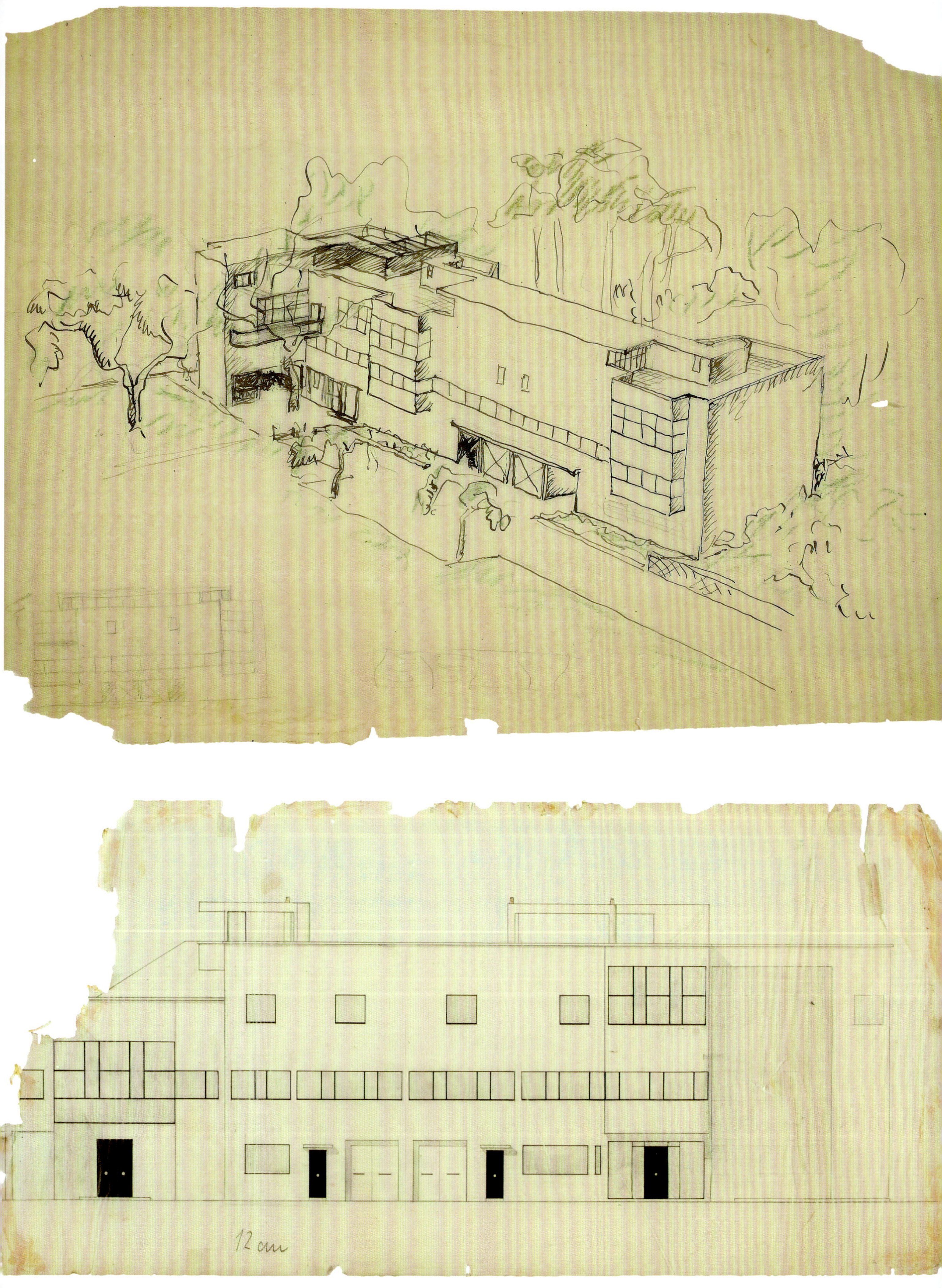
12 cm

One building, many uses: Villa La Roche–Jeanneret, Paris, 1923–25

Le Corbusier initiated the scheme for building two adjoining houses on an L-shaped site at the end of a cul-de-sac: one for his brother, Albert Jeanneret, and the other for the banker and modern art collector Raoul La Roche. While Albert's part of the structure had a simple program—salon, dining room, bedrooms, study, kitchen, maid's room, garage—the part belonging to La Roche featured dramatic spaces for entertaining and for displaying the banker's growing collection. Here Le Corbusier created a triple-height entry hall as well as a double-height gallery with a grand ramp running along a curved wall articulated on the front facade. The complex interplay of volumes and circulation perfectly embodies the principle Le Corbusier called the *promenade architecturale*, a meticulously conceived procession through a series of spaces.

The Villa La Roche–Jeanneret is now the home of the Fondation Le Corbusier.

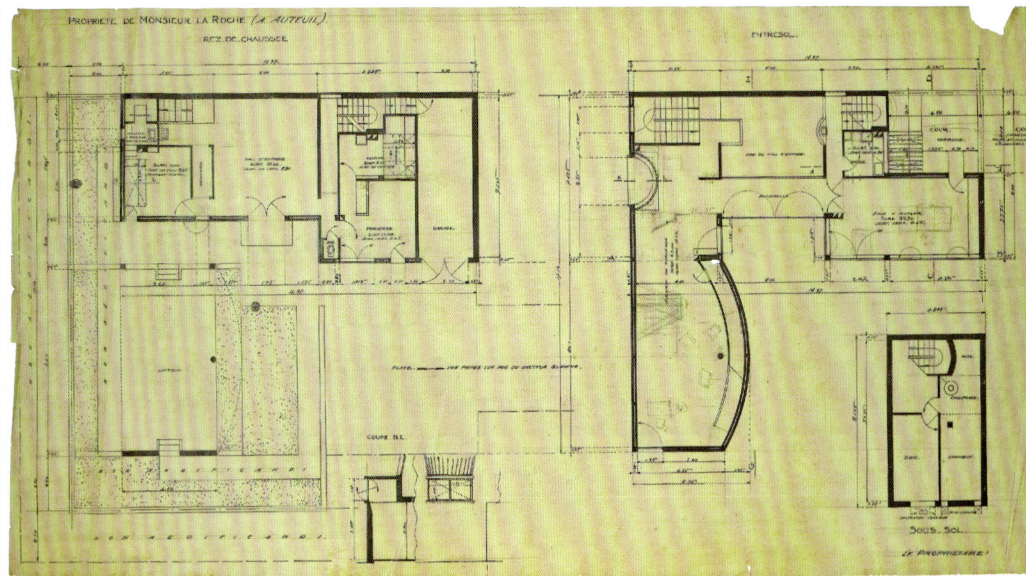

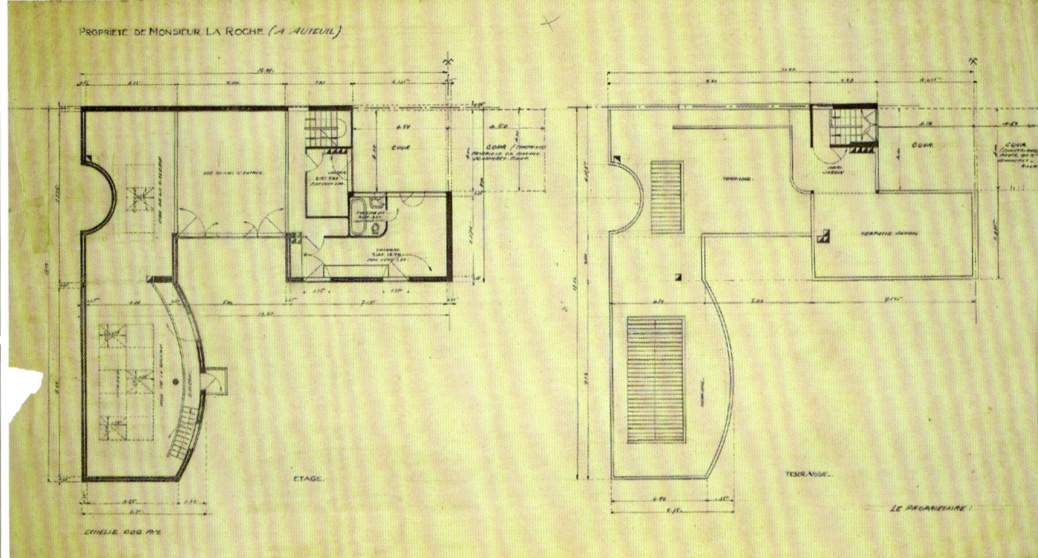

pposite, top. ketch, c. 1923, of early design for lla La Roche–anneret, Paris, 23–25

pposite, bottom. levation, Villa La oche–Jeanneret

p. Ground-floor d mezzanine ans, Villa La oche

iddle. Plans of the cond floor and rrace, Villa La oche

ottom. Perspective etch of a rejected lor scheme for e gallery, Villa La oche

Left. Entry hall under construction, Villa La Roche

Below. Principal entrance, Villa La Roche

Opposite, top. South facade of Villa La Roche–Jeanneret, facing the square du Docteur Blanche

Opposite, bottom. Roof terrace, Villa La Roche–Jeanneret

"And so this second house [Villa La Roche] will be a little like an architectural stroll. You enter and the architectural spectacle is there before your eyes: you follow an itinerary where perspectives follow each other with enormous variety: one plays with an inflow of light illuminating the walls or creating penumbrae."

—Oeuvre complète: Volume 1, 1910–29

420

Opposite, top. Hand-colored photograph of the salon viewed from the dining room, Villa Jeanneret

Opposite, bottom. The "Purist" bedroom, Villa La Roche, with paintings by Amédée Ozenfant and Le Corbusier

Above. View from the first floor to the entry hall, Villa La Roche

Below left. The gallery, Villa La Roche

Below right. The gallery after renovation (1928) and the acquisition of paintings by Juan Gris

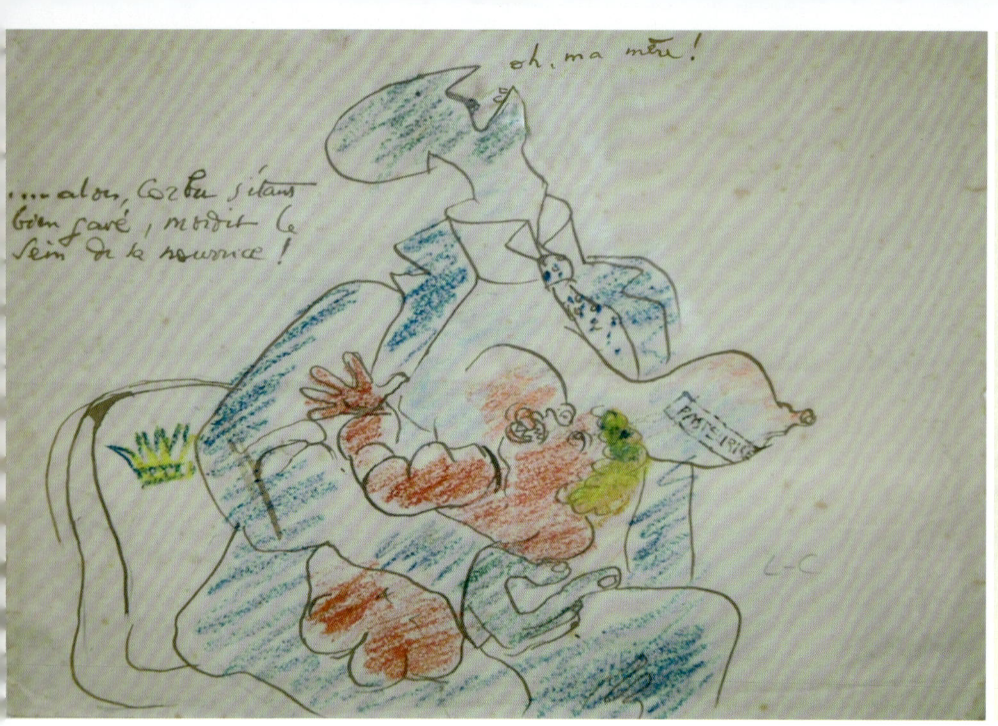

Bitter break with Ozenfant, 1925

The completion of the Villa La Roche also marked the end of the intense personal friendship and creative collaboration between Le Corbusier and Ozenfant. The rift—triggered by Ozenfant's altering the installation that Le Corbusier had designed to display La Roche's art collection in the gallery of the house—proved irreparable.

Above left. Amédée Ozenfant's caricature of Le Corbusier being suckled by a wet nurse (Ozenfant). The note on the left reads "… then, Corbu having drunk his fill, bit the breast of the wet nurse!" Written on the breast is the word "pasteurized."

Above right. Le Corbusier's caricature of Amédée Ozenfant

Below left. Le Corbusier to Amédée Ozenfant, November 1926, "Dedication for the Almanac." "Come, come amédée, let's not ruin our fine Sundays with imaginary bitternesses"

Below right. Le Corbusier to Amédée Ozenfant, 14 December 1928, accusing Ozenfant of falsifying dates and credit in *L'Esprit Nouveau*.

Opposite. Le Corbusier, c. 1920–22

Dédicace de l'Almanach

à Amédée Ozenfant

hommage d'un fourbe
d'un mufle
d'un ingrat

à cet homme détaché des contingences

qui depuis quinze ans s'est consacré à la rénovation d'une architecture nouvelle

à l'auteur de Vers une architecture et consorts et du Pavillon de l'EN

Allons, allons, amédée, ne troublons point nos beaux dimanches par des amertumes imaginaires.

Il y avait deux gars qui ont travaillé ensemble pendant sept années. Ils se trouvaient l'un l'autre, et réciproquement, intelligents.

Par quelle dépravation du raisonnement, se déclareraient-ils, désormais, des abrutis?

Un peu de tenue ne messied pas, même sous le pli du pantalon

votre [illegible]

nov 1926.

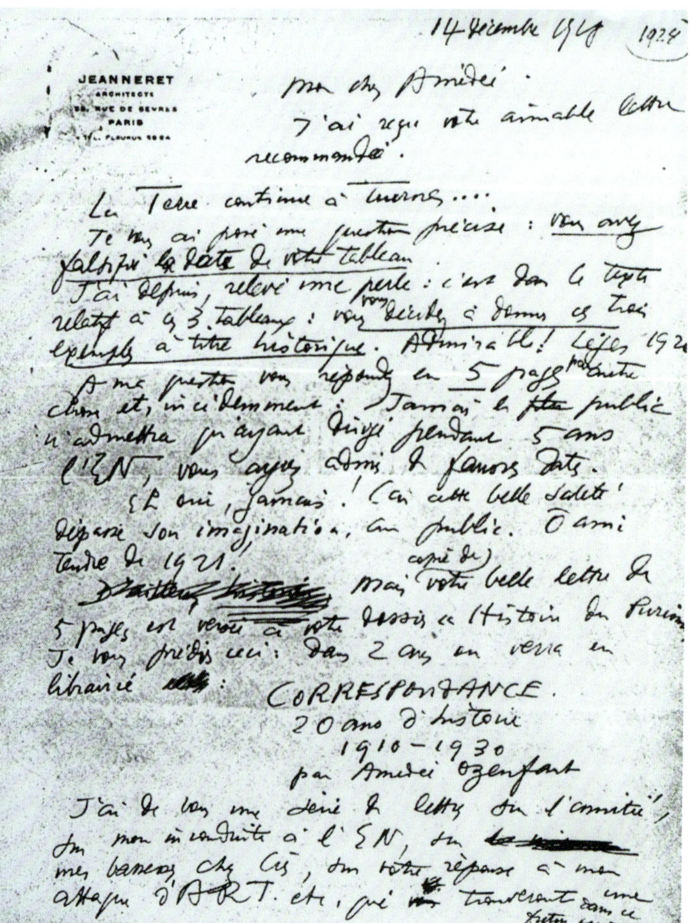
14 décembre 1928 1928

JEANNERET
ARCHITECTE
20, RUE DE SEVRES
PARIS
TEL. FLEURUS [illegible]

Mon cher Amédée.

J'ai reçu votre aimable lettre recommandée.

La Terre continue à tourner....

Je vous ai posé une question précise: vous avez falsifié la date de votre tableau.

J'ai depuis, relevé une perle: c'est dans le texte relatif à ces 3 tableaux: [illegible] à donner ces trois exemples à titre historique. Admirable! [illegible]

A ma question vous répondez en 5 pages [illegible] et, incidemment: Jamais le grand public n'admettra qu'ayant dirigé pendant 5 ans l'EN, vous ayez admis de fausses dates.

Eh oui, jamais! Car cette belle saleté dépasse son imagination, au public. Ô ami tendre de 1921.

[illegible] Mais copie de votre belle lettre de 5 pages est versée au dossier de l'Histoire du Purisme. Je vous prédis ceci: dans 2 ans on verra en librairie [illegible]:

CORRESPONDANCE.
20 ans d'histoire
1910–1930
par Amédée Ozenfant

J'ai de vous une série de lettres sur l'amitié, sur mon inconduite à l'EN, sur [illegible] mes bassesses chez Crès, sur votre réponse à mon attaque d'ART. etc, qui [illegible] trouveront dans ce [illegible] une [illegible]

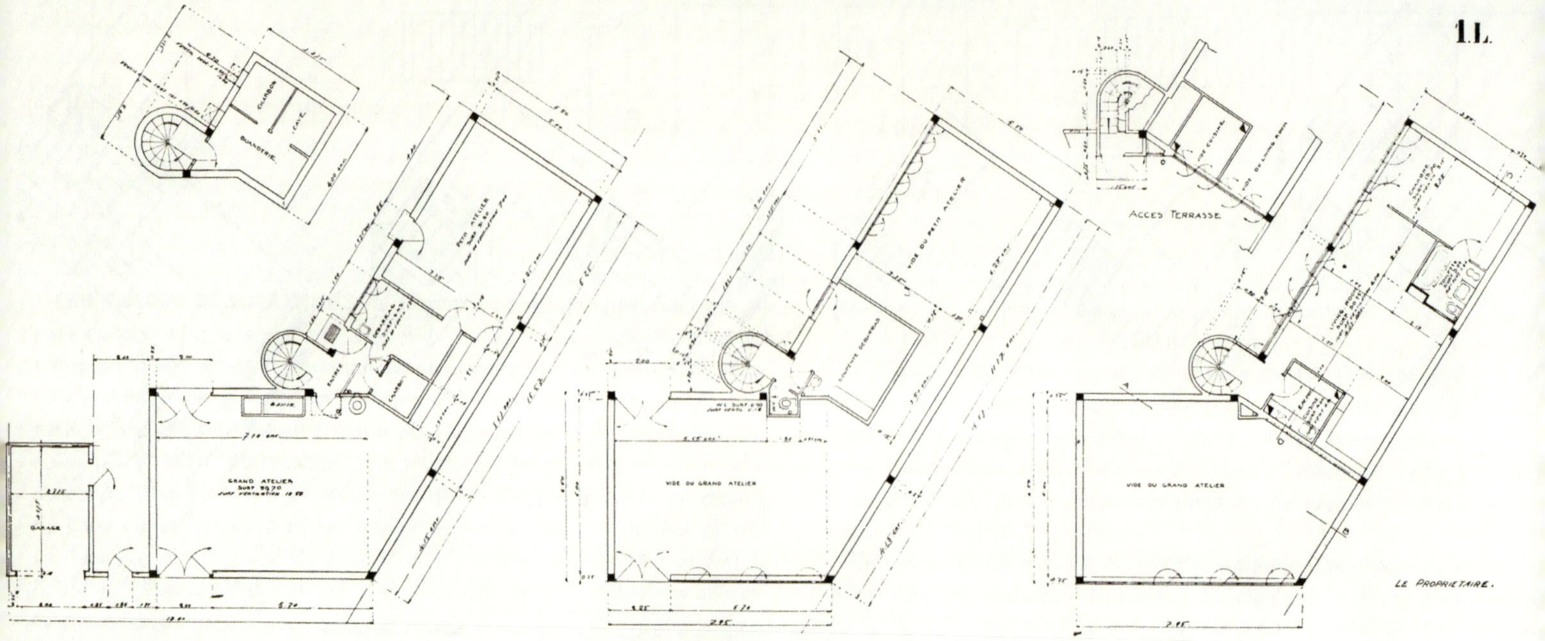

1L.

LE PROPRIETAIRE.

Rez-de-chaussée

Etage intermédiaire

1er étage

Plans de la maison Lipchitz

Commissions for two sculptors: Maison Lipchitz and Maison Miestchaninoff, Boulogne-sur-Seine, France, 1923–24

In these adjacent houses and studios designed for two sculptors, Le Corbusier placed the studio spaces below the living spaces. This inversion of the arrangement he had used in the Maison Citrohan and the Ozenfant studio made it possible to move heavy sculpture materials in and out easily. At the same time that he was completing these and other commissions secured through artistic circles in Paris, Le Corbusier successfully promoted his reputation as an architect through the publication of his book *Vers une architecture* (*Toward an Architecture*) and by exhibiting projects at the annual Salon d'Automne.

Opposite, clockwise from top:

Ground-floor plan, mezzanine plan, and first-floor plan, Maison Lipchitz, Boulogne-sur-Seine, France, 1923–24

Two views of the garden, Maison Lipchitz and Maison Miestchaninoff Entrance, Maison Lipchitz

Right. Maison Lipchitz and Maison Miestchaninoff, view from allée des Pins

Below. Tinted photograph of Maison Miestchaninoff, view from rue des Arts

"The little house will be like an ancient temple at the water's edge."

—Letter to Yvonne Gallis, 11 September 1924

A lakeside haven for his parents: La Petite Maison, Lac Léman, Switzerland, 1924–25

In 1923 Le Corbusier's parents asked him to design a house for them on a lake near Vevey, Switzerland. Unlike the house he had built for them in La Chaux-de-Fonds, La Petite Maison would be completed on time and within budget. The house was small—only four by sixteen meters—and its design was dictated by efficiency. Open to the lake on one side via a long ribbon window running nearly its entire length, the house demonstrated the architect's sensitivity to both the natural and the modern.

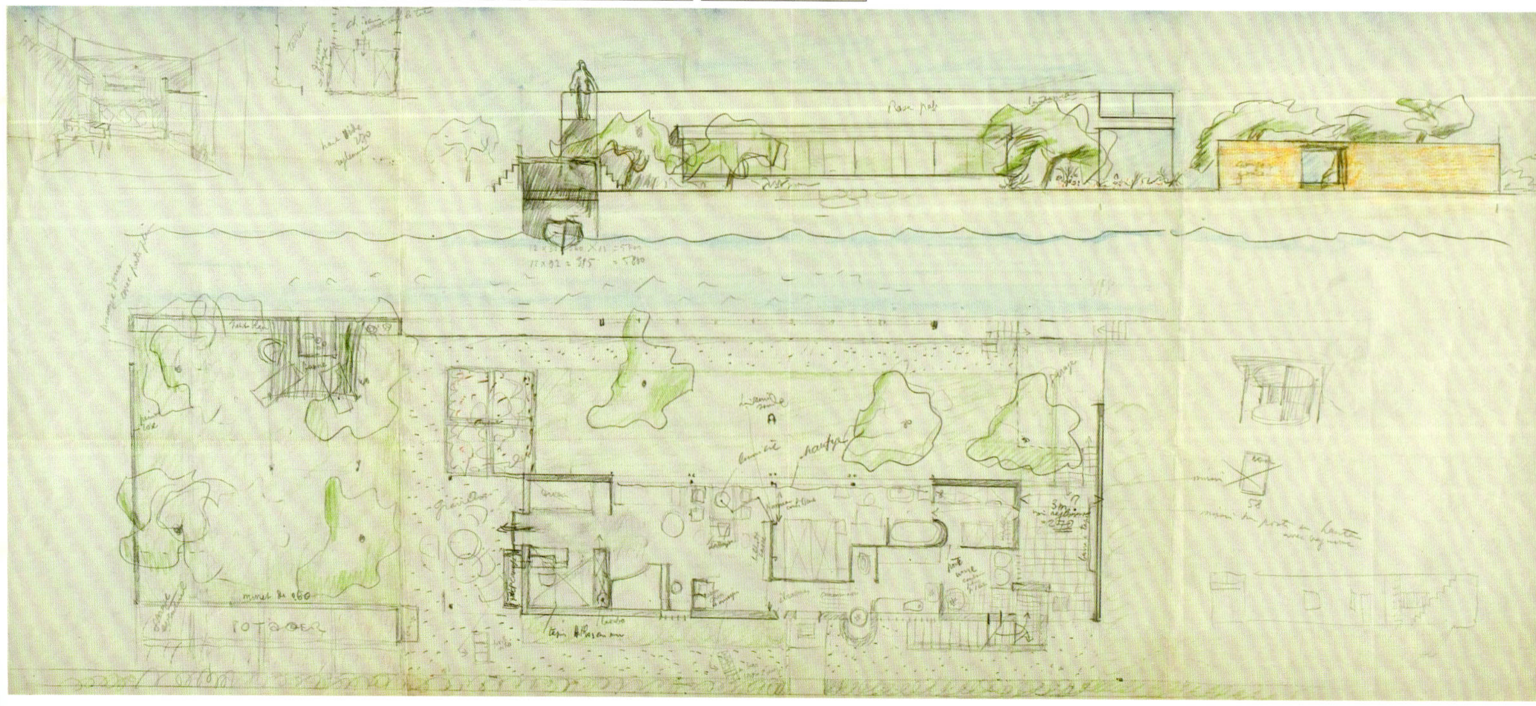

Opposite, top and middle. Sketches of La Petite Maison, Lac Léman, Switzerland

Opposite, bottom. Facade (top) and plan sketches

Clockwise from top left:

View of the lake from the terrace

La Petite Maison viewed from Lac Léman

Street facade

View of Lac Léman

View from south-east, showing the porch topped by a small terrace

View from east

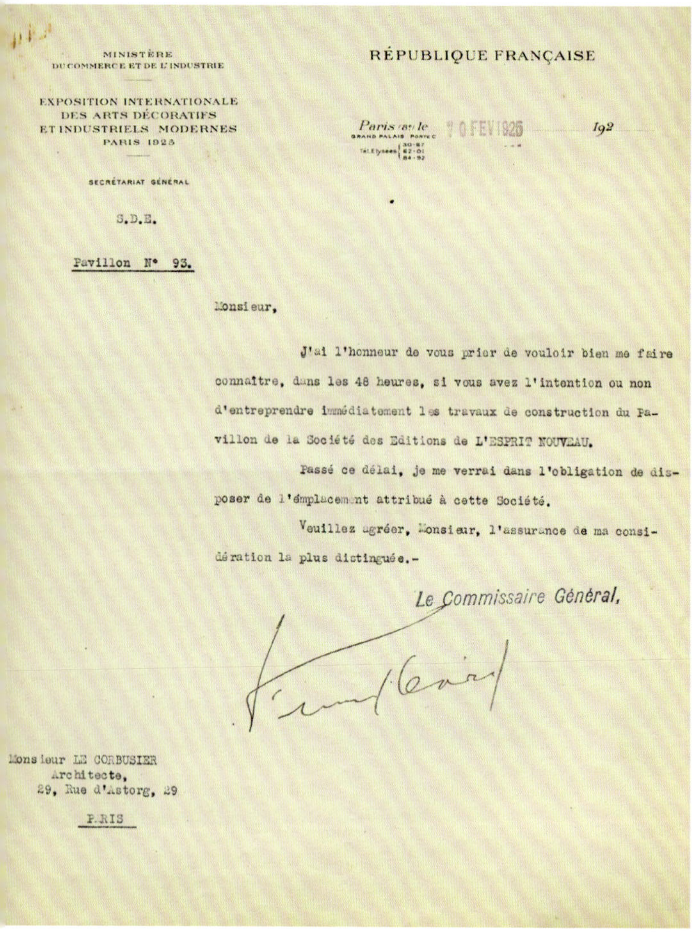

MINISTÈRE
DU COMMERCE ET DE L'INDUSTRIE

EXPOSITION INTERNATIONALE
DES ARTS DÉCORATIFS
ET INDUSTRIELS MODERNES
PARIS 1925

SECRÉTARIAT GÉNÉRAL

S.D.E.

Pavillon N° 93.

RÉPUBLIQUE FRANÇAISE

Paris, le 10 FEV 1925

Monsieur,

J'ai l'honneur de vous prier de vouloir bien me faire connaître, dans les 48 heures, si vous avez l'intention ou non d'entreprendre immédiatement les travaux de construction du Pavillon de la Société des Editions de L'ESPRIT NOUVEAU.

Passé ce délai, je me verrai dans l'obligation de disposer de l'emplacement attribué à cette Société.

Veuillez agréer, Monsieur, l'assurance de ma considération la plus distinguée.-

Le Commissaire Général,

Monsieur LE CORBUSIER
Architecte,
29, Rue d'Astorg, 29
PARIS

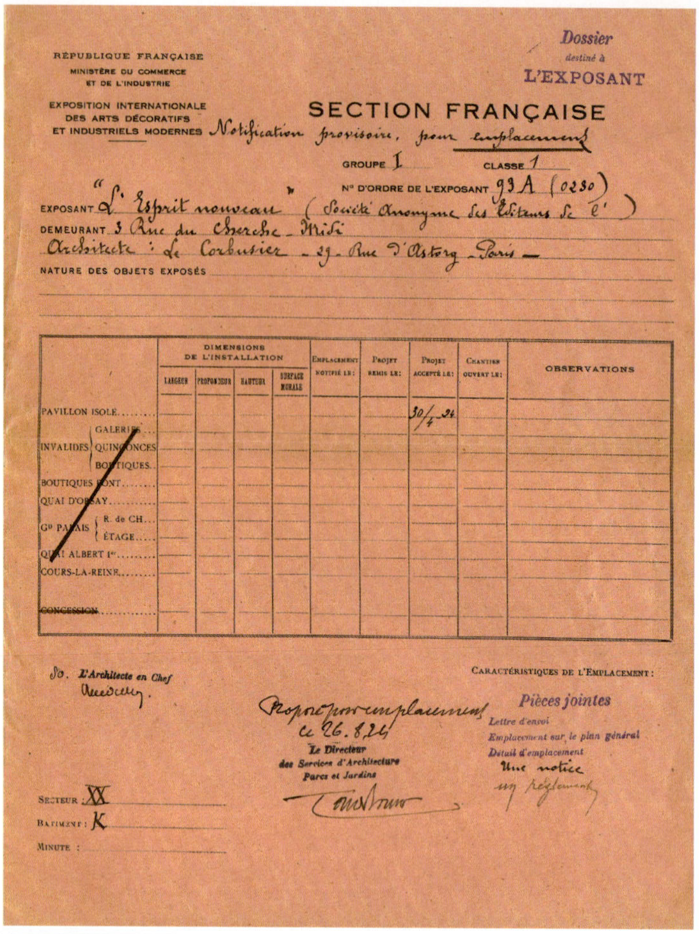

RÉPUBLIQUE FRANÇAISE
MINISTÈRE DU COMMERCE ET DE L'INDUSTRIE
EXPOSITION INTERNATIONALE DES ARTS DÉCORATIFS ET INDUSTRIELS MODERNES

Dossier destiné à L'EXPOSANT

SECTION FRANÇAISE

Notification provisoire, pour emplacement

GROUPE I CLASSE 1

N° D'ORDRE DE L'EXPOSANT 93 A (0230)

EXPOSANT "L'Esprit nouveau" (Société Anonyme des Editions de l')

DEMEURANT 3 Rue du Cherche-Midi

Architecte : Le Corbusier – 29 Rue d'Astorg – Paris –

NATURE DES OBJETS EXPOSÉS

	DIMENSIONS DE L'INSTALLATION				EMPLACEMENT NOTIFIÉ LE:	PROJET REMIS LE:	PROJET ACCEPTÉ LE:	CHANTIER OUVERT LE:	OBSERVATIONS
	LARGEUR	PROFONDEUR	HAUTEUR	SURFACE MURALE					
PAVILLON ISOLÉ							30/4-24		
INVALIDES GALERIES									
INVALIDES QUINCONCES									
INVALIDES BOUTIQUES									
BOUTIQUES PONT									
QUAI D'ORSAY									
Gd PALAIS R. de CH.									
Gd PALAIS ÉTAGE									
QUAI ALBERT 1er									
COURS-LA-REINE									
CONCESSION									

Vu. L'Architecte en Chef

CARACTÉRISTIQUES DE L'EMPLACEMENT :

Proposé pour emplacement le 26.8.24

Le Directeur des Services d'Architecture Parcs et Jardins

Pièces jointes
Lettre d'envoi
Emplacement sur le plan général
Détail d'emplacement
Une notice
un règlement

SECTEUR XX
BATIMENT : K
MINUTE :

State-of-the-art housing for the masses: Pavillon de l'Esprit Nouveau, 1925

Le Corbusier created the Pavillon de l'Esprit Nouveau for the 1925 *Exposition des arts décoratifs et industriels modernes*. Built as one in a series of temporary structures erected between Les Invalides and the Grand Palais on either side of the Seine, the Pavillon de l'Esprit Nouveau was intended to demonstrate the potential for standardizing residential construction with industrial materials. It was presented as a residential unit to be included within the Plan Voisin—Le Corbusier's revolutionary, and highly controversial, master plan for Paris.

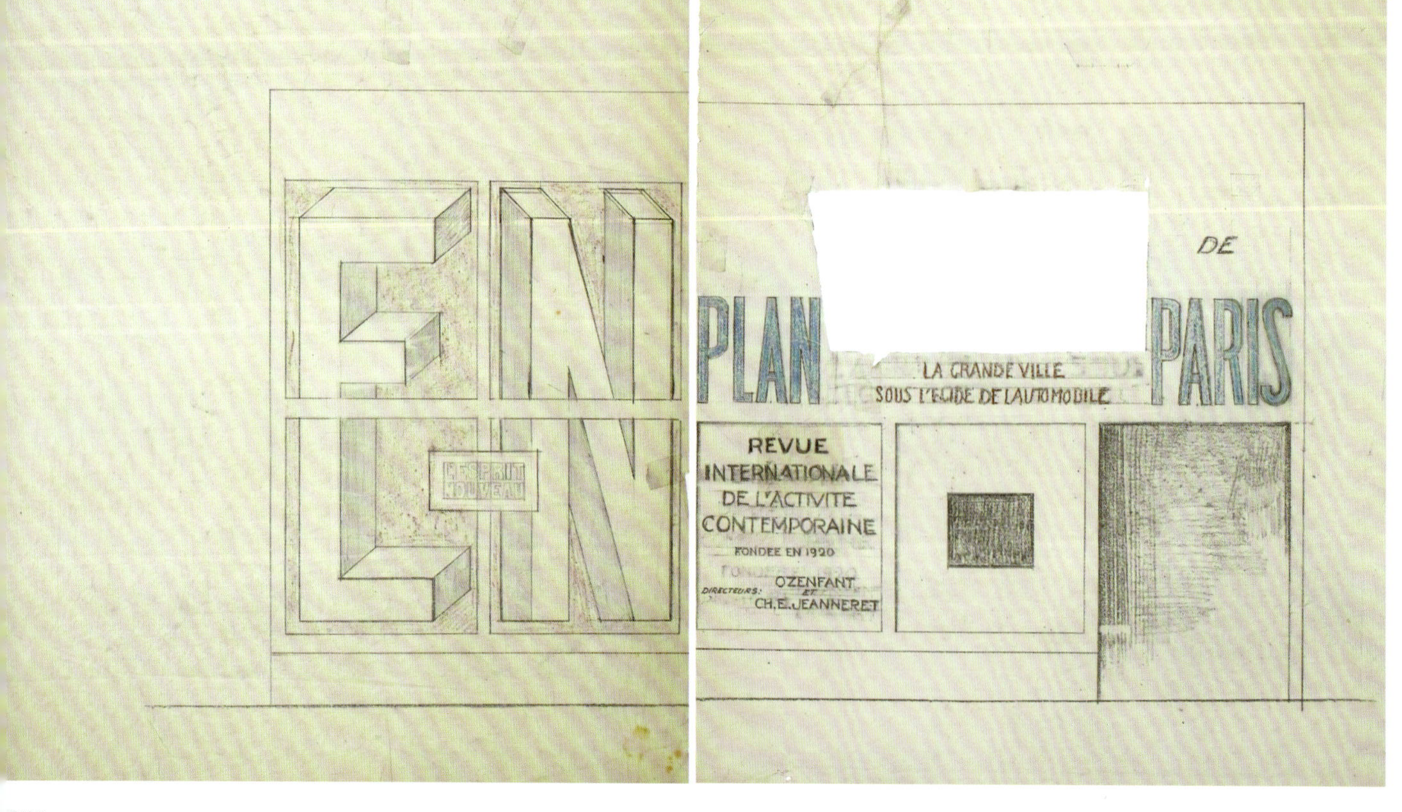

"I built the Pavillon de l'Esprit Nouveau, which is a fantastic avant-garde work for the period. The entire modular order of housing was created in it, with surprising pomp yet without any sumptuosity... The pavilion was ready in 1922, but the outside was shocking and naturally everybody screamed at the outside without bothering to see what was inside."

—Interview, 1962, *The Oral History of Architecture*

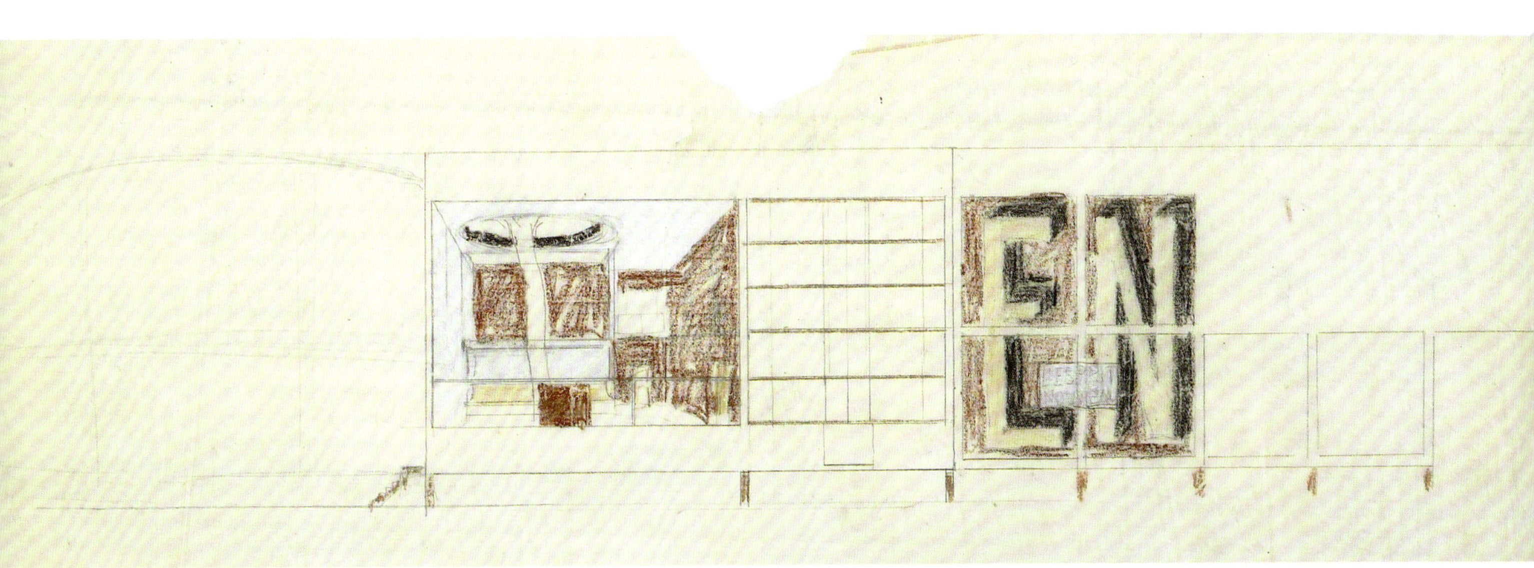

Opposite, top left. Letter from the commissioner general of the *Exposition des arts décoratifs et industriels modernes* to Le Corbusier, 10 February 1925, advising him that construction is about to begin on the Pavillon de l'Esprit Nouveau

Opposite, top right. Notification of specifications for the Pavillon de l'Esprit Nouveau, signed by the director of architecture services for the exposition

Opposite, bottom. Sketches of principal facade and signage

Top. Perspective sketch and elevation

Above. Facade study

L'ESPRIT
NOUVEAU

L'ESPRIT
NOUVEAU

Opposite, top. Garden terrace facade, Pavillon de l'Esprit Nouveau, Paris

Opposite, bottom left. Detail of entry facade, with mural by Le Corbusier

Opposite, bottom right. Corner detail

Right. Two views of garden with sculpture by Jacques Lipchitz

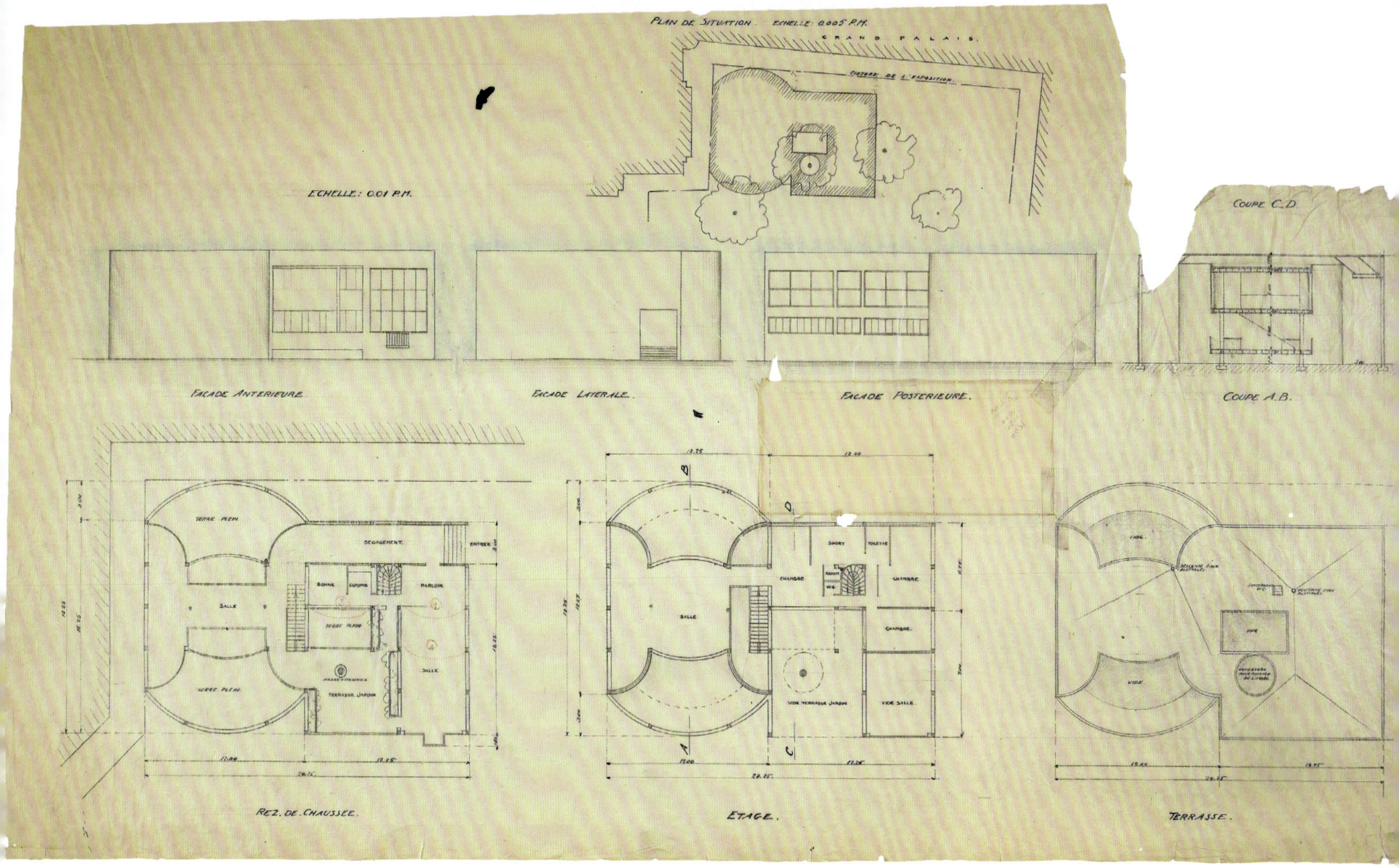

PLAN DE SITUATION . ECHELLE: 0.005 P.M.

GRAND PALAIS

ECHELLE: 0.01 P.M.

COUPE C.D.

FACADE ANTERIEURE

FACADE LATERALE

FACADE POSTERIEURE

COUPE A.B.

REZ. DE. CHAUSSEE

ETAGE

TERRASSE

Above. Site plan, elevations, section, and plans, Pavillon de l'Esprit Nouveau, Paris

Left. Detail of salon with paintings by Fernand Léger (left) and Le Corbusier, and furniture by Thonet

Opposite, top. Double-height salon

Opposite, bottom left. Staircase from ground floor to first floor

Opposite, bottom right. Dining room

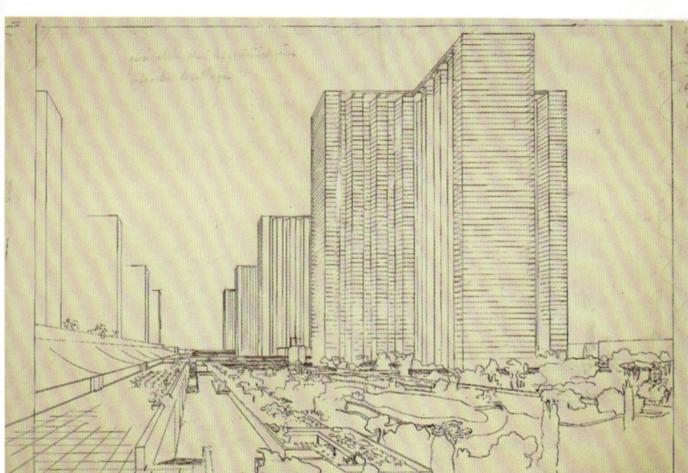

Metropolis as manifesto: Plan Voisin, 1925

Le Corbusier's Plan Voisin was named after the automobile manufacturer that partially funded the Pavillon de l'Esprit Nouveau. This radical proposal for Paris called for the destruction of hundreds of acres on the Right Bank, including the ancient Marais district, to accommodate towering apartment blocks and vast parks. In addition, a new large-scale highway would obliterate even more of the city. Observers then and ever since have decried the ambitious plan as outrageous. But some architectural historians, while acknowledging th plan's excesses, have also pointed out the prescienc of Le Corbusier's vision of the mod ern city.

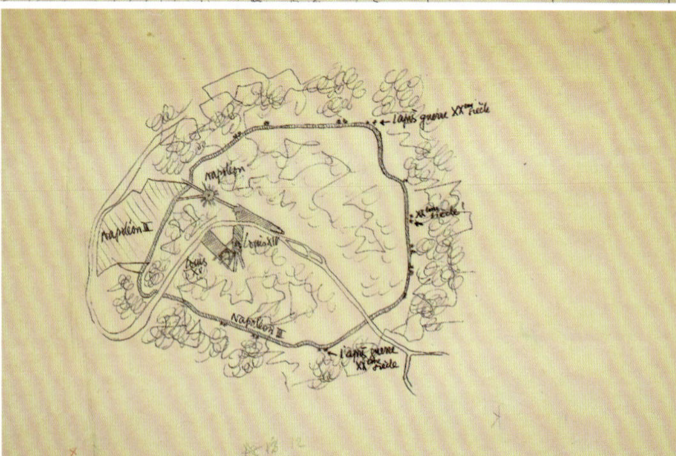

Opposite, top. Perspective sketch, Plan Voisin, 1925. Titled "Une ville contemporaine," showing the plan's main features: skyscrapers, parks and gardens, and elevated highways

Opposite, middle left. Plan of Paris indicating location of the ancient city walls and major construction projects throughout history

Opposite, middle right. Site plan, showing the Plan Voisin's location on the Right Bank, along the axis of boulevard Sébastopol

Right. Bird's-eye-view axonometric, showing typical cruciform skyscrapers

Below. Photograph of panorama, Plan Voisin

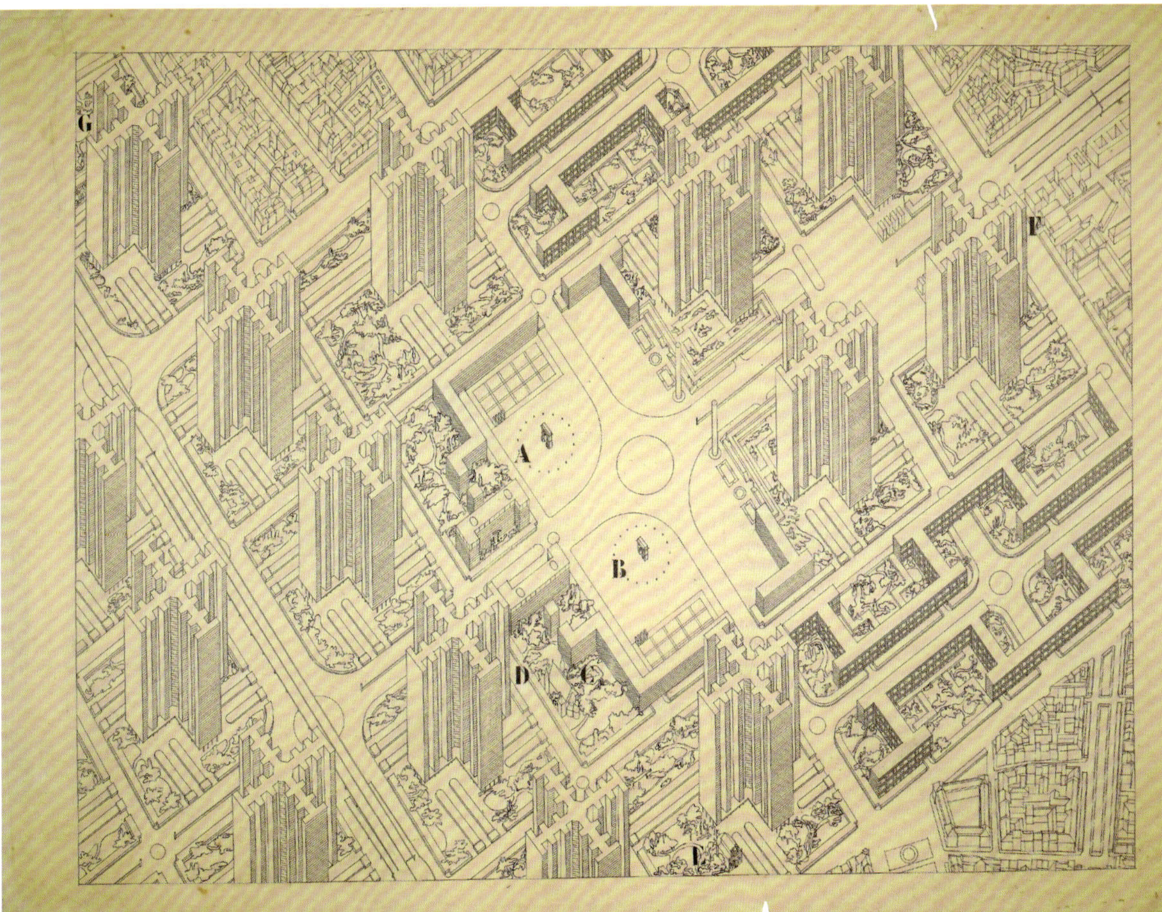

His father's death, January 1926: Georges-Edouard Jeanneret-Gris (1855–1926)

The slow physical decline of Georges Jeanneret, and his excruciating terminal illness, became a source of great emotional pain to his family. Although Le Corbusier unflinchingly sketched his father on his deathbed (as he would do with his mother and wife decades later), the grief of losing him under such difficult circumstances would haunt Le Corbusier for years to come.

Above. Le Corbusier's father, Georges-Edouard Jeanneret-Gris

Below left. First page of letter from Le Corbusier to William Ritter and Janko Czadra, 18 January 1926, about the recent death of his father, "in perfect peace"

Below right. Le Corbusier to his mother, 3 May 1927, about his design for his father's grave

Opposite, top and bottom left. Le Corbusier's sketches of his father

Opposite, bottom right. Le Corbusier's father on his deathbed, 11 January 1926

"If only you knew how sad, heartbreaking and pitiful it is to see my poor dad... He feels that life is abandoning him and that he's going downhill fast. My poor mother is stouthearted. She smiles and cajoles, she makes him think all's going well. Then she goes into the kitchen and cries." —Letter to Yvonne Gallis, 24 December 1925

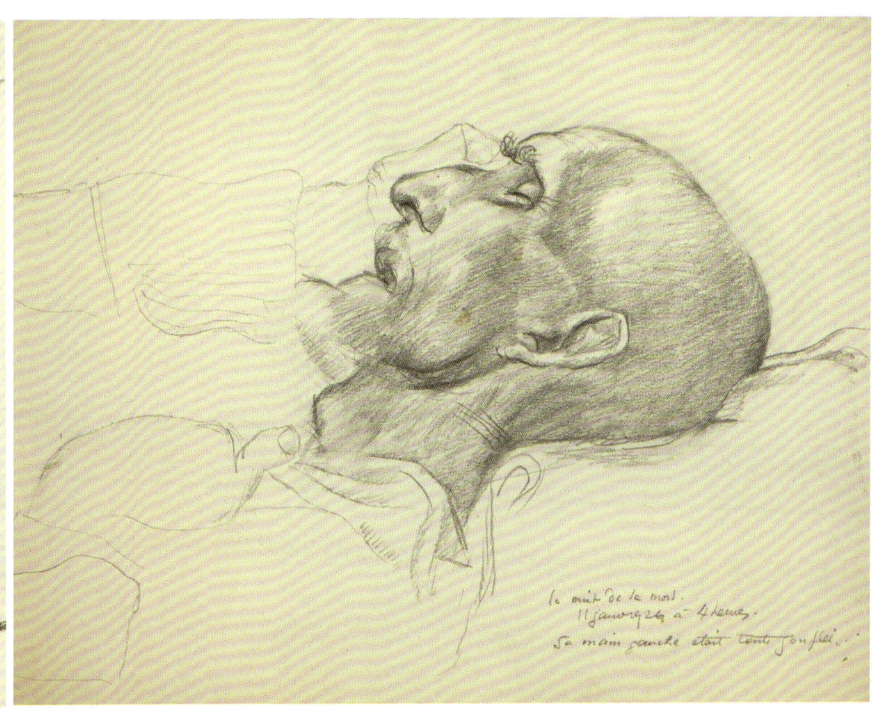

"The pool is a restful sight: its subtlety of line and delicacy of color, and the houses crammed together around the edge dazzled us from the start, and still delight us." —Letter to his mother, August 1926

On holiday in Le Piquey, France, with Yvonne, summer 1926

In 1926 Le Corbusier and Yvonne Gallis spent their summer holiday at the seaside resort of Le Piquey, on the Bassin d'Arcachon, a region in southwestern France that Amédée Ozenfant had introduced him to several years earlier. In addition to his delight in the simple vernacular beach cottages that lined the hillsides of Le Piquey, the trip was noteworthy for another reason: it was here that, at age thirty-eight, Le Corbusier finally learned to swim.

Opposite, top. Sketch of typical wooden cottage at Le Piquey, France

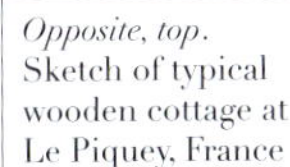

Opposite, bottom. Yvonne and Le Corbusier at Le Piquey

Above. Sketch of wooden cottage construction

Right. Sketch of outdoor scene, Le Piquey

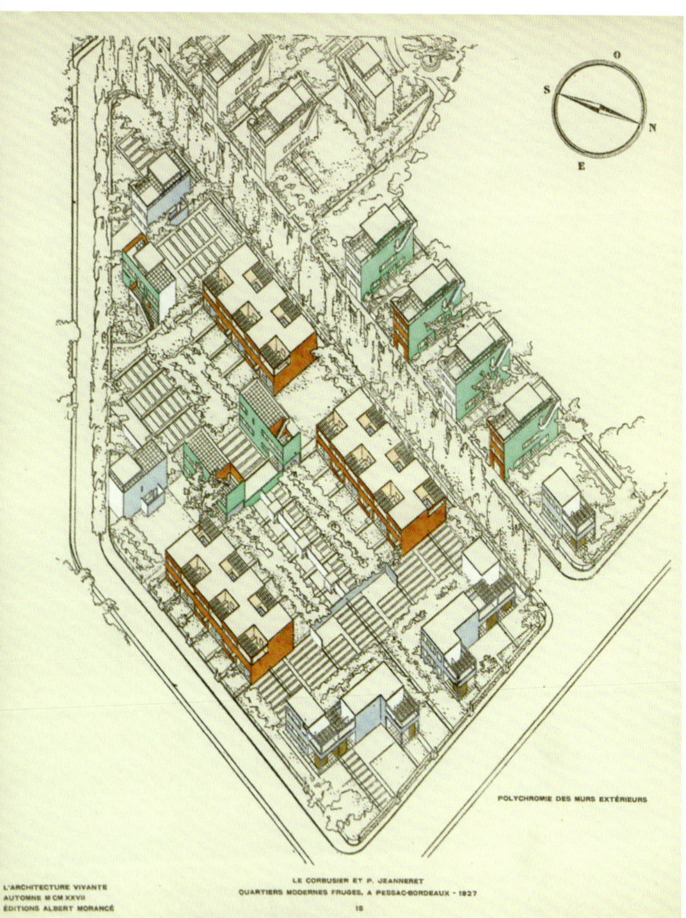

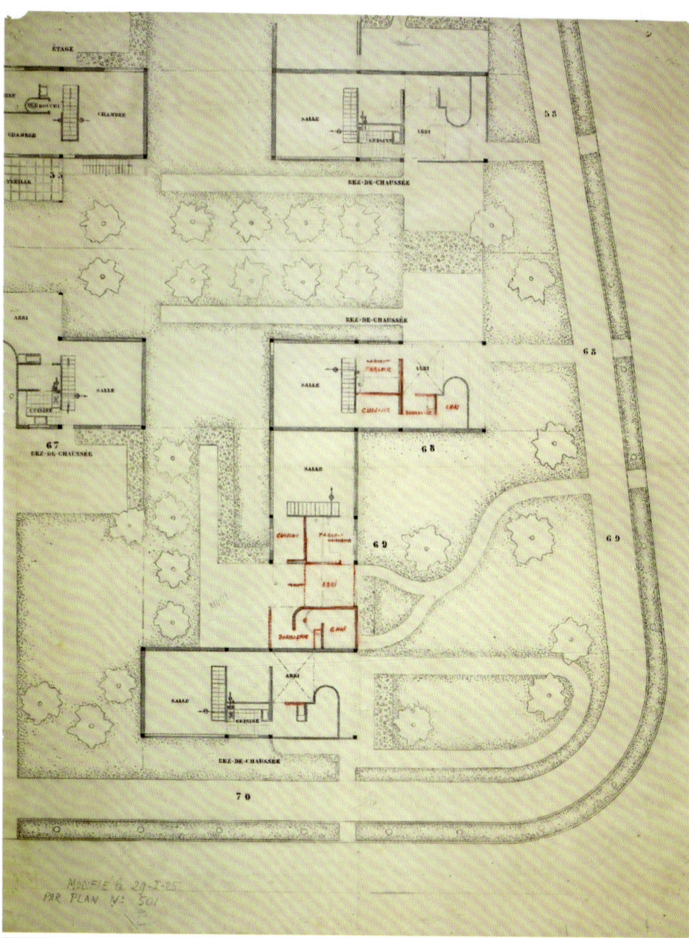

An expensive experiment with low-cost housing: Quartier Moderne Frugès, Pessac, France, 1925–28

The Quartier Moderne (modern neighborhood) Frugès in Pessac, near Bordeaux, was commissioned by Henri Frugès, who also partially funded the Pavillon de l'Esprit Nouveau. Frugès wanted to provide decent, inexpensive housing for his employees, a program that fit in neatly with Le Corbusier's research into the Garden City movement and the ideas of French urban designer Tony Garnier; it also related to the workers' housing he had seen in Berlin.

Le Corbusier's solution, a variation on the Maison Citrohan, was to be constructed of standardized components that would be arranged in different configurations, such as terrace houses or apartment blocks. All the streets would be lined with trees, and residents would have access to private gardens and roof terraces. However, standardizing the structural components proved challenging, and the costs became prohibitive. Nevertheless, the project emerged as an influential experiment in affordable housing.

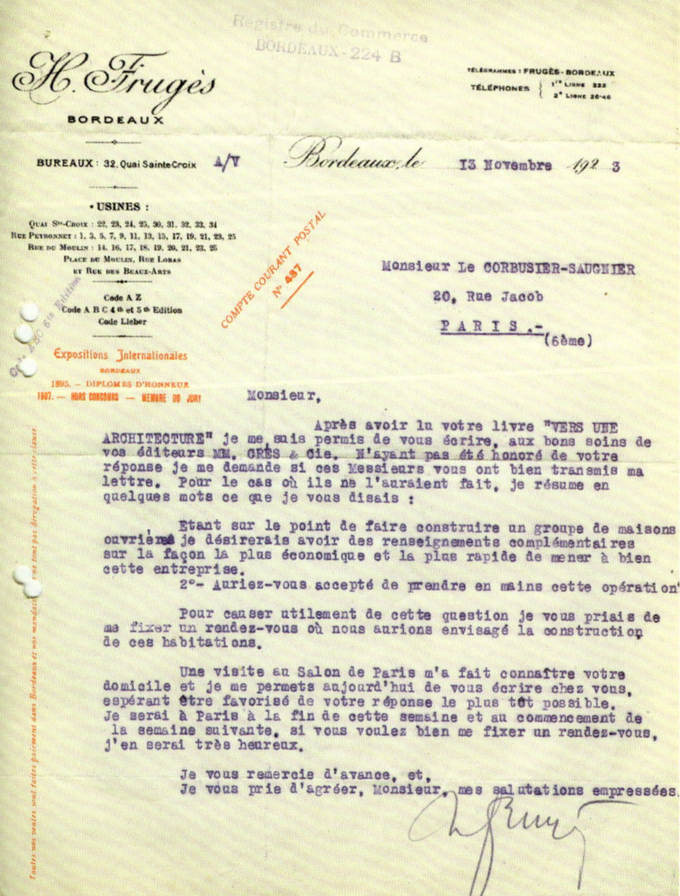

Registre du Commerce
BORDEAUX-224 B

H. Frugès
BORDEAUX

TÉLÉGRAMMES : FRUGÈS-BORDEAUX
TÉLÉPHONES { 1re Ligne 332 / 2e Ligne 26-46

BUREAUX : 32, Quai Sainte-Croix

USINES :
Quai Ste-Croix : 22, 23, 24, 25, 30, 31, 32, 33, 34
Rue Peyronnet : 1, 3, 5, 7, 9, 11, 13, 15, 17, 19, 21, 23, 25
Rue du Moulin : 14, 16, 17, 18, 19, 20, 21, 23, 25
Place du Moulin, Rue Lobas et Rue des Beaux-Arts

Code A Z
Code A B C 4e et 5e Edition
Code Lieber

Expositions Internationales
BORDEAUX
1895. – DIPLOMES D'HONNEUR
1907. — HORS CONCOURS — MEMBRE DU JURY

COMPTE COURANT POSTAL N° 487

A/V   Bordeaux, le 13 Novembre 1923

Monsieur Le CORBUSIER-SAUGNIER
20, Rue Jacob
PARIS.-
(6ème)

Monsieur,

Après avoir lu votre livre "VERS UNE ARCHITECTURE" je me suis permis de vous écrire, aux bons soins de vos éditeurs MM. CRÈS & Cie. N'ayant pas été honoré de votre réponse je me demande si ces Messieurs vous ont bien transmis ma lettre. Pour le cas où ils ne l'auraient fait, je résume en quelques mots ce que je vous disais :

Etant sur le point de faire construire un groupe de maisons ouvrières je désirerais avoir des renseignements complémentaires sur la façon la plus économique et la plus rapide de mener à bien cette entreprise.

2°- Auriez-vous accepté de prendre en mains cette opération?

Pour causer utilement de cette question je vous priais de me fixer un rendez-vous où nous aurions envisagé la construction de ces habitations.

Une visite au Salon de Paris m'a fait connaître votre domicile et je me permets aujourd'hui de vous écrire chez vous, espérant être favorisé de votre réponse le plus tôt possible. Je serai à Paris à la fin de cette semaine et au commencement de la semaine suivante, si vous voulez bien me fixer un rendez-vous, j'en serai très heureux.

Je vous remercie d'avance, et,
Je vous prie d'agréer, Monsieur, mes salutations empressées.

AUX « QUARTIERS MODERNES » DU MONTEIL

UNE VISITE DE M. DE MONZIE

Ministre des travaux publics

Nous avions été convié à nous joindre, dimanche, au cortège qui devait accompagner M. de Monzie, ministre des travaux publics, dans sa visite des « quartiers modernes Frugès », situés au Monteil, deux kilomètres après le bourg de Pessac, à deux cents mètres environ de la route départementale.

Il est dix heures quand le ministre des travaux publics fait son entrée dans les « quartiers modernes ». Il est accompagné par MM. Arnault, préfet de la Gironde; H. Frugès, Le Corbusier et Pierre Jeanneret, architectes des quartiers; Masse, chef de cabinet du ministre, etc.

M. de Monzie est salué par M. Cordier, maire de Pessac; Barrès, président de la Chambre de commerce; Charles Cazalet, Mongermon, Bourdon, Dubois, Girardet, Caillet, Petitjean, Maurice Raynal, Albert Jeanneret, directeur de l'Ecole française de rythmique et d'éducation corporelle; Lallier, Victor de La Fortelle, Leniel, Badovici, Zervos, Me Laborderie, avocat à la cour d'appel; plusieurs adjoints et conseillers municipaux de Pessac, Brezzi, président du Syndicat d'initiative de Pessac, etc.

Le ministre visite les « quartiers modernes », cependant que les photographes prennent des clichés et que les opérateurs de cinémas tournent des films.

De chaque côté d'une allée se terminant à la ligne du chemin de fer se dressent des maisons comprenant un ou deux étages et toutes construites dans un style uniforme. Il y a là une évocation d'un paysage oriental. De fait, les immeubles, de forme cubique, ont l'aspect de ceux que l'on trouve au Maroc par exemple. Les toitures sont remplacées par des terrasses sur lesquelles des jardins ont été aménagés. Les murs sont peints en blanc, en bleu ou en terre de sienne brûlée, ce qui ne fait qu'accentuer, semble-t-il, la vision d'un de ces pittoresques tableaux comme on en voit sous le ciel d'Afrique.

Tout d'abord, les conceptions de l'architecte étonnent, surprennent, puis bientôt l'œil s'habitue et l'on finit par trouver de l'agrément et du charme à des constructions qui en premier lieu avaient dérouté les esprits même les plus avertis. C'est, en un mot, un quartier de Rabat ou de Fez comme miraculeusement posé sur un coin de notre jolie banlieue bordelaise.

M. de Monzie et les personnes de sa suite visitent plusieurs maisons, du sous-sol à la terrasse. Quelques-unes sont achevées et meublées dans le goût moderne. On observe que dans toutes les pièces il y a de l'air et de la lumière.

La visite terminée, le ministre des travaux publics se rend à la villa n. 14, sur la terrasse de laquelle des allocutions sont prononcées.

M. Frugès remercie le ministre d'être venu et explique pourquoi et comment il a été lui, industriel, amené à entreprendre des travaux de construction. Il a été guidé, dit-il, par la seule pensée de trouver dans une certaine mesure une solution à la crise du logement.

Ayant rendu hommage à MM. Le Corbusier et Pierre Jeanneret, les deux architectes du groupe, M. Frugès a remercié tous ceux qui se sont associés de près ou de loin à cette expérience, et il a fait ressortir que la présence du ministre des travaux publics en cette circonstance était pour lui le plus précieux des encouragements.

M. Le Corbusier, prenant la parole, explique ensuite sa technique. Ses développements sont suivis par tous avec le plus vif intérêt.

Le ministre des travaux publics a dit combien il était heureux d'avoir pu répondre à l'invitation qui lui a été faite. Toutes les questions se rapportant à la crise du logement retiennent son attention. Il a félicité tous ceux qui, à un titre quelconque, s'emploient dans la mesure de leurs moyens à résoudre cet angoissant problème.

Cette réunion, d'un caractère à la fois aimable et intime, a été suivie d'un champagne d'honneur.

Les maisons des « quartiers modernes ».
Dans le centre du médaillon : *M. de Monzie, ministre des travaux publics.*
(Photo « Petite Gironde ».)

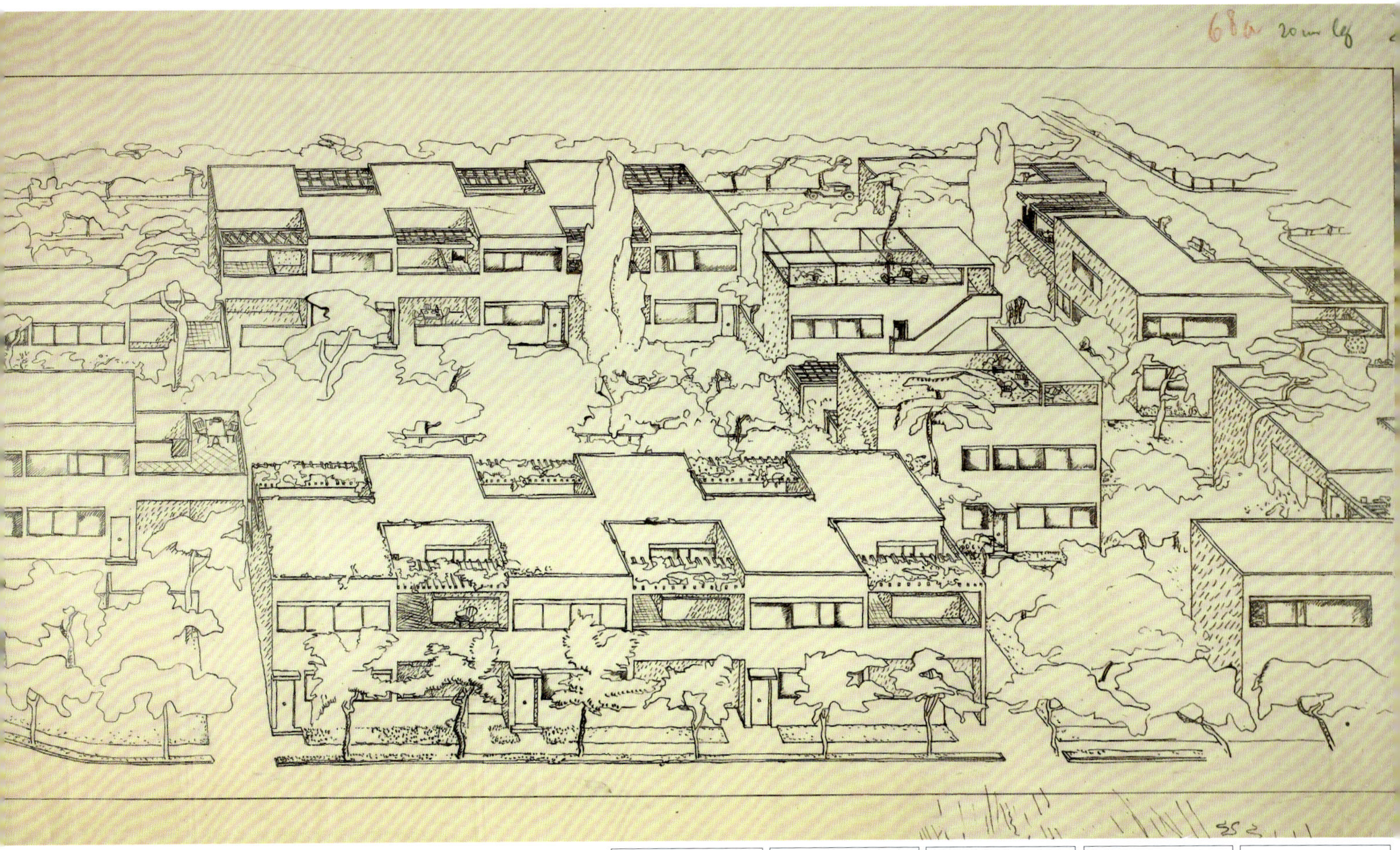

Opposite, top left. Axonometric, Quartier Moderne Frugès, Pessac, near Bordeaux, France, 1925–28, showing scheme for polychrome exterior walls

Opposite, top right. Ground-floor plan of typical unit, 29 February 1925

Opposite, bottom left. Henri Frugès to Le Corbusier, from Bordeaux, 13 November 1923.

Frugès mentions that he has read *Vers une architecture* and requests a meeting with Le Corbusier to discuss housing for his workers.

Opposite, bottom right. Undated newspaper article recounting visit by Anatole de Monzie, minister of public works, to the inauguration of the Quartier Moderne Frugès

Above. Bird's-eye perspective

Below. Perspective from the street

Above left and right, and left. Quartier Moderne Frugès, Pessac, shortly after completion

Below. Inauguration of the Quartier Moderne Frugès, June 1926

Opposite, top. Le Corbusier and Yvonne on one of the terraces

Opposite, bottom. Le Corbusier in front of one of the houses

An unconventional house for an American expatriate: Villa Cook, Boulogne-sur-Seine, France, 1926-27

William Cook, an American journalist in Gertrude Stein's circle, commissioned a house for a difficult site near the Bois de Boulogne. Le Corbusier transposed the conventional arrangement by placing bedrooms and service rooms on the ground floor, and public rooms on the second level. This inverted arrangement, which he repeated in numerous projects, produced a *promenade architecturale* that culminated in views of the treetops in the Bois de Boulogne.

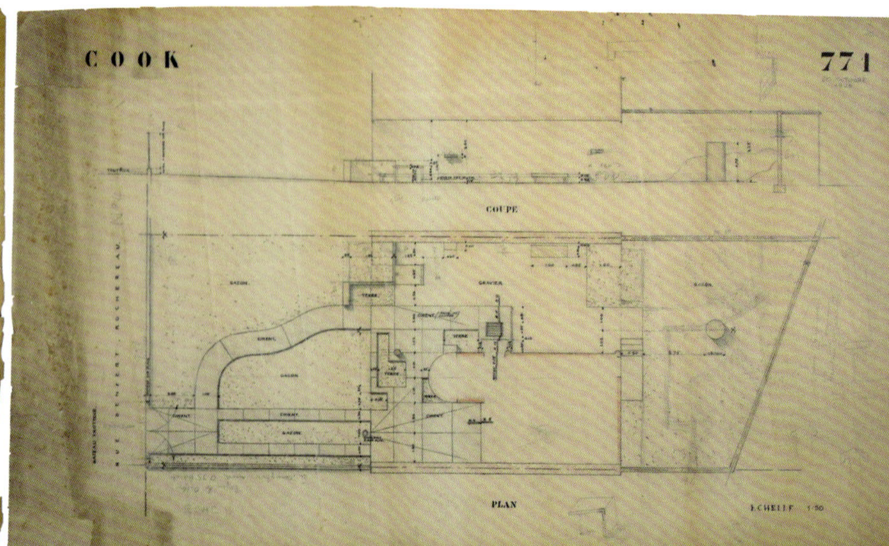

Opposite, top. Cutaway axonometric, Villa Cook, Boulogne-sur-Seine, France, 1926–27

Opposite, bottom. Elevation of principal facade (left) and longitudinal section and ground-level plan (right), 20 October 1926

Clockwise from top left: Ground-floor entrance;

Principal facade, rue Denfert-Rochereau

Double-height salon with curved wall enclosing a niche

The salon

Salon, with door onto balconette and stairs to terrace

View of terrace from third-floor library

PROPRIETE DE Mme DE MONZIE

879

A house for collectors: Villa Stein–de Monzie, Garches, France, 1926–27

Like the Villa Cook, the Villa Stein–de Monzie embodied Le Corbusier's "Five Points of a New Architecture," though with a good deal more complexity. The house was built for Michael Stein (brother of Gertrude Stein); his wife, Sarah; and their close friend Gabrielle de Monzie—all wealthy collectors of modern art. The Villa Stein–de Monzie was Le Corbusier's most ambitious residential project of the 1920s—a modernist expression of the classical ideal villa.

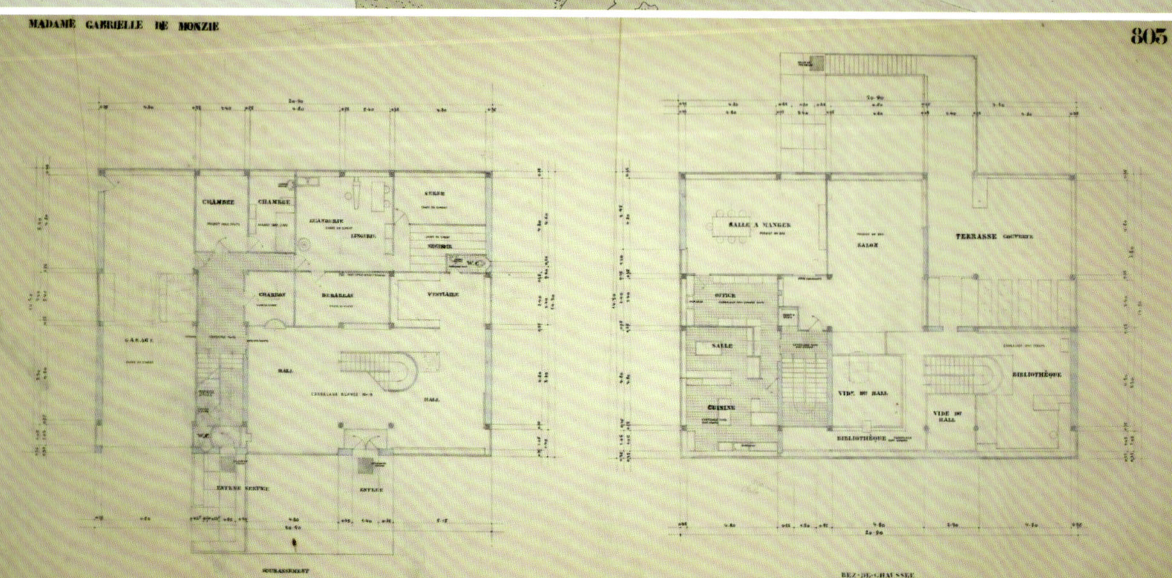

Above. Axonometric, Villa Stein–de Monzie, Garches, France, 1926–27

Left. Ground-floor and first-floor plans

Right. Villa Stein–de Monzie under construction, view of rear facade with garden

Below. Completed villa

516.X6

Opposite. Detail of the principal facade, Villa Stein–de Monzie, Garches

Below and right. A gathering on the terrace, with Piet Mondrian (right, hand on step) and El Lissitzky (right, second from left at top of stairs), c. 1926

Bottom. Main entrance, with the caretaker's house at right

Clockwise from top left:

Garage interior, Villa Stein–de Monzie, Garches, France, 1926–27

View of garden level from below the terrace

Two views of the kitchen

Interior of salon, with window at right looking out to the first-floor terrace

Ground-level entry hall, with stairs to the first floor

Right. Ground-floor hallway

"Architectural emotion: that's when the work resounds inside us in tune with a universe whose laws we are subject to, recognize, and admire. When certain relationships are achieved, we are apprehended by the work. Architecture is a matter of 'relationships,' a 'pure creation of the mind.'"

—*Toward an Architecture*, 1923

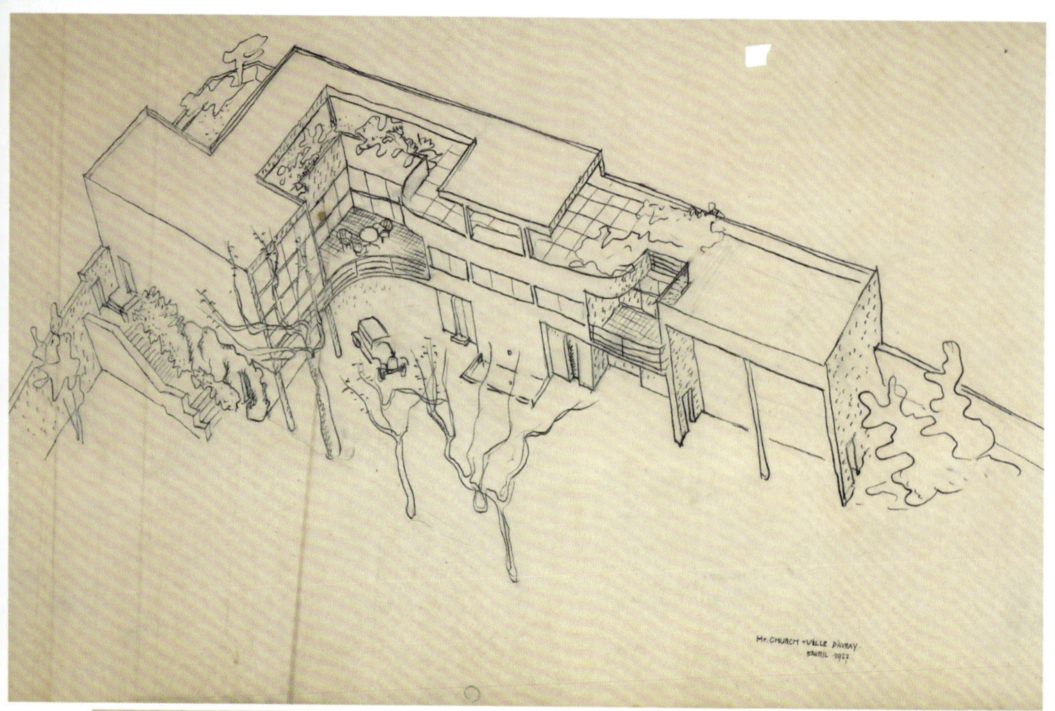

A sophisticated house for a conservative neighborhood: Villa Church, Paris, 1926–27

Built for the wealthy Americans Henry and Barbara Church, the Villa Church was sited in a uniformly neo-classical block. Faced with this setting, Le Corbusier developed a cubic volume with a strongly classical profile that featured a symmetrical facade and a formal entry sequence. Inside, however, the spatial complexity of the ascending *promenade architecturale* echoed Le Corbusier's other residential projects of the time.

Top. Bird's-eye perspective, 5 April 1927, of an early scheme for Villa Church, Paris, 1926–27

Middle. Principal facade

Bottom. Interior perspective

Opposite, top. View of the principal facade

Clockwise from bottom left: View of stairs

Two views of the library

The terrace

View from entry hall

Gardens and glass: Villa Meyer (unbuilt), Paris, 1925–26

The dominant feature of the proposed scheme for the Villa Meyer was its roof garden—a standard feature in Le Corbusier's residential designs of the period, envisioned here with extravagant aplomb. His sketches for the roof garden, the lower garden, and the generous glazing of the Villa Meyer demonstrate the degree to which Le Corbusier intended modern materials and finishes to be employed to encourage a profound reengagement with nature.

Left. Le Corbusier and Pierre Jeanneret to Madame Meyer, October 1925. The text of the letter is woven through sketches of the Villa Meyer, describing and depicting the entrance, front hallway, living room, bedroom, and roof.

Opposite, top left. Axonometric of garden facade

Opposite, top right. Principal elevation

Opposite, middle. Two elevations

Opposite, bottom. Plans of the second scheme for Villa Meyer

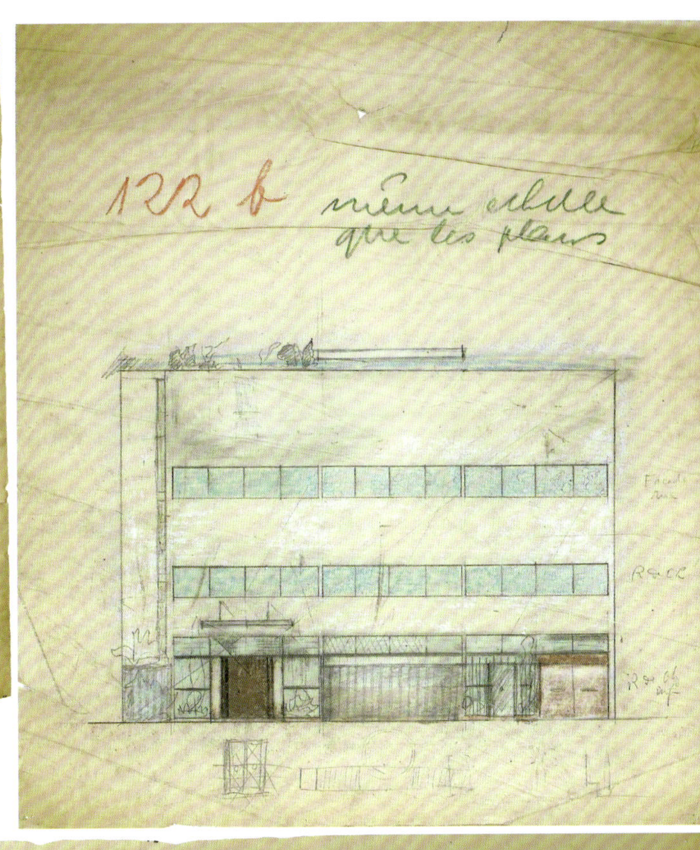
122 b même échelle
que les plans

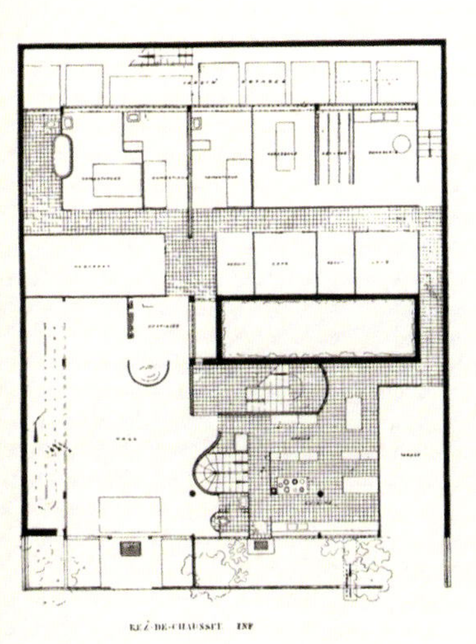
REZ-DE-CHAUSSEE INF

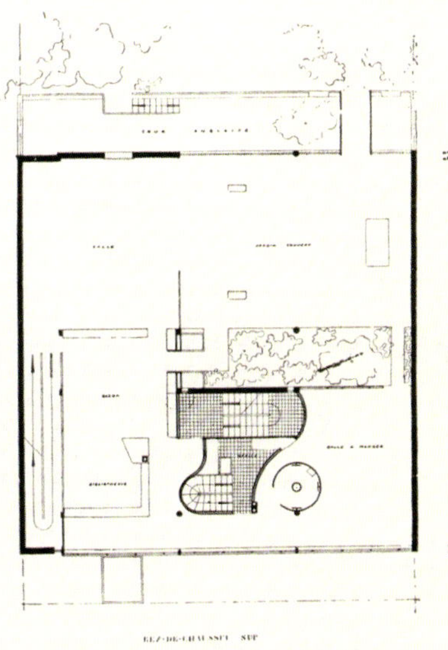
REZ-DE-CHAUSSEE SUP

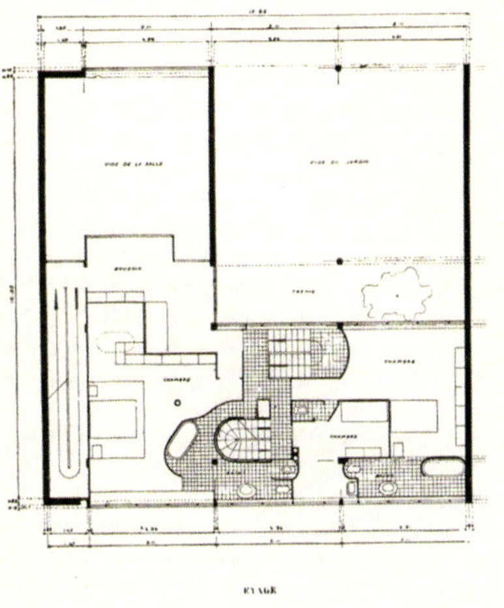
ETAGE

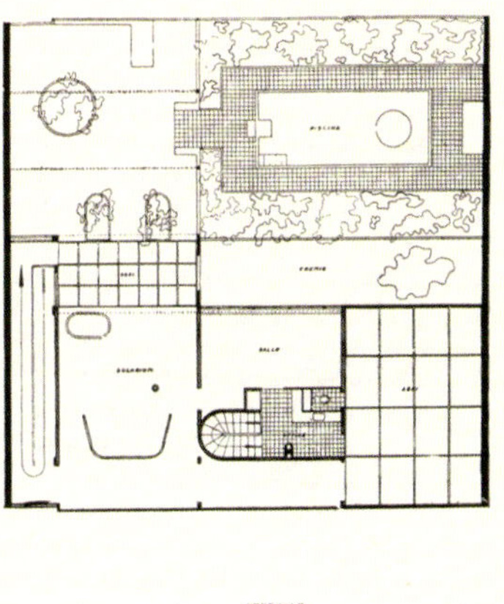
TERRASSE

Annex for the Palais du Peuple, Salvation Army dormitory, Paris, 1926

A dormitory annex for the Palais du Peuple (people's palace) was the first of three projects designed by Le Corbusier for the Salvation Army in Paris. It was followed by the Asile Flottant (floating haven, a barge converted to house the homeless) and the Cité de Refuge (city of refuge), one of his major projects to be completed during the 1930s.

Below. Plan of a dormitory floor, 22 September 1926, annex for the Palais du Peuple, Salvation Army, Paris, 1926

Bottom left. Axonometric, 2 September 1926

Bottom right. Longitudinal and transverse sections, 30 September 1926

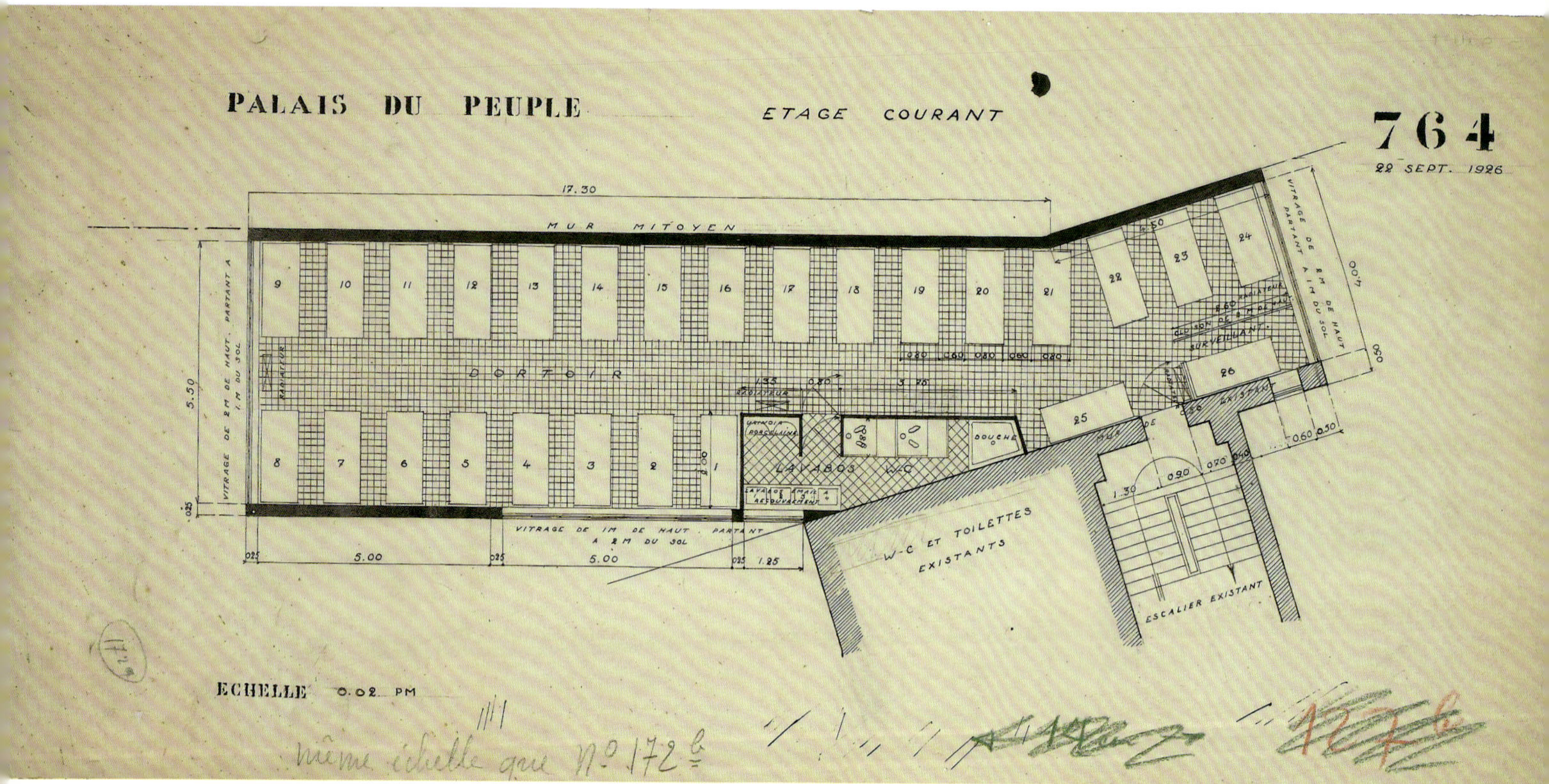

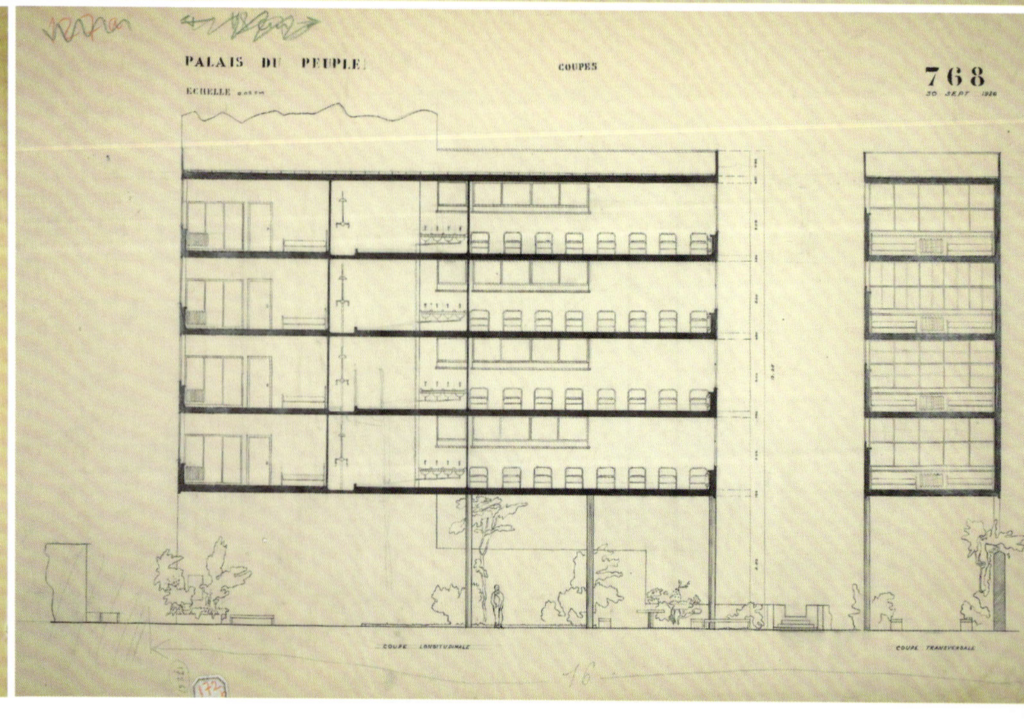

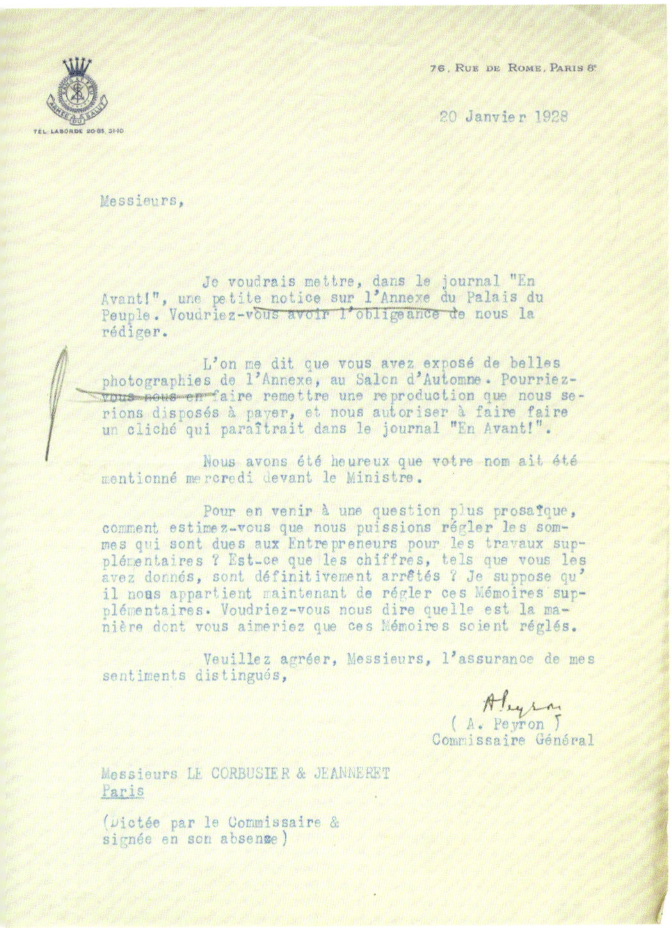

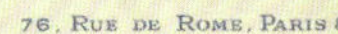

76, RUE DE ROME, PARIS 8e

TÉL. LABORDE 20-85, 31-10

20 Janvier 1928

Messieurs,

Je voudrais mettre, dans le journal "En Avant!", une petite notice sur l'Annexe du Palais du Peuple. Voudriez-vous avoir l'obligeance de nous la rédiger.

L'on me dit que vous avez exposé de belles photographies de l'Annexe, au Salon d'Automne. Pourriez-vous nous en faire remettre une reproduction que nous serions disposés à payer, et nous autoriser à faire faire un cliché qui paraîtrait dans le journal "En Avant!".

Nous avons été heureux que votre nom ait été mentionné mercredi devant le Ministre.

Pour en venir à une question plus prosaïque, comment estimez-vous que nous puissions régler les sommes qui sont dues aux Entrepreneurs pour les travaux supplémentaires ? Est-ce que les chiffres, tels que vous les avez donnés, sont définitivement arrêtés ? Je suppose qu'il nous appartient maintenant de régler ces Mémoires supplémentaires. Voudriez-vous nous dire quelle est la manière dont vous aimeriez que ces Mémoires soient réglés.

Veuillez agréer, Messieurs, l'assurance de mes sentiments distingués,

A Peyron
(A. Peyron)
Commissaire Général

Messieurs LE CORBUSIER & JEANNERET
Paris

(Dictée par le Commissaire & signée en son absence)

Top left. Albin Peyron, commissioner general of the Salvation Army, to Le Corbusier, 20 January 1928, concerning a statement and photographs for press coverage of the dormitory annex of the Palais du Peuple, as well as payment arrangements for the contractors

Top right. Exterior

Above. View underneath the building, showing *pilotis*

Right. View from a dormitory room

A traveling advertisement: Pavillon Nestlé, 1927–28

Le Corbusier's design for a mobile exhibition pavilion for the Nestlé corporation represented a strange marriage of the architect's social ideals—low-cost, universally applicable construction—with commerce.

Opposite, top left and right. Perspectives of the Pavillon Nestlé

Opposite, middle. Elevation and signage studies

Opposite, bottom. Tinted photograph of the principal facade, Paris fairgrounds, 1928

Right. The side elevation with public entrance

Below. The *passarelle*, the public passage through the pavilion

"The naked man is for him who has overcome himself and satisfied his body. He is a complex of firm, rectilinear planes. For me the naked man is architecture. When I'm not doing architecture, I see everything as women." —Letter to William Ritter, 6 April 1915

Returning to the nude: Paintings of the late 1920s and early 1930s

Le Corbusier considered painting to be a way to access the creative corners of his subconscious. Through the 1920s and into the 1930s, his paintings evolved from mainly still lifes in the Purist aesthetic to a repertoire of abstracted figurative forms.

Above. Le Corbusier painting

Opposite, top left. L'équipe: "La victorieuse" (Team Victorious), 1928

Opposite, top right. Lignes de la main (Lines of the Hand), 1930

Opposite, bottom. Pêcheuse d'Arcachon (Fisherwoman of Arcachon), 1932

L'équipe: "la Victorieuse"
1928
Pierre Jeanneret
Le Corbusier

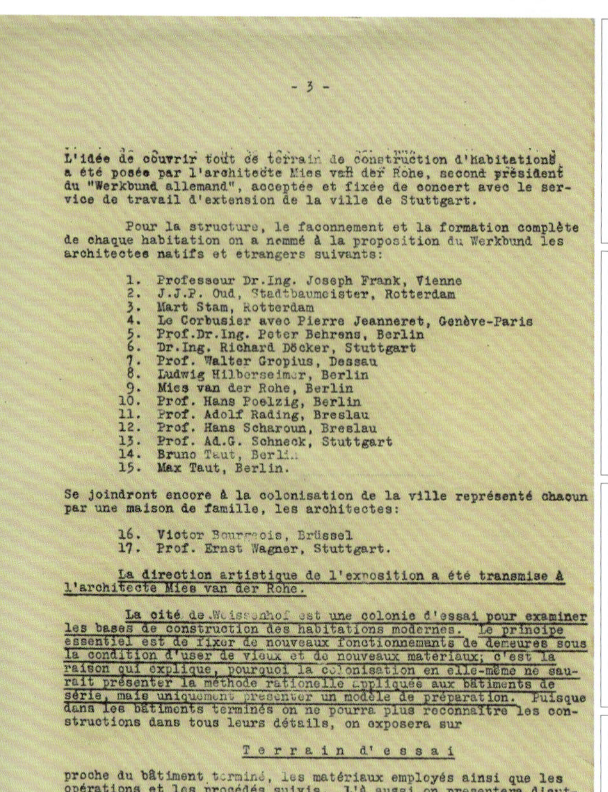

\- 3 -

L'idée de couvrir tout ce terrain de construction d'habitations a été posée par l'architecte Mies van der Rohe, second président du "Werkbund allemand", acceptée et fixée de concert avec le service de travail d'extension de la ville de Stuttgart.

Pour la structure, le faconnement et la formation complète de chaque habitation on a nommé à la proposition du Werkbund les architectes natifs et etrangers suivants:

1. Professeur Dr.Ing. Joseph Frank, Vienne
2. J.J.P. Oud, Stadtbaumeister, Rotterdam
3. Mart Stam, Rotterdam
4. Le Corbusier avec Pierre Jeanneret, Genève-Paris
5. Prof.Dr.Ing. Peter Behrens, Berlin
6. Dr.Ing. Richard Döcker, Stuttgart
7. Prof. Walter Gropius, Dessau
8. Ludwig Hilberseimer, Berlin
9. Mies van der Rohe, Berlin
10. Prof. Hans Poelzig, Berlin
11. Prof. Adolf Rading, Breslau
12. Prof. Hans Scharoun, Breslau
13. Prof. Ad.G. Schneck, Stuttgart
14. Bruno Taut, Berlin
15. Max Taut, Berlin.

Se joindront encore à la colonisation de la ville représenté chacun par une maison de famille, les architectes:

16. Victor Bourgeois, Brüssel
17. Prof. Ernst Wagner, Stuttgart.

La direction artistique de l'exposition a été transmise à l'architecte Mies van der Rohe.

La cité de Weissenhof est une colonie d'essai pour examiner les bases de construction des habitations modernes. Le principe essentiel est de fixer de nouveaux fonctionnements de demeures sous la condition d'user de vieux et de nouveaux materiaux; c'est la raison qui explique, pourquoi la colonisation en elle-même ne saurait présenter la méthode rationelle appliquée aux bâtiments de série, mais uniquement presenter un modèle de préparation. Puisque dans les bâtiments terminés on ne pourra plus reconnaître les constructions dans tous leurs détails, on exposera sur

T e r r a i n d' e s s a i

proche du bâtiment terminé, les matériaux employés ainsi que les opérations et les procédés suivis. L'à aussi on presentera d'autres nouvelles constructions dignes d'observation, des méthodes de construction et des matériaux et autant que possible, les machines de constructions en mouvement qui permettront de montrer ainsi les moyens d'emploi progressifs du travail.

Bien que les constructions d'habitations seront entièrement montées, établies, il est impossible, par elles seûles, de de-

Top left. Cover of the second Bauhaus yearbook, February–March 1928

Top right. Description of the Weissenhof-Siedlung housing exhibition, with list of participating architects.

Bottom. Plan of the Weissenhof-Siedlung site, with portraits of participating architects keyed to their respective projects

Opposite, top left. Le Corbusier with Walter Gropius in Paris, 1930

Opposite, top right. Le Corbusier with Ludwig Mies van der Rohe in Stuttgart, 1927

Opposite, bottom. Le Corbusier with Mies (middle) and others, Stuttgart, 1927

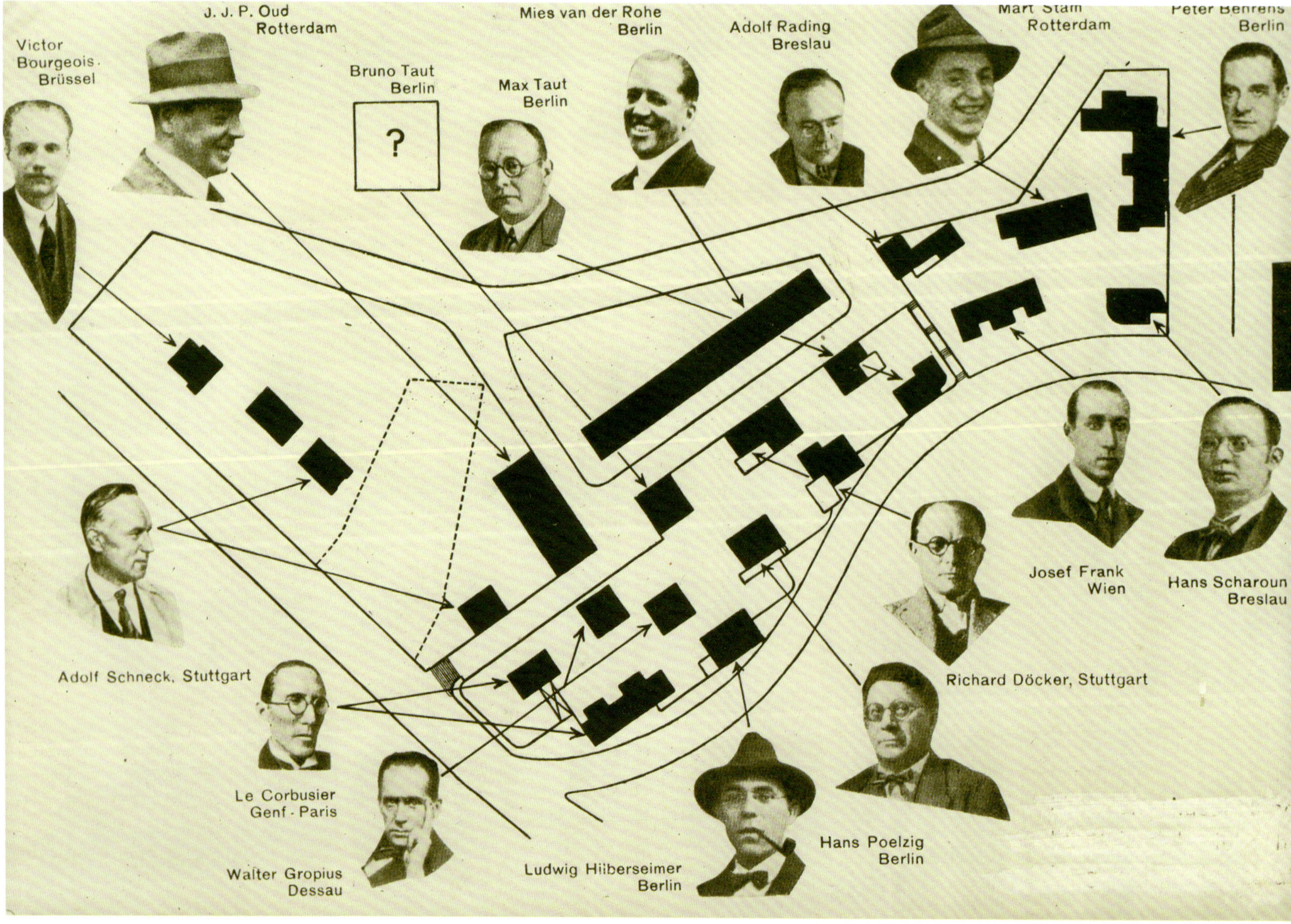

Creating a modernist neighborhood: Weissenhof-Siedlung housing exhibition, Stuttgart, Germany, 1927

After only limited success with his workers' housing at Pessac, Le Corbusier found another opportunity to experiment with variations on the Maison Citrohan, at the *Weissenhof-Siedlung*, an exhibition of full-size houses created for a neighborhood in Stuttgart. Organized by the Deutscher Werkbund and Ludwig Mies van der Rohe, who built an apartment block for the project, it also included contributions by Peter Behrens, Walter Gropius, J. J. P. Oud, and several other modernists. Le Corbusier was assigned two lots, on which he erected one single-family Citrohan-derived structure and another with two units.

P.S. Pour la bibliothèque en BL C2 en terrasse, il faudrait bien d'arranger encore une étagère pour livres etc. comme en BL. C1, mêmes divisions peut-être sans tôles coulissantes. Quand vous y pensez?

Bibliothèque.

Pierre vois J.P.

Above. Postcard from Le Corbusier to Pierre Jeanneret regarding details of his design for the Weissenhof-Siedlung housing exhibition, Stuttgart, Germany, 1927

Below. Unsigned letter from the Weissenhof construction office to Le Corbusier and Pierre Jeanneret, 7 July 1927, concerning progress on the construction of their Weissenhof project

Opposite, top. Axonometric, 6 June 1927

Opposite, bottom. Axonometric, section, and construction details

DIE WOHNUNG
WERKBUND-AUSSTELLUNG STUTTGART 1927

DIE BAULEITUNG:
BÜRO DR. DÖCKER STUTTGART
NUSSKLINGE 7 TELEF. 26176

Weissenhof le 7 juillet 1927

Messieurs
Le Corbusier & P. Jeanneret
architectes
Paris
Rue de Sèvres 35

Chers messieurs,

j'ai bien reçu les 2 lettres de Mr Le Corbusier, je vous en remercie beaucoup.

Par le même courrier je vous envoie: les esquisses pour la peinture intérieure (veuillez excuser leurs inexactitudes et leurs fautes) pour BL. C2. J'espère qu'elles vous servent. La semaine prochaine on va commencer avec la peinture intérieure, donc je vous prie de me les retourner aussitôt que possible.

Pour la peinture en BL. C1 je vous envoie les developpements la semaine suivante, je n'avais pas le temps de les préparer déjà maintenant.

Ici il y a du travail énorme. Nous sommes arrivés au „tempo presto" mais je peux vous assurer que nos 2 Blocs seront terminés pour le 23 juillet.

BL C1 avance rapidement. Il y a dans les deux blocs une foule d'ouvriers.

J'ai été enthousiasmé de vos indications pour peinture de façade, je me réjouis beaucoup de la commencer bientôt. J'ai encore une question sur ce point pour BL. C2:

blanc

vert pâle

vert pâle

aussi vert pâle ou blanc?

TYPOGRAPHIE WILLY BAUMEISTER
DIN 4 A

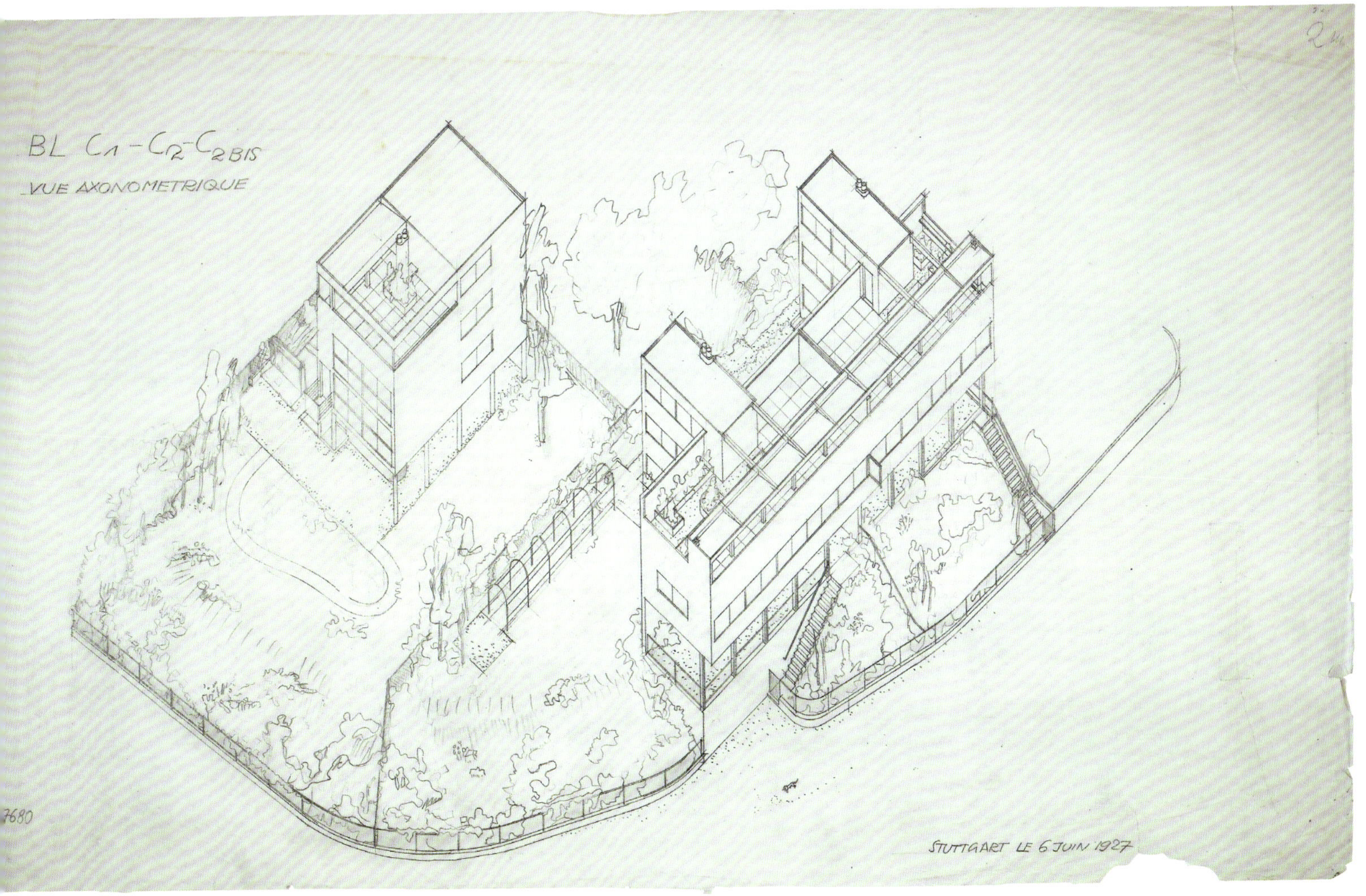

BL C1-C2-C2BIS

VUE AXONOMETRIQUE

7680

STUTTGART LE 6 JUIN 1927

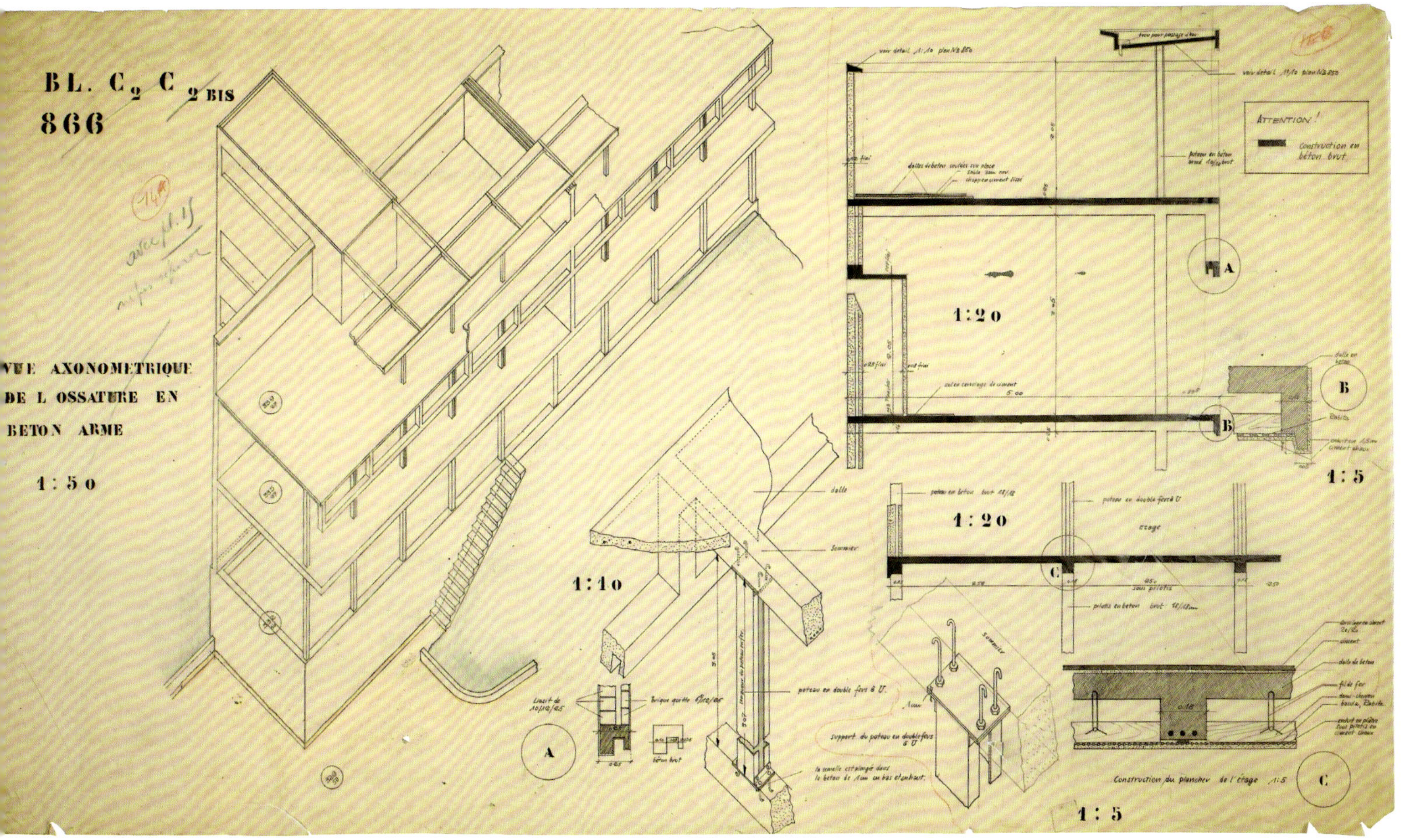

BL. C2 C2 BIS

866

VUE AXONOMETRIQUE DE L OSSATURE EN BETON ARME

1:50

ATTENTION! Construction en béton brut

1:20

A

B

1:5

1:20

C

1:10

A

1:5

C

Above. Elevation of the principal facades of Le Corbusier's two villas for the Weissenhof-Siedlung housing exhibition, Stuttgart, 1927

Left. View of the villas under construction

Below. Aerial view of the exhibition, with Le Corbusier's two houses at upper left

Above. West facades of the Villas Weissenhof-Siedlung

Right. South facade of the two-unit villa

"Architecture is the masterful, correct, and magnificent play of volumes brought together in light. Our eyes were made for seeing forms in light; shadow and light reveal forms; cubes, cones, spheres, cylinders, and pyramids are the great primary forms that light reveals well; the image is clear and tangible for us, without ambiguity. That is why these are ***beautiful forms, the most beautiful forms.***" —*Toward an Architecture*, 1923

Opposite, top. Living room on the ground floor of the double house, Weissenhof-Siedlung housing exhibition, Stuttgart, 1927

Opposite, bottom. Library fireplace and stairs on the terrace level of the double house

Above. Living room of the single house

MM. LE CORBUSIER, P. JEANNERET et
CH. PERRIAND ont l'honneur de vous inviter à venir
voir à leur Stand au Salon d'Automne (Grand Palais)

UN ÉQUIPEMENT INTÉRIEUR
D'UNE HABITATION

le Mardi 10 Décembre, de 2 heures à 6 heures.

Cette carte tiendra lieu d'entrée le Mardi 10, de 2 à 6 heures
(Porte Avenue Victor-Emmanuel).

Le Corbusier
et P. JEANNERET
ARCHITECTE
35, RUE DE SÈVRES
PARIS
TÉL. FLEURUS 39-84

Certificat

Je certifie que Madame Charlotte Perriand, architecte de Paris, travaille avec nous en tant qu'associée, depuis plusieurs années, tout particulièrement dans les travaux relatifs à l'équipement de la vie domestique.

Madame Perriand possède dans ce domaine des qualités exceptionnelles d'invention, d'initiative et de réalisation.

C'est elle qui avait l'entière responsabilité dans la réalisation de nos équipements domestiques.

Elle peut entreprendre toute étude relative à la réforme de l'habitation et en suivre la réalisation

Paris 17 mai 1932

Le Corbusier

SOCIÉTÉ
DU
SALON D'AUTOMNE
RECONNUE D'UTILITÉ PUBLIQUE
GRAND PALAIS
Porte B
SECRÉTARIAT GÉNÉRAL

Paris 15 Juin 1931

Cher Monsieur,

Le Trésorier et le Comité me prient d'insister auprès de vous pour que vous nous fassiez régler la somme de 9.733 f 50, montant de votre participation (en collaboration avec Mlle Perriand) aux ensembles de 1929 qui ne nous a pas encore été payée. Nous devons arrêter nos comptes ces jours-ci.

avec nos remerciements veuillez agréer, Cher Monsieur, l'expression de nos sentiments les plus distingués

Le Secrétaire Général

[signature]

Creating classic modern furniture: Charlotte Perriand, 1927, and the Salon d'Automne, Paris, 1929

One of the challenges encounter by Le Corbusier a the Weissenhof-Siedlung housing exhibition was the production of tub lar metal furnitur for his interiors. Almost immedi-

ately after comple tion of the exhibition houses Le Corbusier hire designer Charlott Perriand to overse fabrication of furn iture prototypes and their eventua manufacture.

Prior to her arriva Le Corbusier had been engaged in the design of seat ing, and over the next two years the firm would refine his schemes for a chaise longue, sma and large club

chairs, and a chair with a pivoting back, as well as Perriand's designs for a round dining chair and stool, an a small vanity stoo The first public showing of the tubular metal furn

ture took place at the 1929 Salon d'Automne, where the firm's expense were underwritter by the furniture manufacturer Thonet. It would add the furniture its existing line of

modernist metal furniture designed by Ludwig Mies van der Rohe and Marcel Breuer.

L. C. ET P. J.
SALON D'AUTOMNE, A PARIS, 1929

L'ARCHITECTURE VIVANTE
PRINTEMPS MCMXXX
ÉDITIONS ALBERT MORANCÉ

9

Opposite, top left. Le Corbusier with Charlotte Perriand and her first husband, Percy Scholefield, at the Bar sous le Toît, the rooftop bar that she created for the Salon d'Automne, Paris, 1927

Opposite, top right. Pierre Jeanneret, holding card, with Charlotte Perriand and Bruno Weil, director of Thonet, November 1929

Opposite, middle. Invitation to view the installation of furniture at the Salon d'Automne, 10 December 1929

Opposite, bottom left. Document by Le Corbusier certifying that Charlotte Perriand has worked as an associate at the rue de Sèvres office for several years, especially on "household equipment," 17 March 1932

Opposite, bottom right. E. Bonifay, secretary general of the Salon d'Automne, to Le Corbusier, 15 June 1931, demanding payment for the cost of participation in the 1929 Salon

Above. Rendering and photo-collage of the installation of furniture at the Salon d'Automne, 1929

Below. Sketches of the Grand Confort chair by Le Corbusier and Charlotte Perriand

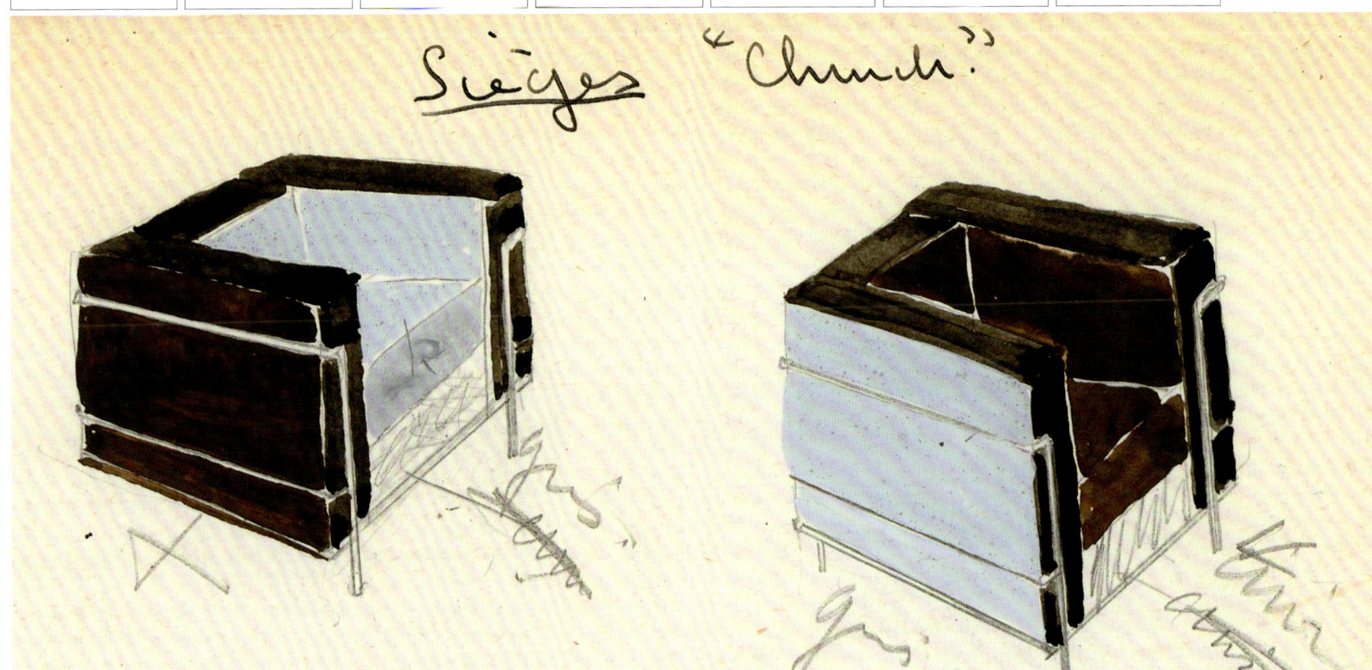

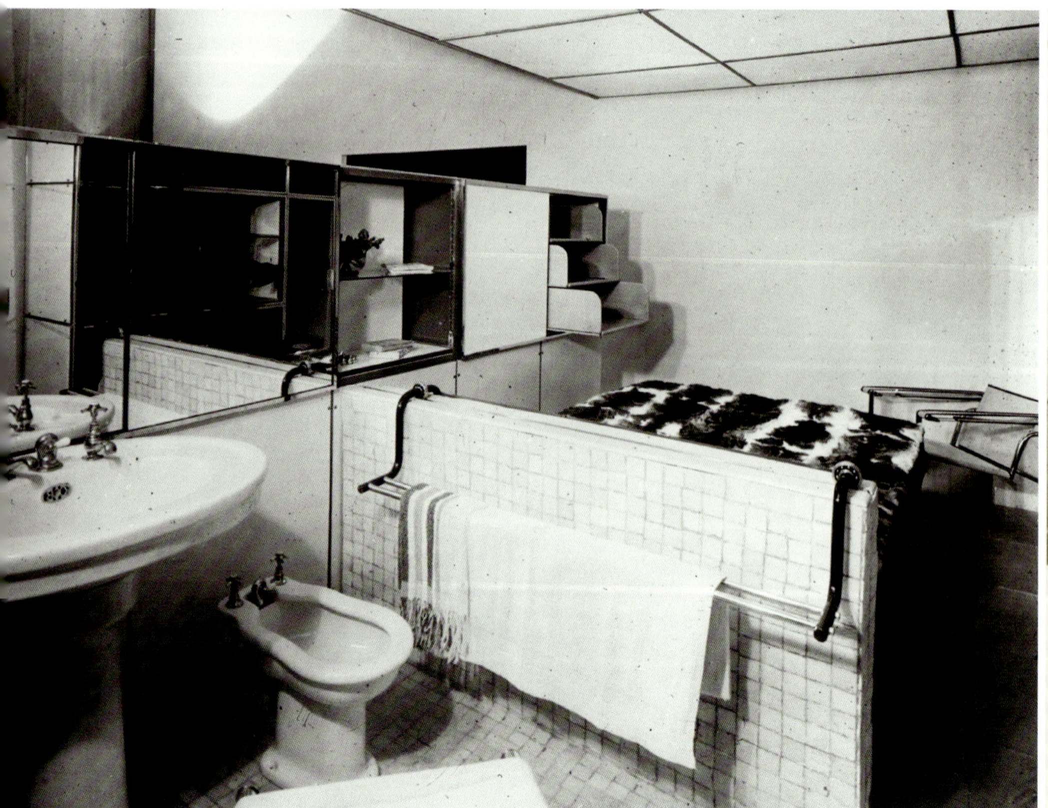

9. **L'ÉLÉMENT BIOLOGIQUE :**
LA CELLULE
DE 14 M² PAR HABITANT

B. 307
table.

CES
MODÈLES
DE

LE CORBUSIER
P. JEANNERET
CH. PERRIAND

SONT
ÉDITÉS
EXCLUSIVEMENT
PAR

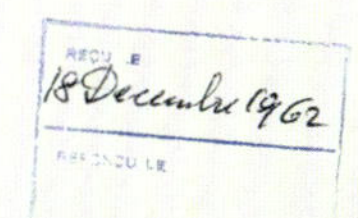

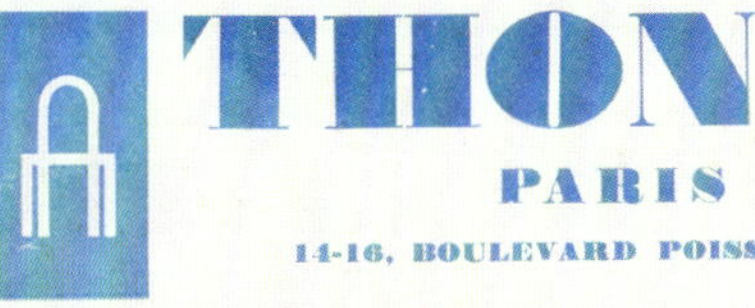

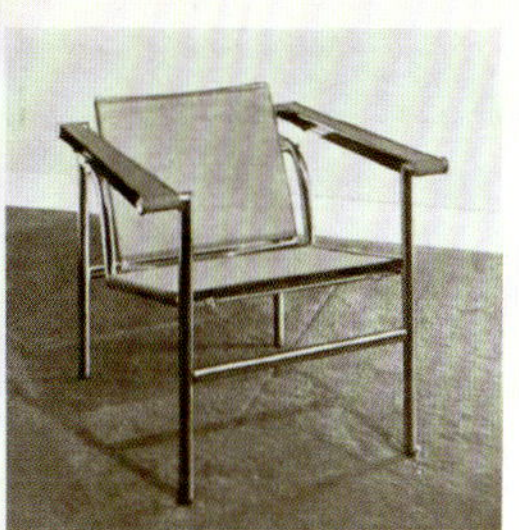

B. 301
fauteuil
à
dossier
basculant

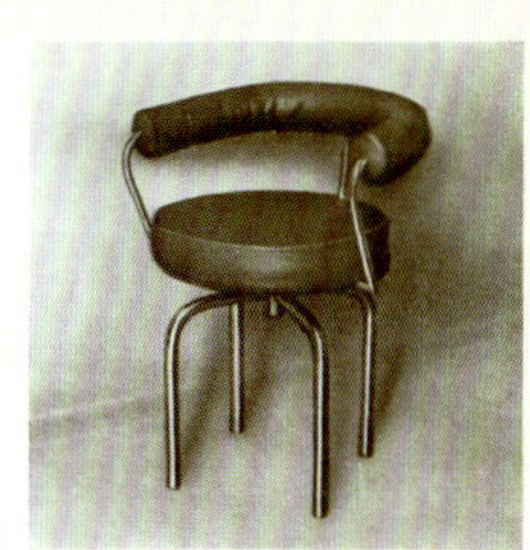

B. 302
fauteuil
tournant

B. 305
tabouret
de salle
de bain
recouvert
de tissu
éponge
inter-
changeable

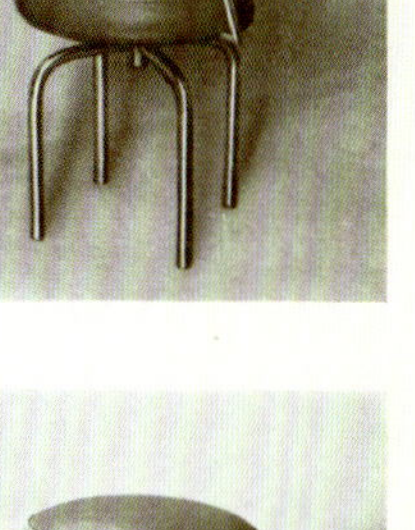

B. 303
chaise
tournante

B. 304
tabouret
tournant

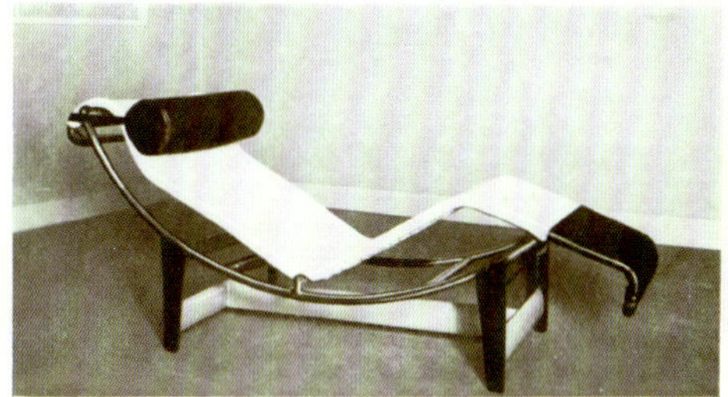

B. 306
chaise longue
à position
variable

"We cannot revise the plans for contemporary houses effectively unless we take a new look at the furniture question... Furniture, apart from chairs and tables, consists almost entirely of storage space. And existing storage units generally have the wrong dimensions and are practically unusable. I condemn such a waste of space." —***Précisions*, 1930**

Opposite, top. Furniture installation at the Salon d'Automne, Paris, 1929

Opposite, bottom left. View of bathroom, Salon d'Automne, 1929

Opposite, bottom right. Bedroom "cell of 14m² per person" with furniture by Le Corbusier, Charlotte Perriand, and Pierre Jeanneret, as reproduced in Le Corbusier's book *La ville radieuse* (*The Radiant City*), 1935

Above. Thonet sales brochure, with furniture by Le Corbusier, Pierre Jeanneret, and Charlotte Perriand, 1930. These pieces are still in production with Cassina.

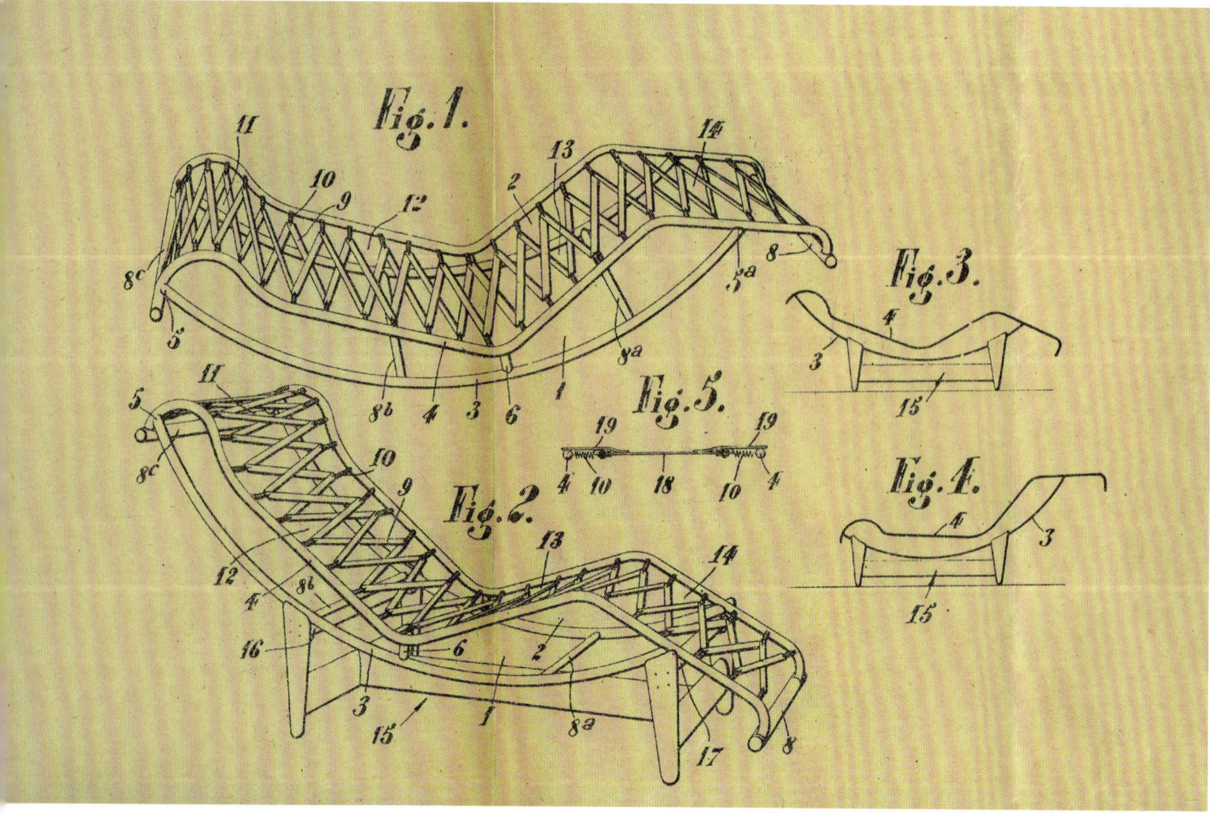

Above. Studies by Charlotte Perriand or Pierre Jeanneret of the chaise longue, 1928

Left. Patent application drawings of the structure of the chaise longue, 1929

Opposite. Published photographs of Perriand's seating for the Salon d'Automne, 1929

Premières recherches

EQUIPEMENT INTERIEUR D'UNE HABITATION. DEMONSTRATION AU SALON D'AUTOMNE 1929

Le Corbusier, Pierre Jeanneret, Charlotte Perriand

1. Vue de la salle de séjour sur la cuisine, les chambres et la salle de bains. Des casiers normalisés juxtaposables et empilables forment des cloisons totales ou partielles entre les pièces.
2. Fauteuils, châssis métallique, coussins en cuir.

4. à 7. Chaise-longue, armature en tube d'acier, sangles tendues par des ressorts (4) ou des peaux posées sur des lames d'acier (5). Piètement indépendant en tubes ovoïdes laqués. L'inclinaison du siège est donnée par un simple glissement de celui-ci sur le piètement, sans moyen mécanique. Permet plusieurs positions, de repos normal (6) ou de grand délassement, les pieds au-dessus du niveau de la tête (7).

8. Chaises en tube d'acier chromé, dossier basculant, housse amovible tendue par des ressorts.

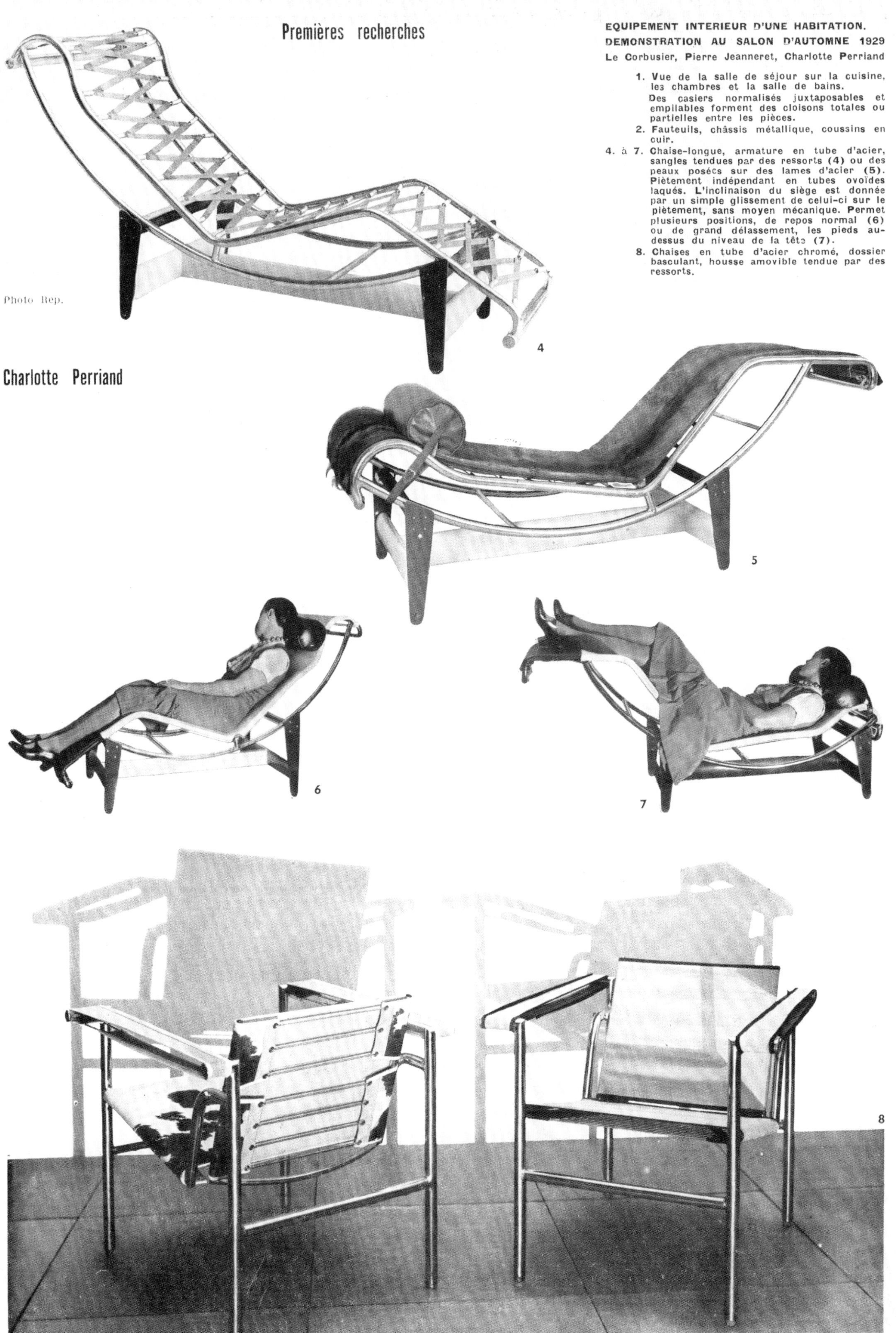

Photo Rep.

4

Charlotte Perriand

5

6

7

8

Right. Le Corbusier at work in his rue Jacob apartment, Paris, 1931

PERNOD FIL
FEVRIER
11
PLANS

1. Les pilotis. Des recherches assidues, obstinées, ont abouti à des réalisations partielles qui peuvent être considérées comme des acquits de laboratoire. Ces résultats ouvrent des perspectives neuves à l'architecture; celles-ci s'offrent à l'urbanisme qui peut y trouver des moyens d'apporter la solution à la grande maladie des villes actuelles.

La maison sur pilotis! La maison s'enfonçait dans le sol: locaux obscurs et souvent humides. Le ciment armé nous donne les pilotis. La maison est en l'air, loin du sol; le jardin passe sous la maison, le jardin est aussi sur la maison, sur le toit.

2. Les toits-jardins. Depuis des siècles un comble traditionnel supporte normalement l'hiver avec sa couche de neige, tant que la maison est chauffée avec des poêles.

Dès l'instant où le chauffage central est installé, le comble traditionnel ne convient plus. Le toit ne doit plus être en bosse mais en creux. Il doit rejeter des eaux à l'intérieur et non plus à l'extérieur.

Vérité irrécusable: les climats froids imposent la suppression de comble incliné et provoquent la construction des toits-terrasses creux avec écoulement des eaux à l'intérieur de la maison.

Le ciment armé est le nouveau moyen permettant la réalisation de la toiture homogène. Le béton armé se dilate fortement. La dilatation apporte la fissuration de l'ouvrage aux heures de brutal retrait. Au lieu de chercher à évacuer rapidement les eaux de pluie, s'efforcer au contraire à maintenir une humidité constante sur le béton de la terrasse et par là une température régulière sur le béton armé. Mesure particulière de protection: sable recouvert de dalles épaisses de ciment, à joints écartés; ces joints sont semés de gazon. Sable et racines ne laissent filtrer l'eau que lentement. Les jardins-terrasses deviennent opulents: fleurs, arbustes et arbres, gazon.

Des raisons techniques, des raisons d'économie, des raisons de confort et des raisons sentimentales nous conduisent à adopter le toit-terrasse.

3. Le plan libre. Jusqu'ici: murs portants; partant du sous-sol, ils se superposent, constituant le rez-de-chaussée et les étages, jusqu'aux combles. Le plan est esclave des murs portants. Le béton armé dans la maison apporte le plan libre! Les étages ne se superposent plus par cloisonnements. Ils sont libres. Grande économie de cube bâti, emploi rigoureux de chaque centimètre. Grande économie d'argent. Rationalisme aisé du plan nouveau!

4. La fenêtre en longueur. La fenêtre est l'un des buts essentiels de la maison. Le progrès apporte une libération. Le ciment armé fait révolution dans l'histoire de la fenêtre. Les fenêtres peuvent courir d'un bord à l'autre de la façade. La fenêtre est *l'élément mécanique-type* de la maison; pour tous nos hôtels particuliers, toutes nos villas, toutes nos maisons ouvrières, tous nos immeubles locatifs...

5. La façade libre. Les poteaux en retrait des façades, à l'intérieur de la maison. Le plancher se poursuit en porte-à-faux. Les façades ne sont plus que des membranes légères de murs isolants ou de fenêtres.

La façade est libre; les fenêtres, sans être interrompues, peuvent courir d'un bord à l'autre de la façade.

Le Corbusier et *Pierre Jeanneret*

"With reinforced concrete you do away with walls entirely. The floors are borne by narrow, widely separated posts. The ground beneath the house is liberated, the roof is reclaimed, the facade is completely free. An end to our paralysis." ***—Oeuvre complète: Volume 1, 1910–29***

Jusqu'au béton armé et au fer, pour bâtir une maison de pierre, on creusait de larges rigoles dans la terre et l'on allait chercher le bon sol pour établir la fondation.

On constituait ainsi les caves, locaux médiocres, humides généralement.

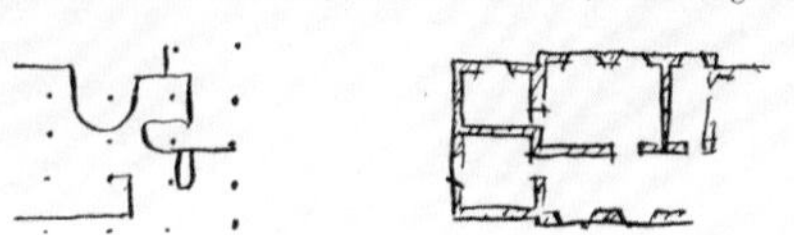

Puis on montait les murs de pierre. On établissait un premier plancher posé sur les murs, puis un second, un troisième; on ouvrait des fenêtres.

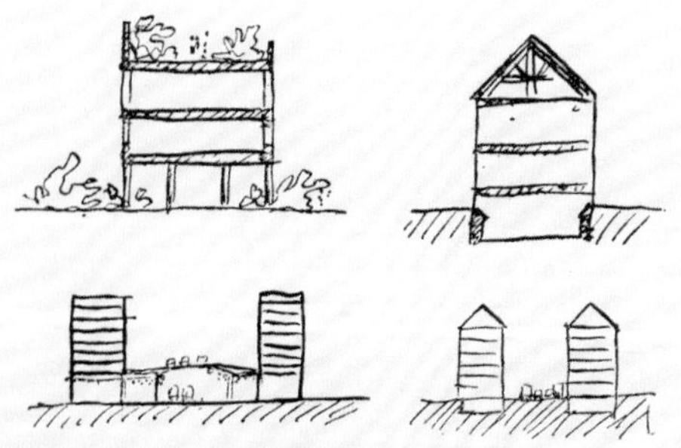

Avec le béton armé on supprime entièrement les murs. On porte les planchers sur de minces poteaux disposés à de grandes distances les uns des autres.

Le sol est libre sous la maison, le toit est reconquis, la façade est entièrement libre. On n'est plus paralysé.

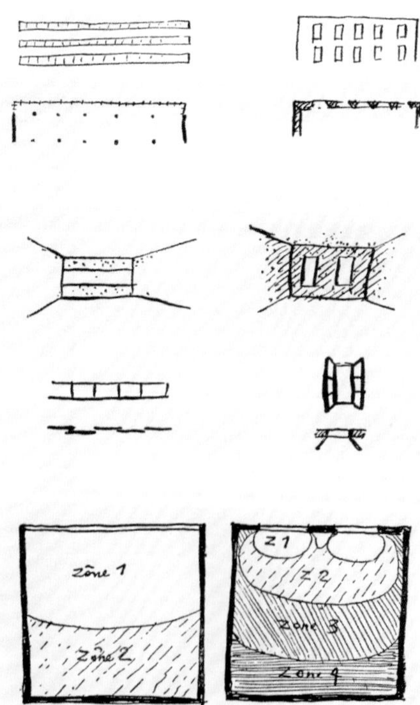

La tabelle dit ceci: à surface de verre égale, une pièce éclairée par une fenêtre en longueur qui touche aux deux murs contigus comporte deux zones d'éclairement: une zone, très éclairée; une zone 2, bien éclairée.

D'autre part, une pièce éclairée par deux fenêtres verticales déterminant des trumeaux, comporte quatre zones d'éclairement: la zone 1, très éclairée, la zone 2, bien éclairée, la zone 3, mal éclairée, la zone 4, obscure.

he Five oints of a New chitecture"

Le Corbusier developed a set of principles that had begun to emerge in the Dom-ino system and were refined in his villas of the 1920s, culminating in the Villa Savoye (completed in 1929). These principles were articulated as "The Five Points of a New Architecture": the use of *pilotis*, or vertical piers, to raise structural volumes; the *toît-jardin* (roof garden); the *plan libre* (free plan); the *fenêtre en longueur* (ribbon window); and the *façade libre* (free facade).

Opposite. Pages from *Oeuvre complète: Volume 1, 1910–29*, explaining "The Five Points of a New Architecture"

Right. Description of Le Corbusier's "twelve little inventions" from *Le Corbusier lui-même*, 1970. Third on his list are *pilotis* and the other five points.

Below. Diagram of Le Corbusier's "Five Points" from *La ville radieuse* (*The Radiant City*), 1935

12 petites inventions

Le Corbusier inventeur ?... Pourquoi pas. Il n'est besoin que choisir dans son œuvre et ses projets... Voici donc, parmi d'autres, douze petites inventions...

— TUYAU D'EVERITE, 1919 : Application absolument nouvelle du fibro-ciment (évérit-éternit), Le Corbusier inventeur du tuyau d'évérite. Actuellement d'un usage courant.

— TYPOGRAPHIE, 1920 : Utilisation de la pleine page dans l'impression (Imprimerie Arrault à Tours). Dans le domaine courant actuellement.

— LES PILOTIS - L'OSSATURE INDEPENDANTE - LE PLAN LIBRE - LA FAÇADE LIBRE - LE TOIT JARDIN !

Cinq points également bien connus actuellement des architectes.

— MOBILIER 1927 : Les casiers forment l'équipement du logis. Avec une carcasse standard, possibilité de création d'équipements extrêmement différents suivant la destination des casiers.
Usage extrêmement courant actuellement.

— AUTOMOBILE 1928 : Le Corbusier et Pierre Jeanneret dessinent une « voiture maximum » : moteur à l'arrière, formes aérodynamiques, faible encombrement et grand confort intérieur, grands emplacements pour les bagages, possibilité de transformer les sièges en couchettes. Les formes extérieures sont déduites de ces considérations de confort. Les surfaces de carrosserie sont toutes à simple courbure (tôle emboutie, plane, légèrement gaufrée). Toiture décapotable par panneau coulissant vers l'arrière. Egalement d'un usage courant actuellement.

— LE MUR NEUTRALISANT, 1929 : Créés à l'occasion des plans du Centrosoyus de Moscou, les murs neutralisants formés d'une double membrane laissant entre elles un vide de quelques centimètres, permettent une ventilation et un chauffage constants. Jamais appliqué jusqu'alors.

— CANOT DE SAUVETAGE, 1930 : Conception d'un canot de sauvetage intégré dans la coque même du bateau et largué automatiquement en cas de naufrage. Non utilisé.

— BRISE-SOLEIL, 1930-1965 : Création d'un dispositif permettant au soleil de donner plein effet en hiver et d'être jugulé en été aux périodes caniculaires. Trente-cinq années de mise au point.
Dispositif actuellement très connu des architectes du monde entier.

— MUSEE A CROISSANCE ILLIMITEE, 1931 : Le musée commence par le centre et se développe au fur et à mesure en spirale carrée ; on entre, par dessous, au centre. Un seul type de poutre, un seul type de vitrage. Réalisé depuis par Le Corbusier aux Indes, à Ahmédabad et au Japon, à Tokio.

— AERATEURS, 1945 : Fentes verticales dans un mur, fermées d'une toile métallique moustiquaire et munies d'un volet pivotant. Assurent une parfaite ventilation des locaux.

— LE MODULOR, 1942, 1948, 1945 : Une gamme de dimensions de construction à usage humain. Système de proportionnement mathématique basé sur la stature humaine. Employé par quantité d'architectes et de créateurs.

— PANS DE VERRE ONDULATOIRES, 1957 : Solution raisonnable au vitrage moderne.
La pellicule vitrée des façades indépendantes de la structure portante est raidie par des membrures fines en béton armé. L'emploi du Modulor permet de grandes variations de densité des membrures.

Si cette liste est loin d'être complète, il est impossible de passer sous silence une invention à usage personnel de Le Corbusier : l'élastique porte-crayons. On sait peut-être que Le Corbusier a utilisé énormément les crayons de couleurs, dans ses notes, ses études, ses préparations de conférences. Plusieurs élastiques permettront de réunir les crayons pour les tenir dans la main gauche, dans la poche, dans la rue, en voyage. Mais, attention, là est le secret ! Il s'agit de connaître un réseau particulier d'enchevêtrements... Seul Le Corbusier le connaissait !...

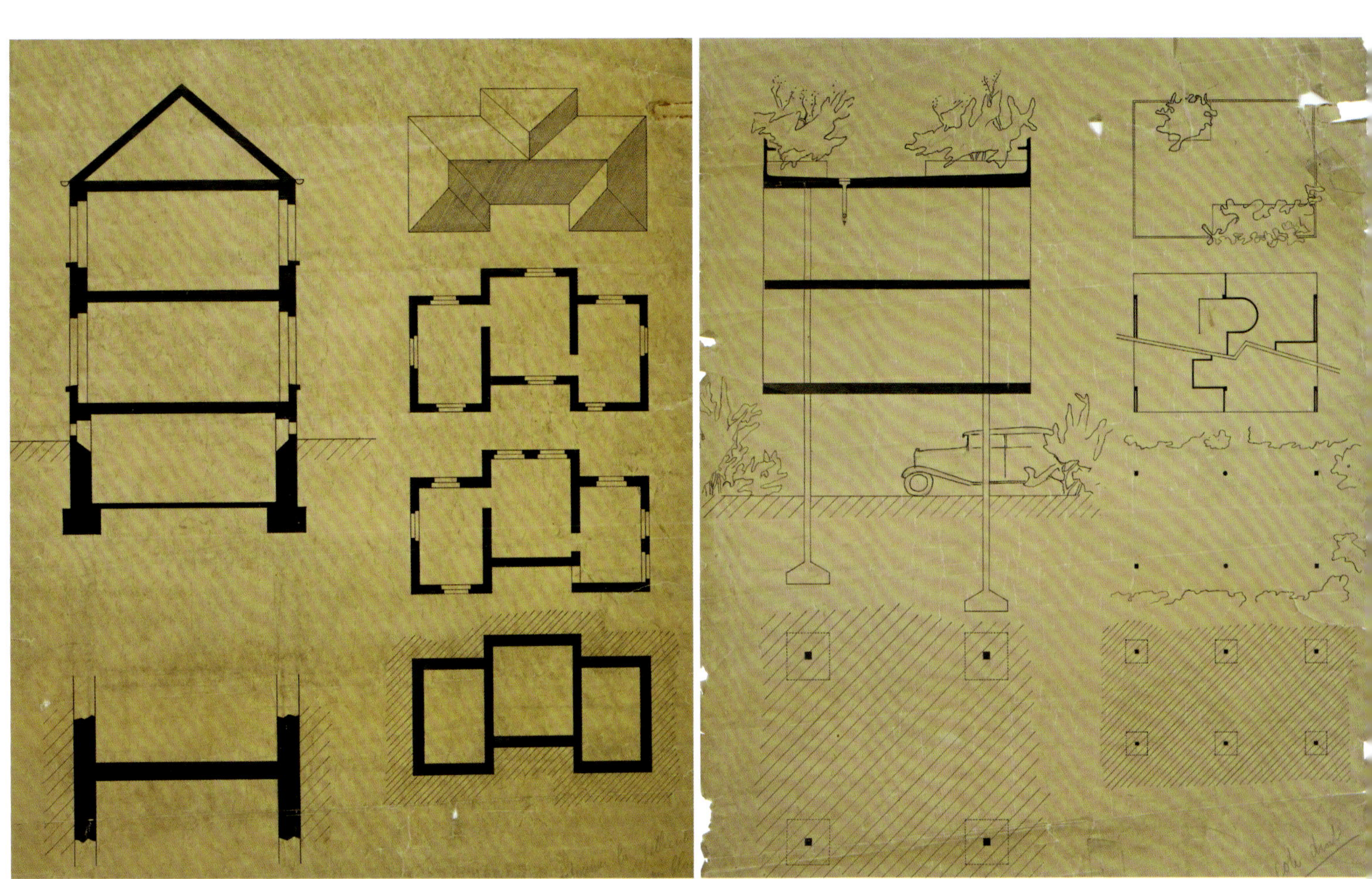

An icon of modern design: Villa Savoye, Poissy, France, 1928–31

The Villa Savoye is the most sophisticated embodiment of Le Corbusier's "Five Points of a New Architecture." It combines the complex *promenade architecturale* of the Villa La Roche–Jeanneret with the strong geometry of the Villa Stein–de Monzie, and it introduces a greater attenuation of form than in the canonical villas of the 1920s. The Villa Savoye also brings to an end Le Corbusier's exploration of pristine white volumes with ribbon windows, set on *pilotis*. While he was completing construction of the Villa Savoye for Pierre Savoye and his wife, Eugénie, Le Corbusier embarked on a new course with the commission for the Villa de Mandrot in Provence.

Above left. Pierre Savoye to Le Corbusier, 24 March 1930, outlining problems encountered on a visit to Villa Savoye in bad weather

Above right. Le Corbusier to Mr. Crépin, landscape contractor, 17 July 1930, insisting he repair the road next to Villa Savoye

Middle left. Le Corbusier to Pierre Savoye, 15 October 1930, requesting his final payment for Villa Savoye

Middle right. Le Corbusier to Eugénie Savoye, 28 June 1931, advising her to plant perennials at the entrance that are "tall, prolific and disorderly"

Bottom left. Pierre Savoye to Mr. Cormier, contractor, 7 September 1936, demanding that he fix numerous leaks at the Villa Savoye

Bottom right. Eugénie Savoye to Mr. Goudeau, chairman of the construction firm for the villa, 11 October 1937, telling him to make the Villa Savoye habitable "urgently," and at his own expense

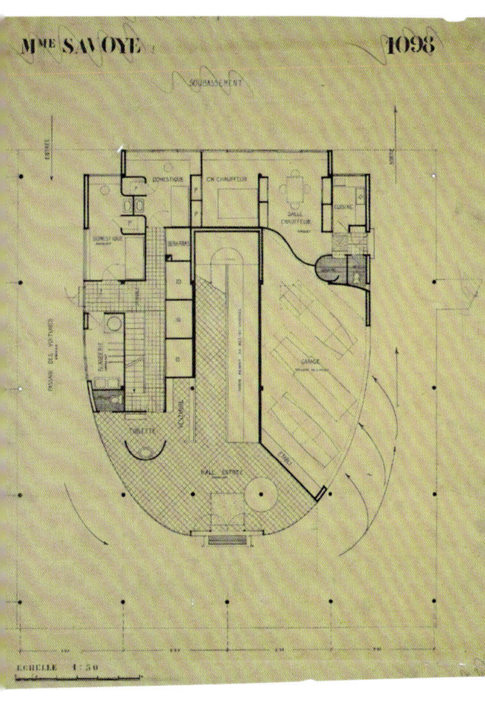

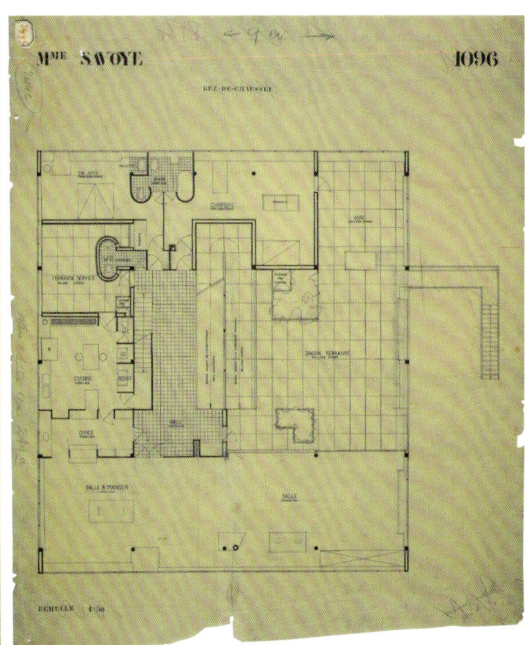

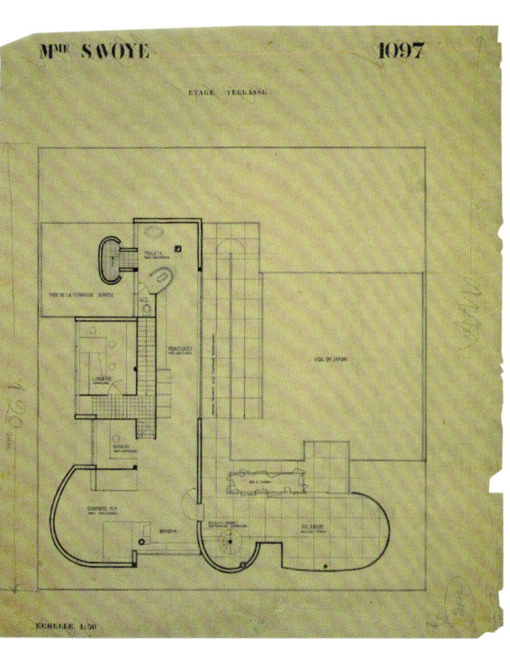

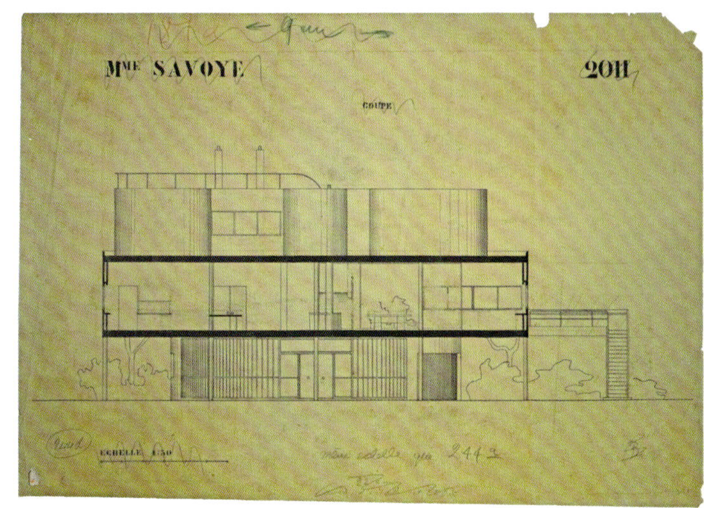

Above. Plans, October 1928. Left to right: basement, ground floor, terrace, Villa Savoye, Poissy, 1928–31

Right. Section, October 1928

Below. Perspective of the roof garden, 1928

Opposite, top. Le Corbusier with a model of the Villa Savoye, 21 October 1935, New York

Opposite, bottom. Roof garden under construction, summer 1929

Above and right. Two views of the Villa Savoye

Above. Terrace-level garden, Villa Savoye, Poissy

Left. Ground floor under the *pilotis* of the principal facade

Above. Ramp (center) from terrace level to the roof

Right. A "composition" on the terrace by Le Corbusier

Above. Entry hall on the ground floor, Villa Savoye, Poissy, 1928–35

Below left. Kitchen

Below right. Bathroom

Opposite, top. Salon on the terrace level

Opposite, bottom. Interior, with staircase

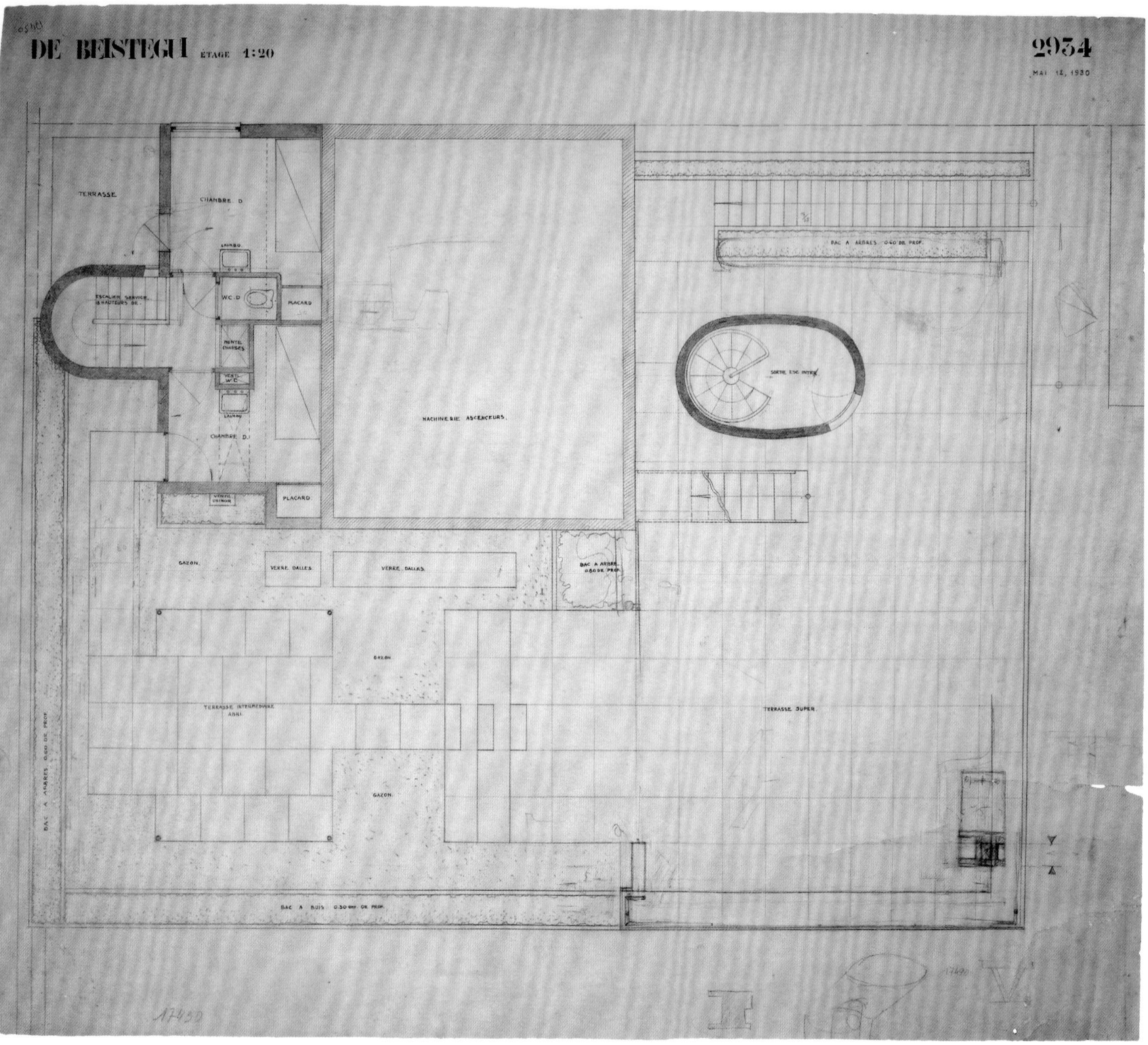

A surreal penthouse: Beistegui apartment, Paris, 1929–31

The extravagant rooftop apartment for Charles de Beistegui, on the Champs-Elysées, may be seen as an ironic catalog of the developments in Le Corbusier's villas of the 1920s. Here the ethos of the machine age is expressed by such surreal flourishes as motorized hedges and an outdoor room complete with rococo mantelpiece and a full carpet of grass. The effect is of an absurd, elegant, and decadent farewell to the principles that had guided Le Corbusier through the 1920s.

Above. Plan, first floor and terrace, 12 May 1930, Bestegui apartment, Paris, 1929–31

Below right. Ground-floor plan, 30 November 1929

Below left. Plan, roof garden and terrace, 30 November 1929

Opposite, clockwise from top left:

Beistegui apartment and roof terrace

Salon with spiral stairs to the roof terrace

Upper terrace with a fireplace and the Arc de Triomphe in the background

The garden

View from the living room to the terrace

Upper terrace with fireplace and the Eiffel Tower in the background

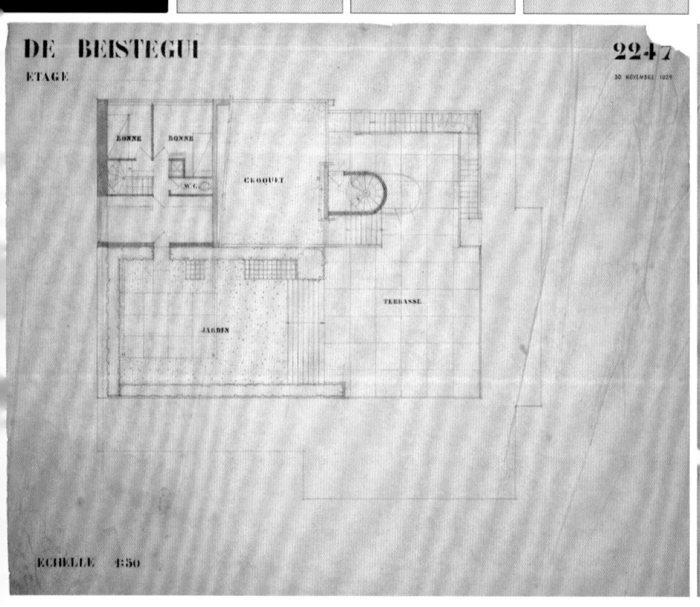

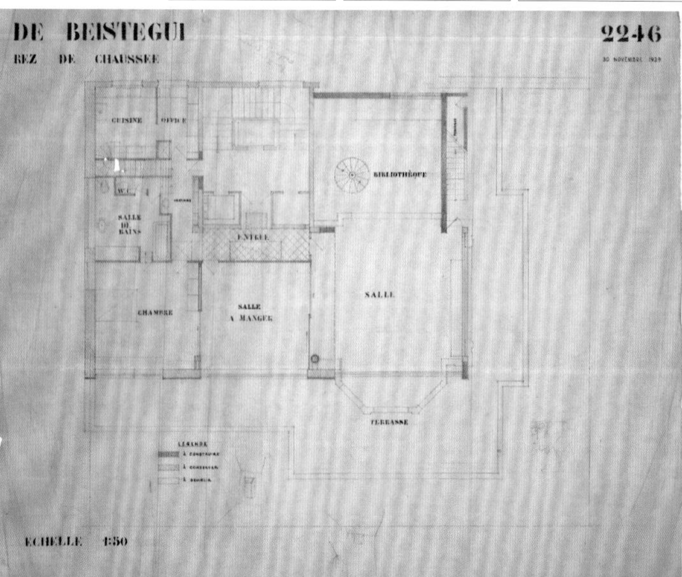

"A spectacle orchestrated to honor Paris. Solitary forms would suddenly become visible beyond the greenery in the foreground, coming up through the large slabs of stone: the Arc de Triomphe and next the Eiffel Tower. Then the hill of Sacré Coeur, and, finally, as an ivy hedge is moved electronically, one sees the very axis of the city, the Tuileries and Notre Dame, set between Saint-Gervais and the Panthéon."—*Croisade*, 1933

SALUBRA S.A. / BÂLE

Notre: H/Si.Gp.5g
Votre:

25 Avril 1931.

Cher Monsieur,

Comme convenu nous vous soumettons par ce même courrier – comme papiers d'affaires recommandés – ce qui suit:

1.) Une maquette de la marque Salubra et à votre choix quatre maquettes "Le Corbusier" (dont celle marquée d'une croix nous conviendrait le mieux) ainsi qu'une couverture d'album, sur laquelle veuillez placer les maquettes choisies, les coller et nous retourner la couverture ainsi munie des deux maquettes "Salubra" et "Le Corbusier".

2.) Un jeu complet des harmonies de couleurs ainsi qu'il sera présenté dans les albums. Aucune marge au haut, 4 m/m au bas et du côté libre, marge suffisante pour onglet.

3.) Echantillons d'autres cartons pour les harmonies de couleurs. (NB. Le carton brun du jeu ci-dessus nous semble le meilleur, la couleur brune nous paraît agréable et, la partie visible étant presque nulle, ne peut guère gêner.)

4.) Deux lunettes en carton brun, qui pourraient aussi être exécutées en un des cartons d'autres couleurs selon les échantillons mentionnés ci-dessus.

5.) Un échantillon de la nuance 70: terre de Sienne nature claire qui – probablement par erreur – ne figure sur aucune des harmonies de couleurs. Veuillez s.v.p. nous indiquer où elle doit être placée ou si elle peut être supprimée.

Nous vous serions très obligés si vous vouliez bien nous donner vos instructions au sujet de ces cinq questions aussitôt qu'il vous sera possible.–

./.

Télégrammes: Salubra Bâle. Code: ABC 6th Edition. Téléphone: Safran 3222.
Case postale: 28 Bâle 16. Compte de chèques postaux: V 2526.

Les papiers peints Le Corbusier - Salubra

C'est en 1932 que Le Corbusier créa la première collection de papiers peints Salubra qu'il baptisa „Le clavier des couleurs". Il en écrivit personellement le commentaire, dans lequel il décrit très clairement sa conception de l'emploi des couleurs pour les papiers peints. Voici, entre autres, ce qu'il dit:

„Salubra est la peinture à l'huile en rouleaux. Les papiers peints Salubra résistent à la lumière et sont lavables. Au lieu d'étendre plusieurs couches de peinture sur les parois et les plafonds dans l'atmosphère d'un chantier bruyant et poussiéreux, on peut désormais procéder en dernier lieu et en toute quiétude à la pose de la peinture à l'huile en rouleaux.

A l'architecte, toujours plus ou moins à la merci d'une malfaçon d'un ouvrier-peintre, Salubra offre une grande tranquillité, assurant avec une proportion d'huile et de couleur toujours exacte, une qualité constante de ton et de matière.

Le choix des couleurs ne se fait plus au milieu du fracas et des incommodités d'un chantier. Grâce à la „peinture à l'huile en rouleaux", il se fait avec sécurité, posément, dans un recueil raisonné d'échantillons qui sont les morceaux même de l'exécution."

— C'est ainsi que s'exprima Le Corbusier en 1932.

Le Corbusier a, de tout temps, milité en faveur de la pureté et de l'esthétique des matériaux. Si, bien que sollicité aux quatre coins du monde, il trouve aujourd'hui le temps de créer une nouvelle collection Salubra, cela démontre l'importance qu'il accorde aux papiers peints et constitue une preuve des expériences concluantes faites avec Salubra.

Demandez à voir chez votre fournisseur la collection Le Corbusier-Salubra 1959 ou écrivez directement pour la documentation complète à

Salubra S.A., Fabrique de papiers peints, Bâle/Suisse.

Papiers peints Salubra-Le Corbusier, Dessin: „Marbre I" 4322 B, Uni 4320 F

The importance of color in architecture: Salubra color key, 1931–32

For the Swiss manufacturer Salubra, Le Corbusier created a series of wallpapers, which came with special sample books that outlined a system intended to make color selection foolproof. Called "Color Keyboards," these books offered forty-three "architectural" shades arrayed so that complementary shades could be easily identified with a special viewing device.

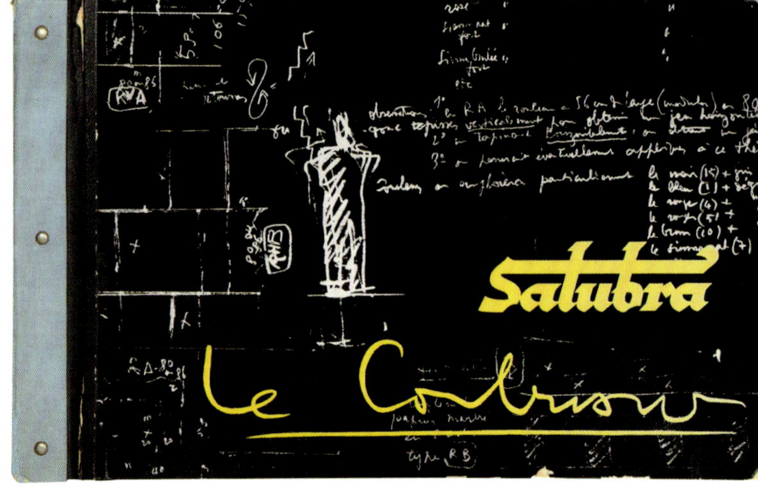

Opposite, top left. Salubra to Le Corbusier, 25 April 1931, cover letter accompanying a maquette of a color sample book and a complete set of color samples

Opposite, top right. Advertisement for Le Corbusier's Salubra wallpaper

Opposite, middle. Cover of Salubra sample book featuring Le Corbusier's wallcoverings and colors, c. 1931–32

Opposite, bottom. Color keys from Salubra sample book

This page. Samples of wallcoverings for Salubra, c. 1931–32.

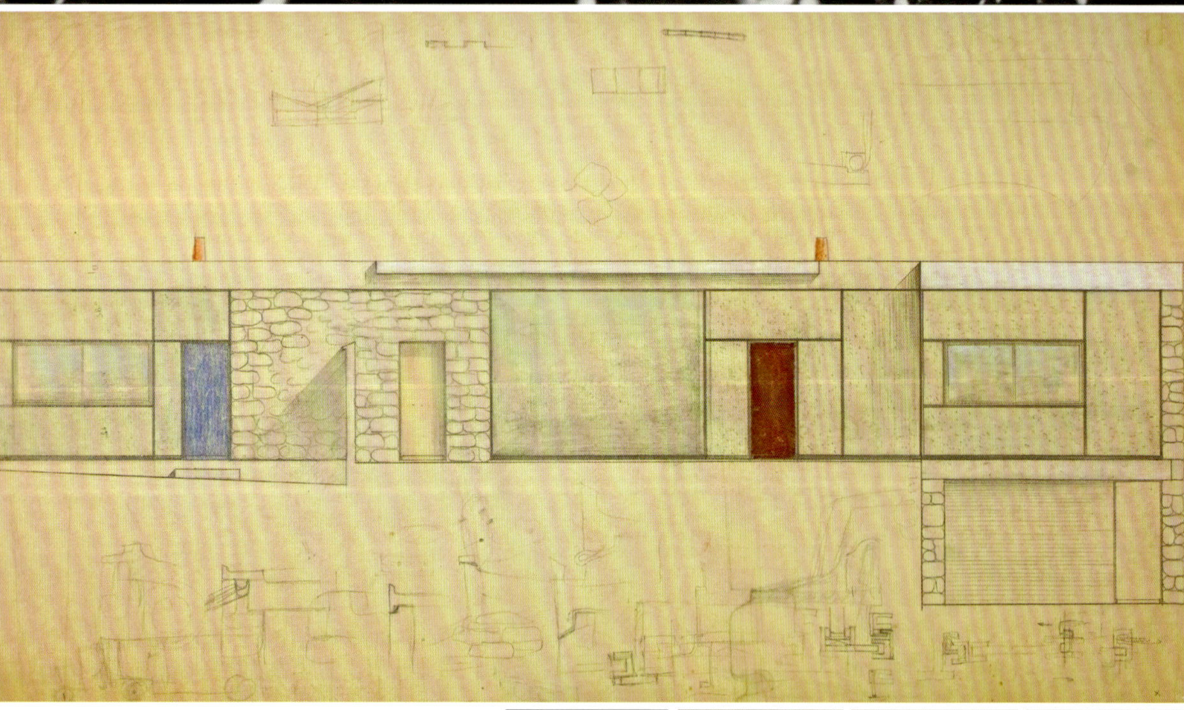

Above. Principal facade, Villa de Mandrot, Le Pradet, France, 1929–31

Left. Principal facade elevation

A new rustic style: Villa de Mandrot, Le Pradet, France, 1929–31

Hélène de Mandrot hosted the first Congrès Internationaux de l'Architecture Moderne (CIAM) at her château in La Sarraz, Switzerland, in 1928.

Le Corbusier's Villa de Mandrot, a vacation house he designed for her in a remote part of Provence, was constructed of masonry walls (in deference to its traditional neighbors) within a metal frame that permitted an open plan. The result is a union between a machine-age aesthetic and the "primitive" integrity of local vernacular construction methods.

Petite Maison de Weekend, La Celle, France, 1934–35

The primitivism of the Villa de Mandrot found more refined expression in the Petite Maison de Weekend. It was commissioned by a M. Félix, director of the bank Société Henfel, as a private hideaway. Based on the earlier scheme for the Maison Monol (1919), with its rusticated walls and low barrel vaults, the Petite Maison de Weekend featured concrete and glass bricks, simple wood paneling, and a turf roof, achieving a remarkable balance between machine and cave.

Top. Main entrance to the Petite Maison de Weekend, La Celle, France, 1934–35

Middle and bottom left. Interior perspectives

Above right. View of the garden "kiosk" from the dining area

Marries Yvonne Gallis, 1930

Le Corbusier and Yvonne Gallis wed on 18 December 1930, after living together for nearly ten years. For the rest of his life Le Corbusier would carefully compartmentalize the main components of his life: home, painting, and architecture. Together he and Yvonne agreed that this left no room for children. Despite Le Corbusier's extensive travels and occasional infidelities, the marriage survived to the end of Yvonne's life, nearly thirty years later.

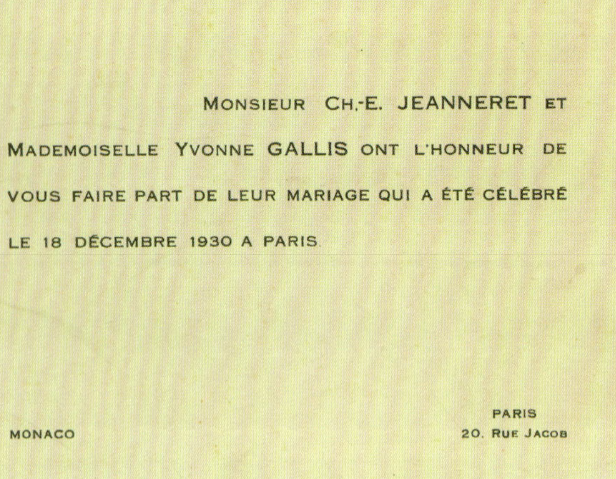

Monsieur Ch.-E. Jeanneret et Mademoiselle Yvonne Gallis ont l'honneur de vous faire part de leur mariage qui a été célébré le 18 décembre 1930 a Paris.

Monaco

Paris
20. Rue Jacob

"If there are no hitches, everything is ready for our marriage on Thursday 18th. In the evening a little banquet in an inn 35 km from Paris, with friends and Albert." —Letter to his mother, 15 December 1930

ACTES DE L'ÉTAT CIVIL

Naissances.

Les actes de naissance doivent être dressés dans les trois jours de l'accouchement (non compris le jour de la naissance), à la Mairie de l'arrondissement dans lequel a eu lieu l'accouchement.

La déclaration de naissance est faite par le père, ou, à son défaut, par les docteurs en médecine ou en chirurgie, sages-femmes ou officiers de santé ou autres personnes qui auront assisté à l'accouchement et, lorsque la mère sera accouchée hors de son domicile, par la personne chez qui elle sera accouchée.

A Paris, l'acte de naissance peut être immédiatement rédigé en présence du déclarant muni du présent livret sur simple production d'un certificat de constatation de naissance signé du docteur, de la sage-femme ou de l'officier de santé qui aura procédé à l'accouchement.

Mariages.

On peut demander à la Mairie des renseignements sur les formalités à remplir pour contracter mariage.

Le mariage doit être précédé d'une publication.

La publication dure dix jours.

(Voir au second recto de la couverture.)

Adj. 1923. 9e Lot. No 7008.

Année 1930

RÉPUBLIQUE FRANÇAISE
Liberté — Égalité — Fraternité

Numéro 1088 VILLE DE PARIS 6e Arrondissement

Du 18 décembre mil neuf centtrente

Mariage

Entre : Charles Edouard JEANNERET- GRIS
Né le 6 octobre 1887 à La Chaux-de-Fonds
Arrondt d d Suisse
Profession : artiste-peintre
Domicilié à Paris, rue Jacob, 20
Fils de Georges Edouard
et de Marie Charlotte Amélie Perret } mariés.
Veuf de

Et Jeanne Victorine GALLIS
Née le 1 janvier 1892 à Monaco
Arrondt d d Principauté
Profession : sans
Domiciliée à Paris, rue Jacob, 20
Fille de Jean Baptiste
et de Marie Joséphine Crovetto } mariés.
Veuve de

Contrat de mariage reçu le 16 décembre 1930 par Me Charles Tollu, notaire à Paris.

Signature de l'Époux, Signature de l'Épouse,

Jeanneret

Délivré le 18 décembre 1930

L'Officier de l'État civil,

République Française — Mairie du Luxembourg VIe Arrondt Paris — Liberté, Égalité, Fraternité

Above left. Announcement of the marriage of Charles-Edouard Jeanneret and Yvonne Gallis, 18 December 1930, Paris

Above right. Photograph of Yvonne, with her inscription "To M [?] with my best compliments, Yvonne Le Corbusier"

Left. Marriage certificate, Charles Edouard Jeanneret-Gris and Jeanne Victorine [Yvonne] Gallis, 18 December 1930

Opposite, top left. Le Corbusier with Yvonne and others

Opposite, top right. Pierre Jeanneret and Yvonne seated on the running board of a car

Opposite, bottom. Le Corbusier, Yvonne, Yvonne's mother (second from right), and friends, in front of the flower shop owned by Yvonne's mother, Monaco, 1930

EXPEDITIONS
AU PANIER

Left. Le Corbusier, portrait of Yvonne, 1932

Below. Le Corbusier to Yvonne, writing about "doing nothing at all" while visiting his parents

Opposite. Yvonne and Le Corbusier, c. 1930

Opposite. Le Corbusier in Antwerp, Belgium, presenting ideas on his Ville Radieuse, 1933

4 In Search of the Big Commission (1926–1942)

Starting in 1928, Le Corbusier set his sights on what he called "Les Grands Projets" (The Great Projects). A tremendous increase in his international visibility resulted from the competition for the League of Nations headquarters in Geneva, held in the winter of 1926–27. The design by Le Corbusier and Pierre Jeanneret was one of nine finalists for the top honor, and it nearly won outright. As the only modernist among the potential winners, Le Corbusier spearheaded an international campaign, orchestrated by his friend Sigfried Giedion, to denounce as a scandal the award of the final commission to a seventy-year-old French academician and his Swiss colleague. This rousing campaign—pursued in articles, lectures, and the book *Une maison, un palais* (1928; A House, a Palace)—led directly to the founding of the *Congrès Internationaux d'Architecture Moderne* (CIAM) in a château in Switzerland in 1928.

Le Corbusier was soon being asked to design the Centrosoyuz ministry building in Moscow, the Salvation Army headquarters in Paris, the Pavillon Suisse (a dormitory for Swiss students at the Cité Universitaire in Paris), and two apartment blocks, one in Paris (where he moved into a penthouse suite in 1935) and one in Geneva, where many of his friends bought apartments. Despite all this productivity, by 1935 the bailiffs were in the studio, repossessing the office furniture against unpaid debts. For the rest of the 1930s, Le Corbusier built almost nothing, except two small houses and the Pavillon des Temps Nouveaux at the Paris world's fair in 1937. But even as the commissions diminished, his ambitions grew ever more expansive.

Le Corbusier's intentionally provocative ideas for "a city for three million people," originally embodied in the diorama at the 1922 Salon d'Automne, had been further developed in a lecture in Strasburg six months later. There he announced that the only way to save Paris was to destroy the Right Bank and replace it with his city of towers. Le Corbusier would deploy variations on this plan for the rest of his life, and they were guaranteed to provoke fury and adulation in equal measure. Between 1930 and 1935 he developed what he called La Ville Radieuse (The Radiant City), in which a city center of office towers would radiate out into a zigzag pattern of housing blocks spaced far apart in open parkland. His watchwords were: "space, sun, and greenery." His plans for Montevideo, Rio de Janeiro, and Algiers took shape as free-form "ribbon developments" combining circulation and housing that exploited each city's distinctive terrain to release pressure on the urban center.

From 1929 on, Le Corbusier was in constant motion, traveling, lecturing, spreading the word of modern architecture. He tried to conquer North America in a whirlwind visit in 1935, when he lectured to most of the leading universities on the East Coast and in the Midwest. Despite his happy marriage to Yvonne Gallis, these long periods abroad led him to seek "tenderness" elsewhere. During his U.S. tour he found solace in a close friendship with Marguerite Tjader Harris—they exchanged letters until the end of his life, and he confided in her about many of his disappointments, especially the generally cool reception of his paintings. He was also intimate with Helena Simkhovitch, with whom he exchanged coded love letters in the 1940s and 1950s. And there were others. On 23 February 1949, he even asked Tjader Harris to arrange a dinner, at his expense, in a good restaurant, for "The New York women from my 1946–7 years, to wit Marguerite [Tjader Harris], Helena [Simkhovitch], Barbara [Joseph] and perhaps, if the others will agree, Mitzi the sculptress [Mitzi Solomon] (up to you)." As he noted in his sketchbook "A gigolo like me (63 years old) doesn't exist in the USA (or hardly)!!!"

A competition, a disappointment: League of Nations headquarters, Geneva, 1926–28

By the end of the 1920s, Le Corbusier was focused on obtaining major commissions – what he termed "Les Grands Projets." For the two-part competition to design a group of buildings for the League of Nations headquarters in Geneva, he adapted his revolutionary "Five Points of a New Architecture" to a greatly expanded public scale. His loss of the competition and the ensuing controversy were the source of tremendous personal bitterness, but it also generated worldwide celebrity for the ambitious architect.

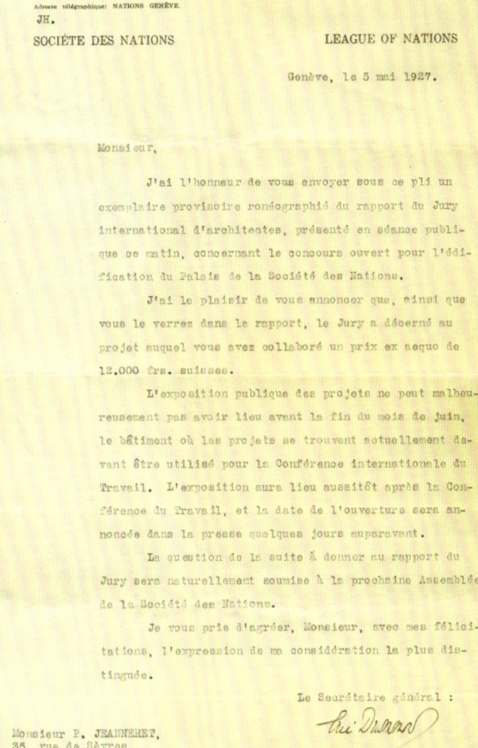

Adresse télégraphique: NATIONS GENÈVE.
JH.

SOCIÉTE DES NATIONS — LEAGUE OF NATIONS

Genève, le 5 mai 1927.

Monsieur,

J'ai l'honneur de vous envoyer sous ce pli un exemplaire provisoire ronéographié du rapport du Jury international d'architectes, présenté en séance publique ce matin, concernant le concours ouvert pour l'édification du Palais de la Société des Nations.

J'ai le plaisir de vous annoncer que, ainsi que vous le verrez dans le rapport, le Jury a décerné au projet auquel vous avez collaboré un prix ex aequo de 12.000 frs. suisses.

L'exposition publique des projets ne peut malheureusement pas avoir lieu avant la fin du mois de juin, le bâtiment où les projets se trouvent actuellement devant être utilisé pour la Conférence internationale du Travail. L'exposition aura lieu aussitôt après la Conférence du Travail, et la date de l'ouverture sera annoncée dans la presse quelques jours auparavant.

La question de la suite à donner au rapport du Jury sera naturellement soumise à la prochaine Assemblée de la Société des Nations.

Je vous prie d'agréer, Monsieur, avec mes félicitations, l'expression de ma considération la plus distinguée.

Le Secrétaire général :

Monsieur P. JEANNERET,
35, rue de Sèvres,
PARIS.

…posite: clockwise …m top.

…onometric, 1927, …owing Grand …sembly Hall (left) …d Secretariat …ght), competition …try for the League … Nations, Geneva

Letter from the secretary general of the League of Nations, Geneva, 5 May 1927, to Pierre Jeanneret, congratulating him on the jury's decision to award him and Le Corbusier

a prize of 12,000 Swiss francs for their submission

View of rear of Secretariat and enclosed garage (left) with *pilotis*, 1927

Principal facade of the Secretariat, 1927

Canopied entrance to the Grand Assembly Hall and covered walkway for journalists, 1927

Above. Photo-collage, 1927, the Secretariat (left) and Grand Assembly Hall (right), seen from Lake Geneva

Right. Bird's-eye view of Secretariat and Grand Assembly Hall, with surrounding grounds, 1927

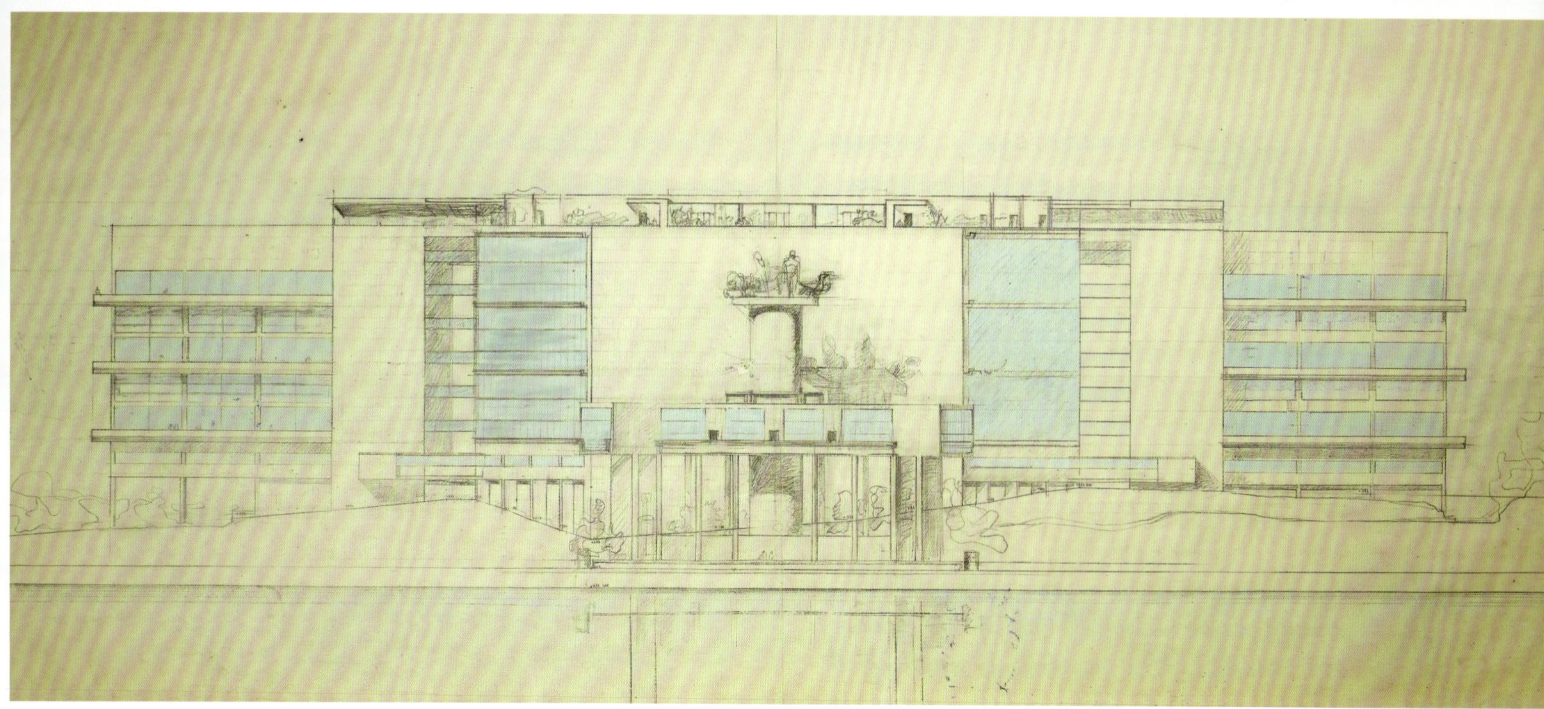

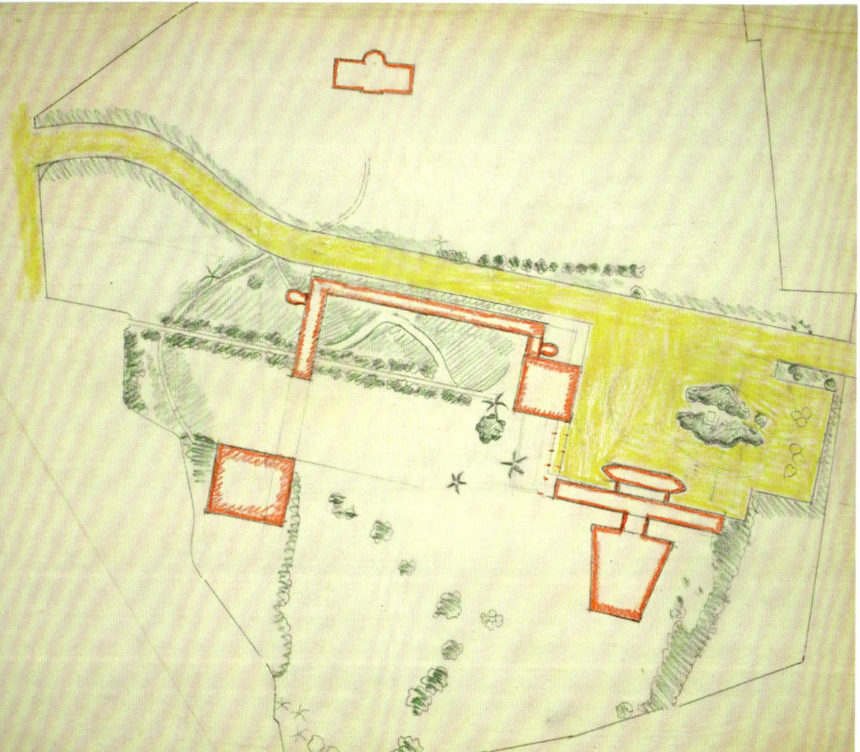

Above. Facade, 1927, Grand Assembly Hall, League of Nations competition

Left. Site plan, second competition for the League of Nations, 1928.

The site was moved from Lake Geneva to Ariana Park, and a World Library was added.

Below left. Sketch for second competition, 1928

Below right. Winning design for the League of Nations, by a team led by Julien Flegenheimer (Switzerland) and Henri-Paul Nénot (France)

Du 1er au 21 juin 1928

Galerie Georges Bernheim, 109, Faubourg St-Honoré

EXPOSITION DU PROJET DE PALAIS DES NATIONS

de Le Corbusier et P. Jeanneret

Ce que le public ignore

au sujet du

Projet de Palais des Nations

de Le Corbusier et P. Jeanneret

Mai 1927. — A la majorité relative, le jury des *professionnels* a désigné ce projet pour le premier prix et l'exécution (entre 377 projets représentant 14 kilomètres de plans).

A la 63e séance du jury, M. Lemaresquier (juré français délégué par l'Académie) *fait tomber ce projet, prétextant qu'il est reproduit par un moyen mécanique* (au lieu d'être directement dessiné à l'encre).

Neuf prix égaux sont alors décernés, chaque juré désignant un lauréat. Résultat : un mélange incongru de cinq projets académiques et de quatre modernes — reflet exact de la composition du jury

Juin 1927. — Exposition publique des projets, à Genève. L'intérêt général se concentre sur ce projet L.-C. et P. J. car il représente l'esprit moderne (innombrables articles de journaux et de revues.)

Septembre 1927. — Assemblée générale des Nations. Coup de théâtre. L'Assemblée décide, préalablement à tout choix, d'élever de 50% le crédit alloué. Protestation des Associations professionnelles contre cette *rupture de contrat. C'est que la lutte est ouverte entre l'Académie et l'esprit moderne.*

Seul le projet L. C. et P. J. ne dépasse pas le crédit alloué de 13 millions de francs-or (condition *sine qua non* du concours).

Les quatres projets académiques coûtent 27 millions, 40 millions, 45 millions, 50 millions ; leurs auteurs ont déclaré 13 millions, mais des experts ont dénoncé le mensonge. Le nouveau crédit (19 ½) porté enfin à 24 millions, permettra de se rapprocher des projets académiques.

L'arbitraire règne : Six *ambassadeurs* sont chargés par l'Assemblée des Nations de désigner le projet à exécuter *suivant un mandat précis*, coût de la construction et efficacité de fonctionnement.

Les experts techniques consultés par les ambassadeurs désignent le projet L. C. et P. J. : l'expert tchécoslovaque, l'expert du gouvernement fédéral suisse ; l'expert du gouvernement genevois.

27 décembre 1927. — Les *ambassadeurs* ne désignent pas un *projet* mais ils désignent *un architecte* : M. Nénot, membre de l'Institut et Président du Salon des Artistes Français (27 millions) et lui adjoignent trois confrères académiques : MM. Broggi (italien) 40 m., Vago (Italo-Hongrois) 40 m., Lefebvre (Français) 50 m..

Protestation mondiale contre cette seconde rupture de contrat : des Associations professionnelles de Suisse, Tchécoslovaquie, Hollande, France, Suède, Danemark, Allemagne, Autriche, etc;

des plus hautes personnalités techniques de France, Allemagne, Amérique, Scandinavie, Suisse, etc.

appel par les chefs du *Redressement Français*, à l'élite mondiale;

avertissements innombrables de la grande presse et des revues à la S. D. N.

L. C. et P. J. envoient au Conseil de la S. D. N. une requête établie par Me Prudhomme avocat à la Cour, professeur aux Facultés de Droit, *demandant l'annulation du verdict des Ambassadeurs.* Cette requête limite ses arguments aux *fautes d'ordre purement juridique*, flagrantes, commises par la S. D. N. dans l'affaire du Palais.

5 mars 1928. — Le *Conseil des Nations* se réunit. La requête à lui adressée, *n'est pas remise* par Sir Eric Drummond, secrétaire général de la S. D. N. (La requête imprimée sur 30 pages était envoyée à raison de 25 exemplaires recommandés.)

Le Conseil confirme la décision des Ambassadeurs : *quatre cabinets d'architecture sont chargés d'établir le plan définitif du Palais sur un programme qui n'a rien de commun avec les projets de ces quatre cabinets.* **Au contraire, le nouveau programme est inspiré directement du projet L. C. et P. J.** L'un des Ambassadeurs a déclaré : « Le projet L. C. et P. J. nous sera très utile pour construire le nouveau Palais. »

Le *Secrétaire général* n'a pas jugé utile d'accuser réception de la requête à M. Prudhomme. Aussi celle-ci est-elle envoyée à nouveau au Conseil des Nations pour la session de juin.

Toutefois, un mois plus tard, en réponse à une lettre recommandée de M. Prudhomme, le Secrétariat Général de Genève lui fait savoir que la S. D. N. n'a à connaitre que les affaires entre nations et non pas celles des particuliers (!).

La requête est la première instance juridique intentée contre la S. D. N. depuis la fondation. Il n'existe pas de juridiction qui puisse juger la S. D. N., *organe suprême de la justice humaine.* Ce cas intéresse vivement les milieux juridiques. Quelle suite peut être donnée à une telle requête?

Une personnalité mêlée, dès ses origines, à l'affaire du concours a déclaré: «Ce concours était arrangé dès le début; l'Académie était désignée pour l'exécution; le concours n'était qu'une façade. De plus des ambitions nationales s'étant manifestées avec violence, on a établi le compromis des quatre architectes pour satisfaire des appétits politiques. On a désigné des pays, des architectes de l'Académie *et non pas un des projets du concours* (la comédie du concours a coûté plus de 20 millions aux 377 concurrents!) En des articles importants, la grande presse mondiale a qualifié la manœuvre : « Le Scandale du Palais. »

Les projets n'ont jamais été discutés objectivement, *sauf par le jury des professionnels* et ensuite par les experts. Car les projets (en moyenne 30 à 40 mètres de plans chacun) étaient dans des caisses.

On a, derrière le rideau des communiqués brefs, fait de la diplomatie *occulte:* quatre architectes académiques sont désignés ; quatre architectes modernes sont écartés. Le cinquième architecte académique (M. Labro) n'a pu être décemment admis, par suite des ses relations avec M. Lemaresquier, architecte du Nouveau Cercle Militaire de Paris, juré au concours et metteur en scène de l'incident (63e séance du jury) qui a permis, dans la suite, de faire triompher l'Académie et de vaincre l'esprit moderne.

L'exposition du projet L. C. et P. J. permettra à ceux que la question architecturale intéresse, d'étudier ce plan de palais dont il a été tant parlé et que personne, pour ainsi dire, n'a jamais vu.

IMP. UNION, PARIS

Protesting a lost competition: *Une maison, un palais*, 1928

Le Corbusier's submission for the League of Nations competition was the only modernist scheme among the nine finalists, and the awarding of the commission to a team of academic architects gave him a platform to launch an extended protest campaign. He publicized the details of the competition in various lectures and articles, some of which were published in his book *Une maison, un palais* (A House, a Palace).

Above, left and right. "What the Public Doesn't Know about the Project for the League of Nations," a broadside by Le Corbusier and Pierre Jeanneret, published by Galerie Georges Bernheim, Paris, 1928

Left. Cover of *Une maison, un palais*, Le Corbusier's book explaining the ideas behind his League of Nations competition entry, 1928

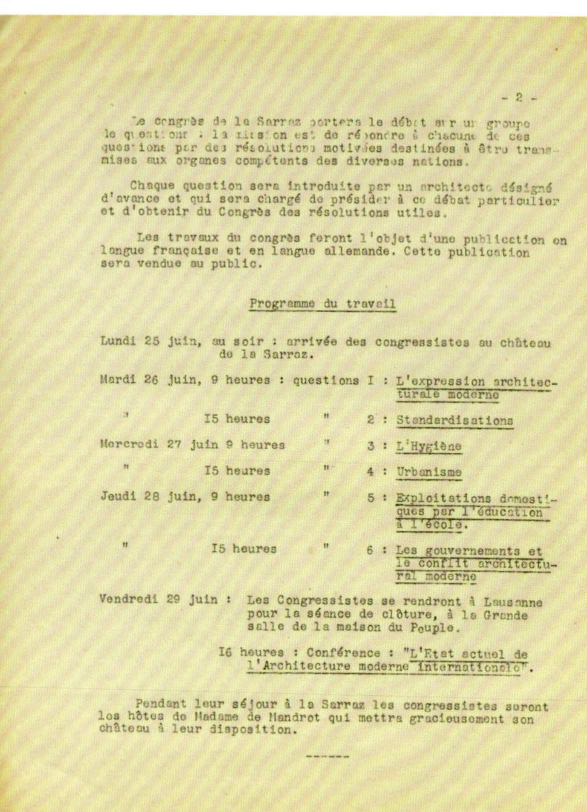

- 2 -

Le congrès de la Sarraz portera le débat sur un groupe de questions : la mission est de répondre à chacune de ces questions par des résolutions motivées destinées à être transmises aux organes compétents des diverses nations.

Chaque question sera introduite par un architecte désigné d'avance et qui sera chargé de présider à ce débat particulier et d'obtenir du Congrès des résolutions utiles.

Les travaux du congrès feront l'objet d'une publication en langue française et en langue allemande. Cette publication sera vendue au public.

Programme du travail

Lundi 25 juin, au soir : arrivée des congressistes au château de la Sarraz.

Mardi 26 juin, 9 heures : questions I : L'expression architecturale moderne

" I5 heures " 2 : Standardisations

Mercredi 27 juin 9 heures " 3 : L'Hygiène

" I5 heures " 4 : Urbanisme

Jeudi 28 juin, 9 heures " 5 : Exploitations domestiques par l'éducation à l'école.

" I5 heures " 6 : Les gouvernements et le conflit architectural moderne

Vendredi 29 juin : Les Congressistes se rendront à Lausanne pour la séance de clôture, à la Grande salle de la maison du Peuple.

I6 heures : Conférence : "L'Etat actuel de l'Architecture moderne internationale".

Pendant leur séjour à la Sarraz les congressistes seront les hôtes de Madame de Mandrot qui mettra gracieusement son château à leur disposition.

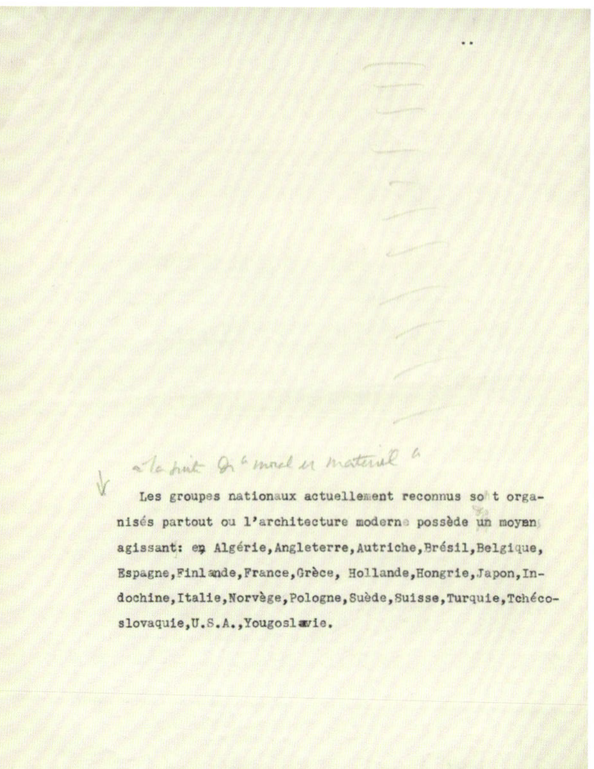

Les groupes nationaux actuellement reconnus soit organisés partout ou l'architecture moderne possède un moyen agissant: en Algérie, Angleterre, Autriche, Brésil, Belgique, Espagne, Finlande, France, Grèce, Hollande, Hongrie, Japon, Indochine, Italie, Norvège, Pologne, Suède, Suisse, Turquie, Tchécoslovaquie, U.S.A., Yougoslavie.

An international forum for architects: CIAM I and IV, 1928 and 1933

Another result of the League of Nations controversy was the establishment of the Congrès Internationaux de l'Architecture Moderne (CIAM), a forum in which the leading figures of modern architecture would share their ideas throughout the following three decades. The first meeting was hosted by Le Corbusier's client for the Villa de Mandrot at her château in La Sarraz. CIAM IV was held in Athens and on board the *SS Patris II*. There were seven more conferences before the group disbanded after CIAM XI (1959).

"You'll have a visit from Madame de Mandrot, owner of the Château de la Sarraz… A goodhearted, decent woman, knows a thing or two, as artists do. And as I set up the program for an international architecture congress she's organizing at La Sarraz on 26–30 June, she's very grateful. The congress will bring together 45 of Europe's best-known architects for 5 days of discussion of questions crucial to the future of architecture."

—Letter to his mother, 29 March 1928

Above left. Program from CIAM I, 25–29 June 1928, La Sarraz, Switzerland

Above right. List of the twenty-two nations represented at CIAM I

Left. Le Corbusier's schematic drawing of the six topics of discussion at the first conference; these were focused on techniques rather than aesthetics

Opposite, top. Official CIAM I group photograph, 1928. Le Corbusier is standing in the middle row, center (partially obscured). Other attendees included Sigfried Giedion, Pierre Chareau, Alfred Roth, and Pierre Jeanneret.

Opposite, bottom. Le Corbusier (far right), Hélène de Mandrot, and others at CIAM I

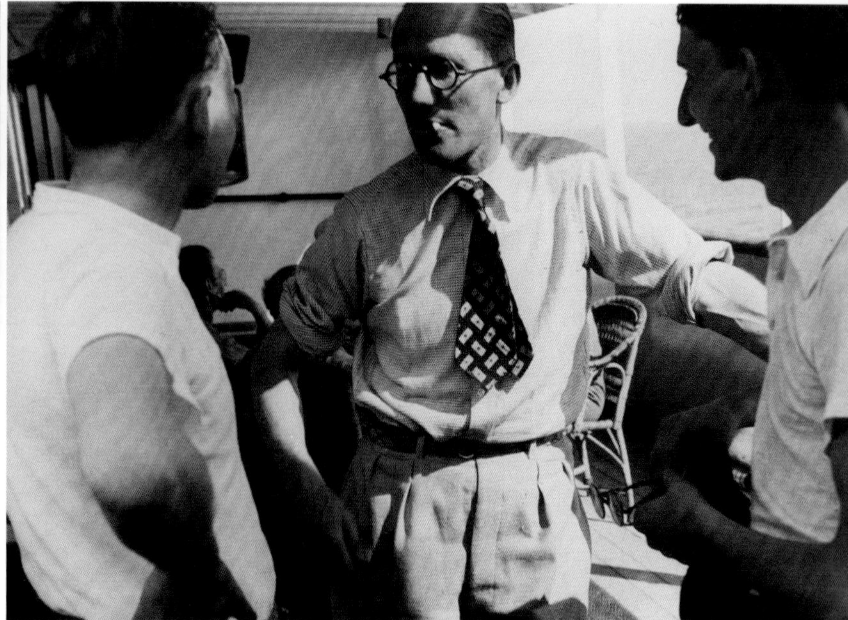

Left. Left to right: Fernand Léger, Charlotte Perriand, Le Corbusier, Albert Jeanneret, Pierre Jeanneret, and Jean Badovici (?) at CIAM IV, Athens, 1933

Above, below, and opposite. Le Corbusier and others on board the *SS Patris II*, from Marseille to Athens, CIAM IV, 1933

Informacions de «La Publicitat»

Le Corbusier a Barcelona

El cèlebre arquitecte comenta la ciutat

Com que he tingut l'honor, conjuntament amb uns amics, d'acompanyar Le Corbusier durant els pocs dies que ha estat entre nosaltres, amb motiu de donar dues conferències, he cregut que seria d'un gran interès transcriure alguns comentaris que feia el genial arquitecte tot passejant i coneixent les nostres coses.

Les converses que hem tingut han estat sempre en un to de confiança amical, defugint tota preocupació en la recerca de la frase i, per tant, hem pogut saborejar l'encant del comentari espontani. Aquest fet ens obliga a reconèixer, abans que tot, la nostra indiscreció. Però, la temptació de transcriure alguns caires de la seva profunda visió i la conveniència de satisfer l'interès actual que ha motivat la seva visita, pot servir per justificar la facècia que faig a Le Corbusier, a qui, des d'ara, presento les meves excuses.

Al voltant de la seva obra s'ha escrit i teoritzat amb quantitat i de tota manera. Ell mateix alterna constantment la tasca de constructor amb la polèmica. Els seus llibres, els seus articles i les seves conferències, apassionen els cenacles intellectuals de tot el món. Le Corbusier és prou fort per resistir tota mena de crítica. Es ell qui ens ha contat — tot rient — una opinió apareguda a *L'Intransigeant*, de París. Transcriurem el sentit, ja que no ens ha estat possible adquirir el diari: "El trio que fa moure més la joventut d'avui dia és Josefina Baker, Charlot i Le Corbusier."

* * *

Volgut lector: Com que és evident que la causa primordial que t'ha fet decidir a llegir aquest article ha estat la seva capçalera, el més enraonat serà que faci un resum de les converses que he tingut amb Le Corbusier, sense afegir-hi, de la meva part, altres comentaris que les necessàries aclaracions. Crec així obtenir, si més no, el teu agraïment. I ja que Le Corbusier estima el sistema de compartiments classificadors, permeteu que l'acapti en aquesta ocasió.

Diu Le Corbusier:

TOT DINANT A LA FONT DEL LLEO. —En la gestació d'un projecte constructiu, el més gran enemic de l'arquitecte és el dibuix. Si en pensar un projecte determinat hom dibuixa tot seguit, la limitació determinada que dóna el llapis fa que la idea se subjecti a la imatge i privi la intelligència de treballar lliurement. Cal pensar molt temps abans de decidir-se a dibuixar, perquè així, sense la influència de cap figura, el cervell plasma la concepció en tots sentits i en tots els ordres, per dintre i per fora, per dalt i per baix de la construcció.

A LA CASA DEL BARO DE GUELL. — Aquests porxos de les vostres masies són encantadors. La vostra tradició regional és una font inesgotable d'inspiracions. He notat, però, i no parlo per aquesta casa, que massa sovint copieu l'ornament tradicional, i no copseu el vostre racial sentit del passat. Formós jardí. No conec cap ciutat que la iguali en aquest sentit.

MONESTIR DE PEDRALBES.— Quina simplicitat més moderna! Aquesta austeritat de motllures és impressionant. Això és del més bo que he vist a la vostra terra. Tinc una peritable sorpresa amb el vostre gòtic.

ESCALA DEL PALAU DE LA LLOTJA. — Imagineu-vos aquestes voltes d'escala realitzades amb guix i de la mateixa forma; a ben segur que no ens plaurien. El seu encant prové del traçat estereotòmic de la pedra, que fa treballar la intelligència i en resulta un goig de l'esperit.

SANTA MARIA DE LA MAR. — Es un dels interiors d'església més formosos que he vist. El criteri de mostrar interiorment el major espai possible, és un gran encert.

LA CATEDRAL. — L'arquitecte d'això tenia el sentit de la ponderació de volums molt afinat. El vostre gòtic m'ha conquistat del tot, i m'atreveixo a dir que el prefereixo al nostre.

CARRER DEL BISBE.—Nota.— Fou una llàstima no haver pogut conèixer l'opinió del nostre hoste, referent al pont gòtic recentment inaugurat. Encara que va esguardar-lo una bona estona, tot seguit la seva atenció va quedar concentrada en un aparador de figuretes religioses on es va encantar ho i dient: "ça est joli, ça..." i després no vaig atrevir-me a preguntar, i vaig preferir respectar el seu silenci.

Continua parlant Le Corbusier.

PLAÇA DEL REI. — Aquest recó té un cert regust florentí que el fa encisador.

SOPANT AL RITZ. — El vostre país crec que és molt apropiat per a germinar la nova modalitat de l'arquitectura viva. A Alemanya trobem l'obstacle en el sentit d'ostentació luxosa, i en la confusió nòrdica, a Rússia lluitem amb les seves complicacions cerebrals, a França ens trobem amb un mal entès refinament tradicional.

L'arquitectura que preconitzo és essencialment llatina perquè és relació matemàtica i té claredat de concepció. ¿Compreneu per què la crec adequada en la vostra terra on hi ha una mica de solucions estructurals, clares i ben raonades?

PEL CAMI DE SITGES. — La visita que he fet a Madrid i Toledo m'ha agradat molt. ¡Són gentils els madrilenys! ¡Quin altre món més diferent del vostre allò d'allà dalt! Les planures de Castella són força interessants i hi ha un sentit del patètic profund. M'ha semblat veure a Madrid un fet insòlit; crec que han passat tent un salt, del llum d'oli a l'electricitat, sense aturar-se gaire en els intermedis del petroli i el gas. (*Nota:* interpreti's la frase amb les seves equivalències d'ordre estètic.)

Una cosa que m'ha frapat, de les terres castellanes, són els ases. ¡Fa bo de contemplar la fila que fa l'home rural a dalt d'un ase!

La dansa andalusa i el cant flamenc els he trobat molt emotius. Comença el cant amb una corba melòdica pregona i sentimental. Es com l'ondulació del seu paisatge; de sobte surt la trepidació persistent i harmònica que fa els peus del "bailaor"; la individualitat humana que lluita i es manifesta en el diapasó de la natura. Convivència harmònica en el fet integral de la nostra existència.

PASSEJANT PER SITGES. — Un flagell que hem de suportar en tots els països, és el dels arquitectes mal orientats. ¡Mireu quin paper més deplorable fan en aquests carrers admirables les cases construïdes amb pretensions artístiques! Ah! Això, dieu que se'n diu "Mar i Cel"... nom bonic i ben trobat... es necessita ésser americà per empescar-se una cosa d'aquestes. Mireu aquella casa al costat de l'església; allí s'acaba l'arqueologia i continua la vida, interrompuda per aquesta fastuositat arqueològica. Fa bo de contemplar el vostre paisatge; el trobo més fort que el d'Itàlia.

GAUDI.—Hi ha grandiositat ponderada en aquesta casa (la d'En Milà i Camps.)

Es interessant de trobar "chez Gaudí" la mateixa solució de la biga treballant en sistema "de bàscula" que jo practico en les construccions de ciment armat.

En un carrer fet amb cases d'aquestes potser no podríem dormir.

SAGRADA FAMILIA.—¡Cal descobrir-se davant d'aquesta meravella constructiva! Es de doldre, però, que el sentit decoratiu ofegui el raonament matemàtic. Hi ha un contrasentit estrany en l'obra d'aquest geni. Potser influència de l'època? Devia ésser formidable la personalitat de Gaudí. Recordo que deu fer una quinzena d'anys vam sentir a París un gran entusiasme en descobrir aquesta arquitectura.

* * *

Podria continuar, si l'espai ho permetés, recordant altres converses de diverses matèries prou interessants, venint d'una personalitat tan intelligent, però, ben segura que ja n'he fet massa. Per acabar, em plau anotar que Le Corbusier ha sortit de Barcelona per la via aèrea en viatge cap a Marsella. Això vol dir que és un home conseqüent. No solament teoritza el maquinisme, sinó que també el practica.

MARIUS GIFREDA

LES EXCAVACIONS D'HERCULANO

Roma, 17. — El "Messagero" anuncia que les obres d'exploració d'Herculano continuen activament.

Recentment han estat descobertes diverses estàtues de bona factura, entre elles un París en marbre rosa i una Diana, alguns gots de terra cuita i utensilis en bronze i alguns trossos de pa i altres comestibles carbonitzats. — Fabra.

Saps que pensava, noia? Que aquesta mena de treball ha d'ésser molt higiènic, però ja no hi sóc a temps.

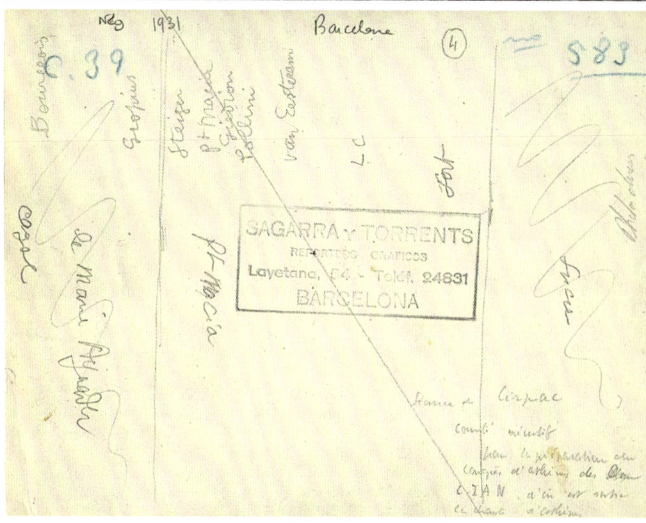

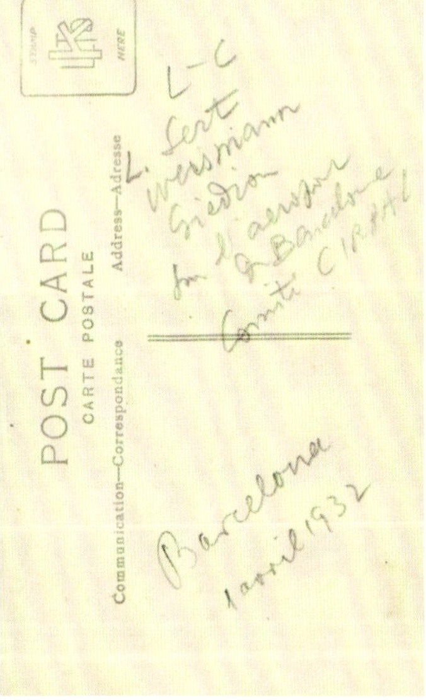

Discovering Spain, 1928–33

During the late 1920s and early 1930s, Le Corbusier made several trips to Spain. His first visit, in 1928, was under the auspices of an aristocratic circle in Madrid, which invited him to lecture. Subsequent trips offered opportunities to tour the country in the company of his brother, Albert, his cousin Pierre, and Fernand Léger. It was during that first trip to Spain that Le Corbusier encountered, in Barcelona, the work of Antonio Gaudí, which he greatly admired.

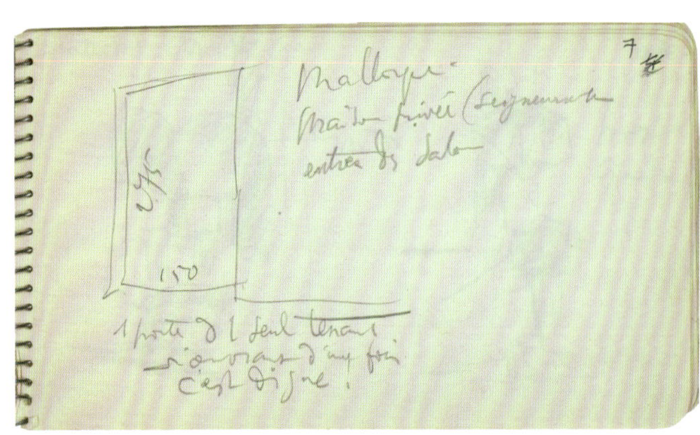

Opposite page

Top left. "Le Corbusier in Barcelona," *La Publicitat* (Barcelona), 18 May 1928. The author summarizes Le Corbusier's comments on a number of the city's sites and landmarks.

Top right. Two sides of a photograph marked "Barcelona 1931." Notes identify Walter Gropius, Sigfried Giedion, Le Corbusier, and others in this group portrait.

Bottom left. Two sides of a postcard, 1 April 1932. The note identifies Le Corbusier, José Luis Sert, Ernest Weismann, and Sigfried Giedion, at the Barcelona airport.

Bottom right. Meeting of CIRPAC (International Committee for the Resolution of Problems in Contemporary Architecture), the elected executive body of CIAM, Barcelona, 29 March 1932

Above. Cover and pages from Le Corbusier's notebook, dated 1932–33. The notebook contains sketches from Barcelona and Mallorca, including the drawing above left (second from top) of Antonio Gaudí's cathedral in Palma, Mallorca.

A successful competition for the USSR: Centrosoyuz, Moscow, 1928–35

In the summer of 1926 the Soviet Union invited Le Corbusier to participate in the competition to design a new office building in Moscow. He was delighted to secure the commission for the Centrosoyuz project—for the Central Union of Consumer Cooperatives—which included offices for 3,500 employees and amenities that would function as what the Soviets called a "social condenser." This commission gave Le Corbusier the perfect opportunity to use concrete slab construction, *pilotis*, ramps, and glazed facades to express his vision of social cooperation and technical optimization.

Above. Left to righ Le Corbusier, with the architects Andrei Burov and Alexander Vesnin

Left. Le Corbusier "Five Points of a New Architecture, translated into Russian and published in *Sovremennaia Arkhitektura* 3, no. 1, 1928

Opposite, top. Le Corbusier with filmmaker Sergei Eisenstein (middle and Andrei Burov (right), Moscow, October 1928

Opposite, bottom. Le Corbusier with group of Soviet architects. Left to right: Nikolai Sobolev, Georgi Golts, unidentified Andrei Burov, Le Corbusier, and Nikolai Kolli, Moscow, October 1928

ОСЕНЬЮ ПРОШЛОГО ГОДА ЭКСКУРСИЯ СТУДЕНТОВ АРХИТЕКТУРНЫХ И СТРОИТЕЛЬНЫХ ФАКУЛЬТЕТОВ МОСКОВСКИХ ВУЗ'ов ПОСЕТИЛА ГЕРМАНИЮ. ЭКСКУРСИЯ, ПРОБЫВШАЯ В ГЕРМАНИИ МЕСЯЦ, ВСТРЕТИЛА ТАМ СРЕДИ АРХИТЕКТОРОВ РАДУШНОЕ ОТНОШЕНИЕ К СЕБЕ И ЖИВОЕ УЧАСТИЕ В РАБОТЕ.

В СОСТАВЛЕНИИ МАРШРУТА, В ВЫБОРЕ ОБЪЕКТОВ ОСМОТРА: — АРХИТЕКТУРНЫХ СООРУЖЕНИЙ И Т. Д., АРХИТЕКТОРЫ: ГУГО ЭРИНГ, ЛЮДВИГ ГИЛЬБЕРЗЕЙМЕР, АРТУР КОРН, МАКС ТАУТ, ВАЛЬТЕР ГРОПИУС, ГАННЕС МАЙЕР, АДОЛЬФ МАЙЕР, И ОТТО ЭЙЗЛЕР ОКАЗАЛИ ЭКСКУРСИИ БОЛЬШУЮ ПОМОЩЬ; МНОГИЕ ИЗ НИХ ЛИЧНО ДАВАЛИ ОБЪЯСНЕНИЯ ПО СВОИМ РАБОТАМ.

МЫ—УЧАСТНИКИ ЭКСКУРСИИ—ПРИНОСИМ ГЛУБОКУЮ БЛАГОДАРНОСТЬ НАЗВАННЫМ ВЫШЕ ЛИЦАМ.

ХОЧЕТСЯ ОТМЕТИТЬ ОСОБЕННО СЕРДЕЧНОЕ ОТНОШЕНИЕ К НАМ АРХИТЕКТОРА ГУГО ЭРИНГА.

МУРАВЬЕВ И., КЕЛЬМИШКАЙТ А., КОЧАР Г., БАБУРОВ В., КОЗЕЛКОВ Г., МОРДВИНОВ А., СУВОРКИН, КАРЫГИН, СЕЛИВАНОВ Н.

IM HERBST DES VERFLOSSENEN JAHRES VERANSTALTETEN DIE BAUABTEILUNGEN DER MOSKAUER HOCHSCHULEN EINE EXCURSION NACH DEUTSCHLAND, WO SIE EIN MONAT VERWEILTE. SIE FAND EIN REGES INTERESSE SEITENS DER DEUTSCHEN ARCHITEKTEN, VON DENEN SIE SEHR WARM AUFGENOMMEN WURDE. DIE WAHL DES FAHRPLANES UND DER ARCHITEKTUROBIEKTE WAR VON DEN HERREN ARCHITEKTEN HUGO HERING, LUDWIG HILBERSEIMER, ARTUR KORN MAX TAUT, WALTER GROPIUS, HANNES MEYER, ADOLF MEYER UND OTTO EISLER BESTIMMT, WODURCH SIE DEN EXCURSANTEN EINE GROSSE HILFE LEISTETEN. EINIGE DER GENANNTEN HERREN WAREN SO LIEBENSWÜRDIG, PERSÖNLICH DAZU NOCH ERKLÄRUNGEN UBER IHRE ARBEITEN ZU ERTEILEN.

DIE ECXCURSANTEN SENDEN HIERMIT IHREN HEISSEN DANK DEN OBEN GENANNTEN HERREN, INSBESONDERE ABER FÜR SEIN ÄUSSERST, HERZLICHES ENTGEGENKOMMEN—DEM HERRN ARCHITEKTEN HUGO HERING.

UNTERZEICHNET: MURAWIEFF, KELMISTKEIT, KOTZAR, BABUROFF, KOSELKOFF, MORDWINOFF, SSUWORKIN, KARYGIN, SSELIWANOF.

5 ТЕЗИСОВ КОРБЮЗЬЕ

Нижеизложенные теоретические соображения основываются на долголетнем практическом опыте в области строительства.
Теории требуют ясной формулировки. Не эстетические фантазии, не стремление к модным эффектам, а архитектоническая реальность ставит вопросы нового строительства от жилого дома до дворца.

1. СТОЛБЫ

Разрешить проблему научным путем, значит прежде всего проанализировать ее элементы. В постройке можно поэтому отделить конструктивные части, несущие нагрузку от неконструктивных частей здания. Применяемый без точного технического и экономического расчета, сплошной фундамент заменяется отдельными основаниями, прежние стены—отдельными столбами. И столбы и основания имеют точный расчет на их нагрузку, на их работу. Столбы расставлены с определенными промежутками, независимо от внутреннего плана дома. Столбы поднимаются над землей на 3—4—6 метров и несут здание, в котором благодаря этому устраняется сырость от земли и увеличиваются свет и воздух. Участок же остается свободным для сада, который таким образом расположен частью под домом. Таких же размеров сад получается на плоской крыше.

WEISSENHOFSIEDLUNG STUTTGART. ZWEIFAMILIENHAUS VON LE-CORBUSIER UND P. JEANNERET

2. САД НА КРЫШЕ

Плоская крыша прежде всего требует соответственного ее использования для жилищных целей, террасы, сада. Железобетон нуждается в защите от перемен внешней температуры. Слишком сильное изнашивание железобетона устраняется сохранением постоянной влажности на бетоне крыши. Терраса на крыше удовлетворяет обоим требованиям: жилья и материала. Пропитанный дождями слой песку покрыт бетонными плитами с дерном во швах. Земля для клумб насыпана непосредственно на песчаный слой. Таким образом, дождевая вода чрезвычайно медленно стекает. Сточные трубы расположены внутри дома, так чтобы на поверхности крыши сохранялась постоянная влажность. Сады на крыше дают роскошную растительность, там сажают не только кусты, но даже небольшие деревья от 3-4 метров вышиною. Такой сад становится излюбленным местопребыванием в доме. **Сады на крыше как бы возвращают городу застроенную площадь.**

3. СВОБОДНАЯ ФОРМА ПЛАНА

Система столбов поддерживает междуэтажные перекрытия и проходит насквозь до самой крыши. Перегородки устанавливаются произвольно, в зависимости от назначения помещений, причем ни один этаж не зависит от другого.
Нет больше несущих капитальных стен,—есть лишь изолирующая мембрана необходимой толщины. Следствие этого абсолютная свобода формы плана, то есть свободное использование площади, что возмещает довольно дорогую железобетонную конструкцию.

4. ГОРИЗОНТАЛЬНО-ПРОТЯЖЕННЫЕ ОКНА

Столбы и междуэтажные перекрытия образуют в фасаде прямоугольные отверстия, через которые входит масса света и воздуха. Окно идет от столба к столбу—горизонтально-протяженное окно. Ходульные окна, неприятные междуоконные пилястры и рамы исчезли, помещения равномерно освещены от одной стены до другой.
Опыт показал, что помещения с такими окнами получают в 8 раз больше света, чем те же помещения с высокими окнами.
Вопрос оконных отверстий—один из основных вопросов в истории архитектуры. Железобетонная конструкция и горизонтально-протяженное окно дают возможность максимального освещения.

5. СВОБОДНАЯ КОМПОЗИЦИЯ ФАСАДА

Пол верхних этажей, выступающих за плоскость несущих столбов на подобие террасы вокруг всего здания, создает новую плоскость фасада, независимую от плоскости основных конструкций, то есть фасад теряет значение несущей стены, и окна свободно расширяются в любом направлении, независимо от внутреннего распределения помещений.
Окно может достигнуть 10 метров ширины для жилого дома и 200 метров для общественного здания. (Наш проект Дворца народов в Женеве.)

Перевел И. Гуревич

ВЫСТАВКА ЖИЛЬЯ В ШТУТГАРТЕ. ДОМА ЛЕ-КОРБЮЗЬЕ И П. ЖАННЕРЕ

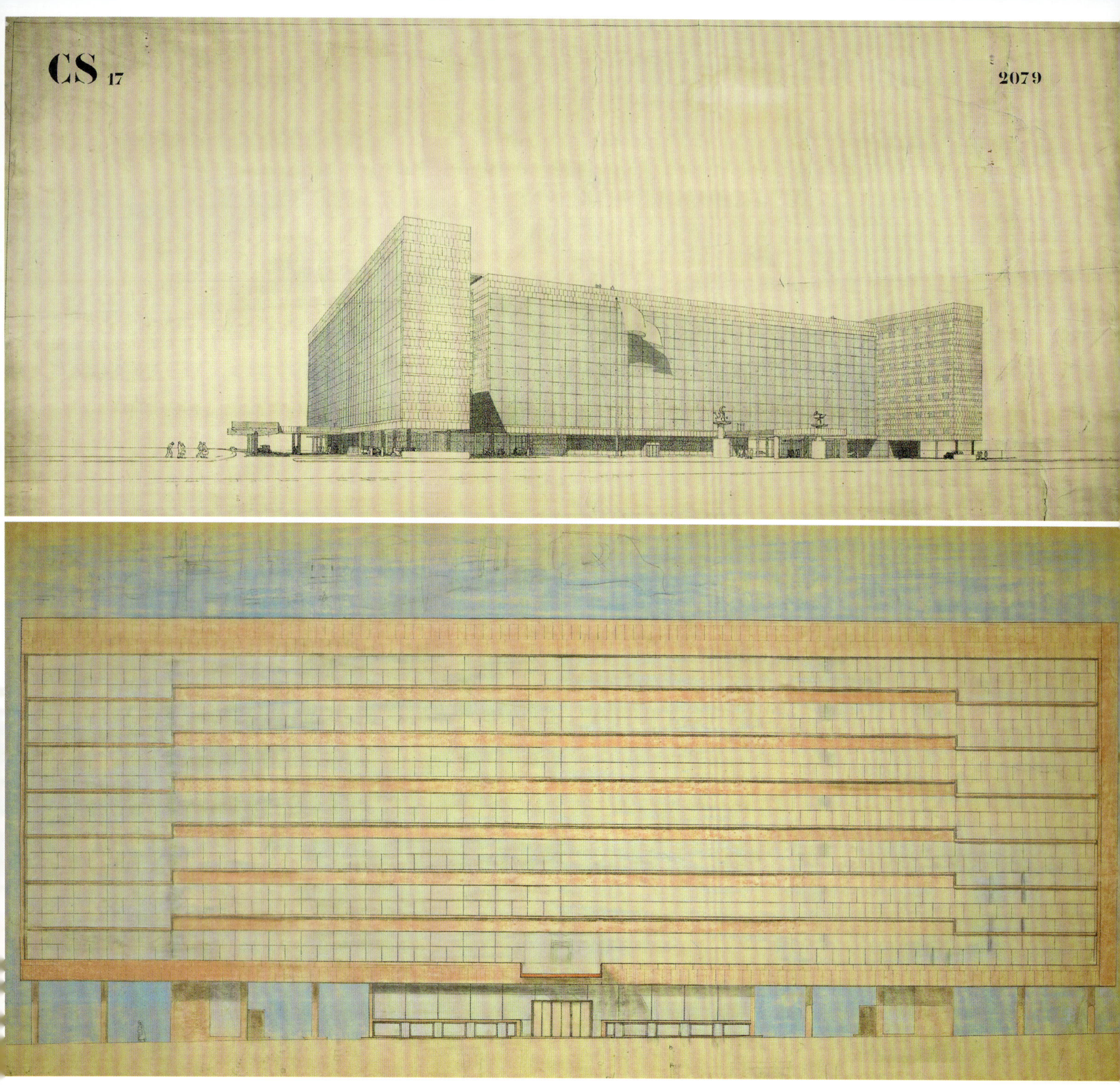

"I thought that under the aegis of 'constructivism' (a Russian architecture movement) I would find enemies on the lookout—all the more so since I was here to try for an enormous commission. Surprise, surprise, I'm proclaimed the great father—the father, no less! And signs of affection and esteem endlessly, endlessly, for the last ten days." —Letter to his mother, 16 October 1928

Top. Perspective, Centrosoyuz, Moscow

Above. Elevation, 1929

Opposite, top left. Facade study

Opposite, top right. Section of an office wing, 1929

Opposite, middle. Front and rear elevations

Opposite, bottom left. Office interior, 20 October 1928

Opposite, bottom right. Axonometric

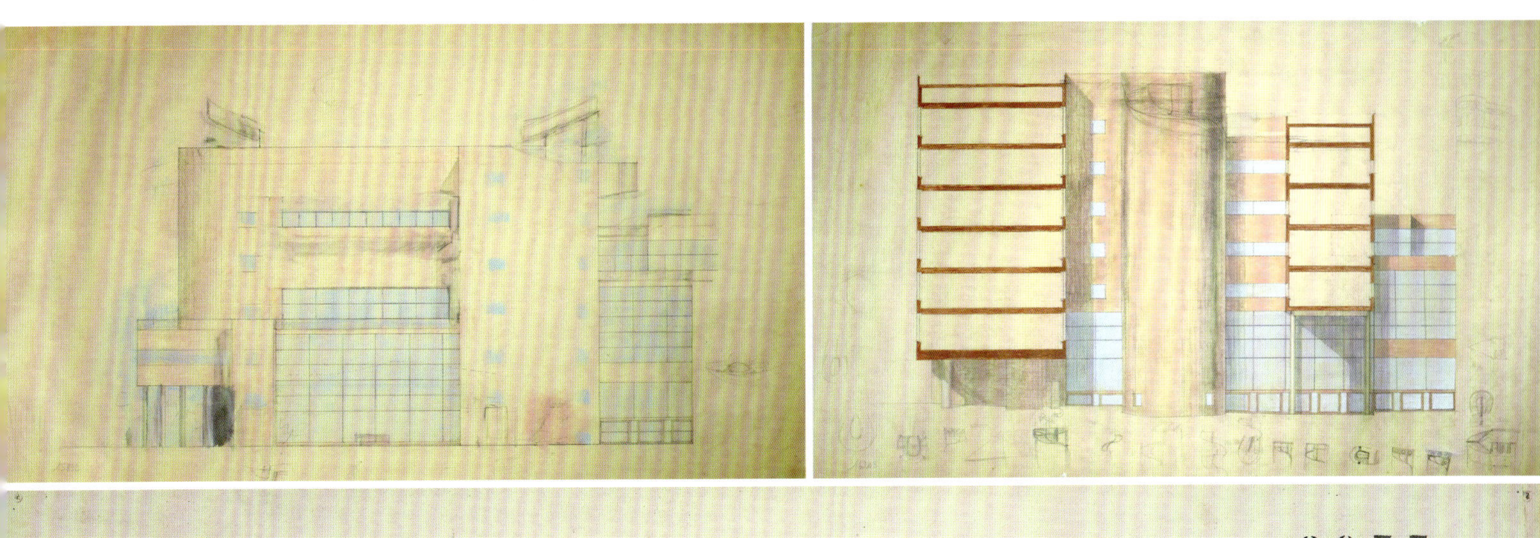

CS 15
2077

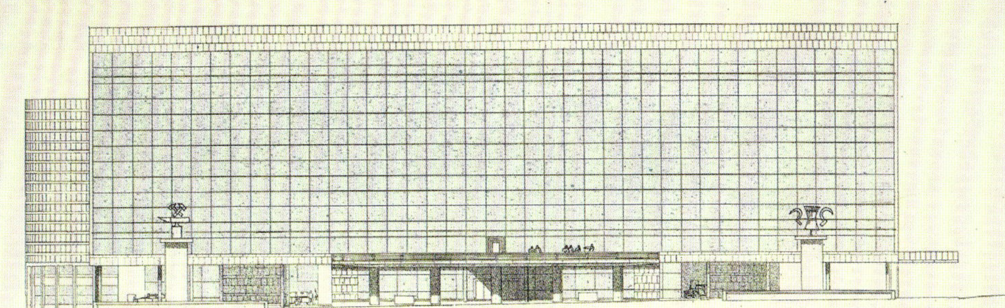

FACADE SVR LE BOVLEVARD

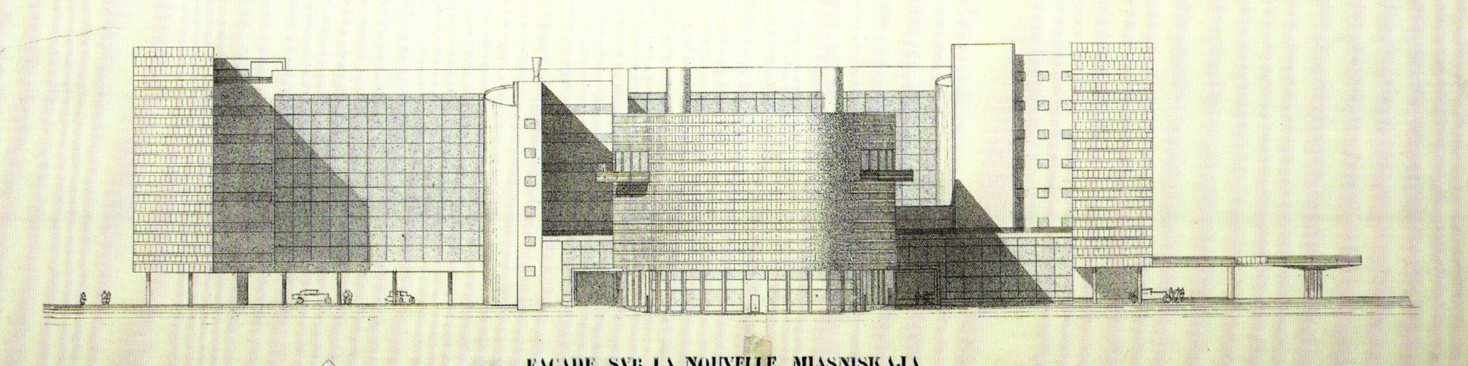

FACADE SVR LA NOUVELLE MIASNISKAJA

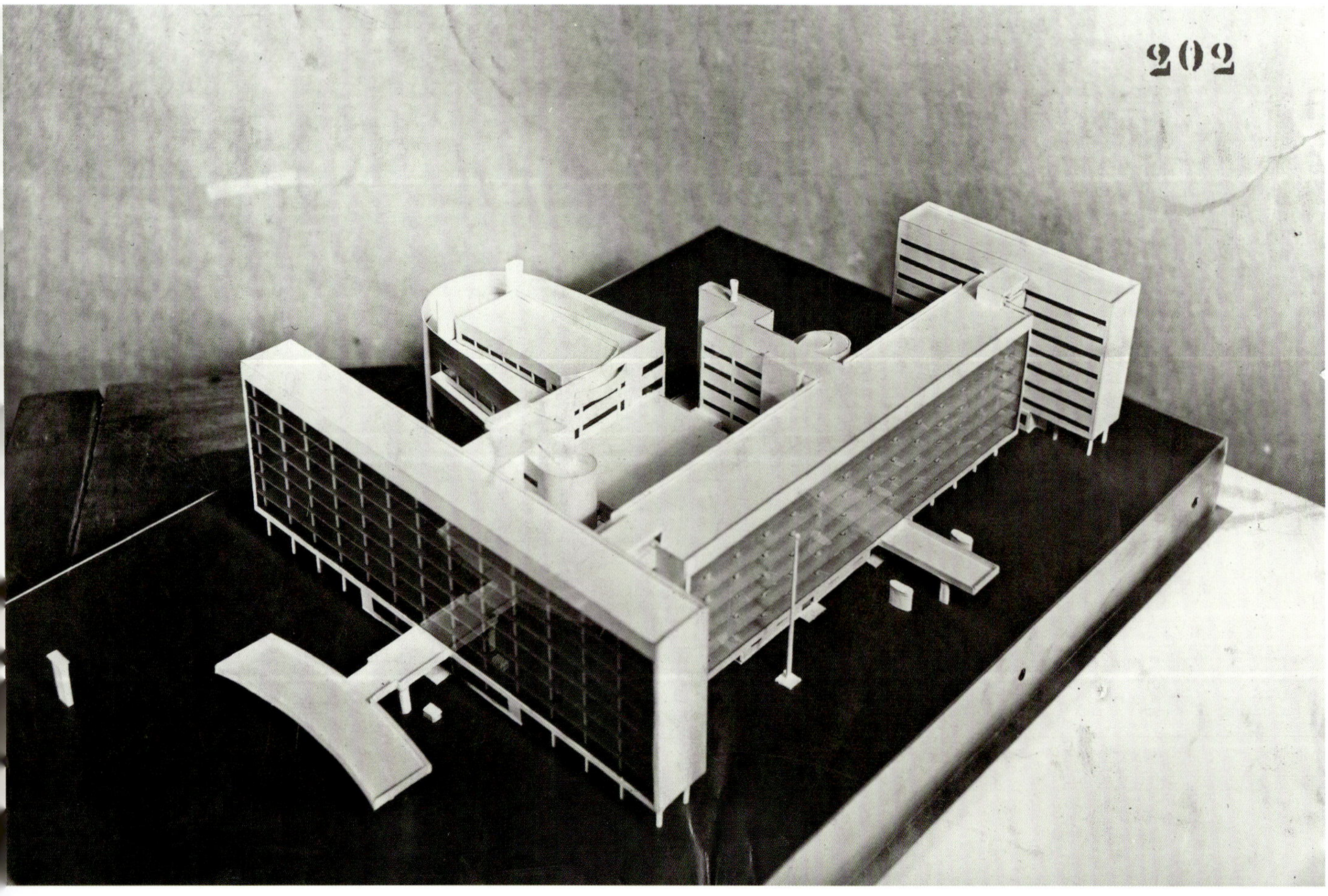

202

Opposite. Two views of a study model of penultimate scheme for Centrosoyuz, Moscow, 1929

Above. A ramp under construction, c. 1932

Following pages. Le Corbusier (right center, in glasses) and construction workers for Centrosoyuz, Moscow, with a wooden mold, 1929

Opposite, top. Facade, Centrosoyuz, Moscow, 1934

Opposite, bottom. Centrosoyuz in 1936, showing *pilotis*

Right. Le Corbusier at the Centrosoyuz site, Moscow, March 1930

Below. Street view of Centrosoyuz

Rejected by the USSR: Palais des Soviets competition, Moscow, 1930–31

Following the success of the Centrosoyuz project, Le Corbusier was one of a handful of Western modernists (including Auguste Perret and Walter Gropius) invited by the Soviet Union to participate in a competition to design for a building composed of offices, restaurants, libraries, and two large auditoriums. The complex was intended to be a venue for entertainment and political rallies to commemorate the First Five Year Plan. The spectacularly sculptural scheme developed by Le Corbusier—with an immense parabolic arch and auditoriums suspended from girders that resembled twentieth-century versions of flying buttresses—was ultimately rejected in favor of a neoclassical entry by two Soviet architects.

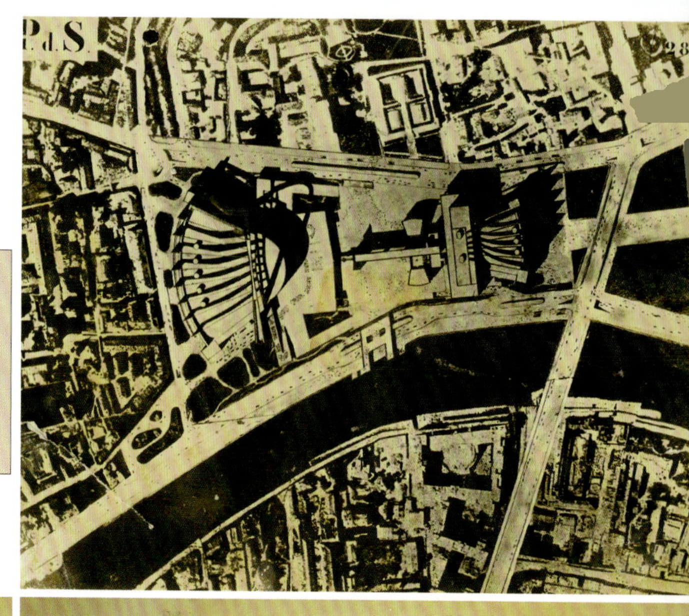

Opposite, top. Photo-collage, aerial view, c. 1931, Palais des Soviets and its surroundings, Moscow, 1930–31

Opposite, middle left. Cutaway perspective, 1931, showing the main entry to the Great Hall (right) and cloakroom (bottom left)

Opposite, middle right. Entrance facade elevation, 15 December 1931, Great Hall

Opposite, bottom. Model, 1931, including the Great Hall (left), an open-air platform for speeches, and an administration building (middle and right)

Above. Site plan, c. 1931

Below. Sheet of photographs showing building of the model for the Palais des Soviets, c. 1931. Le Corbusier's note at lower left says "this model is in New York, stolen by the museum."

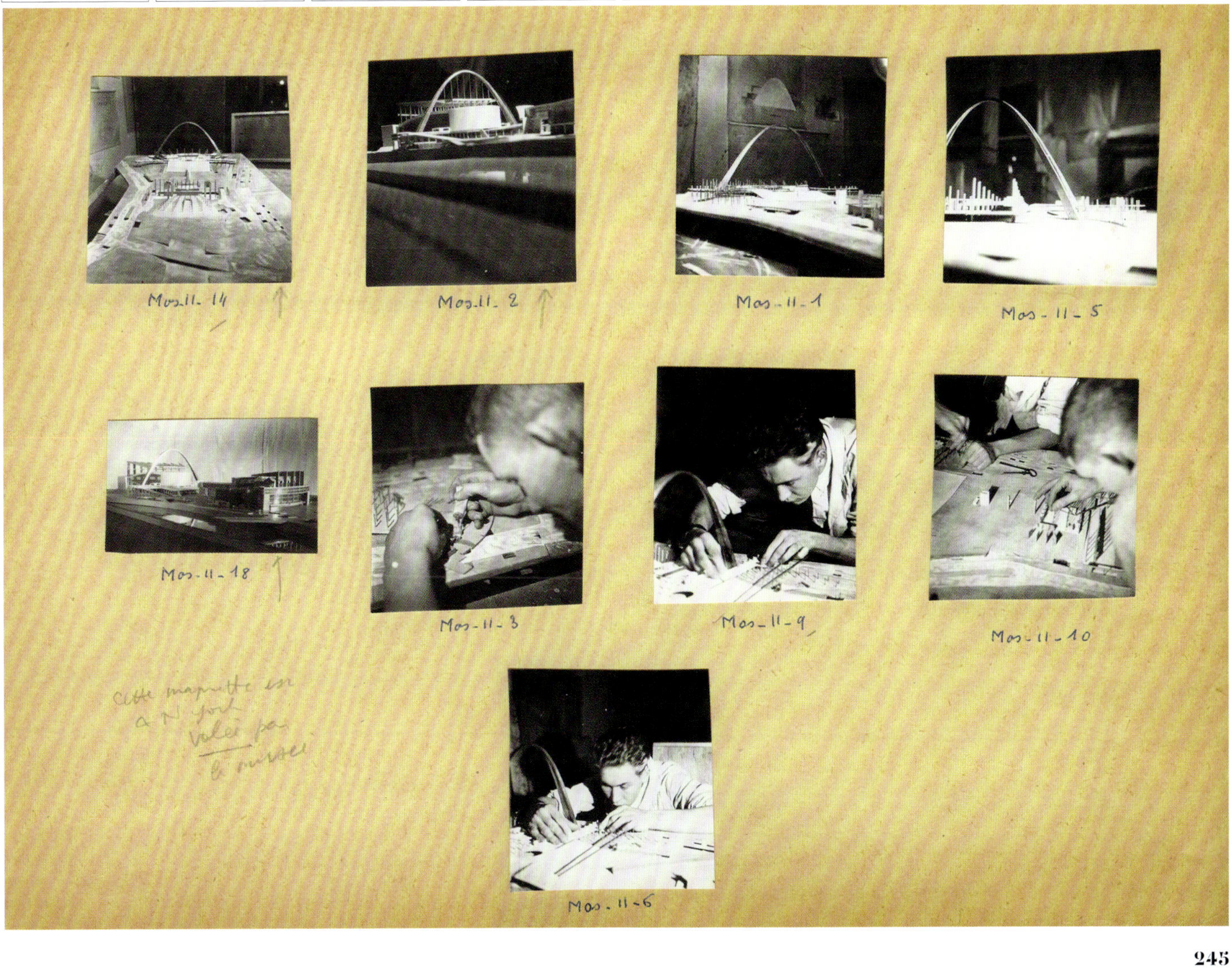

Mos.11. 14

Mos.11. 2

Mos-11-1

Mos-11-5

Mos-11-18

Mos-11-3

Mos-11-9

Mos-11-10

Mos-11-6

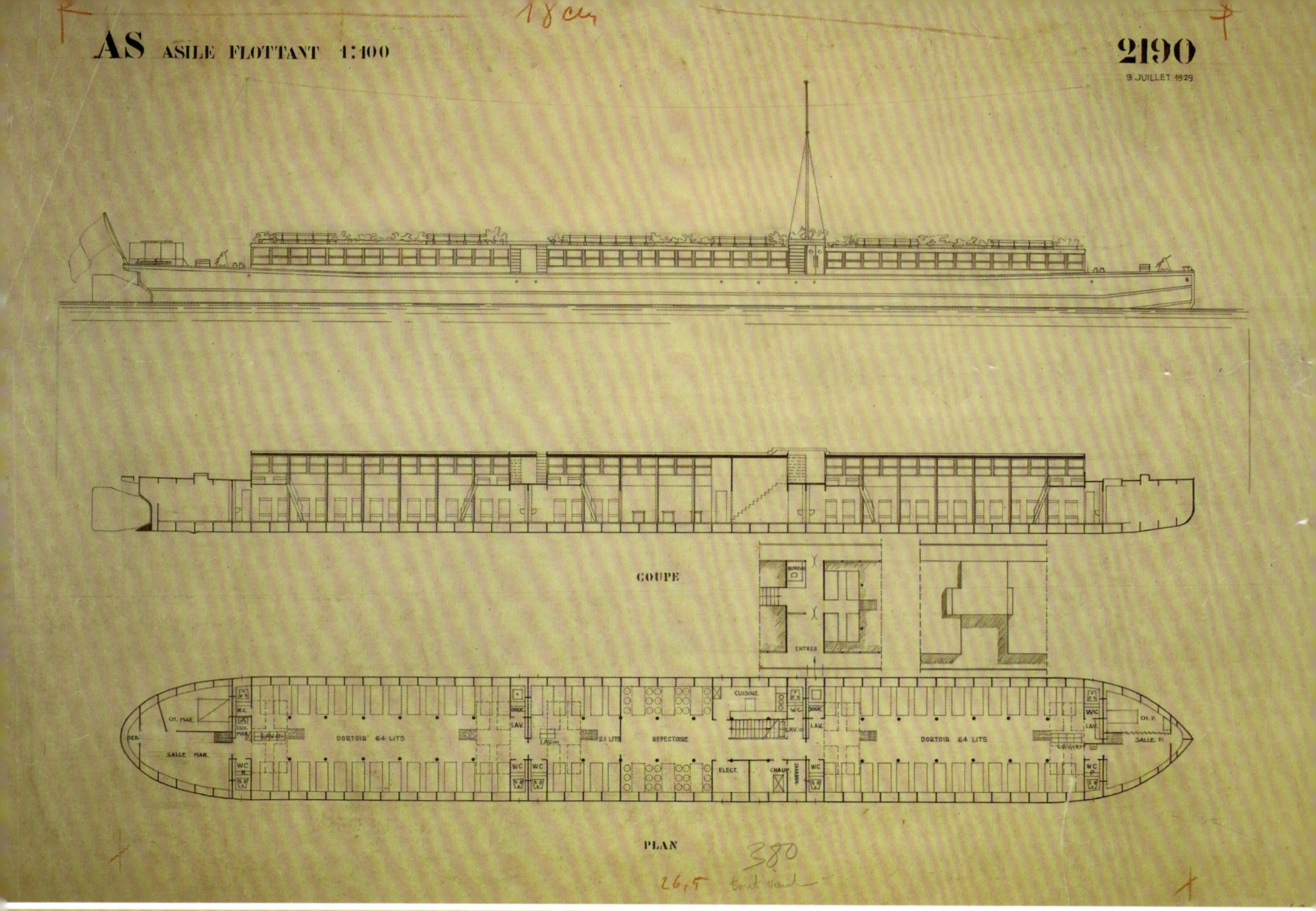

AS ASILE FLOTTANT 1:100

2190
9 JUILLET 1929

COUPE

ENTREE

CH. MAR
DEB.
SALLE MAR.
W.C.
CUI. MAR
LAV.
W.C. M.
DORTOIR 64 LITS
DOUC.
LAV.
W.C.
W.C.
LAV.
21 LITS
REFECTOIRE
CUISINE
LAV.
W.C.
DOUC.
LAV.
ELECT.
CHAUF.
CHARBON
W.C.
DORTOIR 64 LITS
W.C.
CH. P.
LAV.
SALLE P.
LAV. (9)
W.C. P.

PLAN

ASILE FLOTTANT

pposite, top.
levation, section,
nd plan, 9 July
929, Asile Flottant
loating haven),
aris, 1928–30

pposite, bottom.
endering of the
arge on
ne Seine, 1929

lockwise from above
ft. Barge under
onstruction, detail
f prow, gangplank,
nd interior

A floating refuge: Asile Flottant, Salvation Army, Paris, 1928–30

After Le Corbusier had completed his Palais du Peuple dormitory for the Salvation Army in 1926, the organization commissioned him again, this time to outfit a river barge as a housing shelter for homeless men.

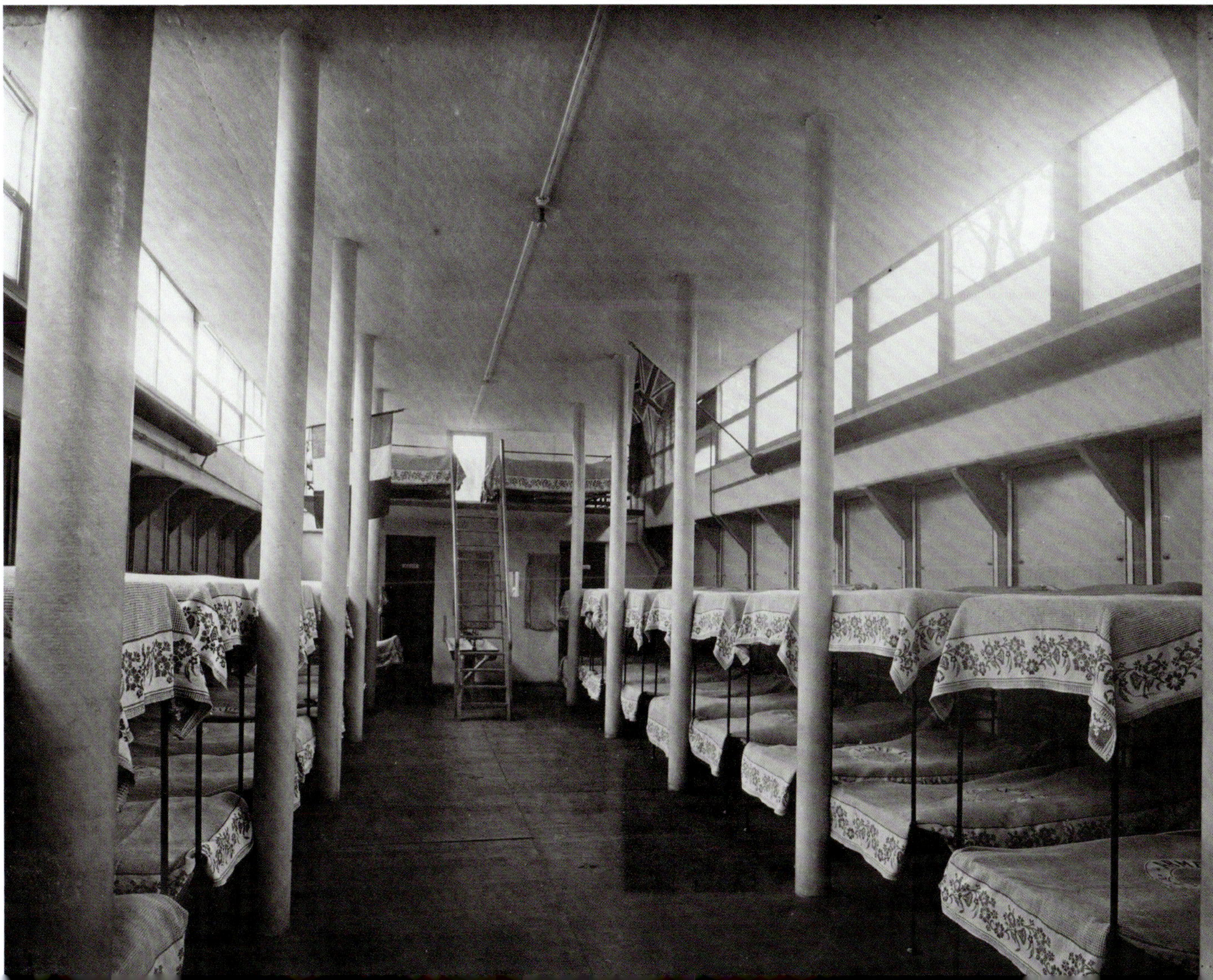

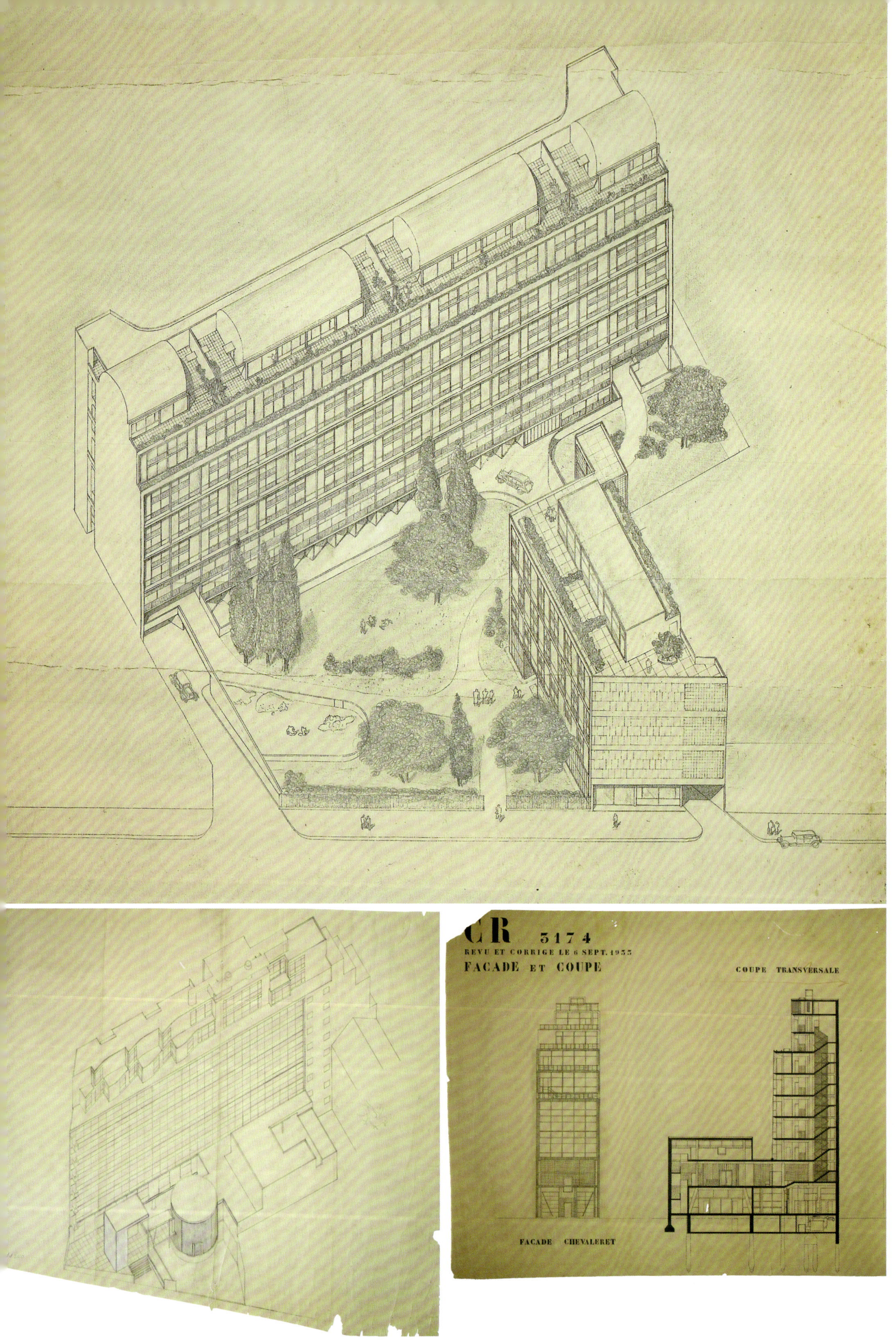
CR 3174
REVU ET CORRIGE LE 6 SEPT. 1933
FACADE ET COUPE
COUPE TRANSVERSALE
FACADE CHEVALERET

multipurpose
ıelter: Cité
› Refuge,
ılvation Army
eadquarters,
aris, 1929–33

For his third and final project for the Salvation Army, Le Corbusier designed a housing shelter for homeless men and women that also accommodated a nursery for working mothers, a cafeteria, and classrooms and studios for employment training. Le Corbusier envisioned the Cité de Refuge as an opportunity to realize a Western example of the Soviet "social condenser" as well as a chance to experiment with nautical metaphors inspired by his work on the Salvation Army's Asile Flottant and his ocean voyage to South America in 1929.

Opposite, top. Axonometric, c. 1929, preliminary design for the Salvation Army headquarters, Paris, 1929–33

Opposite, bottom left. Axonometric of final design, c. 1929

Opposite, bottom right. Elevation and transverse section, c. 1929

Above. Construction photographs showing reinforced-concrete columns

Below. Principal (south) facade with double-glazed curtain wall

LA CITÉ DE REFUG

12, RUE CANTAGREL (ENTRÉE PRINCIPALE) et 37, RUE DU CHEVALERET, PARIS (XIIIe)

LE CORBUSIER & JEANNERET, Architectes

LA CITÉ DE REFUGE A ÉTÉ INAUGURÉE LE 7 DÉCEMBRE 1933 PAR M. ALBERT LEBRUN, PRÉSIDENT DE LA RÉPUBLIQUE ASSISTÉ DU MINISTRE DE LA SANTÉ ET EN PRÉSENCE D'AMBASSADEURS ET DU GÉNÉRAL HIGGINS, GÉNÉRALISSIME DE L'ARMÉE DU SALUT

LA CITÉ DE REFUGE

La Maquette photographiée

La Princesse de Polignac signant le procès verbal de la pose de la 1re pierre

Madame la Commissaire Peyron et le Ministre de la Santé Publique

Une Chambre pour Mère et Enfant.

Un Dortoir pour homme.

Sa Raison d'être :

A la fois Maison d'accueil, Centre de triage et de reclassement, Bureau d'informations et de renseignements, en relation directe et ultra-rapide avec les Œuvres d'Assistance Publique et Privée, Bureau de placement, Œuvre d'assistance par le travail, d'Hospitalité de nuit, et de secours pour l'homme, pour la femme, pour la mère et pour l'enfant, la **Cite de Refuge** sera l'Usine du Bien où l'on révisera les rouages de la machine humaine usés par la vie.

« A l'armée de la misère sans drapeau, il faut une espérance, une maison où, en même temps que le pain et le lit, on donnerait le conseil et le travail; une Cité de Refuge où chaque misère aurait son confident, son défenseur et son guide, où chacun retrouverait sa joie... Et ce sera la grandeur de cette œuvre de n'être point bâtie pour servir de retraite, mais au contraire, pour créer des lendemains nouveaux. » (André LABARTHE).

« ...Pourquoi un édifice de plus, pourquoi une sollicitation de plus dans le domaine de la Charité qu'on morcelle au risque d'en diminuer les récoltes ou de les voir mal employées si on les dissémine ? Parce que ce qui va s'offrir ici ne se trouve nulle part. Et il est indispensable de le créer.

« Lorsque le malheur atteint une famille, contre le mauvais sort, contre l'abandon, contre la faute, où est le refuge ? A quelle porte frapper ? Que de pas à ajouter aux pas vite fatigués, dans les recherches sans guide : et le découragement arrête souvent dans son effort pour son relèvement, celui qui n'a pu aller droit et rapidement vers ceux qui s'occupent de son cas.

« Il s'arrête alors au bord de la route douloureuse qui lui parait sans fin, et il trouve dans le fossé des compagnons toujours prêts à l'accueillir sans formalité : la mendicité, l'alcoolisme et le vice.

« Demain, ici, dans la vaste demeure, à la moindre crainte, à la plus légère menace, comme aussi après le lourd passé, quiconque se présentera sera reçu fraternellement. Avec une affectueuse familiarité on démêlera les causes de sa misère, on tirera au clair les troubles de sa vie, on épouillera les corps et les consciences, et une fois la volonté réveillée, réconfortée, une fois la confiance en soi et dans les autres ranimée, on orientera, on conduira vers l'œuvre où l'administration qui conviendront, ceux qui ont besoin de leur aide. Dans les hôpitaux, il y a ce qu'on appelle le service de la porte. On y amène les victimes d'accidents de la rue ; ils reçoivent un pansement sommaire et après examen sont dirigés exactement où ils doivent être traités. La Cité de Refuge sera un service pour les victimes d'elles-mêmes ou de la société. En vérité elle réalisera avec les méthodes pratiques de classement les plus modernes, les plus hautes aspirations d'un idéal devant lequel tout le monde s'incline. » (Justin GODART).

« Cet état-major et sa petite armée en action sont l'une des plus claires manifestations **du produit social que peut fournir un groupe, de la puissance de réalisation d'un homme et de la sublime force de l'enthousiasme.** »

AIMEZ-VOUS LES UNS LES AUTRES.

Above left. Entrance, Salvation Army headquarters, Paris

Above. Pamphlet commemorating the inauguration of the Cité de Refuge on 7 December 1933 and outlining the Salvation Army's goals for the new building

Left. Courtyard off the men's library

Opposite, top. Nursery and day-care center

Opposite, bottom. Entrance lobby with semicircular wall of Nevada glass tiles

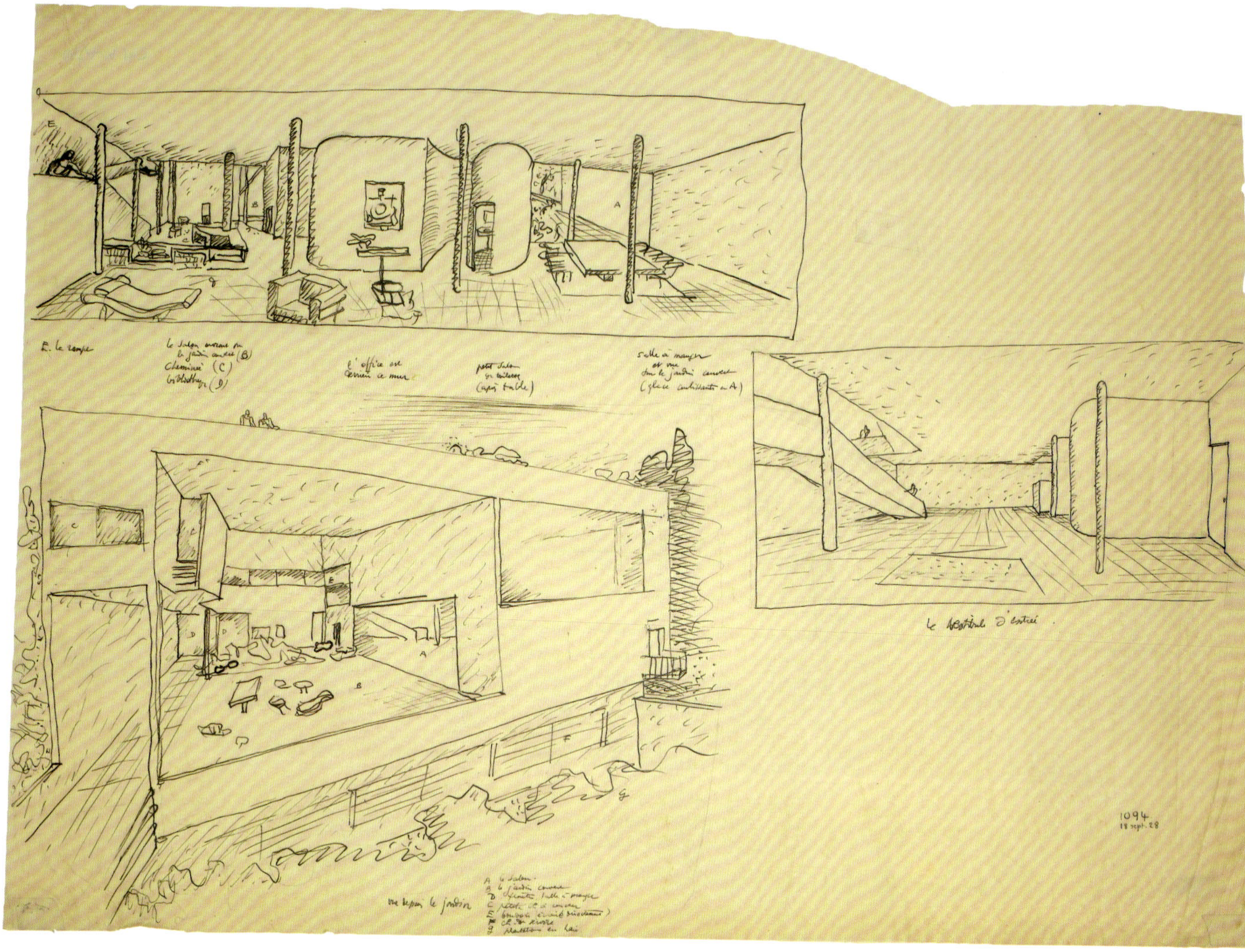

House for an Argentine patron: Villa Ocampo (unbuilt), 1928

Le Corbusier got to know the Buenos Aires–born patron of the arts, writer, and publisher Victoria Ocampo during her extended stays in Paris. She was responsible for organizing series of lectures that he would give in Argentina in 1929, under the auspices of Los Amigos del Arte (Friends of Art), and she met him at the boat when he arrived in Buenos Aires. In 1928, in advance of the architect's trip to South America the following year, Ocampo asked Le Corbusier to design a house for her, and he began to draw up plans. The house would remain unbuilt, however, opposed by Ocampo's family.

Above. Interior sketches, Villa Ocampo, Argentina, 18 September 1928

Below left. Ground-floor plan, 18 September 1928

Below right. Terrace plan, with pool, 18 September 1928

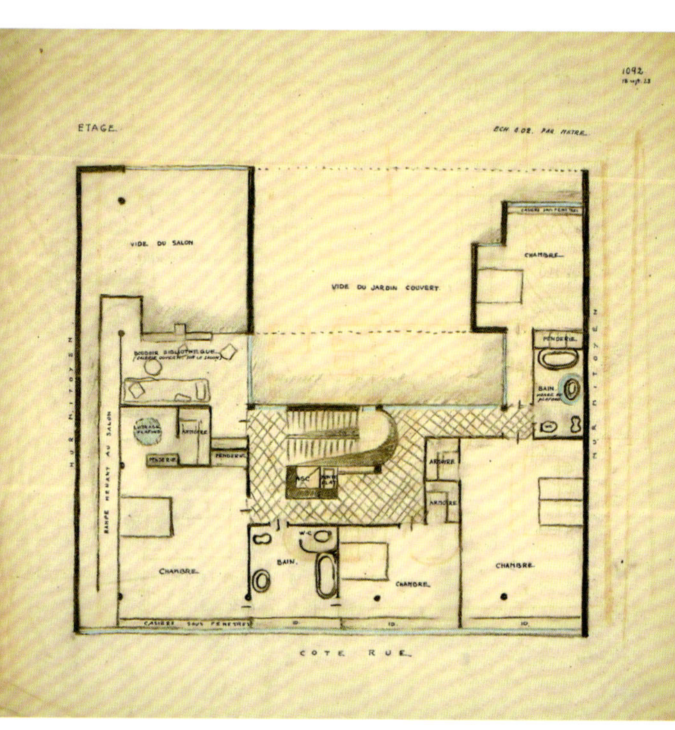

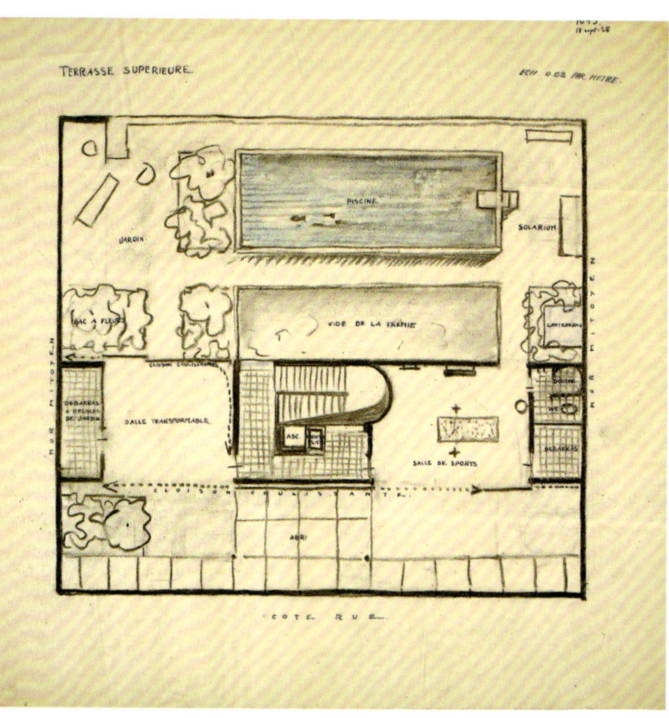

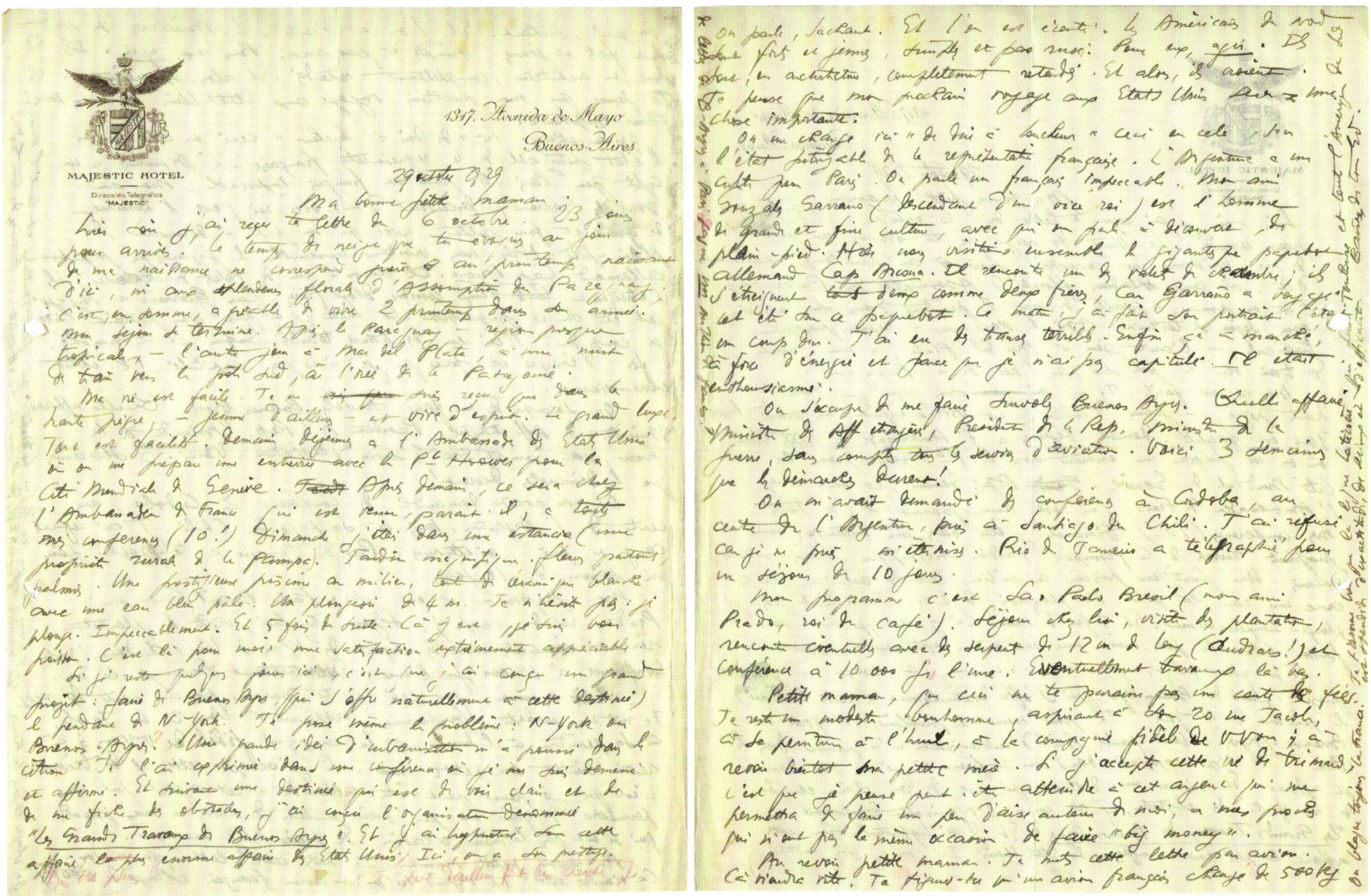

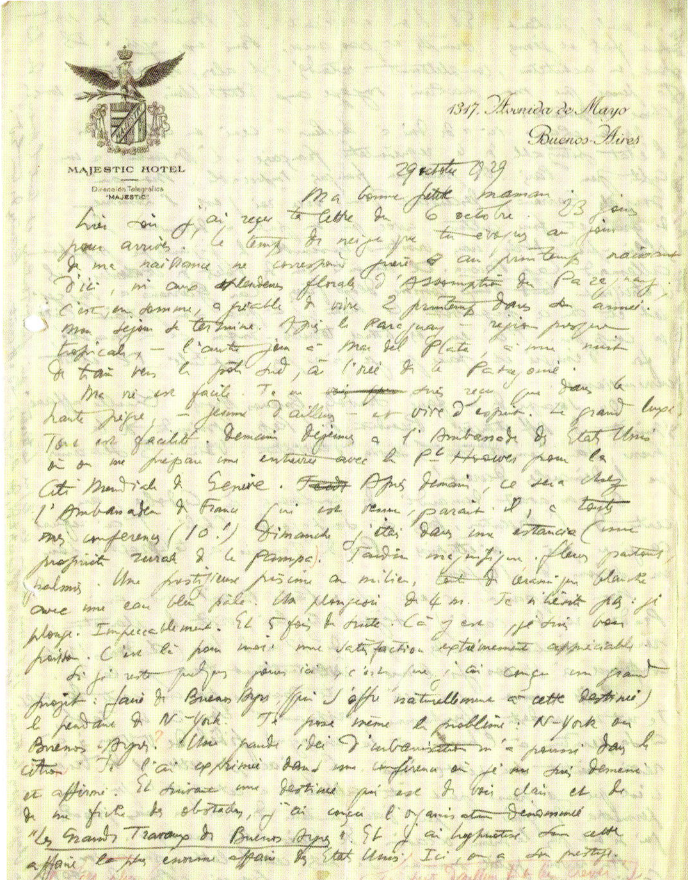

MAJESTIC HOTEL

1317, Avenida de Mayo
Buenos Aires

29 octobre 1929

Ma bonne petite maman

First trip to South America: Argentina and Brazil, 1929

The ostensible purpose for Le Corbusier's journey to South America was a series of ten lectures in and around Buenos Aires and Rio de Janeiro. The lectures yielded significant fees as well as an opportunity for Le Corbusier to cultivate his image as a creative force on the world stage. But their true value was as a catalyst both for his new master plan for Buenos Aires and for the publication in 1930 of his book *Précisions sur un état présent de l'architecture et de l'urbanisme* (*Precisions on the Present State of Architecture and City Planning*).

Top. Le Corbusier's depiction of Rio de Janeiro at night, as seen on his approach to the city by boat, 1929

Above. Le Corbusier to his mother, from Buenos Aires, 29 October 1929. He writes that his time in South America is coming to an end, and discusses his city plan for Buenos Aires. "I've come up with a big project: to make Buenos Aires… a counterpart to N-York"

AMIGOS DEL ARTE

FLORIDA 659

Buenos Aires, Octubre de 1929.

"Amigos del Arte", tiene el placer de invitar a Vd. a las conferencias, que en sus salones, dará el Señor M. LE CORBUSIER, los dias 3 y 5 de Octubre a las 18 y 30 horas.

1.ª conferencia. *Tema:* Libertarse de todo espíritu académico.

2.ª conferencia. *Tema:* Las técnicas son el fundamento del lirismo. Abren un nuevo siglo de arquitectura.

Left. Invitation to lectures by Le Corbusier hosted by the group Amigos del Arte (Friends of Art), Buenos Aires, 3 and 5 October 1929

Below left. Advertisement for *Hacia una arquitectura*, the Spanish translation of Le Corbusier's book *Vers une architecture*. The ad touts Le Corbusier as "the prophet of the new architecture," and the book as "the bible of the perfect dwelling."

Below right. Photograph of Le Corbusier from an undated Argentine newspaper. The caption gives the topic of his lectu "Can Buenos Aire be one of the world's great capitals?"

UN GRAN EXITO EDITORIAL

Ya está en prensa la segunda edición castellana de la extraordinaria obra de

LE CORBUSIER

el profeta de la nueva arquitectura

HACIA UNA ARQUITECTURA

Traducida directamente del francés por el prestigioso escritor y crítico de arte

Luis A. Romero

ESTA OBRA, JUSTAMENTE CALIFICADA POR LA PRENSA TECNICA MUNDIAL COMO

LA BIBLIA DE LA PERFECTA HABITACION

Hallábase agotada desde hace seis años, y al reeditarla, accedemos a insistentes requerimientos de miles de arquitectos, ingenieros y constructores de toda la América Latina.

Le Corbusier (Carlos Eduardo Jeanneret) es, el gran lírico de la arquitectura moderna. Y, por lo tanto, un revolucionario. Un reformador. Quiere adaptar los principios eternos de la arquitectura a la técnica actual de la vida.

Le Corbusier ha defendido su credo en todos los congresos. Ha escrito numerosos libros. Su postulado se concreta en esta fórmula; Los principios arquitectónicos más puros, los nuevos medios de edificación y las condiciones prácticas y morales de la sociedad actual.

Es la Esencia Misma de las Nuevas Doctrinas Arquitectónicas

Precio, en todos los países de América (incl. franqueo) Rústica $ 4.20, Tela $ 5.75

El Distribuidor Americano

RECONQUISTA 972 BUENOS AIRES

Adjunto la suma de $ ....

en cheque, giro, ... para que me remitan, enseguida de su aparición, y libre de todo otro gasto, un ejemplar de, HACIA UNA ARQUITECTURA.

Nombre ....

Calle ....

Localidad .... F. C. ....

DERECHOS EXCLUSIVOS DE LA TRADUCCION CASTELLANA

EL DISTRIBUIDOR AMERICANO

RECONQUISTA 972

BUENOS AIRES

DESCUENTOS A LOS SEÑORES LIBREROS Y REVENDEDORES

En Venta en Todas las Buenas Librerías

M. Le Corbusier, que dió en Los Amigos del Arte una conferencia sobre: "¿Podrá llegar a ser Buenos Aires una de las grandes capitales del mundo?"

Right. Sketches from Le Corbusier's lectures in Buenos Aires, 3–19 October 1929, and Brazil, December 1929. The drawing in the top row, center, which compares Buenos Aires to New York, was published in Le Corbusier's book *Précisions*, 1930.

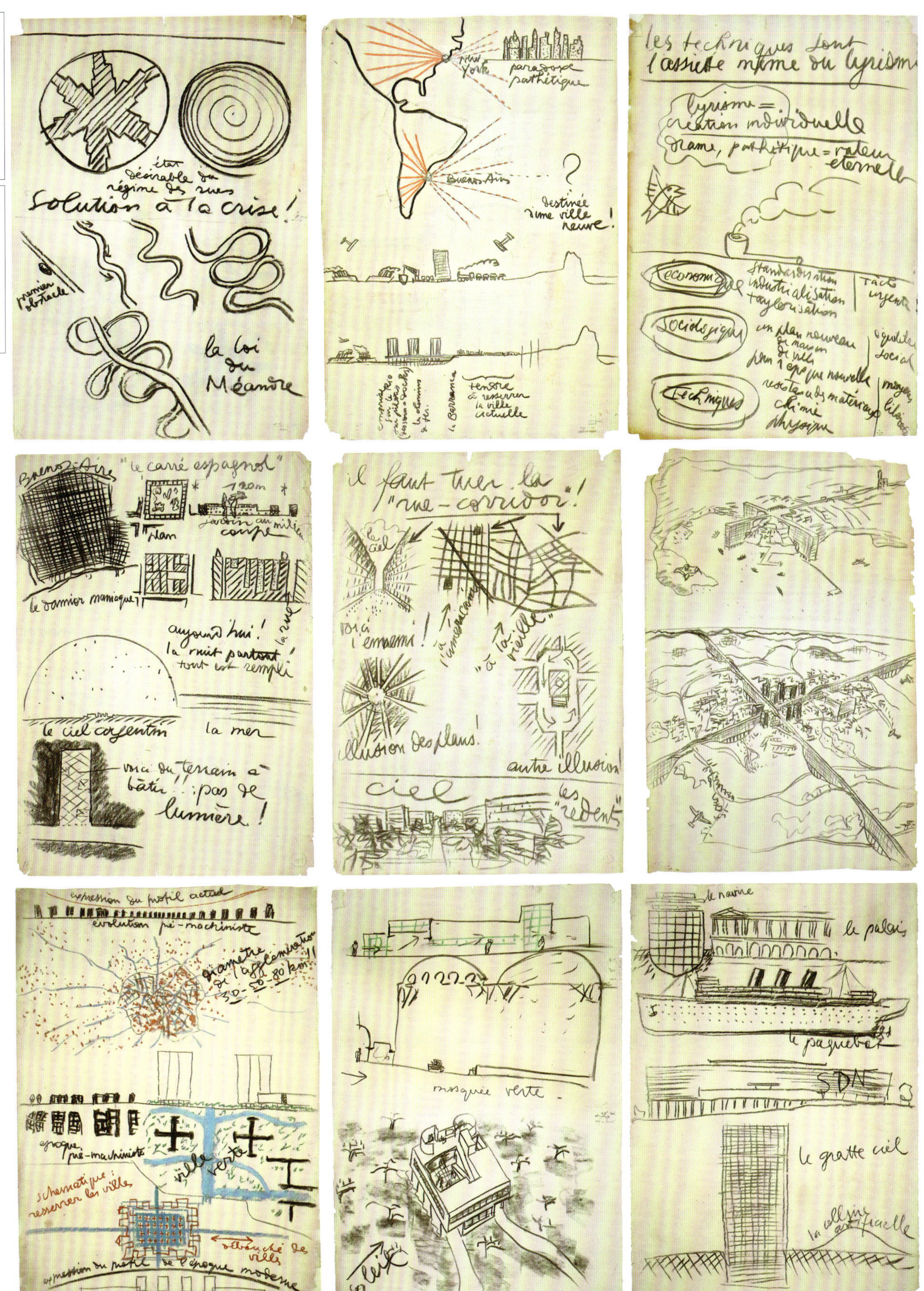

"I remain a modest little guy, hoping to get back to his 20 rue Jacob, to his oil painting, to the faithful company of Yvon; and to see my little mother again soon. If I put up with this wandering life, it's because I think maybe I'll get the money that will mean I can make life easier for those around me, for my family who haven't had the same chance to make 'big money.'"

—Letter to his mother, 29 October 1929

FACULTAD DE CIENCIAS EXACTAS, FISICAS Y NATURALES

CONFERENCIAS

DEL

ARQUITECTO M. LE CORBUSIER

Imp. Esteve y Gené, Perú 247

1929

El Decano de la Facultad de Ciencias Exactas, Físicas y Naturales de la Universidad de Buenos Aires, tiene el agrado de invitar a usted a las conferencias que dará en el local de la misma, Perú 222, el arquitecto M. LE CORBUSIER, de acuerdo al programa adjunto.

Buenos Aires, 2 de octubre de 1929.

PROGRAMA

I.—Martes 8 de octubre a las 18 horas.

Urbanismo en todo. Arquitectura en todo.

II.—Jueves 10 de octubre a las 18 horas.

Una célula en la escala humana.

III.—Martes 15 de octubre a las 18 horas.

La aventura del mobiliario.

IV.—Jueves 17 de octubre a las 18 horas.

Una casa. Un palacio. En busca de una unidad arquitectural.

"Buenos Aires is an enormous city; bigger than Paris. And not 'small beer'; it's marvelously alive, the beginnings of a great capital. My urbanism projects are steadily taking shape. As are the financial means. I think we're going to have a hive of activity here." —Letter to his mother, 2 November 1929

ew visions for e New World: ·ban plans for ·gentina and ·azil, 1929

Le Corbusier's trip to Argentina and Brazil greatly informed his thinking about urbanism. The rapidly developing cityscapes of Buenos Aires, São Paulo, and Rio de Janeiro inspired a new vision for port cities in mountainous landscapes. This was a departure from the flat landscape of his plan for Paris, the Ville Contemporaine, which concentrated on urban elements such as large-scale highways and high-rise construction.

Opposite, top. Annotated program for lectures at the Faculty of Exact and Natural Sciences, University of Buenos Aires, October 1929. On the program (far right), Le Corbusier noted six additional lectures he gave for the Amigos de la Ciudad (Friends of the City), 3–19 October 1929

Opposite, bottom. Le Corbusier on board the *SS Lutétia*, 1929, working on his book *Précisions*, which was based on his lectures in Buenos Aires

Above. Le Corbusier in bathing attire in Rio de Janeiro, on his return for a conference in 1936

Sketches from Le Corbusier's notebook, Rio de Janeiro, 1929

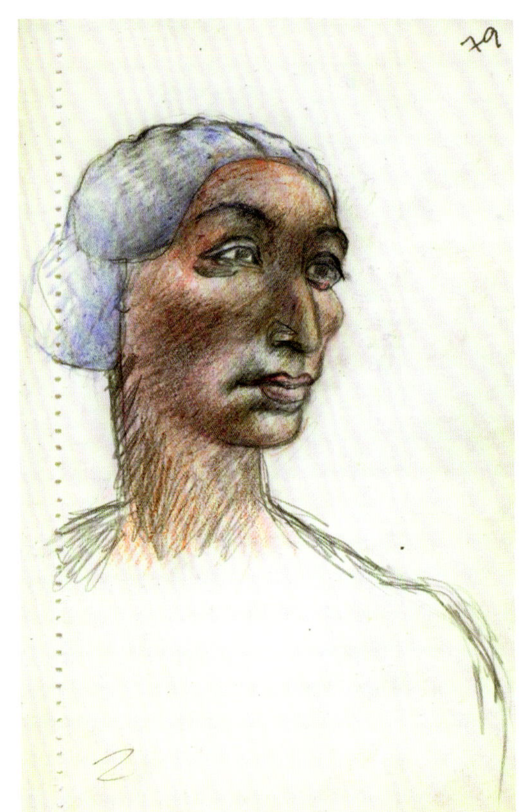

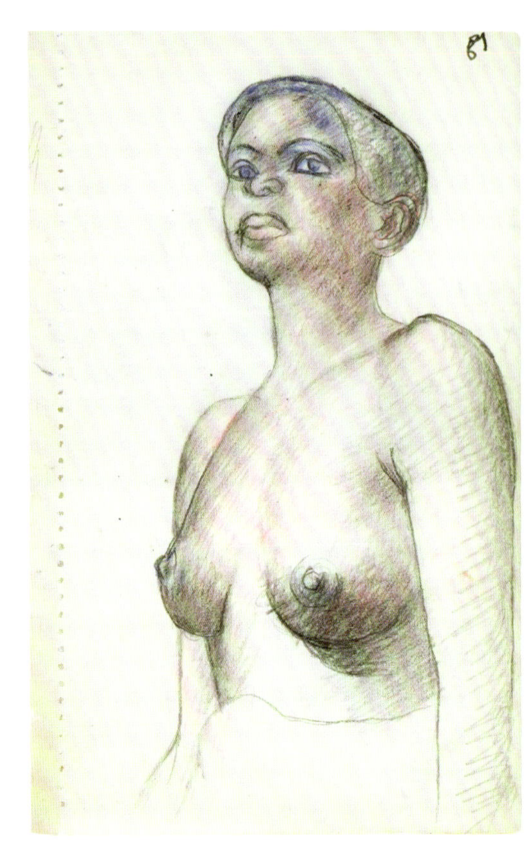

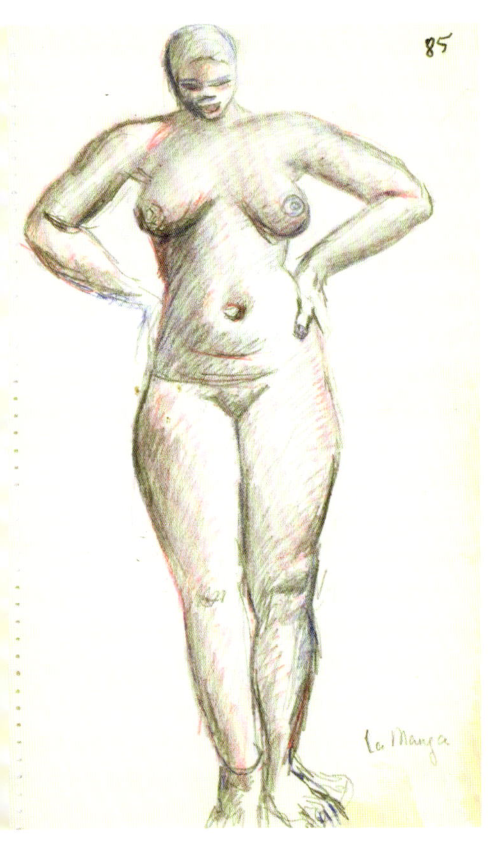

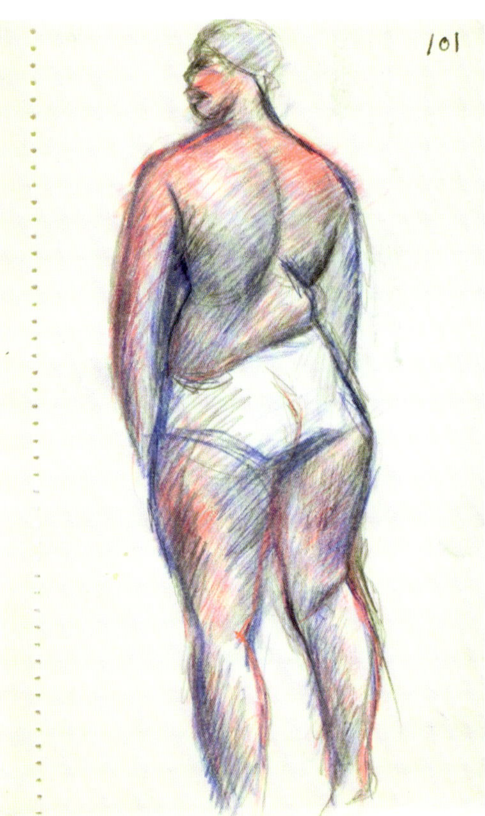

Top. Sketch of Rio de Janeiro, 1929

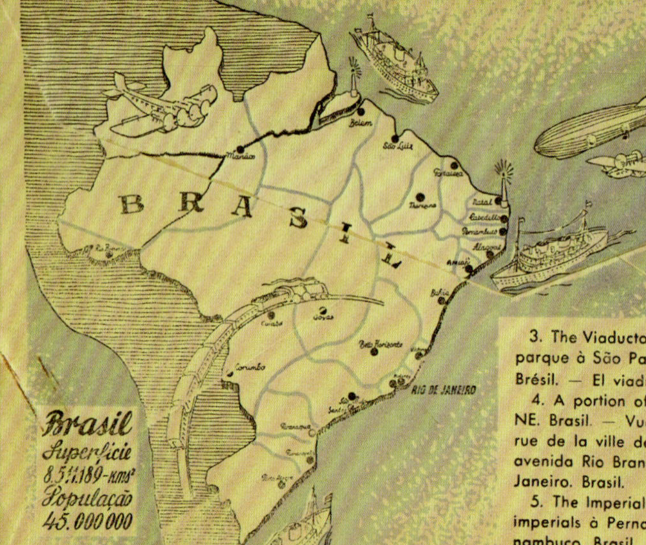

Middle. Souvenir envelope with map of Brazil and descriptions of key sites, 1936. Le Corbusier, who had a lifelong fascination with flying machines, traveled to Rio de Janeiro on the *Graf Zeppelin* when he returned in 1936.

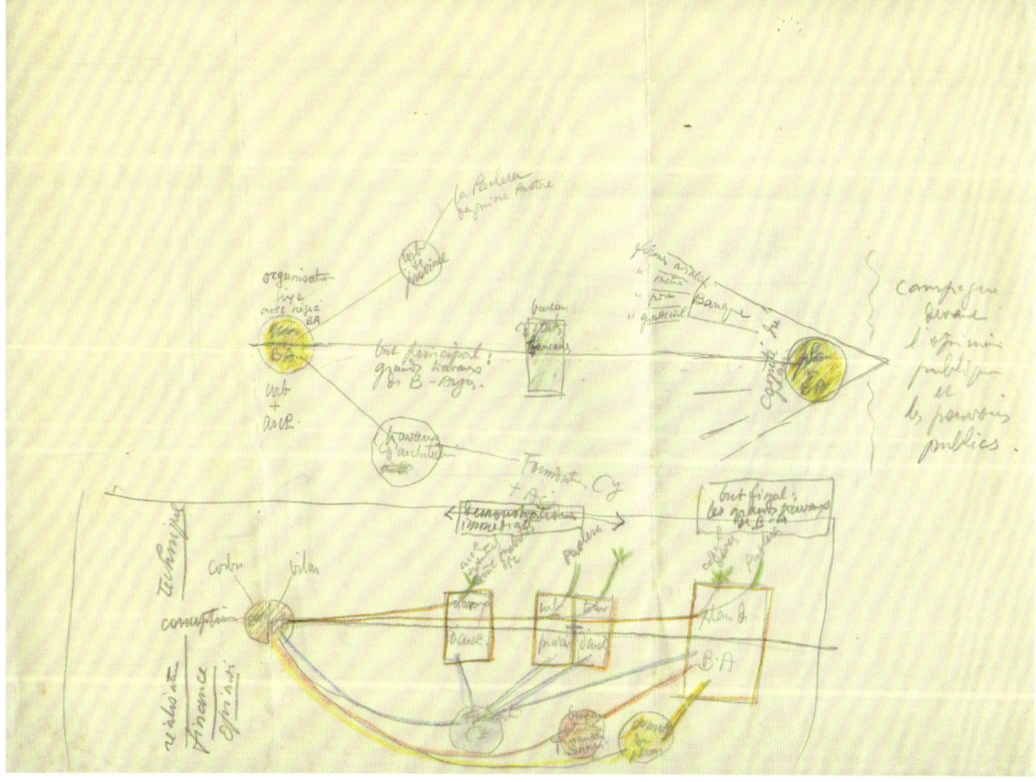

Bottom. Diagram of strategy for organizing public works in Buenos Aires, from Le Corbusier's South American lecture tour, 1929

Opposite. Le Corbusier (left) and unidentified man, Rio de Janeiro, 1929

LE CORBUSIER
&
P.

PARIS, le 4 Février 1935

Madame Joséphine BAKER

Théâtre Marigny - Avenue Marigny

PARIS VIII°

Chère Joséphine,

Je pense à vous quelques fois avec beaucoup de plaisir, mais j'ai des sentiments mélancoliquesque vous m'avez laissé parfaitement tomber.

Ce sentiment m'est venu tout particulièrement l'autre jour où, chez des amis, une personne m'a annoncé que vous faisiez bâtir des maisons locatives les unes après les autres.

Souvenez-vous du voyage en Amérique du Sud où j'étais en mission d'architecture et où vous m'aviez si gentiment demandé de vouloir collaborer avec vous à la rentrée en Europe, dans vos entreprises de construction.

Vous n'êtes pas une cliente ordinaire ; c'est pour cela que je me désole de ne pas être votre architecte à l'occasion.

Voulez-vous me faire un plaisir : ce serait de venir visiter une maison locative que j'ai terminée 24 rue Nungesser et Coli et que j'habite moi-même.

Je vous ferai voir quelques appartements et le mien, et nous aurions ainsi le plaisir de vous revoir un instant.

Dites à Pepito mes amitiés et faites-moi signe, vous me ferez le plus vif plaisir.

PARIS, le 2 Janvier 1936

35, rue de Sèvres - VI°

Madame Joséphine BAKER

App. 8 62

43 East - 60th Street

NEW - YORK

Chère Joséphine,

Vous serez peut-être étonnée, mais l'envoi de votre Merry Christmas avec votre signature m'a fait un très vif plaisir.

Nous jouons de malheur ensemble : je viens de passer deux mois aux Etats-Unis. Je savais que vous y étiez. J'ai prié des amis de découvrir votre retraite. Cela n'a pas réussi et c'est le jour de mon arrivée à Paris que je trouve votre adresse à la 60th rue, alors que, moi, j'habitais à la 55e. Pourtant, vous apprécierez quel plaisir j'aurais eu à vous revoir, vous qui êtes si jolie, si gentille et nous aurions pu nous rappeler dans l'Amérique du Nord les bons souvenirs de l'Amérique du Sud.

Je disais que je n'avais pas de chance avec vous. Parce que vous m'aviez fait promettre à Rio de Janeiro que je ne vous laisserais pas tomber ; or c'est vous qui m'avez laissé tomber parfaitement et je ne vous pardonnerais pas si je ne savais que vous être une travailleuse acharnée. Comme je fais exactement la même chose, les minutes libres n'existent pas et seuls les bons souvenirs demeurent. Vous m'aviez fait promettre que je consentirais à vous construire un village pour les petits enfants. Vous n'avez pas construit le village et je pense que vous avez construit autre chose et que vous vous êtes passée de moi. Cela n'est pas gentil aussi je vous envoie ce mot comme un aiguillon du remords pour qu'il vous touche à vif.

Est-ce que vous êtes de la sorte des Héros qui rapportent des dollars d'U.S.A. ? Moi pas ! En tous cas si vous en avez de trop au retour, mettez-les dans la pierre et à ce sujet j'ai toujours, dans mon atelier, des études extrêmement intéressantes pour les placements d'argent.

Vous voyez, chère Joséphine, que ma lettre finit par des arguments de commis-voyageurs. Il faut bien se dire tout puisque nous ne pouvons nous voir que par lettre.

Quand vous reviendrez à Paris, soyez assez gentille pour me faire signe et en attendant je vous salue bien amicalement.

LC

A shipboard encounter: Josephine Baker, 1929

On the boat from Buenos Aires to Rio de Janeiro, Le Corbusier began an affectionate friendship with the performer Josephine Baker, whom he sketched several times. They also sailed back to Paris on the same ship, the *SS Lutétia*, in December 1929.

**esigns a
oject for
viss clients:
avillon Suisse,
aris, 1930–33**

In the late 1920s the Swiss community in Paris commissioned Le Corbusier to build a dormitory for Swiss students at the Cité Universitaire. His original scheme, which was another example of a box set on slender *pilotis*, met with considerable resistance from the structural engineers, who claimed that such thin supports would be unable to withstand strong winds. Faced with these objections, Le Corbusier developed sculptural supports that looked more solid. By reaching this compromise, he was able to maintain the open space at ground level characteristic of the Ville Radieuse, and the Pavillon Suisse became a realized prototype for his vision of the ideal city.

Below left. Plan of a typical room, Pavillon Suisse, Paris, 1930–33

Below right. Ground-floor plan

Middle left. North facade

Middle right. Entry hall

Bottom left. Terrace and *pilotis*

Bottom right. Fourth-floor student room

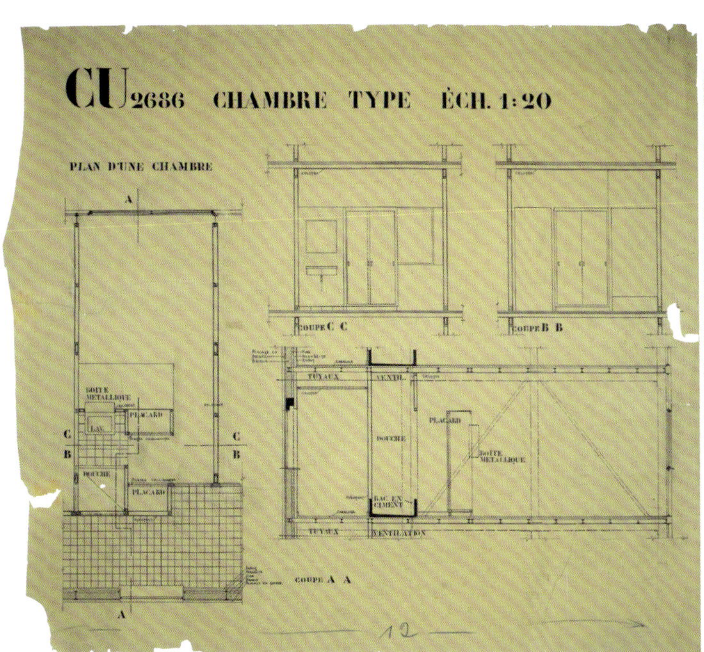

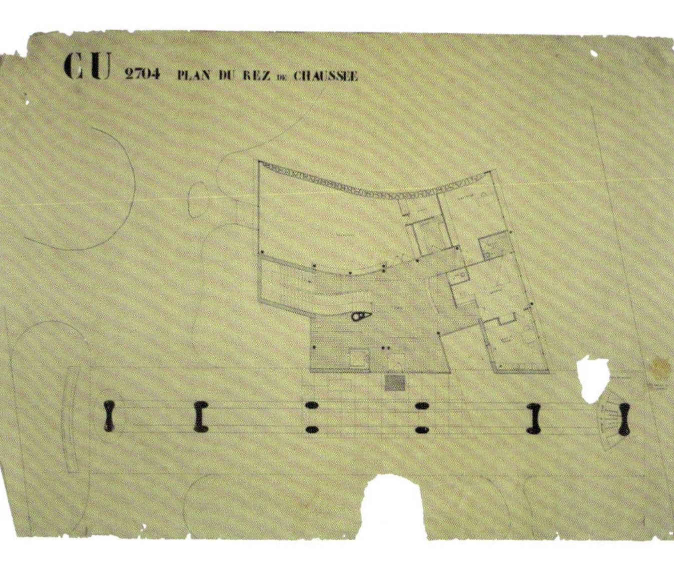

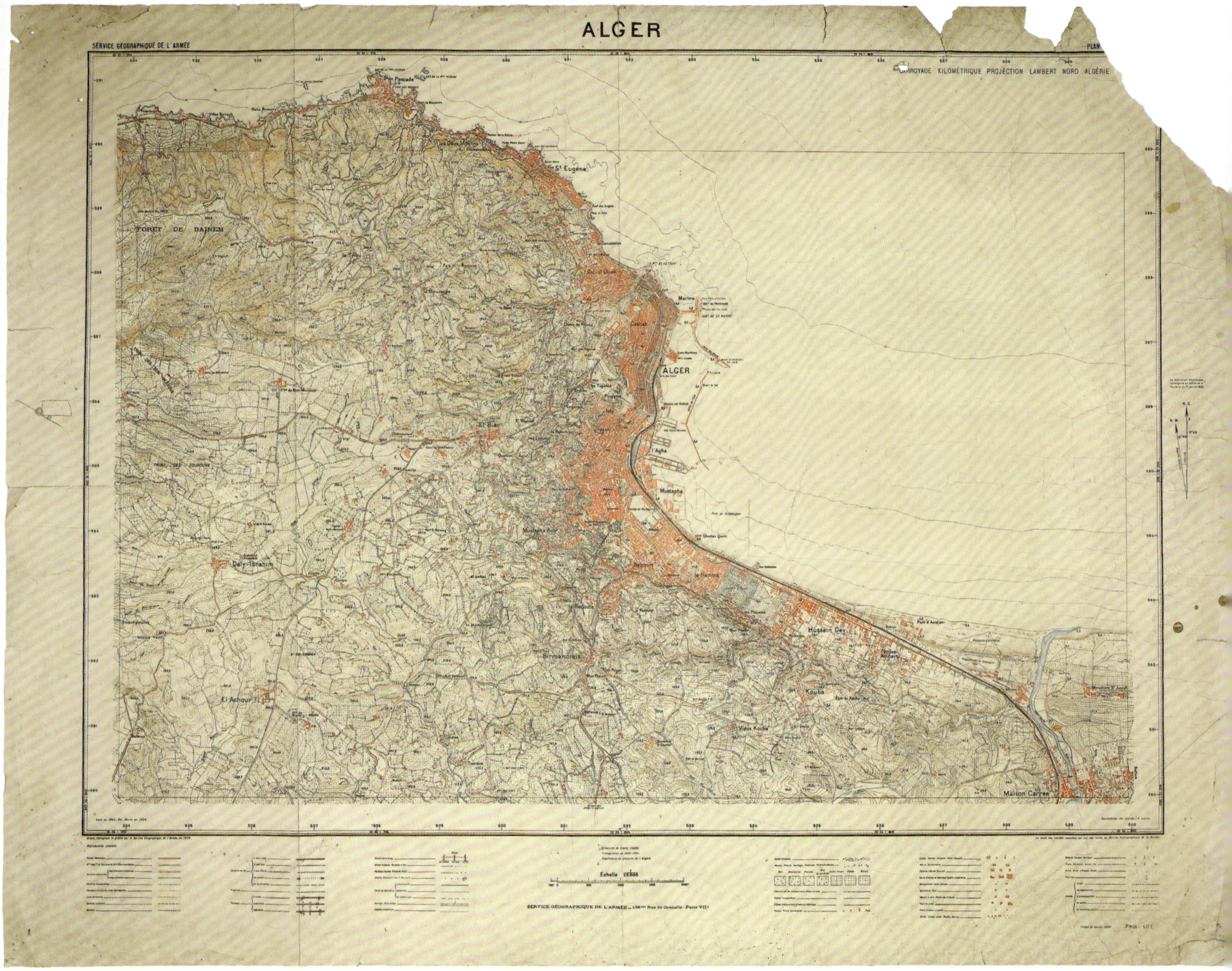

First visit to North Africa: Discovering the city of Algiers, 1931

In 1931 Le Corbusier, with his wife, Yvonne, made his first trip to North Africa. He instantly felt a deep affinity with the city of Algiers and with the entire region, marveling at its lush vegetation and the extraordinary qualities of light. The more remote oasis towns impressed him with their coherent density and integration into the natural landscape. His dream of developing a new master plan for Algiers became something close to an obsession that would endure for more than a decade.

Opposite, top. Map of Algiers used by Le Corbusier

Opposite, bottom. Postcard of Algiers, general view from the Admiralty, c. 1931

Right. Postcards of North Africa collected by Le Corbusier

Bottom. Sketch from Algeria, *2 femmes au turban et chameaux* (Two Women in Turbans with Camels)

"The springtime is dazzling. I've been through a fairly typical part of Algeria. It's a splendid country whose agreeable characteristics and beauties accumulate from its handsome shores to its snowcapped mountains and deserts."

—Letter to his mother, 29 March 1931

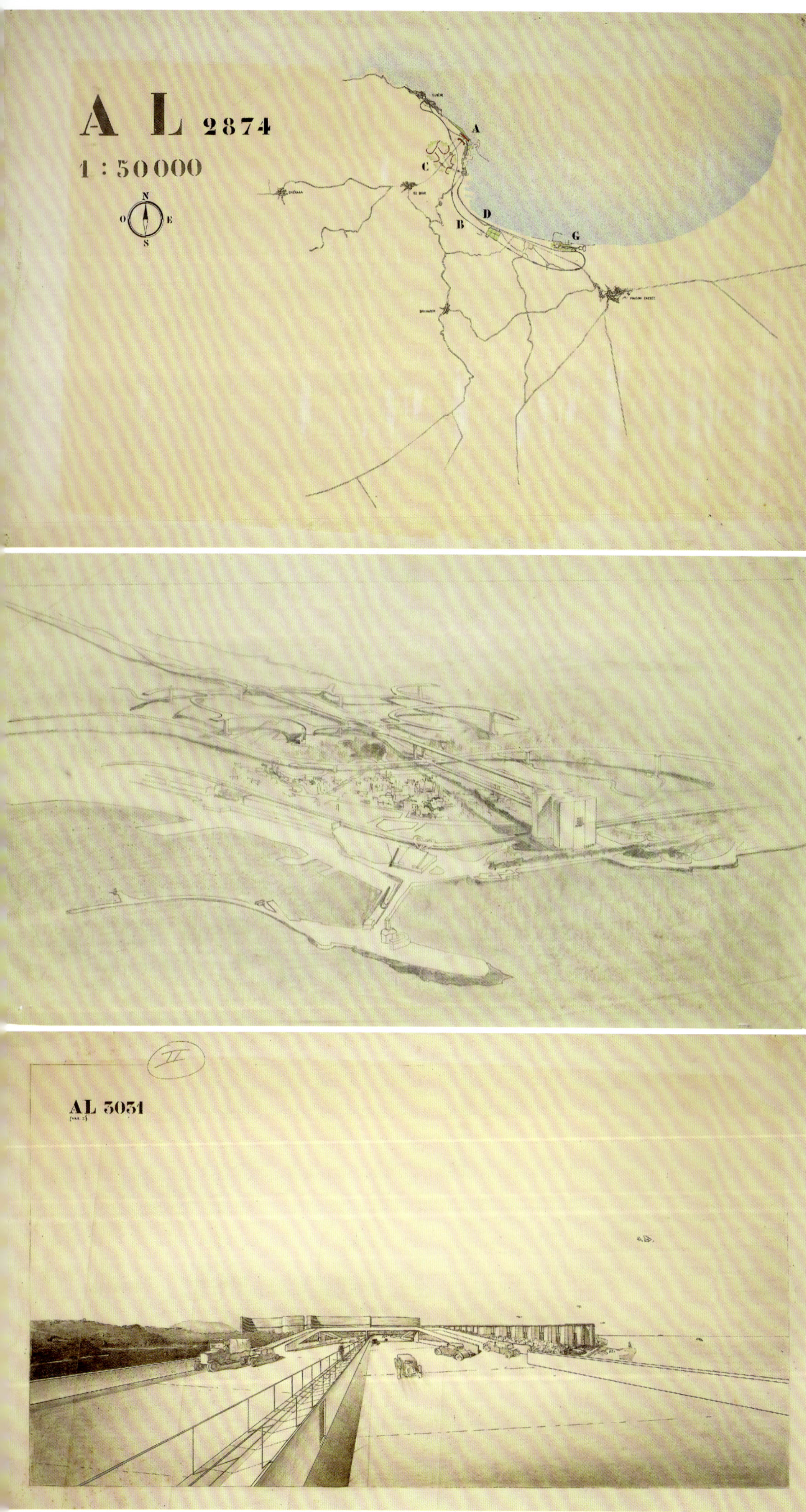
A L 2874
1 : 50000
N
O
E
S
A
C
D
B
G
II
AL 3031

uturistic ision for a ity in tran- ition: Plans or Algiers, 931–42

uring his visit to lgiers in 1931, Le orbusier sensed hat the region was ntering a period of reat transition. he following year e unveiled an nsolicited plan for he city, called the "Plan Obus," encompassing an administrative center and a residential enclave linked by an elevated highway. The most striking of the plan's components was an undulating viaduct, raised 100 meters above ground, that contained shops and promenades as well as low-cost housing to be constructed according to the Dom-ino system. Dismissed by the colonial administration as unfeasible, the Plan Obus was never adopted, though Le Corbusier would recast it in different iterations throughout the 1930s.

Opposite, top. Master plan of Algiers, "Plan Obus," Project A, 1932. The plan included an office high-rise on the waterfront linked by an elevated highway to a residential neighborhood on the hills of Fort l'Empereur.

Opposite, middle. Bird's-eye view, master plan of Algiers, Project B, 1933–34.

Opposite, bottom. Perspective of elevated highway, Project B, 1933–34

Above left. Rendering of apartment interior, master plan of Algiers

Above right. Perspective, master plan of Algiers

Below. Bird's-eye view, master plan of Algiers, Project B, c. 1934

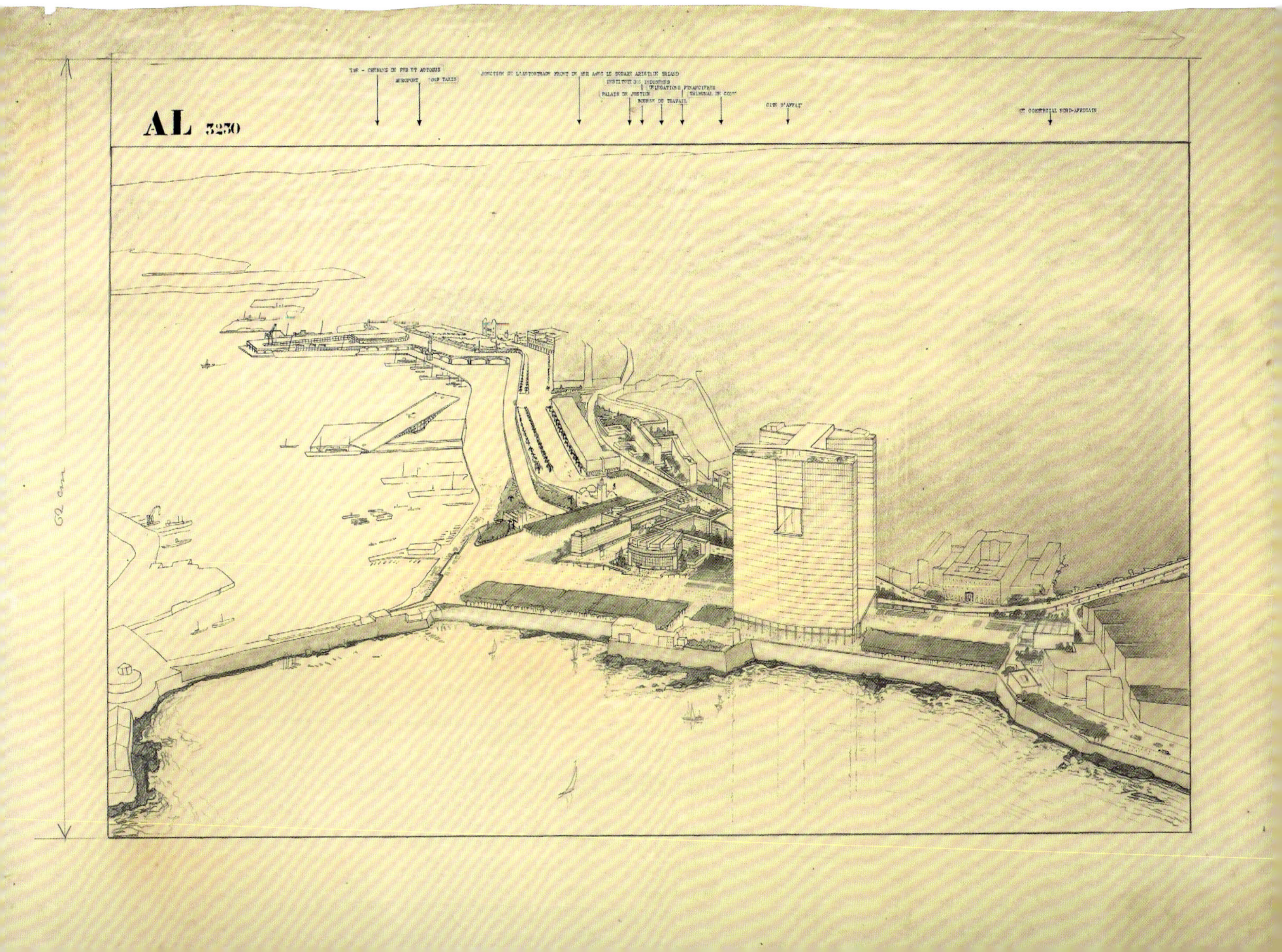

"Algiers was a major phase for me. Faced with that imposing natural setting I opened up my urbanism to new, flexible splendors, parts of the elements, as it were: sea, sun, cliffs, vegetation. I've a notebook packed with these violent utterances, revealers of a fresh phase. A phase adding prodigious poetry to our energy." — Letter to his mother, 4 April 1931

Below. Model, master plan of Algiers, "Plan Obus," Project A, 1932. An elevated highway connects apartment blocks on the hills (left) to an office high-rise on the waterfront (right).

Opposite, top. Aerial views of the model

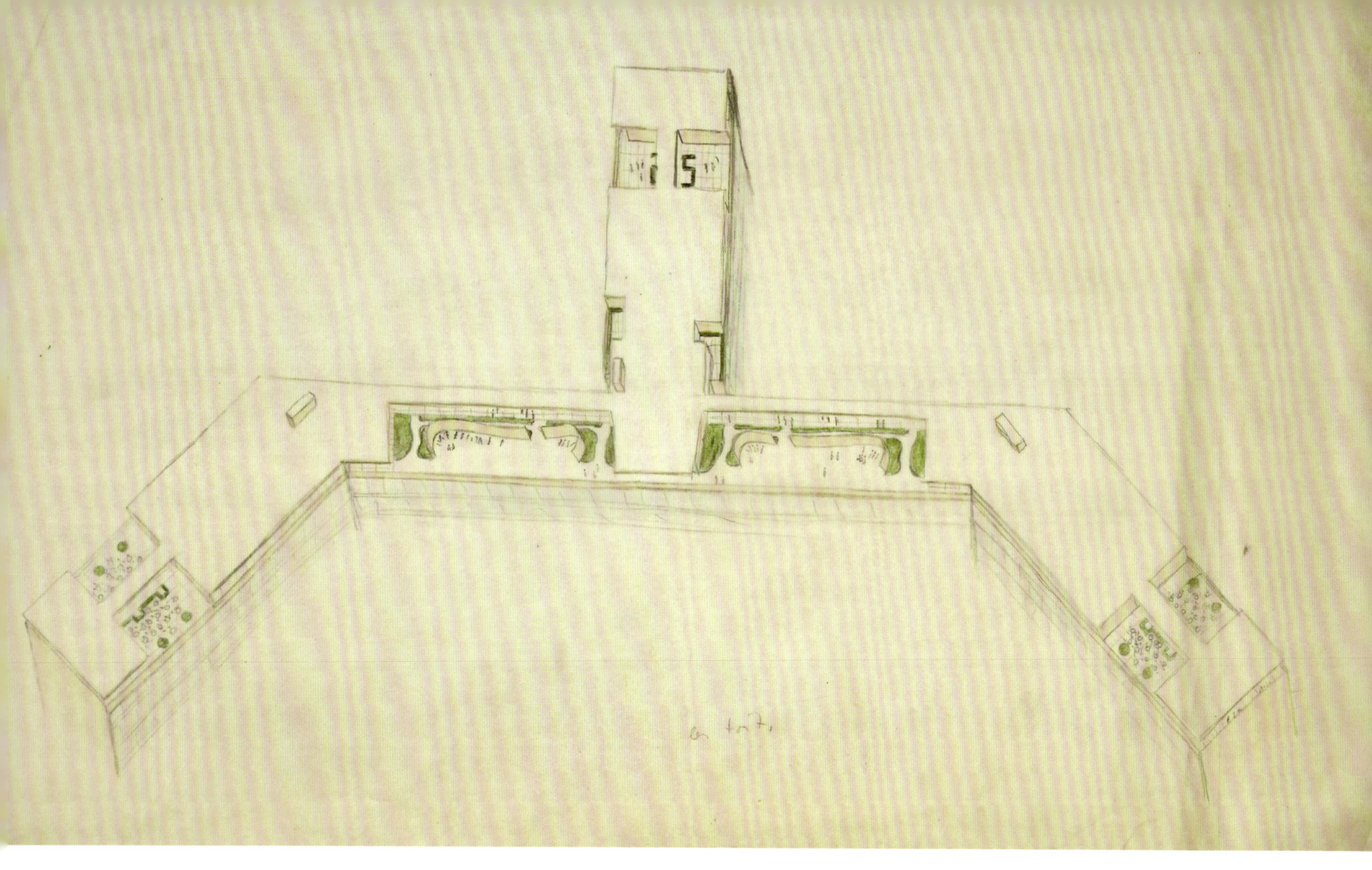

"In opposition to New York, to Chicago, we offer the Cartesian skyscraper—translucent, cleancut, gleamingly elegant against the sky of the Ile-de-France.

In place of the porcupine and Dante's inferno, we propose an organized, serene, forceful, airy, ordered entity. From below, it could be sublime. From the air (we are all now learning to look at cities from above), it will be a symbol of the spirit...

Instead of New York (magnificent and milling clamour of the machine age in its adolescence), I propose the Cartesian city." —***The Radiant City*, 1935**

A French concept for the U.S. cityscape: The Cartesian Skyscraper (unbuilt), 1937

During his 1935 visit to New York and Chicago, Le Corbusier found himself increasingly seduced by the skyscraper. He soon developed a scheme he called "The Cartesian Skyscraper," which he originally conceived specifically for the American landscape, with its vast reserves of space: each Cartesian skyscraper would be set within large parks surrounded by superhighways. Le Corbusier later applied this typology to his urban plan for Algiers.

Above. Bird's-eye view of the Cartesian Skyscraper, 1937, showing the roof garden

Right. Perspective of the principal facade

100
50
20
50

Transplanting the concept to Algiers: Skyscraper for the Quartier de la Marine, Algiers (unbuilt), 1938–42

As Le Corbusier continued to pursue his preoccupation with Algiers, his schemes became increasingly scaled back, ultimately reduced to a single skyscraper for the Quartier de la Marine. The tower was distinguished by the large-scale *brises-soleil*, or sunshades, which Le Corbusier had been developing as a method of controlling solar heat. The screens gave texture to the facade and expressed interior functions through varied scales and articulation on the exterior.

Left. Model, skyscraper for the Quartier de la Marine, Algiers, 1938–42. The project was to include a hotel, restaurant, offices, and archives.

Below left. Drawing of another version of the skyscraper for Algiers, superimposed on an aerial photograph of the city, c. 1938

Below right. Model of alternate version of the skyscraper, photographed on a site plan, c. 1938

Opposite. Le Corbusier in front of model of the skyscraper for Algiers, Paris, c. 1947

Above. Four views of the model, Ville Radieuse, Paris, 1930

Below. Cover of Le Corbusier's book, *La ville radieuse* (*The Radiant City*), Editions de l'Architecture d'aujourd'hui, Boulogne, France, 1935

Opposite. Le Corbusier, with *La ville radieuse*, in his Paris apartment, c. 1935

A concept and a book: La Ville Radieuse, Paris, 1930–35

A decade after gaining international notoriety for his Ville Contemporaine, Le Corbusier published a reconsideration of his vision for the ideal city: La Ville Radieuse (The Radiant City). Like the Ville Contemporaine, it relied on high-density construction within generous green spaces. However, he abandoned the centralization of the Ville Contemporaine in favor of a linear organization with all the structures raised on *pilotis* to create an uninterrupted public real at ground level.

LA VILLE RADIEUSE

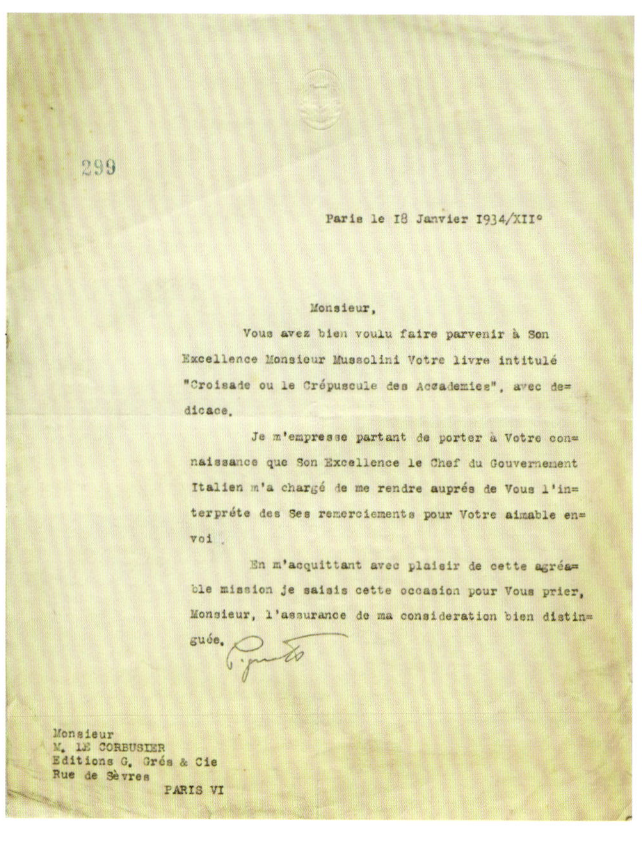

299

Paris le 18 Janvier 1934/XII°

Monsieur,

Vous avez bien voulu faire parvenir à Son Excellence Monsieur Mussolini Votre livre intitulé "Croisade ou le Crépuscule des Accademies", avec dedicace.

Je m'empresse partant de porter à Votre connaissance que Son Excellence le Chef du Gouvernement Italien m'a chargé de me rendre auprés de Vous l'interpréte des Ses remerciements pour Votre aimable envoi .

En m'acquittant avec plaisir de cette agréable mission je saisis cette occasion pour Vous prier, Monsieur, l'assurance de ma consideration bien distingué.

Monsieur
M. LE CORBUSIER
Editions G. Crés & Cie
Rue de Sèvres
PARIS VI

Une autre planche de l'album lui apparut parallèlement à des images concomitantes... « Eupalinos, songeait-il, recherchait la raison des choses. »

Il fut frappé par les analogies qui, dans cette présente époque, lient l'une à l'autre toutes les œuvres entreprises pour obtenir l'efficacité des gestes et atteindre à la glorification de l'esprit.

Et il était persuadé que l'architecture a ce don miraculeux de mettre toutes les choses en harmonie.

Toujours appuyé au bastingage de la galère, Le Corbusier se souvint qu'un soir, après qu'il avait harangué une foule de gens venus pour s'informer, il avait eu la sensation que quelqu'un s'était levé. Et, qu'ayant évoqué les leçons de l'histoire, l'interrupteur l'avait désigné du doigt et s'était écrié : « Cet homme ment-il ? Cet homme qui prêche à son tour une croisade ? »

Spreading the word: Books, 1930–35

Le Corbusier considered publishing his work to be of paramount importance. His publications ranged from early sketchbooks recording observations made during his travels to later manifestos such as *Précisions sur un état présent de l'architecture et de l'urbanisme* (1930), which developed out of his lectures in South America. By far his most ambitious publishing project was his *Oeuvre complète*, with ultimately eight volumes surveying his entire career.

Top left, and above left and right. Le Corbusier, *Croisade ou le crépuscule des académies* (Crusade or the Twilight of the Academies), Crès, Paris, 1933, cover and interior pages

Top right. Giuseppe Bottai to Le Corbusier, 18 January 1934 (Anno XII of Fascist rule in Italy), thanking the architect on behalf of "His Excellency Mister Mussolini," for sending him a copy of the book *Croisade*.

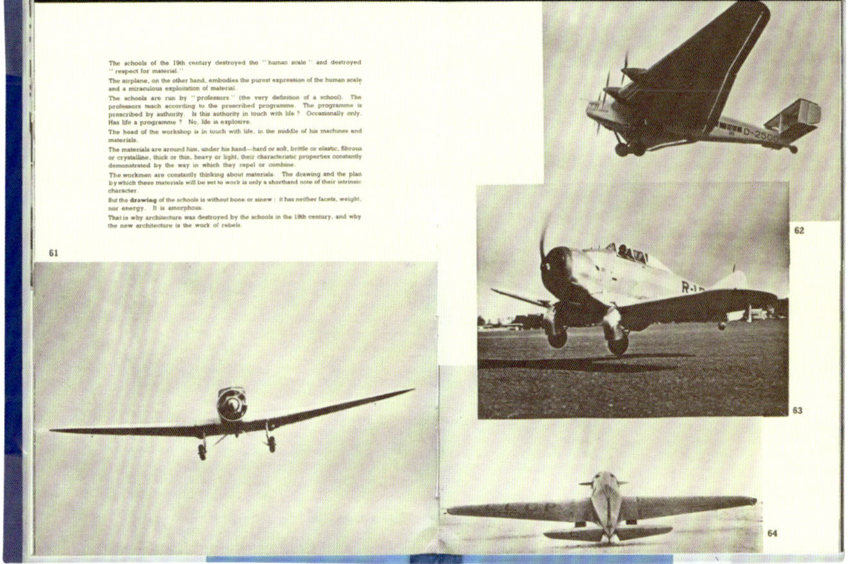

The schools of the 19th century destroyed the "human scale" and destroyed "respect for material."

The airplane, on the other hand, embodies the purest expression of the human scale and a miraculous exploitation of material.

The schools are run by "professors" (the very definition of a school). The professors teach according to the prescribed programme. The programme is prescribed by authority. Is this authority in touch with life? Occasionally only. Has life a programme? No, life is explosive.

The head of the workshop is in touch with life, in the middle of his machines and materials.

The materials are around him, under his hand—hard or soft, brittle or elastic, fibrous or crystalline, thick or thin, heavy or light, their characteristic properties constantly demonstrated by the way in which they repel or combine.

The workmen are constantly thinking about materials. The drawing and the plan by which these materials will be set to work is only a shorthand note of their intrinsic character.

But the **drawing** of the schools is without bone or sinew: it has neither facets, weight, nor energy. It is amorphous.

That is why architecture was destroyed by the schools in the 19th century, and why the new architecture is the work of rebels.

61

62

63

64

…p left. Le …orbusier, *Précisions …r un état présent de …architecture et de …urbanisme …Precisions on the …resent State of …rchitecture and City …lanning).* Crès, …aris, 1930

Top right. Le Corbusier and Pierre Jeanneret, *Ihr gesamtes Werk von 1910–1929* (Their Complete Works 1910–1929), Verlag Dr. H. Girsberger, Zurich, 1930. Later published in an eight-volume edition known as the *Oeuvre complète.*

Above and right. Cover and interior pages, *Aircraft: The New Vision* The Studio, London and New York, 1935

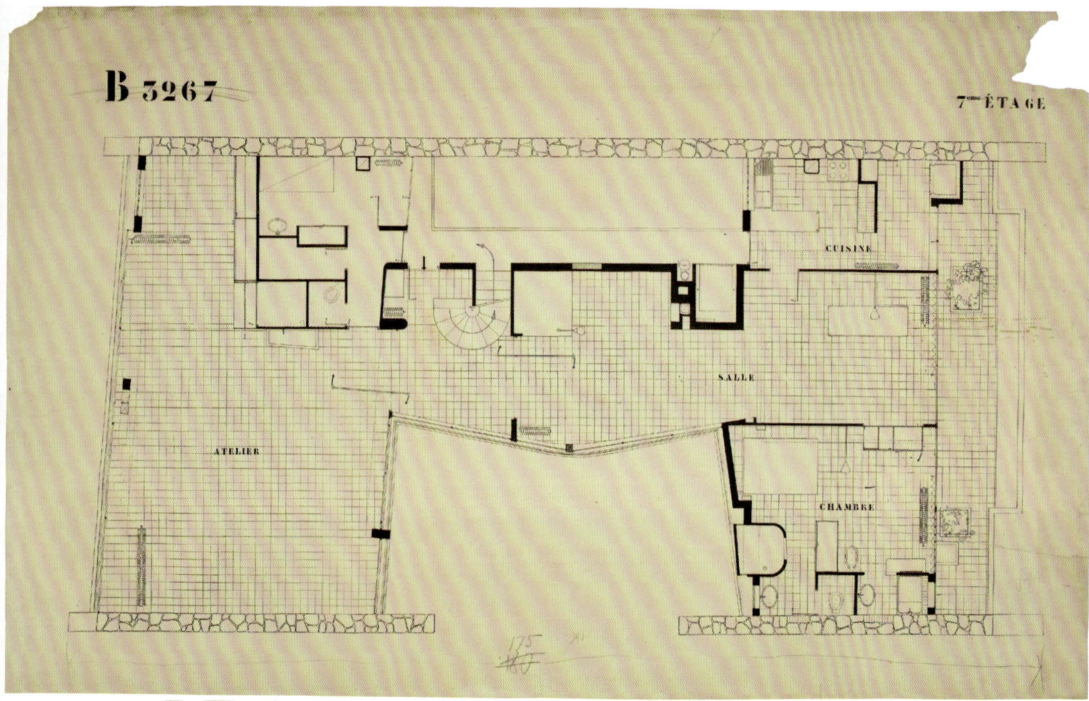

Designs and builds his own apartment, 24 rue Nungesser-et-Coli, Paris, 1931–34

The commission to design an apartment building in Paris's sixteenth arrondissement gave Le Corbusier another opportunity to experiment with the principles of his Ville Radieuse. On the top two floors of the building, he designed an apartment for Yvonne and himself. In addition to a roof garden, it featured a spectacular vaulted studio with rusticated walls, where he would paint for a few hours each morning before journeying across the city to his office on the rue de Sèvres.

Opposite, top. Seventh-floor plan (apartment and studio of Le Corbusier and Yvonne), 5 June 1934, apartment building at 24 rue Nungesser-et-Coli, Paris, 1931–34

Opposite, bottom. Perspective of street facade, c. 1932

Above left and right. 24 rue Nungesser-et-Coli

Left and below. Prospectus from the Société Immobilière, Paris, advertising the new apartment building

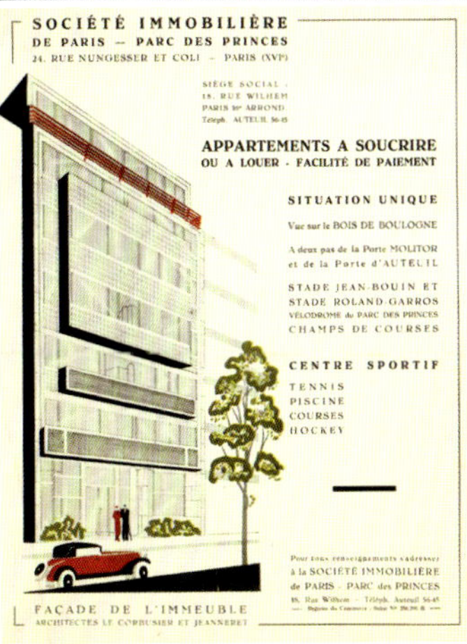

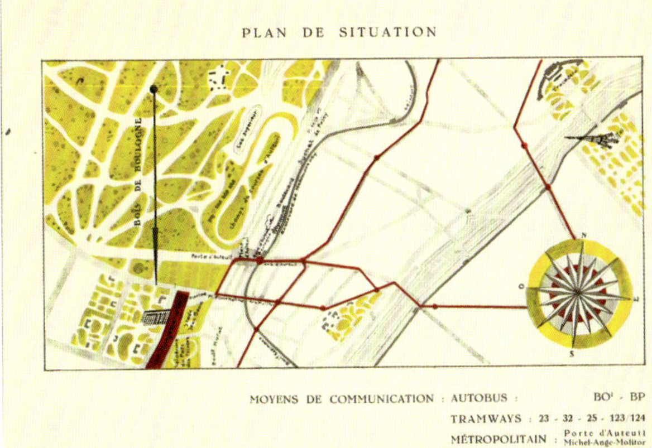

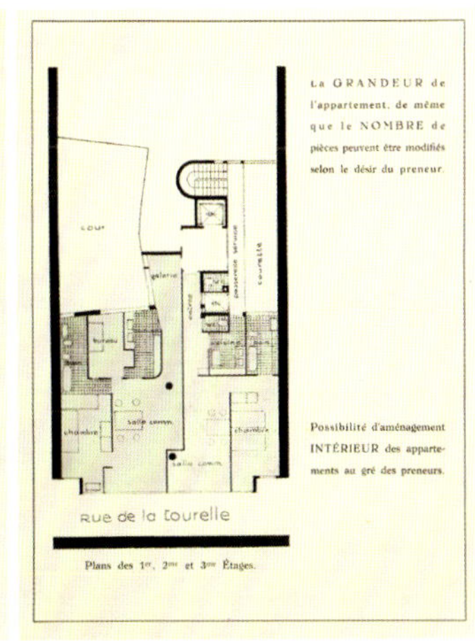

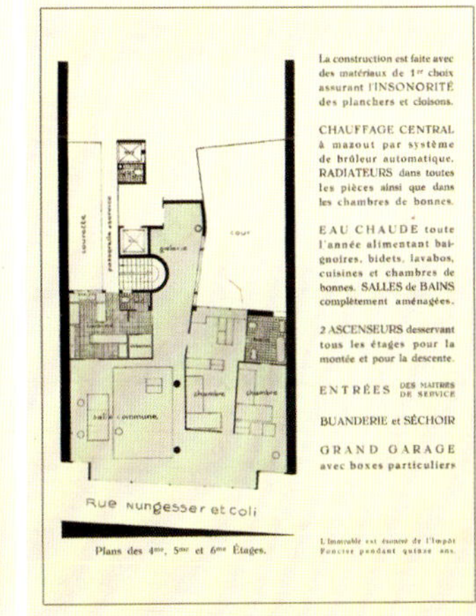

"The apartment is great. It was dangerous for me to go live in a building of my own. Really, it's magnificent. There's a view over the countryside with no sense of being perched up on the 7th or 8th floor, thanks to architectural stratagems."

—Letter to his mother, 29 April 1934

Above left. Stairs leading from Le Corbusier's apartment to the roof terrace, 24 rue Nungesser-et-Coli, Paris

Left. Bathroom

Opposite, top. Dining room, with marble table and Alvar Aalto's Savoy vase

Opposite, bottom. Living room with view toward dining room and terrace

Above. Rooftop terrace, Le Corbusier's apartment at 24 rue Nungesser-et-Coli, Paris

Far left. Stairs leading to the roof terrace

Left. Le Corbusier with his dog Pinceau ("paintbrush") on the terrace

Opposite, top left. Sculpture by Jacques Lipchitz, *Marin à la guitare* (Sailor with Guitar), 1917

Opposite, top right. Collection of objects Le Corbusier used for research and inspiration

Opposite, bottom. Bowl, pipe, and painting on the terrace bench

Top, left and middle. Le Corbusier to his mother, 29 April 1934, regarding his move from rue Jacob to rue Nungesser-et-Coli, Paris, including a list of his neighbors in the building

Top right, and middle. Le Corbusier and Yvonne to his mother, 28 May 1934, explaining how much they like the new apartment, "everything is sky and light, space and simplicity."

Bottom. Desk in Le Corbusier's apartment

Above. Le Corbusier with his dog Pinceau

Below. Le Corbusier and Yvonne to his mother, 11 February 1935, reminiscing about his father, and discussing Pinceau, who is "goodhearted and loving …less crazy, but more violent."

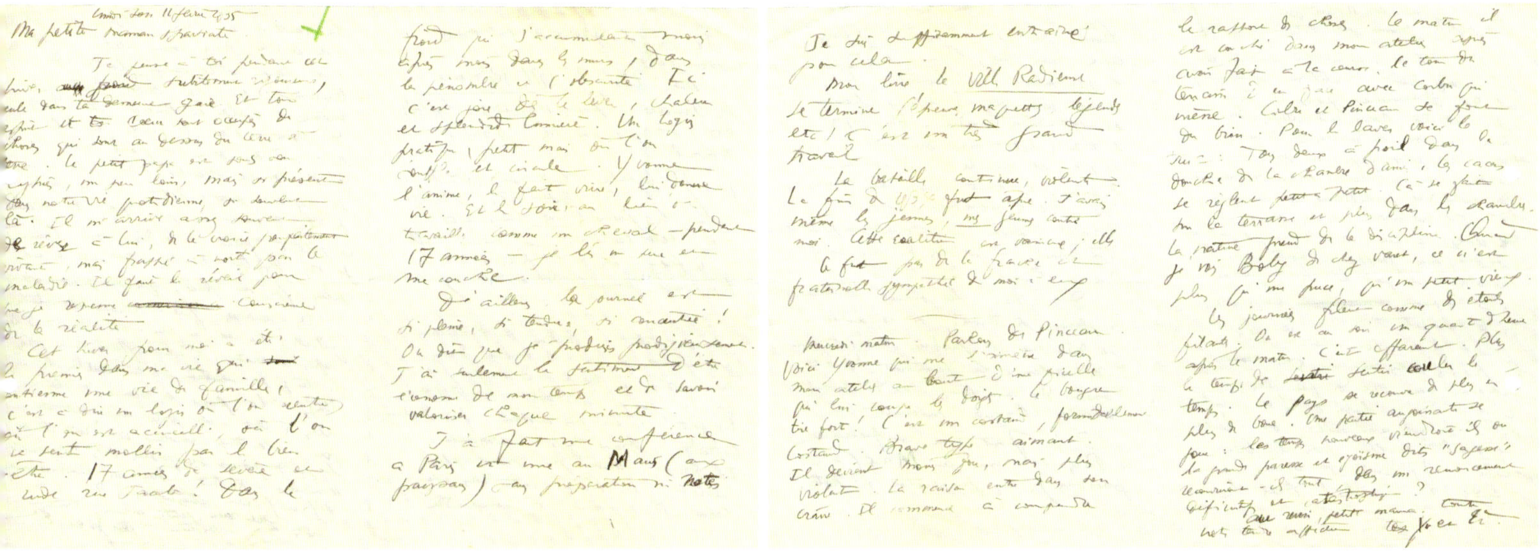

"Mrs. Cuttoli came to choose an Aubusson tapestry cartoon she's going to have made at the Royal manufactory. So there I am with Picasso, Léger, Braque, Matisse, and Rouault. I'm delighted!"

—Letter to his mother, 10 January 1937

Exploring a new medium: Tapestries and paintings, 1930s

Le Corbusier's extensive travels to South America, North Africa, and the United States were driven by multiple ambitions: to attract new clients, to establish an international reputation, and to export worldwide his vision of creating architectural solutions to the problems of the modern city. Concurrent with these goals were his ongoing efforts to create more modest, two-dimensional forms through painting. In 1935 he met Marie Cuttoli, who collaborated with him, as well as with Matisse, Picasso, and other well-known artists, to translate modern paintings into tapestries. Le Corbusier would later design tapestries on a grand architectural scale for the High Court at Chandigarh, India.

Above. Tapestry design by Le Corbusier, executed by Marie Cuttoli in silk and wool, 1936

Right. Etude pour tapisserie (Study for Tapestry), 1927–30

Below. Femme, cordage, bateau et porte ouverte (Woman, Rope, Boat and Open Door), 1935

BA 3432

URBANISATION D'HELLOCOURT

ECHELLE 0,2 M M P. M.

From workers' housing to shoe stores: Bat'a projects, 1935–36

Le Corbusier was approached by Tomàs Bat'a, a Czech owner of footwear factories, to design a master plan for workers' communities in Zlín, Czechoslovakia, and Hellocourt, France. Unlike the similar commission for Pessac, no aspect of the Bat'a project was ever realized. Le Corbusier also designed facades and interiors, including vitrines and other display fixtures, for the Bat'a chain of shoe stores.

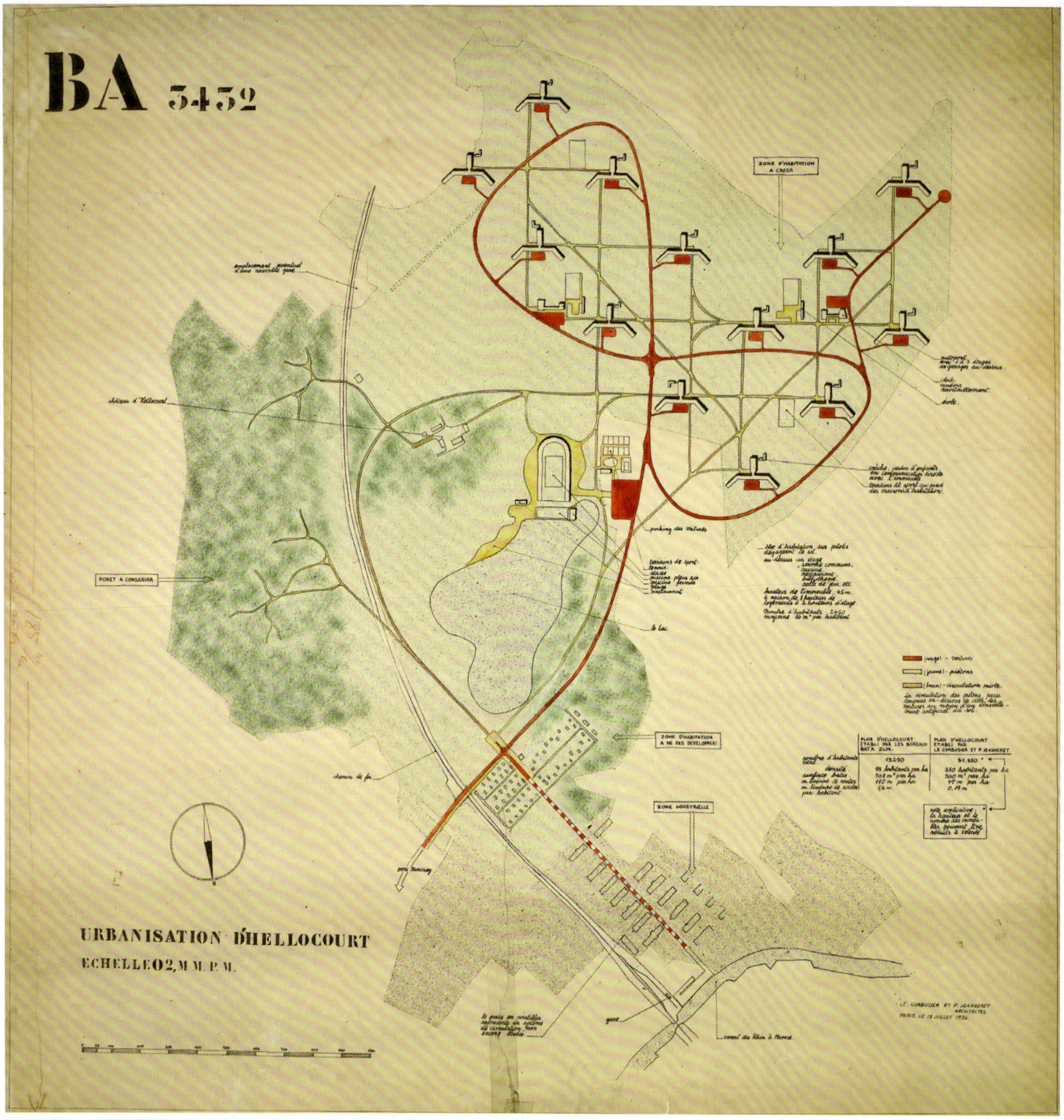

Above. Urban plan for Hellocourt, in the Lorraine region, France, 18 July 1936

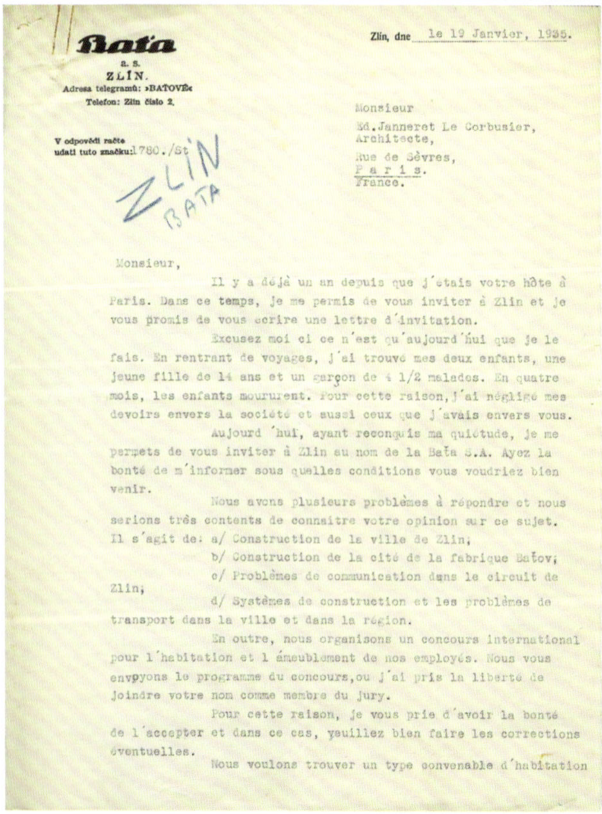

Bata
a. s.
ZLÍN.
Adresa telegramů: »BAŤOVĚ«
Telefon: Zlín číslo 2.

Zlín, dne le 19 Janvier, 1935.

V odpovědi račte udati tuto značku: 1780./St

ZLÍN BATA

Monsieur
Ed.Janneret Le Corbusier,
Architecte,
Rue de Sèvres,
P a r i s.
France.

Monsieur,

Il y a déjà un an depuis que j'étais votre hôte à Paris. Dans ce temps, je me permis de vous inviter à Zlin et je vous promis de vous écrire une lettre d'invitation.

Excusez moi ci ce n'est qu'aujourd'hui que je le fais. En rentrant de voyages, j'ai trouvé mes deux enfants, une jeune fille de 14 ans et un garçon de 4 1/2 malades. En quatre mois, les enfants moururent. Pour cette raison, j'ai négligé mes devoirs envers la société et aussi ceux que j'avais envers vous.

Aujourd'hui, ayant reconquis ma quiétude, je me permets de vous inviter à Zlin au nom de la Baťa S.A. Ayez la bonté de m'informer sous quelles conditions vous voudriez bien venir.

Nous avons plusieurs problèmes à répondre et nous serions très contents de connaitre votre opinion sur ce sujet. Il s'agit de: a/ Construction de la ville de Zlin;

b/ Construction de la cité de la fabrique Baťov;

c/ Problèmes de communication dans le circuit de Zlin;

d/ Systèmes de construction et les problèmes de transport dans la ville et dans la région.

En outre, nous organisons un concours international pour l'habitation et l'ameublement de nos employés. Nous vous envoyons le programme du concours, ou j'ai pris la liberté de joindre votre nom comme membre du jury.

Pour cette raison, je vous prie d'avoir la bonté de l'accepter et dans ce cas, veuillez bien faire les corrections éventuelles.

Nous voulons trouver un type convenable d'habitation

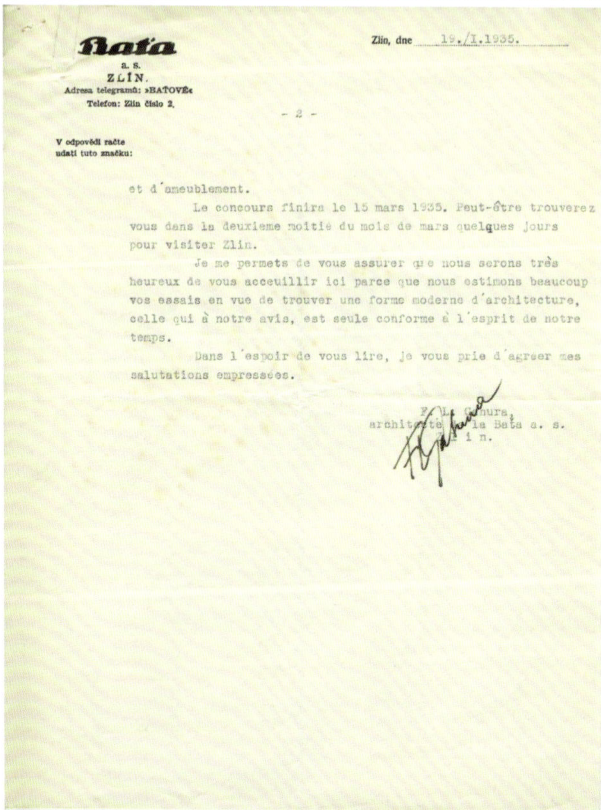

Bata
a. s.
ZLÍN.
Adresa telegramů: »BAŤOVĚ«
Telefon: Zlín číslo 2.

Zlín, dne 19./I.1935.

V odpovědi račte udati tuto značku:

- 2 -

et d'ameublement.

Le concours finira le 15 mars 1935. Peut-être trouverez vous dans la deuxieme moitié du mois de mars quelques jours pour visiter Zlin.

Je me permets de vous assurer que nous serons très heureux de vous acceuillir ici parce que nous estimons beaucoup vos essais en vue de trouver une forme moderne d'architecture, celle qui à notre avis, est seule conforme à l'esprit de notre temps.

Dans l'espoir de vous lire, je vous prie d'agréer mes salutations empressées.

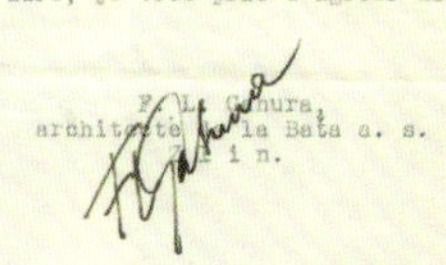

F. L. Ganura,
architecte de la Bata a. s.
Z l i n.

Left. F. L. Ganura to Le Corbusier, from Zlín, Czechoslavakia, 19 January 1935, inviting him to visit Zlín on behalf of Bat'a to discuss redesigning the town and building a Bat'a factory.

He also invites him to participate in the competition for Bat'a employee housing and furniture.

Opposite, top. Master plan for Zlín, along the Drevnice River, 1934

Opposite, middle. Plan for the Zlín Valley, 1935

Opposite, bottom. Facade (left) and interior (right) for a Bat'a boutiq 1936

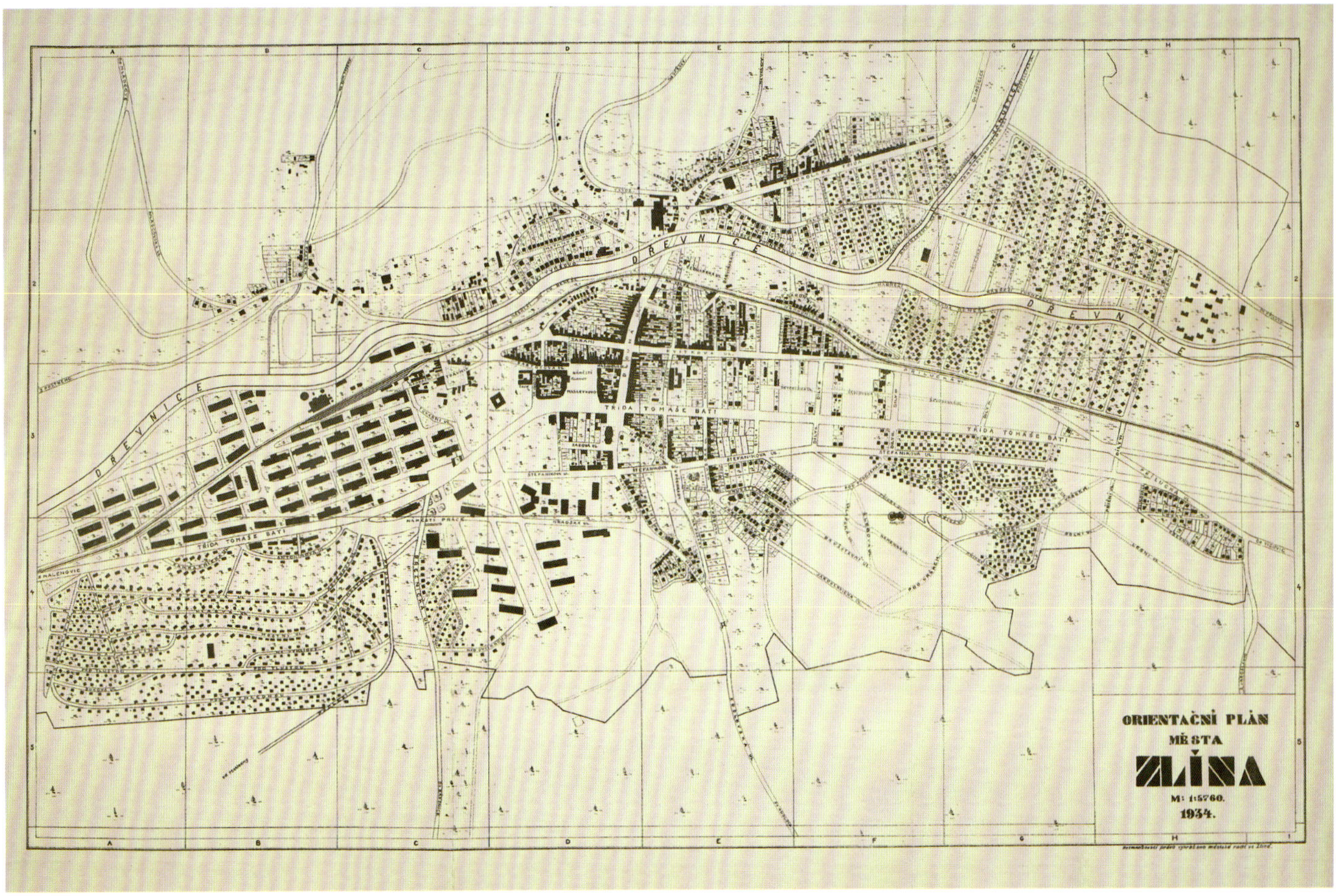

ORIENTAČNÍ PLÁN
MĚSTA
ZLÍNA
M: 1:5760.
1934.

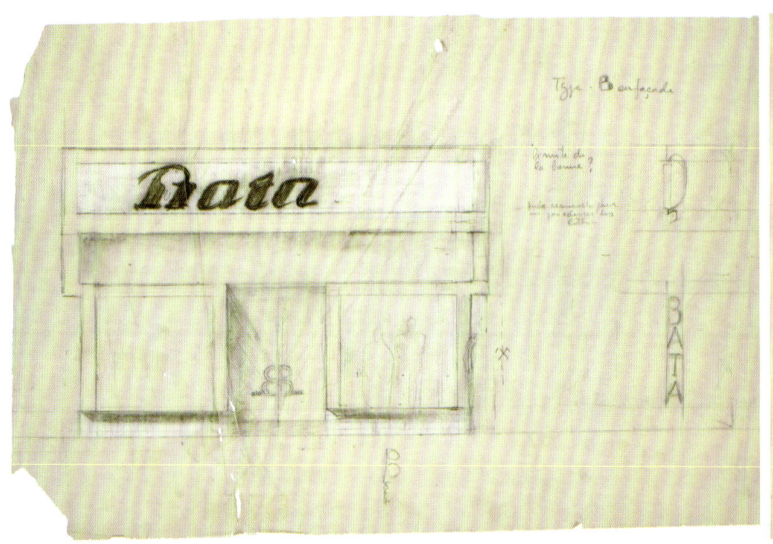

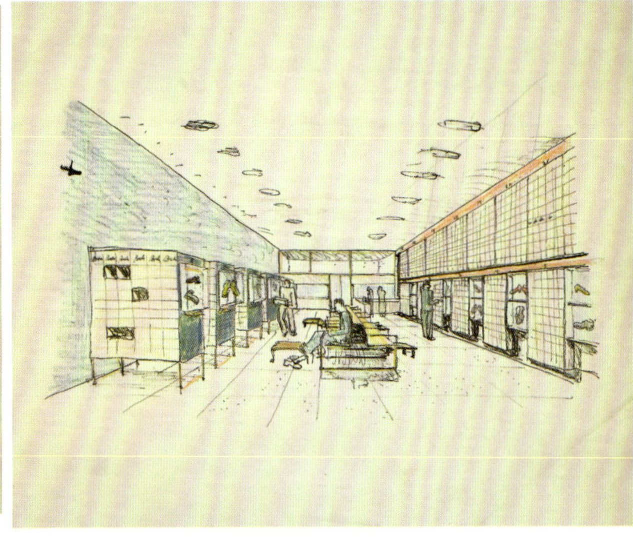

First trip to the United States, 1935: A two-month lecture tour

With the invitation to give a series of lectures in the United States, sponsored in part by the Museum of Modern Art, New York, Le Corbusier's status as a world-famous oracle of modernism seemed assured. His audiences, and the popular press, were not disappointed by the European genius brimming with impossible ideas. Le Corbusier's schedule during his tour of the United States was demanding, with lectures at various Ivy League universities and cultural institutions. In his lectures he focused on outlining the principles of the Ville Radieuse and showing recent projects, including the villas La Roche and Savoye.

Left. Le Corbusier in a playful moment on a TWA flight from Chicago to New York, 28 November 1935

SCHEDULE OF LE CORBUSIER LECTURE TOUR 10/11/35

5-12- [illegible]
16-23 - Cranbrook 19 wrote as [illegible]
27-4 - Madison [illegible]

October 21	Arrival of Le Corbusier
October 23	Luncheon at the Knickerbocker Club
October 24	Museum of Modern Art
October 25	Wadsworth Atheneum, Hartford
October 28	Columbia University
October 29	Wesleyan University, Middletown, Conn.
October 30	Yale University
November 1	Vassar College
November 4	Princeton University
November 5	Princeton University
November 6	Princeton University
November 8	Philadelphia Art Alliance
November 12	Bowdoin College, Brunswick, Maine
November 14	Massachusetts Institute of Technology
November 15	Harvard University
November 18	Municipal Art Society of Baltimore
November 19	Columbia University
November 21	Cranbrook Academy of Art, Bloomfield, Michigan
November 22	Kalamazoo Institute of Arts, Kalamazoo, Mich.
November 25	Arts Club of Chicago
November 25	Renaissance Society, University of Chicago
November 26	Madison Union, Madison, Wisconsin
November 27	Illinois Society of Architects and American Institute of Architects, Chicago.

Architect Speaks On Future Cities

Lecturing in French to an audience of about two hundred in the lounge of the Union last night, Monsieur Le Corbusier, noted French prophet of modern architecture, explained the essentials of his revolutionary theories and illustrated his ideas with crayon sketches, lantern slides, and moving pictures.

The principal features of Le Corbusier's conception of the ideal modern house are elevation of the entire structure on stilt-like columns which would give room underneath the first floor for passage of autos and pedestrians, ventilation, and possibly gardening; far greater window space on every floor—to be facilitated by making the walls which hold the structure up internal, and the external walls largely of glass; and a roof garden capping the building, drainage for the roof to run down through the center of the house.

After explaining his model house Le Corbusier went on to his plans for a modern city, which include housing the population in apartment buildings raised above the ground, and leaving over 80% of the actual terrain free for parks, sport facilities, and other municipal projects.

Plans Model City

As the most widely known of the founders of the International Style for architecture, Le Corbusier's influence has been felt in architecture throughout civilized countries. In Germany and in Russia whole aspects of modern architecture have crystallized around the word "corbusierism-us"—obviously formed from his name as a convenient designation for his theories and practice.

Le Corbusier, whose real name is Charles-Edouard Jeanneret, was born in 1888 at La Chaux-de-Fonds, near Geneva, Switzerland. He is now a naturalized French citizen. His father was a watch manufacturer with many intellectual interests; his mother was musical. After a youth devoted to study of the various arts, he traveled over the Continent, studying

(Continued on page 3)

FRENCH ARTIST GIVES LECTURE

(Continued from page 1)

and working in Vienna, Berlin, Constantinople, Asia Minor, Greece, and Rome.

Was Factory Manager

Shortly before the war he established himself as an architect in Paris. Unable to find work in his profession, he obtained a position as manager of a factory. He did some building, however, putting his advanced architectural principles into practice in a small way in a house in Switzerland and devoting much attention to the problems of modern housing.

After the War Le Corbusier turned for a time to painting and also began writing on all the arts. In 1921 he began the practice of architecture in Paris. It was then that he adopted his mother's maiden name, Le Corbusier, preferring to use his own name, Jeanneret, only for his painting.

Above. Itinerary of Le Corbusier's U.S. lecture tour, 11 October 1935

Above right. Press clipping from the *Bowdoin Orient*, 13 November 1935

Below. Postcards of New York City collected by Le Corbusier

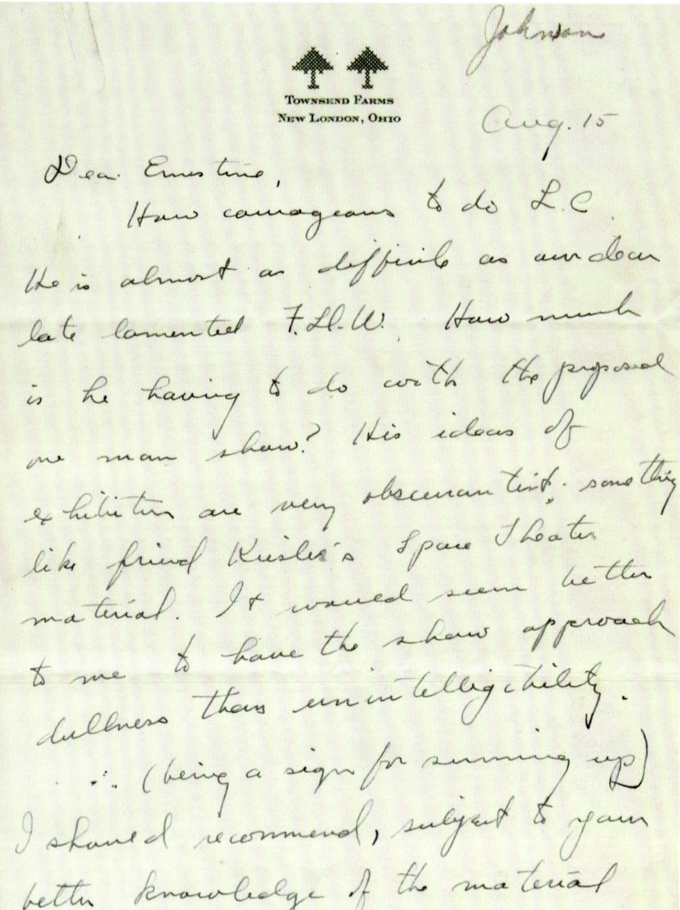

Johnson

TOWNSEND FARMS
NEW LONDON, OHIO

Aug. 15

Dear Ernestine,

How courageous to do L.C. He is almost as difficult as our dear late lamented F.Ll.W. How much is he having to do with the proposed one man show? His ideas of exhibition are very obscurantist, something like friend Kiesler's Space Theater material. It would seem better to me to have the show approach dullness than unintelligibility.

∴ (being a sign for summing up) I should recommend, subject to your better knowledge of the material

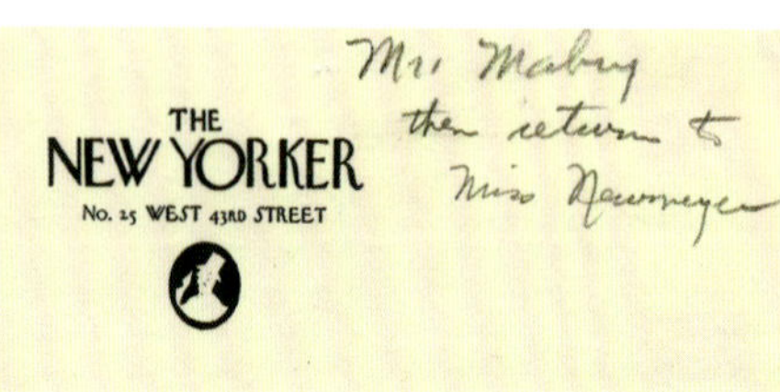

Mrs Mabry
then return to
Miss Newmeyer

THE NEW YORKER
No. 25 WEST 43RD STREET

EDITORIAL OFFICES
BRYANT 9-8200

October 10, 1935

Dear Miss Newmeyer:

Thanks for suggesting it, but we would not be interested in a PROFILE of Le Corbusier.

Very truly yours,

Stanley Walker

Stanley Walker

Miss Sarah Newmeyer
Museum of Modern Art
11 West 53rd Street
New York

The New York Times
"All the News That's Fit to Print."

TELEPHONE: LAckawanna 4-1000

TIMES SQUARE, NEW YORK
September 12, 1935.

TIMES BUILDING — TIMES ANNEX

Miss Sara Newmyer
11 West 53rd Street
New York City.

Dear Miss Newmyer:

Mr. Turpin has told me of his conversation with you and I think we might well work out a highly interesting Corbusier article. My idea would be to have Mr. Brock accompany M. Corbusier on his inspection of our sky-line and our architecture, making the thing a sort of running interview, done against the background of the man's career and his personality. I should be glad to hear that such a piece can be arranged.

Yours, sincerely,
Lester Markel
Lester Markel
Sunday Editor.

LM.G

Top left. First page of letter from Philip Johnson, curator of architecture at the Museum of Modern Art, New York, to his secretary, Ernestine Fantl, 15 August 1935, regarding Le Corbusier's forthcoming MoMA exhibition, to be held 24 October 1935 to 2 January 1936

Top right. Sketch of Le Corbusier by Fernand Léger, c. 1930s

Above left. Stanley Walker of the *New Yorker* magazine to Sarah Newmeyer of MoMA, 10 October 1935

Above right. Lester Markel of the *New York Times* to Sara Newmeyer, 12 September 1935

…hibition and …cture, Museum … Modern Art, …w York, 1935

In addition to sponsoring Le Corbusier's tour of the United States, the Museum of Modern Art also mounted an exhibition of the architect's work. Finding himself an honored guest in the American temple of modernist high culture, Le Corbusier set his sights on securing a commission that would have an international impact. He was particularly hopeful that Nelson Rockefeller, son of one of the founders of MoMA, could help him realize such a project, perhaps a new League of Nations or the next world's fair.

But none of these plans would be realized; on the contrary, Le Corbusier would find himself in a dispute with MoMA over unpaid lecture fees.

Finds American Skyscrapers 'Much Too Small'

Herald Tribune photo—Acme

Charles Edouard Le Corbusier, the famous French architect, with a model of his Villa Savoye, which he recently designed

Skyscrapers Not Big Enough, Says LeCorbusier at First Sight

French Architect, Here to Preach His Vision of 'Town of Happy Light,' Thinks They Should Be Huge and a Lot Farther Apart

Right. Clipping from *New York Herald Tribune*, 22 October 1935

Below. Installation view of Le Corbusier's work, including a model of the Villa Savoye, in the 1932 MoMA exhibition *Modern Architecture: International Exhibition*; Philip Johnson was co-curator of the show

The Gotham
5TH AVE. AT 55TH ST.
NEW YORK CITY

Labatut

Eh bien cher ami, voici la lettre annoncée. Elle dit merci aux braves gens de Princeton, à vous et à Madame, bien particulièrement. A vos collègues et à vos élèves si gentils.

Princeton, même sans feuilles est jolie et nous encourage à faire des villes vertes.

Et bientôt, le 14, je passerai l'eau avec regret, et le désir très vif

Shaking up the Ivy League: Lecture, Princeton University, 1935

During his U.S. lecture tour, Le Corbusier was particularly fascinated by the institutions of higher education he visited. He viewed the splendid isolation of schools such as Princeton University as remarkable essays in creating an earthly Eden, despite their preference for historicist architecture. The communal solidarity of Princeton's eating clubs struck him as a potent example of the American elite's social cohesion, but he preferred the more independent approach to academic life practiced by Europeans.

Above and left. Letter and drawing from Le Corbusier in New York to Jean Labatut, Director of Graduate Studies in Architecture at Princeton University, New Jersey, 4 December 1935, expressing gratitude for his visit in November. The drawing shows Le Corbusier striding across the Atlantic on the way back to Paris, wearing his "melon [bowler hat] de Princeton."

n my seminar at Princeton I am discussing the plans or a villa. I say: 'It is necessary to choose and limit, you must make the good design, the true one, the right ne!' Expressing myself (modestly!) in the manner of Iontaigne, I conclude: 'Gentlemen, you never have nore than one bottom to sit on!' The teacher and the hairman of the department are present. Silence and mbarrassment.—'Will you translate that, please?'—No, ou will not translate such a remark in the beautiful, reen, Gothic town of Princeton."

***Vhen the Cathedrals Were White: Journey to the Land of the imid People*, 1937**

Above. Detail of a drawing for Princeton University lecture, 16 November 1935, showing Le Corbusier's Villa Savoye (left and center), and his Villa le Sextant (1934–35), on the Atlantic coast of France (right)

Below. A drawing for Princeton University lecture, 14–15 November 1935, showing, at right, Le Corbusier's proposal for a vertical garden city, with sporting activities and the separation of cars and pedestrians

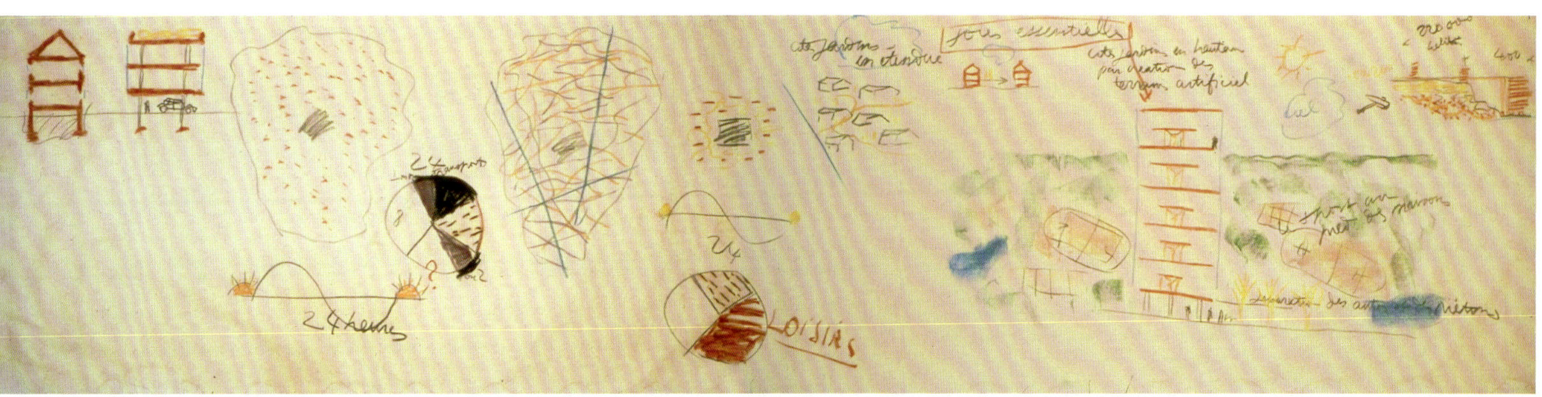

Le Corbusier with Eliel Saarinen, Cranbrook Academy, Michigan, November 1935

CHAMP MONTANEY
BLONAY
S/VEVEY

Le 25 avril

Cher Monsieur Le Corbusier :

Il y a une semaine, j'ai reçue cett/e lettre que j'avais adressée à vous il y a plus qu'un mois. Comme vous voyais, j'avais fait une stupide faute d'adresse, en écrivant Rue de Seine, au lieu de Sevre. Ainsi, j'espère que vous pardonnerez mon silence.

Maintenant j'ai de tres mauvaises nouvelles de l'Amérique. Toute ma famille est dans un état financier très critique, et je ne pourrais avoir que la moitié de la somme nécessaire pour construire la maison. J'ai pas encore abandonner/ l'espoir de la construire cependant, et je fais des plans pour quitter cette grande maison, pour vivre très simplement cet été, et peutêtre xxxxxxxxxxxxxxxxxxxx xxxxxxxxxxx je pourrais tout de meme commencer de construire une maison encore plus petite de ce que j'ai pensé, dans deux ou trois mois. Est-ce que la construction pourrait se faire pendant les mois d'autonne, et pensez vous que je pourrais avoir une maison pour 25,000, ou 30,000 ?

Si vous avez le temps, je serais très reconnaisante si vous pourriez reponcre à ces questions, et je vous supplie de ne pas perdre patience avec mon indécision. Je viendrai à Paris au commencement du mois de Juin, et alors j'espère xxxxxx avoir tout arrangé de point de vue financière, et alors pouvoir parler avec vous de plans définitives.

J'ai eu le plaisir de voir Madame votre mère dernièrement, et l'ai trouvé toujours en excellente santé, avec son admirable gaité d'esprit.

Je vous écrirai avant de venir à Paris, et, en attendant, veuillez croire à mes sentiments les xxxxxx meilleurs,

Sincèrement —

Marguerite Tjader Harris

CHAMP MONTANEY
BLONAY
S/VEVEY

Le 2 Mai

Cher M. Le Corbusier :

Encore un petit mot, pour vous remercier mille fois pour les merveilleux plans ! J'ai signé mon bail pour le petit appartement près de la plage de Vevey qui me ferait des grands economies, et, j'espère, sera le primier pas dans xxxx la réalisation de mes rêves, que vous avez si bien cristalisés........

Encore merci, et merci.....

Marguerite Tjader Harris

Les plans sont tellement beaux comme pures dessins !

Far left and below left. Marguerite Tjader Harris to Le Corbusier, 25 April 1932, explaining that her family is in a "very critical financial condition," and can only secure "half the amount necessary to build the house." She asks if she can have it built for less money.

Left. Marguerite Tjader Harris to Le Corbusier, 2 May 1932, thanking him profusely for the "marvelous plans" for a villa at Vevey, Switzerland

Below right. Marguerite Tjader Harris with her son, Hilary, Vevey, 1932

Opposite, top. Elevation, Villa Tjader Harris, 1932

Opposite, bottom. Axonometric

Client, lover, friend: Marguerite Tjader Harris

In 1932 a Swedish-American heiress and divorcée named Marguerite Tjader Harris, who lived in Vevey, Switzerland, found herself admiring the house belonging to Marie Jeanneret. Mrs. Tjader Harris and Mme. Jeanneret struck up a friendship, and a month later Tjader Harris had the pleasure of meeting the house's designer, and the owner's son, Le Corbusier. After she told him of her intention to settle permanently in the area, he designed a sprawling lakeside villa for her, built on *pilotis* of varying heights and featuring a grand entry sequence from the street. Though the house was never built, Le Corbusier and Marguerite Tjader Harris embarked on an affair, which developed into a friendship that would thrive for decades.

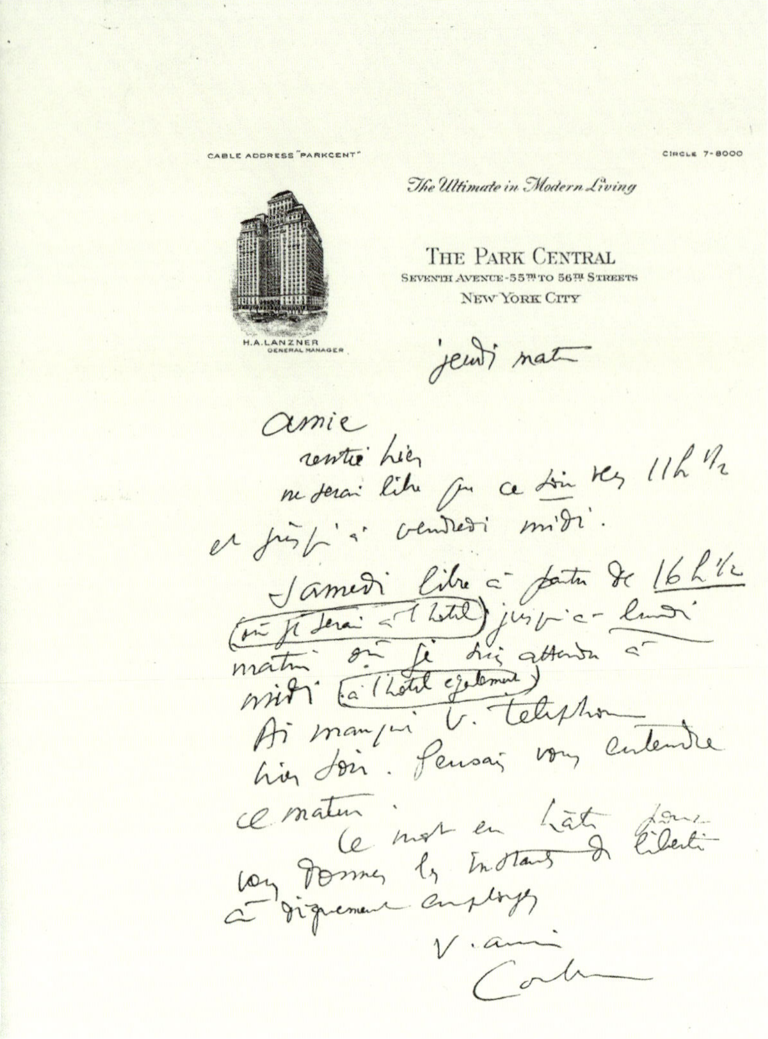

CABLE ADDRESS "PARKCENT" CIRCLE 7-8000

The Ultimate in Modern Living

THE PARK CENTRAL
SEVENTH AVENUE-55TH TO 56TH STREETS
NEW YORK CITY

H. A. LANZNER
GENERAL MANAGER

jeudi matin

amie
rentré hier
ne serai libre que ce soir vers 11h ½
et jusqu'à vendredi midi.
Samedi libre à partir de 16 h ½
(où je serai à l'hôtel) jusqu'à lundi
matin où je suis attendu à
midi (à l'hôtel également)
Ai manqué v. téléphone
hier soir. Pensais vous entendre
ce matin
Ce mot en hâte pour
vous donner les instants de liberté
à dignement employer
V. ami
Corbu

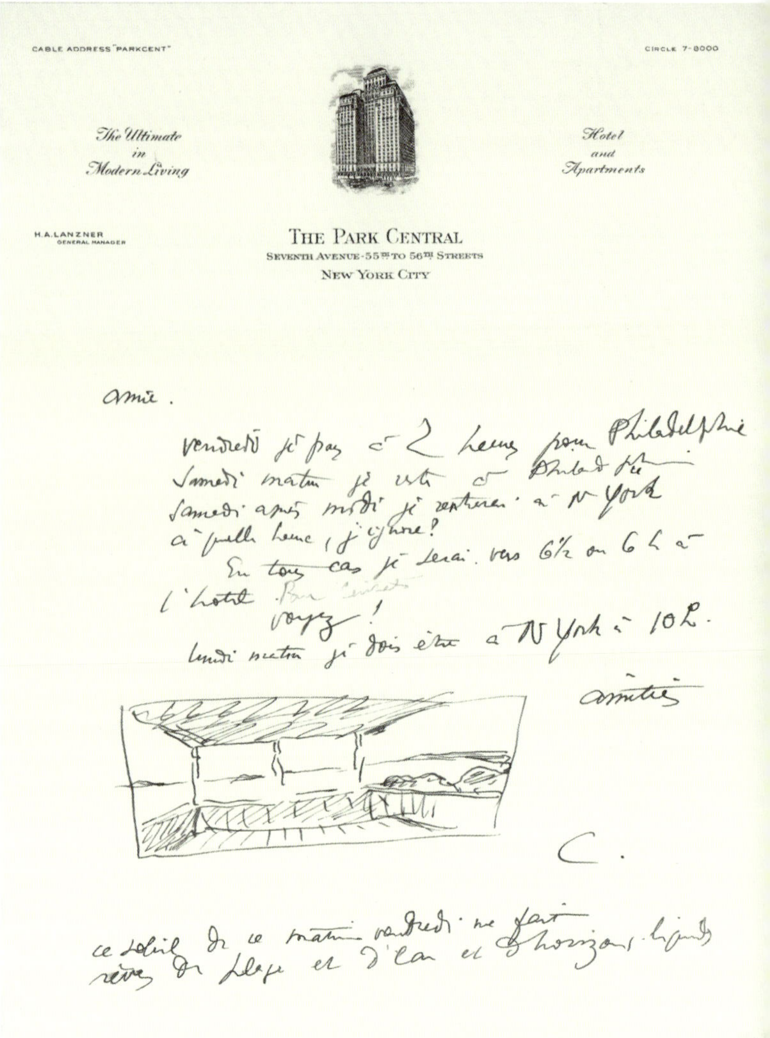

CABLE ADDRESS "PARKCENT" CIRCLE 7-8000

The Ultimate in Modern Living *Hotel and Apartments*

H. A. LANZNER
GENERAL MANAGER

THE PARK CENTRAL
SEVENTH AVENUE-55TH TO 56TH STREETS
NEW YORK CITY

amie.
vendredi je pars à 2 heures pour Philadelphie
Samedi matin je suis à Philadelphie
Samedi après midi je rentrerai à N York
à quelle heure, j'ignore?
En tous cas je serai vers 6½ ou 6 h à
l'hôtel Park Central
voyez!
lundi matin je dois être à N York à 10h.
amitiés
C.
ce soleil de ce matin vendredi me fait rêver de plage et d'eau et d'horizons lignes

"Everything was beautiful and fine and right, and fitting and loving. Why shouldn't the heart have the right to love in places where things cause it to open up, lay itself bare, and receive its full dose of joy and wellbeing? ...goodbye darling"

—Letter to Marguerite Tjader Harris, from on board the *MS Lafayette*, 14 December 1935

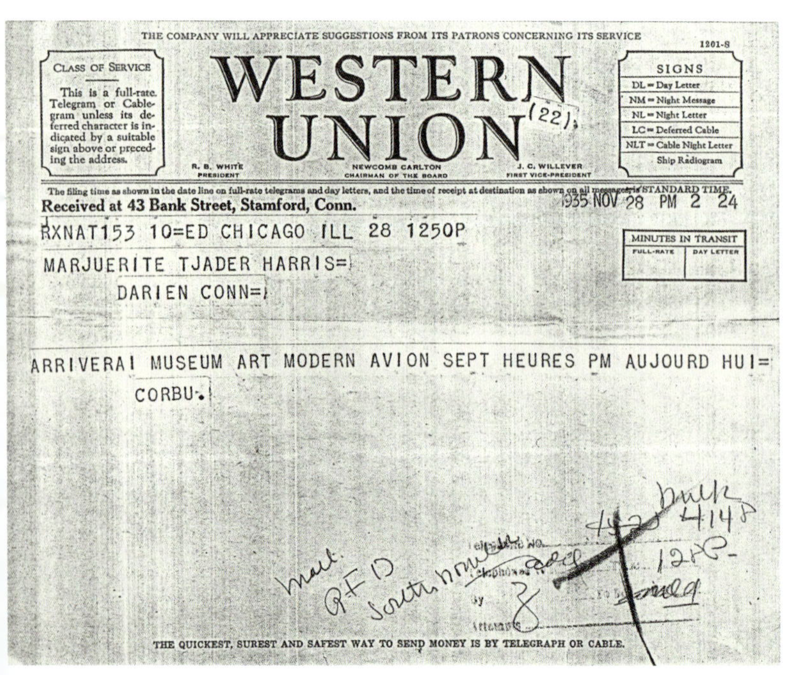

THE COMPANY WILL APPRECIATE SUGGESTIONS FROM ITS PATRONS CONCERNING ITS SERVICE

1201-S

CLASS OF SERVICE
This is a full-rate Telegram or Cablegram unless its deferred character is indicated by a suitable sign above or preceding the address.

WESTERN UNION (22)

R. B. WHITE, PRESIDENT — NEWCOMB CARLTON, CHAIRMAN OF THE BOARD — J. C. WILLEVER, FIRST VICE-PRESIDENT

SIGNS
DL = Day Letter
NM = Night Message
NL = Night Letter
LC = Deferred Cable
NLT = Cable Night Letter
Ship Radiogram

The filing time as shown in the date line on full-rate telegrams and day letters, and the time of receipt at destination as shown on all messages, is STANDARD TIME.

Received at 43 Bank Street, Stamford, Conn. 1935 NOV 28 PM 2 24

RXNAT153 10=ED CHICAGO ILL 28 1250P

MINUTES IN TRANSIT — FULL-RATE — DAY LETTER

MARJUERITE TJADER HARRIS=
DARIEN CONN=

ARRIVERAI MUSEUM ART MODERN AVION SEPT HEURES PM AUJOURD HUI=
CORBU.

mail RFD Southworth

THE QUICKEST, SUREST AND SAFEST WAY TO SEND MONEY IS BY TELEGRAPH OR CABLE.

Above left. Le Corbusier to Marguerite Tjader Harris, 31 October 1935, giving the times when he is free to meet ("will only be free this evening around 11:30")

Above right. Le Corbusier to Marguerite Tjader Harris, 8 November 1935, informing her when he will be in New York next. Included is a drawing of Long Island Sound from the porch of her *baraque*, or cabin, on Pratt's Island, Connecticut

Left. Telegram from Le Corbusier to Marguerite Tjader Harris, 28 November 1935, notifying her that he will be arriving at MoMA later that day

LC / TADJER HARRIS

M.S. LAFAYETTE

A Bord le 14 Dec 1935

Amie.

Le bateau est parti. La mer, les vagues. Plus rien ou ville. Et la marche côté France.

Mon dernier geste a été pour vous, à N York et je vous ai dit "au revoir" sur un papier d'hôtel, avec vous dessinée dessus. Wall Street et le bateau déjà loin.

Voilà!

Tout a été beau et bien et propre, et digne et [illegible]. Pourquoi le coeur n'aurait-il pas [illegible] d'aimer là où les choses font qu'il s'ouvre, se découvre et reçoit pleine charge de joie et de bienfait?

Le chemin qu'il parcourt est petit à petit escarpé, vif, dangereux et il conduit sur les arêtes d'où l'on voit un peu de la vie. Pourquoi ne pas regarder la vie?

Je vous ai vue et pas regardée, puis vue et connue, et reconnue. Vous êtes forte, saine, juste et bonne. Vous êtes aimante et ouverte. Pas fermée. Autour de vous, ce sont des affections qui se groupent. Vous êtes forte et gaie. Bonne.

Tonton est votre fils; je l'aime beaucoup.

Je n'imagine pas, faute de capacité d'imaginer l'inconnu, ce qu'aurait été mon N York et mon USA sans vous, sans la mer, sans votre mère, sans Tonton et Baby, sans la cabane et sans la maison coloniale, sans les routes du Connecticut et l'amazone rouge qui conduit.

Cela aurait été quelque chose, mais quoi? des aventures rapides de Broadway, ou quelque autre évasion ou [illegible] Park Avenue ou n'importe où. Vous avez été le paysage de N York, la petite Jeanne d'Arc de [illegible] ferraillant dans le vide. Un soutien. Le paysage, en opposition à l'autre de Chicago, qui est la femme des gratte-ciel, hardis mais peureux, téméraires mais ~~[illegible]~~ irraisonnés, une autre Jeanne d'Arc sans victoire possible, [illegible] l'artifice va vers [illegible], alors que la Santé et la Bonté [illegible] la lumière.

Blonde lumière, gentille.

Amie, je vous dis merci, merci.

Et maintenant, volontairement je vais cesser de penser à là-bas. Et ma vie va reprendre. Ainsi un coeur vif et croyant et propre et [illegible] que je respecte beaucoup.

Imaginons un lieu de froid, les chaleurs d'été, ou les tiédeurs du printemps. Et la mer douce, l'eau tout près et vite profonde. Des nuits dans l'eau et sur le sable. Des ébats. De la joie honnête et des gestes tendres. De la tendresse!

Quelle chose, quel mot, quel rare événement.

De la tendresse au pays des gratte ciel, à deux doigts de N York.

L'avenir ne nous appartient pas. Les années passent, vont passer. Pauvre vieux [illegible] près de l'automne et dont le coeur est celui d'un enfant

au revoir, amie. ~~[illegible]~~

C

M.S. LAFAYETTE

A Bord le

Je vous envoie par même courrier, 4 dessins faits pour vous.

2 ~~[illegible]~~ expriment l'idée naissante du Tableau de la barque. Je les ~~[illegible]~~ préciserai avec tous les yeux, les coquillages dont la couleur est si belle

Above. Le Corbusier to Marguerite Tjader Harris, after the departure of his boat from New York back to Paris, 14 December 1935: "I can't imagine what my New York and my USA would have been without you" and "Around you affection accumulates." The last page reads, "I'm sending with this letter 4 drawings done for you."

Right. One of the drawings included in the above letter

Machines for driving in: Voitures "Minimum" and "Maximum," 1936

During much of 1936, Le Corbusier aggressively promoted his concept for a truly modern automobile, the impetus for which was a competition sponsored by the French Society of Automobile Engineers (SIA). Le Corbusier submitted two proposals, for both the minimum and the maximum specifications for a two-seater coupe. Once the designs were published in the society's yearbook, he contacted FIAT founder Giovanni Agnelli regarding production of his designs. FIAT, however, did not pursue the concept.

LE CORBUSIER
&
P.

PARIS, le 31 Mars 1936

Monsieur B E R G E R

Secrétaire Général de la S I A

3, avenue Friedland

PARIS VIII°

Cher Monsieur,

Nous avons l'honneur de vous envoyer le dessin de la voiture que nous avons établi, au nom de LE CORBUSIER & Pierre JEANNERET, architectes.

Nous joignons une Note descriptive, expliquant les raisons pour lesquelles nous sommes intervenus dans cette question.

Je vous serais très obligé s'il vous était possible de reproduire notre dessin tel qu'il est établi dans le plan en question et de ne pas le faire redessiner, car nous avons mis un soin précis à établir les profils exacts qui ont une grande importance.

Je me permets de vous rappeler la conclusion de notre conversation de Samedi dernier : s'il vous était possible d'établir un contact avec une firme automobile désireuse de faire appel à notre collaboration pour l'aménagement confortable d'une voiture et pour son esthétique (sa ligne), nous vous en serions infiniment reconnaissants.

Veuillez agréer, cher Monsieur, nos salutations les meilleures.

Top left. Le Corbusier and Pierre Jeanneret to Mr. Berger, Secretary General of SIA, 31 March 1936, explaining that they have enclosed drawings of a car they designed

SOCIÉTÉ DES INGÉNIEURS DE L'AUTOMOBILE

FONDÉE EN 1927
PRÉSIDENT D'HONNEUR FONDATEUR
A. RATEAU
MEMBRE DE L'INSTITUT
PRÉSIDENTS D'HONNEUR
Mr CH. FAROUX
Mr LÉON GUILLET
MEMBRE DE L'INSTITUT

SIA - 3 AVE FRIEDLAND
PARIS (8)
ÉLYSÉES 72-90 · 72-91
CHÈQ. POST. PARIS 338-89

Monsieur LE CORBUSIER
35, rue de Sèvres
PARIS

Paris le 7 Avril 1936

Cher Monsieur,

Je vous remercie vivement de votre lettre du 31 Mars ainsi que des dessins joints. Ce dessin et la notice descriptive seront publiés dans l'Album "Voiture SIA" qui va paraître dans quelques semaines, et j'espère que, dans ces conditions, les différentes firmes d'automobiles désireuses de faire appel à votre collaboration, ne manqueront pas de s'adresser directement à vous-même.

Selon votre demande, le dessin sera reproduit intégralement sans retouche.

Je vous prie d'agréer, Cher Monsieur, l'assurance de mes meilleurs sentiments.

Le Secrétaire-Général :

M. Berger

M. BERGER

Top right. Mr. Berger to Le Corbusier, 7 April 1936, thanking him for the drawings and explaining that they will be published in the upcoming SIA catalog

PARIS - 35 rue de Sèvres - VI°

le 6 Octobre 1936

Petite Auto

MONSIEUR LE SENATEUR AGNELLI

Usines Fiat

TURIN

Cher Monsieur,

Vous vous souvenez peut-être de l'aimable accueil que vous m'avez fait lors de ma visite des Usines Fiat en 1934.

J'ai eu l'occasion, à la demande de la Société S I A (Société des Ingénieurs de l'Automobile) d'étudier une voiture automobile minimum. Notre projet a été publié dans l'album consacré au Concours que cette Société avait ouvert entre ses ingénieurs pour la construction d'une voiture à deux places. Nous n'avons toutefois pas admis la base du concours, notre intention n'étant pas de paraître au palmarès, mais étant au contraire de montrer ce que, à notre point de vue, nous jugeons comme nécessaire, minimum et maximum, pour confort véritable d'une voiture moderne.

Nous avons donc établi les plans d'une petite voiture, mais suffisante pour un usage qui nous paraît être le véritable usage d'une automobile.

Je suis persuadé que vos services possèdent l'ALBUM publié par la SIA. Notre projet est sous le chiffre 108.

Je viens donc vous demander si, éventuellement, il vous intéresserait d'examiner notre projet et de voir si vos Etablissements seraient susceptibles d'en tirer un parti quelconque, en collaboration avec nous. J'en serais personnellement très heureux.

Je pars à Rome le 23 de ce mois, pour assister comme délégué français à la Réunion VOLTA de l'Academia Reale d'Italia et, si vos nouvelles me parvenaient en temps utile, il me serait certainement possible, au retour, de m'arrêter à Turin.

Veuillez agréer, cher Monsieur, l'expression de mes sentiments très distingués.

P.S. - L'adresse de la Société des Ingénieurs de l'Automobile, éditrice de L'ALBUM "VOITURE SIA", est : 3, avenue Friedland - Paris VIII° (France)

Middle left. Le Corbusier to Giovanni Agnelli, president of FIAT, 6 October 1936, asking if the company would be interested in his designs for a new car

96 6552

FIAT
IL PRESIDENTE

TORINO 9 Ottobre 1936 XIV
SEDE: VIA NIZZA 250

Petite Voiture

Monsieur
LE CORBUSIER
35 rue de Sèvres
PARIS (VI°)

Monsieur,

Je vous remercie pour votre aimable lettre du 6 crt. mais, comme vous savez, notre Société a étudié une voiturette qui a été produite soit en Italie, soit en France sous notre licence par la SIMCA.

Dans ces conditions, bien en appréciant votre ambition, je ne vois pas la possibilité de donner suite à votre proposition.

Veuillez bien agréer, Monsieur, l'assurance de mes meilleurs sentiments.

Middle right. Giovanni Agnelli to Le Corbusier, 9 October 1936, politely declining his proposal

Below. Le Corbusier on the roof track at the FIAT car factory, Milan, 1934

Right. Le Corbusier and Pierre Jeanneret, drawings and plans for Voiture Minimum, 1936

Below. Sketch of Voiture Minimum, 1936

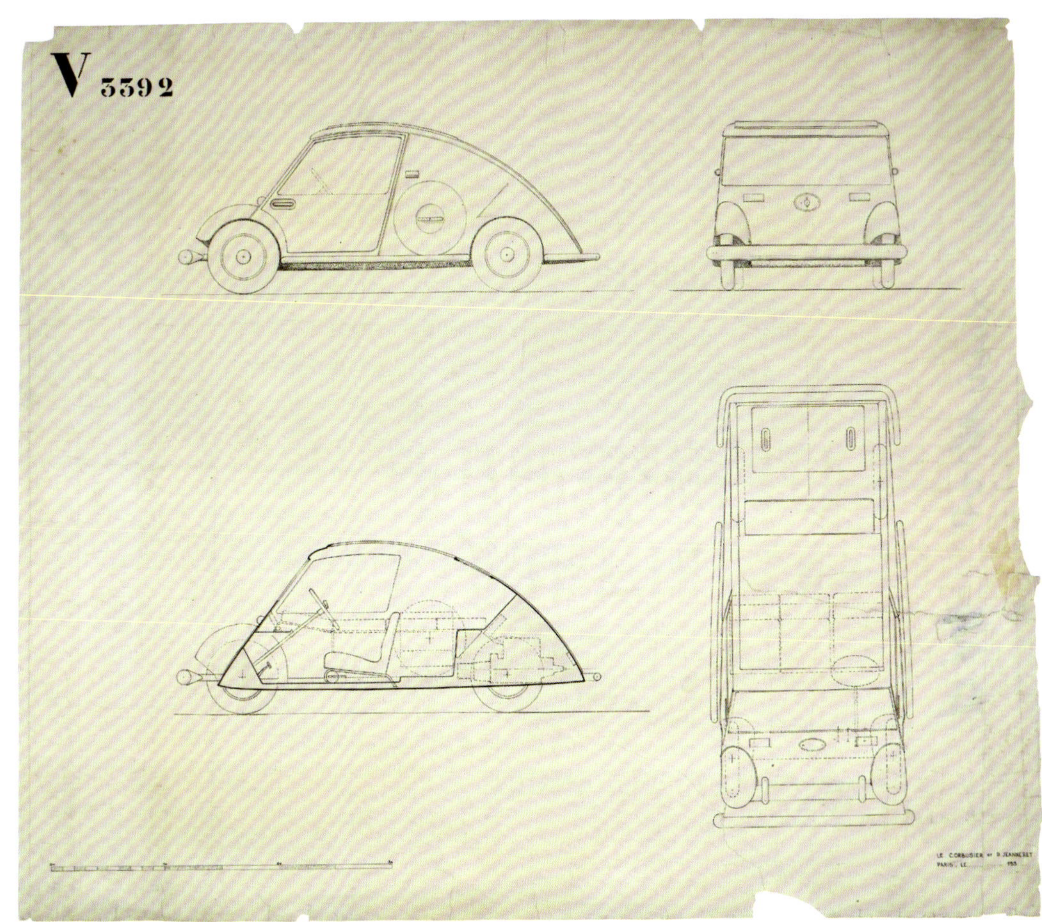

Reflection and recrimination: *Quand les cathédrales étaient blanches*, 1937

In 1937 Le Corbusier published his impressions of the United States in *Quand les cathédrales étaient blanches: Voyage au pays des timides*, a meditation on the intense ambivalence he felt toward the home of the skyscraper and of suburban sprawl.

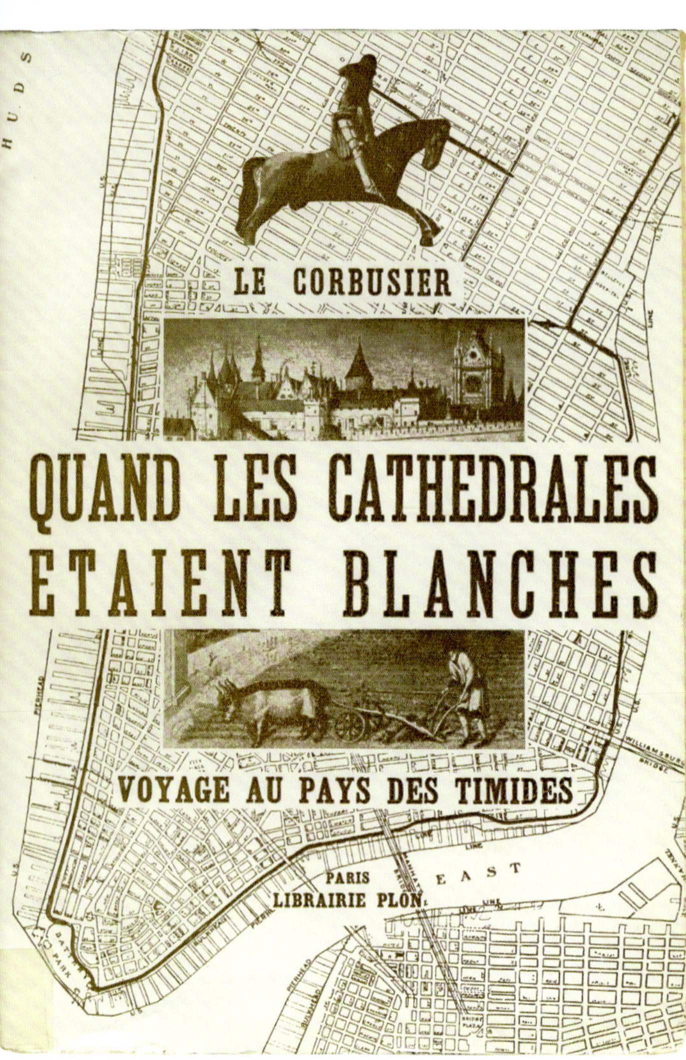

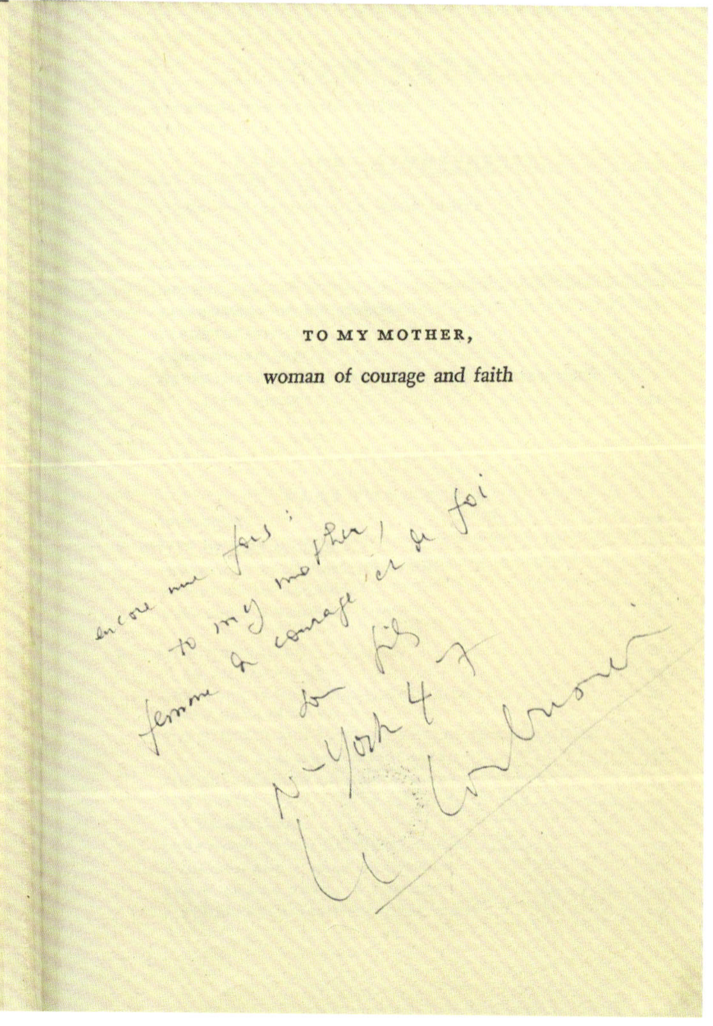

Left. Cover of *Quand les cathédrales etáient blanches* (*When the Cathedrals Were White*), by Le Corbusier, a rumination on his 1935 U.S. tour, Plon, Paris, 1937

Below. Le Corbusier's signed copy to his mother of *When the Cathedrals Were White*, published in the United States in 1947. Le Corbusier dedicated the book to his mother, "woman of courage and faith," and translated the dedication into French in his mother's copy of the book.

274 QUAND LES CATHÉDRALES ÉTAIENT BLANCHES

dans l'ordre des sensations psycho-physiologique, quelque chose d'important. On a ça dans le cou et dans l'estomac. Une chose belle en soi.

Pourtant la raison s'inquiète. J'ai dit : « les gratte-ciel de

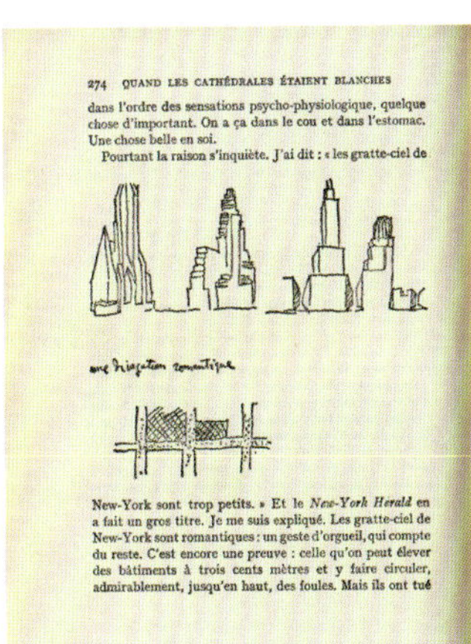

New-York sont trop petits. » Et le *New-York Herald* en a fait un gros titre. Je me suis expliqué. Les gratte-ciel de New-York sont romantiques : un geste d'orgueil, qui compte du reste. C'est encore une preuve : celle qu'on peut élever des bâtiments à trois cents mètres et y faire circuler, admirablement, jusqu'en haut, des foules. Mais ils ont tué

NÉCESSITÉ DES PLANS ET ENTREPRISES 275

la rue et ils ont rendu la ville folle. Ils sont déraisonnables du bas en haut et la faute en est à un règlement de voirie qui est un contresens étonnant : on s'inquiète que l'autorité ait pu souscrire à de tels postulats et légiférer dessus.

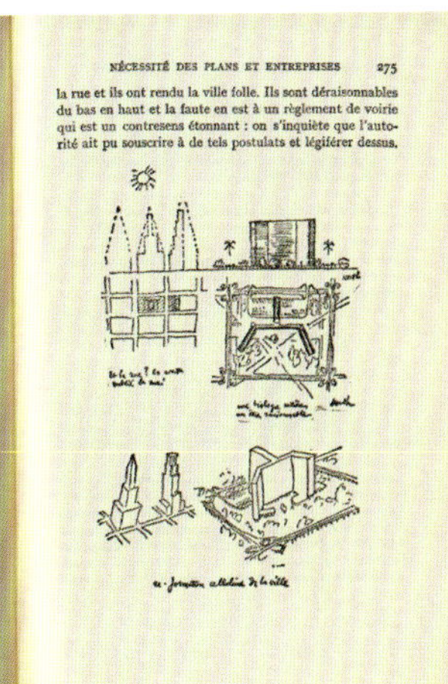

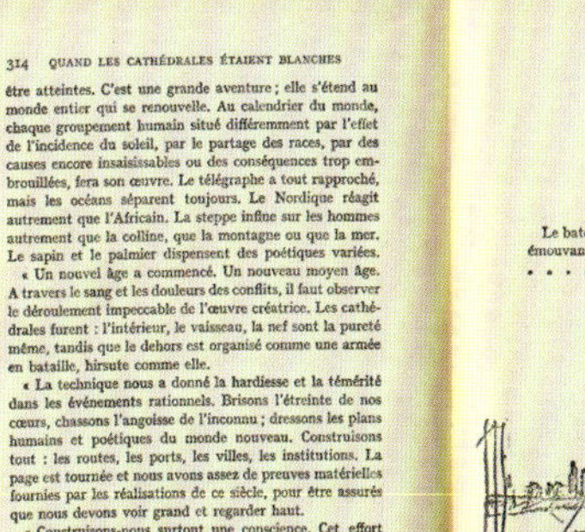

314 QUAND LES CATHÉDRALES ÉTAIENT BLANCHES

être atteintes. C'est une grande aventure ; elle s'étend au monde entier qui se renouvelle. Au calendrier du monde, chaque groupement humain situé différemment par l'effet de l'incidence du soleil, par le partage des races, par des causes encore insaisissables ou des conséquences trop embrouillées, fera son œuvre. Le télégraphe a tout rapproché, mais les océans séparent toujours. Le Nordique réagit autrement que l'Africain. La steppe influe sur les hommes autrement que la colline, que la montagne ou que la mer. Le sapin et le palmier dispensent des poétiques variées.

« Un nouvel âge a commencé. Un nouveau moyen âge. A travers le sang et les douleurs des conflits, il faut observer le déroulement impeccable de l'œuvre créatrice. Les cathédrales furent : l'intérieur, le vaisseau, la nef sont la pureté même, tandis que le dehors est organisé comme une armée en bataille, hirsute comme elle.

« La technique nous a donné la hardiesse et la témérité dans les événements rationnels. Brisons l'étreinte de nos cœurs, chassons l'angoisse de l'inconnu ; dressons les plans humains et poétiques du monde nouveau. Construisons tout : les routes, les ports, les villes, les institutions. La page est tournée et nous avons assez de preuves matérielles fournies par les réalisations de ce siècle, pour être assurés que nous devons voir grand et regarder haut.

« Construisons-nous surtout une conscience. Cet effort n'est pas de raison, ni d'ordre collectif. Il s'appuie au fond de chacun, dans le silence de l'examen individuel ; il peut impliquer de grands sacrifices pour que cette conscience, partout éveillée, soit la grande conscience universelle, levier des actes féconds. »

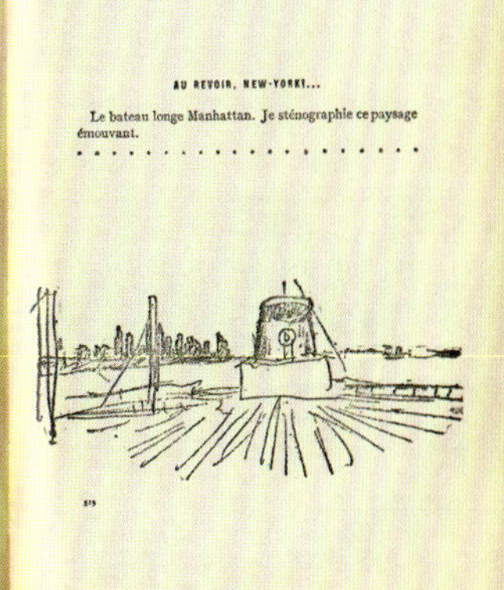

AU REVOIR, NEW-YORK !...

Le bateau longe Manhattan. Je sténographie ce paysage émouvant.

. . . .

316 QUAND LES CATHÉDRALES ÉTAIENT BLANCHES

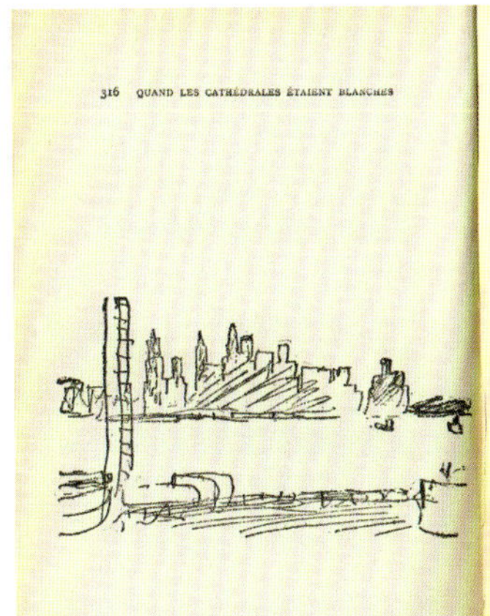

AU REVOIR, NEW-YORK !... 317

318 QUAND LES CATHÉDRALES ÉTAIENT BLANCHES

AU REVOIR, NEW-YORK !... 319

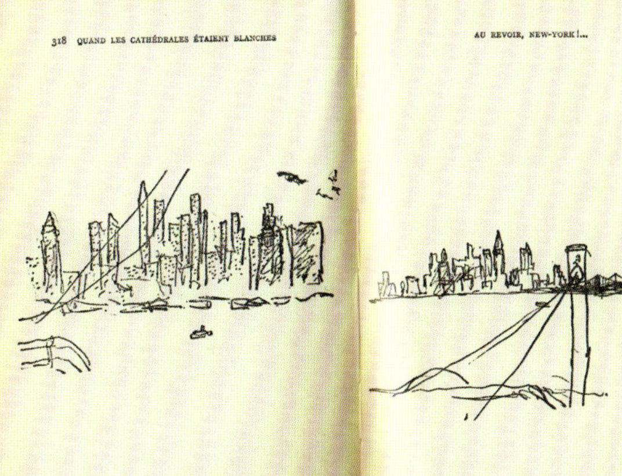

320 QUAND LES CATHÉDRALES ÉTAIENT BLANCHES

AU REVOIR, NEW-YORK !... 321

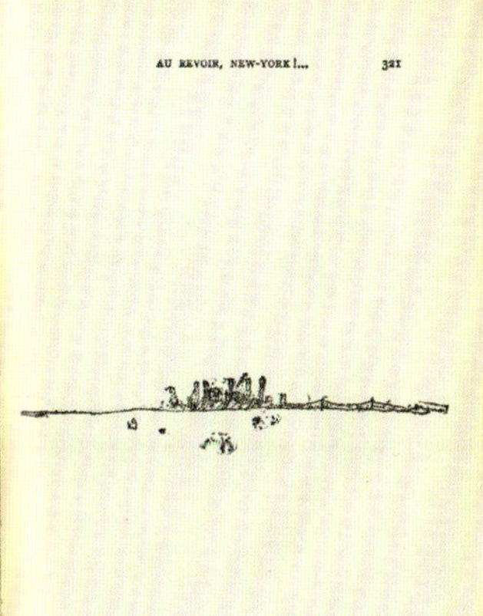

322 QUAND LES CATHÉDRALES ÉTAIENT BLANCHES

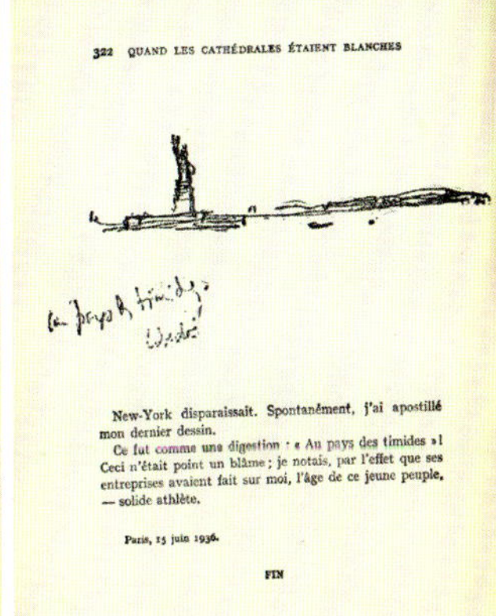

New-York disparaissait. Spontanément, j'ai apostillé mon dernier dessin.

Ce fut comme une digestion : « Au pays des timides »! Ceci n'était point un blâme ; je notais, par l'effet que ses entreprises avaient fait sur moi, l'âge de ce jeune peuple, — solide athlète.

Paris, 15 juin 1936.

FIN

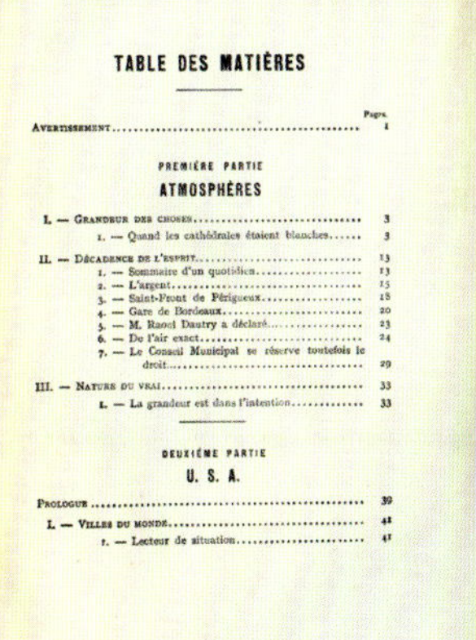

TABLE DES MATIÈRES

Pages.

Avertissement 1

PREMIÈRE PARTIE

ATMOSPHÈRES

I. — Grandeur des choses 3
1. — Quand les cathédrales étaient blanches 3

II. — Décadence de l'esprit 13
1. — Sommaire d'un quotidien 13
2. — L'argent 15
3. — Saint-Front de Périgueux 18
4. — Gare de Bordeaux 20
5. — M. Raoul Dautry a déclaré 23
6. — De l'air exact 24
7. — Le Conseil Municipal se réserve toutefois le droit 29

III. — Nature du vrai 33
1. — La grandeur est dans l'intention 33

DEUXIÈME PARTIE

U. S. A.

Prologue 39

I. — Villes du monde 41
1. — Lecteur de situation 41

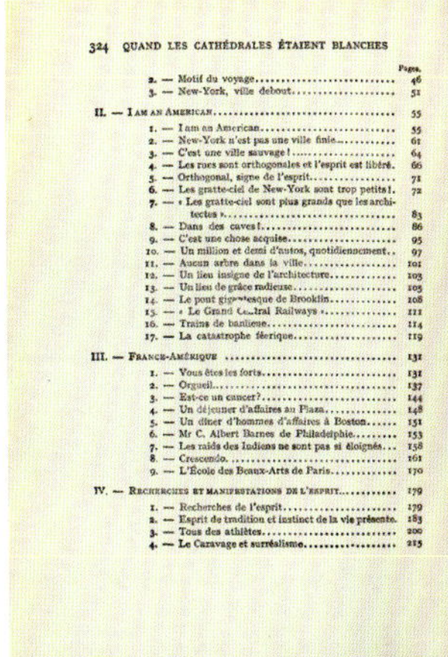

324 QUAND LES CATHÉDRALES ÉTAIENT BLANCHES

Pages.
2. — Motif du voyage 46
3. — New-York, ville debout 51

II. — I am an American 55
1. — I am an American 55
2. — New-York n'est pas une ville finie 61
3. — C'est une ville sauvage ! 64
4. — Les rues sont orthogonales et l'esprit est libéré. 66
5. — Orthogonal, signe de l'esprit 71
6. — Les gratte-ciel de New-York sont trop petits !. 72
7. — « Les gratte-ciel sont plus grands que les architectes » 83
8. — Dans des caves ! 86
9. — C'est une chose acquise 95
10. — Un million et demi d'autos, quotidiennement.. 97
11. — Aucun arbre dans la ville 101
12. — Un lieu insigne de l'architecture 103
13. — Un lieu de grâce radieuse 105
14. — Le pont gigantesque de Brooklin 108
15. — « Le Grand Central Railways » 111
16. — Trains de banlieue 114
17. — La catastrophe féerique 119

III. — France-Amérique 131
1. — Vous êtes les forts 131
2. — Orgueil 137
3. — Est-ce un cancer? 144
4. — Un déjeuner d'affaires au Plaza 148
5. — Un dîner d'hommes d'affaires à Boston 151
6. — Mr C. Albert Barnes de Philadelphie 153
7. — Les raids des Indiens ne sont pas si éloignés... 158
8. — Crescendo 161
9. — L'École des Beaux-Arts de Paris 170

IV. — Recherches et manifestations de l'esprit 179
1. — Recherches de l'esprit 179
2. — Esprit de tradition et instinct de la vie présente. 183
3. — Tous des athlètes 200
4. — Le Caravage et surréalisme 215

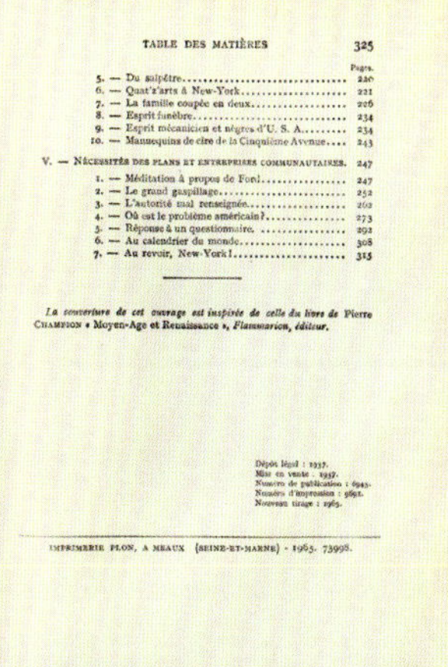

TABLE DES MATIÈRES 325

Pages.
5. — Du salpêtre 220
6. — Quat'z'arts à New-York 221
7. — La famille coupée en deux 226
8. — Esprit funèbre 234
9. — Esprit mécanicien et nègres d'U. S. A. 234
10. — Mannequins de cire de la Cinquième Avenue.... 243

V. — Nécessités des plans et entreprises communautaires. 247
1. — Méditation à propos de Ford 247
2. — Le grand gaspillage 252
3. — L'autorité mal renseignée 262
4. — Où est le problème américain? 273
5. — Réponse à un questionnaire 292
6. — Au calendrier du monde 308
7. — Au revoir, New-York ! 315

La couverture de cet ouvrage est inspirée de celle du livre de Pierre Champion « Moyen-Age et Renaissance », *Flammarion, éditeur.*

Dépôt légal : 1937.
Mise en vente : 1937.
Numéro de publication : 6943.
Numéro d'impression : 9692.
Nouveau tirage : 1965.

IMPRIMERIE PLON, A MEAUX (SEINE-ET-MARNE) - 1965. 73998.

This page. Selected pages from *Quand les cathédrales étaient blanches*, including sketches of New York City disappearing as Le Corbusier sails away

Opposite.
Le Corbusier in his apartment, 24 rue Nungesser-et-Colli, Paris, 1 May 1946

Paris, Vichy, and the War (1937–1943)

Le Corbusier was unwise in his political affiliations, and he had an unfortunate knack for making people believe that he was an ardent advocate of whatever they opposed. Labeled a proto-Communist and the "Trojan Horse of Bolshevism" by his compatriot Alexander von Senger, Le Corbusier also came under attack by his friend Karel Teige as a liberal idealist, and as a bourgeois capitalist dilettante by the Moscow press and the adherents of the Comintern in Paris. Despairing of ever getting official commissions from the French government, Le Corbusier turned to the neo-Fascist Redressement Français, delivering talks in the group's lecture hall in 1929 and publishing articles in its journal. He also tried to ingratiate himself with Benito Mussolini in 1934, presenting lectures in Rome, Venice, and Milan and unsuccessfully seeking an audience with Il Duce.

Political differences played a major role in ending Le Corbusier's partnership with Pierre Jeanneret. Both Pierre and Charlotte Perriand had moved to the left during the 1930s, and matters came to a head in 1937, when Le Corbusier was forced to collaborate with Les Jeunes (The Young Ones)—a group of young Communists and Socialists, in which Pierre and Charlotte played a leading role—in order to build the Pavillon des Temps Nouveaux at the Paris world's fair. Even though Le Corbusier and Pierre would live in neighboring houses in the little village of Ozon in the French Pyrenees during the first months of World War II, their partnership was effectively over. (It was eventually revived in India, where Pierre served as Le Corbusier's site architect on the Chandigarh project.)

More positive was Le Corbusier's association with the Syndicalist movement, for which he had helped edit the journals *Plans* and *Préludes* in the early 1930s. His resulting contact with a group of farmers led to a theory about the industrialization of agriculture, to which he devoted the Ferme Radieuse (Radiant Farm) project in 1935. Eventually this evolved into his theory of land use, published as *Les trois établissements humains* (1945; *The Three Human Establishments*). The idea, which became the leitmotif of his lectures on urbanism until the end of his life, was to link cultural and administrative cities (to be spaced 200 kilometers apart) with industrial cities that would be supported by industrial-agricultural settlements. This seemed to offer a synthesis of all his thinking about urbanism, facilitating industrial growth without the strangulation of cities, and giving more people direct access to unspoiled countryside.

During the Occupation, Le Corbusier ended up with an office in Vichy, where for several miserable months he attempted to impose his ideas for reconstruction on a demoralized and reactionary administration. He also designed some modular log huts, known as Constructions Murodins, to be erected for refugees by members of the Vichy youth movement. He wrote several books that could be seen as giving at least tacit approval to the Vichy regime, but he quickly became disillusioned after none of his major reconstruction projects in France or Algeria were accepted. By 1942, Le Corbusier was back in Paris, building political bridges with the left and founding a collective of architects and engineers known as ASCORAL to plan for postwar reconstruction.

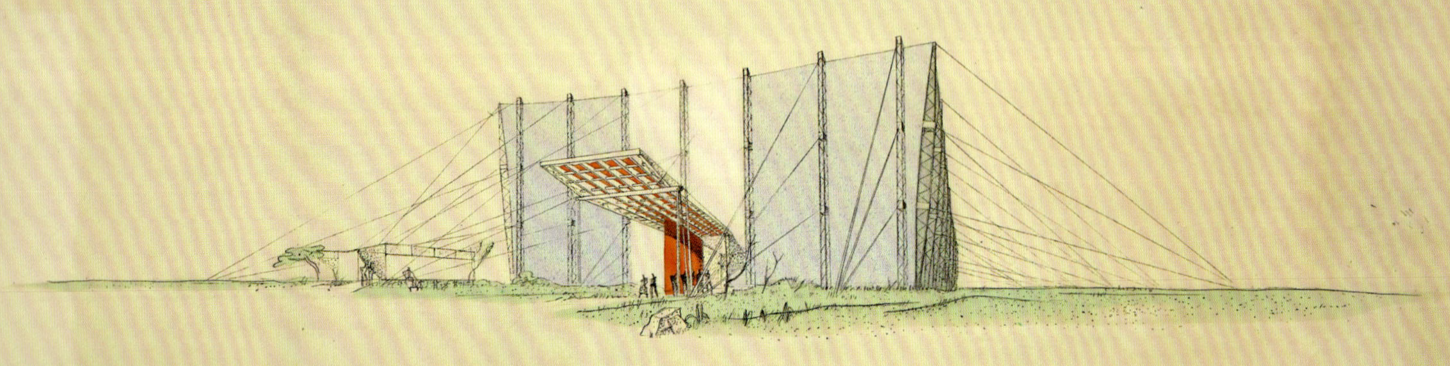

Innovation at the world's fair: Pavillon des Temps Nouveaux, Paris, 1937

Le Corbusier produced three schemes for a pavilion at the 1937 Paris world's fair, all of which were rejected. After intervention by Prime Minister Léon Blum, he received approval and funding to erect the novel tent-like Pavillon des Temps Nouveaux. Its structural components consisted of a tensile steel-truss system and multicolored cloth roof and walls. The interior featured a suspended airplane and murals created by the architect and painter José Luis Sert. Upon completion of the pavilion, Le Corbusier accepted the Legion of Honor, an award he had refused on four previous occasions.

Above and below. Perspective renderings, principal elevation, Pavillon des Temps Nouveaux, Paris, 1937

Opposite, clockwise from top:

Elevations of display panels for "Agrarian Reform" exhibit

Sketch of exhibit circulation scheme

Interior perspective, 6–7 February 1936

Interior sketch

Site plan

Plans, elevations, and sections

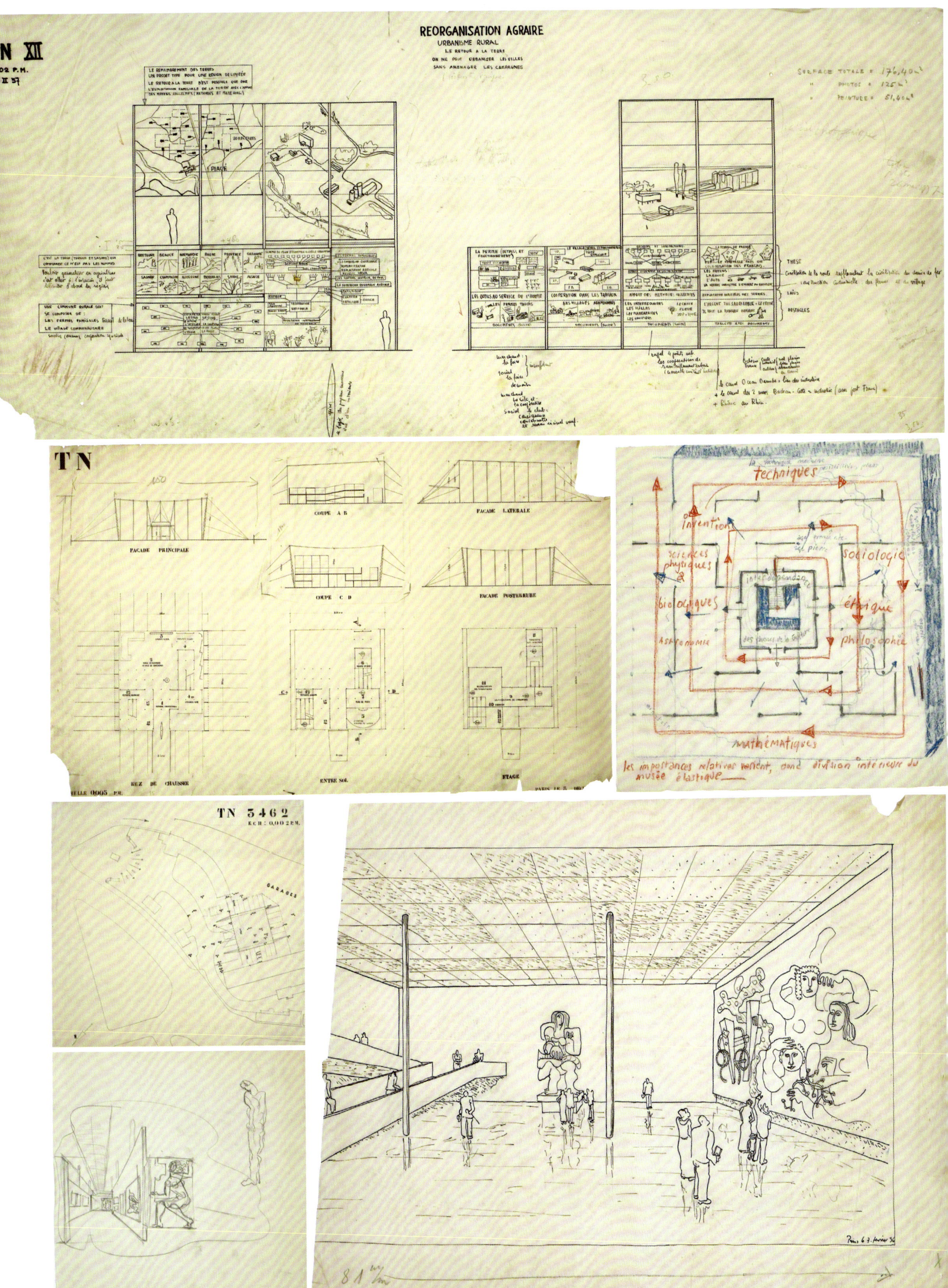

N XII
REORGANISATION AGRAIRE
URBANISME RURAL
LE RETOUR A LA TERRE
ON NE PEUT URBANISER LES VILLES
SANS AMENAGER LES CAMPAGNES
TN
FACADE PRINCIPALE
COUPE A B
FACADE LATERALE
COUPE C D
FACADE POSTERIEURE
REZ DE CHAUSSEE
ENTRE SOL
ETAGE
techniques
invention
sciences physiques
sociologie
biologiques
éthique
astronomie
philosophie
mathématiques
les importances relatives varient, donc division intérieure du musée élastique
TN 3462
GARAGES

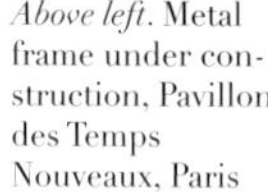

Above left. Metal frame under construction, Pavillon des Temps Nouveaux, Paris

Above right. Detail of anchorages for structural cables

Below. Principal facade, with cladding of blue, white, and red canvas

Opposite. Two views of main entrance, with door pivoting on a central axis

PAVILLON DES TEMPS NOUVEAUX
LE CORBUSIER ET P. JEANNERET ARCHITECTES
ESSAI DE MUSÉE D'ÉDUCATION POPULAIRE (URBANISME)
VISITEUR, C'EST ICI LA SCIENCE SEVERE DE L'URBANISME
L'URBANISME PORTEUR DU MALHEUR DES VILLES ET DES CAMPAGNES, OU PORTEUR,- DEMAIN DES JOIES ESSENTIELLES
L'URBANISME, MANIFESTATION TOTALE DU LYRISME D'UNE EPOQUE.
ENTRÉE
PAVILLON DES TEMPS NOUVEAUX 
VISITEUR, EN T'EN ALLANT, SAIS-TU MAINTENANT QUE TOUTES CES CHOSES SONT POSSIBLES?
ELLES SONT LA TÂCHE MÊME DU TEMPS PRÉSENT.

DES LOGIS
LES GRANDES ZONES INDUSTRIELLES EUROPÉENNES PACIFICATRICES

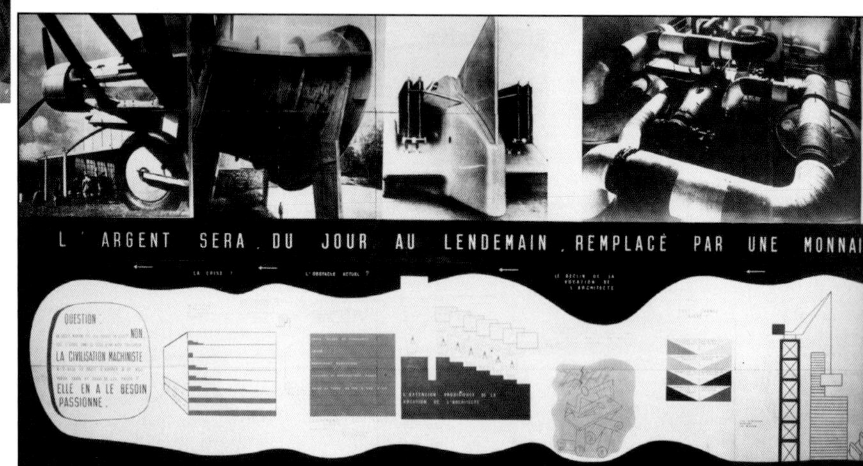
L'ARGENT SERA, DU JOUR AU LENDEMAIN, REMPLACÉ PAR UNE MONNAI
QUESTION
NON
LA CIVILISATION MACHINISTE
ELLE EN A LE BESOIN PASSIONNÉ

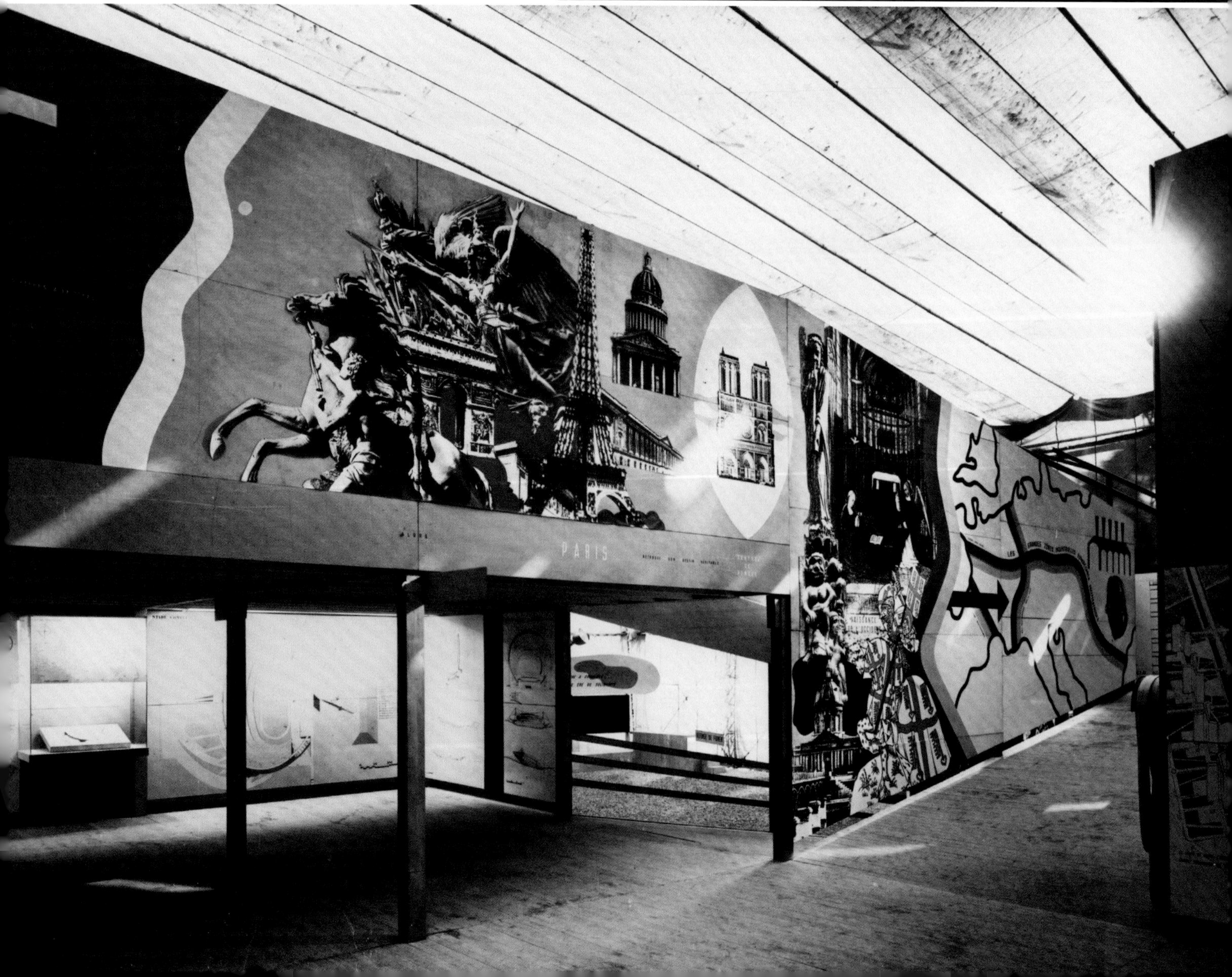

Opposite, top left and right. Exhibits, Pavillon des Temps Nouveaux, Paris

Opposite, bottom. "Plan de Paris 1937," panels depicting the "Spiritual Force of Paris"

Above. Main exhibition hall with panels at upper left representing the four functions of architecture; dwelling, recreation, work, and circulation

Left. First page of a letter from Le Corbusier to his mother, 19 February 1937, describing how much time he has spent working on the Pavillon des Temps Nouveaux

Below. Two pages of a letter from Le Corbusier to his mother, 25 June 1937, discussing the opening of his pavilion at the world's fair

Opposite. Le Corbusier, 1942

"Despite the despicable criticisms of all those bastards, it's marvelous to think that we've done this, in the heart of Paris, and in the midst of a social revolution. It's very instructive. Everything's possible! You can create a new city right in the vigorous heart of an ancient one, without wrecking its life, without halting its life."

—Letter to his mother, 25 June 1937

COLLECTION DE L'ÉQUIPEMENT DE LA CIVILISATION MACHINISTE

DES CANONS, DES MUNITIONS ?

LE CORBUSIER

MERCI ! DES LOGIS... S.V.P.

ÉDITIONS DE L'ARCHITECTURE D'AUJOURD'HUI, 5, RUE BARTHOLDI, BOULOGNE (SEINE)

A call for peace, just before the war: *Des canons, des munitions? Merci! Des Logis ... S.V.P.*, 1938

In 1938 Le Corbusier published *Des canons, des munitions? Merci! Des Logis ... S.V.P.* (Guns, Ammunition? Thanks! Housing ... Please), which argued for the peaceful application of methods of mass production. Ironically, after World War II began the following year, the French government awarded Le Corbusier a commission to build a munitions factory.

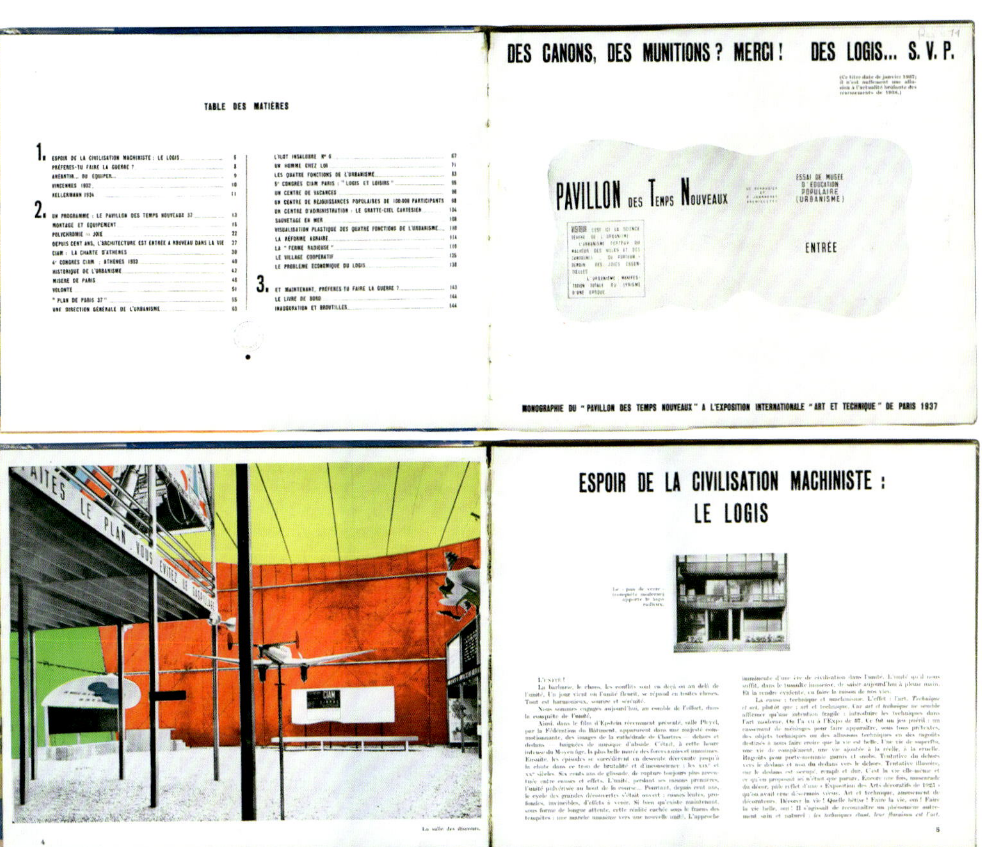

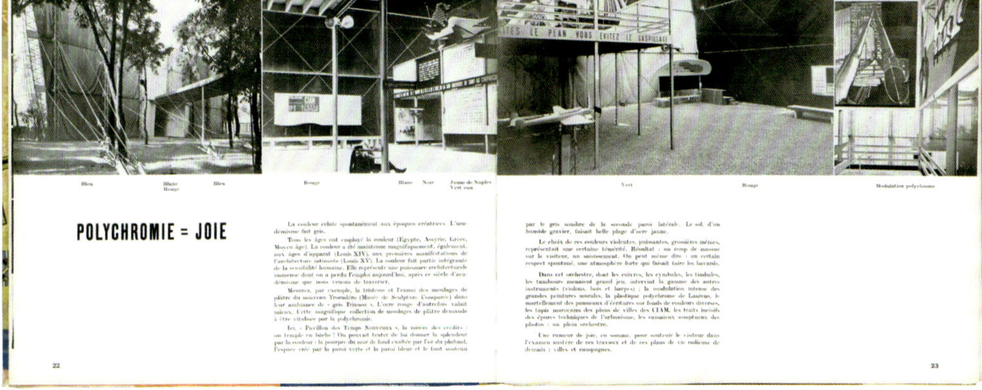

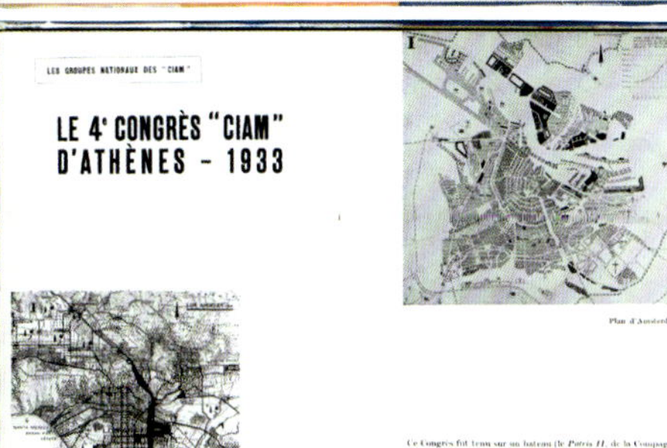

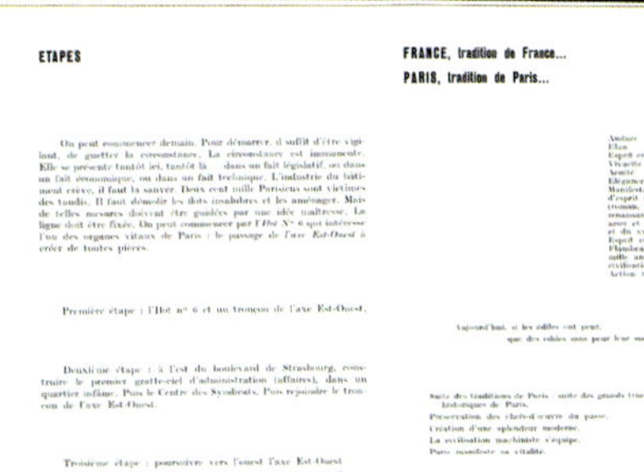

Opposite, top. Sketches of cover designs, c. 1937–38, for *Des canons, des munitions? Merci! Des Logis ... S.V.P.* (Guns, Ammunition? Thanks! Housing ... Please), Editions de l'Architecture d'Aujourd'hui, Paris, 1938. The book documented the Pavillon des Temps Nouveaux.

Opposite, bottom. Cover, *Des canons, des munitions?*

Right. Selected pages from *Des canons, des munitions?*

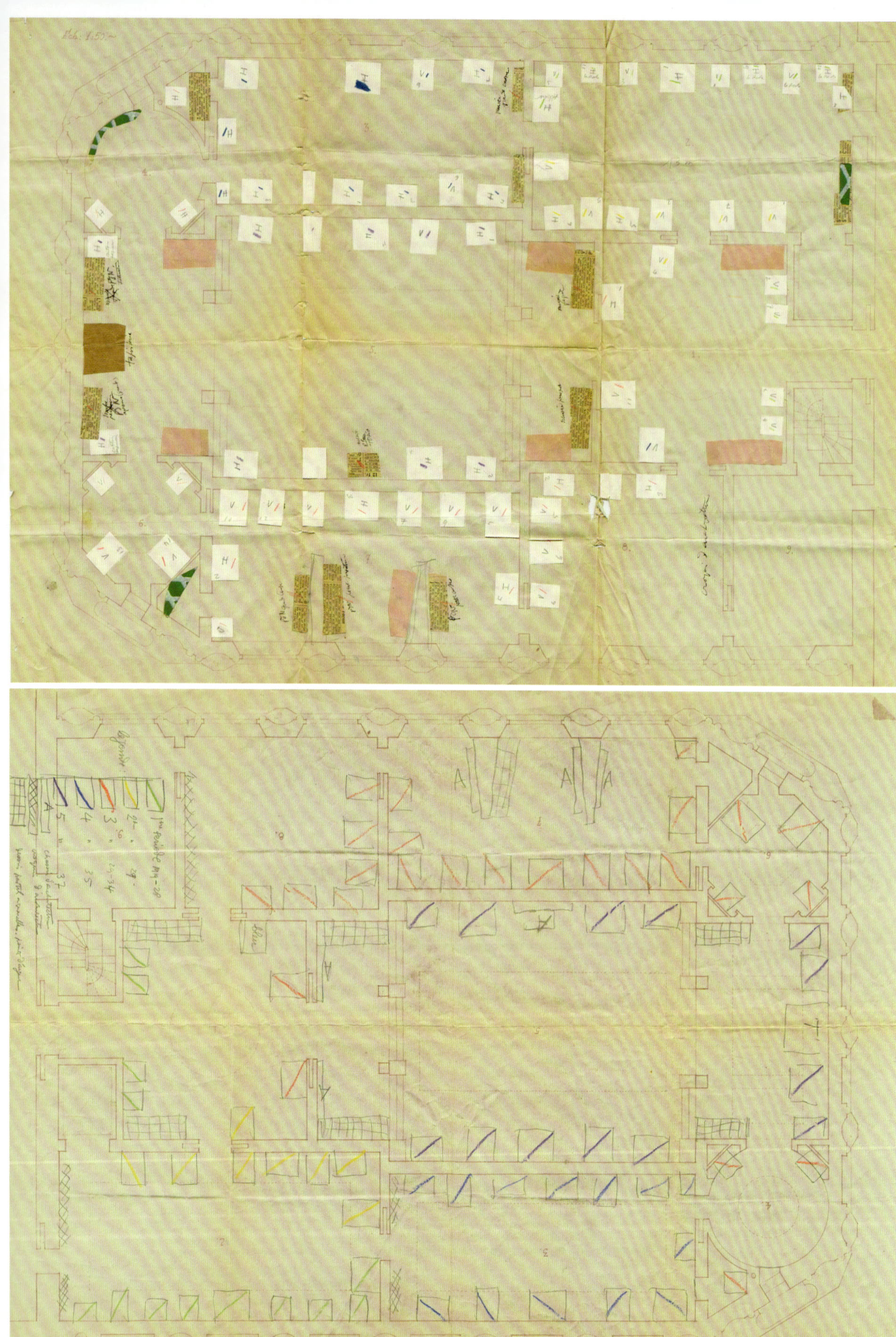

***Le Corbusier: Oeuvre plastique, 1919–1937, Tableaux et architecture,* Kunsthaus, Zurich, 1938**

Le Corbusier found himself increasingly discouraged by political developments in Europe as the 1930s progressed, particularly with regard to the grim outlook for making new architecture. He was therefore optimistic when the Kunsthaus in Zurich mounted an exhibition of his paintings spanning the previous two decades. Largely ignored by the Swiss press and public, the exhibition proved to be a disappointment for Le Corbusier.

Opposite. Installation plans for exhibition *Le Corbusier: Oeuvre plastique, 1919–1937, Tableaux et architecture* (Le Corbusier: Plastic Art, 1919–1937, Paintings and Architecture).

Kunsthaus Zurich, 1938

Right. Sketch of a gallery interior with notes on the installation of works

Below. Sketch of cover (left) and collage of cover design (right) for the exhibition catalog

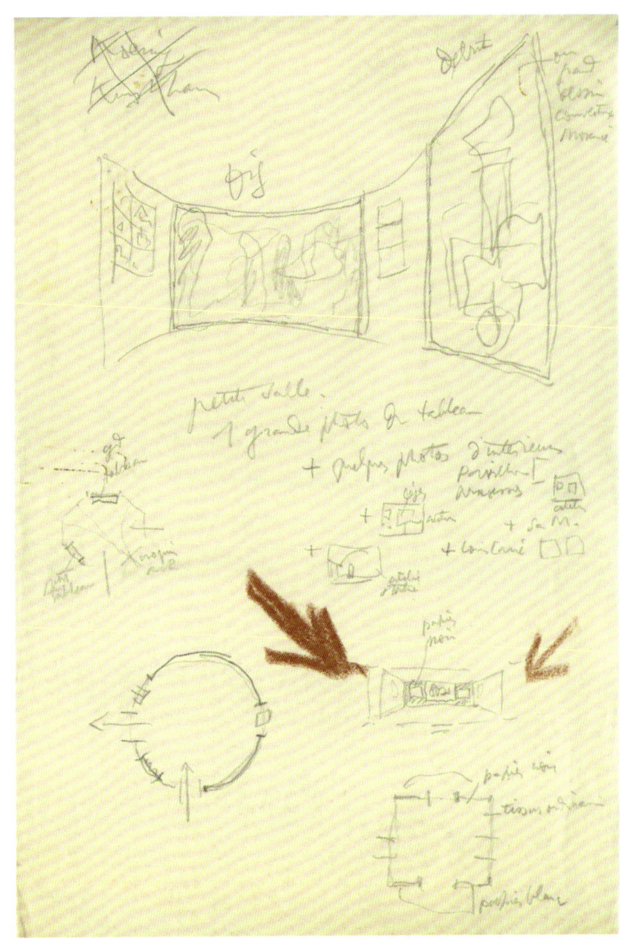

"Hate is everywhere and the struggle is as hard as ever. For the moment total 'depression,' no work. I paint... In January–February I'm having a serious exhibition of painting at the Kunsthaus in Zurich (known here as the Salzburg of plastic art). 10 rooms. Big pictures, 120 drawings. 17 years of work. *unknown*, because I've not exhibited since 1923."

—Letter to Marguerite Tjader Harris, 8 December 1937

Above and opposite, top. Installation views, *Le Corbusier: Oeuvre plastique, 1919–1937, Tableaux et architecture*, Kunsthaus Zurich, 1938

Below. Le Corbusier to Marguerite Tjader Harris, 8 December 1937, discussing his upcoming exhibition of paintings in Zurich and his struggle to find architectural work

Opposite, bottom left. La femme au guéridon et au fer à cheval (Woman with Table and Horseshoe), 1928

Opposite, bottom right. La main rouge (The Red Hand), 1930–32

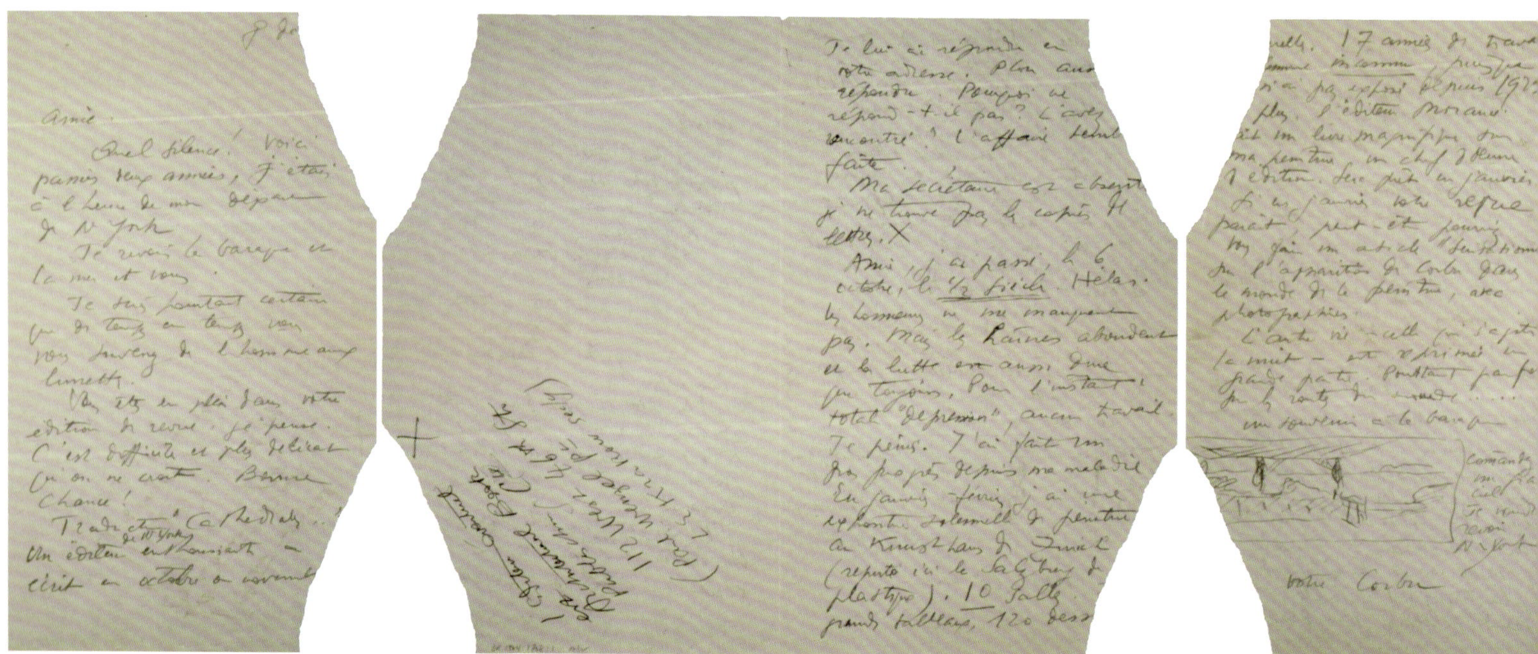

Amie.

Quel silence ! Voici passées deux années, j'étais à l'heure de mon départ de N York.

Je revois le barrage et la mer et vous.

Je suis pourtant certain que de temps en temps vous vous souvenez de l'homme aux lunettes.

Vous êtes en plein dans votre édition de revue, je pense. C'est difficile et plus délicat qu'on ne croit. Bonne chance !

Traduction « Cathédrales » ! Un éditeur de N York enthousiaste m'a écrit en octobre ou novembre. Je lui ai répondu en votre adresse. Plus aucune réponse. Pourquoi ne répond-t-il pas ? L'avez-vous rencontré ? L'affaire semble faite.

Ma secrétaire est absente je ne trouve pas les copies de lettres. X

Ainsi j'ai passé, le 6 octobre, le ½ siècle. Hélas. Les honneurs ne me manquent pas. Mais les haines abondent et la lutte est aussi dure que toujours. Pour l'instant : total « dépression », aucun travail. Je peins. J'ai fait un gros progrès depuis ma maladie. En janvier-février j'ai une exposition solennelle de peinture au Kunsthaus de Zurich (reprise ici le salle [illegible] de plastique). 10 salles, grands tableaux, 120 dessins[...]

[...]elles. 17 années de travail presque inconnu, puisque je n'ai pas exposé depuis 1923. Plus, l'éditeur Morancé fait un livre magnifique sur ma peinture, un chef d'œuvre d'édition. Sera prêt en janvier.

Si vous faisiez votre revue paraître, peut-être pourriez-vous faire un article sensationnel sur l'apparition de Corbu dans le monde de la peinture, avec photographies.

L'autre [illegible] – est exprimé en grande partie. Pourtant partout par les routes du monde...

un souvenir de la barque

Comment va [illegible] N York

Votre Corbu

(Pour Madame M. Tjader Harris, 112 West 16th St, New York)

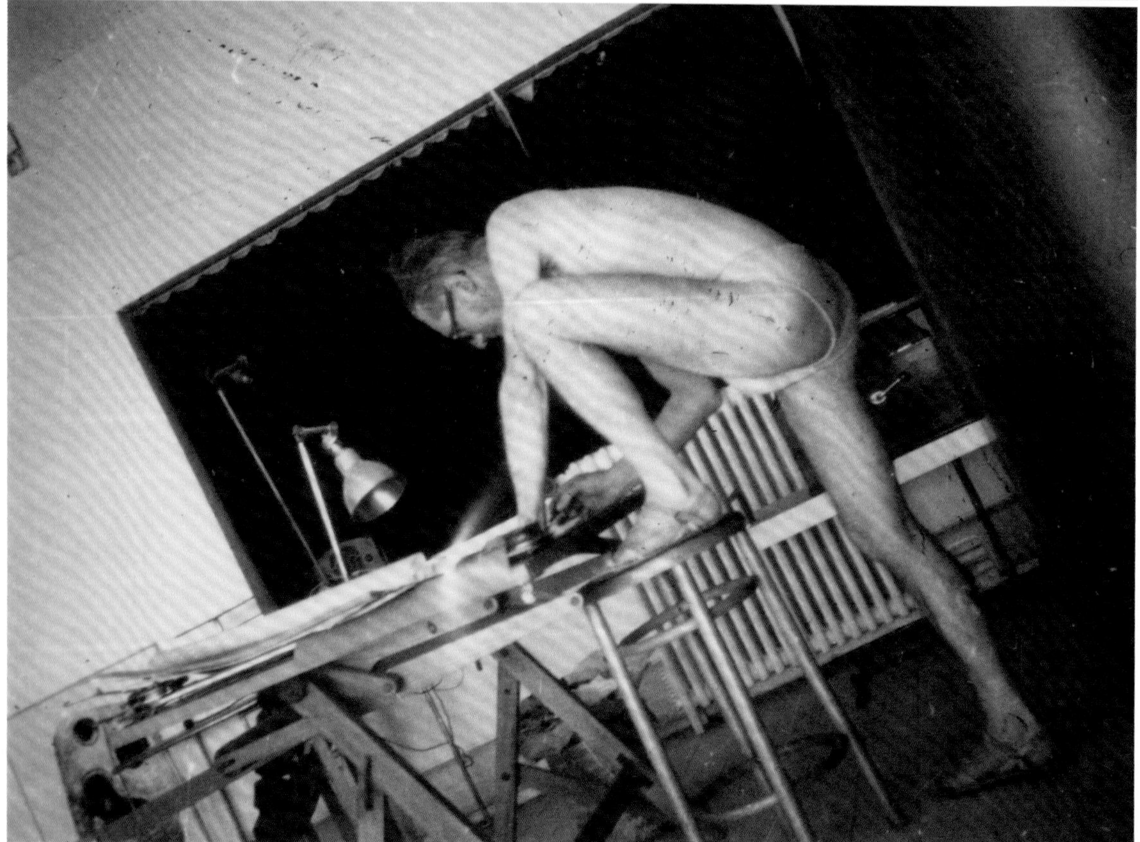

**urals for
e Eileen
ray/Jean
adovici house,
oquebrune-
ap-Martin,
rance,
938–39**

Irish architect and furniture designer Eileen Gray was part of a circle of avant-garde artists, designers, and critics in Paris that included Fernand Léger, Amédée Ozenfant, and José Luis Sert. While Le Corbusier and Gray admired each other's work, they were not close friends. And whatever mutual admiration did exist nearly vanished after a short stay by Le Corbusier and Yvonne Gallis at Villa E.1027, the house in Roquebrune-Cap-Martin, in the south of France, that Gray had designed for architect and publisher Jean Badovici. As a gift, Le Corbusier spontaneously applied several large murals to the house's walls, angering Gray, though pleasing Badovici.

Opposite. Le Corbusier at work on murals for Villa E.1027, home of Jean Badovici and Eileen Gray, Roquebrune-Cap-Martin, France, c. 1938

Above. View of some of the murals painted by Le Corbusier at Villa E.1027

Right. First page of letter from Le Corbusier to Jean Badovici, 1 January 1950, discussing preservation plans for the murals

1 janvier 1950

Mon cher Bado.

Enfin un mot de vous!

" NARCISSE, fils du fleuve Céphise et de la nymphe Liriope, méprisa l'amour de la nymphe Echo; épris de sa propre image, il se laissa mourir ou se tua près de la fontaine qui reflétait ses traits; il fut changé en une fleur qui a gardé son nom et qui était consacrée aux dieux infernaux. Cette fable a fourni à Malfilâtre le sujet d'un petit poème. Le musée de Naples possède une très belle statue de bronze à laquelle on attribue, mais peut-être à tort, le nom de Narcisse "

(Dictionnaire de géographie et d'Histoire)

Si je lis bien votre pensée, vous enlèverez mes peintures pour restituer à v. maison "le sens profond d'une attitude d'esprit qui bannissait formellement la peinture." Mais je vous demande, formellement aussi, de faire photographier mes peintures avant de les effacer.

Je comprends peut-être mal le sens profond de votre pensée, car bien que vous habitiez Paris depuis 30 années vous n'avez pas encore été conduit à pouvoir faire comprendre aux autres ce que vous écrivez.

Vous réclamez une mise au point de mon "contentement de mon autorité mondiale", démontrant

Below.
Le Corbusier, Yvonne, and Jean Badovici at Villa E.1027, Roquebrune-Cap-Martin, c. 1939

"The mural paintings brightened only the most unpleasing walls of the house. The 'good walls' remained white. The paintings created space in cramped places; at the entrance, within the porch, and at the bar." —*New World of Space*, **1948**

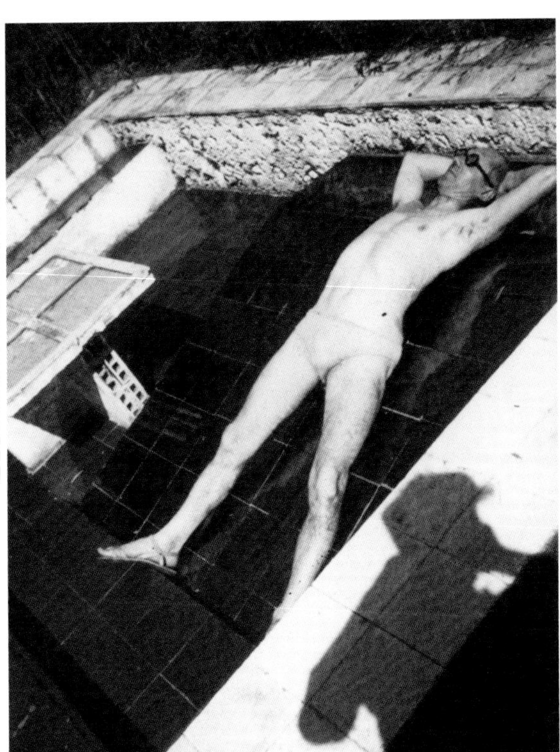

Right. Le Corbusier sunbathing in Roquebrune-Cap-Martin, n.d.

Far right. Interior of Villa E.1027, Roquebrune-Cap-Martin, with one of Le Corbusier's paintings in the background

Below. Le Corbusier at Villa E.1027, c. 1939

Boating accident, Saint-Tropez, France, 1938

Le Corbusier and his wife, Yvonne, spent the summer of 1938 in the south of France, as usual. While he was swimming off the beach at Saint-Tropez, a large motorboat rode over him, its propeller nearly slicing off his thigh. Le Corbusier required two operations and, as he frequently noted, two meters of stitches.

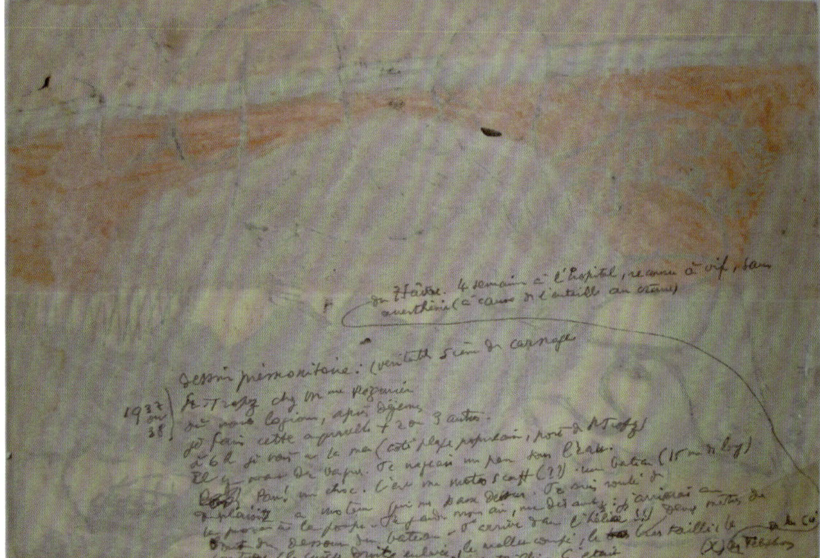

Opposite. Le Corbusier at work on a mural at Villa E.1027, Roquebrune Cap-Martin, n.d. His right thigh bears the scar from his boating accident.

Top. Dessin prémonitoire (Premonitory Drawing), 1938. Le Corbusier completed this painting hours before being hit by a motorboat in the ocean off Saint-Tropez.

Above. Verso of *Dessin prémonitoire*, with Le Corbusier's hand-written description of his accident and hospitalization

Below left. Le Corbusier to his mother, from central hospital, Saint-Tropez, 23 August 1938

Below middle. First page of letter from Le Corbusier to his mother, from Saint-Tropez, 21 September 1938

Below right. First page of a letter from Le Corbusier to Marguerite Tjader Harris, 22 December 1938, mentioning his accident

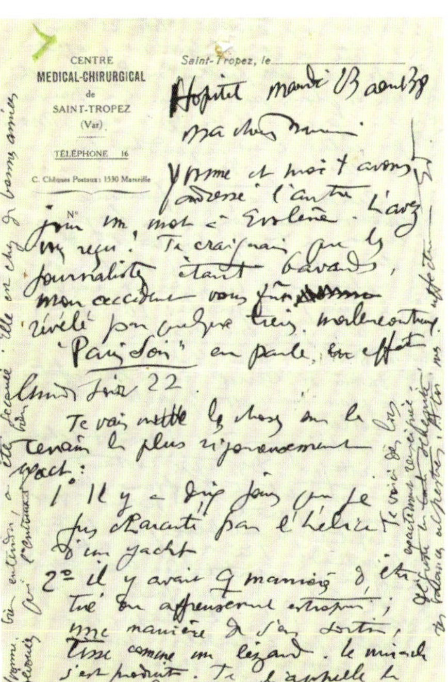

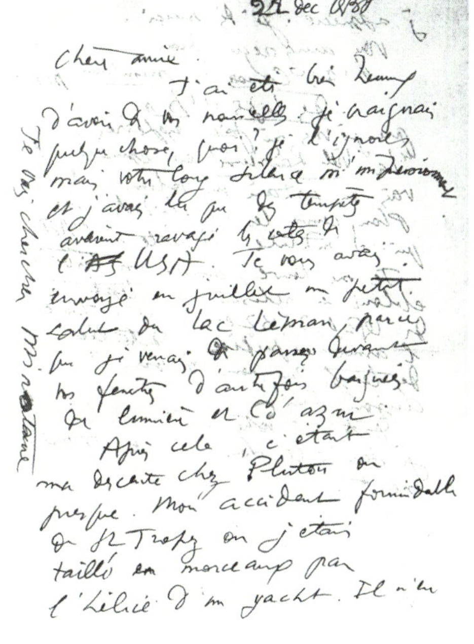

Premonitions of war: Correspondence with his mother, 1938–39

Le Corbusier was initially sanguine in response to his mother's mounting fears about the rise of Hitler and the start of World War II. However, as Paris emptied out, Le Corbusier's optimism faded. He and Yvonne ultimately fled Paris on 4 September 1939, taking refuge in a house belonging to Jean Badovici in Vézelay, France.

Opposite, top, and middle left. Le Corbusier to his mother, 18 November 1938, describing the outlook for war in Europe and his hopes for work in London, including the possibility of opening an office there

Opposite, middle right. Le Corbusier to his mother and brother, from Paris, 3 September 1939, describing his return to occupied Paris and plans to settle temporarily in Vézelay

Opposite, bottom. Le Corbusier to his mother and brother, from Vézelay, 9 September 1939, describing conditions in occupied France

Above. Le Corbusier in his apartment, 24 rue Nungesser-et-Coli, Paris, 1944

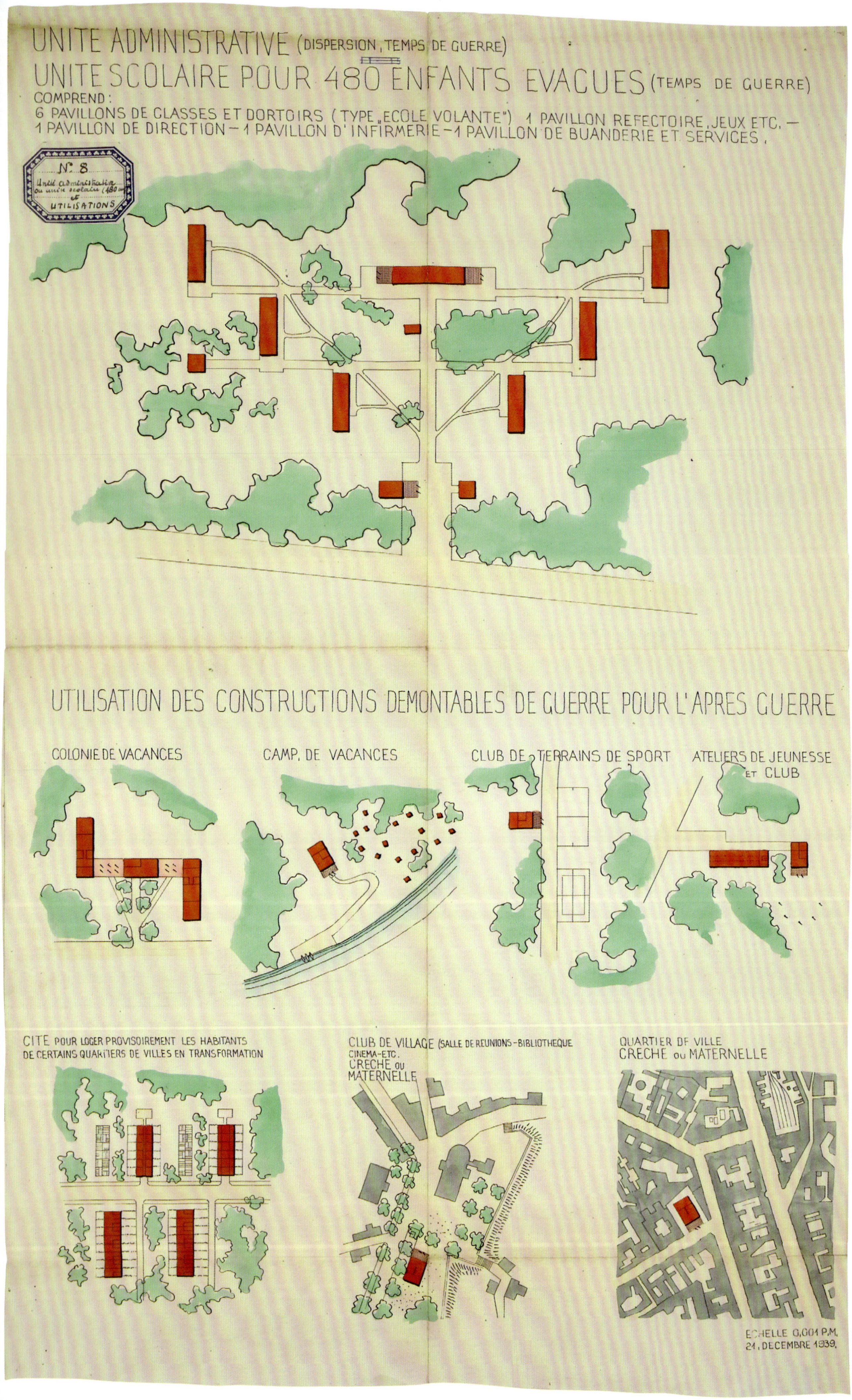

UNITE ADMINISTRATIVE (DISPERSION, TEMPS DE GUERRE)
UNITE SCOLAIRE POUR 480 ENFANTS EVACUES (TEMPS DE GUERRE)
COMPREND:
6 PAVILLONS DE CLASSES ET DORTOIRS (TYPE „ECOLE VOLANTE") 1 PAVILLON REFECTOIRE, JEUX ETC. —
1 PAVILLON DE DIRECTION — 1 PAVILLON D'INFIRMERIE — 1 PAVILLON DE BUANDERIE ET SERVICES.
N° 8
UTILISATIONS
UTILISATION DES CONSTRUCTIONS DEMONTABLES DE GUERRE POUR L'APRES GUERRE
COLONIE DE VACANCES
CAMP. DE VACANCES
CLUB DE TERRAINS DE SPORT
ATELIERS DE JEUNESSE ET CLUB
CITE POUR LOGER PROVISOIREMENT LES HABITANTS DE CERTAINS QUARTIERS DE VILLES EN TRANSFORMATION
CLUB DE VILLAGE (SALLE DE REUNIONS - BIBLIOTHEQUE CINEMA - ETC.
CRECHE ou MATERNELLE
QUARTIER DE VILLE
CRECHE ou MATERNELLE
ECHELLE 0,001 P.M.
21, DECEMBRE 1939.

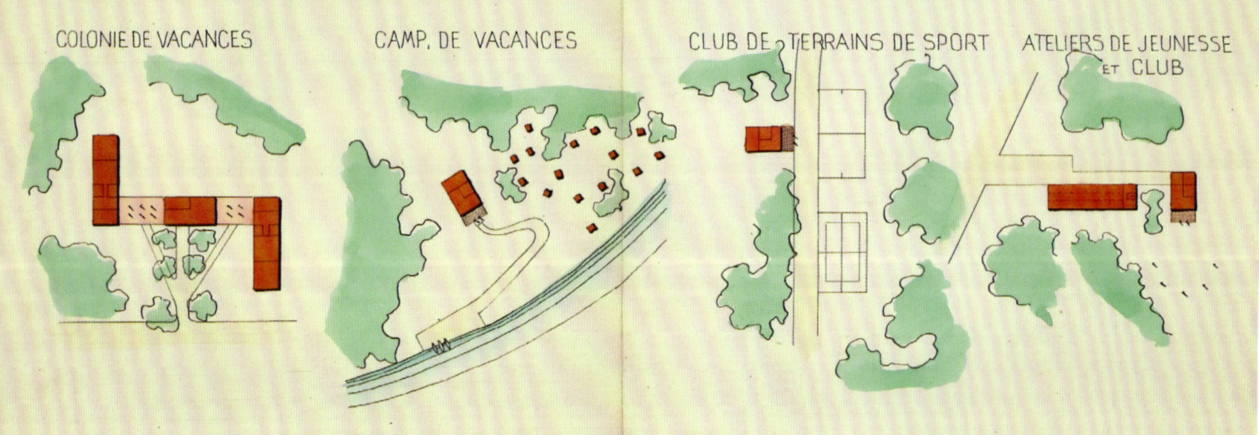

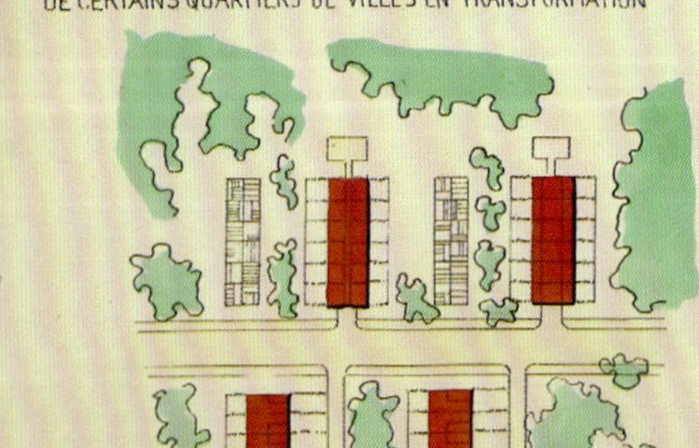

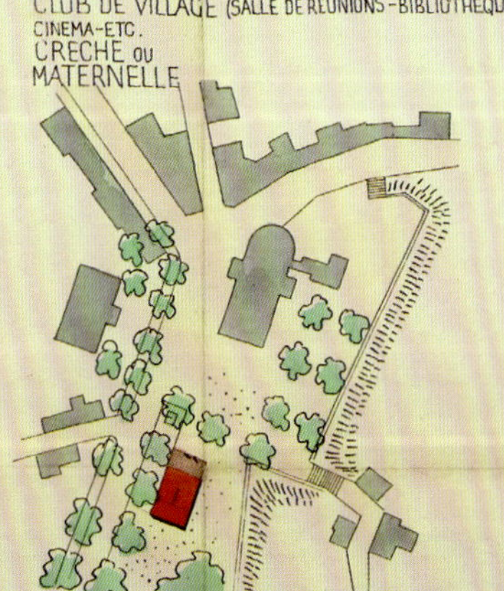

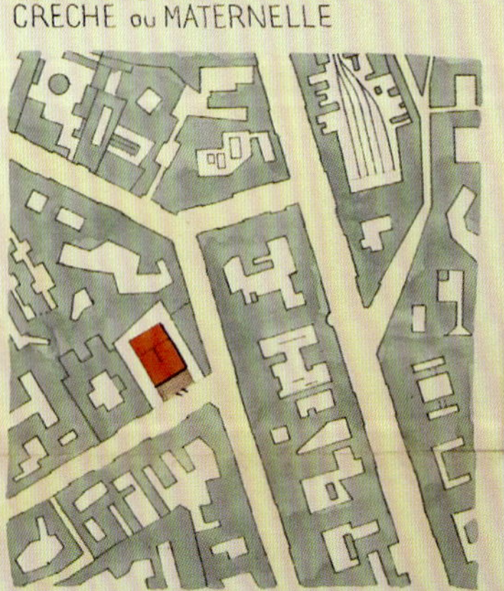

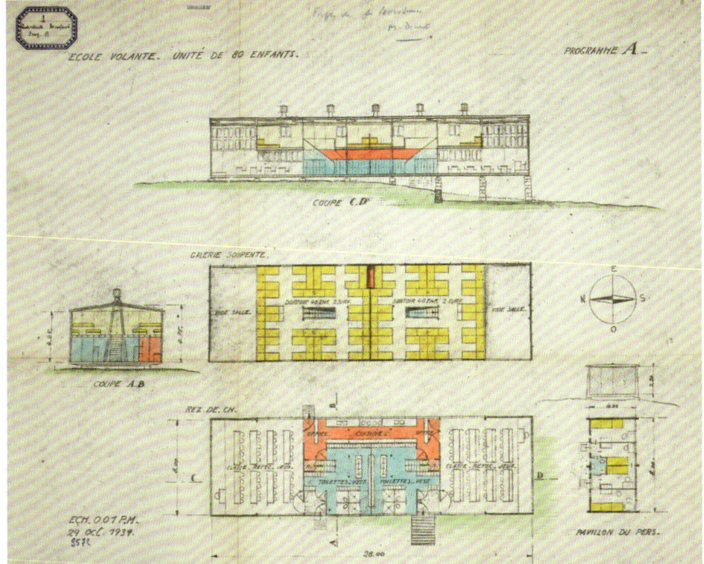

Wartime projects: Ecoles Volantes, 1939–40

Soon after relocating to Vézelay, Le Corbusier was dividing his time between Vézelay and Paris while working on plans for a munitions factory. He and the designer Jean Prouvé also designed a scheme commissioned by the Ministry of Education for temporary structures called Ecoles Volantes (Flying Schools). These would be mobile, easily reassembled, and used as schools, nurseries, workshops, or barracks.

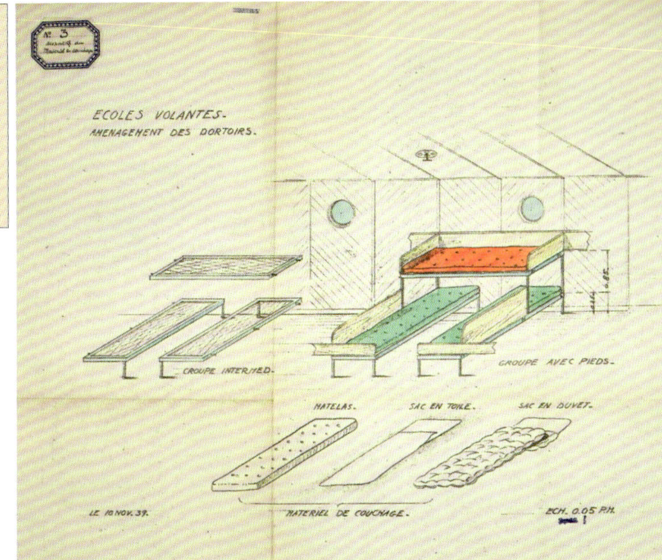

Opposite. Plan, 21 December 1939, showing wartime and postwar uses of Ecoles Volantes, portable structures developed in collaboration with Jean Prouvé

Above left. Plans and sections, Ecoles Volantes for eighty children, 29 October 1939

Above right. Perspective of a classroom

Right. Axonometric of the components of a dormitory, 10 November 1939

Below. Perspective

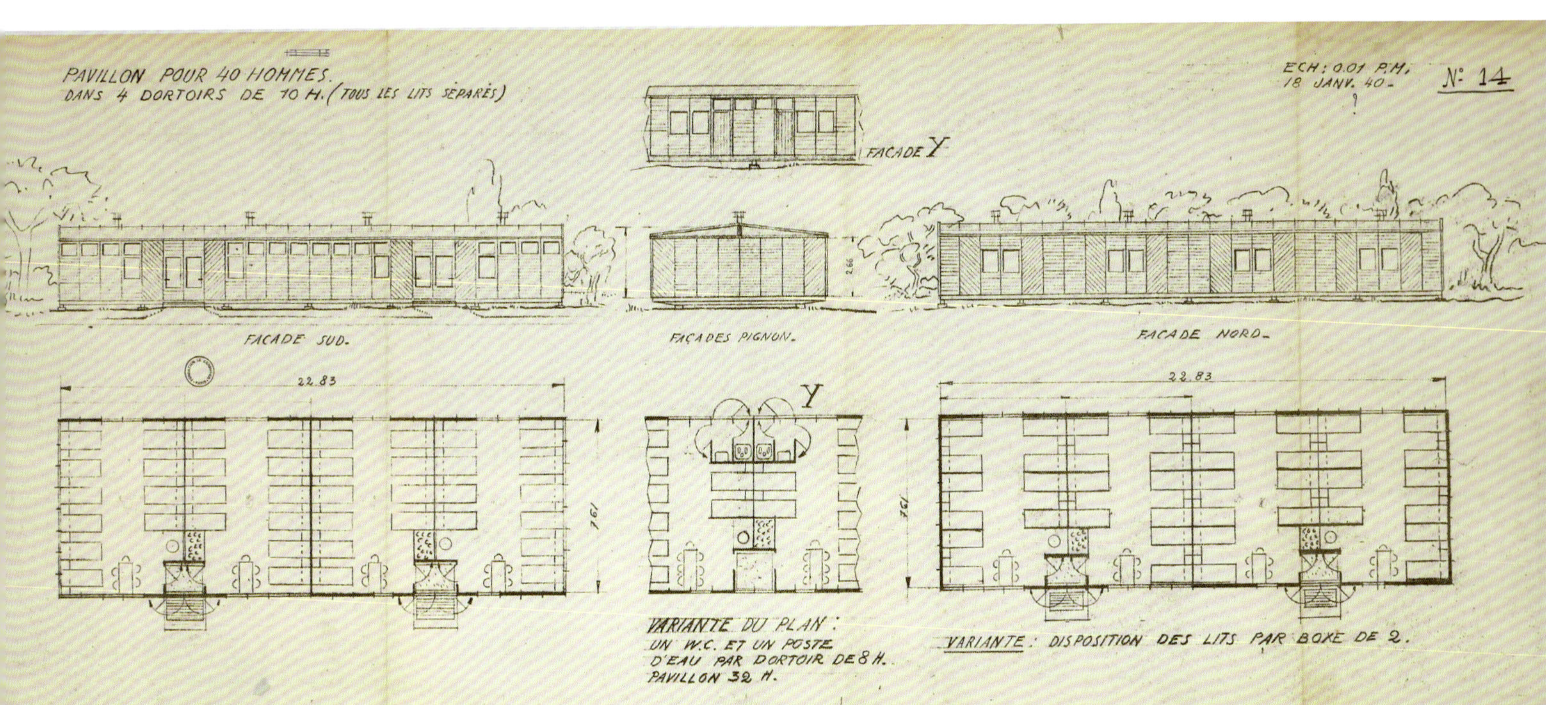

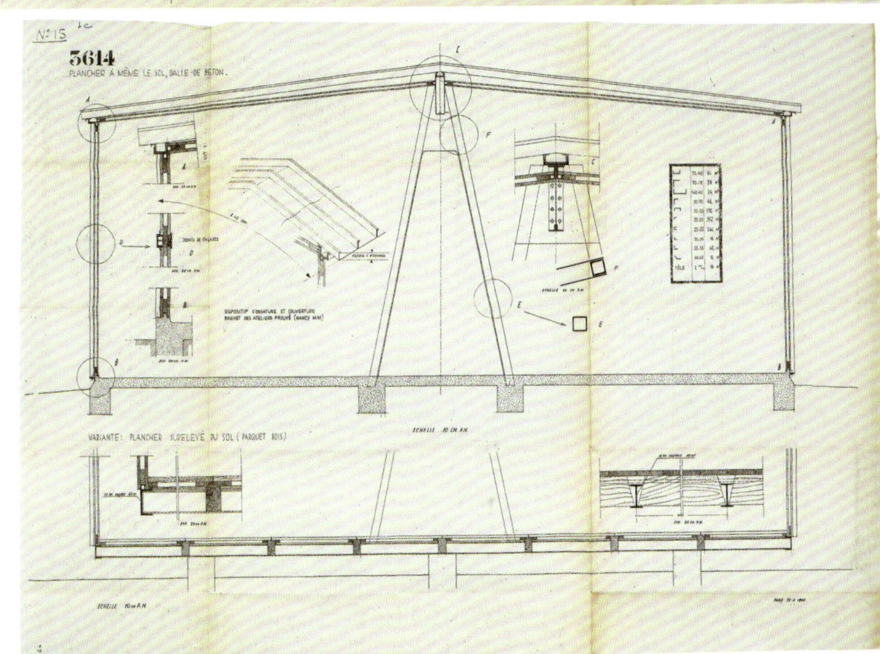

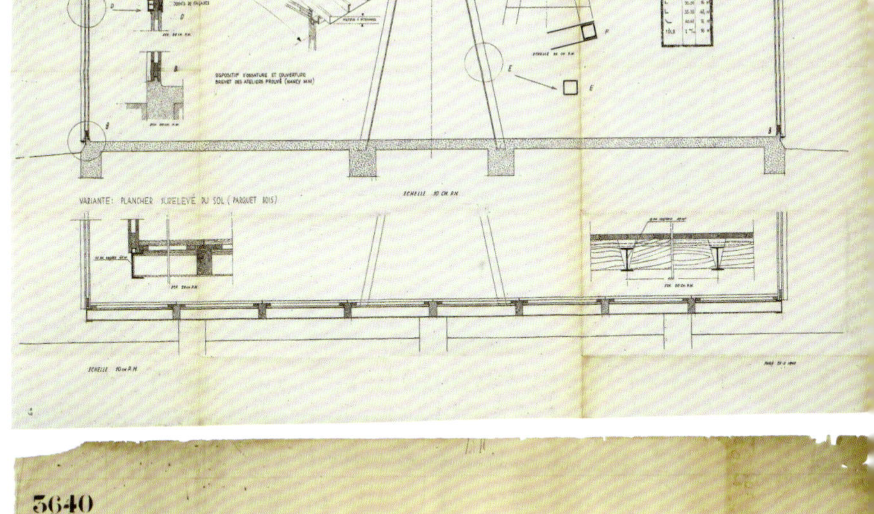

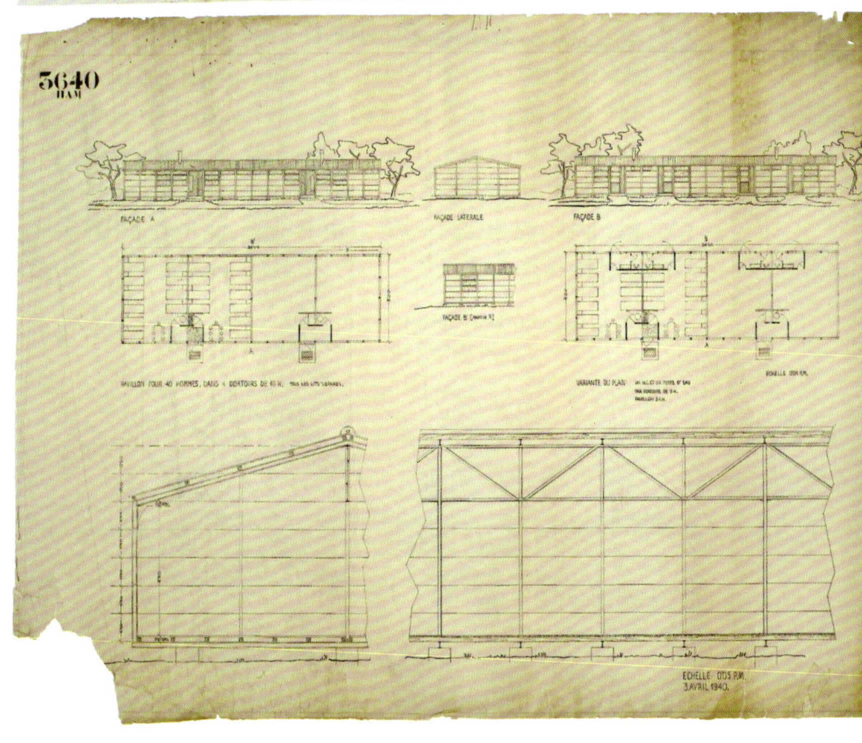

Opposite. Le Corbusier, October 1945

Top. Plans and elevations of a variation of the Ecoles Volantes, a dormitory for forty men, 18 January 1940

Middle. Section with construction details for bending sheet metal, 2 February 1940

Right. Elevations, plans, and sections of a dormitory for forty men, 3 April 1940

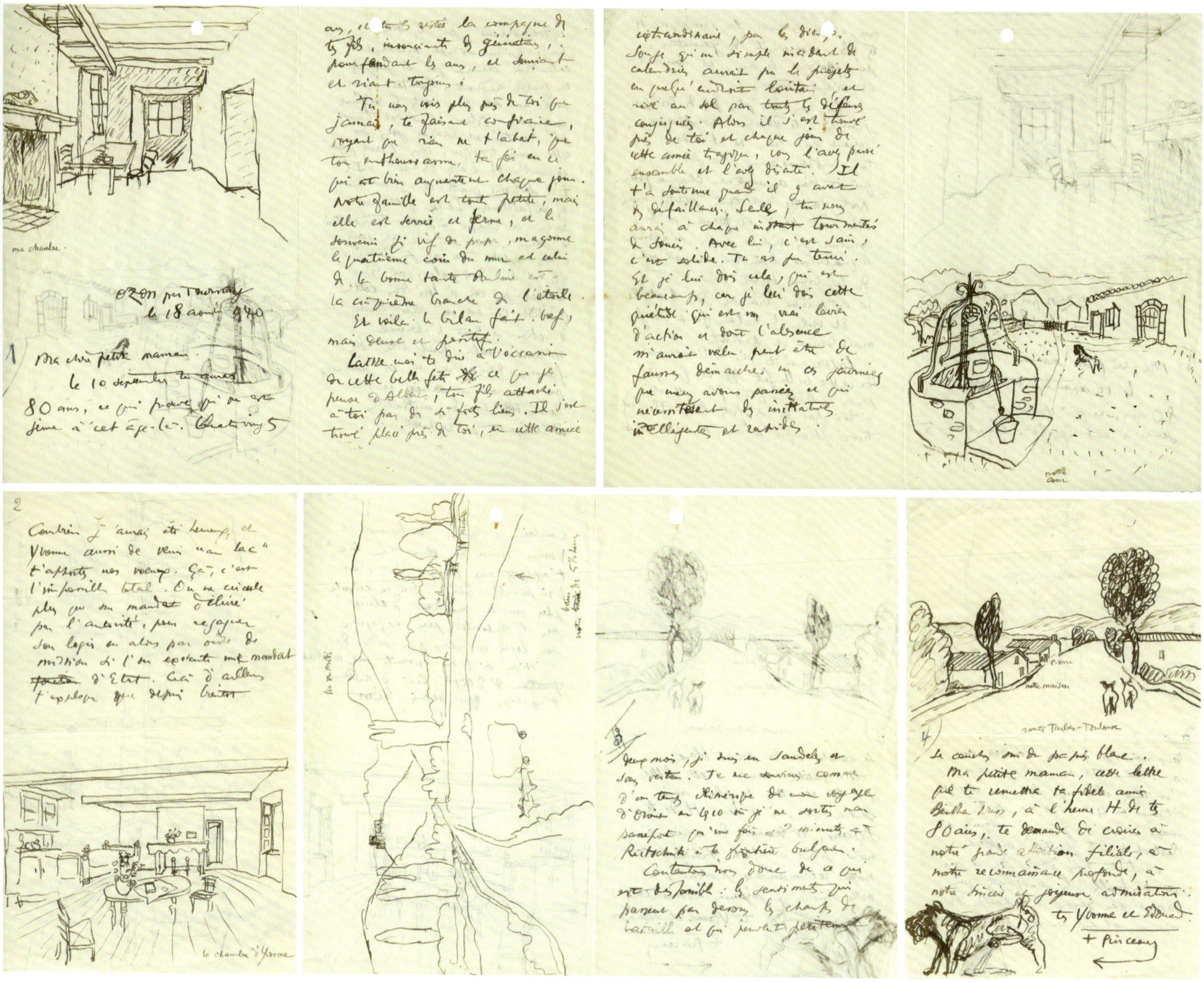

“How happy I would have been, and Yvonne too to come ‘to the Lake’ and bring you my best wishes, that’s totally impossible. You can only travel with a pass issued by the authorities, to return home or under orders for a state mission. This is also why for nearly two months, I’m in sandals without a jacket. I remember as if in a dream my trip to the East in 1910 when I only ever got my passport out once for 2 minutes at Rutschuk on the Bulgarian border.”

—Letter to his mother, from Ozon, France, 18 August 1940

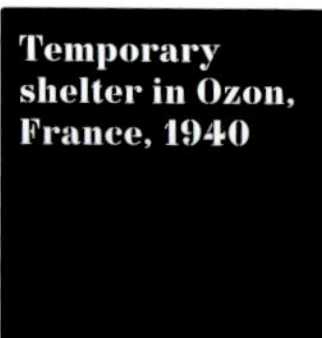

Temporary shelter in Ozon, France, 1940

Just a few days before the Germans invaded Paris in June 1940, Le Corbusier and Yvonne moved from Vézelay to the mountain village of Ozon, France. There Le Corbusier came to the decision that he should assist the Vichy government in the reconstruction of France, rather than joining the French Resistance, as his cousin and partner Pierre Jeanneret did.

Above. Le Corbusier to his mother, from Ozon, France, 18 August 1940. He writes in anticipation of her eightieth birthday in September, and illustrates the letter with images of his and Yvonne’s temporary home.

Opposite. Le Corbusier with Yvonne back home, 24 rue Nungesser-et-Coli, Paris, 1944

"Subject of the Vichy lecture: the citizen – the family – the household – housing, children = childcare = playgrounds and buildings – urb[anism]"

— Notes for a lecture to a Vichy women's group, December 1940

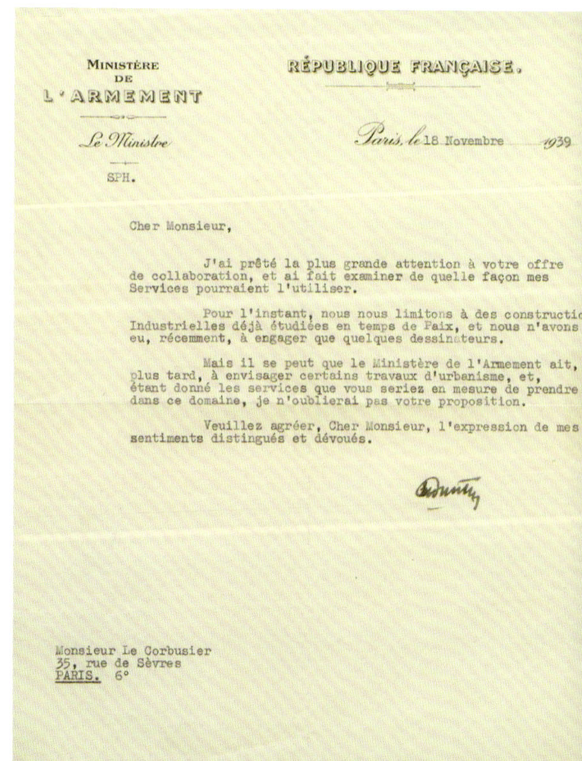

MINISTÈRE
DE
L'ARMEMENT

RÉPUBLIQUE FRANÇAISE.

Le Ministre

Paris, le 18 Novembre 1939

SPH.

Cher Monsieur,

J'ai prêté la plus grande attention à votre offre de collaboration, et ai fait examiner de quelle façon mes Services pourraient l'utiliser.

Pour l'instant, nous nous limitons à des constructi
Industrielles déjà étudiées en temps de Paix, et nous n'avons eu, récemment, à engager que quelques dessinateurs.

Mais il se peut que le Ministère de l'Armement ait, plus tard, à envisager certains travaux d'urbanisme, et, étant donné les services que vous seriez en mesure de prendre dans ce domaine, je n'oublierai pas votre proposition.

Veuillez agréer, Cher Monsieur, l'expression de mes sentiments distingués et dévoués.

Monsieur Le Corbusier
35, rue de Sèvres
PARIS. 6°

Above and opposite page. Le Corbusier's sketches and notes for a lecture entitled "Le citoyen, la famille, le foyer, le logis" (The citizen, the family, the household, housing), delivered to a Vichy women's group, December 1940, synthesizing his urban planning research

Right. French Minister of Munitions to Le Corbusier, 18 November 1939, explaining that he might employ the architect's services in the future, but not at present, for urban planning projects

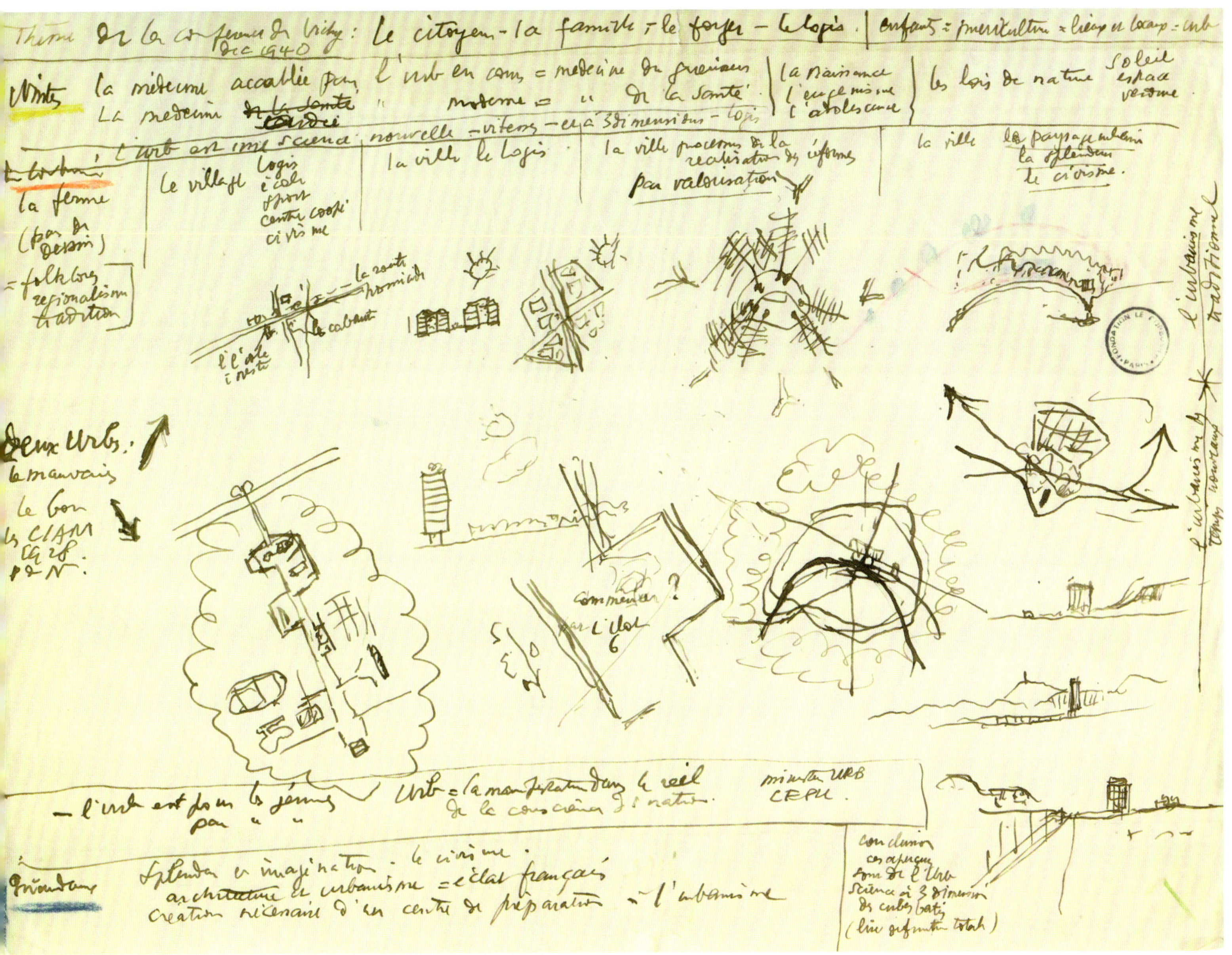

Thème de la conférence de Vichy : Le citoyen – la famille – le foyer – le logis | enfants = puériculture = lieux et loisirs – urb
Déc 1940

Vérités
la médecine accablée par l'urb en cours = médecine des guérisons
La médecine de la santé " moderne = " de la santé
la naissance
l'enfance
l'adolescence
les lois de nature: soleil, espace, verdure

l'urb est une science nouvelle – vitesse – et à 3 dimensions – logis

tradition
la ferme
(par des [illegible])
= folklore
régionalisme
tradition

le village
logis
école
sport
centre coopé
civisme

la ville le logis

la ville processus de la réalisation des réformes
par valorisation

la ville le paysage urbain
la splendeur
le civisme

la route nomade
le cabaret
l'état
i [illegible]

Deux Urbs:
le mauvais
le bon
les CIAM
[illegible]

commencer?
par l'état
6

l'urbanisme traditionnel

l'urbanisme [illegible]

– l'urb est pour les jeunes
pas " "

Urb = la manifestation dans le réel de la conscience d'une nation.

ministère URB
CEPU

Grandeur
Splendeur et imagination – le civisme.
architecture et urbanisme = éclat français
création nécessaire d'un centre de préparation à l'urbanisme

Conclusion
[illegible]
forme de l'Urb
Science à 3 dimensions
des cubes bâtis
(une définition totale)

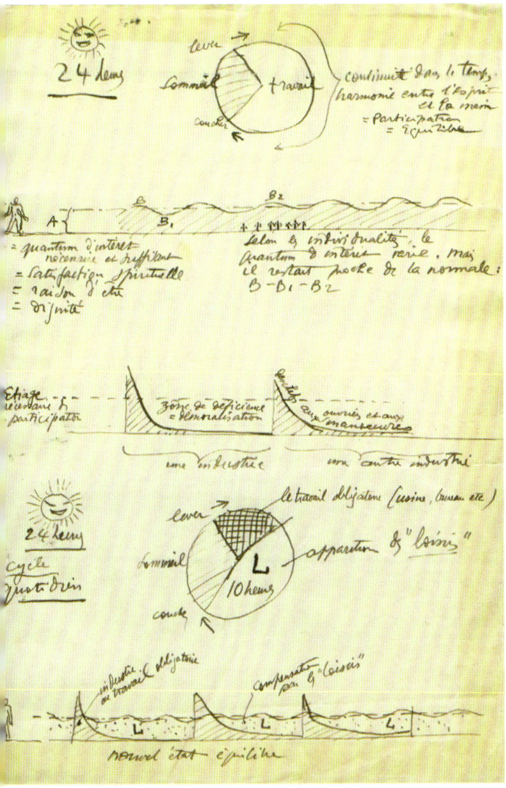

24 heures
lever
sommeil
travail
coucher
continuité dans le temps,
harmonie entre l'esprit et la main
= participation
= équilibre

A B B1 B2
= quantum d'intérêt nécessaire et suffisant
= satisfaction spirituelle
= raison d'être
= dignité

selon les individualités, le quantum d'intérêt varie, mais il restant proche de la normale: B – B1 – B2

Étiage nécessaire de participation
zone de déficience = démoralisation
ouvriers et aux manœuvres
une industrie
une autre industrie

24 heures
cycle quotidien
le travail obligatoire (usine, bureau etc)
lever
sommeil
coucher
L
10 heures
apparition des "loisirs"

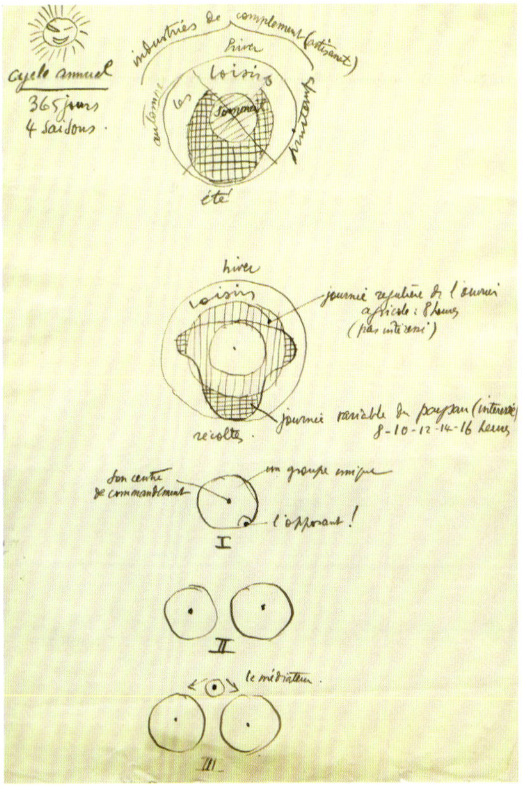

industrie de travail obligatoire
compensation par les "loisirs"
L L L
nouvel état équilibre

cycle annuel
365 jours
4 saisons
industries de complément (artisanat)
hiver
loisirs
sommeil
automne
printemps
été

hiver
loisirs
journée régulière de l'ouvrier agricole: 8 heures (pas intéressé)
journée variable du paysan (intéressé) 8-10-12-14-16 heures
récolte

son centre de commandement
un groupe unique
l'opposant!
I
II
le médiateur
III

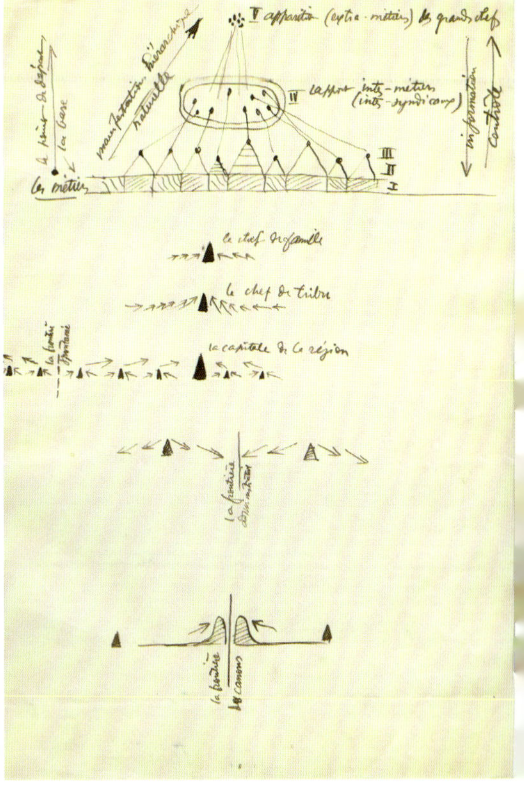

V apparition (sortie métiers) des grands chefs
manifestation hiérarchie naturelle
la trame de départ
la base
les métiers
IV rapport inter-métiers (inter-syndicats)
III
II
I
information
contrôle

le chef de famille
le chef de tribu
la capitale de la région
la frontière
la frontière
la frontière des cantons

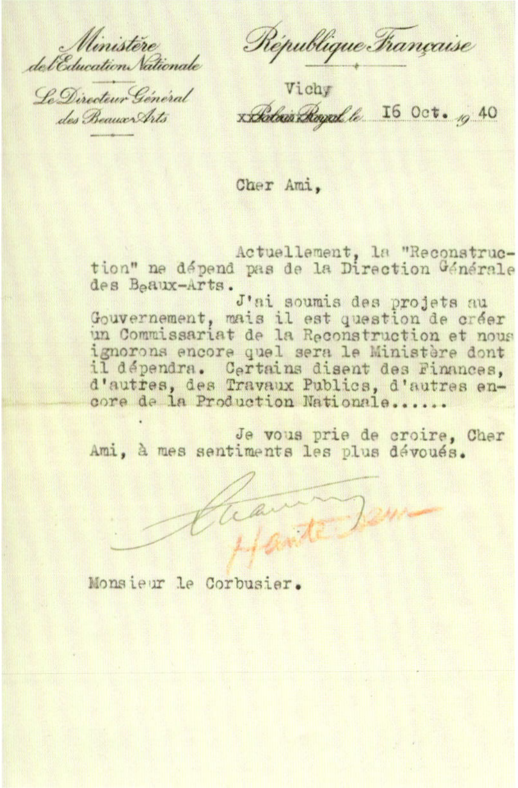

An unsuccessful collaboration: Life in Vichy, France, 1941–42

In January 1941 Le Corbusier and Yvonne moved to the French spa town of Vichy, which had become the seat of Prime Minister Philippe Pétain's collaborationist government

in the so-called Free Zone of France. For decades after the war, Le Corbusier would be haunted by his association with the Vichy government.

Ministère de l'Éducation Nationale
Le Directeur Général des Beaux-Arts

République Française

Vichy ~~Palais-Royal~~, le 16 Oct. 1940

Cher Ami,

Actuellement, la "Reconstruction" ne dépend pas de la Direction Générale des Beaux-Arts.

J'ai soumis des projets au Gouvernement, mais il est question de créer un Commissariat de la Reconstruction et nous ignorons encore quel sera le Ministère dont il dépendra. Certains disent des Finances, d'autres, des Travaux Publics, d'autres encore de la Production Nationale......

Je vous prie de croire, Cher Ami, à mes sentiments les plus dévoués.

Hautecœur

Monsieur le Corbusier.

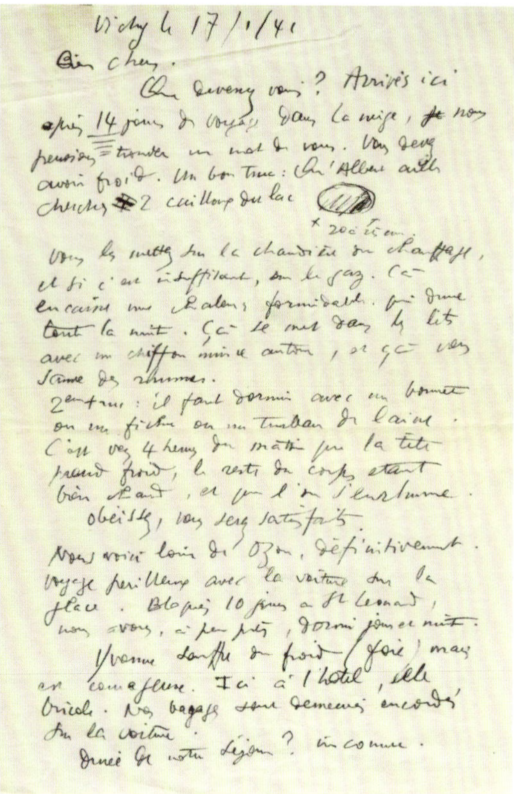

"Here we are a long way from Ozon, for good. Perilous journey in the car on the ice... Length of our stay? unknown."

—Letter to his mother and brother, from Vichy, France, 17 January 1941

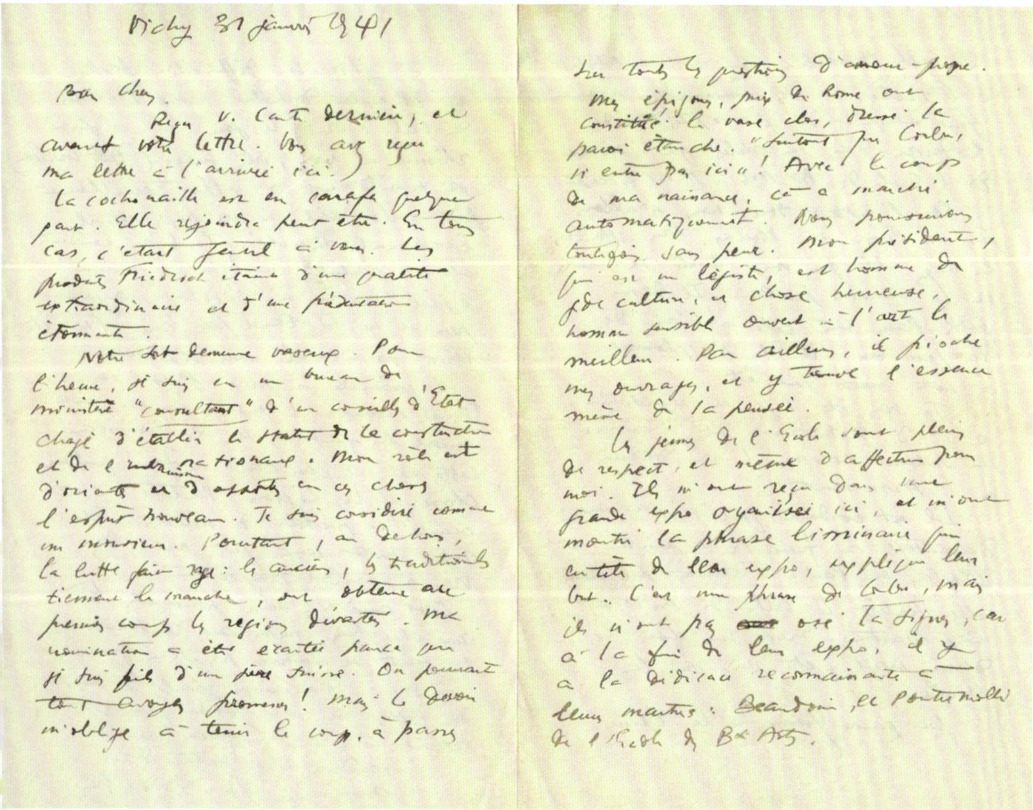

Above left. General Director of Fine Arts to Le Corbusier, Vichy, 16 October 1940, about establishing a Ministry of Reconstruction for the Vichy government

Above right. First page of letter from Le Corbusier to his mother and brother, from Vichy, 17 January 1941, about coping with the cold and Yvonne's illness

Left. First two pages of a letter from Le Corbusier to his mother and brother, from Vichy, 31 January 1941, about the difficulties of reconstruction plans for the Vichy government

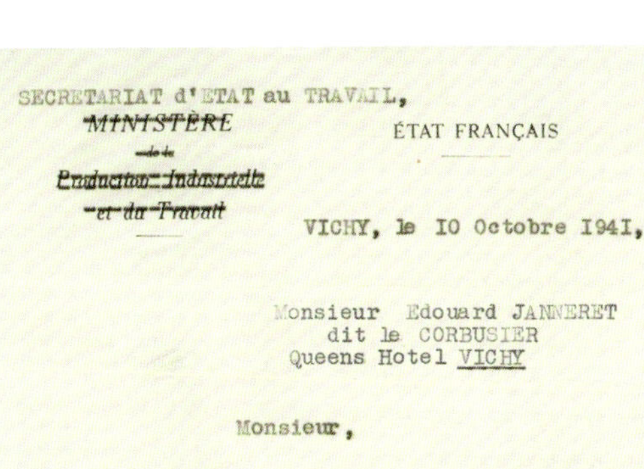

SECRETARIAT d'ETAT au TRAVAIL,
~~MINISTERE de la Production Industrielle et du Travail~~

ÉTAT FRANÇAIS

VICHY, le 10 Octobre 1941,

Monsieur Edouard JANNERET
dit le CORBUSIER
Queens Hotel VICHY

Monsieur,

J'ai le plaisir de vous faire connaître que la demande de laissez passer que vous aviez présentée le 20 septembre a été acceptée.

Ci-joint, le laissez passer en question.

Croyez Monsieur, à l'assurance de ma parfaite considération.

Le Chef de Cabinet,

Cycliste

Secrétariat d'État au Travail

AUSWEIS

CABINET SECRÉTARIAT D'ÉTAT AU TRAVAIL

Monsieur Edouard JEANNERET
dit Le CORBUSIER

QUEENS Hotel

VICHY

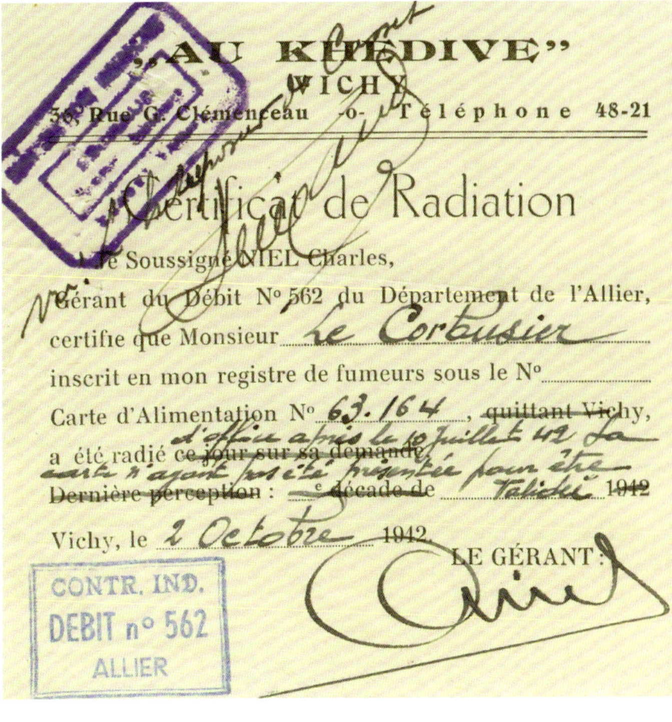

„AU KHÉDIVE"
VICHY
36, Rue G. Clémenceau -o- Téléphone 48-21

Certificat de Radiation

Je Soussigné NIEL Charles,
Gérant du Débit N° 562 du Département de l'Allier,
certifie que Monsieur *Le Corbusier*
inscrit en mon registre de fumeurs sous le N°
Carte d'Alimentation N° *63.164*, ~~quittant Vichy~~,
a été radié *d'office après le 10 juillet 42 la carte n'ayant pas été présentée pour être validée* ~~ce jour sur sa demande~~.
Dernière perception : ~~e décade de~~ 1942
Vichy, le *2 Octobre* 1942.

LE GÉRANT :

CONTR. IND.
DEBIT n° 562
ALLIER

Top left and middle left. Secretary of State for Labor to Le Corbusier, Vichy, 10 October 1941, approving his application for a travel permit

Above right. Certificate of Le Corbusier's removal from Vichy's food rationing roster, 2 October 1942

Below left. Letter from the office of Philippe Pétain to Le Corbusier, 4 November 1942, confirming a meeting with a Monsieur Lallemant, member of the Vichy cabinet

Below right. Le Corbusier's permit to travel from Paris to Vienna, c. 1942

DÉLÉGATION GÉNÉRALE
DU
GOUVERNEMENT FRANÇAIS
DANS LES
TERRITOIRES OCCUPÉS

SECRÉTARIAT PARTICULIER
DU
MARÉCHAL PÉTAIN

8, BOULEVARD DES INVALIDES (7e)
INVALIDES : 71-52 & 71-53

Paris, le 4 Novembre 1942

Monsieur,

Monsieur LALLEMANT, du Cabinet Civil du Maréchal à Vichy serait très heureux de vous rencontrer demain jeudi vers 9 heures, chez vous.

Si ce rendez-vous ne pouvait avoir lieu, nous vous serions obligés de bien vouloir nous téléphoner à l'adresse ci-dessus, à moins que vous ne puissiez répondre directement au garde, porteur de ce pli.

Je vous prie de croire, Monsieur, à l'expression de mes sentiments distingués.

Le Chargé de mission au Secrétariat particulier du MARÉCHAL de FRANCE, CHEF de l'ÉTAT
et par son ordre,

Monsieur LE CORBUSIER, 24,rue Nungesser & Coli, Paris

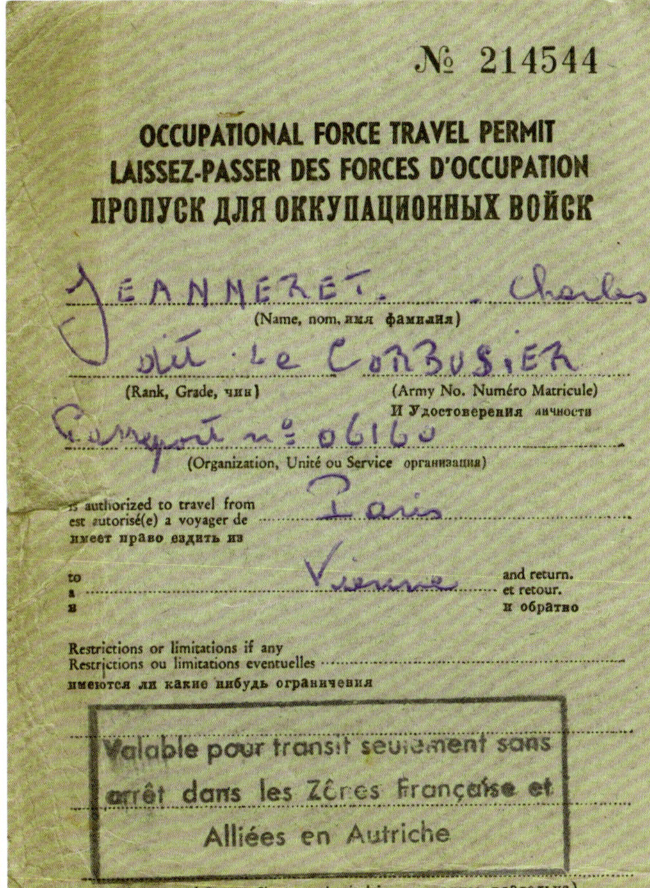

№ 214544

OCCUPATIONAL FORCE TRAVEL PERMIT
LAISSEZ-PASSER DES FORCES D'OCCUPATION
ПРОПУСК ДЛЯ ОККУПАЦИОННЫХ ВОЙСК

JEANNERET. Charles
(Name, nom, имя фамилия)

dit Le CORBUSIER
(Rank, Grade, чин) (Army No. Numéro Matricule)
И Удостоверения личности

Passeport n° 06160
(Organization, Unité ou Service организация)

is authorized to travel from
est autorisé(e) a voyager de
имеет право ездить из Paris

to
a
в Vienne
and return.
et retour.
и обратно

Restrictions or limitations if any
Restrictions ou limitations eventuelles
имеются ли какие нибудь ограничевия

Valable pour transit seulement sans arrêt dans les Zônes Française et Alliées en Autriche

(Signature of Bearer, Signature du titulaire, подпись владельца)

COLLECTION PRÉLUDES « THÈMES PRÉPARATOIRES A L'ACTION »

LE CORBUSIER

DESTIN DE PARIS

Destin de Paris and _Sur les quatre routes_, 1941

In 1941 Le Corbusier published two volumes that demonstrate how he had begun thinking about the future of France during the uncertainty of the Vichy regime. Both *Destin de Paris* (Destiny of Paris) and *Sur les quatre routes* (*The Four Routes*) articulated a rather ominous vision of a France where architectural planning policies would be dictated by a single powerful individual. Concurrent with the publication of these volumes, Le Corbusier attempted to revive the Plan Obus as the way forward for Vichy urban planning at home and in Algiers.

Ozon le 31 oct 1940

LE CORBUSIER

SUR LES 4 ROUTES

—

Depuis des années que le problème de l'urbanisme est, en quelque sorte à l'ordre du jour, jamais il n'a été exposé dans son ensemble.

De ce fait il est ignoré et du public et des professionnels et souvent même des autorités.

Le dernier livre de Le Corbusier vient donc à son heure.

Ecrit en automne 1939, un an avant la défaite ce livre auquel l'auteur n'a pas jugé devoir changer une ligne, démontre l'urgence des tâches à accomplir une fois la paix revenue.

Tâches gigantesques qui se doivent de résoudre l'équipement d'une civilisation ayant tourné la page et pour laquelle tout peut, tout doit être préparé sous peine de retomber, une fois de plus, dans la plus complète incohérence, car non seulement les cadres sont inexistants et les responsabilités mal définies, mais en outre le trouble le plus grand règne dans les idées puisqu'il s'agit de marier ce qu'il y a de valable dans le passé avec les exigences impérieuses de la vie nouvelle, deux éléments on ne peut plus contradictoires, sur lesquels néanmoins il est indispensable de se mettre d'accord.

Mais cet accord ne saurait intervenir si le public le plus vaste est tenu en marge du débat et s'il manque des éléments essentiels d'information lui permettant de se formuler à lui même une opinion. Lui ouvrir les yeux, lui montrer de quoi il s'agit - rien de moins que de son bonheur ou de son malheur - tel est le but poursuivi par Le Corbusier dans son livre qui ne manquera pas de soulever de nombreuses et violentes polémiques, trop de gens aujourd'hui comme hier ayant intérêt à ce que rien ne change, car les ennemis de la révolution architecturale sont les mêmes que ceux de la Révolution nationale, à ce point qu'on peut dire qu'il n'y aura pas de Révolution nationale sans révolution architecturale.

—

Top. Cover of *Destin de Paris* (Destiny of Paris), Paris/Clermont-Ferrand, Sorlot, 1941

Middle left and bottom. Le Corbusier to his mother, from Ozon, France, 31 October 1940, writing about his recently completed book, *Destin de Paris*

Middle right. Text for a radio presentation about *Sur les quatre routes* (*The Four Routes*), c. 1942, Gallimard, Paris, 1941

Right. Cover and selected pages from *Sur les quatre routes*, 1941

Bottom. Front and back of a postcard from French physician and scientist Alexis Carrel, to Le Corbusier, 19 February 1942. Carrel, an advocate of eugenics and euthanasia, was close to the Vichy government. He tells Le Corbusier that he would be "very interested" in reading *Sur les quatre routes*: "As you know, I attach a very great importance to the effect of the surroundings upon the human being."

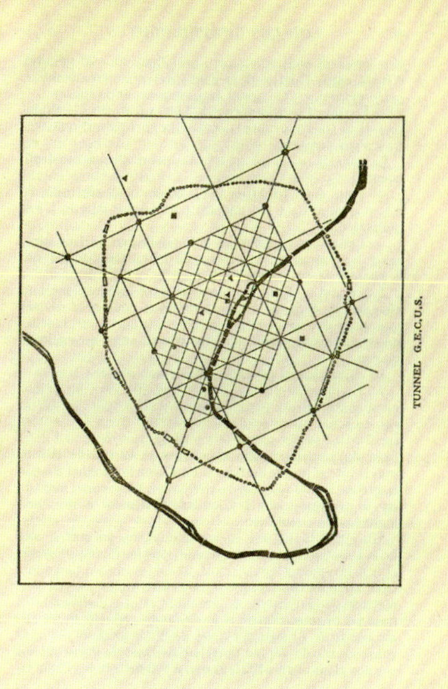

pas l'exil dans les banlieues sordides du Bourget ou de Croydon ; à Rio, les avions descendent du ciel sur le front même de la ville.

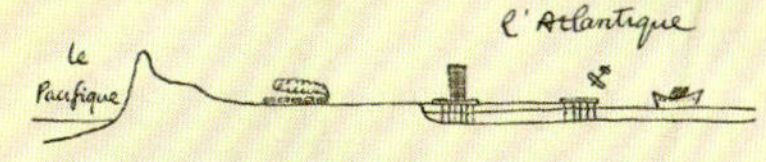

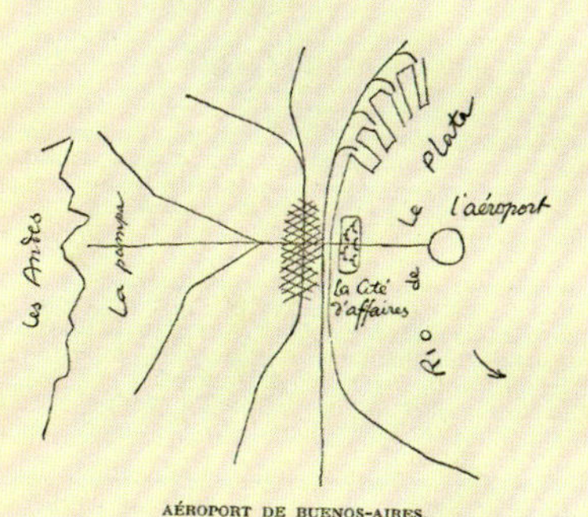

AÉROPORT DE BUENOS-AIRES.

A Buenos-Aires, en 1929, cherchant devant mon public où bien placer les quatre routes, je pensai *géographie* et *monde* et je tirai de cette pensée et des lignes qui l'expriment, le lieu de leur croisement fatidique : en un endroit

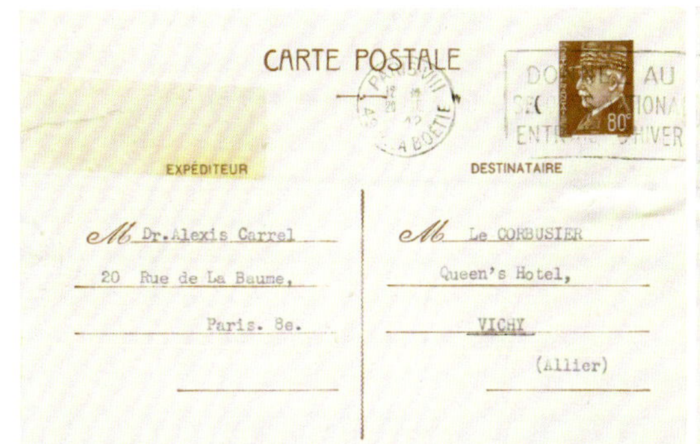

Cher Monsieur, Paris, 19/2/42.

J'ai bien reçu votre carte et je serai très intéressé par la lecture de votre dernier ouvrage "Sur les 4 Routes" que vous devez me faire parvenir par l'intermédiaire de la N.R.F. Ainsi les 4 livres que vous pensez terminer prochainement compléteront, sans nul doute, vos travaux entrepris depuis tant d'années, sur l'urbanisme et l'architecture, et je vous félicite de l'ardeur que vous ne cessez de consacrer à ces problèmes.

Parmi ses diverses activités, la Fondation Française pour l'Etude des Problèmes Humains se propose de dégager quelques règles essentielles d'habitation, et j'attache, comme vous le savez, une très grande importance à l'influence du milieu sur l'être humain.

Les temps présents posent de nombreux problèmes, et nous devons les étudier très profondément avant d'apporter les remèdes indispensables.

Croyez, cher Monsieur, à mes sentiments les meilleurs.

Green designs for a modern factory: L'Usine Verte (unbuilt), 1940–44

Though not yet completely disillusioned by the politics of the Vichy government, Le Corbusier became increasingly frustrated with the bureaucratic obstacles that prevented the realization of his building projects. A commission (never built) for an ammunitions factory in 1940, in Moutiers-Rozeille, France, led the architect to develop a concept for a healthier, more joyous work environment: the Usine Verte (Green Factory). This new kind of factory would restore dignity to workers by providing them with access to sun, space, and greenery, or in his words, "restore nature's conditions to work."

Above. Schematic site plan with circulation routes, Usine Verte, 1944

Below. Site plan

Opposite, top. Site plan, showing the surrounding green landscape

Opposite, bottom. Bird's-eye perspective

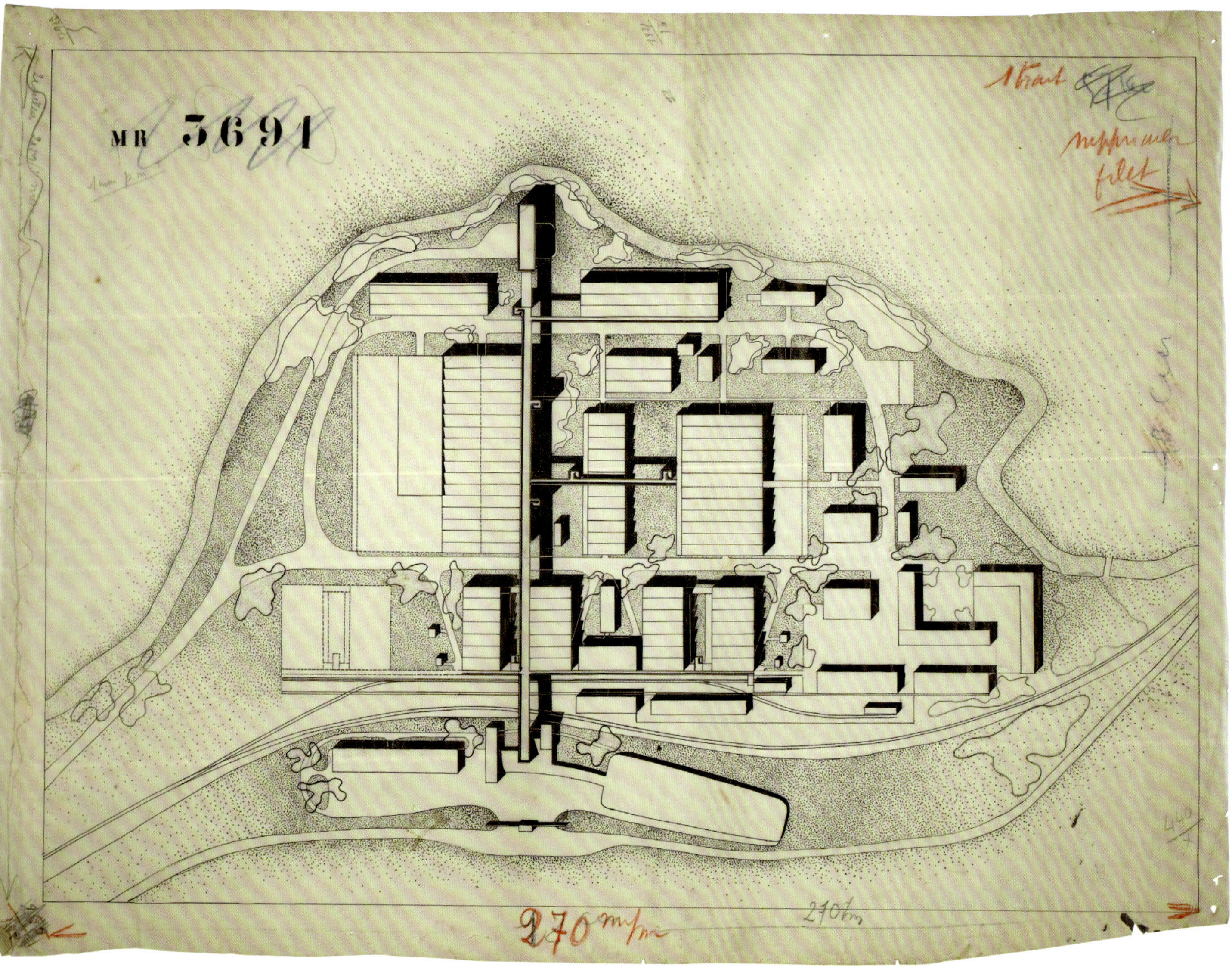

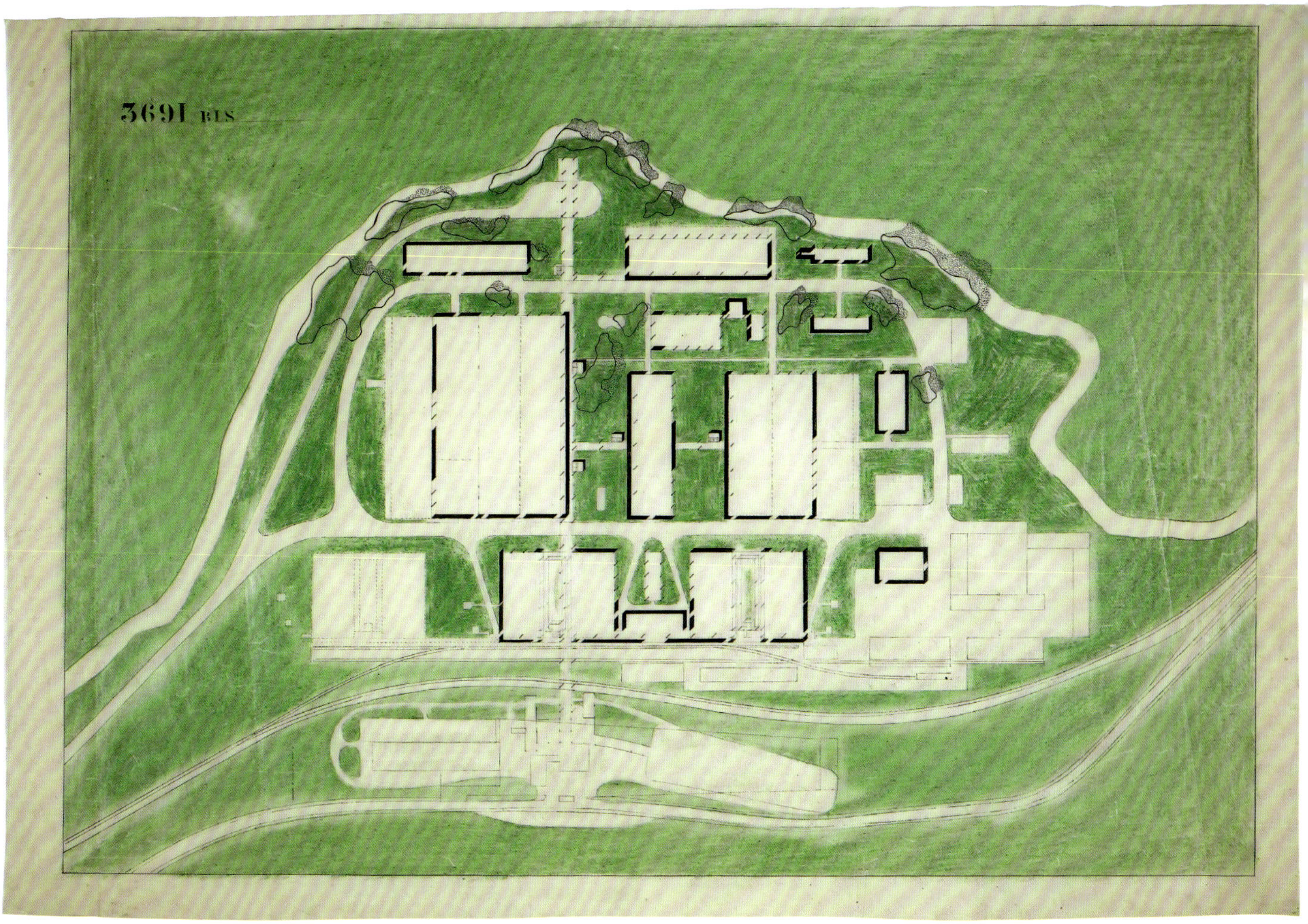

3691 BIS

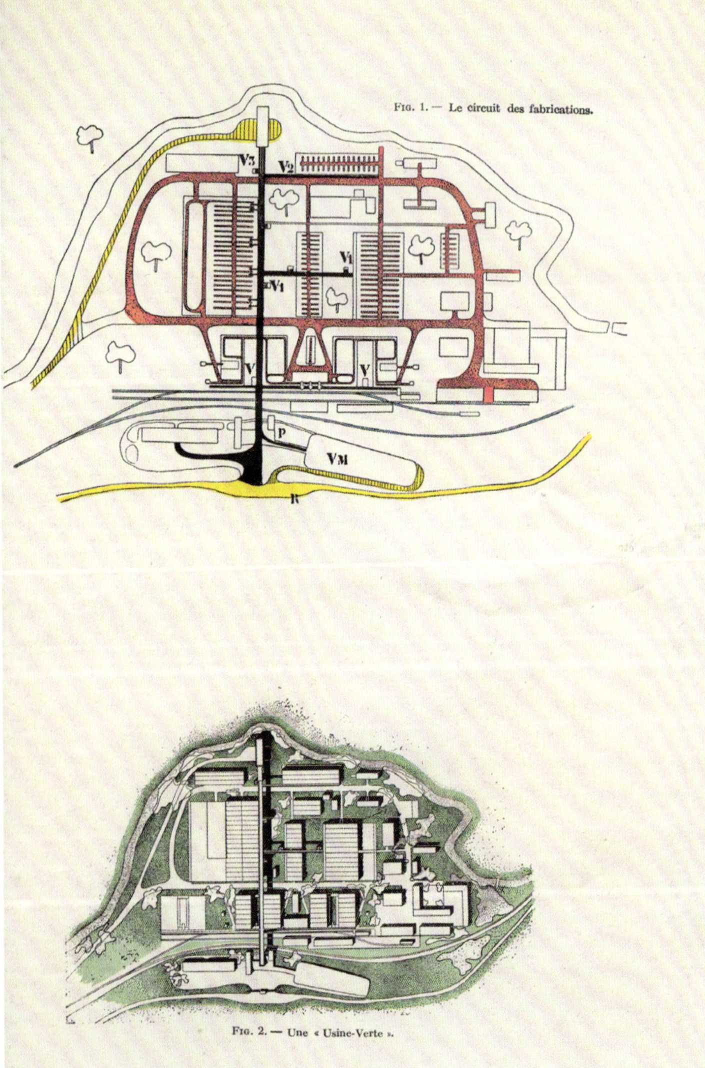

Fig. 3. — Un établissement industriel de grandeur conforme (Un grand moulin).

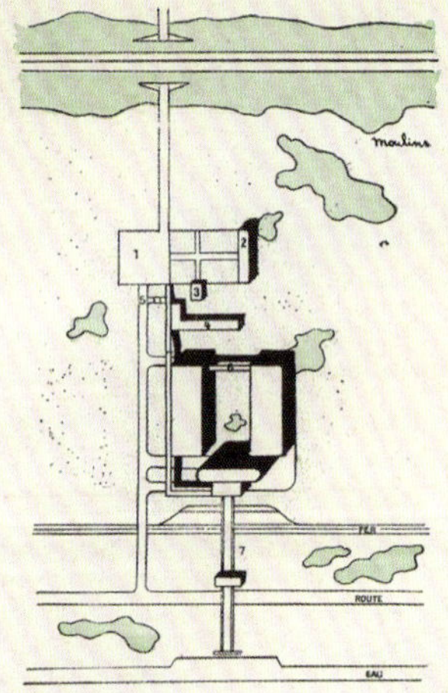

1. Parquement : vélos, motos, autos.
2. Administration.
3. Services sociaux.
4. Réfectoires.
5. Pointage.
6. Les ateliers, etc.
7. Le transbordeur.

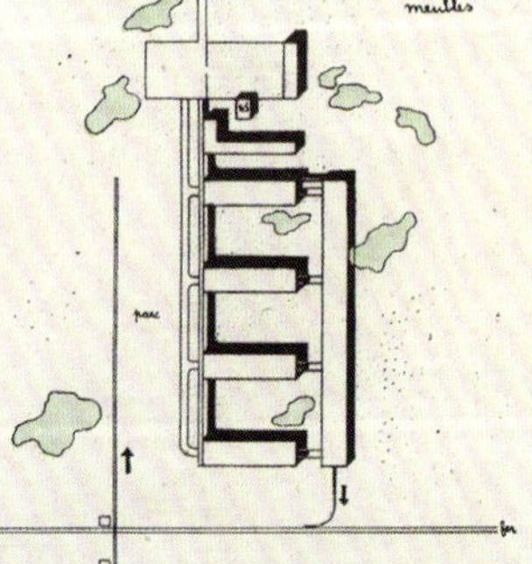

Fig. 4 — Un établissement industriel de grandeur conforme (Manufacture de meubles).

Above. Drawing contrasting a typical "Black Factory," at left, with Le Corbusier's proposed "Green Factory," c. 1944

Left. Plans and details from Le Corbusier's "L'Usine Verte: Work-place Architecture," published in the journal *Hommes et techniques*, July 1945

Opposite, top left. Le Corbusier's hand-written notes describing plans for a "green factory" and a forthcoming publication, *La maison des hommes* (The House of Men), 22 July 1941

Opposite, top right, middle, and bottom. Le Corbusier's "L'Usine Verte: Workplace Architecture," extracted from *Les trois établissements humains* (*The Three Human Establishments*),

Formes et couleurs, Lausanne, 1944

Pendant la guerre, double Mark of Time (ingénieur)
Le Corbusier fut chargé comme (chef de groupe)
de la construction de la grande cartoucherie d'Aubusson (3000 ouvriers)
pour laquelle il établit les plans modèle d'usine moderne (circulation indépendante des produits et de celle du personnel ouvrier) Type de "usine-verte" répondant des conditions de travail exceptionnellement favorable. Le bâtiment n'a pas été achevé.

Après une retraite (dans la solitude [illegible]), il a pris la direction de [illegible] par les problèmes de reconstruction [illegible] qui pouvaient être envisagés.

Chargé d'une mission temporaire, il a participé à la création d'un service d'État précisément voué à cet objet : "Comité d'études de l'habitation et de la construction immobilière" (décret du 27 mai 1941 signé du Maréchal Pétain)

Pendant les six mois de sa mission, avec deux jeunes anciens camarades, François de Pierrefeu et André Boll, il a mis au point une "doctrine du domaine bâti de la France". Cette doctrine va paraître dans un volume signé de François de Pierrefeu et de Le Corbusier intitulé « La maison des hommes », ouvrage qui sera certainement traduit en plusieurs langues et particulièrement en USA, espérons-le (1)

Cette doctrine envisage la société moderne dans les fonctions qui manifestent son activité par l'architecture et

(1) À la suite de son voyage d'études en USA, Le Corbusier avait fait paraître à Paris (Édition Plon et Cie) un livre exprimant les réactions personnelles en face de l'événement américain : "Quand les cathédrales étaient blanches", livre traduit à New York [illegible]

Architecture des lieux de travail

L'USINE VERTE

par LE CORBUSIER

L'usine est un grand établissement affecté à la fabrication de produits. On y transforme en objets la matière première ou seconde. Les machines sont maîtresses, porteuses d'infiniment plus de puissance, de vitesse, d'exactitude que les mains des hommes. Les métaux, les pâtes, les fibres, les grains, les liquides, les gaz y subissent des manipulations et des combinaisons. Le bruit, voire le vacarme, les trépidations, la poussière, les odeurs, voire les puanteurs, y entretiennent une atmosphère parfois démoniaque à laquelle s'ajoutent les flammes et la chaleur, les fumées et les buées.

La lumière tombe des toitures ou des grandes baies, rayonnant des températures froides ou chaudes selon la saison.

Les machines réalisent l'exagération de tous les gestes humains, atteignant souvent à la grimace : broyage et mastication, pilonnage, roulage, étirage, soufflage et martelage. Tant de gesticulation impressionne. Parfois, des lenteurs de géants : les grands marteaux pilons, les grandes presses ; parfois des vitesses d'êtres dangereux : serpents ou éclairs, galops et glissades ; des membres fantasques ou maniaques partout profilent leurs gestes inquiétants.

Sur eux, sur le sol, sur les murs et les charpentes, la poussière et les déchets se répandent.

Et ainsi de suite et de fil en aiguille, le travail moderne a institué des conditions hors de l'humain, bien faites pour agir sur le comportement des gens partageant l'aventure des machines. Réactions morales et physiques. De ces conditions anormales, l'homme ne peut supporter les effets que d'une partie seulement. Les autres le dominent, l'asservissent, le molestent.

Si bien que le travail moderne pourrait, à une certaine lumière, être considéré comme la grande pénitence, la rançon de quelque crime, inconsciemment perpétré.

Charge qui pèse sur notre société moderne, le travail, dans l'esprit de beaucoup, apparaît comme un châtiment.

En opposition à ce tableau décevant peut être entreprise la description joyeuse, enthousiaste et stimulante du travail moderne, placé par l'effet des dispositions inventées de toutes pièces, dans les conditions les plus dignes, en plein accord avec le respect dû à la personne humaine. Car le travail moderne peut donner à ceux qui l'accomplissent le sentiment de sa grandeur, la perception de sa beauté.

Si tout est à régler encore, sur le plan social, relativement à la juste interprétation des droits et devoirs du travail, les constructeurs doivent, sans tarder, prendre en charge l'aménagement des lieux de production : l'occupation utile du sol, les réserves rurales, les cités d'industrie, leur texture, les lieux d'échange, enfin, la biologie de leurs circulations, de l'assemblage de leurs bâtiments, l'efficience de ceux-ci.

Et particulièrement en ce qui concerne l'industrie, l'usine des cent années du premier cycle machiniste, l'usine noire pourra être remplacée par « l'Usine Verte ».

M. Le Corbusier nous a réservé la publication de cette étude qui est extraite d'un livre à paraître aux Éditions Denoël, ayant pour titre : "Les trois établissements humains". Cet ouvrage est publié sous l'égide de "Urbanisme des C.I.A.M." (Congrès Internationaux des Architectes Modernes) et appartient à la collection Ascoral (Association des Constructeurs pour le Renouvellement Architectural).

DÉFINITION DE « L'USINE VERTE »

L'Usine Verte réinstalle à nouveau autour du travail les « conditions de nature ». Soleil, espace, verdure (1) apportent ici, comme dans les quartiers de résidence (2), les influences cosmiques, la réponse aux pulsations du poumon, la vertu de l'air, ainsi que la présence de ce milieu naturel qui présida à la longue et minutieuse élaboration de l'être humain.

Une telle intention pourra paraître présomptueuse. Est-il bien nécessaire, possible, de mettre en jeu, dans la dure vie du travail quotidien, des éléments de distraction, voire même d'introduire dans l'implacable rigueur du travail moderne des facteurs de détente, plus encore, par des dispositions précises et préméditées, d'introduire la joie de vivre ? Il s'agit, en fait, de transformer radicalement, de contrition en joie vaillante, ce temps de la vie qui en est le plus long, qui en occupe la part la plus vaste, le temps du travail : heures, journées, années, vie. Ici s'insère la tâche la plus vraie incombant à la civilisation machiniste.

C'est une question d'éthique, une décision de l'esprit, l'adoption d'un point de vue. Les moyens sont tous présents, à la disposition de l'élaborateur du plan.

D'une part, le logis retrouve par des aménagements décisifs ses conditions de nature ; le travail en fait de même, sans pour cela provoquer la moindre gêne, entraîner la moindre perte. Au contraire, l'harmonie est un facteur d'efficience dans la production.

(1) Charte d'Athènes des CIAM.

(2) Travaux des Sections 3a, 3b et 3c de l'ASCORAL : *Une Science du logis* (équipement domestique, normalisation et construction, industrialisation).

DESCRIPTION DE « L'USINE VERTE »

Il s'agit ici, plus précisément, d'une grande usine de guerre, construite pour l'Armement dans des délais optimes, en 1940, et malheureusement stoppée par la défaite de juin.

Le ministre de l'Armement avait manifesté le désir que des soins particuliers fussent apportés à l'élaboration des plans et qu'une intention s'y manifestât pour servir éventuellement d'usine-pilote, en cas de réussite, aux entreprises industrielles suivantes.

Une grande part des établissements industriels actuels est caractérisée par un certain désordre troublant la succession naturelle des opérations. Une règle peut s'y opposer, coordonnant toutes choses dans le temps et dans l'espace. Une expression l'illustre bien : la chaîne, qualifiant, en effet, un véritable système imposé aux fabrications pour en solidariser toutes les phases, mais se contentant aussi d'imaginer, sous ce vocable, la contiguïté et la continuité des opérations d'une fabrication.

Rigueur acquise par une sévère organisation du travail et qui deviendra l'armature même de l'Usine Verte.

On l'a dit, « l'Usine Verte » prétend à introduire dans cette discipline matérielle un facteur moral éminent : la joie de vivre. Celle-ci est bannie par le désordre.

Le tyranneau diabolique du désordre ne manque pas une occasion d'agir ; il suffit que l'occasion lui en soit fournie par des dispositions malencontreuses de bâtiments et d'accès, par exemple, la rupture des continuités ou l'existence inopportune des surfaces de routes, rues, esplanades, allées, etc., ne servant à rien, à rien d'autre qu'à devenir prétextes à promenades incontrôlables du personnel, à circulation incontrôlable de produits ou de matière, à entreposage d'un provisoire vite promu définitif de toutes sortes de résidus : roues cassées, poutrelles ou poitrails, pièces lourdes ou légères de mécaniques fatiguées, etc., tous objets qui vont acquérir des droits de séjour à l'ancienneté, au pied des bâtiments, dans l'herbe, ou sur l'asphalte ou le sable des avenues.

Une "Usine Verte" de 3.000 ouvriers environ.

Pour bannir le désordre, il suffit de lui interdire l'accès (question de circulations) d'espaces déclarés *a priori* inoccupables (question de disposition réciproque des bâtiments).

Ces espaces seront déclarés inoccupables, afin que personne ni quoi que ce soit ne s'y puisse rendre ou installer. Ces espaces seront donc affectés à une fonction hors de la fabrication ; ce seront des espaces architecturaux et paysagistes tout ensemble.

On estime donc que le travail s'effectuera dans une ambiance préparée, réservée ou aménagée, faite des perspectives heureuses des bâtiments sortant des gazons ou de l'herbe, de plantations d'arbres, et des découpures heureuses du ciel.

Précisons encore :

La suite des opérations de fabrication peut être ordonnée selon une ligne continue, véritable voie de transport à sens unique où tout rebroussement est évité. Cette voie de transport unique va, par des dispositions habiles, mériter son qualificatif : faite d'une piste dure et lisse de ciment, installée à travers les territoires de l'usine, donc à travers les herbages, elle recevra exclusivement les wagonnets électriques ou autres, transportant les produits depuis la bascule réceptrice des matières premières, les hangars qui abritent celles-ci, les ateliers et les halls de transformation, jusqu'au magasin des produits terminés et le quai de leur embarquement. Cette piste relie un bâtiment à un autre ; à l'intérieur des ateliers, elle s'est ramifiée, desservant chaque machine.

Toutes les opérations se font au sol, sur le sol, à même le béton de la piste ou l'aire des ateliers. Ce circuit matières et marchandise est absolument interdit au personnel, ouvriers ou autres.

Quel est donc le cheminement prescrit à ceux-ci ? Et tout d'abord, d'où viennent-ils ?

Ils viennent de chez eux par la route qui passe devant la porte de l'usine.

Où vont-ils ? Au garage des vélos, motos, autos ; au pointage, à l'entrée de l'usine, et de là, sans perdre une minute en alternatives diverses, ils se rendent à leur travail, c'est-à-dire chacun à sa place, devant sa machine, après avoir passé aux vestiaires et lavabos.

En fin de journée, ils feront le chemin inverse. En cours de journée, certains auront pu être appelés aux services centraux de l'administration ou auront eu à se rendre aux services sociaux (assistantes, médecin, etc.). Ils ne divagueront pas, pour cela, dans l'usine ou alentour.

L'itinéraire qui vient d'être décrit reproduit étonnamment les phases d'un circuit sanguin ou lymphatique dans le corps d'un être organisé. Sa forme expressive, ponctuellement ramifiée, est celle d'un tronc avec ses branches, forme économie d'effort s'il en est, sobre, concise, rigoureusement exacte. Nous sommes loin, dès lors, du quadrillage traditionnel des rues ou avenues qui sert presque toujours de lit aux circulations dans les usines, — circulations confondues des matières, des produits, des ouvriers, du personnel et des cadres.

Trois schémas vont donc, pour l'établissement industriel que nous analysons ici, permettre d'illustrer la théorie des Usines-Vertes.

LE CIRCUIT DES MATIÈRES PREMIÈRES

Rappelons tout d'abord succinctement l'essentiel de la fabrication ici considérée.

Trois matières premières essentielles y sont consommées : le plomb, le laiton, l'acier.

L'acier est requis plus encore par les nécessités de l'outillage.

Par ailleurs, les explosifs sont stockés dans une poudrière située loin de l'usine, et ils n'y viennent que par petites livraisons, heure par heure.

Les aciers, plombs et laitons, arrivés par fer, sont déchargés et pesés en A.P.L. La piste de béton part de là et s'en va en P1, au hangar des plombs, en A1 et L1, au dépôt des aciers et laitons ; elle se ramifie pour entrer en P2 dans l'atelier de façonnage, en A2 au chromage, à l'atelier d'outillage, à l'atelier de précisions, à l'atelier de mécanique ; en L2 à l'autre atelier de façonnage ; ayant servi les diverses machines, elle poursuit sa route en P3 et en L3 aux ateliers de chargement, d'étiquetage et d'empaquetage.

Elle finit enfin en P4 L4 au magasin ouvrant sur le quai d'embarquement du chemin de fer. Sur cette piste de béton ne roulent que des wagonnets électriques ; hormis leurs conducteurs, aucune personne (ouvriers ou employés) n'y doit circuler. La piste est coulée dans les herbages et son tablier compact et dur rejette toute mauvaise herbe.

Le circuit des matières.

CIRCUIT DU PERSONNEL

(ouvriers et employés)

Trois mille cinq cents ouvriers, ouvrières et employés viennent par la route à l'usine, au cours de la journée (voir planche couleurs, fig. 1).

VM est le garage de leurs vélos et motos ou autres.

P est le pointage d'entrée.

S, l'accès aux services sociaux (assistantes sociales, médecin et réfectoire), bâtiment faisant vis-à-vis à P.

A partir de là, la piste quitte le sol, restant à peu près horizontale, tandis que celui-ci s'abaisse vers la rivière.

La piste se transforme donc en passerelle à niveau des toitures des ateliers (sheds). Cette passerelle est close par des parois et un plafond : c'est un tube carré.

En V, la passerelle se ramifie, et des escaliers conduisent aux vestiaires des ateliers de chargement. En V1, même opération alimentant les ateliers de façonnage et de mécanique. En V2, l'outillage est desservi. En V3 enfin, le bâtiment d'administration.

On peut dire que là où passent les hommes doivent passer aussi les alimentations en lumière, en eau, en chauffage. Par conséquent, la passerelle sera tout en même temps l'abri des canalisations de lumière, d'eau et de chauffage. Celles-ci se trouveront alignées sous plafond, visibles, accessibles facilement. Elles aussi, pour remplir utilement leurs fonctions, suivent la route la plus économe.

Des vestiaires situés en entre-sol, le personnel descendra aux lavabos à rez-de-chaussée dont les nombreuses portes ouvrent de plain-pied sur les ateliers.

La piste du personnel est indiquée en noir plein sur le dessin.

Le circuit des wagonnets électriques est indiqué en rouge.

Enfin, marquée de hachures, la piste automobile, avec son aire de parquage, dessert directement le bâtiment d'administration.

Ce schéma des circulations est révolutionnaire, correspondant aux propositions de l'urbanisme moderne des grandes villes dans lequel doit se réaliser utilement la séparation du piéton et de l'automobile.

Ces circulations expriment la plus stricte économie. Elles procèdent du dedans au dehors, discipline qui est celle même de la vie.

PLAN DE MASSES DE L'ÉTABLISSEMENT INDUSTRIEL CONÇU EN "USINE VERTE"

Les bâtiments sont disposés selon les nécessités du terrain et les exigences de la fabrication ; leurs formes, leurs dimensions sont, chaque fois, proportionnées aux fonctions. La lumière est largement et systématiquement distribuée dans les ateliers par des dispositifs appropriés.

Mais, par place, des baies verticales seront ouvertes, quand le soleil ne gênera pas, sur des perspectives paysagistes judicieusement réservées ou aménagées. Les espaces entre les bâtiments et les murailles de ceux-ci constitueront des ensembles harmonieux avec de vastes étendues de ciel et des perspectives sur les lointains. L'herbe est au pied même de ces vitrages ouverts sur la campagne : les arbres sont maintenus et d'autres sont plantés pour habiller le site (voir planche couleurs, fig. 2).

L'une des parois de la passerelle est vitrée, offrant ce spectacle agreste aux foules qui y circulent.

L'administration ouvre ses trois étages sur le cours de la rivière.

... Des baies verticales seront ouvertes sur des perspectives paysagistes.

TOUT EST ORDONNÉ ET PROPRE

Les charges de l'entretien sont assumées par la nature même, ce qui est rassurant : cet entretien est fait d'herbages, de feuilles ou de ramures changeant au cours des saisons.

Les objecteurs n'ont plus qu'un argument : les fenêtres des ateliers seront sales et brisées, ainsi qu'il est d'usage depuis cent ans dans l'industrie.

Réponse : Déjà Bata, en Tchécoslovaquie, a entouré de verdure les bâtiments de ses manufactures dont les fenêtres sont rigoureusement entretenues, aussi propres que celles d'une demeure.

On sent bien que le monde moderne prenant possession de ses outils de travail, au cours de la grande mutation présente, a déjà tourné le dos à cette cruelle indifférence du XIXe siècle machiniste qui nous a valu les villes tentaculaires, les villes noires de suies, l'épouvante du machinisme.

★

Tel est un exemple tout à fait occasionnel d'usine verte. Occasion fournie par l'exceptionnel temps de guerre, démonstration qui devait servir d'exemple. La débâcle arrêta les travaux en cours d'exécution.

Le principe peut être considéré comme recommandable et servir de jalon lors de la constitution des cités linéaires industrielles.

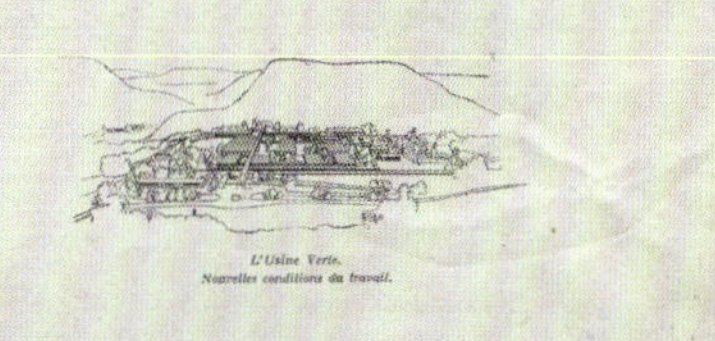

L'Usine Verte.
Nouvelles conditions du travail.

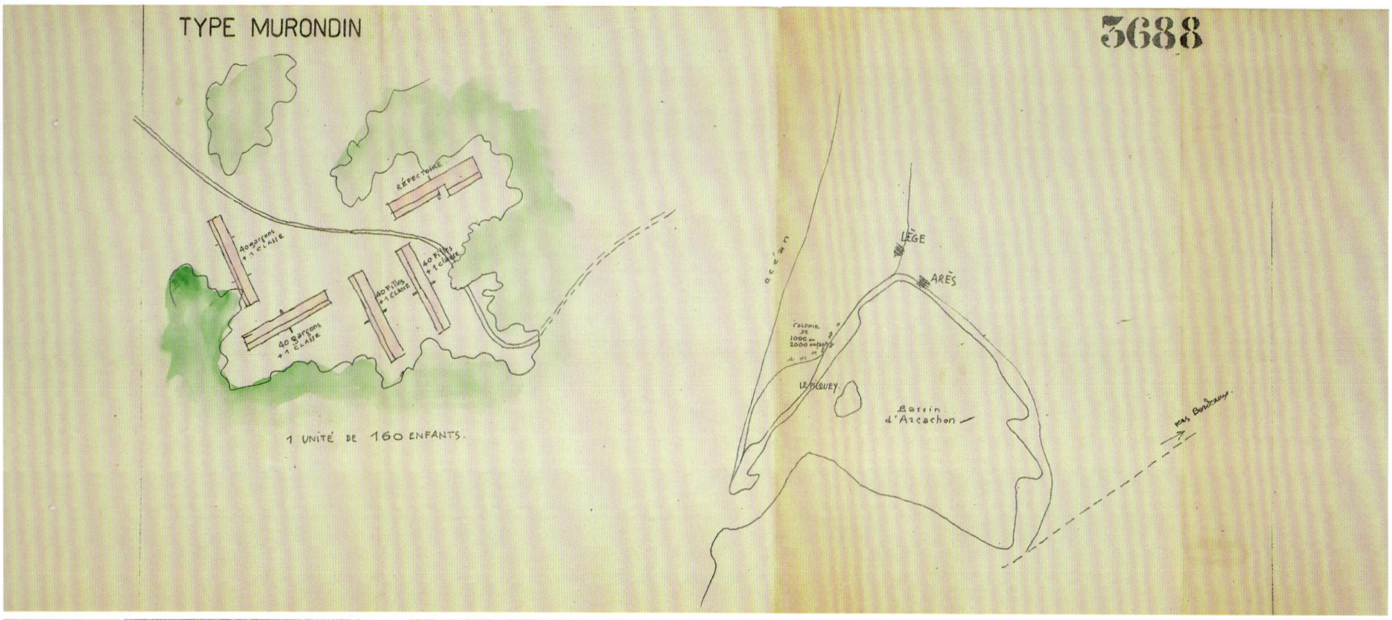

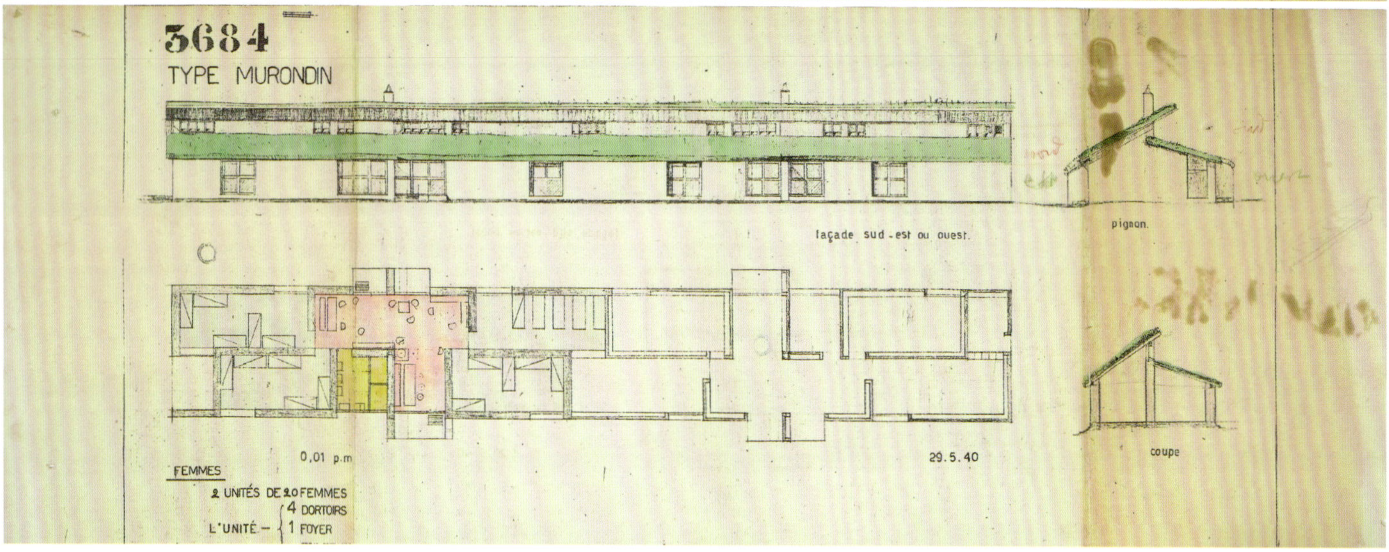

TYPE MURONDIN

3688

1 UNITÉ DE 160 ENFANTS.

3684

TYPE MURONDIN

façade sud-est ou ouest.

pignon.

coupe

0,01 p.m

29.5.40

FEMMES

2 UNITÉS DE 20 FEMMES

L'UNITÉ – 4 DORTOIRS
1 FOYER

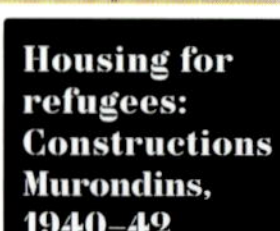

Housing for refugees: Constructions Murondins, 1940–42

While working for the Vichy government, Le Corbusier developed a scheme for making easily assembled buildings that he called "Constructions Murondins" (an invented word combining *mur* [wall] with *rondin* [log]). The simple structures—made of adobe, logs, and tin roofs—were intended as standardized housing for war refugees, to be erected by members of the Vichy youth corps.

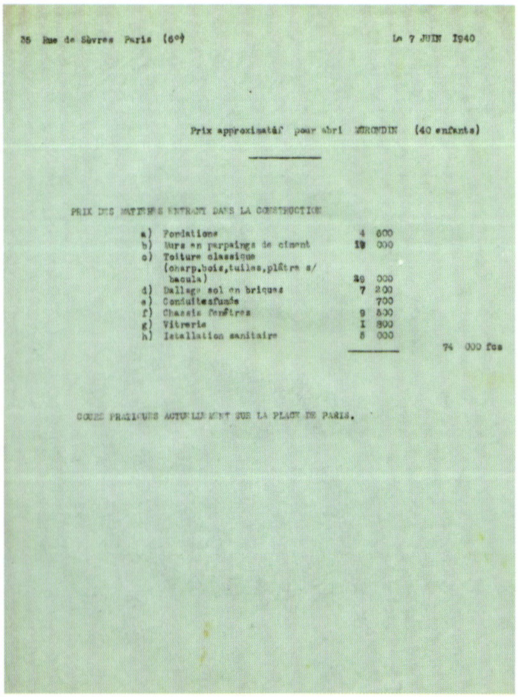

35 Rue de Sèvres Paris (6e) Le 7 JUIN 1940

Prix approximatif pour abri MURONDIN (40 enfants)

PRIX DES MATIÈRES ENTRANT DANS LA CONSTRUCTION

a)	Fondations	4 000
b)	Murs en parpaings de ciment	19 000
c)	Toiture classique (charp.bois,tuiles,plâtre s/ bacula)	29 000
d)	Dallage sol en briques	7 200
e)	Conduitesfumée	700
f)	Chassis fenêtres	9 500
g)	Vitrerie	I 800
h)	Istallation sanitaire	5 000
		74 000 fcs

COURS PRATIQUÉS ACTUELLEMENT SUR LA PLACE DE PARIS.

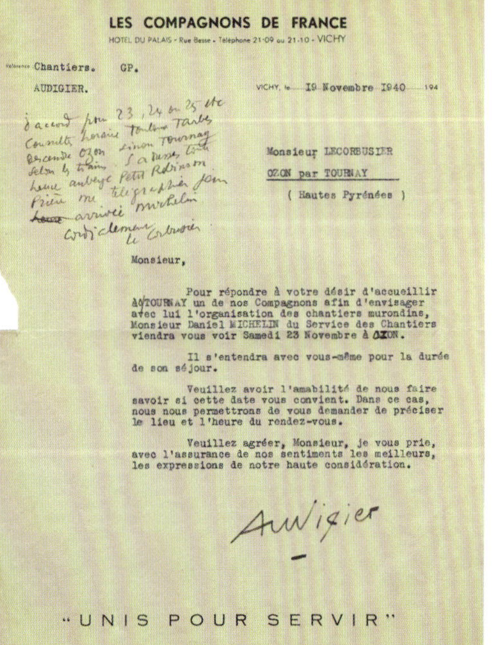

LES COMPAGNONS DE FRANCE

HOTEL DU PALAIS - Rue Besse - Téléphone 21-09 ou 21-10 - VICHY

Référence Chantiers. GP.
AUDIGIER.

VICHY, le 19 Novembre 1940

Monsieur LECORBUSIER
OZON par TOURNAY
(Hautes Pyrénées)

Monsieur,

Pour répondre à votre désir d'accueillir à TOURNAY un de nos Compagnons afin d'envisager avec lui l'organisation des chantiers murondins, Monsieur Daniel MICHELIN du Service des Chantiers viendra vous voir Samedi 23 Novembre à OZON.

Il s'entendra avec vous-même pour la durée de son séjour.

Veuillez avoir l'amabilité de nous faire savoir si cette date vous convient. Dans ce cas, nous nous permettrons de vous demander de préciser le lieu et l'heure du rendez-vous.

Veuillez agréer, Monsieur, je vous prie, avec l'assurance de nos sentiments les meilleurs, les expressions de notre haute considération.

Audigier

"UNIS POUR SERVIR"

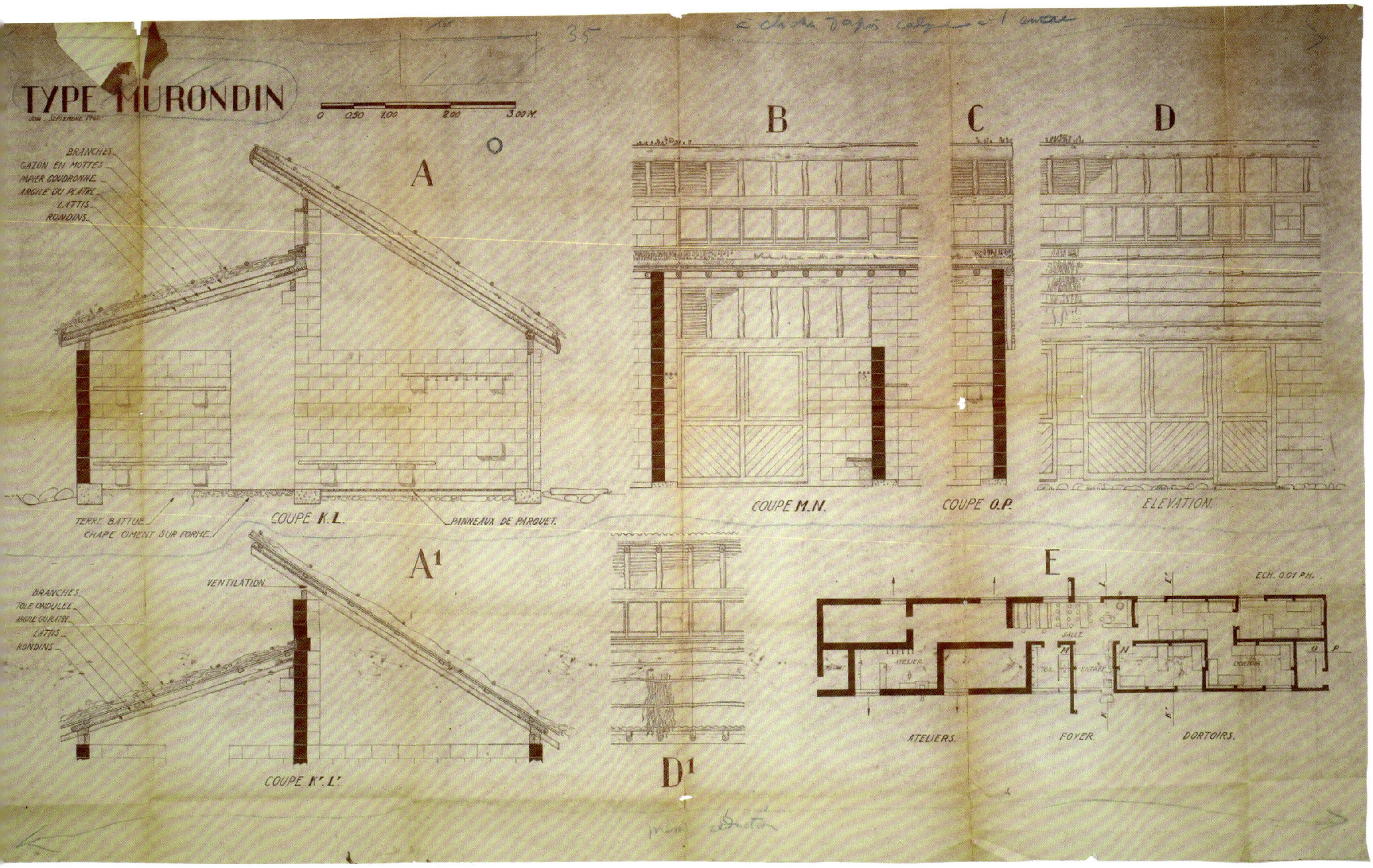

pposite, top. Site an, 5 June 1940, urondin housing r 160 children ear Arcachon, rance

pposite, middle. levations, plan, nd section, 29 May 1940, Murondin housing for twenty women

Opposite, bottom left. Cost estimates, dated 7 June 1940, for Murondin housing for forty children

Opposite, bottom right. Architect Raymond Audigier to Le Corbusier, 19 November 1940. In response to Le Corbusier's request, Audigier writes that one of the "Compagnons de France" (Companions of France, a Vichy youth organization) will meet with Le Corbusier to help him plan the Murondin building sites.

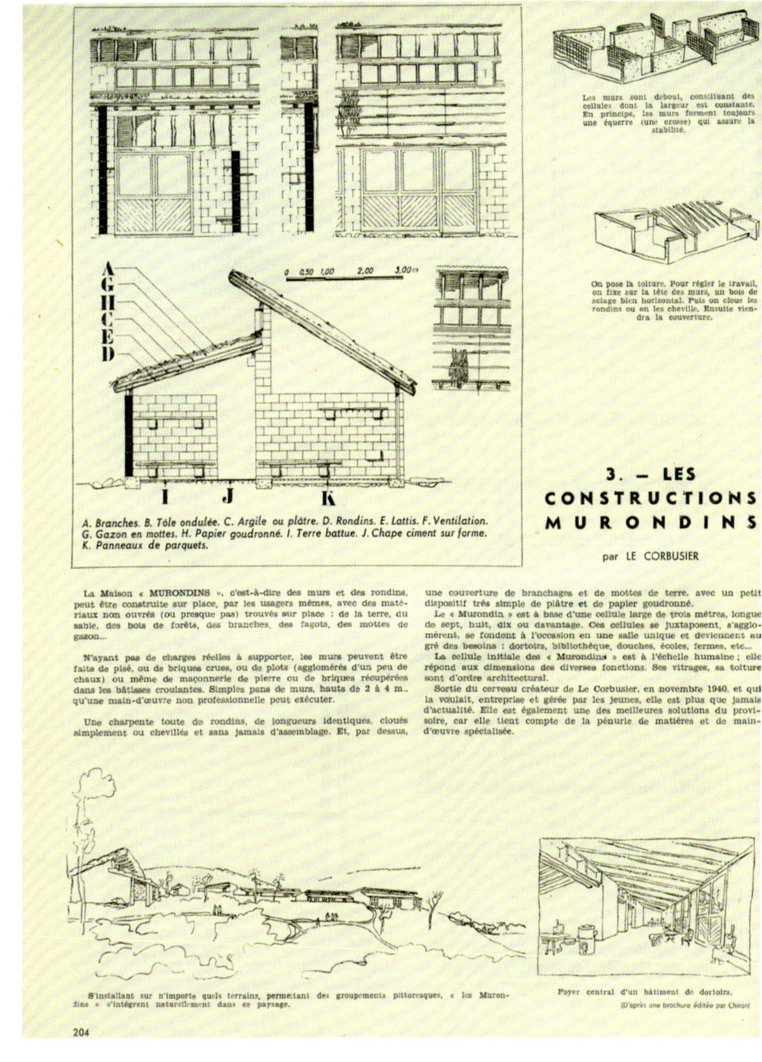

A. Branches. B. Tôle ondulée. C. Argile ou plâtre. D. Rondins. E. Lattis. F. Ventilation. G. Gazon en mottes. H. Papier goudronné. I. Terre battue. J. Chape ciment sur forme. K. Panneaux de parquets.

Les murs sont debout, constituant des cellules dont la largeur est constante. En principe, les murs forment toujours une équerre (une crosse) qui assure la stabilité.

On pose la toiture. Pour régler le travail, on fixe sur la tête des murs, un bois de sciage bien horizontal. Puis on cloue les rondins ou on les cheville. Ensuite viendra la couverture.

3. — LES CONSTRUCTIONS MURONDINS

par LE CORBUSIER

La Maison « **MURONDINS** », c'est-à-dire des murs et des rondins, peut être construite sur place, par les usagers mêmes, avec des matériaux non ouvrés (ou presque pas) trouvés sur place : de la terre, du sable, des bois de forêts, des branches, des fagots, des mottes de gazon...

N'ayant pas de charges réelles à supporter, les murs peuvent être faits de pisé, ou de briques crues, ou de plots (agglomérés d'un peu de chaux) ou même de maçonnerie de pierre ou de briques récupérées dans les bâtisses croulantes. Simples pans de murs, hauts de 2 à 4 m., qu'une main-d'œuvre non professionnelle peut exécuter.

Une charpente toute de rondins, de longueurs identiques, cloués simplement ou chevillés et sans jamais d'assemblage. Et, par dessus, une couverture de branchages et de mottes de terre, avec un petit dispositif très simple de plâtre et de papier goudronné.

Le « Murondin » est à base d'une cellule large de trois mètres, longue de sept, huit, dix ou davantage. Ces cellules se juxtaposent, s'agglomèrent, se fondent à l'occasion en une salle unique et deviennent au gré des besoins : dortoirs, bibliothèque, douches, écoles, fermes, etc...

La cellule initiale des « Murondins » est à l'échelle humaine ; elle répond aux dimensions des diverses fonctions. Ses vitrages, sa toiture sont d'ordre architectural.

Sortie du cerveau créateur de Le Corbusier, en novembre 1940, et qui la voulait, entreprise et gérée par les jeunes, elle est plus que jamais d'actualité. Elle est également une des meilleures solutions du provisoire, car elle tient compte de la pénurie de matières et de main-d'œuvre spécialisée.

S'installant sur n'importe quels terrains, permettant des groupements pittoresques, « les Murondins » s'intègrent naturellement dans ce paysage.

Foyer central d'un bâtiment de dortoirs.

(D'après une brochure éditée par Chiron)

204

Above. Sections, elevation, and plan showing construction details and materials, June September 1940

Right. Page from Le Corbusier's article "Les Constructions Murondins" published in *Techniques et architecture*, July 1945

CARTE POSTALE

EXPÉDITEUR

M. J. GROSPERRIN.
Délégué Départemental à
la Jeunesse
24 Rue Werly 24
BAR.LE.DUC.
(Meuse)

DESTINATAIRE

M. Etienne CHIRON
Editeur
8 Rue Rameau
CLERMONT.FERRAND.

Monsieur,

Votre brochure : " Les constructions Murondins par le Corbusier.

Ayant lu avec un très grand intérêt votre brochure, je vous serais obligé de me faire savoir à qui je puis m'adresser pour me procurer les plans, coupes, projets divers de constructions Murondins, spécialement pour les Maisons des Jeunes.

Attendant le plaisir de vous lire à ce sujet, je vous prie d'accepter, Monsieur, l'expression de mes sentiments distingués.

Above. Two sides of a postcard from J. Grosperrin, Delegate for Youth, Meuse, France, to Etienne Chiron, publisher of Le Corbusier's pamphlet *Les constructions "Murondins,"* 29 March 1942, seeking copies of drawings for Murondin housing for children

Below left. Sketches for cover and one page of *Les constructions "Murondins"*

Below right. Deputy Regional Commissioner, Lyon, France, to Etienne Chiron, 20 March 1942, saying he is "keenly interested" in *Les constructions "Murondins"*

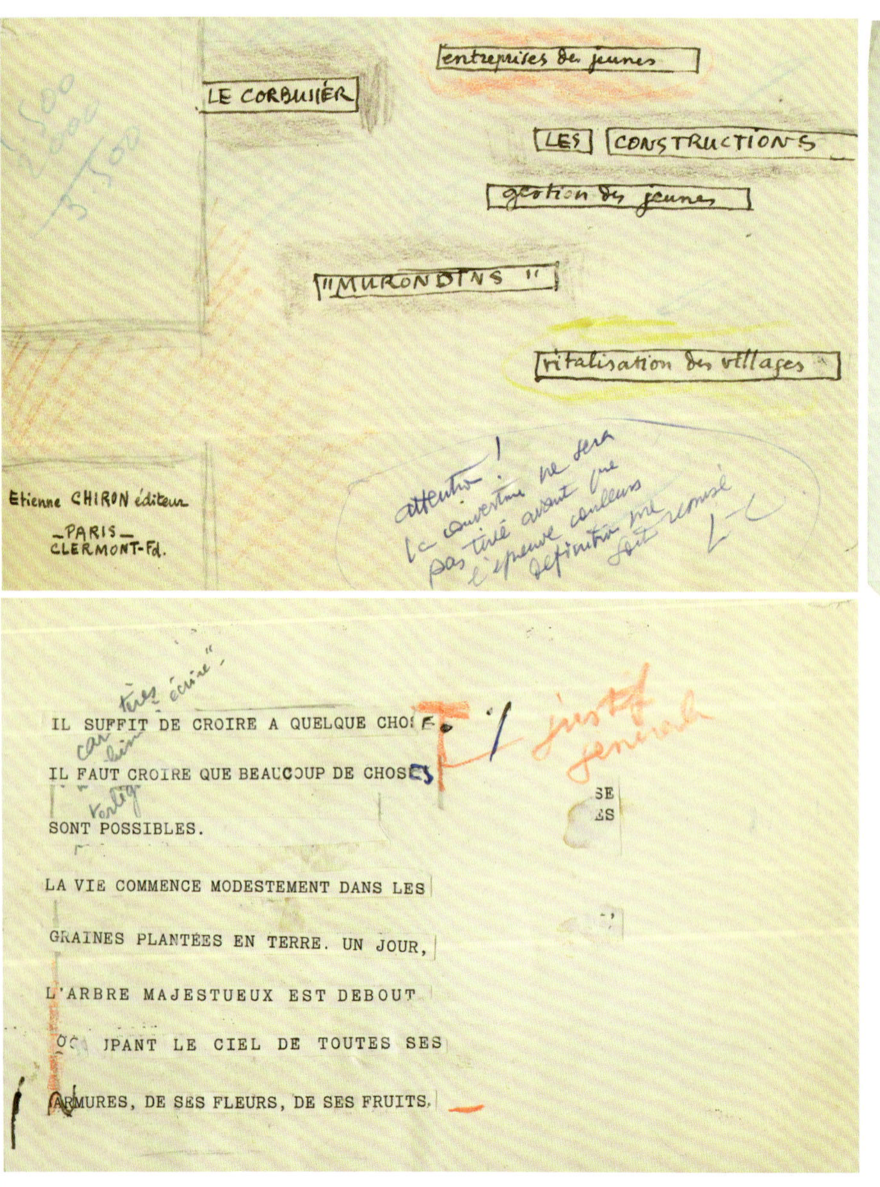

IL SUFFIT DE CROIRE A QUELQUE CHOSE
IL FAUT CROIRE QUE BEAUCOUP DE CHOSES
SONT POSSIBLES.
LA VIE COMMENCE MODESTEMENT DANS LES
GRAINES PLANTÉES EN TERRE. UN JOUR,
L'ARBRE MAJESTUEUX EST DEBOUT
OCCUPANT LE CIEL DE TOUTES SES
RAMURES, DE SES FLEURS, DE SES FRUITS.

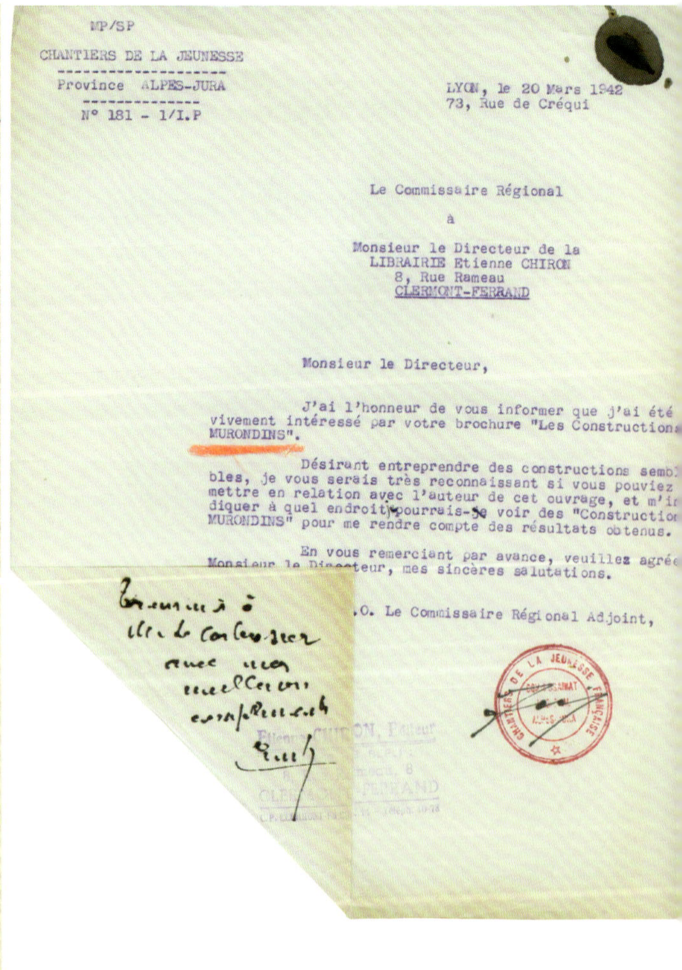

MP/SP
CHANTIERS DE LA JEUNESSE
Province ALPES-JURA
N° 181 - 1/I.P

LYON, le 20 Mars 1942
73, Rue de Créqui

Le Commissaire Régional
à
Monsieur le Directeur de la
LIBRAIRIE Etienne CHIRON
8, Rue Rameau
CLERMONT-FERRAND

Monsieur le Directeur,

J'ai l'honneur de vous informer que j'ai été vivement intéressé par votre brochure "Les Constructions MURONDINS".

Désirant entreprendre des constructions semblables, je vous serais très reconnaissant si vous pouviez mettre en relation avec l'auteur de cet ouvrage, et m'indiquer à quel endroit pourrais-je voir des "Constructions MURONDINS" pour me rendre compte des résultats obtenus.

En vous remerciant par avance, veuillez agréer Monsieur le Directeur, mes sincères salutations.

P.O. Le Commissaire Régional Adjoint,

LE CORBUSIER

entreprises des jeunes

LES CONSTRUCTIONS

manuel technique publié sous le patronage du Secrétariat Général de la Jeunesse

gestion par les jeunes

"MURONDINS"

vitalisation des villages

Etienne Chiron éditeur Paris - Clermont-Fd

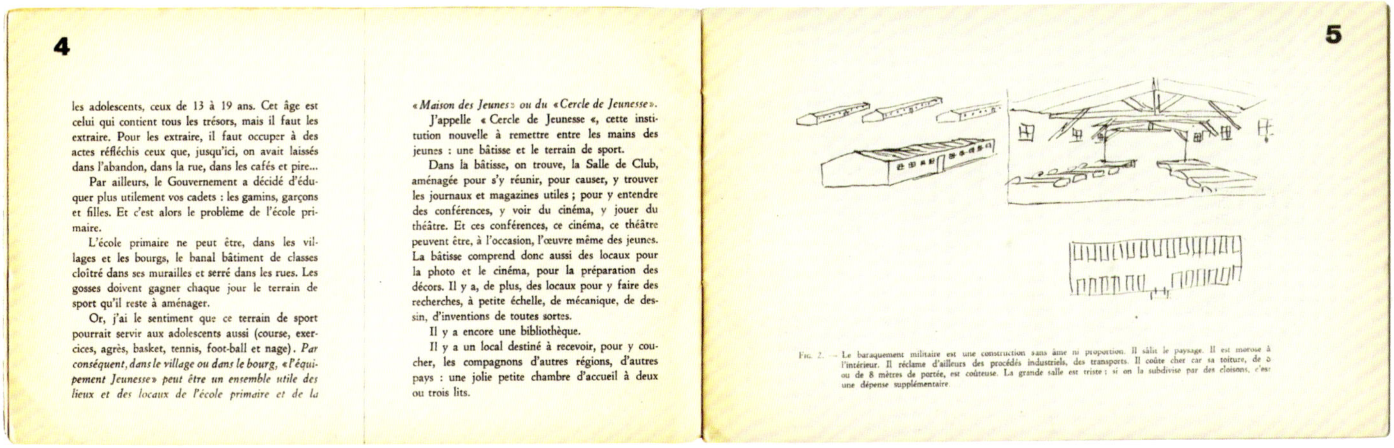

4

les adolescents, ceux de 13 à 19 ans. Cet âge est celui qui contient tous les trésors, mais il faut les extraire. Pour les extraire, il faut occuper à des actes réfléchis ceux que, jusqu'ici, on avait laissés dans l'abandon, dans la rue, dans les cafés et pire...

Par ailleurs, le Gouvernement a décidé d'éduquer plus utilement vos cadets : les gamins, garçons et filles. Et c'est alors le problème de l'école primaire.

L'école primaire ne peut être, dans les villages et les bourgs, le banal bâtiment de classes cloîtré dans ses murailles et serré dans les rues. Les gosses doivent gagner chaque jour le terrain de sport qu'il reste à aménager.

Or, j'ai le sentiment que ce terrain de sport pourrait servir aux adolescents aussi (course, exercices, agrès, basket, tennis, foot-ball et nage). *Par conséquent, dans le village ou dans le bourg, «l'équipement Jeunesse» peut être un ensemble utile des lieux et des locaux de l'école primaire et de la «Maison des Jeunes» ou du «Cercle de Jeunesse».*

J'appelle « Cercle de Jeunesse «, cette institution nouvelle à remettre entre les mains des jeunes : une bâtisse et le terrain de sport.

Dans la bâtisse, on trouve, la Salle de Club, aménagée pour s'y réunir, pour causer, y trouver les journaux et magazines utiles ; pour y entendre des conférences, y voir du cinéma, y jouer du théâtre. Et ces conférences, ce cinéma, ce théâtre peuvent être, à l'occasion, l'œuvre même des jeunes. La bâtisse comprend donc aussi des locaux pour la photo et le cinéma, pour la préparation des décors. Il y a, de plus, des locaux pour y faire des recherches, à petite échelle, de mécanique, de dessin, d'inventions de toutes sortes.

Il y a encore une bibliothèque.

Il y a un local destiné à recevoir, pour y coucher, les compagnons d'autres régions, d'autres pays : une jolie petite chambre d'accueil à deux ou trois lits.

5

Fig. 2. — Le baraquement militaire est une construction sans âme ni proportion. Il sâlit le paysage. Il est morose à l'intérieur. Il réclame d'ailleurs des procédés industriels, des transports. Il coûte cher car sa toiture, de 6 ou de 8 mètres de portée, est coûteuse. La grande salle est triste ; si on la subdivise par des cloisons, c'est une dépense supplémentaire.

12

Fig. 11. — Voici les matériaux de la toiture : on coupe du bois de défriche ; on en fait des rondins de dimension unique. Avec les branches, on prépare des lattis. Avec les brindilles, on fait des fagots. Par ailleurs, dans la prairie, on a découpé à la bêche, des mottes de gazon.

Fig. 12. — Voici, toutefois, quelques produits de scierie ou de grosse menuiserie, fabriqués en série quelque part, ou commandés à l'artisan du village ; des bastings sciés droits, le panneau standard des vitrages, la porte, les lucarnes.

13

Fig. 13. — On commence la bâtisse : une fouille en rigole, qu'on remplit d'un béton maigre. C'est le socle de la maison. On badigeonne au goudron pour éviter la montée de l'eau par porosité.

Cover and selected pages from *Les constructions "Murondins,"* Etienne Chiron, Paris/Clermont-Ferrand, 1942

"Sprung from the creative brain of Le Corbusier in November 1940, and taken up and managed by young people, as he wished, it is now more relevant than ever. It is also one of the best temporary solutions, in that it takes account of the shortage of materials and specialist manpower." —Les Constructions "Murondins," July 1945

Below. Le Corbusier and boy, Vichy stadium, 31 August 1941

Right. Secretary General of Fine Arts to Le Corbusier, from Vichy, 27 February 1942, noting his interest in Le Corbusier's writings and "campaigns"

Below right. First page of letter from Le Corbusier to Charles Trochu, president of the Paris City Council, 7 March 1942, concerning detailed reconstruction plans in Le Corbusiers's forthcoming book, *La maison des hommes* (The House of Men)

Opposite. Le Corbusier at home with his dog, Pinceau, 24 rue Nungesser-et-Coli, Paris, 1944

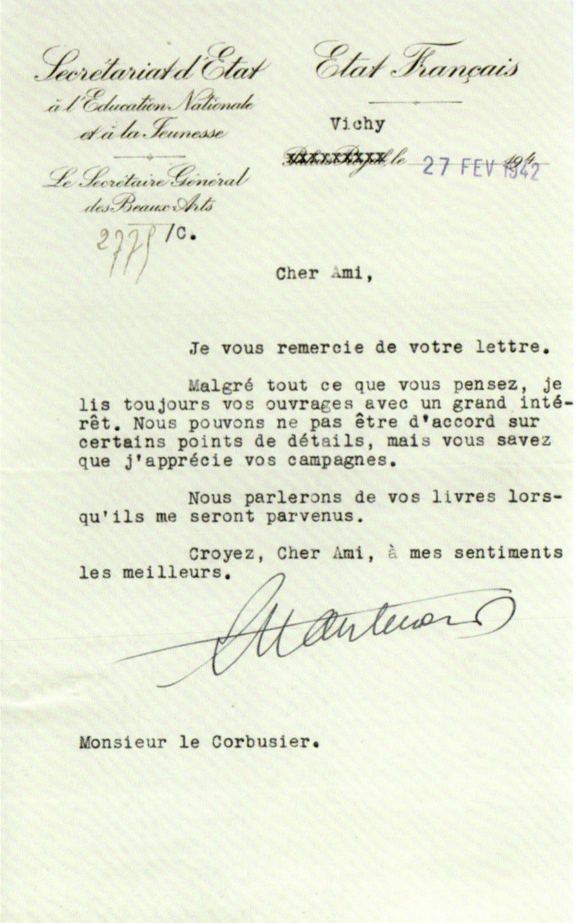

Secrétariat d'Etat à l'Education Nationale et à la Jeunesse

Le Secrétaire Général des Beaux Arts

2778 IC.

Etat Français

Vichy, le 27 FEV 1942

Cher Ami,

Je vous remercie de votre lettre.

Malgré tout ce que vous pensez, je lis toujours vos ouvrages avec un grand intérêt. Nous pouvons ne pas être d'accord sur certains points de détails, mais vous savez que j'apprécie vos campagnes.

Nous parlerons de vos livres lorsqu'ils me seront parvenus.

Croyez, Cher Ami, à mes sentiments les meilleurs.

Hautecœur

Monsieur le Corbusier.

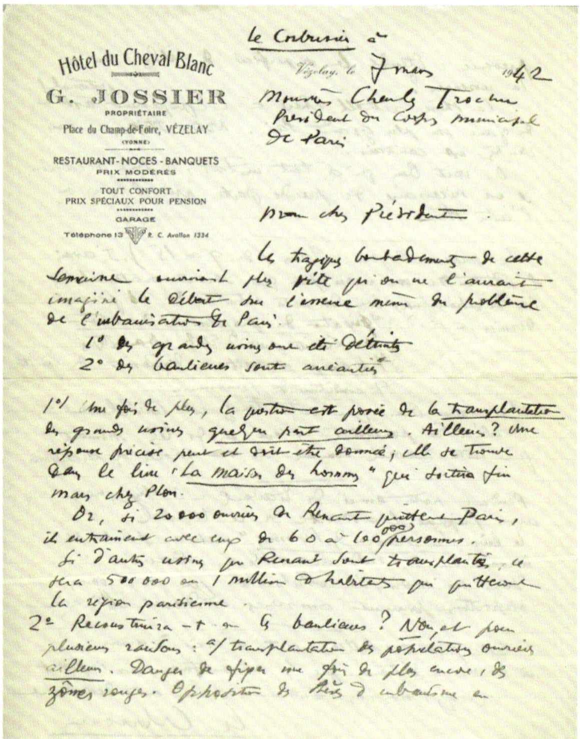

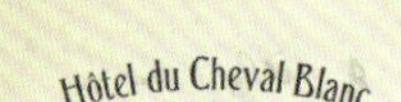

Hôtel du Cheval Blanc

G. JOSSIER

PROPRIÉTAIRE

Place du Champ-de-Foire, VÉZELAY (YONNE)

RESTAURANT-NOCES-BANQUETS

PRIX MODÉRÉS

TOUT CONFORT

PRIX SPÉCIAUX POUR PENSION

GARAGE

Téléphone 13 R. C. Avallon 1334

Le Corbusier à

Vézelay, le 7 mars 1942

Monsieur Charles Trochu
Président du Conseil municipal de Paris

Mon cher Président.

Les tragiques bombardements de cette semaine ouvriront plus vite qu'on ne l'aurait imaginé le débat sur l'essence même du problème de l'urbanisation de Paris.

1° des grandes usines ont été détruites
2° des banlieues sont anéanties

1° Une fois de plus, la question est posée de la transplantation des grandes usines quelque part ailleurs. Ailleurs? Une réponse précise peut et doit être donnée; elle se trouve dans le livre "La maison des hommes" qui sortira fin mars chez Plon.

Or, si 20 000 ouvriers de Renault quittent Paris, ils entraînent avec eux de 60 à 100 000 personnes.

Si d'autres usines que Renault sont transplantées, ce sera 500 000 ou 1 million d'habitants qui quitteront la région parisienne.

2° Reconstruira-t-on les banlieues? Non, et pour plusieurs raisons: a/ transplantation des populations ouvrières ailleurs. Danger de figer une fois de plus encore, des zones rouges. Opposition des lois d'urbanisme au

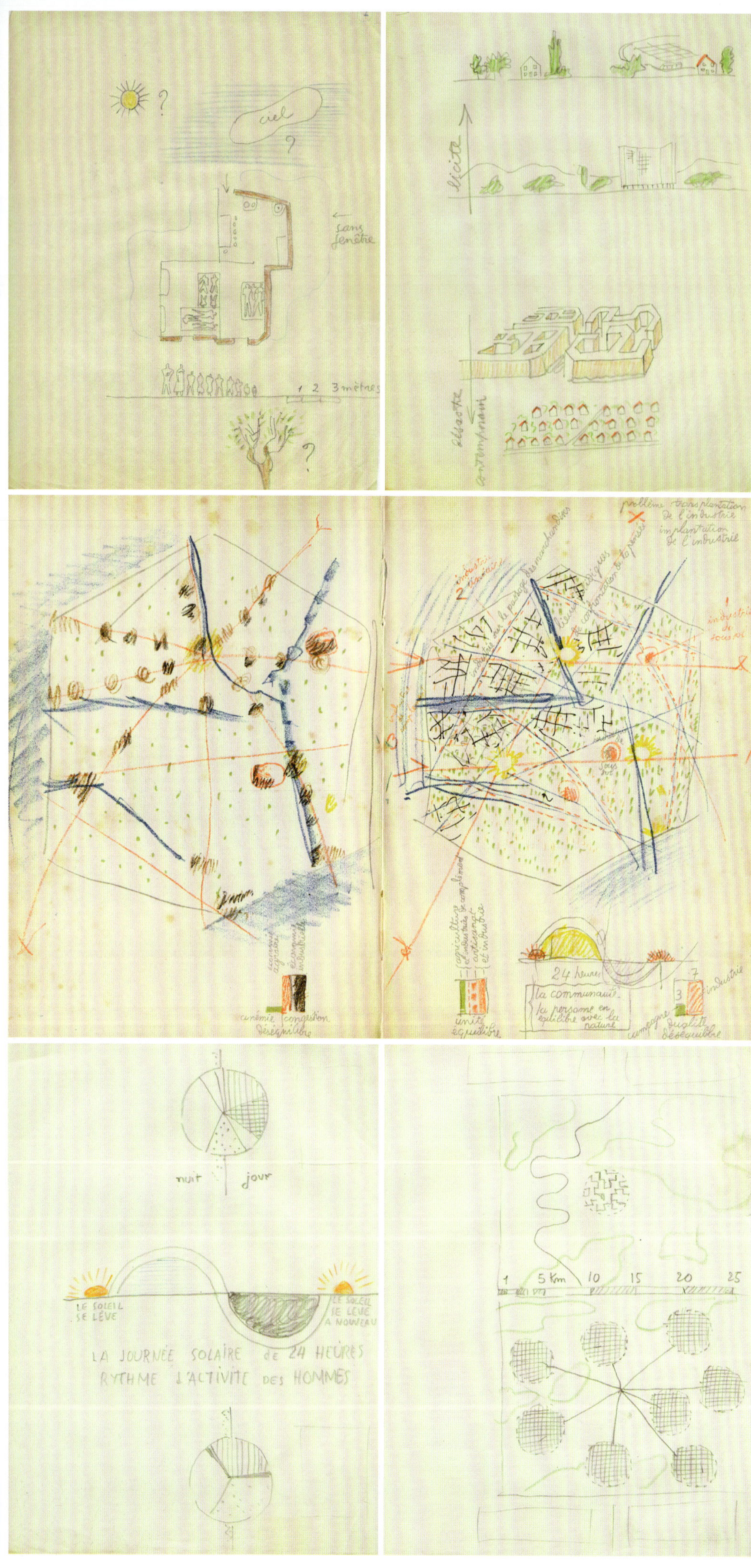

Concepts for the reconstruction: *La maison des hommes*, 1942

La maison des hommes (The House of Men)—co-authored by François de Pierrefeu, a friend who provided Le Corbusier with many valuable connections within the Vichy regime—presents plans for the reconstruction of postwar France.

This page and opposite. Preparatory sketches analyzing the distribution of industry within the "hexagon" of France, for *La maison des hommes (The House of Men)*, written with François de Pierrefeu, Plon, Paris, 1942

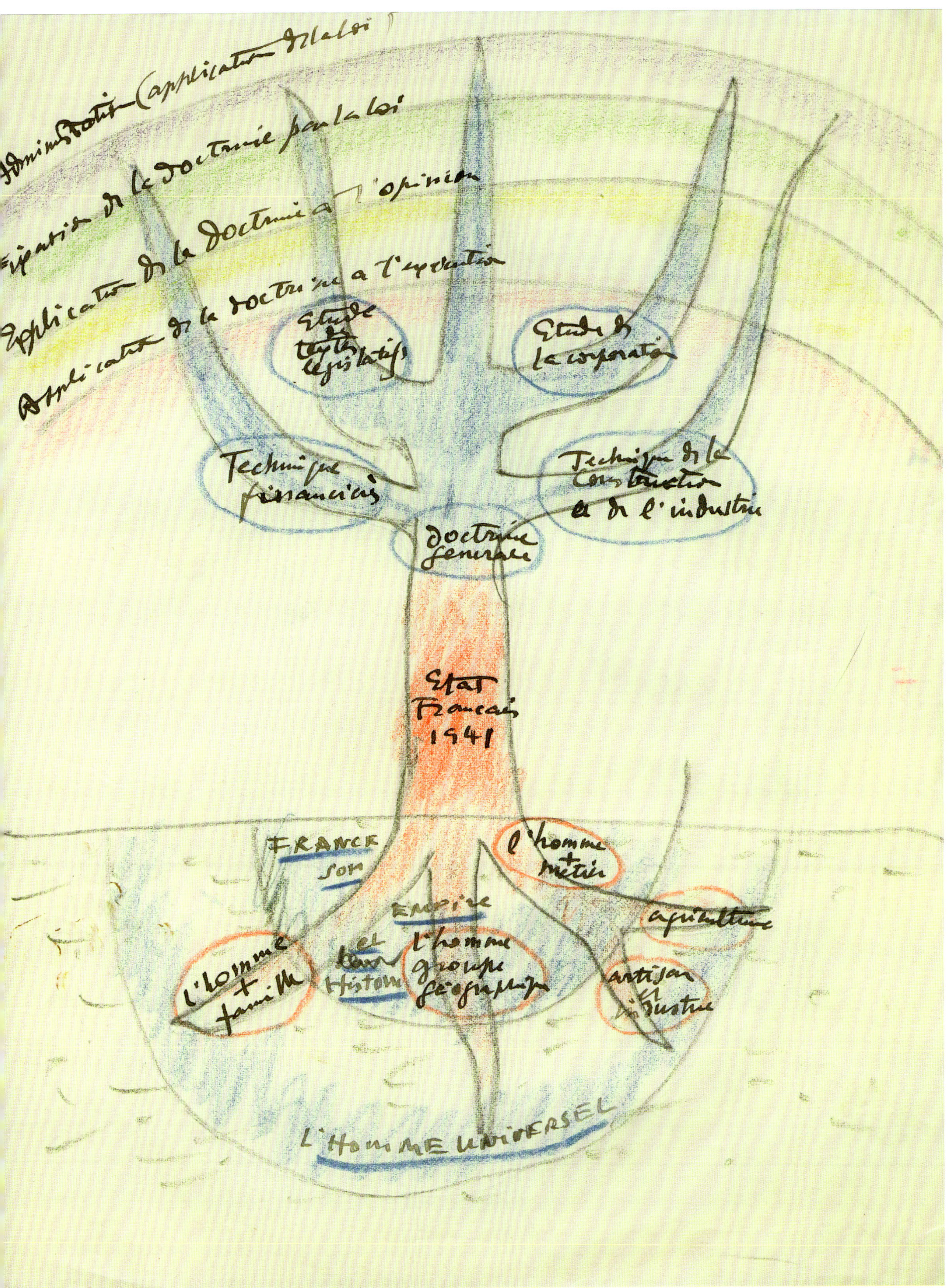
Administration (application de la loi)
Expression de la doctrine par la loi
Explication de la doctrine à l'opinion
Application de la doctrine à l'exécution
Etude des textes législatifs
Etude de la corporation
Technique financière
Technique de la construction et de l'industrie
doctrine générale
Etat Français 1941
FRANCE sol
l'homme + métier
EMPIRE
agriculture
l'homme + famille
l'homme groupe géographique
artisan et industrie
L'HOMME UNIVERSEL

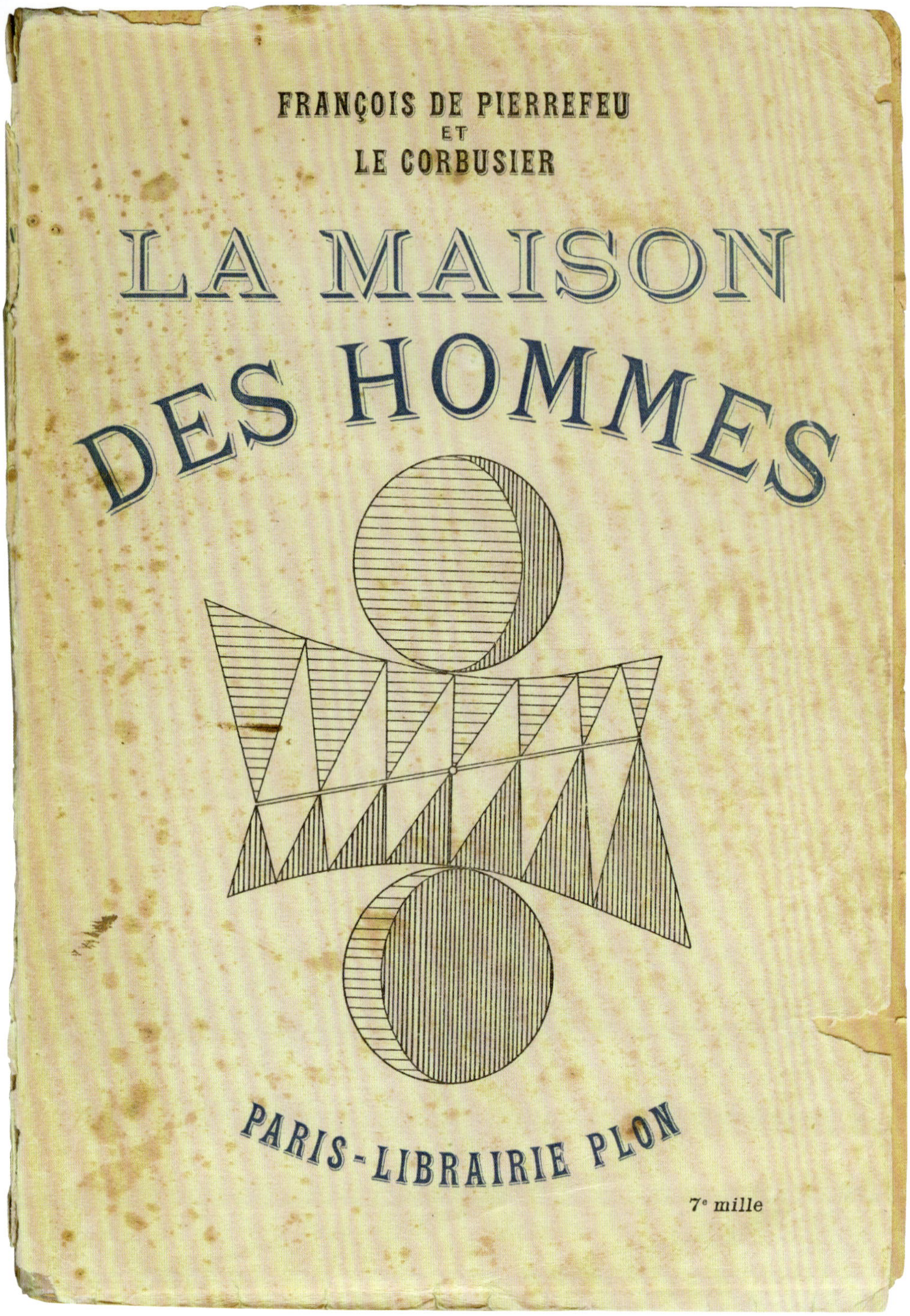

FRANÇOIS DE PIERREFEU
ET
LE CORBUSIER

LA MAISON DES HOMMES

PARIS-LIBRAIRIE PLON

7e mille

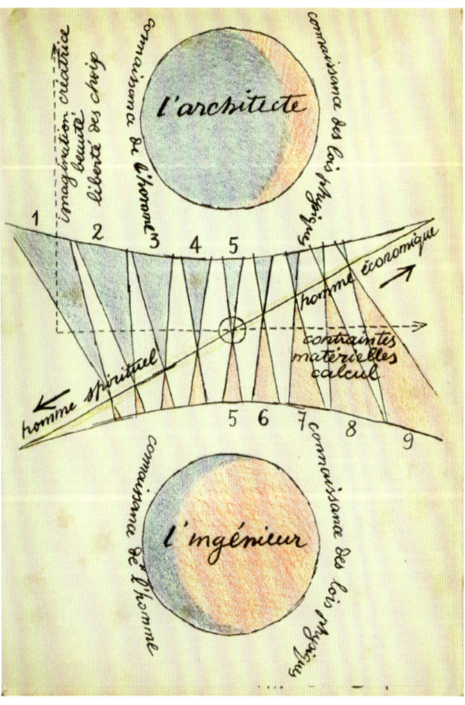

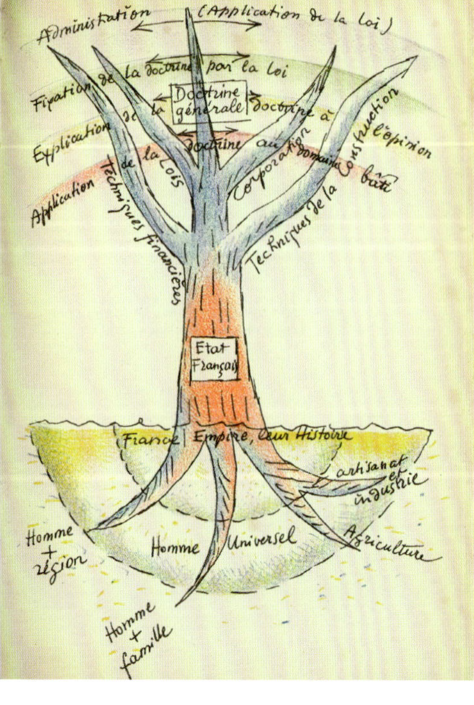

This page and opposite. Cover and selected pages of La maison des hommes, 1942

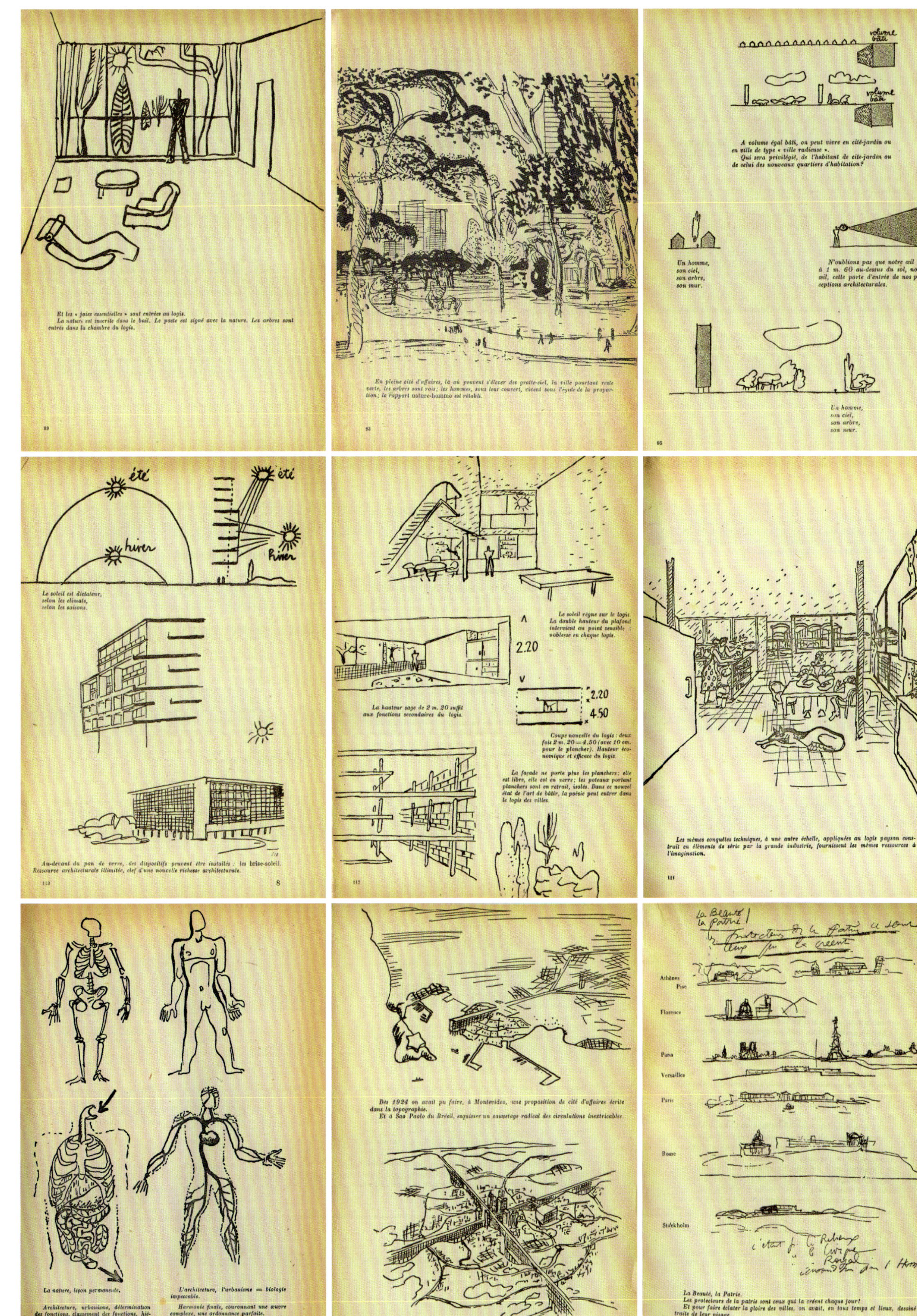

Et les « joies essentielles » sont entrées au logis.
La nature est inscrite dans le bail. Le pacte est signé avec la nature. Les arbres sont entrés dans la chambre du logis.

En pleine cité d'affaires, là où peuvent s'élever des gratte-ciel, la ville pourtant reste verte, les arbres sont rois; les hommes, sous leur couvert, vivent sous l'égide de la proportion; le rapport nature-homme est rétabli.

93

A volume égal bâti, on peut vivre en cité-jardin ou en ville de type « ville radieuse ».
Qui sera privilégié, de l'habitant de cité-jardin ou de celui des nouveaux quartiers d'habitation?

Un homme,
son ciel,
son arbre,
son mur.

N'oublions pas que notre œil est à 1 m. 60 au-dessus du sol, notre œil, cette porte d'entrée de nos perceptions architecturales.

Un homme,
son ciel,
son arbre,
son mur.

95

Le soleil est dictateur,
selon les climats,
selon les saisons.

Au-devant du pan de verre, des dispositifs peuvent être installés : les brise-soleil. Ressource architecturale illimitée, clef d'une nouvelle richesse architecturale.

113 8

Le soleil règne sur le logis. La double hauteur du plafond intervient au point sensible : noblesse en chaque logis.

La hauteur sage de 2 m. 20 suffit aux fonctions secondaires du logis.

Coupe nouvelle du logis : deux fois 2 m. 20 = 4.50 (avec 10 cm. pour le plancher). Hauteur économique et efficace du logis.

La façade ne porte plus les planchers; elle est libre, elle est en verre; les poteaux portant planchers sont en retrait, isolés. Dans ce nouvel état de l'art de bâtir, la poésie peut entrer dans le logis des villes.

117

Les mêmes conquêtes techniques, à une autre échelle, appliquées au logis paysan construit en éléments de série par la grande industrie, fournissent les mêmes ressources à l'imagination.

121

La nature, leçon permanente.

Architecture, urbanisme, détermination des fonctions, classement des fonctions, hiérarchie.

L'architecture, l'urbanisme = biologie impeccable.

Harmonie finale, couronnant une œuvre complexe, une ordonnance parfaite.
« Jeu savant, correct et magnifique des formes sous la lumière ».

129

Dès 1924 on avait pu faire, à Montevideo, une proposition de cité d'affaires écrite dans la topographie.
Et à Sao Paolo du Brésil, esquisser un sauvetage radical des circulations inextricables.

175

La Beauté, la Patrie.
Les protecteurs de la patrie sont ceux qui la créent chaque jour!
Et pour faire éclater la gloire des villes, on avait, en tous temps et lieux, dessiné les traits de leur visage.

183

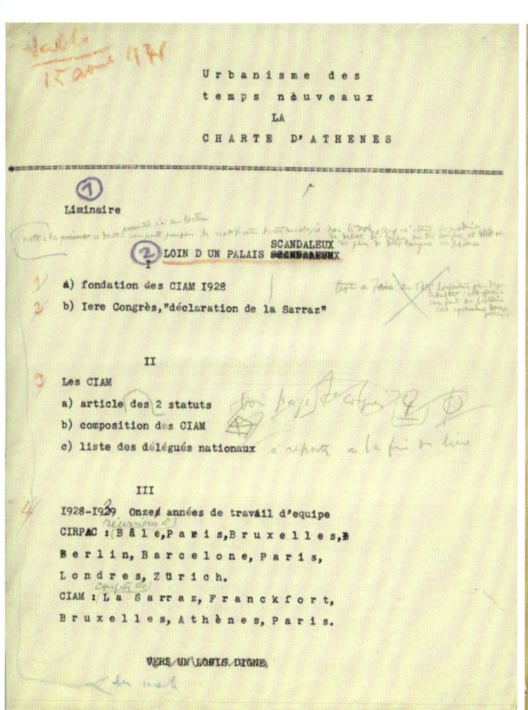

Urbanisme des
temps nouveaux
LA
CHARTE D'ATHENES

(1) Liminaire

(2) LOIN D UN PALAIS SCANDALEUX

a) fondation des CIAM 1928
b) 1ere Congrès,"déclaration de la Sarraz"

II

Les CIAM
a) article des 2 statuts
b) composition des CIAM
c) liste des délégués nationaux

III

1928-1939 Onze années de travail d'equipe
CIRPAC : Bâle, Paris, Bruxelles, Berlin, Barcelone, Paris, Londres, Zürich.
CIAM : La Sarraz, Francfort, Bruxelles, Athènes, Paris.

VERS UN LOGIS DIGNE

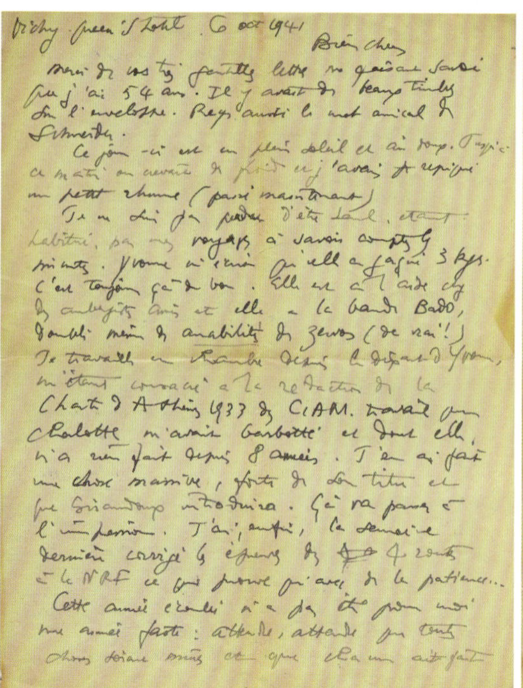

Ideas from the 1930s for the post-war era: *La charte d'Athènes*, 1943

In 1943 Le Corbusier edited and published the proceedings of the 1933 CIAM conference as the book *La charte d'Athènes*. The Athens Charter outlined a program for the rational planning and construction of cities, with particular emphasis given to the creation of zones based on four functions: living, working, recreation, and circulation. The concepts in the charter were widely adopted by European planners during reconstruction efforts following World War II.

"I've been working in my room since Yvonne left, devoting myself to writing up CIAM's 1933 Athens Charter. A job Charlotte stole from me and which she's done nothing on for 8 years. I've made it into something huge, with its impressive title, and Giraudoux will do the introduction."

—Letter to his mother and brother, 6 October 1941

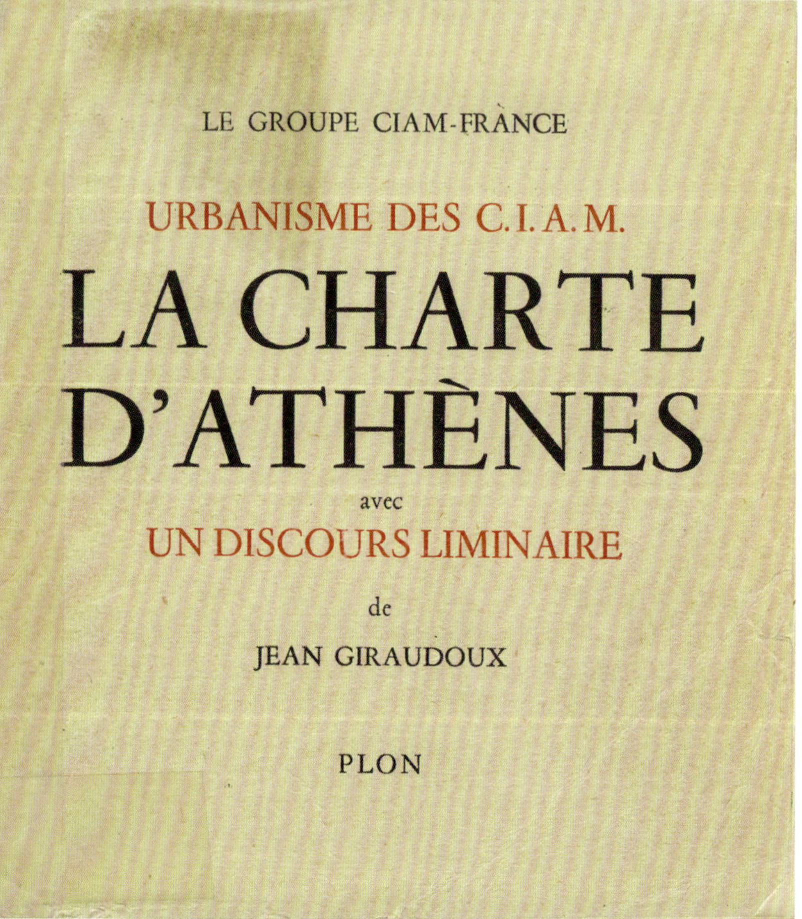

LE GROUPE CIAM-FRANCE

URBANISME DES C.I.A.M.

LA CHARTE D'ATHÈNES

avec

UN DISCOURS LIMINAIRE

de

JEAN GIRAUDOUX

PLON

Opposite, top left. Typescript of *La charte d'Athènes* with Le Corbusier's notes, c. 1941

Opposite, top middle and right. Le Corbusier to his mother and brother, from Vichy, 6 October 1941, describing the editing of *La charte d'Athènes*

Opposite, bottom. Sketch of the cover design (left) and the final cover (right), *La charte d'Athènes*, Plon, Paris, 1943

Right and below. Mock-ups of individual pages from *La charte d'Athènes*, 1943

ESSAI THÉORIQUE SUR LES BASES DE LA CHARTE D'ATHÈNES

LE PROJET RÉPOND AUX ARTICLES 23 .... 63 DE LA CHARTE D'ATHÈNES

LA VILLE ET SA RÉGION — ARTICLES 1 · 3 · 4 · 5 · CARACTÈRE ÉCONOMIQUE, GÉOGRAPHIQUE ET POLITIQUE DE LA VILLE
POUR ORLÉANS : CARACTÈRES DOMINANTS
1 ORLÉANS VILLE CARREFOUR, CENTRE D'ÉCHANGES
2 LA LOIRE
3 CENTRE ADMINISTRATIF DE LA RÉGION

HABITATION — ARTICLES 23 · 24 · 25 · 26 · 27 · 28 · 29 · HYGIÈNE, ENSOLEILLEMENT, SURFACES VERTES, DÉGAGEMENT DES VOIES DE COMMUNICATION, TECHNIQUES MODERNES ·

LOISIRS — ARTICLES 35 · 36 · 37 · 38 · 39 · 40 · AMÉNAGEMENT DES JEUX ET DES SPORTS, AMÉNAGEMENT DE PARCS, TERRAINS DE SPORTS, STADES, PLAGES ETC ....

TRAVAIL — ARTICLES 46 · 49 · 50 · DISTANCES ENTRE LIEUX DE TRAVAIL ET LIEUX D'HABITATION, ARTISANAT A L'INTÉRIEUR DE LA VILLE LIAISON DE LA CITÉ D'AFFAIRES AVEC LES QUARTIERS D'HABITATION ET L'ARTISANAT

CIRCULATION — ARTICLES 59 · 60 · 61 · 62 · 63 · ANALYSE DE L'ENSEMBLE DE LA CIRCULATION DANS LA VILLE ET DANS SA RÉGION, CROISEMENT DES VOIES DE CIRCULATION, PRIORITÉ DU PIÉTON, ETC ....

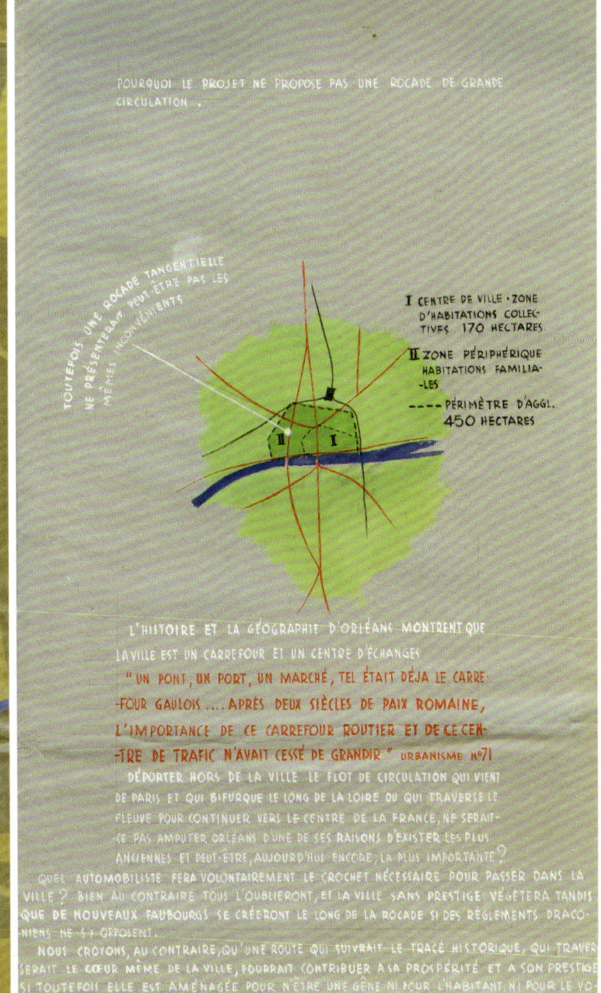

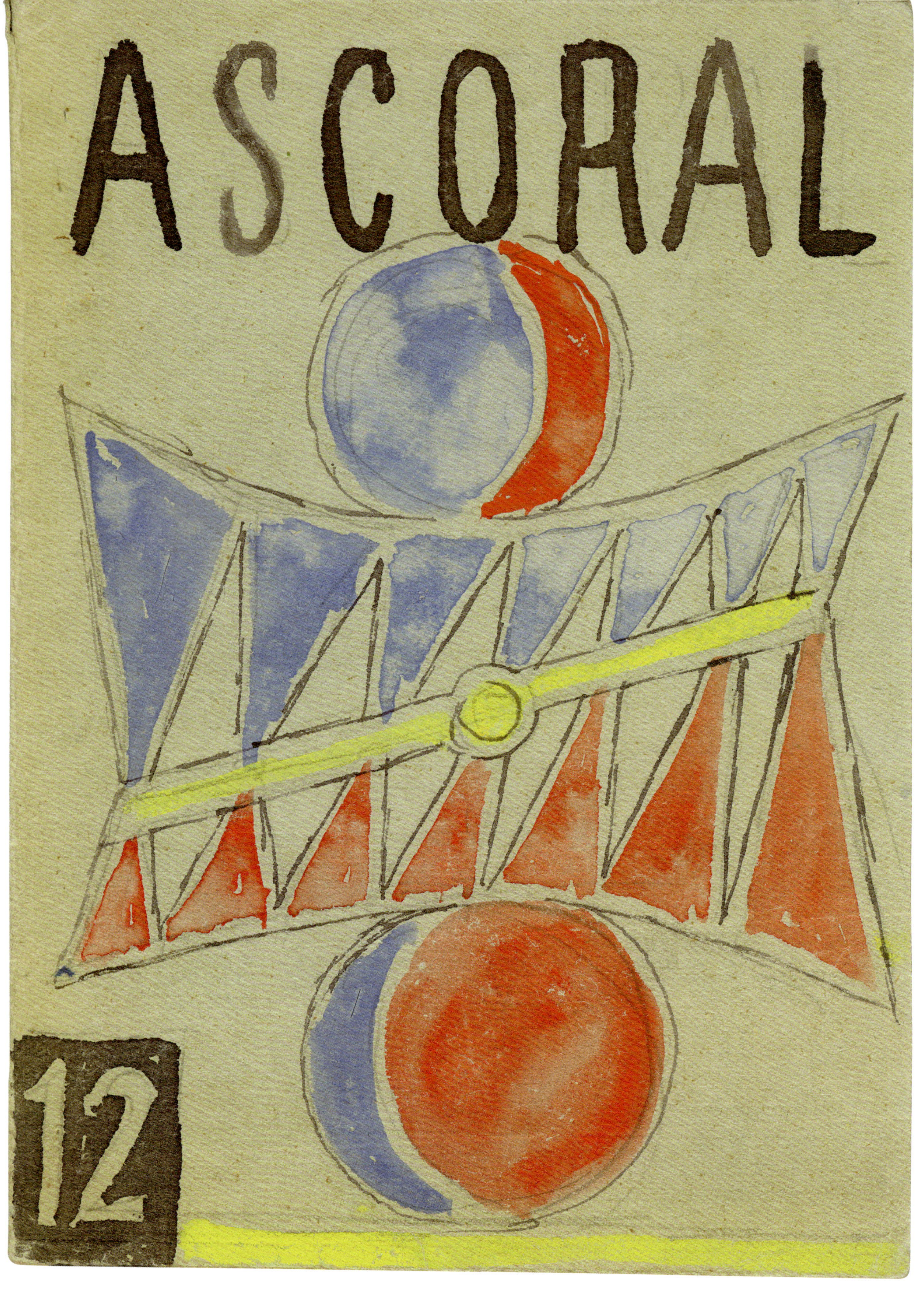
ASCORAL
12

Plans for the future: ASCORAL, 1943

In late 1942 Le Corbusier thought his luck within the Vichy regime was changing when he was appointed to a committee to study housing and urbanism in Paris. However, the abrupt and final rejection of his Plan Obus for Algiers left him without hope that his visions would ever be realized under Marshal Philippe Pétain, and he left Vichy for good.

Looking ahead to postwar reconstruction, Le Corbusier established the Assemblée de Constructeurs pour une Rénovation Architecturale, or ASCORAL. With these colleagues and students gathered at his rue de Sèvres office, he would develop his newest concept for the creation of rational structures, one that he would continue to refine for the rest of his life: the Modulor.

L'assemblée générale
GROUPE DE PARIS
GROUPES DES PROVINCES
GROUPES ÉTRANGERS
DOCTRINE
Le conseil de direction
ACTION
Secrétariat et Trésorerie
LES SECTIONS DE TRAVAIL
1 Idées générales
2 "Savoir hat. ter"
3 Sciences du logis équipement normalisat. industrialis.
4 Équipement Santé maladie
5 Travail agriculture industrie échanges
6 Ethique & Esthétique
7 Entreprise A B
8 Financement
9 Législation
10 Synthèse des arts majeurs
LES LIVRES "ASCORAL"
ASsemblée de COnstructeurs pour une Rénovation ArchitecturaLe
LES COMITÉS
Presse
petites grandes Conférences
Club
Bulletin
Radio
Liaisons inter-associations
Projections
Films
Microfilms
Rayon
Ascoral chez les libraires
Bibliothèque
Photothèque
Cinémathèq.
Discothèque

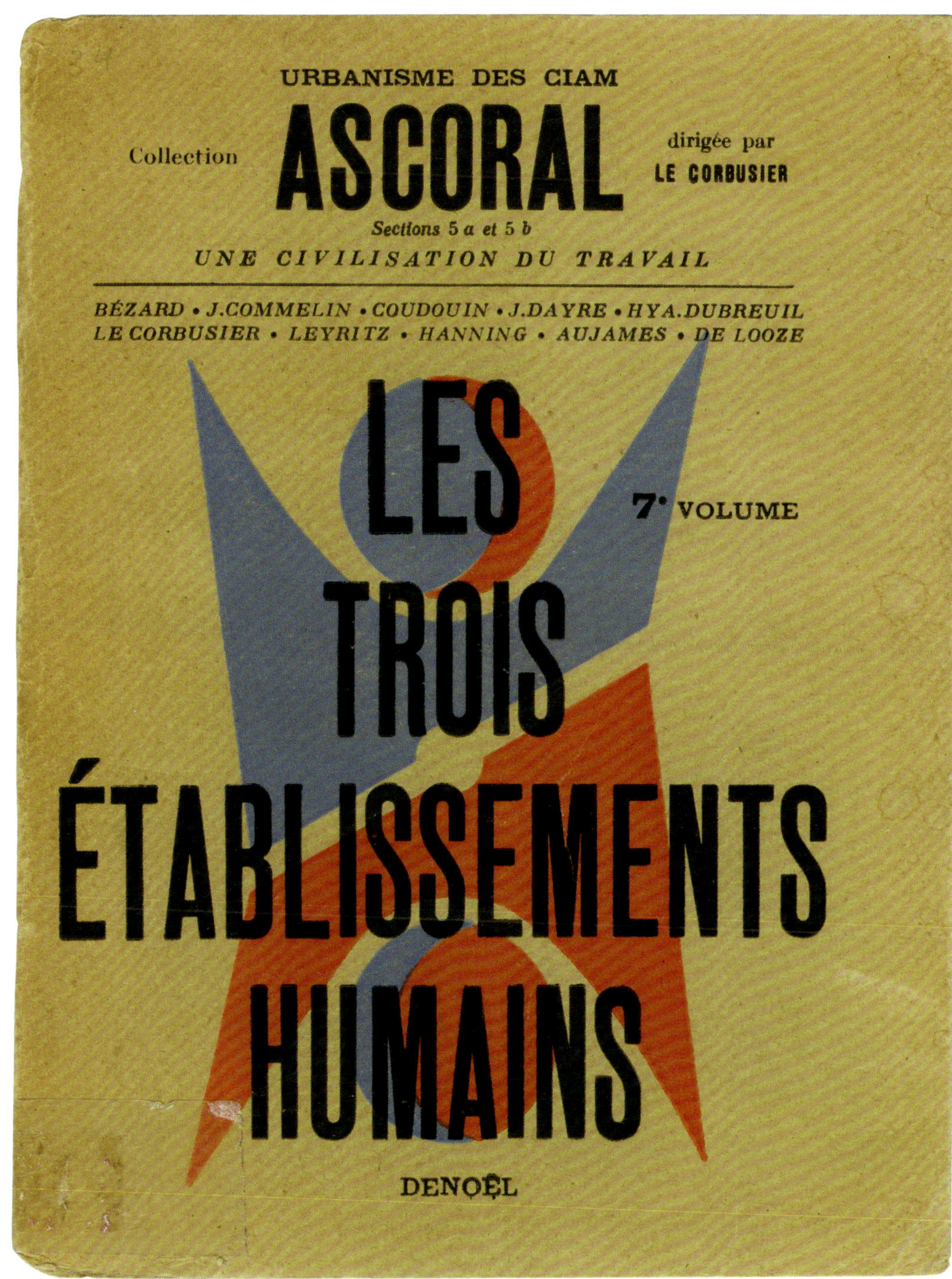

Top. Structure of work sections and committees of the CIAM group Assemblée de Constructeurs pour une Rénovation Architecturale (ASCORAL; Assembly of Builders for an Architectural Renovation)

Opposite and right. Sketch and cover of the book *Les trois établissements humains* (*The Three Human Establishments*), a collection of city planning studies by ASCORAL, Denoël, Paris, 1945

HEBREW GRAMMAR
WOOD
OS JUDEUS
MODULOR

Le Corbusier returned to Paris in 1942 and began to rebuild his reputation. In addition to ASCORAL, he founded an association of engineers, architects, urbanists, and designers—ATBAT—to work on every aspect of reconstruction. None of his ambitious plans to rebuild cities devastated in the war were accepted, but ATBAT became a potent force in post-war architectural debates about housing for those displaced by the war.

Le Corbusier's humiliating loss of the League of Nations competition twenty years earlier repeated itself in 1946–47 in New York, where he spent many months trying to impose his views on the committee responsible for designing the United Nations head-quarters. Although he was not allowed to take charge of the project, he never ceased to assert that the finished building was based on the model numbered 23A, which he claimed was his design. After the debacle, Le Corbusier complained to his New York-based friend Helena Simkhovitch: "Every expectation reversed by this extraordinary New York attitude. I'm talking about gangsters, and their conspiracies. It seems that the matter is closed. Abramovitz replaces Le Corbusier. Why not? I call this childishness, thoughtlessness, theft, amoral business practice, filthy morality, friendship trampled underfoot; a sense of justice receives a kick up the ass. Very New York, 'your honorable city.'"

Much of the thinking that went into his plans for postwar cities was incorporated into the Unité d'Habitation de Grandeur Conforme (Dwelling Unit at an Appropriate Scale), the first of which was built in Marseille in 1947–52. Here he combined his urban and domestic theories: these large-scale apartment blocks incorporating hundreds of apartments were intended to provide not only the basic needs of the inhabitants (shops, schools, gymnasium, running track) inside each block, but also a private domestic space in which every dweller would be assured perfect quiet and a splendid view. He also took great pride in the design of the kitchen, on which Charlotte Perriand was a consultant, and in the double-height space of the living room.

Grand Projects on a Human Scale (1942–1952)

The Unité design was reproduced, with a few variations, on four other sites in France and Germany.

Built as a research project, the Marseille Unité attracted a torrent of criticism in the national press, but it also became a standard around which postwar modern architects rallied. In the course of the design, Le Corbusier developed his postwar style of *béton brut* (raw concrete), with the concrete surface revealing the rough texture of the planks that formed the molds. This was part of Le Corbusier's move away from machine-like finishes and toward a celebration of tactile craftsmanship.

Another step toward a more humanist practice was the development of his proportional system, the Modulor. A system of measurements based on the human body, the Modulor became an article of faith for Le Corbusier.

Opposite. Le Corbusier discussing his Modulor system at the Metropolitan Museum of Art, New York, 1950

Back in Paris, 1942

In 1942 life in Paris started to become bearable again for Le Corbusier and Yvonne. Food rationing was still severe, but there was heat in their penthouse on rue Nungesser-et-Coli. Le Corbusier was eager to reopen his office on the rue de Sèvres, but the absence of new projects made this difficult.

Vichy officials granted him permission to open the office to students enrolled at the Ecole des Beaux-Arts, and four of them elected him as adviser, following a curriculum approved by Vichy. This gave Le Corbusier not only the opportunity to continue the work and research that had been interrupted by the war but also the chance to "correct" the education being provided by the Ecole des Beaux-Arts, an institution whose tenets he had long rejected.

"And did I tell you there's going to be a Corbu workshop at the Ecole des Beaux Arts? It's the young ones, the rebels, who are summoning me. So the connection will be made between the School, which needs a shot in the arm, and major works in Paris, where I'll push my youngsters into the breach. And so my rue de Sèvres studio that pulled in young people from all countries is going to be revived in the Mecca of Architecture, in the midst of the youth of France."

—Letter to his mother, 28 March 1942

Below. Le Corbusier working in his office on the rue de Sèvres, 1950s. The office would remain his headquarters for the rest of his life.

Opposite. Le Corbusier painting in the studio of his apartment on rue Nungesser-et-Coli, May 1946

WALKER ART CENTER

LE CORBUSIER

ARCHITECT
WRITER
PAINTER

DEC 15 TO FEB 20

THE NEW SPIRIT

LE CORBUSIER

STORM CENTER
OF
CONTROVERSY
........NEVERTHELESS

***The New Spirit:* *Le Corbusier—Architect, Writer, Painter*, Walker Art Center, Minneapolis, 1944**

The Walker's retrospective of Le Corbusier's work introduced him to a Midwestern audience and initiated an ongoing relationship. Two years later the museum co-sponsored a show of his work at the Rockefeller Center in New York.

ARCHITECT

OF LeCORBUSIER

WRITER

AN EXHIBITION

30 YEARS OF HIS WORK

PAINTER

Opposite, top. Entrance to the Walker Art Center, Minneapolis, where the exhibition *The New Spirit: Le Corbusier—Architect, Writer, Painter* was held in 1944

Opposite, bottom. Entrance to the exhibition

Right. Invitation to the exhibition

Below. Installation view, with photograph of Le Corbusier's Villa Weissenhof, Stuttgart, Germany, 1927 (left), and a model and photograph of Villa Savoye, Poissy, France, 1928–31 (right)

LET US STATE THE PROBLEM
LE CORBUSIER
LET US STATE THE PROBLEM
PAINTING
WRITING
ARCHITECTURE

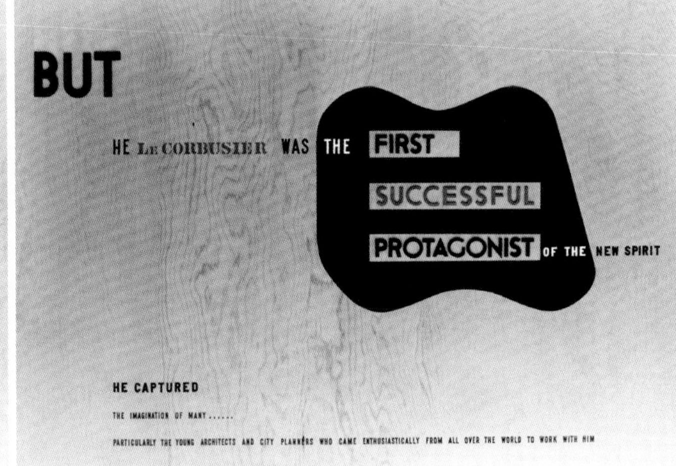

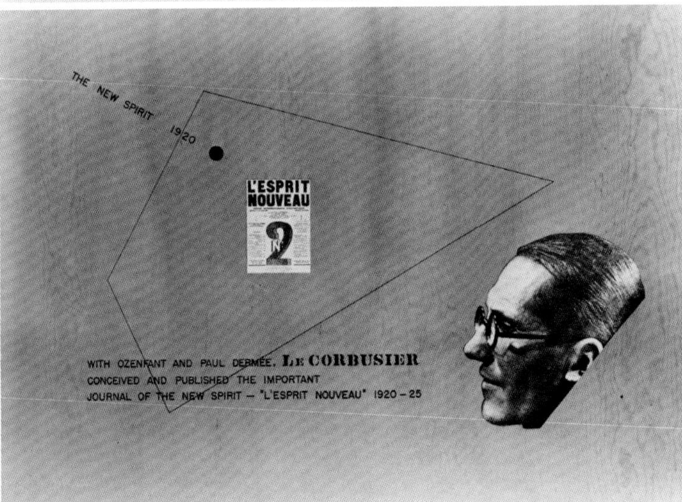

Opposite and this page. Images from the Walker Art Center's exhibition on Le Corbusier

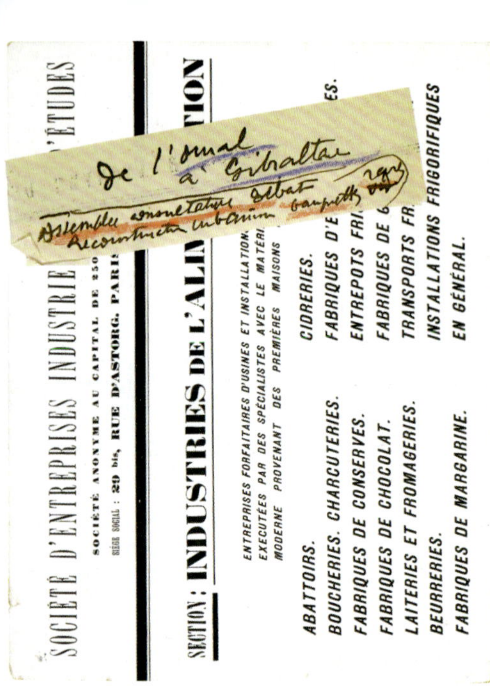

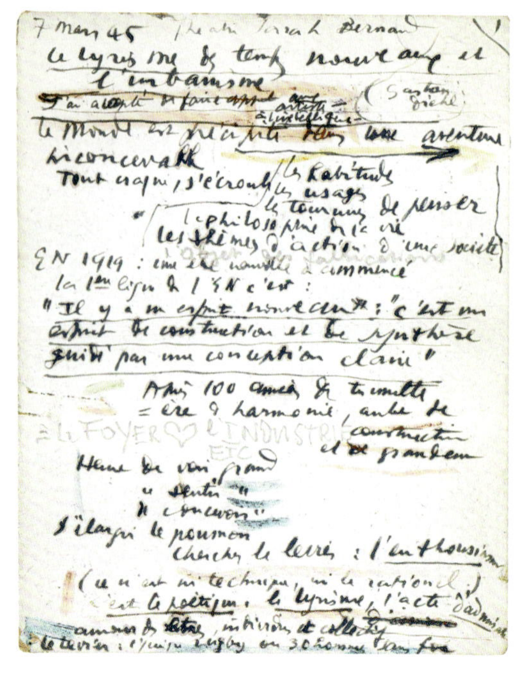

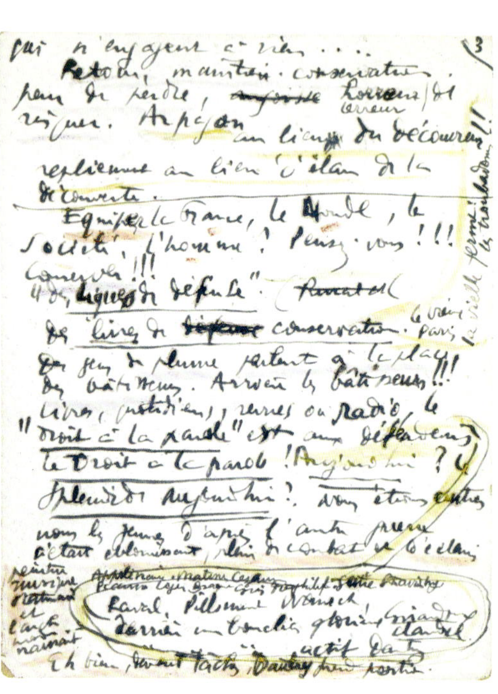

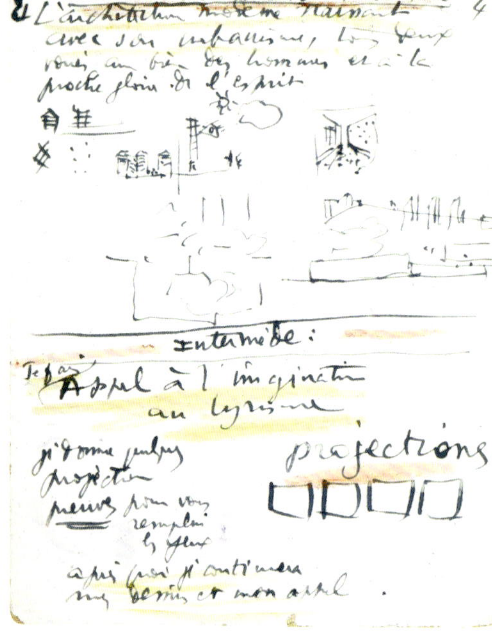

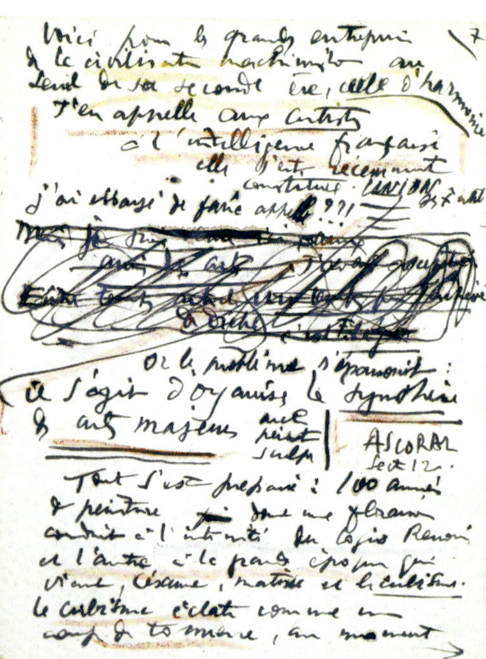

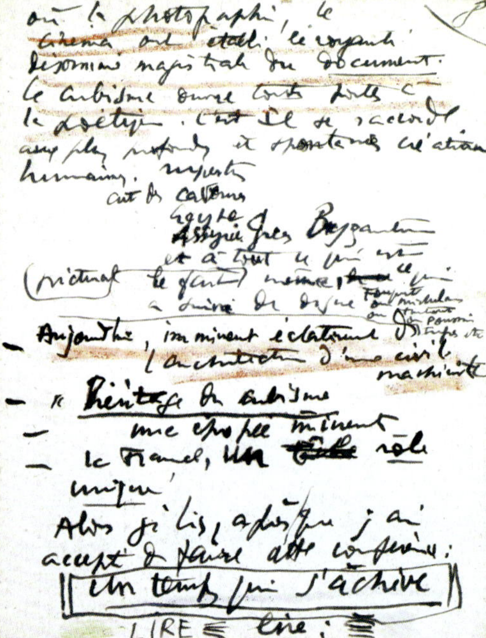

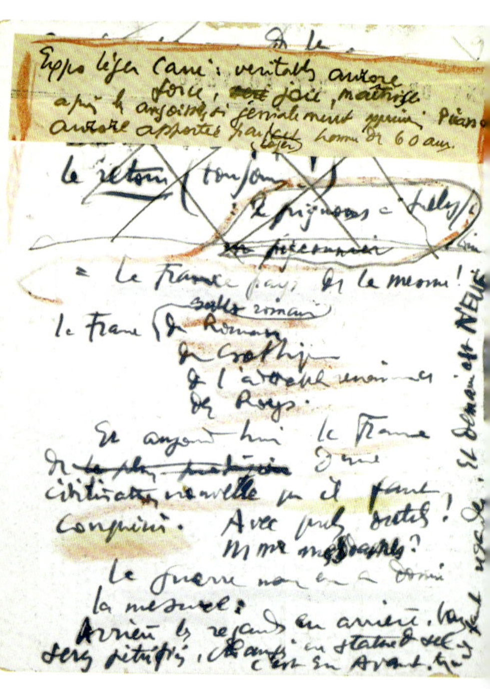

Le Corbusier the lecturer

Throughout his career Le Corbusier remained an energetic teacher and lecturer, from his tour of South America in 1929 to his whirlwind circuit through the elite institutions of North American higher education in 1935, to his international appearances after the war as the world's preeminent proselytizer for modern architecture and urban planning.

"*The architectural revolution has been accomplished* and modern Architecture is being born with its urbanism, both dedicated to human wellbeing and the imminent glory of the spirit."

—Lecture at the Théâtre Sarah Bernhardt, Paris, 7 March 1945

Opposite. Notes for a lecture at the Théâtre Sarah Bernhardt, Paris, 7 March 1945

Below. Le Corbusier giving a presentation at the Milan Triennale, 1951

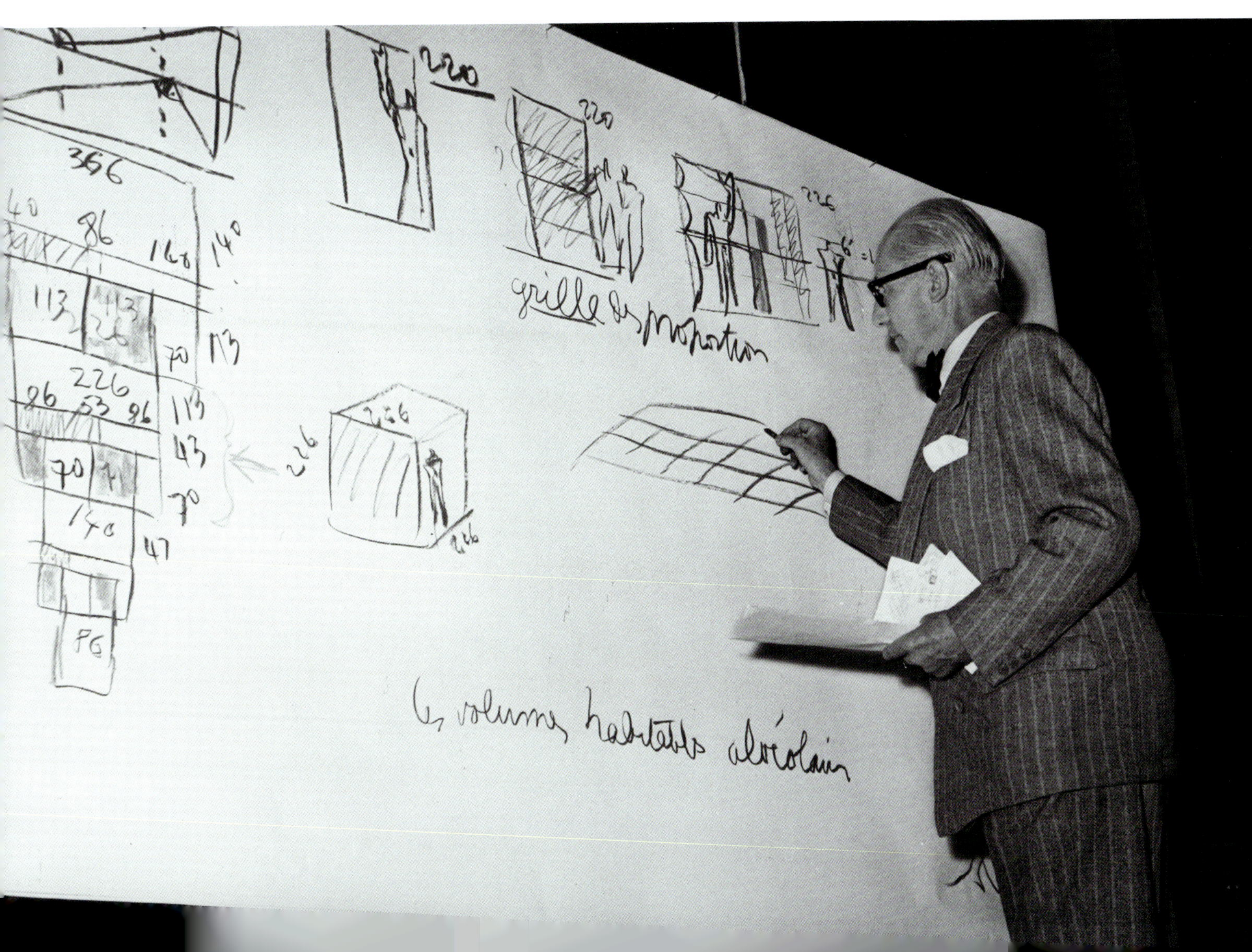

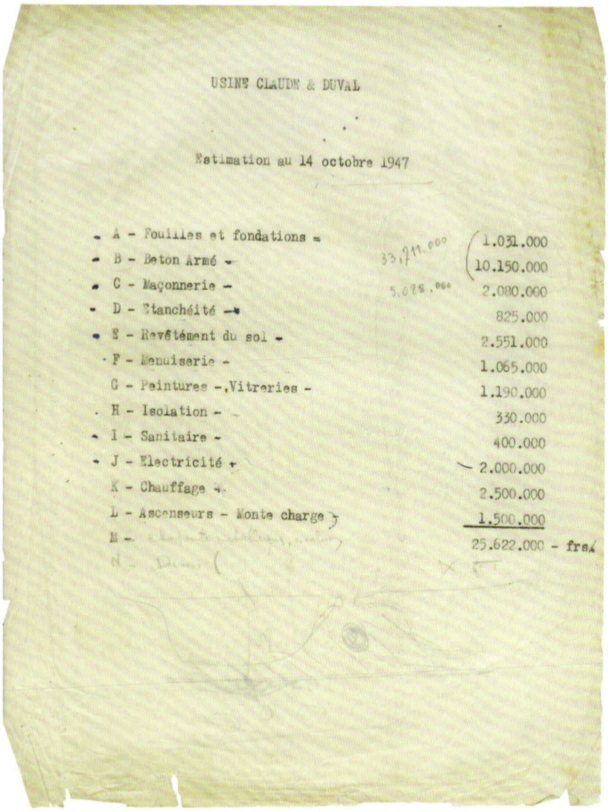

USINE CLAUDE & DUVAL

Estimation au 14 octobre 1947

A - Fouilles et fondations	1.031.000
B - Beton Armé	10.150.000
C - Maçonnerie	2.080.000
D - Etanchéité	825.000
E - Revêtement du sol	2.551.000
F - Menuiserie	1.065.000
G - Peintures - Vitreries	1.190.000
H - Isolation	330.000
I - Sanitaire	400.000
J - Electricité	2.000.000
K - Chauffage	2.500.000
L - Ascenseurs - Monte charge	1.500.000
M -	25.622.000 - frs.

Rebuilding postwar France: City plan and a hat factory, Saint-Dié, 1945–50

One of the first commissions Le Corbusier received after the war was for a master plan for the badly damaged town of Saint-Dié in northeastern France. Even though construction of the plan never materialized, it did lead to a commission for a hat factory in Saint-Dié. For the factory, Le Corbusier began to explore the methods and materials that would characterize his work through the 1950s, including the use of *brises-soleil* (sunshades), *béton brut* (raw concrete), and the Modulor system, which he had been developing with his staff of students/apprentices ever since his return to Paris.

Vue du Centre Civique de Saint-Dié avec le Centre administratif en gratte-ciel

Une élévation avec les édifices de la première et seconde étape

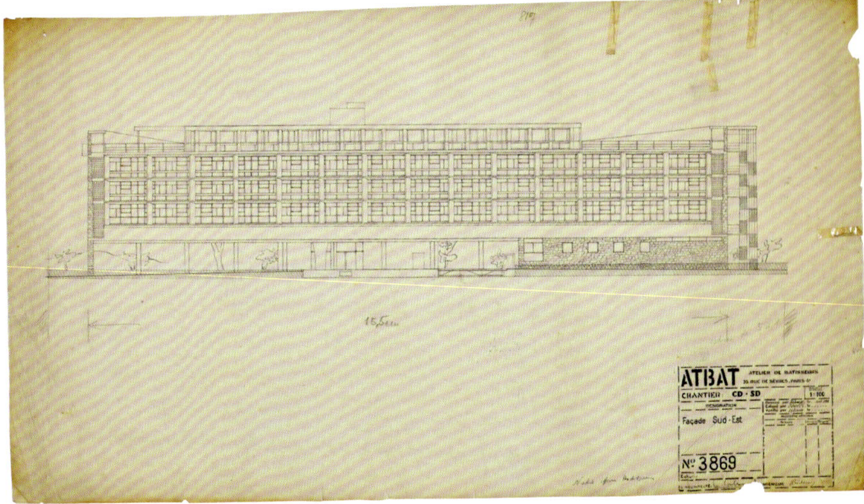

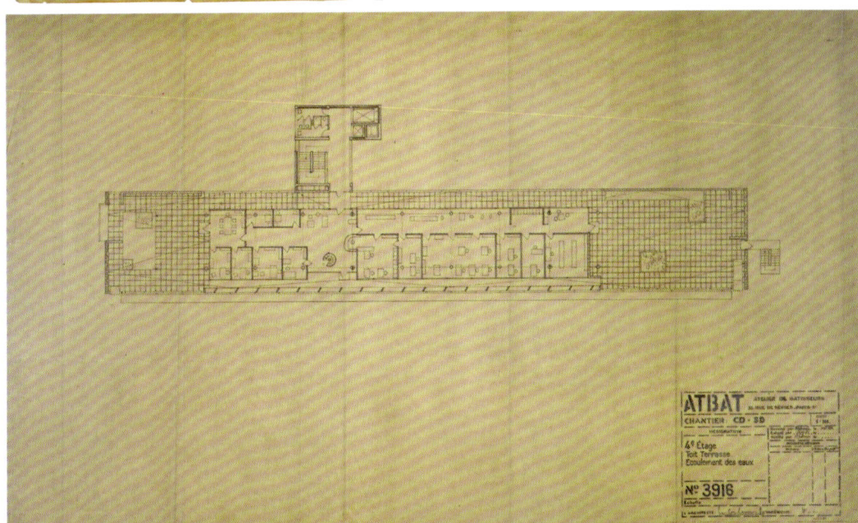

pposite, top left. stimate of onstruction costs, 4 October 1947, or building the hat actory in Saint-Dié

Opposite, top right. Photograph of Saint-Dié, showing the massive destruction from World War II

Opposite, bottom. Sketch of the Saint-Dié civic center, c. 1946, with the administrative center and tower (top) and elevation of buildings at the first and second stages (bottom)

bove left. Sketch f tower for Saint-ié's civic center, 1946 — part of e Corbusier's econstruction plan

Above right. Southeast elevation, 1945, Saint-Dié factory

Right. Fourth-floor plan, roof and terrace, 1945, Saint-Dié factory

Below. Le Corbusier (right), with his client, Jean-Jacques Duval, at the Saint-Dié factory work site, 1946

Above. Saint-Dié factory, 1946–47

Opposite. Photographs of the Saint-Dié factory, including the roof garden and client Jean-Jacques Duval's office (bottom left), with a photographic enlargement on the wall of a detail from a painting by Le Corbusier

A new measure of man: The Modulor system

The Modulor system of proportions that Le Corbusier had been laboring over for so long was represented by a male figure with one arm raised. Not only was this figure a tool to achieve harmonious proportions, by uniting the measurements of a man of average height with the classical golden section, but the Modulor also embodied a design philosophy in which structure was generated by the needs of its inhabitants. In Le Corbusier's vision, the human scale would henceforth determine every aspect of architecture, planning, and design, from the width of city boulevards to the height of door handles.

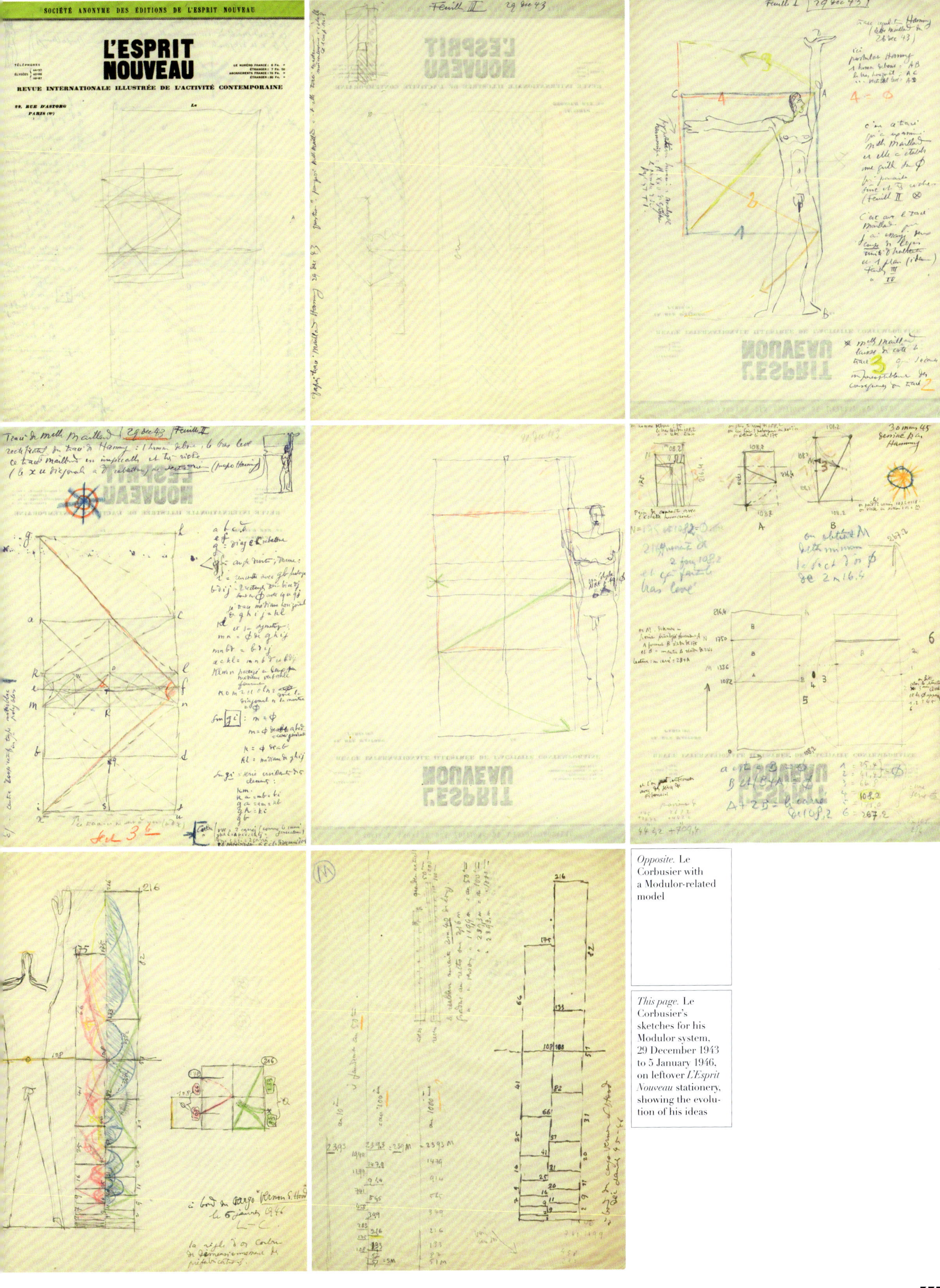

Opposite. Le Corbusier with a Modulor-related model

This page. Le Corbusier's sketches for his Modulor system, 29 December 1943 to 5 January 1946, on leftover *L'Esprit Nouveau* stationery, showing the evolution of his ideas

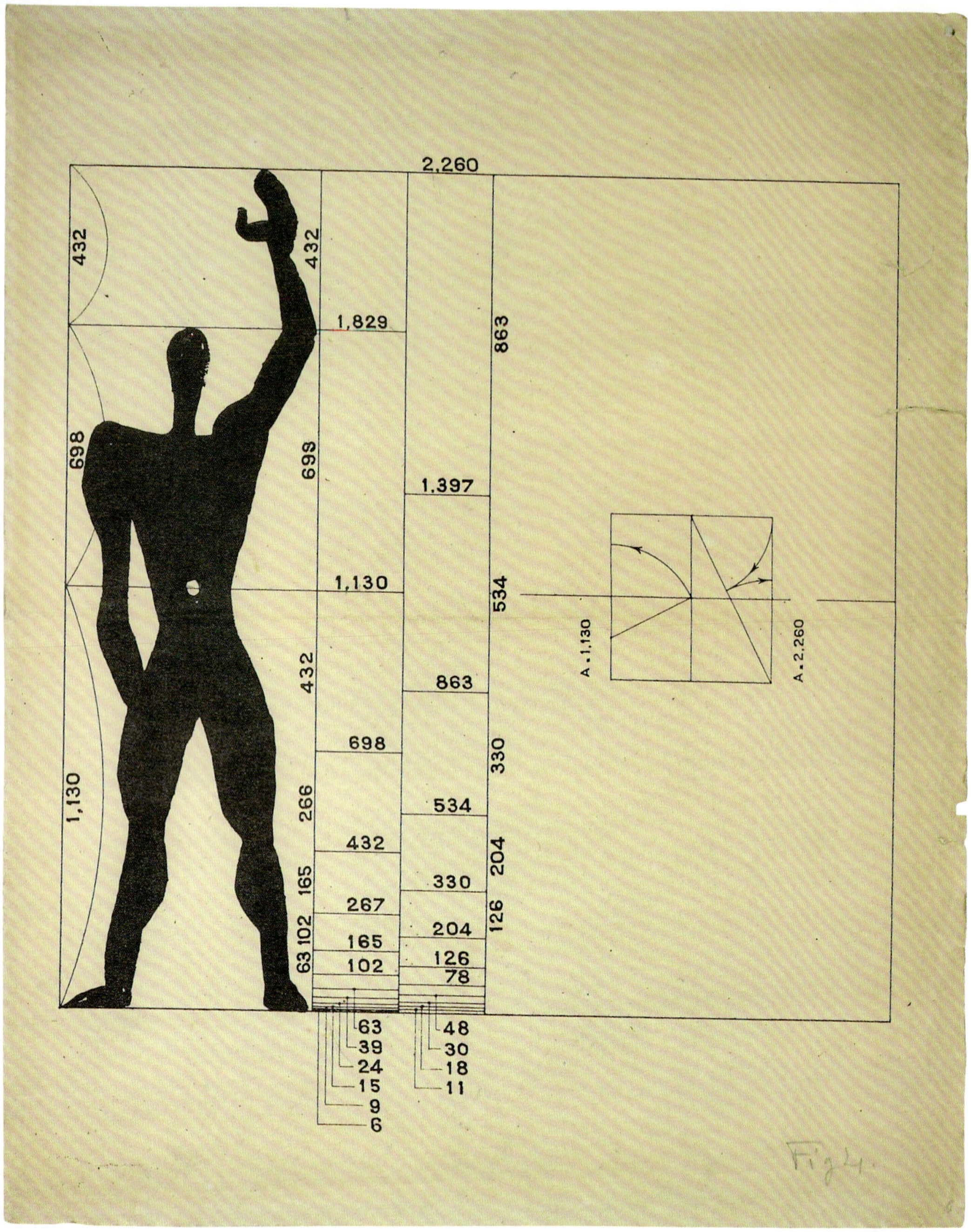

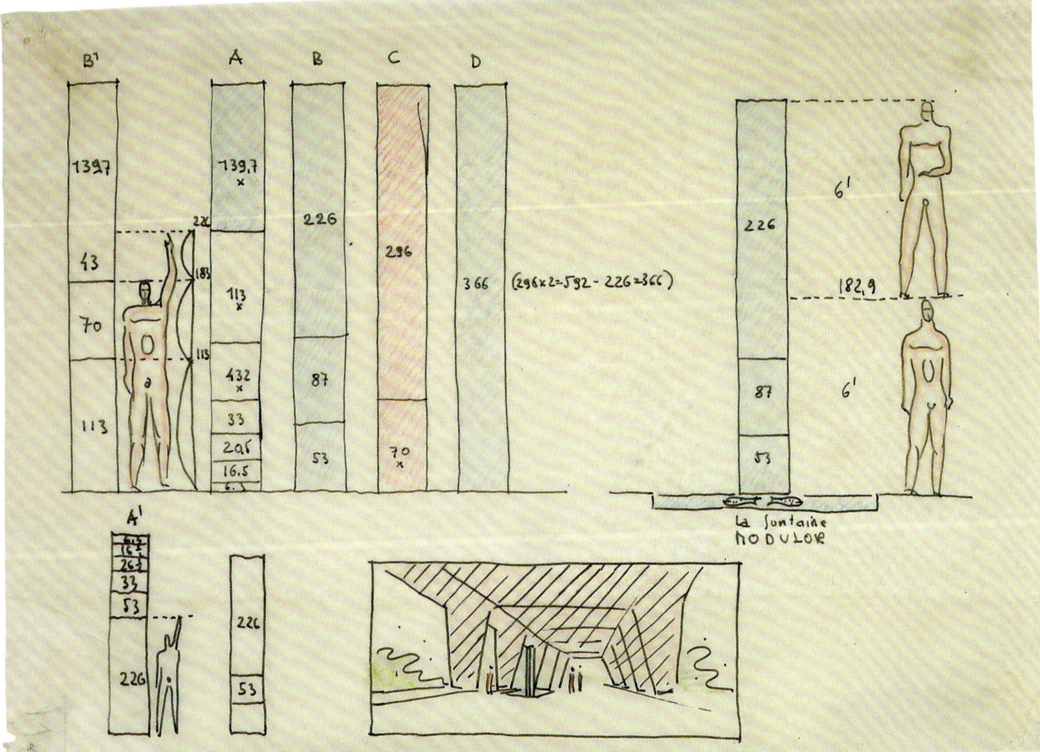

Left. Modulor measurements, 1950, featuring the figure of "Modulor man"

Below left. Modulor sketches, 1945, for the Unité d'Habitation, Marseille (sketch at the bottom shows the building's tapered piers)

Opposite. Drawing, "Modular Woman," by Justino Serralta, 1952, which features Le Corbusier's notes as he attempts "to show clearly the relationships between the Modular and the proposed 3-4-5 system"

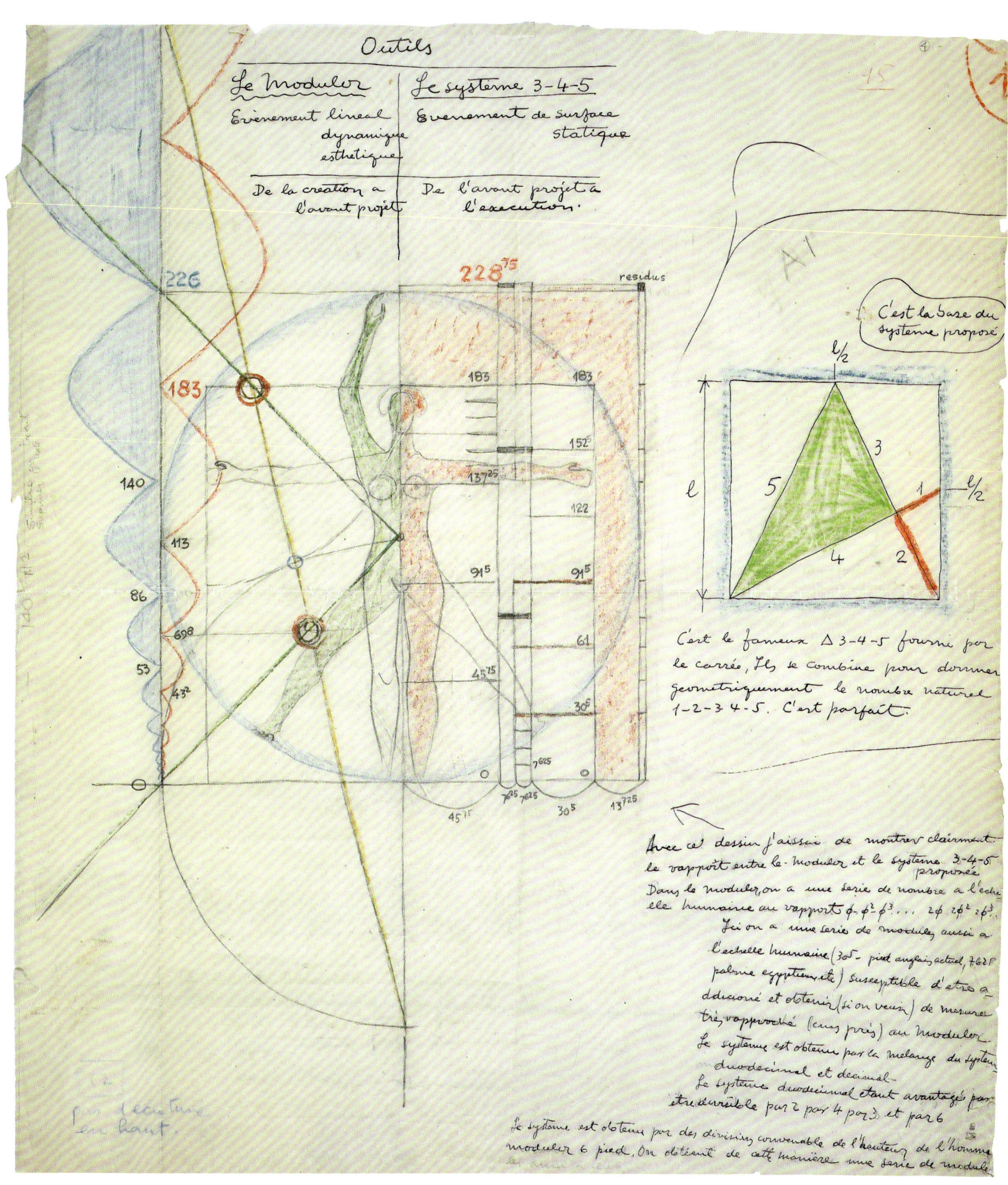

“This is the wonderful 3-4-5 provided by the square. They combine to give geometrically the natural number 1-2-3-4-5. It's perfect.”

—Note on drawing, with a “Modulor woman,” 1952

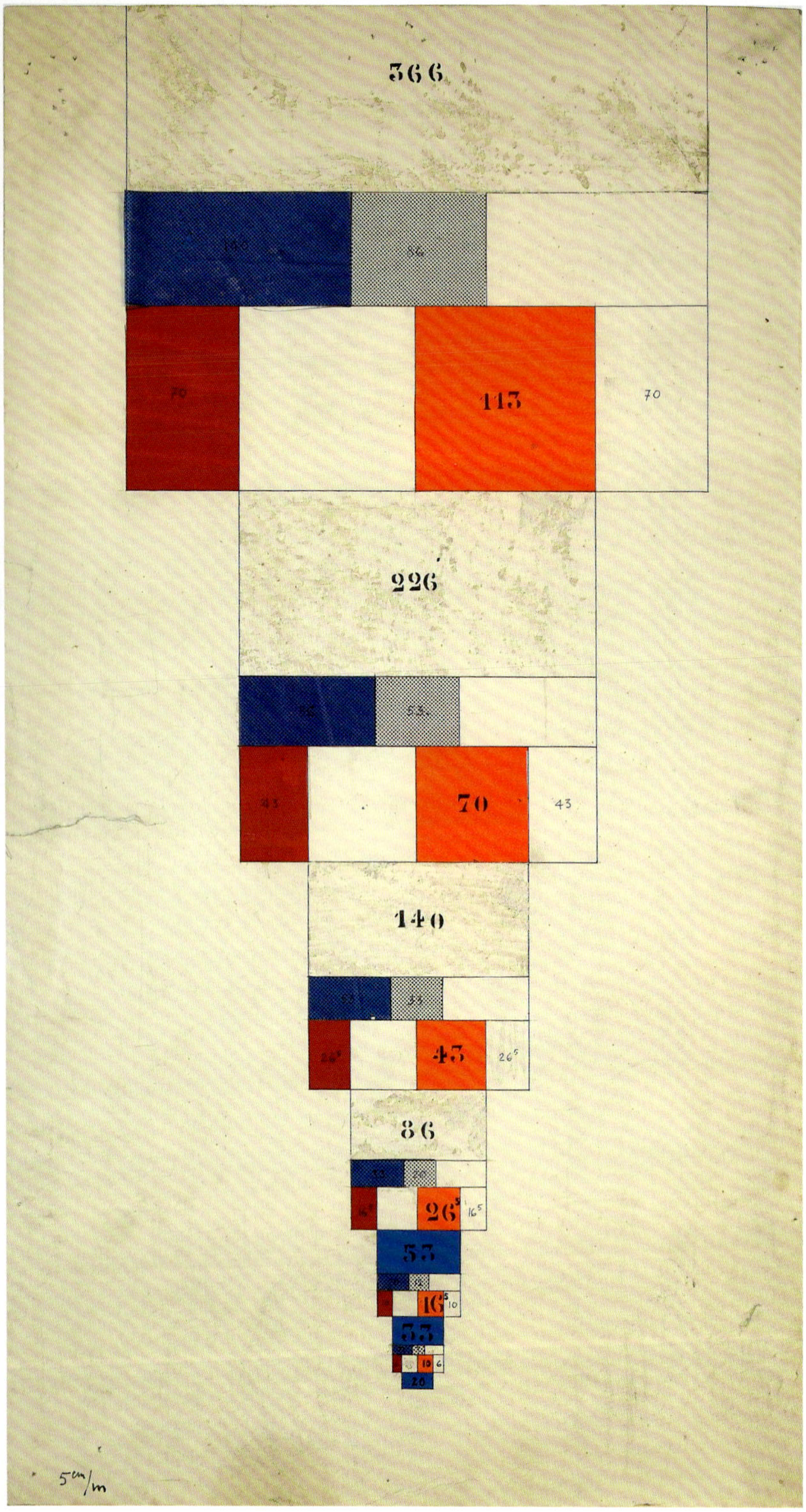

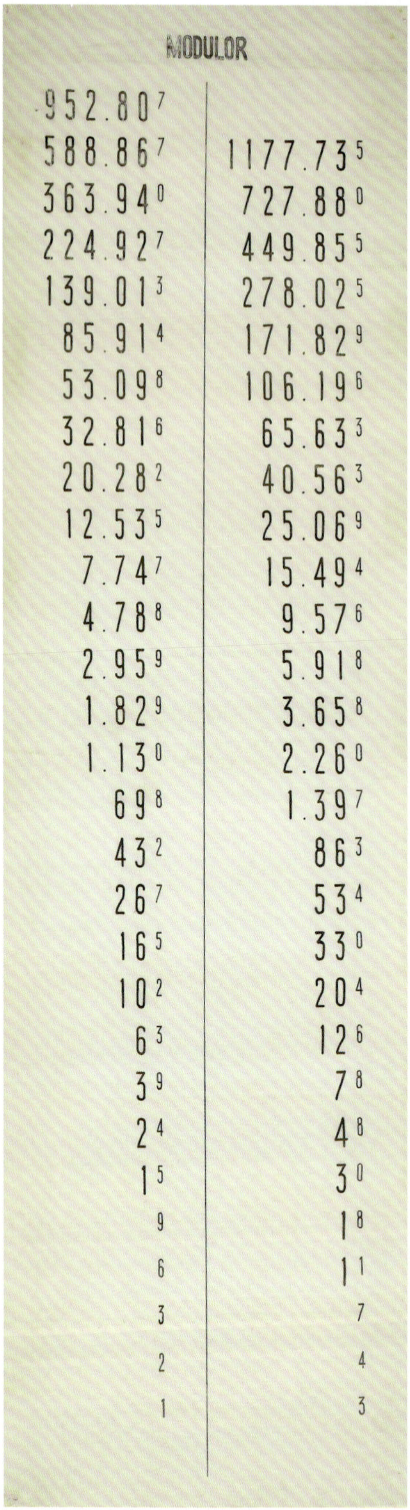

MODULOR

952.80^{7}	
588.86^{7}	1177.73^{5}
363.94^{0}	727.88^{0}
224.92^{7}	449.85^{5}
139.01^{3}	278.02^{5}
85.91^{4}	171.82^{9}
53.09^{8}	106.19^{6}
32.81^{6}	65.63^{3}
20.28^{2}	40.56^{3}
12.53^{5}	25.06^{9}
7.74^{7}	15.49^{4}
4.78^{8}	9.57^{6}
2.95^{9}	5.91^{8}
1.82^{9}	3.65^{8}
1.13^{0}	2.26^{0}
69^{8}	1.39^{7}
43^{2}	86^{3}
26^{7}	53^{4}
16^{5}	33^{0}
10^{2}	20^{4}
6^{3}	12^{6}
3^{9}	7^{8}
2^{4}	4^{8}
1^{5}	3^{0}
9	1^{8}
6	1^{1}
3	7
2	4
1	3

Far left and left. Drawing showing Modulor proportions and a list of Modulor units of measurement, both 1950

Below. Covers of Le Corbusier's books *Le Modulor*, 1950, and *Modulor 2*, 1955; both published by L'Architecture d'Aujourd'hui. The first volume explained the system; the second published selected public debates around it plus evidence of the system's success in various design projects.

Opposite. Le Corbusier presenting Modulor man at the Milan Triennale, 1951

113

Le Corbusier and Albert Einstein, 1946–47

Le Corbusier's faith in the power of his Modulor system was validated during a 1946 visit to the United States as a goodwill ambassador for the French Ministry of Foreign Affairs. While visiting Princeton, New Jersey, he met Albert Einstein. According to Le Corbusier, who often repeated the comment, Einstein signaled his approbation of the Modulor system with the simple declaration that it "makes the bad difficult and the good easy."

"I had the pleasure of quite a long chat about the 'Modulor' with Professor Albert Einstein at Princeton. At the time I was very unsure of myself, and anxious, explaining myself badly, explaining the idea badly, getting bogged down in 'cause and effect.'... At one point Einstein took a pencil and started doing a calculation. Foolishly I interrupted him, the conversation changed its course and the calculation went nowhere. The friend who had brought me was terribly distressed. That same evening Einstein kindly wrote to me of the 'Modulor,' 'It's a set of proportions that makes the bad difficult and the good easy.' Some see this assessment as lacking in scientific rigor. Personally I find it extraordinarily clear-sighted. It's a gesture of friendship from a great scientist to those of us who are in no way scientists, but rather soldiers on the battlefield."

—*Le Modulor*, 1950

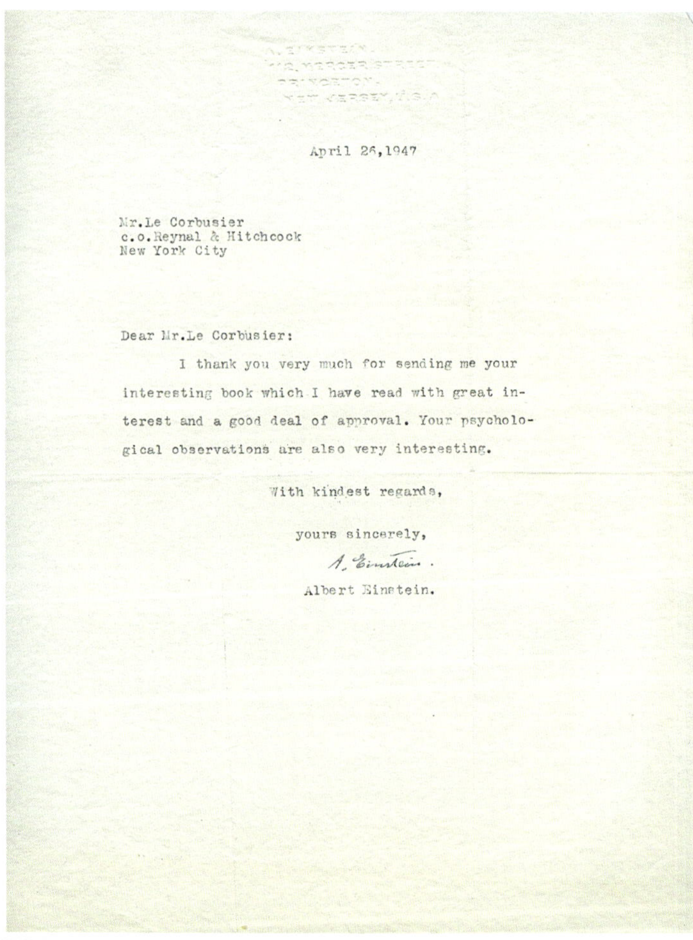

A. EINSTEIN
112 MERCER STREET
PRINCETON
NEW JERSEY, U.S.A.

April 26,1947

Mr.Le Corbusier
c.o.Reynal & Hitchcock
New York City

Dear Mr.Le Corbusier:

I thank you very much for sending me your interesting book which I have read with great interest and a good deal of approval. Your psychological observations are also very interesting.

With kindest regards,

yours sincerely,

A. Einstein.

Albert Einstein.

Top, left and right. Postcard from Princeton University professor Jean Labatut, while teaching at the Fontainebleau School of Fine Arts, 10 August 1947; Labatut's students were "delighted with their visit to rue de Sèvres."

Above. Letter from Albert Einstein, 26 April 1947, responding to Le Corbusier's book *When the Cathedrals Were White*, just published in English translation

Opposite. Le Corbusier with Albert Einstein in Princeton, New Jersey, 1946

Following pages. Photograms of Le Corbusier's profile with "grill" (left page) and with "sticks" (right page) by New Zealand artist Len Lye, 1947

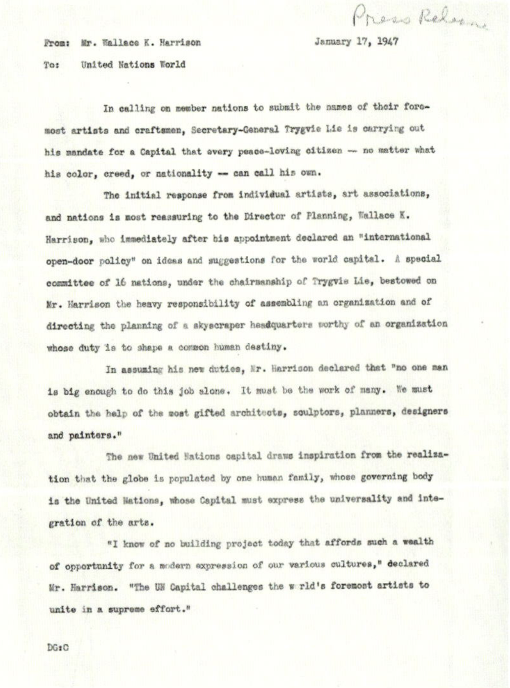

Press Release

From: Mr. Wallace K. Harrison January 17, 1947

To: United Nations World

In calling on member nations to submit the names of their foremost artists and craftsmen, Secretary-General Trygvie Lie is carrying out his mandate for a Capital that every peace-loving citizen -- no matter what his color, creed, or nationality -- can call his own.

The initial response from individual artists, art associations, and nations is most reassuring to the Director of Planning, Wallace K. Harrison, who immediately after his appointment declared an "international open-door policy" on ideas and suggestions for the world capital. A special committee of 16 nations, under the chairmanship of Trygvie Lie, bestowed on Mr. Harrison the heavy responsibility of assembling an organization and of directing the planning of a skyscraper headquarters worthy of an organization whose duty is to shape a common human destiny.

In assuming his new duties, Mr. Harrison declared that "no one man is big enough to do this job alone. It must be the work of many. We must obtain the help of the most gifted architects, sculptors, planners, designers and painters."

The new United Nations capital draws inspiration from the realization that the globe is populated by one human family, whose governing body is the United Nations, whose Capital must express the universality and integration of the arts.

"I know of no building project today that affords such a wealth of opportunity for a modern expression of our various cultures," declared Mr. Harrison. "The UN Capital challenges the world's foremost artists to unite in a supreme effort."

DG:C

Designing the United Nations headquarters, New York, 1946–47

To Le Corbusier, his invitation to participate in the design of the United Nations headquarters in 1946 confirmed, once and for all, the irrelevance of the classicist academy. However, his elation ultimately turned to bitterness when his designs were passed over. His scheme remained the property of the UN selection committee, which ultimately commissioned American architect Wallace K. Harrison to complete the project.

pposite, top. ommittee to hoose the UN eadquarters te, San Francisco,)46

pposite, bottom left. ress release from Vallace K. arrison, Director UN Head-uarters Planning ffice, 17 January)47

Opposite, bottom right. Le Corbusier's UN identification card, issued 20 June 1946

Above. Meeting in New York of UN's Board of Design Consultants, including Wallace K. Harrison (speaking), Oscar Nitzchke and Vladimir Bodiansky (standing in back row, left to right), Julio Vilamajo and Sven Markelius (both seated, in profile, center and center right), and Oscar Niemeyer (seated, second from right, in profile), 1947

Right. Le Corbusier in a meeting of UN architects in New York, 1947

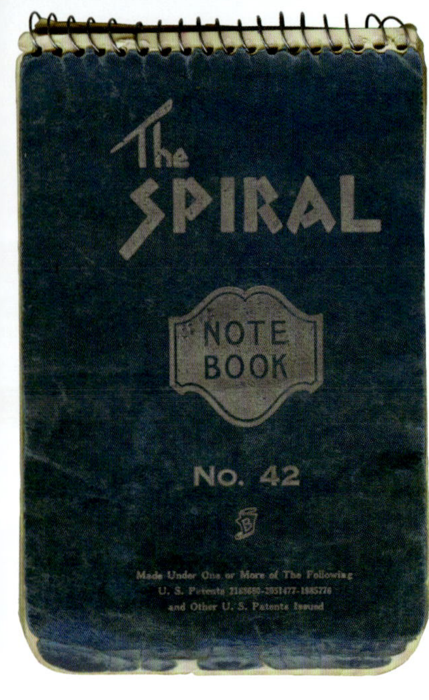
The
SPIRAL
NOTE
BOOK
No. 42
Made Under One or More of The Following
and Other U. S. Patents Issued

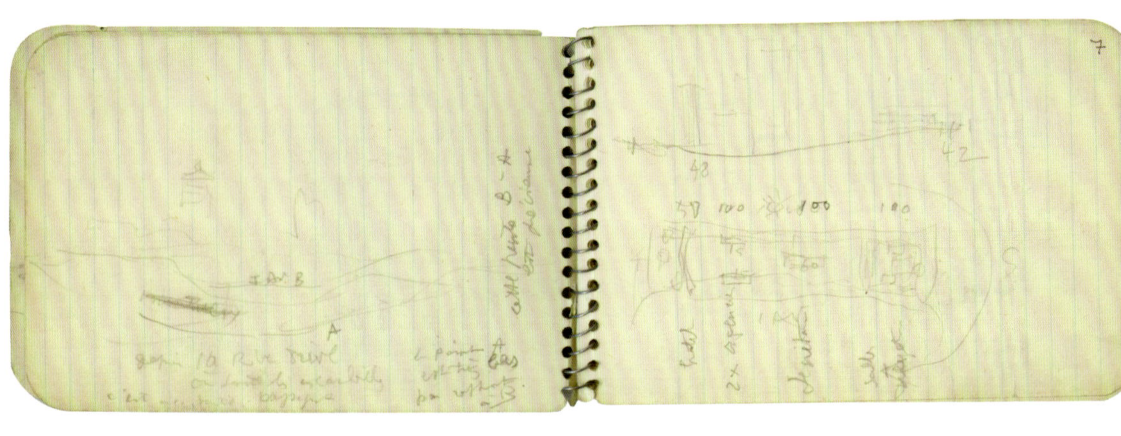

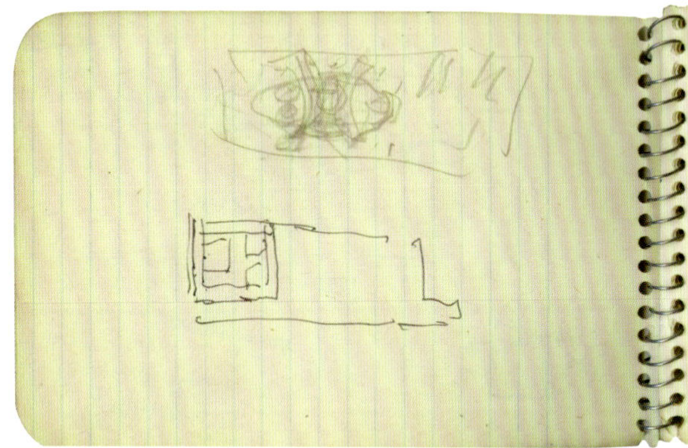

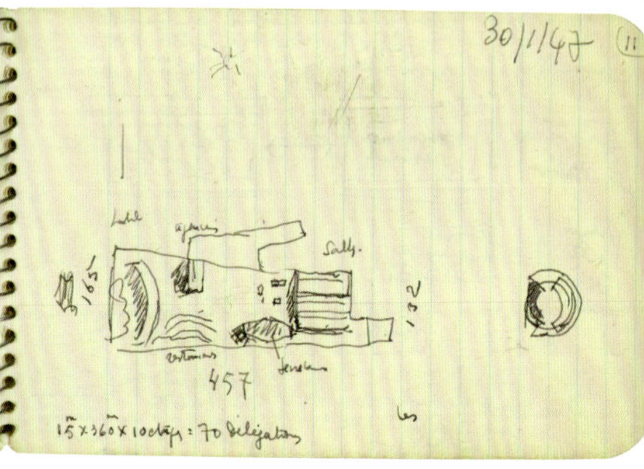
30/1/47
457

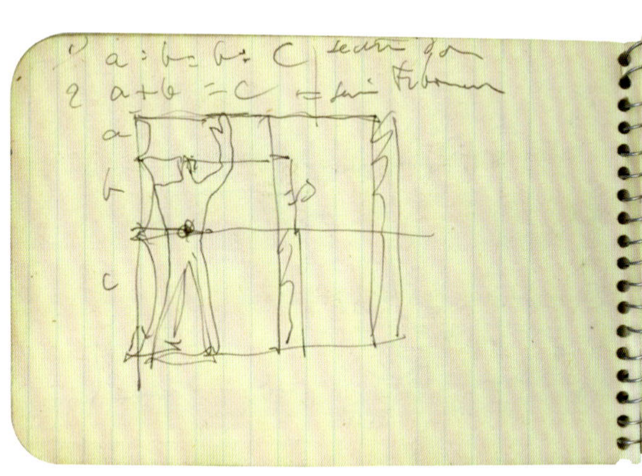

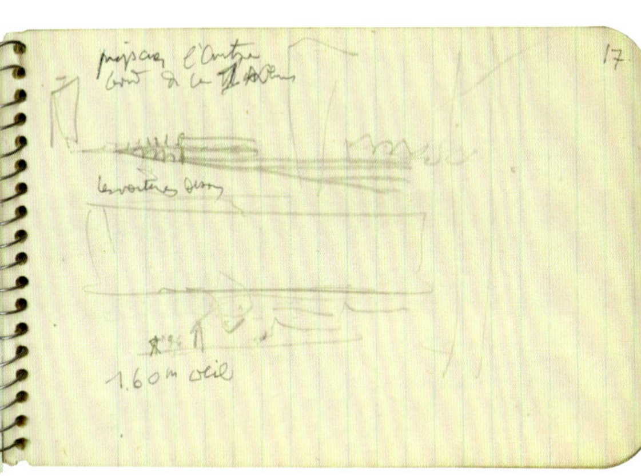
1.60m oeil

25/2/47

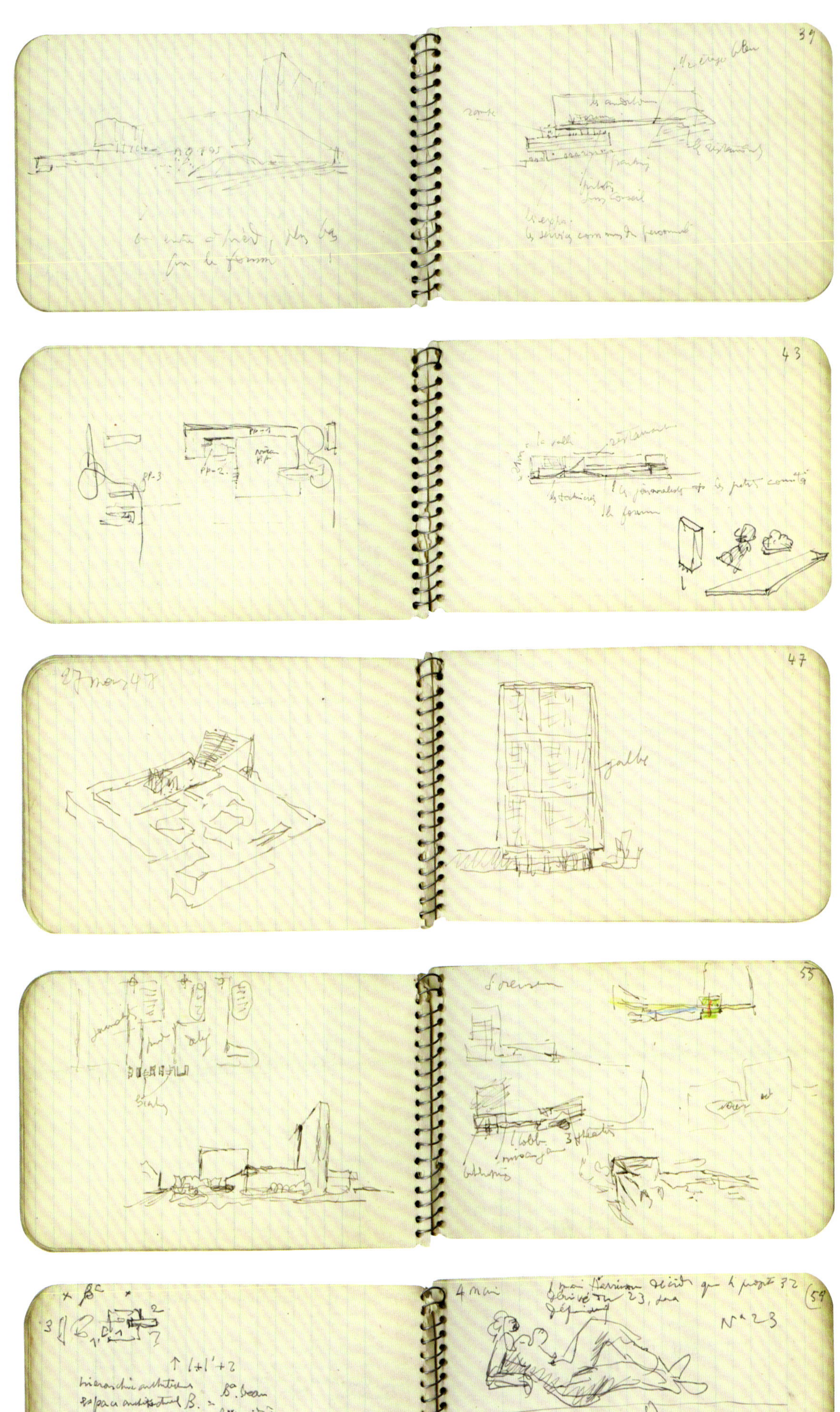

Opposite and this page. Le Corbusier's notebook containing his ideas and plans for the UN headquarters, 1947

"For 10 months I've been carrying on a relentless struggle. And now it's total Victory: the World Center is being built to my ideas in New York... March 47 will see the Corbu explosion everywhere. It must be written in the stars, and will be a kind of symphony. I don't like announcing outcomes, because each time fate laughs mockingly and does what it pleases." —Letter to his mother, 20 February 1947

Opposite. Official UN photograph of Le Corbusier, c. 1947

Right and below. Scheme 23/32, 3–4 May 1947, by Le Corbusier, Oscar Niemeyer, and the engineers Vladimir Bodiansky and Ernst Weissmann. Presented at the May meeting of the UN's Board of Design Consultants, 23/32 combined elements of Le Corbusier's Scheme 23 and Niemeyer's Scheme 32, and eventually led to the final Scheme 42G.

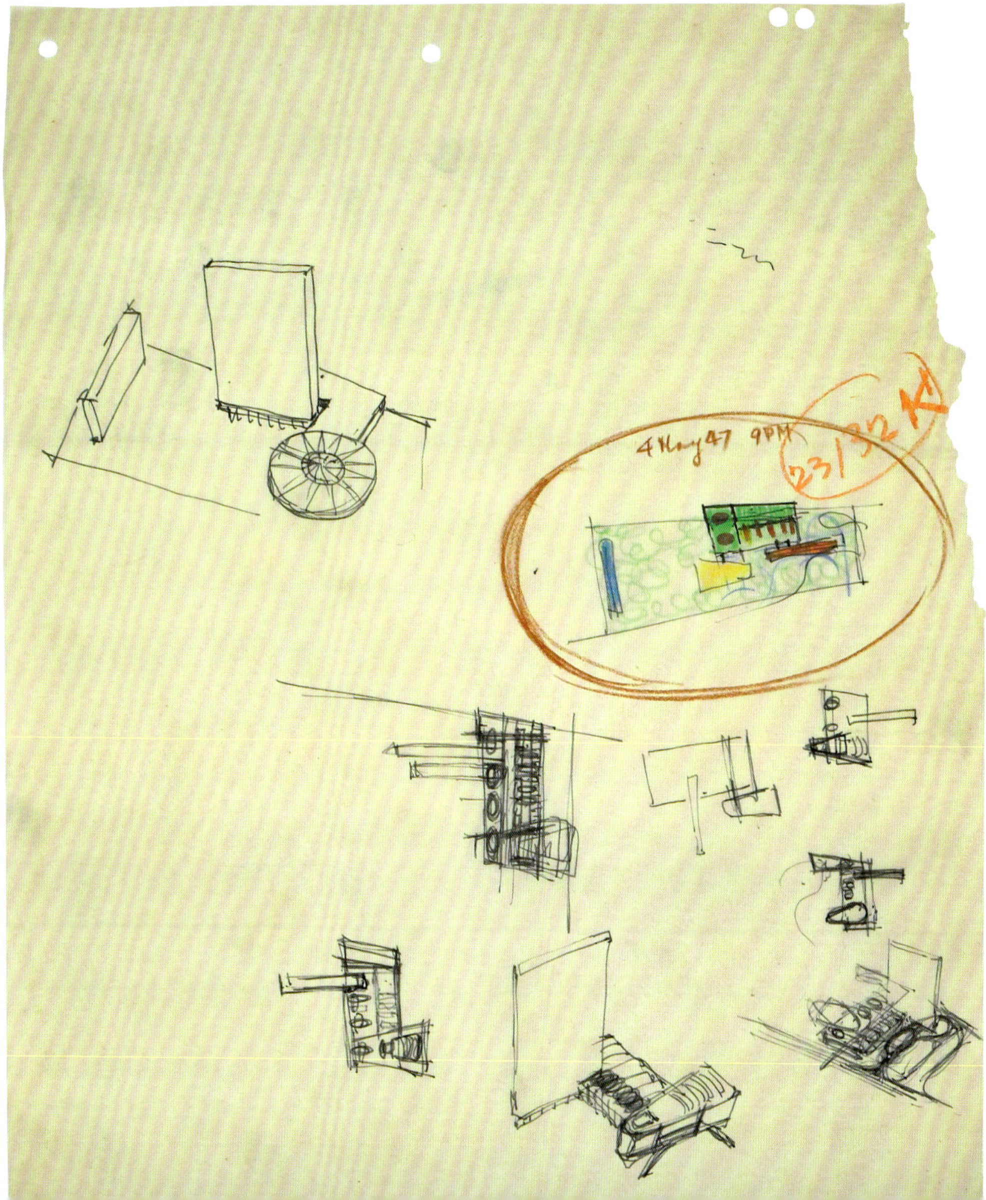

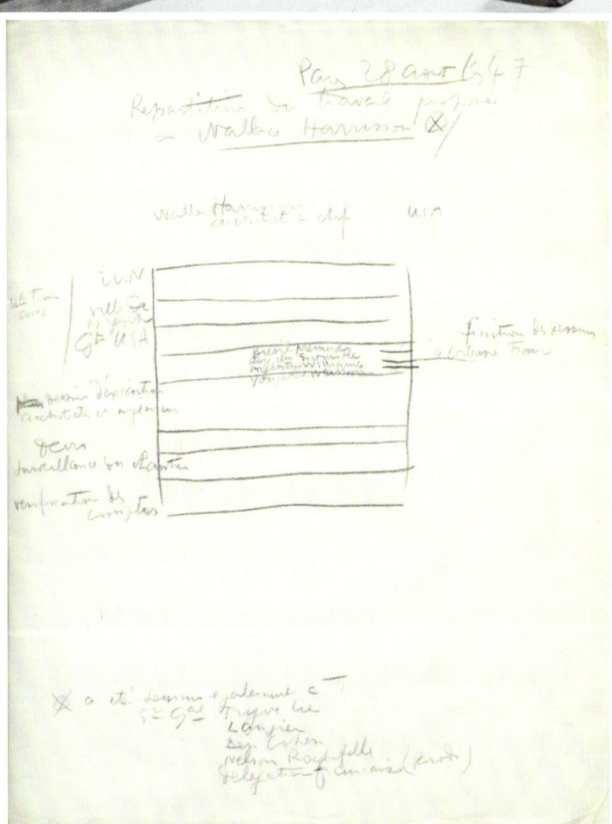

Above. Le Corbusier and Vladimir Bodiansky, engineering consultant from France, working on designs for the UN in Le Corbusier's office in the RKO building, New York, 1947

Left. Le Corbusier included this diagram in a letter to Wallace K. Harrison, 28 August 1947, expressing his belief that he is solely in charge of the design studio, as "mandated by the U.N."

"Those who pursue an ideal and fight for it have to be made of steel."

—Letter to Yvonne, 22 April 1947

ight. "Outline of he Headquarters' ommission eport," from the oint Advisory ommittee on the lan of United ations leadquarters. e Corbusier's hand-written notes include "America *Academie*!" referring to the four organizations mentioned in the letter (including the American Institute of Architects), that were charged with choosing a site for the UN and establishing a committee of architects to design the headquarters.

America ACADEMIE!

COMITE CONSULTATIF MIXTE

sur

LE PLAN ET L'AMENAGEMENT DU SIEGE DES NATIONS UNIES

EXPOSE

SUR LE RAPPORT DE LA COMMISSION DU SIEGE

Au début de cette année, les quatre sociétés techniques nationales, l'Institut américain des Architectes, l'Institut américain des Urbanistes, la Société américaine des Architectes paysagistes et la Société américaine des Ingénieurs civils, ont offert leurs services au Secrétaire général des Nations Unies et à la Commission du Siège. Pour rendre ce geste immédiatement utile et efficace, ces quatre sociétés ont constitué, au mois de mars, un Comité mixte composé des principaux membres de chaque profession en vue de coopérer avec la Commission du Siège des Nations Unies, qui était chargée de choisir des sites dans la région de Westchester-Fairfield, selon les directives données en février dernier par l'Assemblée générale des Nations Unies.

Le premier acte de coopération a consisté, pour le Comité, à répondre à la demande que lui avait faite le Secrétaire général de présenter des noms de candidats compétents au poste de directeur de la Section du personnel des bâtiments du Siège du Secrétariat des Nations Unies.

Below. Brazilian architect Oscar Niemeyer, studying plans for the UN in Le Corbusier's New York office, c. 1947. Niemeyer, one of ten architectural delegates working on the project, had been Le Corbusier's associate on the Ministry of Education building in Rio de Janeiro ten years earlier.

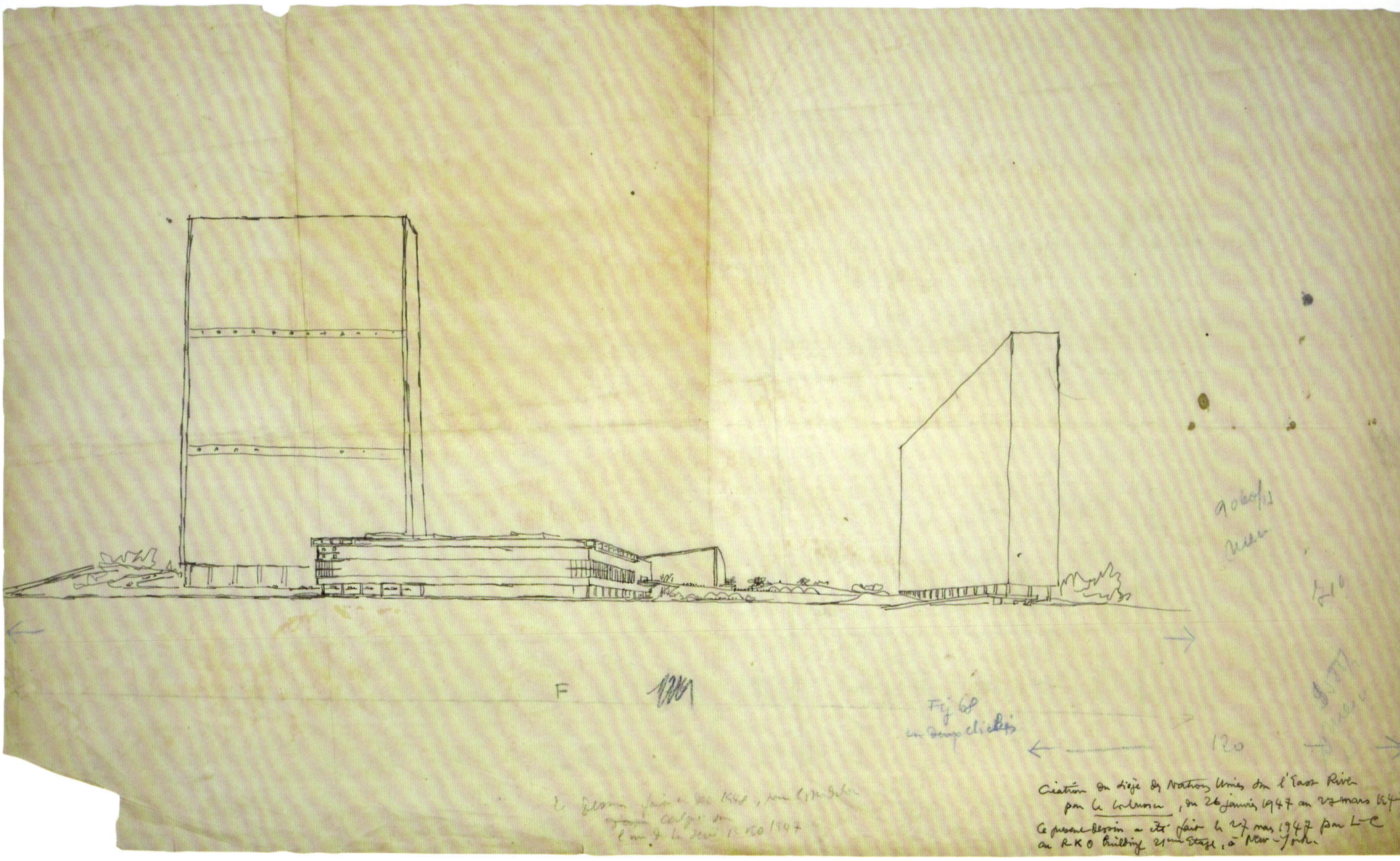

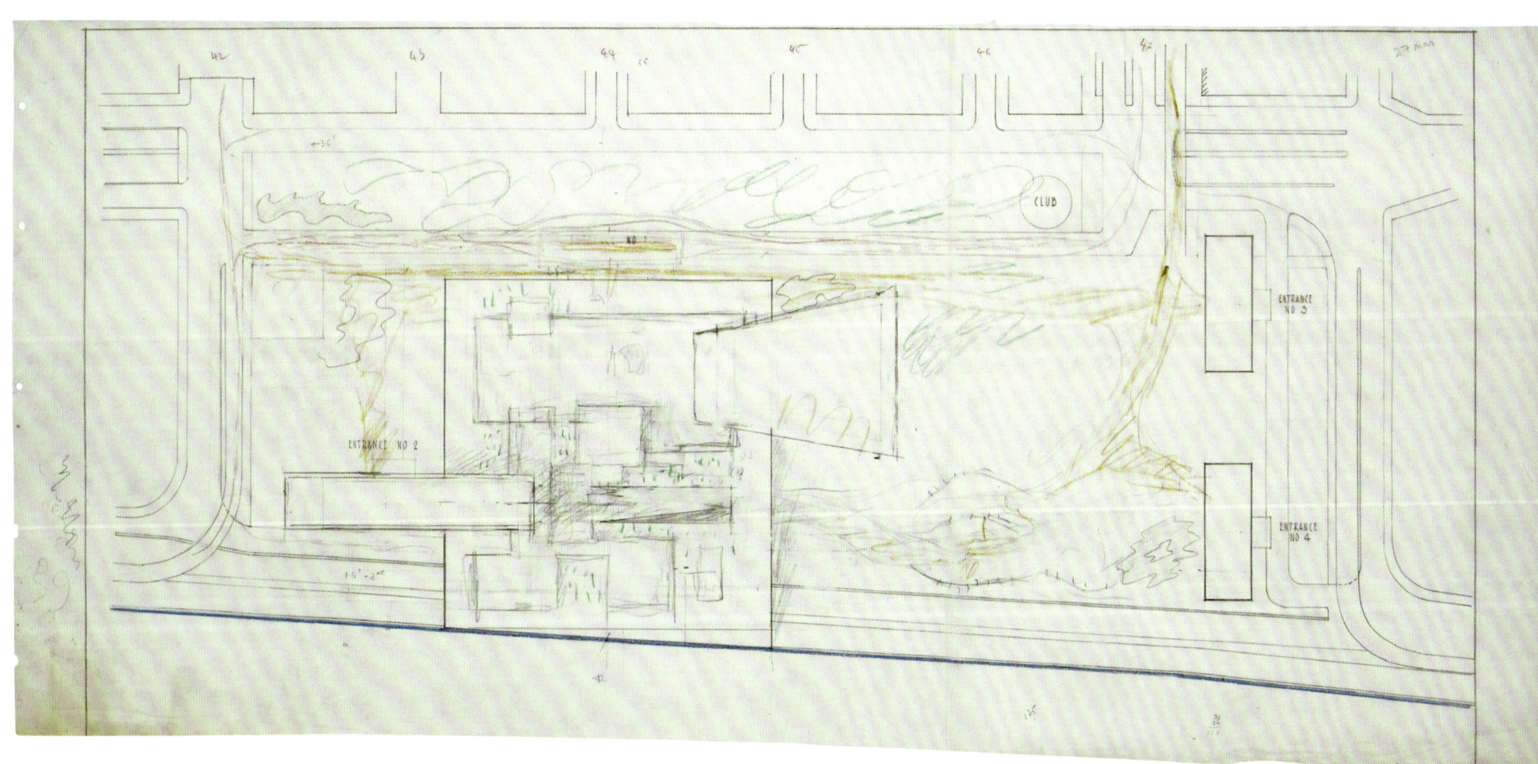

"I'm working here with Harrison, an American who's a fraction jealous, and 14 architects from different nations. 1/3 hostile, 2/3 in favor. The draftsmen have become my friends. We can do something magnificent, and that's why I forge on." —Letter to his mother, 6 May 1947

Opposite, top. Perspective, proposal for the UN headquarters, including the General Assembly and Secretariat, 27 March 1947

Opposite, bottom. Site plan, UN headquarters, 1947

Below. Two models of Plan 23A (left), presented to the Board of Design Consultants on 28 April 1947, devised by Le Corbusier and Vladimir Bodiansky as an alternative to Oscar Niemeyer's Scheme 32 (model at right)

Bottom. Le Corbusier, standing behind a display of models for the UN complex with Wallace K. Harrison (left) and Vladimir Bodiansky right), 1947

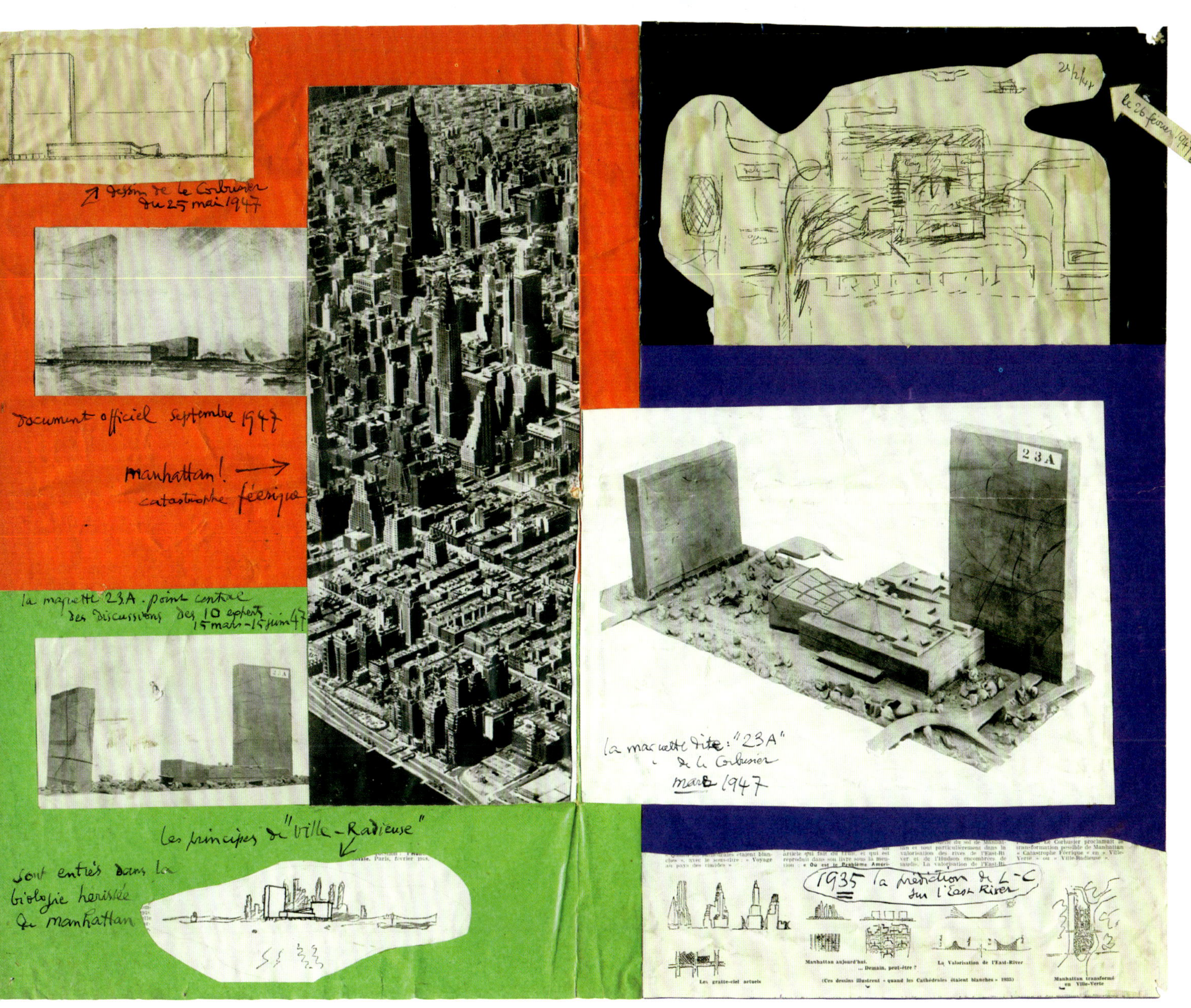

pposite. Le orbusier, during ork on the UN roject, 1947

bove. A 1947 ollage of plans, odels, and draw- ngs for Project 3A, with an aerial hotograph of Manhattan encom- assing the proj- ct's site. At bottom s a sketch of the omplex labeled the principles of Ville-Radieuse'" nd a page from *uand les athédrales étaient lanches* with the otation "1935 -C's prediction or the East River."

Right. Letters from Wallace K. Harrison and Nelson Rockefeller to Le Corbusier, 9 and 18 December 1947. Rockefeller participated in the founding conference of the UN in 1945 and donated money for the UN headquarters. His father, John D. Rockefeller, Jr., donated the land on which to build the UN

Letter mailed 12/17/47 after approval by Mr. Feller and Mr. Rockefeller

December 9, 1947.

Dear Mr. Corbusier:

Your notes have remained unanswered for reasons which you understand perfectly.

I am delighted that you feel that you are the one who designed the United Nations Headquarters. It pleases me equally that other members of the Board have that same satisfaction. After all, the combined work was to be symbolic of the unity and selflessness of the United Nations.

The decision as to how the building of the Headquarters is to be carried on is in the hands of the United Nations. Whatever they decide, I will abide by.

Believe me,

Yours respectfully,

Wallace K. Harrison
Director of Planning

M. Charles Le Corbusier
35 rue de Sevres
Paris 6, France

[illegible]:J

CC - Trygve Lie, Senator Austin, Nelson A. Rockefeller

Room 5600
30 Rockefeller Plaza
New York 20, N. Y.

COPY.

December 18, 1947

Dear M. LeCorbusier:

Please forgive my delay in acknowledging your letter of November tenth.

In view of the fact that you enclosed a copy of the documents which you sent to Mr. Harrison, he has been good enough to show me a copy of the letter which he has written you in reply to your communication to him. Frankly, it seems to me that his letter justly answers the questions which you raise and that there is nothing further I can contribute to the situation.

This letter brings very best wishes for a Merry Christmas and a Happy New Year from Mrs. Rockefeller and myself.

Sincerely,

NELSON A. ROCKEFELLER DEC 19 1947

Nelson A. Rockefeller

M. Charles LeCorbusier
35 Rue de Sevres
Paris 6, France

NAR:GE/sc
Cleared with: Mr. Harrison
Mr. Jamieson

HARRISON & ABRAMOVITZ
ARCHITECTS
630 FIFTH AVENUE, NEW YORK, N. Y. 10020

November 20, 1973

The other day while cleaning up old files my secretary came upon the attached news item and the letter referring to it.

This led to my decision to put on paper what I remembered of the episode.

Without minimizing or commenting on the contribution and influence of Corbusier and the other architects of the 14 countries of the Board of Design to the final design solution for the United Nations Complex, I will concentrate on the reference in the third
& 4th paragraph of the attached newspaper article by Mary Burnet in which Corbusier refers to his notebook. (See postscript dated Nov. 15, 1986)

Under the direction of Wallace K. Harrison and myself (Max Abramovitz) as Deputy Director a design office was set up. This consisted of a design drafting room and a large conference room adjacent. The entire group of architects met in the Conference Room during the many weeks to contribute and review design ideas as the space program for the U.N. Headquarters developed.

It had been agreed that the consultants would not get directly involved in the "back room" drafting activities but would review the sketches developed. This was done to discourage partisanship and encourage fair and unbiased appraisal of the ideas developed.

The transmission of instructions from the consultants' room to the "back room" was one of my duties even though I was also intimately involved in the daily meetings and participated actively in the critical discussions.

In the consultants room were posted the latest schemes as well as plastecene

Page 1 - continue

HARRISON & ABRAMOVITZ
ARCHITECTS
630 FIFTH AVENUE, NEW YORK, N. Y. 10020

\- 2 -

models of the schemes under discussion.

This process continued for many weeks until a concensus was arrived at as to the most plausible solutions for the forms of the Secretariat Building and the Assembly Hall and Conference Block.

The final accepted scheme (the one essentially as has been built)-- I think it was 23 or 23A was the outgrowth of sketches and studies reviewed and refined for several days by all the architects and drawn up in the "back room" (as were all other schemes) to reflect the group's feeling that the plans and forms would be an articulation of the three important elements; i.e. the Secretariat, the General Assembly Room, and the Council and Conference Room group (with the Secretariat to the South and the Assembly Hall to the North) rather than a large square mass advanced by Corbusier which would have contained within it the large Assembly Hall and the various Council and Conference Rooms with the rectangular office form protruding from it.

After several days of discussion and review the day arrived when all the consultants accepted Scheme 23 as the one!

That day, or the day after, I was present in the room and I saw Mr. Corbusier take off the wall the sketch of the plan referred to above, redraw it in his own hand and style, redate it, initial it, and put it back on the wall.

This was the sketch which was later reproduced in various periodicals and which he refers to as his own claiming it evolved from sketches in his notebook. (Note: I was aware, as I assume were others, that he carried a small notebook in which he made notes and sketches).

HARRISON & ABRAMOVITZ
ARCHITECTS
630 FIFTH AVENUE, NEW YORK, N. Y. 10020

\- 3 -

An additional item---while the exhibition referred to in the December 10,1948 news item was in the planning stage in Boston under the direction of Mr. Plaut, Harmon Goldstone who had been for a time in the Planning Office and a friend of Mr. Plaut, telephoned me and asked about the statement made by Mr. Corbusier as to the authorship of the famous plan #23. At that time I related to Harmon Goldstone the information put down above.

I also told this story to Russell Lynes in the late 1950s or the early 1960s.

Although I have mentioned portions of this personal story to friends a few times during several years I have never put it on paper.

At the time of the studies and execution of the UN group of buildings and at the time the statements of Corbusier were attracting attention and for several years thereafter and officially until this day it was the unspoken understanding that the UN Planning Office would not offer any rebuttal nor enter into any controversy related to architecture in the interests of the general purpose of the UN.

November 20, 1973

Max Abramovitz

P.S. - November 15, 1986 The referred to notebook was uncovered a few years ago among Corbusier's own papers in the Corbusier Archives in Paris, France.

Max Abramovitz

Above. Signed affidavit from Max Abramovitz, dated 20 November 1973, with his account of the planning of the UN headquarters, rebutting Le Corbusier's claim to have been the principal creator of the basic design

Below left. Sketch by Le Corbusier for the cover of his book on the UN headquarters

Below right. Final cover, *UN Headquarters: Practical Application of a Philosophy of the Domain of Building*, Reinhold Publishing, New York, 1947

Opposite. The UN Secretariat, 23 October 1951, illuminated to mark the sixth anniversary of the United Nations

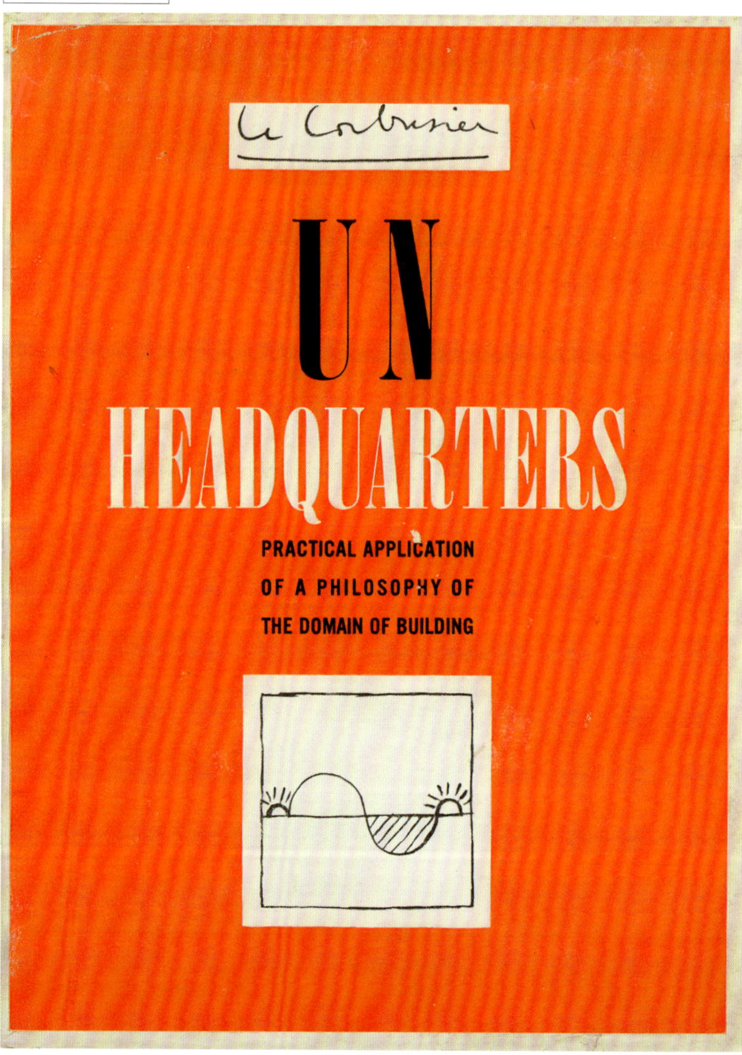

Opposite. Photographs of Le Corbusier and the newly constructed UN Secretariat, New York, c. 1950

Right. Le Corbusier holds a photograph of model 23A, comparing it with the built Secretariat, c. 1950. To the end of his life, he remained bitterly insistent that the building was based on his design.

36

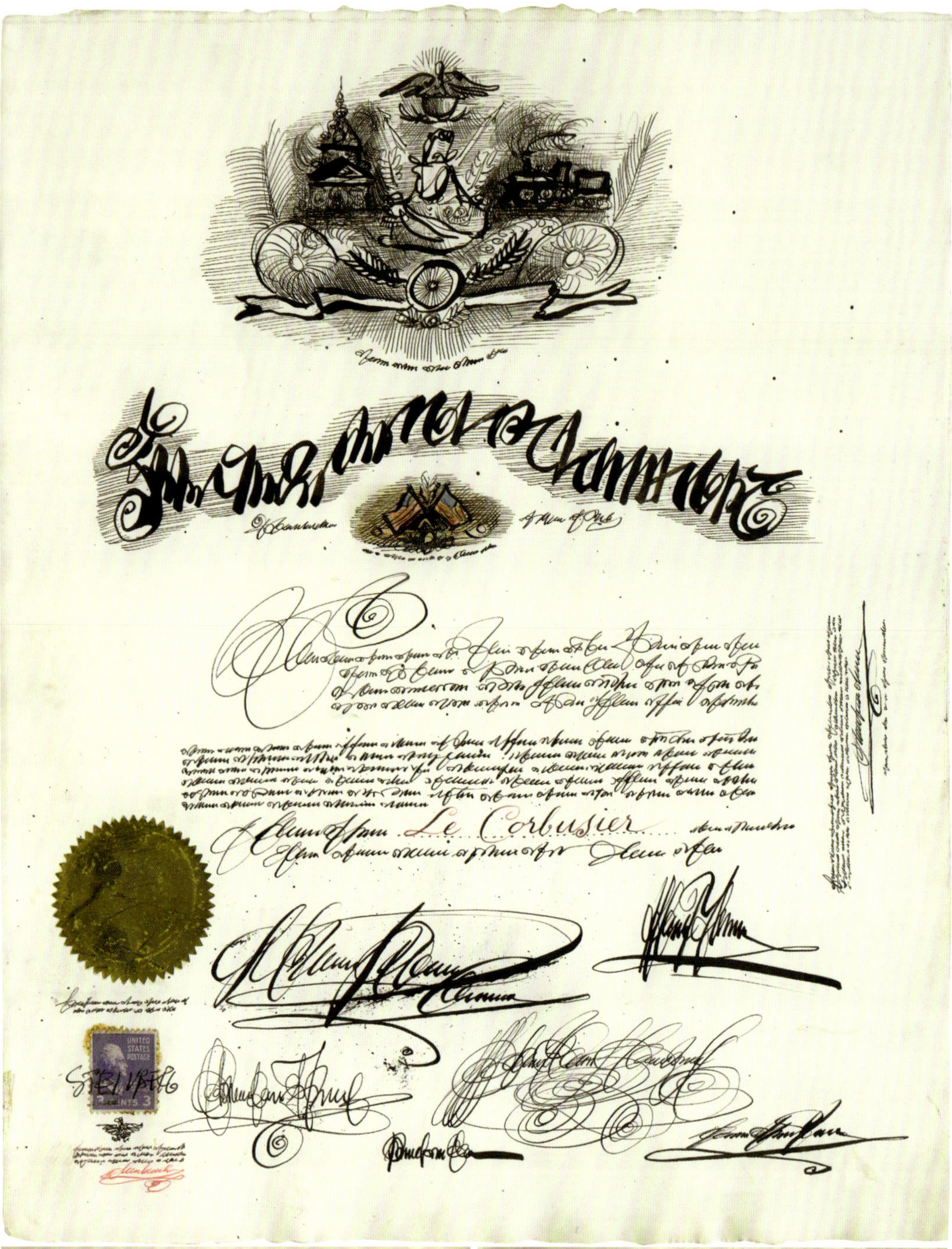

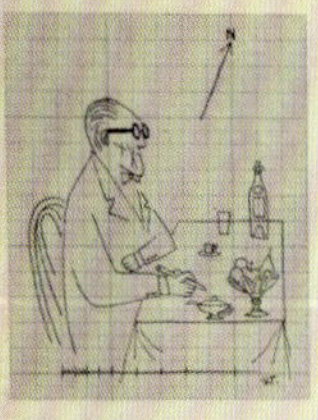

PROFILES

FROM WITHIN TO WITHOUT—II

Le Corbusier, the Swiss-born French architect who for over twenty-five years has been the world's most articulate and influential exponent of modern architecture, is rarely satisfied with anything that happens in building circles, but he was delighted, last December, when the East River site was accepted by the United Nations for its headquarters. As a member of the United Nations Headquarters Commission, he delivered a speech to this group's parent body, the General Assembly's Headquarters Committee, in which he intimated that he had, in a way, foreseen this decision long before the United Nations came into existence. Le Corbusier, who visited this country on a lecture tour in 1935, bases his claim to prescience on an article he wrote while he was here. Under the title "What Is America's Problem?" it appeared, in translation, in the *American Architect*. The passage that he likes to point out reads:

> Manhattan—great unfilleted sole spread out on a rock—is no good except along the backbone; the edges are slums.... The edges along the East River and the Hudson are inaccessible. The ocean is inaccessible, invisible.... Yet all that ocean and those great rivers are invisible, and the advantages of their beauty, their space, their movement, and their lovely light under the sun, all that belongs to no one. New York, the immense ocean port, is for its inhabitants as inland as Moscow! And those splendid sites along the river, destined, it would seem, to receive immense apartment houses with windows opening on space, these sites are desolating—for they are slums. By a well-advised municipal development, it would be easy to rehabilitate these districts and the profit would be sufficient to permit going ahead with rehabilitation of the center of the city, now all violence and anarchy.

Today, a well-advised development—although not a municipal one—is in hand for one of these sites, and Le Corbusier has a good deal to do with it. His conception of what the United Nations Headquarters ought to look like is revealed in the projects, never realized, that he has drawn up for a dozen cities, in Europe, North Africa, and South America, and in a series of buildings that the French government is about to construct, from his plans, in La Rochelle, a war-devastated town in western France, and La Pallice, its port, which during the war was a German submarine base. This conception calls for a group of glass-walled structures perched well above the ground on huge, reinforced-concrete piles, or *pilotis*, and set a few hundred yards apart to provide space in between for parks and athletic fields. Le Corbusier calls a group like this a vertical garden city. Wallace K. Harrison, the eminent American architect who is director of planning for the United Nations headquarters, admires Le Corbusier professionally and selected him as one of ten members of the United Nations Board of Design Consultants, which has been set up to help him design the United Nations buildings. However, Robert Moses, City Construction Coördinator and Mayor O'Dwyer's representative in United Nations negotiations, has little use for him. Moses is the possessor of an intransigence rivalled only by Le Corbusier's. His chauvinism is intense. As one of the chief plumpers for locating the United Nations headquarters in Flushing, he was distressed, last fall, when Le Corbusier, airing his views on that site in a report of the Headquarters Commission, said:

> New York is a terrifying city. For us, it is menacing. We are not wrong in keeping it at a distance!... Flushing Meadow is not the site for the Headquarters of the United Nations, because Flushing Meadow is inescapably a suburb of New York, a dependency of New York. Now, the United Nations is neither a dependency of New York, nor of the United States of America. Freedom—not constraint—must at every minute be the dominant feeling. In no case must the United Nations become a corollary to America. To implant its Headquarters in the very shadow of the skyscrapers of Manhattan is inadmissible. The Manhattan skyscrapers are by their very nature too precarious; New York is a thrilling city but so questionable that it cannot take the Headquarters of the United Nations into its lap. This is a question of moral proportion. In fact, a question of "respectability."

The Rockefeller offer, paradoxically, seems to have dissipated Le Corbusier's terror of the city, and he now believes that a few East River skyscrapers, especially if designed on vertical-garden-city principles, might not be too precarious after all. Moses is still in favor of keeping Le Corbusier at a distance. "What do these foreign fellows know about our foundations, our hard-rock problems?" he said recently. It is probable that the United Nations buildings will show traces of Le Corbusier's influence, but it is also probable that they will rest on old-fashioned, orthodox foundations rather than on *pilotis*.

Along with the other consultants, Le Corbusier is working on plans in a drafting room on the twenty-seventh floor of the R.K.O. Building. He puts in his mornings on sketches and models. Afternoons, he and his colleagues attend staff meetings with Harrison and others. Harrison knows that Le Corbusier is one of the greatest designers in the world and also one of the most temperamental, and he has been handling him accordingly. Le Corbusier has responded with a great show of sweet reasonableness. "I am in complete calm here," he told a visitor to his working quarters the other day. "I think God has come down to earth. I don't even mind working in a room with other people. An architect shouldn't be alone. He can't do his best work without talking. Talking stimulates you. You develop ideas when you have an audience. And anyway, you don't have to listen to what the other man says." After spending the morning not listening to his colleagues, Le Corbusier usually repairs for lunch to Del Pezzo's, a casual Italian restaurant on West Forty-seventh Street, where he politely ignores the remarks of various friends.

Le Corbusier has spent many years in the study of *urbanisme*, a word that he feels embraces not only living in a city but the sociological and economic problems living in a city creates. His present benign state of mind about New York notwithstanding, this study has strengthened his conviction that he exists in a world of idiots, fools, and paupers who haven't the sense to realize how badly off they are. He is sure that slum dwellers, by and large, are not as unhappy as they ought to be. "I know that a proper plan can make New York the city par excellence of modern times," he wrote in "Quand les Cathédrales Etaient Blanches," a fairly trenchant book about the United States that was one result of his lecture tour of this country in 1935, "can actively spread daily happiness for these oppressed families—children, women, men stupefied by work, stunned by noise of the rails of the subways or elevateds—who sink down each evening, at the end of their appointed tasks, in the impasse of an inhuman hovel." Nevertheless, he has noted with annoyance that some of the oppressed millions actually seem to perk up toward evening and go bowling or to the movies. His own capacity for moral indignation is boundless.

37

Le Corbusier's trip in 1935 seems to have been made under a misapprehension. That summer, Philip L. Goodwin, a trustee of the Museum of Modern Art, and at that time chairman of its Committee on Architecture, visited Le Corbusier in Paris and invited him to come here for a lecture tour. Goodwin said that the Museum would sponsor the tour and pay all expenses, and that the entire favorable difference, if any, between these costs and the lecture fees would go to Le Corbusier. The architect accepted this offer, but upon his arrival in New York he acted as though he hadn't completely understood it and was simply on a sightseeing junket in the course of which he would make a mint of money. His ship was met at Quarantine by Robert A. Jacobs, a young Manhattan architect who had served an apprenticeship with the Parisian architectural firm of Le Corbusier & P. Jeanneret a year before, and whom the Museum had engaged to act as Le Corbusier's interpreter on his American tour. "Jacobs," said Le Corbusier, "where are the photographers?" Jacobs, an obliging man who also admires Le Corbusier intensely, found that the press cameramen on board were busy taking pictures of other celebrities. He slipped a newspaperman five dollars and implored him to take a picture of Le Corbusier. "I've used up all my film," said the photographer, returning the money. Being an obliging fellow himself, however, he snapped his empty camera at Le Corbusier, who looked mollified. The Museum had arranged with the French Institute to put Le Corbusier up in a suite that this organization then maintained on its premises to accommodate visiting French notables, but when Le Corbusier heard about this plan, on his way uptown, he shook his head. "*Je m'en fiche de l'Institut Français*," he said. "*Je vais au Waldorf.*" Jacobs suggested that this might be too expensive, and Le Corbusier, who has always called the Modern Museum the Rockefeller Foundation, said that Mr. Rockefeller would foot the bill. Instead, Jacobs took him and his baggage direct to the Museum, where a press conference had been arranged. Le Corbusier's English is poor, and Joseph Alsop, of the *Herald Tribune*, undertook to help interpret it for the benefit of the less cultured reporters. "Your skyscrapers are too small," Le Corbusier said in the course of the conference, during which it quickly turned out that he knew at least enough English to be able to complain bitterly when he felt that Jacobs or Alsop had translated him inadequately. He also complained when the press photographers started to take pictures of him. According to witnesses, he pulled some studio portraits of himself out of a suitcase and offered to supply them to the newspapermen for five

"*Look, Daddy—a swimming pool!*"

Mutual admiration society: Saul Steinberg and Le Corbusier

Saul Steinberg made a drawing of Le Corbusier to accompany a *New Yorker* profile in 1947. The rather mocking tone of the article infuriated Le Corbusier, but the experience marked the start of a long friendship with Steinberg.

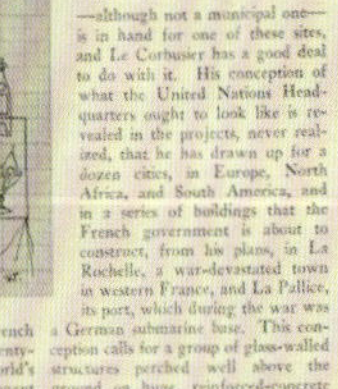

Above. "Diploma" for Le Corbusier by Saul Steinberg, late 1940s

Left. Profile of Le Corbusier, with sketch by Saul Steinberg (top left corner), in the *New Yorker*, 3 May 1947

Opposite, top left. Le Corbusier to Saul Steinberg, 5 January 1956, wishing him a happy new year

Opposite, top right. Postcards from Saul Steinberg to Le Corbusier, one from Cape Cod, Massachusetts, July 1955, and one from Marseille Unité, 18 May 1953 (the back of which reads "Greetings, and thanks, Steinberg")

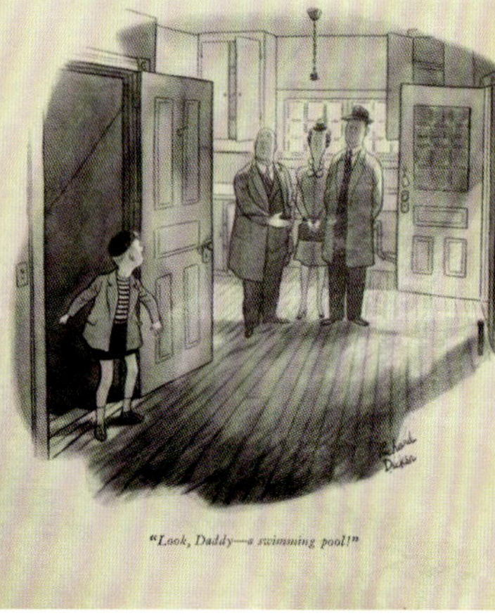

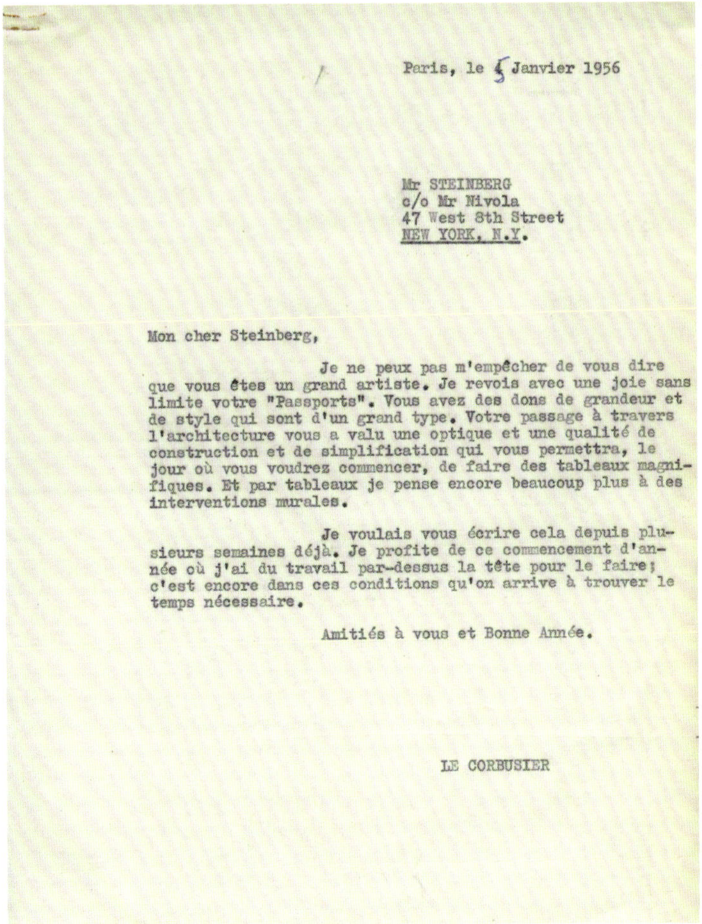

Paris, le 5 Janvier 1956

Mr STEINBERG
c/o Mr Nivola
47 West 8th Street
NEW YORK, N.Y.

Mon cher Steinberg,

Je ne peux pas m'empêcher de vous dire que vous êtes un grand artiste. Je revois avec une joie sans limite votre "Passports". Vous avez des dons de grandeur et de style qui sont d'un grand type. Votre passage à travers l'architecture vous a valu une optique et une qualité de construction et de simplification qui vous permettra, le jour où vous voudrez commencer, de faire des tableaux magnifiques. Et par tableaux je pense encore beaucoup plus à des interventions murales.

Je voulais vous écrire cela depuis plusieurs semaines déjà. Je profite de ce commencement d'année où j'ai du travail par-dessus la tête pour le faire; c'est encore dans ces conditions qu'on arrive à trouver le temps nécessaire.

Amitiés à vous et Bonne Année.

LE CORBUSIER

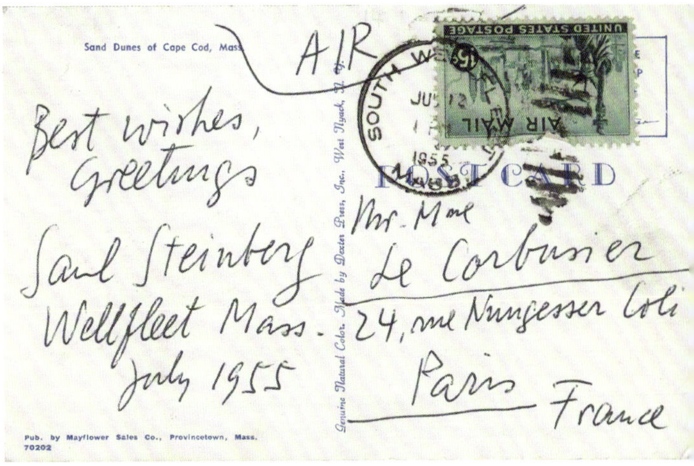

Sand Dunes of Cape Cod, Mass.

AIR

POST CARD

Best wishes,
Greetings
Saul Steinberg
Wellfleet Mass.
July 1955

Mr. Mme
Le Corbusier
24, rue Nungesser Coli
Paris
France

Pub. by Mayflower Sales Co., Provincetown, Mass.
70202

"My dear Steinberg, I simply have to tell you that you are a great artist... You are gifted with immense grandeur and style. The time you spent as an architect has given you a viewpoint and a capacity for construction and simplification that will enable you, once you decide to start, to produce magnificent paintings."

—Letter to Saul Steinberg, 5 January 1956

Creation and recreation away from home: Costantino Nivola

While working on the UN project in New York, Le Corbusier frequently socialized with a circle that included his old friend José Luis Sert and Italian-born sculptor Costantino Nivola. Le Corbusier often spent weekends during the summer at the Nivolas' house in Amagansett, on Long Island, for which he painted a series of murals and made a sand-cast sculpture.

Above. Le Corbusier making a sand-cast sculpture with Costantino Nivola, in the Nivolas' garden, Long Island, New York, 1950

Below left. On the beach with the Nivolas' children, Pietro and Claire, 1950

Below right. With the completed sand-cast, 1950

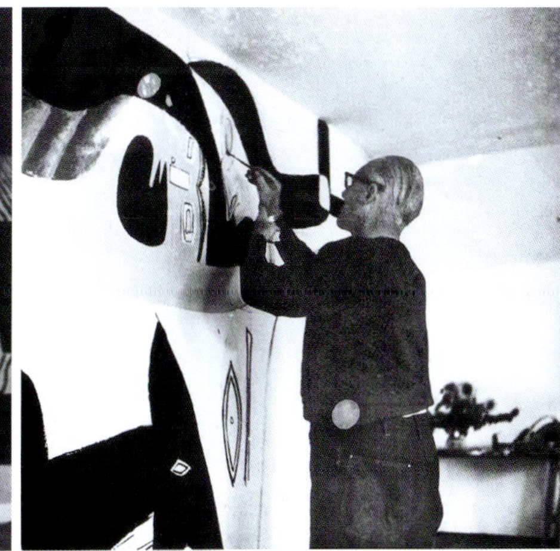

Top. Sketch, 29 June 1950, for the mural that Le Corbusier painted for Costantino Nivola and his wife, Ruth, in their Long Island home

Bottom. Le Corbusier painting the mural, which was completed 1 October 1950. The photograph at left shows the Nivola children, Pietro and Claire, in front of the mural.

Painting a mural at the rue de Sèvres office, 1947

Invigorated by his trips to New York and optimistic about new creative directions, Le Corbusier painted a mural on one of the walls of his Paris office. He also added several new American-made work tables for his growing staff.

Left. Le Corbusier sketching the mural onto the back wall of his office on the rue de Sèvres, 1947

Below. His studio staff working at their drafting tables after completion of the mural, 1947 (left), and with Le Corbusier (right)

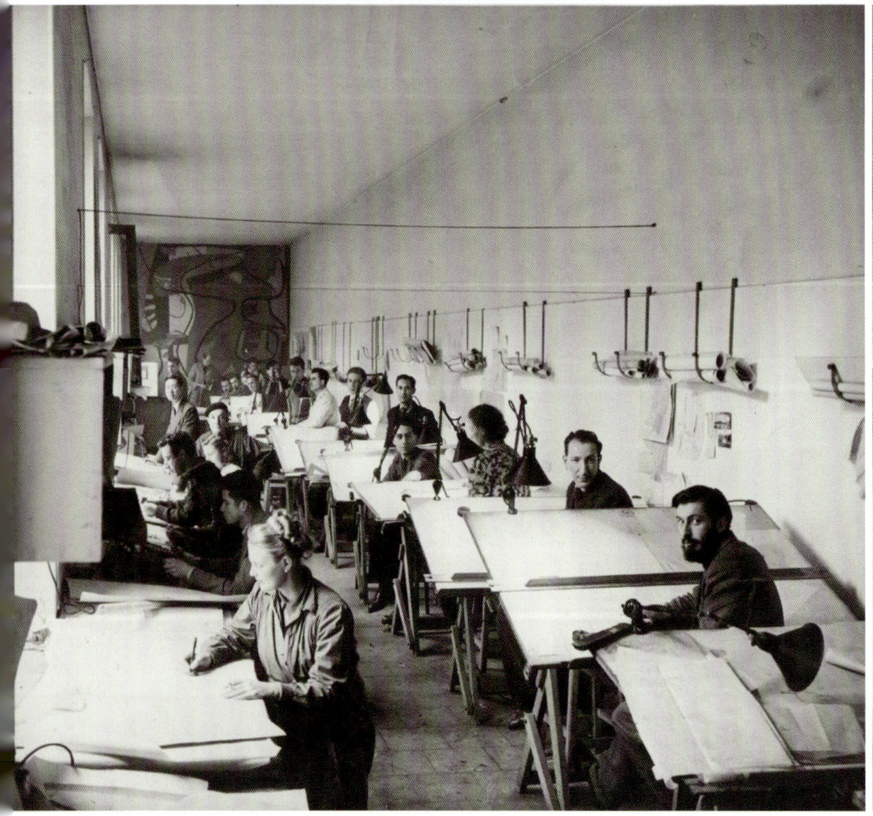

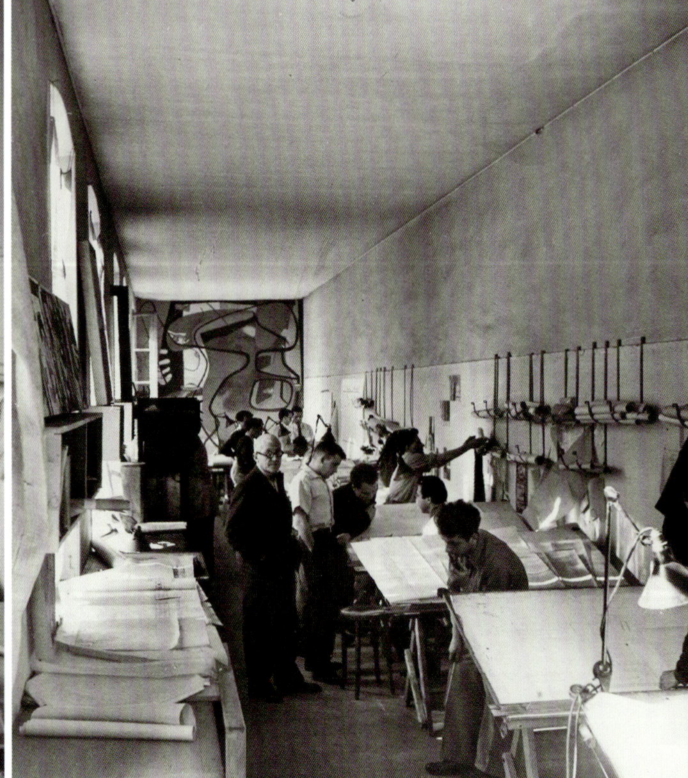

Above. Back wall of the studio with the mural, 1959

Right. An earlier painting by Le Corbusier with similar colors and motifs, *Femme et coquillage* (Woman and Shellfish), 1939–43

Below. Charcoal drawing, *Femme et coquillage*, with a Modulor man to indicate scale, 1948

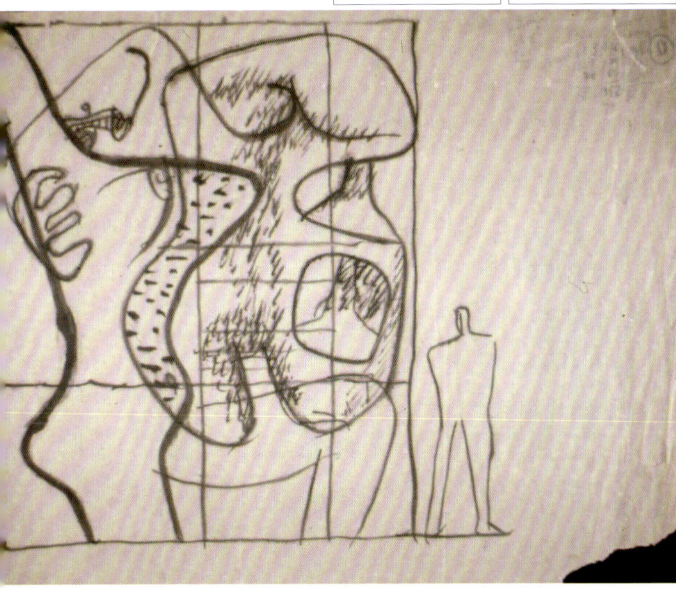

lousing for the uture: Unité l'Habitation, larseille, 945–52

After being summoned to meet with French President Charles de Gaulle, Le Corbusier received a request from Minister of Reconstruction Raoul Dautry to build an apartment complex in Marseille. This commission to design what would be the first in a small group of Unités d'Habitation marked a turning point in Le Corbusier's career.

Here, finally, was a project sufficiently ambitious to permit the mature expression of ideas that he had been exploring for more than a decade: the *brise-soleil*, *béton brut*, and the Modulor.

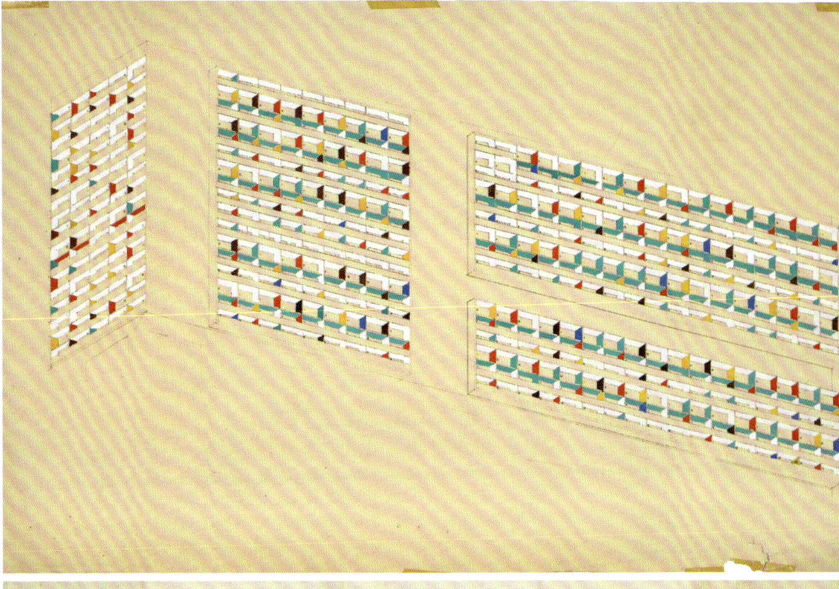

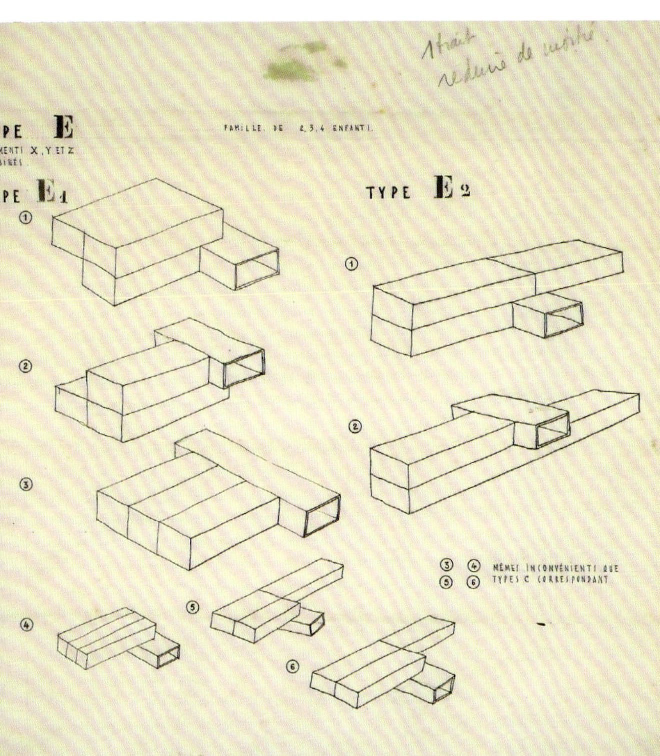

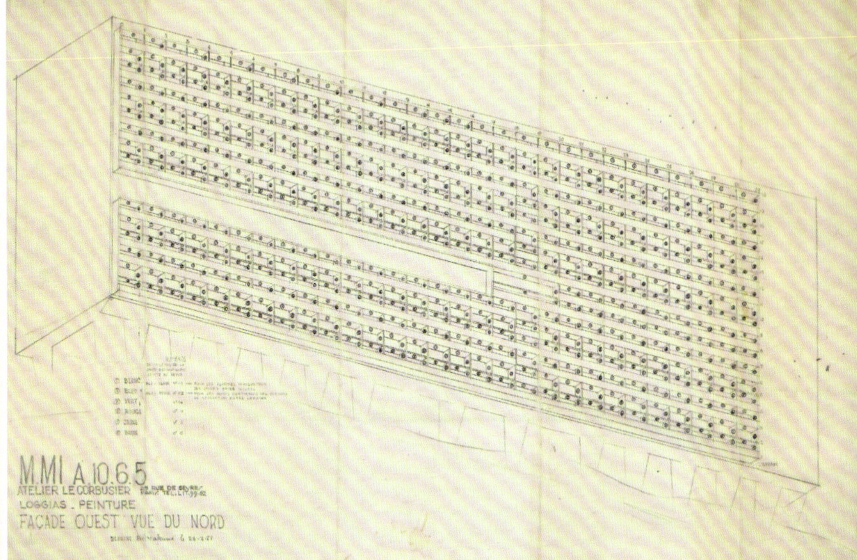

Opposite. Le Corbusier, January 1946, with a model of an apartment module for the Unité d'Habitation, Marseille, 1947–52

Top right. Drawing showing the facades "colorized" to indicate the different colors of paint for the building's balconies, 1945

Above left. Schematic drawing of "type E elements," 1945

Above right. Drawing of west facade keyed to indicate the colors of the balconies, 26 February 1951

Left. Schematic models of apartment modules, c. 1946

Below. Photo illustrating the "bottle" and "wine rack" assembly, c. 1946, devised by Alfred Roth in the 1920s and used by Le Corbusier to lower costs in constructing the Unité and future projects

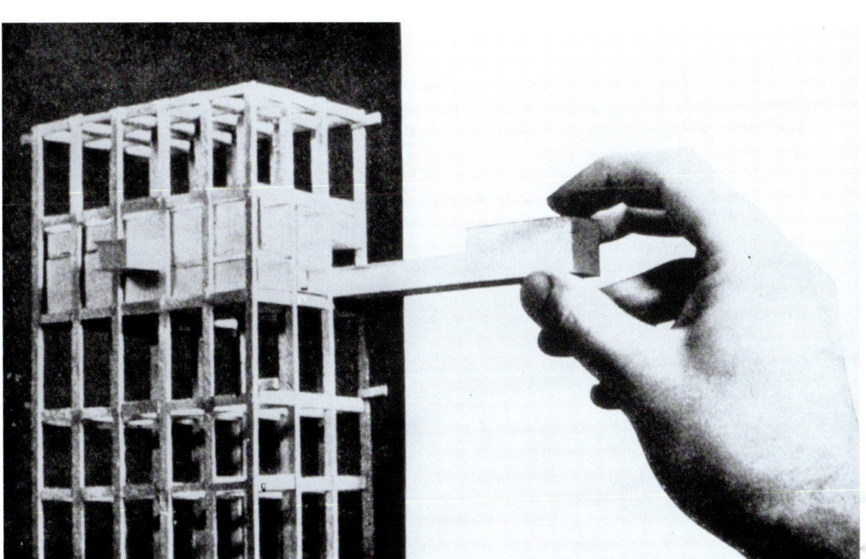

Above. Perspective, east facade, c. 1945, Unité d'Habitation, Marseille

Left. Drawing for the enormous tapered piers that support the building, 1945

Opposite, top. Map of Marseille and environs with drawing for "Marseille La Grande," an unrealized city plan for the client Léon Trouin, 1948–49

Opposite, middle. Proposed elevation and plan of the rooftop

Opposite, bottom. Sections of the south facade (left) and west facade (right)

"Marseille La Grande" – projet de Trouin-Montalte – 1948-49

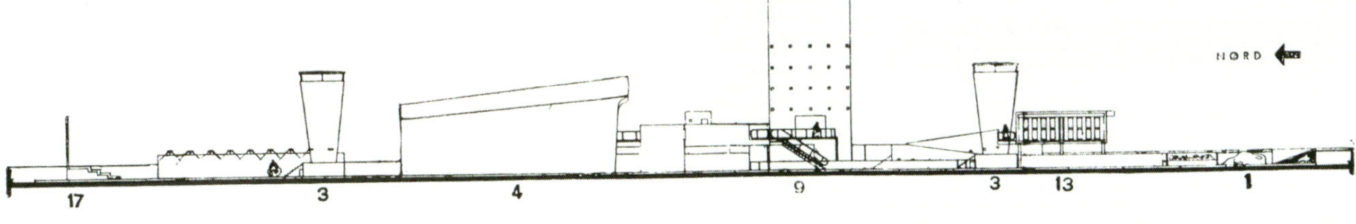

Elévation

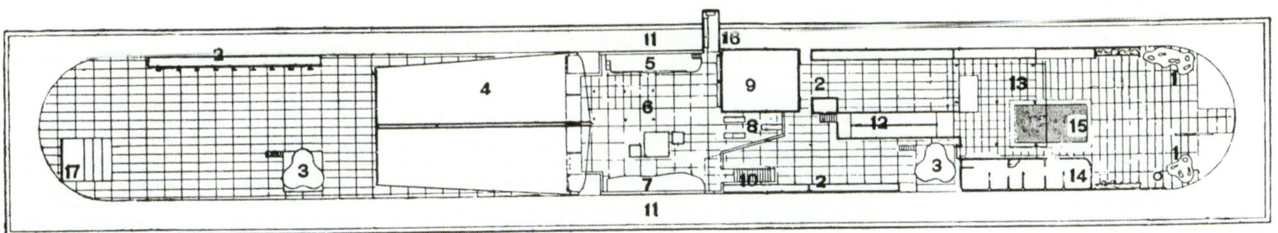

Plan du toit-terrasse

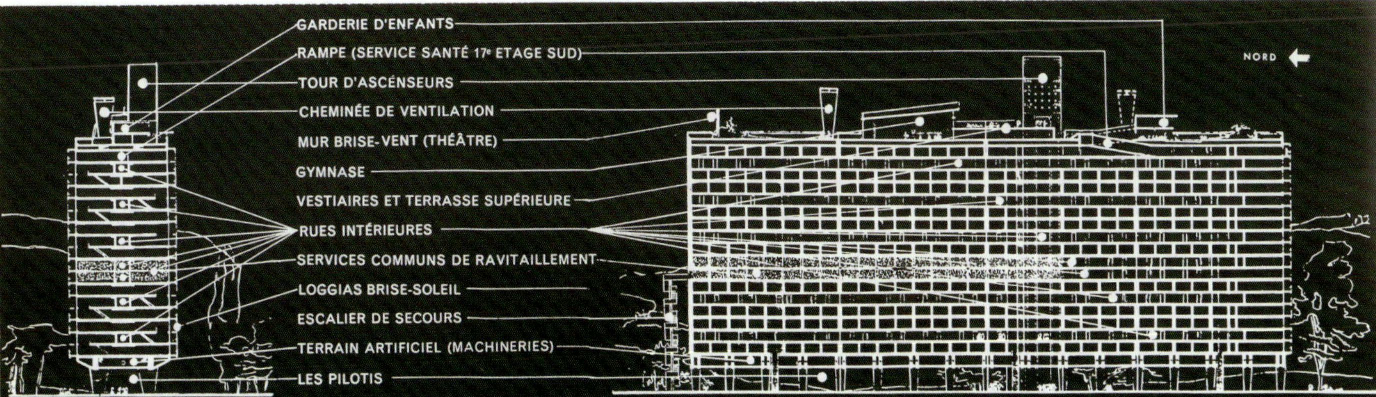

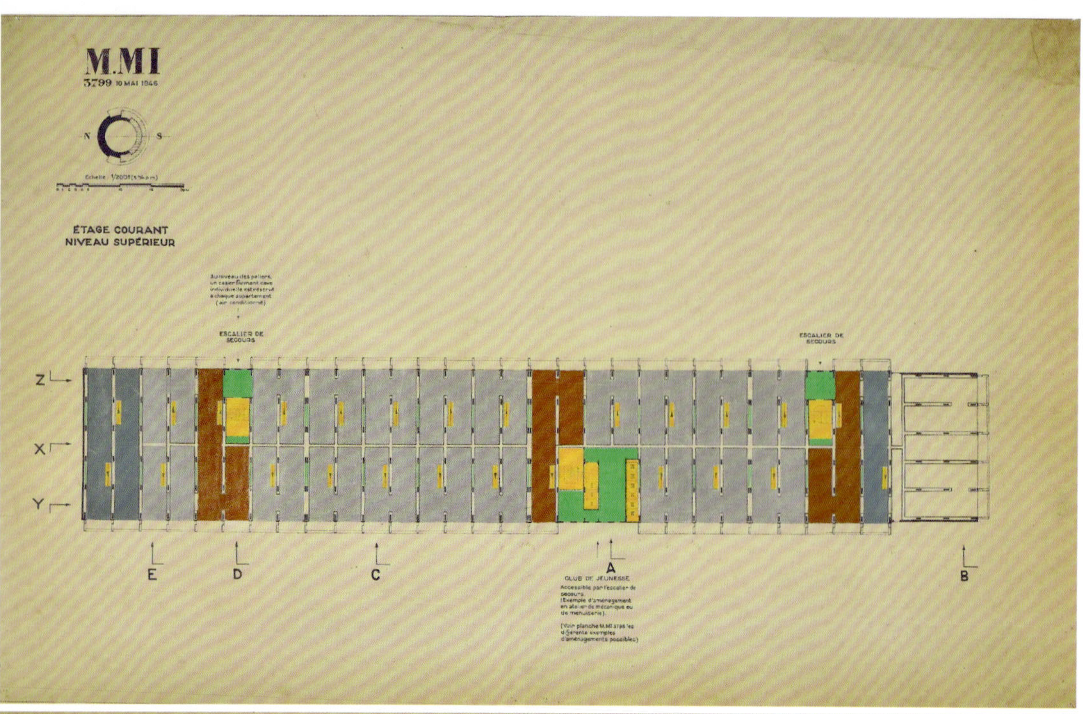

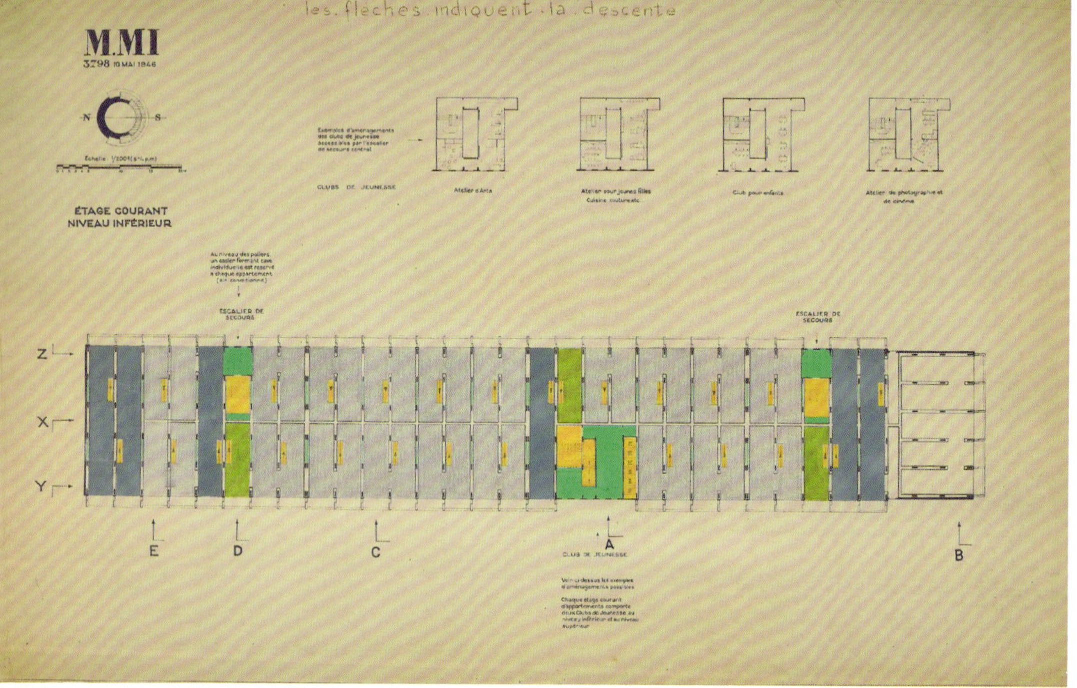

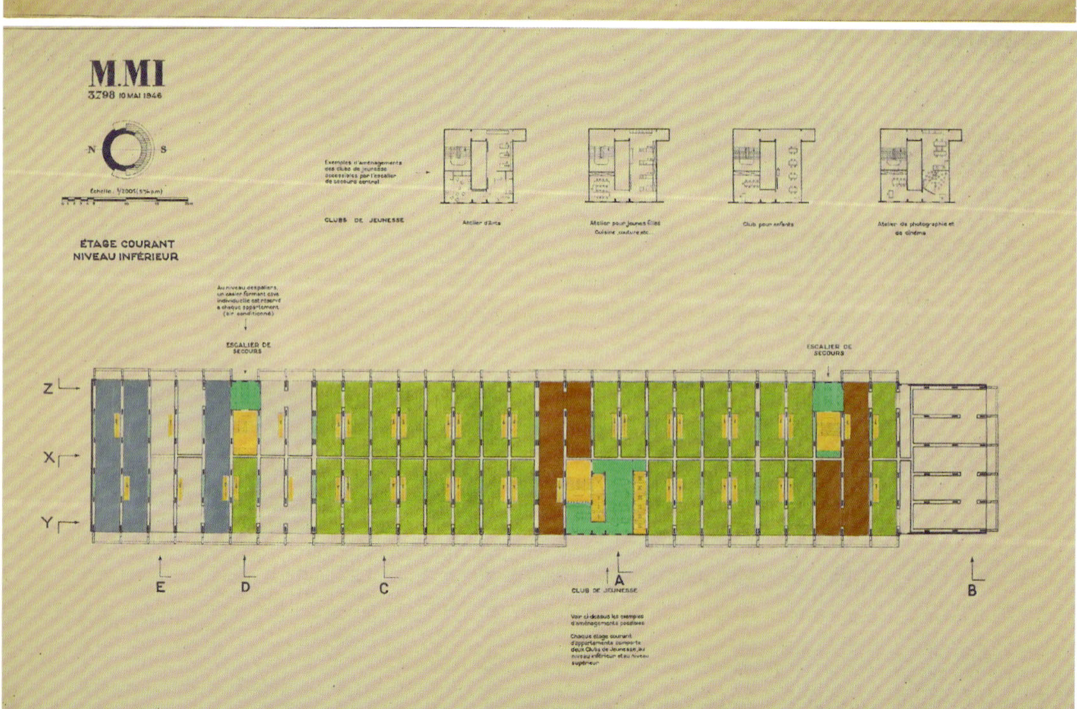

Left. Three general plans, 10 May 1946, for a typical floor in the Unité d'Habitation, Marseille, showing the two apartment levels, "Niveau Supérieur" and "Niveau Inférieur."

Most apartments consisted of two stories, with a double-height living room.

Opposite, top. Schematic drawing of the organization of communal services for the Unité, 1946. Part of the note at right reads "encourage residents to buy their provisions in the building."

Opposite, bottom left. Le Corbusier to Charlotte Perriand, 2 May 1946, asking her to help with "a little fine tuning" of the Unité project

Opposite, middle right. General perspective, August 1945

Opposite, bottom right. Side elevations, 1945

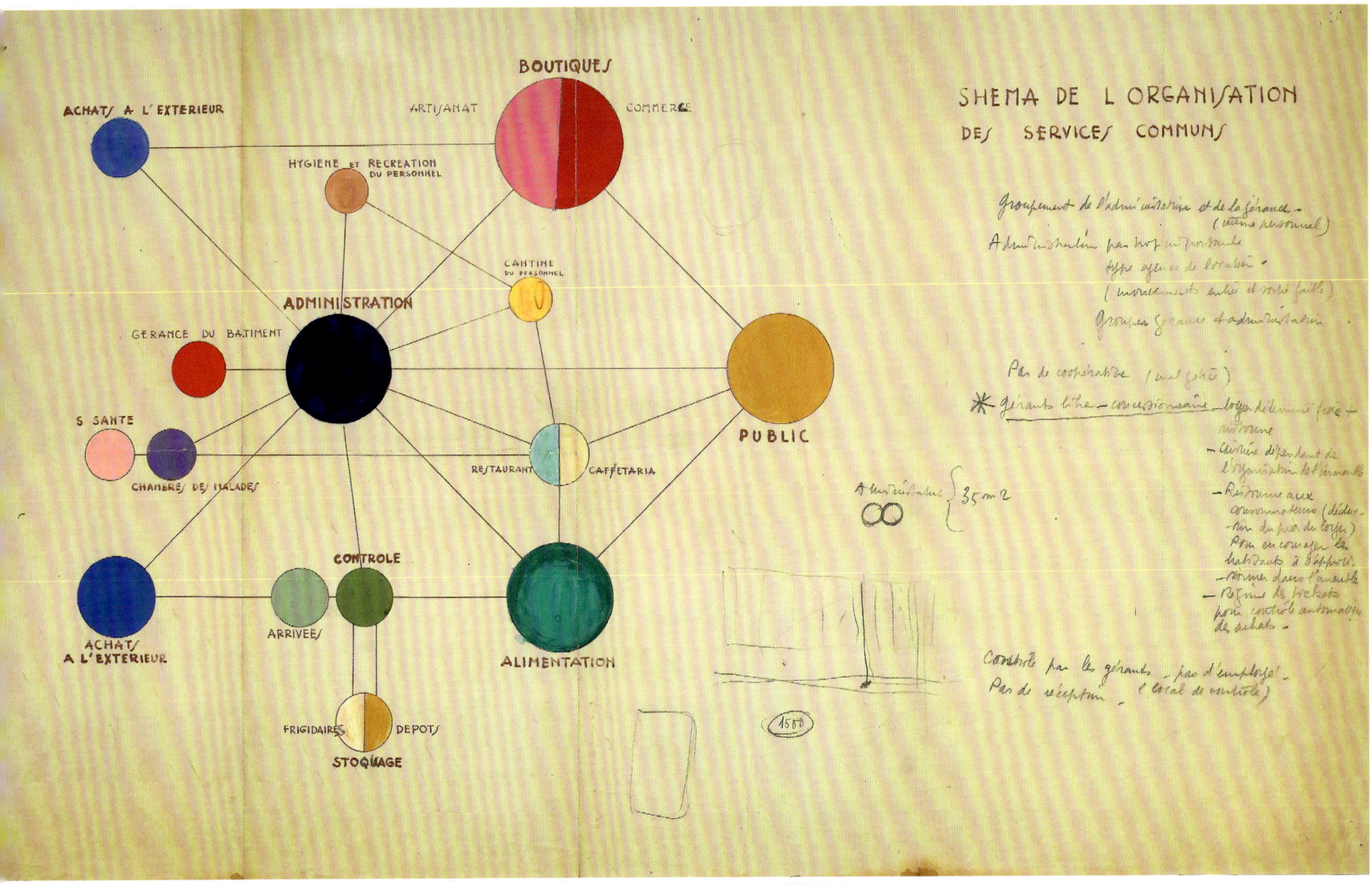

SHEMA DE L ORGANISATION DES SERVICES COMMUNS

BOUTIQUES
ARTISANAT
COMMERCE
ACHATS A L'EXTERIEUR
HYGIENE ET RECREATION DU PERSONNEL
CANTINE DU PERSONNEL
ADMINISTRATION
GERANCE DU BATIMENT
S SANTE
CHAMBRES DES MALADES
RESTAURANT
CAFFETARIA
PUBLIC
CONTROLE
ACHATS A L'EXTERIEUR
ARRIVEES
ALIMENTATION
FRIGIDAIRES
DEPOTS
STOQUAGE

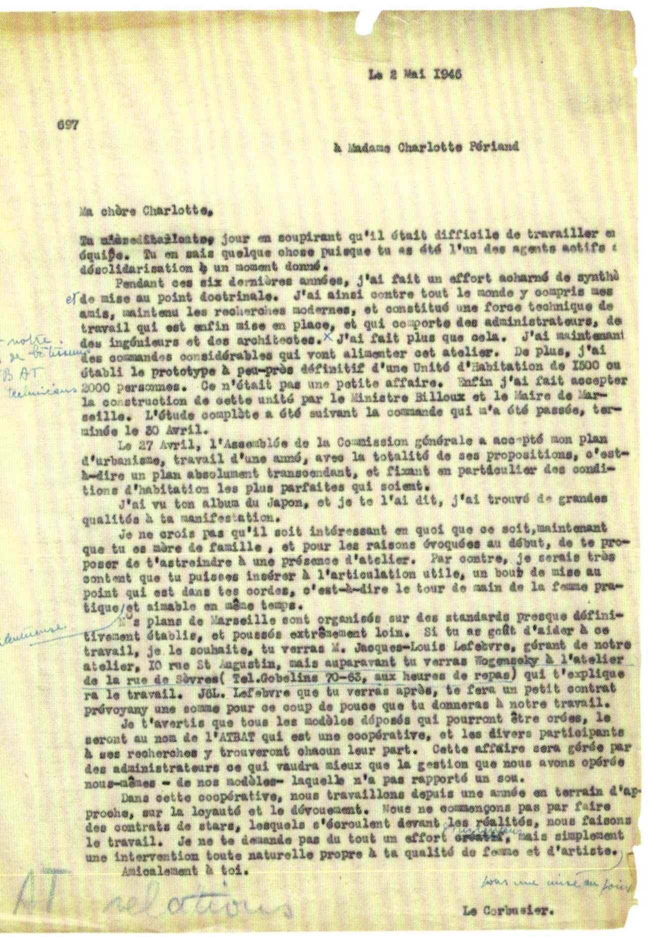

Le 2 Mai 1946

697

à Madame Charlotte Périand

Ma chère Charlotte,

Un mûsediaahiantse jour en soupirant qu'il était difficile de travailler en équipe. Tu en sais quelque chose puisque tu as été l'un des agents actifs de désolidarisation à un moment donné.

Pendant ces six dernières années, j'ai fait un effort acharné de synthèse de mise au point doctrinale. J'ai ainsi contre tout le monde y compris mes amis, maintenu les recherches modernes, et constitué une force technique de travail qui est enfin mise en place, et qui comporte des administrateurs, des ingénieurs et des architectes. J'ai fait plus que cela. J'ai maintenant des commandes considérables qui vont alimenter cet atelier. De plus, j'ai établi le prototype à peu-près définitif d'une Unité d'Habitation de 1500 ou 2000 personnes. Ce n'était pas une petite affaire. Enfin j'ai fait accepter la construction de cette unité par le Ministre Billoux et le Maire de Marseille. L'étude complète a été suivant la commande qui m'a été passée, terminée le 30 Avril.

Le 27 Avril, l'Assemblée de la Commission générale a accepté mon plan d'urbanisme, travail d'une année, avec la totalité de ses propositions, c'est-à-dire un plan absolument transcendant, et fixant en particulier des conditions d'habitation les plus parfaites qui soient.

J'ai vu ton album du Japon, et je te l'ai dit, j'ai trouvé de grandes qualités à ta manifestation.

Je ne crois pas qu'il soit intéressant en quoi que ce soit, maintenant que tu es mère de famille, et pour les raisons évoquées au début, de te proposer de t'astreindre à une présence d'atelier. Par contre, je serais très content que tu puisses insérer à l'articulation utile, un bout de mise au point qui est dans tes cordes, c'est-à-dire le tour de main de la femme pratique et aimable en même temps.

Nos plans de Marseille sont organisés sur des standards presque définitivement établis, et poussés extrêmement loin. Si tu as goût d'aider à ce travail, je le souhaite, tu verras M. Jacques-Louis Lefebvre, gérant de notre atelier, 10 rue St Augustin, mais auparavant tu verras Wogensky à l'atelier de la rue de Sèvres(Tel.Gobelins 70-63, aux heures de repas) qui t'expliquera le travail. JöL. Lefebvre que tu verras après, te fera un petit contrat prévoyany une somme pour ce coup de pouce que tu donneras à notre travail.

Je t'avertis que tous les modèles déposés qui pourront être crées, le seront au nom de l'ATBAT qui est une coopérative, et les divers participants à ses recherches y trouveront chacun leur part. Cette affaire sera gérée par des administrateurs ce qui vaudra mieux que la gestion que nous avons opérée nous-mêmes - de nos modèles- laquelle n'a pas rapporté un sou.

Dans cette coopérative, nous travaillons depuis une année en terrain d'approche, sur la loyauté et le dévouement. Nous ne commençons pas par faire des contrats de stars, lesquels s'éroulent devant les réalités, nous faisons le travail. Je ne te demande pas du tout un effort créateur, mais simplement une intervention toute naturelle propre à ta qualité de femme et d'artiste.

Amicalement à toi.

Le Corbusier.

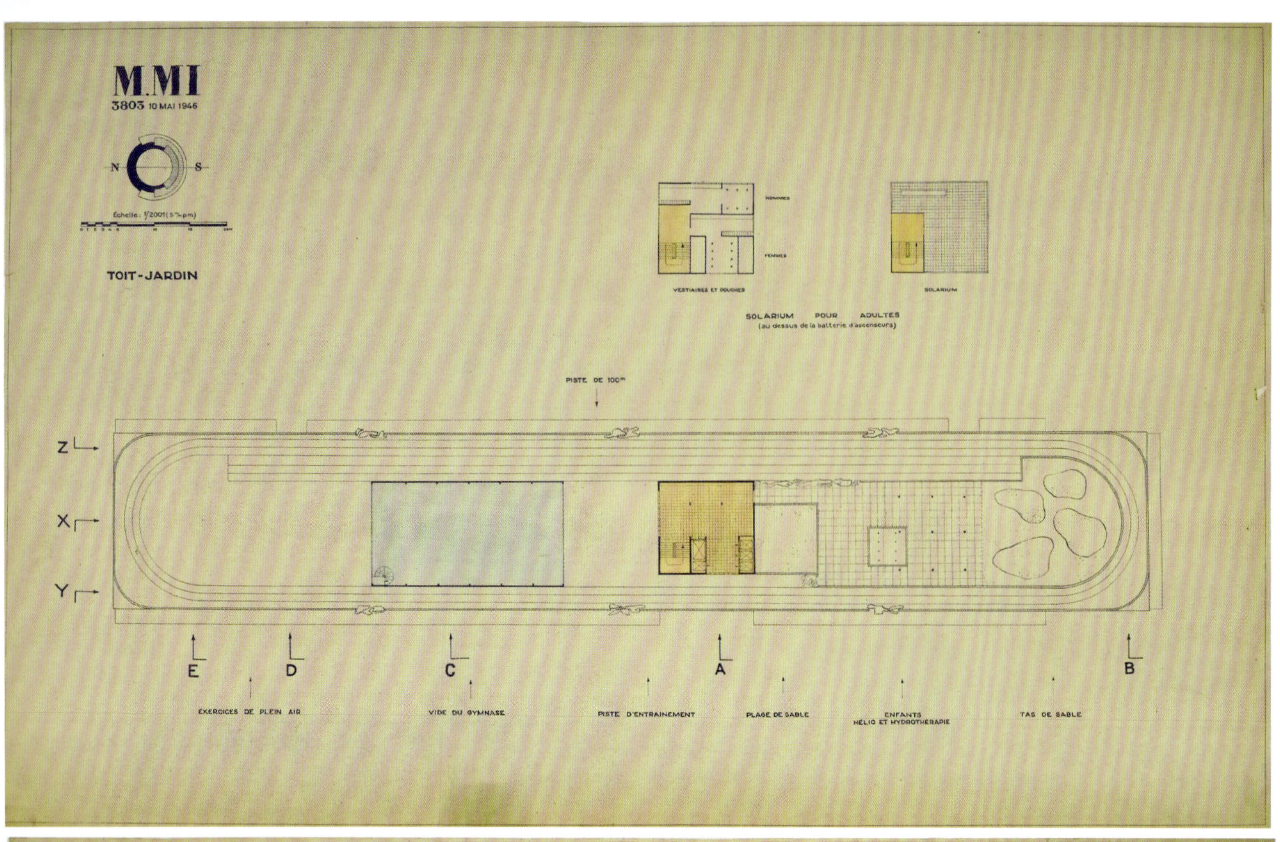
M.M.I
3803 10 MAI 1946
N
S
TOIT-JARDIN
VESTIAIRES ET DOUCHES
SOLARIUM
SOLARIUM POUR ADULTES
(au dessus de la batterie d'ascenseurs)
PISTE DE 100m
Z
X
Y
E
D
C
A
B
EXERCICES DE PLEIN AIR
VIDE DU GYMNASE
PISTE D'ENTRAINEMENT
PLAGE DE SABLE
ENFANTS
HELIO ET HYDROTHERAPIE
TAS DE SABLE

M.M.I. APPARTEMENTS
3814 10 MAI 1946
TYPE A
CHAMBRE D'HÔTEL
GAINE
LIT
LAVABO
DOUCHE
W.C.
ARMOIRE PENDERIE
BRISE-SOLEIL
LOGGIA
RUE INTÉRIEURE
TABLE A MANGER
ARMOIRE PENDERIE
TYPE B
CELIBATAIRE
OU COUPLE
TABLE
ET CASIERS
FOURNEAU
EVIER
VIDE-ORDURES
W.C.
LAVABO
DOUCHE
LIT
CUISINE

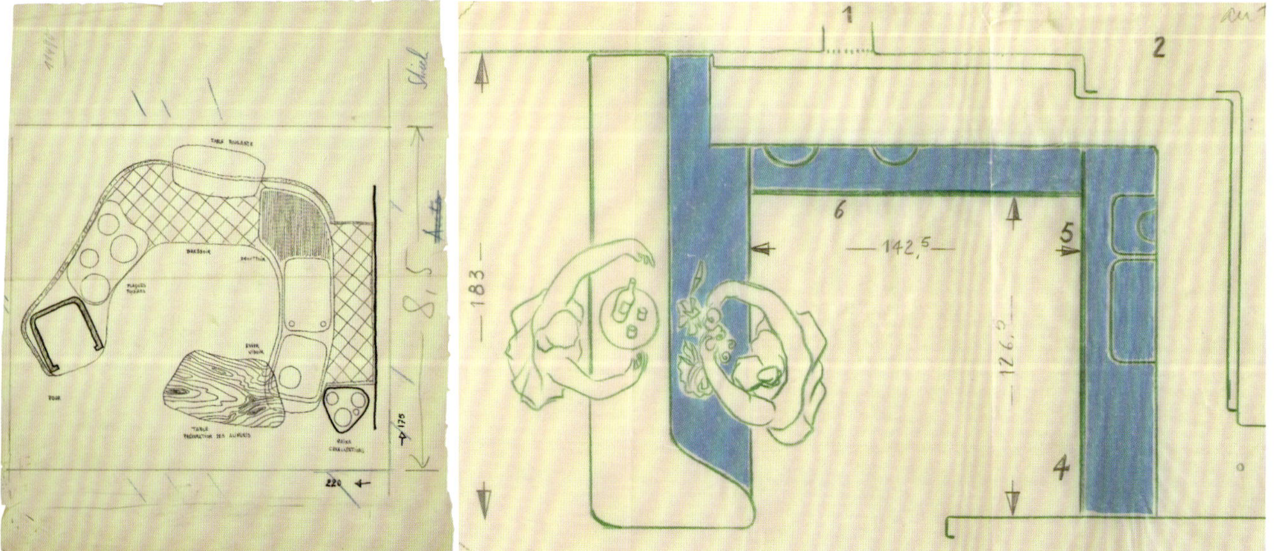
8,5
220
1
2
183
142,5
6
5
126,5
4

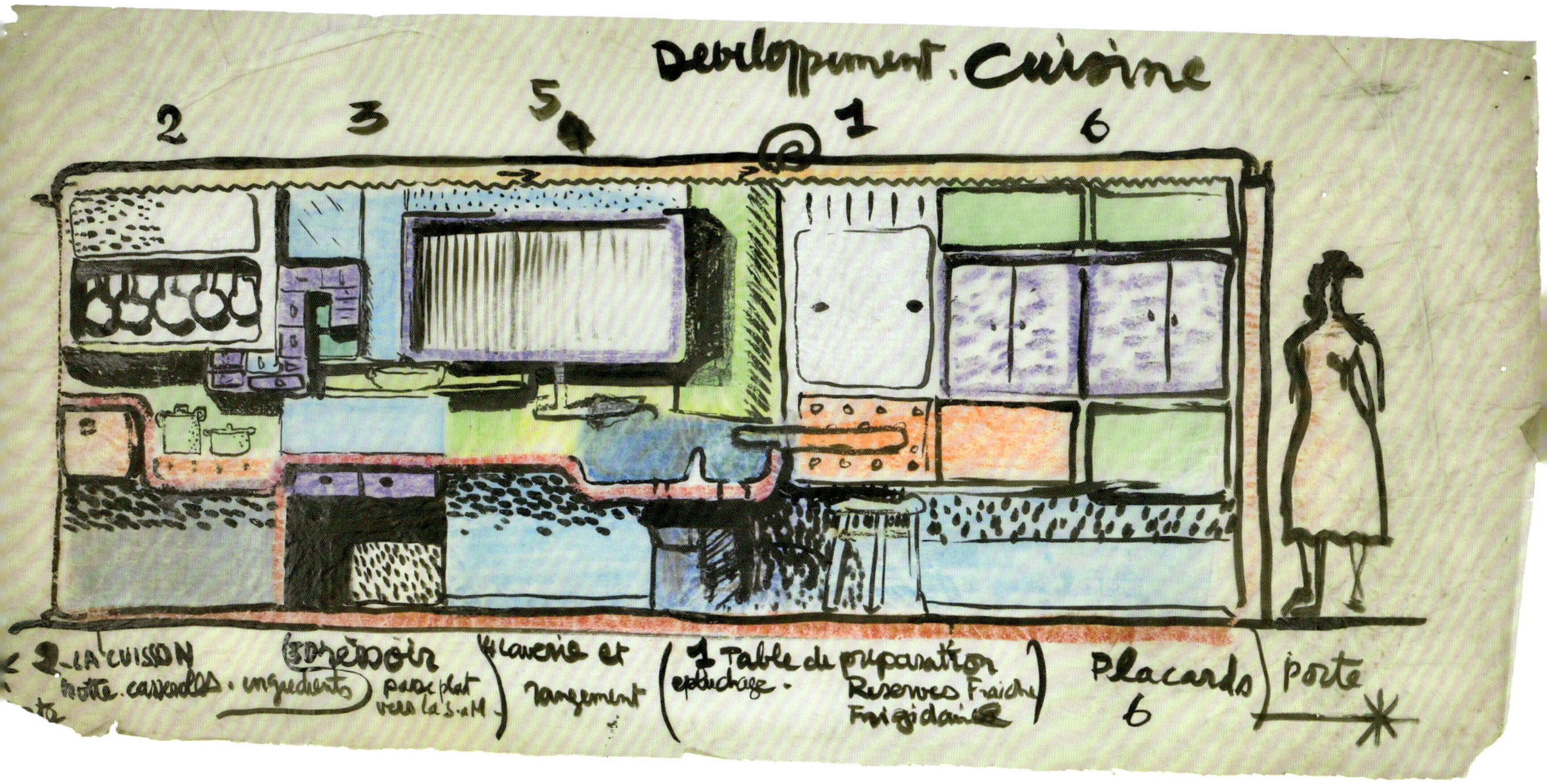

Opposite, top. Plan of the roof garden, 1945, Unité d'Habitation, Marseille

Opposite, middle. Plans for a Type A hotel room (top), and Type B apartment for one or two people (bottom), 1945

Opposite, bottom left. Functional scheme for the kitchen, with a rolling table that could be moved around the space

Opposite, bottom right. Charlotte Perriand's prototype for the Unité kitchen, 1949

Above. Kitchen prototype for Unité d'Habitation, Marseille, including an area to plate food and a pass-through window to the dining room, a preparation table, and shelves for storage

Below. Plan for a Unité kitchen. The curvature was meant to facilitate an efficient and ergonomic workstation for food preparation

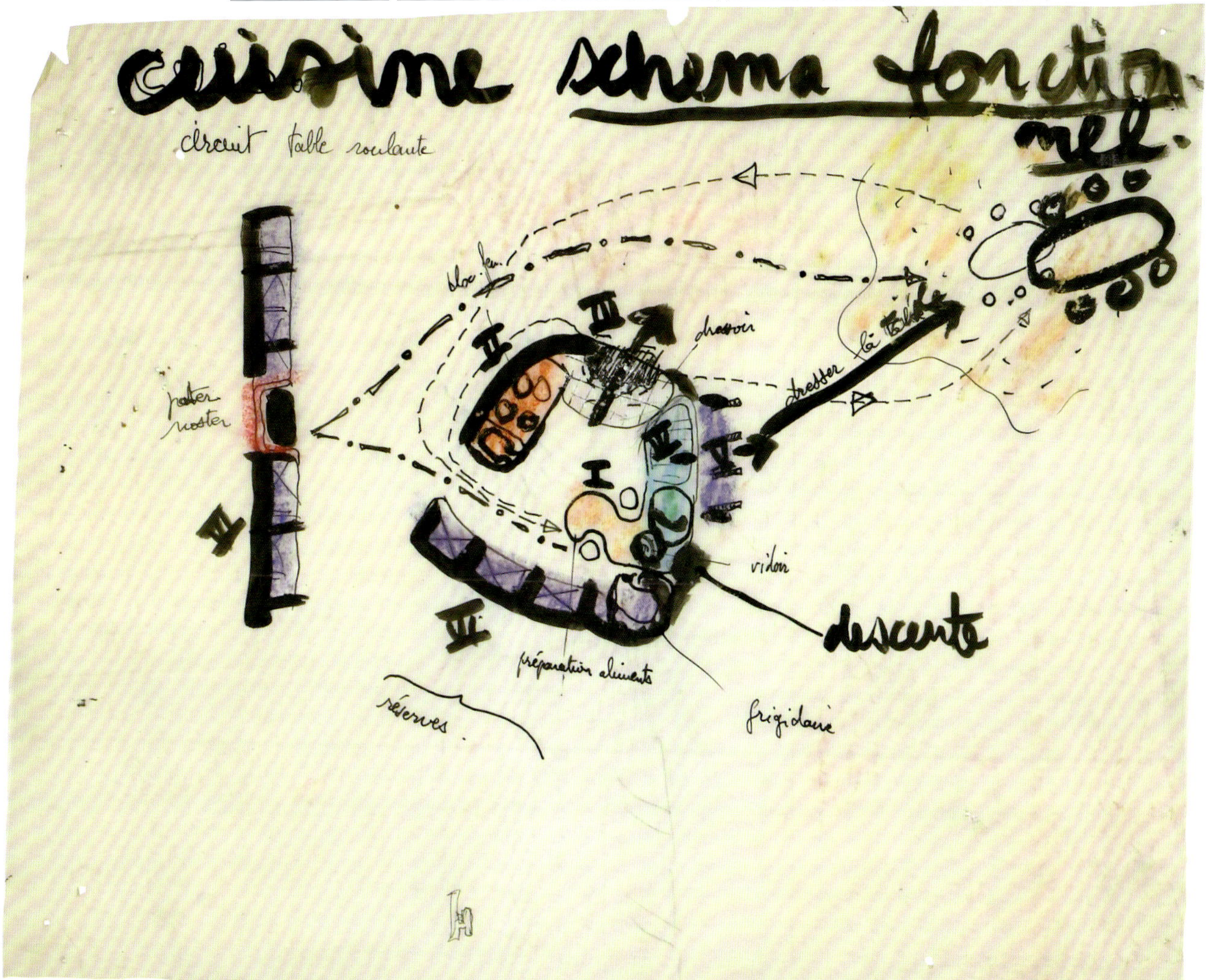

Above left. Detail of facade, Unité d'Habitation, Marseille, 1946

Above right. Construction worker on an upper floor, 1946

Below left. Sinks stacked at the work site

Below right. Workers preparing to lay concrete

Opposite, top. Upper level during construction, 1948

Opposite, bottom left. Tapered piers supporting the building, 1948

Opposite, bottom right. View down the light shaft

15 Nov.
Nº 159
19 Août 1948
N°106

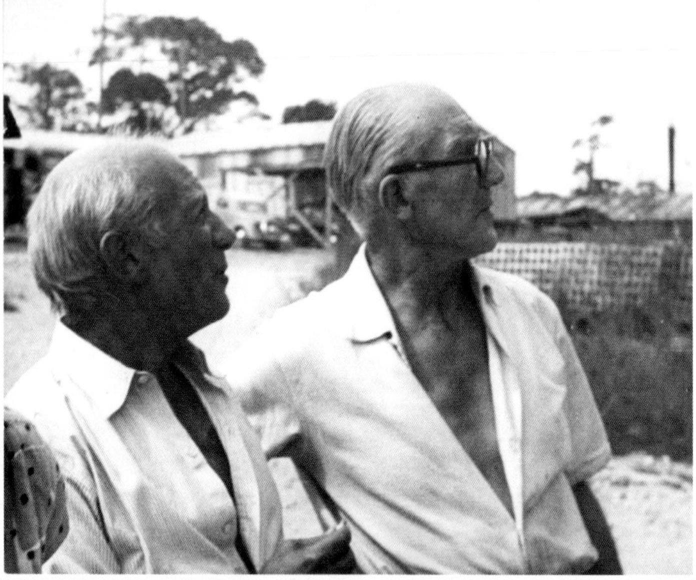

Left. Three views of Pablo Picasso and Le Corbusier touring the work site of the Unité d'Habitation, Marseille, September 1952

Right. Le Corbusier to Pablo Picasso, 21 May 1952, authorizing Picasso's visit to the Unité

Opposite. Le Corbusier in front of the south facade, September 1949

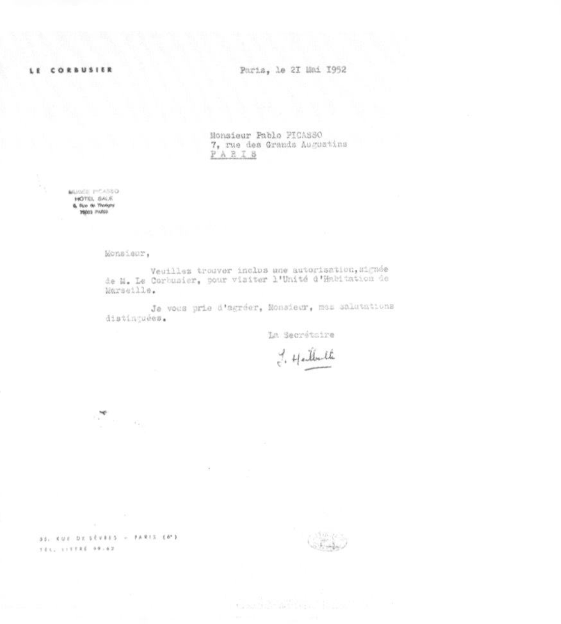

LE CORBUSIER

Paris, le 21 Mai 1952

Monsieur Pablo PICASSO
7, rue des Grands Augustins
PARIS

Monsieur,

Veuillez trouver inclus une autorisation, signée de M. Le Corbusier, pour visiter l'Unité d'Habitation de Marseille.

Je vous prie d'agréer, Monsieur, mes salutations distinguées.

La Secrétaire

J. Heilbuth

35, RUE DE SÈVRES – PARIS (6e)
TÉL. LITTRÉ 99-62

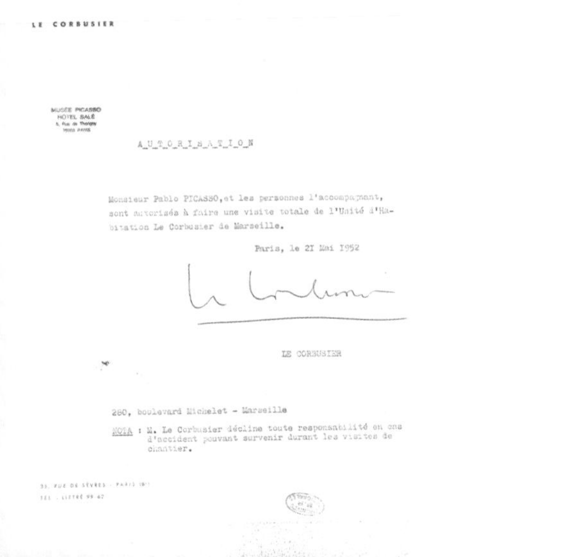

LE CORBUSIER

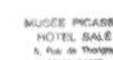

A U T O R I S A T I O N

Monsieur Pablo PICASSO, et les personnes l'accompagnant, sont autorisés à faire une visite totale de l'Unité d'Habitation Le Corbusier de Marseille.

Paris, le 21 Mai 1952

Le Corbusier

LE CORBUSIER

280, boulevard Michelet – Marseille

NOTA : M. Le Corbusier décline toute responsabilité en cas d'accident pouvant survenir durant les visites de chantier.

35, RUE DE SÈVRES – PARIS (6e)
TÉL. LITTRÉ 99-62

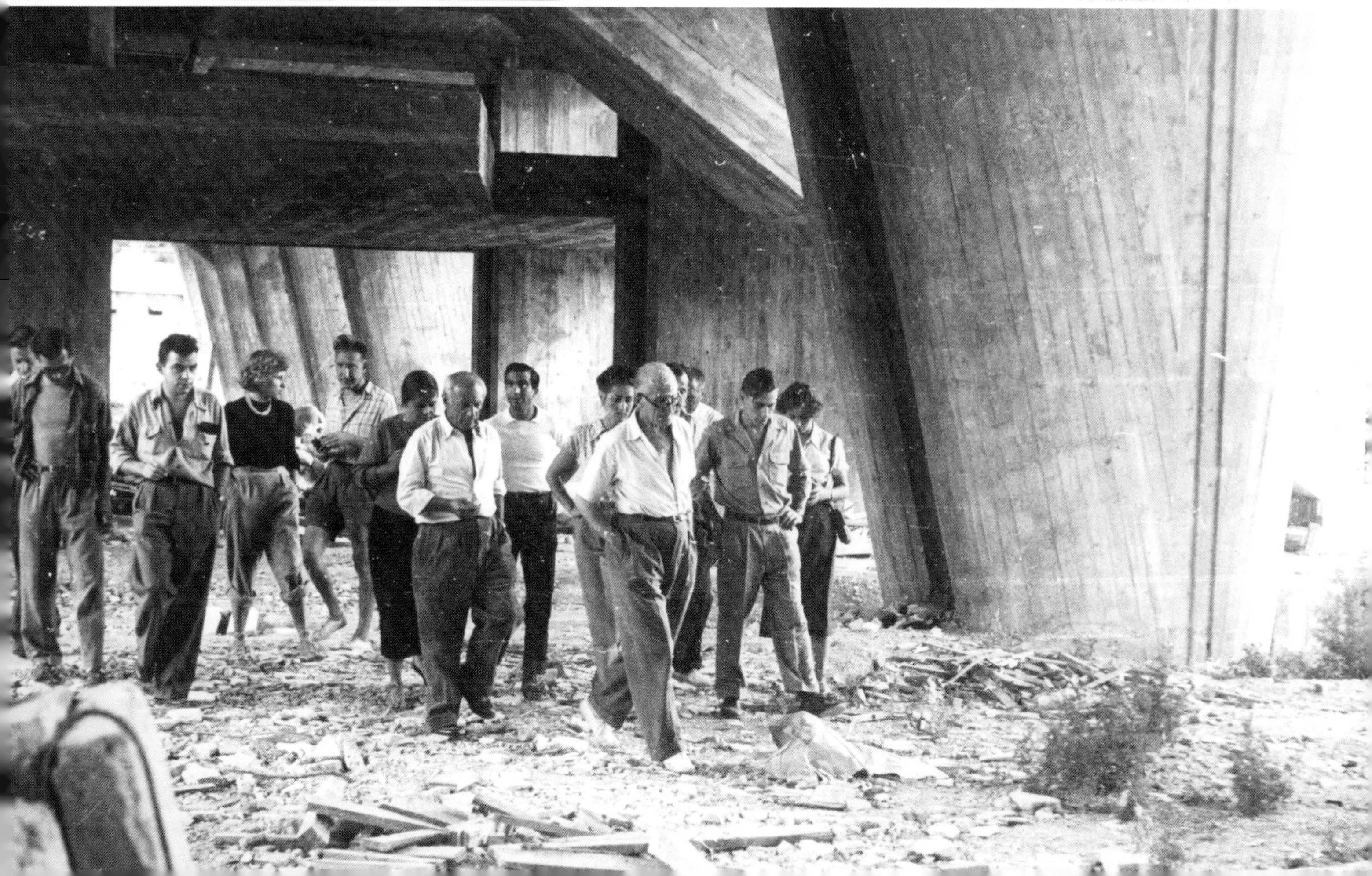

L'ARCHITECTE LE CORBUSIER CONTRUIT À MARSEILLE LA « CITÉ-JARDIN VERTICALE »

Une ville radieuse!

ANNONCENT LES "BATISSEURS"

Une caserne! PROTESTENT LES "BARBUS"

Le Corbusier est un adversaire déclaré de la cité-jardins horizontale — comme celles qu'on rencontre dans la banlieue parisienne. Il la tient pour *le plus grand gaspillage des temps moder-*

Procès d'« esthétique » à Marseille

« La cité Le Corbusier est une immense cage-cimetière »

déclare M. Vergnolle

(De notre correspondant part.)

MARSEILLE 4 décembre.

M. Clauzier ajoute que les is sues de l'immeuble sont insuffi

LA SOCIÉTÉ POUR L'ESTHÉTIQUE GÉNÉRALE DE LA FRANCE demande 20 millions de dommages et intérêts à M. Le Corbusier

Marseille, 25 septembre. — Le 3 octobre prochain sera appelé pour fixation

sur les chantiers mêmes de la construction : « Cette œuvre demandait beaucoup

une prison !... tion !... C'est taient les aut et l'éloigneme Le fait le p bureau géré p struction (M.F cement des ce tements resta travaux : tou Innovation administratif, des services p bien entendu ce fait de su

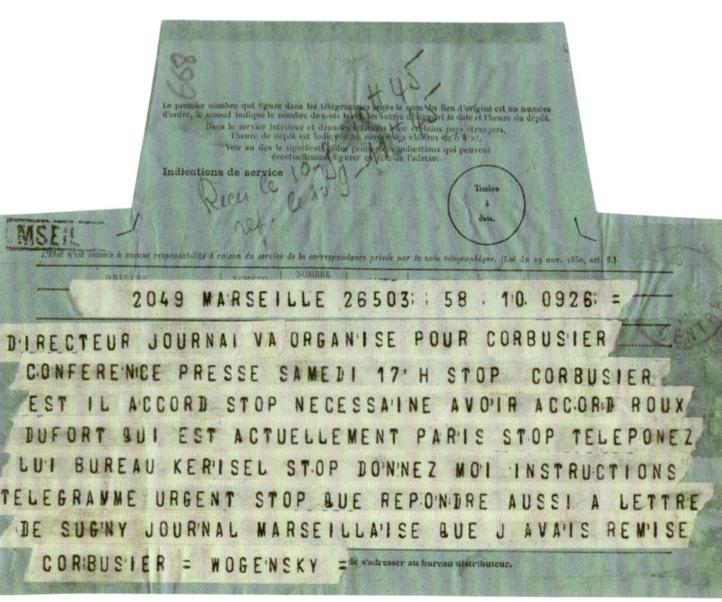

2049 MARSEILLE 26503 58 10 0926 =

DIRECTEUR JOURNAI VA ORGANISE POUR CORBUSIER CONFERENCE PRESSE SAMEDI 17 H STOP CORBUSIER EST IL ACCORD STOP NECESSAINE AVOIR ACCORD ROUX DUFORT QUI EST ACTUELLEMENT PARIS STOP TELEPONEZ LUI BUREAU KERISEL STOP DONNEZ MOI INSTRUCTIONS TELEGRAMME URGENT STOP QUE REPONDRE AUSSI A LETTRE DE SUGNY JOURNAL MARSEILLAISE QUE J AVAIS REMISE CORBUSIER = WOGENSKY =

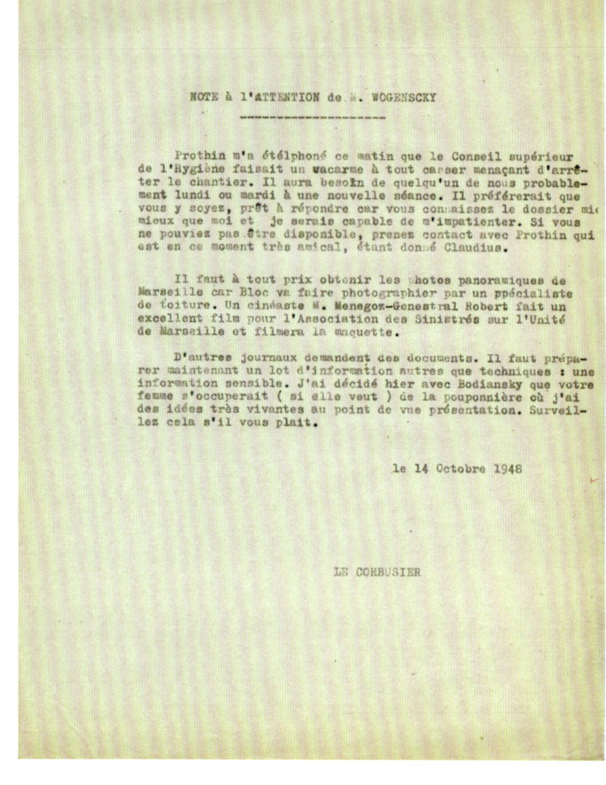

NOTE à l'ATTENTION de M. WOGENSCKY

Prothin m'a ételphoné ce matin que le Conseil supérieur de l'Hygiène faisait un vacarme à tout casser menaçant d'arrêter le chantier. Il aura besoin de quelqu'un de nous probablement lundi ou mardi à une nouvelle séance. Il préférerait que vous y soyez, prêt à répondre car vous connaissez le dossier mieux que moi et je serais capable de m'impatienter. Si vous ne pouviez pas être disponible, prenez contact avec Prothin qui est en ce moment très amical, étant donné Claudius.

Il faut à tout prix obtenir les photos panoramiques de Marseille car Bloc va faire photographier par un spécialiste de toiture. Un cinéaste M. Menegoz-Genestral Robert fait un excellent film pour l'Association des Sinistrés sur l'Unité de Marseille et filmera la maquette.

D'autres journaux demandent des documents. Il faut préparer maintenant un lot d'information autres que techniques : une information sensible. J'ai décidé hier avec Bodiansky que votre femme s'occuperait (si elle veut) de la pouponnière où j'ai des idées très vivantes au point de vue présentation. Surveillez cela s'il vous plait.

le 14 Octobre 1948

LE CORBUSIER

La Société pour l'esthétique de la France perd le procès qu'elle avait engagé contre Le Corbusier

Left to right, top to bottom. Undated newspaper headlines about the Unité d'Habitation, Marseille:

"A radiant city! declare the 'Builders'"

"'Aesthetics' on trial in Marseille: 'Le Corbusier's city is an immense cemetery-cage'"

"The Society for the General Aesthetics of France demands 20 million in damages and interest from M. Le Corbusier"

Telegram from André Wogenscky, an associate in Le Corbusier's office, about a press conference where Le Corbusier can address the controversy over the Unité, Marseille

Le Corbusier to André Wogenscky, 14 October 1948, about meeting with the "Hygiene Committee" at the Unité, who are "kicking up a terrible fuss"

"The Society for the Aesthetics of France loses the suit it brought against Le Corbusier"

Right. Ticket to a public lecture given by Le Corbusier, 2 June 1950, on modern industry's response to France's housing crisis

Below. Le Corbusier in front of a window in the Unité d'Habitation, Marseille, September 1949

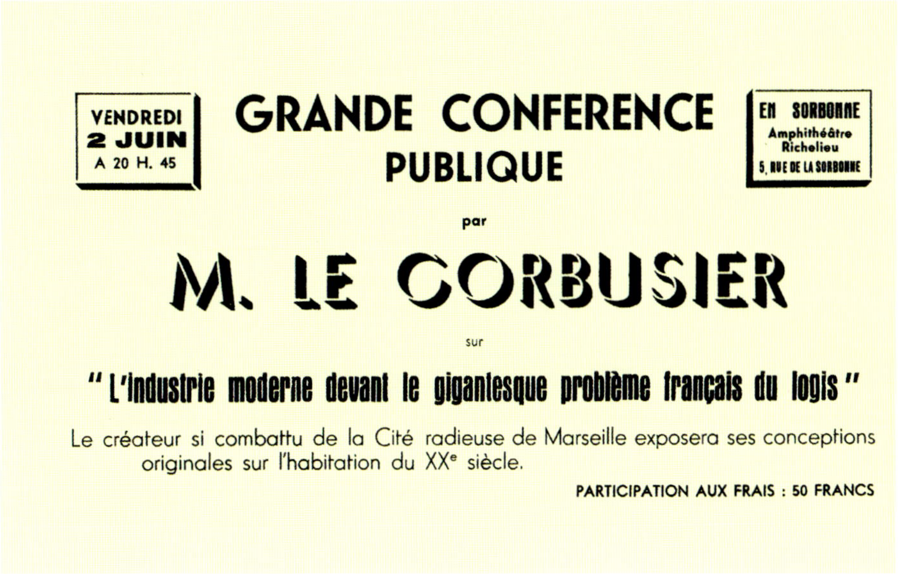

VENDREDI
2 JUIN
A 20 H. 45

GRANDE CONFERENCE
PUBLIQUE

EN SORBONNE
Amphithéâtre
Richelieu
5, RUE DE LA SORBONNE

par

M. LE CORBUSIER

sur

" L'industrie moderne devant le gigantesque problème français du logis "

Le créateur si combattu de la Cité radieuse de Marseille exposera ses conceptions originales sur l'habitation du XXe siècle.

PARTICIPATION AUX FRAIS : 50 FRANCS

"The park has an imperial splendor. And the humans live in it as in a mirage. The silence is total. Yesterday the elevators took 500 guests 56 meters up in 13 minutes. The indoor streets are an invitation to the life of the future. The kids have already got the message of this future life given over to gaiety and warm-heartedness."

—Letter to his mother, 15 October 1952

Opposite, top. Unité d'Habitation, Marseille, and its surroundings

Opposite, bottom. West facade, 1959

This page, clockwise from top left:

Detail of facade and *pilotis*

Carport entrance, 1959

Le Corbusier at the Unité, 3 December 1949

Cars arriving at Unité

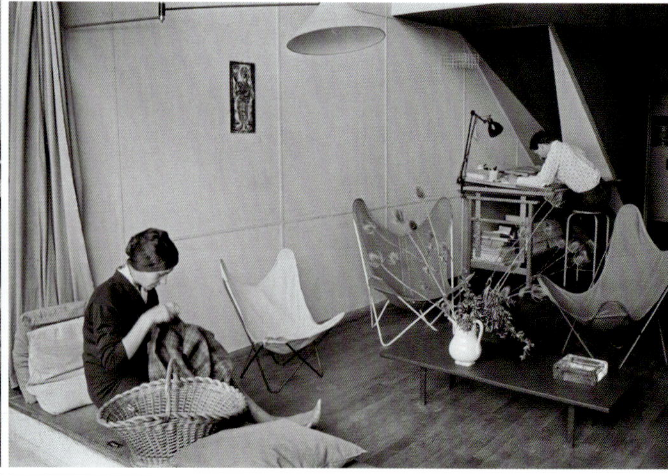

Living in the Unité d'Habitation, Marseille

To design the Unité d'Habitation, Marseille, Le Corbusier called on an array of sources, ranging from the monastery at Val d'Ema, Italy, to an ocean liner to a vertical Garden City—all touchstones he had used before. He created an elevated structure that accommodated 1,600 residents, included an interior shopping avenue located halfway up its seventeen-story height, and offered an elaborate recreation complex on its roof. Residents could choose from twenty-three apartment configurations housing up to six inhabitants, with most featuring double-height living spaces, exposure on both of the building's long main facades, and private terraces.

Above. Interiors in the Unité, Marseille, including the living area and terrace with its *brise-soleil* (sunshade)

Below. View from the bedroom balcony to the living area and terrace, 1959

op left. Pablo icasso (at left), uring his tour of ne Unité, eptember 1952

op right. Bedroom f the most "luxuri- us" apartment ailable

Iiddle left. Chairs n the foreground esigned by Charlotte Perriand nd Pierre eanneret; low table y Perriand; table n background y Jean Prouvé

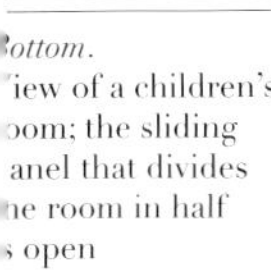

Iiddle right. Typical itchen, based n the prototype esigned by Charlotte Perriand

ottom. iew of a children's oom; the sliding anel that divides ne room in half s open

Grappes
LIBRE

Opposite, top. Gymnasium on the roof terrace, Unité d'Habitation, Marseille, 1959

Opposite, middle left. Children playing in the wading pool on the roof terrace, 1959

Opposite, middle right. The kindergarten, 1959. Nursery and kindergarten facilities were located on the roof terrace and the seventeenth floor.

Opposite, bottom left, and above. Children playing on the roof terrace, 1959

Opposite, bottom right. Entrance to a retail shop on the communal services level

Opposite, top. Children on the roof, Unité d'Habitation, Marseille

Opposite, bottom. Three views of the roof terrace. The terrace also accommodated communal water tanks, two ventilation shafts, and a running track.

Right. Le Corbusier receiving an award at the inauguration ceremony for the Unité, 14 October 1952

Below. Festivities at the inauguration ceremony

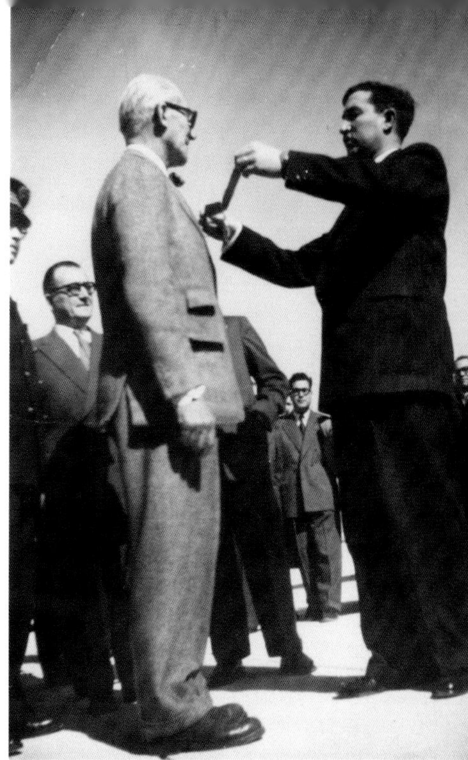

"Yesterday a great day. It was beautiful... The object, the house, is one of the great works of architecture (of any and every period). It's moving by day and magical by night... In the evening, at night, the house is enchanting below, above, top, bottom, on the walls, with three windows lit up."

—Letter to his mother, 15 October 1952

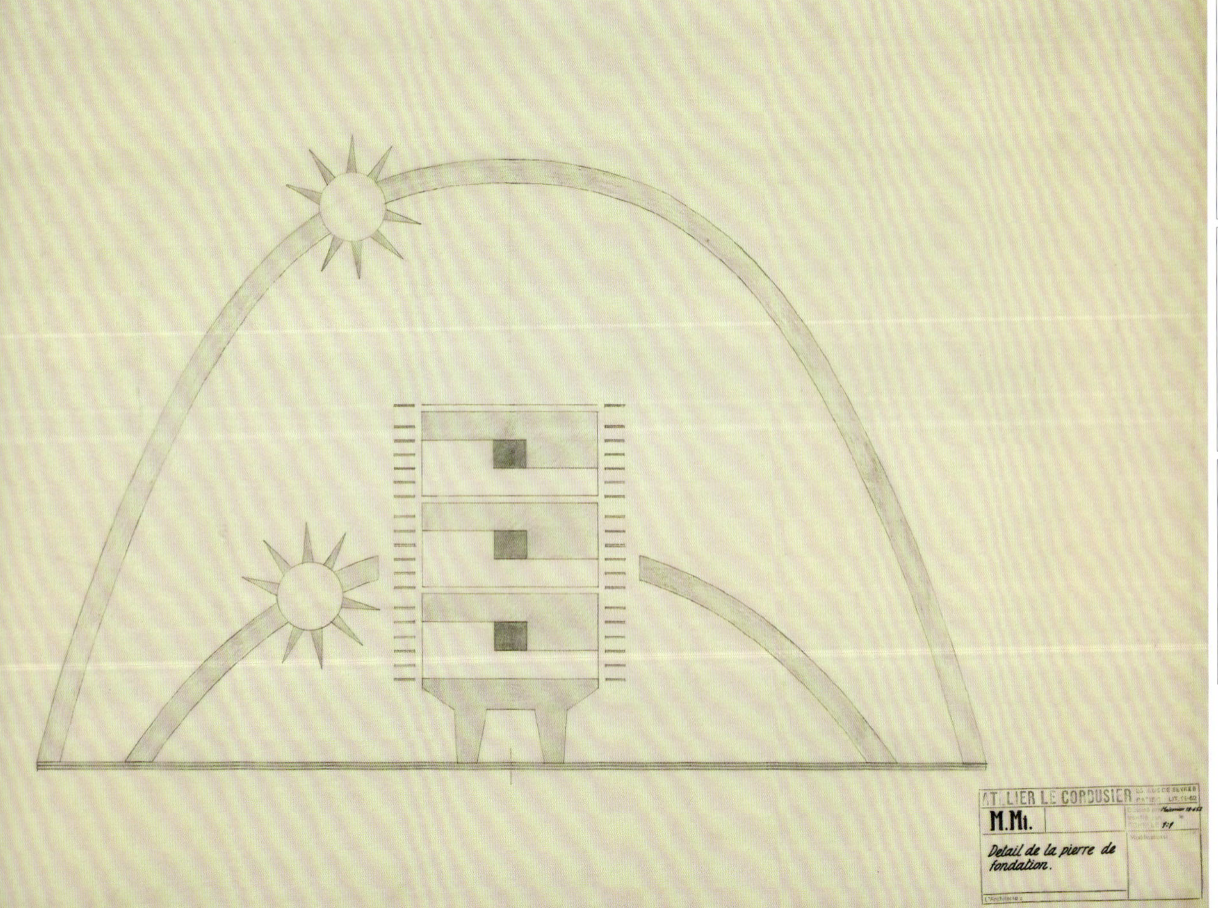

Above. Foundation stone at the entrance to the Unité d'Habitation, Marseille, 1959

Left. Le Corbusier's drawing for the foundation stone, showing the path of the summer and winter sun in relation to the Unité, 1945

Opposite. Le Corbusier and his relief of Modulor man near the entrance to the Unité, 1950

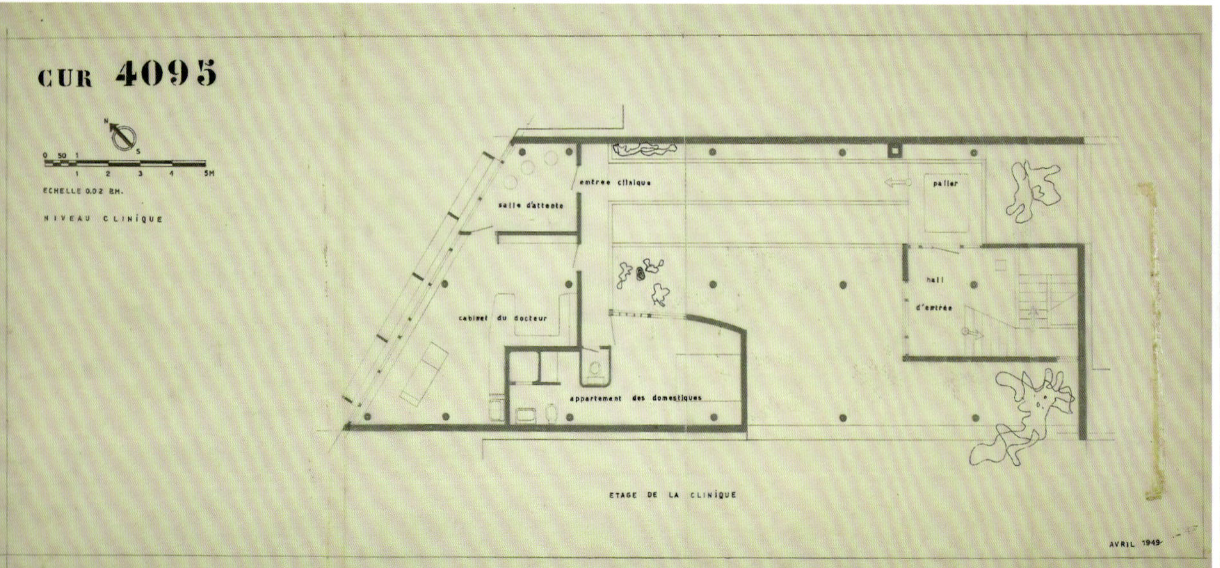

Designing for a tropical climate: Maison Curutchet, La Plata, Argentina, 1949–50

The commission to design a large house with a consulting office for a physician in La Plata, Argentina, gave Le Corbusier the opportunity to reconsider the strategies for residential design he had employed during the 1920s and to adapt them to the South American climate. Le Corbusier would soon refine and recast these strategies in a series of projects in India.

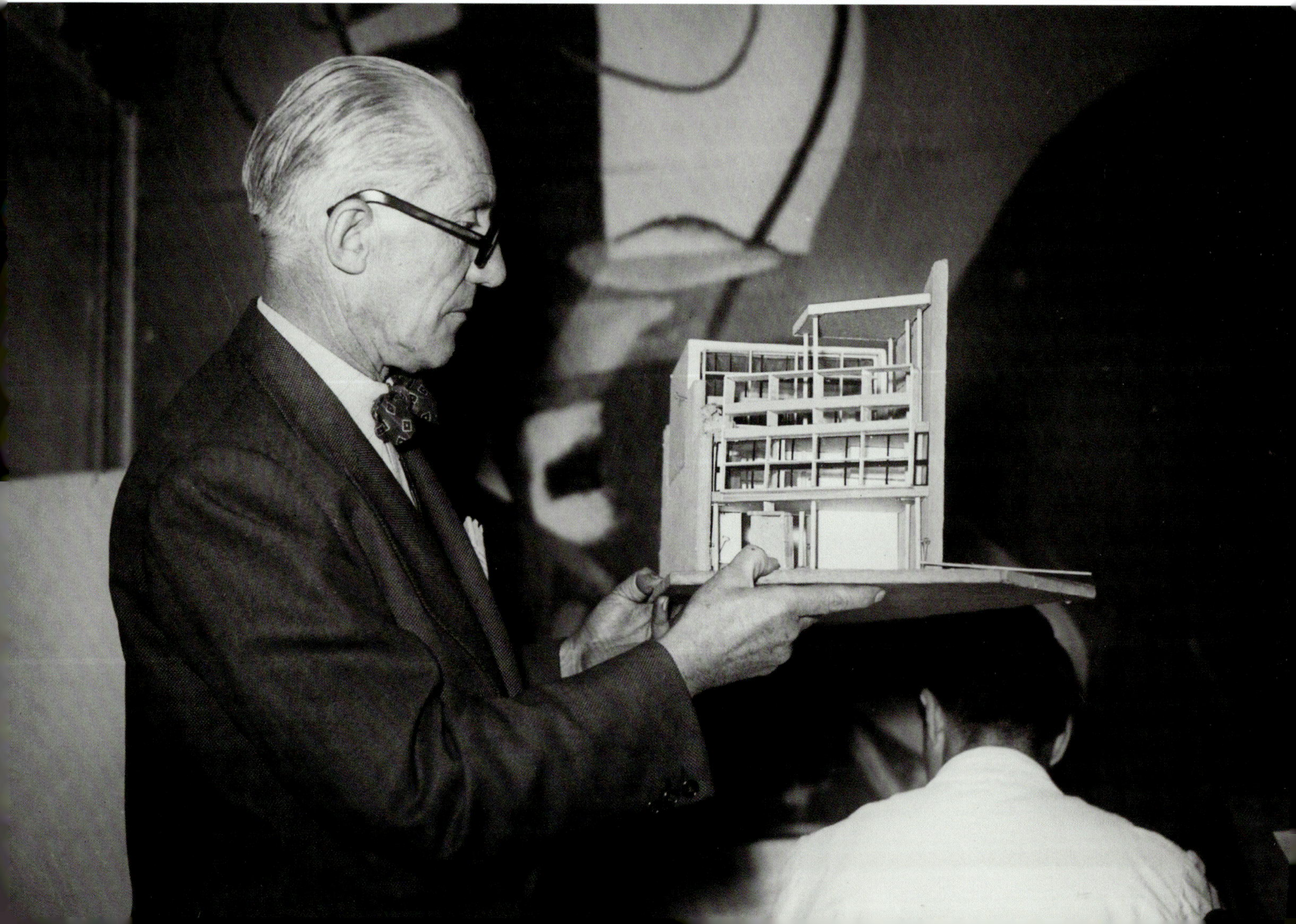

Opposite, top. Plan, April 1949, mezzanine-level clinic, Maison Curutchet, La Plata, Argentina, 1949

Opposite, middle left. Photo-collage of model and bird's-eye perspective, c. 1950

Opposite, middle right. Photo-collage of model and facade perspective, c. 1950

Opposite, bottom. Le Corbusier with a model of Maison Curutchet, c. 1950

Top. Ramp leading from the ground floor to the second floor

Left. Entrance hall

Above. Exterior view

Planning a new Bogotá, 1950

Le Corbusier's plan for Bogotá, Colombia, aspired to impose a linear rigor on the sinuous subtropical landscape. The project was repeatedly and indefinitely postponed,

but it helped prepare the way for the next major phase of Le Corbusier's career.

Top left. Le Corbusier to Helena Simkhovitch, 24 February 1950, from Bogotá (illustrated with a sketch of the city), notifying her that he will be in New York on 9 March

Top right. Le Corbusier to Helena Simkhovitch, 11 July 1950, playfully referring to their encounter on 4 July 1936

Middle and bottom. Le Corbusier's sketchbook notes and drawings from Bogotá, including an early version of his Open Hand motif

ight. Plan for a
ivic center in
ogotá, 1950

elow. Le Corbusier
second from right),
ith José Luis Sert
ar right) and oth-
rs, Baranquilla,
olombia, 1950

Bottom left.
Le Corbusier and
bullfighters,
Bogotá, 1950

Bottom, middle and right. Le Corbusier
with Sert, architect
Paul Wiener, and
others, Colombia,
1950

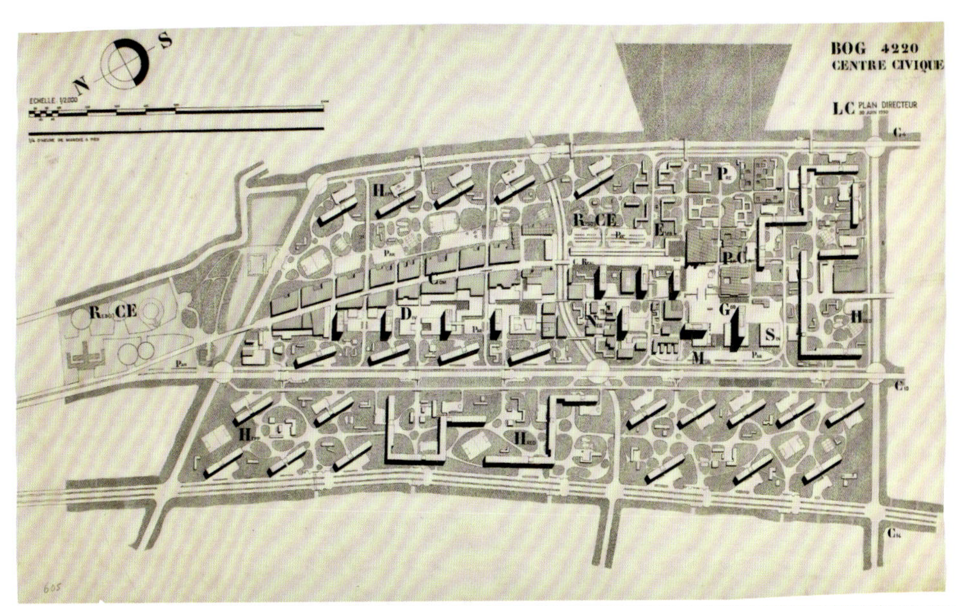

INDIA
AIR-INDIA
Fly with me!
AIR-INDIA International

Opposite. Le Corbusier at Air India counter, 1950s

Passage to India (1950–1962)

In 1950 Le Corbusier and Pierre Jeanneret were asked to join the English architects Maxwell Fry and Jane Drew in creating the new city of Chandigarh, which was established following the 1947 partition of India. Le Corbusier recognized this as the opportunity he had been waiting for all his life. In India he finally found a head of state, Prime Minister Jawaharlal Nehru, who was prepared to support his ideas on a grand scale. Le Corbusier told Nehru: "I did not come to India to make money. I am bringing this country a doctrine of architecture and urbanism, technological know-how, a particular architectural and urban philosophy, in short, the fruit of a 65-year-old man's long experience." And he later added, in the draft of a letter in March 1955: "Make one modern adventure of the spirit… lead to something solid that will endure in your country. A sign of harmony, born of a desire for good, of an unremitting struggle, of patience and perseverance, a spiritual sign, a monastic architecture with mountains and flowers and also a spirit of power and rough simplicity."

Le Corbusier's adventure in India, which he would visit twice a year during the project, was a mixture of a personal crusade and a new beginning, for he saw in India the possibility of resistance to the madness of modern capitalism and urban development: "Calm, dignity and contempt for covetousness: Perhaps India can hold out, and place herself at the head of civilization." He left his mark most firmly on the three main buildings constituting the capitol: the imposing High Court, the eight-story slab of the Secretariat, and the extraordinary Palace of the Assembly. "The Capitol will be a splendid park, with mountains, trees, flowers and architecture. It is dedicated to the pedestrian: man his own master, on foot, walking and living without fear."

The High Court achieves a monumentality that invokes the majesty of the law yet conveys a sense of open access to the legal system for all people. Le Corbusier regarded his colleagues (Maxwell Fry, Jane Drew, and Pierre Jeanneret) as having no concept of the symbolic—unlike himself. "When the mind can express itself by a sign comprehensible to him (and to others) as an algebraic value, then thought has made a great leap forward." The most symbolic of the Chandigarh designs, the Governor's Palace, was never constructed. But the Palace of the Assembly combines the shapes of an industrial cooling tower with an astrological symbolism invoking the power of the sun and moon to guide the deliberations of the politicians. As Le Corbusier himself said, "It's a magnificent and terrible building. Terrible in the sense that it has no fear."

To build a modern city that could accommodate all levels of Indian society was probably a chimera. In fact, the planners were unable to avoid the shanty towns and unplanned disorder that almost inevitably plague a city during periods of growth. Le Corbusier was certainly aware of the problem; he made an admiring sketch of the bamboo and tarpaulin shacks that sprang up around the High Court building and labeled it "The housing solution."

In Ahmedabad, a textile center north of Bombay, Le Corbusier built the Millowners' Association Building and two houses for textile industrialists who were members of the local elite. The two houses, Villa Sarabhai and Villa Shodhan, combine a richness of material and an intimacy of domestic space that contrast starkly with Le Corbusier's Purist villas of the 1920s. Describing one of these houses, he wrote: "What have I given Shodan? A palace = a functional house… I have given him shade in summer and sun in winter… Is it a chateau on the Loire? Yes, for an intelligent prince."

LE CORBUSIER

Paris, le 30 Novembre 1950

Monsieur José Luis SERT
33 West 42sd Street
NEW YORK 18 N.Y.

Mon cher Sert,

Le Secrétaire Général du Gouvernement du Punjab vient d'avoir de longues discussions avec moi/ j'ai à Paris, me demandant conseil pour la construction de la nouvelle capitale du Punjab aux Indes.

Ce mandataire du Gouvernement hindou est allé à Londres, en Suisse, en Belgique et son enquête bien orientée a fini par le conduire à des décisions intéressantes pour notre politique des C.I.A.M. Cette décision est celle-ci :

1º) Le Corbusier sera nommé "Architectural Advisor to the Government of Punjab - Capital Project.
2º) Maxwell Fry et Pierre Jeanneret seront nommés "Senior Architects" sur place pour diriger l'Office du Plan qui sera formé d'un collège de jeunes architectes hindous diplômés en U.S.A., en Angleterre ou ailleurs.
3º) Un certain circuit s'établira entre les dessinateurs de l'Office du Plan et l'Atelier Le Corbusier à Paris afin qu'il en résulte une certaine "instruction."
4º) D'autres membres des C.I.A.M., par exemple Alfred Roth de Zurich, un ou deux Milanais, un ou deux Français etc.. pourront compléter au fur et à mesure ce premier équipage.
Jane Drew rejoindra Maxwell Fry dès qu'elle le pourra.

Cet arrangement de principe a satisfait pleinement le mandataire hindou accompagné de l'ingénieur en chef de l'entreprise.

J'ai eu deux conversations téléphoniques avec Londres avec Maxwell Fry et Jane Drew hier et aujourd'hui. Hier Maxwell Fry avait compris que son collègue serait Emery et il n'était pas d'accord. Aujourd'hui j'ai rectifié en disant qu'il s'agissait de Pierre Jeanneret.

..../...

35, RUE DE SÈVRES – PARIS (6e)
TÉL. LITTRÉ 99-62

LE CORBUSIER

Les délégués hindous seraient ravis de la solution Jeanneret - Maxwell Fry car ce dernier, disent-ils "sait rédiger des rapports". En effet, l'un de ses rapports est resté par mégarde sur ma table ici et j'ai pu voir qu'il s'agissait d'un parfait travail administratif. Mais Fry est très déçu; il espérait être seul avec Jane Drew. En dernier ressort aujourd'hui il disait qu'il accepterait une équipe à égalité: Le Corbusier, Pierre Jeanneret, Maxwell Fry et Jane Drew.

Et voilà encore les susceptibilités, le personnalisme qui surgit: on parle d'"équipes" toute sa vie et quand l'occasion est là, on se récuse!

J'ai dit à Jane Drew et à Maxwell Fry de demander à Sert et Wiener si je sais travailler en équipe et garder ma place sans prendre celle des autres. J'ajoute que Charlotte Perriand est enchantée pour Pierre de cette solution à sa vie difficile (il s'est séparé de Blanchon); il avait peur de partir aux Indes mais Charlotte l'a secoué.

Mon avis serait donc que vous Sert, et par retour du courrier, écriviez à Maxwell Fry en lui disant qu'il doit accepter cette discipline et cette hiérarchie et ne pas considérer humiliant pour lui de ne pas être exactement au même titre que moi. Ma place reste à Paris avec un ou deux voyages par an aux Indes. Maxwell Fry et Pierre Jeanneret, eux, seront installés totalement sur place aux Indes pendant trois ans. Le climat est excellent, le paysage magnifique, le terrain vide de maisons.

Je pense que c'est là l'aventure C.I.A.M. caractéristique et définie qui se situe en l'un des points essentiels du monde actuel. J'avais pensé à vous et à Wiener mais devant les délégués j'ai mesuré immédiatement que le problème réel de présence sur place était le seul qui comptait pour eux.

Les deux délégués partent demain pour soumettre le projet à leur Gouvernement. Claudius Petit a été mêlé à l'affaire pendant quelques jours et n'a pu qu'approuver la marche des évènements. Les Beaux Arts avaient été présents pendant quelques journées avec quelques très bons éléments mais toutefois d'une autre nature que les ressortissants des C.I.A.M.

Amicalement.

LE CORBUSIER

35, RUE DE SÈVRES – PARIS (6e)
TÉL. LITTRÉ 99-62

LE CORBUSIER

P.S. J'ai eu la visite de Mazet et je lui ai conseillé de fai encore une bonne période d'Amérique; il vous écrit.

Je crois que vous avez beaucoup de travail mai tenant pour vos villes d'Amérique du Sud. Mazet a de grandes qualités; n'hésitez pas à le secouer jusqu'à ce qu'il ait un rendement "à l'Américaine." Il se contentera d'une paie courante; il aura à manger un peu de vache en ragée, cela lui fera du bien.

L-C

35, RUE DE SÈVRES – PARIS (6e)
TÉL. LITTRÉ 99-62

A new capital for the Punjab: Creating Chandigarh, India, 1950–62

After the partition of colonial India into modern India and Pakistan in 1947, the Indian province of Punjab required a new capital. Its name, Chandigarh (after Chandi, a goddess of power and transformation in Hindu cosmology), came from one of the seventeen villages that had previously occupied the site. With the vigorous support of French Minister of Reconstruction and Urbanization Eugène Claudius-Petit, Le Corbusier was selected to head a team—which also included Pierre Jeanneret and British CIAM members Maxwell Fry and Jane Drew—to design and build the new capital.

Le Corbusier's plans for the capitol complex comprised four major structures: the Governor's Palace (unbuilt), High Court, Palace of the Assembly, and Secretariat, at the center of which would be the Monument of the Open Hand.

AIR-INDIA
International

in flight

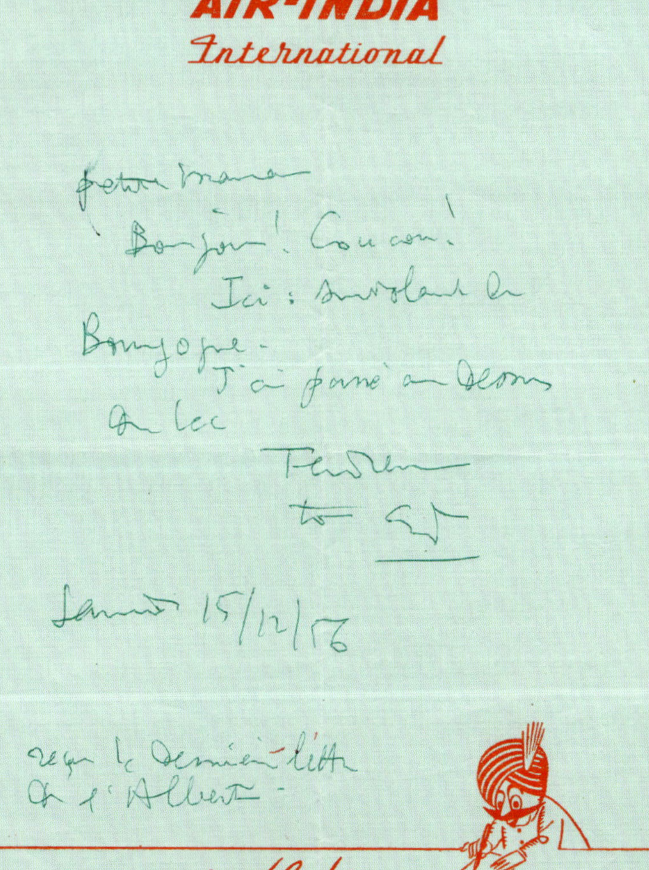

pposite, top. e Corbusier to fel- w CIAM member osé Luis Sert,) November 1950, escribing the team 'architects r Chandigarh

Opposite, bottom left. Le Corbusier to Yvonne, while flying to Bombay, "Sunday evening"; he notes that over the last thirteen days he has spent eighty-seven hours in a plane

Opposite, bottom right. Le Corbusier to his mother, en route to India from Burgundy, France, 15 December 1956

Below left. "From Le Corbusier's design, Chandigarh—the ultra-modern capital of 500,000 inhabitants—will spring up at the foot of the Himalayas," from *Le Franc Tireur,* 8 May 1950, regarding Le Corbusier's press conference announcing the commission to design Chandigarh

Below right. Le Corbusier' multiple-entry visa for India, issued February 1951

Bottom. Le Corbusier's Air India plane ticket from Geneva, 20 February 1951

Sur les plans de Le Corbusier

CHANDIGARH capitale ultra-moderne de 500.000 habitants va surgir au pied de l'Himalaya

Revenant de la nouvelle République du Punjab, l'architecte Le Corbusier a tenu hier une conférence de presse pour expliquer ce que sera la capitale de cette République : Chandigarh.

C'est une ville prévue pour 500.000 habitants, qui va s'élever sur un magnifique plateau campagnard, à proximité du chemin de fer et des routes. Delhi-Simla, Simla-Lahore et Carral-Latiala. Le plateau est légèrement incliné. Il monte doucement, face aux grandioses montagnes de l'Himalaya.

Déjà depuis un an les approvisionnements en canalisations, les stocks de matériaux de constructions, briques, ciment, etc., s'accumulent sur le vaste terrain.

C'est dans le sens de la compréhension des traditions et de l'éthique indiennes que Le Corbusier a préparé les plans de Chandigarh.

Tout est prévu pour apporter aux futurs habitants les « joies essentielles », c'est-à-dire le soleil, l'espace, la verdure. Il y aura une séparation très nette entre le piéton et l'automobiliste.

Si la construction de quelques buildings a été prévue, en revanche la grande majorité des maisons ne comportera qu'un seul étage. Et les indiens qui ont, paraît-il, l'habitude de coucher à la belle étoile, pourront, tout à leur aise, transporter leur lit sur les terrasses — recouvertes d'une toiture — qui domineront les maisons.

Enfin, Chandigarh, grâce à des dispositions d'urbanisme et d'architecture, sera mis à l'abri des bassesses de la spéculation et de ses corollaires désastreux : la banlieue. Il n'y aura pas de banlieue dans la cité ultra-moderne de la nouvelle République du Punjab.

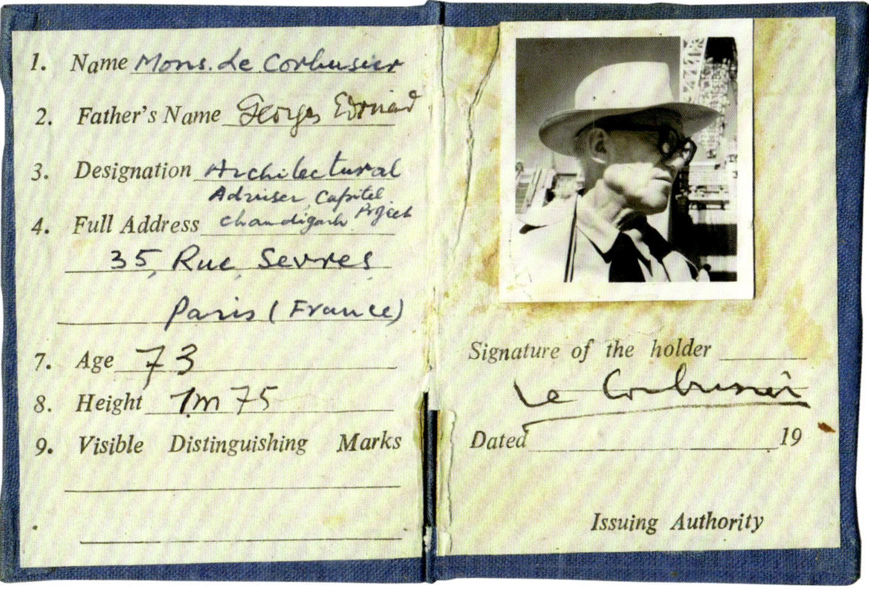

1. Name Mons. de Corbusier
2. Father's Name Georges Edouard
3. Designation Architectural Adviser, Capital Project
4. Full Address Chandigarh 35, Rue Sevres Paris (France)
7. Age 73
8. Height 1m75
9. Visible Distinguishing Marks

Signature of the holder Le Corbusier

Dated 19

Issuing Authority

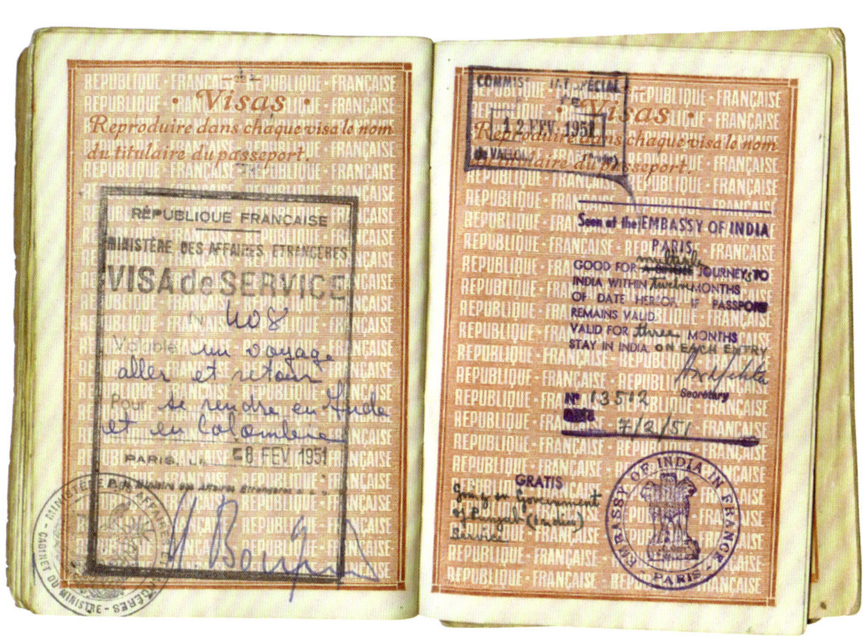

AIR-INDIA International

V. I. P.

PASS

BAG

Name of Passenger Mr LE CORBUSIER

AIR-INDIA INTERNATIONAL LTD

FORM 0982

211596

Convocation :
le 20.2.51. à 12.30.
Air India International
7 Rue Chantepoulet.
Geneve.

Issued By AIR-INDIA INTERNATIONAL LTD.
SUBJECT TO CONDITIONS OF CONTRACT ON PAGE (2)

PASSENGER TICKET AND BAGGAGE CHECK
PASSENGER COUPON

FORM 0982P 211596

Conjunction Ticket(s) Form Number(s) | Expiring Date | Fare Basis | Baggage | Issued in Exchange for- Form and No. | Date Originally Issued

Fare

Equivalent Am't Pd. | Pcs | Wt

Tax

Complete Routing (This Ticket and Conjunction Tickets)

Total

From · To · To · To · To · To · To · To · To · To

Form of Payment

Via Carrier | Flight No. | Date | Time | Used to Point Indicated

FROM GENEVA

TO

TO DELHI

Place and Date of Issue. Not good unless officially validated

AII PARIS

Free Baggage Allowance

Endorsement below revalidates ticket cancelled by indication in this column Revalidated from By:

NOT TRANSFERABLE

Name of Passenger

Signature:

Carriage/Transportation under this Passenger Ticket and Baggage Check, hereinafter called "ticket", is subject to the rules relating to liability established by the Convention for the Unification of Certain Rules Relating to International Carriage/Transportation by Air signed at Warsaw October 12, 1929, and contained in the First Schedule to the Carriage by Air Act, 1934, if such carriage/transportation is "international carriage/transportation" as defined by said Convention and Act.

Below and opposite. Le Corbusier traveling in India

"Let me tell you, here I'm at last going to do my life's work among people, the Indians, who are extraordinarily Civilized." —Letter to Yvonne, 26 February 1951

2797

"I've prepared everything carefully, with sensational benefits from my experiences of a lifetime. Here I'm pouring everything out onto the work table, as if from a horn of plenty." —Letter to Yvonne, 9 or 10 May 1951

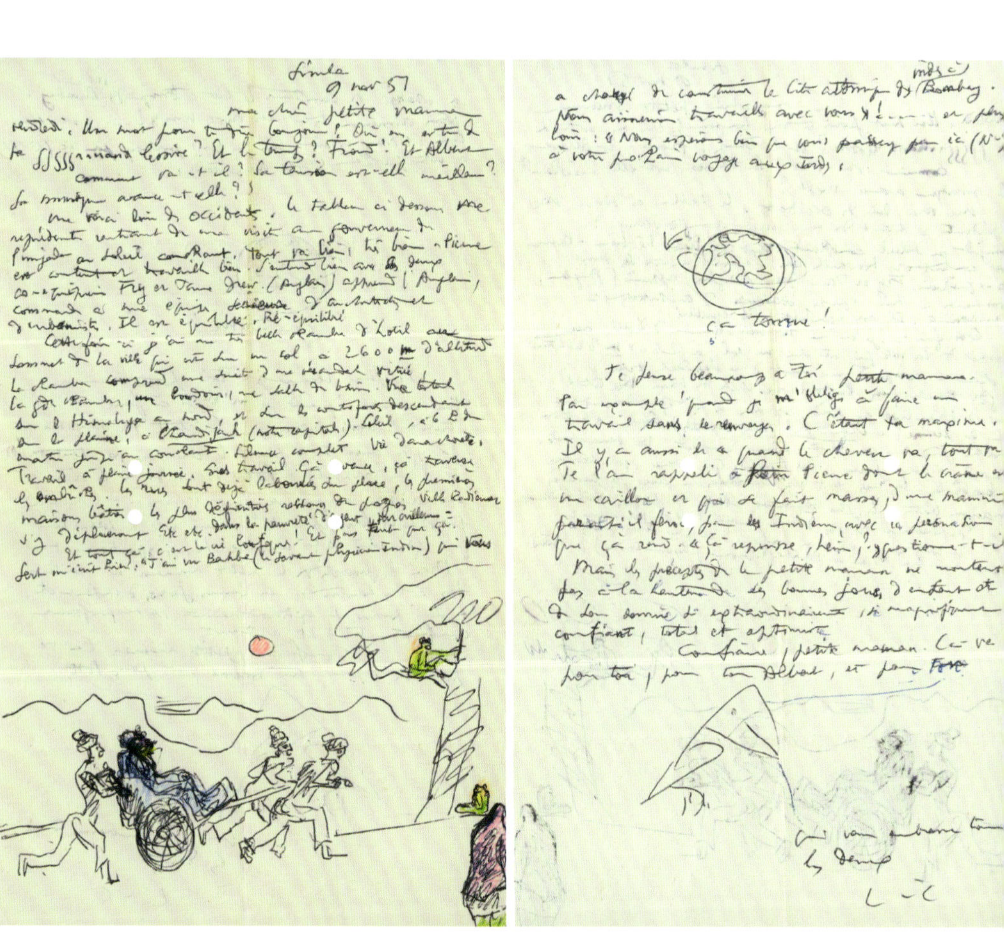

Above. Le Corbusier to Yvonne, from Simla, India, site of the Chandigarh design team office dated "9 or 10 May 1951." The letter describes working conditions at Simla.

Right. Le Corbusier to his mother, from Simla, India, 9 November 1951 He notes: "The streets are already ploughed, the first houses built."

Below. Sketches of site plan of Chandigarh, with Himalayas in the background, and note to Marguerite Tjader Harris, 4 May 1952

Bottom. Sketch from Chandigarh, 15 December 1952, inscribed "Marguerite Happy New Year '53"

Inspiration from the animal world

Virtually from the moment he arrived in India in 1951, Le Corbusier was fascinated and inspired by the close relationship of the people to their animals and, by extension, to the land. He was particularly captivated by the breed of bulls that he encountered in India, admiring their combination of strength and serenity.

Opposite, top left and right. Le Corbusier greeting animals in Chandigarh

Opposite, bottom. Le Corbusier with British architect Jane Drew, a member of the planning team for Chandigarh

Below. Pages of development sketches for the design of Chandigarh, from Le Corbusier's sketchbook, annotated with the handwritten title "Punjab, Simla, Chandigarh, March 1951"

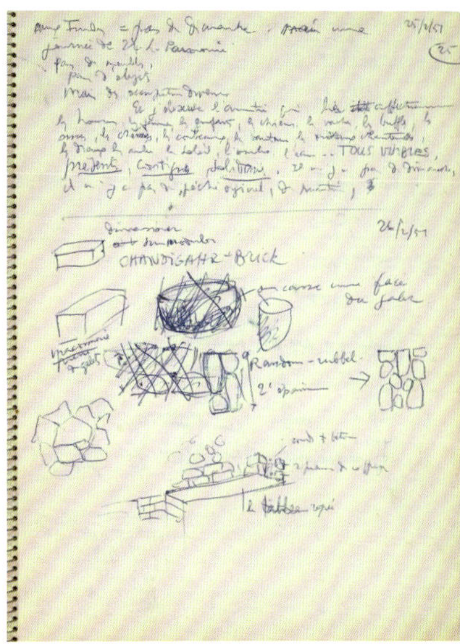

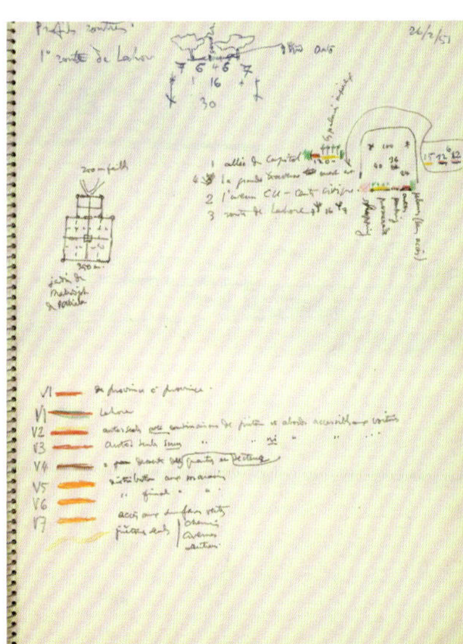

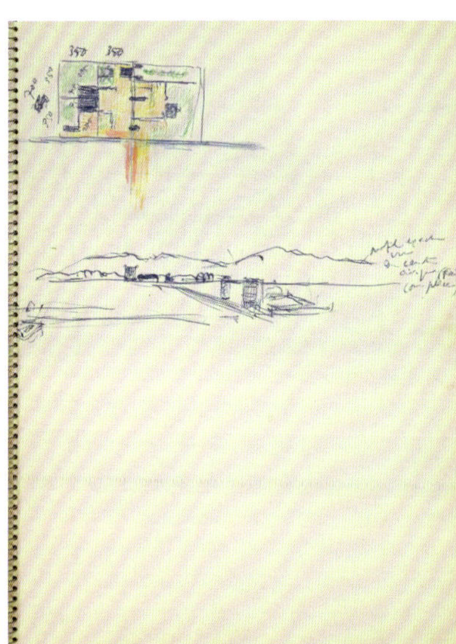

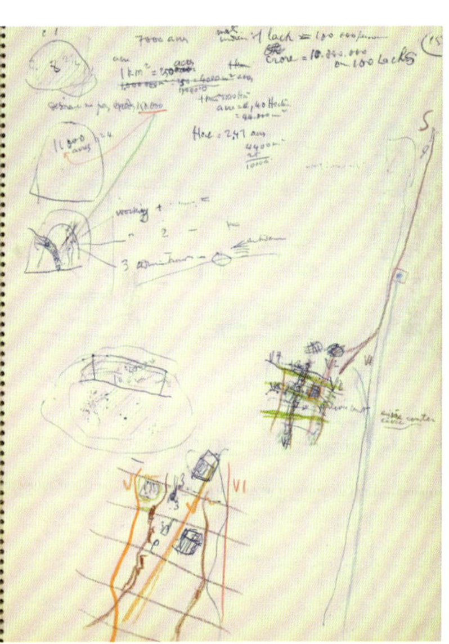

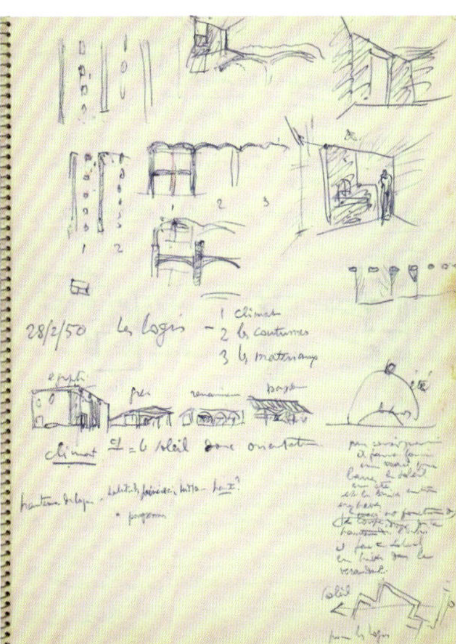

Above. Le Corbusier in a dry riverbed in India with sculpture made from sand castings. In 1960 he dedicated this photograph to his literary agent Helena Strassova, sending her a print inscribed with a personal note.

Opposite. Le Corbusier in India with sculpture of foot made from sand casting, c. 1950

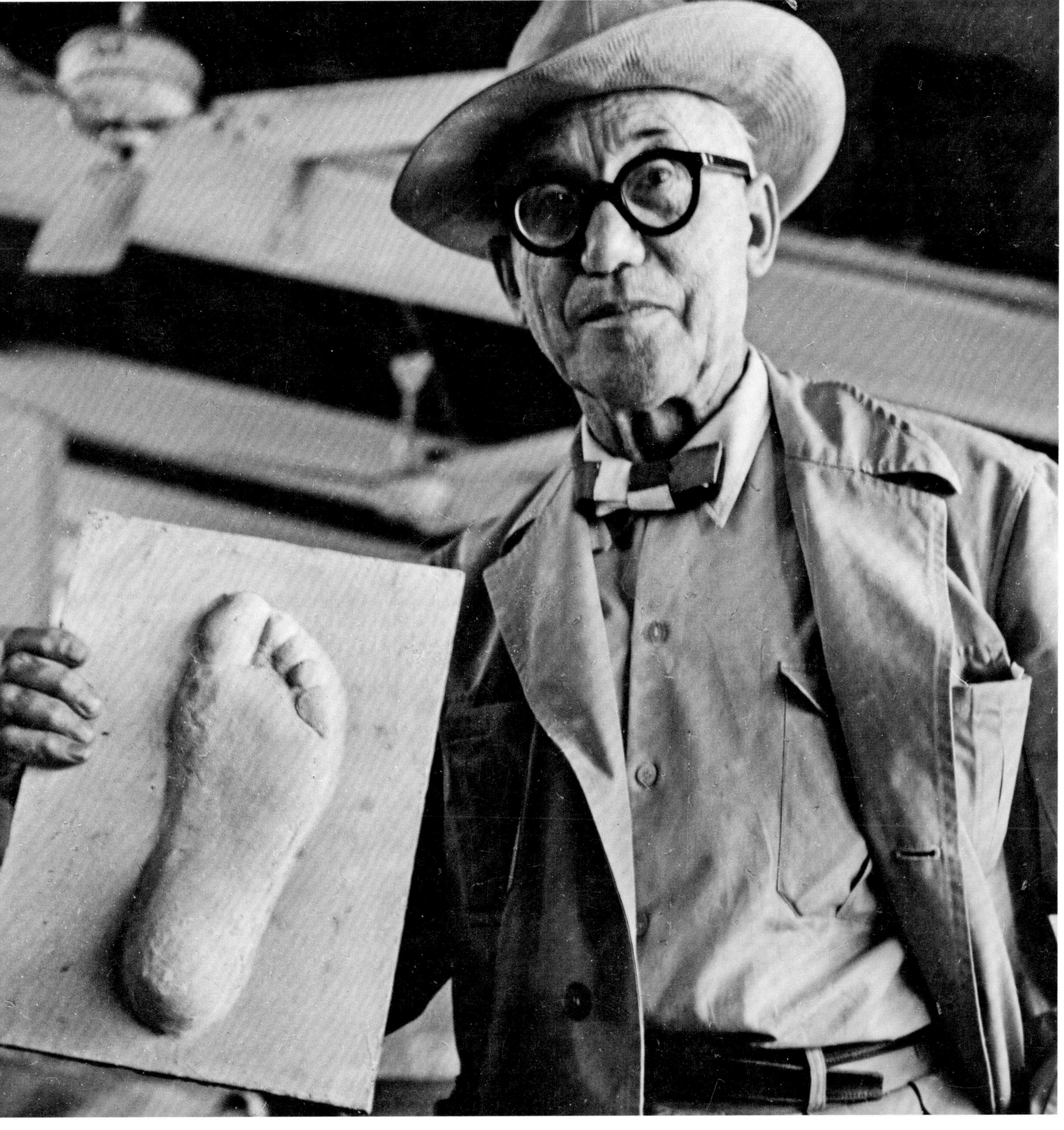

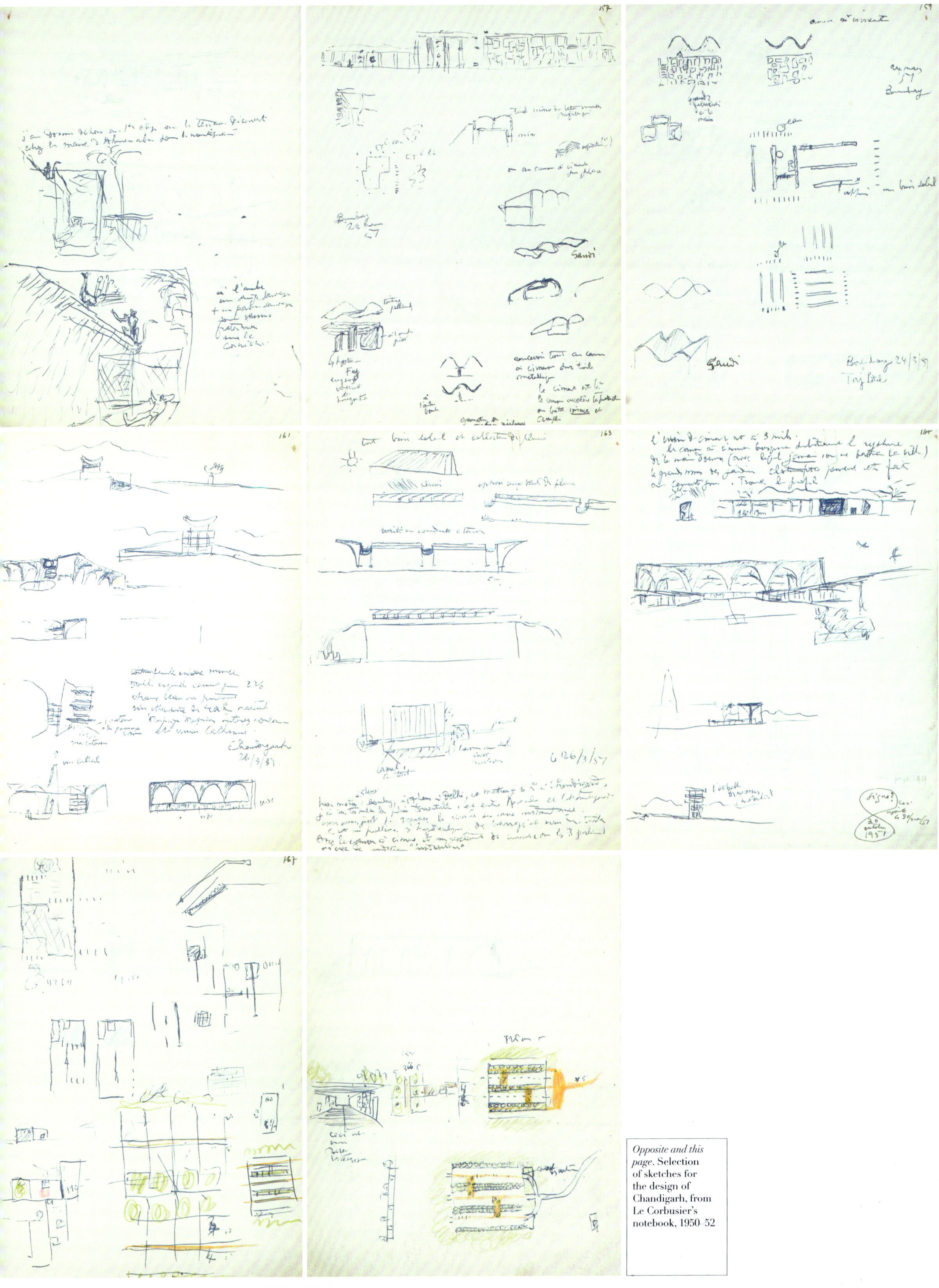

Opposite and this page. Selection of sketches for the design of Chandigarh, from Le Corbusier's notebook, 1950–52

PLAN OF
C H A

Opposite. Le Corbusier on the site of Chandigarh, with the master plan of the new city and a maquette of the Modulor man

"The final touch has been put to a plan of what is going to become a city unique in the world, built for people to live in joie de vivre and simplicity."

—Letter to Yvonne, 26 February 1951

The master plan for Chandigarh

The site chosen for Chandigarh occupied a wide plateau between two rivers, which were dry most of the year—a literal tabula rasa. Though Le Corbusier was not contractually the city's planner, the final master plan for Chandigarh followed only loosely an earlier scheme by American planner Albert Mayer. It was composed of an orthogonal grid with few curving roads, all organized along an axis arranged in the manner of the Ville Radieuse, but without any high-rise towers.

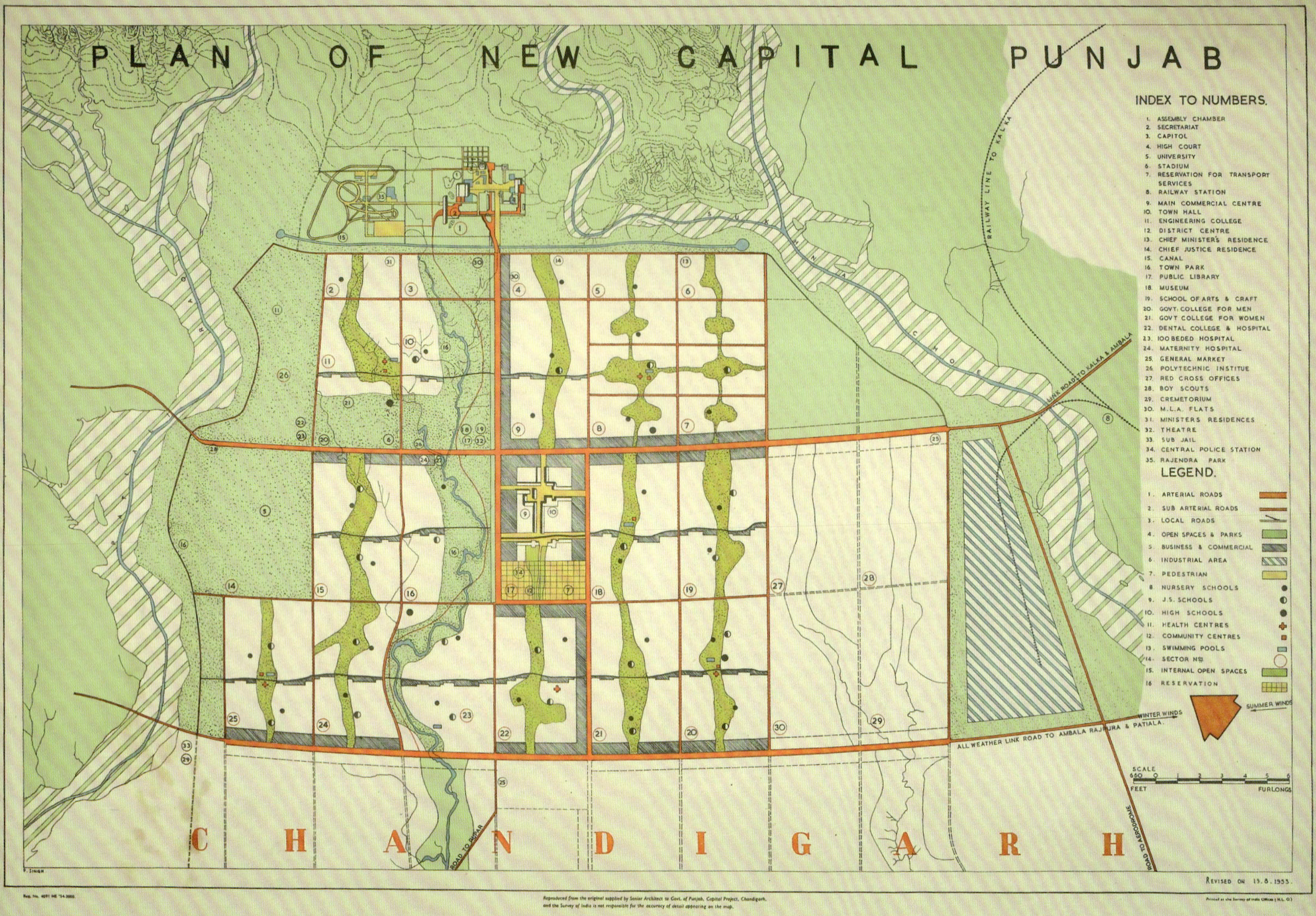

Above. Master plan of Chandigarh, showing numbered sectors, drawn 1951; revised 19 August 1953

Below left. Chandigarh master plan overlaid with bus lines, 17 February 1952

Below middle. Plan of Chandigarh showing distribution of population in thousands, by numbered categories, 15 March 1951

Below right. Chandigarh, general plan no. 3

Opposite, top. Diagram of circulation systems within the city, 24 April 1951

Opposite, bottom. Le Corbusier reviewing plans with a colleague

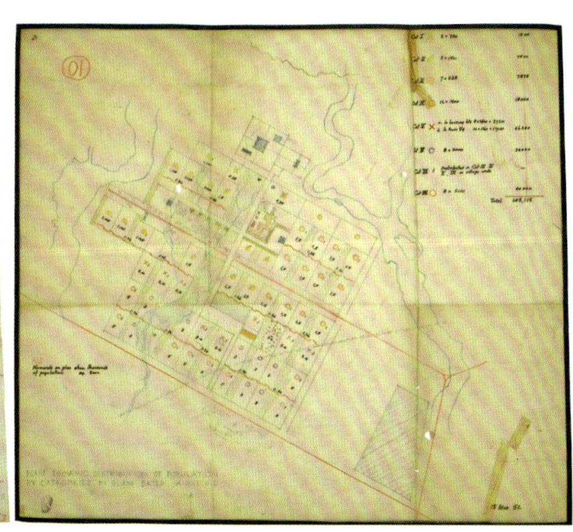

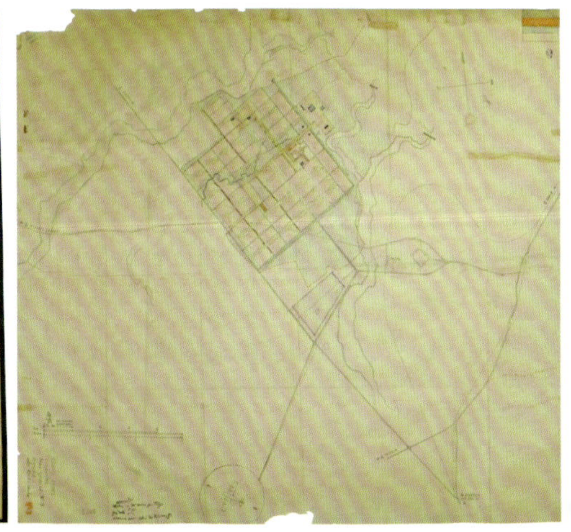

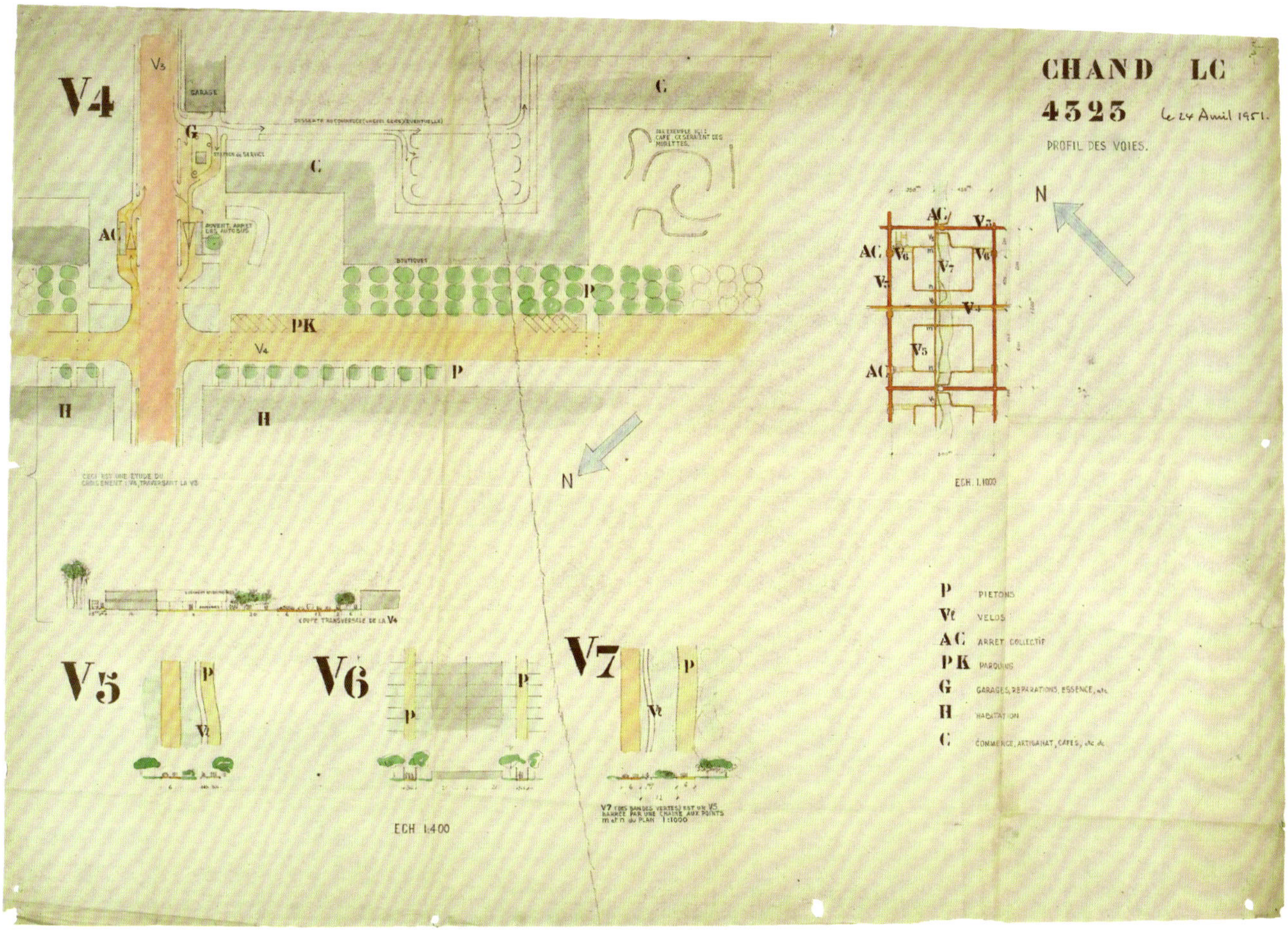

CHAND LC
4323 le 24 Avril 1951.
PROFIL DES VOIES.
V4
V5
V6
V7
ECH. 1:400
ECH. 1:1000
P PIETONS
Vl VELOS
AC ARRET COLLECTIF
PK PARQUING
G GARAGES, REPARATIONS, ESSENCE, etc.
H HABITATION
C COMMERCE, ARTISANAT, CAFES, etc &

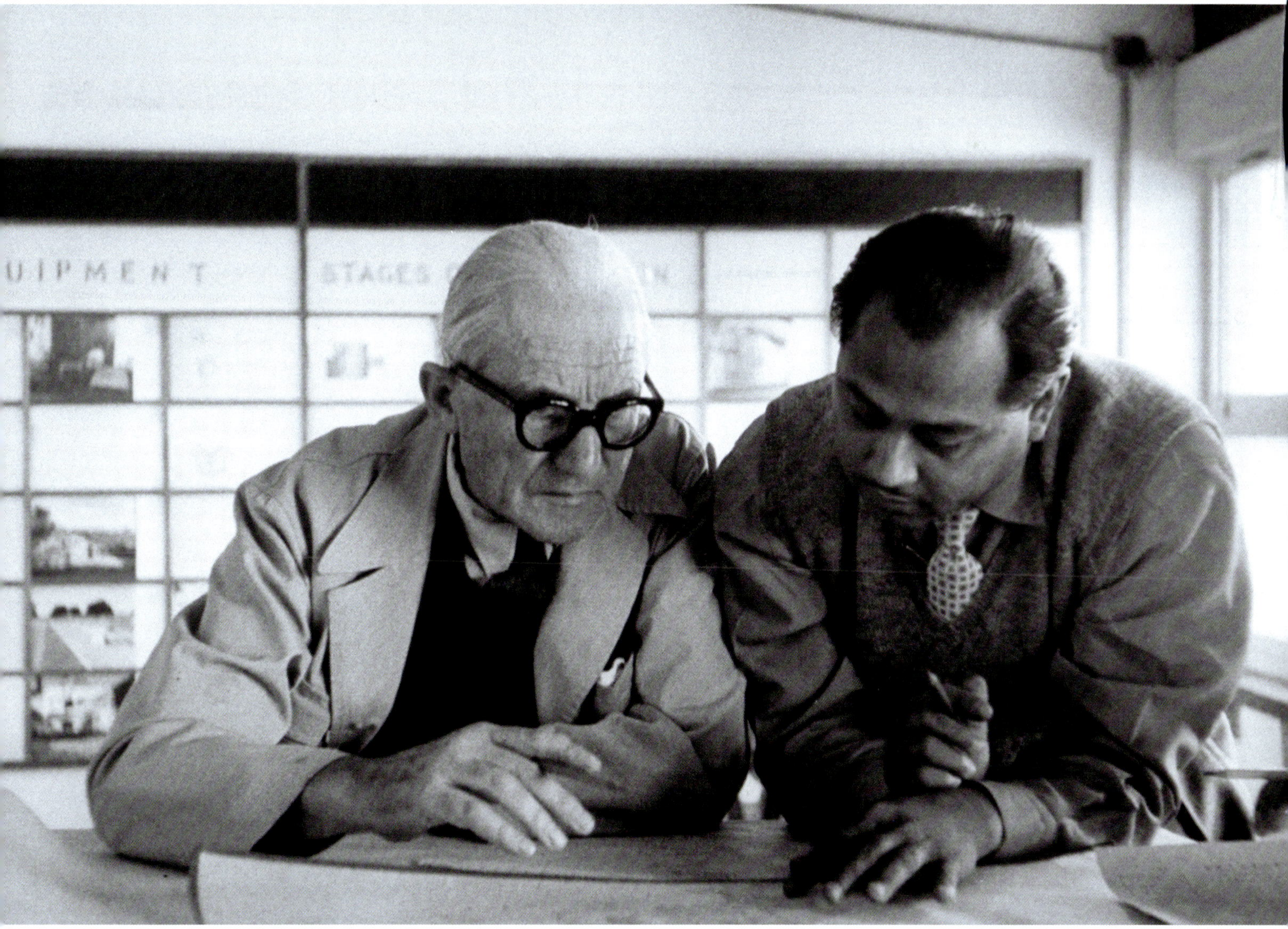

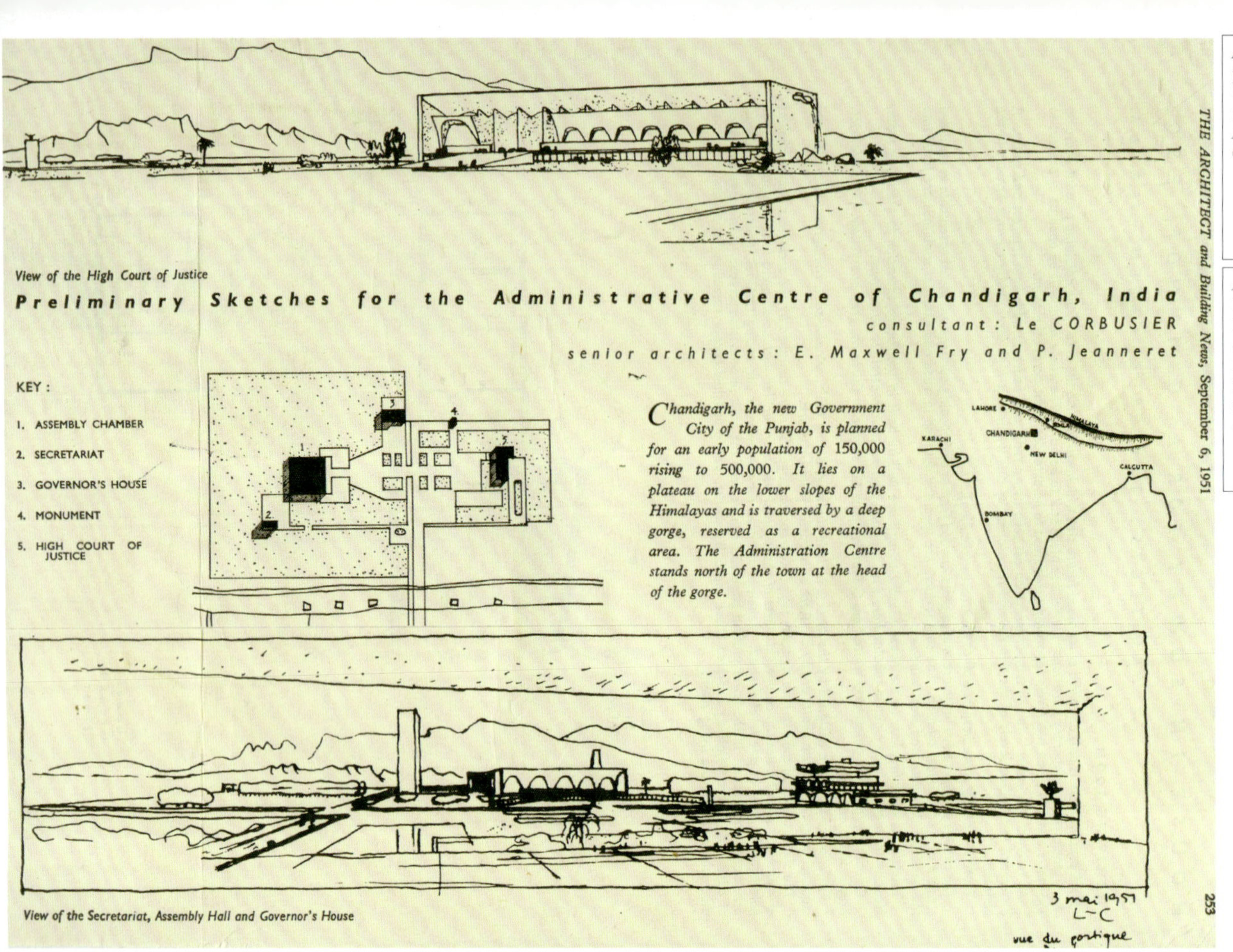

View of the High Court of Justice

Preliminary Sketches for the Administrative Centre of Chandigarh, India

consultant: Le CORBUSIER

senior architects: E. Maxwell Fry and P. Jeanneret

KEY:

1. ASSEMBLY CHAMBER
2. SECRETARIAT
3. GOVERNOR'S HOUSE
4. MONUMENT
5. HIGH COURT OF JUSTICE

Chandigarh, the new Government City of the Punjab, is planned for an early population of 150,000 rising to 500,000. It lies on a plateau on the lower slopes of the Himalayas and is traversed by a deep gorge, reserved as a recreational area. The Administration Centre stands north of the town at the head of the gorge.

View of the Secretariat, Assembly Hall and Governor's House

THE ARCHITECT and Building News, September 6, 1951

Left. Sketches and plans of Chandigarh in *The Architect and Building News*, 6 September 1951

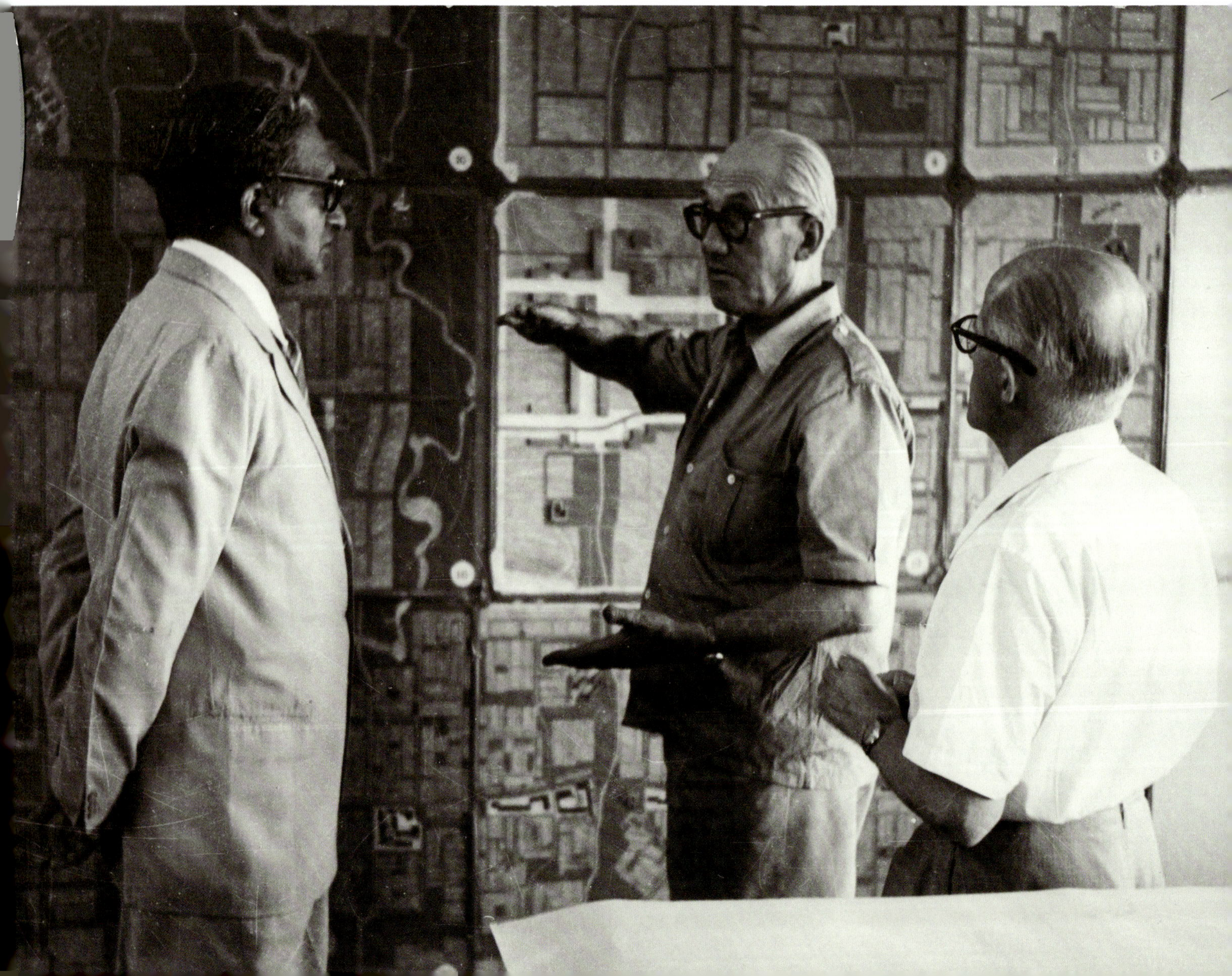

Below and opposite. Le Corbusier with P. L. Varma, chief engineer of the Punjab (left), and Pierre Jeanneret, in front of a map of Chandigarh

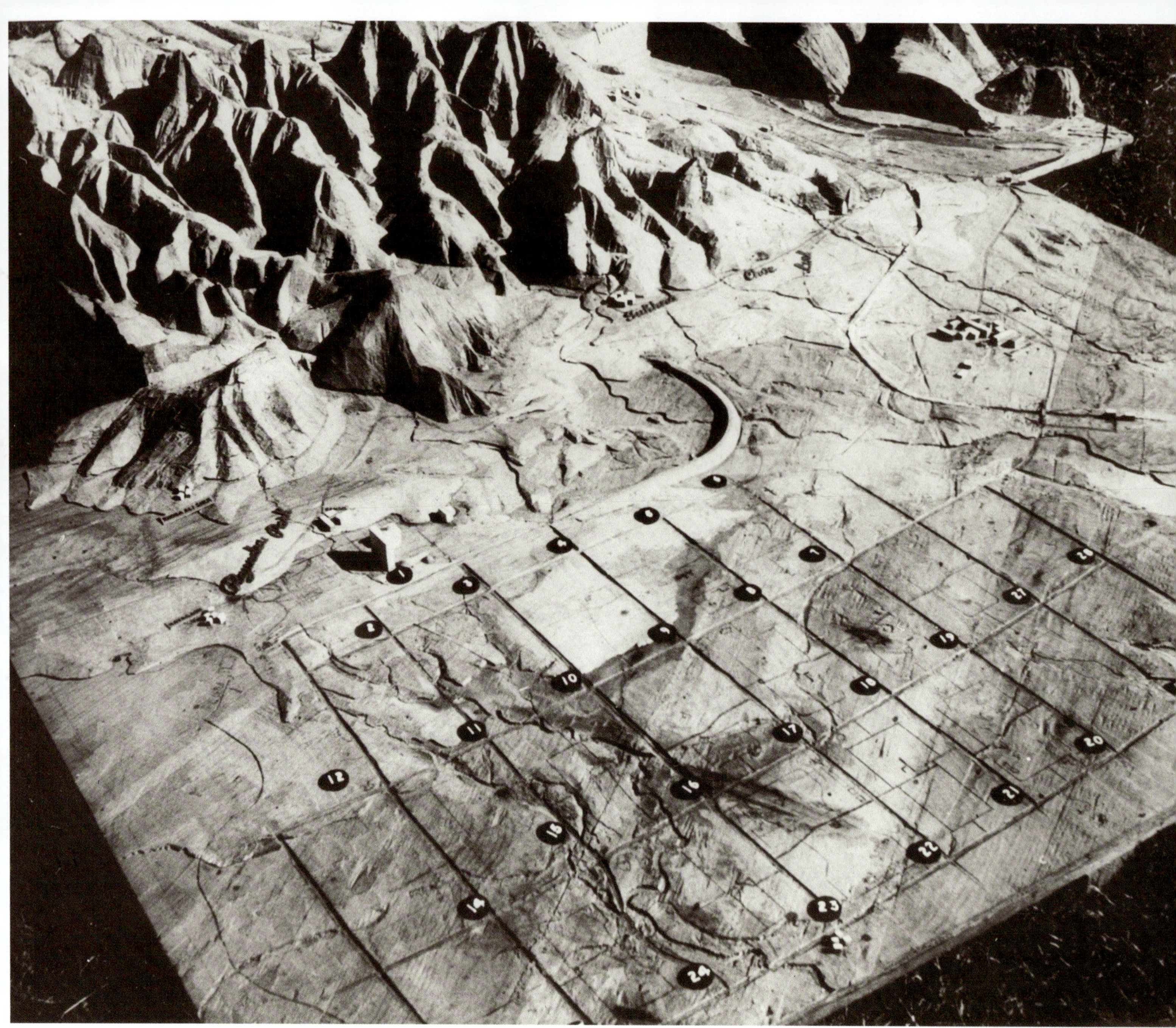

CHANDIGARH - URBANISME - PLANS GENERAUX

Auteur		Référence	Sujet	Description	Echelle	Date	Dessinateur
IND	I	Original L-C. Emporté par LC avril I95I	Plan général	Ière esquisse - Ier ensemble sans définition de secteurs	4inch/Imile	I7/3/5I	L-C
IND	2	Maxwell Fry? Emporté par LC4/5I	Plan général	Zones vertes avec définition de secteurs	4inch/Imile	?	Maxwell Fry
IND	3	Maxwell Fry? Emporté par LC 4/5I	Plan général	Zonage	4inch/Imile	?	M. Fry ?
IND	4	Tirage M.Fry? Emporté par LC 4/5I	Plan général	Vallée d'érosion + surfaces civiques: Capitol, Université, centre commercial, centre hôtelier, etc...	4inch/Imile	?	M.Fry ?
L-C	5	Plan 4.3I8	Plan général	Ensemble définitif de la ville	4inch/Imile	I8/4/5I	Samper
L-C	6		Plan général	[illegible] Etude comparative de Chandigarh & New Delhi	Echelle graphique	I8/4/5I	Taka
IND	7		Plan général	Master Plan for the New Capital	4inch/Imile		
IND	8	Drawing N° 2/6	Plan général	Imprimé de plan définitif	4inch/Imile		
IND	9	Drawing N°7. Job	Plan général	Tirage définitif accepté par LC le I0/2/53	4inch/Imile		
IND	I0	Drawing N°43/5I 2/2	Plan général	Categories of housing density houses per acre, population in thousands	4inch/Imile		
IND	11	Plan signé par LC	Plan général	Idée concernant le développement de surfaces agricoles près du Capitol		8 juin 53	
IND	I2	Drawing N°7. Job N°2. Reçu le 9 Mai I952	Plan général	Blue-print. Master Plan for New Capital at Chandigarh	4inch/Imile		

../...

- 2 - 19

CHANDIGARH - URBANISME - PLANS GENERAUX

Auteur		Référence	Sujet	Description	Echelle	Date	Dessinateur
IND	I3	Original L-C emporté le I2/5I	Plan général	Rectification urbanisme Etude des antichambres du Capitol Etude du City Center Etude des services publics	I60 feet = I inch	I9/11/5I	L-C

Opposite, top. Site model of Chandigarh labeled with numbered sectors

Opposite, bottom. Schedule for construction drawings of Chandigarh, 1951

Below. Aerial view of Chandigarh under construction, 1 September 1958

Following pages. Le Corbusier demonstrating the "Open Hand" motif

"Work all day, a lot of work. It's going ahead, cutting through the obstacles. The streets are already ploughed, the first houses built. The most definitive resources of the Ville Radieuse progress will be put into action there Etc. etc. But amidst a shortage of money."

—Letter to his mother, 9 November 1951

Monument of the Open Hand, Chandigarh

While developing forms for the various public structures of Chandigarh, Le Corbusier also worked to develop a symbolic vocabulary that would express the spirit of the new city. Central to this was the Monument of the Open Hand, which would occupy the most public space in the city, between the Palace of the Assembly and the High Court. The form of the open hand had for a long time held great symbolic significance for Le Corbusier, who had sketched a related image as early as 1943. The monument was not erected until 1985.

ATELIER LE CORBUSIER 35, RUE DE SEVRES PARIS-6e
ÉPURE DE LA "MAIN OUVERTE"
COUPE VERTICALE DANS L'AXE DU MÂT.
VUE EN PLAN
Mât : Construction métallique
Socle en béton

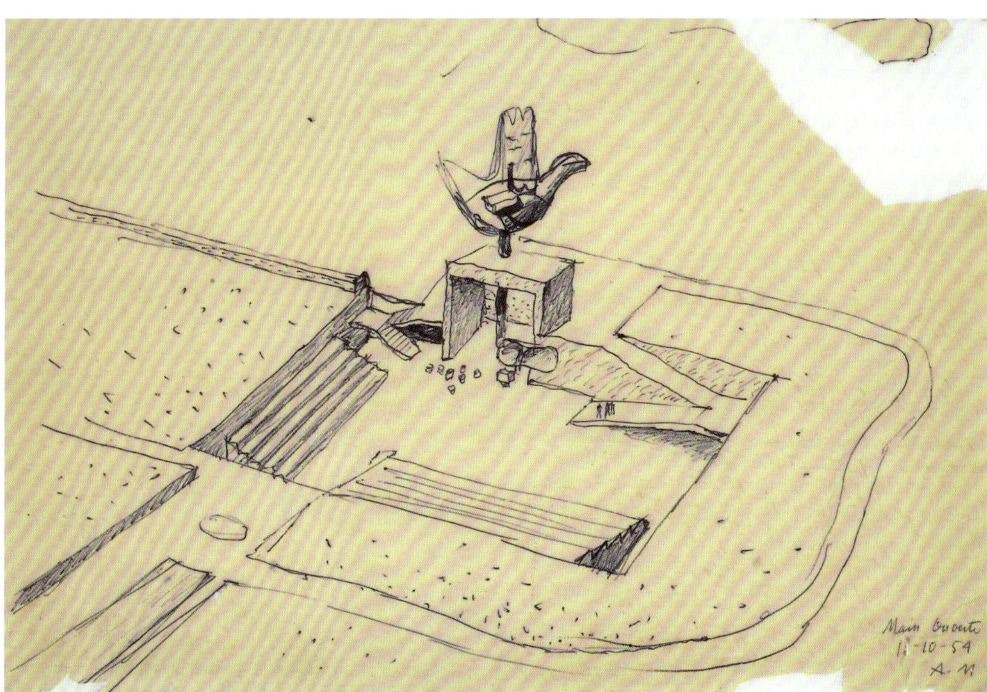

Opposite, top. Sketches of the Monument of the Open Hand, drawn by Le Corbusier on the plane between Karachi and Cairo, 27 February 1954

Opposite, bottom. Technical drawing of the Monument of the Open Hand, 14 January 1955

Above left. Sketch of the Monument of the Open Hand, 6 August 1951, Roquebrune-Cap-Martin, France

Above right. Study for the Monument of the Open Hand, 18 October 1954

Below. Photo-collage showing the proposed Monument of the Open Hand before the "Pit of Contemplation," c. 1955

Below. "The Open Hand," by Le Corbusier, copy in English for Jawaharlal Nehru, December 1954

Opposite. Le Corbusier, with unidentified man, in his office in Simla, India

Le Corbusier

168

pour M. Nehru

" THE OPEN HAND "

The world is under going a fever of clasping mortal contradictions.

It is agreed ! The world may burst ! It is possible !

The machinist civilisation for its hundred years of scientific and technical conquest will shortly have the fruits for its efforts. The balance sheet is eloquen-t.

(a) One science universally researched, practised and developed.

An unprecidented technical equipment, revolutionary in the human history, is capable of producing the unlimited products for fruitful consumption.

A sensational information owing to the progress in photography, cinema and sound recording embraces an extensive domain between the astronomic spaces and the microscopic profounders.

This information through the effects of printing, Radio and television clothed with precision and exactitude, is responded all over the World with the rapidity of lightening. Every day the world is instructed of its proper palpitation.

The science of aeronautics is added to the means of land and naval transports. The air route has introduced a major modification in the relations between human groups.

At last the fission of the atom will upset the sources of energy and thus the production. The human pain the want would then be one day set aside ....

(b) The abundence seems to be the sign of the epoch. The open hand to receive, the open hand to give could be chosen as a symbolic materialization of all thes victories !

.....2

169

- 2 -

Is it that, at this precise moment today, a contrary destiny will claim to hold us in the terror of possible Wars ?

India did not have to live the first centary of the machinist troubles, passed today. On the contrary she is awakening, intact, at the hours of all the possibilities. But India is not a new country; She has lived the highest and the most ancient civilisations. She possess an intelligence, an ethics and a conscience.

India could estimate precisely the conjuncture of dressing in the Capital of Chandigarh, actually under construction, in the midst of palaces sheltering her institutions and her authority, the symbolic and evocatin sign of " THE OPEN HAND ".

Open for receiving the created richness ...

Open for the distribution to her people and to -others ....

'THE OPEN HAND ' will affirm that the second era of the machinist civilization - the era of harmony - has started.

Chandigarh today, offers providentially to bring this witness.

(Le. Corbusier.)
Chandigarh, dated the Dec.' 54

Le Corbusier

"'The Open Hand' will affirm that the second era of the machinist civilization—the era of harmony—has started."

—"The Open Hand," December 1954

Translation

Paris, July 22nd, 1955

Mr J. NEHRU
Prime Minister
Prime Minister's Secretariat
NEW DELHI

Dear Mr Nehru,

I was so glad your miraculous venture through Asia and Europe met such a success. Let me express my deep admiration.

Today I make an appeal to your authority in regard to Chandigarh. I am enclosing an accurately drawn sky-line of the Capitol to make my argument more substantial. The five component elements of the Capitol stand out against the background of the Himalaya :

- the Secretariat
- the Assembly
- the Governor's House
- "The Open Hand"
- the High Court

(An incident: I have been told by Pierre Jeanneret that a certain number of the judges have removed the tapestries from their court of justice. On the other hand, the Chief Judge is keeping his tapestry and his enthusiasm, which is precious to me.

I wonder as a question of principle if the taste of M/S the Subaltern Judges has a right to intervene in a venture such as the Capitol of Chandigarh. You have entrusted its plans to an architect whose works and especially the work of Chandigarh have given him the reputation of being actually the first architect). (I beg your pardon for this lack of modesty).

I am now coming back to the purpose of this letter. The High Court has reached completion. The Secretariat (for 3.000 officers) will be finished at the end of the year. The drawings of the Governor's House are completely finished and the works are going to start. I am beginning the drawings of the Assembly.

...

- 2 -

"The Open Hand"

Quite in the beginning of Chandigarh I was asked by the authorities to consider the possibility of evolving a symbol to crown the Capitol. I spoke to them of "The Open Hand", - the symbol of modern times, - the symbol of future times. I am enclosing as proofs a photostat and the translation of the declaration I made on April 17th, 1949 at the World Congress of the Upholders of Peace.

At that time they laid a frightful pressure on me. They tried to use and misuse my name and practised the threat of the bullet in the nape of the neck. I replied by a written declaration to the World Congress of the Upholders of Peace (Refer to the enclosed document) :

"They wish to place us on the horns of a USA - URSS dilemma. This is the result of a lack of information which can only be obtained by an enquiry on the spot regarding the differences and similitudes which condition the fast developing present machinist phenomenon."

"I refuse to play into your hands and accept the conditions of the dilemma which may be terrible."

....

This document dated April 17th, 1949 has its proper value. But its consequence is even more interesting.

I was possessed by the tragic quandary which was offered here and there under the outrageous term of "TO COMMIT ONESELF". I picked up a drawing of 1948 representing an open hand above the sky-line; five women grouped on the ground see it rise to view. From then onwards I only kept the hand in my drawing its outline getting more and more pure. I drew it during my travels. It took shape.

In 1951 I finished in a month the town planning of Chandigarh (at Simla and in the Rest House on the road leading from Kalka to Delhi). I then instituted the notion of "La Fosse de la Considération": a pit with sides of 40 meters and 5 meters deep, 2 amphitheatres at right angles, a tribune of modest height, an acoustic conch and "The Open Hand" which overlooks the debates. Those who take part in the debates are not politicians but have the liking and the need to discuss public interests.

...

- 3 -

Then "The Open Hand" was created, full of meaning. It gained a size of great dignity. Its summit is 23 metres high and its dimensions are 12m x 7m. It is made of enamelled welted sheet iron and it turns in the wind like a weathercock.

Dear Mr Nehru, I think that such a manifestation of the modern conception: TO RECEIVE AND TO GIVE is worthy of your country, especially worthy of yourself and also worthy of the great effort I am making to realise Chandigarh with very poor material and financial means which are however the most capable of provoking creation.

I have asked Mr P.N. Thapar who is now a great friend and who had the courage to choose me as the architect for Chandigarh to look out for a good opportunity to give you these documents.

Mr P.L. Varma, Chief Engineer to the Punjab Government who is a splendid character and a remarkable leader, would also like to see "The Open Hand" realised.

I explained this project before the Cabinet Sub-Committee meeting on November 16th, 1954 and I was asked to let this Administration have a detailed note. I sent you a copy and even gave you an explanation written by hand at the Opening Ceremony of the High Court, on March 19th, 1955.

I must also add that all the material studies for the execution of the monument are finished. I have obtained extremely low prices from two French firms (very devoted friends of mine) for the making of the hand in enamelled metal as well as its metallic bracket. This low price is really amazing. I do not see the possibility of ever reaching such low prices for a public monumen

The decision lays in your hands and I request the honour of asking you to confer to Chandigarh, the city who is clear of behind the times traditions and open on tomorrow, this symboli materialisation at the foot of the Himalaya. This monument will have far reaching ethical consequences. I am sure that by dressir in this place "The Open Hand", India will make a gesture which w corroborate your intervention which is so decisive at the crucial moment of the machinist evolution and its threats.

I will thus, by the prolongation of my architectural

...

- 4 -

tasks, be close to you. I end this letter with the declaration I have made for one of my books: "Architecture is the expression of the spirit of an era."

Believe me, dear Mr Nehru,

yours most faithful,

LE CORBUSIER

Copy is addressed to :
Mr P.N. Thapar
Mr P.L. Varma
M. Pierre Jeanneret, Senior Architect

Opposite, top. Silhouette of the capitol buildings, with the Monument of the Open Hand at center. Chandigarh, 17 September 1954

Opposite, bottom. Le Corbusier in front of an oversize silhouette and plans of the capitol

Above. Le Corbusier to Jawaharlal Nehru, 22 July 1955, seeking support for the Monument of the Open Hand

"The task that is mine: the city (urbanism),then the Capitol (5 administrative blocks) will be a historical landmark... If we get through without the interruptions and disasters that have accompanied all my ventures."

—Letter to his mother, 30 November 1952

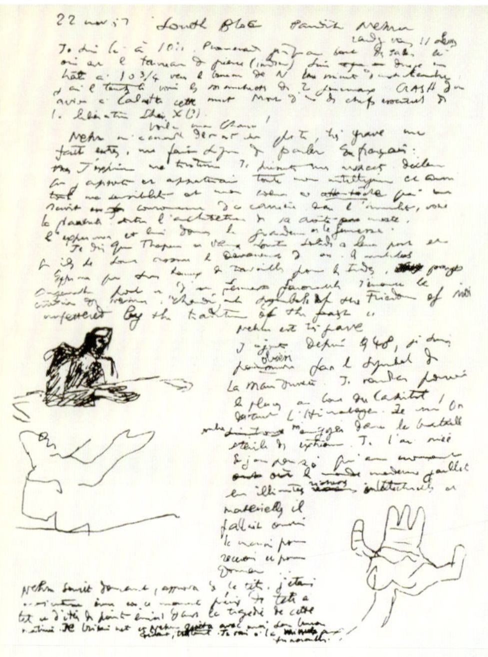

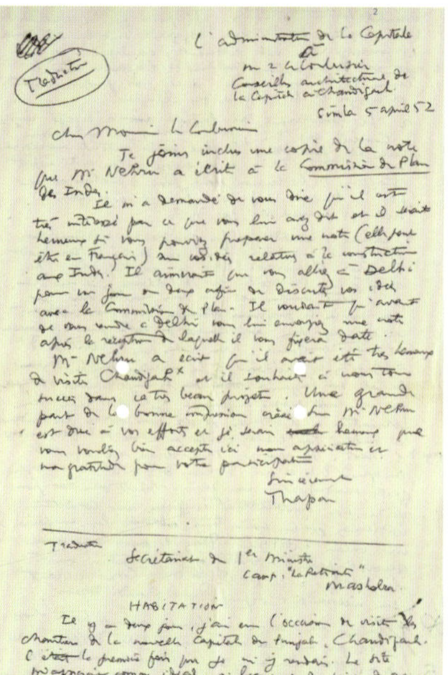

J. NEHRU
4/4/52

The ideal patron: Jawaharlal Nehru

Le Corbusier saw in Prime Minister Jawaharlal Nehru an enlightened client, and indeed the visionary politician gave nearly unequivocal support to the architect's most ambitious plans (a welcome reversal of his experience in Vichy France). For his part, Nehru always saw the establishment of the new capitol as an opportunity to create a potent symbol for a modern era in Indian politics and society.

Paris, September 22nd 1953

To His Excellency
Mr J. NEHRU
in CHANDIGARH
On the occasion of the
Opening Ceremony of Chandigarh
October 7th, 1953

Your Excellency and Friend,

I think you should be acquainted on the day of the Opening Ceremony of Chandigarh - a halcyon day full of lightheartedness - of the sad financial plight of your Architect, your Town Planner, Le Corbusier, the animating spirit of the town. He is in debt of several millions because :

1°) the Punjab Government has not yet payed him,

2°) his wealthy Ahmedabad clients (the Municipal Corporation, the Millowners' Association and several private and very rich clients) have not yet payed him.

Since two years and ten months I have devoted nearly the whole of my activity to India thereby neglecting to undertake more profitable surveys. Despite all my efforts I have n't yet succeeded in being paid. Who is the real responsible ? Since June last, my creditors have become exacting and I have been obliged to leave off paying my draftsmen in my architectural office. At 66 years of age I have never been in such a desperate financial plight.

Meanwhile, all over the world, the public opinion praises Chandigarh, India and the Indians.

I will say no more. My grief is immeasurable. I hope this letter will be handed over to you on October 7th.

I remain,

ever your most truly,

LE CORBUSIER

P.S. Repeatedly Chandigarh has asked me to send innumerable plans for the Governor's House, the Assembly, the Capitol Park and the National Park, the Monument, etc.. How am I supposed to pay my draftsmen ?

Opposite, top left. Notes by Le Corbusier, 22 November 1951, about his meeting with Nehru as well as his obsession with the Open Hand symbol

Opposite, top middle and right. Le Corbusier to his mother, from India, April 1952, enclosing French translations of letters from P.N.Thapar, administrator of the Punjab, and Jawaharlal Nehru about the prime minister's interest in Le Corbusier's ideas for the architecture of Chandigarh

Opposite, bottom. Le Corbusier to Jawaharlal Nehru, from Paris, 22 September 1953, notifying the prime minister that he has not been paid for his work on Chandigarh

Right, top to bottom. Jawaharlal Nehru, Le Corbusier, and others at Chandigarh

"Everything's for the best. The 16th I'll be at Nehru's in Delhi... I think we're doing something good here."—Letter to his mother, April 1952

Above and opposite. Le Corbusier with Jawaharlal Nehru in Chandigarh

La ville s'élève devant un horizon de montagnes.

L'architecte français célèbre Le Corbusier et son collaborateur Pierre Jeanneret construisent la capitale nouvelle du Pendjab, Chandigarh, « ville radieuse » des Indes située à 150 milles au Nord de Delhi, capitale de la République indienne. Les relations amicales franco-indiennes ont une longue histoire, spécialement avec le Pendjab. Des généraux de Napoléon — Ventura, Court, Avitabile, Allard — aidèrent le Maharajah Ranjit Singh, roi des Indes du Nord-Ouest, à former la meilleure armée indienne au XIXe siècle. Aujourd'hui, des architectes français aident le Pendjab à construire une capitale qui sera, nous l'espérons, la meilleure ville des Indes.

Le besoin d'une nouvelle capitale pour l'Etat divisé du Pendjab résulta du partage des Indes, en 1947, qui laissa Lahore, son ancienne capitale, au Pakistan. Simla, centre de villégiature dans l'Himalaya et capitale temporaire du Pendjad oriental, n'est pas favorable à un centre administratif par son climat extrême et sa grande distance des plaines. Le gouvernement décida de construire une cité nouvelle. Les capitales créées de toute pièce sont bien rares dans le monde : Saint-Pétersbourg fut bâtie par Pierre le Grand sur des marais inhabités ; Washington, sur les marécages du Potomac ; tandis que Canberra, en Australie, convertit une station de moutons en une ville florissante. Aux Indes, New-Delhi ne fut qu'un supplément à la ville ancienne de Delhi.

Une des considérations les plus importantes dans le projet d'une capitale nouvelle est le choix du terrain à bâtir. Après avoir examiné nombre de lieux, on décida de construire la ville nouvelle dans la région située au pied des montagnes de l'Himalaya, près de la route qui mène d'Ambala à Simla. Le terrain a beaucoup d'avantages naturels : situation centrale, climat modéré, accessibilité, abondance des matériaux, écoulement naturel des eaux, sol ferme (pour construire) et fertile. Il est bordé sur ses deux flancs par des rivières qui n'ont d'eau que dans la saison des pluies et que l'on a l'intention de convertir en tapis de verdure. En outre, ce terrain bénéficie d'un panorama splendide avec les cimes couronnées de neige de l'Himalaya à l'arrière-plan. Il offre à Le Corbusier une occasion magnifique d'expérimenter sa philosophie de l'architecture — philosophie qui insiste sur « le soleil, l'espace, la verdure, et un silence possible » pour tous les citoyens.

1

CHANDIGARH - VILLE

UNE CAPITALE CONSTRUITE PAR DES ARCHITECTES FRANÇAIS

On a prévu la cité pour une population d'un demi-million d'habitants. Le premier plan directeur était dû à un urbaniste américain, Albert Mayer. Puis ce plan fut discuté et modifié par une équipe d'architectes comprenant, outre Le Corbusier et Pierre Jeanneret, Maxwell Fry et son associée, Mlle Jane Drew. Habilement aidés par des ingénieurs indiens, dont le chef est M. Varma, ces techniciens ont mis la dernière main au plan.

L'aménagement des villes exerce une grande influence sur l'organisation de la vie contemporaine. En projetant comment bâtir ou grouper les bâtiments, l'architecte gouverne aussi la manière de vivre des citoyens. Réciproquement, il doit observer à fond la manière actuelle de vivre des gens et combiner ses plans de façon à ce qu'ils puissent y être heureux. Peut-être Chandigarh sera la première cité des Indes où ces deux points de vue opposés seront respectés. Bien que cela semble paradoxal, les architectes étrangers ont garanti que Chandigarh serait une cité réalisée dans « l'esprit indien ».

On a décrit le plan de la capitale nouvelle comme « le rêve de l'architecte ». La cité est divisée en secteurs, chacun de ces secteurs $1/2 \times 3/4$ milles. Clôturés par un réseau de routes, ces secteurs seraient des unités quasi indépendantes, s'ils n'étaient pas reliés entre eux par des bandes de verdure allant du Sud-Ouest au Nord-Est et par des rues commerciales allant du Sud-Est au Nord-Est. Chaque secteur fournit les logements pour 5.000 personnes dans les régions de densité basse et pour 20.000 personnes dans les régions les plus populeuses. Quoique facilement accessible du système majeur routier de la ville, les secteurs seront complètement protégés des dangers de la circulation, de la poussière, du bruit et du relent d'essence, etc. Tous les secteurs seront des unités complètes, ayant leurs propres écoles, cours de récréation, parcs, quartiers commerçants, bibliothèques et clubs, en plus des maisons d'habitation.

Chaque secteur est, en outre, subdivisé en nombre de communautés comprenant environ 150 maisons avec six à sept cents habitants — la dimension d'un village ordinaire du Pendjab. Il sera meilleur marché de construire de tels centres communautaires et ils conserveront aussi cette vie communale et ces environs salubres avec des espaces libres et plantés d'arbres, ce qui est une des caractéristiques des villages du Pendjab. Les

Le Pandit Nehru et Le Corbusier.

Opposite. First page of article from unidentified French journal regarding the design and construction of Chandigarh

This page. "Mr. Nehru Visits Chandigarh," *Tribune* (Arbala, India), 2 April 1952

AMBALA, THURSDAY, APRIL 3, 1952 THE TRIBUNE

Mr. Jawaharlal Nehru arrived in Ambala on Wednesday by air on his way to Nangal. The pictures taken at the Ambala airport show (1) Mr. Nehru with L. Bhim Sen Sachar, Chief Minister-designate and some Congress leaders; (2) Mr. Nehru and Lady Mountbatten, who accompanied him, with Wing Commander B.K. Sen Gupta, Commanding Officer of the I.A.F. Station.

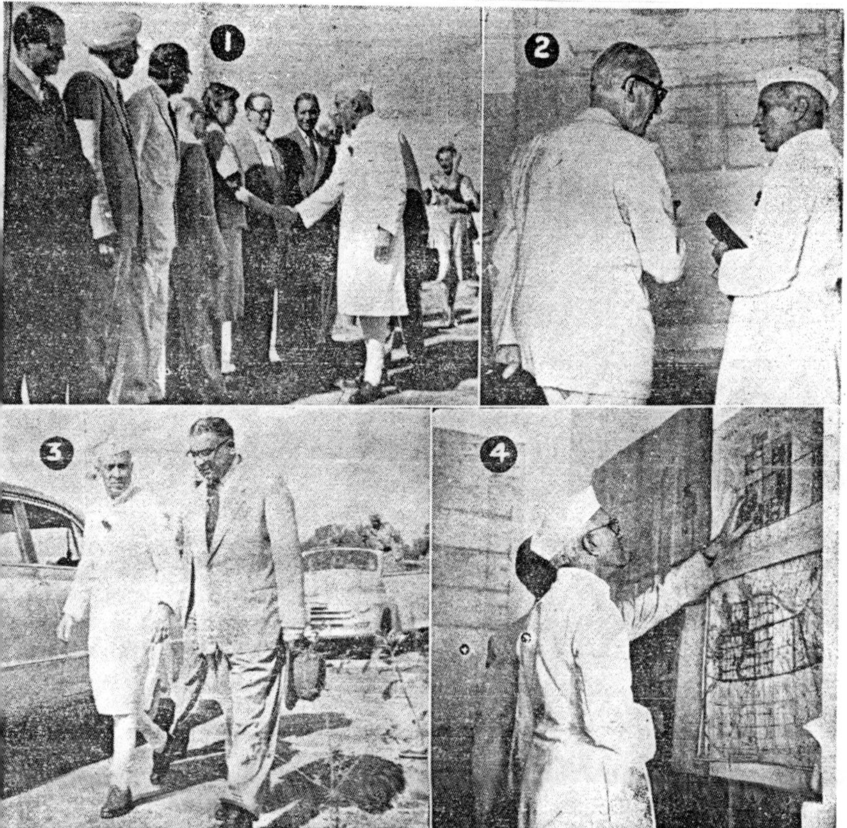

The Prime Minister, Mr. Jawaharlal Nehru, visited the capital site at Chandigarh on Wednesday morning. Pictures show (1) Mr. Nehru shaking hands with Miss Jane Drew, the woman architect and other engineers of the capital project; (2) M. Le Corbusier, the world famous architect explaining the lay-out of the capital; (3) Mr. Nehru with Mr. P. N. Thapar, Administrator of the Capital; (4) Mr. Nehru inspecting a plan of the capital.

Mr. Jawaharlal Nehru at the capital site at Chandigarh. Mr. Bhim Sen Sachar, Chief Minister-designate, Lady Mountbatten, Mrs. Vijayalakshmi Pandit, Miss Jane Drew and Miss Mridula Sarabhai are also seen in the picture.

MR. NEHRU VISITS CHANDIGARH

(*From Our Special Representative*)

CHANDIGARH, April 2.

INDIA'S Prime Minister, Pandit Jawaharlal Nehru, visited Punjab's New Capital in the making for the first time to-day.

This visit of the Prime Minister resulted in creating unbounded confidence among the people and those engaged in the stupendous task of building a new home for a refugee Government of the State of Punjab which is also designed to provide shelter to the refugee population of the State and an asylum for all the uprooted institutions of the Provincial status including the High Court, the University, the Legislature and a few vocational colleges besides serving as a nucleus for collecting together the best talent of the Punjab which having been uprooted after the partition has not been able to come together as it was in Lahore. Pt. Nehru's visit certainly is expected to result in removing the cloud of uncertainty which had been hanging over the future of this project of the Punjab State.

The Prime Minister who was scheduled to have spent only half-an-hour at Chandigarh was so keenly interested in the future home of the Government of the Border State that he actually remained there for over an hour and a half. This in spite of the fact that he is so punctual and always so keen on observing his programme. It was whispered that the Prime Minister might stay on at the Capital site for 10 minutes beyond the scheduled time and therefore those incharge of the arrangements were naturally anxious to rush through the scheduled programme. Pt. Nehru however, on arriving at the Administrative Offices of the Chandigarh Capital Project was so much engrossed in knowing about what had been done and in making certain very useful suggestions for expediting the building up and completion of the Capital project that he did not seem to very much worry about the time schedule. He went into minor detail of every item to which his attention was drawn by the Administrator of the Project Shri P.N. Thapar and the Chief Architect. Pandit Nehru made his own enquiries about everything which was being done and posted himself fully with regard to the details about which he appeared to know so much even before.

Reception

On arrival at the site of the New Capital where he was accompanied by Lady Mountbatten, Mrs. Vijay Lakshmi Pandit, Shri Bhim Sen Sachar, Chief Minister-designate of the Punjab and Miss Mridula Sarabhai, the Prime Minister was received by the Administrator of the Project Shri P.N. Thapar. The Deputy

(Continued on page 3)

MR. NEHRU VISITS CHANDIGARH

(Continued From Page I)

Commissioner of Ambala, Mr. R.P. Kapur and the District Police Chief, Shri C.L. Malhotra were with the Prime Minister as also the D.I.G. Police Mr. Holliday besides Khan Abdul Ghaffar Khan, M.L.A., President Ambala District Congress Committee and Gyani Rajendra Singh, Advocate, M.L.A., Shri Kidar Nath Sehgal, M.L.A. also joined the party here.

Shri Thapar introduced to the Prime Minister the various officers connected with the building of the Project including the Chief Engineer Shri P.L. Varma, the Architectural Adviser Mr. Carbeauser, Mr. Fry, Town Planner, M. Jeaunneret, Miss Drew architectural experts and planners, Shri Gyan Chand Vig, Superintending Engineer, Capital Project, Additional Deputy Commissioner, Executive Engineer, Junior Architects and Junior Town Planners.

A large crowd of the local population including those connected with the Administrative Officers and their kith and kin had collected and they greeted the Prime Minister with loud shouts of 'Pandit Jawaharlal Zindabad.' Panditji acknowledged their greetings with cheerful smile and folded hands.

Plan Explained

Immediately after he was conducted into one of the office rooms where plans and charts had been put up showing the whole project. Here the Architectural Adviser Mr. Carbeauser explained to the Prime Minister in French the whole plan and the architectural designs of the various buildings meant for housing the Punjab Secretariat, the High Court, the University, the various colleges, and the residential quarters both bungalows and houses meant for the Government officers and other employees. The only three persons from among the visitors who could understand what was being explained were Pt. Nehru, his sister Mrs. Vijay Lakshmi Pandit and Lady Mountbatten. Pandit Nehru took very keen interest in what was told to him by the grey-haired French Architectural Adviser and he examined minor details of the whole plan and made many enquiries.

Why High Court First?

Pandit Nehru on being shown the plan for the High Court Building asked rather astonishingly why was it necessary to build the High Court building immediately.

Shri P.L. Varma, Chief Engineer replied saying that the High Court was keen to come down from the heights of Simla.

As the whole talk between the Prime Minister and the Architectural Adviser had taken place in French Pandit Nehru humorously asked a distinguished member of the party, "I hope you have understood all that has been told here to me. The distinguished companion with added humour replied saying "Yes of course" while another member of the party said "Ignorance is Bliss."

At the bottom of the Master Plan of Punjab's Capital was quoted the following Psalm:—

"I will lift up mine eyes unto the mountains from where shall my help come"—Psalm 121-1.

Pandit Nehru read this and was moved on reading this Psalm as it conveyed significantly enough the situation at the Capital Site.

At The Tower

The Prime Minister and the party were then taken in an open truck conducted by Shri P. N. Thapar followed by other officers around the actual site where the Capital is to be built. The party passed through the University Road which is under construction and looked at the Government Printing Press whose building is half-ready and then went upto the Observatory Tower. The Prime Minister and the party were conducted by Mr. Thapar to the top of this 36 feet high tower from where one can have a very clear idea of the whole site with a very fine background provided by the mountainous and submontane area. The landscape is exhilarating and it seemed to have gladdened Pt. Nehru's heart. Lady Mountbatten was full of praise for the Project.

Houses For Govt. Employees

From the Observatory Tower the Prime Minister was conducted to Sector No. 22 where residential quarters are being built for Government employees of the ranks of Superintendents and Assistants. Shri M.R. Sethi, Contractor who is building these quarters and his staff accorded a welcome to the Prime Minister and the party and conducted Pt. Nehru to the buildings which are under construction. Pandit Nehru went into the houses which are still under construction and enquired about the accommodation and other facilities which would be provided to those who are to live in these houses. Here also Pandit Nehru was heard making certain suggestions which he said should be incorporated in view of the special requirements of the houses to be built here in the Punjab. Special attention had to be paid to the need of providing air and sun in these houses which was an equally good need for the houses to be built anywhere in India.

Visibly Moved

As the Prime Minister came out after seeing the houses a huge crowd of labourers including men, women and their children gathered on the road and as a token of their affection for "Our Raja Maharaj" these ignorant but innocent and loving people raised slogans of "Pandit Jawaharlal Ki Jai." They were wearing dirty clothes and yet the Prime Minister got into their crowd and exchanged greetings with them and looked at their children. He was visibly moved to see many children suffering from sore eyes. The Prime Minister asked for Shri P.N. Thapar and as he came up he was advised by Pandit Nehru to get all those children examined by the Doctor and treated for their eye trouble. The labourers were mighty pleased to see Pandit Nehru meeting them and talking to them. A woman with a small child in her lap went upto the truck on which Pandit Nehru was going about and said something which was not audible. She probably referred to some ailment from which her little child was suffering. Pandit Nehru asked that the boy should be taken to the hospital and given proper treatment.

How Time Changes

Before getting into his car to motor to Nangal the Prime Minister of India came to the spot where a little more than a year ago those engaged in the agitation against the building up of the Capital used to hold demonstrations. This was the place where these villagers used to shout 'Murdabad' and in their excitement sometime had to face Police lathis also. Today, however, these very people shouted 'Zindabad' (Long Live) for India's Prime Minister and the people's beloved leader Pandit Jawaharlal Nehru. He went up to the crowd which had lined along the road side and acknowledged their greetings. It was a pleasant site and some one remarked, "Time is a great healer and a great teacher. Those who shouted 'Murdabad' are shouting 'Zindabad' today, having realized the importance of the project which is to benefit the whole State." There prevailed an atmosphere of cordiality and affection.

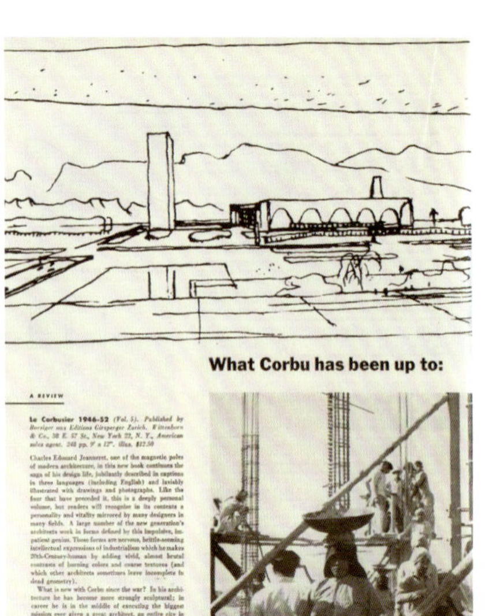

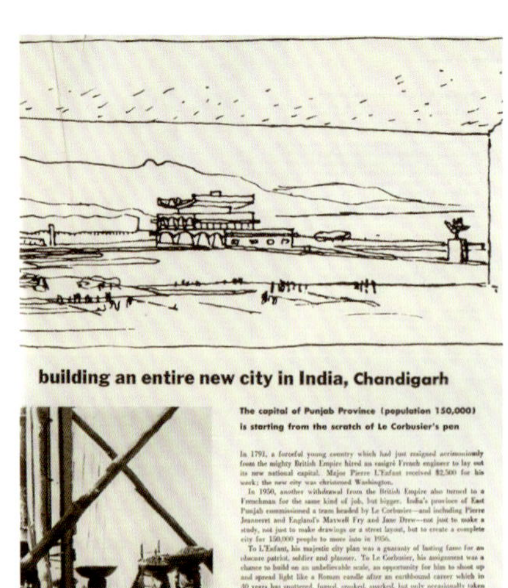

What Corbu has been up to: building an entire new city in India, Chandigarh

The capital of Punjab Province (population 150,000) is starting from the scratch of Le Corbusier's pen

Chandigarh is a 14-square-mile city:

"40 miles of roads, with no buildings facing them"

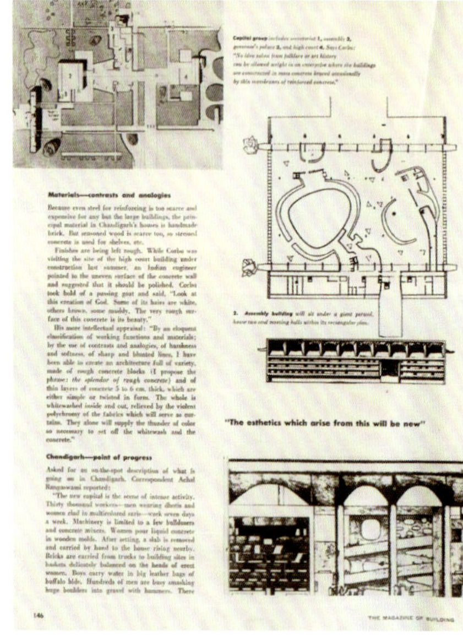

"The esthetics which arise from this will be new"

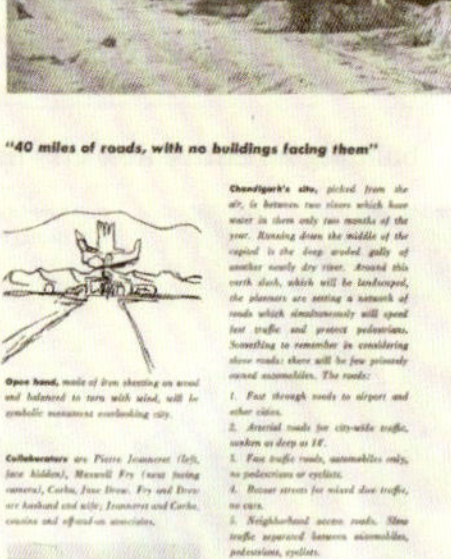

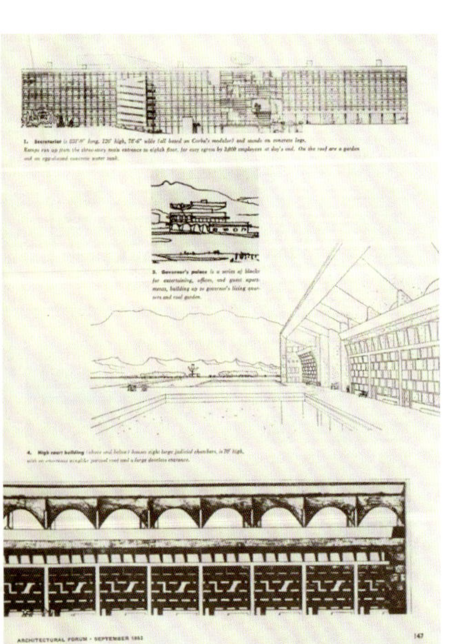

"India's true wealth is its poverty. It makes wonders succeed"

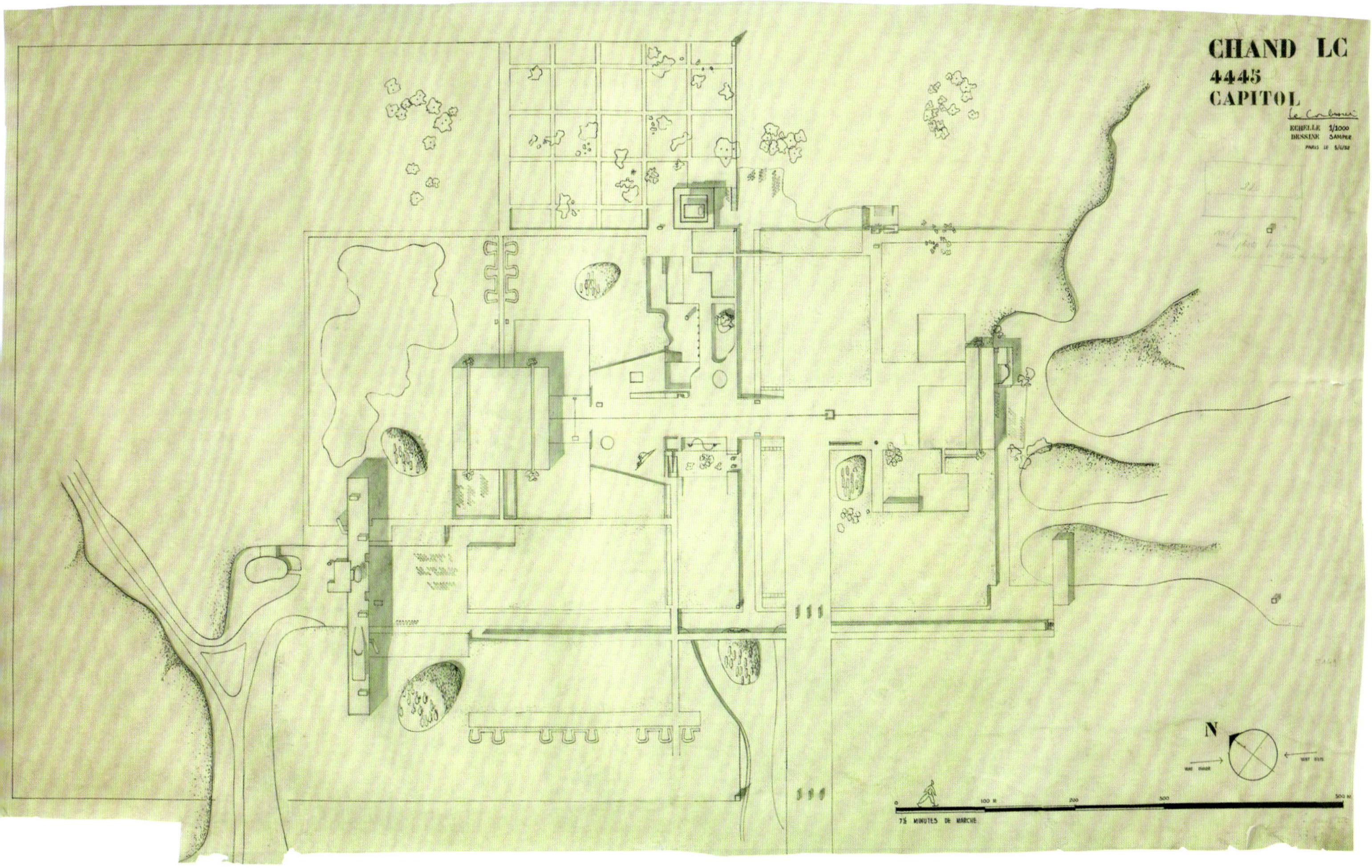

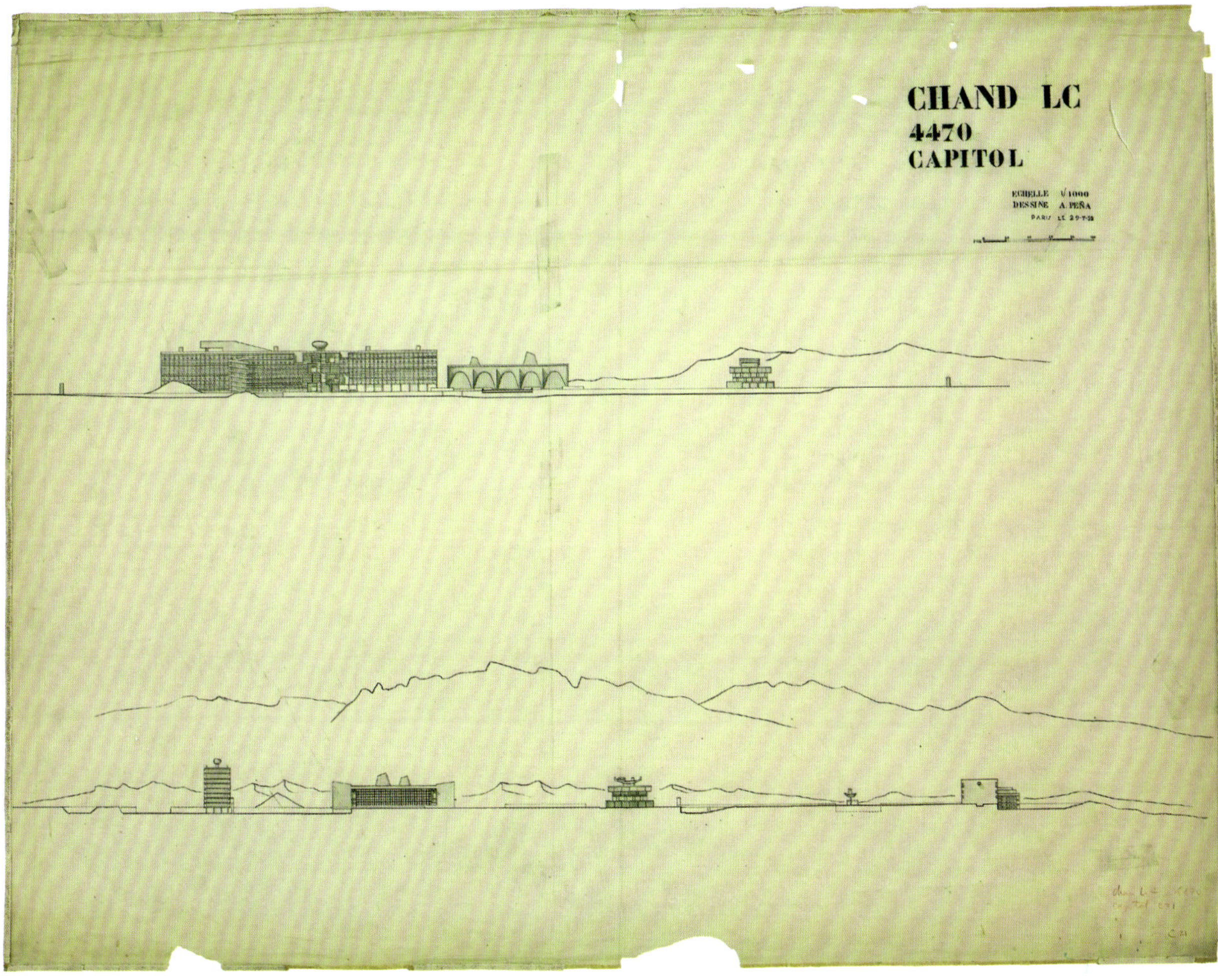

CHAND LC
4445
CAPITOL

ECHELLE 1/1000

N

75 MINUTES DE MARCHE

CHAND LC
4470
CAPITOL

ECHELLE 1/1000
DESSINE A PEÑA

pposite. "What
Corbu Has Been
p To: Building an
ntire New City in
ndia, Chandigarh,"
rchitectural Forum,
eptember 1953

bove. Plan of the
apitol complex,
Chandigarh,
June 1956

ight. Elevations of
he capitol com-
lex, 29 July 1952

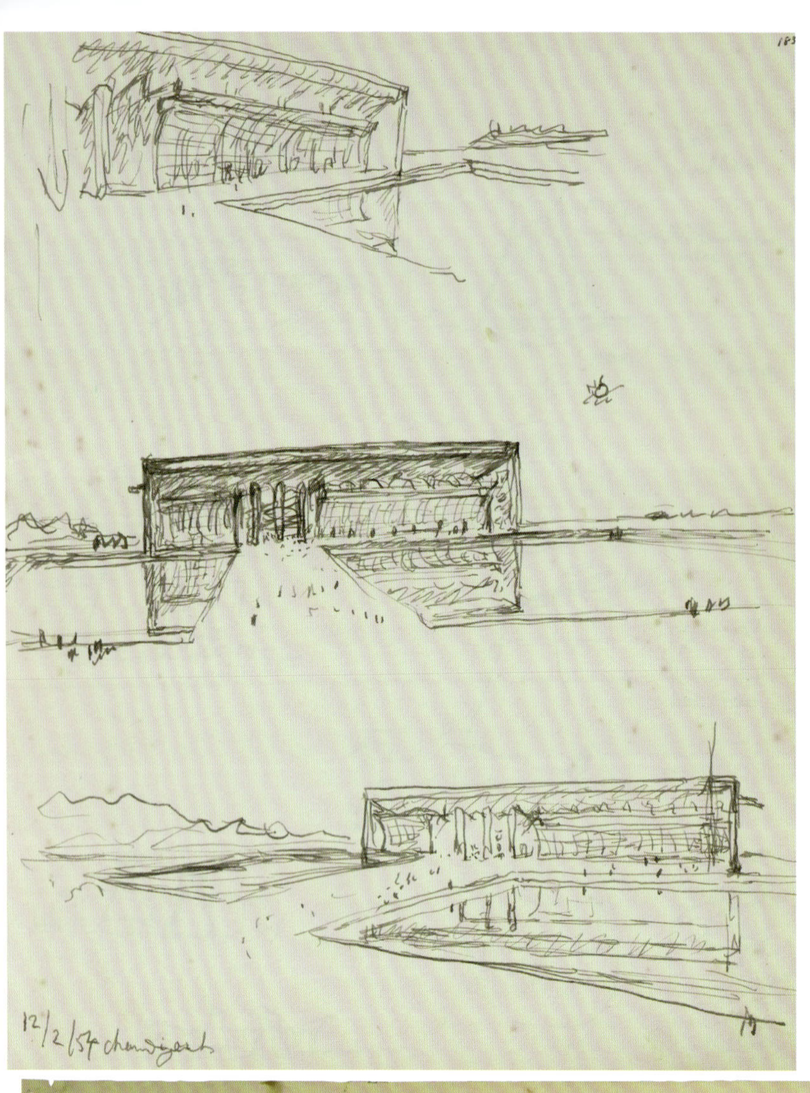

High Court, Palace of Justice, Chandigarh, 1951–55

In the High Court, Le Corbusier employed the concept of the *parasol*, a large-scale overhanging roof structure, to provide a visual metaphor for the law's power to protect. Beneath it a series of concrete piers, reminiscent of the muscular *pilotis* of the Unité d'Habitation, support the overhanging roof. The first of the capitol buildings to be completed, the High Court functioned as a sort of laboratory for working out strategies, such as the *brise-soleil* (sunshade) and *parasol*, that would be employed again within the capitol complex.

CHAND LC
4333

ÉCHELLE 1/200
LE 4-5-1951

FAÇADE PRINCIPALE

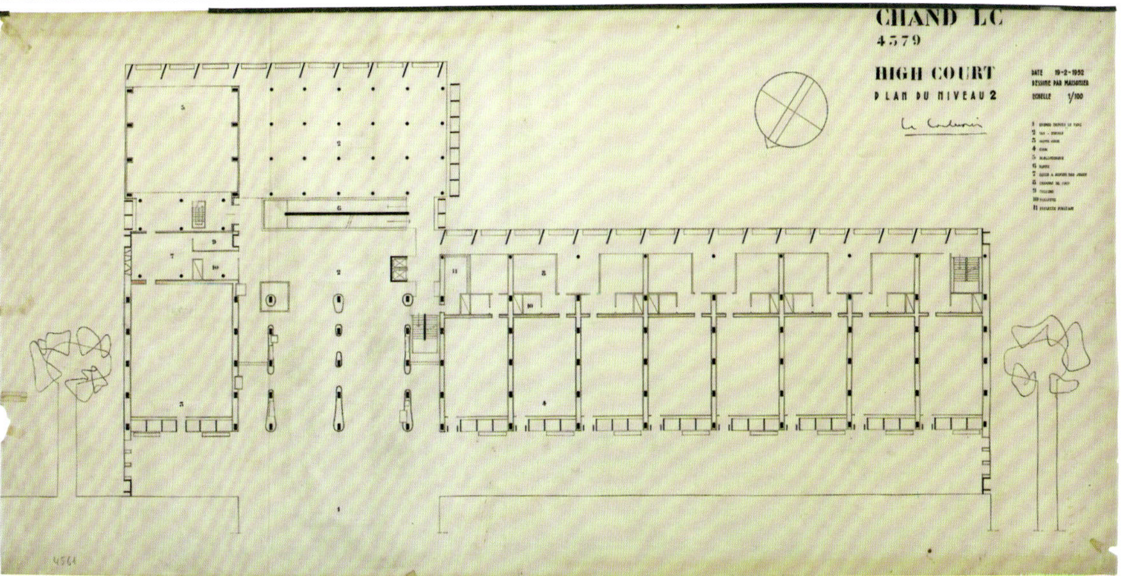

pposite, top. ketches, 2 February 1954, ligh Court, Palace f Justice, Chandigarh, 951–55

pposite, bottom. erspective f principal facade nd reflecting ools, 4 March 1952

bove. Study of rincipal facade, May 1951

Above middle. Model, showing principal facade

Right. Second-floor plan

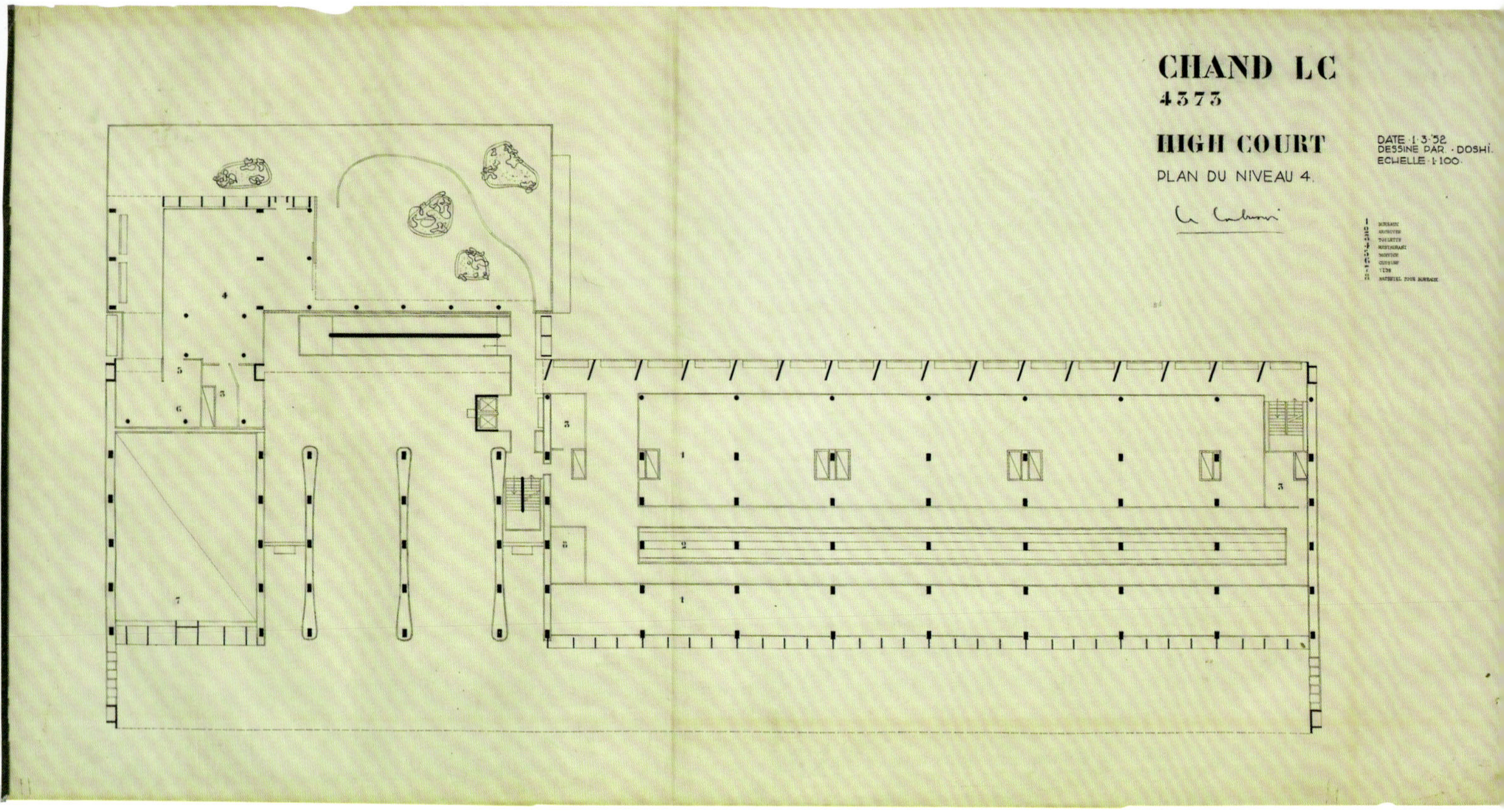

CHAND LC
4373

HIGH COURT

PLAN DU NIVEAU 4.

DATE 1·3·'52
DESSINE PAR. · DOSHI.
ECHELLE · 1·100·

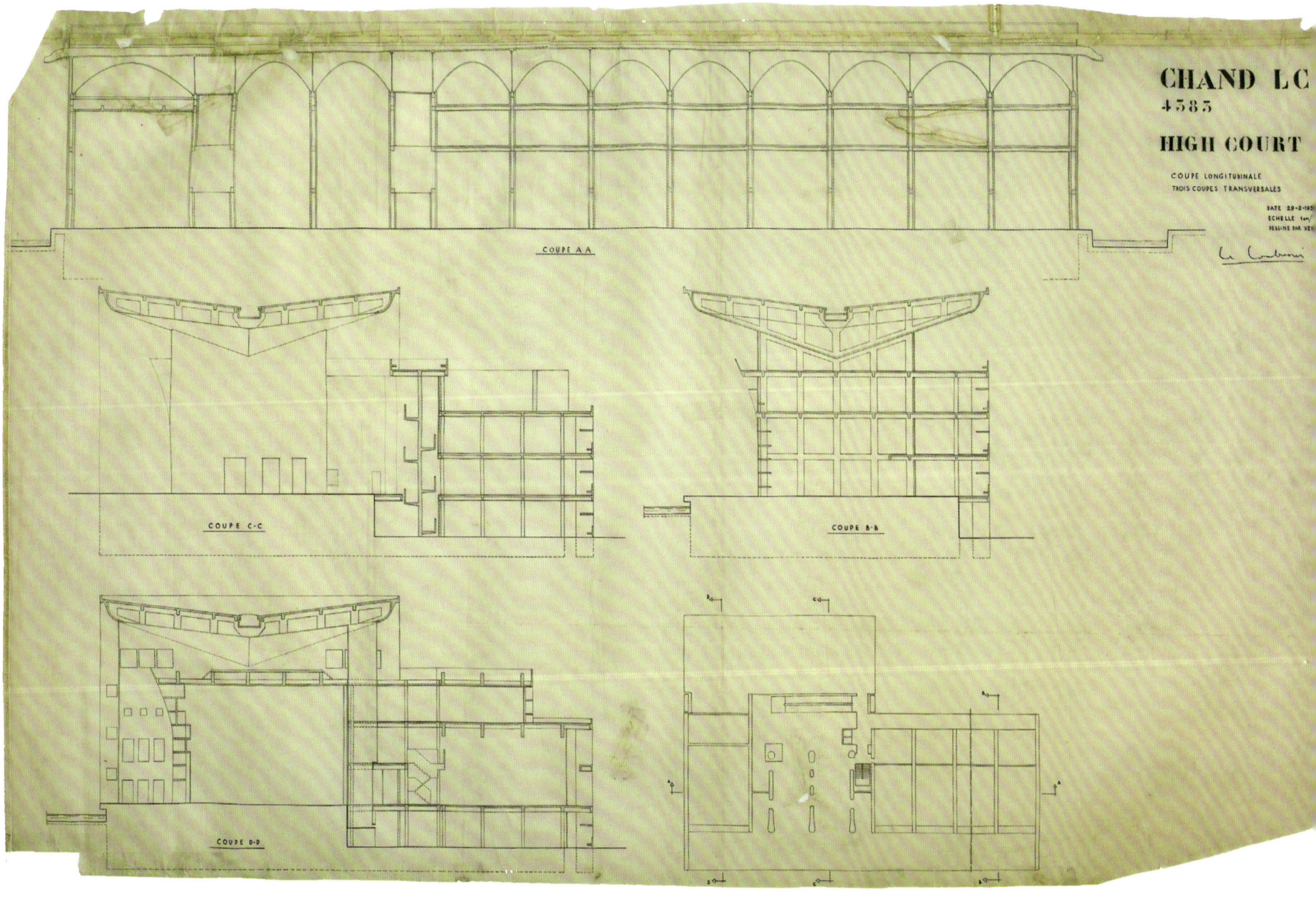

1 BUREAUX
2 ARCHIVES
3 TOILETTE
4 RESTAURANT
5 [illegible]
6 CUISINE
7 VIDE
8 MATERIEL POUR BUREAUX

CHAND LC
4383

HIGH COURT

COUPE LONGITUDINALE
TROIS COUPES TRANSVERSALES

DATE 29-2-195
ECHELLE 1cm/
DESSINE PAR XE

COUPE A-A

COUPE C-C

COUPE B-B

COUPE D-D

Opposite, top. Fourth-floor plan, 1 March 1952, High Court, Chandigarh

Opposite, bottom. Longitudinal and transverse sections and plan detail, 28 February 1952

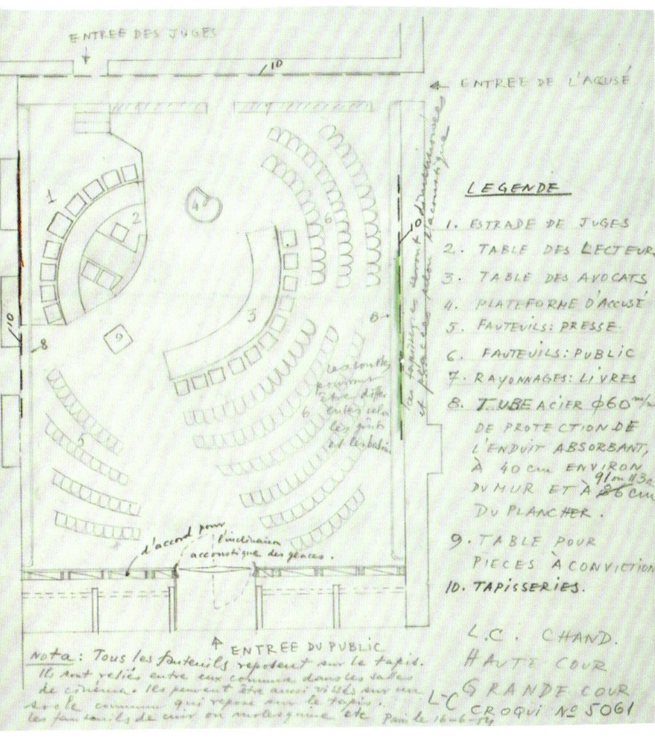

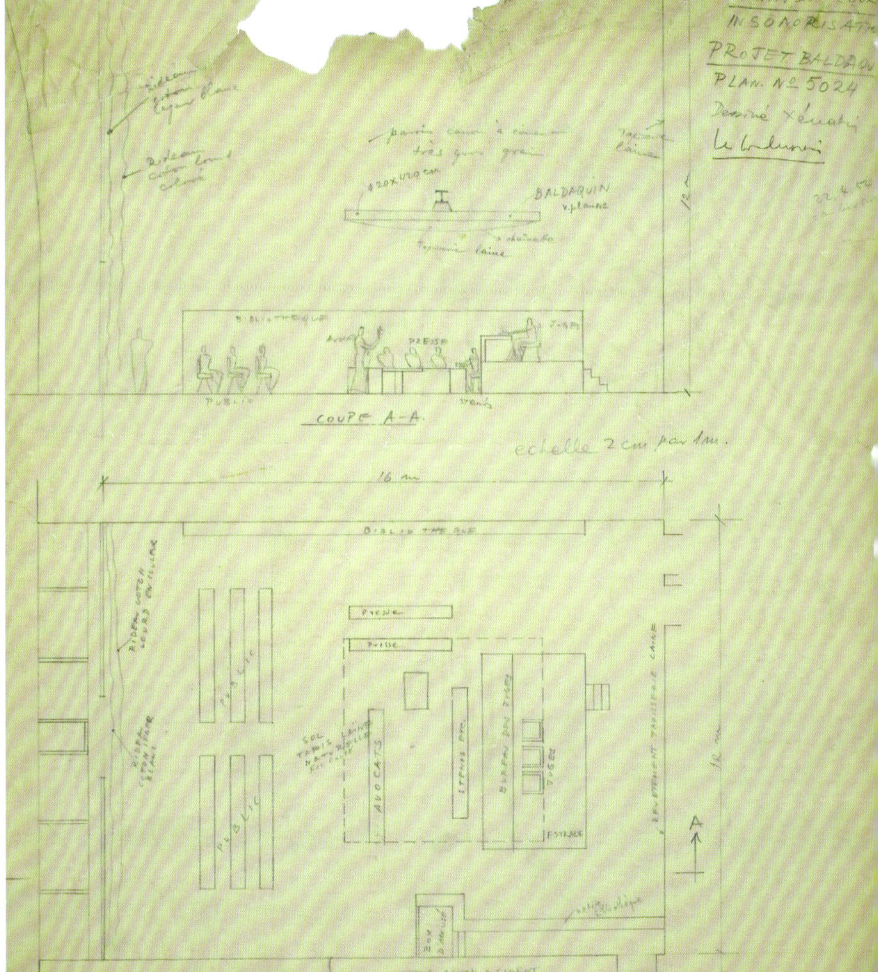

Top. Perspective of main entrance, 4 March 1952

Above. Sketched plan of a courtroom showing access for judges, the public, and the accused, 16 June 1954

Right. Sketches of courtroom section and plan

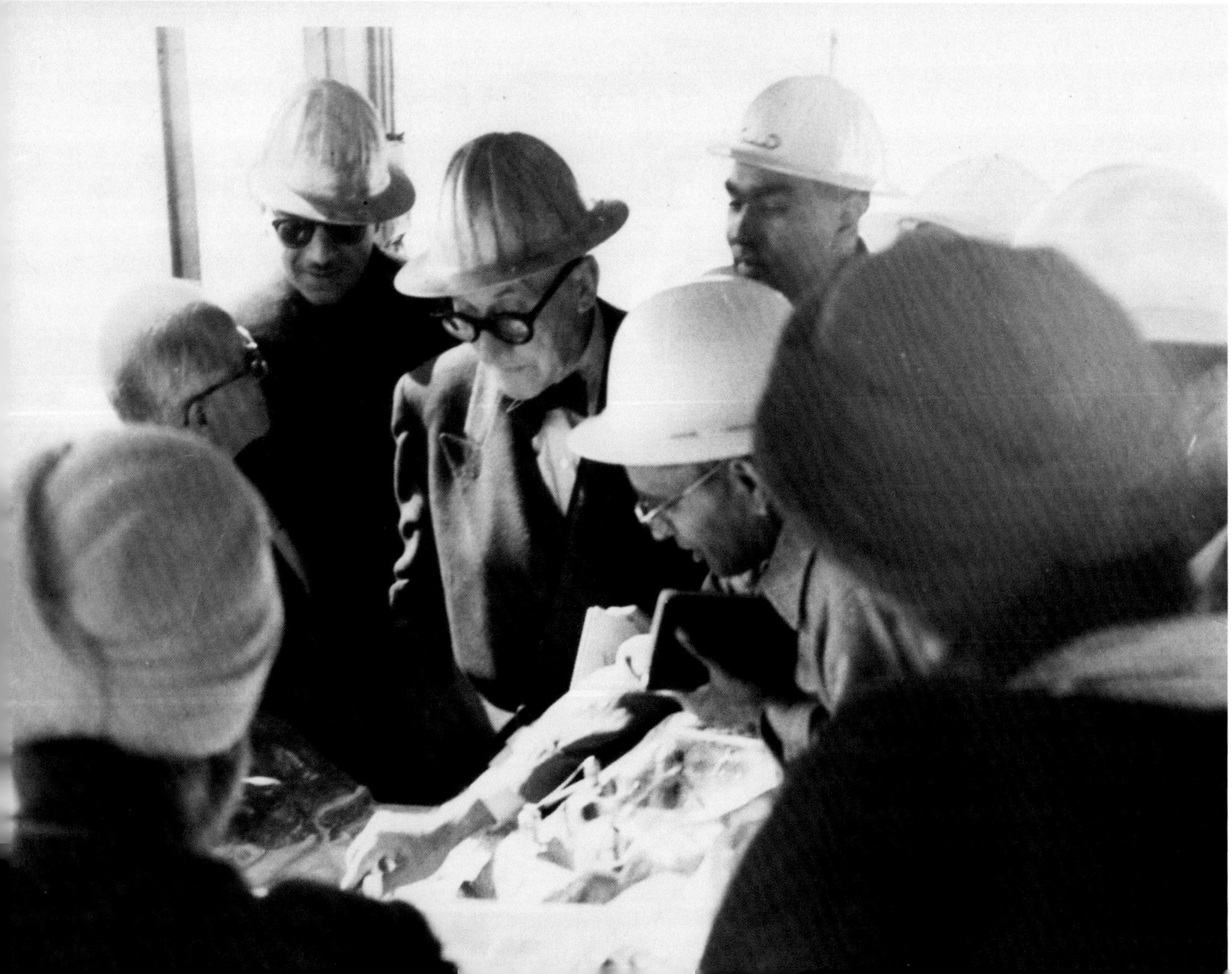

Opposite, top and bottom.
Le Corbusier and his team at the High Court construction site, Chandigarh

Above and right.
Two views of the High Court under construction

Opposite. Principal facade and entrance portico, High Court, Chandigarh

Top left. Man sweeping the plaza, 1 September 1958

Top right. Entrance portico with concrete pylons and roof overhang, or *parasol*. The pylons were to be painted – one green, one white, and one red-orange.

Above left. Residents of Chandigarh in front of the principal facade

Above right. Principal facade

Opposite. Le Corbusier, front row, at the formal opening ceremonies of the High Court, Chandigarh, 1 March 1955

Top, left and right. Detail of *brise-soleil* (sunshade) on the facade of the High Court

Above. Le Corbusier and Pierre Jeanneret on Sukhna Lake, Punjab, in a pedalo designed by Jeanneret, 1958

Right. Le Corbusier with Pierre Jeanneret, arriving for the dedication of the High Court, 1 March 1955

Above. First two pages of a letter from Le Corbusier to his mother, 30 November 1952, expressing excitement about progress at Chandigarh

Below. Le Corbusier in front of the entrance to the High Court, Chandigarh

Opposite. Le Corbusier at a construction site in Chandigarh, with the High Court in the distance

Tapestries and murals, High Court, Chandigarh

Inside the High Court, large-scale ramps link the various levels containing courtrooms and administrative offices. For the courtrooms Le Corbusier designed a series of brightly colored abstract tapestries. Most of the judges presiding over these courtrooms felt the tapestries were not sufficiently respectful of the law and insisted that they be removed.

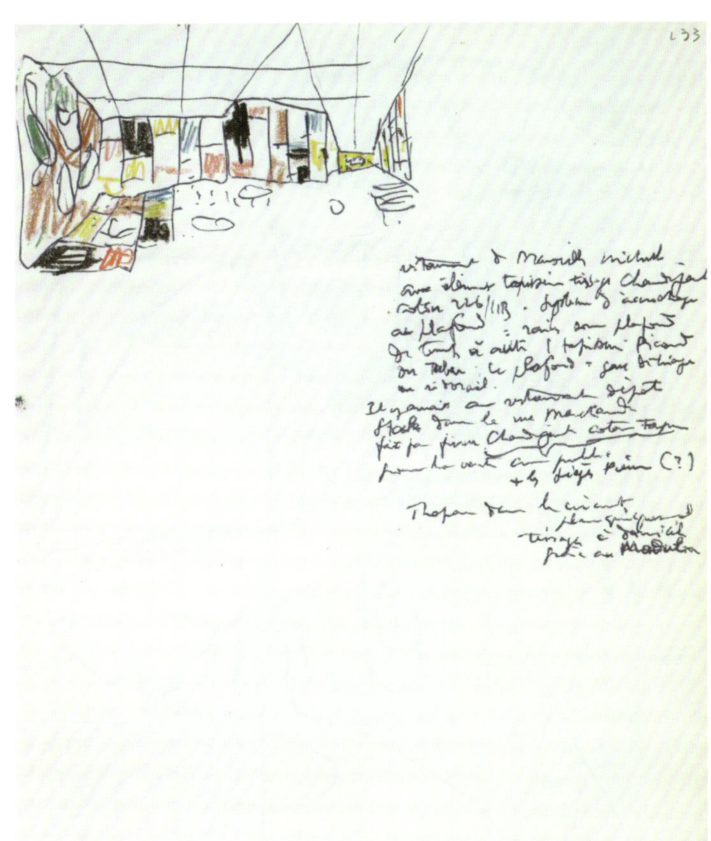

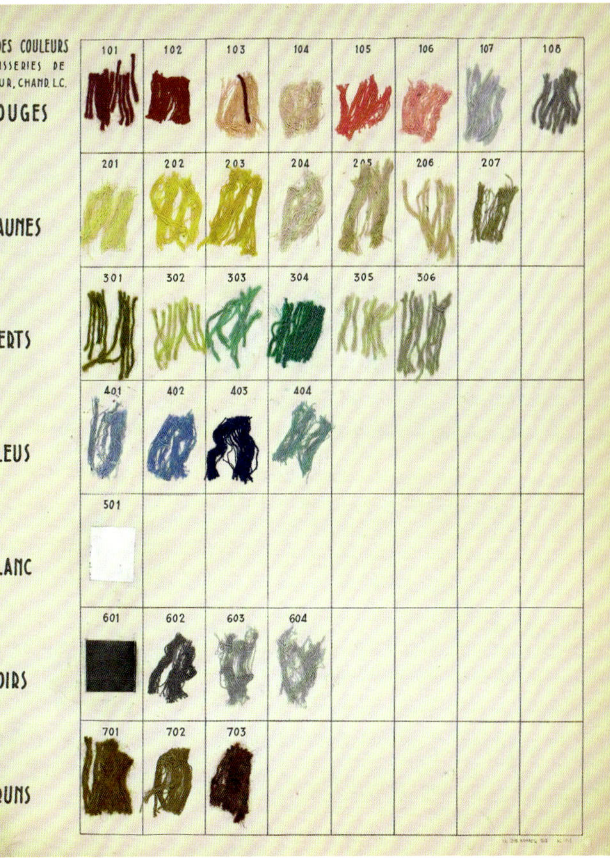

Opposite, top. Le Corbusier's cartoon, 10 March 1954, for a tapestry for a small courtroom in the High Court, Chandigarh

Opposite, bottom. Study for interior mural for the High Court

Above left. Sketch by Le Corbusier of a Marseille restaurant interior with a tapestry woven from Chandigarh cotton

Above right. Wool samples for High Court tapestries, 23 March 1954

Right. Detail of tapestry cartoon for "6th small court," signed by Le Corbusier, 1 April 1954

Far right, top to bottom. Three details of tapestry cartoons, signed by Le Corbusier, 1 April, 2 April, and 1 April 1954, respectively

"The High Court, where close to 1000 workers and women and donkeys are preparing for the opening on 3 January 55, is quite simply extraordinary. It's an architectural symphony that surpasses all my hopes, gleaming and taking shape in the light in an unwearyingly unimaginable way. Seen close up or from afar it's a surprise, it knocks you out. It's been made of raw concrete, with a cement gun."

—Letter to his mother, 17 November 1954

Opposite. Interior circulation ramps, High Court, Chandigarh

Above, left and right. Courtroom with Le Corbusier tapestry, 1 September 1958

Secretariat, Chandigarh, 1951–58

Le Corbusier originally conceived the Secretariat as a skyscraper in the manner of the hotel he designed for Algiers, with its filigree of *brises-soleil*. He soon realized, however, that such a looming tower would be out of scale with the other capitol structures, so he turned the tower scheme on its side. Drawing from his experience with the Unité d'Habitation in Marseille, Le Corbusier developed an 800-foot-long structure with an extensive sunshade that is intricately varied in scale, following Modulor proportions.

Left. Study model of principal facade of the Secretariat, Chandigarh

Below. Sheet of construction photographs of the Secretariat

Opposite. Secretariat under construction

CS_156

CS.157

CS_154

CS_155

CS_125

CS_153

CS_117

CS_116

Below. Principal facade, Secretariat, Chandigarh

Opposite. Roof garden

Following pages.
View from south-
east, Secretariat

Governor's Palace (unbuilt), Chandigarh, 1952–55

Le Corbusier planned a Governor's Palace to occupy the most prominent position in the capitol complex, to be surrounded by a series of gardens, pools, and ramps.

Originally he intended to crown it with a crescent-shaped sculptural form, inspired by the horns of the bulls he so frequently depicted. Instead, it was ultimately incorporated into the Palace of the Assembly. Because Nehru decided that the presence of the Governor's Palace would be undemocratic, it remained unbuilt.

Opposite, top. Sketch of oxen and cart in India, 5 April 1952, from Le Corbusier's notebook, 1950–52

Opposite, bottom. Undated sketches of oxen in India, from his notebook, 1952–59

Above. Sketch of gardens at Chandigarh, with the unbuilt Governor's Palace in the background, 12 April 1952, from his notebook, 1950–52

Palace of the Assembly, Chandigarh, 1951–62

Two bold and powerful sculptural forms distinguish the Palace of the Assembly: the towering conical roof of the Assembly chamber and the crescent-sectioned roof of the monumental portico. The first was inspired by the cooling tower of a power station in Ahmedabad, India, which Le Corbusier saw while pursuing several projects in the area. The second refers to the horns of a bull, an animal that captivated Le Corbusier from his earliest days in India.

Opposite, top left. Sketches of Chandigarh showing the High Court and the Palace of the Assembly, from Le Corbusier's notebook, 1950–52

Opposite, top right. Sketches showing the unbuilt Governor's Palace and sunken garden, from his notebook, 1950–52

Opposite, bottom left. Sketches of Chandigarh, including the Monument of the Open Hand, from his notebook, 1952–59, inscribed "Bombay, 19 June 1953"

Opposite, bottom right. Sketches of the Palace of the Assembly, from his notebook, 1952–59, inscribed "Bombay, 19 June 1953"

Above. Three views of the model of the Palace of the Assembly

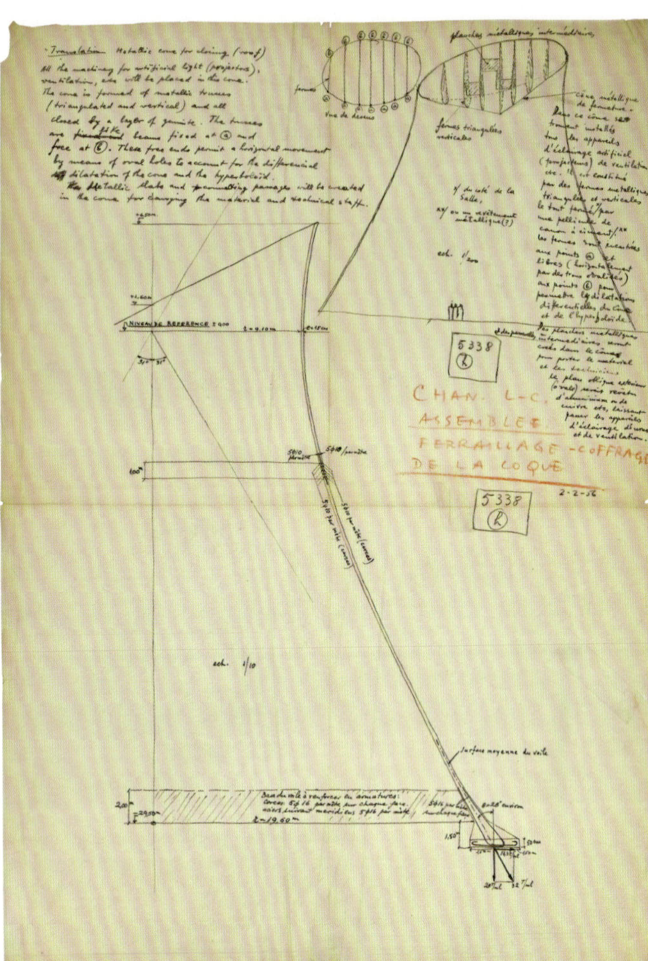

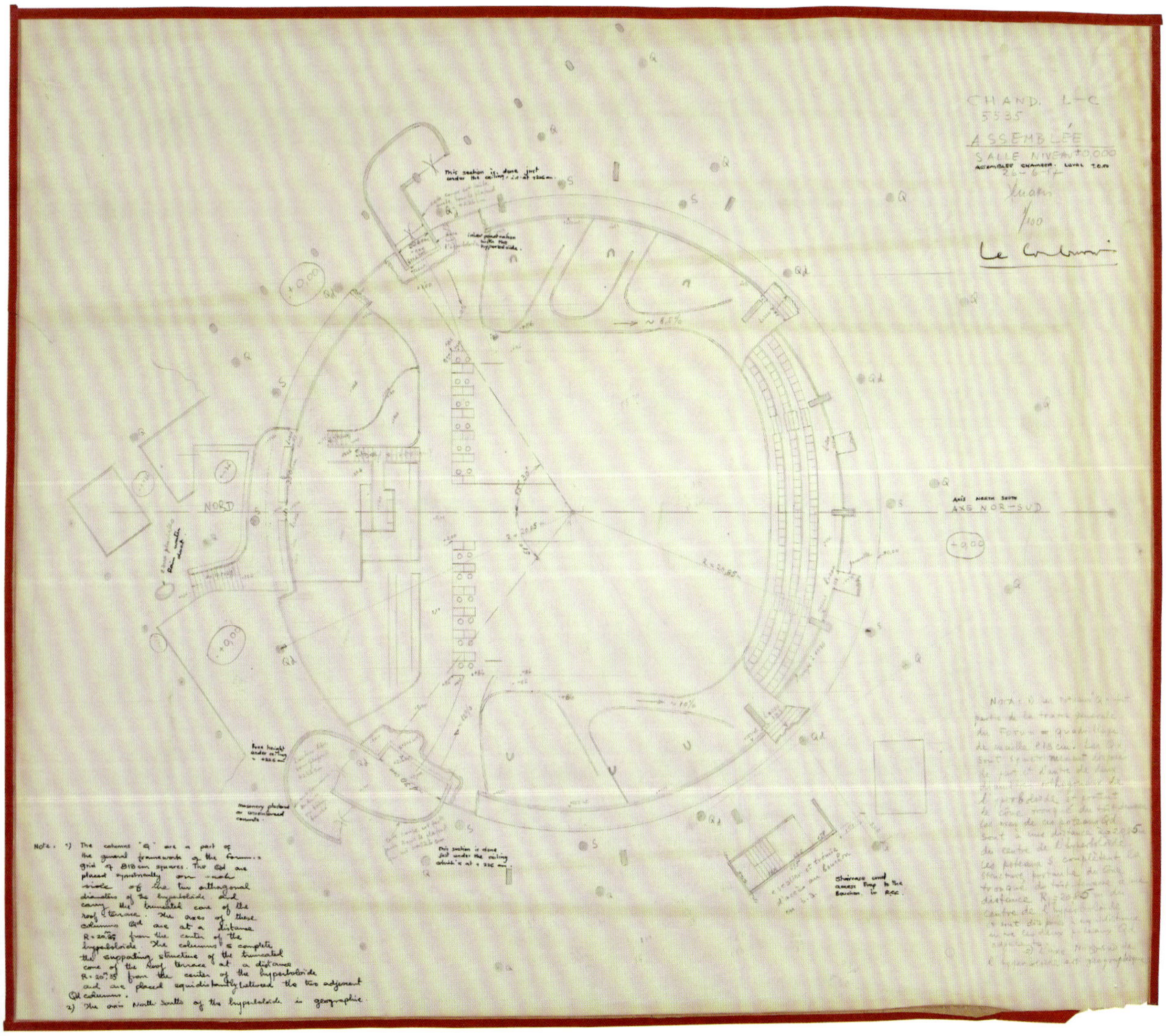

Above left. Detail sketches of conical Assembly chamber, Palace of the Assembly, 12 January 1954, from Le Corbusier notebook, 1952–59

Above right. Structural framing study, Assembly chamber, 2 February 1956

Left. Plan of audito rium level, Assembly chamber 26 June 1957

Opposite, top. Shee of photographs of study model for Assembly chambe

Opposite, bottom. Details of structura framing system for Assembly chambe 5 November 1956.

The structure is in the form of a hyperbolic shell topped with alumi num framework, intended to reduce weight and con struction costs.

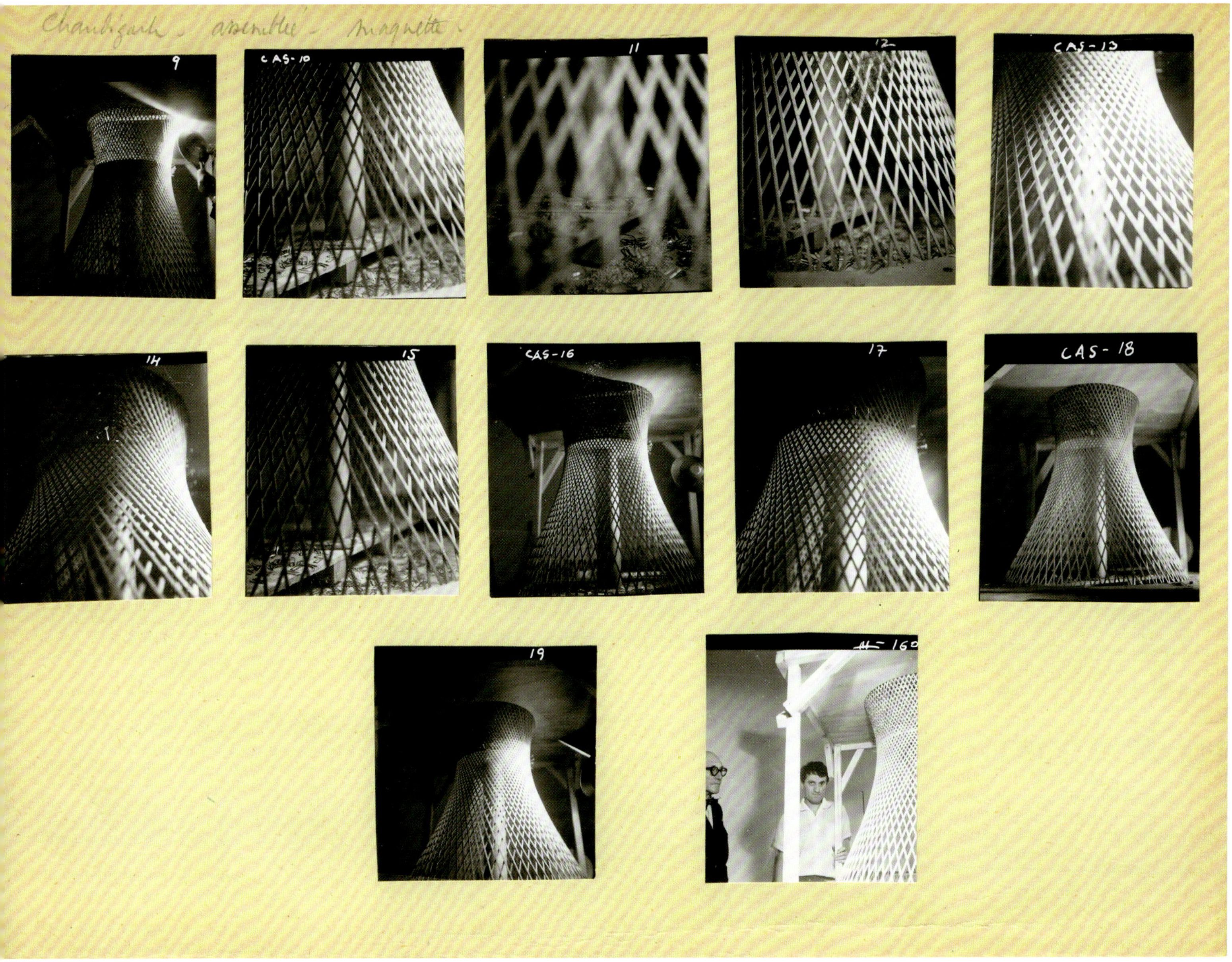

Chandigarh - assemblée - maquette

9 CAS-10 11 12 CAS-13

14 15 CAS-16 17 CAS-18

19 H-160

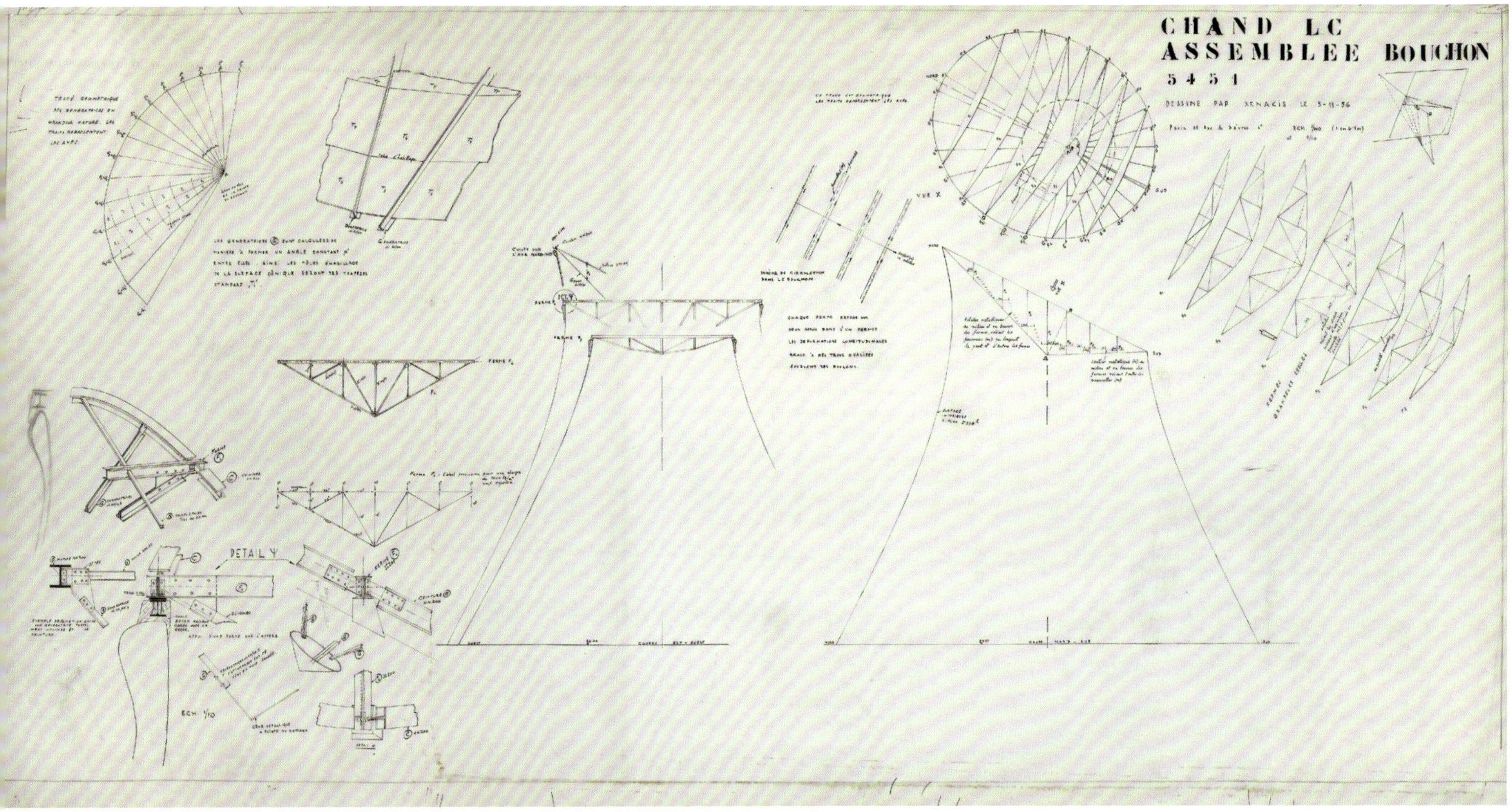

CHAND LC
ASSEMBLEE BOUCHON
5451

DESSINE PAR XENAKIS LE 5-11-56

DETAIL 4

Above. Palace of the Assembly, Chandigarh, under construction

Left. Assembly chamber under construction

Opposite, top. South facade

Opposite, bottom. Detail of west facade under construction

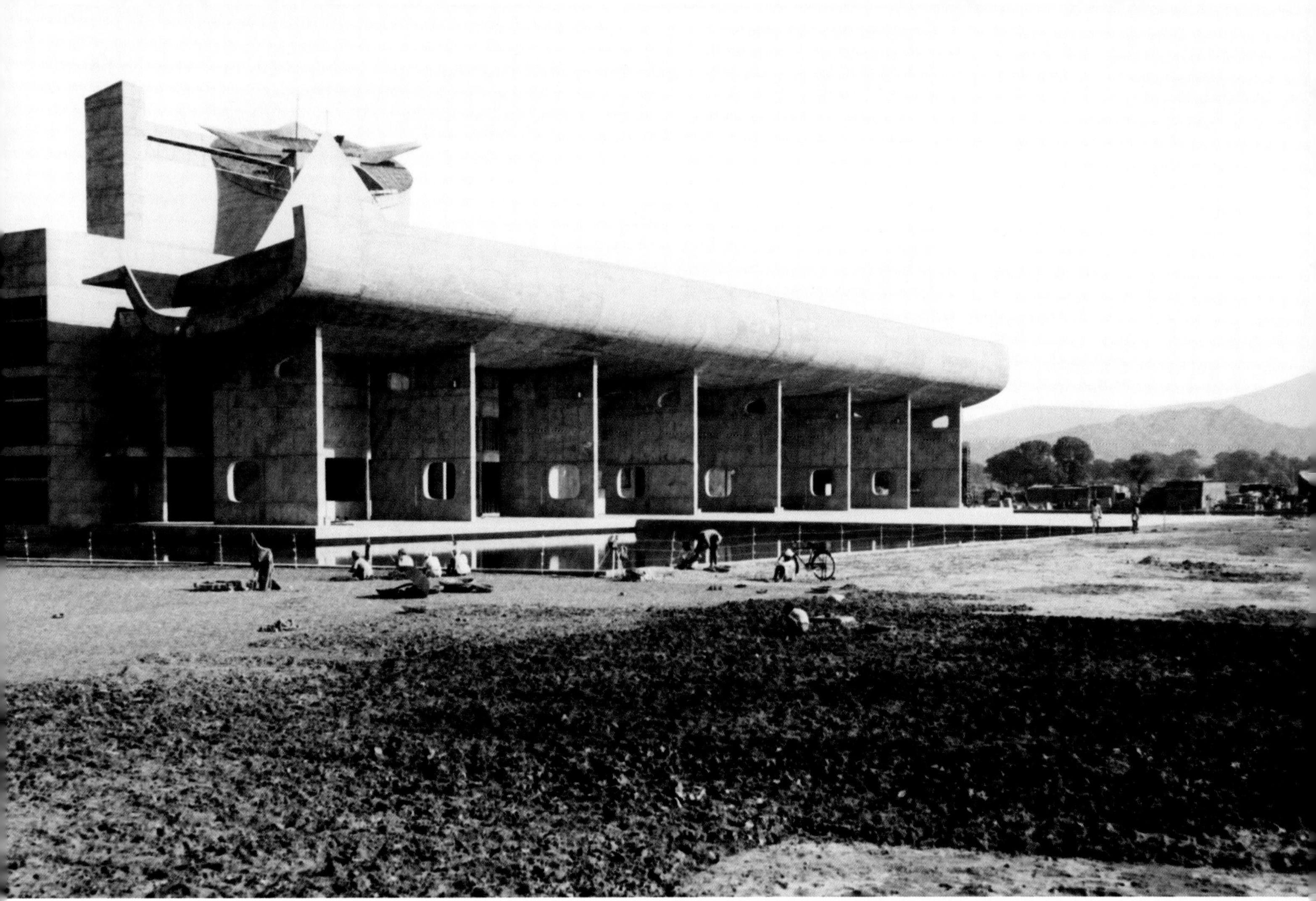

Above. South facade with reflecting pool, Palace of the Assembly, Chandigarh

Opposite, top. South facade, Palace of the Assembly, with Secretariat in the background

Opposite, bottom. The Assembly viewed from a nearby hill

Interior, Palace of the Assembly, Chandigarh

The Palace of the Assembly is dominated by the soaring walls of its conical structure. Le Corbusier shifted the orientation of the room to align with the cardinal points rather than with the grid used to organize both the city and the Assembly building. This gesture toward solar orientation related to murals depicting diagrams of the sun as well as to the *promenade architecturale* that circulates through a main hall of columns.

Above. Interior, Assembly chamber, Palace of the Assembly, Chandigarh

Right. Main hall

Opposite. Detail of interior walls, Assembly chamber

Above. Cartoon for tapestry for southwest wall, 24 November 1961, Punjab Legislature Council Chamber, Palace of the Assembly, Chandigarh

Left and below. Two views of tapestries designed by Le Corbusier for the Palace of the Assembly, Chandigarh

Bottom, left and right. Circulation ramps

Above. Enameled door of main entrance to the Palace of the Assembly, view from exterior

Right. View from interior of the door in open position

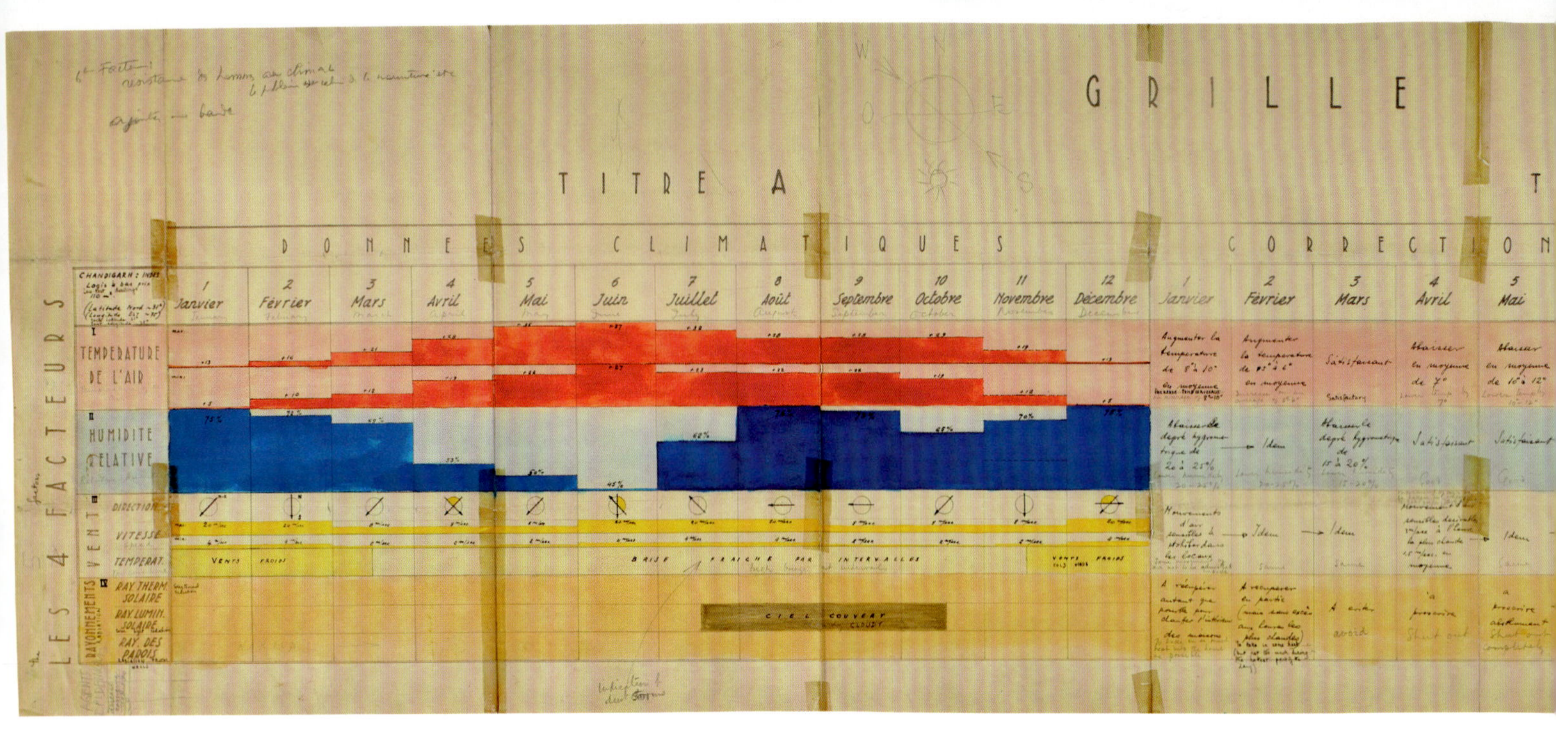

GRILLE CLIMATIQUE

TITRE C

Chandigarh Maisons 110 m²

Atelier Le Corbusier

35 Rue de Sèvres Paris 6e

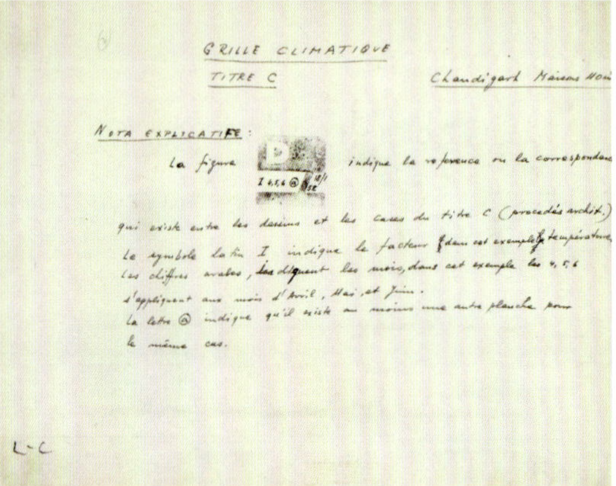

18 Janvier 1952

GRILLE CLIMATIQUE

TITRE C

Chandigarh Maisons 110 m²

NOTA EXPLICATIF:

La figure indique la référence ou la correspondance qui existe entre les dessins et les cases du titre C (procédés archit.)

Le symbole latin I indique le facteur (dans cet exemple température). Les chiffres arabes, indiquent les mois, dans cet exemple les 4, 5, 6 s'appliquent aux mois d'Avril, Mai et Juin.

La lettre ⓐ indique qu'il existe au moins une autre planche pour le même cas.

L-C

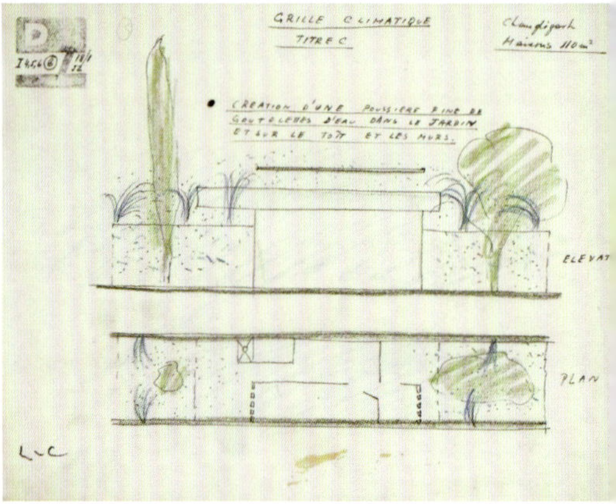

GRILLE CLIMATIQUE TITRE C Chandigarh Maisons 110 m²

• Création d'une poussière fine de gouttelettes d'eau dans le jardin et sur le toit et les murs.

ELEVAT. PLAN L-C

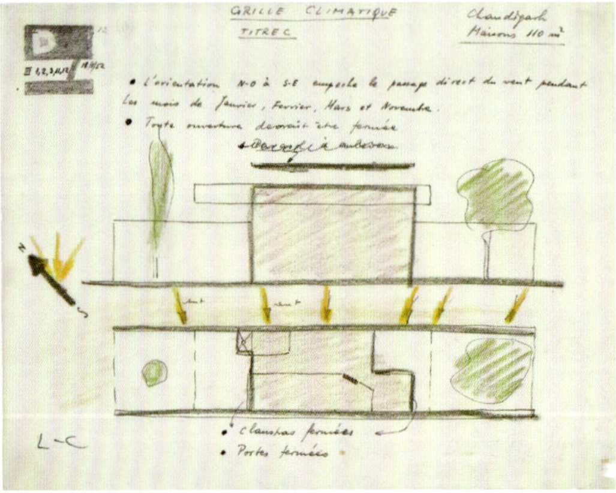

GRILLE CLIMATIQUE TITRE C Chandigarh Maisons 110 m²

• L'orientation N-O à S-E empêche le passage direct du vent pendant les mois de Janvier, Février, Mars et Novembre.

• Toute ouverture devra être fermée

• Claustras fermées

• Portes fermées

L-C

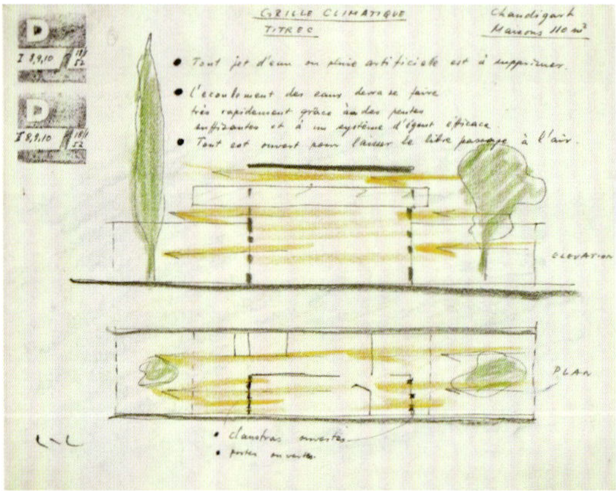

GRILLE CLIMATIQUE TITRE C Chandigarh Maisons 110 m²

• Tout jet d'eau ou pluie artificielle est à supprimer

• L'écoulement des eaux devra se faire très rapidement grâce à des pentes suffisantes et à un système d'égout efficace

• Tout est ouvert pour laisser le libre passage à l'air.

ELEVATION PLAN

• Claustras ouvertes

• Portes ouvertes

L-C

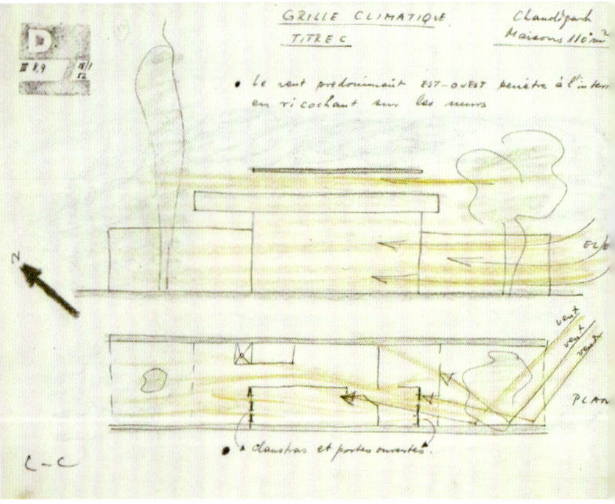

GRILLE CLIMATIQUE TITRE C Chandigarh Maisons 110 m²

• Le vent prédominant EST-OUEST pénètre à l'intérieur en ricochant sur les murs

PLAN

• Claustras et portes ouvertes.

L-C

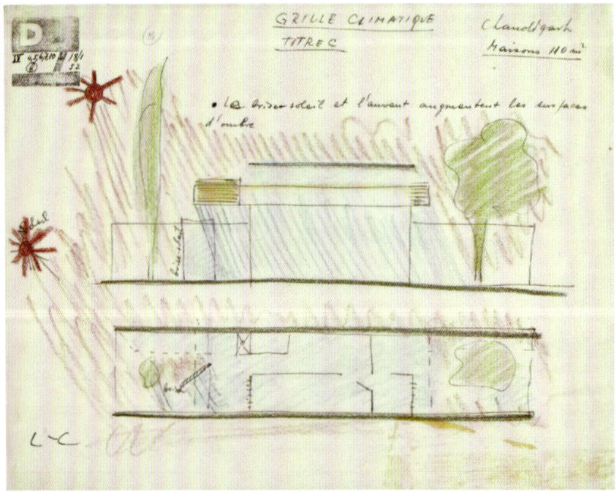

GRILLE CLIMATIQUE TITRE C Chandigarh Maisons 110 m²

• Les brise-soleil et l'auvent augmentent les surfaces d'ombre

L-C

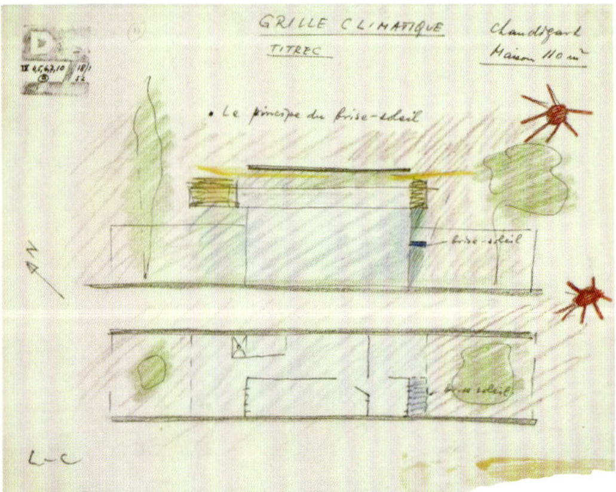

GRILLE CLIMATIQUE TITRE C Chandigarh Maison 110 m²

• Le principe du brise-soleil

brise-soleil

L-C

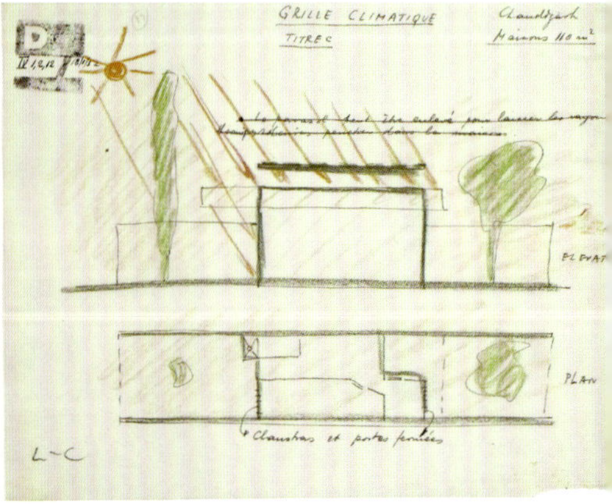

GRILLE CLIMATIQUE TITRE C Chandigarh Maisons 110 m²

ELEVAT. PLAN

• Claustras et portes fermées

L-C

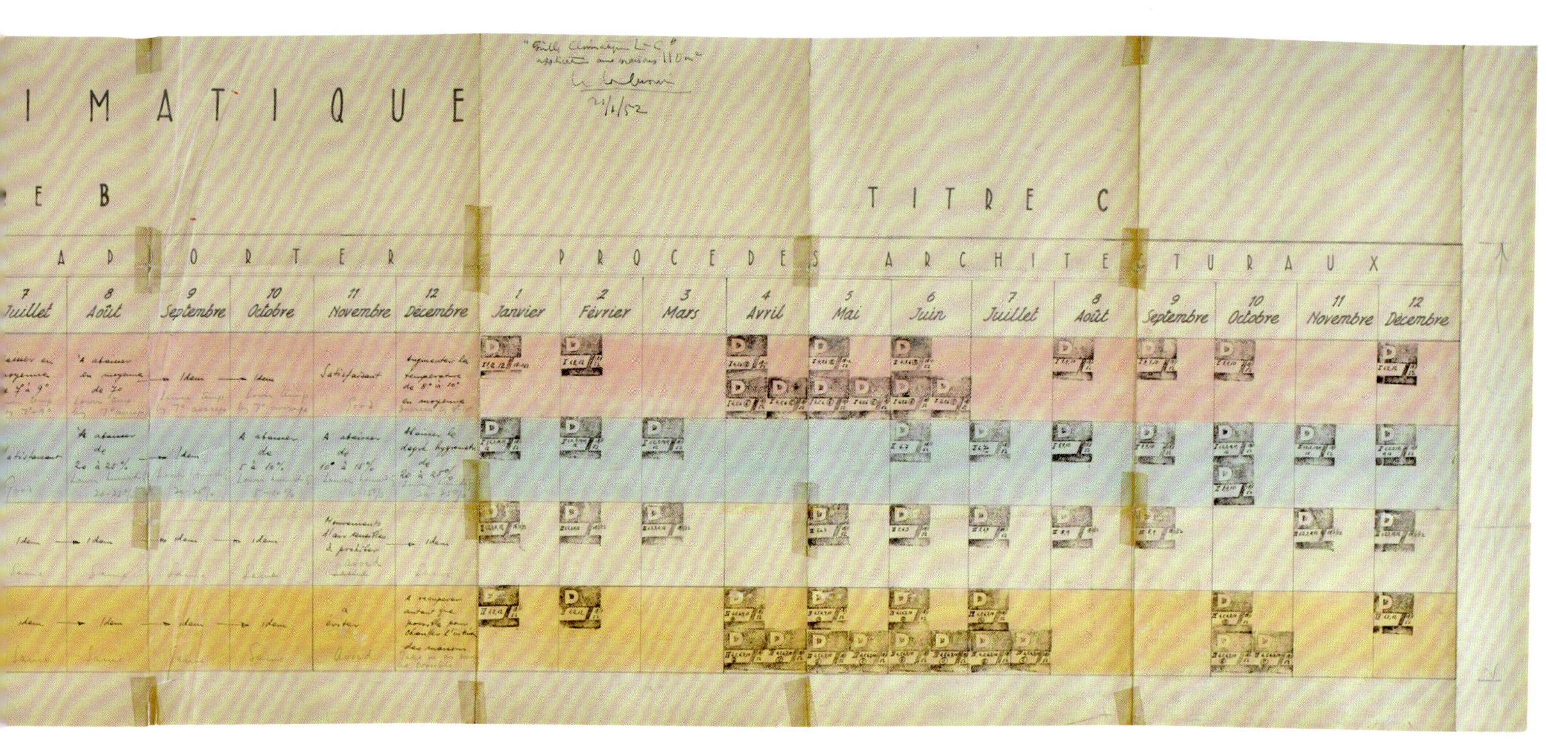

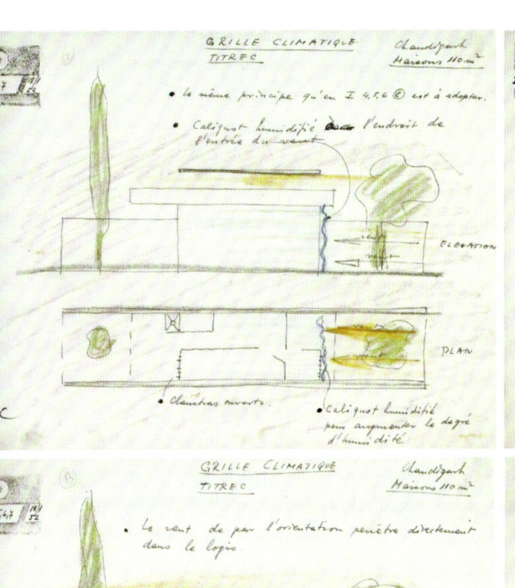

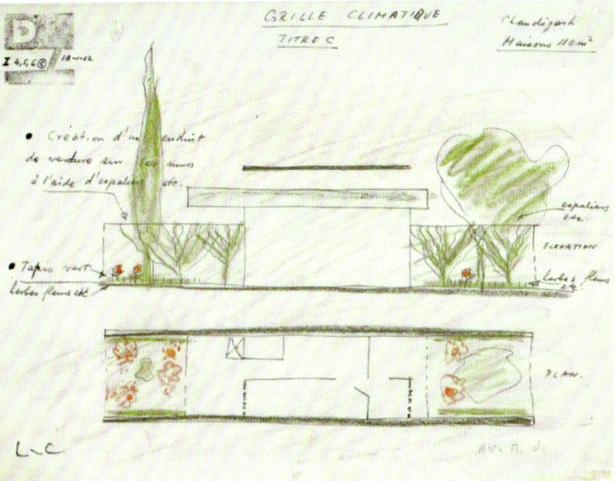

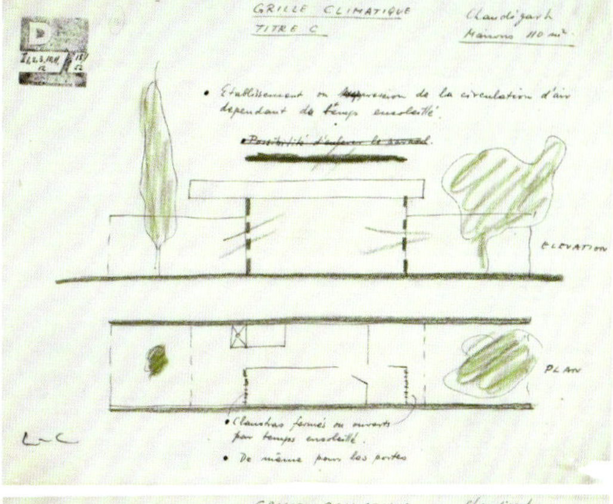

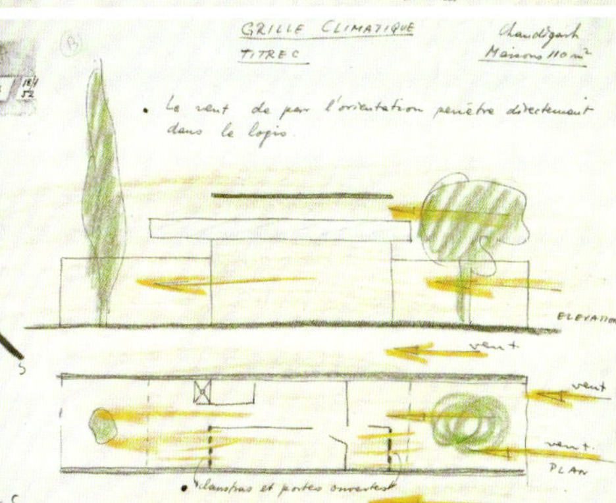

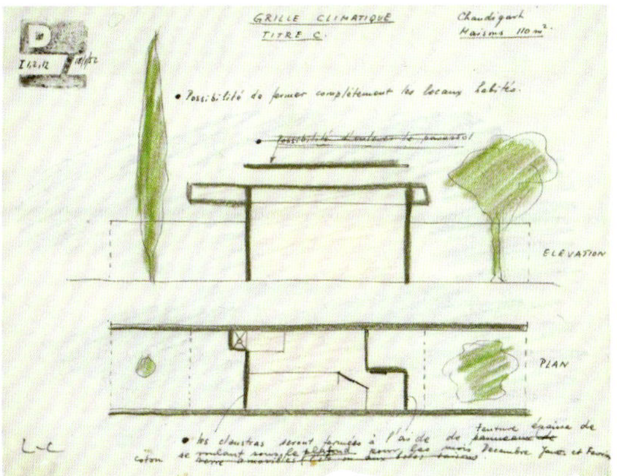

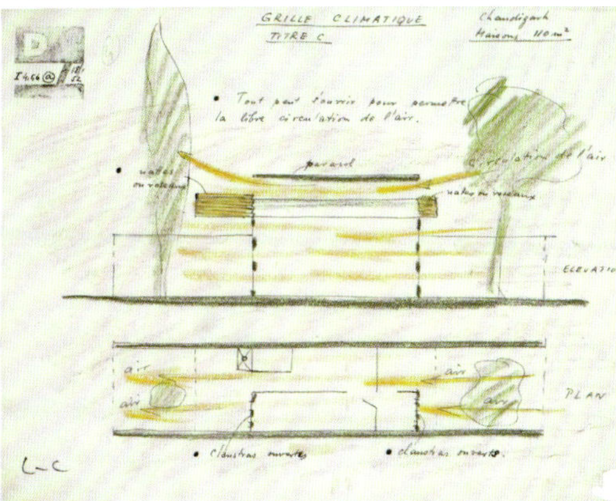

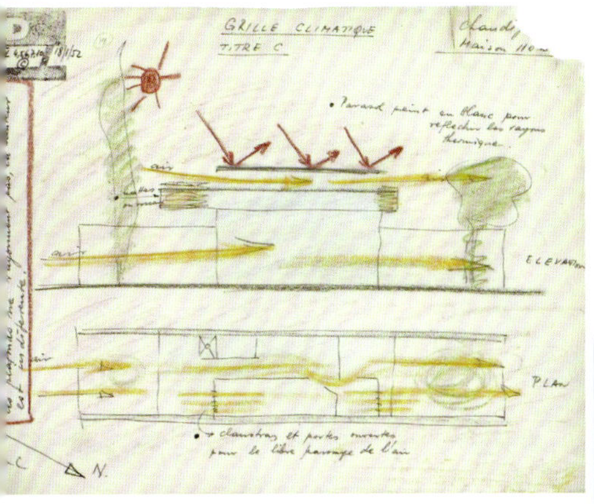

Workers' housing, Chandigarh, 1952

While working in India, Le Corbusier undertook studies for low-cost housing for workers. However, because the two British members of the Chandigarh team, Maxwell Fry and Jane Drew, were contractually responsible for the housing component of the project, he was not able to realize these studies. He confided to his colleague Balkrishna V. Doshi some dissatisfaction with the housing schemes at Chandigarh, promising to build earthen mounds to conceal them, which he did.

Opposite and this page. Le Corbusier's Grille Climatique (top) analyzing temperature, humidity, and wind conditions in Chandigarh, with his sketches (bottom) showing various architectural responses to those conditions, January 1952

Following pages. Workers' housing by various architects, Chandigarh

THE TRIBUNE (Inde) 7 octobre 1953

"Chandigarh supplement"

The Tribune

CHANDIGARH Supplement

AMBALA, WEDNESDAY, OCTOBER 7, 1953

THE STORY OF CHANDIGARH

Land-Mark In History Of The Punjab

Chandigarh A City With A Difference

HOUSING AT CHANDIGARH

A DREAM COMES TRUE

Source Of Poetry

ARCHITECTURE OF CHANDIGARH

By Mr MAXWELL FRY (Senior Architect)

CHANDIGARH—THE NEW CITY

By P. L. VARMA (Chief Engineer Capital)

HOUSING AT CHANDIGARH

TOWN PLANNING IN CHANDIGARH

CHANDIGARH—THE NEW CITY

THE STORY OF CHANDIGARH

ARCHITECTURE OF CHANDIGARH

PUNJAB'S NEW CAPITAL

PLANNING

THEY BUILT CHANDIGARH

THE NEW CAPITAL

BIRTH OF A CAPITAL

THE CAPITOL OF CHANDIGARH

CHANDIGARH'S ARCHITECTURE

Ambala, Wednesday, October 7, 1953

THE TRIBUNE

LANDSCAPING THE CITY OF CHANDIGARH

By M. S. RANDHAWA, I.C.S.

CHANDIGARH—A CITY OF TOMORROW

By PIERRE JEANNERET

Chandigarh—Punja New Capital

By Mrs. Urmila Choudhry, Junior Architect.

THE CAPITOL OF CHANDIGARH

PUNJAB'S FIVE YEAR PLAN

WATER SUPPLY AT CHANDIGARH

Le Corbusier On Town Planning

City of Tomorrow: Chandigarh and Le Corbusier in the news

By the time of the commission for Chandigarh, Le Corbusier had become a celebrity whose latest projects garnered worldwide press coverage. Chandigarh proved to be no exception, with Le Corbusier's vision disseminated by the international architectural press and with milestones such as Nehru's visits to the site detailed in the popular press.

Above. Clippings from the "Chandigarh Supplement" in the *Tribune* (Ambala, India), 7 October 1953

Opposite. Le Corbusier with a full-size model of the Modulor

(Minette de Silva)

Décembre 1955

Cher Corbu.
Un petit coin de mon atelier.
Quand viendrez-vous pour en voir vous-même? En Janvier? J'espère beaucoup visiter Chandigarh en Janvier – le dernier part. et vous? Serez-vous là aussi à même temps? Après, peut-être, à Ceylon pour quelques jours? Écrivez-moi bientôt, Corbu. Il n'y a pas les nouvelles de Doshi! J'écrit deux lettres et envoyé un telegramme! Minnette

A corner of my studio

Left. Photograph of Minnette de Silva in her studio in Ceylon with letter on verso to Le Corbusier, December 1955, suggesting a meeting in Chandigarh in February

Middle. Le Corbusier to Minnette de Silva, 30 November 1951, writing about the establishment of a Chandigarh group for the CIAM meeting in 1953 and a bulletin entitled *CHAND*

Bottom left. Minnette de Silva to Le Corbusier, 29 August 1956, detailing her plans to study French in order to be able to talk with him

Bottom right. First page of a letter from Minnette de Silva to Le Corbusier, 26 November 1956, inviting him to Ceylon when he is next in India

Opposite top. Le Corbusier with Minnette de Silva

Opposite below. Le Corbusier with Minnette de Silva and others

A friend from Ceylon: Minnette de Silva

Le Corbusier met Minnette de Silva, a Ceylonese architecture student, in 1946, and the two would enjoy a lasting relationship that paralleled in many ways the friendship between Le Corbusier and Marguerite Tjader Harris. His relationship with de Silva had creative significance as well: she embodied for him an idealized vision of the East.

TRANSLATION

Paris, November 30th 1951

Miss Minnette de SILVA
The Studio of Modern Architecture
St Georges
KANDY
Ceylon

Dear Friend,

I am back this morning 35 rue de Sèvres after four weeks of intensive work in India (most thrilling). I found your letter of November 5th and I suppose you received mine from Simla.

We had a very pretty meeting in a Simla Club where I proposed to gather a Chandigarh Group who, if it is accepted could step into the CIAM of 53 (you know that in 53 the CIAM is to be altered to give way to the young). I explained to those Indians, all very nice and willing to do their work properly, that they must keep in touch with you and tell you about their work and progress and tell you that I consider as an impossible dream to try to associate for active work places so far away as Bombay, Ceylon and Chandigarh. I suggested they should start a little bulletin entitled "CHAND".

I intend also to start here, in Paris, a little bulletin called "35 RUE DE SEVRES" in which my boys will write. It will be the next step taken by the CIAM, that is to say an heritage taken on by the young ones.

It is a good thing to know that your house is nearly finished, I am waiting eagerly for photographs.

Your letter is the first one I have dictated since I am back in Europe this morning.

Sincerely yours

LE CORBUSIER

THE STUDIO OF MODERN ARCHITECTURE
architecture · arts · crafts

MINNETTE DE SILVA, A.R.I.B.A.
ARCHITECT
telephone 849 Ambassador 8853

ST. GEORGE'S
KANDY
CEYLON

3. Hyde Park Crescent
Hyde Park Street
London W.2.
England –

29 Août 1955

Corbu, you see I'm in London now. I shall be in Mentone staying with Mimi de Gielgud (you remember her?) at the "Villa Regina" Mentone – in September – early. I hope to come to "La Sarraz". Where will you be this month – I want to see you so much – Comment-allez vous? Ça va? Bien? J'ai prends des leçons Française, seulement pour parler avec vous, Corbu! J'ai rencontré Doshi à Bombay quand j'etait en passant à Londre – Avec beaucoup de mon coeur, Minnette

THE STUDIO OF MODERN ARCHITECTURE
architecture · arts · crafts

MINNETTE DE SILVA, A.R.I.B.A.
ARCHITECT
telephone 849

ST. GEORGE'S
KANDY
CEYLON

30 Novembre 1956

26th November, 1956.

Corbu, je suis désolée puisque vous n'avez pas reçu ma lettre écrit en Janvier cet année. Votre livre merveilleuse, plein de vos pensées secrète, me donnée beaucoup de joie, beaucoup de plaisir, aussi une vraie nouvelle sympathie très près, avec vous. Je vous remercie avec tout mon coeur pour ce cadeau très rare. Pour l'honneur de le recevoir.

J'ai été seul sans aucune nouvelles de vous – Comment? Quand vous viendrez aux Indes? de me montrer Chandigarh? Je ne l'ai pas vue encore. Venez à Ceylon aussi à même temps. si invité. Je serais très

AIR INDIA

A young colleague from India: Balkrishna V. Doshi

Indian architect Balkrishna V. Doshi began working at Le Corbusier's office in Paris as soon as he learned about the plans for Chandigarh. He worked for Le Corbusier not only in Chandigarh but also on his major projects in Ahmedabad. Doshi is among the most prominent of a generation of Indian architects who refashioned the Indian architectural landscape by following the lessons they learned from Le Corbusier.

vastu/shilpa town planning architecture industrial design old balentine's haveli near three gates ahmedabad

REÇU LE 4 Juillet 1957
RÉPONDU LE

june 29th 57

my dear mons.le corbusier

i am enclosing herewith a copy of a letter addressed to me by dr. dr.giedion on behalf of the graham foundation.

as you know i have hardly begun my independant practice.before i settle down i feel that it would be a great opportunity for me to broaden my experience and ourlook by spending one year in the states.

since they have asked me to submit a resume of my career and work,i thought it would be best if you would give me a letter of recommendation stating your opinion of my work done under your direction in paris and in india.also i would like to have your permission to take the photographs of the details and the furniture i did on your behalf for the buildings in ahmedabad.this will help me give them an idea of what i have done so far under your guidance.this is particularly necessary because having so recently started my independant practice i have little else completed.

i should perhaps not trouble you,however,the opportunity to travel and to spend one year abroad will be of great value to my education.

i shall indeed be very happy to receive your letter before you go on your holidays.

how is mrs.le corbusier now ?

my wife and i send you both our respects.

yours

encl:one copy

balkrishna v. doshi ariba aita

Opposite, top. Two photographs of Le Corbusier with Balkrishna V. Doshi

Opposite, bottom. Le Corbusier and Doshi with the office team, 35 rue de Sèvres, Paris

Above. Balkrishna V. Doshi to Le Corbusier, 29 June 1957, seeking a letter of recommendation and permission to photograph Le Corbusier's work in Ahmedabad, for a grant application

Below. Letter to Balkrishna V. Doshi from Le Corbusier's secretary, 13 July 1957, enclosing a letter of recommendation and giving the requested permission

Paris, July 13th, 1957

Mr Balkrishna V. DOSHI
Vastu-Shilpa Town Planning
Architecture Industrial Design
Old Balentine's haveli
near Three Gates
A H M E D A B A D

My dear Doshi,

Kindly find enclosed a copy of the letter M. Le Corbusier wrote in your behalf to Mr Jose Luis Sert.

I hope you will spend a happy and useful year in the States.

None of us have forgotten you and we shall also miss Talati when he will soon leave us.

Of course M. Le Corbusier quite agrees you should take the photographs of the details and the furniture you did for him for the buildings in Ahmedabad.

All our very best regards to you and your wife.

Yours sincerely,

the Secretary

Encl.: 1

"I was once in [Le Corbusier's] office with Mr. Varma, then the Chief Engineer of Chandigarh. And Le Corbusier asked, 'What is truth really?' Then he drew two parallel lines, with a wavy line in between. 'Truth is like a river,' he said, 'it flows continuously, changing course, modifying itself, without ever touching either bank.'"

—Balkrishna V. Doshi, 1986, *Le Corbusier and Louis I. Kahn: The Acrobat and the Yogi of Architecture*

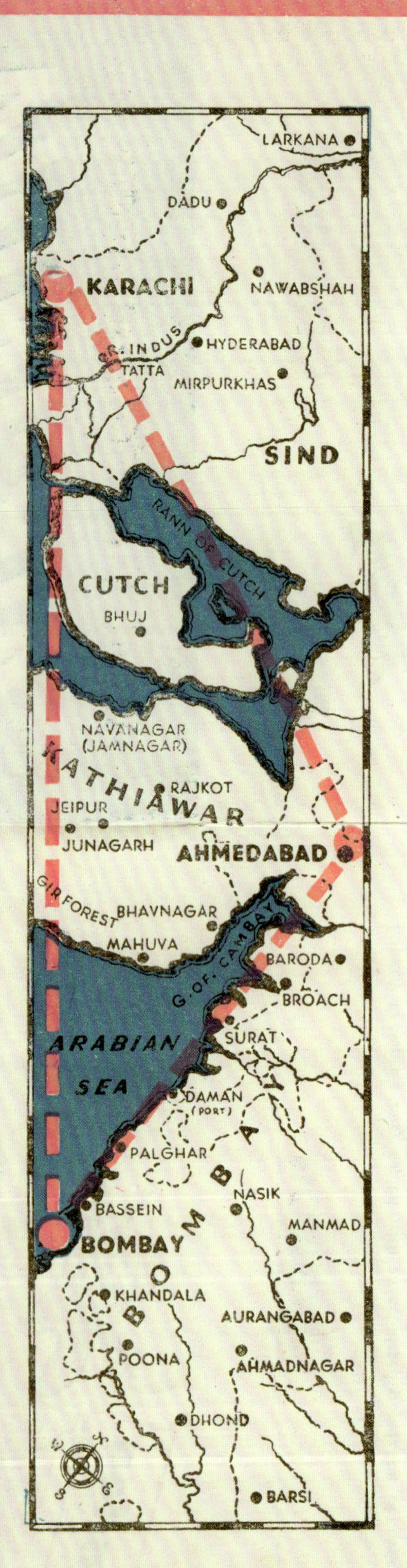

No. Recu & Cul. 71. of 1950-51. MUNICIPAL CORPORATION.

AHMEDABAD, 10th March 1951.

15 Mars 1951

From

The Chairman,
Recreational & Cultural Committee,
Municipal Corporation,
AHMEDABAD.

To

Mr. Les Corbusier,
C/o East Punjab Capital Project,
SIMLA.

Dear Sir,

This City is the second largest in Bombay State and has a population of about a million people. It has been the centre of brocades and textiles for the past several centuries and is well known for its distinctive architecture of the middle ages in which there is a synthesis both of the Hindu and Muslim styles.

The Municipal Corporation has a scheme for starting a museum of Painting, Sculpture and Archaeology. There will be a well-equipped library of books, photographs, latern slides, cine-films and gramophone records and an auditorium with a fully equipped stage in addition to the usual amenities that are provided by a modern museum. We want to erect a building of roughly 30,000 Sq.Ft.

We understand that you have come to India to consult with the East Punjab Government and will stay here for about a month. We write this to enquire whether you would be interested in designing the building including the interiors, display cases, lighting, etc., and if so what would be your terms. We would suggest that you visit Ahmedabad on your way back from Delhi to Bombay. Ahmedabad is on the air-route from Delhi to Bombay and can be conveniently visited. Your visit would give us an opportunity to discuss the details of the problem with you.

Yours faithfully,

M. B. Kadri

CHAIRMAN,
Recreational & Cultural Committee.

GMP.
10.3.

Form 101.

THOS. COOK & SON, LTD.

WORLD-WIDE TRAVEL SERVICE

ESTABLISHED 1841

NEW DELHI—SIMLA.

Mr Le Corbusier ITINERARY No. 17. 3 1951.

The undermentioned dates and times are taken from the latest information in the possession of Thos. Cook & Son, Ltd., but are not guaranteed; all times and sailing dates are subject to alteration without notice and should be verified *en route*.

March 1951

22nd	Delhi Palam air Port	Leave	14.30
"	Ahmedabad	arrive	18.05
23rd	Ahmedabad	Leave	16.20 } applied for
23rd	Bombay	arrive	18.15
25th	Bombay	Leave	17.00
26th	Rome	arrive	08.40
26th	Rome	Leave }	accommodation applied for by Connecting Plane
26th	Paris	arrive }	

WITH BEST COMPLIMENTS FROM:—
THE GUJARAT INSTITUTE OF CIVIL ENGINEERS & ARCHITECTS; AHMEDABAD.

Projects for an elite clientele, Ahmedabad, India, 1951–56

Very soon after Le Corbusier's arrival in India, the mayor of Ahmedabad invited the architect to come to the city to discuss building a museum and cultural center. The prosperous and culturally rich city—center of the country's textile industry—offered multiple opportunities for new commissions. Not all of these were realized, but the four that were completed—the museum, the Millowners' Association Building, the Villa Sarabhai, and the Villa Shodhan—gave Le Corbusier the opportunity to develop his subtropical modernism on a more modest scale than at Chandigarh. The clients for the projects were all part of the same wealthy and refined coterie linked to the local textile industry.

Opposite, left. Detail of map of India, showing the geographic relationship of Bombay, Ahmedabad, and Karachi (now Pakistan)

Opposite, top right. M.B. Kadri, chairman of the Recreational and Cultural Committee of the Municipal Corporation of Ahmedabad, to Le Corbusier, 10 March 1951, proposing that he design a new museum of painting, sculpture, and archaeology

Opposite, bottom right. Itinerary of 22–26 March 1951 for Le Corbusier's return to Paris from Bombay by way of Ahmedabad

Above. Le Corbusier and members of the Gujarat Institute of Civil Engineers and Architects on his arrival in Ahmedabad

Regional and rustic: Villa Sarabhai, Ahmedabad, 1951–56

Built for a wealthy widow and her two sons, the Villa Sarabhai is composed of a series of vaulted bays derived from the simultaneously mechanical and rustic aesthetic of the Maison Monol, designed in 1919 but never built. The roof of the Villa Sarabhai features a garden with grass lawn, and the entire house is so engulfed in lush greenery that it nearly vanishes into the site. A long slide extends from the roof garden to the swimming pool.

Le Corbusier considered the Villa Sarabhai to be a "regionalist hypothesis," employing techniques for structure, shading, and ventilation that would find expression in his other Indian projects, ranging from the public buildings at Chandigarh to studies for low-cost housing.

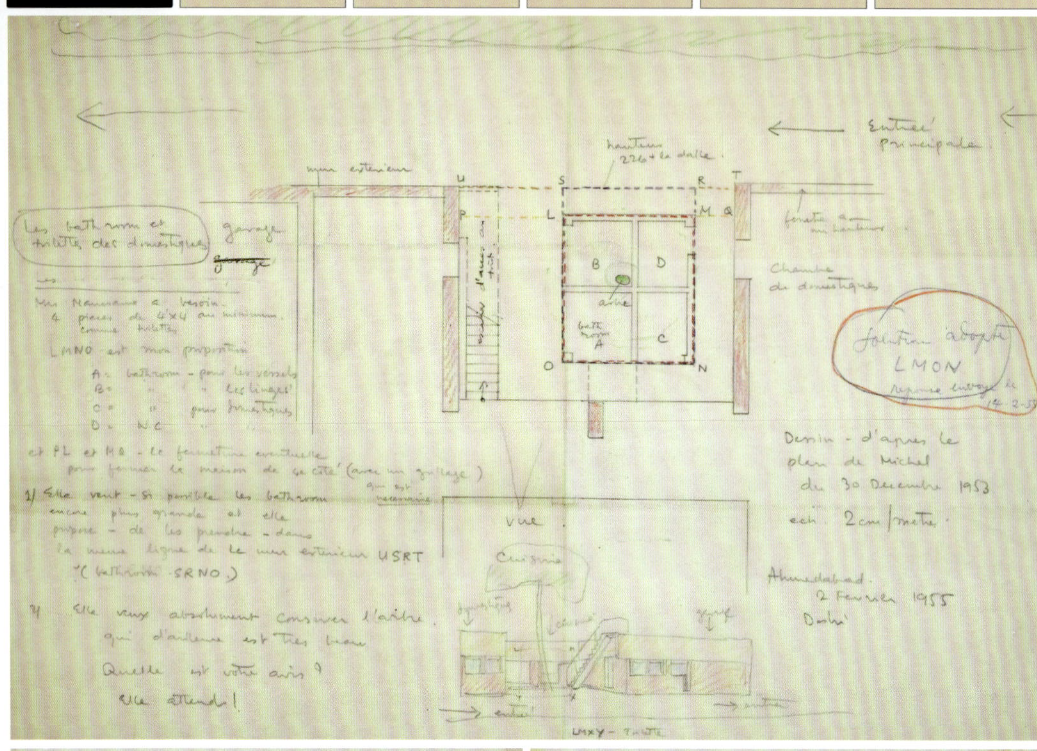

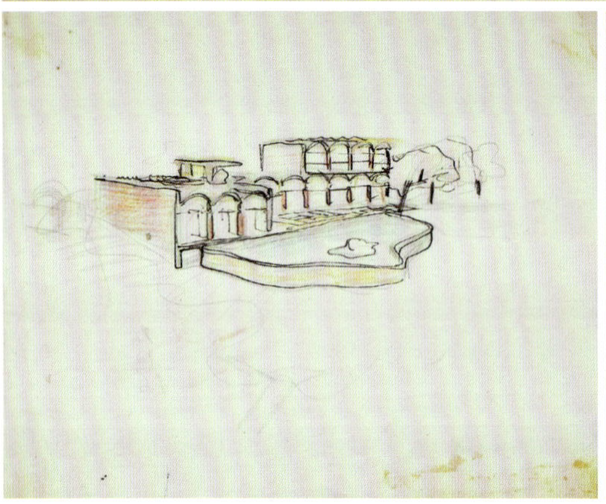

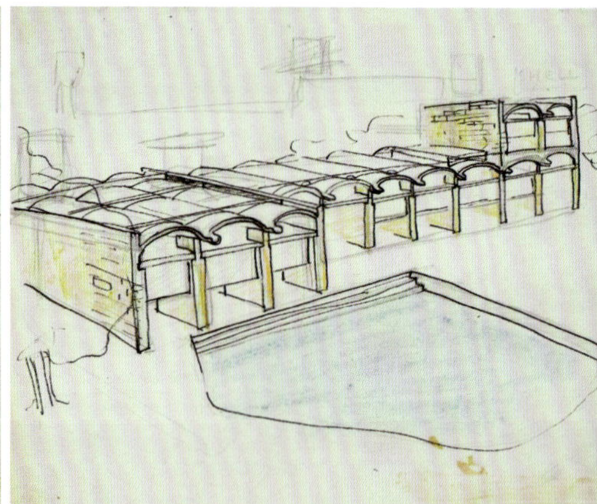

TELEGRAMS: BUSINESS.

GIRA SARABHAI

POST BOX 28
AHMEDABAD

May 19, 1951

Dear Mr.Corbusier,

Thank you very much for your letter. I am very happy to learn that you have finished the initial drawings for the museum and also for the two houses. I have arranged with the Municipal Engineer here for sending you all the materials that you wanted in this connection and I understand that they are being airmailed to you in Paris.

We are greatly looking forward to receiving the plans and also to meeting you when you are next in India.

It was very kind of you to have arranged for my brother to see the building at Marseilles. He was greatly impressed.

With kindest regards,

Yours sincerely,

Mr.Le Corbusier,
35, Rue De Sevres,
Paris 16e

Translation

Paris, May 3rd 1954

Mrs Manorama SARABHAI
The Retreat
Shahibag
AHMEDABAD

Dear Mrs Sarabhai,

I am in receipt of your letters dated April 22nd and 23rd, 1954.

1st point : the parapet
I cannot agree to a "galic" in brick, it would destroy the harmony of the front of the house. But we can reduce the parapet to 3' as you have required (see enclosed sketch which shows the 2 solutions).

2nd point : the stone
I have spoken of this matter with Gira when she dined at my home. I repeat most earnestly that this stone is of rustic appearance, it is not polished but simply smoothed and the color is dark grey, light grey and blackish. You have a typical demonstration of this stone in Veret's bungalow. Our pattern of parallel bands will give it a lot of personality.

3rd point : ceramic tiles of the bath rooms
I will send my answer in a few days.

4th point : the rear windows
I maintain the drawing of the rear windows I made with Veret on my last visit. The ventilation will be ensured by the vertical openings. As the whole house will open (visually) on the front I think you will not have the feeling of suffocation.

Yours sincerely,

LE CORBUSIER

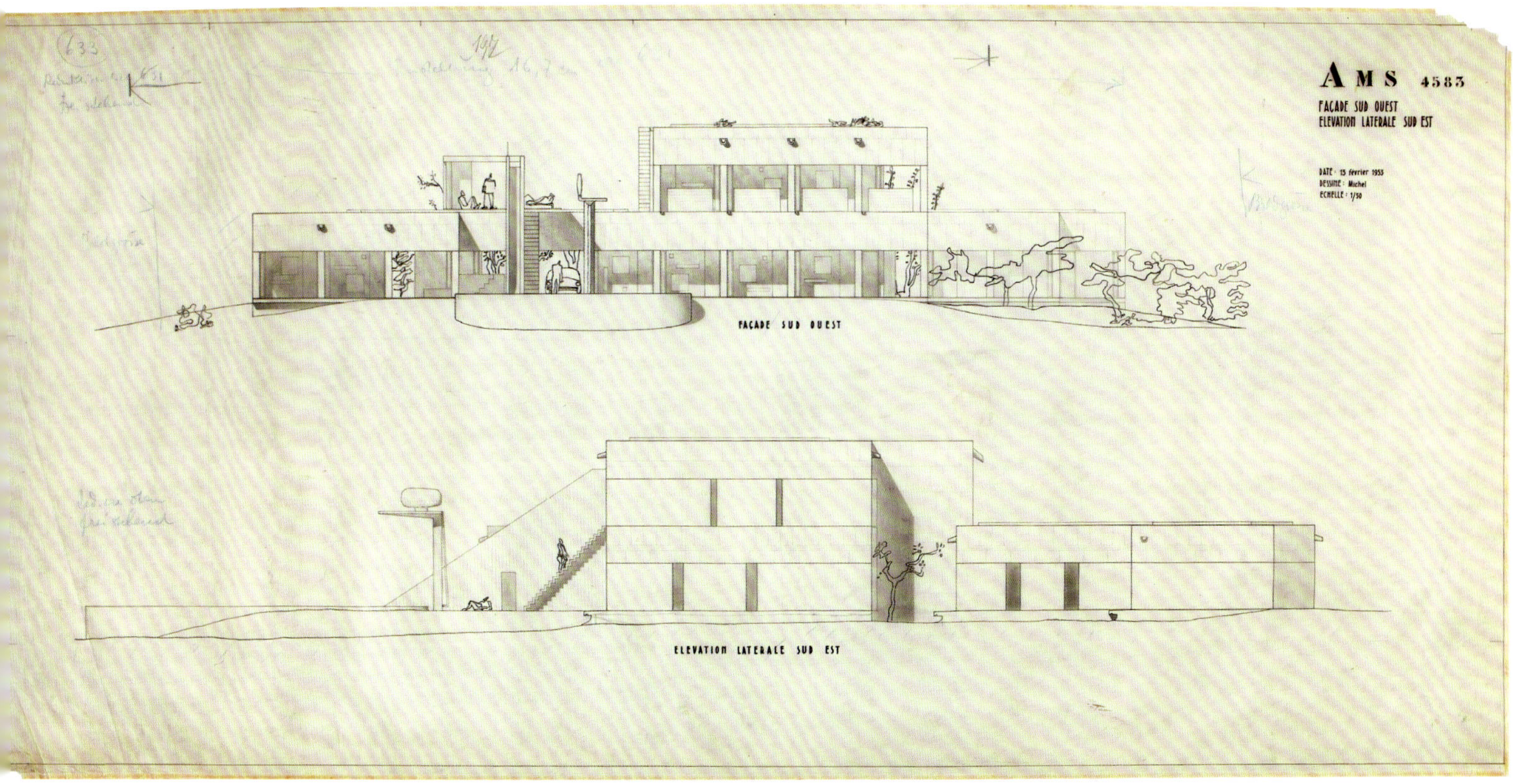

Opposite, top. Detail of plan, Villa Sarabhai, Ahmedabad, February 1955

Opposite, middle. Perspective sketches of various schemes for the Villa Sarabhai

Opposite, bottom left. Gira Sarabhai to Le Corbusier, 19 May 1951, confirming receipt of drawings for the museum project and two houses in Ahmedabad

Opposite, bottom middle. Le Corbusier to Manorama Sarabhai, 3 May 1954, regarding the construction and finishing details of the Villa Sarabhai

Opposite, bottom right. Le Corbusier to Manorama Sarabhai, 1 May 1956, complaining that her furnishings are "killing" the new house

Above. Southwest facade and southeast elevation, 13 February 1953

Below. Northeast facade and northwest elevation, 8 November 1953

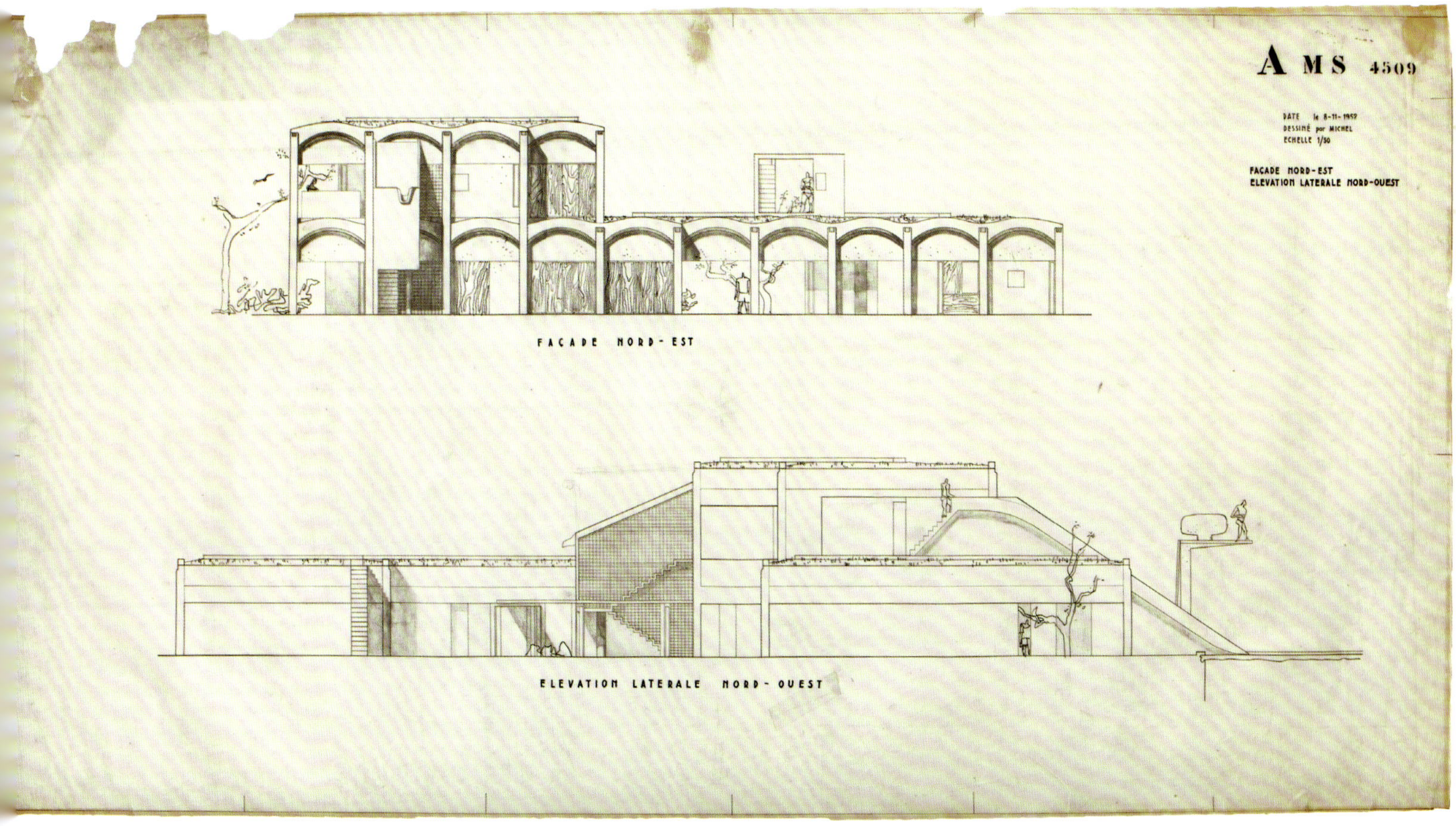

Opposite, left and bottom right. Three views of the south facade, Villa Sarabhai, Ahmedabad

Opposite, top right. Construction view with peacock

Opposite, middle right. Detail of drainage spouts, roof terrace

Below. Gardens on the roof terrace

Above. Interior view, looking south, with diagonal drainage channel from roof garden, Villa Sarabhai, Ahmedabad

Opposite, top left. Bedroom interior showing Catalan vault and Le Corbusier's mural on the far wall

Opposite, top right and bottom. Two views of the main living area

Surottam Hutheesing

TELE {GRAM: 'HUTHEESING'
PHONE: 2009 : 2910
SHAHIBAG,

Ahmedabad, 19th March 1951

Dear Monsieur Le Carbusier,

I have been given to understand that you have come up from France to design the Capital of the East Punjab and that you will stay in this country for some time. I am desirous of building a residential house and I woudd like you to design the house for me. I wonder whether you will be willing to do the job and if so, what will be the terms and your fees. On hearing from you, I shall be pleased to give you such details as you require.

Thanking you for your early reply,

Yours faithfully,

Surottam Hutheesing

Monsieur Le Carbusier,
C/o Shri P.L. Varma,
Capital Project Chief Engineer,
East Punjab, Simla.

A return to the cube: Villa Shodhan, Ahmedabad, 1951–56

While the Villa Sarabhai reinterpreted the cavelike vaults of the Maison Monol, the Villa Shodhan evolved out of the cubic geometry of the Dom-ino system and the Maison Citrohan. Here, too, *brises-soleil* (sunshades) protect interior spaces from the harsh sun, while their diagonal orientation encourages cooling breezes. A complex section that recalls the Maison Curutchet in Argentina is bisected by ramps and stairs culminating in a fantastical rooftop garden.

Above. Plans, section, and site plan, with directional arrow indicating prevailing winds, 24 October 1951, Villa Shodhan, Ahmedabad, 1951–56

Left. Surottam Hutheesing, the client for what would later become the Villa Shodhan, to Le Corbusier, 19 March 1951

Opposite, top left. Sketch of northwest facade

Opposite, top right. Site plan sketch, 6 June 1952

Opposite, middle. Southwest elevation

Opposite, bottom. Southwest facade, 18 May 1953; revised 30 January 1954

N-O-G

HUTTESING. FAÇADE SUDEST

ASH 4705
FAÇADE SUD-OUEST
ech. 1/50

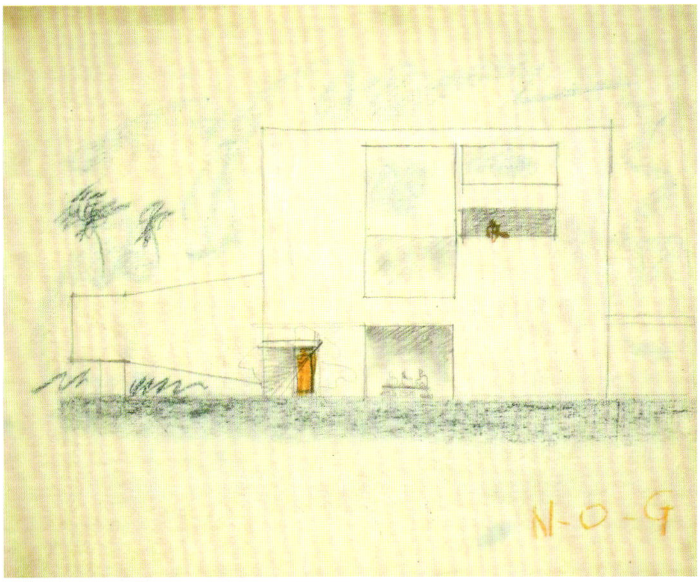

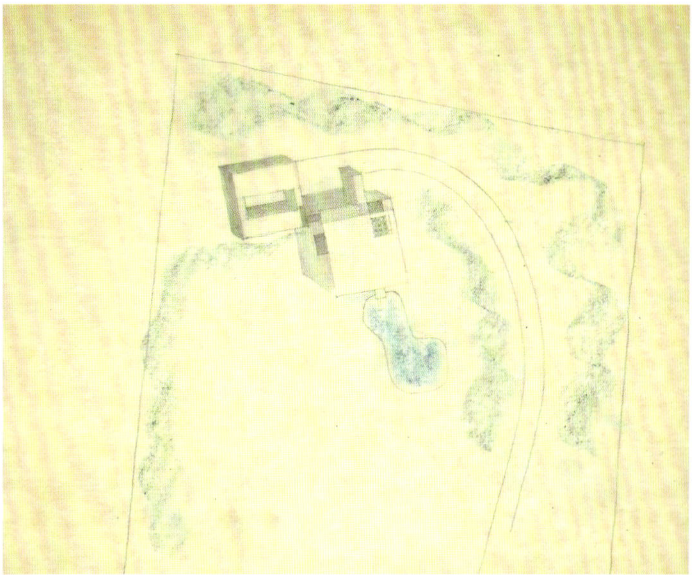

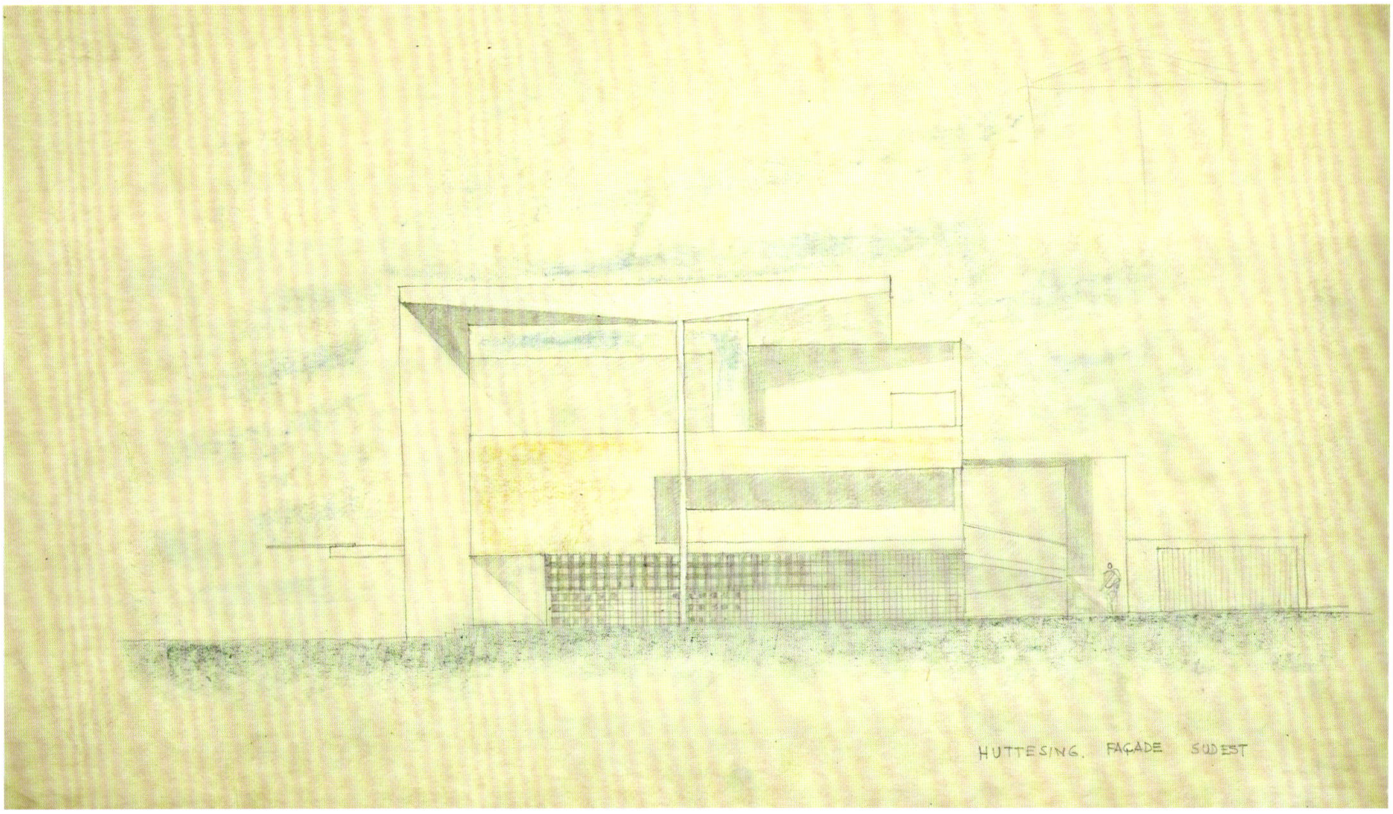

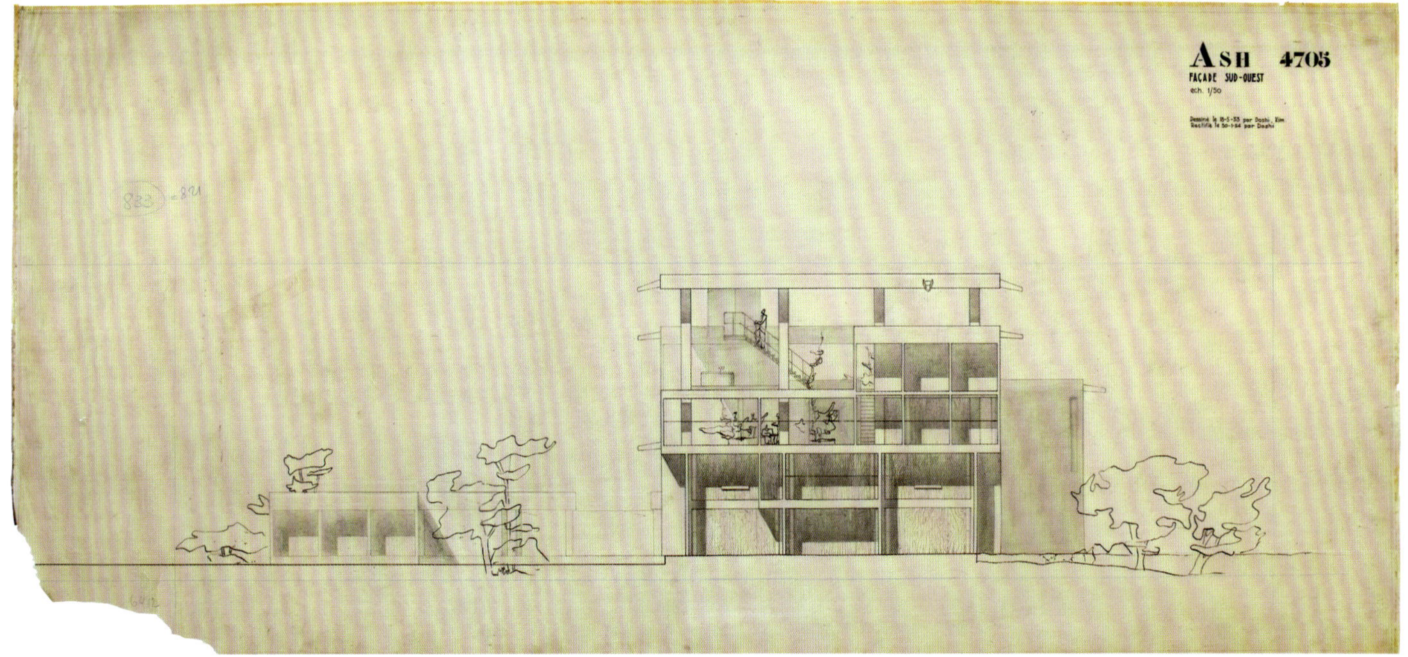

Translation

Paris, June 26th 1952

Mr Surottam P. HUTHEESING
Shahibag
AHMEDABAD

Dear Mr Hutheesing,

My fees for the architectural surveys of your villa not having been yet settled, I availed myself of my meeting with Mr Nehru last April 17th to ask him to kindly allow my clients to realize their payments.

Mr Nehru asked Mr BajpMy, of his private secretariat, to handle this matter.

Therefore I take liberty to enclose a duplicate of the extract, which concerns you, of the letter I addressed to Mr BajpMy at New Delhi. I assume in this letter that you could write to Mr BajpMy yourself and ask him to help you to forward my fees.

Believe me,

most sincerely

LE CORBUSIER

Left. Le Corbusier to Surottam Hutheesing, 26 June 1952, regarding delayed payment of fees

Below. Interior of the main living area, with Le Corbusier's flexible floor lamp to the left, Villa Shodhan, Ahmedabad

Opposite. View from west

"This museum is a modern tool that should, in my view, exist in many different regions... It is my honest opinion that the invention of the 'Museums of the Knowledge' will seem to you useful for your country, and this would please me enormously."

—Letter to Jawaharlal Nehru, 27 December 1954

Museum and Cultural Center, Ahmedabad, 1951–58

In his Museum and Cultural Center for Ahmedabad, Le Corbusier first explored the concept of the *parasol* that would figure so powerfully in his designs for Chandigarh.

A horizontal slab shaded the structure, beneath which the galleries were elevated on *pilotis*.

Above. Le Corbusier with drawings of the proposed Museum of Ahmedabad (now known as the Museum of the City)

Opposite, top. Installation view of an exhibition about the design and construction of the museum

Opposite, middle and bottom. Panels from the exhibition

SCOPE OF THE CENTRE
The centre will be a place where people can
meet
No passive spectator but active participant
MIRACLE-BOX: theatre for professionals
-two stages [one inside
-Auditorium [inside outside
OPEN AIR THEATRE: for „spontaneous theatre"
only for amateurs
WORK-SHOP: for improving the standard of craftsm
CONFERENCE-ROOM: for lectures and cultural fil
READING-ROOM: for journals, art & scientific liter

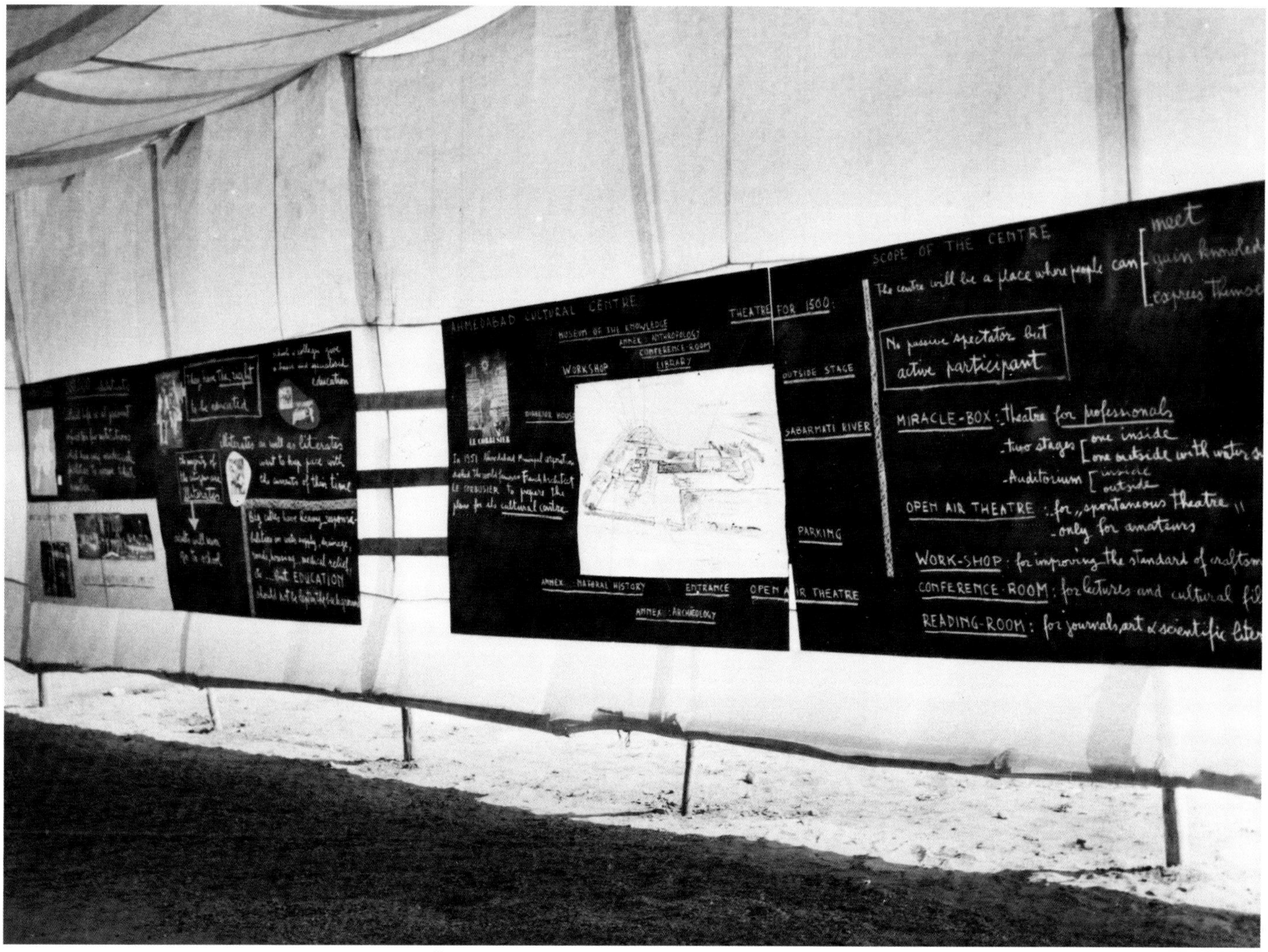

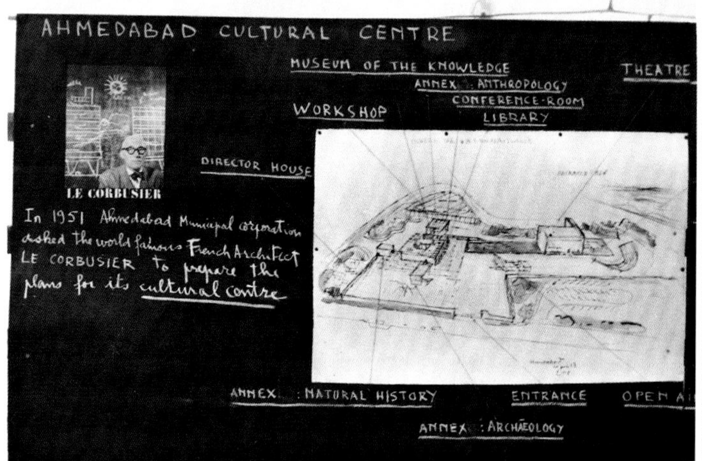

AHMEDABAD CULTURAL CENTRE
MUSEUM OF THE KNOWLEDGE
ANNEX: ANTHROPOLOGY
CONFERENCE-ROOM
LIBRARY
WORKSHOP
THEATRE
DIRECTOR HOUSE
LE CORBUSIER
In 1951 Ahmedabad Municipal corporation
asked the world famous French Architect
LE CORBUSIER to prepare the
plans for its cultural centre
ANNEX: NATURAL HISTORY
ENTRANCE
ANNEX: ARCHÆOLOGY

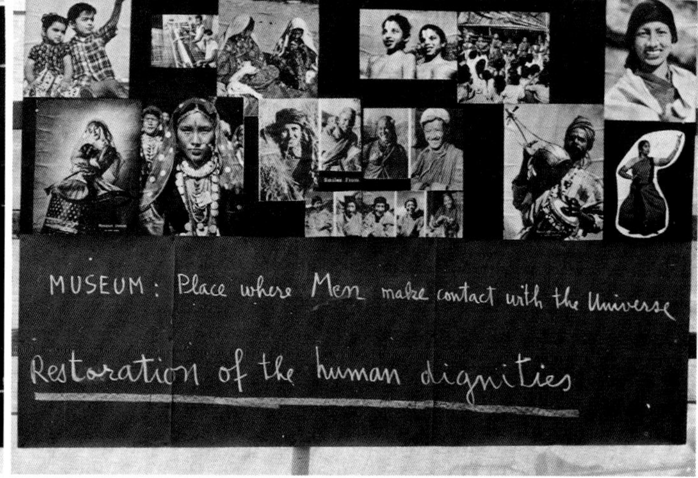

MUSEUM: Place where Men make contact with the Universe
Restoration of the human dignities

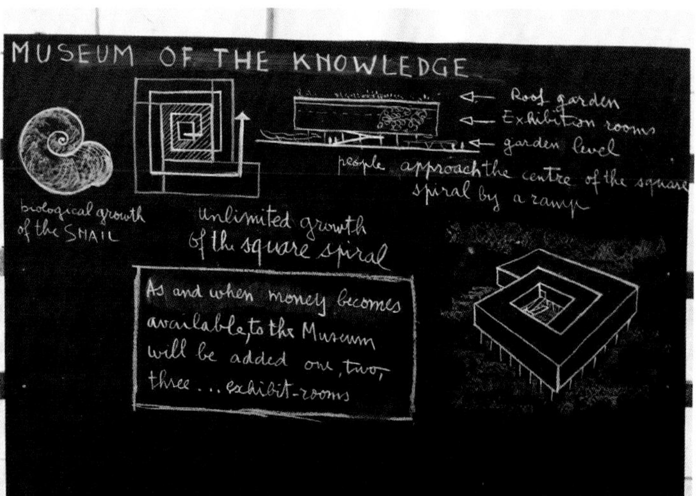

MUSEUM OF THE KNOWLEDGE
Roof garden
Exhibition rooms
garden level
people approach the centre of the square spiral by a ramp
biological growth of the SNAIL
unlimited growth of the square spiral
As and when money becomes available, to the Museum will be added one, two, three ... exhibit-rooms

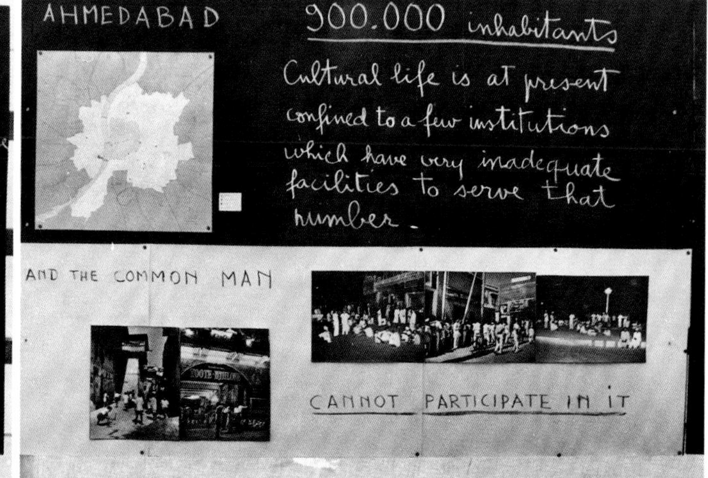

AHMEDABAD
900.000 inhabitants
Cultural life is at present confined to a few institutions which have very inadequate facilities to serve that number.
AND THE COMMON MAN
CANNOT PARTICIPATE IN IT

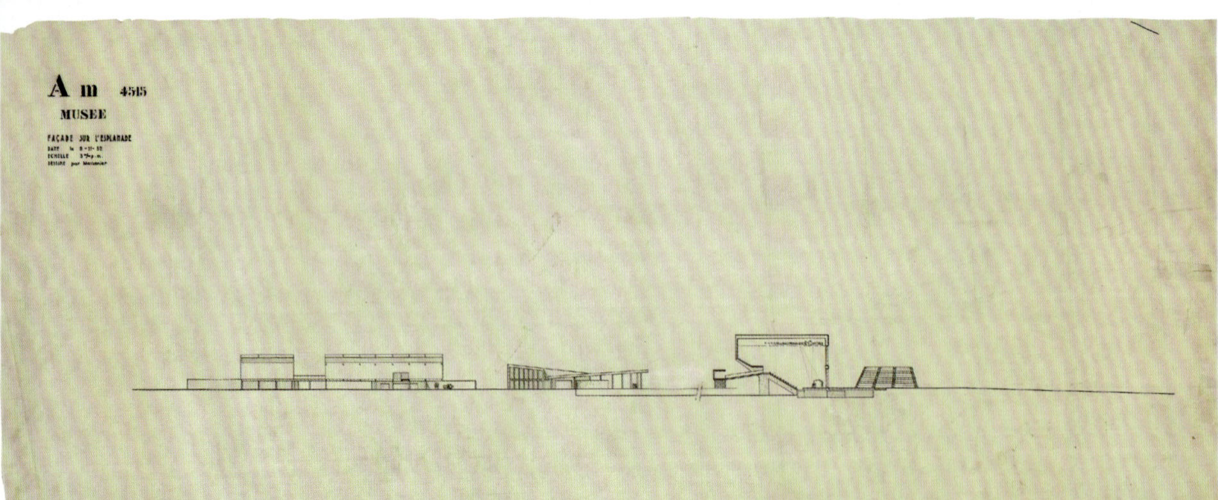

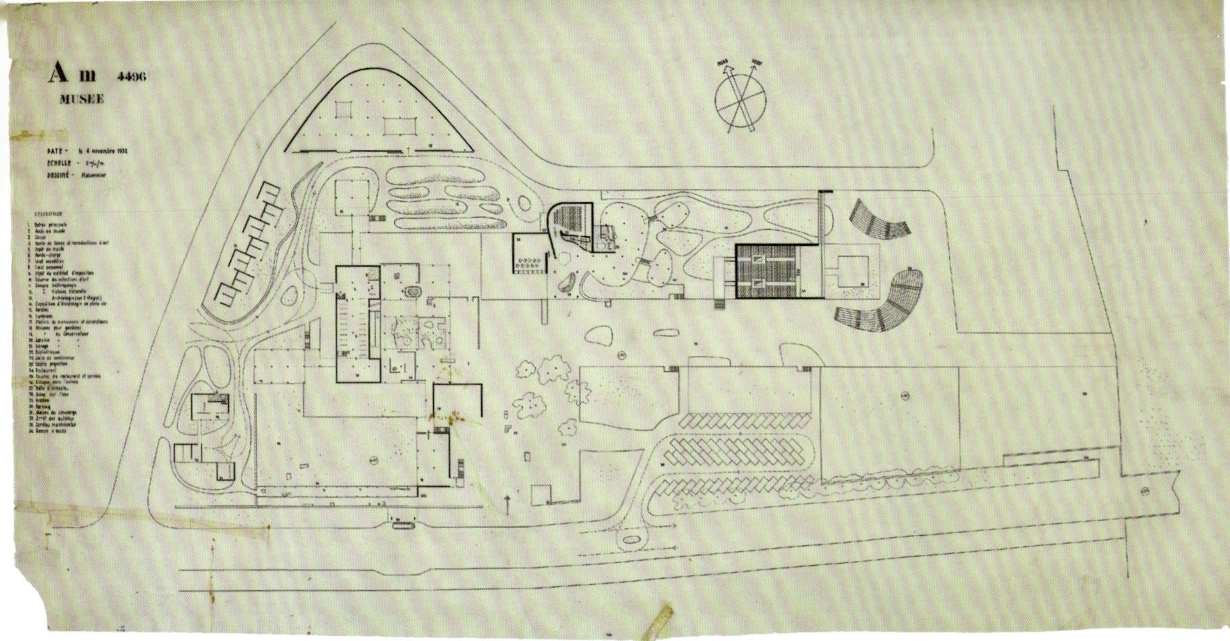

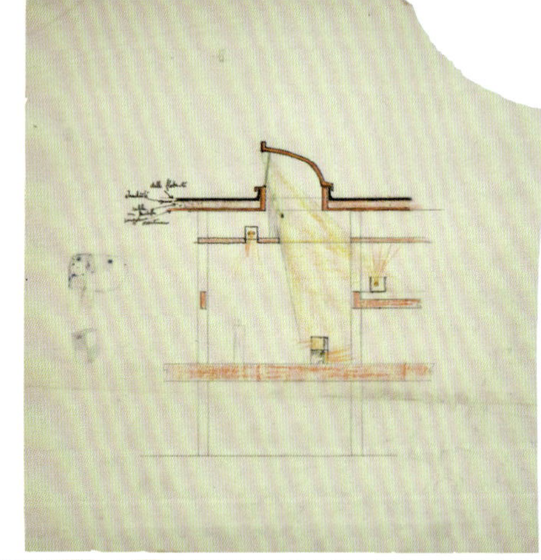

Top. Facade and sections along the esplanade, 9 November 1952, Museum and Cultural Center, Ahmedabad, 1951–58. The esplanade is the central circulation spine through the complex.

Above. Site plan with first-floor plans, 4 November 1952

Right. Section detail with natural and artificial light study

Below left. Section, museum, 9 November 1952

Below right. Site plan, 6 October 1951

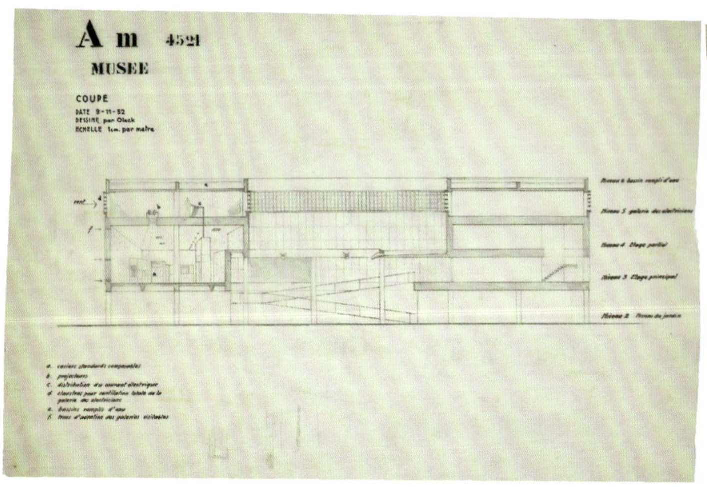

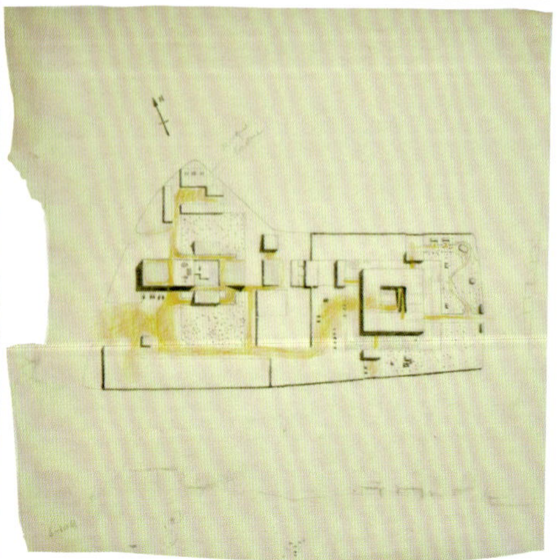

Above. View of Museum under construction

Below. Three-page proposal by Gautam Sarabhai, 23 March 1951, for a municipal museum for Ahmedabad, to include sections devoted to regional archaeology, Indian art, art in daily life, natural history, anthropology in India, the natural resources of Gujarat, and a library

Below right. Le Corbusier to Jawaharlal Nehru, 27 December 1954, concerning the proposal for the Musée de la Croissance, which would become the Museum and Cultural Center, Ahmedabad

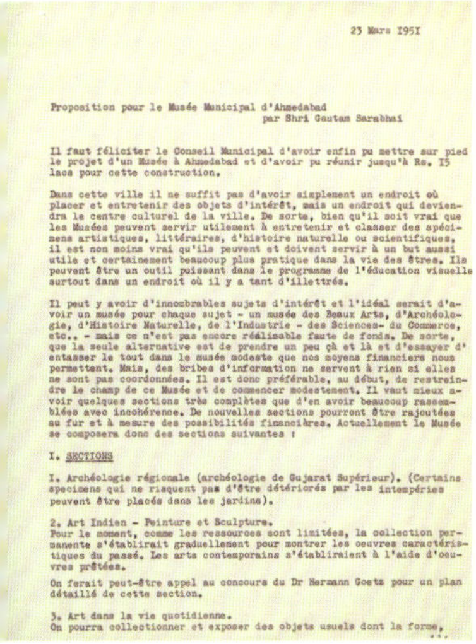

23 Mars 195I

Proposition pour le Musée Municipal d'Ahmedabad
par Shri Gautam Sarabhai

Il faut féliciter le Conseil Municipal d'avoir enfin pu mettre sur pied le projet d'un Musée à Ahmedabad et d'avoir pu réunir jusqu'à Rs. I5 lacs pour cette construction.

Dans cette ville il ne suffit pas d'avoir simplement un endroit où placer et entretenir des objets d'intérêt, mais un endroit qui deviendra le centre culturel de la ville. De sorte, bien qu'il soit vrai que les Musées peuvent servir utilement à entretenir et classer des spécimens artistiques, littéraires, d'histoire naturelle ou scientifiques, il est non moins vrai qu'ils peuvent et doivent servir à un but aussi utile et certainement beaucoup plus pratique dans la vie des êtres. Ils peuvent être un outil puissant dans le programme de l'éducation visuelle surtout dans un endroit où il y a tant d'illettrés.

Il peut y avoir d'innombrables sujets d'intérêt et l'idéal serait d'avoir un musée pour chaque sujet - un musée des Beaux Arts, d'Archéologie, d'Histoire Naturelle, de l'Industrie - des Sciences- du Commerce, etc.. - mais ce n'est pas encore réalisable faute de fonds. De sorte, que la seule alternative est de prendre un peu çà et là et d'essayer d'entasser le tout dans le musée modeste que nos moyens financiers nous permettent. Mais, des bribes d'information ne servent à rien si elles ne sont pas coordonnées. Il est donc préférable, au début, de restreindre le champ de ce Musée et de commencer modestement. Il vaut mieux avoir quelques sections très complètes que d'en avoir beaucoup rassemblées avec incohérence. De nouvelles sections pourront être rajoutées au fur et à mesure des possibilités financières. Actuellement le Musée se composera donc des sections suivantes :

I. SECTIONS

I. Archéologie régionale (archéologie de Gujarat Supérieur). (Certains specimens qui ne risquent pas d'être détériorés par les intempéries peuvent être placés dans les jardins).

2. Art Indien - Peinture et Sculpture.
Pour le moment, comme les ressources sont limitées, la collection permanente s'établirait graduellement pour montrer les oeuvres caractéristiques du passé. Les arts contemporains s'établiraient à l'aide d'oeuvres prêtées.

On ferait peut-être appel au concours du Dr Hermann Goetz pour un plan détaillé de cette section.

3. Art dans la vie quotidienne.
On pourra collectionner et exposer des objets usuels dont la forme, ...

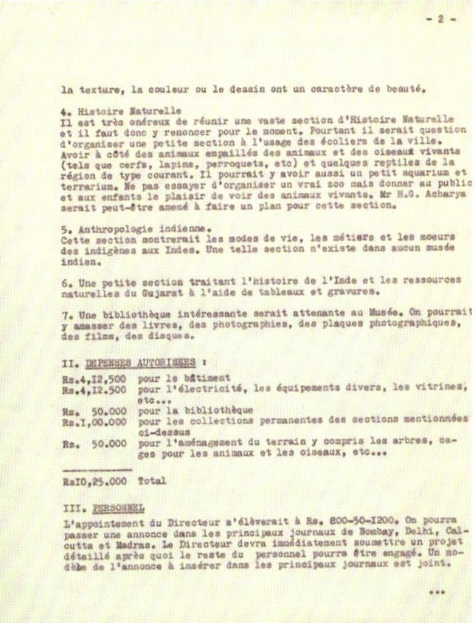

- 2 -

la texture, la couleur ou le dessin ont un caractère de beauté.

4. Histoire Naturelle
Il est très onéreux de réunir une vaste section d'Histoire Naturelle et il faut donc y renoncer pour le moment. Pourtant il serait question d'organiser une petite section à l'usage des écoliers de la ville. Avoir à côté des animaux empaillés des animaux et des oiseaux vivants (tels que cerfs, lapins, perroquets, etc) et quelques reptiles de la région de type courant. Il pourrait y avoir aussi un petit aquarium et terrarium. Ne pas essayer d'organiser un vrai zoo mais donner au public et aux enfants le plaisir de voir des animaux vivants. Mr H.G. Acharya serait peut-être amené à faire un plan pour cette section.

5. Anthropologie indienne.
Cette section montrerait les modes de vie, les métiers et les moeurs des indigènes aux Indes. Une telle section n'existe dans aucun musée indien.

6. Une petite section traitant l'histoire de l'Inde et les ressources naturelles du Gujarat à l'aide de tableaux et gravures.

7. Une bibliothèque intéressante serait attenante au Musée. On pourrait y amasser des livres, des photographies, des plaques photographiques, des films, des disques.

II. DEPENSES AUTORISEES :

Rs.4,I2,500	pour le bâtiment
Rs.4,I2.500	pour l'électricité, les équipements divers, les vitrines, etc...
Rs. 50.000	pour la bibliothèque
Rs.I,00.000	pour les collections permanentes des sections mentionnées ci-dessus
Rs. 50.000	pour l'aménagement du terrain y compris les arbres, cages pour les animaux et les oiseaux, etc...
RsI0,25.000	Total

III. PERSONNEL

L'appointement du Directeur s'élèverait à Rs. 800-50-I200. On pourra passer une annonce dans les principaux journaux de Bombay, Delhi, Calcutta et Madras. Le Directeur devra immédiatement soumettre un projet détaillé après quoi le reste du personnel pourra être engagé. Un modèle de l'annonce à insérer dans les principaux journaux est joint.

...

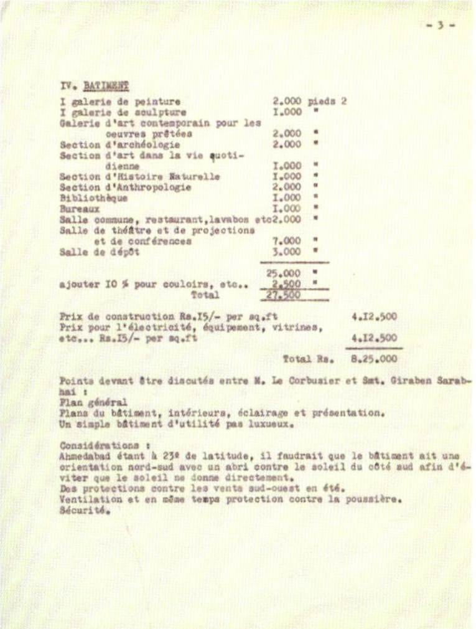

- 3 -

IV. BATIMENT

I galerie de peinture	2.000	pieds 2
I galerie de sculpture	I.000	"
Galerie d'art contemporain pour les oeuvres prêtées	2.000	"
Section d'archéologie	2.000	"
Section d'art dans la vie quotidienne	I.000	"
Section d'Histoire Naturelle	I.000	"
Section d'Anthropologie	2.000	"
Bibliothèque	I.000	"
Bureaux	I.000	"
Salle commune, restaurant,lavabos etc	2.000	"
Salle de théâtre et de projections et de conférences	7.000	"
Salle de dépôt	3.000	"
	25.000	"
ajouter I0 % pour couloirs, etc..	2.500	"
Total	27.500	

Prix de construction Rs.I5/- per sq.ft	4.I2.500
Prix pour l'électricité, équipement, vitrines, etc... Rs.I5/- per sq.ft	4.I2.500
Total Rs.	8.25.000

Points devant être discutés entre M. Le Corbusier et Smt. Giraben Sarabhai :
Plan général
Plans du bâtiment, intérieurs, éclairage et présentation.
Un simple bâtiment d'utilité pas luxueux.

Considérations :
Ahmedabad étant à 23º de latitude, il faudrait que le bâtiment ait une orientation nord-sud avec un abri contre le soleil du côté sud afin d'éviter que le soleil ne donne directement.
Des protections contre les vents sud-ouest en été.
Ventilation et en même temps protection contre la poussière.
Sécurité.

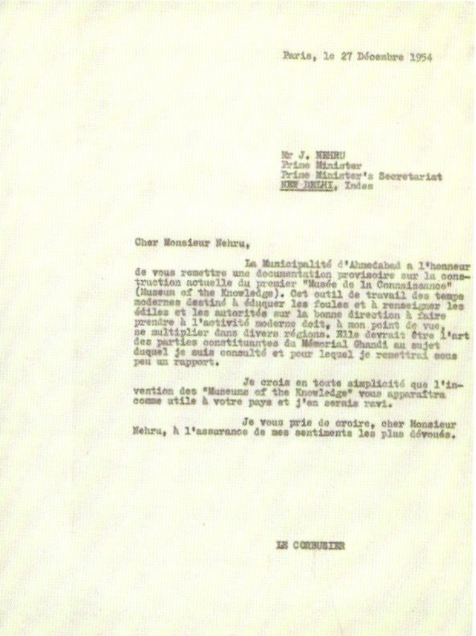

Paris, le 27 Décembre 1954

Mr J. NEHRU
Prime Minister
Prime Minister's Secretariat
NEW DELHI, Indes

Cher Monsieur Nehru,

La Municipalité d'Ahmedabad a l'honneur de vous remettre une documentation provisoire sur la construction actuelle du premier "Musée de la Connaissance" (Museum of the Knowledge). Cet outil de travail des temps modernes destiné à éduquer les foules et à renseigner les édiles et les autorités sur la bonne direction à faire prendre à l'activité moderne doit, à mon point de vue, se multiplier dans divers régions. Elle devrait être l'art des parties constituantes du Mémorial Ghandi au sujet duquel je suis consulté et pour lequel je remettrai sous peu un rapport.

Je crois en toute simplicité que l'invention des "Museums of the Knowledge" vous apparaîtra comme utile à votre pays et j'en serais ravi.

Je vous prie de croire, cher Monsieur Nehru, à l'assurance de mes sentiments les plus dévoués.

LE CORBUSIER

Opposite. Northwest corner of the Museum of Ahmedabad (now known as The Museum of the City)

Top right. Principal stairs to the roof

Middle right. Circulation ramp

Below right. Ground-level pools below the museum

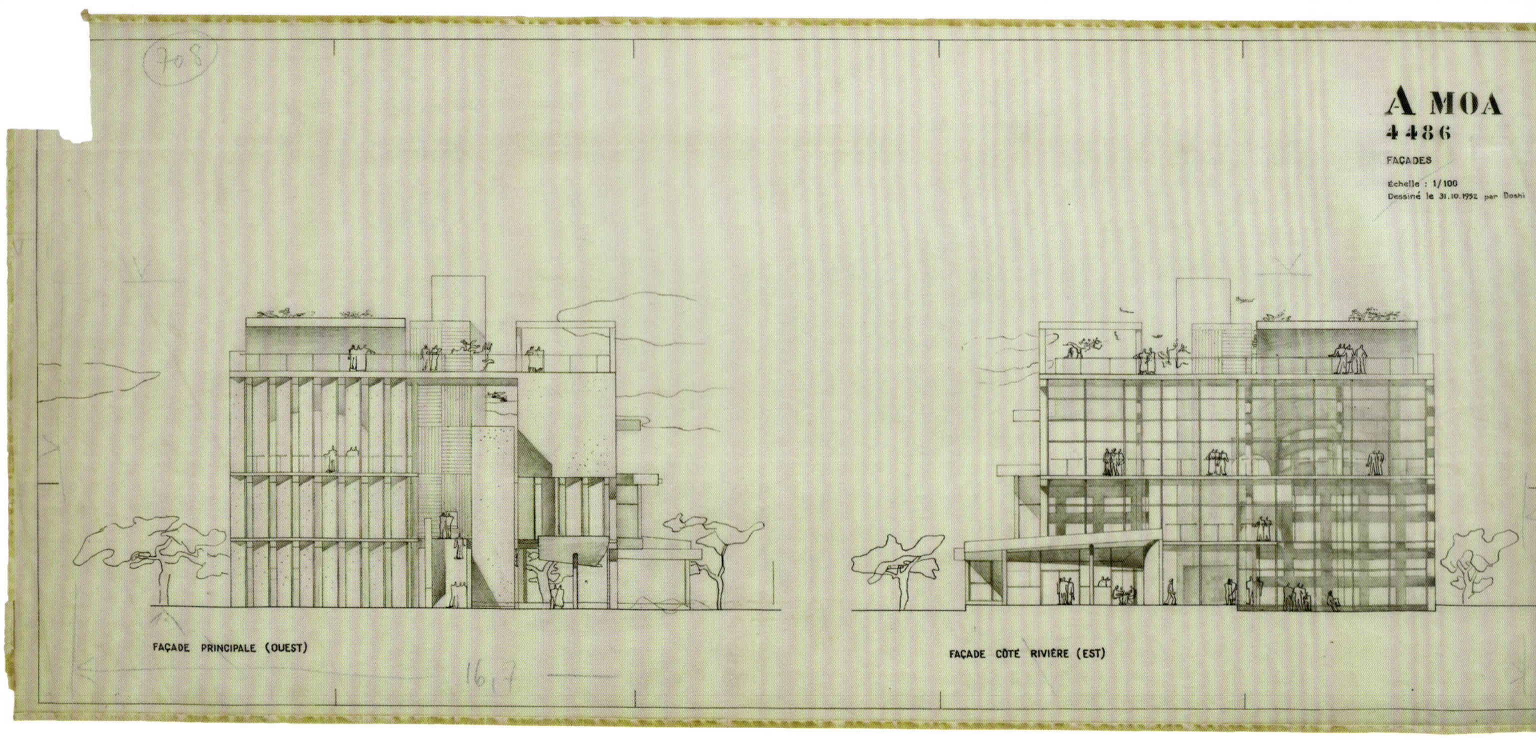

Millowners' Association Building, Ahmedabad, 1951–54

The Millowners' Association Building was conceived for an organization that had been founded in 1891 to bring together members of Ahmedabad's merchant class. The program included a dining room, auditorium, offices, and spaces for exhibitions and entertaining. Here *brises-soleil* and a complex *promenade architecturale*, punctuated by a monumental entrance ramp, are realized in the raw concrete and intricately articulated facades that characterize Le Corbusier's later work.

"The situation of a building in a garden dominating the river furnishes a picturesque spectacle of cloth dyers washing and drying their cotton materials on the sand in the company of herons, cows, buffalo, and donkeys half immersed in water to keep cool. Such a panorama was an invitation to... frame views from each floor of the building."

—Oeuvre complète: Volume 6, 1952–57

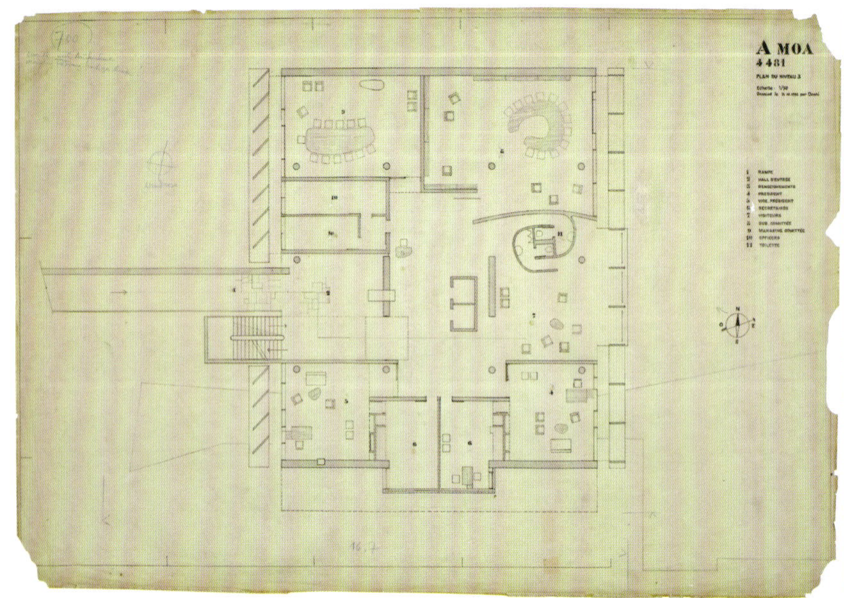

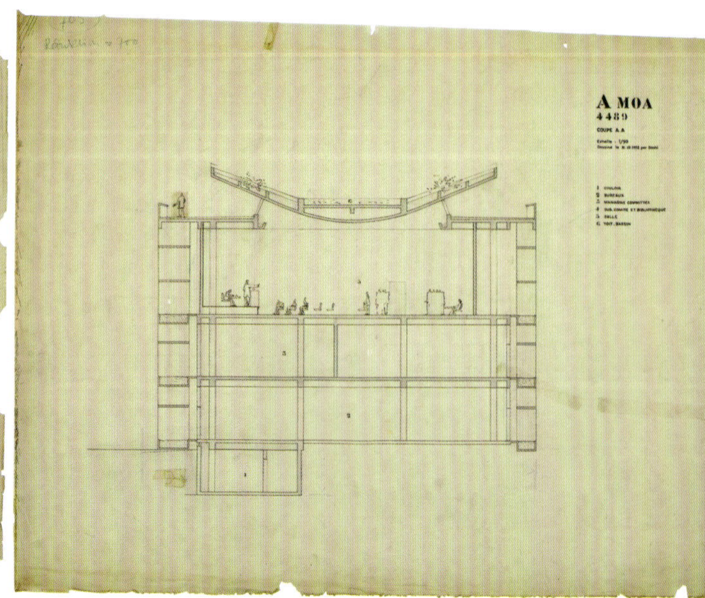

Opposite, top. West and east facades, 31 October 1952, Millowners' Association Building, Ahmedabad, 1951–54

Opposite, bottom left. Third-floor plan, 31 October 1952

Opposite, bottom right. Section, 31 October 1952

Above. View of the Millowners' Association Building from across the river

Below, left. Le Corbusier to Surottam Hutheesing, 18 January 1952, regarding terms of the contract and fees for the design of the building

Below, right. H. G. Acharya, secretary of the Ahmedabad Millowners' Association, to Le Corbusier, 15 October 1953, regretting that Le Corbusier has contacted Prime Minister Nehru about payment of his fees

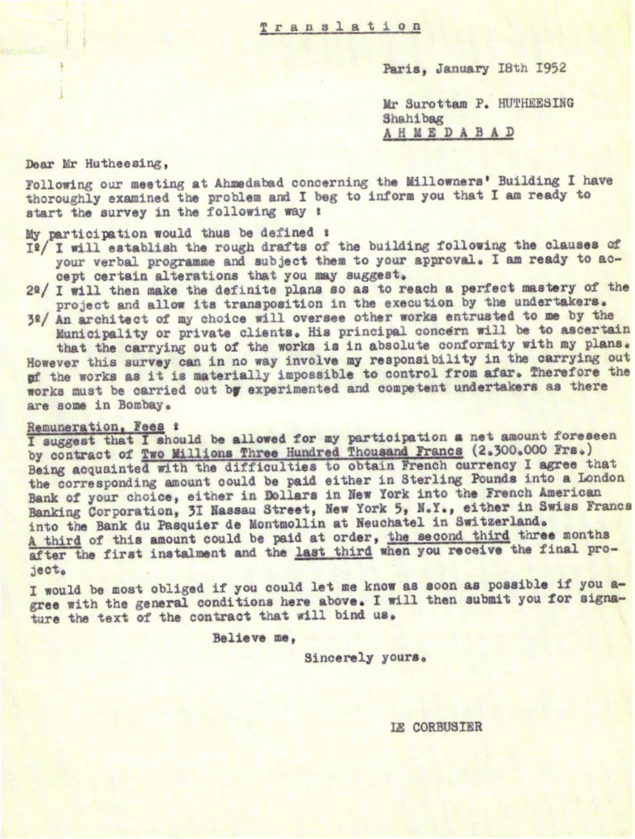

T r a n s l a t i o n

Paris, January I8th I952

Mr Surottam P. HUTHEESING
Shahibag
A H M E D A B A D

Dear Mr Hutheesing,

Following our meeting at Ahmedabad concerning the Millowners' Building I have thoroughly examined the problem and I beg to inform you that I am ready to start the survey in the following way :

My participation would thus be defined :
Iº/ I will establish the rough drafts of the building following the clauses of your verbal programme and subject them to your approval. I am ready to accept certain alterations that you may suggest.
2º/ I will then make the definite plans so as to reach a perfect mastery of the project and allow its transposition in the execution by the undertakers.
3º/ An architect of my choice will oversee other works entrusted to me by the Municipality or private clients. His principal concern will be to ascertain that the carrying out of the works is in absolute conformity with my plans.
However this survey can in no way involve my responsibility in the carrying out of the works as it is materially impossible to control from afar. Therefore the works must be carried out by experimented and competent undertakers as there are some in Bombay.

Remuneration, Fees :
I suggest that I should be allowed for my participation a net amount foreseen by contract of Two Millions Three Hundred Thousand Francs (2.300.000 Frs.)
Being acquainted with the difficulties to obtain French currency I agree that the corresponding amount could be paid either in Sterling Pounds into a London Bank of your choice, either in Dollars in New York into the French American Banking Corporation, 3I Nassau Street, New York 5, N.Y., either in Swiss Francs into the Bank du Pasquier de Montmollin at Neuchatel in Switzerland.
A third of this amount could be paid at order, the second third three months after the first instalment and the last third when you receive the final project.

I would be most obliged if you could let me know as soon as possible if you agree with the general conditions here above. I will then submit you for signature the text of the contract that will bind us.

Believe me,

Sincerely yours.

LE CORBUSIER

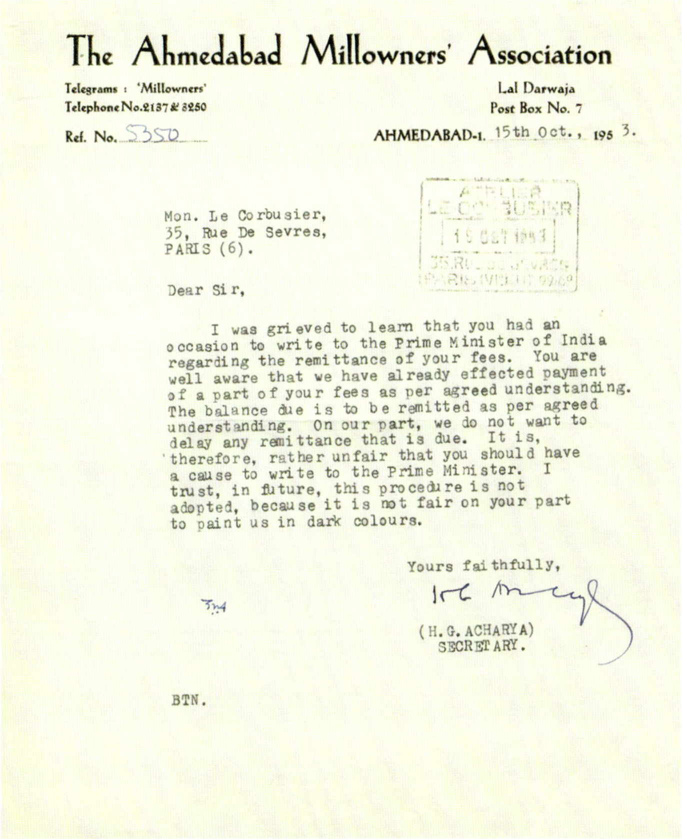

The Ahmedabad Millowners' Association

Telegrams : 'Millowners'
Telephone No. 2137 & 3250

Lal Darwaja
Post Box No. 7

Ref. No. 5350

AHMEDABAD-1. 15th Oct., 1953.

Mon. Le Corbusier,
35, Rue De Sevres,
PARIS (6).

Dear Sir,

I was grieved to learn that you had an occasion to write to the Prime Minister of India regarding the remittance of your fees. You are well aware that we have already effected payment of a part of your fees as per agreed understanding. The balance due is to be remitted as per agreed understanding. On our part, we do not want to delay any remittance that is due. It is, therefore, rather unfair that you should have a cause to write to the Prime Minister. I trust, in future, this procedure is not adopted, because it is not fair on your part to paint us in dark colours.

Yours faithfully,

(H. G. ACHARYA)
SECRETARY.

BTN.

Left. Principal (west) facade under construction, Millowners' Association Building, Ahmedabad

Below. View from across the river

Opposite. Detail of principal facade, showing recessed entry, underside of stairs, and concrete structural elements

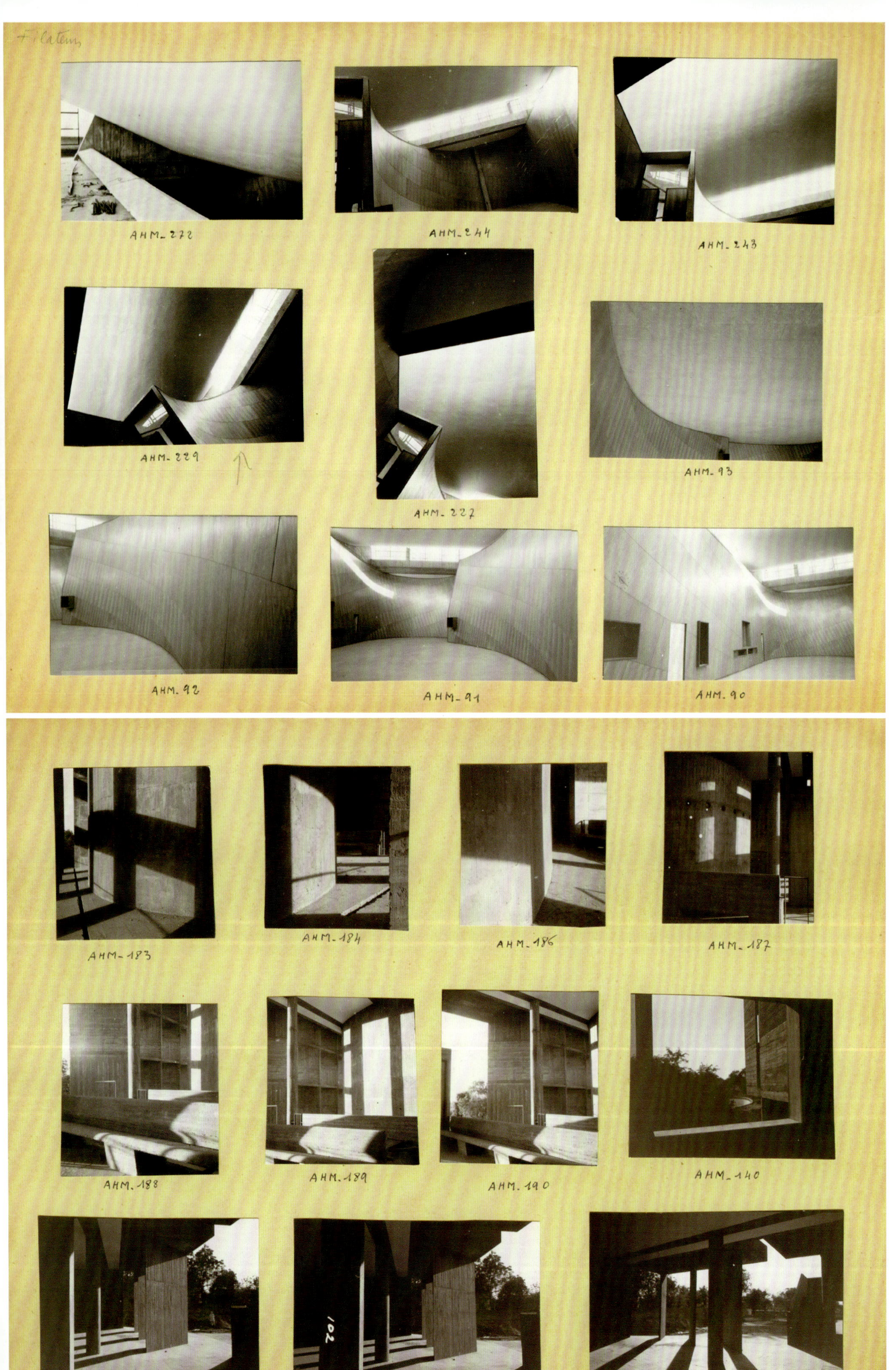
AHM-272
AHM-244
AHM-243
AHM-229
AHM-227
AHM-93
AHM-92
AHM-91
AHM-90
AHM-183
AHM-184
AHM-186
AHM-187
AHM-188
AHM-189
AHM-190
AHM-140
AHM-102
AHM-101
AHM-99

Opposite. Sheets of photographs of the conference room (top) and main entrance and ramp (bottom), Millowners' Association Building, Ahmedabad

Below. Le Corbusier with Balkrishna V. Doshi (right) and unidentified man in the Millowners' Association Building

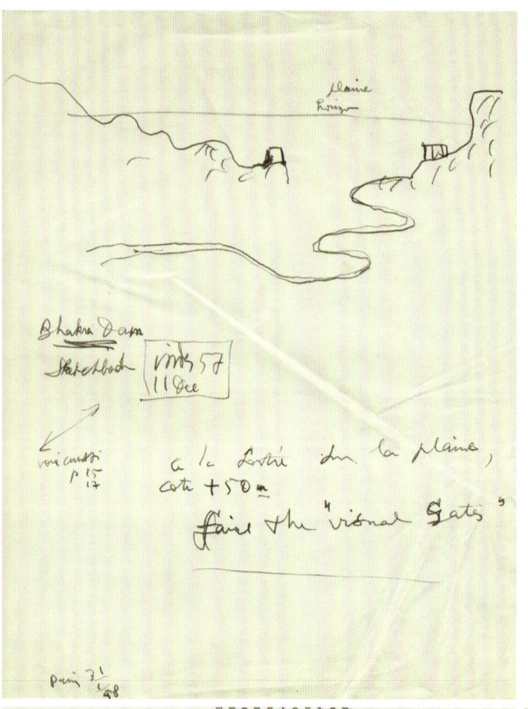

T_r_a_n_s_l_a_t_i_o_n

Paris, April 16th, 1958

Mr S.D. KHUNGAR
General Manager
Bhakra Dam
NANGAL TOWNSHIP

Dear Mr Khungar,

To my astonishment, the contract Bhakra - Le Corbusier has not yet been signed and returned.

I am willing to be patient but you will notice that I have been correct in doing the main part of my work during December 1957 and March 1958. I hope we shall be able to settle this question easily. There is no object in changing the earlier terms of the contract which you accepted yourself. I would not like to have to acquaint Mr Nehru with this shortcoming of your offices. Before an audience of 50.000 people, Mr Nehru spoke in terms which cannot be misinterpreted of my work for Chandigarh and Bhakra.

Thanking you beforehand,

Yours sincerely,

LE CORBUSIER

T_r_a_n_s_l_a_t_i_o_n

Paris, May 21st, 1958

Mr S.D. KHUNGAR
General Manager
Bhakra Dam
NANGAL TOWNSHIP

Dear Mr Khungar,

I am just back in Paris and have found your letter dated the 8th of May answering mine dated the 16th of April, 1958.

1º/ Dear Sir, I do not wish to put my finger in the intricate network of disputes with lawyers or Finance officers. I am an honest architect and town-planner who knows his job and I cannot accept the three paragraphs i) ii) iii) of your proposition dated the 8th of May which opens every door to disloyal discussions, disputes, etc... I cannot work under such conditions.

I am sending a copy of this letter to Mr P.L. Varma asking him to give you his own opinion and, if necessary, I shall write to Mr Nehru so that he may arbitrate this question between Government officers (Finance) who do not know these problems and myself who knows them.

By refusing the three above-mentioned paragraphs, the previous figures of my compensation shall be maintained and shall be drafted accordingly to your draft agreement of November 4th, 1957 :

i) Half the amount (Rs. 50.000 - Rupees Fifty thousand) immediately this agreement is signed by the Employee and the Government.

ii) One fourth of the amount (Rs. 25,000 - Rupees Twenty-five thousand) after one year from the date of execution of this agreemen

iii) One fourth of the amount (Rs. 25,000 - Rupees Twenty-five thousand) after two years from the date of execution of this agreement.

This drafting is a gentlemen's agreement whereas the result of the drafting proposed on the 8th of May, 1958 is a complete incomprehension of the technicality of the problem and it would have as future effect ceaseless contestations and discussions.

I am also changing the paragraph b) of your draft agreement dated the 8th of May, 1958 by adding the following sentences which set forth clearly the events of a practical nature which have taken plac in the interval :

...

- 2 -

"The Employee shall receive from the Government 360 fr per working hour for his office charges only in the case he has to m certain drawings in Paris. If so he shall make a bill giving the det of the working hours of his staff.

"But it has been agreed that the Architects' Office, w has M. Pierre Jeanneret at its head, shall furnish the necessary dra per the instructions given by M. Le Corbusier during his two annual sits to Chandigarh or sent by him from Paris.

"This agreement has already practically taken effect s December 1957 when M. Le Corbusier was at Chandigarh. The necessary velopment took place in April during M. Le Corbusier's next visit to Chandigarh."

I am therefore enclosing a draft agreement (two copies signed by me) with the new amendments. I am sure you will accept the Will you kindly sign one of these copies and return it to me.

Yours sincerely,

LE CORBUSIER

Enc.: 2

From

Shri M.R. Chopra, I.S.E.,
General Manager, Bhakra Dam,
Nangal Township.

To

Mons: Le Corbusier,
Architect,
Chandigarh.

No. 3565/GMBD, dated Nangal Township, the 11th Dec.1958

Agreement with Mons. Le Corbusier.

An agreement for your employment as architectural adviser for architectural treatment of Bhakra Dam and the two Power Plants with the connected works at Nangal Township also, has been signed this day- the 11th December, 1958, in your presence. A copy of the same has been handed over to you personally.

Kindly acknowledge.

General Manager, Bhakra Dam,
Nangal Township.

Bhakra Dam, Nangal Township, India, 1955–58

Le Corbusier had been fascinated with great works of civil engineering ever since visiting the Barberine hydroelectric dam in the Alps in 1924. He was therefore delighted to be offered the commission to add some architectural motifs to the Bhakra dam, which supplied water to Chandigarh.

Top left. Sketch of the Bhakra Dam site, Nangal Township, India, 1955–58

Middle left. Le Corbusier to S. D. Khungar, general manager of the Bhakra Dam project, 16 April 1958, complaining about the delay of his contract and threatening to contact Prime Minister Nehru about it

Middle center and right. Le Corbusier to S. D. Khungar, 21 May 1958, reiterating the terms of his agreement

Bottom left. R. Chopra, general manager of the Bhakra Dam project, to Le Corbusier, 11 December 1958, confirming that the agreement has been signed

Above. Model of the Bhakra Dam

Right. Views of the Bhakra Dam site

1 A WORKING MODEL OF BHAKRA DAM

2 RIVER SUTLEJ FLOWING PAST THE DAM SITE IN THE PRE-DIVERSION STAGE

4 A VIEW OF RIVER SUTLEJ UPSTREAM OF THE DAM SITE AND OVERLOOKING THE VILLAGE BHAKRA FROM WHICH THE DAM DERIVES ITS NAME

5 BLASTING OPERATIONS IN PROGRESS AT SITE OF THE DAM (LOOKING UPSTREAM)

Opposite. Pierre Jeanneret and Le Corbusier at the Bhakra Dam construction site, Nangal Township

Above. Two views of the Bhakra Dam under construction

Below left. Le Corbusier to Talati, apologetically telling him that the Architects' Office in Chandigarh will be the Bhakra-Paris liaison, and not Talati

Below right. Le Corbusier and Pierre Jeanneret (?) at the Bhakra Dam construction site

10 dec 57

Mon cher Talati

[illegible]

PUNJAB

André Malraux visits Chandigarh, December 1958

French Minister of Culture André Malraux visited both the Bhakra Dam and Chandigarh during his 1958 trip to India. A few years later, Le Corbusier appealed to Malraux to facilitate completion of the Monument of the Open Hand, which ultimately would not be erected until 1985—twenty years after the architect's death.

Avant de quitter ce soir l'Inde pour le Japon

André Malraux a visité Chandighar

(la capitale la plus moderne du monde)

en compagnie de Le Corbusier

(De notre envoyé spécial Serge MAFFERT.)

NEW-DELHI, 7 décembre (par câble).

M. ANDRE MALRAUX quitte ce soir l'Inde pour Tokio. Il devait avoir hier soir un dernier entretien avec le président Nehru, au cours d'un dîner offert par l'ambassadeur de France, M. Ostrorog.

Le ministre délégué à la présidence du Conseil avait consacré la fin de la semaine à visiter l'Inde de demain — et même d'après-demain. Il s'est rendu vendredi à 200 kilomètres au nord de Delhi, à Chandigahr, capitale de l'Etat du Pendjab, construite de toutes pièces par le célèbre architecte franco-suisse Le Corbusier.

L'expédition ministérielle était partie la veille au soir par un de ces extraordinaires trains indiens sortis tout droit des livres de Kipling. Locomotive de type Far-West, wagons de bois où chacun est censé apporter son **bedding** (matériel de literie).

Après la matinée consacrée à la visite du barrage géant de Bhakra, symbole de la volonté d'industrialisation de l'Inde, André Malraux et sa suite partirent par la route pour Chandighar.

Une ville entièrcment artificielle

Chandighar est la nouvelle capitale de l'Etat indien du Pendjab (30 millions d'habitants). Commencée il y a huit ans, cette ville entièrement artificielle, irréelle, prodigieuse par son étendue, sera peut-être terminée un jour. Elle constitue l'expérience la plus audacieuse d'urbanisme jamais tentée. En compagnie de Le Corbusier, André Malraux visita le cadre existant de cette capitale, dont les lignes, les formes et la conception générale sont très éloignées de l'Inde traditionnelle et probablement de toute véritable humanité.

Opposite, top. Le Corbusier with André Malraux (center) and others in Chandigarh, 1958

Opposite, bottom. Le Corbusier with André Malraux (left) and others, Chandigarh, 1958

Above. Le Corbusier and André Malraux, 1958

Right. "André Malraux visited Chandigarh," by Serge Maffert, *Le Journal du Dimanche* (France), 7 December 1958. The article calls Chandigarh "the boldest experiment in urban planning ever attempted."

à remplir en vue de l'obtention d'un visa pour l'Inde

Fee

Receipt No.

Checked

NOTE : Si les détails donnés ci-dessous sont incorrects, le visa est susceptible d'être annulé.

1. NOM (en capitales) (Surname) LE CORBUSIER

2. PRENOM (Name) Charles Edouard

3. Nom à la naissance, s'il est différent Jeanneret

4. Né à (lieu) (Born at) La Chaux-de-Fonds, Suisse

Le (date) 6.10.1887

5. Profession Architecte

6. ADRESSE :

(a) Présente: 24, rue Nungesser et Coli, Paris (16º)

(b) Permanente: id

Téléphone: MOLitor 32-52

7. Nationalité actuelle (Present nationality) Française

8. Nationalité d'origine (Nationality at birth) Suisse

9. Nationalité d'origine du père Suisse

10. Si vous êtes titulaire d'un passeport :

(a) Numéro du passeport: 258083

(b) Date d'émission 28.10.1959

(c) Lieu d'émission Paris

(d) Date d'expiration 26.11.1962

11. Avez-vous déjà été en Inde ? (Répondez par OUI ou NON) OUI
Si oui, lieux et dates de séjour: Chandigarh, Delhi, Bombay, Ahmedabad, 3.51, 11.51, 3.52, 11.52, 5.53, 1.54, 11.54, 3.55, 11.55, 3.56, 11.56, 4.57, 12.57, 3.58, 11.58, 3.59, 11.59, 4.60

12. Si l'autorisation de visiter l'Inde ou de proroger votre séjour dans ce pays vous a été refusée, indiquez dans ce cas la date du refus.

Copie pour L-C.

M. Le Corbusier,
Architectural Adviser,
Capital Project,
Chandigarh.

D.O.No.
Chandigarh.
Dated 1st January, 1960.

Subject: Preservation of the Capitol at Chandigarh.

Dear Mr. Vohra,

A most important part of the problem to be solved, by creation of a necessary by-law which is to save the future of Chandigarh, is the one of the protection of Capitol at Chandigarh (Sector No.1) which extends in its limit to the Rajindra Park in the west and to the approach to the Lake in the east and to the Himalayas to the north.

Protection of the Capitol:

The Capitol is an architectural and urbanistic composition which has to be considered as a whole. It is an ensemble of perspective views, of harmony and contrast, with the unity in the spirit and facts etc. This ensemble of the High Court, the Knowledge Museum, the Assembly and the Secretariat is made by the same mind and the same man. It constitutes an attraction for tourism and perhaps also an educational means in the country. It must be protected and my opinion is that this protection can be determined by its designation as a historic monument. Such protection was given in France by the designation of the Villa at Poissy designed by me and Mons. P. Jeanneret as a national monument. The same was made by the city of Stuttgart recently to preserve two houses designed by us which were exceptionally remarked in the housing exhibition of 1928 and in the same manner, recently, the Palace of Centro-Soyus in Moscow designed also by us in the year 1928-30. An instrument of protection officially exists for the buildings of New Delhi created by Sir Edwin Luttyens.

The modern life is so full of unknown things that a very small initiative of inoffensive appearance can destroy important and

-2-

valuable things significant for the population.

I would like to add that the buildings of the Capitol represent an important step in the employment of concrete which became for the first time a total element of architecture. That is an important event not only for India when it concerns public buildings of importance signification.

You must not take this letter as a manifestation of immodesty. Chandigarh, for the foreign people, represents something which belongs to India and I am very happy to be a contributor in this enterprise.

With best wishes,

Yours sincerely,

Le Corbusier

(Le Corbusier)

Shri B.B.Vohra, IAS,
Secretary to Government Punjab,
Capital Project,
Chandigarh.

P.S. I have an interview with the Prime Minister, Shri Jawaharlal Nehru on Tuesday the 5th at 3.0 P.M. I permit myself to hand him a copy of this letter at the time of this interview.

(Le Corbusier)

Above left. Le Corbusier's Indian visa application form, c. 1960, referencing sixteen previous visits to the country

Above right. Le Corbusier to B. B. Vohru, secretary to the government of Punjab for the Capitol Project, 1 January 1960, seeking to protect Chandigarh as a historic monument

Below. Cover and two pages from an issue of the Indian art journal *Revue Marg*, devoted to Chandigarh, 8 July 1958

Opposite. Le Corbusier at the airport in Chandigarh

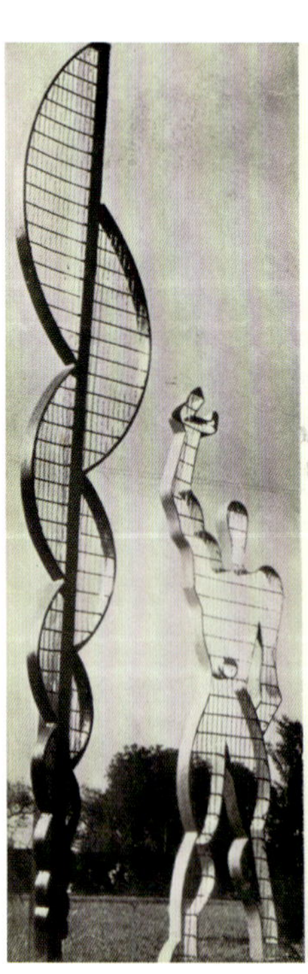

Modulor in steel based on human height

Le Corbusier has indeed carried on the bourgeois revolution in Indian architecture, by enabling the middle and lower middle classes to expand themselves into the four to five-roomed life. And if he could not get over the class system, and divided the rich from the poor, all the same he released a social revolution in the lives of the poor by giving them verandahs, smokeless kitchens, flush lavatories, front gardens and the urges to demand a classless and casteless society. And to all the obtuse clerks of the secretariat and the abject lawyers of the High Court he revealed the vision of gateways as stately as the Buland Darwaza, fountains which are like question marks, and tapestries which fill the soul with pleasure beyond dry as dust considerations of *de jure* and *de facto* logic chopping.

It is true that Le Corbusier and his associates did not give the Punjabies the open verandahs they love, perhaps because he saw them in English striped pyjama suits and not in tunics and helmets, he nevertheless caught the movement of the sun in his open hand, arrested the glow of the moon and the stars in his raised eyes, and he caught the blue tints of the lower Himalayas above his raised eyebrows.

No other painter-poet-architect could have done more than this remarkable man of our century, specially in choosing his associates, each of whom recognised himself into greatness in the free world of his own choice.

Anyhow Le Corbusier and his associates, got away with it. And considering the hindrances offered by ignorance, routine behaviour, official machinery and the mediocre thinking inevitable to the democratic structure, this town of the future seems like a miracle. Wrung out of the heritage of indifference and bad taste left by the Victorian British minds who ruled us for two centuries.

The Prime Minister of India Jawaharlal Nehru, has said, in an inspired moment that: 'Chandigarh represents the most powerful idea in Indian architecture of our time, inspite of the many things in it with which one may disagree'. Almost all the enlightened young architects of India will endorse this statement. And they would add: 'Chandigarh has become the best laboratory for the experiments in town planning and building for the cities and towns of India as well as a platform for a continuous modern symposium on the principles and practice of architecture in our time.

I. THE MASTER PLAN

by Le Corbusier

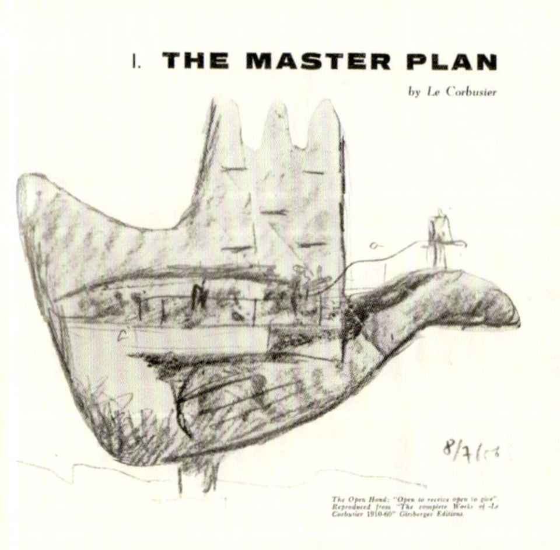

The Open Hand: "Open to receive open to give". Reproduced from "The complete Works of Le Corbusier 1910-60" Girsberger Editions

In November 1950, Messrs. P. N. Thapar and P. L. Varma came from Simla to see me in Paris, asking me to name two architects who could be appointed by the Punjab Government in view of building the new capital of the East-Punjab, on a plateau situated at 400 m, at the foot of the Himalaya. Discussion, conversations, etc...: a month later, my visitors returned asking me to accept to be, in this concern, the "Government Architectural Adviser". In London they had appointed Maxwell Fry and his wife, Jane Drew, as permanent architects at Simla and Chandigarh. I asked them to engage Pierre Jeanneret with whom I had worked 35 rue de Sevres in perfect friendship from 1922 to 1939. And this was realized.

a. The Secretariat
b. The High Court
c. The Assembly

5

AIR-INDIA
International
AIR-INDIA
International
LIGHT INFORMATION
COMMANDER FROM VIA
MATHEN DELHI BOMBAY BEIRUT ZURICH PARIS
Constellation

Opposite. Le Corbusier en route from Paris to La Tourette, France, 1950s

8 The Sacred and the Sublime (1950–1959)

Le Corbusier's religious buildings have puzzled critics and historians from the moment they were built. The pilgrimage chapel Notre-Dame-du-Haut in Ronchamp, France—commissioned to replace a church bombed in 1944—stimulated the sixty-three-year-old architect to design his most unexpected building. But for many of the architects and critics first seeing it in 1955, Ronchamp seemed a betrayal of the fundamental ideas of modern architecture. Highly expressive and sculptural, the building appeared to commit the cardinal sin (for modern architects) of disguising its structure.

Le Corbusier's involvement with Ronchamp and with the Dominican monastery at La Tourette was nurtured by his friendship with Father Marie-Alain Couturier (a Dominican monk who had been trained as an artist) and with Pierre Régamey. They were cofounders of the review *L'Art Sacré*, whose aim was to involve modern artists in commissions for religious art. Although not religious himself, Le Corbusier recognized the power of spirituality and developed a personal iconography based on natural metaphors and alchemical references. "I accept signs, I believe in signs, because they are the expression of a lived reality or the evocation of unanswered questions. Symbols and the metaphysical give me pause = [they signify] imagination, worthwhile creativity in any given time and place, objects and fetishes that man can exploit, a sanctuary for those who have escaped, are escaping or are trying to escape [the physical world] and lovers of the mythic."

For Le Corbusier, natural forms had a profound spiritual charge. It was being sensitive to nature, and imposing an order on it, that was for him the essential artistic act. He had collected natural objects—shells, bones, driftwood, stones—all his life. In a radio interview in 1960, he explained why. "These objects exist everywhere ... and it's all a question of seeing them, observing them, recognizing them and realizing that they are admirable because as a general rule they express and embody the laws of nature... The only one education I have had, consists in taking nature into account, studying it and learning its lessons." He said that the shape of the roof at Ronchamp was based on a crab shell he had picked up on a beach on Long Island, New York, but it also suggests an airplane wing or water flowing over a dam. The sharp white edge of the building on the southeast corner creates the "place of the right angle"—absolutely crisp and vertical—that brings order and precision to the counterpoint of the rough-textured inclined walls and the dark bulbous shape of the roof.

Le Corbusier often referred to himself as a monk and stated his intentions in designing the monastery of La Tourette in terms that could have applied to the life of the intellectual as much as to that of a Dominican monk: "I tried to make a place of meditation, research, and prayer for the preaching brothers... The brief was to house monks while trying to give them what people of today need more than anything: silence and peace." Describing the elevation of the monastery on stilts, Father Bonnet explained that since Le Corbusier "could not build from the ground up [because of the steeply inclined site], he built from the sky downward, and from the sky he reached the ground." Asked about the architect's attitude to religion, Bonnet recalled: "He took part in the solemn inaugural Mass of the church with which he brought the construction of the monastery to its conclusion. I saw him weep, in fact really weep, like a man profoundly moved, and I heard him say as he emerged from the Mass: 'Now I have understood what I have done; this is what I was trying to achieve.'"

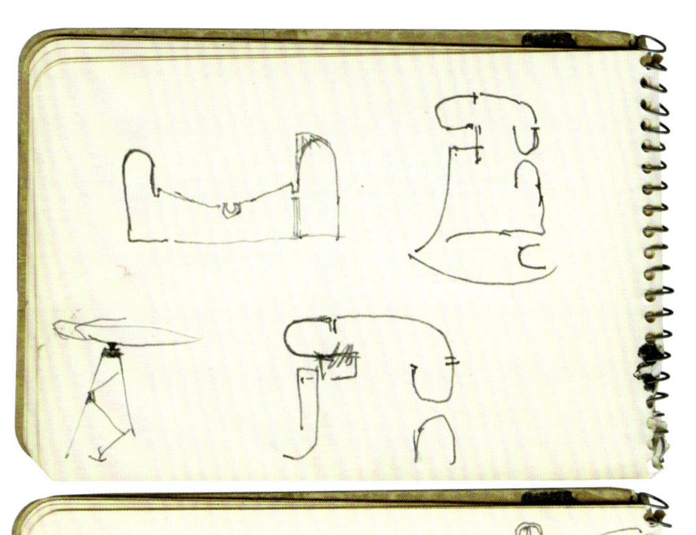

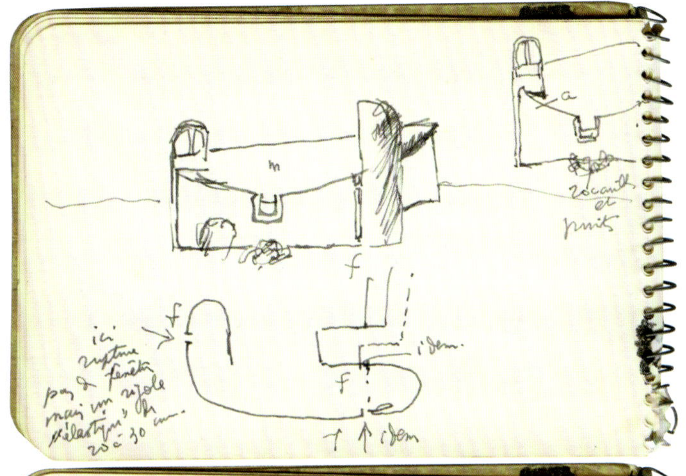

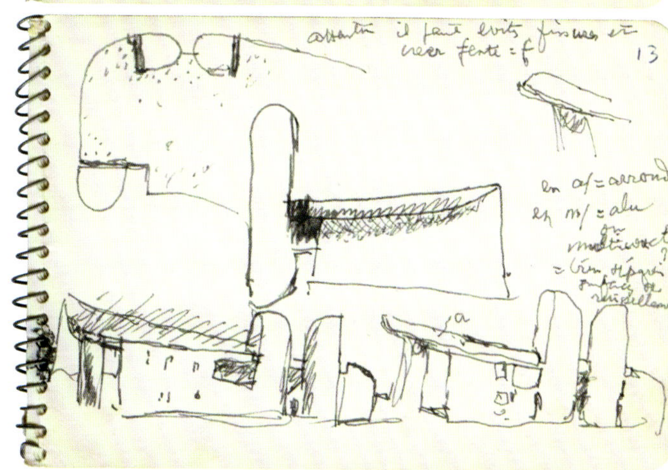

A new form of spirituality: Notre-Dame-du-Haut, Ronchamp, France, 1950–55

Le Corbusier's chapel at Ronchamp, which replaced a traditional chapel that had been bombed during World War II, is a complex composition of simple elements. Walls of varying shape and thickness, a curved roof, and a series of three towers contribute to a richness of visual experience that is reinforced by modulated light and scale. One of the most effective of these visual strategies is a sliver of light that runs along the top of one wall, which makes the massive curved ceiling appear to hover.

This page and opposite. Notebook sketches of Notre-Dame-du-Haut, Ronchamp, 1950–51

Visions of a chapel for Ronchamp, France, 1950–51

With the commission to design the pilgrimage chapel of Notre-Dame-du-Haut in Ronchamp, France, Le Corbusier continued his experiments with "primitivist" architectural forms, which had begun with such projects as the Maison Monol and the Petite Maison de Weekend. Le Corbusier's work in Chandigarh facilitated this exploration of vernacular sources, at a time when he was also turning to mysticism as a source of inspiration.

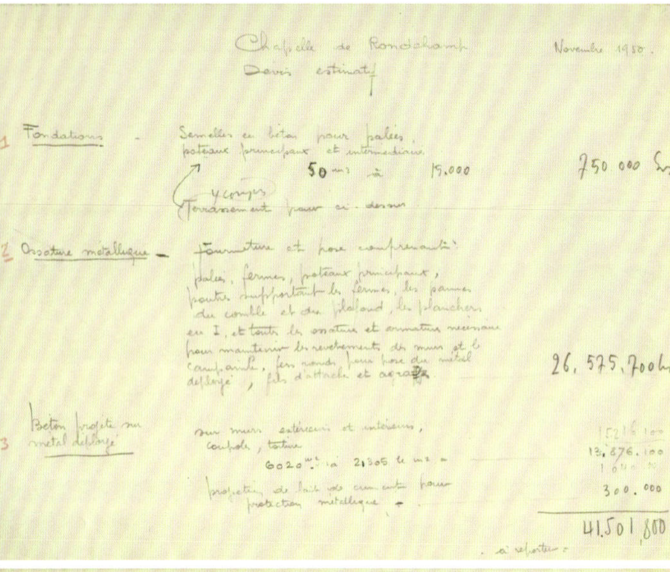

Chapelle de Ronchamp
Devis estimatif
Novembre 1950

1 Fondations — 750 000
2 Ossature métallique — 26.575.700
3 Béton projeté sur métal déployé — 300.000
41.501.800

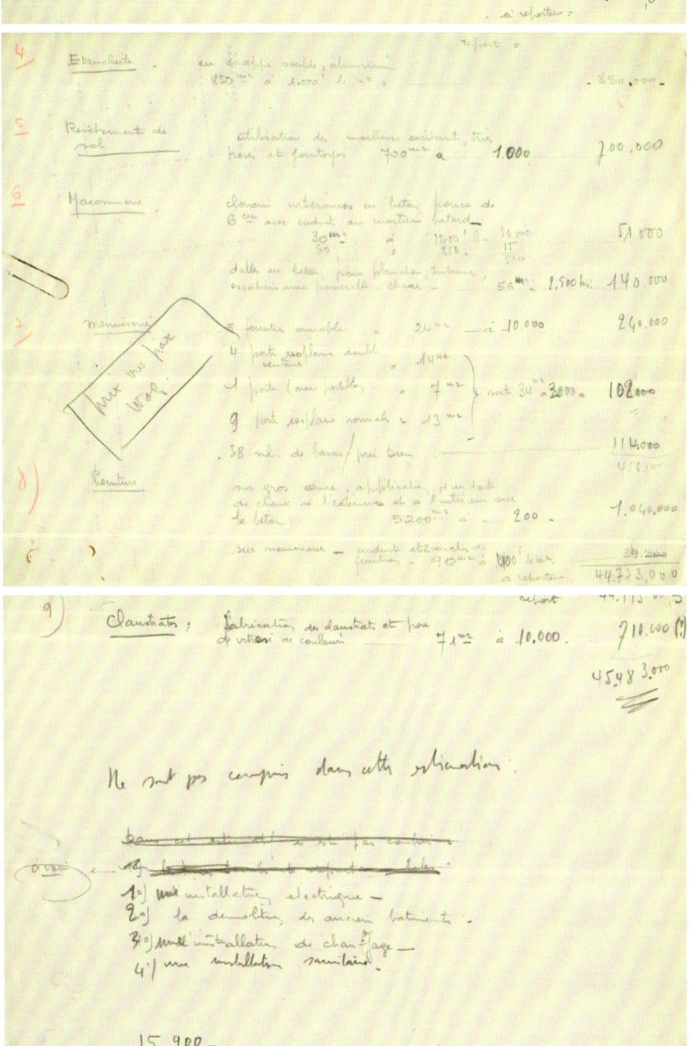

Ne sont pas compris dans cette estimation

1°) une installation électrique —
2°) la démolition des anciens bâtiments —
3°) une installation de chauffage —
4°) une installation sanitaire

15 900 —

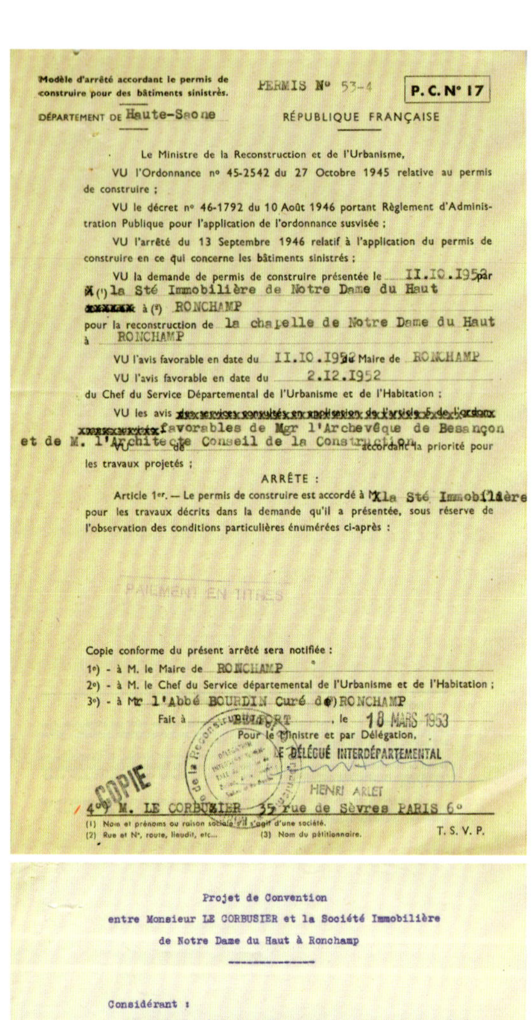

Modèle d'arrêté accordant le permis de construire pour des bâtiments sinistrés.

PERMIS N° 53-4

P. C. N° 17

DÉPARTEMENT DE Haute-Saone

RÉPUBLIQUE FRANÇAISE

Le Ministre de la Reconstruction et de l'Urbanisme,

VU l'Ordonnance n° 45-2542 du 27 Octobre 1945 relative au permis de construire ;

VU le décret n° 46-1792 du 10 Août 1946 portant Règlement d'Administration Publique pour l'application de l'ordonnance susvisée ;

VU l'arrêté du 13 Septembre 1946 relatif à l'application du permis de construire en ce qui concerne les bâtiments sinistrés ;

VU la demande de permis de construire présentée le II.IO.1952 par M (1) la Sté Immobilière de Notre Dame du Haut xxxxxx à (2) RONCHAMP pour la reconstruction de la chapelle de Notre Dame du Haut à RONCHAMP

VU l'avis favorable en date du II.IO.1952 du Maire de RONCHAMP

VU l'avis favorable en date du 2.I2.1952 du Chef du Service Départemental de l'Urbanisme et de l'Habitation ;

VU les avis ~~des services consultés en application de l'article 5 de l'ordonnance~~ favorables de Mgr l'Archevêque de Besançon et de M. l'Architecte Conseil de la Construction ~~VU de~~ accordant la priorité pour les travaux projetés ;

ARRÊTE :

Article 1er. — Le permis de construire est accordé à M. la Sté Immobilière pour les travaux décrits dans la demande qu'il a présentée, sous réserve de l'observation des conditions particulières énumérées ci-après :

PAIEMENT EN TITRES

Copie conforme du présent arrêté sera notifiée :

1°) - à M. le Maire de RONCHAMP

2°) - à M. le Chef du Service départemental de l'Urbanisme et de l'Habitation ;

3°) - à Mr l'Abbé BOURDIN Curé de RONCHAMP

Fait à BELFORT, le 18 MARS 1953

Pour le Ministre et par Délégation,

LE DÉLÉGUÉ INTERDÉPARTEMENTAL

HENRI ARLET

COPIE

4°) M. LE CORBUSIER 35 rue de Sèvres PARIS 6°

(1) Nom et prénoms ou raison sociale s'il s'agit d'une société.
(2) Rue et N°, route, lieudit, etc...
(3) Nom du pétitionnaire.

T. S. V. P.

Projet de Convention

entre Monsieur LE CORBUSIER et la Société Immobilière

de Notre Dame du Haut à Ronchamp

Considérant :

d'une part I/ le caractère religieux et artistique de la Chapelle de Notre Dame du Haut à Ronchamp
2/ le travail qui peut être fait à l'occasion du pélérinage pour la cause d'un art sacré authentique.

d'autre part le financement non commercial de la construction et la charge énorme qui pèse sur la Société Immobilière.

Il est entendu ce qui suit :

I/ Monsieur LE CORBUSIER garde sa vie durant la propriété artistique sur son oeuvre.

2/ Monsieur LE CORBUSIER concède à la Société Immobilière et à elle seule le droit de reproduire et d'autoriser toute reproduction de son oeuvre, qu'il s'agisse de journaux, films ou éditions proprement dites - son droit de regard artistique étant sauf.

3/ A l'exception de celles qui pourraient illustrer ses livres ou propres articles, Monsieur LE CORBUSIER abandonne à la Société Immobilière sur toutes ces reproductions :

x % des revenus de Droits d'Auteurs pendant la période de financement de la construction,

y % dans la suite pour l'entretien et l'aménagement de la chapelle.

4/ La Société Immobilière se donnera pour règle stricte de n'éditer que des objets de bon aloi.

5/ Pour permettre à la Société Immobilière d'atteindre ce but avec plus de sécurité et d'autorité, Monsieur LE CORBUSIER lui cède formellement à son décès la propriété artistique sur la Chapelle avec les droits d'auteurs et de controle y afférents.

Opposite top. Original chapel of Notre-Dame-du-Haut, Ronchamp, France, after bombing by Nazis, October 1944

Opposite, left. Cost estimates for construction of Le Corbusier's Notre-Dame-du-Haut, November 1950

Opposite, top right. Building permit issued by the Ministry of Reconstruction and Town Planning, 18 March 1953

Opposite, bottom right. Agreement between Le Corbusier and the development corporation for Notre-Dame-du-Haut

Right. Schematic site plan

Below. Site plan of Notre-Dame-du-Haut and associated buildings, 15 December 1952

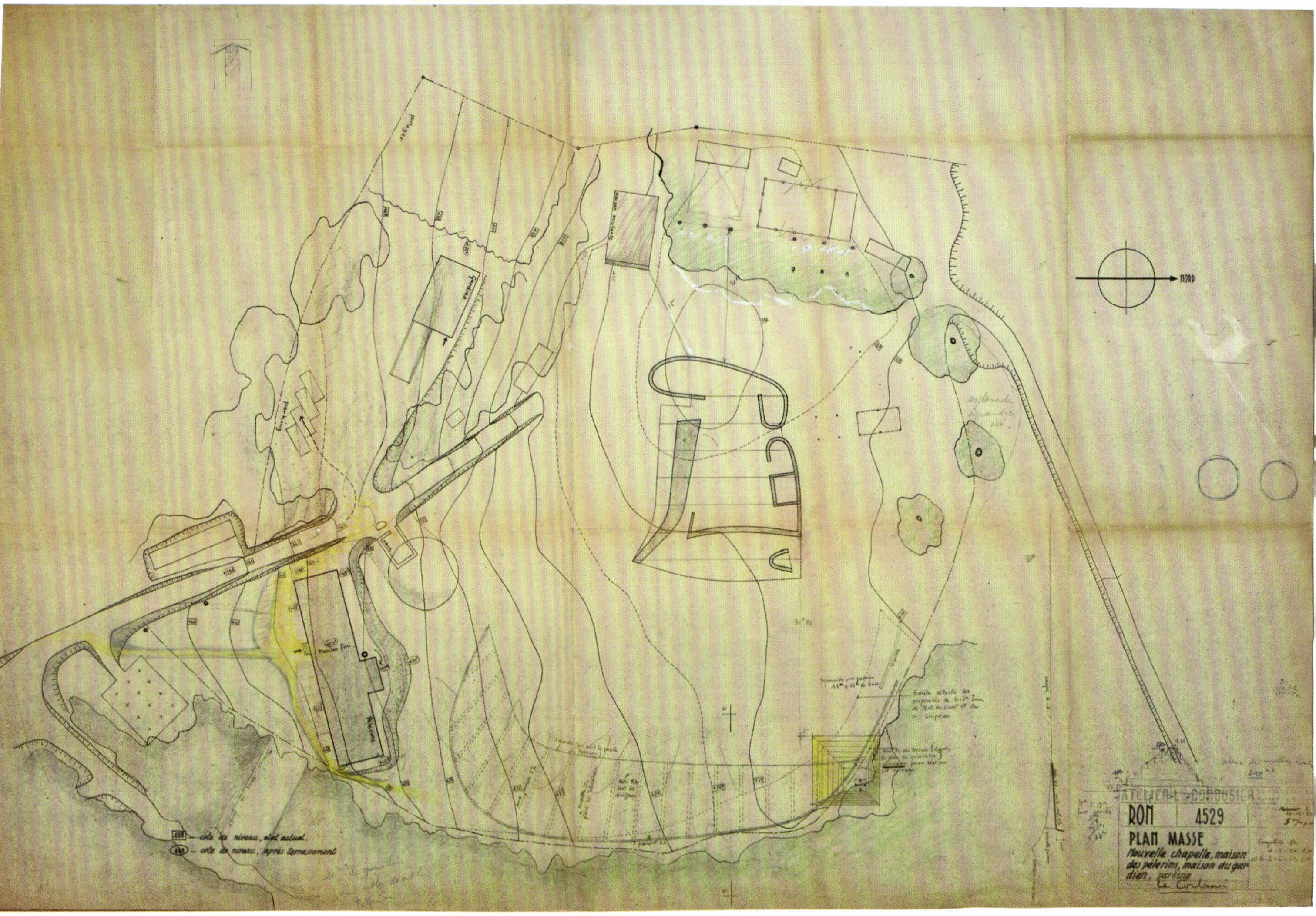

Paris, le I7 Octobre I95I

Monsieur l'Abbé BOURCHIS *Bourdin*
Curé de Ronchamp
RONCHAMP
Haute Saône

Monsieur le Curé,

Je me suis rendu Vendredi dernier, I2 Octobre, sur la colline de Ronchamp avec mon adjoint André Wogensky, c'était le seul jour possible pour moi avant mon départ pour les Indes.

Je vais, bien entendu vous faire parvenir, dès que possible, le devis de la Chapelle afin que vous puissiez en discuter les termes et apporter les éventuels changements que vous jugerez utiles.

J'envoie ces jours-ci à Ronchamp un ingénieur pour l'examen des conditions de mise en chantier.

Partant le 27 pour les Indes il m'était malheureusement impossible de reporter mon passage à Ronchamp mais comme nous allons bientôt entrer dans une phase active je me réjouis à la pensée des occasions fréquentes qui me seront offertes de vous rencontrer.

Je vous prie de croire, Monsieur le Curé, à mes sentiments les plus dévoués.

LE CORBUSIER

P.S. J'ai frappé à la Cure Vendredi mais M. le Vicaire était absent.

Ronchamp ce 21 Janvier 1952

Monsieur l'Architecte 23/1/52

Vous voudrez bien excuser cette simple carte (je suis seul en ce moment) destinée à vous accuser réception de votre bonne lettre du 17 Ct.

Je vous avertis que la démolition de la chapelle actuelle se fera par nos soins, et nous pourrons, d'après vos prescriptions, faire le pavage en pierres de récupération.

Je vous demande de prévoir le permis de construire, démarche qui est de votre ressort s'il vous plaît.

Il faut aussi descendre le prix total de votre chapelle à 40.000.000. ou à peu près en réduisant les proportions sans nuire à l'harmonie de l'édifice. 250 places suffiront largement. Prévoir également une protection parfaitement étanche pour la statue en hiver.

Quelle somme nous sera demandée au comptant?

Enfin je voudrais avoir une dizaine de grandes photos et une centaine de cartes postales de notre future chapelle.

Je vous prie d'agréer, Mr l'Architecte, l'expression de mes sentiments [illegible]

Above, left. Le Corbusier to Father Bourdin, parish priest of Notre-Dame-du-Haut, Ronchamp, 17 October 1951, about the architect's visit to the site on 12 October

Above, right. Front and back of an unsigned note, 23 January 1952, concerning demolition of the damaged original Chapel of Notre-Dame-du-Haut and costs of constructing the new one

Below. Le Corbusier to Father Bourdin, 17 January 1952, outlining terms for the contract

Opposite, top. Four views of plaster models of Notre-Dame-du-Haut

Opposite, bottom. Le Corbusier to Father Bourdin, 31 July 1952, concerning his discussions with Father Couturier about financing for Notre-Dame-du-Haut. Le Corbusier enclosed five photographs of the first model of the new building, but cautioned the priest to use great prudence in showing them to anyone.

Paris, le I7 Janvier I952

Monsieur l'Abbé BOURDIN
Curé de Ronchamp
RONCHAMP
(Haute Saône)

Monsieur le Curé,

L'état d'avancement de nos études concernant la construction de la Chapelle de Ronchamp est actuellement parvenu à un stade où je suis en mesure de vous préciser le montant des dépenses qu'il y a lieu d'envisager en vue de la réalisation de cette construction, telle qu'elle est définie par les plans.

Les prix qui vous sont indiqués ci-dessous et qui ont été étudiés par une entreprise parisienne très sérieuse ont fait l'objet de notre examen et de notre contrôle

Iº) Travaux de démolition.
Ces travaux entraînent une dépense nette et forfaitaire de Deux Millions de Francs.

2º) Travaux de construction.
Les travaux peuvent être exécutés pour le prix net et forfaitaire de 49.800.000 Frs. (Quarante Neuf Millions Huit Cent Mille Francs).
Ce prix comprend tout le travail de fouilles, fondations, gros-oeuvre, étanchéité, menuiserie, vitrerie, peinture, y compris le pavage en pierres de récupération.

Ces prix sont établis sur la base des salaires et du coût des matériaux en vigueur à la date de ce jour et devront être assortis d'une formule de variation tenant compte des fluctuations éventuelles des salaires et du coût des matériaux.

Je serai particulièrement heureux de prendre un contact avec vous et ceux qui, autour de vous, s'intéressent particulièrement au programme, afin de fournir toutes ex-

../...

plications utiles et de tenir compte des observations que vous pourriez être appelés à formuler.

Dès qu'un accord de principe aura été réalisé nous ~~pourrons~~ constituer le dossier ~~peuvant passer les marchés des travaux~~. *devant permettre de passer les marchés de travaux*

Je vous prie d'agréer, Monsieur le Curé, l'expression de mes sentiments les plus dévoués.

LE CORBUSIER

COPIE

Paris, le 3I Juillet 1952

Monsieur l'Abbé BOURDIN
Curé de Ronchamp
R O N C H A M P
Haute Saône

Monsieur le Curé,

J'ai eu la visite du Révérend Père Couturier qui m'a dit le plaisir qu'il avait eu à vous voir et à faire votre connaissance, et il m'a dit également toute sa certitude que notre entreprise se réaliserait harmonieusement grâce à votre précieux concours ainsi qu'à celui de M. Canet.

Le Révérend Père Couturier, le Chanoine Ledeur et moi-même sommes d'avis qu'il ne faut en aucun cas livrer à la presse courante les documents photographiques de la maquette de la chapelle de Ronchamp. Vous n'avez pas idée de ce que certains milieux intéressés possèdent d'armes perfides!

J'ai eu une conversation de matin avec le Ministre de la Reconstruction qui m'a dit avoir remis au Révérend Père Couturier les précisions qui seront utiles à M. Canet et à vous-même pour assurer le financement de la construction.

Je vous envoie inclus 5 photographies I2 x 24 de la première maquette en vous priant d'en faire état avec la plus grande prudence et en ne les montrant qu'à des personnes qui méritent votre confiance comme la mienne également.

Je quitte Paris pour un mois à partir du 2 août. Ce délai vous permettra certainement d'assurer le financement demeuré en suspens, et c'est avec

../...

plaisir que je recevrai de vos nouvelles à mon retour à Paris.

Veuillez agréer, Monsieur le Curé, l'assurance de mes sentiments les meilleurs.

LE CORBUSIER

P.S. J'envoie à M. Canet copie de cette lettre et je lui fournis également une série de 5 photographies.

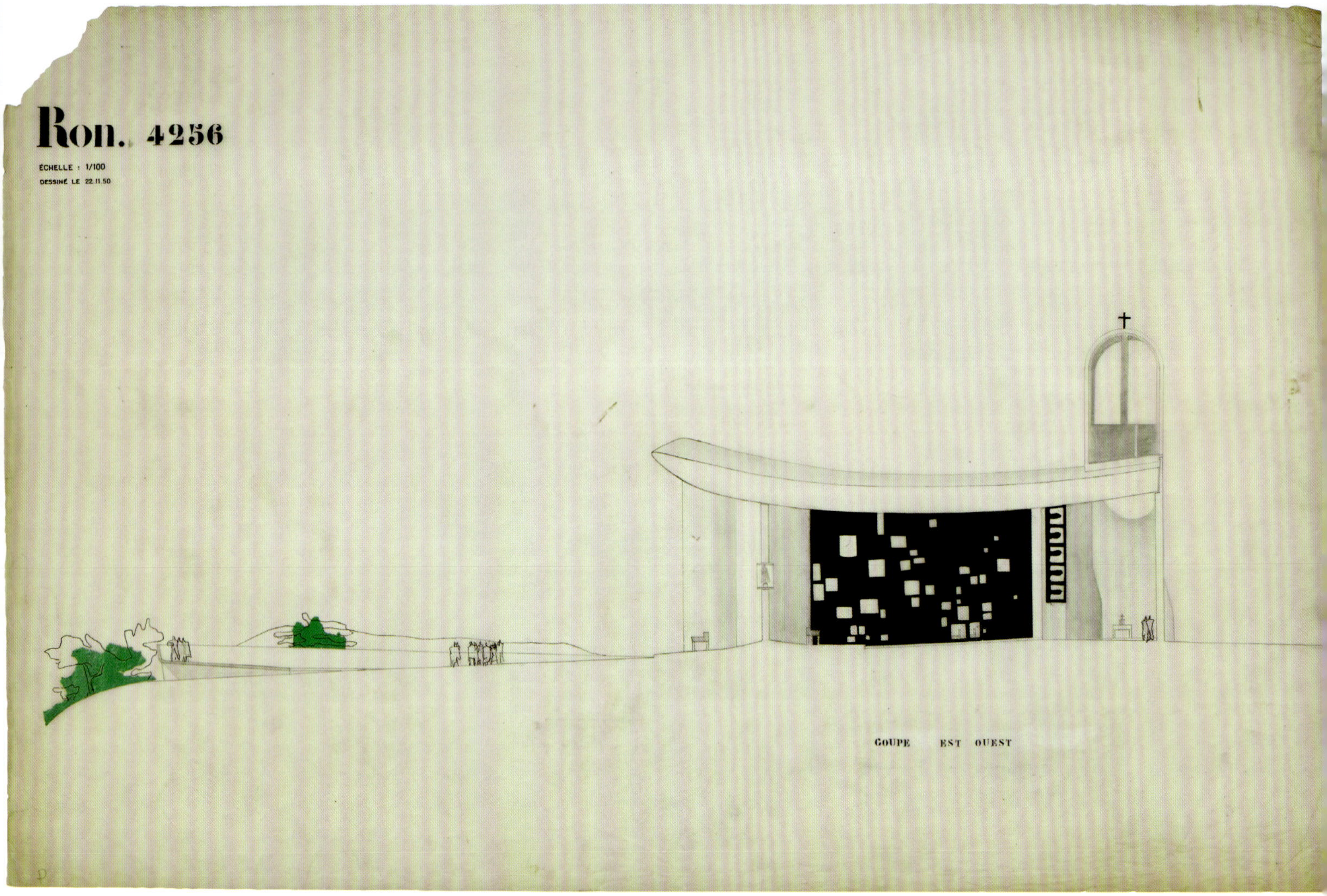

Ron. 4256
ÉCHELLE : 1/100
DESSINÉ LE 22.11.50
COUPE EST OUEST

FAÇADE NORD

ATELIER LE CORBUSIER
Axonometrique
Vue du Nord

Facade Sud

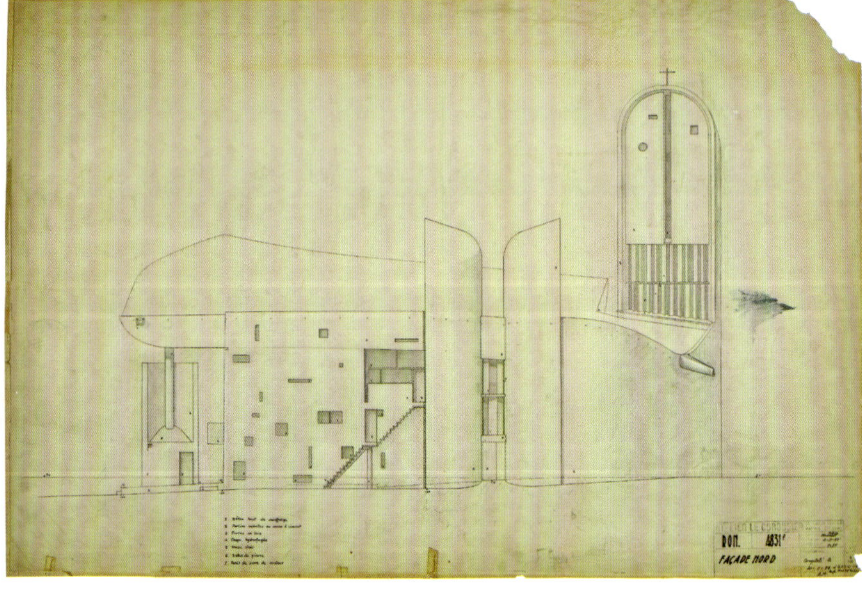

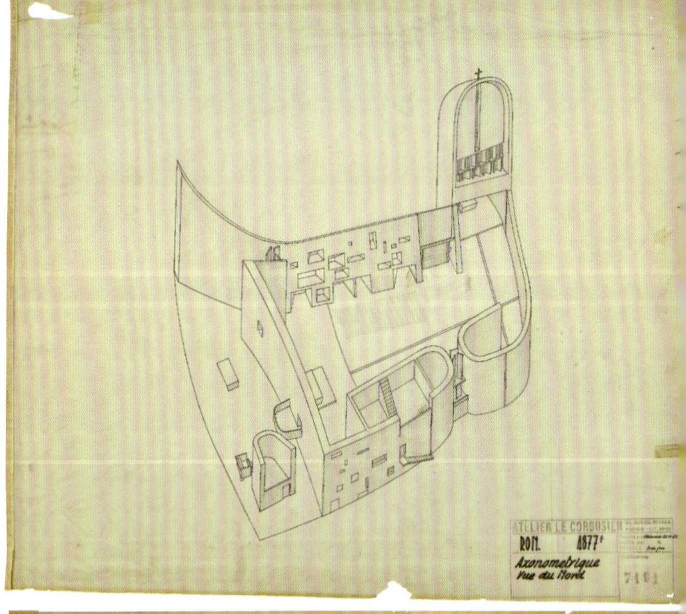

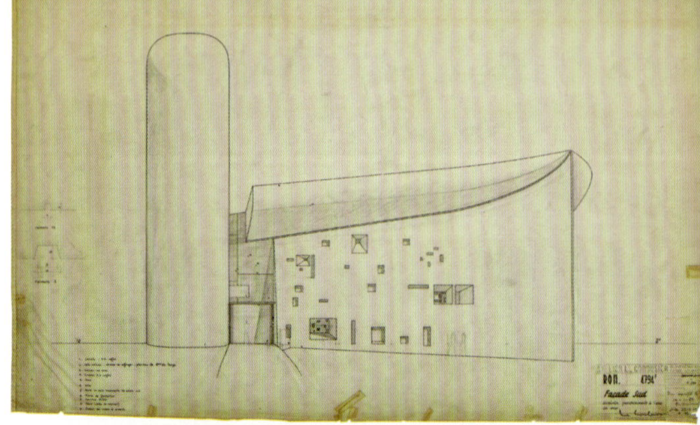

Top. East-west section, 22 November 1950, Notre-Dame-du-Haut, Ronchamp

Above, left. North elevation, 4 November 1953

Above, right. Cutaway axonometric, view from north, 22 November 1953

Right. South elevation, 26 June 1953

Right. Interior elevation of south wall with a figure of the Modulor man

Below. Le Corbusier with a paper study model

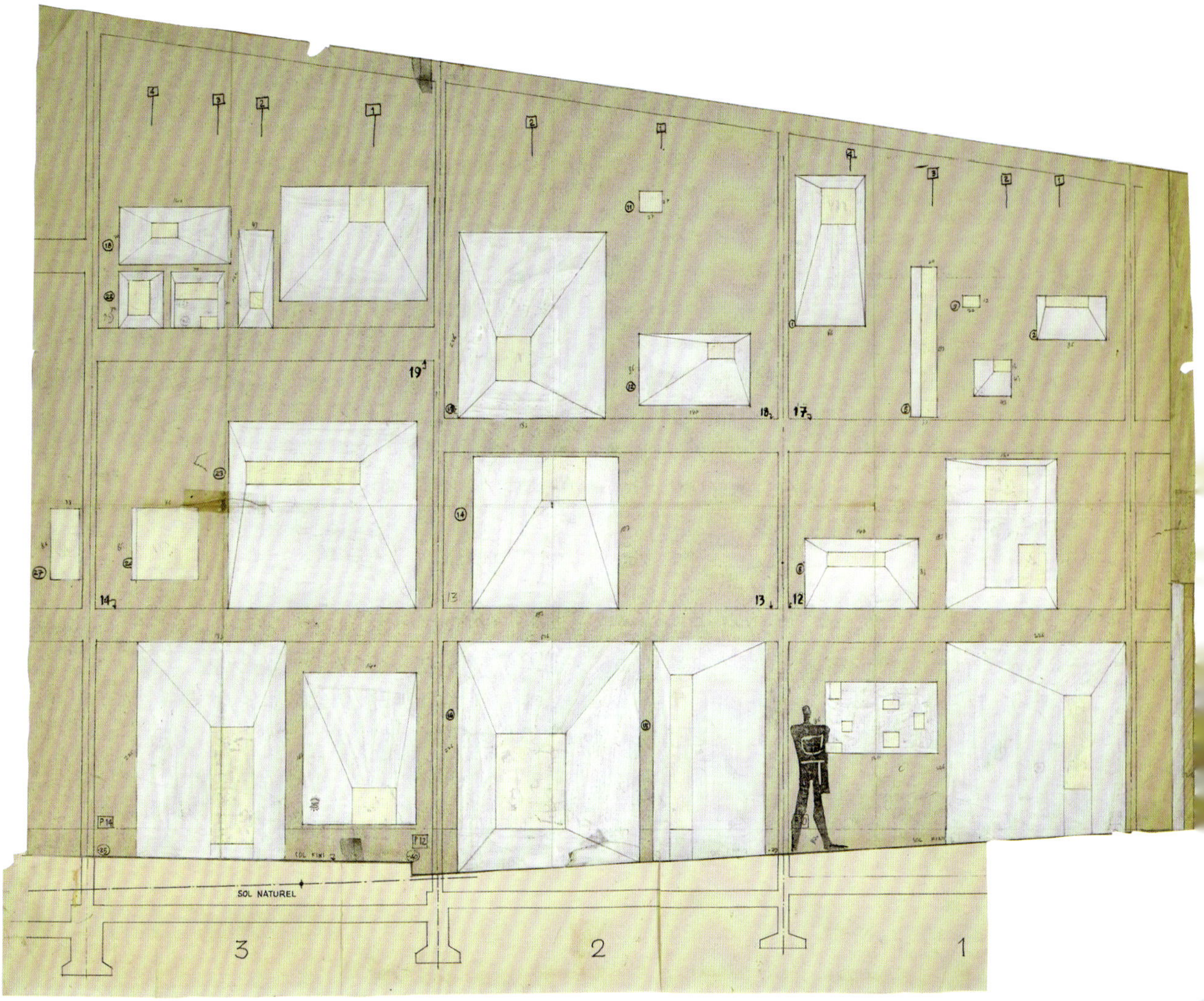

Building the Ronchamp chapel

With the exception of metal joists, virtually all of the structural components of the chapel consisted of sand and cement mixed into concrete on-site; stones and rubble found on the site were used as infill. The curved roof was made of reinforced concrete with a structure based on the same principles as an airplane wing, in a tour de force of engineering.

"Under no circumstances should the press be given photographs of the model of the Ronchamp Chapel. You have no idea of how treacherous and dangerous certain self-interested circles can be... I include with this letter five 12x24 photographs of the first model, requesting that you mention them in the most prudent terms and show them only to people worthy of your trust and mine."

—Letter to Father Bourdin, 31 July 1952

Above. Notre-Dame-du-Haut, Ronchamp, under construction

Opposite, top. Workers on the wooden formwork of the chapel roof

Opposite, bottom. Contact sheet of construction views of Notre-Dame-du-Haut

E-1-68 E-1-164 E-1-182 E-1-160

E-1-73 E-1-141 E-1-119 E-1-87

E-1-67 E-1-12 E-1-176 E-1-70

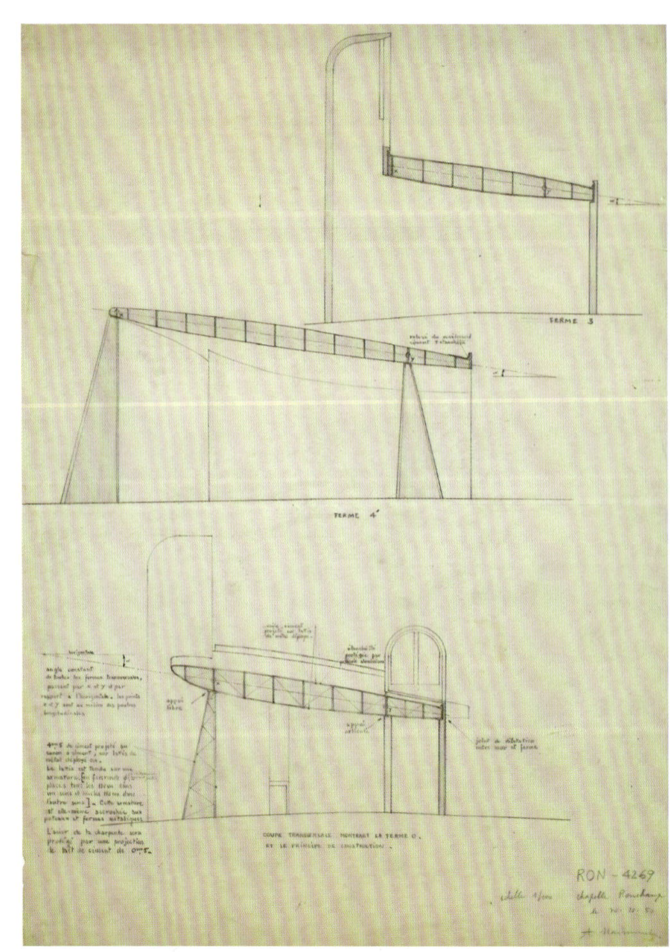
FERME 3
FERME 4
COUPE TRANSVERSALE MONTRANT LA FERME C.
ET LE PRINCIPE DE CONSTRUCTION.
RON - 4269
chapelle Ronchamp

Opposite, top, and bottom left. Notre-Dame-du-Haut, Ronchamp, under construction

Opposite, bottom right. Transverse sections, 20 October 1950, showing girders and principles of construction

Right. Notre-Dame-du-Haut under construction

Below. Unidentified man sitting in the chapel's foundation

Opposite. Aerial views of Notre-Dame-du-Haut, Ronchamp

Top. North and west facades

Left. Outdoor altar built into the east facade

Above. North facade

Left. Le Corbusier at the inauguration of Notre-Dame-du-Haut, Ronchamp, 25 June 1955

Below. View from southeast on inauguration day

Opposite. Southeast corner with a view of the outdoor altar and pulpit

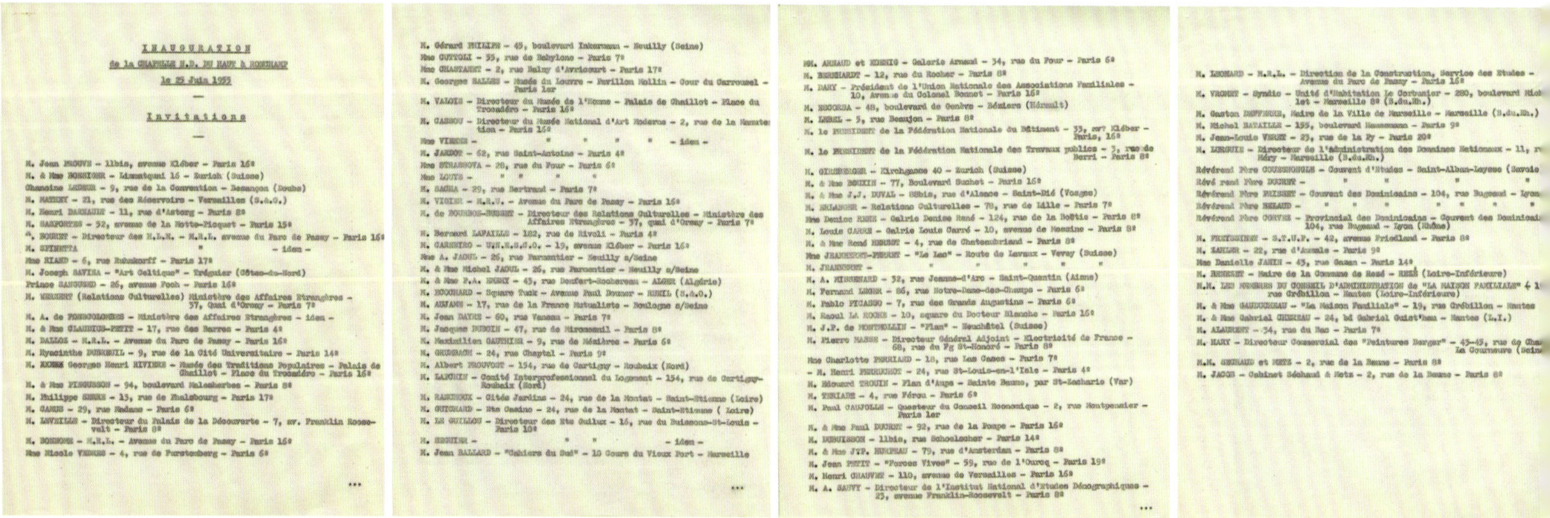

INAUGURATION

de la CHAPELLE N.D. DU HAUT à RONCHAMP

le 25 Juin 1955

—

Invitations

—

M. Jean PROUVE - 11bis, avenue Kléber - Paris 16e
M. & Mme BOESIGER - Limmatquai 16 - Zurich (Suisse)
Chanoine LEDEUR - 9, rue de la Convention - Besançon (Doubs)
M. MATHEY - 21, rue des Réservoirs - Versailles (S.&.O.)
M. Henri DARNAUDET - 11, rue d'Astorg - Paris 8e
M. SASPORTES - 52, avenue de la Motte-Picquet - Paris 15e
M. BONNET - Directeur des H.L.M. - M.R.L. avenue du Parc de Passy - Paris 16e
M. SPINETTA " - idem -
Mme RIAND - 6, rue Ruhmkorff - Paris 17e
M. Joseph SAVINA - "Art Celtique" - Tréguier (Côtes-du-Nord)
Prince SANGUSKO - 26, avenue Foch - Paris 16e
M. WERNERT (Relations Culturelles) Ministère des Affaires Etrangères - 37, Quai d'Orsay - Paris 7e
M. A. de FONSCOLOMBE - Ministère des Affaires Etrangères - idem -
M. & Mme CLAUDIUS-PETIT - 17, rue des Barres - Paris 4e
M. DALLOZ - M.R.L. - Avenue du Parc de Passy - Paris 16e
M. Hyacinthe DUBREUIL - 9, rue de la Cité Universitaire - Paris 14e
M. Georges Henri RIVIERE - Musée des Traditions Populaires - Palais de Chaillot - Place du Trocadéro - Paris 16e
M. & Mme PINGUSSON - 94, boulevard Malesherbes - Paris 8e
M. Philippe SERS - 13, rue de Phalsbourg - Paris 17e
M. CASSE - 29, rue Madame - Paris 6e
M. LEVEILLE - Directeur du Palais de la Découverte - 7, av. Franklin Roosevelt - Paris 8e
M. BONHOMME - M.R.L. - Avenue du Parc de Passy - Paris 16e
Mme Nicole VEDRES - 4, rue de Furstenberg - Paris 6e

...

M. Gérard PHILIPE - 45, boulevard Inkermann - Neuilly (Seine)
Mme CUTTOLI - 55, rue de Babylone - Paris 7e
Mme CHASTANET - 2, rue Balny d'Avricourt - Paris 17e
M. Georges SALLES - Musée du Louvre - Pavillon Mollien - Cour du Carrousel - Paris 1er
M. VALOIS - Directeur du Musée de l'Homme - Palais de Chaillot - Place du Trocadéro - Paris 16e
M. CASSOU - Directeur du Musée National d'Art Moderne - 2, rue de la Manutention - Paris 16e
Mme VIENOT - " " " " - idem -
M. JARDOT - 62, rue Saint-Antoine - Paris 4e
Mme STRASSOVA - 20, rue du Four - Paris 6e
Mme LOUYS - " " " "
M. SACHA - 29, rue Bertrand - Paris 7e
M. VIGIER - M.R.U. - Avenue du Parc de Passy - Paris 16e
M. de BOURBON-BUSSET - Directeur des Relations Culturelles - Ministère des Affaires Etrangères - 37, quai d'Orsay - Paris 7e
M. Bernard LAFAILLE - 182, rue de Rivoli - Paris 4e
M. CARNEIRO - U.N.E.S.C.O. - 19, avenue Kléber - Paris 16e
Mme A. JAOUL - 26, rue Parmentier - Neuilly s/Seine
M. & Mme Michel JAOUL - 26, rue Parmentier - Neuilly s/Seine
M. & Mme P.A. EMERY - 43, rue Denfert-Rochereau - ALGER (Algérie)
M. BOUCHARD - Square Tuck - Avenue Paul Doumer - RUEIL (S.&.O.)
M. AUJAME - 17, rue de la France Mutualiste - Boulogne s/Seine
M. Jean DAYRE - 60, rue Vaneau - Paris 7e
M. Jacques DUBOIS - 47, rue de Miromesnil - Paris 8e
M. Maximilien GAUTHIER - 9, rue de Mézières - Paris 6e
M. GRUNBACH - 24, rue Chaptal - Paris 9e
M. Albert PROUVOST - 154, rue de Cartigny - Roubaix (Nord)
M. LAMCHIN - Comité Interprofessionnel du Logement - 154, rue de Cartigny-Roubaix (Nord)
M. RAMBOUX - Cités Jardins - 24, rue de la Montat - Saint-Etienne (Loire)
M. GUICHARD - Sté Casino - 24, rue de la Montat - Saint-Etienne (Loire)
M. LE GUILLOU - Directeur des Ets Guilux - 16, rue du Buisson-St-Louis - Paris 10e
M. SEGUIN - " " - idem -
M. Jean BALLARD - "Cahiers du Sud" - 10 Cours du Vieux Port - Marseille

...

MM. ARNAUD et HOENIG - Galerie Arnaud - 34, rue du Four - Paris 6e
M. BERNHARDT - 12, rue du Rocher - Paris 8e
M. DARY - Président de l'Union Nationale des Associations Familiales - 10, Avenue du Colonel Bonnet - Paris 16e
M. BECCERRA - 48, boulevard de Genève - Béziers (Hérault)
M. LEBEL - 5, rue Beaujon - Paris 8e
M. le PRESIDENT de la Fédération Nationale du Bâtiment - 33, av. Kléber - Paris, 16e
M. le PRESIDENT de la Fédération Nationale des Travaux publics - 3, rue de Berri - Paris 8e
M. GIRSBERGER - Kirchgasse 40 - Zurich (Suisse)
M. & Mme BEZIKIN - 77, Boulevard Suchet - Paris 16e
M. & Mme J.J. DUVAL - 88bis, rue d'Alsace - Saint-Dié (Vosges)
M. ERLANGER - Relations Culturelles - 78, rue de Lille - Paris 7e
Mme Denise RENE - Galrie Denise René - 124, rue de la Boëtie - Paris 8e
M. Louis CARRE - Galrie Louis Carré - 10, avenue de Messine - Paris 8e
M. & Mme René HERBST - 4, rue de Chateaubriand - Paris 8e
Mme JEANNERET-PERRET - "Le Lac" - Route de Lavaux - Vevey (Suisse)
M. JEANNERET - " " " " "
M. A. MISSENARD - 32, rue Jeanne-d'Arc - Saint-Quentin (Aisne)
M. Fernand LEGER - 86, rue Notre-Dame-des-Champs - Paris 6e
M. Pablo PICASSO - 7, rue des Grands Augustins - Paris 6e
M. Raoul LA ROCHE - 10, square du Docteur Blanche - Paris 16e
M. J.P. de MONTMOLLIN - "Plan" - Neuchâtel (Suisse)
M. Pierre MASSE - Directeur Général Adjoint - Electricité de France - 68, rue du Fg St-Honoré - Paris 8e
Mme Charlotte PERRIAND - 18, rue Las Cases - Paris 7e
- M. Henri PERRUCHOT - 24, rue St-Louis-en-l'Isle - Paris 4e
M. Edouard TROUIN - Plan d'Aups - Sainte Baume, par St-Zacharie (Var)
M. TERIADE - 4, rue Férou - Paris 6e
M. Paul CAUJOLLE - Questeur du Conseil Economique - 2, rue Montpensier - Paris 1er
M. & Mme Paul DUCRET - 92, rue de la Pompe - Paris 16e
M. DUBUISSON - 11bis, rue Schoelscher - Paris 14e
M. & Mme J.P. HURPEAU - 79, rue d'Amsterdam - Paris 8e
M. Jean PETIT - "Forces Vives" - 59, rue de l'Ourcq - Paris 19e
M. Henri CHAUVET - 110, avenue de Versailles - Paris 16e
M. A. SAUVY - Directeur de l'Institut National d'Etudes Démographiques - 23, avenue Franklin-Roosevelt - Paris 8e

...

M. LEONARD - M.R.L. - Direction de la Construction, Service des Etudes - Avenue du Parc de Passy - Paris 16e
M. VRONET - Syndic - Unité d'Habitation Le Corbusier - 280, boulevard Michelet - Marseille 8e (B.du.Rh.)
M. Gaston DEFFERRE, Maire de la Ville de Marseille - Marseille (B.du.Rh.)
M. Michel BATAILLE - 155, boulevard Haussmann - Paris 9e
M. Jean-Louis VERET - 23, rue de la Py - Paris 20e
M. LURGUIN - Directeur de l'Administration des Domaines Nationaux - 11, r Méry - Marseille (B.du.Rh.)
Révérend Père COUSSONGLE - Couvent d'Etudes - Saint-Alban-Leysse (Savoie
Révé rend Père DUCROT - " " " "
Révérend Père BRISSET - Couvent des Dominicains - 104, rue Bugeaud - Lyon
Révérend Père BELAUD - " " " " " " "
Révérend Père CORVEZ - Provincial des Dominicains - Couvent des Dominicai 104, rue Bugeaud - Lyon (Rhône)
M. FREYSSINET - S.T.U.P. - 42, avenue Friedland - Paris 8e
M. ZAHLER - 22, rue d'Aumale - Paris 9e
Mme Danielle JANIN - 43, rue Gazan - Paris 14e
M. BERNERT - Maire de la Commune de Rezé - REZÉ (Loire-Inférieure)
M.M. LES MEMBRES DU CONSEIL D'ADMINISTRATION de "LA MAISON FAMILIALE" - 1 rue Crébillon - Nantes (Loire-Inférieure)
M. & Mme GAUDUCHEAU - "La Maison Familiale" - 19, rue Crébillon - Nantes
M. & Mme Gabriel CHEREAU - 24, bd Gabriel Guist'hau - Nantes (L.I.)
M. ALAURENT - 34, rue du Bac - Paris 7e
M. HARY - Directeur Commercial des "Peintures Berger" - 43-45, rue de Cha La Courneuve (Sein
M.M. SECHAUD et METZ - 2, rue de la Baume - Paris 8e
M. JACOB - Cabinet Séchaud & Metz - 2, rue de la Baume - Paris 8e

Top. Open-air Mass at Notre-Dame-du-Haut, Ronchamp, 1957

Above. Le Corbusier's guest list for the inauguration, 25 June 1955

Opposite. Young visitors sitting on the steps to the outdoor pulpit

Left. Le Corbusier with priest at the inauguration of Notre-Dame-du-Haut, Ronchamp, 25 June 1955

Below. Le Corbusier delivering a speech at the inauguration

Opposite. Procession of worshipers

"Everything went off wonderfully at Ronchamp on Saturday—all joy, beauty and spiritual splendor.

Your Corbu was in the place of honor, at the top. Well regarded, liked. Respected. This was a difficult game to play. It's the most revolutionary work of architecture for a long time."

—Letter to his mother, 27 June 1955

"Corbu painted on glass the 2 Ronchamp facades to be inaugurated 25 June. This Saturday am going to a factory near Tours to paint on enamel 2 x 9m2 doors = 18m2. The time spent learning from L'Eplattenier is bearing fruit: I'm really ready for this kind of thing." –Letter to his mother, 15 May 1955

ecorating the hapel

Le Corbusier conceived the chapel's interior as a catacomb-like chamber for contemplation and meditation. To achieve this effect he created an entry sequence that moves from the colorful enameled mural on the large pivoting door into a startlingly dark space furnished with rough-hewn wooden pews and a stone altar. Illumination is deliberately modulated to create otherworldly effects, as in a niche punctuated by pinpoint apertures that evoke the celestial sphere.

Opposite. Le Corbusier with enameled door panels for Notre-Dame-du-Haut, Ronchamp

Right. Design for door, 24 December 1954

Below. Congratulatory note to Le Corbusier from British architects Peter and Alison Smithson, with photograph of the enameled door

Je vous salut Corbu. Peter Smithson et moi aussi Alison Smithson

Above. Le Corbusier in front of the closed enameled door of Notre-Dame-du-Haut, Ronchamp

Right. Door in the open position, 1955

Opposite. Door of Notre-Dame-du-Haut, Ronchamp, open to receive visitors

Top left. The main altar

Top right. View from below into the tower

Middle left. View through the nave toward the main altar

Bottom left. Sketch of the nave viewed from the main altar

Bottom right. View through the nave toward the rear of the chapel

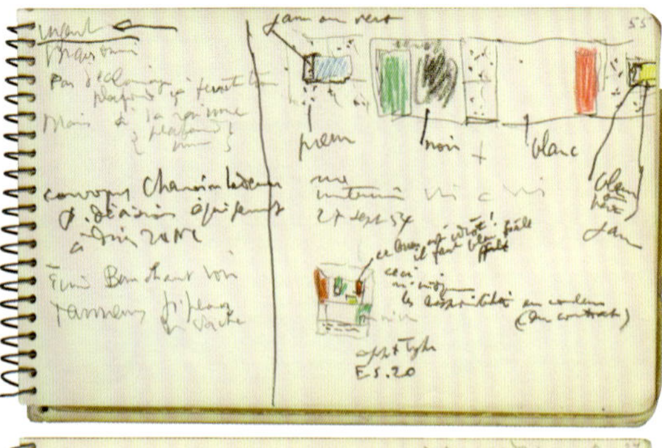

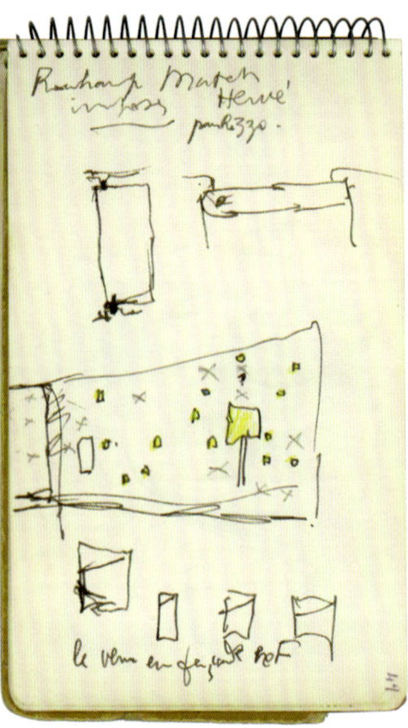

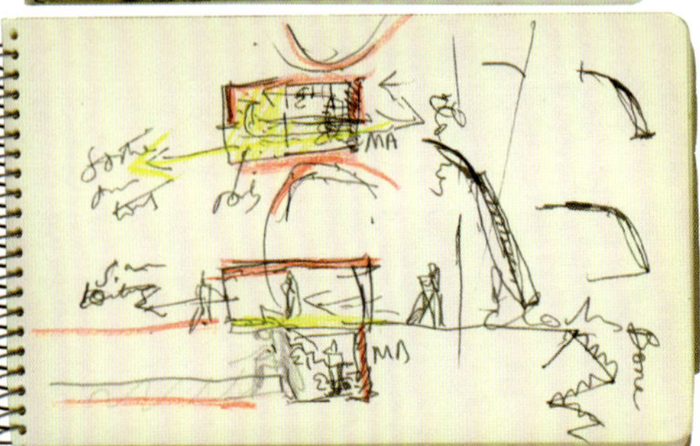

Above. Noteboook studies for the window openings in the south wall, Notre-Dame-du-Haut, Ronchamp

Below. Interior elevation of the south wall, showing patterns for stained glass

Opposite. Interior view of the south wall under construction

Following pages. Interior view of the south wall

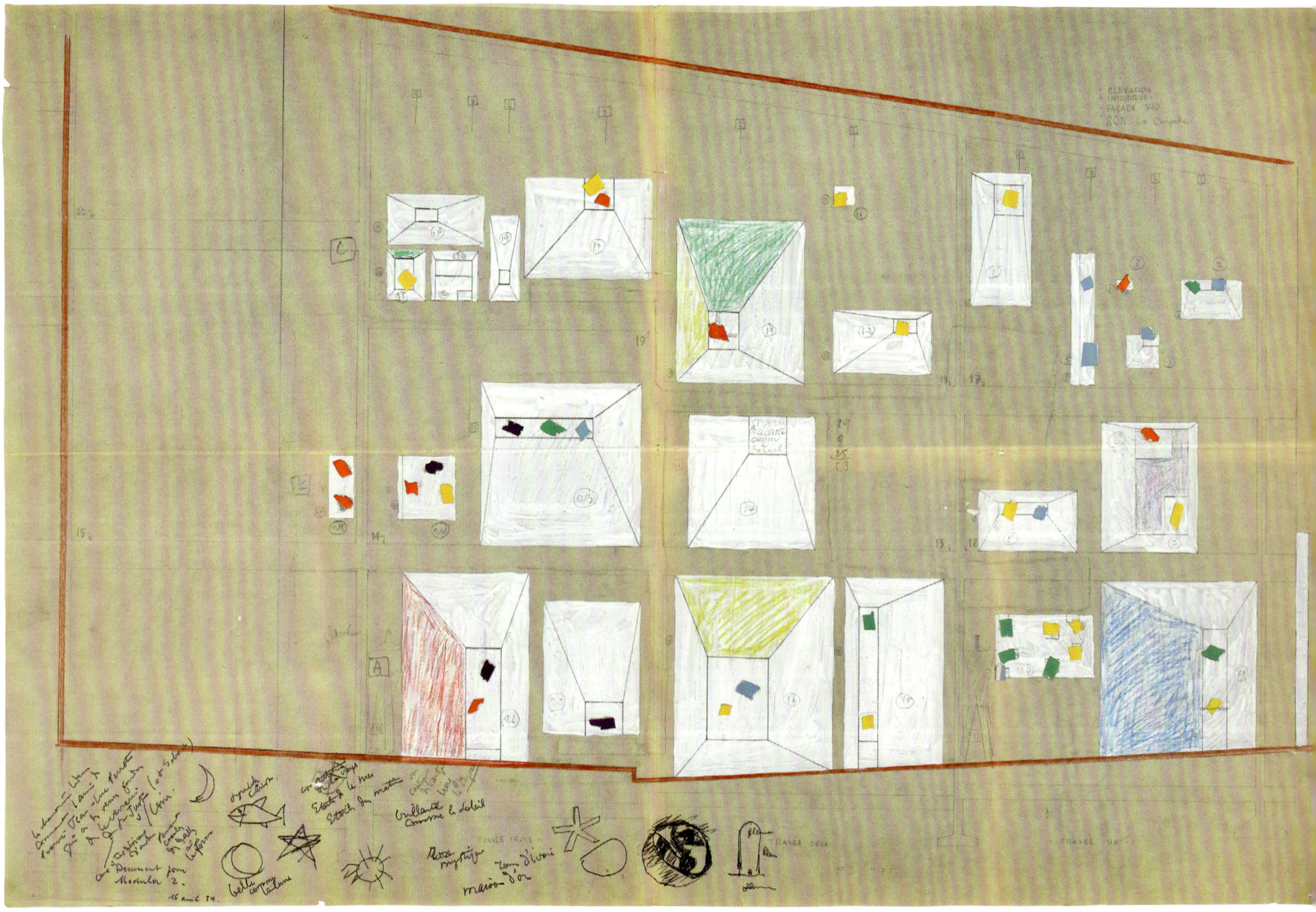

ROUGE
RONCHAMP
CHAPELLE NOTRE-DAME DU HAUT

le 29 Juin 1955

Mr. le Président
de la société immobilière de
Notre Dame du Haut
Ronchamps
Haute Saône

Mr. le Président,

Je ne voudrais pas manquer de vous confirmer la très grande impression que l'inauguration de Notre Dame du Haut a fait sur tous les participants suisses. Il ne faut pas oublier le dîner collectif et je peux vous assurer que l'evènement de Ronchamps et le courage du clergé et de la commune auront une repercussion mondial.

C'est un moment décisive surtout pour tous ceux qui ont travaillé pendant 25 annés dans la "résistance" contre les ennemis de l'architecture contemporaine. Nous avons entendu et vu que même un édifice sacral si tendant vers l'avenir peut êntrer lentement dans la conscience du peuple, qui était pendant des longues années mal informé et séduit par l'autorité, par la presse et tous ceux qui justement "ne veulent pas".

Je me permets de vous écrire ces lignes pas seulement pour vous remercier du charmant accueil, mais comme historien et sécrétaire général des CIAM qui ont veillé depuis un quart de siècle sur le developpement de l'architecture contemporaine.

En dehors de cela j'écris au moment un petit livre sur "L'architecture et la communauté" et je voudrais inserrer, si c'est possible, quelques mots du sermon magnifique de Mr. l'Archevêque de Besançon et si vous avez d'autres documents de l'inauguration pour me faire parvenir je vous serai très reconnaissant.

Acceptez, Monsieur le Président, l'assurance de ma parfaite consideration

S. Giedion
Sécrétaire général

Comunità

LIRE 250 ANNO XI DICEMBRE 1957 SPEDIZIONE IN ABBONAMENTO POSTALE GRUPPO IV n. 55

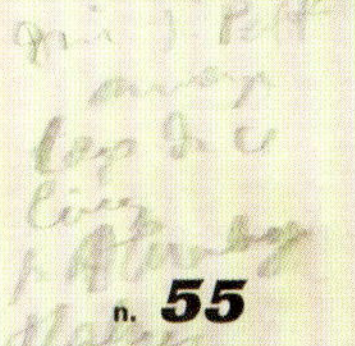

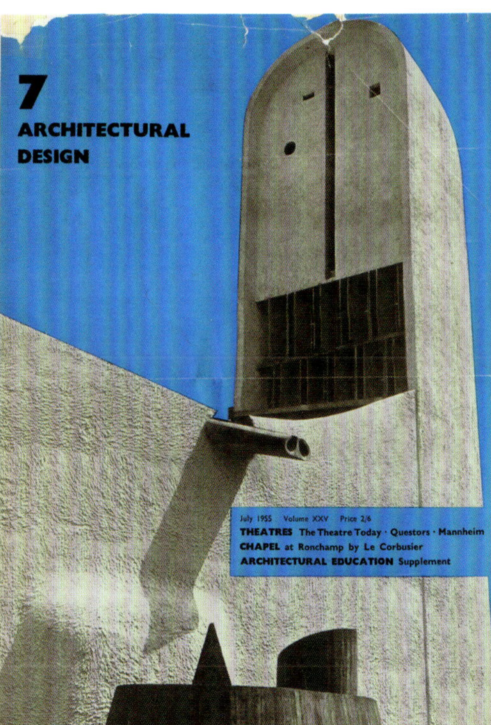

View from the north-west.

CHAPEL

of Notre Dame de Ronchamp

Le Corbusier

Text by M. and H. U. Gasser Photos by René Burri

Ronchamp, a pilgrimage-place, because of its Miraculous Madonna, is situated on the main road between Paris and Basle, on French soil, about a hundred miles from the Swiss frontier. It stands high on top of one of those billowing mountains, characteristic of the countryside and similar to those of Derbyshire. A dominating position, therefore, ideally suited for a sanctuary, ever since mankind built sanctuaries. The original Gothic church was burnt in 1913. In its place a monstrous object was built and gracefully erased by war-time bombs. This produced the opportunity to commission le Corbusier for the design of a church with a credit of a hundred thousand pounds, of which, it is said, the architect spent only £43,500. The church was sanctified on June 25th, 1955.

Site layout. Right: view from the south-east.

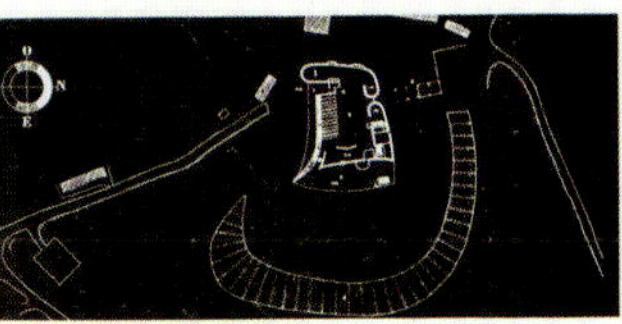

214 • ARCHITECTURAL DESIGN, JULY, 1955

(continued from previous page)

them, the roof rests, or seems to float under the direction of the artist's freely acting hand.

The church is without ornament, as adornment is not needed in a building which is a plastic element in itself. The spiritual interest of the congregation is concentrated on the Miraculous Image and in order to enliven this, the architect has devised a light-effect in the side wall. This he achieved by windows placed at different heights and varying in shape and size, which as in mediæval fortifications, are slit-like on the outside and open up widely within. Light therefore comes into the room from, apparently, all directions. These windows contain different coloured glass-panes, placed in varying angles, to give the glittering, yet mysterious bloom of stained glass windows without resorting to the imitation of an art quite dead since the twelfth century. 'When the cathedrals were white,'—an idea cherished by le Corbusier—is realized here: a gleaming, sparkling sanctuary, glittering in multi-coloured light-effects—and not the grey exteriors which the withered buildings of the Gothic period, and its imitations throughout the ages, present to-day. *(continued opposite)*

Right: the north front with free standing stairs in concrete leading to the conference room at the top and the small rooms in the upper part of the church.
Below: detail of the pool which collects all rain water, a sculpture in concrete.

he response to onchamp

The forms of the chapel troubled some clerics, who found the design too radical a departure from traditional ecclesiastical structures. Moreover, a significant number of secular critics saw architectural heresy in its curving, soaring, asymmetrical walls, roof, and towers, which seemed to express forces closer to the divine than to the structural.

Opposite, top. Le Corbusier with the bishop of Besançon at a meal celebrating the inauguration of Notre-Dame-du-Haut, Ronchamp, 25 June 1955

Opposite, bottom. Le Corbusier signing postcards at the meal

Top left. Sigfried Giedion, secretary general of CIAM, to the president of the chapel's building association, 29 June 1955, congratulating him on the completion of the building: the "decisive moment especially for all those who have worked for 25 years in the 'resistance' against the enemies of contemporary architecture"

Top right. Cover of *Comunità* (Italy), December 1957, featuring the article "Ronchamp" by Le Corbusier

Above. Cover and interior pages of *Architectural Design*, July 1955, with the article "Chapel of Notre Dame de Ronchamp: Le Corbusier" by M. and H. U. Gasser, with photographs by René Burri

Pèlerins !

L'accès à la chapelle vous a coûté 1 F. La méthode peut paraître brutale. Cette participation instituée timidement en 1956-57 s'est avéré le moyen le plus pratique et le plus efficace.

Ceux qui avaient pris les risques de rebâtir pour la deuxième fois en 30 ans le sanctuaire de N.-D. du Haut ont pu faire face aux dettes, équiper la colline et préparer l'avenir.

La chapelle, le Centre d'accueil, la maison du chapelain, les installations de l'Abri du Pèlerin, l'électrification, la distribution d'eau, les sanitaires, le parking, l'achat de plus de quatre hectares de terrain, les intérêts des capitaux prêtés... tout a été possible par cette modeste contribution des bonnes volontés.

Acceptez de bon cœur cet effort pour quelques mois encore.

L'Œuvre de Notre-Dame du Haut sera votre œuvre.

N. B. : Nous tenons à préciser que la chapelle n'est ni responsable, ni bénéficiaire des commerces subsistant tout près du sanctuaire.

Le chapelain.

Les conférences des « Amis de l'Art »

L'APPORT DE LE CORBUSIER DANS L'ART SACRÉ

par le R. P. COCAGNAC
directeur de la revue de l'« Art Sacré »

Le corbusier vu par Len.

C'est un entretien amical plutôt qu'une conférence nous dit le R.P. Cocagnac qui précise, mon métier étant de m'occuper de l'art sacré qui m'intéresse et je laisse à d'autres le soin de parler de son apport dans l'architecture.

Mais, parler d'art sacré, entraîne à souligner la décadence qui, à partir du siècle dernier, a particulièrement affecté ce mode d'expression : influence néfaste d'un académisme à bout de souffle, faux intellectualisme, invasion du temple par les marchands et tous ceux enfin qui ont apporté une pacotille qui satisfaisait le clergé et les fidèles. Et pour couronner le tout, « la triste farce qu'on appelle Saint Sulpice ».

En architecture, on a fait appel à tous les esprits de style : faux

re pèlerinage dans l'église de Ronchamp, tentative audacieuse de Le Corbusier.

Pour le renouveau de l'art sacré, a conclu le R.P. Cocagnac, il nous faut des hommes de « bonne volonté », qui, avec le vrai talent, possède l'humilité qualité complémentaire de la compétence.

Si l'on en juge par les monuments relevés depuis la guerre, nous n'en sommes, hélas, pas encore là.

LEN

RÉPUBLIQUE FRANÇAISE

MINISTÈRE DES POSTES ET TÉLÉCOMMUNICATIONS

INValides 78-60 - SEGur 16-40 • 20, AVENUE DE SÉGUR, PARIS-7e

DIRECTION GÉNÉRALE DES POSTES

3e Bureau
n° III B I453/B.211

PARIS, LE 17 DEC 1963

Monsieur LE CORBUSIER
Architecte
35 rue de Sèvres
PARIS 6ème

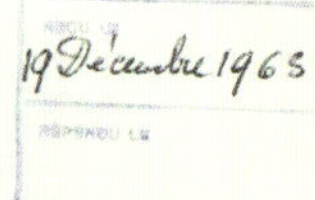

Maître,

M. MARETTE, Ministre des Postes et Télécommunications a été saisi d'une demande tendant à consacrer un timbre-poste à la Chapelle de Notre-Dame du Haut à Ronchamp, conçue et réalisée par vos soins.

M. MARETTE se propose de répondre favorablement à la requête qui lui a été présentée, mais désire au préalable recueillir votre accord étant entendu que votre nom figurera sur le timbre.

Je vous serais donc très obligé de bien vouloir, si ce projet, comme je l'espère, rencontre votre agrément, me retourner après signature l'autorisation ci-jointe.

Je vous prie de croire, Maître, à l'assurance de mes sentiments les meilleurs.

P. le Ministre des Postes et Télécommunications,
Le Directeur Général des Postes,
Le Chef du Bureau des Émissions,

VANET

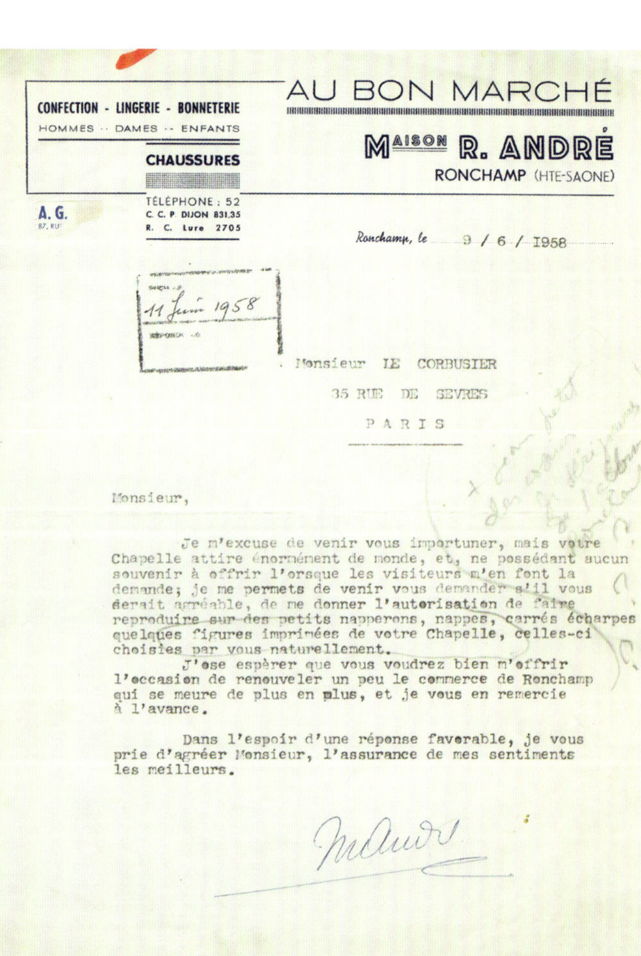

CONFECTION - LINGERIE - BONNETERIE
HOMMES -- DAMES -- ENFANTS
CHAUSSURES

AU BON MARCHÉ
MAISON R. ANDRÉ
RONCHAMP (HTE-SAONE)

A. G.

TÉLÉPHONE : 52
C. C. P. DIJON 831.35
R. C. Lure 2705

Ronchamp, le 9 / 6 / 1958

11 Juin 1958

Monsieur LE CORBUSIER
35 RUE DE SEVRES
PARIS

Monsieur,

Je m'excuse de venir vous importuner, mais votre Chapelle attire énormément de monde, et, ne possédant aucun souvenir à offrir l'orsque les visiteurs m'en font la demande; je me permets de venir vous demander s'il vous serait agréable, de me donner l'autorisation de faire reproduire sur des petits napperons, nappes, carrés écharpes quelques figures imprimées de votre Chapelle, celles-ci choisies par vous naturellement.

J'ose espèrer que vous voudrez bien m'offrir l'occasion de renouveler un peu le commerce de Ronchamp qui se meure de plus en plus, et je vous en remercie à l'avance.

Dans l'espoir d'une réponse favorable, je vous prie d'agréer Monsieur, l'assurance de mes sentiments les meilleurs.

Far left, top. Front and back of card for "pilgrims," announcing a one-franc charge to enter Notre-Dame-du-Haut, Ronchamp

Far left, middle. Postcard of the chapel, with special stamp and "First Day" postmark, 13 June 1964

Left. Clipping from *Ouest France* (Rennes), "The Contribution of Le Corbusier to Sacred Art," by R. P. Cocagnac, with a caricature of the architect and introduction by Len, 4 December 1956

Bottom left. Ministry of Mail and Telecommunications to Le Corbusier, December 1963, announcing approval of a stamp commemorating the opening of the chapel

Bottom right. Proprietor of the store Maison R. André to Le Corbusier, 9 June 1958, seeking approval to produce tablecloths, place mats, and scarves with souvenir images of Notre-Dame-du-Haut, Ronchamp

Opposite. Le Corbusier at Ronchamp, 1955

LE CORBUSIER
RONCHAMP
les carnets de la recherche patiente
2

LE CORBUSIER
Ronchamp
2

LE CORBUSIER
RONCHAMP
VERLAG GERD HATJE
les carnets de la recherche patiente
2

RONCHAMP
2

LE CORBUSIER
RONCHAMP
HATJE VERLAG STUTTGART
les carnets de la recherche patiente
2

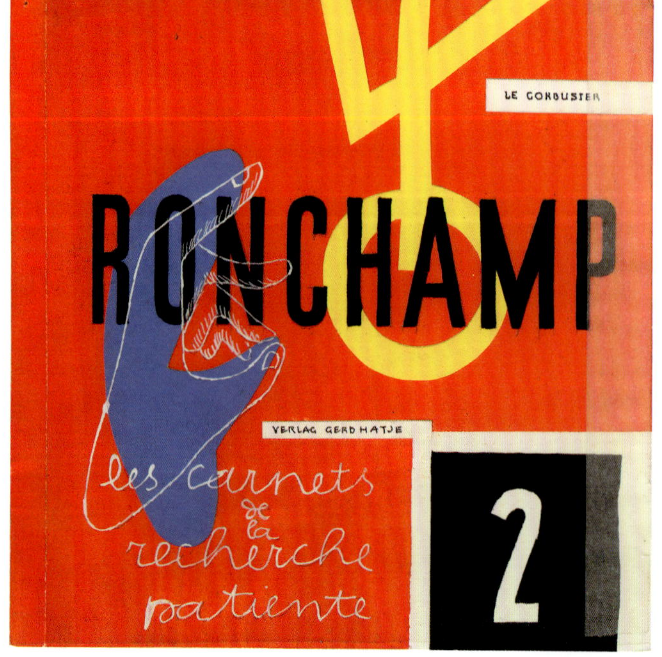
LE CORBUSIER
RONCHAMP
VERLAG GERD HATJE
les carnets de la recherche patiente
2

Opposite. Alternative designs for the cover of Le Corbusier's book *Ronchamp: Les carnets de la recherche patiente* (Ronchamp: The Notebooks of the Patient Research), Hatje Verlag, Stuttgart, 1957. The version at bottom right is the final cover.

This page. Layouts for Le Corbusier's book *Ronchamp*

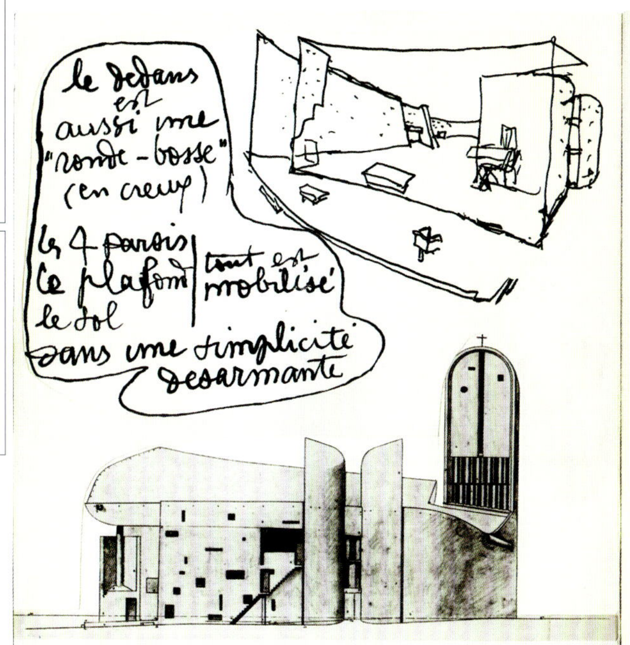

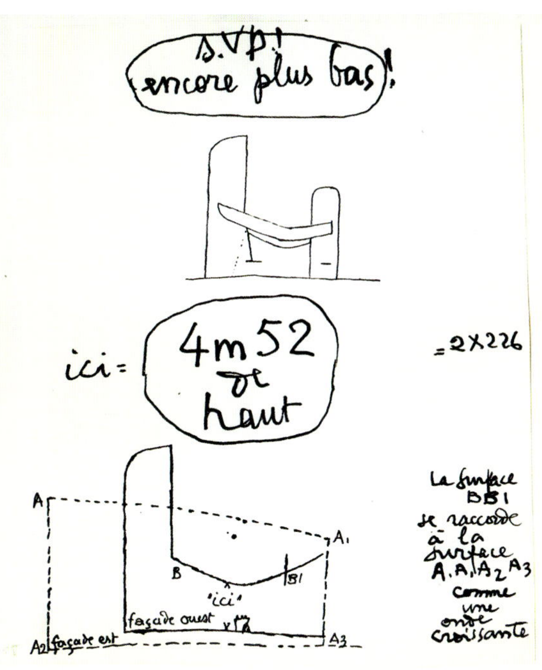

observez le jeu des ombres
jouez le jeu....
Ombres propres, - nettes ou fondues
ombres portées: aiguës
Ombres portées - rigueur du tracé
mais arabesque ou découpage si

ensorcelant! Contrepoint
et fugue Musique
Grande musique!
Essayer de regarder les images
à l'envers, ou tournez-les d'1/4.
Vous découvrirez le jeu!

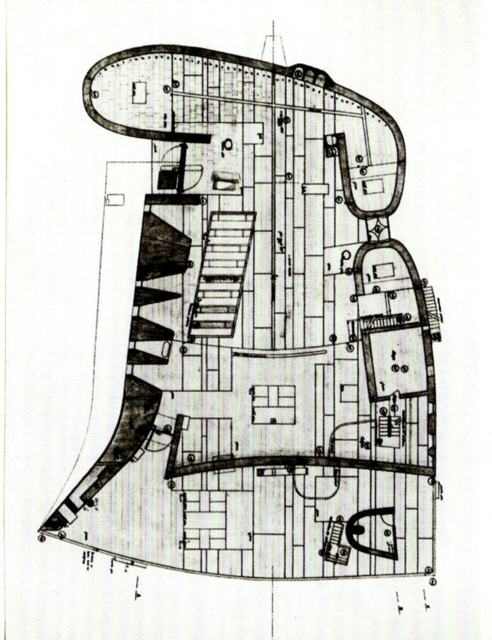

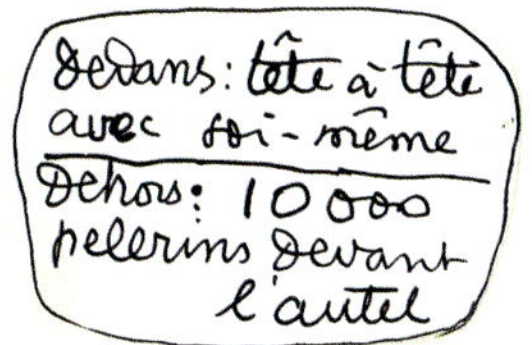

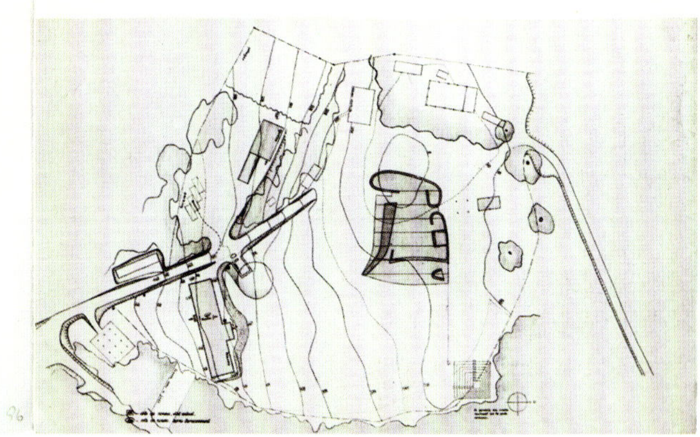

e Corbusier
he painter

Ever since he began painting in 1918, Le Corbusier had spent every available morning at home working in his studio. In 1953 the Musée d'Art Moderne in Paris mounted a retrospective exhibition of his paintings, and four years later the Pierre Matisse Gallery in New York presented his Bull series. The lukewarm popular and critical response to both exhibitions was deeply discouraging to Le Corbusier.

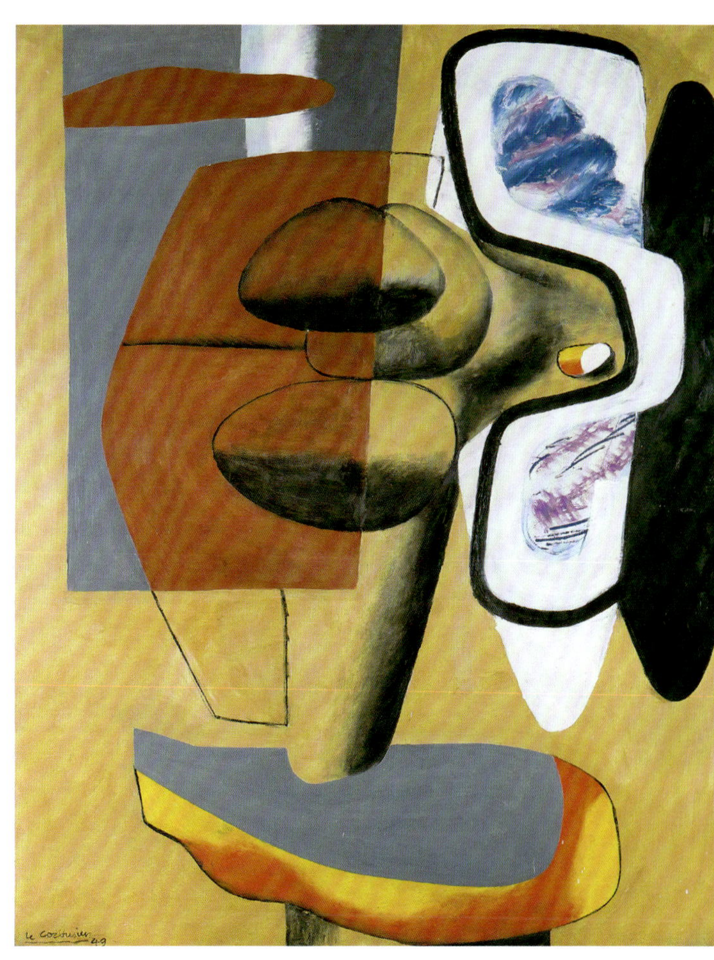

Opposite top, and below. Le Corbusier in the studio at his Paris apartment

Opposite, bottom left. Taureau V (Bull V), 1954

Opposite, bottom right. Taureau II (Bull II), 1928/53

Right. Le grand Ubu (The Large Ubu), 1949

LE CORBUSIER

Paris, le 6 Avril 1957

Monsieur Pierre MATISSE
Pierre Matisse Gallery Corp.
41 East 57th Street
NEW YORK 22, N.Y.

Mon cher Matisse,

J'ai bien reçu votre lettre du 18 mars qui parle :

1º/ de la non vente à Harvard, à Cambridge et au Guggenheim Museum

2º/ de la difficulté d'établir un marché Le Corbusier

3º/ de la clause financière de notre contrat signé le 16 novembre 1955

4º/ de l'Exposition de la Kunsthaus de Zürich et des neuf autres expositions.

Commençons par le nº 3 : mille regrets ! je ne peux pas accepter d'annuler l'une des clauses fondamentales de l'entente que nous avons signée. Ce serait rompre un contrat et enlever toute signification aux accords intervenus.

Par contre, je suis tout à fait disposé à reporter à plus tard la réalisation des paiements prévus dans notre contrat et à porter la somme en "à valoir" pour vous permettre d'attendre le moment où vos efforts et les miens conjugués pourront porter fruit. Je suis sûr que vous accepterez cette manière de faire qui est tout à fait loyale et qui nous permettra de poursuivre un effort dont les lignes suivantes vont s'occuper.

Concernant le point 4 : les circonstances ont provoqué une confusion dans votre esprit. Au début, les organisateurs de l'Exposition de Zürich ne voulaient pas de peinture et j'ai proposé ma baraque militaire. Puis ils ont fait volte-face; ils ont organisé une gigantesque exposition, qui fera dix villes d'Europe et d'Amérique, la préparant par des maquettes, des agrandissements photographiques, etc..., dépensant un budget de 12 millions pour frais d'établissement.

Plus que cela, ils ont exigé que chacune des expositions, à leur ouverture, paient à Le Corbusier 8.000 francs suisses. Total : 80.000 francs suisses dont le premier versement vient d'être effectué.

35, RUE DE SÈVRES - PARIS (6e)
TÉL. : LITTRÉ 99-62

...

- 2 -

De plus encore, une fois récupérés sur les dix expositions les "frais d'établissement", le bénéfice de chacune de ces expositions sera versé à Le Corbusier.

Vous voyez donc que j'ai cessé de tolérer d'être toujours considéré comme honoré par ceux qui veulent bien s'occuper de moi. Il y a un moment donné où celui qui expose honore celui qui l'expose.

Ces dix expositions prendront de deux à trois années. La convention passée avec les promoteurs stipule que les tableaux, tapisseries ou sculptures pourront en cours de tournée être remplacés par l'initiative de L-C. La convention stipule encore que Le Corbusier a le droit de contrôle de la comptabilité de l'Union de Banques Suisses, en ce qui concerne ces expositions.

Vous voyez qu'une attitude ferme a forcé les barrières ou les obstacles qui étaient dressés depuis longtemps contre moi.

Je reçois ce matin une lettre de l'organisation de l'Exposition de Zürich me disant que le comité était très déçu par le nombre trop faible des tableaux que j'avais projeté d'exposer, c'est à dire les tableaux énumérés ci-dessous :

6 Taureaux	Matisse
1 Taureau	24 N.C.
1 Icône 3	24 N.C.
1 Icône 1	Matisse
1 Embrazza	Cassou
1 Ubu G[d]	Cassou
1 Sous un Hangar	Cassou
1 T 20 Fig. Assiettes 1919	Cassou
1 T 20 Fig. 1920	Cassou

soit 14 au total.

Ces MM. ajoutent de plus : "Lors de nos conversations à Paris, il était toujours question d'une trentaine de tableaux (en tenant compte des différentes époques). Il semble que 14 tableaux soit un nombre absolument insuffisant pour une exposition qui devrait donner une impression compréhensive de votre oeuvre. Je vous prie donc de bien vouloir revenir sur cette question et me faire savoir votre décision. En outre, le nombre de sculptures est également très modeste. Dans votre programme de 1955 vous avez fait figurer des dessins originaux, des croquis ainsi que des sketch-books. Il est prévu d'exposer ces documents dans des vitrines fermées".

Venons en à l'autre question, celle du barrage anti-Corbu. Il y a deux barrages. Il y a celui des architectes qui est maintenant

...

- 3 -

renversé. Il y a le second barrage qui est celui des artistes de Montparnasse et qui a été dressé au moment de l'exposition Corbu au Musée National d'Art Moderne, en 1953. En voici l'explication : je suis resté trente années sans exposer, 1923 - 53, à l'exception d'une exposition Louis Carré en 1938. L'Occupation a tout changé du côté Carré. Il avait chez lui la presque totalité de ma peinture. Quand je suis rentré à Paris, en 1942, j'ai appris que mes tableaux avaient émigré chez mon emballeur Robinot. Que s'était-il exactement passé ? La menace de l'Occupant à ce moment-là.

Mais quand dix années plus tard, en 1953, Cassou me demandait d'accepter l'exposition dans son musée; ce fût une grimace unanime chez les artistes. Mes propres amis manifestaient leur humeur. Le silence de trente années avait produit un vide et l'apparition subite de Corbu au Musée d'Art Moderne puis la création de la salle permanente (sous l'initiative exclusive de Cassou et à mon insu) provoqua ce que vous pouvez imaginer : une belle jalousie!

Un autre facteur intervenait : les artistes se sont toujours tenus hors de l'architecture et privés de toute curiosité à l'égard du phénomène impératif qui se saisissait du monde moderne de l'après guerre de 1918. Les architectes, on s'en foutait (et ils le méritaient bien). Mais un jour et d'une manière évidente, autour de Gropius par exemple, on s'aperçut que l'architecte devenait un homme capable de comprendre les arts, d'y être mêlé intimement. Mais à Montparnasse, on resta hors de l'architecture; on fût contre les tracés régulateurs; on se mit à réclamer des murs pour peindre mais on ne s'occupa pas des contacts avec la chose bâtie et on attendait de l'architecte des commandes et non pas des tableaux. La période précédant l'orage est, par exemple, bien illustrée par l'achat que me fit le Musée d'Art Moderne de New York (Barr) de mon septième tableau peint en 1920. Quand j'arrivais en janvier 46, pour la première fois, à New York, je trouvais la salle des Cezanne, Rousseau, Bauchant, Braque, Gris, etc... puis, passant une porte, il y avait "les Demoiselles d'Avignon", le tableau de Corbu de 1920, "Le Grand Déjeuner" de Fernand Léger et, de l'autre côté de la cloison, Mondrian, Van Doesbirg ....

Mais autour de 1950, une revue japonaise publiait l'antichambre du bureau de Zeckendorf à Madison Avenue où, en place d'honneur, et très bien placé par l'architecte chinois de Zeckendorf, se trouvait le tableau Corbu du Musée d'Art Moderne de New York.

x x x

Et petit à petit, tant à Paris, à Montparnasse, qu'à New York, qui suit le mouvement, on crée une véritable vindicte contre Corbu peintre.

Il y eut, en 54, une magnifique exposition à la Kunsthalle

...

- 4 -

de Berne (toute les salles). Puis, l'année suivante, à la Triennale de Milan, à la Villa del Olmo, la même exposition, exposée admirablement dans les superbes salles de cette Villa réservée exclusivement à des manifestations décisives.

En 1956, il y eût l'Exposition Le Corbusier au Musée des Beaux-Arts de Lyon.

Toutes ces expositions avaient des catalogues très sérieusement établis.

En 1948, Frederick S. Wight et James Plaut de l'Institute of Contemporary Art de Boston, faisaient une exposition à la dévotion de Le Corbusier, homme très en vue en 1946 - 47 à New York, très respecté de l'autorité de Washington jusqu'au moment du coup de force organisé dans le second semestre de 47 pour le vol des plans Le Corbusier du Siège de l'U.N.O. sur l'East River. Fait significatif, l'Institute of Contemporary Art de Boston avait établi le programme d'une première exposition à Boston, d'une deuxième à New York, etc... finissant à San Francisco (huit musées de l'U.S.A.) .... Mais la deuxième exposition fila sur San Francisco, bien loin de New York, comme vous le savez, et ne vint jamais dans cette ville. Auparavant, avait eu lieu une exposition "Le Corbusier "honoré" au Radio Building du Rockefeller Center (avec ambassadeurs et personnalités), tableaux et architecture, vers 44 - 45, à la Libération.

En 1945 ou 1946 (?) Sandberg, Directeur du Musée d'Amsterdam, avait fait la première exposition Corbu d'après guerre, peinture comprise.

En 1953, à Londres, l'Institute of Contemporary Arts avait fait une très jolie exposition et la Tate Gallery avait acheté un des tableaux, un "Taureau". (60 Fig.)

Sous la direction de Denise René, le Musée de Helsinki avait acheté un tableau de la même époque. La Confédération Suisse acheta en 54 une tapisserie à Berne. Des collectionneurs, tel que le Dr Friedrich de Zürich qui acheta une grande tapisserie, etc...

Au Japon, en 1955, l'exposition organisée par Charlotte Perriand à Tokio mettait en camaraderie Léger et Corbu. Et Tokio acheta une tapisserie et un tableau, un "Taureau" également.

Kahn Weiler m'estime comme un peintre de second ordre. Il l'ignore, me semble-t-il, ce qui se passe à travers le monde sur le plan de l'immense évolution architecturale et des arts plastiques.

Sont intervenus, après coup, les "abstraits" et particulièrement les "voraces" de l'abstrait disposant et imprimant des masses de papier imprimé et réclamant table rase de tout ce qui est peinture en contact avec une figuration quelconque.

...

- 5 -

Le mot de "mural" fut inventé un jour et mis en pratique par Matisse et Léger chez Rockefeller. Et mon bon ami Fernand, qui me respectait comme architecte, attendait de moi des commandes que je n'ai jamais pu obtenir de mes clients durant toute ma carrière. Il sut manifester pas mal de mauvaise humeur contre mon existence de peintre (c'était son droit, bien entendu).

En 1932, quand j'avais fait le Pavillon Suisse à la Cité Universitaire de Paris, Fueter m'avait sommé de faire contre 50.000 francs suisses une peinture murale de 55 m2 dans la bibliothèque de ce Pavillon. Je refusais, disant :"Vous serez déjà assez embêté avec mon architecture; je ne veux pas faire intervenir un problème d'esthétique murale". Mais en 1948, le même Président Fueter (chic type) me sommait de faire pour 5.000 francs cette même peinture. Ce que j'acceptais et ce que je fis. J'appelle cette peinture "le mural du silence". Il fût bu 50 bouteilles de champagne à l'inauguration et jamais un mot ne fut prononcé ni dans la presse ni ailleurs sur cette peinture que Paul Rosenberg considérait comme seule pouvant être faite par Picasso ou par moi. Teriade l'a considérée également comme un morceau de grande valeur.

J'ai fait pas mal de peintures murales gratuites sur les murs chez divers amis ou au mastroquet. Ceux qui réclamaient des commandes de "murals" n'en ont jamais fait de gratuits sur les murs de leurs amis ou au mastroquet.

Mon cher Matisse, etc, etc....

Je pense que les choses suivent un chemin régulier et compréhensible. Les trente années de silence expliquent tout. Les critiques d'art sont de pauvres types qui, me concernant, ont perdu la piste complètement. A vous de travailler le thème et d'arriver à un résultat.

Donc les dix expositions qui s'ouvrent sous peu peuvent être un prétexte excellent pour vous. Vous avez accepté en principe d'être le vendeur de ces expositions. Avez-vous un programme ? Avez-vous une méthode ? Avez-vous dans chacune des villes qui vous seront désignées un correspondant qui puisse être présent et faire ce qu'il faut ? Il suffira de déclencher une ou deux choses pour que tout s'enclenche. Je vous signale en passant que Khurt Valontin avait vu mon exposition à la Kunsthalle de Berne et avait été profondément frappé. Il avait voulu prendre contact avec moi à sa rentrée à New York. Le pauvre est mort avant de rentrer chez lui.

Pour finir, et pour répondre à la question inquiète des organisateurs de l'Exposition de Zürich, pouvez-vous me faire un programme d'un groupement de toiles comportant une part de ce que vous avez à disposition ? De mon côté, je verrai dans le stock résultant de l'Exposition de Boston de 1948 ce que je pourrai extraire pour établir une chronologie utile (cette Exposition de Boston a été à Boston, San Francisco, Colorado Springs, Saint-Louis, Philadelphie et d'autres villes Cleveland Chicago.

...

- 6 -

que j'oublie). Je n'ai jamais eu une seule ligne sur ces expositions ni un catalogue. Vous voyez que je n'étais pas curieux.

Autre chose encore : les organisateurs des dix expositions à venir réclament des dessins, des croquis, des gouaches. Je dois en avoir pas mal dans la série de l'Exposition de Boston actuellement entreposée quelque part, ici, à Paris. Mais il doit y avoir dans les "superflus" réexpédiés par Boston à Paul Rosenberg, au moment de la formation de l'exposition, un sérieux paquet de dessins très valables. Vous ne m'avez jamais donné nomenclature des tableaux, dessins, gouaches, que Paul Rosenberg, sur ma demande, vous avait remis lors de la conclusion de notre entente. Il faudrait le faire.

Voilà, j'ai fini !!!

Amicalement à vous et réponse S.V.P. le plus vite possible.

Le Corbusier

LE CORBUSIER

je ne fais pas retaper cette lettre, malgré les ratures.

"So you can see that I no longer put up with always being considered as honored by those who want to work with me. There comes a time when he who shows his work honors he who wants it on show."

—Letter to Pierre Matisse, 6 April 1957

Opposite. Installation views of *Le Corbusier: Les Taureaux* (The Bulls) Pierre Matisse Gallery, New York, 1957

Above. Le Corbusier to Pierre Matisse, 6 April 1957, regarding their business arrangements and his exhibitions at other galleries and museums

Le Corbusier the sculptor

Le Corbusier found another creative outlet in sculpture. Starting in 1944, he maintained a longstanding collaboration with Joseph Savina, a Breton cabinetmaker who transformed images from Le Corbusier's paintings into three-dimensional objects, following the architect's detailed instructions.

This page. Le Corbusier working on sculpture with Joseph Savina, 19 March 1963

Opposite. Le Corbusier examining a sculpture

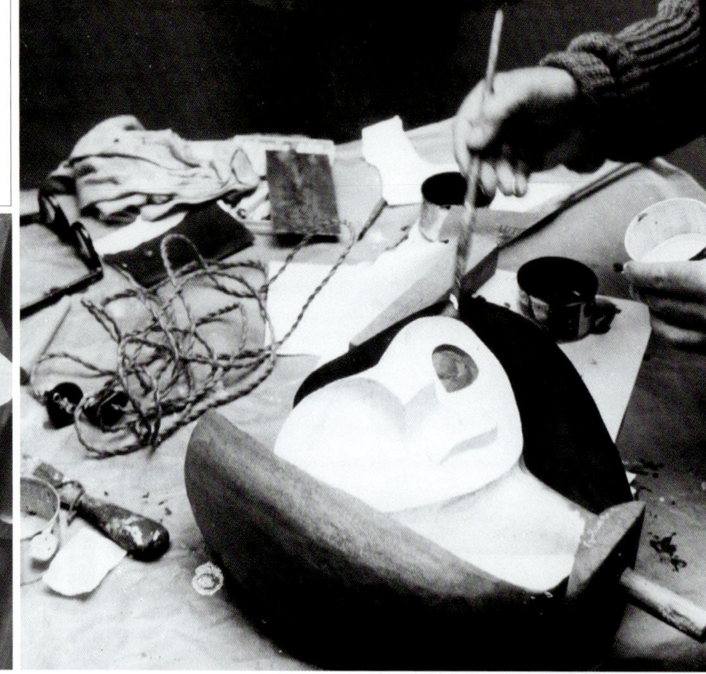

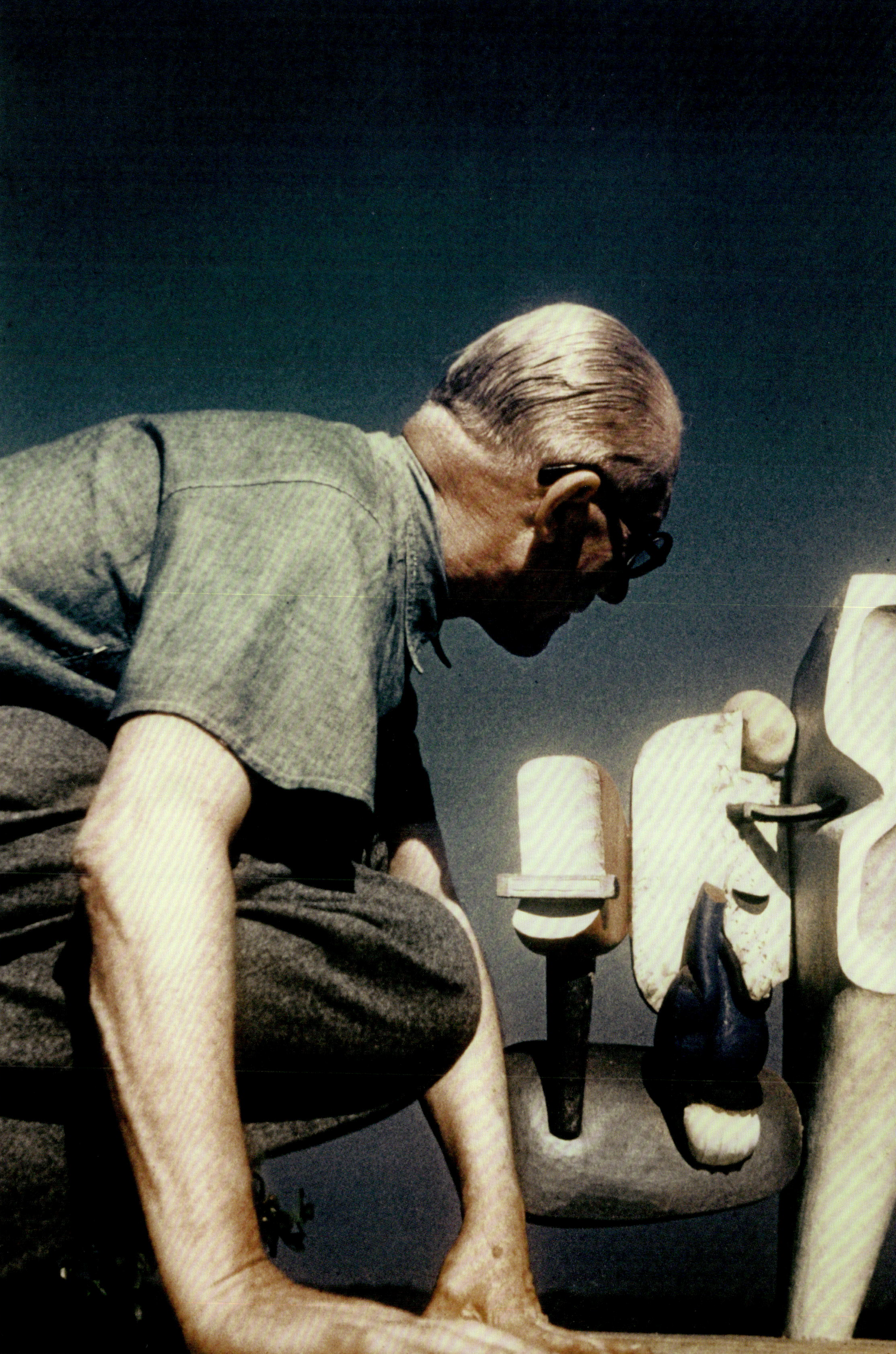

Le Corbusier, créateur célèbre — et encore maudit ? — expose ses œuvres plastiques

POUR le Français moyen, Le Corbusier est l'homme de « l'urbanisme » qui fit à l'époque — 1925 — quelques bruit ; celui des plans de la SDN, du pavillon des Temps nouveaux et, plus récemment, de la Cité Radieuse.

Pourtant l'architecte écrit lui-même qu'une partie de son temps va à la peinture « tremplin essentiel de l'œuvre créatrice qu'il a réalisée dans les domaines de l'organisation bâtie de la société. »

Et il s'élève avec vigueur contre l'opposition arbitraire que l'on fait de ces deux formes d'art :

« La spécialisation, nous déclare-t-il en parcourant la vaste salle du musée d'art moderne où il expose depuis hier ses œuvres plastiques, la spécialisation tue notre temps. Comme si tout ne se tenait pas... Mais d'architecture, toute œuvre d'art en est pleine : un poème, un dessin, une jolie femme... Les mots qui isolent chacune d'elles sont faux — ou peut-être n'ont-ils plus de sens parce que nous ne savons plus [illegible].. Qu'est-ce qu'un architecte ? A coup sûr autre chose qu'un monsieur qui manie le double mètre et le devis. Et la peinture ? On me l'a interdite trente ans durant, et l'on continue... mais le vocabulaire n'est plus en cause : c'est que je ne manie pas le pinceau, la pipe à la bouche et assis dans un fauteuil. »

Rêveur : « J'avais trente et un ans lorsque je fis ma première toile. Je travaillais à heures perdues, la nuit... ». Et rapprochant ces heures précieuses mais dures, de cette autre, si autre qu'il vit actuellement, Le Corbusier ajoute : « Aucune des quatre personnalités officielles que j'attendais ce matin n'est venue... »

« La raison de ma vie, dit-il abruptement, c'est la vision des choses... »

Une quarantaine de toiles, trois sculptures, des plans et des photographies de vastes peintures murales en témoignent. Ils prouvent également, par delà une perception attentive, une puissance créatrice à coup sûr pas assouvie. Et dans ce jaillissement, qui soulèvera encore maints commentaires, il n'y a pas place à la facilité. On y retrouve la rigueur de l'homme habitué à tabler sur le matériau. « Quel que soit le thème choisi, commente-t-il lui-même, il n'y a ici rien d'arbitraire. La spéculation m'est interdite ». C'est évident ; le souci des volumes qui cerne la couleur comme les masses.

Mais dans cette production linéaire l'humain dans sa forme la plus brutale, les viscères, prend pourtant forme d'obsession. On le note avec curiosité.

Mais c'est sur un mot positif que se termine cette visite. Face au décor mural du Cap-Martin, il dit :

« J'aime le mur... »

France RAVENEL.

Voici "la femme" vue par Le Corbusier...

...qui expose, depuis hier, au Musée d'Art moderne, ses anciennes réalisations plastiques (1918-1932) : tableaux et sculptures...

Le Corbusier a « repensé » la femme

LE célèbre architecte Le Corbusier révèle au Musée d'Art moderne le fruit de trente ans de loisirs : ses peintures et ses sculptures. Voici « la femme » telle qu'il la conçoit. Le maître de la cité radieuse a réuni en un seul bloc les principaux « avantages » féminins. Comme on peut s'en rendre compte, si ses appartements sont parfois étroits, il voit large lorsqu'il repense le corps féminin.

AU MUSÉE D'ART MODERNE

Le Corbusier peintre et sculpteur

Urbaniste aussi illustre que discuté, architecte aux vastes conceptions, auteur de la fameuse unité d'habitation que les Marseillais d'abord rebelles ont adoptée, ainsi que de la maquette de la chapelle de Ronchamp, dont la polémique s'est emparée, et bâtisseur de cités radieuses, telle la nouvelle capitale du Penjab, Le Corbusier, alias Jeanneret, nous rappelle aujourd'hui qu'il a manié et manie encore le pinceau et la serpe du tailleur d'images.

C'est avec émotion que nous revoyons ses premières toiles cubistes exposées chez Druet en 1920, où s'affirment ses dons de constructeur ; et que nous contemplons ses toiles récentes, fidèles à sa première discipline, mais où les tons purs éclatent en gammes joyeuses ; ainsi que ses bois polychromes aux robustes volumes.

Le bâtisseur était déjà en puissance dans le peintre, le fresquiste et le sculpteur ; et une unité profonde les relie à l'architecte, ainsi qu'en témoignent les maquettes qui accompagnent et commentent l'œuvre de cet obstiné créateur.

G. JOLY.

Left. French newspaper articles about Le Corbusier's 1953 exhibition at the Musée d'Art Moderne, Paris (clockwise from top left): *Combat*, 18 November 1953; *L'Aurore*, 18 November 1953; and *France Soir*, 21 November 1953

Below, left. Le Corbusier to Joseph Savina, 28 June 1951, about the exhibition of Le Corbusier's work at the Museum of Modern Art, New York, and plans to collaborate on a new sculpture

Below, middle and right. Le Corbusier to Joseph Savina, 1 September 1953, about plans for the forthcoming exhibition of Le Corbusier's work at the Musée d'Art Moderne, Paris

Opposite. Le Corbusier holding a piece of wood

(27)
24

28 juin 5I

Mon cher Savina

Totem

Votre grande sculpture est arrivée, celle d'après le dessin Vézelay I926-42. C'est bien, Savina, fort, nourri ; ilya du coeur et de l'estomac là-dedans ; je parle de la présence du sculpteur. C'est rude, comme je vous l'avais écrit d'après les photos, mais c'est corrigeable. Le Musée d'Art Moderne de N.York, fait en ce moment une expo Corbu (préliminaire) (avant la grande de I952.) La photo agrandie de la sculpture sert d'affiche. J'ai donné votre nom bien entendu.

Je serai au 8e congrès CIAM du 7 au I4 juillet à Londres. Je partirai le 25 juillet pour la côte d'Azur (un mois) - serai à St Dié le 22 juillet.

Il faudrait vous arranger à venir dans un des intervalles, pour travailler la statue. Prendre des outils. J'ai ici Andréou (un des miens du bureau) qui est sculpteur-menuisier, mouleur, d'une habileté de singe. Il pourra nous aider. Programme : il y a un bout de bois à ajouter (vous apporterez un morceau de bois) vous passeriez quelques jours 24 N-C dans la chambred'amis - lit et boustifaille.

Organisez cela, avertissez moi à temps. J'ai préparé deux nouveaux dessins de sculpture polychrome. Et je vous entretiendrai des sculptures sur sable à marée descendante de mon ami Nivola de N York (j'en ai fait moi même aussi).

A l'Atelier 35 Sèvres, boulot gigantesque. Au revoir Savina. Amitiés à Rose à la fifille et à vous, d'Yvonne et de moi.

Voir croquis au dos -----

(34)

Cap Martin Roquebrune
Etoile de mer. 1 sept.53

Mon cher Savina

J'avais emporté ici v. l. du 17 juillet.

Il y eut le congrés CIAM-AIX (19-26 juillet). Ici 10 premiers jours de sommeil total (24 heures). J'étais rentré crevé des Indes.

Content que vous soyez content du Tom V oeuvres complètes. Evidemment si nous pouvions travailler dans la même ville ce serait idéal. Hélas.

L'expo Corbu Novembre 53 sera très importante. Je voudrais exposer 1→ la statue polychrome de 1946-47 (qui est dans mon salon) + celle avec 2→ les clous, monochrome. (Elle fut à Londres à mon expo personnelle de l'Institut d'Art Contemporain, - belle expo). Je crois qu'il faudrait encore disposer de la dernière (démontable il faudrait amener à Paris l'épreuve 2 (dont j'ai des photos) et l'épreuve 3 (à polychromer par moi) ou non ? !) Si vous pouviez l'envoyer à Paris le plus vite possible (fin sept ou début d'octobre, vous pourriez la retoucher avec moi.

Il s'est produit pour Nantes une chose paradoxale et qui montre bien la réalité cruelle des rapports Bâtiment + art majeur voici :

Rentré le 2 juillet des Indes (épuisé) j'avais une semaine de séance à l'UNESCO-Comité des 5. On fermait l'atelier 35 sèvres le 17 juillet. J'avais à revoir les plans des divers chantiers de France + une mise au point formidable pour Chandigarh (2 palais actuellement en construction). Un jour on me dit : "Patron, il faut ce soir même dessiner grandeur nature les "Modulor" du Béton Armé de Nantes, ceux-ci devant être pris dans les coffrages la semaine du 29. Je fis cela en une heure sur le tableau noir. on calqua. On expédia par avion à Barberis à Ajaccio, le menuisier qui a traité Nantes. on ajoute : comme l'Atelier est fermé le 17, le congrès CIAM 19-26 à Aix, Barberis fera parvenir les bois chantournés à Aix, et vous sculpterez çà pendant le congrès. On rectifia : pour que vous ne soyez pas empoisonné par les 300 congressistes CIAM, les bois seront à Marseille, à l'"Unité" Une auto me conduisit 3 matins à Marseille, où, dans"la rue marchande" du 7ème étage, actuellement en installation, je taillai les bois avec le plus adorable des ouvriers menuisiers de Barberis, qui s'en tira admirablement. Ayant quitté Marseille le 27, je n'ai plus entendu parler de tout ceci, sauf que le ferraillage est en plein travail à Rezé. Et voilà comment, les circonstances et les délais implacables font que les bois de coffrage de Nantes-Bretagne, viennent de Corse et ne furent pas taillés par Savina. J'en aurais pleuré. Mais je suis entrainé à l'esprit de sacrifice qui est le lot des vrais du bâtiment et non pas celui de MMr les artistes peintres ou sculpteurs de montparnasse Cote d'Azur.

- Dessins pages 229 + 242 Girsberger Tome V
bas de page milieu — à droite en haut

1 → page 238 Tome V Zurich
2 → p. 245

(34 suite)

p 229. Dessin fait dans l'avion février 1951 avant d'arriver au Caire dans Album I. Je vous enverrai un agrandissement photographique. On finit de tisser une tapisserie à Aubusson sur ce même thème. Je dois avoir plusieurs études de ce thème. Je verrai. Je pense que vous voyez cela en ronde bosse.

p 242. Le thème de droite est beau. En plusieurs pièces mobiles Polychromé. Le socle doit exprimer un paysage (comme par exemple aussi page 242, projet à gauche (en haut). Il faudra que je pousse plus loin l'étude volumétrique (la présence du cadre rectangulaire) le pivotage de diverses pièces etc.)

Deux projets me séduiraient un jour = p 242 en haut, a) à gauche, b) au milieu. Mais il y a là une question de dimensions. Peut-être 140 de haut pour a) (Voyez p. 84, troisième image, servant de face à un bureau)

b) et aussi a) pourraient avoir 2,26 m (Voyez page 84, première image). Mais pour cela, il faudrait avoir une commande dans une maison que je bâtirais (quand) ?

Amitiés d'Y et moi à vous
Rose
+ fille

Corbu

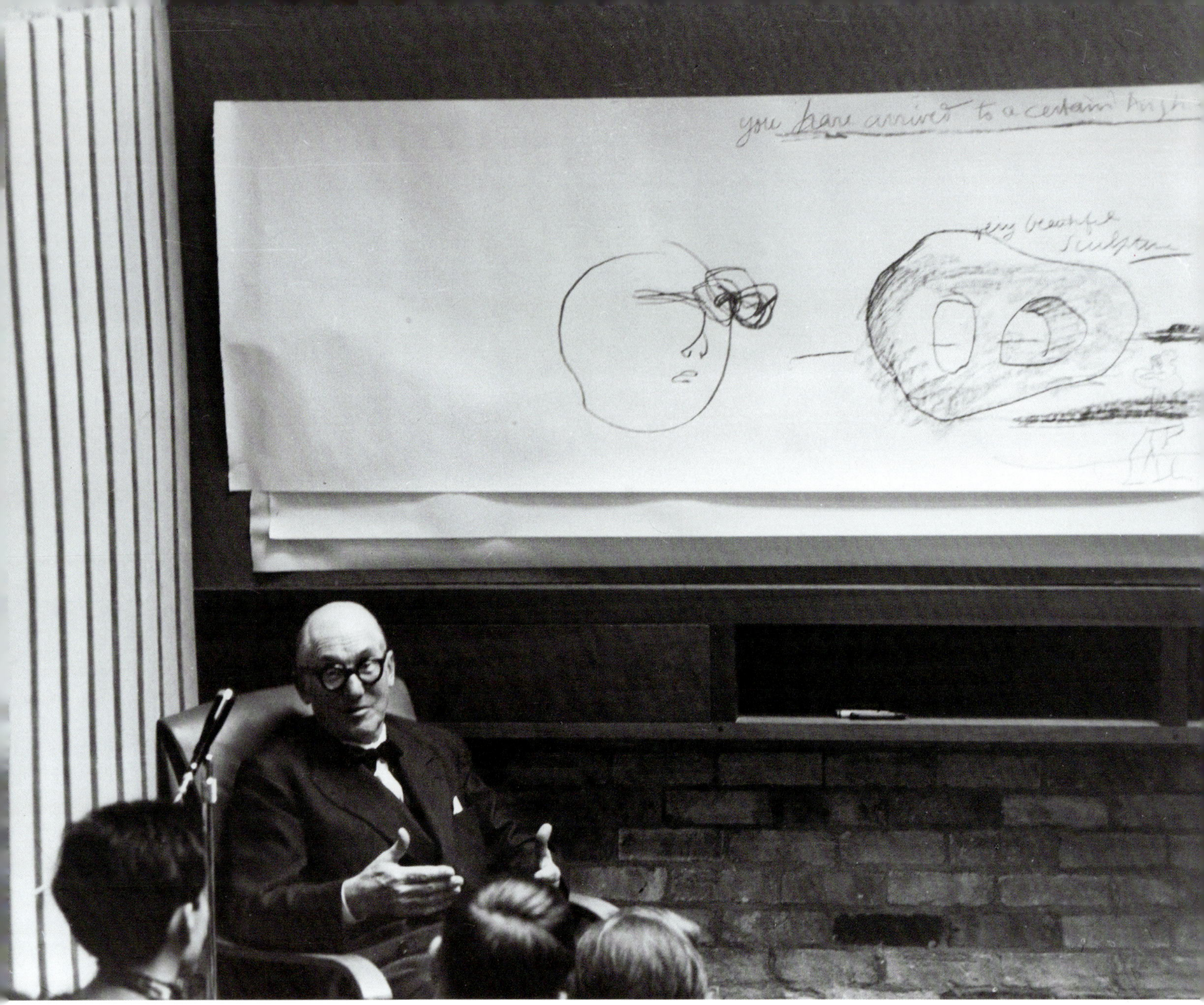

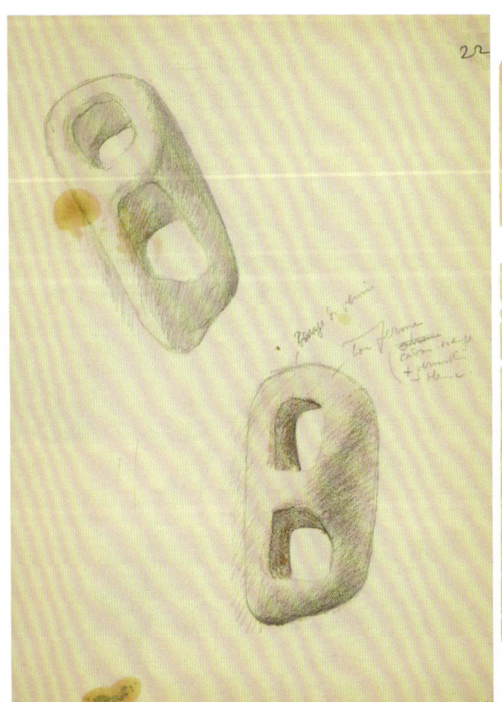

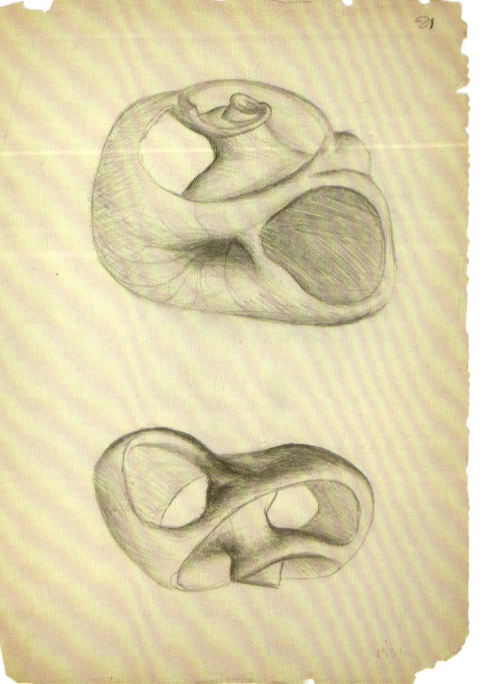

Inspiration from shells, bones, and other natural forms

Le Corbusier famously credited the shape of the chapel roof at Ronchamp to a crab's shell he found on a beach on Long Island, New York. In fact, the architect had collected shells over the course of his entire career. These and other natural forms (such as the bull's horns at Chandigarh) served as a lifelong source of inspiration and a point of departure for much of his later work.

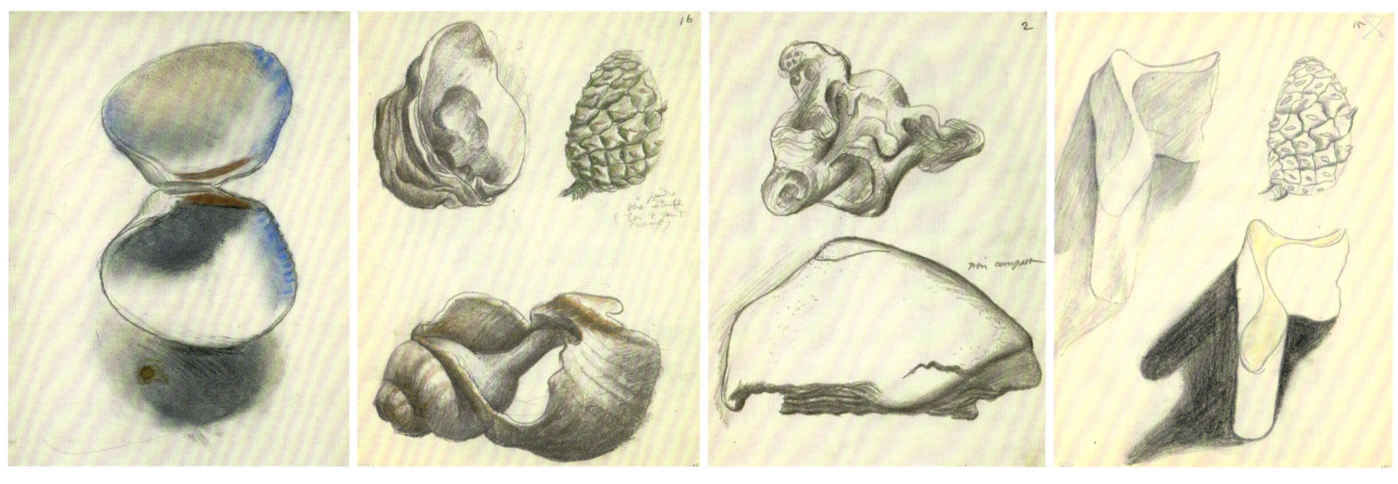

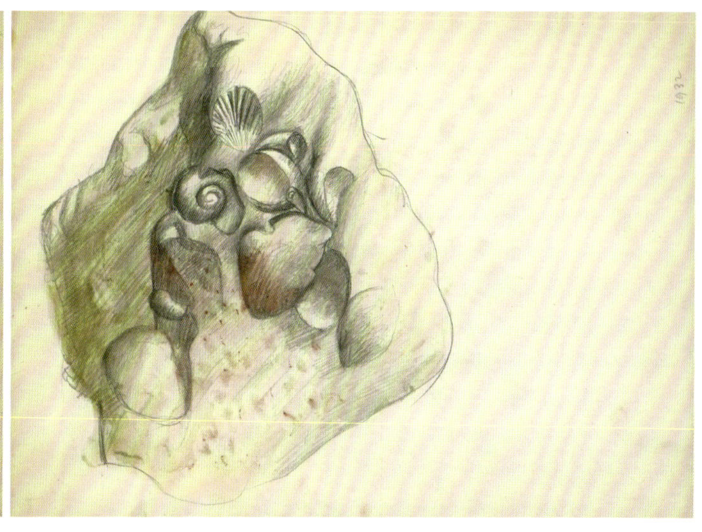

Opposite, top. Le Corbusier in the lecture hall of the School of Architecture, Cambridge University, on the occasion of receiving an honorary doctorate. Behind him is a sketch of a Henry Moore sculpture, 1959.

Opposite bottom, and above. Le Corbusier's sketches of natural forms, from the 1920s and 1930s

Right. Le Corbusier with a shell

Echoes of Val d'Ema: Sainte-Marie-de-La-Tourette, Eveux-sur-l'Arbresle, France, 1953–60

While still designing Notre-Dame-du-Haut at Ronchamp, Le Corbusier was commissioned to design the Dominican monastery of La Tourette, near Lyon, France. The project appealed to his memory of the monastery at Val d'Ema, Italy, the profound impact of which had reverberated through his career. Le Corbusier's concept for La Tourette was shaped by his seminal idea of the box set on *pilotis* and by the use of *béton brut*, as well as by such historical sources as the Cistercian abbey of Le Thoronet, France.

Left. Le Corbusier dining with a Dominican monk

Below. Sketch plans of Sainte-Marie-de-La-Tourette, Eveux-sur-l'Arbresle, 4 August 1953

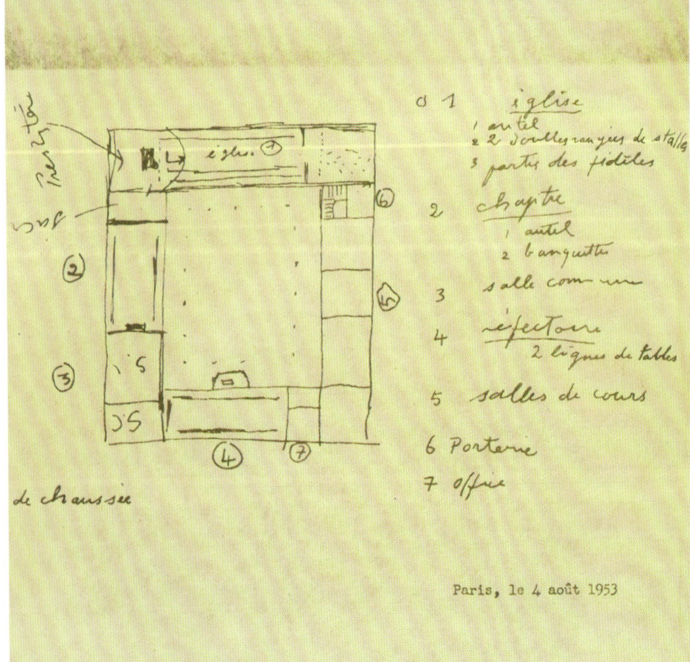

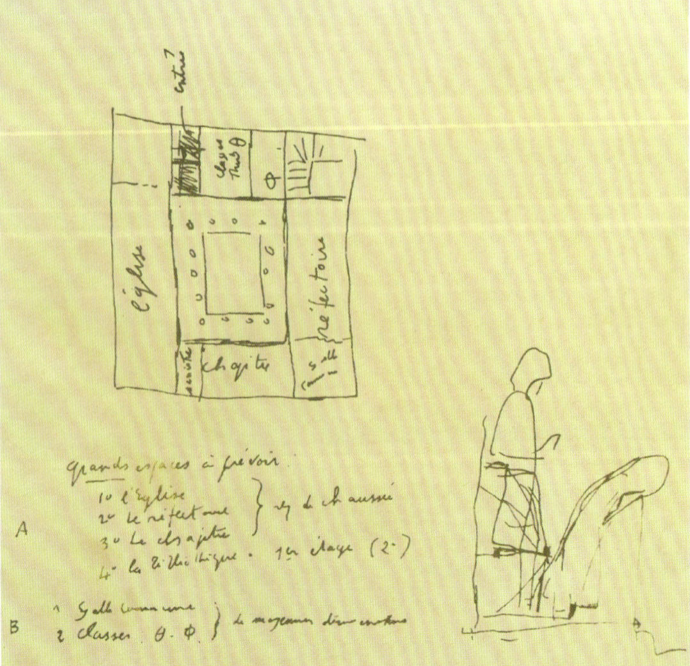

Article sur le R.P. Couturier (ami de LC

L'ART SACRÉ

Revue Mensuelle

Photo Meywald, 1949.

Le Père Couturier

9 - 10

Mai-Juin

L'ART SACRÉ

Revue mensuelle

Le silence

1 - 2

Septembre-Octobre 1954

NOTE pour M. WOGENSCKY dictée par L-C le 9/2/53

Le Père Couturier, qui a obtenu la commande du Couvent près de Lyon, veut me faire visiter l'Abbaye de Toronet (?) qui se trouve derrière Toulon. Il viendrait me retrouver à Marseille le jour où j'y serai et il faudrait frêter une voiture pour aller de Marseille à Toronet et retour.

Conclusion : Envisager une réunion causerie-conférence avec les locataires et préparer auparavant une maquette du bulletin mensuel avec un responsable. Désigner un jeune de l'Atelier qui soit capable de le faire. Je vous laisse préparer cela.

P.S. Préparer la carte des membres avec des compartiments semblables à la carte de l'Ascoral et signaler que le correspondant du bulletin sera 35 rue de Sèvres, mais en tant que Membre de l'Ascoral

L'ART SACRÉ

Revue mensuelle

Ronchamp

RONCHAMP

1-2

Septembre-Octobre 1955

L'ART SACRÉ

Revue mensuelle

En Provence avec Cézanne

7-8

Mars-Avril 1956

Paris, le 11 Mai 1953
LC AW/JD

Révérend Père COUTURIER
"Chalet Sainte-Anne"
S A L A N C H E S
Haute-Savoie

OBJET : Couvent de la Tourette

Mon cher Père,

A la demande du Père Belaud, nous sommes allés, Le Corbusier et moi, visiter le terrain de la Tourette le lundi 4 mai.

Nous avons beaucoup pensé à vous et nous étions bien déçus de ne pas pouvoir faire cette visite en votre compagnie.

Le terrain nous a beaucoup plu. Le Corbusier a décidé de faire d'abord un avant-projet du couvent. Son implantation dans le parc sera ensuite étudiée en fonction de l'avant-projet.

Le Corbusier qui va partir aux Indes la semaine prochaine, veut réfléchir à la question pendant son voyage. Il me demande de lui préparer "une petite étude historique et exacte sur l'abbaye du Thoronet seule, ou sur les couvents de l'époque romane".

Je peux trouver des renseignements dans les livres d'histoire de l'architecture. Mais j'y trouverai surtout une documentation d'ordre architectural. Or, je pense que Le Corbusier désire surtout être documenté sur la vie monastique et sur la façon dont le plan des monastères découle du mode de vie des moines.

J'ai pensé que vous pourriez certainement me dire où je pourrai trouver cette documentation.

En vous adressant tous nos voeux de meilleure santé,

Nous vous prions, Le Corbusier et moi, de croire, mon cher Père, à nos sentiments de sincère amitié.

l'Architecte Adjoint,

A. WOGENSCKY

Révérend Père COUTURIER
Bon-Secours
66, rue des Plantes

PARIS (14e)

Monsieur LE CORBUSIER
35, rue de Sèvres

PARIS (7e)

Paris, le 8 décembre,

Mon cher ami,

Merci de votre lettre. J'ai commencé à faire des croquis, mais l'état de mes mains ne me permet guère d'y joindre les explications nécessaires. Ne vous serait-il pas possible de venir vous-même un de ces jours ? En une heure, je vous aurai donné de vive voix des précisions qui, par lettre n'en finiraient pas et de votre côté, vous pourrez me poser des questions auxquelles je ne pense pas. Venez donc, si vous le pouvez, si-tôt que possible, ce sera mieux.

Je viens de recevoir une bonne lettre du Père BELAUD.

Votre tout dévoué,

M. Couturier

Above. Covers of the journal *L'Art Sacré*, edited by Father Marie-Alain Couturier, Le Corbusier's friend and fellow artist

Top right. Le Corbusier to André Wogenscky, 9 February 1953, making plans for a visit to the monastery at Le Thoronet, France, followed by a meeting with Father Couturier in Marseille

Middle right. André Wogenscky to Father Couturier, 11 May 1953, writing about Le Corbusier's site visit to La Tourette and requesting books on monastic life for Le Corbusier's research

Bottom right. Father Couturier to Le Corbusier, 8 December 1953, requesting a face-to-face meeting to discuss Sainte-Marie-de-La-Tourette

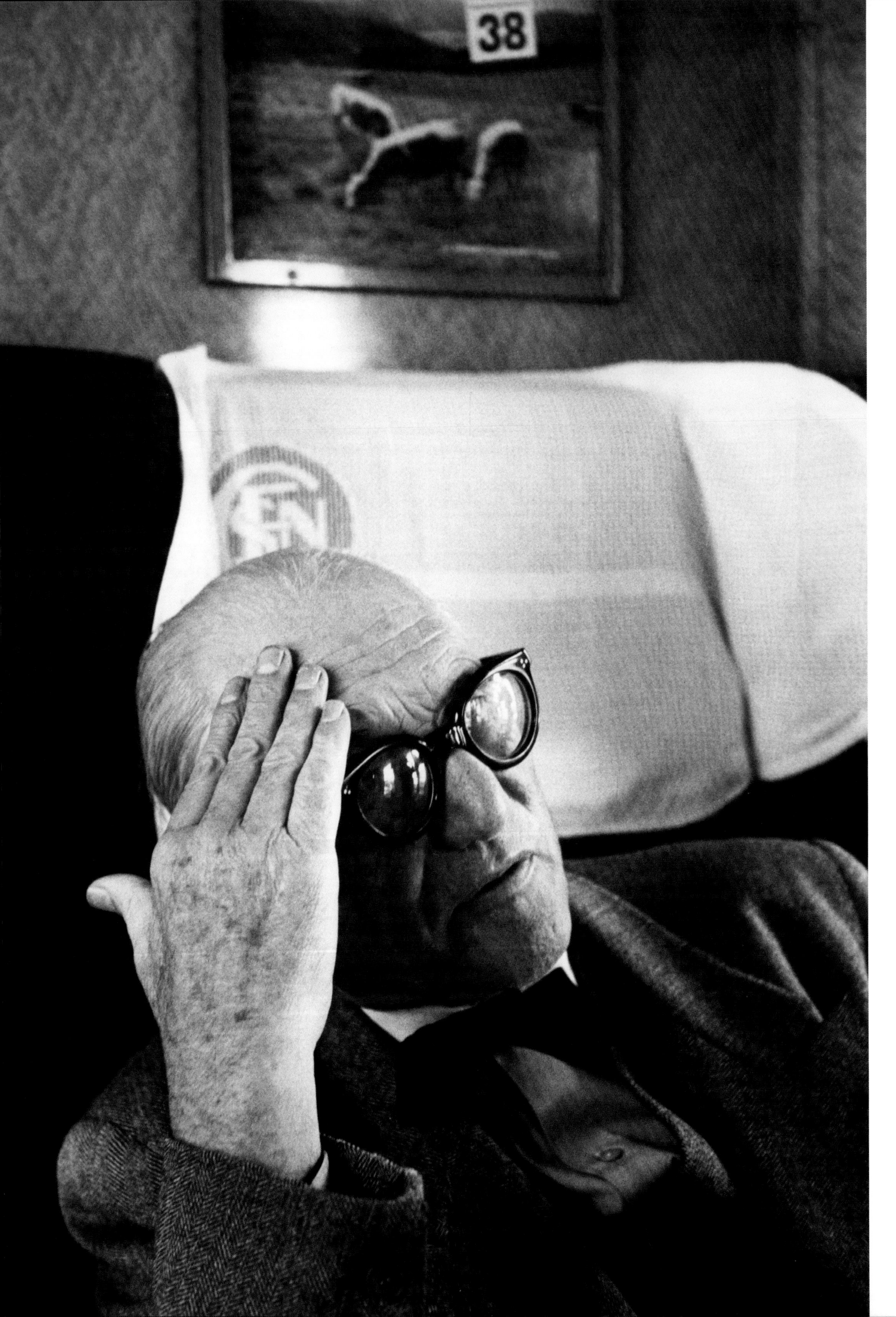
38

Opposite and bottom. Le Corbusier on the train to Sainte-Marie-de-La-Tourette, Eveux-sur-l'Arbresle

Below left. Sketch of the landscape around the monastery site, 4 May 1953

Below right. Perspective sketch of the monastery, 5 May 1953

Following pages. Le Corbusier meeting with the Dominicans of Sainte-Marie-de-La-Tourette

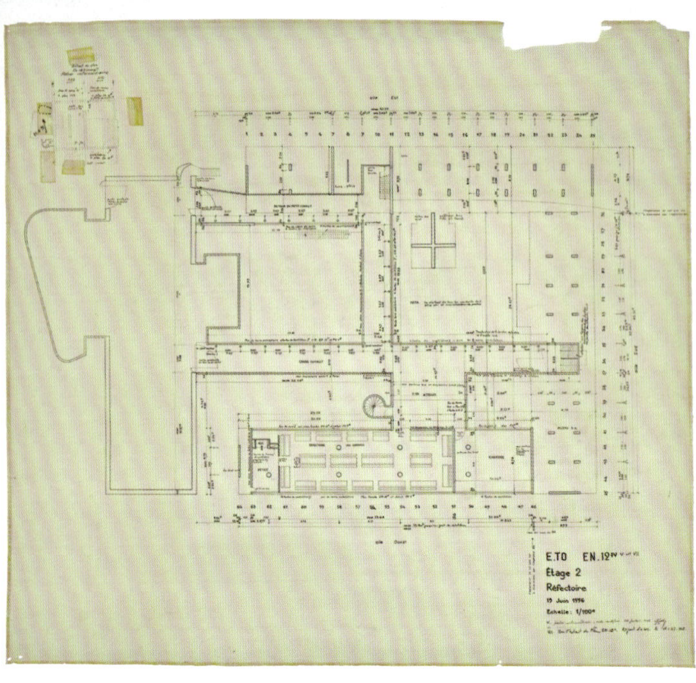

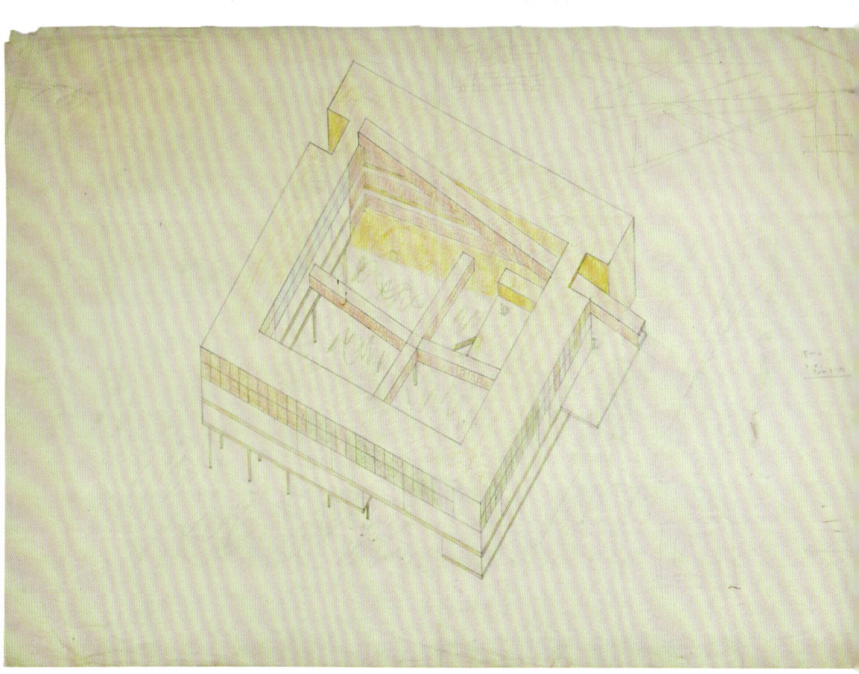

Above left. Plan of the second-floor refectory, Sainte-Marie-de-La-Tourette, Eveux-sur-l'Arbresle, 15 June 1956

Above right. Axonometric

Below and opposite. Le Corbusier with the Dominicans of the monastery

Above. Le Corbusier with Dominicans on the site of Sainte-Marie-de-La-Tourette, Eveux-sur-l'Arbresle

Below. Elevation and transverse and longitudinal sections through the monastery courtyard

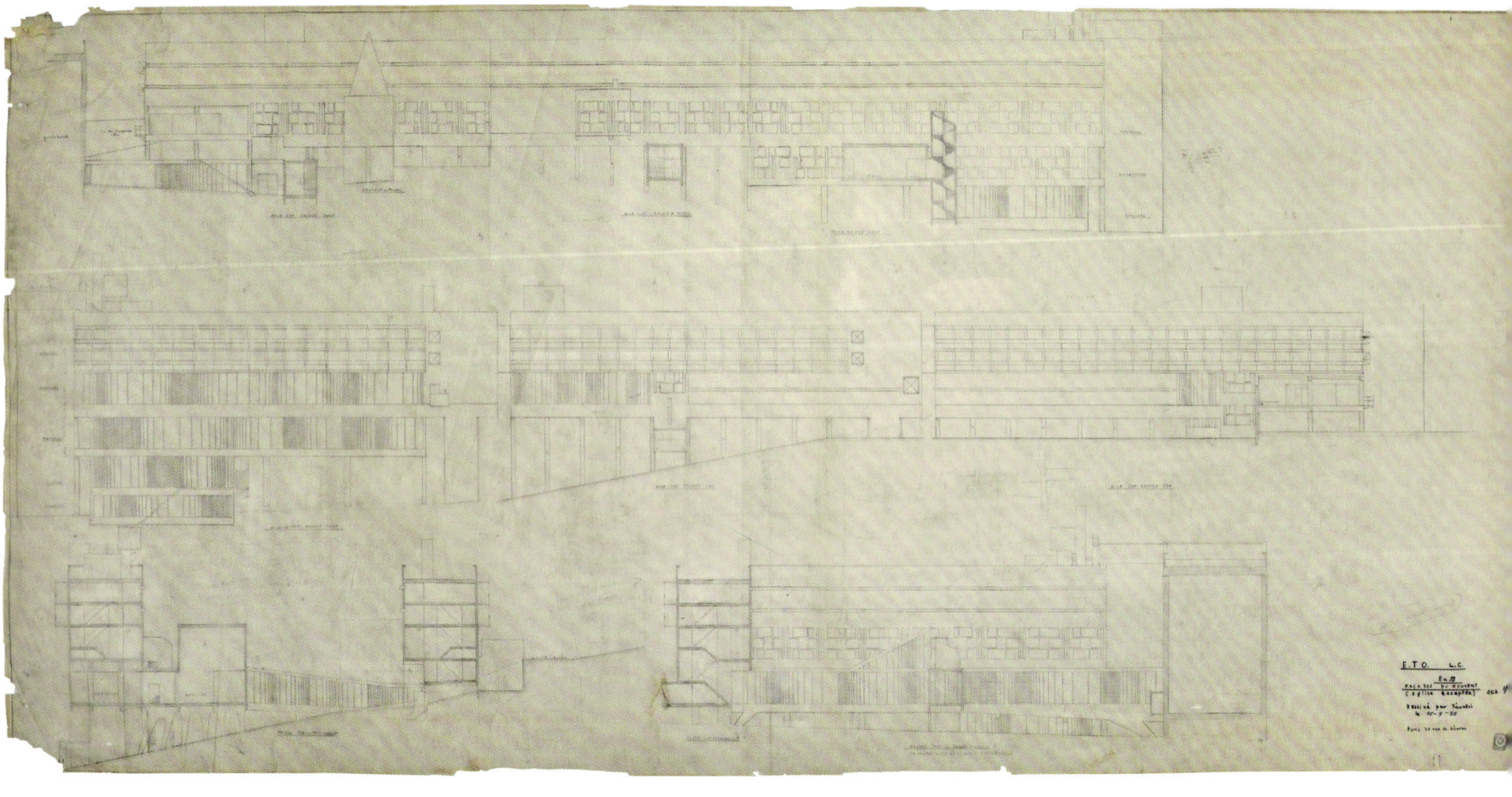

Left and bottom. Le Corbusier on the construction site of the monastery

Below. Aerial view

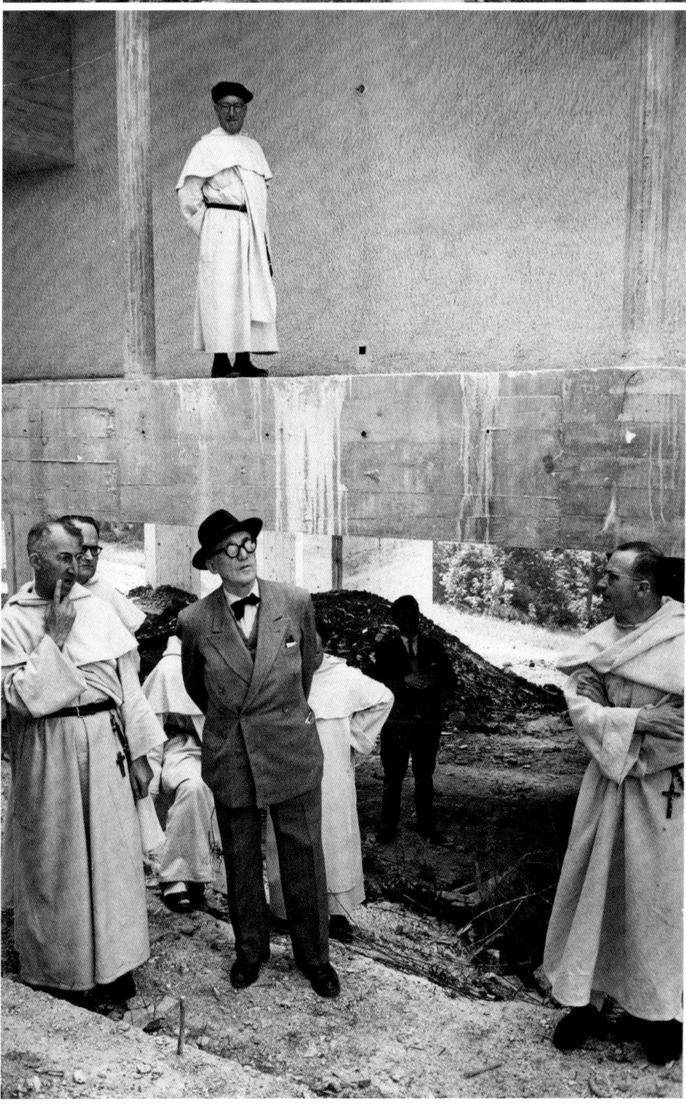

"I have tried to create a place of meditation, questing and prayer for the Dominican friars. The human implications of this problem guided our work… I devised the formal solutions, the points of contact and the channels needed for prayer, liturgy, meditation and study to be at their ease in this building. My profession is to provide lodgings for people. The aim here was to house the monks while trying to give them what people today need most: silence and peace."

—***Le Corbusier et l'architecture sacrée: Sainte-Marie-de-La-Tourette-Eveux***

Opposite, top. Le Corbusier with Dominicans, viewing the newly completed monastery of Sainte-Marie-de-La-Tourette, Eveux-sur-l'Arbresle

Opposite, bottom. West facade

Above. View from southwest

Right. Le Corbusier with Dominicans and others

Opposite. Le Corbusier in front of the stairway enclosure on the roof, Sainte-Marie-de-La-Tourette, Eveux-sur-l'Arbresle, c. 1959

Left. View of the light cannons below the bell tower, north facade

Below. The bell tower

Bottom left. Detail of the light cannons in the courtyard

Bottom right. Roof drainage channel

Left. Altars under the light cannons, Sainte-Marie-de-La-Tourette, Eveux-sur-l'Arbresle

Above. Detail of a light cannon

Below left. Sketch of altar furnishings and lighting, 3 February 1956

Below right. Priests conducting Mass at altars under the light cannons

Opposite. Detail of the light cannons over the chapels

Left. Double-height library, Sainte-Marie-de-La-Tourette, Eveux-sur-l'Arbresle

Below. Courtyard

Bottom. Corridor with glazed wall

Above. A monk reading on the balcony outside a cell

Right. Monastic cell

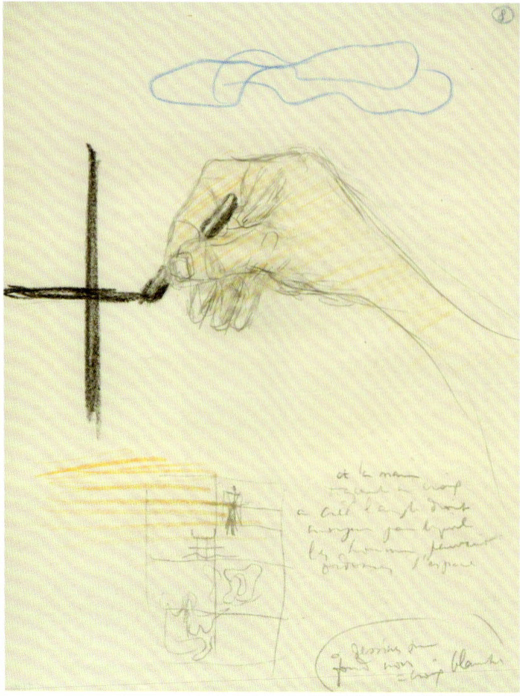

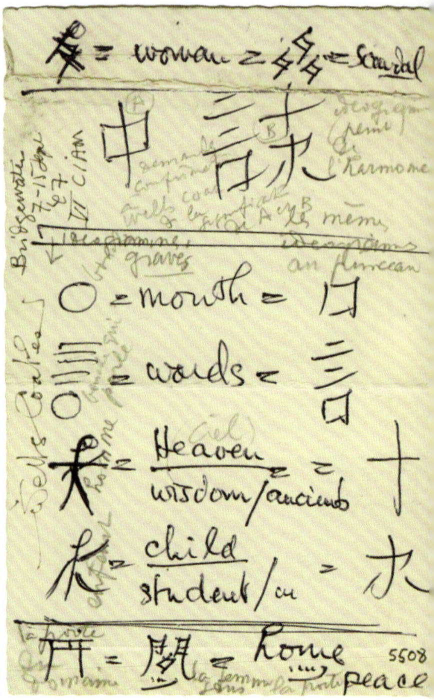

Signs of inspiration: *Le poème de l'angle droit*, 1947–55

Between 1947 and 1955 Le Corbusier composed and published an illustrated prose poem entitled *Le poème de l'angle droit* (*Poem of the Right Angle*). The book was a sort of catalog of his diverse sources of inspiration, including natural forces, the Modulor, the Open Hand, and a female animating force that Le Corbusier had perceived again and again in the women he met around the world.

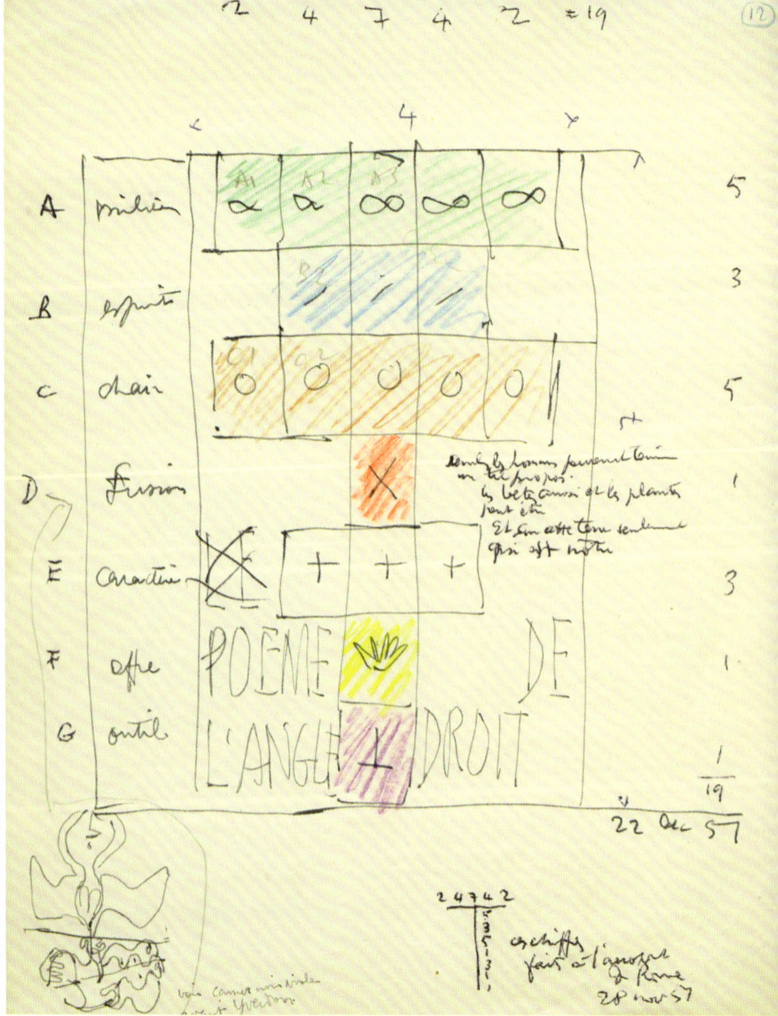

Opposite, top left. Sketch of a cover design for *Le poème de l'angle droit* (*Poem of the Right Angle*), made in Chandigarh, India, 28 March 1952

Opposite, top middle. Sketch of Le Corbusier's hand drawing his symbol for the word *right* in *Le poème de l'angle droit*

Opposite, top right. Preparatory sketch for *Le poème de l'angle droit*, with Chinese ideograms provided by British architect Wells Coates at CIAM VI, Bridgewater, England, 1947

Opposite, bottom. Two schemes for the layout of images in *Le poème de l'angle droit*, 22 December 1951, with seven terms—*environment, spirit, flesh, fusion, nature, offer*, and *tool*—arranged in the same configuration as an Eastern Orthodox iconostasis

Below. Le Corbusier with *Le poème de l'angle droit*

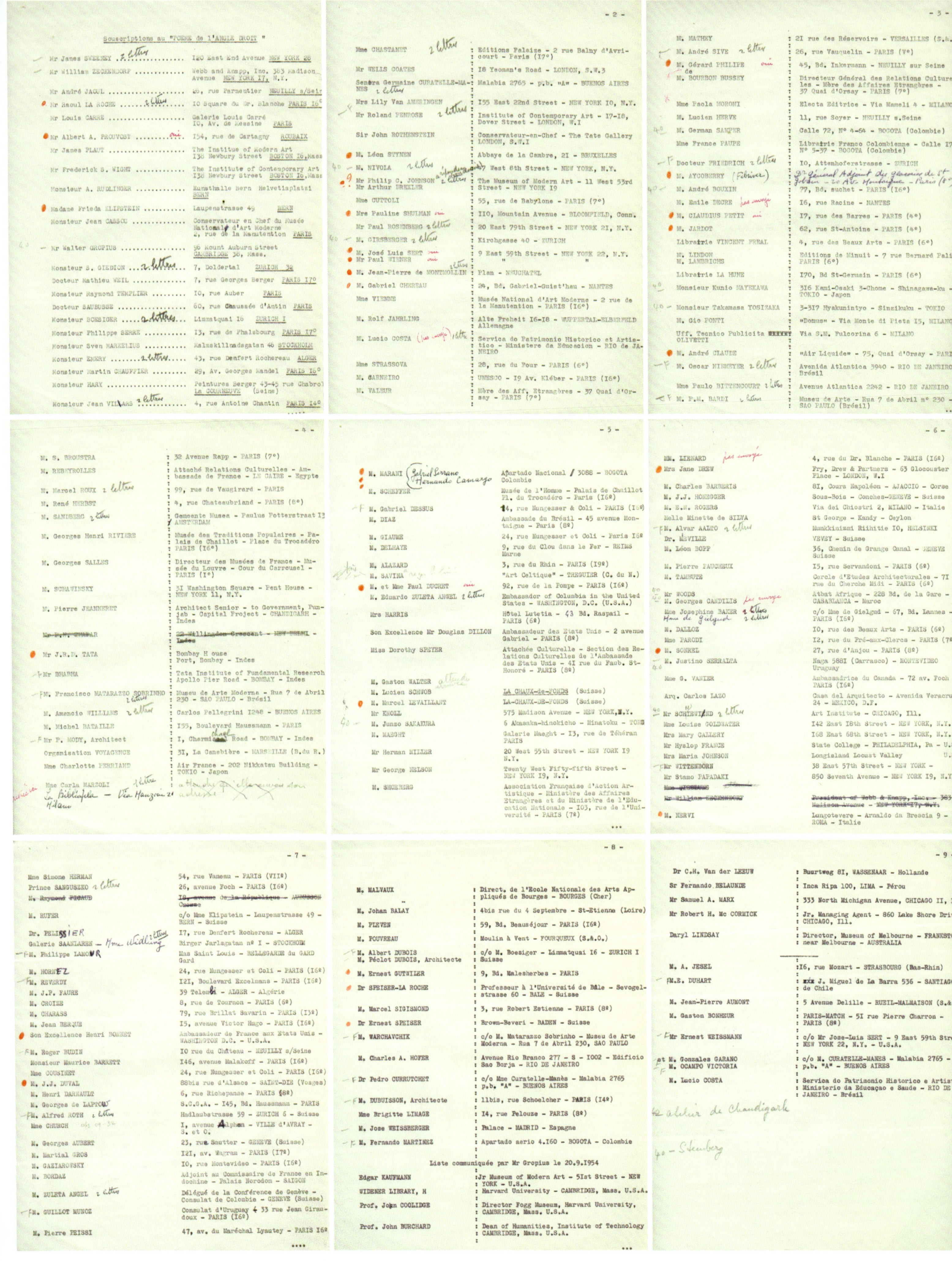

Souscriptions au "POEME de l'ANGLE DROIT "

Mr James SWEENEY	120 East End Avenue NEW YORK 28
Mr William ZECKENDORF	Webb and Knapp, Inc. 383 Madison Avenue NEW YORK 17, N.Y.
Mr André JACOUL	26, rue Parmentier NEUILLY s/Seine
Mr Raoul LA ROCHE	10 Square du Dr. Blanche PARIS 16°
Mr Louis CARRE	Galerie Louis Carré 10, Av. de Messine PARIS
Mr Albert A. PROUVOST	154, rue de Cartagny ROUBAIX
Mr James PLAUT	The Institue of Modern Art 138 Newbury Street BOSTON 16, Mass
Mr Frederick S. WIGHT	The Institute of Contemporary Art 138 Newbury Street BOSTON 16, Mass
Monsieur A. RUDLINGER	Kunsthalle Bern Helvetiaplatz1 BERN
Madame Frieda KLIPSTEIN	Laupenstrasse 49 BERN
Monsieur Jean CASSOU	Conservateur en Chef du Musée National d'Art Moderne 2, rue de la Manutention PARIS
Mr Walter GROPIUS	96 Mount Auburn Street CAMBRIDGE 38, Mass.
Monsieur S. GIEDION	7, Doldertal ZURICH 32
Docteur Mathieu WEIL	7, rue Georges Berger PARIS 17°
Monsieur Raymond TEMPLIER	10, rue Auber PARIS
Docteur SAUBUSSE	60, rue Chaussée d'Antin PARIS
Monsieur BOESIGER	Limmatquai 16 ZURICH I
Monsieur Philippe SERRE	13, rue de Phalsbourg PARIS 17°
Monsieur Sven MARKELIUS	Malmskillnadsgatan 46 STOCKHOLM
Monsieur EMERY	43, rue Denfert Rochereau ALGER
Monsieur Martin CHAUFFIER	29, Av. Georges Mandel PARIS 16°
Monsieur HARY	Peintures Berger 43-45 rue Chabrol LA COURNEUVE (Seine)
Monsieur Jean VILLARS	4, rue Antoine Chantin PARIS 14°

- 2 -

Mme CHASTANET	Editions Falaize - 2 rue Balny d'Avricourt - Paris (17°)
Mr WELLS COATES	18 Yeoman's Road - LONDON, S.W.3
Senõra Germaine CURATELLE-MANES	Malabia 2765 - p.b. "A" - BUENOS AIRES
Mrs Lily Van AMERINGEN	155 East 22nd Street - NEW YORK 10, N.Y.
Mr Roland PENROSE	Institute of Contemporary Art - 17-18, Dover Street - LONDON, W.I
Sir John ROTHENSTEIN	Conservateur-en-Chef - The Tate Gallery LONDON, S.W.I
M. Léon STYNEN	Abbaye de la Cambre, 21 - BRUXELLES
M. NIVOLA	7 West 8th Street - NEW YORK, N.Y.
Mr Philip C. JOHNSON Mr Arthur DREXLER	The Museum of Modern Art - 11 West 53rd Street - NEW YORK 19
Mme CUTTOLI	55, rue de Babylone - PARIS (7°)
Mrs Pauline SHULMAN	110, Mountain Avenue - BLOOMFIELD, Conn.
Mr Paul ROSENBERG	20 East 79th Street - NEW YORK 21, N.Y.
M. GIRSBERGER	Kirchgasse 40 - ZURICH
M. José Luis SERT Mr Paul WIENER	9 East 59th Street - NEW YORK 22, N.Y. " "
M. Jean-Pierre de MONTMOLLIN	Plan - NEUCHATEL
M. Gabriel CHEREAU	24, Bd. Gabriel-Guist'hau - NANTES
Mme VIENNE	Musée National d'Art Moderne - 2 rue de la Manutention - PARIS (16°)
M. Rolf JAHRLING	Alte Freheit 16-18 - WUPPERTAL-ELBERFELD Allemagne
M. Lucio COSTA	Servica do Patrimonio Historico et Artistico - Ministere da Educacion - RIO de JANEIRO
Mme STRASSOVA	28, rue du Four - PARIS (6°)
M. CARNEIRO	UNESCO - 19 Av. Kléber - PARIS (16°)
M. VALEUR	Mère des Aff. Etrangères - 37 Quai d'Orsay - PARIS (7°)

- 3 -

M. MATHEY	21 rue des Réservoirs - VERSAILLES (S.&O.)
M. André SIVE	26, rue Vauquelin - PARIS (V°)
M. Gérard PHILIPE	45, Bd. Inkermann - NEUILLY sur Seine
M. de BOURBON BUSSEY	Directeur Général des Relations Culturelles - Mère des Affaires Etrangères - 37 Quai d'Orsay - PARIS (7°)
Mme Paola MORONI	Electa Editrice - Via Mameli 4 - MILANO
M. Lucien HERVE	11, rue Soyer - NEUILLY s.Seine
M. German SAMPER	Calle 72, N° 4-64 - BOGOTA (Colombie)
Mme France PAUPE	Librairie Franco Colombienne - Calle 17, N° 5-37 - BOGOTA (Colombie)
Docteur FRIEDRICH	10, Attenhoferstrasse - ZURICH
M. AYCOBERRY	
M. André BOUXIN	77, Bd. suchet - PARIS (16°)
M. Emile DECRE	16, rue Racine - NANTES
M. CLAUDIUS PETIT	17, rue des Barres - PARIS (4°)
M. JARDOT	62, rue St-Antoine - PARIS (4°)
Librairie VINCENT FREAL	4, rue des Beaux Arts - PARIS (6°)
M. LINDON M. LAMBRICHS	Editions de Minuit - 7 rue Bernard Palissy PARIS (6°)
Librairie LA HUNE	170, Bd St-Germain - PARIS (6°)
Monsieur Kunio MAYEKAWA	316 Kami-Osaki 3-Chome - Shinagawa-ku - TOKIO - Japon
Monsieur Takamasa YOSIZAKA	3-317 Hyakunintyo - Sinzikuku - TOKIO
M. Gio PONTI	"Domus" - Via Monte di Pieta 15, MILANO
Uff. Tecnico Publicita OLIVETTI	Via S.M. Fulcorina 6 - MILANO
M. André CLAUDE	"Air Liquide" - 75, Quai d'Orsay - PARIS
M. Oscar NIEMEYER	Avenida Atlantica 3940 - RIO DE JANEIRO Brésil
Mme Paulo BITTENCOURT	Avenue Atlantica 2242 - RIO DE JANEIRO
M. P.M. BARDI	Museu de Arte - Rua 7 de Abril n° 230 - SAO PAULO (Brésil)

- 4 -

M. S. BROUSTRA	32 Avenue Rapp - PARIS (7°)
M. REBEYROLLES	Attaché Relations Culturelles - Ambassade de France - LE CAIRE - Egypte
M. Marcel ROUX	99, rue de Vaugirard - PARIS
M. René HERBST	4, rue Chateaubriand - PARIS (8°)
M. SANDBERG	Gemeente Musea - Paulus Potterstraat 13 AMSTERDAM
M. Georges Henri RIVIERE	Musée des Traditions Populaires - Palais de Chaillot - Place du Trocadéro PARIS (16°)
M. Georges SALLES	Directeur des Musées de France - Musée du Louvre - Cour du Carrousel - PARIS (1°)
M. SCHAWINSKY	31 Washington Square - Pent House - NEW YORK 11, N.Y.
M. Pierre JEANNERET	Architect Senior - to Government, Punjab - Capital Project - CHANDIGARH - Indes
~~M. [illegible]AR~~	~~22 Willingdon Crescent - NEW DELHI - Indes~~
Mr J.R.D. TATA	Bombay H ouse Fort, Bombay - Indes
Mr BHABHA	Tata Institute of Fundamental Research Apollo Pier Road - BOMBAY - Indes
M. Francisco MATARAZZO SOBRINHO	Museu de Arte Moderna - Rua 7 de Abril 230 - SAO PAULO - Brésil
M. Amancio WILLIAMS	Carlos Pellegrini 1248 - BUENOS AIRES
M. Michel BATAILLE	155, Boulevard Haussmann - PARIS
Mr P. MODY, Architect	I, Charmichael Road - BOMBAY - Indes
Organisation VOYAGENCE	31, La Canebière - MARSEILLE (B.du R.)
Mme Charlotte PERRIAND	Air France - 202 Nikkatsu Building - TOKIO - Japon
Mme Carla MARZOLI	

- 5 -

M. MARANI (Gabriel Serrano, Hernando Camargo)	Apartado Nacional / 3088 - BOGOTA Colombie
M. SCHEFFER	Musée de l'Homme - Palais de Chaillot Pl. du Trocadéro - Paris (16ª)
M. Gabriel DESSUS	14, rue Nungesser & Coli - PARIS (16ª)
M. DIAZ	Ambassade du Brésil - 45 avenue Montaigne - Paris (8ª)
M. GIAUME	24, rue Nungesser et Coli - Paris 16ª
M. DELHAYE	9, rue du Clou dans le Fer - REIMS Marne
M. ALAZARD	3, rue du Rhin - PARIS (19ª)
M. SAVINA	"Art Celtique" - TREGUIER (C. du N.)
M. et Mme Paul DUCRET	92, rue de la Pompe - PARIS (16ª)
M. Eduardo ZULETA ANGEL	Embassador of Columbia in the United States - WASHINGTON, D.C. (U.S.A.)
Mrs HARRIS	Hôtel Lutetia - 43 Bd. Raspail - PARIS (6ª)
Son Excellence Mr Douglas DILLON	Ambassadeur des Etats Unis - 2 avenue Gabriel - PARIS (8ª)
Miss Dorothy SPEYER	Attachée Culturelle - Section des Relations Culturelles de l'Ambassade des Etats Unis - 41 rue du Faub. St-Honoré - PARIS (8ª)
M. Gaston WALTER	
M. Lucien SCHWOB	LA CHAUX-de-FONDS (Suisse)
M. Marcel LEVAILLANT	LA-CHAUX-DE-FONDS (Suisse)
Mr KNOLL	575 Madison Avenue - NEW YORK, N.Y.
M. Junzo SAKAKURA	6 Akasaka-hinokicho - Minatoku - TOKIO
M. MAEGHT	Galerie Maeght - 13, rue de Téhéran PARIS
Mr Herman MILLER	20 West 55th Street - NEW YORK 19 N.Y.
Mr George NELSON	Twenty West Fifty-fifth Street - NEW YORK 19, N.Y.
M. SHOEBERG	Association Française d'Action Artistique - Ministère des Affaires Etrangères et du Ministère de l'Education Nationale - 103, rue de l'Université - PARIS (7ª)

- 6 -

MM. LIENARD	4, rue du Dr. Blanche - PARIS (16ª)
Mrs Jane DREW	Fry, Drew & Partners - 63 Gloucester Place - LONDON, W.I
M. Charles BARBERIS	81, Cours Napoléon - AJACCIO - Corse
M. J.J. HONEGGER	Sous-Bois - Conches-GENEVE - Suisse
M. E.N. ROGERS	Via dei Chiostri 2, MILANO - Italie
Melle Minette de SILVA	St George - Kandy - Ceylon
M. Alvar AALTO	Munkkiniemi Riihitie 10, HELSINKI
Dr. […]ILLE	VEVEY - Suisse
M. Léon BOPP	36, Chemin de Grange Canal - GENEVE Suisse
M. Pierre FAUCHEUX	15, rue Servandoni - PARIS (6ª)
M. TAMBUTE	Cercle d'Etudes Architecturales - 71 rue du Cherche Midi - PARIS (6ª)
Mr WOODS M. Georges CANDILIS	Atbat Afrique - 228 Bd. de la Gare - CASABLANCA - Maroc
Mme Josephine BAKER	c/o Mme de Gielgud - 67, Bd. Lannes - PARIS (16ª)
M. DALLOZ	10, rue des Beaux Arts - PARIS (6ª)
Mme PARODI	12, rue du Pré-aux-Clercs - PARIS (7ª)
M. SONREL	27, rue d'Anjou - PARIS (8ª)
M. Justino SERRALTA	Naga 5881 (Carrasco) - MONTEVIDEO Uruguay
Mme G. VANIER	Ambassadrice du Canada - 72 av. Foch - PARIS (16ª)
Arq. Carlos LAZO	Casa del Arquitecto - Avenida Veracruz 24 - MEXICO, D.F.
Mr SCHIEWIND	Art Institute - CHICAGO, Ill.
Mme Louise GOLDWATER	142 East 18th Street - NEW YORK, N.Y.
Mrs Mary CALLERY	168 East 68th Street - NEW YORK, N.Y.
Mr Hyslop FRANCE	State College - PHILADELPHIA, Pa - U.S.
Mrs Maria JOHNSON	Longisland Locust Valley U.S.
Mr WITTENBORN	38 East 57th Street - NEW YORK -
Mr Stamo PAPADAKI	850 Seventh Avenue - NEW YORK 19, N.Y.
~~[illegible]~~	
~~Mr William ZECKENDORF~~	~~President of Webb & Knapp, Inc. - 383 Madison Avenue - NEW YORK 17, N.Y.~~
M. NERVI	Lungotevere - Arnaldo da Brescia 9 - ROMA - Italie

- 7 -

Mme Simone HERMAN	54, rue Vaneau - PARIS (VIIª)
Prince SANGUSZKO	26, avenue Foch - PARIS (16ª)
~~M. Raymond PICAUD~~	~~10, avenue de la République - AUBUSSON Creuse~~
M. RUFER	c/o Mme Klipstein - Laupenstrasse 49 - BERN - Suisse
Dr. PELISSIER	17, rue Denfert Rochereau - ALGER
Galerie SAANLAREN	Birger Jarlsgatan nº 1 - STOCKHOLM
M. Philippe LAMOUR	Mas Saint Louis - BELLEGARDE du GARD Gard
M. HORNEZ	24, rue Nungesser et Coli - PARIS (16ª)
M. REVERDY	121, Boulevard Excelmans - PARIS (16ª)
M. J.P. FAURE	39 Telemli - ALGER - Algérie
M. CROIZE	8, rue de Tournon - PARIS (6ª)
M. CHARASS	79, rue Brillat Savarin - PARIS (13ª)
M. Jean BERQUE	15, avenue Victor Hugo - PARIS (16ª)
Son Excellence Henri BONNET	Ambassadeur de France aux Etats Unis - WASHINGTON D.C. - U.S.A.
M. Roger BUDIN	10 rue du Château - NEUILLY s/Seine
Monsieur Maurice BARRETT	146, avenue Malakoff - PARIS (16ª)
Mme COUSINET	24, rue Nungesser et Coli - PARIS (16ª)
M. J.J. DUVAL	88bis rue d'Alsace - SAINT-DIE (Vosges)
M. Henri DARNAULT	6, rue Richepanse - PARIS (8ª)
M. Georges de LAPTOUX	S.C.G.A. - 145, Bd. Haussmann - PARIS
M. Alfred ROTH	Hadlaubstrasse 59 - ZURICH 6 - Suisse
Mme CHURCH	1, avenue Alphen - VILLE d'AVRAY - S. et O.
M. Georges AUBERT	23, rue Sautter - GENEVE (Suisse)
M. Martial GROS	121, av. Wagram - PARIS (17ª)
M. GAZIAROWSKY	10, rue Montevideo - PARIS (16ª)
M. BORDAZ	Adjoint au Commissaire de France en Indochine - Palais Norodom - SAIGON
M. ZULETA ANGEL	Délégué de la Conférence de Genève - Consulat de Colombie - GENEVE (Suisse)
M. GUILLOT MUNOZ	Consulat d'Uruguay - 33 rue Jean Giraudoux - PARIS (16ª)
M. Pierre PEISSI	47, av. du Maréchal Lyautey - PARIS 16ª

- 8 -

M. MALVAUX	Direct. de l'Ecole Nationale des Arts Appliqués de Bourges - BOURGES (Cher)
M. Johan BALAY	4bis rue du 4 Septembre - St-Etienne (Loire)
M. PLEVEN	59, Bd. Beauséjour - PARIS (16ª)
M. POUVREAU	Moulin à Vent - FOURQUEUX (S.&.O.)
M. Albert DUBOIS M. Péclot DUBOIS, Architecte	c/o M. Boesiger - Limmatquai 16 - ZURICH I Suisse
M. Ernest GUTWILER	9, Bd. Malesherbes - PARIS
Dr SPEISER-LA ROCHE	Professeur à l'Université de Bâle - Sevogelstrasse 60 - BALE - Suisse
M. Marcel SIGISMOND	3, rue Robert Estienne - PARIS (8ª)
Dr Ernest SPEISER	Brown-Beveri - BADEN - Suisse
M. WARCHAVCHIK	c/o M. Matarazzo Sobrinho - Museu de Arte Moderna - Rua 7 de Abril 230, SAO PAULO
M. Charles A. HOFER	Avenue Rio Branco 277 - S - 1002 - Edificio Sao Borja - RIO DE JANEIRO
Dr Pedro CURRUTCHET	c/o Mme Curatelle-Manès - Malabia 2765 p.b. "A" - BUENOS AIRES
M. DUBUISSON, Architecte	11bis, rue Schoelcher - PARIS (14ª)
Mme Brigitte LIMAGE	14, rue Pelouze - PARIS (8ª)
M. Jose WEISSBERGER	Palace - MADRID - Espagne
M. Fernando MARTINEZ	Apartado aerio 4.160 - BOGOTA - Colombie

Liste communiquée par Mr Gropius le 20.9.1954

Edgar KAUFMANN	Jr Museum of Modern Art - 51st Street - NEW YORK - U.S.A.
WIDENER LIBRARY, H	Harvard University - CAMBRIDGE, Mass. U.S.A.
Prof. John COOLIDGE	Director Fogg Museum, Harvard University, CAMBRIDGE, Mass. U.S.A.
Prof. John BURCHARD	Dean of Humanities, Institute of Technology CAMBRIDGE, Mass. U.S.A.

- 9 -

Dr C.H. Van der LEEUW	Buurtweg 81, WASSENAAR - Hollande
Sr Fernando BELAUNDE	Inca Ripa 100, LIMA - Pérou
Mr Samuel A. MARX	333 North Michigan Avenue, CHICAGO 11, I
Mr Robert H. Mc CORMICK	Jr. Managing Agent - 860 Lake Shore Driv CHICAGO, Ill.
Daryl LINDSAY	Director, Museum of Melbourne - FRANKSTO near Melbourne - AUSTRALIA
M. A. JESEL	16, rue Mozart - STRASBOURG (Bas-Rhin)
M.E. DUHART	J. Miguel de La Barra 536 - SANTIAGO de Chile
M. Jean-Pierre AUMONT	5 Avenue Delille - RUEIL-MALMAISON (S.&.
M. Gaston BONHEUR	PARIS-MATCH - 51 rue Pierre Charron - PARIS (8ª)
Mr Ernest WEISSMANN	c/o Mr Jose-Luis SERT - 9 East 59th Stre NEW YORK 22, N.Y. - U.S.A.
M. Gonzales GARANO M. OCAMPO VICTORIA	c/o M. CURATELLE-MANES - Malabia 2765 - p.b. "A" - BUENOS AIRES
M. Lucio COSTA	Servica do Patrimonio Historico e Artist Ministerio da Educaçao e Saude - RIO DE JANEIRO - Brésil

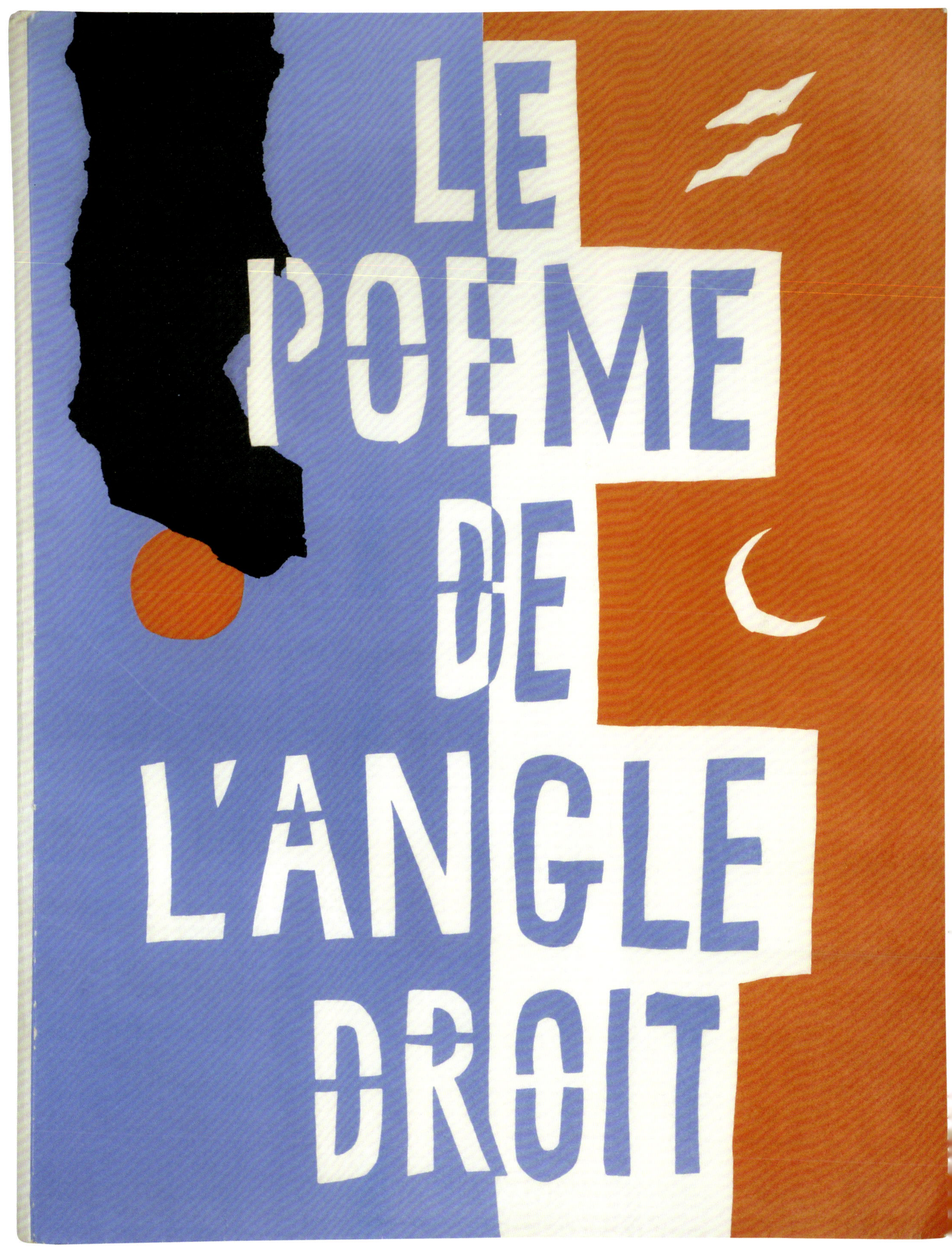

Opposite. Partial subscription list for *Le poème de l'angle droit*

Above. Cover of *Le poème de l'angle droit (Poem of the Right Angle)*, Verve, Paris, 1955

Following pages. Selected illustrations from *Le poème de l'angle droit*

A milieu
B esprit
C chair
D fusion
E Caractere
F offre
G outil

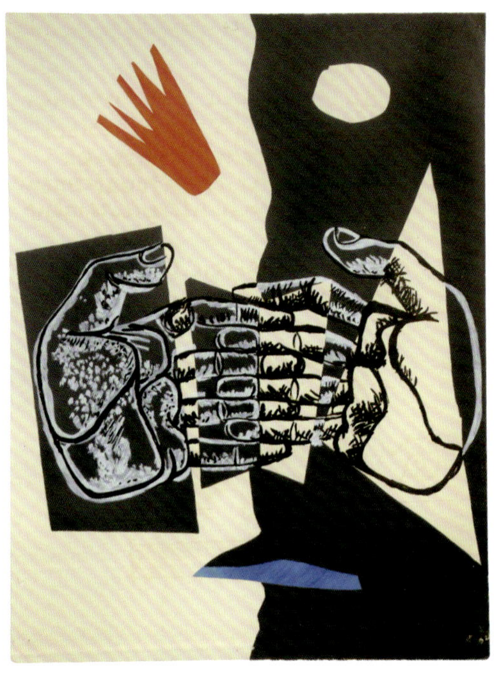

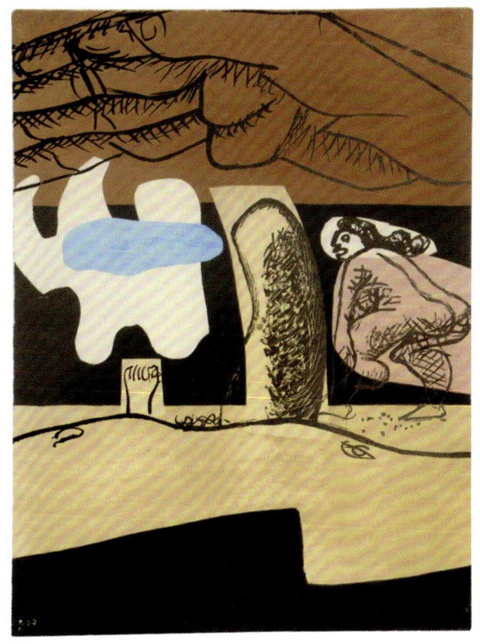

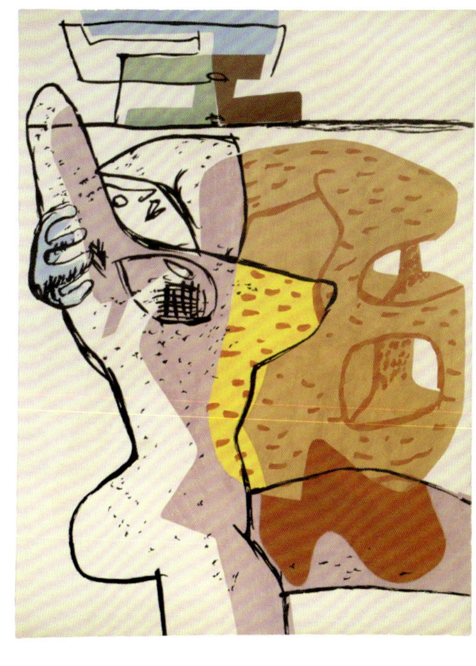

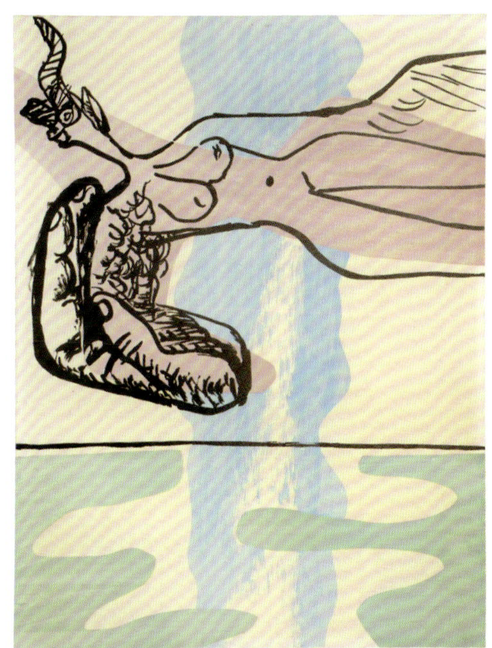

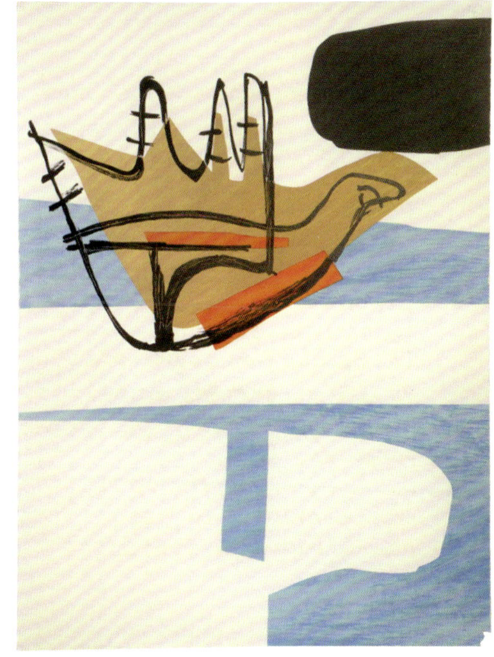

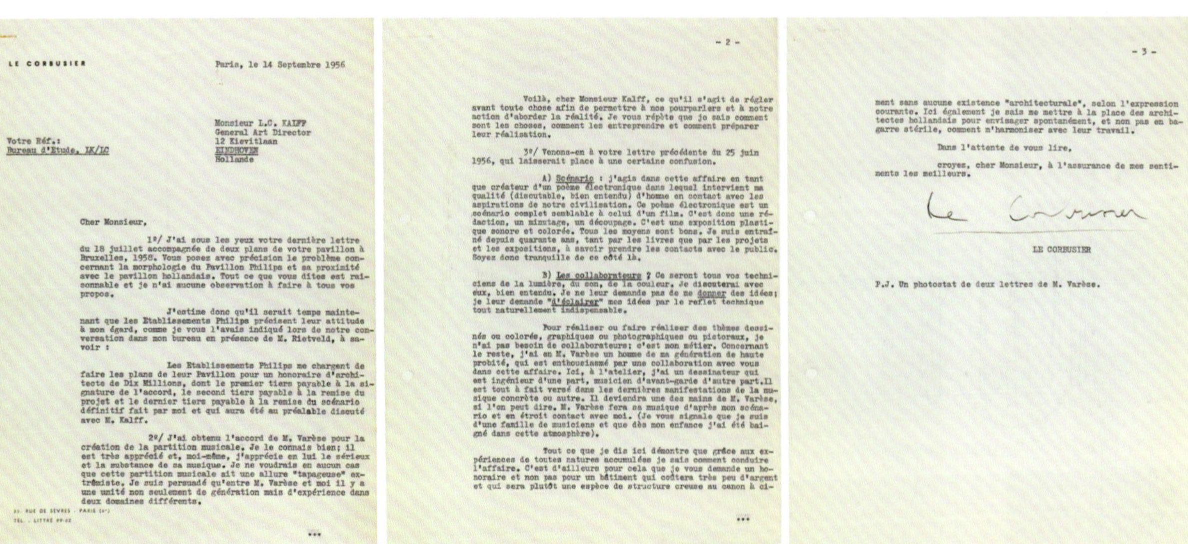

LE CORBUSIER

Paris, le 14 Septembre 1956

Votre Réf.:
Bureau d'Etude, LK/LC

Monsieur L.C. KALFF
General Art Director
12 Kievitlaan
EINDHOVEN
Hollande

Cher Monsieur,

1º/ J'ai sous les yeux votre dernière lettre du 18 juillet accompagnée de deux plans de votre pavillon à Bruxelles, 1958. Vous posez avec précision le problème concernant la morphologie du Pavillon Philips et sa proximité avec le pavillon hollandais. Tout ce que vous dites est raisonnable et je n'ai aucune observation à faire à tous vos propos.

J'estime donc qu'il serait temps maintenant que les Etablissements Philips précisent leur attitude à mon égard, comme je vous l'avais indiqué lors de notre conversation dans mon bureau en présence de M. Rietveld, à savoir :

Les Etablissements Philips me chargent de faire les plans de leur Pavillon pour un honoraire d'architecte de Dix Millions, dont le premier tiers payable à la signature de l'accord, le second tiers payable à la remise du projet et le dernier tiers payable à la remise du scénario définitif fait par moi et qui aura été au préalable discuté avec M. Kalff.

2º/ J'ai obtenu l'accord de M. Varèse pour la création de la partition musicale. Je le connais bien; il est très apprécié et, moi-même, j'apprécie en lui le sérieux et la substance de sa musique. Je ne voudrais en aucun cas que cette partition musicale ait une allure "tapageuse" extrêmiste. Je suis persuadé qu'entre M. Varèse et moi il y a une unité non seulement de génération mais d'expérience dans deux domaines différents.

35, RUE DE SÈVRES . PARIS (6e)
TÉL. . LITTRÉ 99-62

...

\- 2 -

Voilà, cher Monsieur Kalff, ce qu'il s'agit de régler avant toute chose afin de permettre à nos pourparlers et à notre action d'aborder la réalité. Je vous répète que je sais comment sont les choses, comment les entreprendre et comment préparer leur réalisation.

3º/ Venons-en à votre lettre précédente du 25 juin 1956, qui laisserait place à une certaine confusion.

A) Scénario : j'agis dans cette affaire en tant que créateur d'un poème électronique dans lequel intervient ma qualité (discutable, bien entendu) d'homme en contact avec les aspirations de notre civilisation. Ce poème électronique est un scénario complet semblable à celui d'un film. C'est donc une rédaction, un minutage, un découpage. C'est une exposition plastique sonore et colorée. Tous les moyens sont bons. Je suis entraîné depuis quarante ans, tant par les livres que par les projets et les expositions, à savoir prendre les contacts avec le public. Soyez donc tranquille de ce côté là.

B) Les collaborateurs ? Ce seront tous vos techniciens de la lumière, du son, de la couleur. Je discuterai avec eux, bien entendu. Je ne leur demande pas de me donner des idées; je leur demande "d'éclairer" mes idées par le reflet technique tout naturellement indispensable.

Pour réaliser ou faire réaliser des thèmes dessinés ou colorés, graphiques ou photographiques ou pictoraux, je n'ai pas besoin de collaborateurs; c'est mon métier. Concernant le reste, j'ai en M. Varèse un homme de ma génération de haute probité, qui est enthousiasmé par une collaboration avec vous dans cette affaire. Ici, à l'atelier, j'ai un dessinateur qui est ingénieur d'une part, musicien d'avant-garde d'autre part. Il est tout à fait versé dans les dernières manifestations de la musique concrète ou autre. Il deviendra une des mains de M. Varèse, si l'on peut dire. M. Varèse fera sa musique d'après mon scénario et en étroit contact avec moi. (Je vous signale que je suis d'une famille de musiciens et que dès mon enfance j'ai été baigné dans cette atmosphère).

Tout ce que je dis ici démontre que grâce aux expériences de toutes natures accumulées je sais comment conduire l'affaire. C'est d'ailleurs pour cela que je vous demande un honoraire et non pas pour un bâtiment qui coûtera très peu d'argent et qui sera plutôt une espèce de structure creuse au canon à ci-

...

\- 3 -

ment sans aucune existence "architecturale", selon l'expression courante. Ici également je sais me mettre à la place des architectes hollandais pour envisager spontanément, et non pas en bagarre stérile, comment m'harmoniser avec leur travail.

Dans l'attente de vous lire,

croyez, cher Monsieur, à l'assurance de mes sentiments les meilleurs.

LE CORBUSIER

P.J. Un photostat de deux lettres de M. Varèse.

From right angle to parabola: Philips Pavilion, world's fair, Brussels, 1956–58

The Dutch electronics company Philips commissioned Le Corbusier to design a pavilion it would sponsor at the 1958 world's fair in Brussels. The project's modest scale might have dissuaded him from participating had Philips not promised Le Corbusier access to all of its technological resources in order to integrate cutting-edge electronics with visionary architecture, in a multimedia installation called the *Poème électronique* (Electronic Poem). For the pavilion's form he again turned to the shell for inspiration. Starting with that source, an architect working in Le Corbusier's office, Iannis Xenakis, devised the hyperbolic paraboloid structure by making models out of piano wire and cloth.

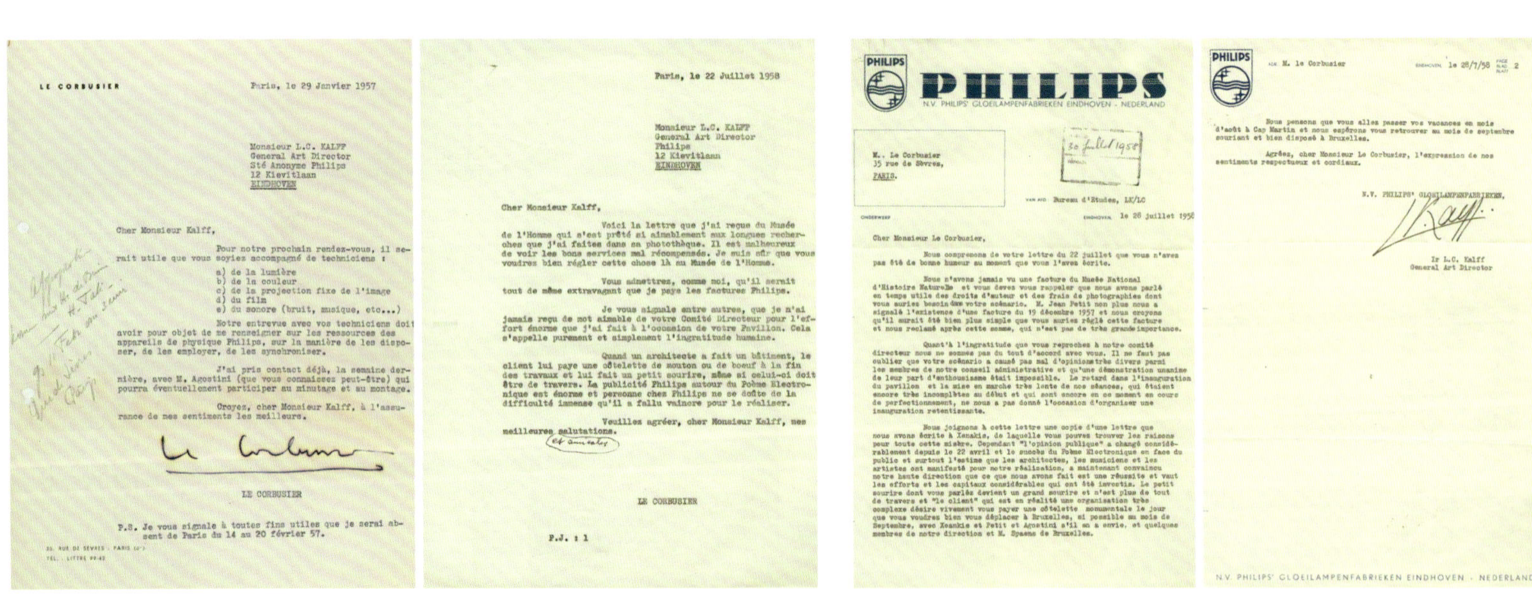

LE CORBUSIER

Paris, le 29 Janvier 1957

Monsieur L.C. KALFF
General Art Director
Sté Anonyme Philips
12 Kievitlaan
EINDHOVEN

Cher Monsieur Kalff,

Pour notre prochain rendez-vous, il serait utile que vous soyiez accompagné de techniciens :

a) de la lumière
b) de la couleur
c) de la projection fixe de l'image
d) du film
e) du sonore (bruit, musique, etc...)

Notre entrevue avec vos techniciens doit avoir pour objet de me renseigner sur les ressources des appareils de physique Philips, sur la manière de les disposer, de les employer, de les synchroniser.

J'ai pris contact déjà, la semaine dernière, avec M. Agostini (que vous connaissez peut-être) qui pourra éventuellement participer au minutage et au montage.

Croyez, cher Monsieur Kalff, à l'assurance de mes sentiments les meilleurs.

LE CORBUSIER

P.S. Je vous signale à toutes fins utiles que je serai absent de Paris du 14 au 20 février 57.

35, RUE DE SÈVRES . PARIS (6e)
TÉL. . LITTRÉ 99-62

Paris, le 22 Juillet 1958

Monsieur L.C. KALFF
General Art Director
Philips
12 Kievitlaan
EINDHOVEN

Cher Monsieur Kalff,

Voici la lettre que j'ai reçue du Musée de l'Homme qui s'est prêté si aimablement aux longues recherches que j'ai faites dans sa photothèque. Il est malheureux de voir les bons services mal récompensés. Je suis sûr que vous voudrez bien régler cette chose là au Musée de l'Homme.

Vous admettrez, comme moi, qu'il serait tout de même extravagant que je paye les factures Philips.

Je vous signale entre autres, que je n'ai jamais reçu de mot aimable de votre Comité Directeur pour l'effort énorme que j'ai fait à l'occasion de votre Pavillon. Cela s'appelle purement et simplement l'ingratitude humaine.

Quand un architecte a fait un bâtiment, le client lui paye une côtelette de mouton ou de boeuf à la fin des travaux et lui fait un petit sourire, même si celui-ci doit être de travers. La publicité Philips autour du Poème Electronique est énorme et personne chez Philips ne se doute de la difficulté immense qu'il a fallu vaincre pour le réaliser.

Veuillez agréer, cher Monsieur Kalff, mes meilleures salutations. (et amitiés)

LE CORBUSIER

P.J. : 1

PHILIPS
PHILIPS
N.V. PHILIPS' GLOEILAMPENFABRIEKEN EINDHOVEN - NEDERLAND

M. Le Corbusier
35 rue de Sèvres,
PARIS.

30 Juillet 1958

VAN AFD. Bureau d'Etudes, LK/LC

ONDERWERP

EINDHOVEN, le 28 juillet 1958

Cher Monsieur Le Corbusier,

Nous comprenons de votre lettre du 22 juillet que vous n'avez pas été de bonne humeur au moment que vous l'avez écrite.

Nous n'avons jamais vu une facture du Musée National d'Histoire Naturelle et vous devez vous rappeler que nous avons parlé en temps utile des droits d'auteur et des frais de photographies dont vous auriez besoin dans votre scénario. M. Jean Petit non plus nous a signalé l'existence d'une facture du 19 décembre 1957 et nous croyons qu'il aurait été bien plus simple que vous auriez réglé cette facture et nous reclamé après cette somme, qui n'est pas de très grande importance.

Quant'à l'ingratitude que vous reprochez à notre comité directeur nous ne sommes pas du tout d'accord avec vous. Il ne faut pas oublier que votre scénario a causé pas mal d'opinions très divers parmi les membres de notre conseil administrative et qu'une démonstration unanime de leur part d'enthousiasme était impossible. Le retard dans l'inauguration du pavillon et la mise en marche très lente de nos séances, qui étaient encore très incomplètes au début et qui sont encore en ce moment en cours de perfectionnement, ne nous a pas donné l'occasion d'organiser une inauguration retentissante.

Nous joignons à cette lettre une copie d'une lettre que nous avons écrite à Xenakis, de laquelle vous pouvez trouver les raisons pour toute cette misère. Cependant "l'opinion publique" a changé considérablement depuis le 22 avril et le succès du Poème Electronique en face du public et surtout l'estime que les architectes, les musiciens et les artistes ont manifesté pour notre réalisation, a maintenant convaincu notre haute direction que ce que nous avons fait est une réussite et vaut les efforts et les capitaux considérables qui ont été investis. Le petit sourire dont vous parlez devient un grand sourire et n'est plus de tout de travers et "le client" qui est en réalité une organisation très complexe désire vivement vous payer une côtelette monumentale le jour que vous voudrez bien vous déplacer à Bruxelles, si possible au mois de Septembre, avec Xeankis et Petit et Agostini s'il en a envie, et quelques membres de notre direction et M. Spaens de Bruxelles.

PHILIPS

AAN M. le Corbusier

EINDHOVEN, le 28/7/58 PAGE 2

Nous pensons que vous allez passer vos vacances en mois d'août à Cap Martin et nous espérons vous retrouver au mois de septembre souriant et bien disposé à Bruxelles.

Agréez, cher Monsieur Le Corbusier, l'expression de nos sentiments respectueux et cordiaux.

N.V. PHILIPS' GLOEILAMPENFABRIEKEN,

Ir L.C. Kalff
General Art Director

N.V. PHILIPS' GLOEILAMPENFABRIEKEN EINDHOVEN - NEDERLAND

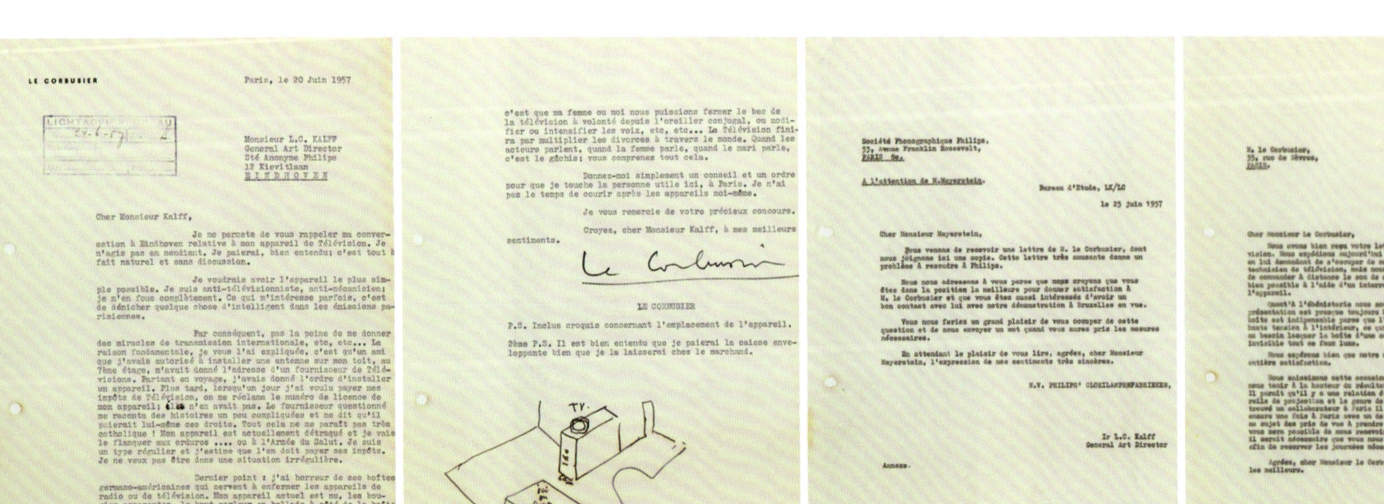

LE CORBUSIER

Paris, le 20 Juin 1957

Monsieur L.C. KALFF
General Art Director
Sté Anonyme Philips
12 Kievitlaan
EINDHOVEN

Cher Monsieur Kalff,

Je me permets de vous rappeler ma conversation à Eindhoven relative à mon appareil de Télévision. Je n'agis pas en mendiant. Je paierai, bien entendu; c'est tout à fait naturel et sans discussion.

Je voudrais avoir l'appareil le plus simple possible. Je suis anti-télévisionniste, anti-mécanicien; je m'en fous complètement. Ce qui m'intéresse parfois, c'est de dénicher quelque chose d'intelligent dans les émissions parisiennes.

Par conséquent, pas la peine de me donner des miracles de transmission internationale, etc, etc... La raison fondamentale, je vous l'ai expliquée, c'est qu'un ami que j'avais autorisé à installer une antenne sur mon toit, au 7ème étage, m'avait donné l'adresse d'un fournisseur de Télévisions. Partant en voyage, j'avais donné l'ordre d'installer un appareil. Plus tard, lorsqu'un jour j'ai voulu payer mes impôts de Télévision, on me réclama le numéro de licence de mon appareil; il n'en avait pas. Le fournisseur questionné me raconta des histoires un peu compliquées et me dit qu'il paierait lui-même ces droits. Tout cela ne me paraît pas très catholique ! Mon appareil est actuellement détraqué et je vais le flanquer aux ordures .... ou à l'Armée du Salut. Je suis un type régulier et j'estime que l'on doit payer ses impôts. Je ne veux pas être dans une situation irrégulière.

Dernier point : j'ai horreur de ces boîtes germano-américaines qui servent à enfermer les appareils de radio ou de télévision. Mon appareil actuel est nu, les bougies apparentes, le haut-parleur en ballade à côté de la boîte de projection.

Enfin, le luxe que je voudrais me payer

35, RUE DE SÈVRES . PARIS (6e)
TÉL. . LITTRÉ 99-62

...

c'est que ma femme ou moi nous puissions fermer le bec de la télévision à volonté depuis l'oreiller conjugal, ou modifier ou intensifier les voix, etc, etc... La Télévision finira par multiplier les divorces à travers le monde. Quand les acteurs parlent, quand la femme parle, quand le mari parle, c'est le gâchis; vous comprenez tout cela.

Donnez-moi simplement un conseil et un ordre pour que je touche la personne utile ici, à Paris. Je n'ai pas le temps de courir après les appareils moi-même.

Je vous remercie de votre précieux concours.

Croyez, cher Monsieur Kalff, à mes meilleurs sentiments.

LE CORBUSIER

P.S. Inclus croquis concernant l'emplacement de l'appareil.

2ème P.S. Il est bien entendu que je paierai la caisse enveloppante bien que je la laisserai chez le marchand.

Société Phonographique Philips,
53, Avenue Franklin Roosevelt,
PARIS 8e.

A l'attention de M.Meyerstein.

Bureau d'Etude, LK/LC

le 25 juin 1957

Cher Monsieur Meyerstein,

Nous venons de recevoir une lettre de M. le Corbusier, dont nous joignons ici une copie. Cette lettre très amusante donne un problème à resoudre à Philips.

Nous nous adressons à vous parce que nous croyons que vous êtes dans la position la meilleure pour donner satisfaction à M. le Corbusier et que vous êtes aussi intéressés d'avoir un bon contact avec lui avec notre démonstration à Bruxelles en vue.

Vous nous feriez un grand plaisir de vous occuper de cette question et de nous envoyer un mot quand vous aurez pris les mesures nécessaires.

En attendant le plaisir de vous lire, agréez, cher Monsieur Meyerstein, l'expression de nos sentiments très sincères.

N.V. PHILIPS' GLOEILAMPENFABRIEKEN,

Ir L.C. Kalff
General Art Director

Annexe.

M. le Corbusier,
35, rue de Sèvres,
PARIS.

Bureau d'Etude, LK/LC

le 25 juin 1957

Cher Monsieur Le Corbusier,

Nous avons bien reçu votre lettre concernant votre poste de télévision. Nous expédions aujourd'hui une copie à M. Meierstein à Paris, en lui demandant de s'occuper de cette affaire. Nous ne sommes pas technicien de télévision, mais nous craignons qu'il sera difficile de commander à distance le son de cet appareil. Il est naturellement bien possible à l'aide d'un interrupteur normale d'allumer ou d'éteindre l'appareil.

Quant'à l'ébénisterie nous sommes complètement d'accord que la présentation est presque toujours horrible, mais nous croyons que la boîte est indispensable parce que l'appareil fonctionne avec de la haute tension à l'intérieur, ce qui est fort dangéreux. On pourrait au besoin laquer la boîte d'une couleur de votre choix afin de rendre invisible tout ce faux luxe.

Nous espérons bien que notre maison à Paris pourra vous donner entière satisfaction.

Nous saisissons cette occasion pour vous demander de bien vouloir nous tenir à la hauteur du résultat de votre contact avec un cinéaste. Il paraît qu'il y a une relation étroite entre le système et les appareils de projection et le genre de film à prendre. Dès que vous aurez trouvé un collaborateur à Paris il sera donc nécessaire que nous venions encore une fois à Paris avec un de nos experts, pour avoir un entretien au sujet des prises de vue à prendre pour le scénario. Nous espérons qu'il vous sera possible de nous recevoir pour cela environ le 15 juillet, mais il serait nécessaire que vous nous avertissiez au plus tôt que possible afin de reserver les journées nécessaires pour notre voyage à Paris.

Agréez, cher Monsieur le Corbusier, l'expression de nos sentiments les meilleurs.

N.V. PHILIPS' GLOEILAMPENFABRIEKEN

Ir L.C.Kalff
General Art Director

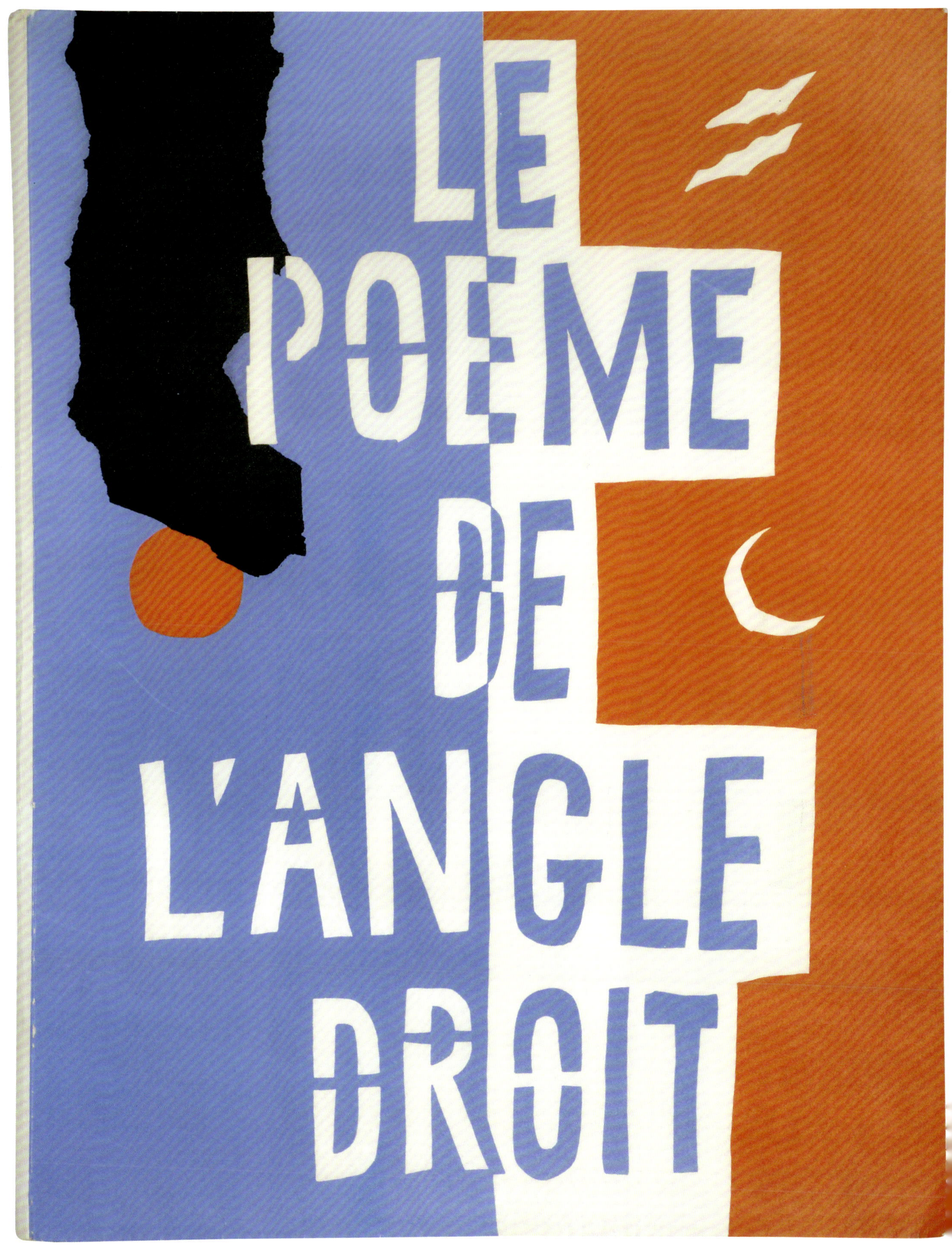

Opposite. Partial subscription list for *Le poème de l'angle droit*

Above. Cover of *Le poème de l'angle droit* (*Poem of the Right Angle*), Verve, Paris, 1955

Following pages. Selected illustrations from *Le poème de l'angle droit*

A milieu
B esprit
C chair
D fusion
E Caractère
F offre
G outil

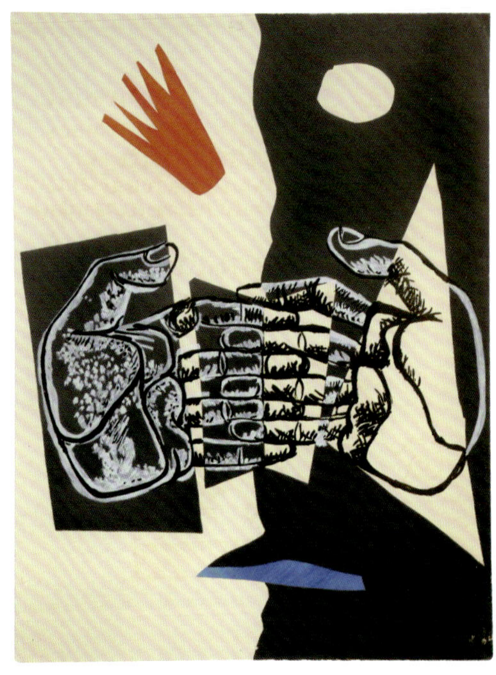

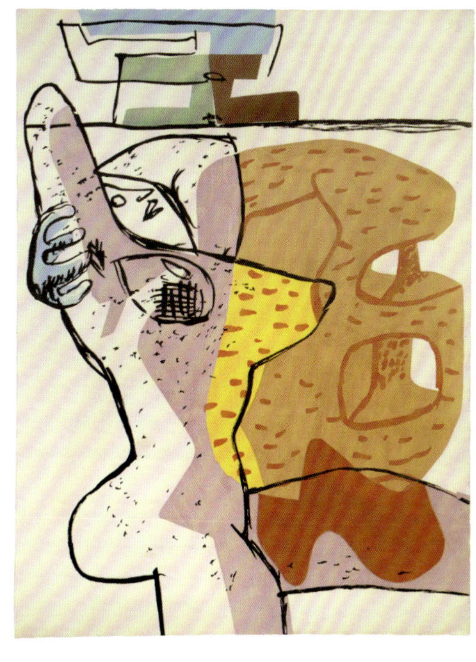

1.
I
48

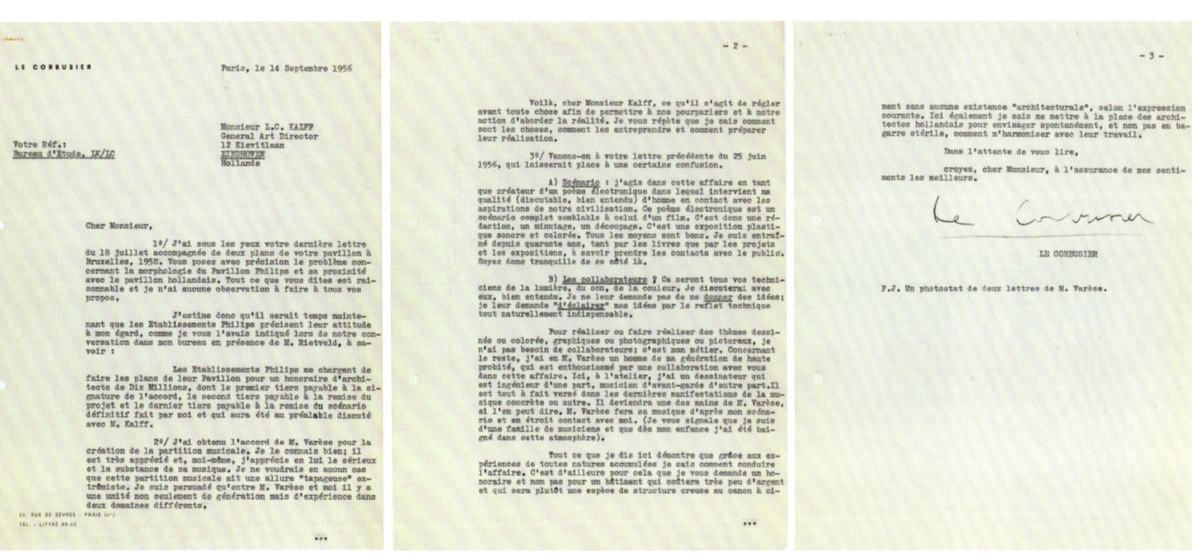

LE CORBUSIER

Paris, le 14 Septembre 1956

Votre Réf.:
Bureau d'Etude, LK/LC

Monsieur L.C. KALFF
General Art Director
12 Kievitlaan
EINDHOVEN
Hollande

Cher Monsieur,

1º/ J'ai sous les yeux votre dernière lettre du 18 juillet accompagnée de deux plans de votre pavillon à Bruxelles, 1958. Vous posez avec précision le problème concernant la morphologie du Pavillon Philips et sa proximité avec le pavillon hollandais. Tout ce que vous dites est raisonnable et je n'ai aucune observation à faire à tous vos propos.

J'estime donc qu'il serait temps maintenant que les Etablissements Philips précisent leur attitude à mon égard, comme je vous l'avais indiqué lors de notre conversation dans mon bureau en présence de M. Rietveld, à savoir :

Les Etablissements Philips me chargent de faire les plans de leur Pavillon pour un honoraire d'architecte de Dix Millions, dont le premier tiers payable à la signature de l'accord, le second tiers payable à la remise du projet et le dernier tiers payable à la remise du scénario définitif fait par moi et qui aura été au préalable discuté avec M. Kalff.

2º/ J'ai obtenu l'accord de M. Varèse pour la création de la partition musicale. Je le connais bien; il est très apprécié et, moi-même, j'apprécie en lui le sérieux et la substance de sa musique. Je ne voudrais en aucun cas que cette partition musicale ait une allure "tapageuse" extrêmiste. Je suis persuadé qu'entre M. Varèse et moi il y a une unité non seulement de génération mais d'expérience dans deux domaines différents.

35, RUE DE SÈVRES . PARIS (6e)
TÉL. . LITTRÉ 99-62

...

- 2 -

Voilà, cher Monsieur Kalff, ce qu'il s'agit de régler avant toute chose afin de permettre à nos pourparlers et à notre action d'aborder la réalité. Je vous répète que je sais comment sont les choses, comment les entreprendre et comment préparer leur réalisation.

3º/ Venons-en à votre lettre précédente du 25 juin 1956, qui laisserait place à une certaine confusion.

A) Scénario : j'agis dans cette affaire en tant que créateur d'un poème électronique dans lequel intervient ma qualité (discutable, bien entendu) d'homme en contact avec les aspirations de notre civilisation. Ce poème électronique est un scénario complet semblable à celui d'un film. C'est donc une rédaction, un minutage, un découpage. C'est une exposition plastique sonore et colorée. Tous les moyens sont bons. Je suis entraîné depuis quarante ans, tant par les livres que par les projets et les expositions, à savoir prendre les contacts avec le public. Soyez donc tranquille de ce côté là.

B) Les collaborateurs ? Ce seront tous vos techniciens de la lumière, du son, de la couleur. Je discuterai avec eux, bien entendu. Je ne leur demande pas de me donner des idées; je leur demande "d'éclairer" mes idées par le reflet technique tout naturellement indispensable.

Pour réaliser ou faire réaliser des thèmes dessinés ou colorés, graphiques ou photographiques ou pictoraux, je n'ai pas besoin de collaborateurs; c'est mon métier. Concernant le reste, j'ai en M. Varèse un homme de ma génération de haute probité, qui est enthousiasmé par une collaboration avec vous dans cette affaire. Ici, à l'atelier, j'ai un dessinateur qui est ingénieur d'une part, musicien d'avant-garde d'autre part. Il est tout à fait versé dans les dernières manifestations de la musique concrète ou autre. Il deviendra une des mains de M. Varèse, si l'on peut dire. M. Varèse fera sa musique d'après mon scénario et en étroit contact avec moi. (Je vous signale que je suis d'une famille de musiciens et que dès mon enfance j'ai été baigné dans cette atmosphère).

Tout ce que je dis ici démontre que grâce aux expériences de toutes natures accumulées je sais comment conduire l'affaire. C'est d'ailleurs pour cela que je vous demande un honoraire et non pas pour un bâtiment qui coûtera très peu d'argent et qui sera plutôt une espèce de structure creuse au canon à ci-

...

- 3 -

ment sans aucune existence "architecturale", selon l'expression courante. Ici également je sais me mettre à la place des architectes hollandais pour envisager spontanément, et non pas en bagarre stérile, comment m'harmoniser avec leur travail.

Dans l'attente de vous lire,

croyez, cher Monsieur, à l'assurance de mes sentiments les meilleurs.

LE CORBUSIER

P.J. Un photostat de deux lettres de M. Varèse.

From right angle to parabola: Philips Pavilion, world's fair, Brussels, 1956–58

The Dutch electronics company Philips commissioned Le Corbusier to design a pavilion it would sponsor at the 1958 world's fair in Brussels. The project's modest scale might have dissuaded him from participating had Philips not promised Le Corbusier access to all of its technological resources in order to integrate cutting-edge electronics with visionary architecture, in a multimedia installation called the *Poème électronique* (Electronic Poem). For the pavilion's form he again turned to the shell for inspiration. Starting with that source, an architect working in Le Corbusier's office, Iannis Xenakis, devised the hyperbolic paraboloid structure by making models out of piano wire and cloth.

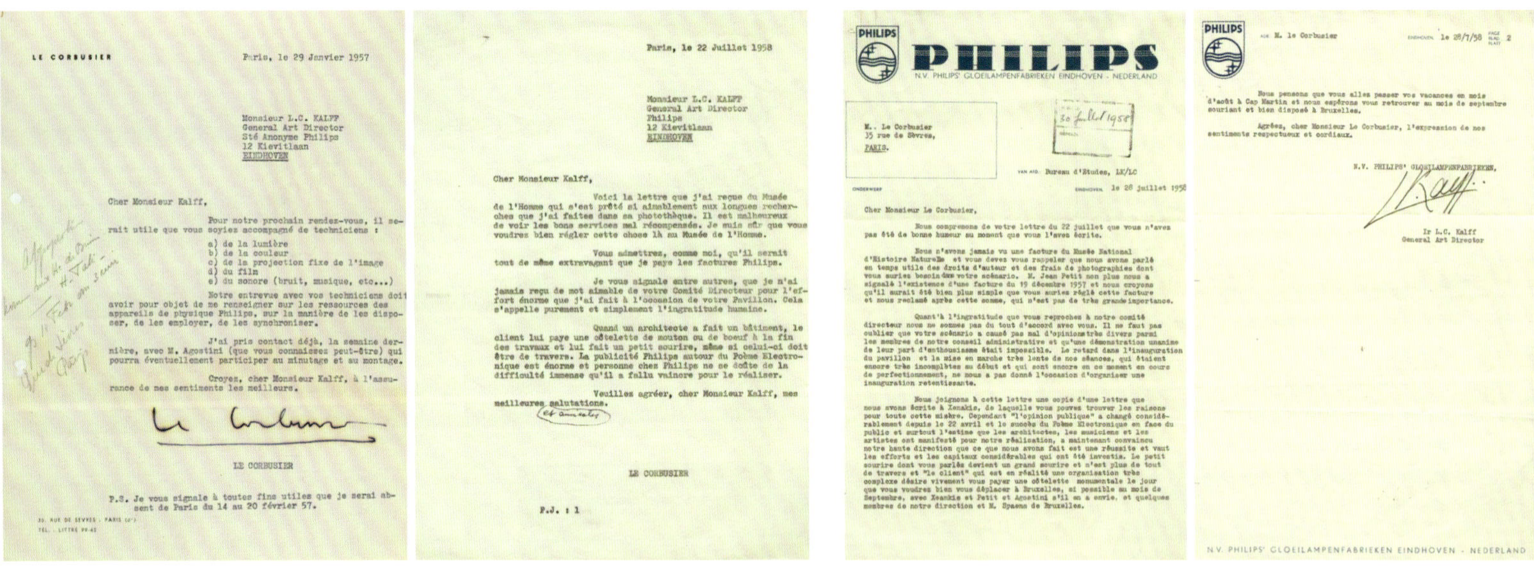

LE CORBUSIER

Paris, le 29 Janvier 1957

Monsieur L.C. KALFF
General Art Director
Sté Anonyme Philips
12 Kievitlaan
EINDHOVEN

Cher Monsieur Kalff,

Pour notre prochain rendez-vous, il serait utile que vous soyiez accompagné de techniciens :

a) de la lumière
b) de la couleur
c) de la projection fixe de l'image
d) du film
e) du sonore (bruit, musique, etc...)

Notre entrevue avec vos techniciens doit avoir pour objet de me renseigner sur les ressources des appareils de physique Philips, sur la manière de les disposer, de les employer, de les synchroniser.

J'ai pris contact déjà, la semaine dernière, avec M. Agostini (que vous connaissez peut-être) qui pourra éventuellement participer au minutage et au montage.

Croyez, cher Monsieur Kalff, à l'assurance de mes sentiments les meilleurs.

LE CORBUSIER

P.S. Je vous signale à toutes fins utiles que je serai absent de Paris du 14 au 20 février 57.

35, RUE DE SÈVRES . PARIS (6e)
TÉL. . LITTRÉ 99-62

Paris, le 22 Juillet 1958

Monsieur L.C. KALFF
General Art Director
Philips
12 Kievitlaan
EINDHOVEN

Cher Monsieur Kalff,

Voici la lettre que j'ai reçue du Musée de l'Homme qui s'est prêté si aimablement aux longues recherches que j'ai faites dans sa photothèque. Il est malheureux de voir les bons services mal récompensés. Je suis sûr que vous voudrez bien régler cette chose là au Musée de l'Homme.

Vous admettrez, comme moi, qu'il serait tout de même extravagant que je paye les factures Philips.

Je vous signale entre autres, que je n'ai jamais reçu de mot aimable de votre Comité Directeur pour l'effort énorme que j'ai fait à l'occasion de votre Pavillon. Cela s'appelle purement et simplement l'ingratitude humaine.

Quand un architecte a fait un bâtiment, le client lui paye une côtelette de mouton ou de boeuf à la fin des travaux et lui fait un petit sourire, même si celui-ci doit être de travers. La publicité Philips autour du Poème Electronique est énorme et personne chez Philips ne se doûte de la difficulté immense qu'il a fallu vaincre pour le réaliser.

Veuillez agréer, cher Monsieur Kalff, mes meilleures salutations.

LE CORBUSIER

P.J. : 1

PHILIPS
N.V. PHILIPS' GLOEILAMPENFABRIEKEN EINDHOVEN - NEDERLAND

M. Le Corbusier
35 rue de Sèvres,
PARIS.

30 Juillet 1958

VAN AFD. Bureau d'Etudes, LK/LC

ONDERWERP

EINDHOVEN le 28 juillet 1958

Cher Monsieur Le Corbusier,

Nous comprenons de votre lettre du 22 juillet que vous n'avez pas été de bonne humeur au moment que vous l'avez écrite.

Nous n'avons jamais vu une facture du Musée National d'Histoire Naturelle et vous devez vous rappeler que nous avons parlé en temps utile des droits d'auteur et des frais de photographies dont vous auriez besoin dans votre scénario. M. Jean Petit non plus nous a signalé l'existence d'une facture du 19 décembre 1957 et nous croyons qu'il aurait été bien plus simple que vous auriez réglé cette facture et nous reclamé après cette somme, qui n'est pas de très grande importance.

Quant à l'ingratitude que vous reprochez à notre comité directeur nous ne sommes pas du tout d'accord avec vous. Il ne faut pas oublier que votre scénario a causé pas mal d'opinions très divers parmi les membres de notre conseil administrative et qu'une démonstration unanime de leur part d'enthousiasme était impossible. Le retard dans l'inauguration du pavillon et la mise en marche très lente de nos séances, qui étaient encore très incomplètes au début et qui sont encore en ce moment en cours de perfectionnement, ne nous a pas donné l'occasion d'organiser une inauguration retentissante.

Nous joignons à cette lettre une copie d'une lettre que nous avons écrite à Xenakis, de laquelle vous pouvez trouver les raisons pour toute cette misère. Cependant "l'opinion publique" a changé considérablement depuis le 22 avril et le succès du Poème Electronique en face du public et surtout l'estime que les architectes, les musiciens et les artistes ont manifesté pour notre réalisation, a maintenant convaincu notre haute direction que ce que nous avons fait est une réussite et vaut les efforts et les capitaux considérables qui ont été investis. Le petit sourire dont vous parlèz devient un grand sourire et n'est plus de tout de travers et "le client" qui est en réalité une organisation très complexe désire vivement vous payer une côtelette monumentale le jour que vous voudrez bien vous déplacer à Bruxelles, si possible au mois de Septembre, avec Xeankis et Petit et Agostini s'il en a envie, et quelques membres de notre direction et M. Spaens de Bruxelles.

PHILIPS

AAN M. le Corbusier

EINDHOVEN le 28/7/58 PAGE 2

Nous pensons que vous allez passer vos vacances en mois d'août à Cap Martin et nous espérons vous retrouver au mois de septembre souriant et bien disposé à Bruxelles.

Agréez, cher Monsieur Le Corbusier, l'expression de nos sentiments respectueux et cordiaux.

N.V. PHILIPS' GLOEILAMPENFABRIEKEN,

Ir L.C. Kalff
General Art Director

N.V. PHILIPS' GLOEILAMPENFABRIEKEN EINDHOVEN - NEDERLAND

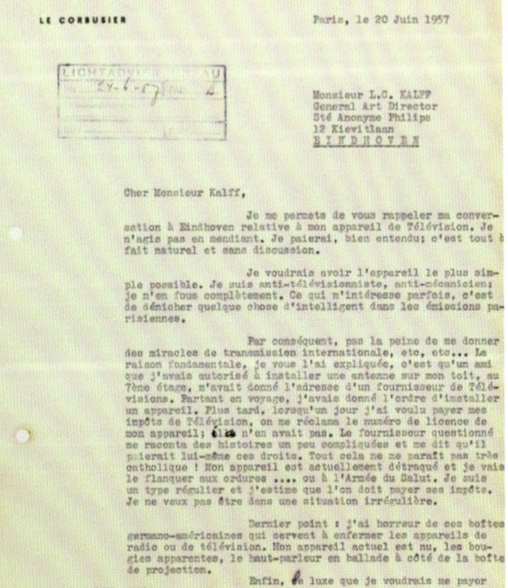

LE CORBUSIER

Paris, le 20 Juin 1957

Monsieur L.C. KALFF
General Art Director
Sté Anonyme Philips
12 Kievitlaan
EINDHOVEN

Cher Monsieur Kalff,

Je me permets de vous rappeler ma conversation à Eindhoven relative à mon appareil de Télévision. Je n'agis pas en mendiant. Je paierai, bien entendu; c'est tout à fait naturel et sans discussion.

Je voudrais avoir l'appareil le plus simple possible. Je suis anti-télévisionniste, anti-mécanicien; je m'en fous complètement. Ce qui m'intéresse parfois, c'est de dénicher quelque chose d'intelligent dans les émissions parisiennes.

Par conséquent, pas la peine de me donner des miracles de transmission internationale, etc, etc... La raison fondamentale, je vous l'ai expliquée, c'est qu'un ami que j'avais autorisé à installer une antenne sur mon toit, au 7ème étage, m'avait donné l'adresse d'un fournisseur de Télévisions. Partant en voyage, j'avais donné l'ordre d'installer un appareil. Plus tard, lorsqu'un jour j'ai voulu payer mes impôts de Télévision, on me réclama le numéro de licence de mon appareil; il n'en avait pas. Le fournisseur questionné me raconta des histoires un peu compliquées et me dit qu'il paierait lui-même ces droits. Tout cela ne me paraît pas très catholique ! Mon appareil est actuellement détraqué et je vais le flanquer aux ordures .... ou à l'Armée du Salut. Je suis un type régulier et j'estime que l'on doit payer ses impôts. Je ne veux pas être dans une situation irrégulière.

Dernier point : j'ai horreur de ces boîtes germano-américaines qui servent à enfermer les appareils de radio ou de télévision. Mon appareil actuel est nu, les bougies apparentes, le haut-parleur en ballade à côté de la boîte de projection.

Enfin, le luxe que je voudrais me payer

35, RUE DE SÈVRES . PARIS (6e)
TÉL. . LITTRÉ 99-62

...

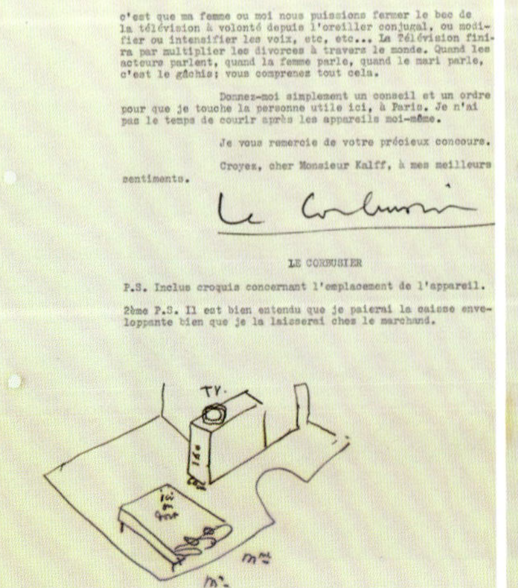

c'est que ma femme ou moi nous puissions fermer le bec de la télévision à volonté depuis l'oreiller conjugal, ou modifier ou intensifier les voix, etc, etc... La Télévision finira par multiplier les divorces à travers le monde. Quand les acteurs parlent, quand la femme parle, quand le mari parle, c'est le gâchis; vous comprenez tout cela.

Donnez-moi simplement un conseil et un ordre pour que je touche la personne utile ici, à Paris. Je n'ai pas le temps de courir après les appareils moi-même.

Je vous remercie de votre précieux concours.

Croyez, cher Monsieur Kalff, à mes meilleurs sentiments.

LE CORBUSIER

P.S. Inclus croquis concernant l'emplacement de l'appareil.

2ème P.S. Il est bien entendu que je paierai la caisse enveloppante bien que je la laisserai chez le marchand.

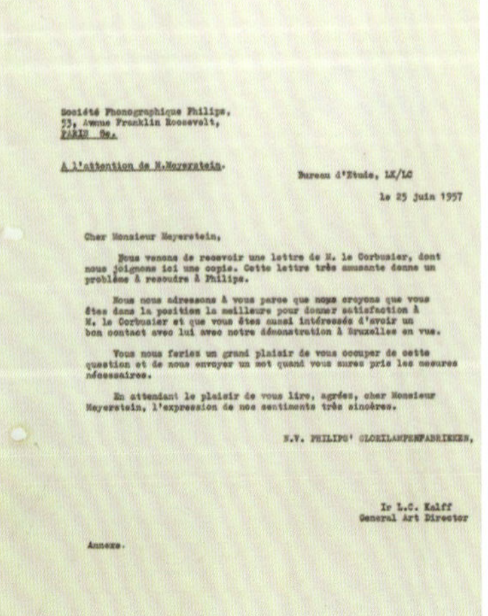

Société Phonographique Philips,
33, Avenue Franklin Roosevelt,
PARIS 8e.

A l'attention de M. Meyerstein.

Bureau d'Etude, LK/LC

le 25 juin 1957

Cher Monsieur Meyerstein,

Nous venons de recevoir une lettre de M. le Corbusier, dont nous joignons ici une copie. Cette lettre très amusante donne un problème à resoudre à Philips.

Nous nous adressons à vous parce que nous croyons que vous êtes dans la position la meilleure pour donner satisfaction à M. le Corbusier et que vous êtes aussi intéressés d'avoir un bon contact avec lui avec notre démonstration à Bruxelles en vue.

Vous nous feriez un grand plaisir de vous occuper de cette question et de nous envoyer un mot quand vous aurez pris les mesures nécessaires.

En attendant le plaisir de vous lire, agréez, cher Monsieur Meyerstein, l'expression de nos sentiments très sincères.

N.V. PHILIPS' GLOEILAMPENFABRIEKEN,

Ir L.C. Kalff
General Art Director

Annexe.

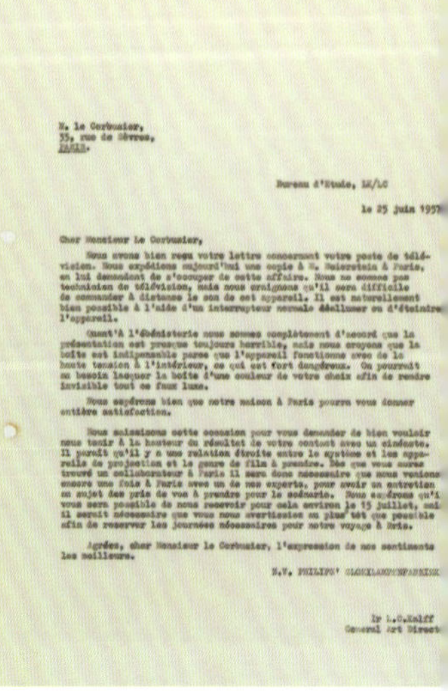

M. le Corbusier,
35, rue de Sèvres,
PARIS.

Bureau d'Etude, LK/LC

le 25 juin 1957

Cher Monsieur Le Corbusier,

Nous avons bien reçu votre lettre concernant votre poste de télévision. Nous expédions aujourd'hui une copie à M. Meierstein à Paris, en lui demandant de s'occuper de cette affaire. Nous ne sommes pas technicien de télévision, mais nous craignons qu'il sera difficile de commander à distance le son de cet appareil. Il est naturellement bien possible à l'aide d'un interrupteur normale d'allumer ou d'éteindre l'appareil.

Quant à l'ébénisterie nous sommes complètement d'accord que la présentation est presque toujours horrible, mais nous croyons que la boîte est indispensable parce que l'appareil fonctionne avec de la haute tension à l'intérieur, ce qui est fort dangereux. On pourrait au besoin laquer la boîte d'une couleur de votre choix afin de rendre invisible tout ce faux luxe.

Nous espérons bien que notre maison à Paris pourra vous donner entière satisfaction.

Nous saisissons cette occasion pour vous demander de bien vouloir nous tenir à la hauteur du résultat de votre contact avec un cinéaste. Il paraît qu'il y a une relation étroite entre le système et les appareils de projection et le genre de film à prendre. Dès que vous aurez trouvé un collaborateur à Paris il sera donc nécessaire que nous venions encore une fois à Paris avec un de nos experts, pour avoir un entretien au sujet des prises de vue à prendre pour le scénario. Nous espérons qu'il vous sera possible de nous recevoir pour cela environ le 15 juillet, mais il serait nécessaire que vous nous avertissiez au plus tôt que possible afin de reserver les journées nécessaires pour notre voyage à Paris.

Agréez, cher Monsieur le Corbusier, l'expression de nos sentiments les meilleurs.

N.V. PHILIPS' GLOEILAMPENFABRIEKEN

Ir L.C.Kalff
General Art Director

Opposite, top row. Le Corbusier to L. C. Kalff, "general art director" of Philips, 14 September 1956, summarizing terms of the collaboration on the *Poème électronique* (Electronic Poem)

Opposite, middle row, far left. Le Corbusier to L. C. Kalff, 29 January 1957, asking that Philips technicians attend a forthcoming meeting

Opposite, middle row, left. Le Corbusier to L. C. Kalff, 22 July 1958, complaining about what he considered rude treatment by Philips, including its failure to give him a meal after completion of the pavilion

Opposite, middle row, right and far right. L. C. Kalff to Le Corbusier, 28 July 1958, assuring him that the management of Philips considered the *Poème électronique* to be a great success

Opposite, bottom row, far left and left. Le Corbusier to L. C. Kalff, 20 June 1957, seeking a no-frills television set with one luxury: to "be able to shut [it] up… from the nuptial bed."

Opposite, bottom row, right. L. C. Kalff to M. Meyerstein, in the Philips design department, Paris, 25 June 1957, passing along Le Corbusier's request

Opposite, bottom row, far right. L. C. Kalff to Le Corbusier, 25 June 1957, about his search for the new television set and progress on securing a filmmaker for the *Poème électronique*

Above. Left to right: Unknown man, Le Corbusier, L. C. Kalff, acoustic consultant Willem Tak, and architect and composer Iannis Xenakis during the positioning of audio speakers in the pavilion

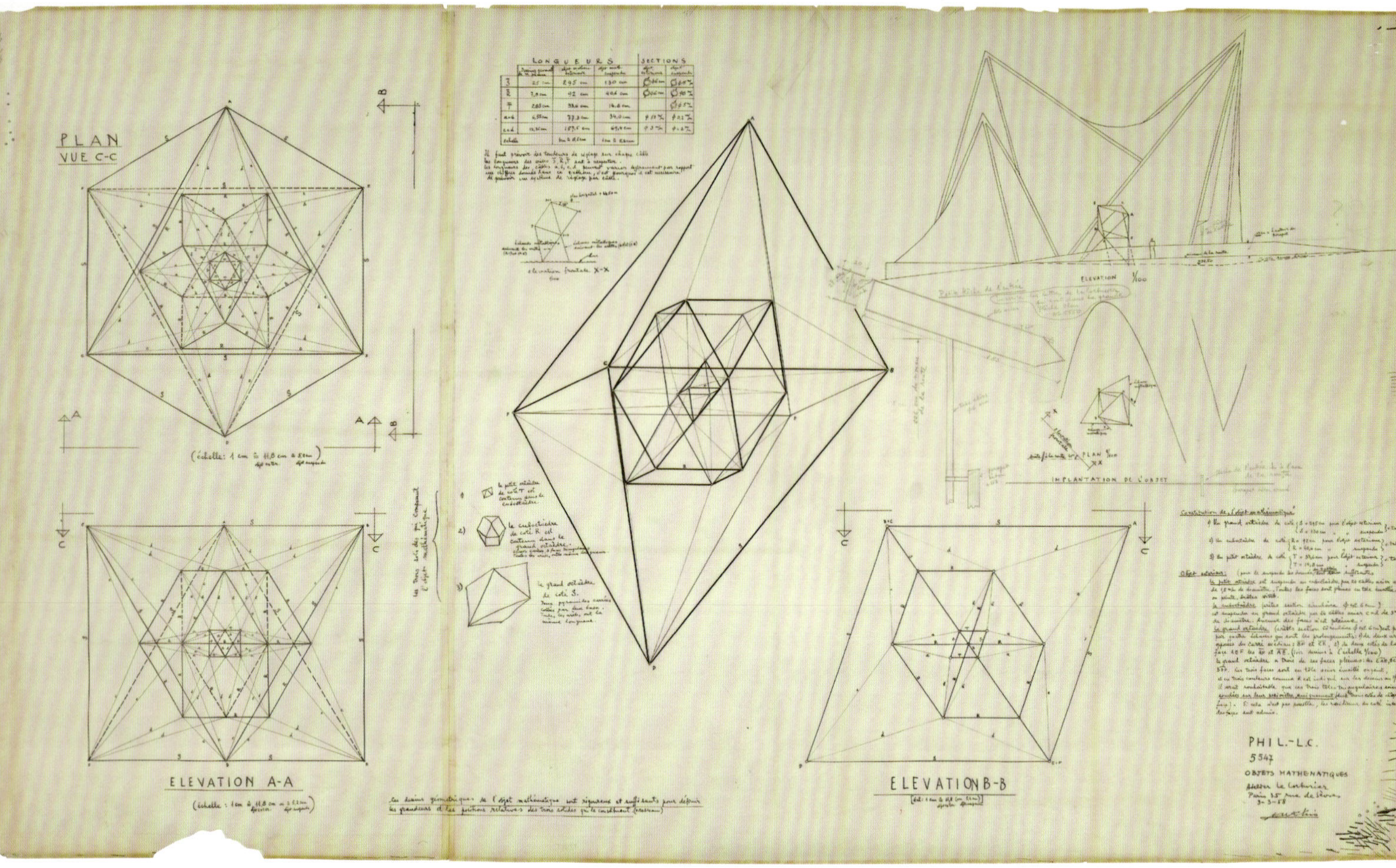

Above. Studies, 3 March 1958, for the *Objet mathématique* (mathematical object), the sculptural element above the entrance to the Philips Pavilion, Brussels

Below. Two views of the wire and thread study model of the first scheme, Philips Pavilion, 1956

"I shall make you not a Pavilion, but an Electronic Poem. A bottle containing the poem
1. Light
2. Color
3. Image
4. Rhythm
5. Sound
6. Architecture brought together as an organic whole accessible to the public and thus displaying the resources of Philips's products."

—Le Corbusier, in Iannis Xenakis, "Le Poème électronique du Pavillon Philips," 1957

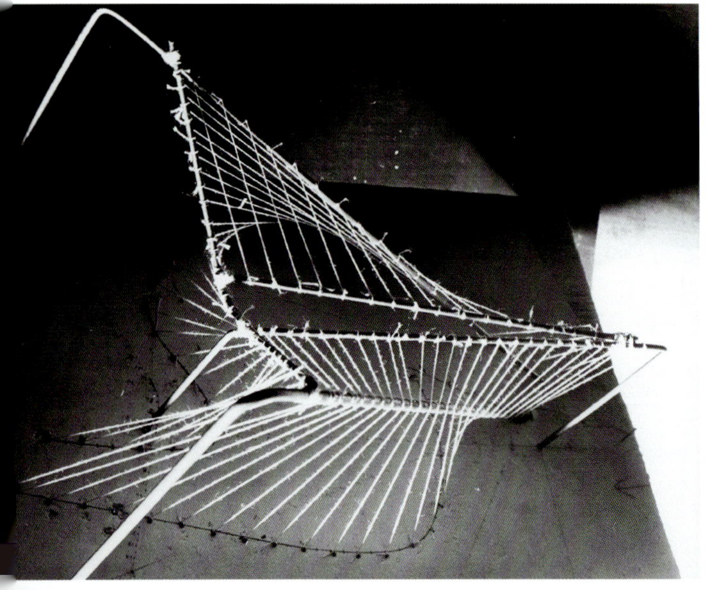

Right. Wire and thread study model of the second scheme, covered with tracing paper, Philips Pavilion, 1956

Below. Model of the Philips Pavilion, with wire figures for scale

STRABED
STRABED

Opposite. Philips Pavilion, Brussels, under construction

Right. Le Corbusier with Philips executive L. C. Kalff (left) and composer Edgard Varèse (right) in front of the Philips Pavilion, 1958

Below. The completed pavilion

LE CORBUSIER

Paris, le 3 Juillet 1956

Monsieur L.C. KALFF
General Art Director
12 Kievitlaan
EINDHOVEN
Hollande

Cher Monsieur,

Rentré de voyage cette nuit, j'ai trouvé votre lettre du 25 juin.

J'ai reçu, le 16 juin, une réponse favorable de M. Edgard Varèse pour la partition.

Il reste, bien entendu, que je serai à la clef du scénario. Je serai ravi de prévoir et de réaliser tous les contacts que vous signalez dans votre lettre afin d'obtenir une exécution parfaite. La raison de mon intervention n'est pas de faire un local de plus dans ma carrière, mais bien de créer avec vous autres un premier "jeu électrique", électronique, synchronique, où la lumière, le dessin, la couleur, le volume, le mouvement et l'idée, font un tout étonnant et accessible, bien entendu, à la foule.

Si je l'ai proposé, c'est que je me sens apte à le faire avec vous. Et ce sera une belle chose à faire.

Croyez, cher Monsieur, à mes meilleurs sentiments.

Le Corbusier

LE CORBUSIER

35, RUE DE SEVRES . PARIS (6e)
TÉL. . LITTRÉ 99-62

ATELIER
LE CORBUSIER
35, rue de Sèvres
Paris-6e - Lit 99-62

COPIE

Paris, le 3 Novembre 1956

Monsieur Edgard VARESE
168 Sullivan Street
NEW YORK 12, N.Y.

Mon cher Varèse,

Je pars aux Indes vers le 12 novembre; je ne rentrerai que vers le 18 ou le 20 décembre. Les événements Nasser ont provoqué tout ce désarroi. C'est donc à la fin de l'année que nous pourrions nous voir et si vous aimez mieux passer la Noël à New York, ne venez qu'en janvier.

J'ai vu M. Kalff, General Art Director, des Ets. Philips de Eindhoven, depuis la lettre que je vous ai adressée le 24 octobre 1956. Il est parfaitement loyalement d'accord pour les droits d'auteur de faire les discriminations nécessaires selon le bon sens. Il viendra certainement à Paris au moment où vous serez ici.

avec Philips x

Je vous ai dit avoir contracté x un "gentleman's agreement" par échange de lettres (dont vous avez eu les extraits utiles le 24 octobre 1956). Mon travail est très avancé: les plans sont faits, acceptés et les ingénieurs calculent. La construction ne peut pas attendre (c'est une exposition universelle et la main d'oeuvre et les matériaux sont très rares). Toute cette affaire ne tient debout qu'à la condition que je puisse remettre le scénario, comme convenu, au début de janvier. Et ce scénario doit être fait avec vous.

J'envoie copie de cette lettre à M. Kalff qui doit prendre des contacts directs avec vous à toutes fins utiles.

Bien amicalement à vous.

LE CORBUSIER

16-VI/56

19 juin 1956

Mon cher Le Corbusier

Votre lettre du 12 est arrivée ce matin – Merci.

Comme vous me le demandez je tiens à vous faire savoir de suite que je trouve votre projet magnifique et que j'accepte avec un vif plaisir la collaboration que vous me proposez.

D'après ce que vous m'écrivez je vois [illegible]

Comme vous et comme les Ets. Philips seul m'intéresse de donner naissance à "la chose la plus extraordinaire possible"

Je serai à Paris fin Automne et me réjouis de vous revoir

En toute amitié

Edgard Varèse

Je vous prie de transmettre mon bon souvenir à Xenakis

30-VII/56

3 Septembre 1956

Mon cher Le Corbusier

J'espère que vous avez reçu mon aérogramme de remerciement et d'acceptation du 30 juin.

Un mot de vous me [illegible] à ce sujet [illegible]

En toute cordialité

Votre

Varèse

Edgard Varèse
188 Sullivan St
New York 12 N.Y.

AIR MAIL 10¢

AIR LETTER
AÉROGRAMME

VIA AIR MAIL
PAR AVION

Monsieur Le Corbusier
35 Rue de Sèvres
Paris 6e
FRANCE

NO TAPE OR STICKER MAY BE ATTACHED

IF ANYTHING IS ENCLOSED, THIS LETTER WILL BE SENT BY ORDINARY MAIL

FIRST FOLD

Edgard Varèse
188 Sullivan St
New York 12 N.Y.

NEW YORK, N.Y. JUN 16 10 PM 1956

CHURCH STREET STATION

AIR MAIL 10¢

AIR LETTER
AÉROGRAMME

VIA AIR MAIL
PAR AVION

Monsieur Le Corbusier
35 Rue de Sèvres
Paris 6e
FRANCE

NO TAPE OR STICKER MAY BE ATTACHED

IF ANYTHING IS ENCLOSED, THIS LETTER WILL BE SENT BY ORDINARY MAIL

SECOND FOLD

Above. Two aerograms from composer Edgard Varèse to Le Corbusier, 16 June and 30 July 1956, agreeing to collaborate with him on the Philips Pavilion

Top left. Le Corbusier to L. C. Kalff, 3 July 1956, concerning Edgard Varèse's agreement to collaborate on the "electric game" at the Philips Pavilion

Middle left. Le Corbusier to Edgard Varèse, 3 November 1956, regarding artists' rights for contributions to the Philips Pavilion

Below left. Le Corbusier to Edgard Varèse, 1 February 1957, assuring him of progress on plans for the Philips Pavilion

Below middle. Le Corbusier to Edgard Varèse, 22 June 1957, describing the twenty-seven plates of the scenario for the *Poème électronique*

Below right. Le Corbusier to Edgard Varèse, 18 February 1958, concerning change to the scenario of the *Poème électonique*

Paris, le 1er Février 1957

Monsieur Edgard VARESE
188 Sullivan Street
NEW YORK 12, N.Y.

Mon cher Varèse,

J'ai bien reçu votre mot du 28.1.57. Ne vous en faites pas; cela continue. Il faut d'abord passer les bulldozers sur le terrain de l'administration et des obstacles. Tout se poursuit et nous avançons. Vous pensez bien que je vous mobiliserai dès que l'heure sera venue. Comptez sur moi.

Bien amicalement à vous.

LE CORBUSIER

Paris, le 22 Juin 1957

Monsieur Edgard VARESE
188 Sullivan Street
NEW YORK 12, N.Y.

Mon cher Varèse,

Comme promis, j'ai établi pour vous les 27 planches du scénario du Poème Electronique du Pavillon Philips, Bruxelles (que je vous envoie par pli séparé en recommandé, par avion.)

Vous n'y comprendrez rien du tout, mille regrets !

Toutefois, vous vous rendrez compte qu'il y a une succession d'ambiances (noire, blanche rouge, jaune, bleue, etc...) qui envahissent tout l'intérieur du pavillon; des rythmes horizontaux ou des rythmes verticaux (circulaires) qui animent le déploiement des couleurs; des apparitions de formes grossissantes ou dégrossissantes au travers de cadences colorées, par exemple, planche 5; des apparitions subites du visage humain, par exemple, planche 6; des présences intermittentes de la mathématique d'une part et de la figure humaine d'autre part dans la planche 11, planche 12; puis dans des multifaces humains, planche 13; puis des évocations animales et brutales ou répugnantes, planche 14; des foules hurlantes, planche 15; beauté sereine, planche 16; de mécanique vivante naturelle, planche 17; de mécanique brutale, planche 18; puis subitement, coupure nette dans une ambiance blanche ineffable sans rien en vue et dans le silence total, planche 19; puis reprise de la vie colorée, planche 20; puis apparition de phénomènes grossissants ou dégrossissants (inquiétude), planche 21; puis sur ambiance rouge, un éclair terrible, planche 22; puis évocation de désastres de toutes sortes, planche 23; puis reprise en mains de la vie des couleurs en zones horizontales et présence humaine et mathématique, planche 24; montée vers l'optimisme et l'épanouissement, planche 25; puis évocation de l'immense cosmos, planche 26; et enfin, éventuellement, Laurel et Hardy pour finir en même temps que le sourire d'un bébé.

C'est idiot; mais il y a moyen de faire quelque chose avec cela.

Je répète : pas de musique coordonnée avec cela; chacun suit sa piste et prend contact dans le silence du 19.

Amitiés.

LE CORBUSIER

Paris, le 18 Février 1958

Monsieur Edgard VARESE
c/o Mrs Sliaker
38 Gragelstraat
EINDHOVEN

Mon cher Varèse,

Inclus vous allez trouver copie des décisions que j'ai prises à Cap Martin la semaine dernière dans mon lit pris par la grippe. Ces décisions sont définitives.

J'ai répondu à tous vos désirs, c'est à dire en vous laissant la primauté des terminaisons musicales (entre 384 et 480). Vous êtes maître chez vous à ce moment là. J'ai supprimé le film Kast. Votre musique se déploiera dans l'ombre, la lumière, la couleur et sans aucune distraction.

Par contre, je me suis replié personnellement à la seconde 241. Malgré ma bonne volonté, je ne peux pas diminuer la période des 40 secondes de silence absolu où seront entendues les paroles nécessaires, soit de 241 à 280 secondes. Donc de 241 à 280 on coupe la musique purement et simplement. Puisqu'il y avait un zéro à 240 (silence) on le prolongera jusqu'à 280. Là, vous pourrez faire un raccord. C'est l'effort que je vous demande ayant fait, de mon côté, l'effort le plus grand.

Pour bien mettre les choses au point, je vous donne copie de ma récapitulation du 15 février 1958 écrite dans mon lit et qui a valeur de décision définitive.

Je prépare pour Mr Jansen, Illuminating Engineer, le nécessaire pour le convoquer à Paris afin de fixer le minutage définitif des ambiances colorées.

Bien amicalement à vous.

P.S. Le livre "Ronchamp" vous est expédié aujourd'hui

LE CORBUSIER

Above. Le Corbusier with Edgard Varèse

Music, motion, and color: *Poème électronique*

The exterior of the Philips Pavilion was undeniably striking, but Le Corbusier had actually conceived the project from the inside out, so that its form was generated from a multimedia *Poème électronique*. For this he engaged modernist composer Edgard Varèse to create an electronic score to accompany a sequence of projected images and colored lights carefully curated by the architect himself.

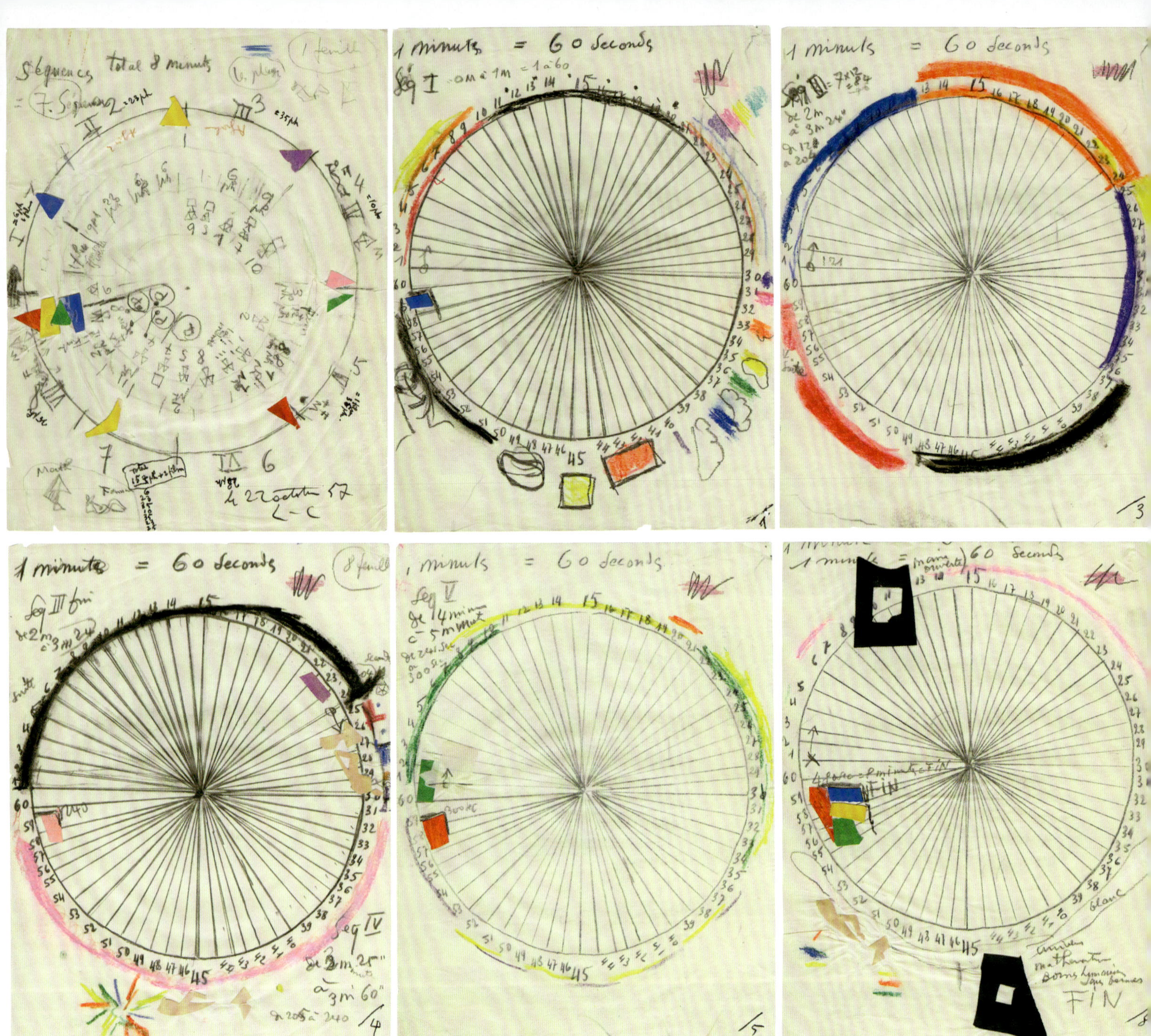

"Scenario: my role here is that of the creator of an electronic poem shaped by my capacities (open to discussion) as a man in contact with the aspirations of our civilization. This electronic poem is a complete scenario similar to that of a film. Thus it contains text, timing and breakdown. It is an exhibition using visuals, sound, and colors. No methods are excluded. I have forty years' experience, via books, projects, and exhibitions, in learning how to make contact with the public. In that respect you may rest easy."

—Letter to L. C. Kalff, 14 September 1956

Opposite. Le Corbusier's scheme, 22 October 1957, for the timing of the images and music in the ten-minute *Poème électronique* at the Philips Pavilion, Brussels

Below. Le Corbusier's schematic renderings, May 1957, for the scenario of the *Poème électronique*

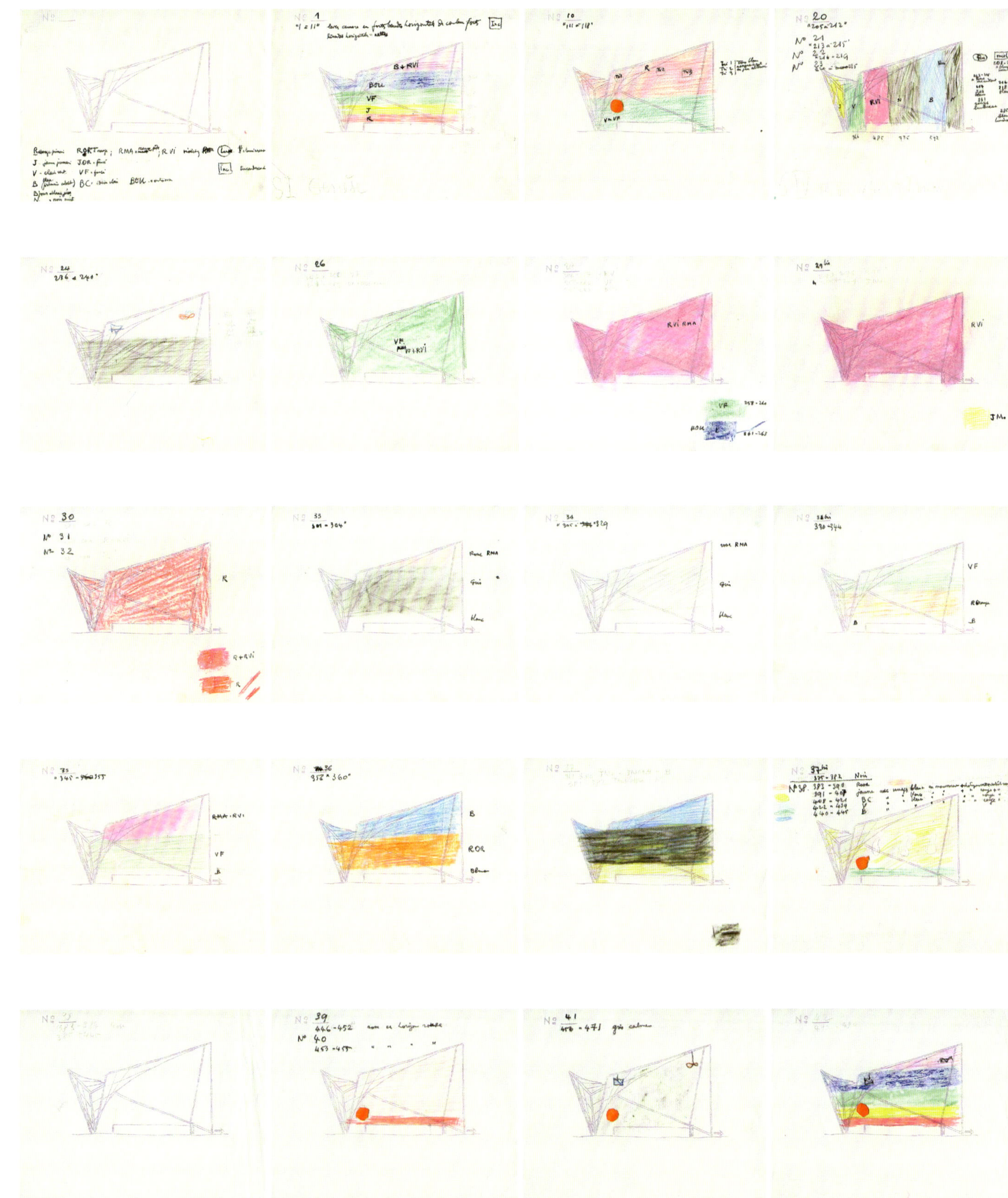

Opposite and above. Le Corbusier's schematic renderings, May 1957, of images for the *Poème électronique* at the Philips Pavilion, Brussels

Opposite. Inauguration of the Philips Pavilion, Brussels, 22 April 1958

Clockwise from top left:

Sculptural element above the entrance to the pavilion

Two images from films shown in the pavilion

Le Corbusier with cinematographer Philippe Agostini (left) and Philips executive L. C. Kalff (right), Eindhoven, the Netherlands

"The aim of my initiative is not to add another building to my career, but to create, with the rest of you, the first 'electric game'—electronic and synchronic—in which light, drawing, color, volume, movement and ideas add up to something both astonishing and, naturally, available to all."

—Letter to L. C. Kalff, 3 July 1956

Above left. Magazine advertisement, "How to dress for the Expo," *Elle* (France), 23 June 1958

Above right. LP record album sleeve for the *Poème électronique* by Edgard Varèse

Below left. Magazine article, "Philips," *Edilizia Moderna* (Italy), August 1958

Below right. Richard Neutra to Le Corbusier, 10 May 1958, thanking him for the "great experience" of attending a "trial presentation" of the *Poème électronique*

Opposite. Demonstration in Brussels in support of Le Corbusier, 1958

Philips

Progetto: *Le Corbusier architetto*
Hanno collaborato alla realizzazione di questo Padiglione un gruppo di specialisti eterogenei: musicisti, cineasti, calcolatori del cemento, tecnici di acustica, tecnici elettronici ecc. Le Corbusier è il creatore non soltanto dell'edificio ma anche del « poema elettronico » della durata di 10 minuti che si svolge all'interno, un poema che interessa la vista e l'udito con suoni, giuochi di colori, di forme, di luci, di ombre, di movimenti.

L'edificio ha una pianta a curve libere ed è costituito da 12 pareti inclinate e a curve paraboloidi iperboliche che si innalzano e si riuniscono in tre vertici. Le pareti sono costruite con elementi di cemento preparate al suolo di circa 1 metro e mezzo di lato e di 5 cm di spessore; esse sono state montate per mezzo di un ponteggio interno e sono sostenute da una doppia maglia di cavi da 8 mm tesa su direttrici cilindriche di cemento fortemento armato.

Gli apparecchi per la realizzazione del « poema » (ci sono 300 altoparlanti e 30.000 saldature di fili elettrici!) sono collocati dietro una barriera di cemento che corre lungo le pareti laterali: queste sono molto alte e integrate da altre superfici curve utili sia per la realizzazione del "poema" sia per ragioni strutturali. Queste pareti sono foderate da materiale fonoassorbente.
All'interno c'è posto per 500 spettatori in piedi.

83

14 Mai 1958

Dear Mr Le Corbusier

It was a great experience to have the Philips people in Brussels let me be present at a trial production of your poème lumineux. It was wonderful to be at this private showing. Let me send you my warm wishes and admiration – also to Mr Varese whom I have known many years ago.

Cordially

Richard Neutra

v. 10 58

Richard Neutra

classer Opinions → Poème électronique

A very popular pavilion

Despite some initial resistance from the Philips management, particularly regarding the choice of Varèse as composer, and despite the inevitable protests against such an unconventional built form, Philips seriously considered re-erecting the pavilion as a corporate museum in Eindhoven, the Netherlands. Ultimately however, the pavilion was permanently dismantled in January 1959.

Le Corbusier always preserved as sacred a full month in August for vacation. In the 1920s and 1930s he went to Le Piquey, on the Bassin d'Arcachon near Bordeaux, or to the medieval town of Vézelay in Burgundy, where his friend Jean Badovici had converted some old stone houses. After the war Le Corbusier took to spending the summer in Roquebrune-Cap-Martin, on France's Côte d'Azur. There the modernist villa designed by Eileen Gray for Jean Badovici, Villa E.1027, gave him a place to relax and to paint his murals, and a modest fish restaurant run by Thomas Rebutato provided convivial meals.

It was for this small village overlooking the sea that Le Corbusier designed a compact log cabin—his *petit cabanon*—where he would live and work each summer until his death. Carefully designed to fulfill his basic needs, with dimensions based on his Modulor system (3.66 meters square and 2.26 meters high), it was constructed in 1951 by his favorite Corsican carpenter, Charles Barbéris, and shipped to Roquebrune for assembly. Many of Le Corbusier's projects of the 1950s and 1960s were conceived in a prefabricated builder's shed that he erected a few meters away, in 1954. "I work here happy as a prince, but in the possession of liberty (and therefore happier than a prince)."

The housing project Roq and Rob (never built), which Le Corbusier devised for the steep hill site above the *cabanon*, would have created a picturesque cascade of vaulted longitudinal spaces with views over the sea. A less ambitious project, to be financed by Marguerite Tjader Harris, consisted of only five houses on the rocks below the *cabanon*; it had to be abandoned after an exceptional storm and high water swamped the site. The only tangible results of these projects were five plywood camping cabins that Thomas Rebutato was able to rent out in the tourist season.

A project with origins dating back to 1935 was the construction in Paris in 1951–55 of two houses for André Jaoul and his son and their families. With these houses, Le Corbusier asked the fundamental question, "How should we live today?" His answer was to offer a simple, rough-and-ready existence close to nature, featuring raw materials and the essential joys of light, space, and greenery. Writing to a Swiss friend for whom he was designing a similar house, he said: "I insist on asserting this most emphatically: these dreadful Swiss irritate me with their notion of perfect finish in architecture. You are a wise man, and so am I. We are not bourgeois, we take pleasure in the crudity of bare bricks, the pointing roughly executed by the mason, the brick walls plastered on the interior, etc… I am certain that your house will be all the better for being rough and you will save at least 20 percent on the cost, which is worth having."

The spirit of the Mediterranean breathes through these houses, constructed by Barbéris and Sardinian mason Salvatore Bertocchi. For the interiors, Le Corbusier used the technique of catalan vaults, which he had admired in Barcelona during visits in 1928 and 1929. Thin tiles laid edge to edge in three layers formed vaults whose warm red surface created the kind of homely atmosphere that the Purist villas of the 1920s lacked.

9 Mediterranean Days (1950–1959)

Opposite. Le Corbusier and one of his murals at Villa E.1027, Roquebrune-Cap-Martin, France, c. 1939

Eden by the sea: Roquebrune-Cap-Martin, France

Starting after World War II, Le Corbusier and Yvonne vacationed regularly at Roquebrune-Cap-Martin on France's Côte d'Azur, not far from Monaco, where Yvonne grew up. To Le Corbusier, Cap-Martin represented an Eden removed from modern urban life. There he could indulge in an ascetic, primitivist manner of living that revolved around the sea and the sun and the myth-infused vision of the Mediterranean that informed his creative life.

Opposite and above. Views of Roquebrune-Cap-Martin on the Côte d'Azur, France, site of Le Corbusier's *petit cabanon* (little cabin)

MARIE BRIZARD

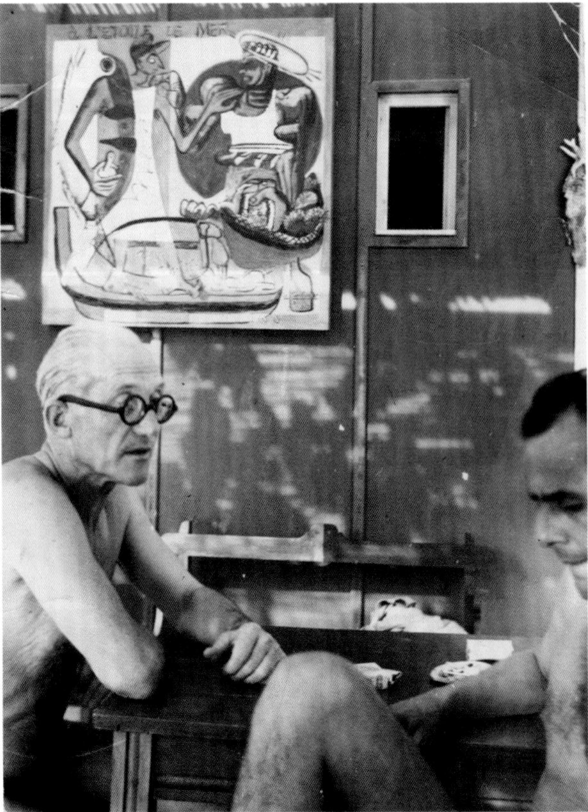

L'Etoile de Mer: The Rebutato restaurant, Roquebrune-Cap-Martin

Thomas Rebutato was a restaurateur and former plumber from Nice, whom Le Corbusier befriended on one of his many trips to Roquebrune-Cap-Martin. During the summer of 1950, which he spent in a nearby rented room, Le Corbusier painted several murals on the walls of Rebutato's modest restaurant, L'Etoile de Mer. The two remained lifelong friends, and Rebutato was Le Corbusier's client for various small projects, mostly unbuilt. Rebutato's son, Robert, would work in Le Corbusier's Paris office.

Opposite, top. Thomas Rebutato and friend in front of Le Corbusier's painting at Rebutato's restaurant, L'Etoile de Mer (starfish)

Opposite, bottom left. Rebutato behind the bar of his restaurant

Opposite, bottom right. Le Corbusier and patron at L'Etoile de Mer

Top. Le Corbusier and Yvonne (far right) at the opening of L'Etoile de Mer, July 1949

Above. Le Corbusier, Yvonne, and others at L'Etoile de Mer, 1950s

Below left. Man on the porch of L'Etoile de Mer

Below right. Woman examining a mural by Le Corbusier on the porch at L'Etoile de Mer

Left and below. Views of Le Corbusier's Modulor man painted on the side of L'Etoile de Mer, Roquebrune-Cap-Martin

Opposite, top left. Photograph of Le Corbusier's painting and mural at L'Etoile de Mer, with a description on the verso

Opposite, top right and bottom. Painting by Le Corbusier on a portable wooden frame in front of his mural

à l'Étoile de Mer Roquebrune Cap Martin
"Chez Rebutato" 1950
murale de Corbu: a/ le panneau Gris moitié 1.13 m
b/ L-C 19
c/ la murale complémentaire
545
722

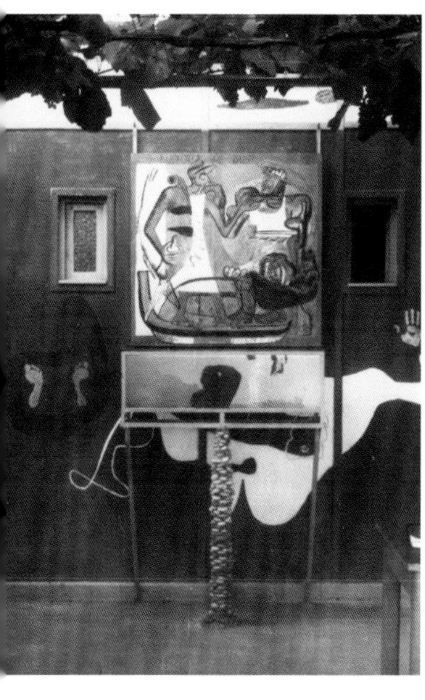

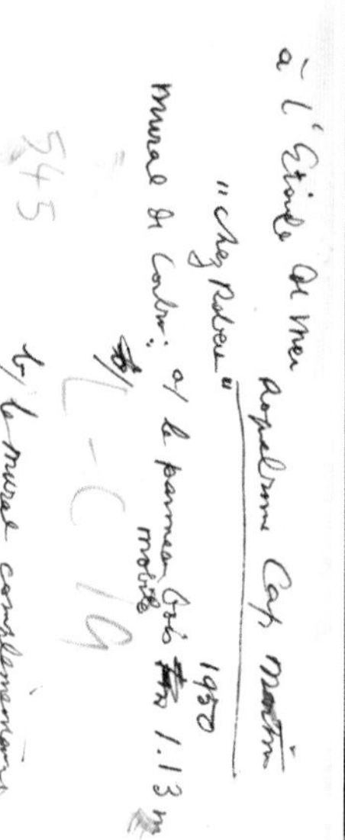

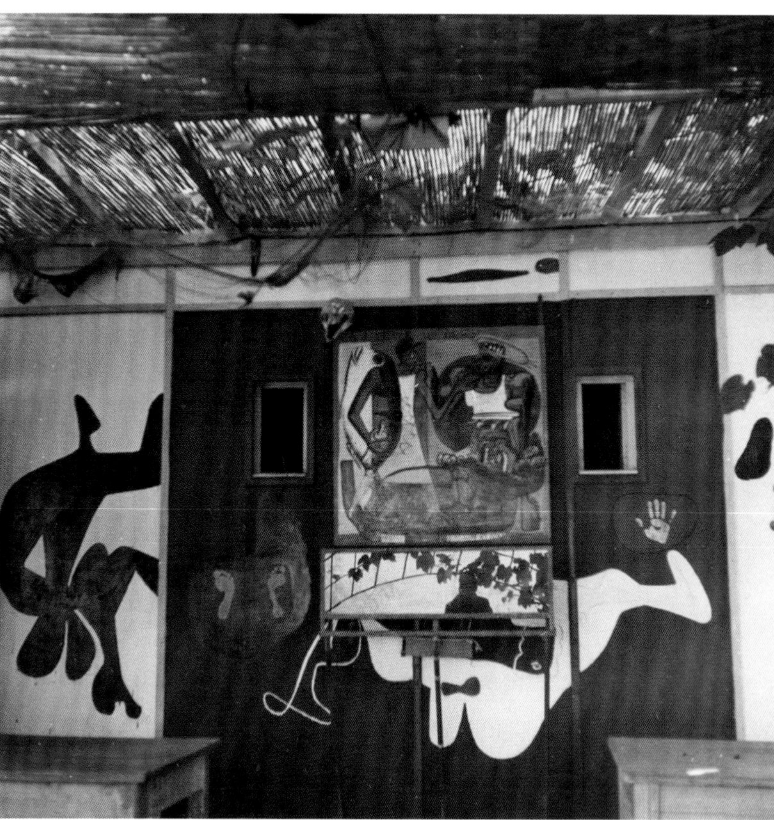

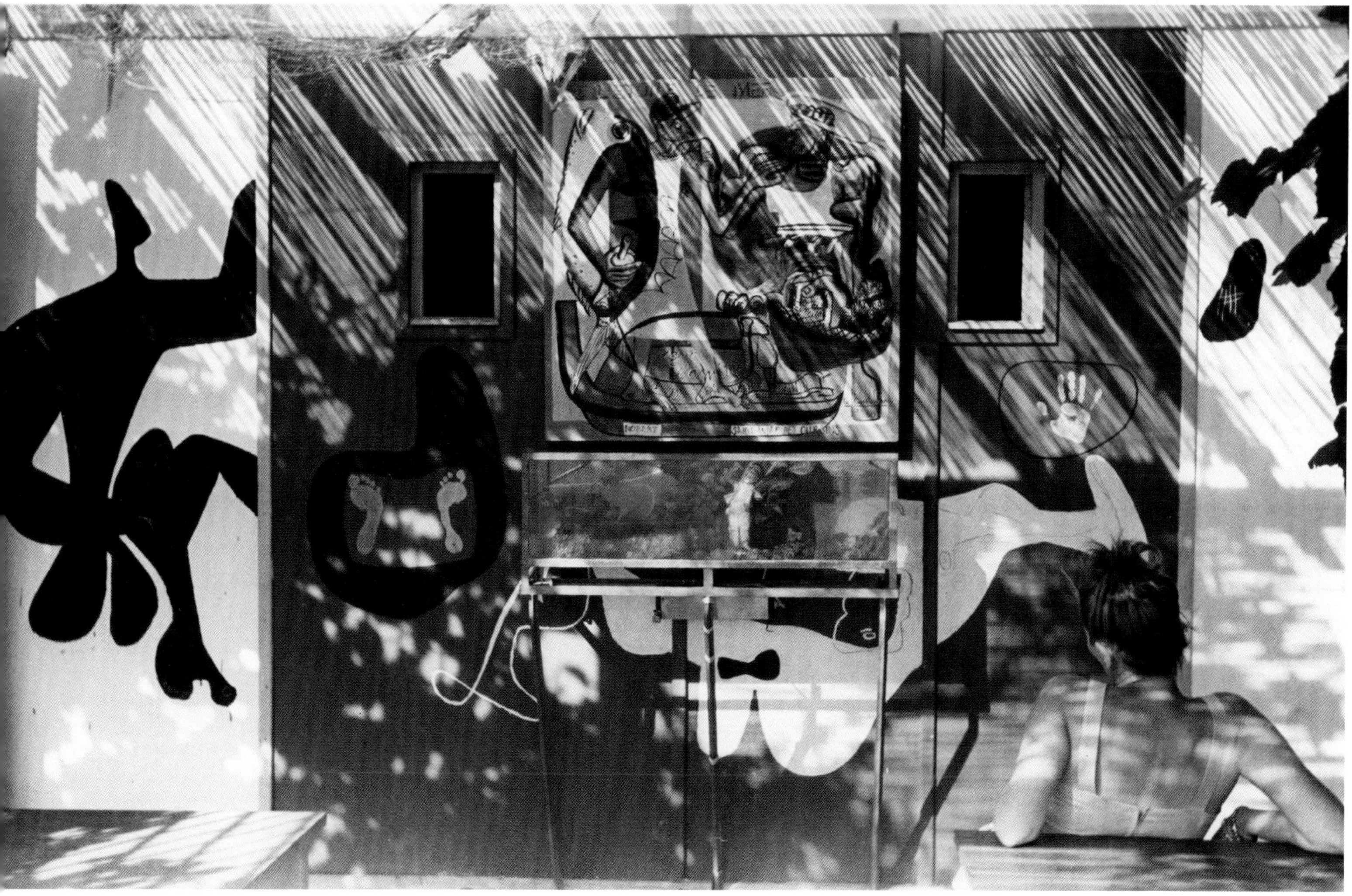

Building the *petit cabanon*, Roquebrune-Cap-Martin, 1951–52

Le Corbusier took all of forty-five minutes to sketch the plans for the rustic cabin he would build for himself, adjacent to L'Etoile de Mer. The Modulor provided all the proportions for the one-room, wood-framed *petit cabanon*, which was a spartan, highly functional space in which Le Corbusier and Yvonne could spend their vacations in absolute simplicity. Le Corbusier had the cabin's structural elements prefabricated, and Thomas Rebutato installed the plumbing. Le Corbusier sketched the plans on 31 December 1951, and the *cabanon* was ready for their August 1952 vacation, at a minimal cost.

Below. Le Corbusier in a restaurant, Marseille

Paris, le 4 Octobre 1954

Madame TJADER HARRIS
Vikingsborg
D A R I E N
Connecticut

Chère Amie,

Ma vie est telle qu'il est impossible de garder des contacts épistolaires avec les amis. Vous savez bien que ce n'est pas par négligence.

J'ai beaucoup pensé à vous cet été à Cap Martin et je vous ai rassemblé un certain nombre de cartes postales vous montrant la situation exceptionnelle du terrain destiné à recevoir nos maisons. Vous y verrez les communications extraordinaires par route, par fer, par eau. Je mets quelques annotations sur les cartes. Vous verrez l'une d'elles qui représente la Procession de la Passion instituée depuis quatre siècles à Roquebrune Village pour perpétuer le miracle qui a arrêté la peste. Ce sont les gens du village qui jouent les rôles sacrés. Vous verrez également le village qui se trouve immédiatement au-dessus de notre terrain. Vous constaterez que ce n'est vraiment pas mal du tout.

Votre banquier vous a confirmé que l'autorisation de bâtir nous a été accordé. Nous avons réexaminé minutieusement tous les plans et je pourrai bientôt vous donner des nouvelles.

Comment allez-vous ? Je commence à vous envier dans vos intentions de vous cloitrer entre quatre murs. J'aimerais bien en faire autant.

Les journaux ici sont optimistes. Mr Eden a ramené le sourire dans les rapports internationaux. Il semble qu'on soit moins décidé à entreprendre des guerres. Ceci a quand même quelque chose de réjouissant.

Que fait votre fils? Quand verrons nous de ses films

Bien amicalement à vous.

LE CORBUSIER

Left. Le Corbusier to Marguerite Tjader Harris, 4 October 1954, telling her about the "remarkable siting of land" on which he is building his cabin in Cap-Martin

Below. Three postcards enclosed with Le Corbusier's letter, showing Harris the cabin's location (below and middle) and the town's annual Easter procession (bottom)

LA COTE D'AZUR
Panorama Aérien
de Nice à la Côte Italienne

(1)

1 notre terrain (Roquebrune-Cap Martin)
2 vieux chemin romain montant à Roquebrune
3. Roquebrune vieille petite ville du moyen âge
4. La route nationale automobile Littorale
5 la "moyenne corniche" (automobile
6 la Grande Corniche Menton - Nice
7 la Promenade des Anglais à Nice

Editions RELLA – Photographie véritable – Reproduction interdite
Fabrication Française

2455

DR 1984:1685

La procession annuelle de la Passion par les habitants du village
Chaque année en août
Faite chaque année depuis 400 ans en commemoration de l'arrêt de la Peste

(17)

DR 1984:1689

"For my personal use I have a château on the Côte d'Azur that measures 3.66 x 3.66 meters. It was for my wife, it was splendid, inside it was extravagantly comfortable and nice. For my personal use, 13 meters away from this same château, next to a flowerbed,

I have my own house, it measures 1.90 x 4 meters, it's made of old planks put together, and it suits me just fine."

—Interview with Georges Charensol, "L'art moderne," Radio France, 1962

Opposite. Le Corbusier's sketch of Roquebrune-Cap-Martin, 15 June 1955, indicating the location of his property—*"notre roche"* (our rock)—in the foreground

Above. Le Corbusier's sketch for his mother, 26 December 1952, showing the location of the *cabanon*

Right. Le Corbusier to his mother and brother, 31 August 1955, with sketches and plan of the *cabanon*

31 août 55

Bien chers

Mercredi matin 8 heures.

Bonjour! Monsieur et dame!

Une nouvelle journée devant soi.

Je pense que vos Vignerons Festival sont déblayés.

Vous avez dû en prendre une purge!

Les journaux en ont beaucoup parlé, en bien.

Et ça recommencera!

A: le cabanon 3m66 x 3.66

B: mon bureau 180 x 380 (en plan)

C: Château de Roquebrune village

D: la Tête de Chien

E: Monaco

F: le bananier

G: Domino le chat

H: Vuki le chien.

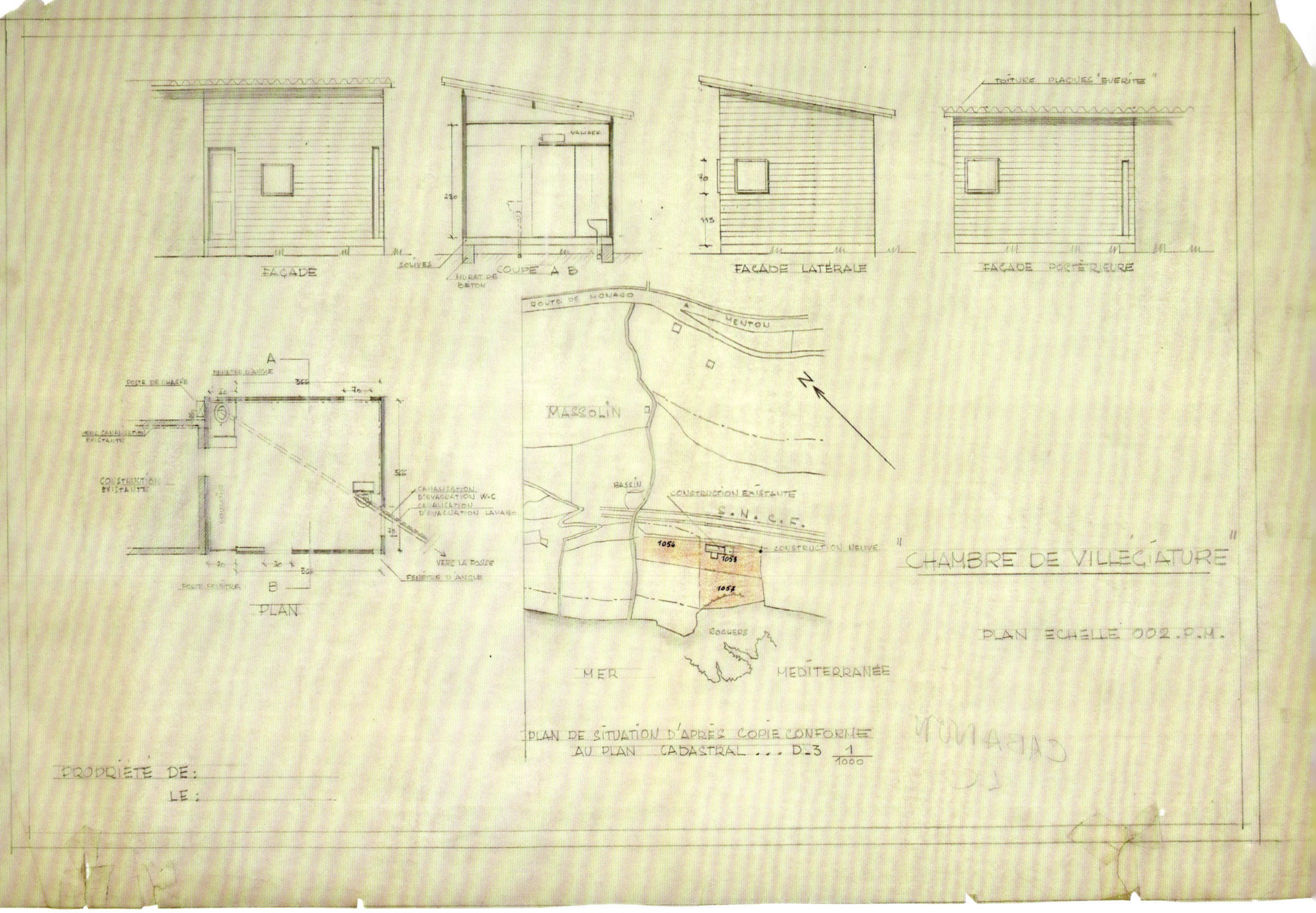

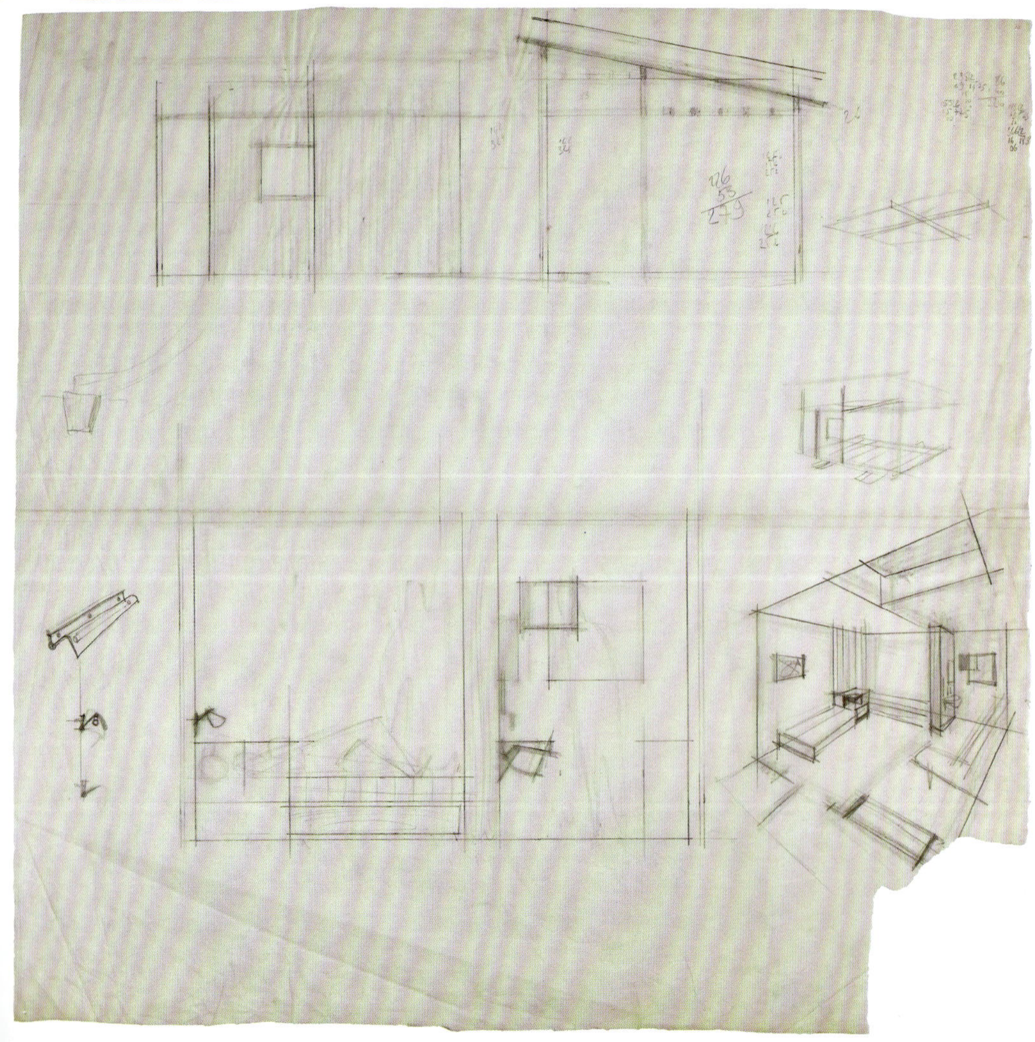

Above. Elevations, section, plan, and site plan of Le Corbusier's *cabanon*, Roquebrune-Cap-Martin, 1951

Left. Two sections and an interior perspective

Right. Perspective sketch showing framing of the *cabanon*

Below. Details of cabinetry. Le Corbusier designed the interior, including built-in furniture, for maximum efficiency

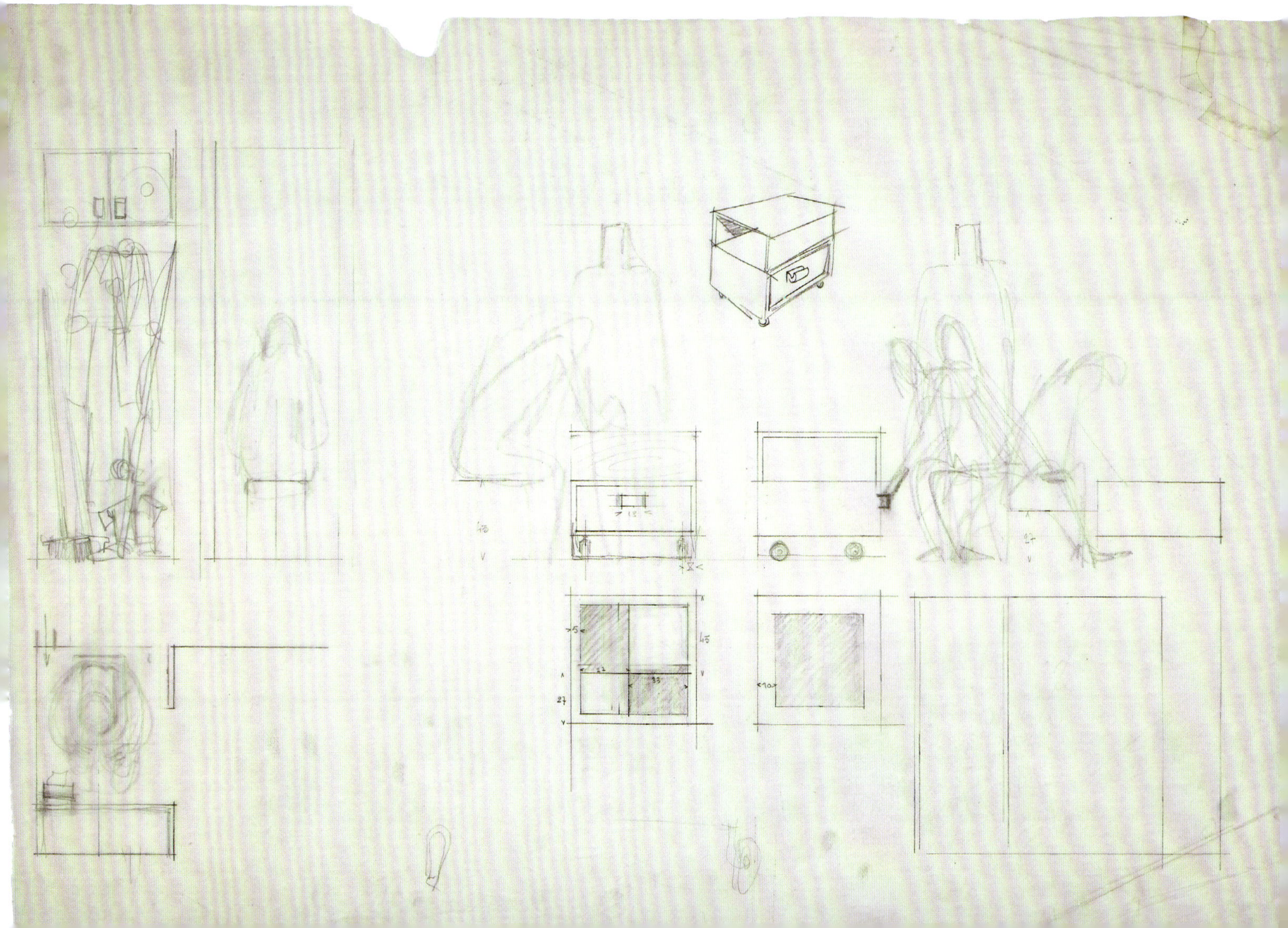

Top. Le Corbusier at the *cabanon*, Roquebrune-Cap-Martin

Above left and opposite. Le Corbusier looking out a window of the *cabanon*

Above right. Corner detail of the *cabanon* showing the *aérature*—the tall, narrow opening for ventilation that is one of Le Corbusier's characteristic design elements

Following pages:

Left page, top. Le Corbusier inside the *cabanon*

Left page, bottom. Sleeping area in the *cabanon*, with one of Le Corbusier's paintings in the background

Right page, top. Interior of the *baraque de chantier* (construction shed) adjacent to the *cabanon*, which Le Corbusier used as a studio

Right page, bottom. Le Corbusier at work inside the construction shed

"She is lying on her bed in the guest room, straight as a recumbent statue, her death mask that magisterial Provençal bone structure. And today, calmly, I have the feeling that death is no horror."

—*"1957," Le Corbusier lui-même*

His wife's death: Yvonne Gallis Le Corbusier (1892–1957)

After a prolonged physical decline, Yvonne Gallis Le Corbusier died at four in the morning on 5 October 1957. The grieving Le Corbusier later recalled her as the "guardian angel of my hearth for over thirty-six years."

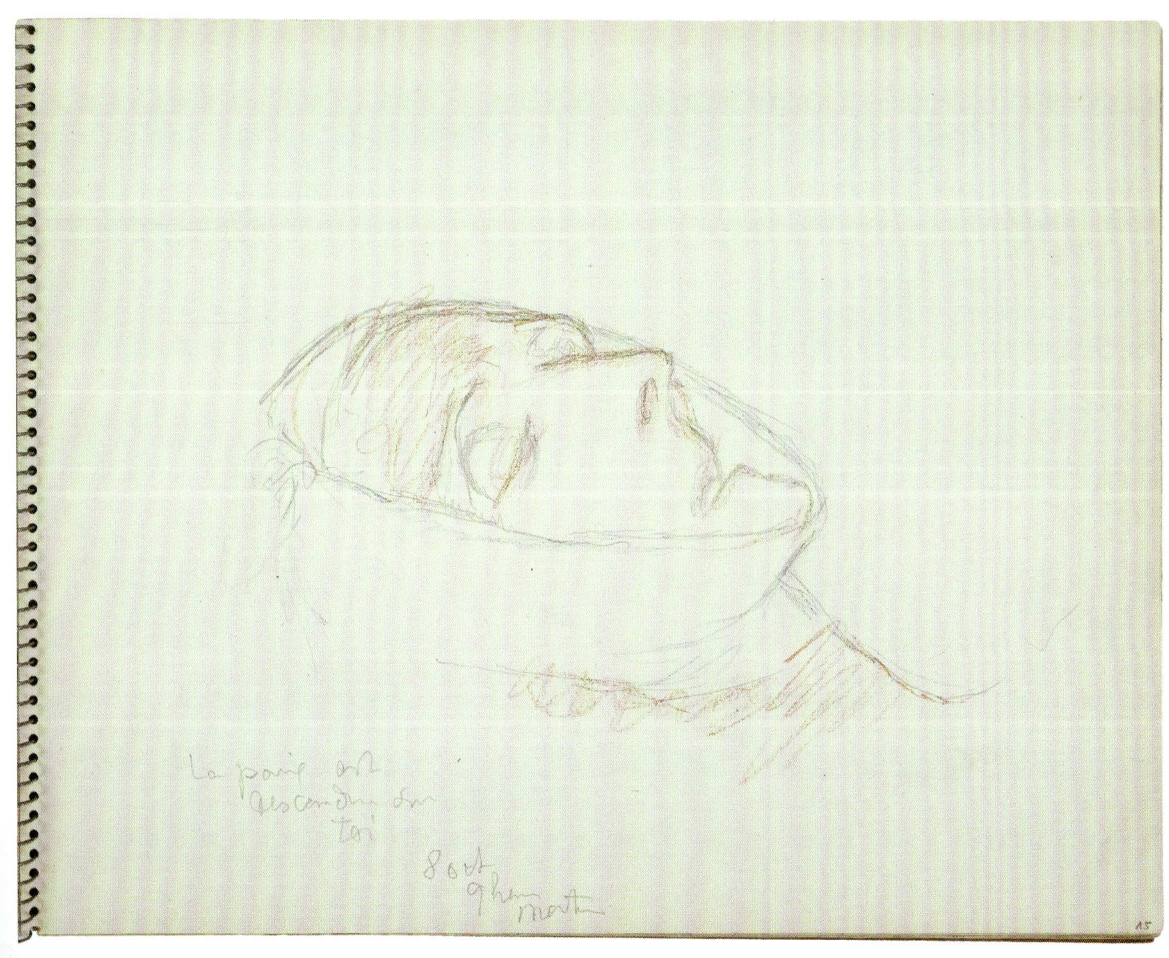

Top. Le Corbusier's sketchbook number 49, with images of Yvonne on her deathbed, October 1957

Left. Sketch of Yvonne after her death, 8 October 1957. The drawing is inscribed, "Peace has descended upon you."

Right. Le Corbusier to the mayor of Roquebrune-Cap-Martin, 9 August 1958, accompanying a donation in memory of Yvonne, "to signal her presence in this Mediterranean countryside she loved so much." He adds, in a post-script, "There should be no flowers on her grave at any time *(please)*"

Far right. Le Corbusier's sketch of Roquebrune-Cap-Martin, 17 June 1958, showing his scheme for a tomb for Yvonne and himself

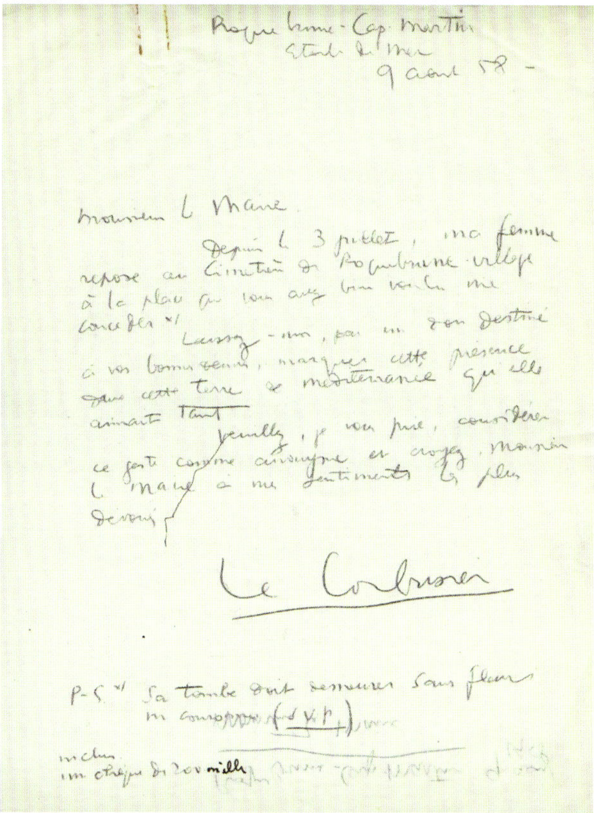

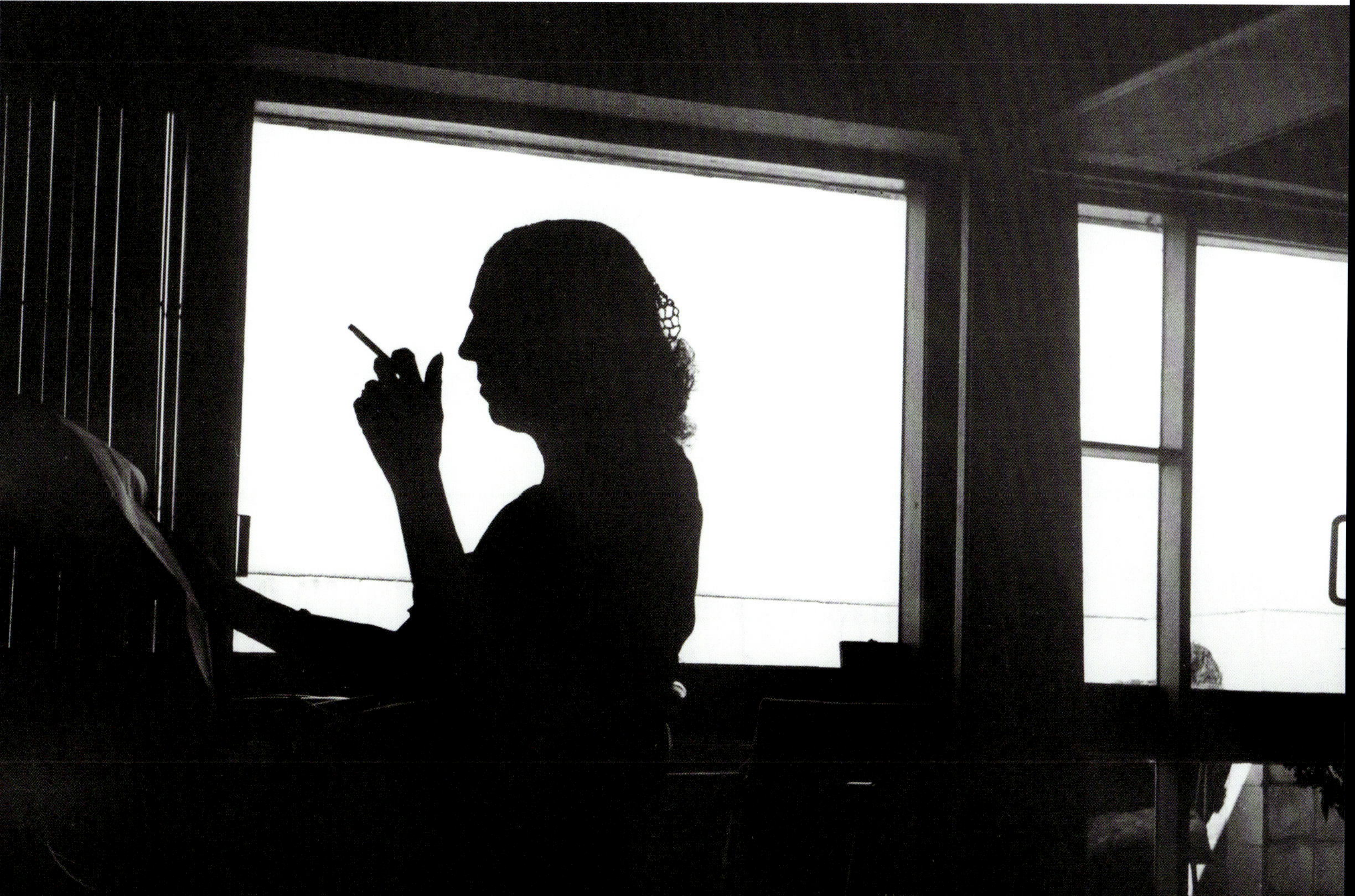

Below. Yvonne in silhouette

17 juin 58

Bien chez tous deux !

Rentré dimanche matin, d'une semaine passée à Roquebrune cimetière pour construire avec Bertocchi (le maçon dont le fils était filleul d'Yvonne) la tombe d'Yvonne. Nid perché à 300 m plus haut que notre cabanon. Pour transports il faut une mule, puis les épaules (les charges) des hommes. De lundi matin à samedi midi, Bertocchi a fait les travaux de fouille, fondation et ciment apparent.

C'est bien !

Y A-T-IL une Crise des Arts?
27 000 f
100
1953
1954
Voici
9 dec 53
avec joie
Coulon salue cet anniversaire
de l'illustre naissance
et il fait confiance à 54
bonne place

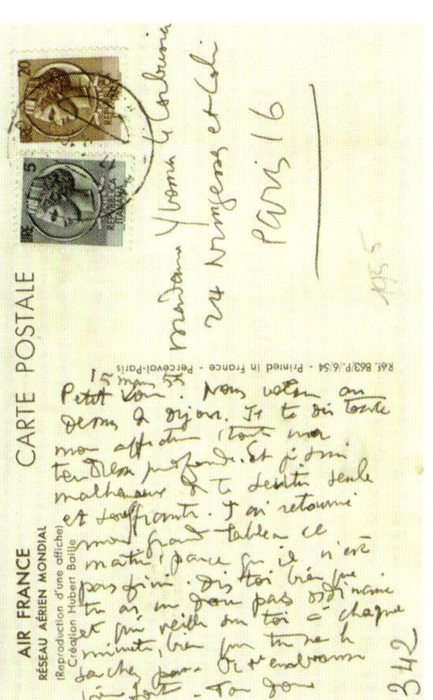

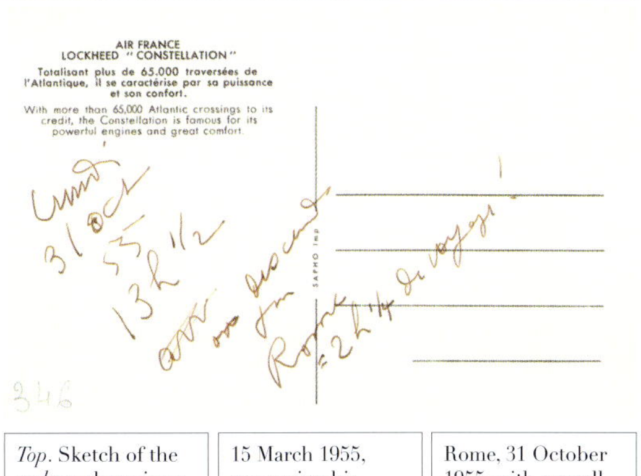

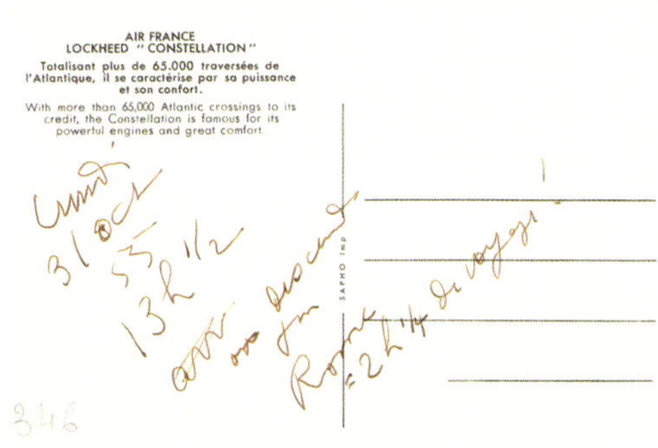

A lifetime of letters to Yvonne

Le Corbusier was a faithful correspondent to Yvonne, if not always a faithful husband. He wittily illustrated his hundreds of postcards and letters to her, sent from all around the world, often signing them with his distinctive crow insignia.

Opposite, top left. Sketch of a bedroom and the Corbusian *corbeau* (crow), from Simla, India, 14 March 1951

Opposite, top right. Le Corbusier's sketch of his hand drawing a scene of Venice, December 1951

Opposite, bottom. Sketch, 9 December 1953, depicting the coming New Year

Top. Sketch of the *corbeau* dropping a gift to Yvonne for the New Year, 1954

Above left. Front and back of postcard from Le Corbusier to Yvonne, from Italy, 15 March 1955, expressing his unhappiness over leaving her alone

Above right. Front and back of Le Corbusier's postcard (unsent) to Yvonne, from Rome, 31 October 1955, with a small sketch of a figure on the airplane's wing

Right. Le Corbusier at work outside his *cabanon* in Roquebrune-Cap-Martin, overlooking the sea

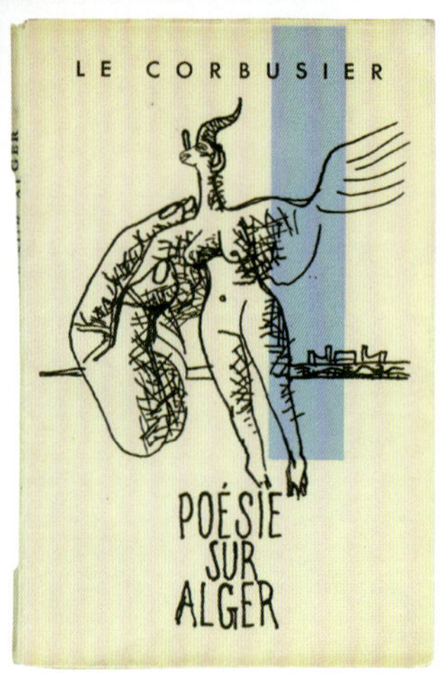

"Poetry shines on Algiers: a master plan—the master plan—will make it known.

This poetry is not subjective, but shot through with North African reality. Laying down rules, the master plan asserts that sources of profoundly human joy will spread if the site's resources are deployed in the interests of people."

—*Poésie sur Alger*, 1950

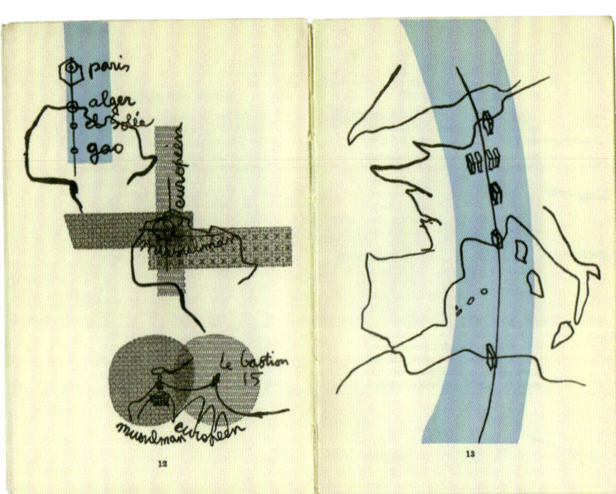

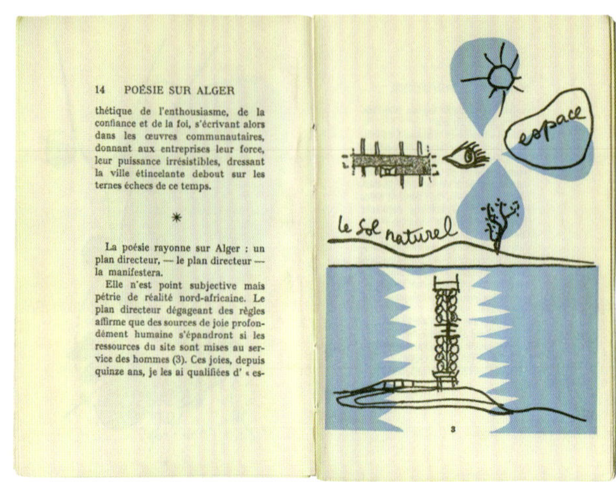
14 POÉSIE SUR ALGER

thétique de l'enthousiasme, de la confiance et de la foi, s'écrivant alors dans les œuvres communautaires, donnant aux entreprises leur force, leur puissance irrésistibles, dressant la ville étincelante debout sur les ternes échecs de ce temps.

*

La poésie rayonne sur Alger : un plan directeur, — le plan directeur — la manifestera.

Elle n'est point subjective mais pétrie de réalité nord-africaine. Le plan directeur dégageant des règles affirme que des sources de joie profondément humaine s'épandront si les ressources du site sont mises au service des hommes (3). Ces joies, depuis quinze ans, je les ai qualifiées d' « es-

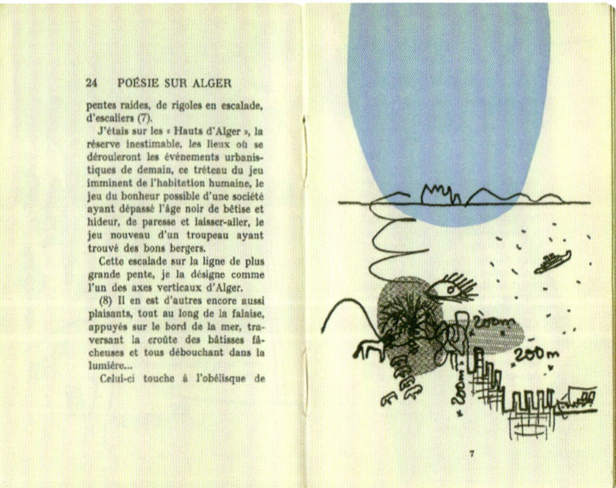
24 POÉSIE SUR ALGER

pentes raides, de rigoles en escalade, d'escaliers (7).

J'étais sur les « Hauts d'Alger », la réserve inestimable, les lieux où se dérouleront les événements urbanistiques de demain, ce tréteau du jeu imminent de l'habitation humaine, le jeu du bonheur possible d'une société ayant dépassé l'âge noir de bêtise et hideur, de paresse et laisser-aller, le jeu nouveau d'un troupeau ayant trouvé des bons bergers.

Cette escalade sur la ligne de plus grande pente, je la désigne comme l'un des axes verticaux d'Alger.

(8) Il en est d'autres encore aussi plaisants, tout au long de la falaise, appuyés sur le bord de la mer, traversant la croûte des bâtisses fâcheuses et tous débouchant dans la lumière...

Celui-ci touche à l'obélisque de

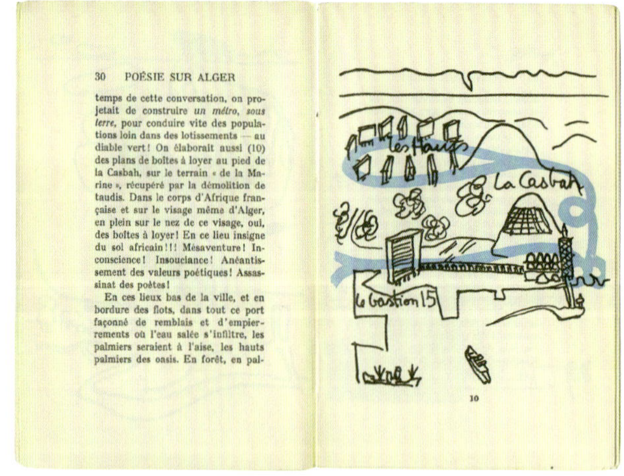
30 POÉSIE SUR ALGER

temps de cette conversation, on projetait de construire *un métro, sous terre*, pour conduire vite des populations loin dans des lotissements — au diable vert! On élaborait aussi (10) des plans de boîtes à loyer au pied de la Casbah, sur le terrain « de la Marine », récupéré par la démolition de taudis. Dans le corps d'Afrique française et sur le visage même d'Alger, en plein sur le nez de ce visage, oui, des boîtes à loyer! En ce lieu insigne du sol africain!!! Mésaventure! Inconscience! Insouciance! Anéantissement des valeurs poétiques! Assassinat des poètes!

En ces lieux bas de la ville, et en bordure des flots, dans tout ce port façonné de remblais et d'empierrements où l'eau salée s'infiltre, les palmiers seraient à l'aise, les hauts palmiers des oasis. En forêt, en pal-

40 POÉSIE SUR ALGER

graphie? Le quartier de « la Marine » est menacé? Le cap d'Alger, ce cap d'Afrique sur méridien de Paris, deviendra péché d'urbanisme? (15).

Pèlerin averti de cette terre des miracles possibles, animé d'une foi maintenue indéfectible par treize années occupées à dégager son potentiel urbanistique, je suis venu parler au Gouverneur, au Préfet, au Maire, m'adressant à chacun de ces sommets de la gestion d'une ville, d'une région, d'une Afrique et leur disant :

M. le Gouverneur, M. le Préfet, M. le Maire, la poésie est sur ce lieu qui s'appelle Alger, sur terre d'Afrique où furent une fois et successivement, trois grandes civilisations : la phénicienne, la romaine, la musulmane. Des vestiges, des témoins partout répandus, nous mettent en garde contre la médiocrité de nos entreprises

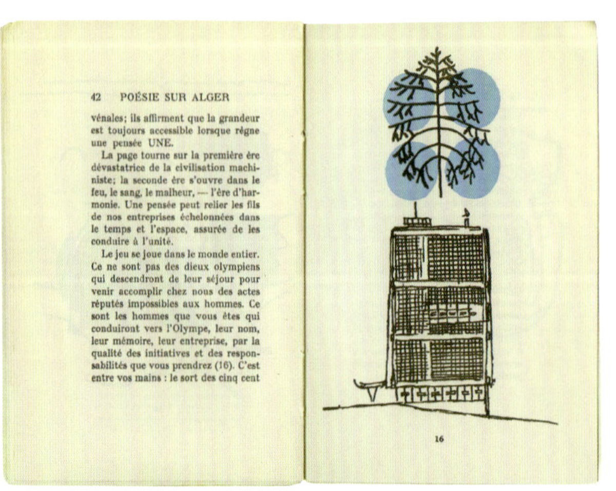
42 POÉSIE SUR ALGER

vénales; ils affirment que la grandeur est toujours accessible lorsque règne une pensée UNE.

La page tourne sur la première ère dévastatrice de la civilisation machiniste; la seconde ère s'ouvre dans le feu, le sang, le malheur, — l'ère d'harmonie. Une pensée peut relier les fils de nos entreprises échelonnées dans le temps et l'espace, assurée de les conduire à l'unité.

Le jeu se joue dans le monde entier. Ce ne sont pas des dieux olympiens qui descendront de leur séjour pour venir accomplir chez nous des actes réputés impossibles aux hommes. Ce sont les hommes que vous êtes qui conduiront vers l'Olympe, leur nom, leur mémoire, leur entreprise, par la qualité des initiatives et des responsabilités que vous prendrez (16). C'est entre vos mains : le sort des cinq cent

Thoughts on a Mediterranean city: *Poésie sur Alger*, 1950

Le Corbusier's *Poésie sur Alger* (Poetry on Algiers) is an impassioned manifesto of urban planning for the city that had so long appealed to his imagination. Written and illustrated by Le Corbusier in 1942, during the war, it was not published until 1950.

Opposite. Cover and selected pages from Le Corbusier's book *Poésie sur Alger* (Poetry on Algiers), Falaize, Paris, 1950

Above. Le Corbusier in Marseille

Plans for a conference in Algiers: CIAM, 1955

Plans were made to hold the tenth CIAM conference in 1955 in Algiers, which would have marked a poignant return to the city for Le Corbusier. However, the conference never took place, and that same year he decided to resign from the group he had helped found, objecting to its growing dependence on English. CIAM X—dominated by a new generation of young architects—ultimately convened in Dubrovnik, Yugoslavia, in 1956; the organization disbanded three years later.

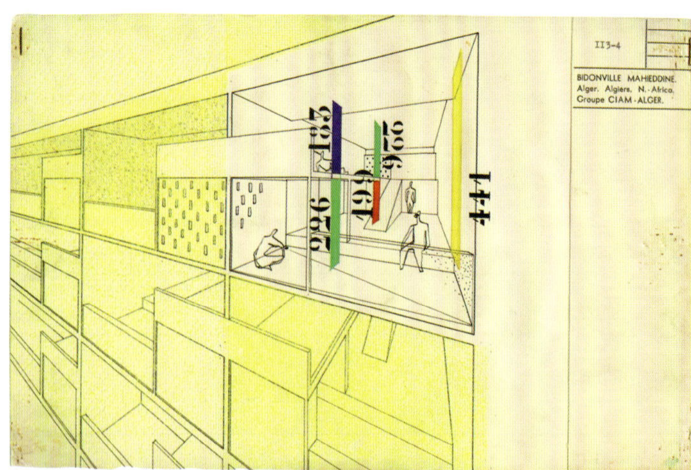

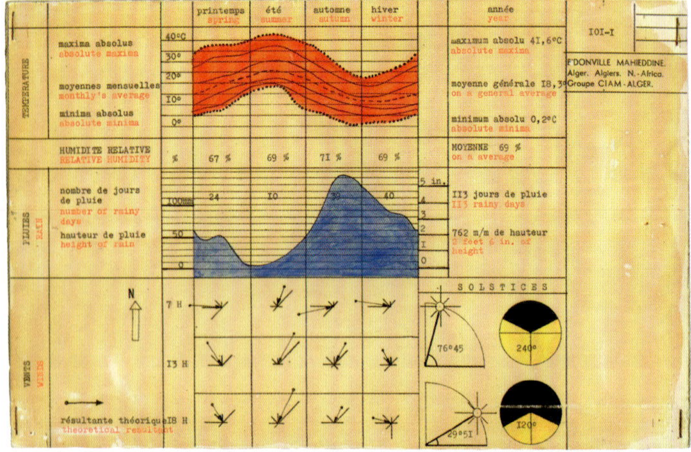

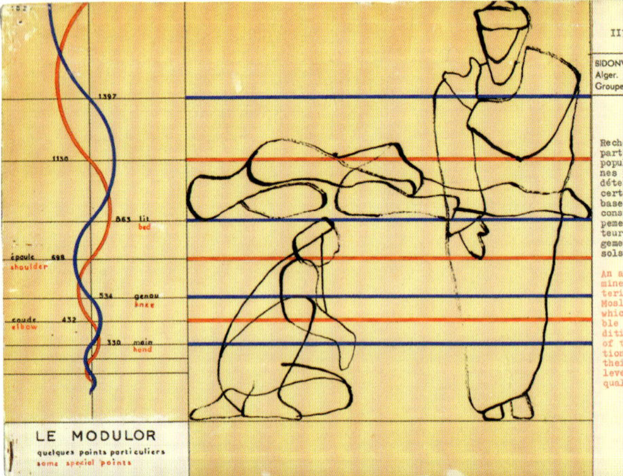

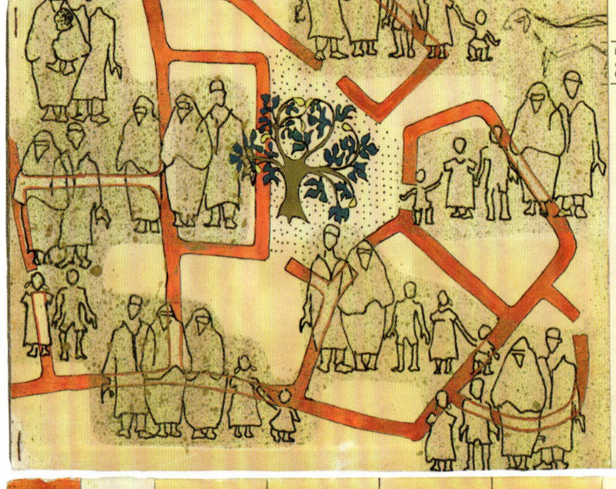

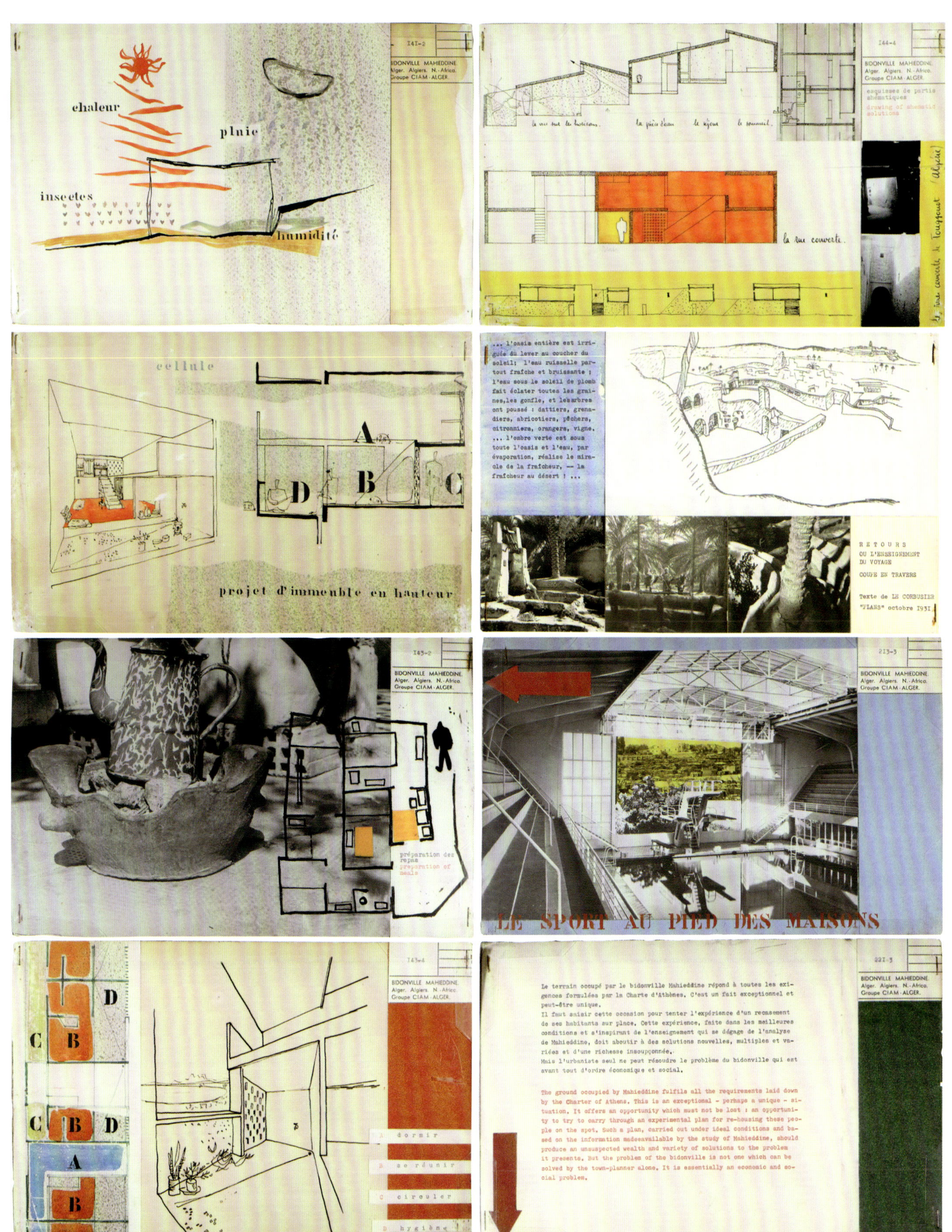

Opposite and this page. Pages from a study prepared by Le Corbusier and others for the CIAM conference planned for Algiers in 1955. The study, for "Bidonville Mahieddine," proposed an urban redevelopment scheme for a shantytown in Algiers, with detailed analyses of the climate, demographics, and living conditions of the residents.

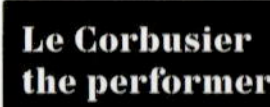

Le Corbusier the performer

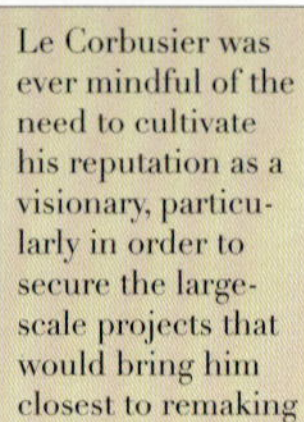

Le Corbusier was ever mindful of the need to cultivate his reputation as a visionary, particularly in order to secure the large-scale projects that would bring him closest to remaking the modern city. This not only meant keeping a vigorous pace as an author but also maintaining an engaging public persona by approaching lectures and other public appearances as opportunities for showmanship.

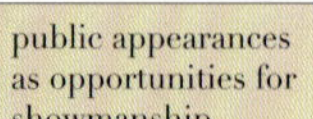

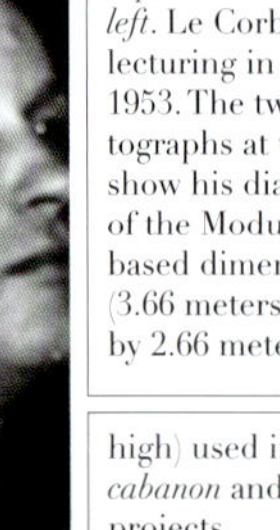

Top, above, and far left. Le Corbusier lecturing in Milan, 1953. The two photographs at top show his diagram of the Modulor-based dimensions (3.66 meters square by 2.66 meters high) used in his *cabanon* and other projects.

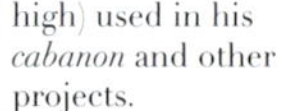

Left and opposite. Le Corbusier at the Milan Triennale, 1951. He wrote on the back of the photograph (opposite), "This was a joke for the photographer who was watching me."

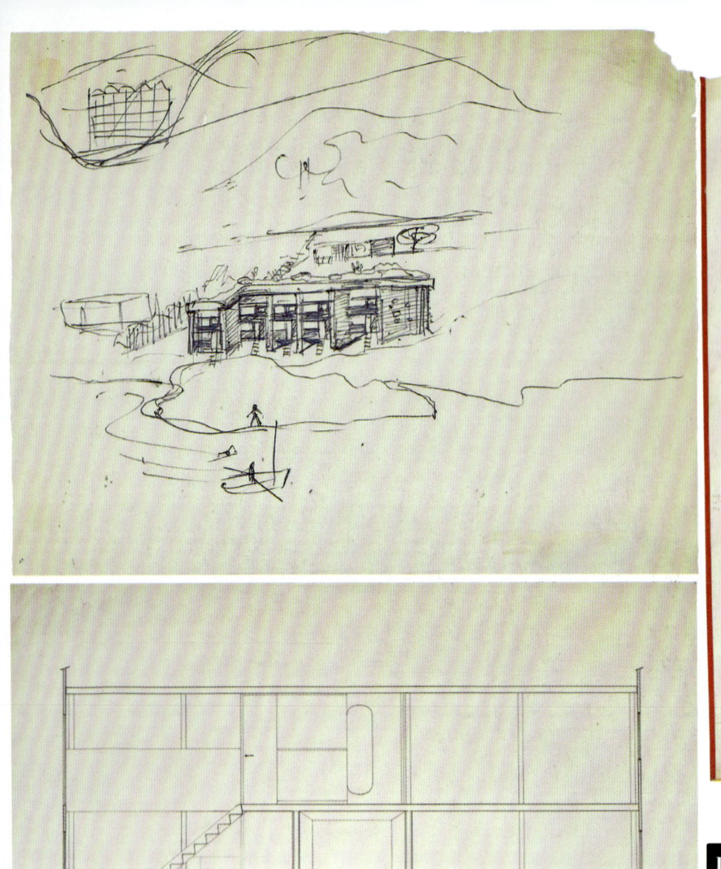

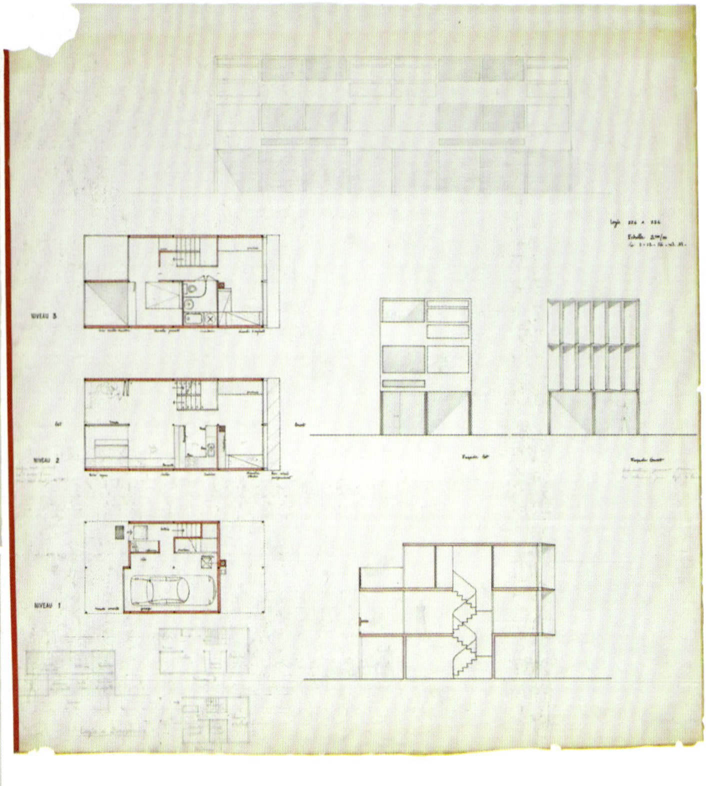

Roq and Rob vacation villas, Roquebrune-Cap-Martin, 1950s

The Roq and Rob vacation villas were Le Corbusier's attempt to introduce urban density to Roquebrune-Cap-Martin, in an effort to stave off suburban sprawl. His goal was to create a complex of living units that would be in harmony with their spectacular natural setting. To accomplish this, he arranged them as a sort of informal Unité, with primitivist vaulted rooms that stretched down the hillside. Only five simple units, the "Unités de Camping," 1954–57, were built on the site, by Thomas Rebutato.

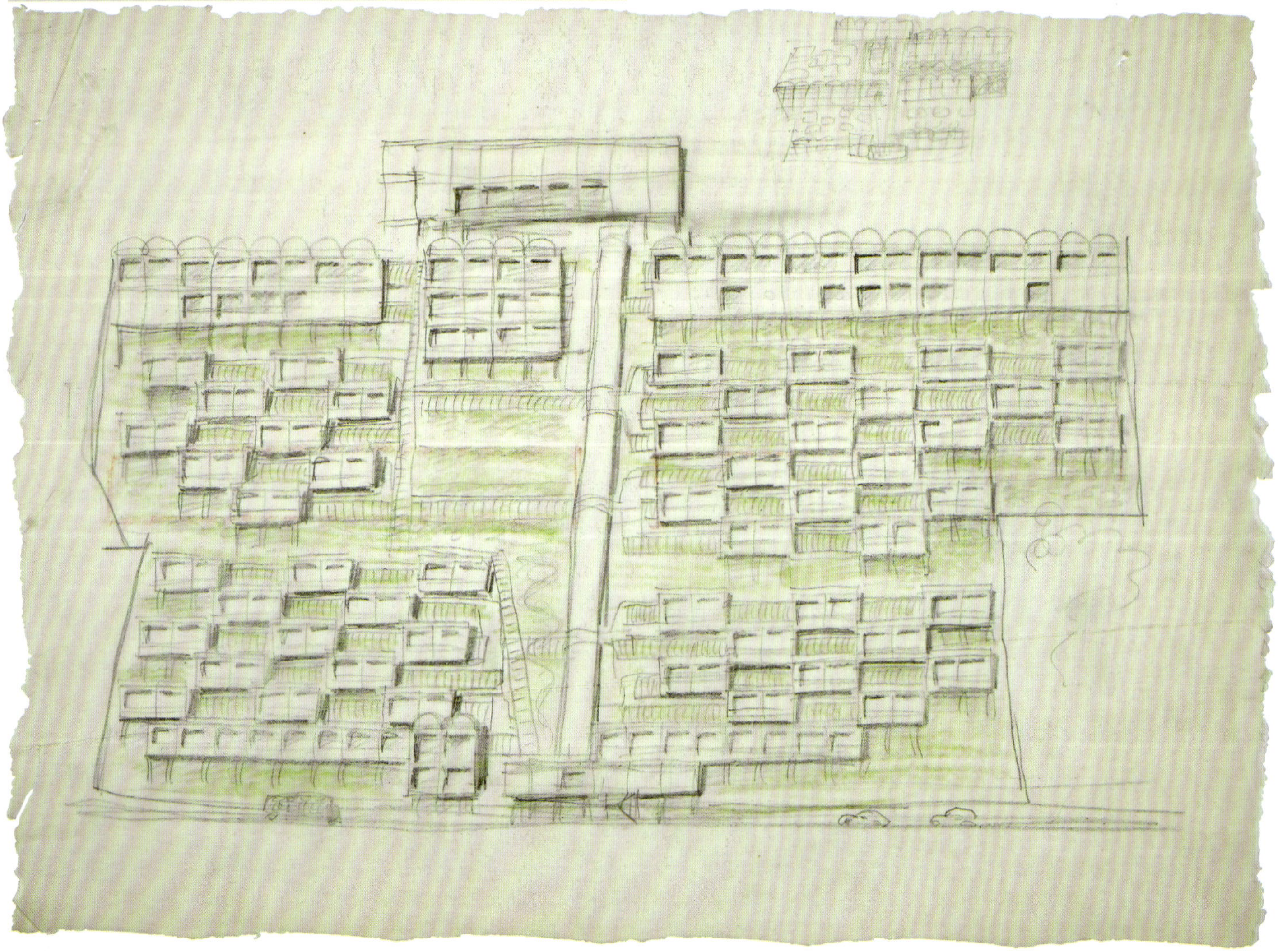

pposite, top left. erspective sketch the Roq and b vacation villas, oquebrune-Cap-artin

Opposite, top right. Plans, section, and elevations of one dwelling, Rob project

Opposite, middle. Section of a dwelling using Modulor proportions: 3.66 meters square by 2.66 meters high

Opposite, bottom. Study of the Roq development, showing its integration into the landscape, c. 1949

This page. Sketches of terraces and various interiors, Roq and Rob vacation villas

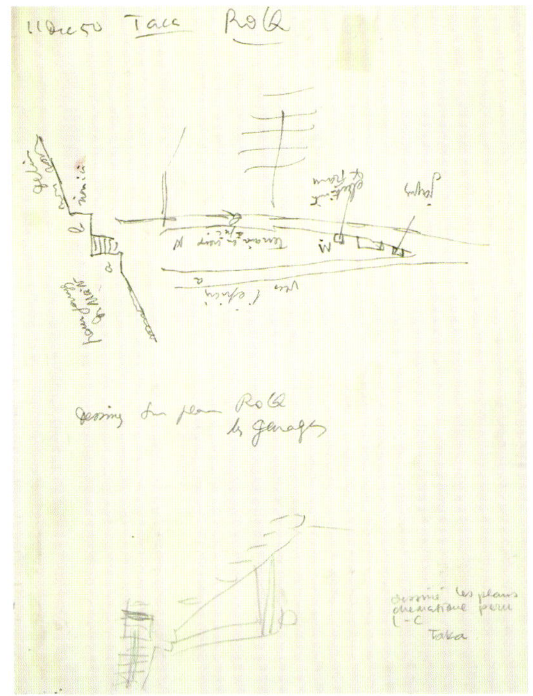

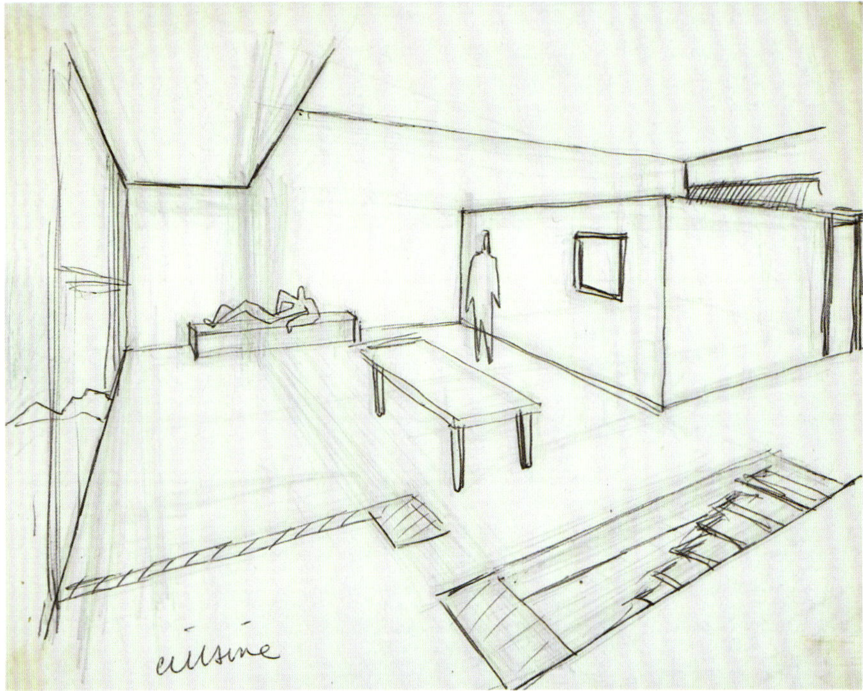

Above. Site plan, 22 December 1953, Rob vacation villas, Roquebrune-Cap-Martin

Opposite, top. Elevation study, showing vegetation on the roofs

Opposite, middle left and bottom left. Sections and plans of a dwelling

Opposite, bottom right. Plan studies for the Rob project

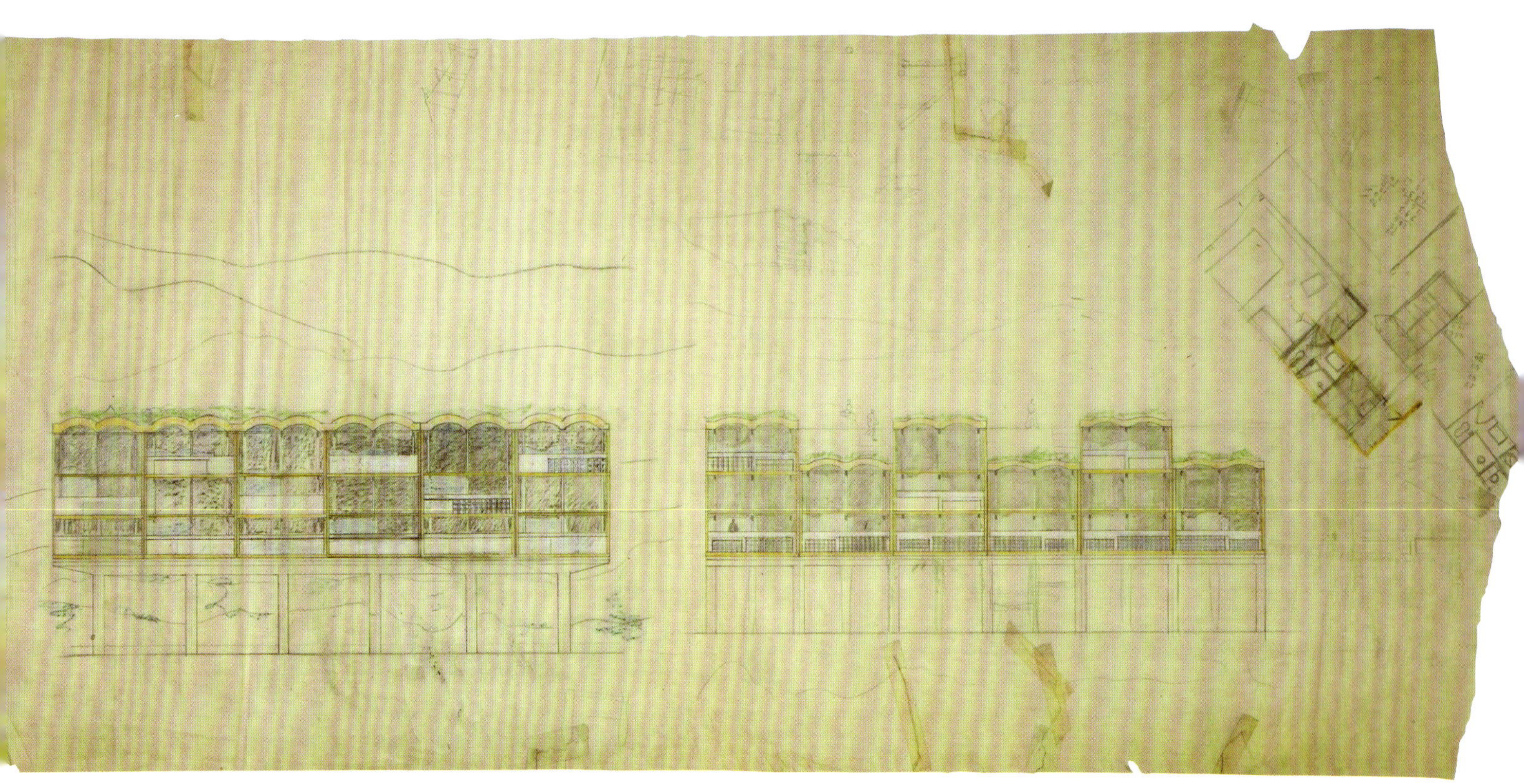

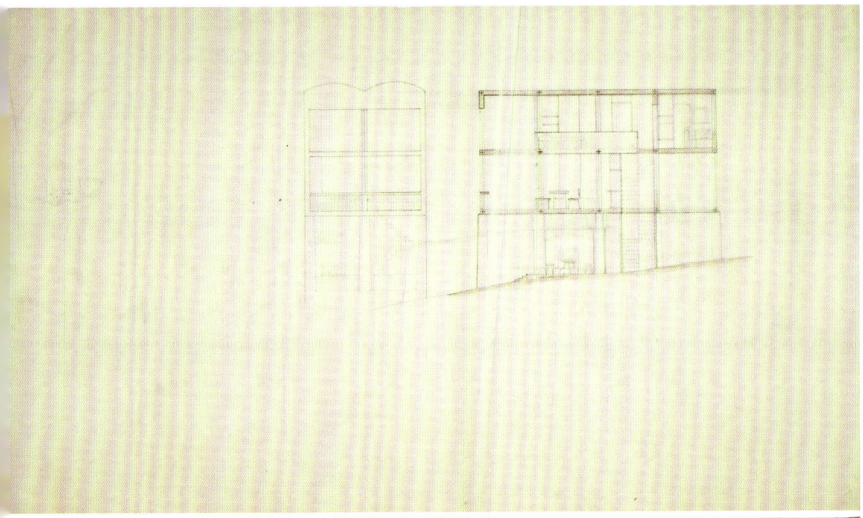

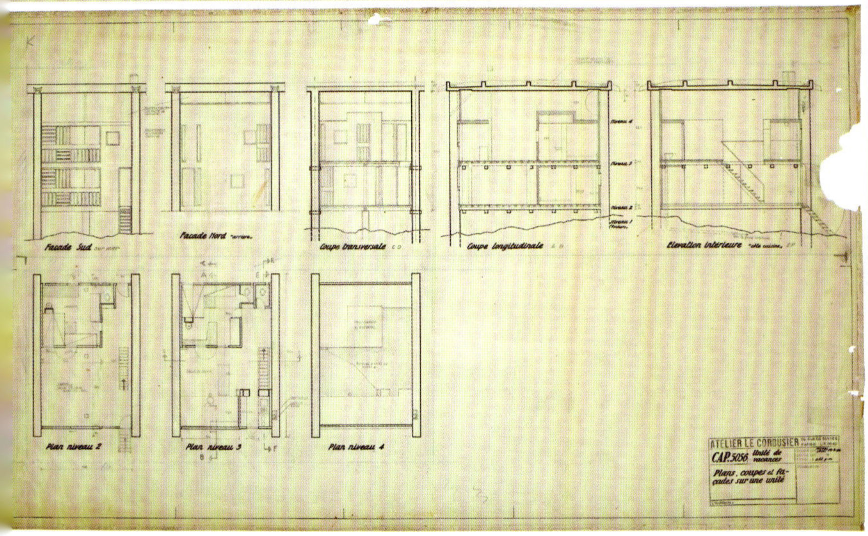

Façade Sud

Façade Nord

Coupe transversale

Coupe longitudinale

Elévation intérieure

Plan niveau 2

Plan niveau 3

Plan niveau 4

ATELIER LE CORBUSIER

CAP. 5056 Unité de vacances

Plans, coupes et façades sur une unité

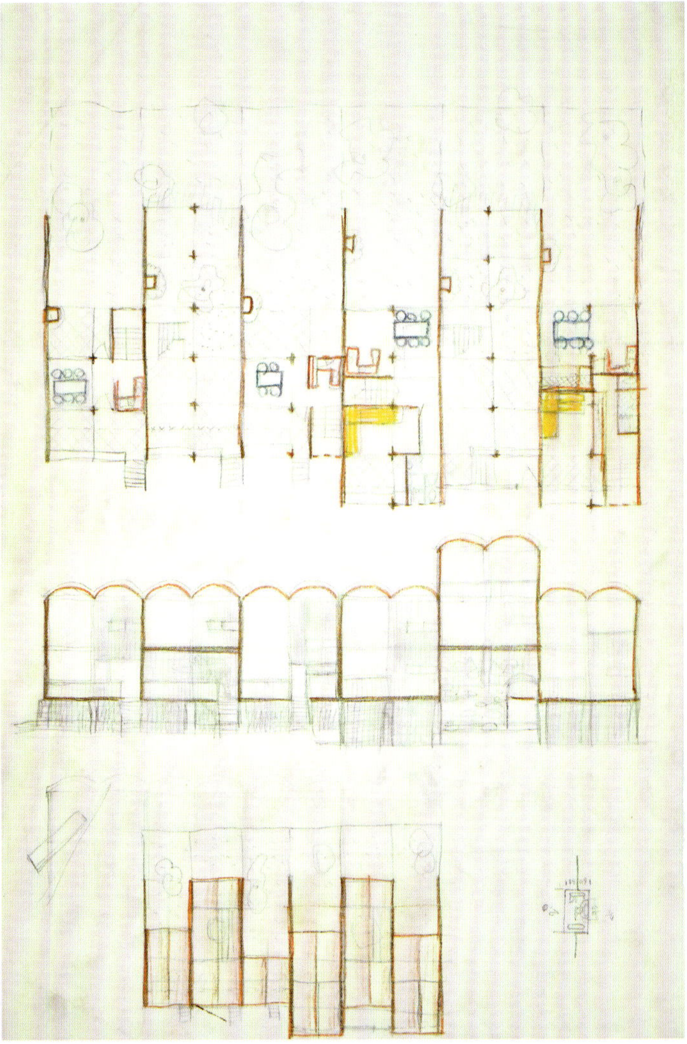

Vernacular villas Maisons Jaoul, Neuilly-sur-Seine, France, 1951–55

Like the Villa Sarabhai in India, the Maisons Jaoul derived from Le Corbusier's forays into a primitivist vernacular style. The two Jaoul houses—Maison A and Maison B—built in suburban Paris for André Jaoul and his son, and their families, are defined by their rough-textured concrete frames and their series of rustic brick vaults.

Paris, le 26 Mai 1952
JA.LC AW/JD

Entreprise Roger BERTRAND
43, rue Emile Ménier
PARIS XVIº

OBJET : Maisons JAOUL à Neuilly s/Seine

Messieurs,

Je tiens à vous confirmer notre entretien du vendredi 23 mai concernant la construction de deux maisons familiales pour M. JAOUL, rue de Longchamp à Neuilly s/ Seine.

Nous vous avons remis un jeu de plans et nous avons donné verbalement les indications nécessaires pour cetté étude. Nous n'avons pas encore rédigé de devis descriptif, mais nous restons à votre entière disposition pour vous fournir tous les renseignements complémentaires qui pourraient vous manquer.

Vous nous avez proposé d'intervenir comme entreprise pilote et nous ne voyons à première vue que des avantages pour cette formule, dont nous sommes de fermes partisans. Toutefois nous tenons à vous préciser que nous voudrions voir de très près avec vous-mêmes le choix des entreprises des différents corps d'état avant que vous ne preniez contact avec certaines d'entre elles. M. Le Corbusier désirerait, en effet, pour la presque totalité des corps d'état, voir les travaux confiés à des entreprises ayant déjà travaillé sous sa direction.

Je reste personnellement à votre disposition pour étudier avec vous cette question,

Et je vous prie de croire, Messieurs, à mes sentiments les plus distingués.

l'Architecte Adjoint,

A. WOGENSCKY

Paris, le 23 Juillet 1952
JA.LC AW/JD

Monsieur André JAOUL
26, rue Parmentier
NEUILLY

Monsieur,

Depuis notre conversation téléphonique de ce matin, j'ai examiné, dès cette après-midi avec notre collaborateur M. Lemarchand, la possibilité de retrancher de l'ensemble des devis établis à votre intention, une certaine partie des aménagements et équipements prévus de manière à présenter au Crédit Foncier un devis total ne dépassant pas la limite fixée par l'arrêté du 7 juin 1952.

Malheureusement cela s'avère impossible.

D'après les renseignements qui m'ont été donnés au M.R.U., le coefficient de juin 1952 est 21,90. Le prix du mètre carré pour maison familiale, de 1.300 francs pour 1939, est donc de : 1.300 x 21,90 = 28.470 francs.

Votre projet compte 715 mètres carrés pondérés hors-oeuvre qui, comptés à 28.470 francs, donnent un total de 20.356.050 francs représentant le devis maximum qui pourrait être accepté par le Crédit Foncier.

Par rapport à la solution la moins chère (voir tableau ci-joint) il faudrait faire apparaître une diminution de plus de 3 millions. Les meubles et équipements, que j'envisageais de supprimer, n'y suffisent pas.

Je reste toutefois persuadé, chaque cas étant examiné, séparément au Crédit Foncier, qu'il y aurait tout intérêt à consulter l'Inspecteur des Finances dont vous m'avez parlé. Je reste pour cela à votre entière disposition.

Je vous adresse ci-joint le tableau résumant les différents devis que je vous avais exposés le vendredi 11 juillet lorsque vous avez bien voulu venir à notre atelier.

...

Enfin, M. Le Corbusier verra le Ministre vendredi soir et lui parlera de votre cas.

Veuillez croire, Monsieur, à mes sentiments sincèrement dévoués.

l'Architecte Adjoint,

A. WOGENSCKY

Paris, le 20 Mai 1953
JA.LC AW/JD

Monsieur JAOUL
26, rue Parmentier
NEUILLY s/Seine

Cher Monsieur,

Nous sommes très ennuyés de l'erreur inexcusable qui s'est glissée dans la note d'honoraires qui vous a été adressée le 14 mai par M. Le Corbusier et nous vous prions de bien vouloir nous en excuser. Nous vous adressons ci-jointe une nouvelle note qui remplace et annule complètement la précédente.

D'autre part, nous avons bien reçu votre lettre du 17 mai et nous avons noté votre ordre de construction concernant les fondations et les sous-sols communs des deux maisons et la construction de la maison B, non compris le deuxième étage partiel qui avait été projeté.

Nous confirmons votre ordre à l'entrepreneur de gros-oeuvre et vous trouverez ci-joint copie de la lettre que nous lui écrivons à ce sujet.

Dès réception de votre lettre, nous avons entrepris les mises au point nécessaires avec l'ensemble des entrepreneurs et nous vous communiquerons incessamment le devis exact de la réalisation telle qu'elle est décidée.

Enfin, nous préparons les pièces de marchés pour les différentes entreprises que nous soumettrons incessamment à votre signature.

En vous renouvelant encore nos excuses, nous vous prions de croire, cher Monsieur, à nos sentiments distingués et dévoués.

l'Architecte Adjoint,

A. WOGENSCKY

P.J. 2

Paris, le 20 Mai 1953

Monsieur André JAOUL
26, rue Parmentier
NEUILLY s/Seine

IMMEUBLE 81 RUE DE LONGCHAMP A NEUILLY
MAISONS A et B

HONORAIRES Nº 1 du 30 AVRIL 1953

\- NOTE D'HONORAIRES Nº 1 -

Honoraires : Application du Barême Minimum des Honoraires dus à l'Architecte (Ordre des Architectes - Edition 1953 - Voir document ci-joint).

A - Calcul des Honoraires sur l'estimation de Vingt Huit Millions Cent Quarante et Un Mille Trois Cent Trente Cinq Francs (28.141.335)

Pour la construction complète les honoraires se monteraient à (barême § A)

Pour les premiers 3.000.000 de Frs, 8 % = 240.000 Frs

Pour la tranche de 3.000.000 à 6.000.000 de Frs. 7 % = 210.000 Frs

Pour la tranche de 6.000.000 à 12.000.000 de Frs. 6,50 % = 390.000 Frs

de 12.000.000 à 28.141.335 de Frs., 6 % soit : 16.141.335 x 6 / 100 = 968.480 Frs

1.808.480 Frs

D - Décomposition des Honoraires
Pour l'étude et l'établissement des plans et dossiers d'exécution (barême § D) soit :
50 % des Honoraires soit : 1.808.480 x 50 / 100 = 904.240 Frs.

(Neuf Cent Quatre Mille Deux Cent Quarante Francs.-)

Top left. Le Corbusier's associate, André Wogenscky, to the builder, Roger Bertrand, 26 May 1952, about the choice of a contractor for the Maisons Jaoul, Neuilly-sur-Seine, France, 1951–55

Left. André Wogenscky to André Jaoul, 23 July 1952, concerning cost estimates

Bottom. André Wogenscky to André Jaoul, 20 May 1953, clarifying an error about Le Corbusier's fees

Opposite, top. Section details of vaults, conduits, and balconies, 18 April 1952

Opposite, middle. Bird's-eye perspective

Opposite, bottom. Northeast elevation and transverse section, 12 March 1952

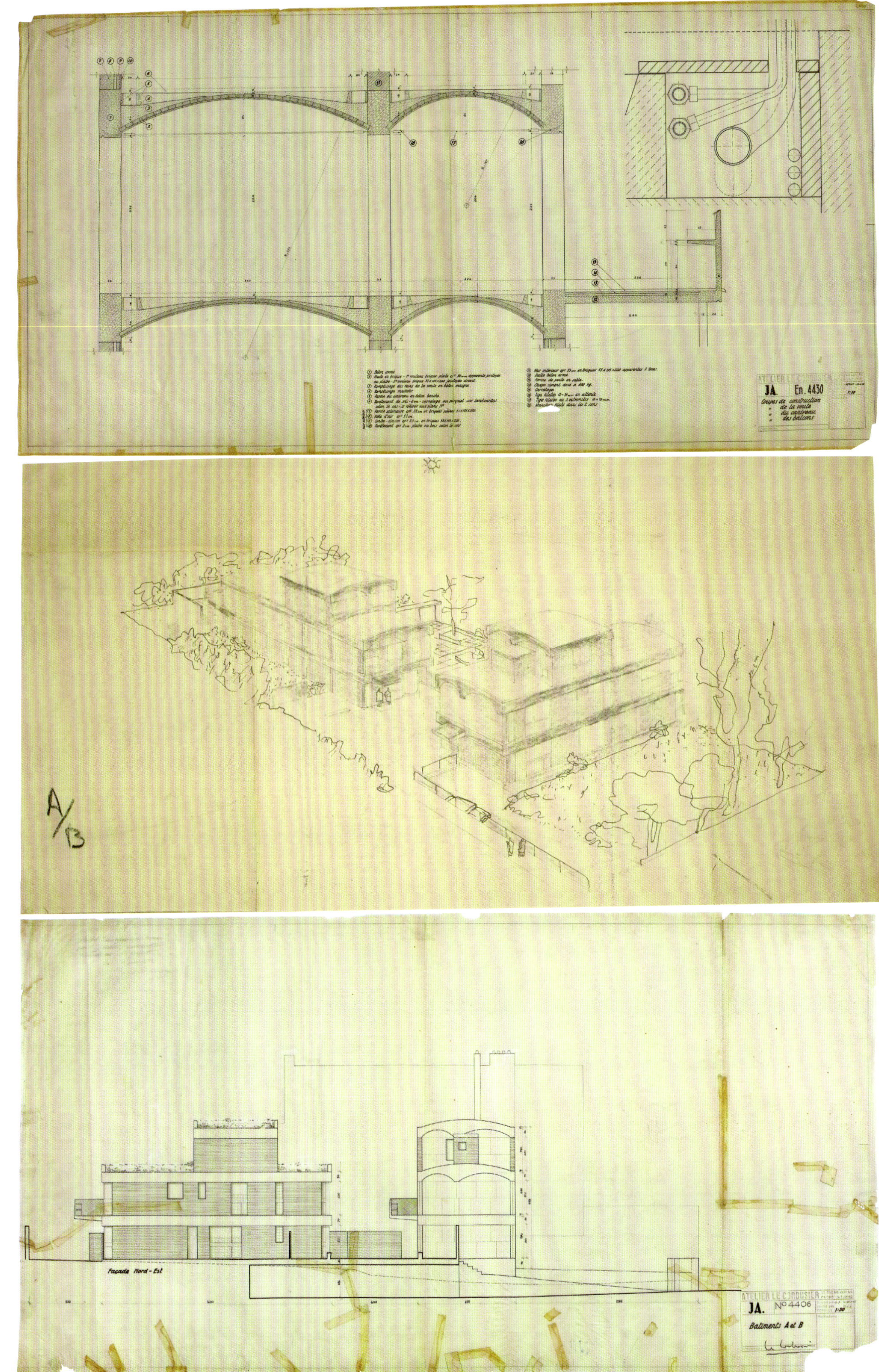
JA. En. 4430
Coupes de construction
de la voute
du caniveau
des balcons
A/B
Façade Nord-Est
ATELIER LE CORBUSIER
JA. N°4406
1:50
Batiments A et B

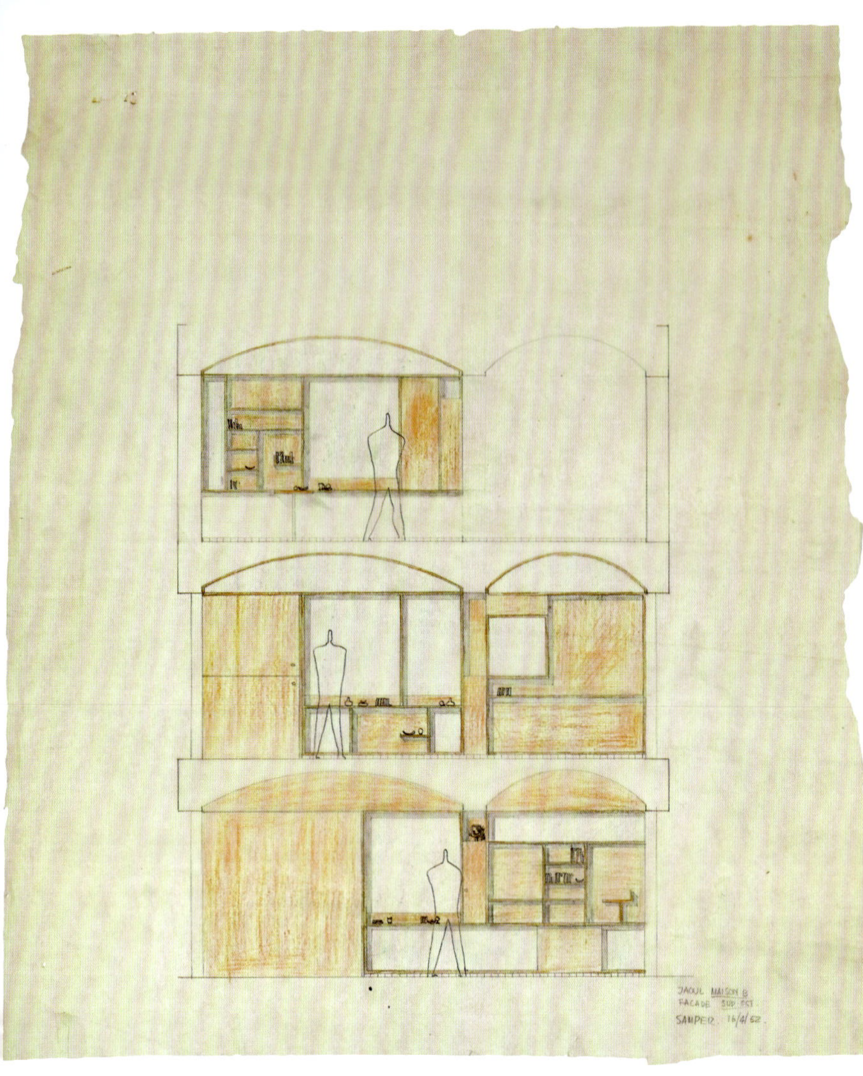

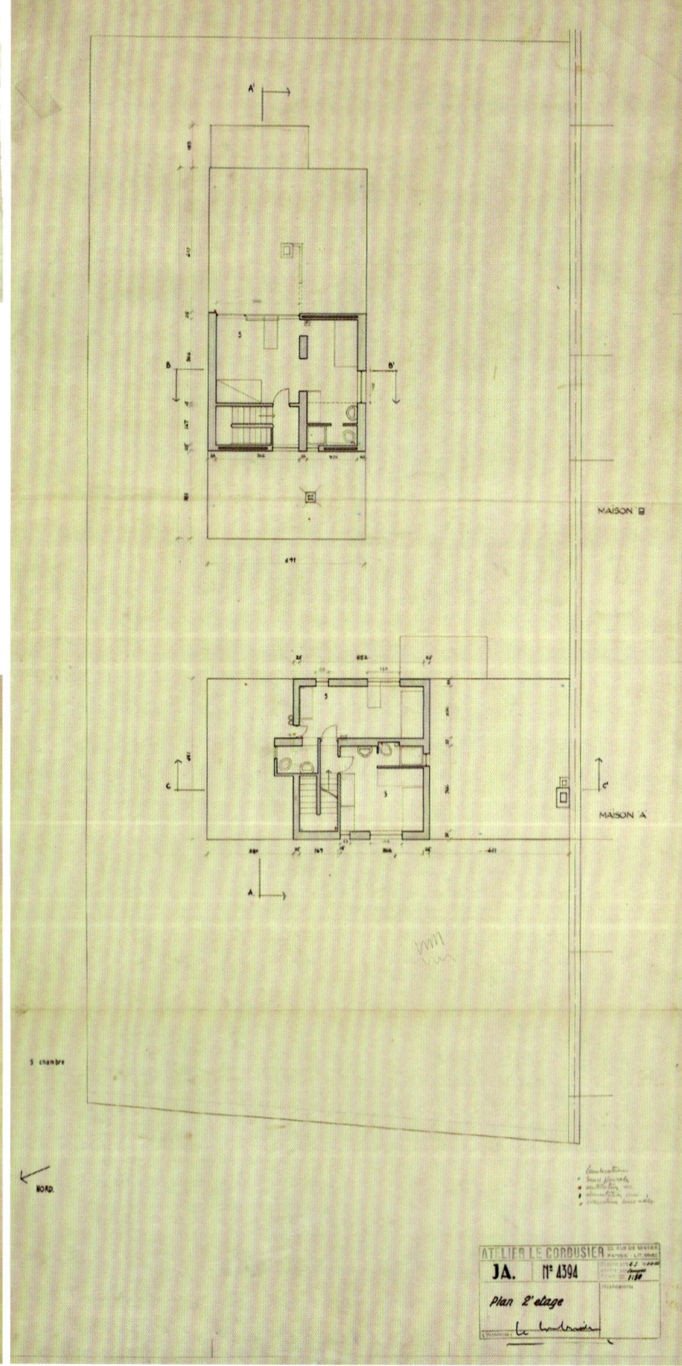

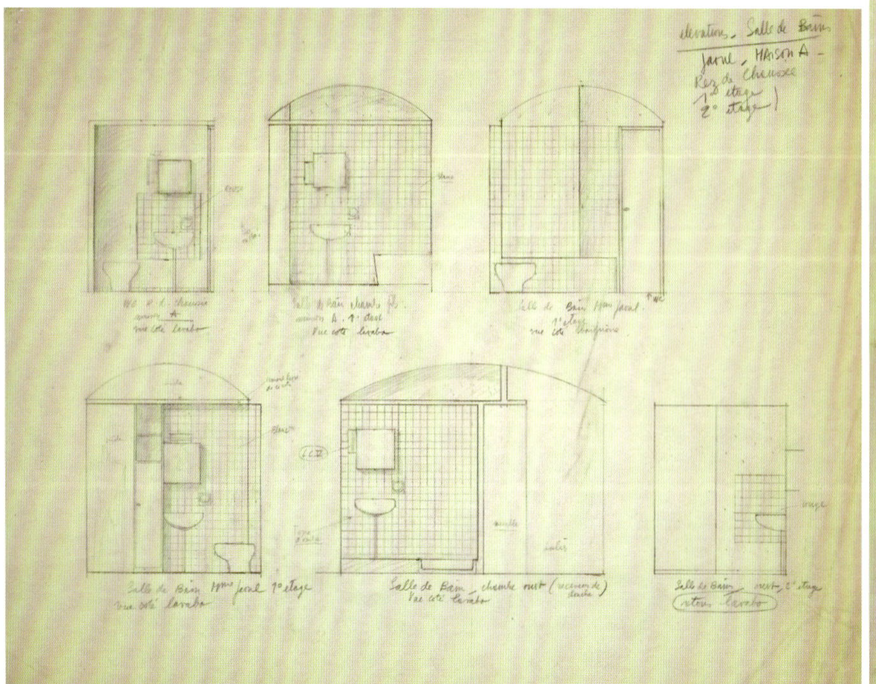

Left. Transverse section through Maison B with interior elevations, 16 April 1952, Maisons Jaoul, Neuilly-sur-Seine

Bottom, left. Elevations of bathroom

Bottom, right. Second-floor plan, 6 March 1952

Opposite. West facade of Maison A, showing the principal entry

Top. Salon with fireplace and pivot door to garden, Maison B, Maisons Jaoul, Neuilly-sur-Seine

Left. Ground-level corridor, view toward entry, Maison A

Above. Entry hall with stairs to upper level, Maison A

Above. Salubra "color keys" for interior wall colors to be used in the Maisons Jaoul

Below. Living and dining areas of Maison A, showing the polychrome treatment of the walls and the Catalan vault

"Dear little hundred-year-old mom. Your boy Edouard thinks of you all the time. And says, 'Keep going!'"

—Letter to his mother, 7 June 1959

Celebrating a milestone birthday, September 1959

Le Corbusier made frequent visits home to his mother, who continued to live in the Petite Maison, which he had designed for her in Corseaux, Switzerland, on Lac Léman. He and his brother, Albert, celebrated her one-hundredth year in 1959—slightly anticipating the official centennial of her birth in 1960.

Opposite, top. Le Corbusier with his brother, Albert, and their mother, at the Petite Maison, Corseaux, Switzerland, on the occasion of her one-hundredth birthday celebration, September 1959

Opposite, bottom. Contact sheet of photographs of the celebration

Right. Marie-Charlotte-Amélie Jeanneret

Below. Le Corbusier's sketch of his mother on her ninety-first birthday, 10 September 1951

HABITER

TRAVAILLER

CULTIVER CORPS ET ESPRIT

CIRCULE

DIVERS

Opposite. Le Corbusier in his Paris office, explaining principles of urban planning, 1950s

Retrospection (1954–1965)

In his final years, as at so many other times during his life, Le Corbusier polarized public opinion, and that of his peers. His project for a new hospital in Venice, on which he was working when he died, offered radical new possibilities for urban planning, surprising even his closest admirers. According to Guillermo Jullian de la Fuente, his principal collaborator on the project: "It is its integration to the life of the city that matters. And Le Corbusier discovered the essence of the city of Venice, its structure and its light—not on the drawing board but... by observing and walking around it for a long time."

For his old friend Eugène Claudius-Petit, formerly minister of reconstruction and planning, and now mayor of the declining French mining town of Firminy, Le Corbusier designed a new civic center comprising a stadium, a youth club, a swimming pool, and a church, as well as a version of the Unité d'Habitation. But as soon as Mayor Claudius-Petit left office, the local left-wing government stopped work on the entire project. It wasn't until 2006 that the church was finally completed by José Oubrerie, who had worked closely with Le Corbusier on the original design.

The Carpenter Center for the Visual Arts at Harvard University in Cambridge, Massachusetts, the only American commission that Le Corbusier ever received, came about through the intervention of his old friend José Luis Sert, dean of Harvard's Graduate School of Design. It seems to have been designed with the intent to upstage the work by other modern architects on campus.

Le Corbusier's philosophy of life was stoic. Unable to sleep because of jet lag one night, he noted in a sketchbook: "There are men, often vain, who are active in the arts, philosophy or literature but who have no idea of the laws of physics and the time it takes for men to work together to create something permanent." The next two sentences were in English: "Its [*sic*] takes a long time. You must be patient. And in the end you realize at the first setback (in the stars) that you are not constituted to understand everything, but that it is better to do something rather than nothing. And to understand that you will die some day and that, having lived a life, it is only normal and reassuring to die."

After Le Corbusier had a fatal heart attack in August 1965, while swimming in the sea near his *cabanon* (cabin) at Roquebrune-Cap-Martin, the verdict on his life's work was far from unanimous. But his friend André Malraux, France's minister of culture, made sure that he was awarded the full splendor of a funeral cortège in the Cour Carré of the Louvre. Tributes came from around the globe; the president of Greece brought earth from the Acropolis to sprinkle on the coffin, and an Indian representative brought holy water from the Ganges.

In a voice trembling with emotion, Malraux delivered the funeral eulogy: "Le Corbusier had some great rivals... But none of them have represented with such power the revolution in architecture because none of them have been so patiently insulted for such a long time. Fame receives its highest praise in the face of outrage, and this fame belongs to the work and not to the man, who cared little for it. Having adopted for his studio over the years the wide corridor of an abandoned monastery, the man who designed capital cities has died in a solitary cabin... His famous phrase, 'The house is a machine for living in' does not get him right at all. Better is his other phrase: 'The house should enshrine life, a machine for emotion.'"

After listing the tributes from Japan, India, and Brazil, Malraux concluded, in the highest rhetorical vein by addressing the dead man directly: "And now it's the turn of France, she who so often ignored you, ... she who says to you now, in the words of her most famous poet: 'I salute you at the solemn threshold of the tomb.' Goodbye, my old master and old friend. Good night."

BAU-FORUM

Opposite and above. Le Corbusier in his private office at 35 rue de Sèvres, 1959

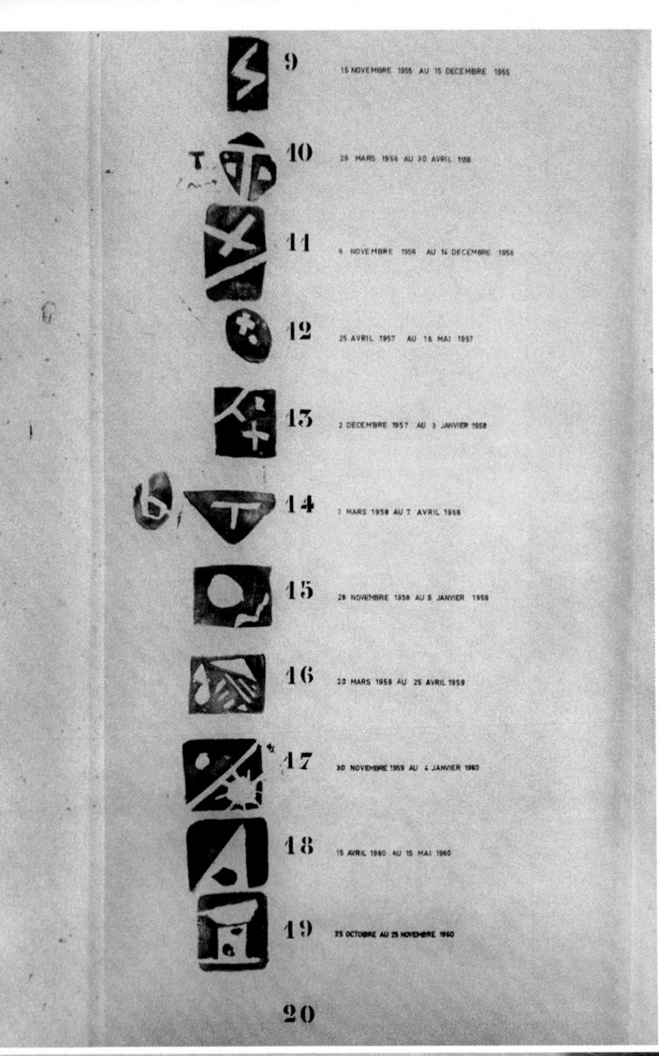

Left. Examples of stamps Le Corbusier made by cutting patterns into erasers, next to a list of his travel dates, 1955–60

Below, and opposite. Le Corbusier in his private office at 35 rue de Sèvres, 1959

Opposite and below. Le Corbusier and colleagues working in his office at 35 rue de Sèvres, Paris, 1960

"Through his arrangement of forms the architect brings into being an order that is a pure creation of his mind. Through these forms he acts intensely on our senses, inducing aesthetic empathy; through the relationships he establishes, he awakens deep echoes in us, giving us the measure of an order we feel to be in harmony with that of the world, and governing the diverse movements of our minds and hearts. It is then that we become aware of beauty."

—"Petit vocabulaire Corbu: Architecte," *Le Corbusier lui-même*

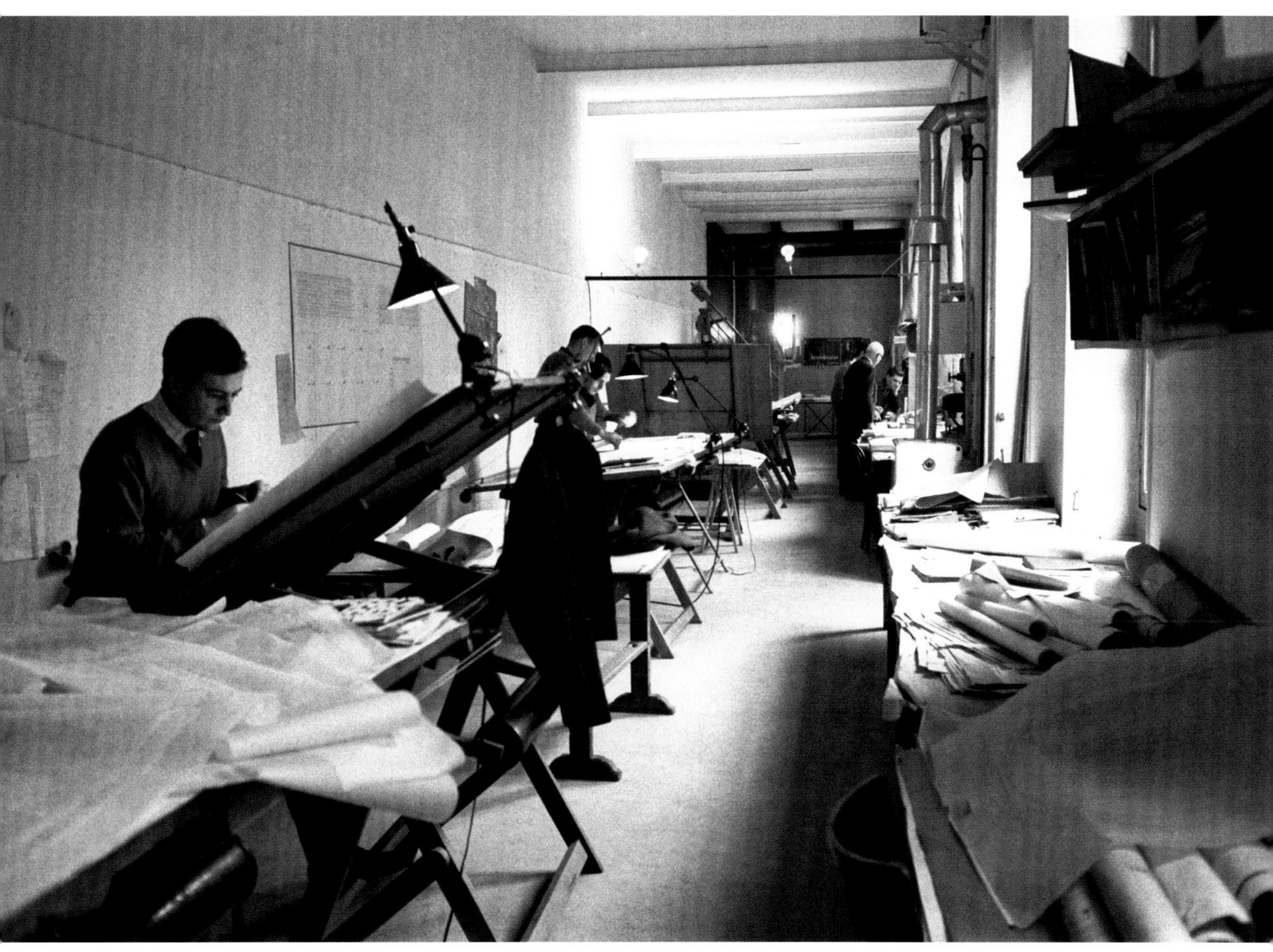

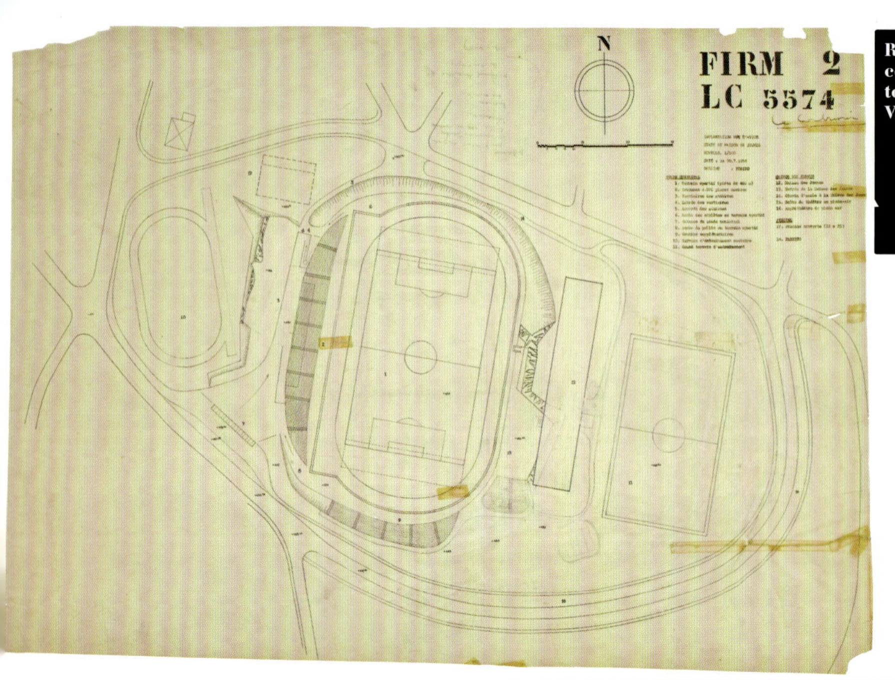

Reviving an old coal-mining town: Firminy-Vert, France

After Le Corbusier's longtime supporter Eugène Claudius-Petit resigned as France's minister of reconstruction and planning, he became mayor of the mining town of Firminy, near Lyon. For a new town next door, to be called Firminy-Vert, Claudius-Petit commissioned Le Corbusier to design a municipal complex with a cultural and youth center (Maison des Jeunes et de la Culture, 1955–65), a Unité d'Habitation (1955–67), a stadium (1966–68), and a church (completed 2006).

165 × 64

FIRM. 2 - L.C. 5573
PERSPECTIVE DE LA MAISON DES JEUNES
Le 30.7.1958
Le Corbusier

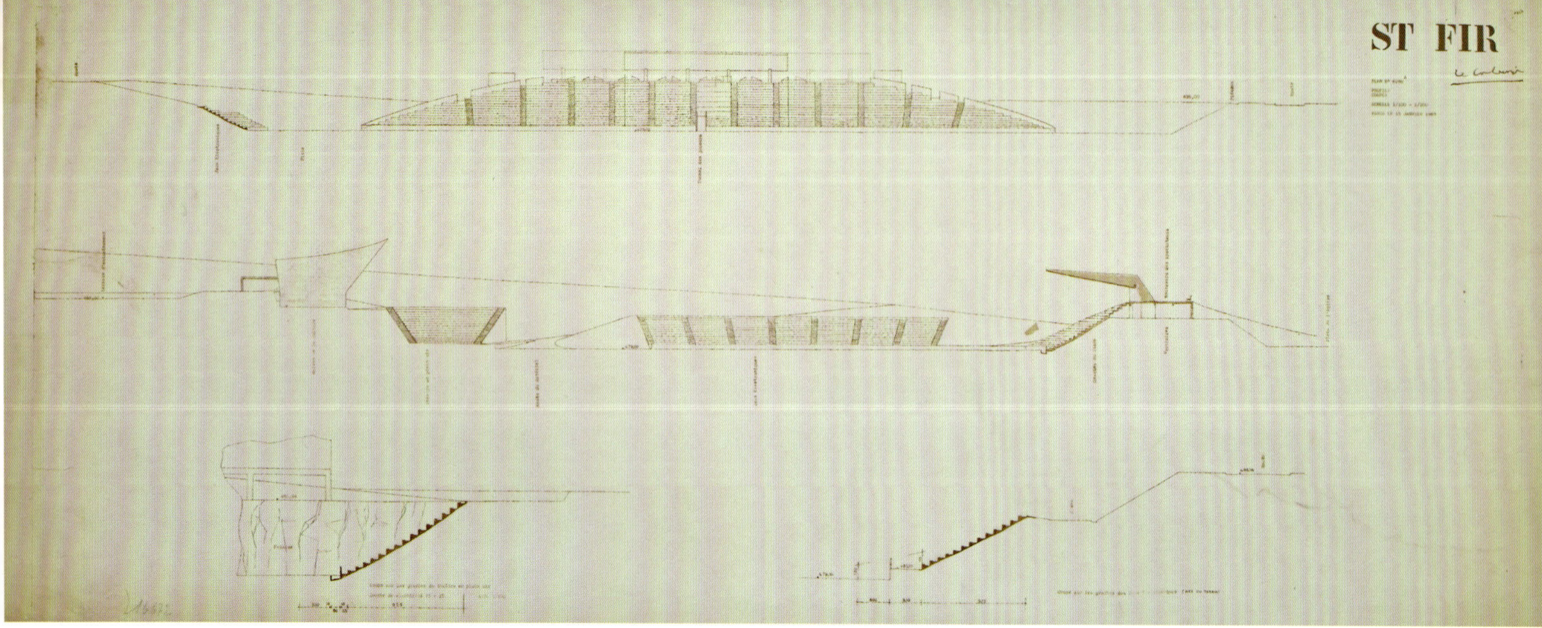

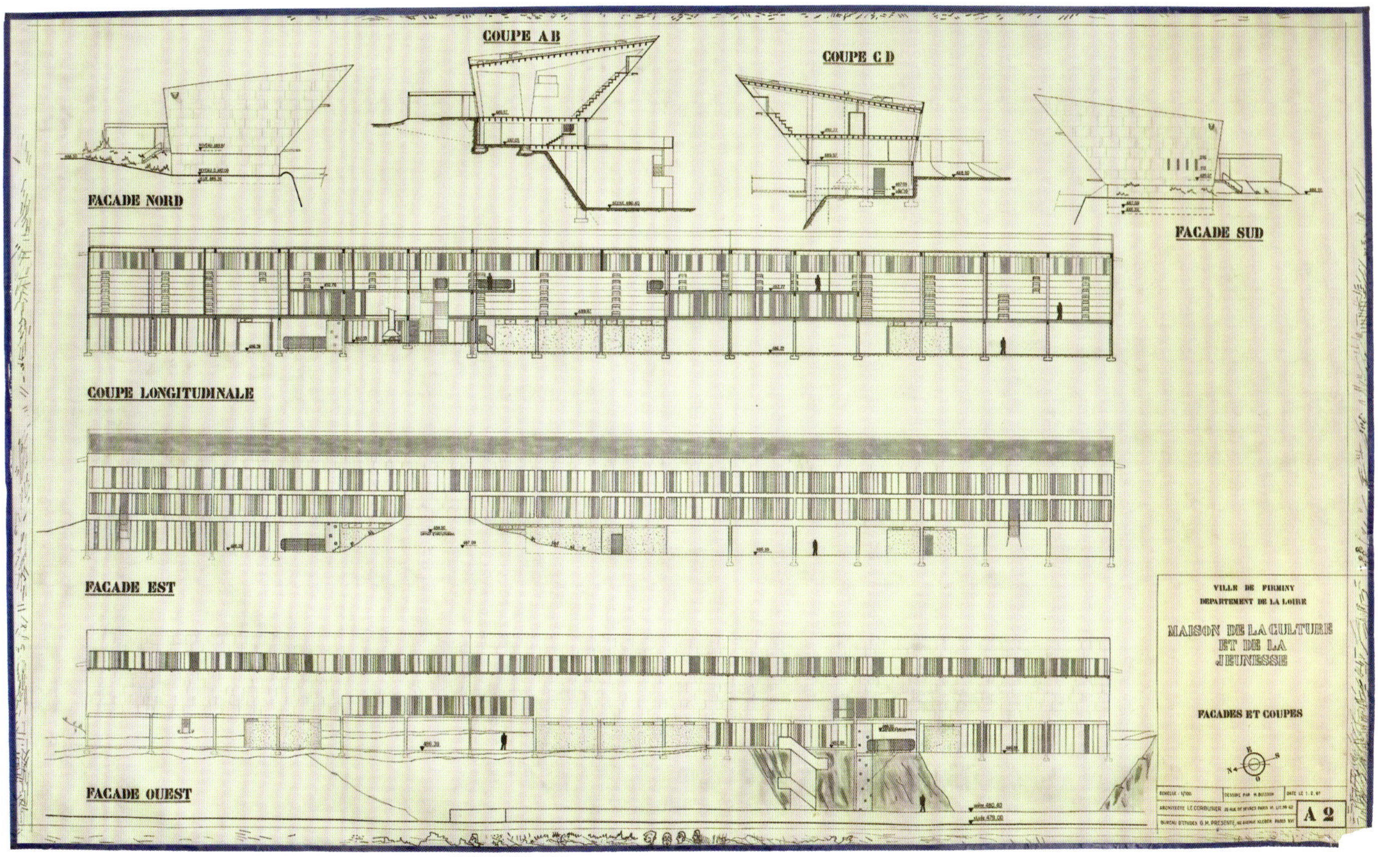

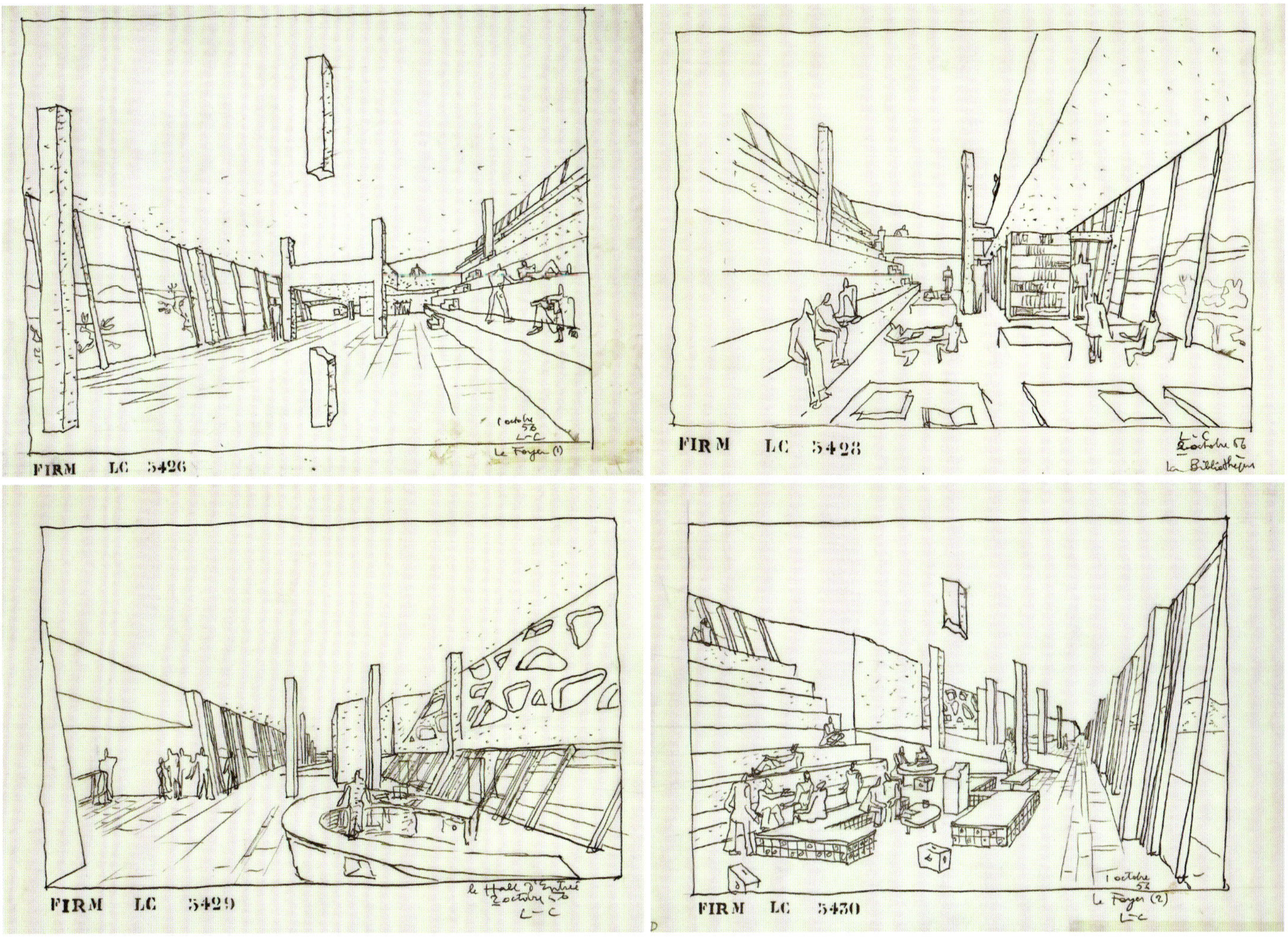

Opposite, top left. Site plan, 1958, Maison des Jeunes et de la Culture (House of Youth and Culture), Firminy-Vert, France, 1955–65

Opposite, middle. Perspective, Maison des Jeunes et de la Culture, 30 July 1958

Opposite, bottom. Stadium sections, 5 January 1965

Above. Facades and sections, Maison des Jeunes et de la Culture

Below. Four drawings of the interior, October 1956, including the lounge (top left and bottom right), library (top right) and entrance hall (bottom left)

Maison des Jeunes et de la Culture, Firminy-Vert, 1955–65

The striking form of the cultural center at Firminy-Vert was adapted from a scheme that Le Corbusier had originally developed to combine the cultural and sports facilities into a single structure. Once these functions were separated, the program for the cultural component (known as the Maison de la Culture) comprised an auditorium, exhibition space, library, and art and music studios.

Above, left and right. Construction views of the Maison de la Culture, Firminy-Vert, 1955–65

Below. Relief wall, south facade

Opposite, top. Open Hand motif, c. 1965

Opposite, bottom left. Interior view showing oblique angle of window-wall and convex ceiling.

Opposite, bottom right. Recreation hall

Left. Le Corbusier's relief on the Maison de la Culture, Firminy-Vert, combining a bull's head, human ear, conch shell, and leaves

Below. Le Corbusier in front of the relief, c. 1965

Opposite. Le Corbusier with Eugène Claudius-Petit (second from right), mayor of Firminy-Vert, and others, 21 May 196

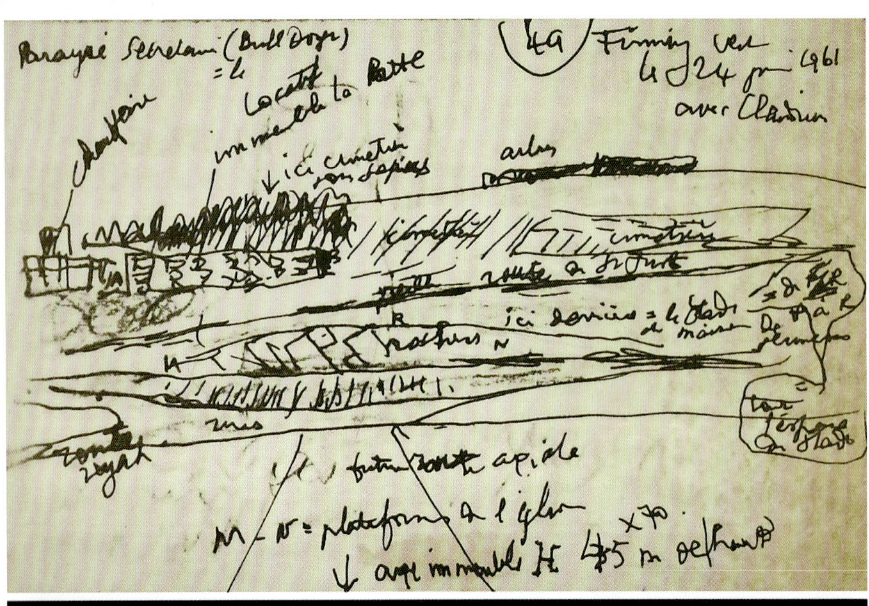

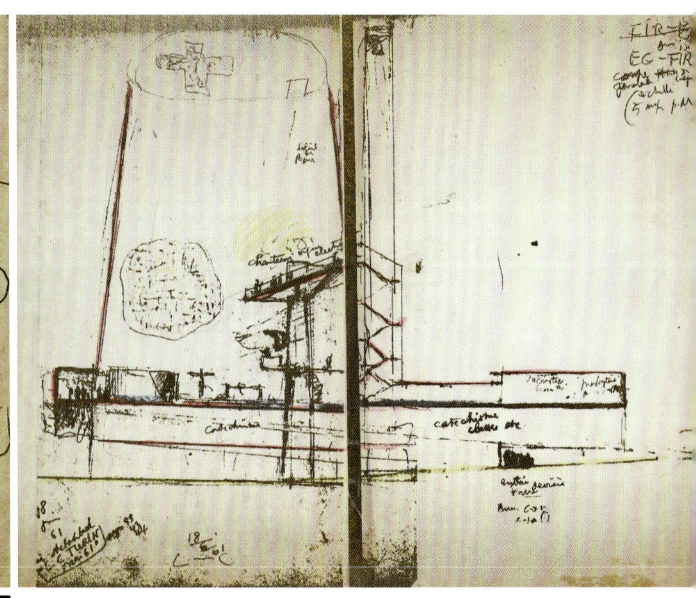

"I can't think of anything else at present other than getting the project underway for the spiritual delight of all."

—Letter to Father Tardy, 28 January 1965

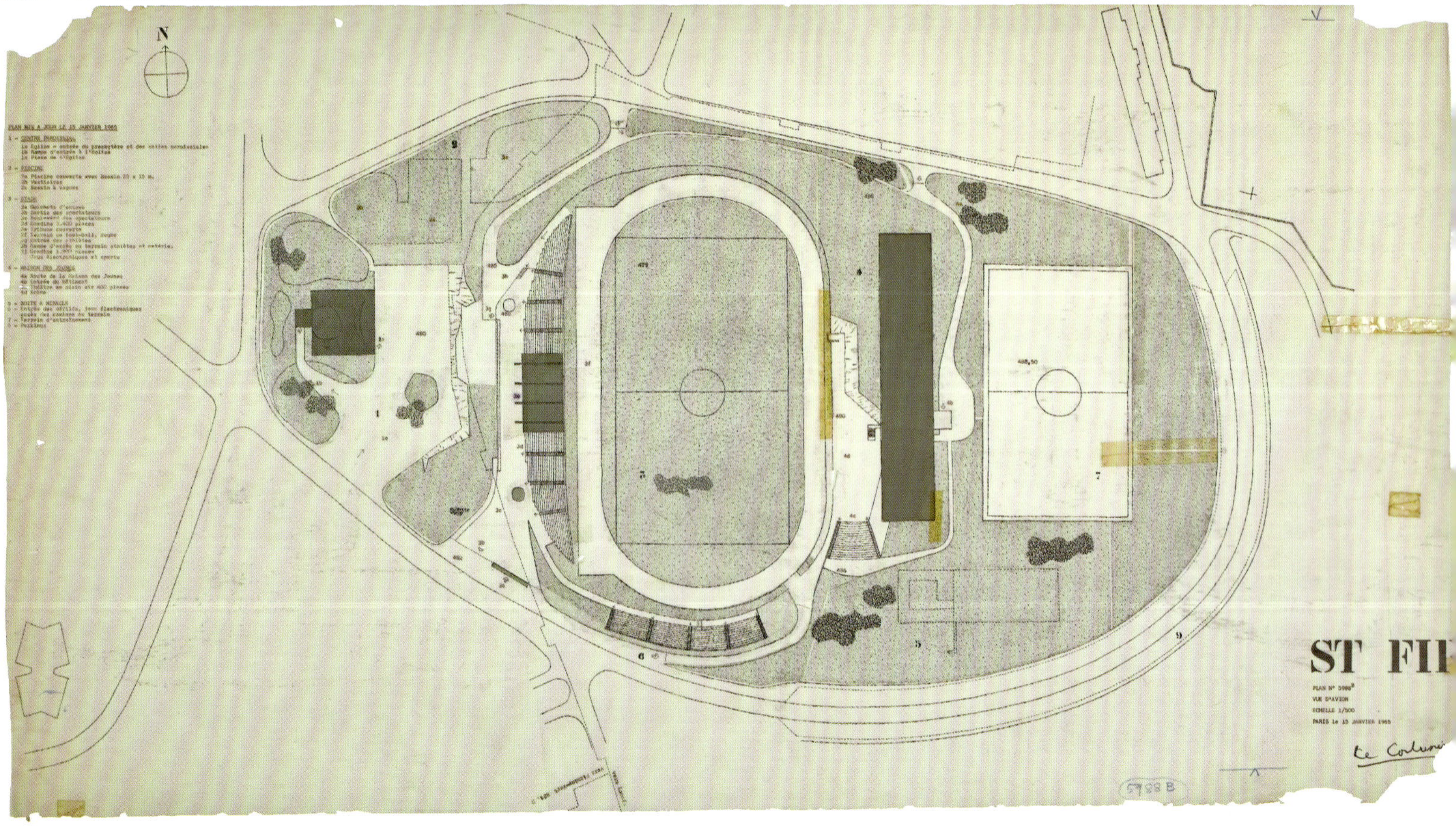

A project for the twenty-first century: Church of Saint-Pierre, Firminy-Vert, completed 2006

Construction on Le Corbusier's projects for Firminy-Vert stopped when Claudius-Petit stepped down as mayor. However, the church was finally completed in 2006 by José Oubrerie, an architect who had worked with Le Corbusier on the original design. The church features a distinctive funnel structure that recalls the Palace of the Assembly at Chandigarh.

Opposite, top. Sketches for the Church of Saint-Pierre, Firminy-Vert, 1960

Opposite, middle. Model, Church of Saint-Pierre, c. 1960

Opposite, bottom. Site plan, Maison des Jeunes et de la Culture, with the Church of Saint-Pierre at left, 15 January 1965

Above. Sections, Church of Saint-Pierre. Left to right: north-south, east-west, south-north

Below. Drawings of the conical structure, 1961, Church of Saint-Pierre

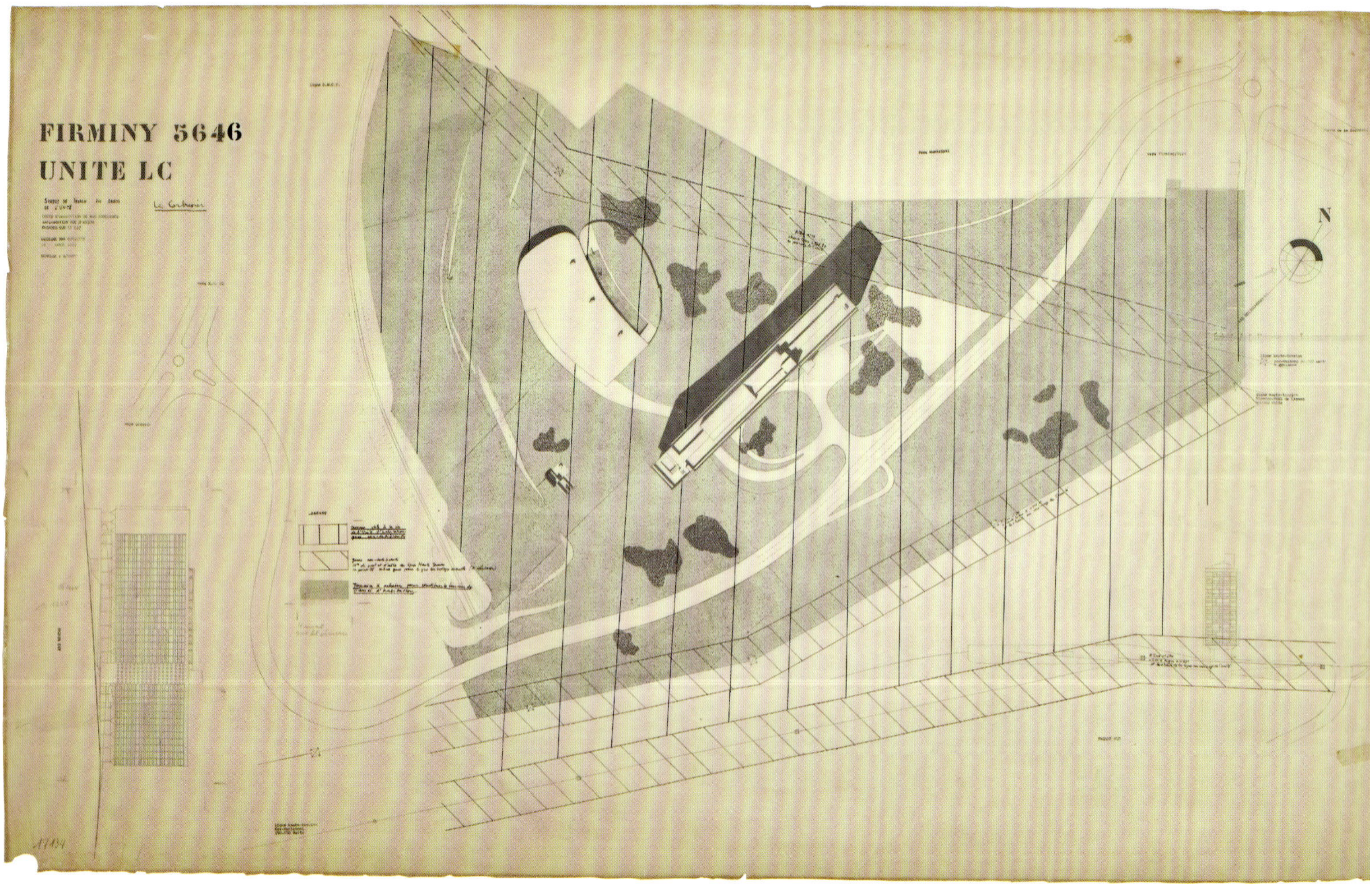

FIRMINY 5646
UNITE LC

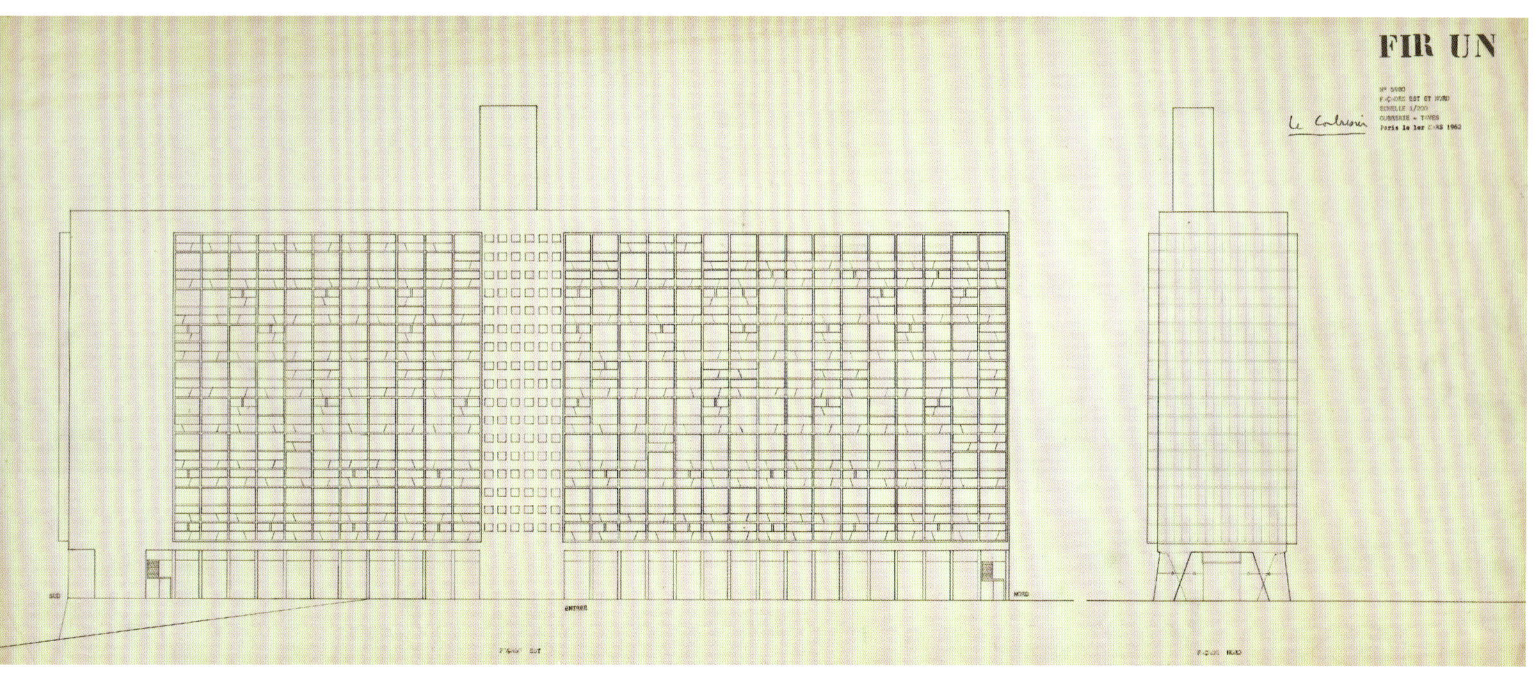

Unité d'Habitation, Firminy-Vert, 1955–67

Le Corbusier's Unité d'Habitation, commissioned by Claudius-Petit for Firminy-Vert, was the second in a series that included three other Unités built in France (Marseille, Briey-en-Forêt, and one near Nantes), plus one in Berlin. Far more modest than the original project in Marseille, the Unité at Firminy accommodated only two hundred inhabitants.

Opposite, top. Perspective drawing of colonnade, c. 1962

Opposite, bottom. Site plan and elevations, 29 April 1960, showing the terrain surrounding the Unité, including land that cannot be built on

Above. East and north elevations, 1962

Below. Sheet of photographs of study model, 20 April 1960

Fir-Un-(Firminy Unité)
photos faites par Gullian le 20 Avril 1960

Fir-Un-13A

Fir-Un-12A

Fir-Un-15A

ATELIER
LE CORBUSIER
35, rue de Sèvres
Paris-6e - Lit. 99-62

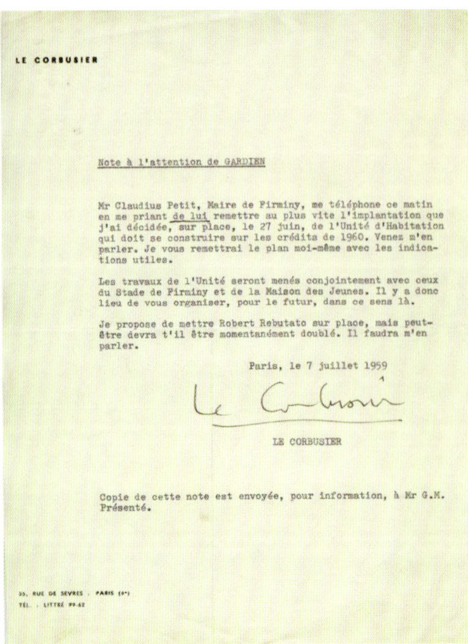

LE CORBUSIER

Note à l'attention de GARDIEN

Mr Claudius Petit, Maire de Firminy, me téléphone ce matin en me priant de lui remettre au plus vite l'implantation que j'ai décidée, sur place, le 27 juin, de l'Unité d'Habitation qui doit se construire sur les crédits de 1960. Venez m'en parler. Je vous remettrai le plan moi-même avec les indications utiles.

Les travaux de l'Unité seront menés conjointement avec ceux du Stade de Firminy et de la Maison des Jeunes. Il y a donc lieu de vous organiser, pour le futur, dans ce sens là.

Je propose de mettre Robert Rebutato sur place, mais peut-être devra t'il être momentanément doublé. Il faudra m'en parler.

Paris, le 7 juillet 1959

LE CORBUSIER

Copie de cette note est envoyée, pour information, à Mr G.M. Présenté.

35, RUE DE SEVRES . PARIS (6e)
TÉL. : LITTRÉ 99-62

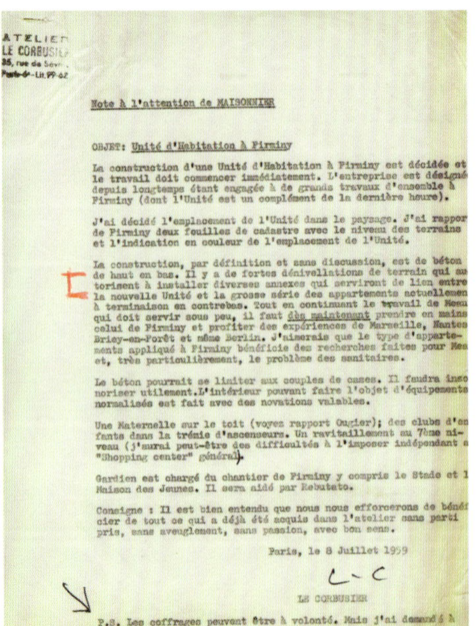

ATELIER LE CORBUSIER
35, rue de Sevres
Paris 6e - Lit. 99-62

Note à l'attention de MAISONNIER

OBJET: Unité d'Habitation à Firminy

La construction d'une Unité d'Habitation à Firminy est décidée et le travail doit commencer immédiatement. L'entreprise est désigné depuis longtemps étant engagée à de grands travaux d'ensemble à Firminy (dont l'Unité est un complément de la dernière heure).

J'ai décidé l'emplacement de l'Unité dans le paysage. J'ai rappor de Firminy deux feuilles de cadastre avec le niveau des terrains et l'indication en couleur de l'emplacement de l'Unité.

La construction, par définition et sans discussion, est de béton de haut en bas. Il y a de fortes dénivellations de terrain qui au torisent à installer diverses annexes qui serviront de lien entre la nouvelle Unité et la grosse série des appartements actuellemen à terminaison en contrebas. Tout en continuant le travail de Meau qui doit servir sous peu, il faut dès maintenant prendre en mains celui de Firminy et profiter des expériences de Marseille, Nantes Briey-en-Forêt et même Berlin. J'aimerais que le type d'appartements appliqué à Firminy bénéficie des recherches faites pour Mea et, très particulièrement, le problème des sanitaires.

Le béton pourrait se limiter aux couples de cases. Il faudra inso noriser utilement. L'intérieur pouvant faire l'objet d'équipements normalisés est fait avec des novations valables.

Une Maternelle sur le toit (voyez rapport Ougier); des clubs d'en fants dans la trémie d'ascenseurs. Un ravitaillement au 7ème niveau (j'aurai peut-être des difficultés à l'imposer indépendant d "Shopping center" général).

Gardien est chargé du chantier de Firminy y compris le Stade et l Maison des Jeunes. Il sera aidé par Rebutato.

Consigne : Il est bien entendu que nous nous efforcerons de béné cier de tout ce qui a déjà été acquis dans l'atelier sans parti pris, sans aveuglement, sans passion, avec bon sens.

Paris, le 8 Juillet 1959

L-C

LE CORBUSIER

P.S. Les coffrages peuvent être à volonté. Mais j'ai demandé à

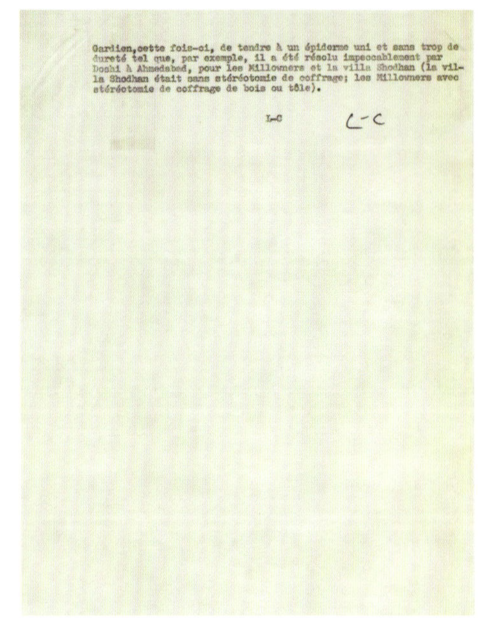

Gardien, cette fois-ci, de tendre à un épiderme uni et sans trop de dureté tel que, par exemple, il a été résolu impeccablement par Doshi à Ahmedabad, pour les Millowners et la villa Shodhan (la villa Shodhan était sans stéréotomie de coffrage; les Millowners avec stéréotomie de coffrage de bois ou tôle).

L-C

L-C

Above left. Le Corbusier to his associate Fernand Gardien, 7 July 1959, regarding the location and schedule for the Unité d'Habitation, Firminy-Vert

Above middle and right. Le Corbusier to his associate André Maisonnier, 8 July 1959, telling him that a Unité will be built in Firminy. "By definition and without being open to discussion, the construction will be concrete from top to bottom."

Right. Cost estimates, May 1962, for flooring, painting, woodwork, glass, and metalwork

Below. Summary of costs, 29 June 1962

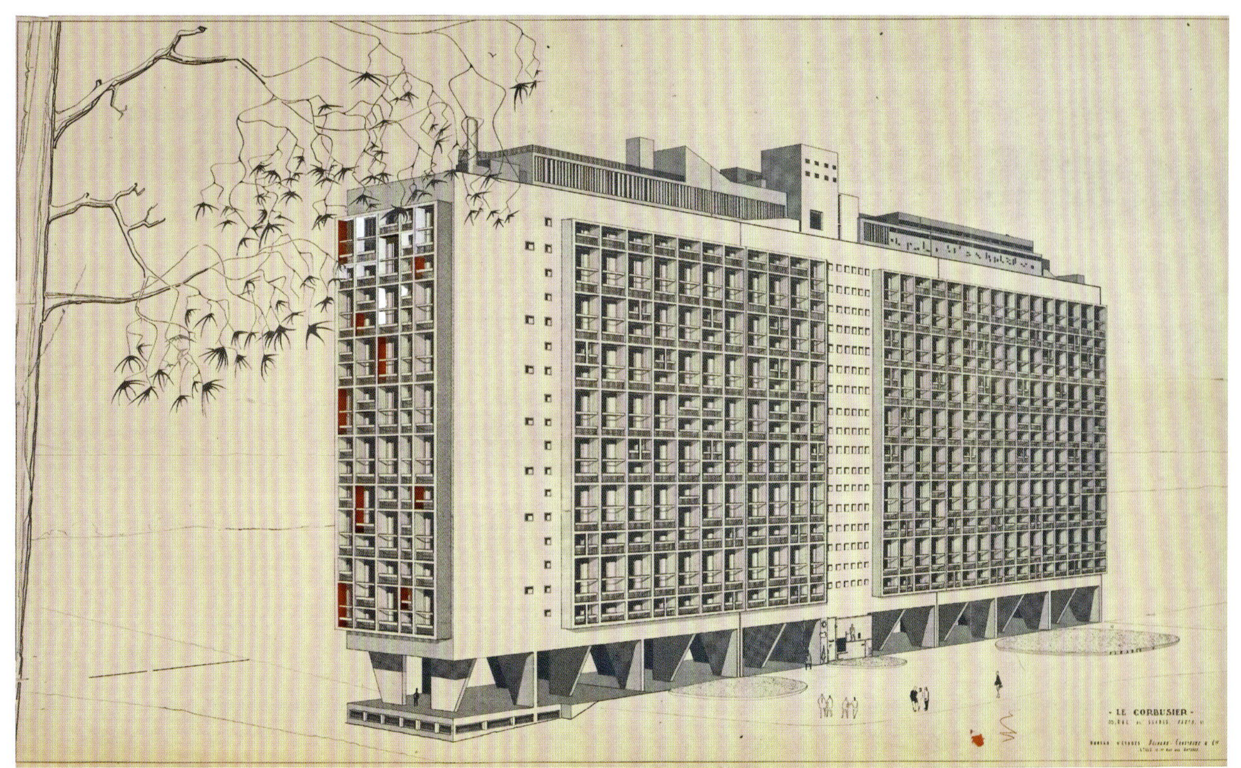

Above. Perspective of east facade

Below. Facade and grounds of the completed building

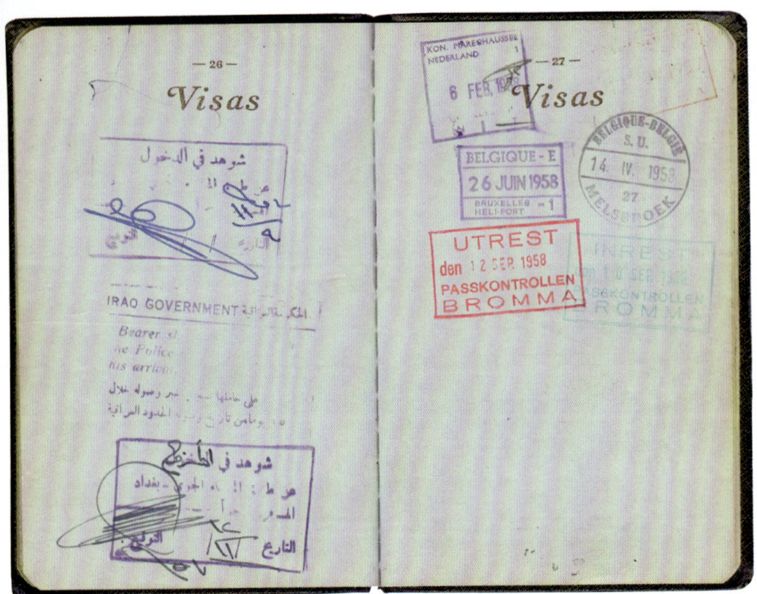

Modernizing an ancient city: Baghdad Sports Center, 1956–64

In the 1950s, Iraq's King Faisal II invited a series of architects—including Le Corbusier, Frank Lloyd Wright, Walter Gropius, and Gio Ponti—to Baghdad in a campaign to modernize the city. The king's assassination in 1958 put a halt to his grand vision of a modernist Baghdad, but a few of the projects were completed nonetheless. Le Corbusier's design for an Olympic stadium for 100,000 spectators was never built, but the smaller gymnasium was erected in 1980 during Saddam Hussein's regime.

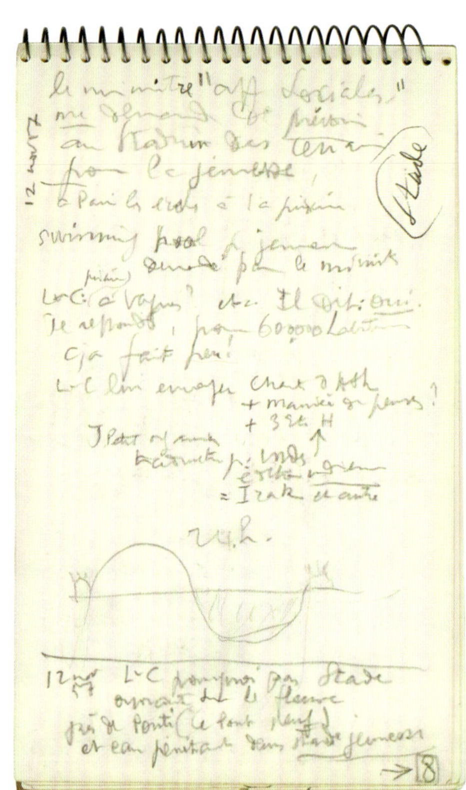

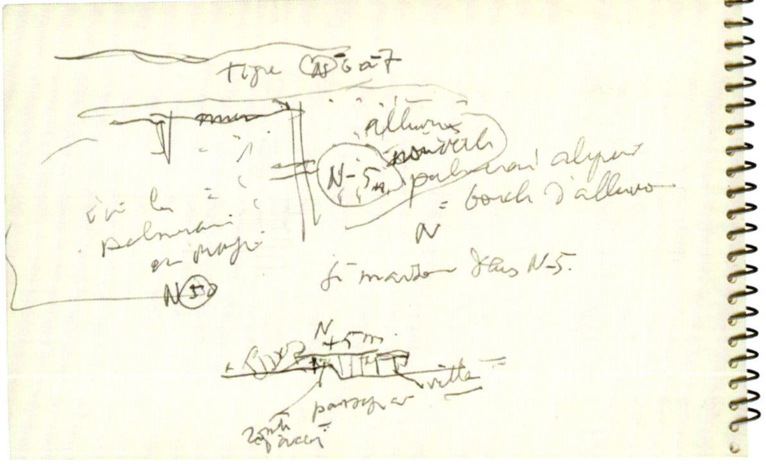

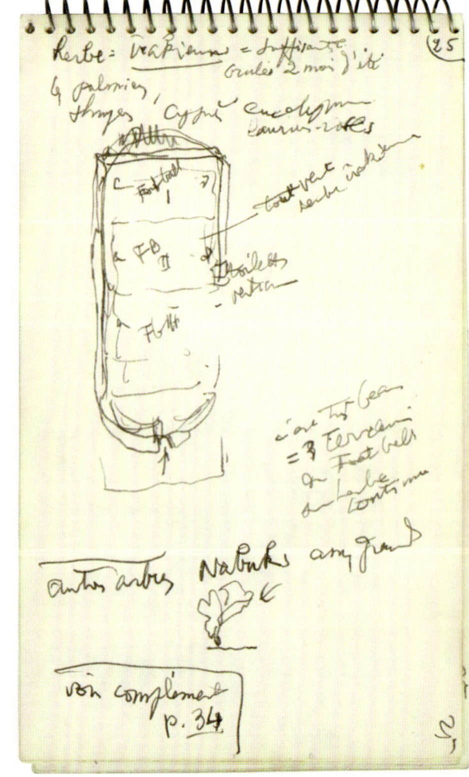

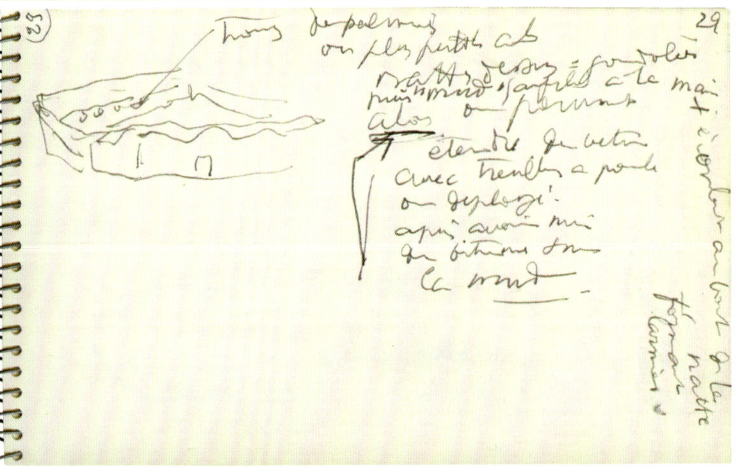

Opposite, top left. Le Corbusier's passport with Iraqi visa

Opposite, bottom left and right. Cover and selected pages from Le Corbusier's sketchbook number 50, from his trip to Baghdad, 8–13 November 1957

Right. Site plan, 5 June 1958, for the stadium (labeled 1) and associated buildings, including the gymnasium (2A), Baghdad, 1956–64

Below left. Study of stadium structure

Below right. Elevations of the stadium and associated buildings, 5 June 1958

Bottom. Model of the gymnasium

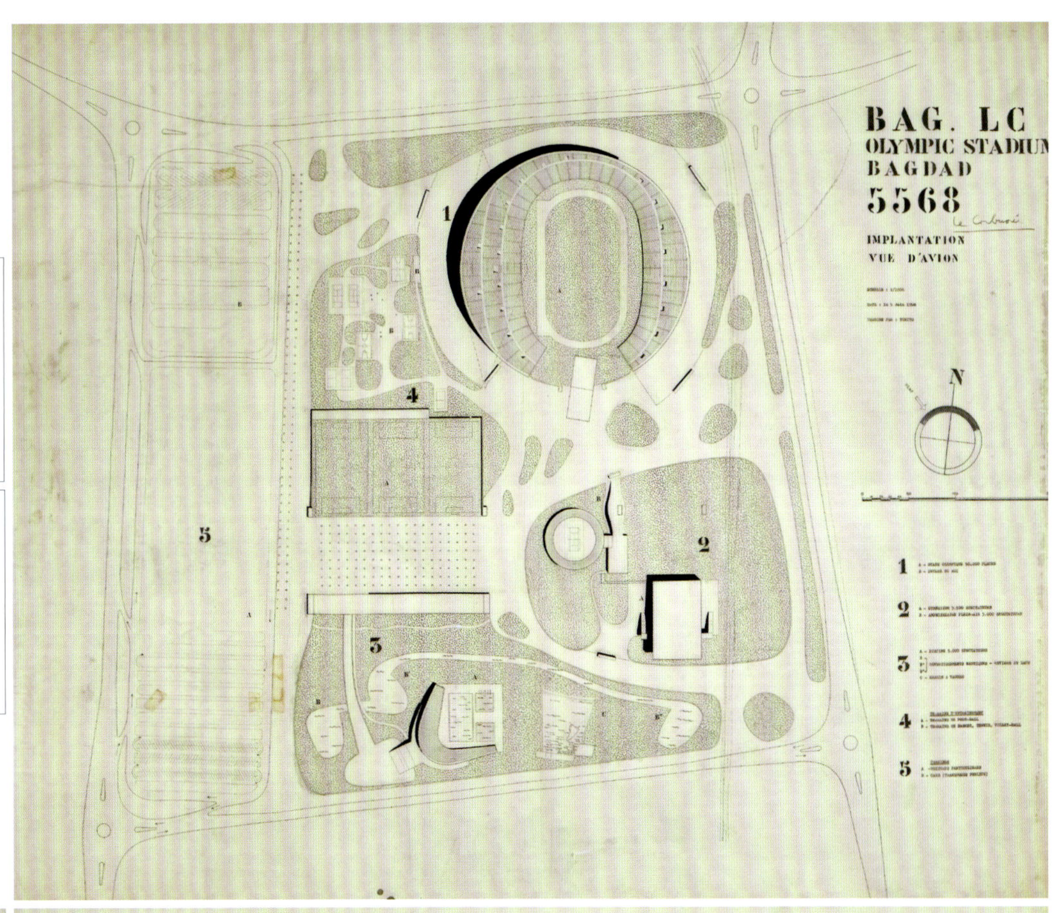

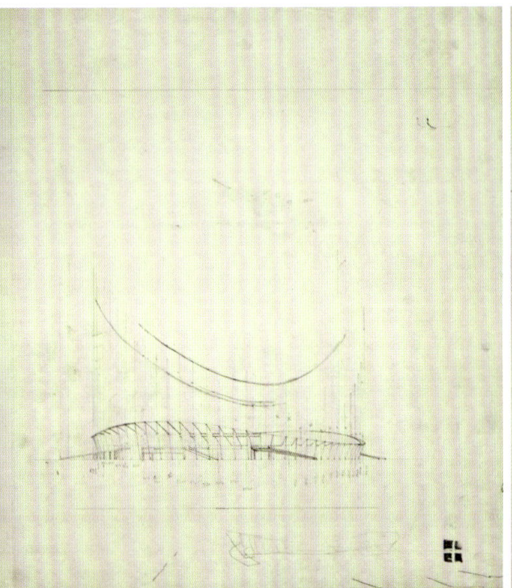

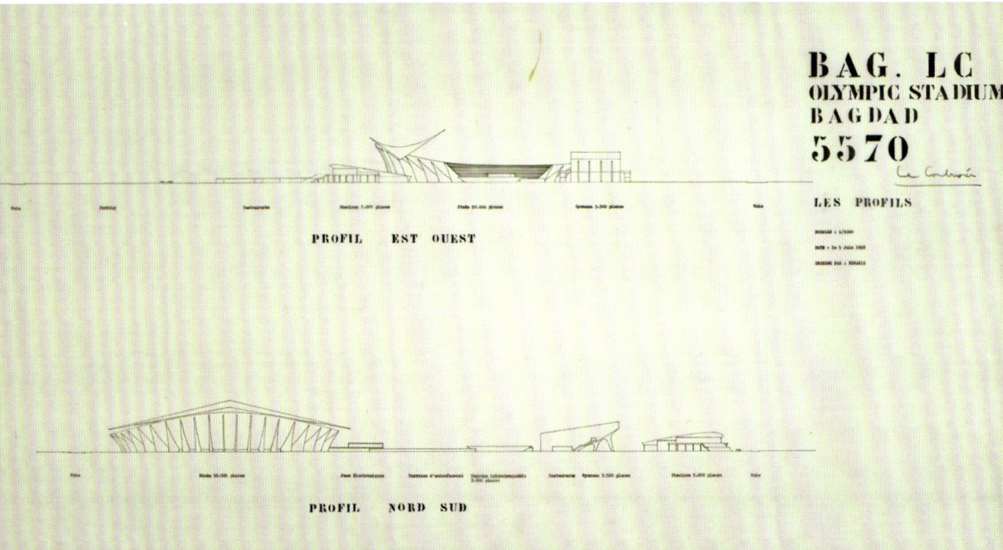

Following pages. Desktop in Le Corbusier's studio, 24 rue Nungesser-et-Coli, Paris, 1960

POST CARD
CORRESPONDENCE ADDRESS

航空 AIR MAIL

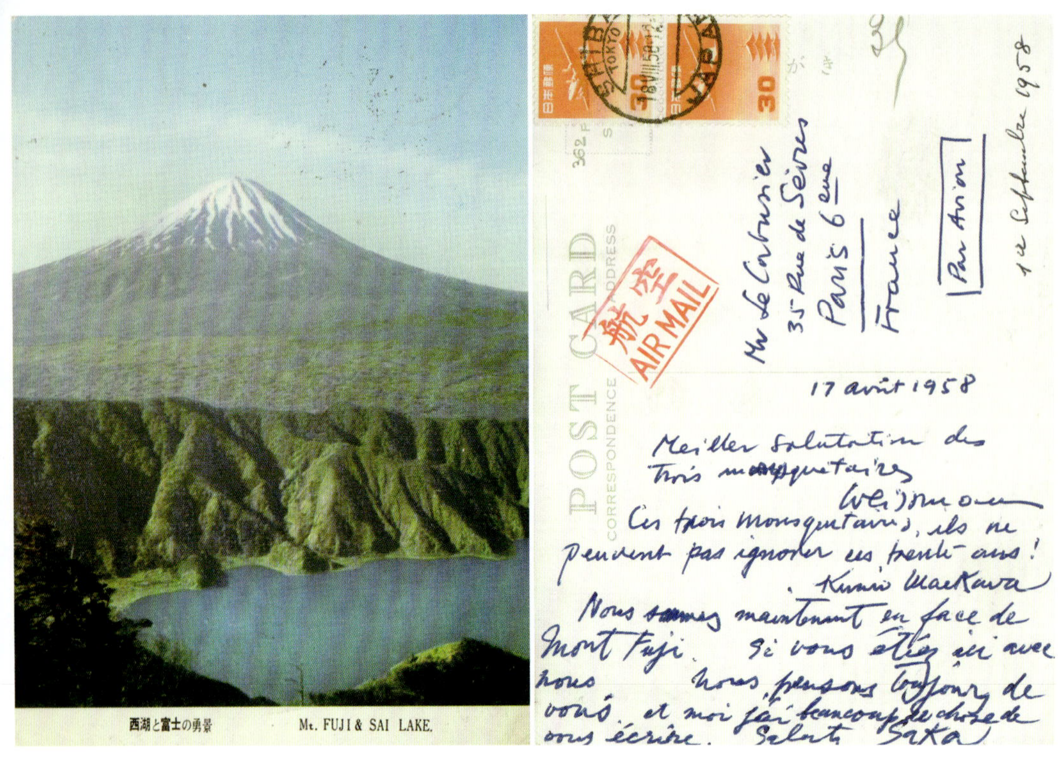

Mr Le Corbusier
35 Rue de Sèvres
Paris 6eme
France

Par Avion

12 Septembre 1958

17 avril 1958

Meilleur salutation des
Trois mousquetaires
Weijou ...

Ces trois Mousquetaires, ils ne
peuvent pas ignorer ces trente ans!
Kunio Maekawa

Nous sommes maintenant en face de
Mont Fuji. Si vous êtes ici avec
nous. Nous pensons toujours de
vous. et moi j'ai beaucoup de chose de
vous écrire. Salut. Saka

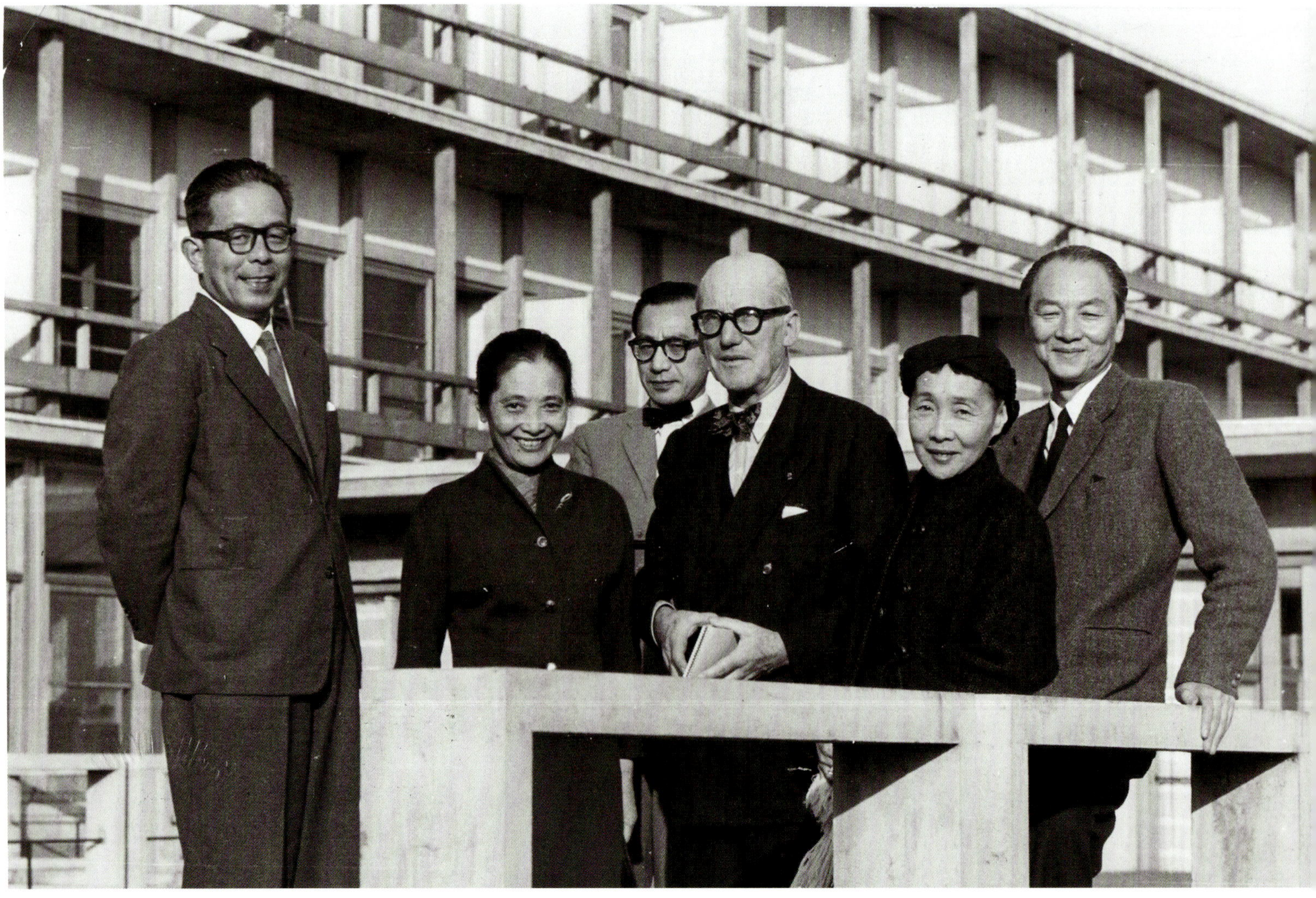

First and only commission in Japan: National Museum of Western Art, Tokyo, 1956–59

The National Museum of Western Art in Tokyo is the third and last of Le Corbusier's museums to be based on his 1939 concept for a Museum of Unlimited Growth. The two others were his museums at Chandigarh and Ahmedabad.

)pposite, top. 'ostcard from the three muske-eers," Ernest Veissmann, Kunio Iaekawa, and unzo Sakakura, to e Corbusier, from It. Fuji, Japan, 7 August 1958. All three were associates in Le Corbusier's office at one time, and Maekawa and Sakakura were the local architects who executed the National Museum of Western Art, Tokyo.

Opposite, bottom. Le Corbusier with Junzo Sakakura behind him, and others, Tokyo, 1955

Right. Le Corbusier and Junzo Sakakura in Katsura, Japan, November 1955

Below. Postcard of the Ryoan-ji garden, Kyoto, Japan, from Le Corbusier's collection

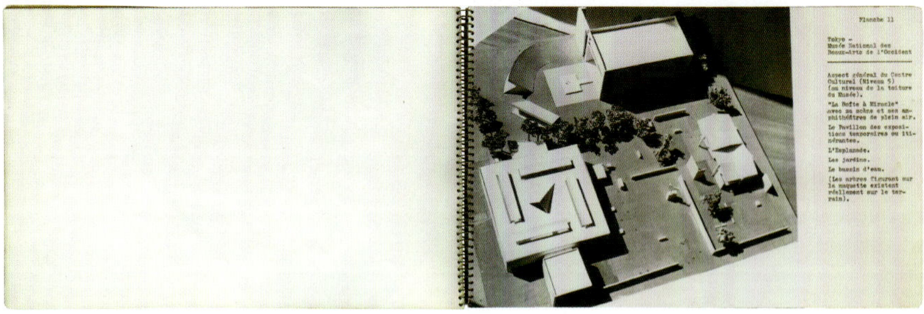
Planche 11
Tokyo –
Musée National des
Beaux-Arts de l'Occident

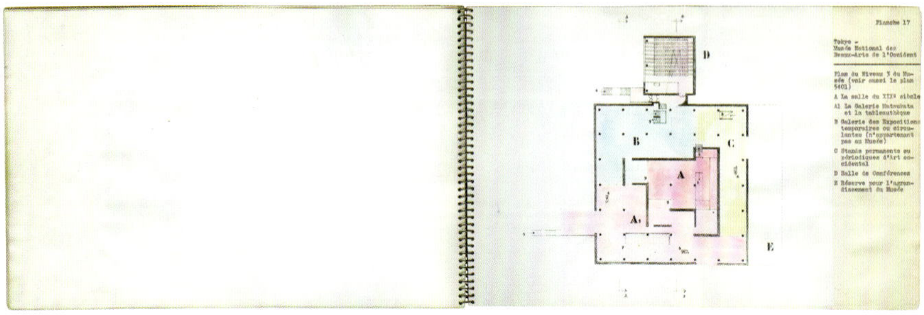
Planche 17
Tokyo –
Musée National des
Beaux-Arts de l'Occident

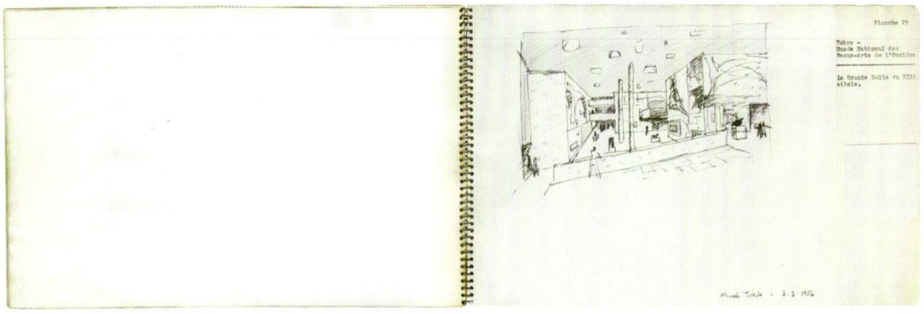
Tokyo –
Musée National des
Beaux-Arts de l'Occident

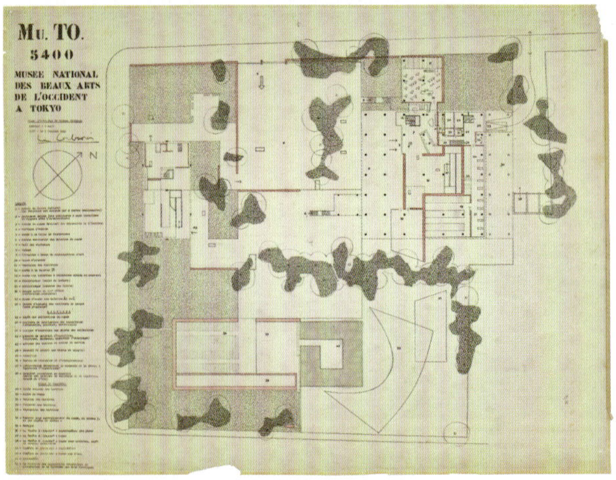
Mu. TO.
5400
MUSEE NATIONAL
DES BEAUX ARTS
DE L'OCCIDENT
A TOKYO

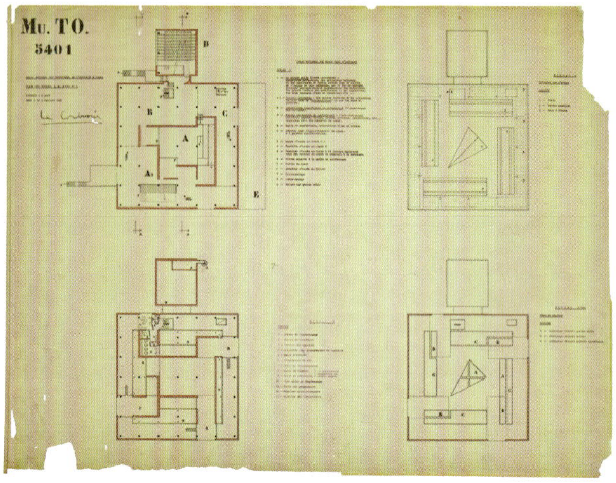
Mu. TO.
5401

Above left. Spreads from a notebook with early plans for the National Museum of Western Art, Tokyo, including (from top to bottom) a model, third-floor plan, and sketch, 7 March 1956, of the Great Hall of the nineteenth century

Top right. Site plan, 9 July 1956

Above right. Plans of the third, fourth, and fifth floors, July 1956

Below. Sections, 9 July 1956

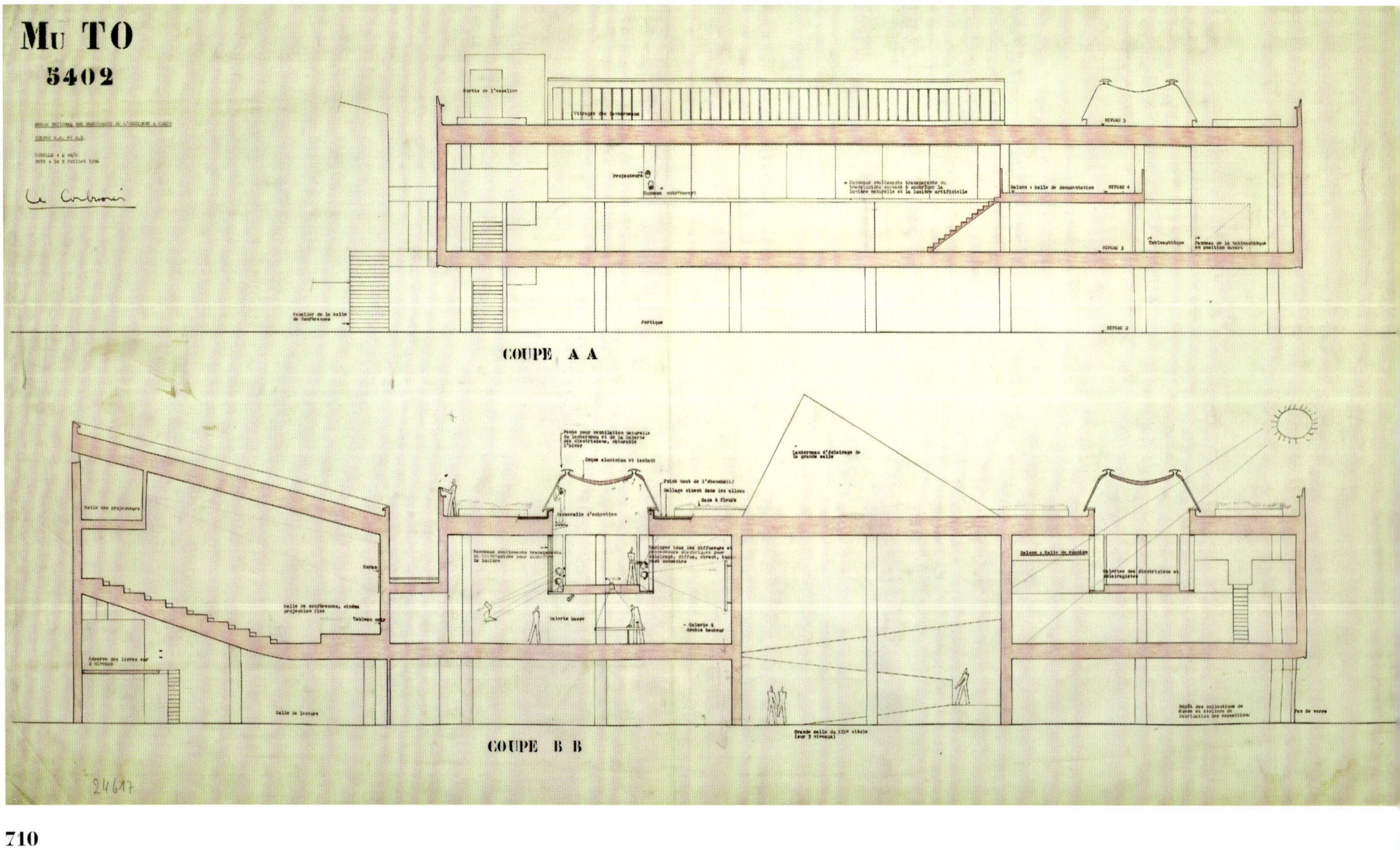
Mu TO
5402
COUPE A A
COUPE B B

Paris, le 7 Septembre 1959

Monsieur Junzo SAKAKURA
6 Akasaka Hinoki-Cho
Minato-Ku
TOKYO

Mon cher Sakakura,

J'ai reçu la revue japonaise Sinkentiku avec de bonnes photographies du Musée.

Je n'ai reçu aucune nouvelle de l'inauguration ni de vous, ni de Maekawa ni de Taka. Je n'ai reçu aucun document photographique, aucun document de presse ! La seule chose qui me concerne est que l'invitation à l'inauguration qui m'était faite par les Affaires Etrangères, et qui m'avait été envoyée également, avait oublié de noter que le bâtiment était fait sur mes plans.

J'ai l'impression que le bâtiment a été très bien exécuté par vous. Je voudrais être renseigné par des documents photographiques car les reproductions des magazines sont insuffisantes; on ne reconnaît pas les matériaux.

Merci d'avance et bien amicalement à vous tous.

LE CORBUSIER

P.S. D'après les quelques documents photographiques que j'ai reçus, il semble que l'exécution du Musée est parfaite et fasse grand honneur à votre capacité professionnelle (à vous trois) et, en plus, à l'intégrité japonaise qui ne transige pas. C'est un des facteurs essentiels de l'âme japonaise que j'avais connu quand j'étais jeune en admirant les travaux d'estampes, de neskés, etc.. Je suis très heureux d'avoir pu réaliser grâce à vous autres ce travail.

Si on m'en laissait le temps, je serais content aussi de faire le mural photographique de la Grande Salle du XIXe Siècle qui devrait être une véritable oeuvre de réhabilitation à l'égard de ce siècle étonnant.

A l'occasion, quelqu'un de vous pourrait-il m'envoyer une traduction de l'article de Kenchiku Bunke qui contient les photos des travaux d'Auguste Perret et de Ronchamp.

L-C

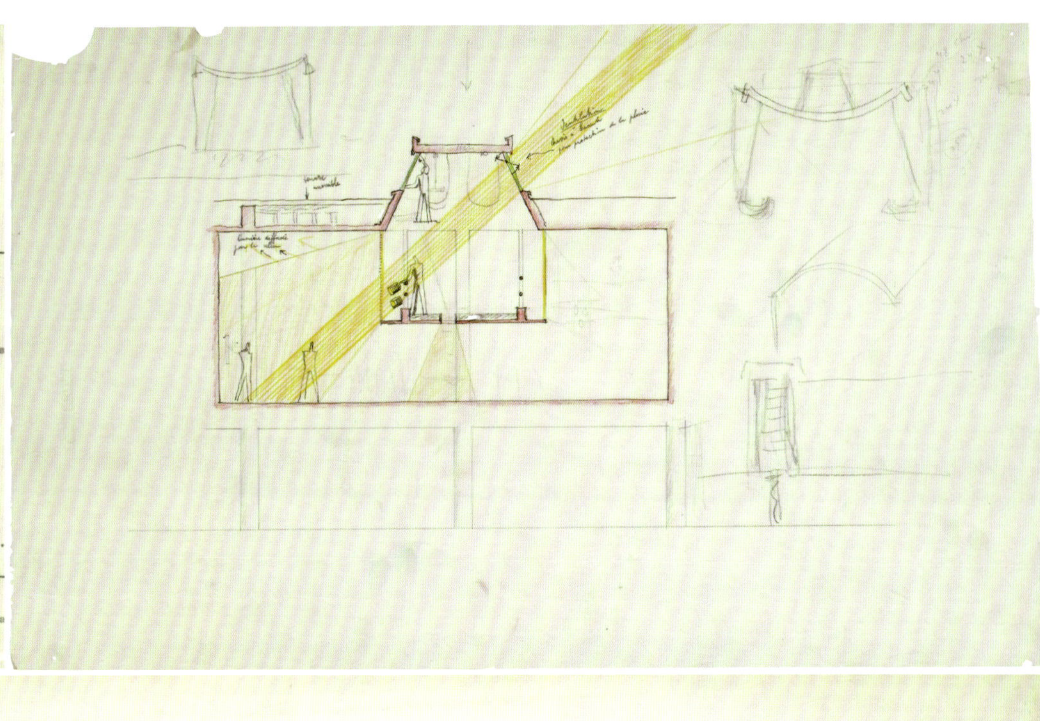

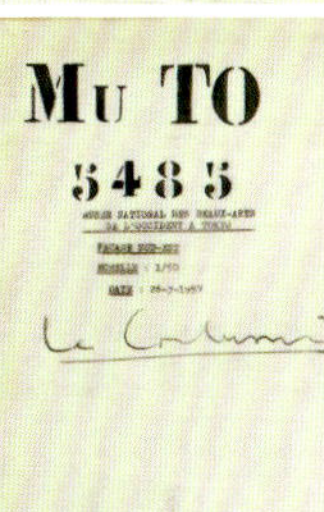

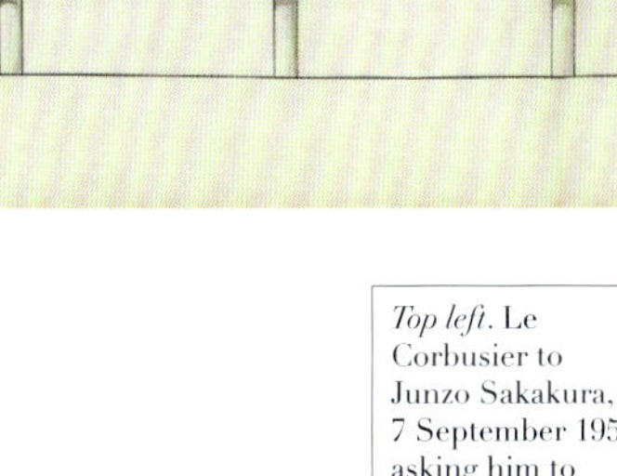

Top left. Le Corbusier to Junzo Sakakura, 7 September 1959, asking him to please send good photographs of the completed museum

Top right. Sketch of the sun's path through a museum gallery

Above. South east elevation, 26 March 1957

Below left. Ground floor, 1962

Below right. Courtyard and main entrance (under *pilotis*)

Top left. Fabric samples from the architect Junzo Sakakura, for a 230-square -meter curtain Le Corbusier was to design for a theater by Sakakura in Tokyo, 1956

Top right. Color study for the theater

Middle. Color samples for the theater tapestry, 21 August 1956, included with letter of 22 August (opposite, middle).

Le Corbusier notes at bottom that he is still waiting for the correct wool samples.

Left. Drawing for tapestry, 18 August 1956, included with letter of 22 August.

Le Corbusier's notes mention that the Modulor helped him establish the composition.

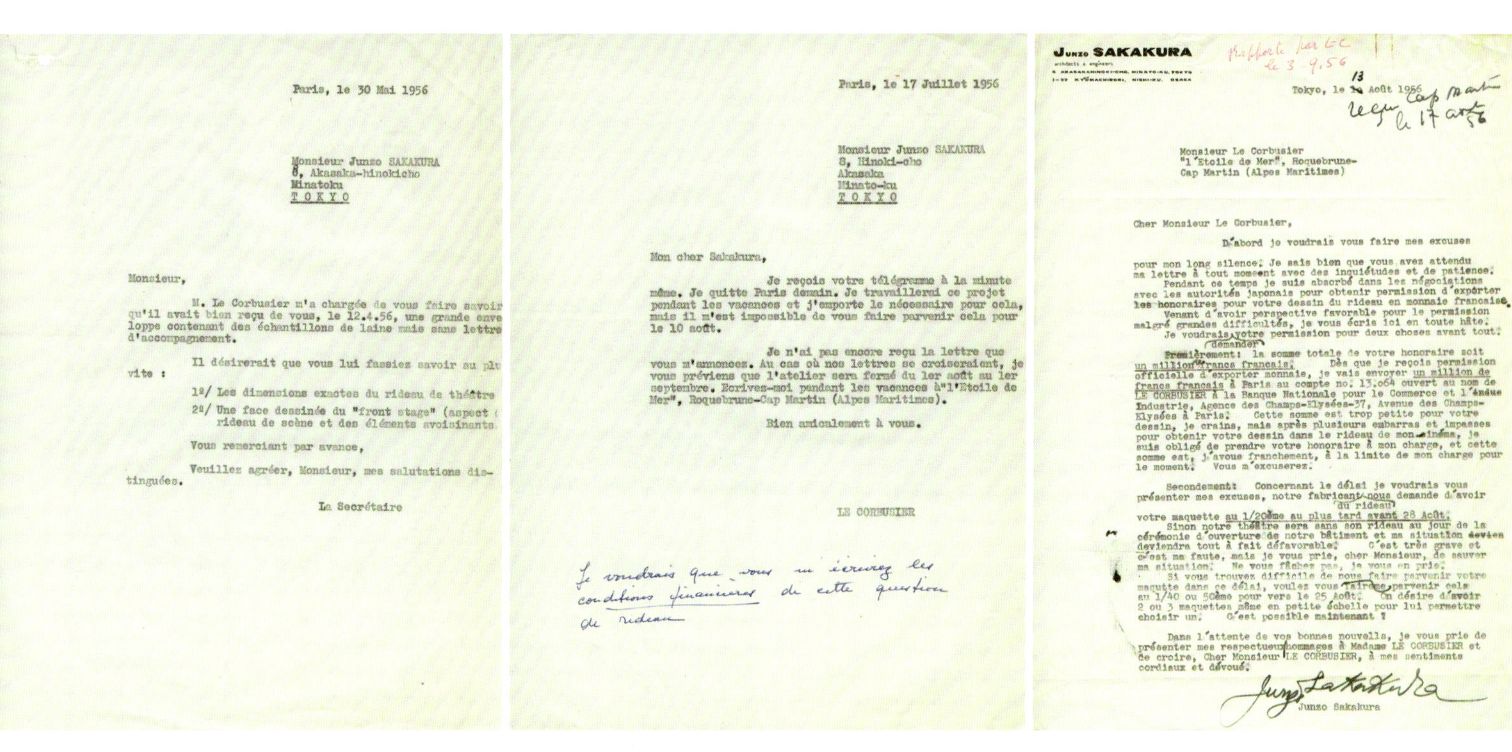

Paris, le 30 Mai 1956

Monsieur Junzo SAKAKURA
8, Akasaka-hinokicho
Minatoku
TOKYO

Monsieur,

M. Le Corbusier m'a chargée de vous faire savoir qu'il avait bien reçu de vous, le 12.4.56, une grande enveloppe contenant des échantillons de laine mais sans lettre d'accompagnement.

Il désirerait que vous lui fassiez savoir au plus vite :

1º/ Les dimensions exactes du rideau de théâtre

2º/ Une face dessinée du "front stage" (aspect du rideau de scène et des éléments avoisinants.

Vous remerciant par avance,

Veuillez agréer, Monsieur, mes salutations distinguées.

La Secrétaire

Paris, le 17 Juillet 1956

Monsieur Junzo SAKAKURA
8, Hinoki-cho
Akasaka
Minato-ku
TOKYO

Mon cher Sakakura,

Je reçois votre télégramme à la minute même. Je quitte Paris demain. Je travaillerai ce projet pendant les vacances et j'emporte le nécessaire pour cela, mais il m'est impossible de vous faire parvenir cela pour le 10 août.

Je n'ai pas encore reçu la lettre que vous m'annoncez. Au cas où nos lettres se croiseraient, je vous préviens que l'atelier sera fermé du 1er août au 1er septembre. Ecrivez-moi pendant les vacances à "l'Etoile de Mer", Roquebrune-Cap Martin (Alpes Maritimes).

Bien amicalement à vous.

LE CORBUSIER

Je voudrais que vous m'écriviez les conditions financières de cette question de rideau

JUNZO SAKAKURA
architects & engineers

Tokyo, le 13 Août 1956

Monsieur Le Corbusier
"l'Etoile de Mer", Roquebrune-
Cap Martin (Alpes Maritimes)

Cher Monsieur Le Corbusier,

D'abord je voudrais vous faire mes excuses pour mon long silence. Je sais bien que vous avez attendu ma lettre à tout moment avec des inquiétudes et de patience.

Pendant ce temps je suis absorbé dans les négociations avec les autorités japonais pour obtenir permission d'exporter les honoraires pour votre dessin du rideau en monnaie française.

Venant d'avoir perspective favorable pour le permission malgré grandes difficultés, je vous écris ici en toute hâte.

Je voudrais demander votre permission pour deux choses avant tout.

Premièrement: la somme totale de votre honoraire soit un million de francs français. Dès que je reçois permission officielle d'exporter monnaie, je vais envoyer un million de francs français à Paris au compte no. 13.064 ouvert au nom de LE CORBUSIER à la Banque Nationale pour le Commerce et l'Industrie, Agence des Champs-Elysées-37, Avenue des Champs-Elysées à Paris. Cette somme est trop petite pour votre dessin, je crains, mais après plusieurs embarras et impasses pour obtenir votre dessin dans le rideau de mon cinéma, je suis obligé de prendre votre honoraire à mon charge, et cette somme est, j'avoue franchement, à la limite de mon charge pour le moment. Vous m'excuserez.

Secondement: Concernant le délai je voudrais vous présenter mes excuses, notre fabricant du rideau nous demande d'avoir votre maquette au 1/20ème au plus tard avant 28 Août.

Sinon notre théâtre sera sans son rideau au jour de la cérémonie d'ouverture de notre bâtiment et ma situation deviendra tout à fait défavorable. C'est très grave et c'est ma faute, mais je vous prie, cher Monsieur, de sauver ma situation. Ne vous fâchez pas, je vous en prie.

Si vous trouvez difficile de nous faire parvenir votre maqutte dans ce délai, voulez vous me faire parvenir cela au 1/40 ou 50ème pour vers le 25 Août. On désire d'avoir 2 ou 3 maquettes même en petite échelle pour lui permettre choisir un. C'est possible maintenant ?

Dans l'attente de vos bonnes nouvells, je vous prie de présenter mes respectueux hommages à Madame LE CORBUSIER et de croire, Cher Monsieur LE CORBUSIER, à mes sentiments cordiaux et dévoué.

Junzo Sakakura

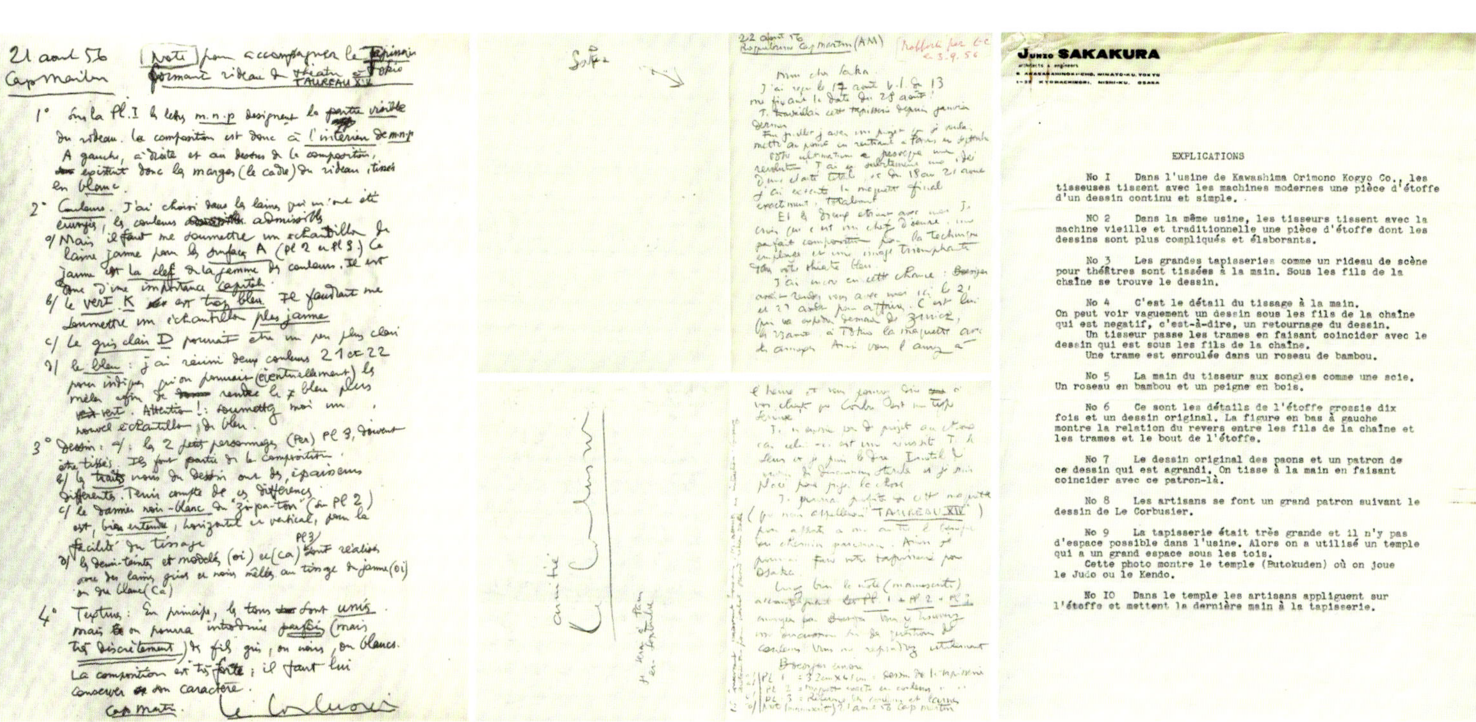

JUNZO SAKAKURA
architects & engineers

EXPLICATIONS

No I Dans l'usine de Kawashima Orimono Kogyo Co., les tisseuses tissent avec les machines modernes une pièce d'étoffe d'un dessin continu et simple.

NO 2 Dans la même usine, les tisseurs tissent avec la machine vieille et traditionnelle une pièce d'étoffe dont les dessins sont plus compliqués et élaborants.

No 3 Les grandes tapisseries comme un rideau de scène pour théâtres sont tissées à la main. Sous les fils de la chaîne se trouve le dessin.

No 4 C'est le détail du tissage à la main. On peut voir vaguement un dessin sous les fils de la chaîne qui est negatif, c'est-à-dire, un retournage du dessin.
Un tisseur passe les trames en faisant coincider avec le dessin qui est sous les fils de la chaîne.
Une trame est enroulée dans un roseau de bambou.

No 5 La main du tisseur aux songles comme une scie. Un roseau en bambou et un peigne en bois.

No 6 Ce sont les détails de l'étoffe grossie dix fois et un dessin original. La figure en bas à gauche montre la relation du revers entre les fils de la chaîne et les trames et le bout de l'étoffe.

No 7 Le dessin original des paons et un patron de ce dessin qui est agrandi. On tisse à la main en faisant coincider avec ce patron-là.

No 8 Les artisans se font un grand patron suivant le dessin de Le Corbusier.

No 9 La tapisserie était très grande et il n'y pas d'espace possible dans l'usine. Alors on a utilisé un temple qui a un grand espace sous les toits.
Cette photo montre le temple (Butokuden) où on joue le Judo ou le Kendo.

No IO Dans le temple les artisans appliguent sur l'étoffe et mettent la dernière main à la tapisserie.

Top left. Le Corbusier's secretary to Junzo Sakakura, 30 May 1956, asking him to send exact measurements of the theater curtain and a drawing of the stage

Top middle. Le Corbusier to Junzo Sakakura, 17 July 1956, saying he can be reached at Roquebrune-Cap-Martin during the month of August

Top right. Junzo Sakakura to Le Corbusier, 13 August 1956, explaining that he will pay him one million French francs for his curtain design and urging him to finish by the 28 August deadline

Above left. Note from Le Corbusier regarding color palette for curtain, 21 August 1956, accompanying letter of 22 August

Above middle. Le Corbusier to Junzo Sakakura, 22 August 1956, explaining that he has finished the design on time. "I think it's a masterpiece, a perfect composition for the medium and a triumphal image for your blue theater."

Above right. An explanation of the hand-weaving process used to make the curtain. Number 9 mentions that the curtain was too big to make the pattern in the factory, so the weavers worked in a large temple instead.

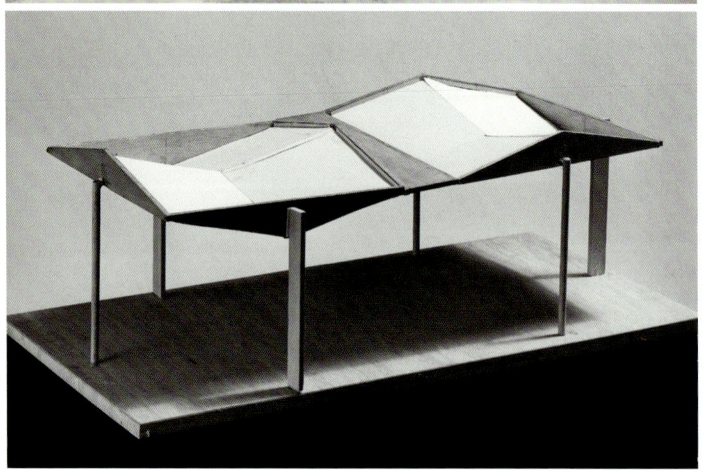

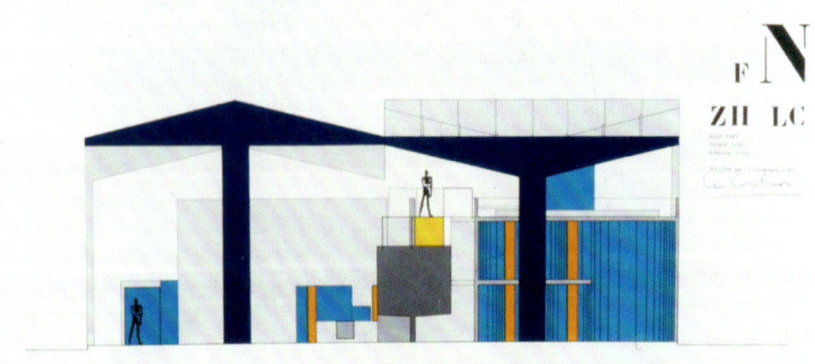

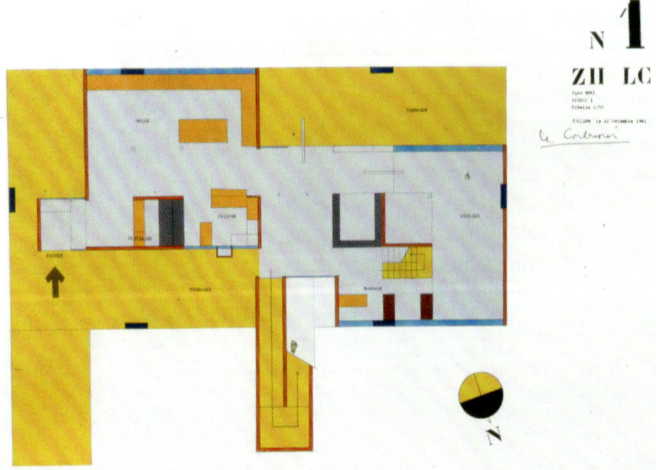

An exhibition pavilion for an art collector: Heidi Weber Pavilion, Zurich, 1962–68

Swiss decorator and art collector Heidi Weber commissioned Le Corbusier to design a gallery in Zurich to house her collection of paintings and sculpture by the architect. For the pavilion, completed three years after his death, Le Corbusier again turned back to an idea from his past. This time it was a series of spaces collected beneath a steel-truss roof, which he had explored in the Pavillon des Temps Nouveaux in 1937.

Top left. Sketches of the tent roof, Heidi Weber Pavilion (now Centre Le Corbusier), Zurich, 1962–68

Top right and middle right. Two views of an elevation model; east elevation facing street (top), west elevation (bottom)

Above. Model showing the tent-roof structure

Middle left. East facade, 12 December 1961

Left. Ground-floor plan, 12 December 1961

Opposite, top. West facade

Opposite, bottom left. Sculpture of the Modulor man outside the pavilion, c. 1964

Opposite, bottom right. The enameled-steel-panel and glass facade with pivoting door

Left. Basement-level exhibition hall, Heidi Weber Pavilion, Zurich

Below. Ground floor, with pivoting enameled-panel door to the left and reception desk to the right

Above. Le Corbusier, Heidi Weber, and Willy Boesiger, editor of the *Oeuvre complète*, at Zurich-Kloten airport, 1960; Le Corbusier had just flown in from Chandigarh

Right. From left to right: Willy Boesiger, Adolf Wasserfallen (architect), Le Corbusier, Pierre Zbinden (inspector of public parks), and Heidi Weber, reviewing plans for the Heidi Weber Pavilion, 1960

First and only commission in the U.S.: Carpenter Center for the Visual Arts, Harvard University, Cambridge, Massachusetts, 1958–63

When José Luis Sert, Le Corbusier's former collaborator and one-time president of CIAM, was appointed dean of the Graduate School of Design at Harvard University, he called on his old friend to design the school's new Carpenter Center for the Visual Arts. The building represents a mature synthesis of elements from Le Corbusier's early and late works, including a concrete structural system descended from the Dom-ino concept, a dramatic *promenade architecturale* defined by a ramp that curves through one side of the building and extends out the opposite side, and angled *brises-soleil* (sunshades) recalling those in his projects in India.

Above. Le Corbusier, 1960s

HARVARD UNIVERSITY
CAMBRIDGE 38
MASSACHUSETTS

GRADUATE SCHOOL OF DESIGN
OFFICE OF THE DEAN

20 Octobre 1958

16 Octobre 58

Michel

Mon cher Corbu:

L'université de Harvard doit bâtir un Centre des arts plastiques (Visual Art Center.) Le president de l'université et le doyen de Harvard College voudrait que tu sois l'architecte de ce bâtiment. Est ce que tu voudrais t'en charger? Il est temps que l'Amerique ai une oeuvre de Le Corbusier et le sujet est, je crois, interessant. Il s'agit des espaces d'exposition et des ateliers pour faire des experiments et enseigner des methodes de travail aux jeunes.

Ci-joint quelques notes sur le Visual Arts Center. Le site doit être choisi dans quelques jours. La surface bâtie sera de 50.000 pieds carrées plus ou moins. Le cout d'un million de dollars.

HARVARD UNIVERSITY
CAMBRIDGE 38
MASSACHUSETTS

GRADUATE SCHOOL OF DESIGN
OFFICE OF THE DEAN

2

Le plan peut être assez libre, et je crois que tu pourrais faire quelque chose vraiment bien. Tes amis ici, seraient bien contents d'avoir une oeuvre de Corbu a Harvard.

Veux-tu me dire si cela t'interesse? Si c'est oui, j'espere te voir bientôt a Cambridge. Tu recevras dans ce cas une communication officielle.

Amitiés

Paris, le 27 Octobre 1958

Mr Jose Luis SERT
Office of the Dean
Graduate School of Design
Harvard University
CAMBRIDGE 38, Mass.

Mon cher Sert,

J'ai reçu le 20 octobre ta lettre du 16 octobre 1958. Je suis actuellement débordé mais la proposition qu'elle contient (Visual Art Center) m'intéresse. Je t'écris aujourd'hui pour te le dire et surtout pour te signaler qu'on ne devrait pas acheter définitivement le terrain sans m'avoir soumis le plan de cadastre car certaines dimensions peuvent être hostiles au projet.

Une telle chose pourrait se faire si l'on admettait, par exemple, que Jacques Michel soit chargé d'une participation dans l'exécution (avec les Américains) tandis que je ne ferai moi-même que les plans "à la française". Ainsi ai-je agi pour le "Musée National des Beaux Arts de l'Occident" à Tokio où les transcriptions en méthodes, matériaux et moyens de mesure et écritures sur les plans ont été faites par Mayekawa, Sakakura et Taka.

Autre question : Quels sont les honoraires que je suis en droit de demander ? Je l'ignore complètement, mon rôle restant de fournir les plans nécessaires et suffisants pour l'exécution du bâtiment par les Américains. Les budgets ne sont pas très gros dans votre affaire.

Bien amicalement à toi et mes amitiés à Muncha.

LE CORBUSIER

MEMORANDUM

For the complete architectural services, the Massachusetts Chapter of the American Institute of Architects schedule of fees provides a fee of 9% of the total construction cost of a building of this type. The construction cost, in turn, is determined by our contract with a general contractor. In this case, the construction cost of the building exclusive of professional fees must be rigidly based on the amount of the gift made for this purpose and cannot exceed $1,200,000. Thus the total architectural fees for the project according to established tariffs would not exceed $108,000. The usual arrangement for compensating an architect for making of preliminary plans is to pay 25% of the total architectural fees for this purpose. In this case, however, we feel that your contributions should not be rigidly measured by the established schedule of fees. Consequently, we suggest that your honorarium for the work that you will do in preparing the preliminary plans for this building be set at 30% of the fee, which will amount to $32,400. We will undertake to adjust the compensation of your collaborating architects accordingly.

The University will be happy to reimburse you for your traveling expenses for two trips to this country including hotel bills while in Cambridge on this business as well as any extra expense items normally provided for in the American Institute of Architects agreement form. In the event that additional trips become necessary, arrangements can be mutually agreed upon for this purpose.

The attached American Institute of Architects agreement sets forth the details of the proposed arrangement and we trust that it will be found satisfactory.

April 22, 1959

Top. José Luis Sert, dean of the Harvard University Graduate School of Design, to Le Corbusier, 16 October 1958, asking if he would be interested in designing a new building for the "Visual Arts Center" at Harvard University.

Above left. Le Corbusier to José Luis Sert, 27 October 1958, explaining that he is interested in the Harvard project, especially if there is a local architect to execute his "French-style' plans"

Above middle. Memorandum from Harvard University to Le Corbusier, 22 April 1959, discussing a fee schedule, with Le Corbusier's notations

Right. "Corbu at Harvard," *Time* magazine, 30 November 1959

Bottom left. Edward Reynolds, administrative vice president of Harvard University, to Le Corbusier, 6 October 1959, informing him that the university will increase his fee

Bottom right. Le Corbusier to Edward Reynolds, 19 October 1959, stipulating additions to his contract

Corbu at Harvard

Now that Frank Lloyd Wright is gone, chief rivals for the title of world dean of international architects are German-born, Chicago-based Ludwig Mies van der Rohe, 73, whose skin-and-bones style (Manhattan's Seagram building) has spread the vogue for glass-curtain walls across the U.S., and France's prickly, Swiss-born Le Corbusier, 72, whose dramatic structures (Ronchamp Chapel) qualify as large-scale sculptures in concrete. Last week "Corbu," who has long been rankled by the fact that U.S. clients have fought shy of his turbulent genius, landed his first U.S. commission—a $1,500,000 Visual Arts Center for Harvard University.

Surrounding himself with all the secrecy of a high diplomatic emissary, Corbu flew in from Paris in person to make a four-day inspection of the site (adjacent to the Fogg Art Museum), was given convincing proof that his absence had long been noted. Architecture students staged an impromptu reception, complete with 16-ft. effigies of Corbu's stylized Modulor figure, cheered him to the rafters. Exclaimed the delighted Corbu: "What spirit! *Une atmosphere morale!*"

Corbu was cozy about his plans for the center, borrowed a line from Wright: "It must grow from the inside out. The concept must be biological, not static. A beautiful seashell is not a façade; it is a shell. This is the essence of architecture." This left Harvard wondering whether it was getting a structure as beautiful as a conch or as homely as a clam. But as it would be his only showpiece in the U.S., Corbu could be counted on to make it impressive.

TIME, NOVEMBER 30, 1959

HARVARD UNIVERSITY
CAMBRIDGE 38, MASSACHUSETTS

ADMINISTRATIVE VICE PRESIDENT
MASSACHUSETTS HALL

10 Octobre 1959

October 6, 1959

Le Corbusier
35 Rue de Sevres
Paris VIe, France

Dear Mr. Le Corbusier:

After discussing with Dean Jose Luis Sert his talks with you in Paris this summer we would like to make this new proposal concerning the Visual Arts Building at Harvard University.

The University is willing to increase the total fee for the architectural services on this project from 9% mentioned in our previous letter to 10% on the total cost of the project, which must not exceed one million two hundred thousand dollars. The total fee may then rise to one hundred twenty thousand dollars. Of this amount we offer you fifty thousand dollars for your work of designing the building and submitting preliminary studies. Dean Sert has agreed that his firm, Sert, Jackson and Gourley, will undertake the production of working drawings and specifications and the supervision of construction, as well as securing necessary engineering consultancy. The compensation for this work will come from the balance of the fee after payment of your honorarium. It is our understanding of this arrangement that upon completion of your design and preliminary studies, your share of the work will be finished and the final payment of your fee will be due as set forth in the next paragraph.

We suggest that the fifty thousand dollar fee paid to you be divided as follows: twenty thousand as a retainer upon execution of the agreement, and the balance upon completion and submittal of your preliminary studies. This division of the preliminary fee is a customary one in the architectural practice of this country. The University anticipates that two trips to the United States will be necessary and will reimburse you your transportation (boat or air ticket) and hotel bills while in Cambridge on this business. If additional trips become necessary they can be arranged by mutual agreement.

-2-

By preliminary studies we understand full plans, sections and elevations at a scale not smaller than one-eighth inch to one foot (1:100 in metric scale) and such larger scale details as you feel are needed to guide the further development of the designs.

We trust that this proposal will be satisfactory to you and that work on this project can soon begin. If so please answer at your earliest convenience, and we will then send you a draft contract (on the same form as previously sent to you) but drawn for the new terms.

We would expect that your initial visit to inspect the site and discuss the program for the building would be made this autumn, preferably not later than November 15th.

Yours sincerely,
Edward Reynolds
Administrative Vice President

Mr Edward REYNOLDS
Administrative Vice President
Massachusetts Hall
Harvard University
CAMBRIDGE 38, Mass.

Monsieur,

Je vous accuse réception de votre lettre du 6 octobre 1959.

Je suis d'accord avec ses termes, en général, mais je désire que soit inscrit, en annexe au contrat, les points dont je vous donne le texte ci-dessous (dans votre projet de contrat imprimé "The Standard Form of Agreement between Owner and Architect" vous avez barré page 1 et page 2 certains paragraphes et en fin de ce contrat vous avez ajouté certaines conditions particulières) :

1. The Architect's Services :
It is understood that the Architect will be responsible only for the completion of preliminary studies. He will work together with the Collaborating Architect, Mr Jose Luis Sert and his partners, who will be retained directly by the Owner and who will be responsible for rendering all services except completion of the preliminary studies.

2. Reimbursement :
Paragraphe en entier

3. Payments :
a) Les honoraires sont fixés à la somme nette et forfaitaire de CINQUANTE MILLE DOLLARS.

b) Ces honoraires sont payables à Paris au compte n° 13.064 ouvert au nom de l'Architecte à la Banque Nationale pour le Commerce et l'Industrie, Agence des Champs Elysées, 37 Avenue des Champs Elysées, Paris, 8°.

c) Ces Honoraires ne subiront aucune retenue ni diminution découlant de l'application des règlements (taxes, impôts, etc..) en vigueur aux Etats Unis étant donné que l'Architecte paie ses impôts en France.

d) Le premier versement de VINGT MILLE DOLLARS aura lieu à la signature du contrat et le solde de TRENTE MILLE DOLLARS sera versé à un compte bloqué au nom de l'Architecte dans une banque à Boston ou à Paris, au choix du Client. Cette somme sera débloquée et versée à Paris, au nom de l'Architecte, le jour de la réception à Boston de ses dessins et plans préliminaires.

Il va de soi que la totalité des honoraires étant payée, l'Architecte se tiendra à la disposition du Client pour les discussions des plans avec Mr Sert répondant à des modifi-
...

- 2 -

cations ou des rectifications nécessaires à la bonne réalisation de l'oeuvre.

....

La rédaction des paragraphes contractuels ci-dessus découlent des expériences vécues à l'occasion de travaux faits à l'étranger. Je vous serais obligé de bien vouloir les accepter.

Vous voudrez bien établir le contrat ~~immédiatement~~ et dès que j'aurai ce contrat signé de vous, je vous retournerai l'exemplaire vous concernant et je réserverai ma place d'avion pour le voyage à Boston au cours du mois de novembre.

Veuillez agréer, Monsieur, l'expression de mes sentiments les meilleurs.

L-C

Right. Sketch, site plan, 29 June 1962, Carpenter Center for the Visual Arts, Harvard University, Cambridge, Massachusetts, 1958–63

Below. Technical drawings, June 1961, for (top to bottom): Section, east elevation, and east facade

Opposite, top. Model, May–June 1960; the Carpenter Center is between the Fogg Art Museum (left) and Harvard Faculty Club

Opposite, bottom. Plan, level 5, which includes the director's studio, 25 April 1961

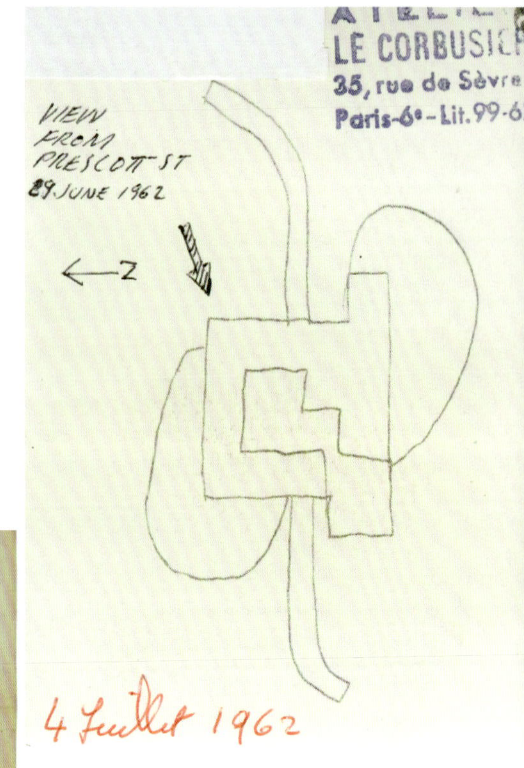

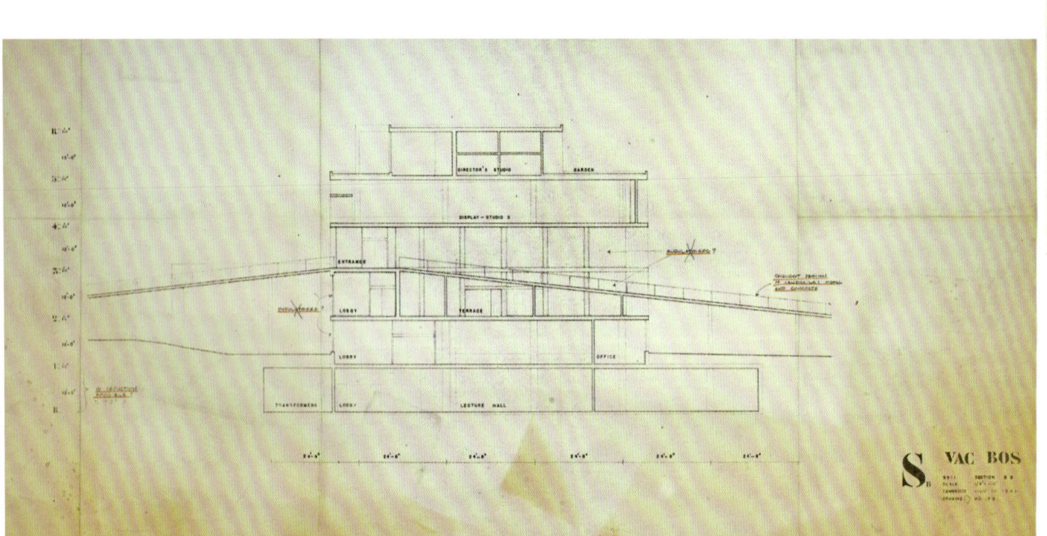

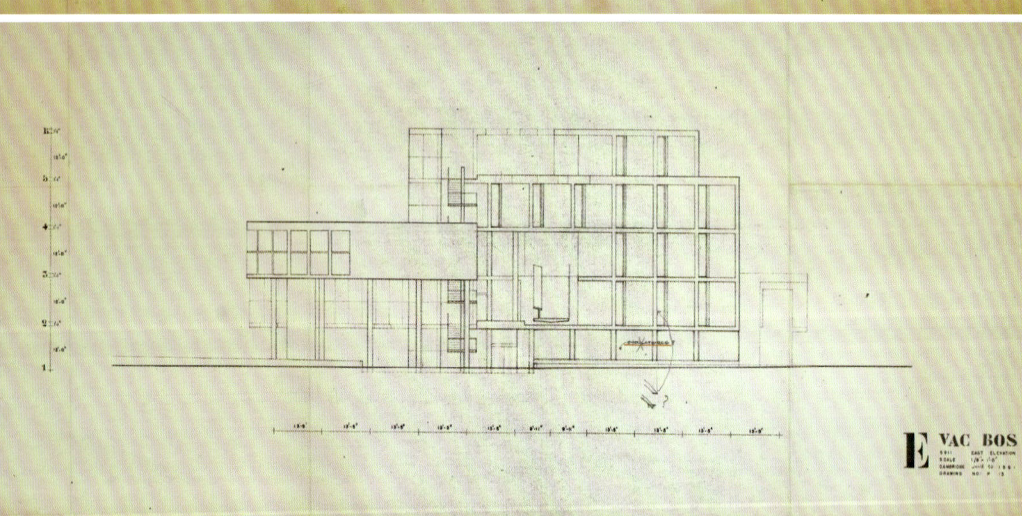

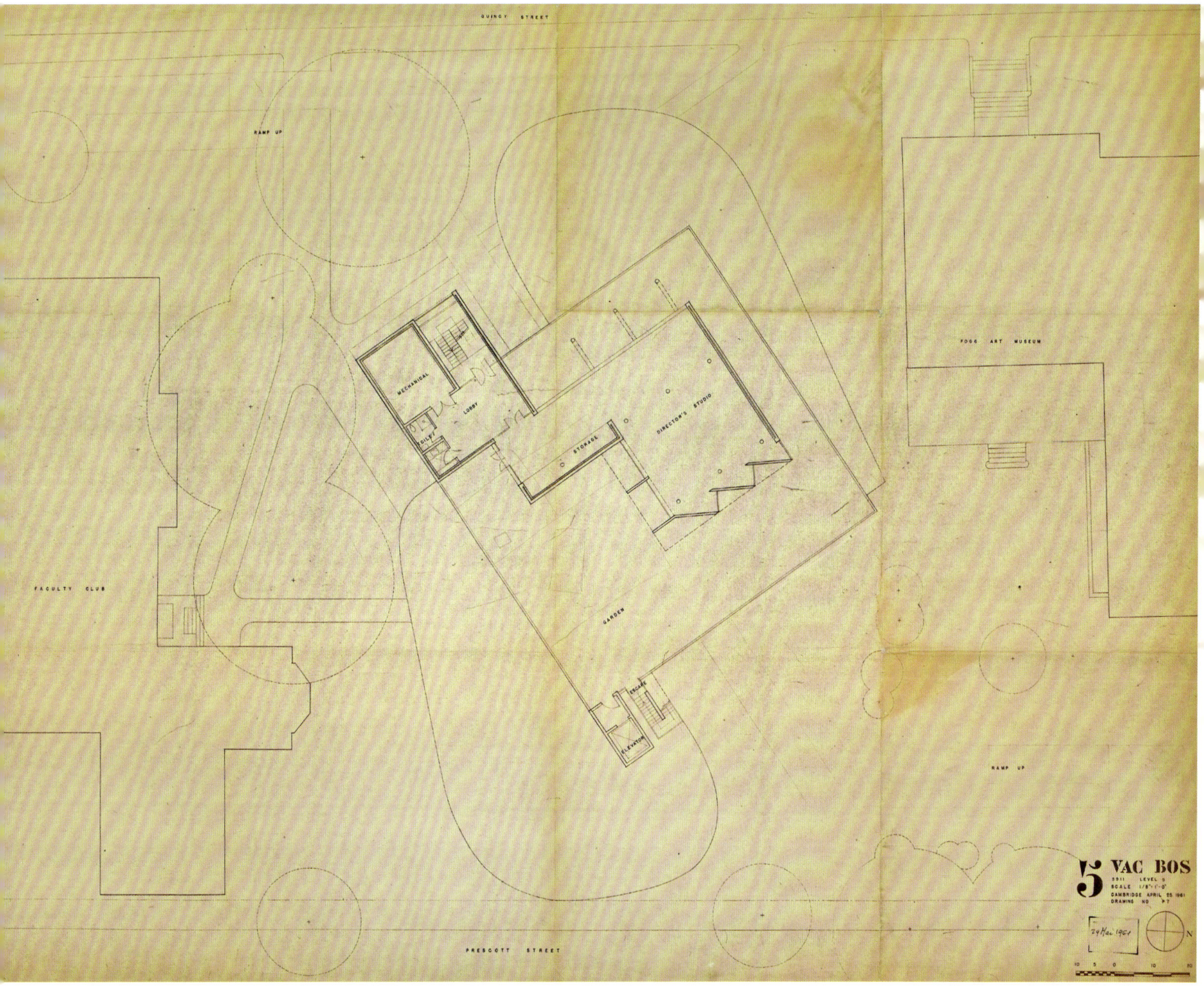

QUINCY STREET

RAMP UP

FACULTY CLUB

MECHANICAL

LOBBY

STORAGE

DIRECTOR'S STUDIO

FOGG ART MUSEUM

GARDEN

ELEVATOR

RAMP UP

PRESCOTT STREET

5 VAC BOS

5911 LEVEL 5

SCALE 1/8"=1'-0"

CAMBRIDGE APRIL 25 1961

DRAWING NO P7

24 Mai 1961

N

10 5 0 10 20

Above. Construction on the Carpenter Center for the Visual Arts, Harvard University, including concrete *brise-soleil* (sunshade)

Opposite, top. Quincy Street (west) facade, c. 1962

Opposite, bottom. Ramp leading to an entrance on level three

"An architecture must be walked *through* and *traversed*... Architecture may be judged as dead or living by the degree to which the rule of *movement* has been disregarded or brilliantly exploited." ***—Talks with Students from the Schools of Architecture, 1945***

"A beautiful seashell is not a façade; it is a shell. This is the essence of architecture."

—"Corbu at Harvard," *Time*, 30 November 1959

Opposite, top. East facade, Carpenter Center for the Visual Arts, Harvard University, March 1964

Opposite, bottom. Northwest view, first-floor lecture hall, February 1963

Above. West facade, February 1963

Right. Southwest view, February 1963

It's a matter of **RECORD**

Of special interest to you:

from the ~~current~~ MARCH issue of

ARCHITECTURAL RECORD

Emerson Goble

Emerson Goble
Editor

ARCHITECTURAL RECORD

Carpenter Center from Quincy Street: each floor has indoor, outdoor terraces. Concrete baffles shield window wall from sun

FIRST U. S. BUILDING BY CORBU COMPLETED

Carpenter Center from Prescott Street: ramp passes between glass-walled workshops and terraces at third floor level. Columns 22 feet high support overhanging third floor lobe

Open studio for two-dimensional drawing shows curving glass wall broken by concrete sun breakers. Columns bear weight of floor above. At upper right is glass-domed skylight

The first North American building by Le Corbusier—the Carpenter Center for the Visual Arts at Harvard University—has opened for student use. The center, given through the Harvard College Program by Alfred St. Vrain Carpenter and the late Mrs. Carpenter of Medford, Ore., will be dedicated in May.

Set between the Fogg Art Museum and the Harvard Faculty Club, the concrete and glass center has a richly complex exterior. The five floors are all different in configuration: rectangles and squares broken by great asymmetrical curves. Each floor has indoor and outdoor terraces, while a pedestrian ramp sweeps through the building at the third floor. Studio and workshop areas are shielded from direct rays of the sun by concrete sun breakers. Supporting the building are concrete columns which vary in diameter with the load each supports.

The building is organized by floors: basement—auditorium, light and communication studios, dark rooms; first floor—administrative areas and common room; second and third floors—two and three dimensional design workshops; fourth floor—seminar rooms; fifth floor—artists' studio.

The architectural firm of Sert, Jackson & Gourley carried out Le Corbusier's design. General contractor was George A. Fuller Construction Company.

10 ARCHITECTURAL RECORD *March 1963*

29 May 63 Wed THE NEW YORK TIMES WESTERN EDI

NEW BUILDING AT CAMBRIDGE: View of Carpenter Center for the Visual Arts, dedicated Monday at Harvard. It was designed by Le Corbusier, the French architect.

HARVARD CENTER ROUSES CRITICISM

Le Corbusier's Structure Clashes With Colonial

By ADA LOUISE HUXTABLE
Special to The New York Times.

CAMBRIDGE, Mass., May 28—This New England stronghold of tradition was the setting yesterday for the dedication of one of the country's most unconventional new buildings.

Harvard University's Carpenter Center for the Visual Arts, the latest work of the architect Le Corbusier, was officially accepted yesterday afternoon by an academic community that, unofficially, either does not accept it at all or is sharply divided on its merits.

The new Harvard art center is the only structure in the United States by the 76-year-old Swiss-born French leader of the modern movement, whose real name is Charles Edouard Jeanneret. He directed every detail of the building's design and construction from Paris but has never seen it.

Its assured, nonconformist rejection of the university's carefully nurtured Colonial charm, both real and synthetic, is the source of most of the criticism. The building could not have been put down in a less sympathetic setting if it had been dropped from the moon.

Obviously Inadequate Site

Situated in Harvard's neo-Georgian heart on Quincy and Prescott Streets, its concrete-and-glass hulk rudely elbows the ivy-draped brick of the faculty club and the Fogg Museum on either side. Architecturally speaking, it virtually thumbs its nose at both from its obviously inadequate site.

To proper Bostonians, this is bad manners, esthetically and otherwise. It has been said that Le Corbusier's buildings violate the street, and this one violates the street and scandalizes the neighborhood. At the same time, the new building manages to make everything around it look stolid and stale.

It does this not because it is brash, or novel, but because it is so remarkably rich in bold ideas. The building itself is an idea—the kind of creative idea that universities traditionally are supposed to deal in.

The architect's commission was for an "inspirational building" that would give impetus and direction to a new, experimental program in visual arts. The obective is "the perception of quality," and the first eye opener is this extraordinary structure.

Inviting Curving Range

What the visitor, approaching from Quincy Street, sees is a curving ramp that invites him into the heart of the five-story building and carried him through it and out again on the Prescott Street side. To the right is a concrete-and-glass-block stiarwell, to the left, the curved procection of a studio workshop, behind it, a series of sunbreaks fronting the upper floors like narrow, angled balconies.

Where the open ramp rises and enters at the third floor, the whole building is suddenly revealed through glass walls that turn studios, workshops and exhibition space into showcases—both of the visual arts and of the architecture itself. The effect is electrifying, for in one sweeping view it becomes apparent that this is indeed a new world.

The many typical Corbusean devices — sunbreaks, balconies, roof gardens, bubble domes, curved walls, angled panels — contribute substantially to the design studies and progress and provide a superb setting for them. The walk "through" Carpenter Center has become Cambridge's favorite Sunday stroll.

Difficult to Grasp

For the stroller, much of the building's quality is, unfortunately, difficult to grasp. From the street, he sees only strong shapes and raw concrete that ivy will never hide. What he cannot sense immediately is the ingenious interplay of indoor and outdoor areas in studios and terraces.

He is not aware of the remarkable manipulation of plan and space that creates the striking curved and angled elements so skillfully dramatized, inside and out.

Nor does he see the pain staking craftsmanship in the deceptively crude, but expert, use of concrete. (Shipbuilders from Nova Scotia executed some of the curved wooden forms that shape the structure.)

Le Corbusier's buildings are a curious and characteristic blend of the deliberately rugged and the artfully primitive, from a mind of unusual subtlety and sophistication. This one is frankly a workshop; there are no slick finishes or rich materials to seduce the viewer; it shares, with the French, the tradition of austerity.

But with all of its virtues, and with due credit to Harvard, the Cambridge architectural firm of Sert, Jackson & Gourley, which executed Le Corbusier's design with dedicated fidelity, and Alfred St. Vain Carpenter, who gave the $1,500,000 for its construction, this is not the architect's best work.

Its weakness is in its aggressive complexity, its over-busy profusion of elements that borders dangerously on the chaotic. Barely contained by the uneasy site, it produces a kind of visual nervous indigestion.

Some choices of interior finish can only be called unfortunate. At present, the ground-floor terrace looks more like a prisoner's exercise yard than an esthetic retreat, an impression reinforced by the overuse of cheerless gray gravel in too many areas.

Proper landscaping, particularly on roof terraces, is still urgently needed to complete the building's concept.

Opposite. Interiors, Carpenter Center for the Visual Arts, Harvard University. Clockwise from top: Third-level curved studio, with skylight, *pilotis*, and *brise-soleil* (sunshade); studio, ground-floor entrance; stairwell

Top, left and right. Emerson Goble, editor, *Architectural Record*, to Le Corbusier, 17 May 1963, with article about the Center for the Visual Arts from the magazine's March issue

Left. "Harvard Center Rouses Criticism," *New York Times*, 28 May 1963. Reviewing the Carpenter Center after its inauguration the previous day, critic Ada Louise Huxtable writes that it is not the architect's best but is "remarkably rich in bold ideas."

A contemporary project at the heart of an ancient city: Venice Hospital (unbuilt), 1963–66

Among the major projects that remained unbuilt after Le Corbusier's death was the Venice Hospital. His concept was a bold agglomeration of low-rise boxes, whose scale was respectful of the surrounding urban context but whose stark facade throws that context into striking relief. The only natural illumination is through a system of skylights.

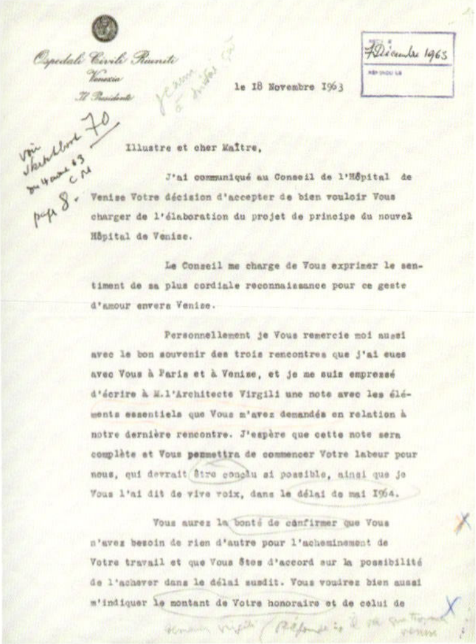

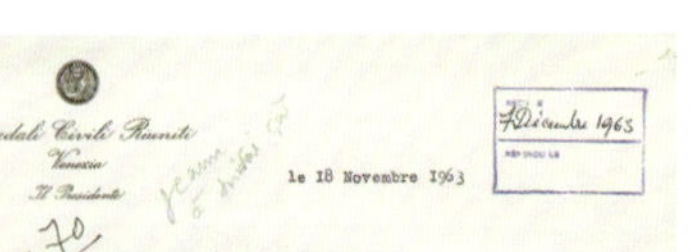

Ospedali Civili Riuniti
Venezia
Il Presidente

le 18 Novembre 1963

Illustre et cher Maître,

J'ai communiqué au Conseil de l'Hôpital de Venise Votre décision d'accepter de bien vouloir Vous charger de l'élaboration du projet de principe du nouvel Hôpital de Venise.

Le Conseil me charge de Vous exprimer le sentiment de sa plus cordiale reconnaissance pour ce geste d'amour envers Venise.

Personnellement je Vous remercie moi aussi avec le bon souvenir des trois rencontres que j'ai eues avec Vous à Paris et à Venise, et je me suis empressé d'écrire à M. l'Architecte Virgili une note avec les éléments essentiels que Vous m'avez demandés en relation à notre dernière rencontre. J'espère que cette note sera complète et Vous permettra de commencer Votre labeur pour nous, qui devrait être conçu si possible, ainsi que je Vous l'ai dit de vive voix, dans le délai de mai 1964.

Vous aurez la bonté de confirmer que Vous n'avez besoin de rien d'autre pour l'acheminement de Votre travail et que Vous êtes d'accord sur la possibilité de l'achever dans le délai susdit. Vous voudrez bien aussi m'indiquer le montant de Votre honoraire et de celui de

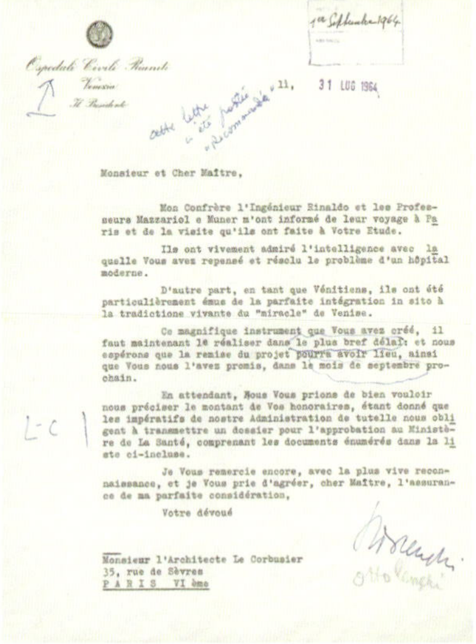

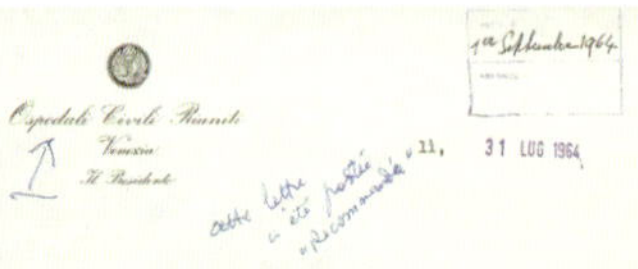

Ospedali Civili Riuniti
Venezia
Il Presidente

..11, 31 LUG 1964

Monsieur et Cher Maître,

Mon Confrère l'Ingénieur Rinaldo et les Professeurs Mazzariol e Muner m'ont informé de leur voyage à Paris et de la visite qu'ils ont faite à Votre Etude.

Ils ont vivement admiré l'intelligence avec laquelle Vous avez repensé et résolu le problème d'un hôpital moderne.

D'autre part, en tant que Vénitiens, ils ont été particulièrement émus de la parfaite intégration in sito à la traditione vivante du "miracle" de Venise.

Ce magnifique instrument que Vous avez créé, il faut maintenant le réaliser dans le plus bref délai: et nous espérons que la remise du projet pourra avoir lieu, ainsi que Vous nous l'avez promis, dans le mois de septembre prochain.

En attendant, Nous Vous prions de bien vouloir nous préciser le montant de Vos honoraires, étant donné que les impératifs de nostre Administration de tutelle nous obligent à transmettre un dossier pour l'approbation au Ministère de La Santé, comprenant les documents énumérés dans la liste ci-incluse.

Je Vous remercie encore, avec la plus vive reconnaissance, et je Vous prie d'agréer, cher Maître, l'assurance de ma parfaite considération,

Votre dévoué

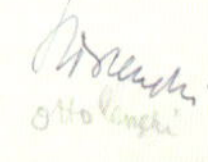

Monsieur l'Architecte Le Corbusier
35, rue de Sèvres
P A R I S VI ème

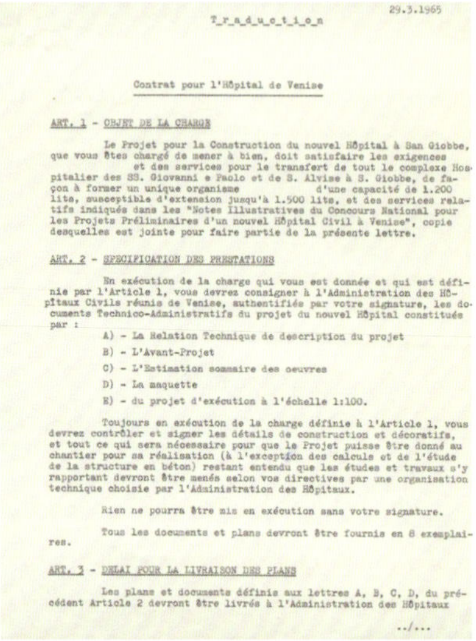

29.3.1965

T_r_a_d_u_c_t_i_o_n

Contrat pour l'Hôpital de Venise

ART. 1 - OBJET DE LA CHARGE

Le Projet pour la Construction du nouvel Hôpital à San Giobbe, que vous êtes chargé de mener à bien, doit satisfaire les exigences et des services pour le transfert de tout le complexe Hospitalier des SS. Giovanni e Paolo et de S. Alvise à S. Giobbe, de façon à former un unique organisme d'une capacité de 1.200 lits, susceptible d'extension jusqu'à 1.500 lits, et des services relatifs indiqués dans les "Notes Illustratives du Concours National pour les Projets Préliminaires d'un nouvel Hôpital Civil à Venise", copie desquelles est jointe pour faire partie de la présente lettre.

ART. 2 - SPECIFICATION DES PRESTATIONS

En exécution de la charge qui vous est donnée et qui est définie par l'Article 1, vous devrez consigner à l'Administration des Hôpitaux Civils réunis de Venise, authentifiés par votre signature, les documents Technico-Administratifs du projet du nouvel Hôpital constitués par :

A) - La Relation Technique de description du projet
B) - L'Avant-Projet
C) - L'Estimation sommaire des oeuvres
D) - La maquette
E) - du projet d'exécution à l'échelle 1:100.

Toujours en exécution de la charge définie à l'Article 1, vous devrez contrôler et signer les détails de construction et décoratifs, et tout ce qui sera nécessaire pour que le Projet puisse être donné au chantier pour sa réalisation (à l'exception des calculs et de l'étude de la structure en béton) restant entendu que les études et travaux s'y rapportant devront être menés selon vos directives par une organisation technique choisie par l'Administration des Hôpitaux.

Rien ne pourra être mis en exécution sans votre signature.

Tous les documents et plans devront être fournis en 8 exemplaires.

ART. 3 - DELAI POUR LA LIVRAISON DES PLANS

Les plans et documents définis aux lettres A, B, C, D, du précédent Article 2 devront être livrés à l'Administration des Hôpitaux

../...

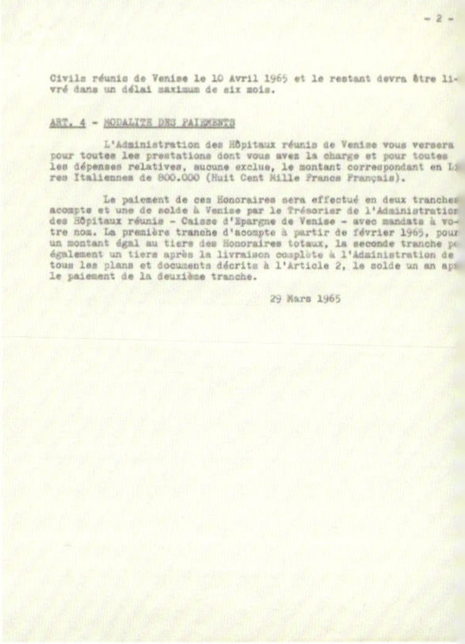

- 2 -

Civils réunis de Venise le 10 Avril 1965 et le restant devra être livré dans un délai maximum de six mois.

ART. 4 - MODALITE DES PAIEMENTS

L'Administration des Hôpitaux réunis de Venise vous versera pour toutes les prestations dont vous avez la charge et pour toutes les dépenses relatives, aucune exclue, le montant correspondant en Li- res Italiennes de 800.000 (Huit Cent Mille Francs Français).

Le paiement de ces Honoraires sera effectué en deux tranches acompte et une de solde à Venise par le Trésorier de l'Administration des Hôpitaux réunis - Caisse d'Epargne de Venise - avec mandats à votre nom. La première tranche d'acompte à partir de février 1965, pour un montant égal au tiers des Honoraires totaux, la seconde tranche p- également un tiers après la livraison complète à l'Administration de tous les plans et documents décrits à l'Article 2, le solde un an ap- le paiement de la deuxième tranche.

29 Mars 1965

pposite, top, far ft. First page of letter from the resident of the ssociation of Iunicipal Hospitals ɔ Le Corbusier, 8 November 1963, xpressing his heartfelt gratitude" that Le Corbusier has accepted the job of designing the new Venice Hospital

Opposite, top, second from left. President of the Association of Municipal Hospitals to Le Corbusier, 31 July 1964, saying how impressed his colleagues were with the plans for the new hospital and urging him to finish it in "the shortest time possible"

Opposite, top right. Contract for the Venice Hospital project, 29 March 1965

Opposite, bottom. Le Corbusier presenting his model of the Venice Hospital, c. 1963–65

Top. Photo-collage of palazzi along the Grand Canal, Venice, c. 1965

Above. Facade sketch and photo-collage, Venice Hospital

Below left. Aerial photograph of Venice. The hospital was to be built in the Cannaregio district, just north of the railway station and the Ponte della Libertà.

Below right. Model, Venice Hospital, 31 October 1964

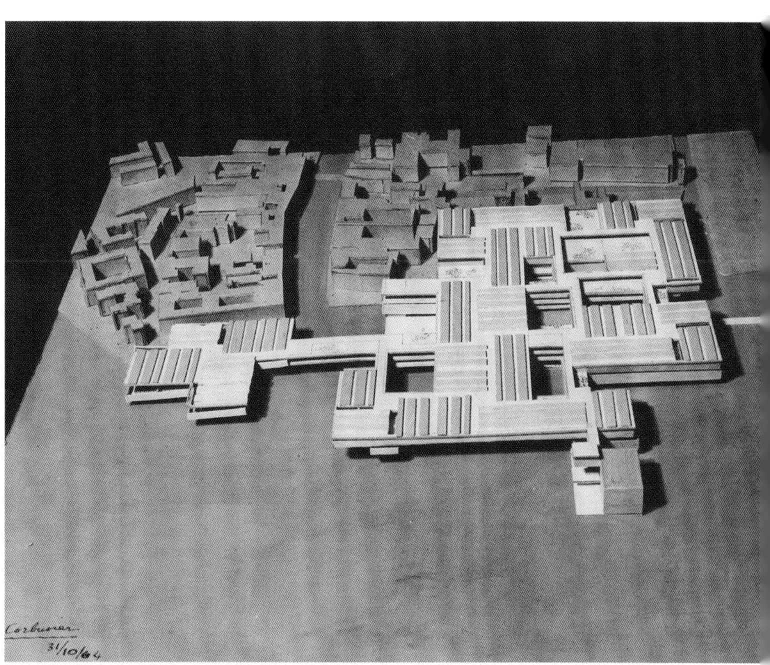

Left. Sketch of Piazza San Marco, Venice

Below and opposite. Le Corbusier in Venice, August 1963, with Giuseppe Mazzariol (second from left), the Venice University professor who was a supporter of Le Corbusier's Venice work

"Venice is one of the world's exceptional cities and a place I have loved since 1907."

—Letter to Giovanni Favaretto Fisco, mayor of Venice, 3 September 1962

Following pages. Le Corbusier, making art in the studio of his apartment at 24 rue Nungesser-et-Coli, Paris, 1960

Ce qu'a dit la Bourse
FRANCE-SOIR
COUPLES
COURSES

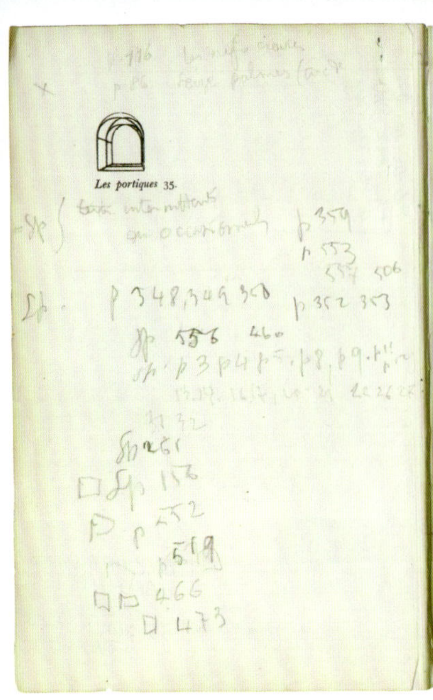

Texte préfacé établi et traduit par PAUL MAZON membre de l'Institut, professeur à l'Université de Paris avec la collaboration de PIERRE CHANTRAINE directeur d'études à l'École des Hautes Études, PAUL COLLART professeur à l'Université de Paris et RENÉ LANGUMIER. Illustrations de JOHN FLAXMAN gravées par SCHULER

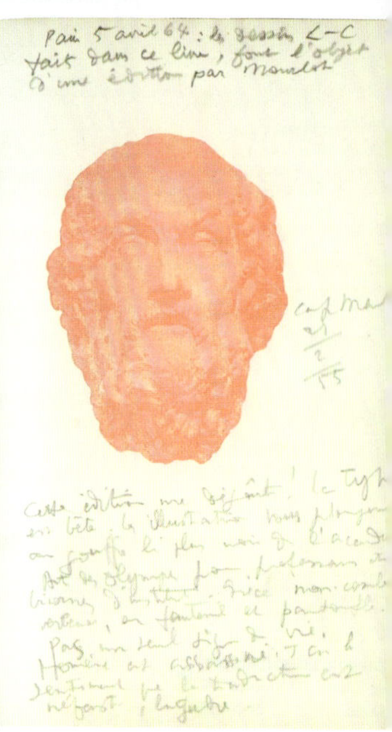

Iliade

sais être l'arrêt des dieux. Non, par Apollon cher à Zeus, à qui, Calchas, va ta prière, lorsque tu veux aux Danaens révéler les arrêts du ciel, non, tant que je vivrai, tant qu'ici-bas j'aurai les yeux ouverts, nul, près de nos nefs creuses, ne portera sur toi sa lourde main, nul entre tous les Danaens, quand tu nommerais même ici Agamemnon, qui aujourd'hui se flatte d'être de beaucoup le premier dans ce camp. »

Le devin sans reproche lors se rassure et dit :

« Ce n'est pas pour un vœu, une hécatombe omise, qu'ici se plaint le dieu. C'est pour son prêtre, à qui Agamemnon a fait affront naguère, en refusant de délivrer sa fille et d'agréer une rançon. Voilà pourquoi l'Archer vous a octroyé des souffrances et vous en octroiera encore. Des Danaens il n'écartera pas le fléau outrageux, avant qu'ils n'aient à son père rendu la vierge aux yeux vifs, sans marché, sans rançon, et mené à Chrysé une sainte hécatombe. Ce jour-là seulement, nous le pourrons apaiser et convaincre. »

Il dit et se rassied. Et voici que se lève le héros, fils d'Atrée, le puissant prince Agamemnon. Il est des plus chagrins; terriblement ses entrailles se gonflent d'une noire fureur; ses yeux paraissent un feu étincelant. Et, d'abord, sur Calchas dardant un œil mauvais, il dit :

« Prophète de malheur, jamais tu n'as rien dit qui fût fait pour me plaire. En toute occasion, ton cœur trouve sa joie à prédire le malheur [3]. Mais, de bonheur, jamais tu n'en annonces, jamais tu n'en amènes. Et tu viens encore aujourd'hui déclarer, au nom des dieux, à la face des Danaens, que, si l'Archer leur cause des souffrances c'est parce que j'ai, moi, refusé d'agréer la splendide rançon de cette fille, Chryséis. Il est vrai : j'aime mieux, de beaucoup, la garder chez moi. Je la préfère à Clytemnestre même, ma légitime épouse. Non, elle ne lui cède en rien, pour la stature ni le port, pour l'esprit ni pour l'adresse.

6

Iliade

mange la fressure; le reste, on le débite en menus morceaux; on enfile ensuite ceux-ci sur des broches, on les rôtit avec grand soin, on les tire enfin tous du feu. L'ouvrage terminé, le banquet apprêté, on festoie, et les cœurs n'ont pas à se plaindre d'un repas où tous ont leur part. Lors donc qu'on a chassé la soif et l'appétit, les jeunes gens remplissent jusqu'au bord les cratères, puis à chacun, dans sa coupe, ils versent de quoi faire libations aux dieux. Et, tout le jour, en chœur, les fils des Achéens, pour apaiser le dieu, chantent le beau péan et célèbrent le Préservateur. Et lui, se plaît à les ouïr.

Le soleil plonge et l'ombre vient. On s'étend le long des amarres; puis, quand, au matin, paraît Aurore aux doigts de rose, on prend le large, pour regagner le vaste camp des Achéens. Apollon le Préservateur envoie la brise favorable. On dresse alors le mât, on déploie la voilure blanche. Le vent gonfle la toile en plein, et, tandis qu'autour de l'étrave en marche, le flot bouillonne et siffle bruyamment, la nef va son chemin, courant au fil du flot. Ils arrivent ainsi au vaste camp des Achéens; là, pour mettre à sec la nef noire, ils la halent, puis, sur le sable, la redressent, enfin l'étayent de longs accores. Après quoi, ils se dispersent par les baraques et les nefs.

Dans l'Olympe

Pendant ce temps, assis près de ses nefs agiles, le divin Péléide, Achille aux pieds rapides, est toujours en courroux. Il ne hante ni l'assemblée, où l'homme acquiert la gloire, ni le combat : il consume son cœur à demeurer là, dans le regret de la huée, de la bataille!

Mais, quand après cela vient la douzième aurore, alors les dieux toujours vivants s'en retournent dans l'Olympe, tous ensemble, et Zeus à leur tête. Thétis alors n'a garde

22

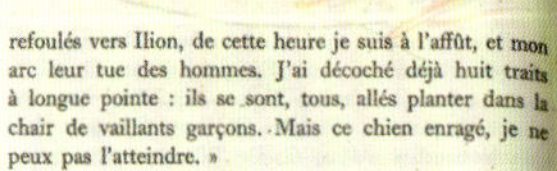

Iliade

refoulés vers Ilion, de cette heure je suis à l'affût, et mon arc leur tue des hommes. J'ai décoché déjà huit traits à longue pointe : ils se sont, tous, allés planter dans la chair de vaillants garçons. Mais ce chien enragé, je ne peux pas l'atteindre. »

Il dit, et, de sa corde, il fait jaillir un nouveau trait, droit sur Hector; son cœur voudrait tant l'atteindre! Mais il le manque, et, à sa place, la flèche va toucher en pleine poitrine Gorgythion sans reproche, le noble fils de Priam, à qui il est né d'une épouse venue d'Ésyme, Castianire la Belle, au corps de déesse. Tel un pavot, dans un jardin, penche la tête de côté, sous le poids de son fruit et des pluies printanières, tel il penche son front par le casque alourdi [12].

Et Teucros, de sa corde, fait jaillir un nouveau trait, droit sur Hector; son cœur voudrait tant l'atteindre! Et, cette fois encore, il le manque : Apollon a fait dévier la flèche. C'est Archéptolème, intrépide cocher d'Hector, en pleine ardeur guerrière, qu'il touche à la poitrine, près de la mamelle. L'homme croule de son char; ses chevaux rapides se dérobent; il reste, lui, sur place, sa vie, sa fougue brisées. Un atroce chagrin serre le cœur d'Hector, à voir mort son cocher. Il le laisse là, pourtant, malgré son déplaisir de perdre un compagnon, et donne l'ordre à Cébrion, son frère, qui est là, tout près, de prendre les rênes du char. Cébrion l'entend et n'a garde de dire non. Pour lui, il saute à terre du char resplendissant, en poussant des cris effroyables. Dans sa main, il prend une pierre, et il va droit à Teucros; son cœur lui enjoint de l'atteindre. Déjà Teucros de son carquois a sorti une flèche amère. Il l'a posée sur la corde, qu'il tire le long de l'épaule, à l'endroit où la clavicule sépare du col la poitrine, là où un coup porte le mieux. C'est là même qu'Hector au casque étincelant l'atteint, en plein élan, de sa pierre aiguë. La corde est brisée. Le

194

Iliade

vient de me porter. C'est le fils de Tydée : à cette heure il combattrait Zeus Père même! »

Elle dit; Arès lui donne ses coursiers au frontal d'or. Elle monte sur le char, le cœur affligé. Iris monte à ses côtés, et, prenant les rênes en main, d'un coup de fouet enlève les chevaux; ceux-ci, pleins d'ardeur, s'envolent. Ils ont vite atteint le séjour des dieux, l'Olympe escarpé. Là, la rapide Iris aux pieds vites comme les vents arrête les chevaux, les dételle du char et place devant eux leur céleste pâture. La divine Aphrodite est cependant tombée aux genoux de sa mère. Dioné serre sa fille dans ses bras, elle la flatte de la main, elle lui parle, en l'appelant de tous ses noms :

« Qui des fils de Ciel, mon enfant, t'a ainsi traitée, sans raison, comme pour te punir d'un méfait notoire? »

Et Aphrodite qui aime les sourires répond :

« C'est le fils de Tydée, le bouillant Diomède, qui vient de me frapper, parce que je voulais soustraire à la bataille Énée, mon fils, qui m'est cher entre tous. Ce n'est plus désormais entre Troyens et Achéens qu'a lieu l'atroce mêlée : les Danaens maintenant font la guerre aux Immortels! »

Dioné, la toute divine, alors lui répond :

« Subis l'épreuve, enfant; résigne-toi, quoi qu'il t'en coûte. Ils sont nombreux chez nous, les maitres de l'Olympe, ceux qui, pour des hommes, ont supporté des épreuves semblables et se sont les uns aux autres infligé de durs chagrins. Arès a subi la sienne, le jour qu'Otos et Éphialte le Fort, les fils d'Aloeus, le lièrent d'un lien brutal. Treize mois enfermé dans une jarre en bronze, il y eût bel et bien péri, Arès, le dieu insatiable de guerre, si leur marâtre, la toute belle Éeribée, n'eût avisé Hermès. Quand celui-ci leur déroba Arès, il était à bout de forces : ses cruelles chaînes avaient eu raison de lui. — Héré a subi la sienne, le jour où le rude

118

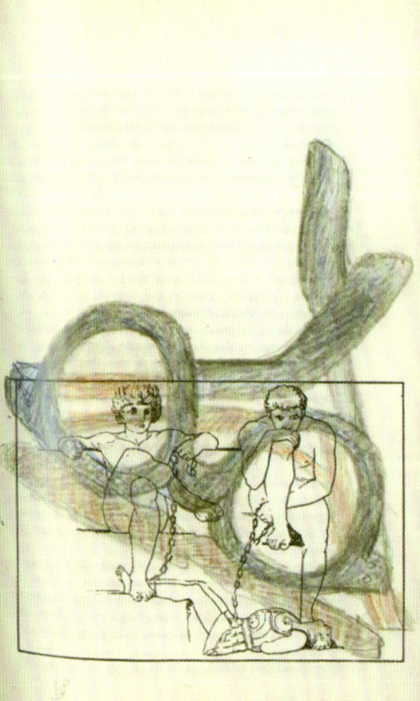

Opposite. Le Corbusier planned to illustrate his copy of Homer's *Iliad*, which contained drawings by the English sculptor and draftsman John Flaxman. He completed only twenty-four drawings before his death, some of which are seen here.

Above. Le Corbusier at Harvard, 1960

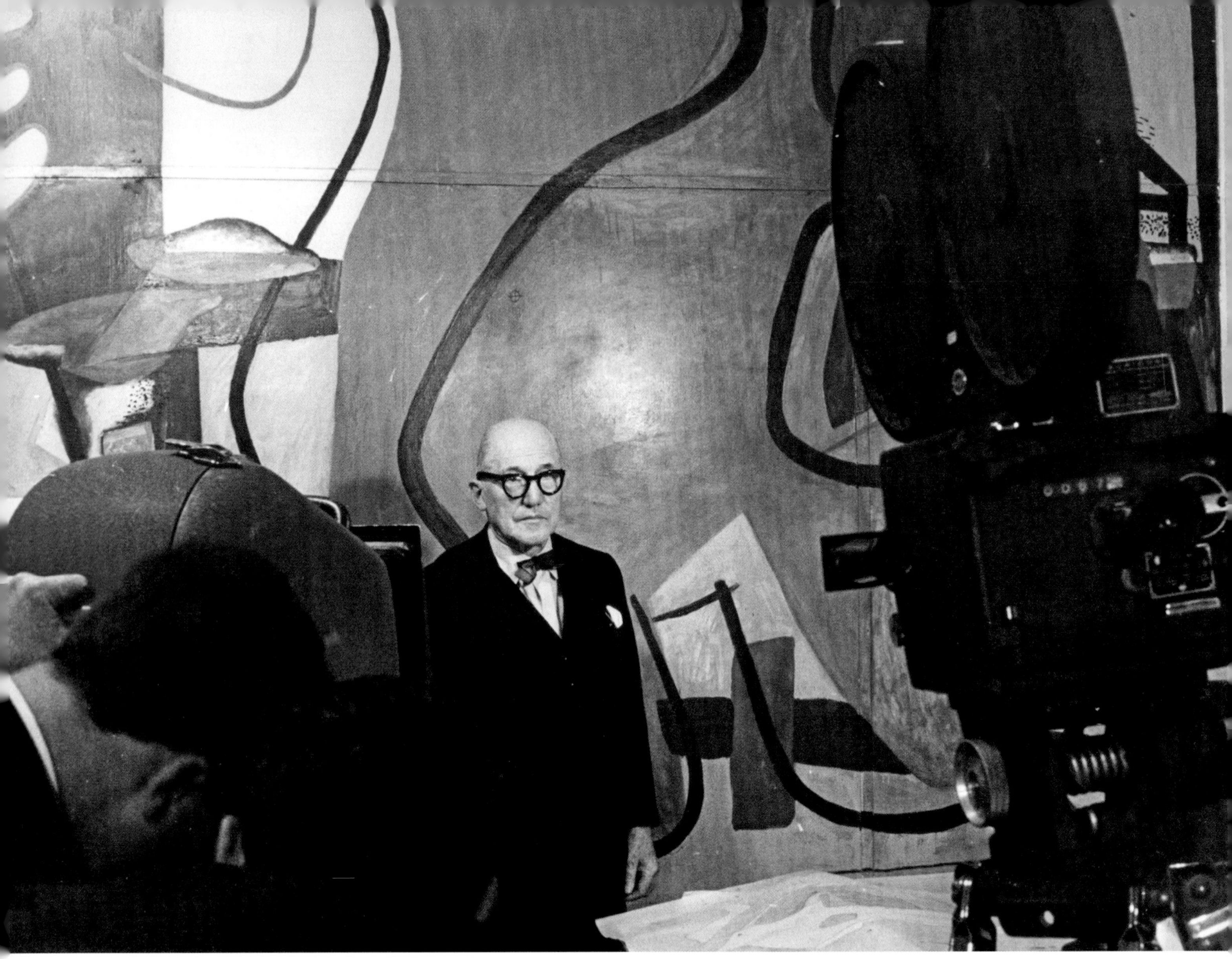

This page and opposite. Le Corbusier, in front of the mural he painted, during filming in his office, 35 rue de Sèvres, Paris, 1960s

PARIS LE CORBUSIER
C
1

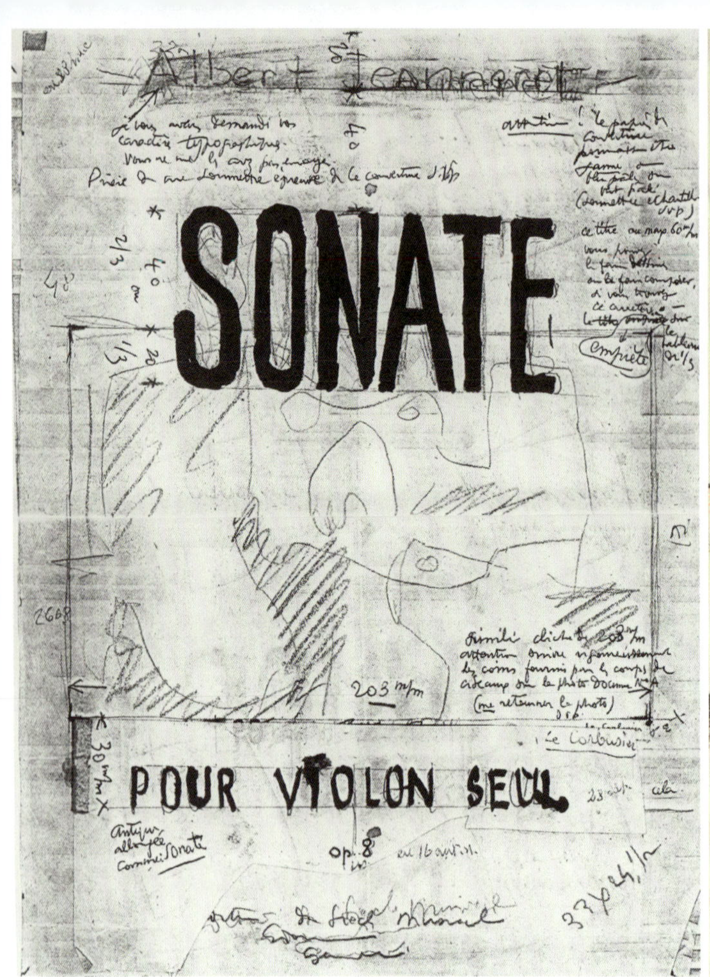

A family's lifelong love of music

Le Corbusier's mother and brother were both accomplished musicians. From them Le Corbusier absorbed a wide-ranging love of music, which would manifest itself throughout his life. In later years he designed the covers for Albert's compositions.

> **"I used the Modulor to establish the typeface for the cover of Albert Jeanneret's 'Sonata for Solo Violin,' a most intimately moving work."**
>
> —***Modulor 2*, 1955**

Opposite. Covers by Le Corbusier for his brother Albert's musical compositions

Clockwise from top left:

Sonate pour violon seul (Sonata for Solo Violin)

Suite brève pour violon et piano (Short Suite for Violin and Piano)

La joie est la clef du bonheur (Joy Is the Key to Happiness) (two versions)

Above. Albert playing the piano at the Petite Maison, Corseaux, Switzerland

Right. Le Corbusier's mother at the piano and Albert playing the violin, late 1950s

His mother's death: Marie-Charlotte-Amélie Perret-Jeanneret (1860–1960)

Le Corbusier was devoted to his mother, Marie-Charlotte-Amélie Jeanneret, and he was devastated by her death in 1960. Throughout her long life he sustained a weekly correspondence with her, from wherever his career took him – Algeria, India, Japan, the United States – and his lively letters home offer vivid insights into his work, his life, and his relationship to his family.

Monsieur Albert JEANNERET, à Corseaux s/Vevey ;

Monsieur LE CORBUSIER, à Paris ;

Monsieur et Madame Rudolf JEANNERET, à Berne ;

Madame Hélène ZWAHLEN, ses enfants et petits-enfants, à La Chaux-de-Fonds et Zurich ;

Madame et Monsieur Otto MULLER et leurs enfants, à Glaris ;

Monsieur et Madame Hermann DELACHAUX, à Zurich ;

Monsieur et Madame Paul DELACHAUX et leurs enfants, à Vernayaz ;

Monsieur et Madame Louis DELACHAUX, à Bâle ;

Monsieur Pierre JEANNERET, à Chandigahr (Indes) ;

Les familles parentes ZIMMERMANN, RIVOIRE, TROTTET et Robert JEANNERET, à Corcelles et Genève ;

Le Dr Adrien MIÉVILLE et Sœur Rose ZENKLUSEN, si dévoués,

ont le chagrin de vous faire part du décès de

MADAME

Marie JEANNERET

née PERRET

leur très chère mère, tante, grand-tante et parente, qui s'est éteinte paisiblement le 15 février 1960, dans sa 100e année.

L'incinération aura lieu à Vevey le mercredi 17 courant.

Culte à 15 h. 15 à la chapelle du crématoire.

Honneurs à 15 h. 45.

Domicile mortuaire : route de Lavaux 21, « Le Lac », Corseaux par Vevey.

Ce que tu fais, fais-le.

Gavillet & Brunet, Vevey

Left. Funeral notice for Marie Jeanneret, who died 15 February 1960

Below left. Le Corbusier to Albert, 18 February 1960, describing their mother's funeral, with a drawing of her as a young woman

Below right. Carola Giedion-Welcker, art historian and wife of Sigfried Giedion, to Le Corbusier, 26 February 1960, extending her condolences

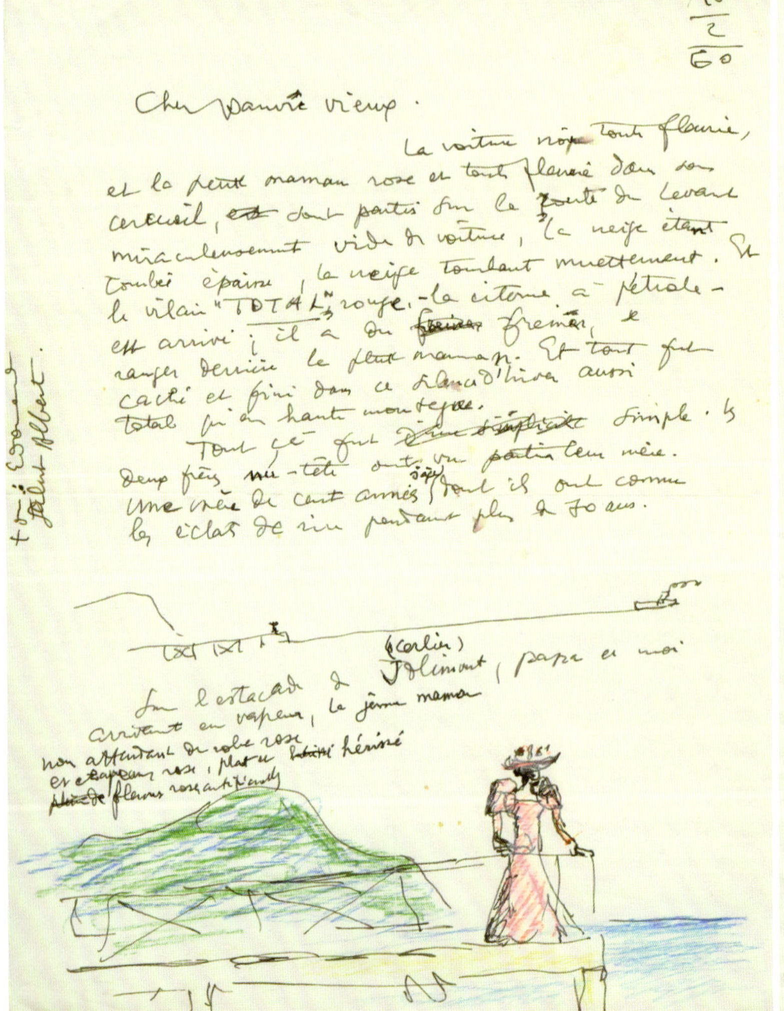

18/2/60

Cher pauvre vieux.

La voiture noire toute fleurie, et la petite maman rose et toute fleurie dans son cercueil, est donc partis sur la route de Lavaux miraculeusement vide de voitures, la neige étant tombée épaisse, la neige tombant muettement. Et le vilain "TOTAL" rouge, – la citerne à pétrole – est arrivé ; il a dû freiner, et ranger derrière la petite maman. Et tout fut caché et fini dans ce blanc d'hiver aussi total qu'en haute montagne.

Tout ça fut simple. Les deux frères nu-tête ont vu partir leur mère. Une mère de cent années, tout il ont connu l'éclat de vie pendant plus de 70 ans.

Sur l'estacade de Jolimont (Corlier), papa et moi attendant la jeune maman arrivant en vapeur, en robe rose et chapeau rose, plat et hérissé de fleurs rose

Zurich 26.II.6

Cher Corbu, ça m'a fait beaucoup de peine de lire dans des journaux Suisse que votre maman est mor

On croyait toujours que la mort ne pouvait pas la toucher et qu'elle restrait vainqueur dan la lutte de l'age.

En esperant de vous revoir une fois à Paris

votre

Carola G-W

"Your kind face—full of sunlight, and so full of good spirits and physical well-being—is part of my view of things, and I thank you for always being for us a bright symbol of strength and courage."

—Letter to his mother, 30 November 1957

Top left. Yvonne and Le Corbusier to his mother, 29 August 1952, writing just to say that "the little lake house is in our eyes and our hearts"

Top right. Le Corbusier to his mother on her birthday, 7 September 1954, expressing his love

Above left. Le Corbusier to his mother and brother, Albert, from Chandigarh, 19 December 1957, adding up their cumulative ages ("238 ½")

Above right. Le Corbusier to his mother, 18 August 1959, reminiscing about twelve days they had just spent together

Le Corbusier
1910 60

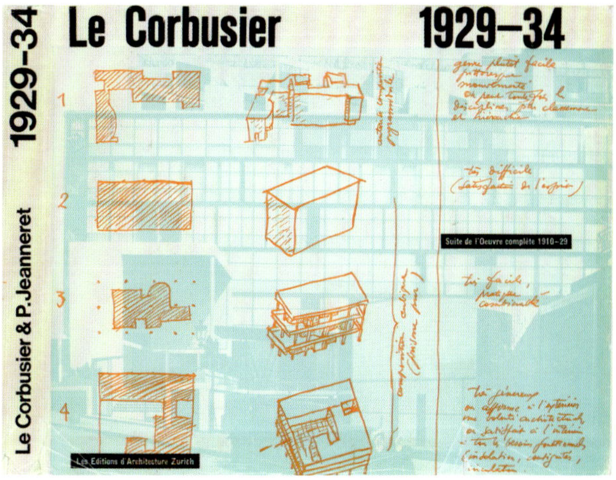

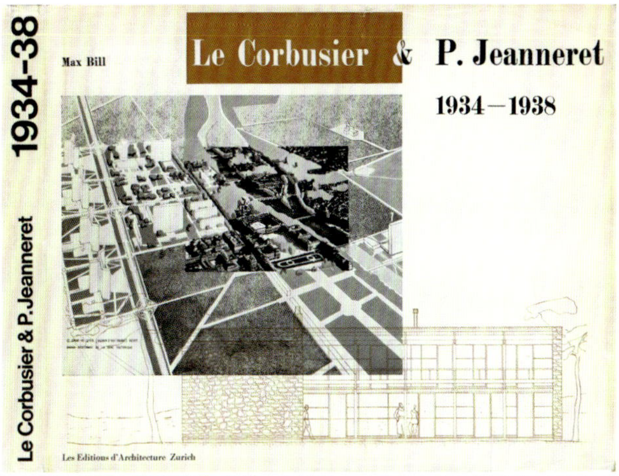

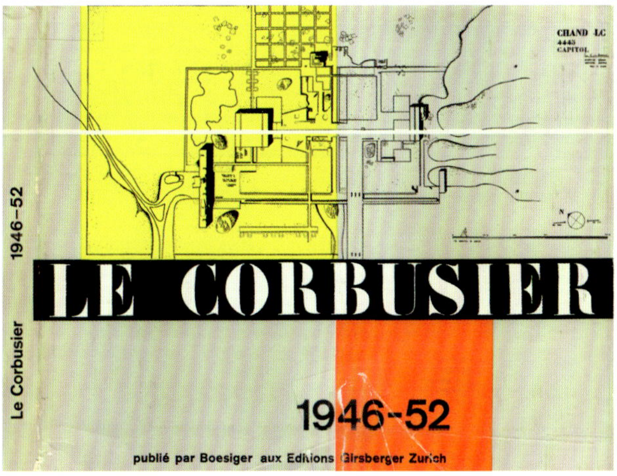

Documenting a life: Fondation Le Corbusier, Paris, 1968, and the *Oeuvre complète*

Following the deaths of his wife and mother, with his own mortality impossible to ignore, Le Corbusier began making plans to establish the Fondation Le Corbusier, which opened in 1968. In the Villa La Roche, which was donated by Raoul La Roche, one of Le Corbusier's earliest patrons, the Fondation archives and displays the architect's architectural records, artworks, library, and personal documents.

During this time Le Corbusier also turned his attention to the final volumes of his complete works, the *Oeuvre complète*; the original six volumes were expanded to eight after his death.

Opposite. Le Corbusier signing copies of the newly published *Le Corbusier 1910–60*, c. 1961, in front of one of his tapestries

Above. Covers of the eight volumes of Le Corbusier's *Oeuvre complète*, 1930–70

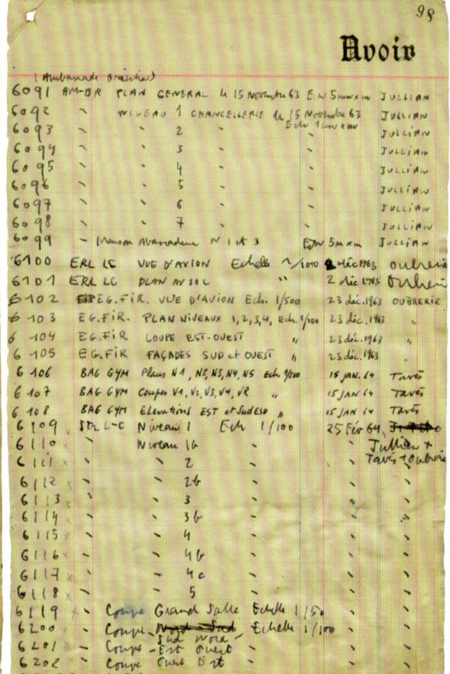

Left. Final pages from Le Corbusier's *Livre noir* (black book), a listing of drawings from the architect's studio spanning forty years, from 1925 to 1965

Opposite. Le Corbusier, 1960s

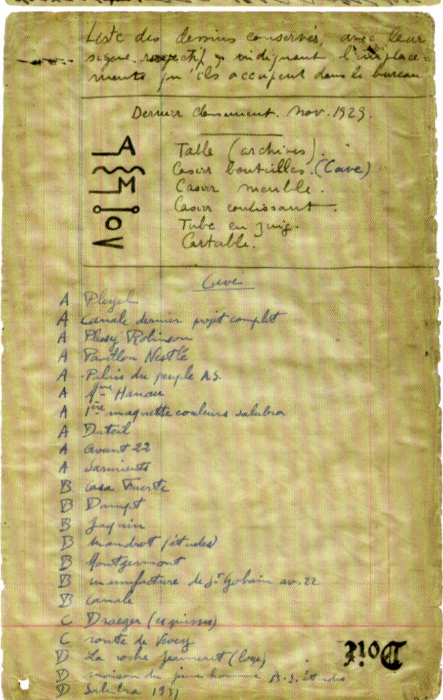

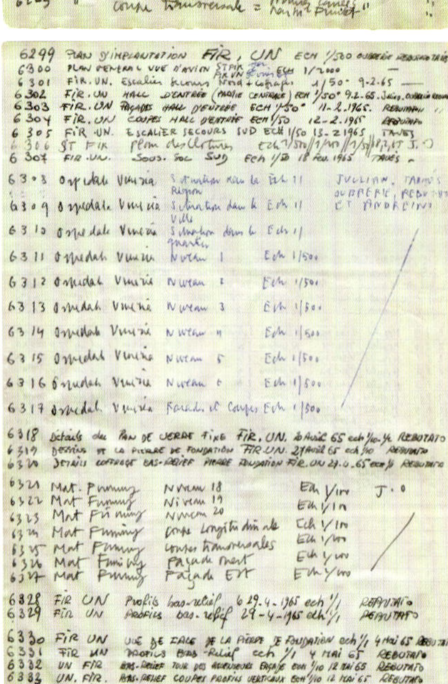

Departure: Roquebrune-Cap-Martin, 27 August 1965

During the summer of 1965 the seventy-seven-year old Le Corbusier vacationed as usual at Roquebrune-Cap-Martin. He stayed in the *cabanon* on his own, though Thomas Rebutato and his family scrupulously looked after their old friend. On 27 August 1965, Le Corbusier died, most likely of a heart attack, while taking his daily morning swim.

Opposite and below. Le Corbusier by the sea, Roquebrune-Cap-Martin, c. 1964

Emotion et consternation dans le monde

LE CORBUSIER EST MORT

HIER A ROQUEBRUNE CAP MARTIN

• Le célèbre architecte a péri noyé dans la petite crique où il passait ses vacances depuis de nombreuses années

MENTON. — L'architecture française, l'architecture mondiale est en deuil. Un deuil auquel s'associe le monde entier. Le Corbusier n'est plus. Celui qui était considéré comme l'un des plus grands architectes du monde, est mort d'hydrocution alors qu'il se baignait dans une petite crique de la Côte d'Azur, la « Plage du Grabet », à Roquebrune - Cap - Martin, dans les Alpes - Maritimes.

Cette crique accueillait chaque année depuis 1957, le vieux bâtisseur qui était âgé de 78 ans. Là, il passait ses vacances en ermite, dans un minuscule bungalow de 4 mètres sur 3. Construite en béton, la bâtisse, peinte en blanc, ne comporte qu'une porte et une fenêtre avec volets verts. Dans le voisinage, on en parlait en disant : **« Le cabanon solitaire »**. L'intérieur, cependant, présente tout le confort et les commodités modernes. Le lit est escamotable dans un mur, ainsi que la table. Les appareils sanitaires eux-mêmes sont logés dans des alvéoles dans un cabinet de toilette miniature.

C'est dans ce décor que Le Corbusier venait se reposer. Il y faisait parfois de courtes visites mais, chaque été, il y séjournait plusieurs semaines.

(Suite en dernière page)

Le Corbusier, le petit horloger suisse devenu le plus grand architecte du monde.

Profonde émotion dans le monde

PARIS. — Profonde émotion dans le monde entier à la suite de la disparition tragique de Le Corbusier.

« Dans la vieille Europe, dans l'Amérique latine en transformation, dans l'Inde immémoriale, partout il faisait jaillir dans le monde des fontaines d'avenir », a déclaré M. René Maheu, directeur général de l'UNESCO, évoquant les grandes réalisations du disparu. « Le Corbusier était un grand esprit. C'est ce qui en avait fait un grand artiste. L'UNESCO n'oublie pas ce qu'elle lui doit. »

M. Jean Cassou, conservateur en chef du Musée d'art moderne : « Nul mieux que Le Corbusier n'aura mérité le beau titre d'humaniste. Il aura été l'un des créateurs de l'humanisme de notre temps. »

« Il n'est pas un architecte de moins de 60 ans qui n'ait été influencé par lui, a dit de son côté M. Richard Sheppard, qui a construit notamment le collège Churchill à Cambridge. Son livre « Vers une architecture », publié en 1922, fut pour nous une révélation. Tout ce qu'il a fait depuis cette date a eu une importance mondiale. »

A Rome, l'architecte Francesco Vacchini, directeur de la fabrique de Saint - Pierre, au Vatican, a déclaré : « Le style de Le Corbusier a eu une grande influence sur le renouveau de l'architecture sacrée. C'est un grand deuil pour l'architecture moderne.

A Stockholm, M. Sven Backstroem, un des plus importants urbanistes suédois : « Le Corbusier était incontestablement un génie. Son œuvre a eu une importance capitale dans le monde entier par la puissance de ses idées créatrices et par l'ampleur de ses vues. Il aura marqué profondément son époque. »

A Helsinki, le professeur Alvar Aalto, célèbre planificateur finlandais a dit : « La mort de Le Corbusier représente pour moi la perte d'un ami cher et d'un architecte de renommée mondiale », tandis que M. Aarne Ervi, représentant de la jeune génération des grands architectes finlandais, ajoutait : « Grâce à Le Corbusier et à son « fonctionnalisme », le monde a hérité d'une nouvelle conception de tout ce que l'architecture peut offrir à l'humanité. »

A New York, à l'annonce du décès du grand architecte, le directeur du département d'architecture du Musée d'art moderne a annoncé sa décision d'ouvrir très prochainement une exposition commémorative à la mémoire du disparu.

Constructeur du « grand navire » du Bd Michelet

Le Corbusier est mort, un peintre, un architecte mais aussi un philosophe qui avait remis en question les fondements de l'urbanisme, disparaît brusquement et les Marseillais ressentiront plus vivement que les autres cette disparition.

Pour eux Le Corbusier ce n'est pas seulement un homme mais un monument : cette « Cité Radieuse » qui dresse ses seize étages comme un puissant navire. Les touristes l'achètent en carte postale et des étudiants en architecture viennent chaque année étudier l'œuvre d'un pionnier. La « Cité Radieuse » n'exprime plus l'avant-garde, les disciples de Le Corbusier ont fait mieux depuis mais ce bloc de béton est un témoignage, l'image d'un effort, d'un espoir.

Il fut un temps où la « maison du fada » faisait sourire, ce n'est pas le genre de choses qu'on peut ignorer et encore maintenant il est difficile de résister à la grandeur d'un édifice dont la beauté rude est à base d'équilibre.

Les grands créateurs ont de la chance : ils continuent à vivre dans leurs œuvres. Le Corbusier sera longtemps bien vivant à travers le monde et tant que son grand navire restera à l'ancre au boulevard Michelet, Edouard Jeanneret-Gris gardera une place de choix dans le souvenir des Marseillais.

J.-P. H.

M. Oscar Niemeyer :

« Le vrai génie de l'architecture contemporaine »

M. Oscar Niemeyer, l'architecte de Brasilia, qui séjourne actuellement à Paris a fait, en apprenant la mort de Le Corbusier, la déclaration suivante :

« C'est avec une profonde tristesse que je vous parle de Le Corbusier. Il fut le plus grand, le vrai génie de l'architecture contemporaine.

« Vers Le Corbusier, je me suis toujours dirigé depuis le temps de l'école d'architecture, lisant ses livres, étudiant son œuvre, attiré par son talent, par sa position d'homme de lutte tant de fois incompris. »

Le chien loup de Le Corbusier attend en vain son maître sur le toit du cabanon où le fanion est en berne.

LE CORBUSIER SE NOIE A ROQUEBRUNE-CAP MARTIN

Le célèbre architecte (78 ans) a été pris d'un malaise au cours d'une baignade

MENTON (C. P.). — Le célèbre architecte Charles-Jeanneret-Gris, mieux connu sous le nom de Le Corbusier, a succombé, hier matin, à Roquebrune Cap-Martin, où il passait ses vacances, des suites d'une crise cardiaque.

Charles Le Corbusier, qui était âgé de 78 ans, se baignait, comme tous les matins, à proximité de la plage du Buse, proche de la villa Casa Del Mare, qui appartient à l'actrice Silvana Mangano et son mari, le producteur Nino de Laurentis, lorsqu'il fut pris de malaise.

Soudain, du rivage, un touriste, M. Simon Auzichio, de Douai (Nord), le vit en difficulté. Il se précipita à la mer et ramena l'architecte, qui, semble-t-il, avait déjà cessé de vivre.

Néanmoins, M. Auzichio tenta l'impossible et lui pratiqua le bouche-à-bouche.

Les sapeurs - pompiers de Menton, qui arrivèrent bientôt, lui insufflèrent des bouffées d'oxygène, mais en vain.

Le docteur Bernard, médecin légiste à Menton, qui avait été alerté, arriva à son tour sur les lieux et injecta dans les veines de l'architecte un stimulant cardiaque qui n'eut pas plus d'effet que les soins prodigués jusqu'alors.

Enfin, après une heure de vains efforts, le corps de Char-

SUITE P. 7 SOUS LE TITRE : LA MORT DU CÉLÈBRE ARCHITECTE

LA MORT DU CÉLÈBRE ARCHITECTE LE CORBUSIER

Une récente photo de Le Corbusier avec le fidèle gardien du petit cabanon de 4 m. sur 3 dans lequel celui qui fut l'un des plus grands architectes du monde aimait se reposer l'été. Ce cabanon ne comportait qu'une porte et une fenêtre. L'intérieur présente tout le confort et les commodités modernes. Le lit est escamotable dans un mur ainsi que la table. Les appareils sanitaires eux-mêmes sont logés dans des alvéoles dans un cabinet de toilette miniature.

★ SUITE DE LA PAGE 1 ★

les Le Corbusier fut transporté au reposoir de l'hôpital de Menton.

Fidèle habitué de Roquebrune-Cap Martin, où il venait passer ses vacances depuis 15 ans déjà, l'architecte était arrivé sur la Côte il y a une quinzaine de jours. Vivant dans un cabanon sans aucun confort, il prenait ses repas de tous les jours dans une modeste pension de famille, « L'Etoile de Mer ».

L'architecture des « Cités radieuses »

Le Corbusier, de son vrai nom Charles-Edouard Jeanneret - Gris était né à la Chaux-de-Fonds (Suisse), le 6 octobre 1887.

Après avoir été graveur et horloger, il se tourne très tôt vers l'architecture. Après avoir visité l'Italie, l'Autriche et l'Allemagne, il se fixe définitivement à Paris en 1916 et sera naturalisé Français.

Il travaille avec les frères Perret et ne cesse alors de préconiser sa conception nouvelle de l'habitation ouverte en terrasse, éclairée horizontalement de mur à mur et montée sur potences en béton.

Il a édifié dans cet esprit de nombreuses villas dans la banlieue parisienne et dans la France entière, avant d'être appelé par des chefs d'Etat étrangers pour réaliser de grands ensembles d'urbanisme parmi lesquels ont peut citer : « La cité universitaire de Rio de Janeiro », « Le plan d'urbanisation de Bogota » (1950), Plan et construction de la nouvelle capitale du Punjab, en Inde (1951 - 1956), etc. Pendant ce temps, s'élevaient en France plusieurs « cités radieuses », notamment celles de Marseille et de Nantes (1945 - 1956).

Membre du comité des cinq experts internationaux chargés de contrôler la construction du Palais de l'Unesco, à Paris, et de l'ONU à New York, c'est lui qui a conçu les plans du musée du XXe siècle qui doit s'élever au Rond-Point de la Défense.

Dans un grand nombre d'articles et de multiples ouvrages, il a exposé ses idées révolutionnaires en matière d'architecture.

« C'est le plus grand architecte du monde » a dit de lui M. André Malraux, lorsque le gouvernement français a élevé l'architecte à la dignité de grand officier de la Légion d'honneur, le 18 décembre 1963.

Le Corbusier était docteur honoris causa de l'Université de Zurich, membre correspondant du Royal institute of british architects et avait reçu, le 27 avril 1965, dans son atelier parisien, du président de la société des architectes de Boston, une médaille de l'Université d'Harward pour les constructions qu'il avait entreprises au Carpenter center de Harward.

M. Bernard Zehrfuss :

« L'un des plus grands de ce siècle »

« Toute la génération actuelle des architectes travaille, en fait, en fonction de ce que Le Corbusier a réalisé », a déclaré en apprenant le décès de Le Corbusier, M. Bernard Zehrfuss, premier grand prix de Rome, architecte conseil au ministère de la Construction.

« L'impulsion que Le Corbusier a donnée à l'architecture moderne, a-t-il ajouté, et l'influence qu'il a eue sur les architectes est énorme. Sa mort est une perte, non seulement française, mais aussi mondiale. Il fut, sans conteste, l'un des des plus grands de ce siècle. »

« Le Corbusier aurait pu apporter encore beaucoup de choses, beaucoup d'idées nouvelles », a conclu M. Zehrfuss.

Il était, une fois, un petit horloger...

« J'ai réalisé en Inde, d'une manière absolue, le contrôle du soleil... ». Phrase étonnante que seul l'homme qu'André Malraux a appelé « le plus grand architecte du monde » pouvait se permettre de prononcer, sans crainte du ridicule.

Contrôle du soleil, contrôle de la couleur, de la lumière, de la pierre, c'est tout cela, Le Corbusier.

Très tôt, Charles-Edouard Jeanneret-Gris, le petit horloger-graveur de La Chaux-de-Fonds, avait compris qu'il était fait pour révolutionner l'architecture, contre vents et marées et malgré l'hostilité, voire la haine, qu'allaient susciter ses conceptions d'un autre monde, un monde « habitable » où l'homme trouverait le bonheur.

Dès son arrivée à Paris, il devient le disciple d'Auguste Perret, « le pape du béton armé ». Le béton armé, que ce soit sous forme de pilotis ou de pare-soleil, sera l'une des clefs de l'univers Le Corbusier.

Fait caractéristique, l'une de ses premières œuvres sera, en 1925, le pavillon de « L'Esprit Nouveau » à l'Exposition des Arts Décoratifs de Paris. Mais s'il commence par Paris, Le Corbusier bien vite sera celui que l'étranger s'arrache et que son propre pays — il s'est fait naturaliser français en 1930 — accable de critiques. Avant que ne soit inaugurée en 1952, la fameuse « Cité radieuse » de Marseille, il aura construit le Palais des Soviets à Moscou (1931), la Cité universitaire de Rio de Janeiro. Il aura conçu le plan d'urbanisation de Bogota et commencé à faire surgir du néant, dans le quasi-désert du Punjab indien, une capitale : Chandigarh.

A Marseille enfin, les Français commencent à « vivre dans du Le Corbusier ». Immeuble révolutionnaire que cette « unité d'habitation de grandeur conforme » qui s'élève vers le soleil sur trente-six pilotis d'acier et de béton, où la rue commerçante est située à mi-hauteur de l'édifice, où les couleurs éclatent, violemment contrastées dans l'abondance de petites surfaces.

« La preuve est faite, a écrit Le Corbusier, qu'un mur s'évade des que des lignes ou des couleurs l'occupent ».

Car ce bâtisseur écrit, et beaucoup. Il a même écrit de livres théoriques au début de sa carrière, avant d'avoir mené à bien de grandes réalisations, qu'un jour le grand architecte américain Frank Lloyd Wright refusa de le recevoir sous prétexte qu'il « ne recevait pas les journalistes ».

Les titres de ses livres sont déjà un programme : « Vers une architecture », « Quand les cathédrales étaient blanches », « La maison des hommes », « le poème de l'angle droit ».

Poète, Le Corbusier l'est aussi, et peintre, sculpteur. De sa peinture, il dira : « J'ai fait de ma peinture une [illegible] et une invention, recherchant avant tout la proportion, cette proportion de nature géométrique et mathématique ».

Pour mettre, en architecture, la proportion à la mesure de l'homme, il invente le « Modulor », « Une gamme de dimensions harmoniques à l'échelle humaine, applicable à l'architecture et à la mécanique ».

Au cours des vingt dernières années, Le Corbusier a construit partout, du Brésil au Japon en passant par l'U.R.S.S. et les Etats-Unis, mais assez peu en France. Le fameux ensemble de Marseille, que les Marseillais eux-mêmes irrévérencieusement appelaient « La Maison du Fada », lui valut d'âpres critiques. La « Société pour l'esthétique générale de la France » alla même jusqu'à lui intenter un procès, qu'elle perdit d'ailleurs.

Bougon, têtu avec son profil grave derrière de sombres lunettes, travaillant comme un fou, Le Corbusier ne s'en émut pas outre mesure. Et bientôt ce fut l'éclatante revanche.

Opposite and above. Press clippings reporting Le Corbusier's death

LE CORBUSIER (78 ans) SE NOIE

A ROQUEBRUNE-CAP-MARTIN

Le Corbusier montrant la maquette de la cité qu'il avait conçue pour la ville de Nantes à Rezé.

L'« architecte de l'an 2000 » avait construit ***entre autres*** une cité à Marseille ("la maison du fada" pour certains) **et la ville** de Chandigar, en Inde

(Voir à la dernière page)

LE CHIEN-LOUP DE LE CORBUSIER attend son maître en vain sur le toit du cabanon

UN GRAND URBANISTE DISPARAIT

LE CORBUSIER EST MORT

Le célèbre architecte s'est noyé

– crise cardiaque –

en se baignant

à Roquebrune Cap-Martin

Il était âgé de 78 ans

L'expérience révolutionnaire de Le Corbusier : « Cité radieuse » du boulevard Michelet, universellement connue.

En page 12 : Nos informations — En page 3 : Le Corbusier et Marseille

C'est le chien fidèle du disparu ; lorsque celui-ci était absent, l'animal attendait toujours son maître sur le toit du cabanon de Roquebrune-Cap-Martin ; victime d'une crise cardiaque en prenant son bain quotidien — c'était un excellent nageur — Le Corbusier, âgé de 78 ans, était marié, sans enfants.

"L'Espoir" du 4 Sept 1965

Les cendres de LE CORBUSIER ont été inhumées dans le petit cimetière de Roquebrune

Une simple plaque indique que c'est là que repose un des plus grands architectes de notre époque... (Photo Morel)

Hier après-midi, a eu lieu l'inhumation des cendres de Le Corbusier, dans le petit cimetière de Roquebrune-Cap-Martin, où il reposera aux côtés de sa femme, sous une tombe d'une grande simplicité.

Une assistance nombreuse, formée d'amis connus ou inconnus de Le Corbusier, de Roquebrunois et de Mentonnais, entourait les personnalités nationales et départementales, pour rendre un dernier hommage au célèbre architecte.

Parmi celles-ci, nous avons noté : M. Anthonioz, représentant M. André Malraux ; M. René Cassin, vice-président du Conseil d'Etat ; M. Fournerot, directeur du cabinet du préfet ; M. Lottier, maire de Roquebrune-Cap-Martin, et l'ensemble du conseil municipal ; M. Lucien Rostin, premier adjoint, représentant M. Francis Palmero, député-maire de Menton ; le général Morel, commandant la subdivision ; le lieutenant-colonel Mangeot, de la base aérienne 943.

M. Jeanneret, frère de Le Corbusier, reçoit les condoléances des autorités (Photo Morel)

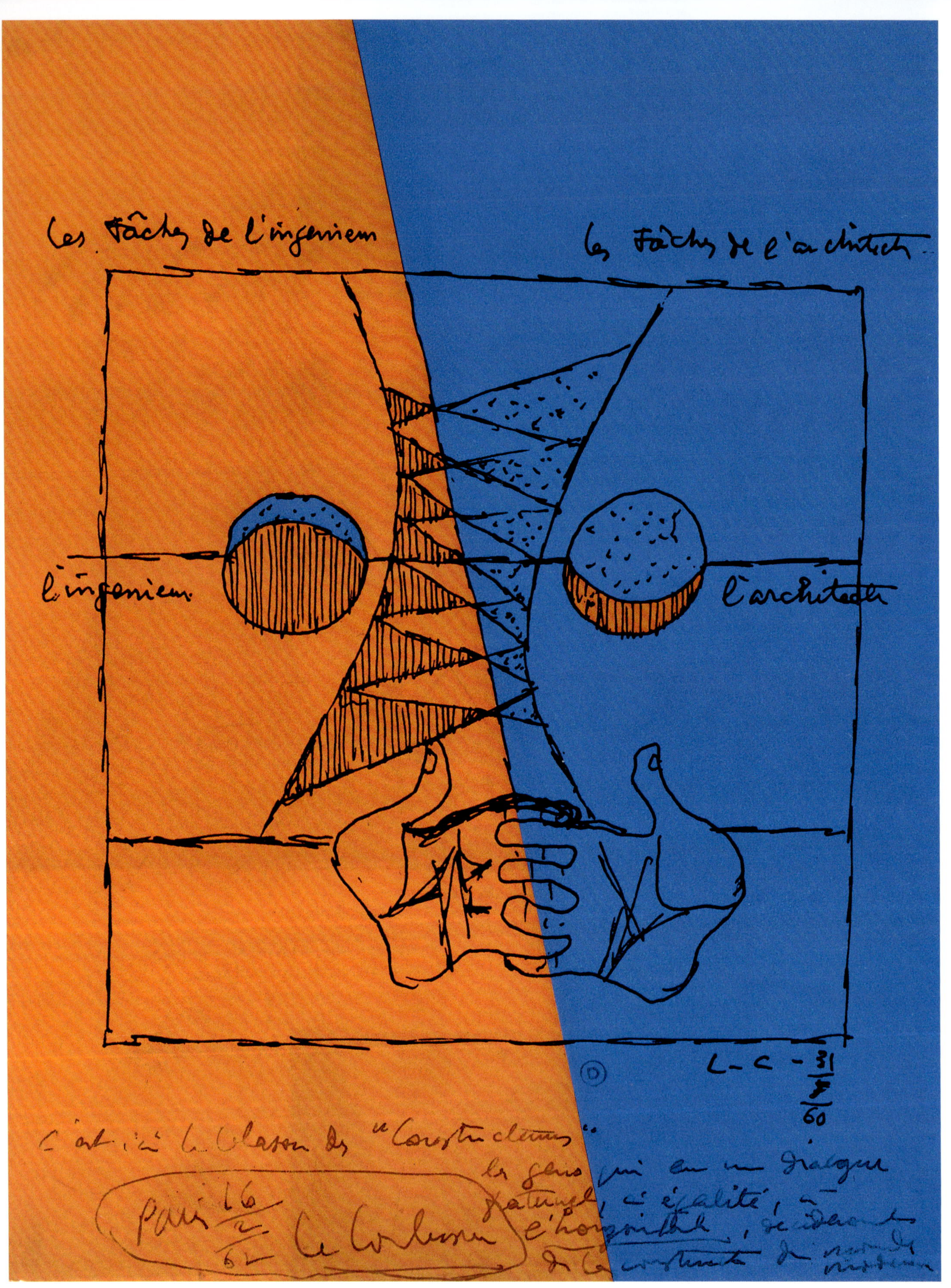

"He fought only for architecture. With a vehemence he felt for nothing else, because architecture alone ans-wered his passionate hope for what can be done for man."
—André Malraux, eulogy for Le Corbusier, 2 September 1965

A formal farewell: André Malraux's eulogy, Paris, 2 September 1965

French Minister of Culture André Malraux delivered the sole eulogy at Le Corbusier's funeral, as well as reading tributes from dignitaries ranging from architects Alvar Aalto and Richard Neutra to the presidents of the United States and Brazil.

Opposite. Drawing by Le Corbusier showing the relationship of the engineer and the architect, 1960, which he gave to André Malraux, 16 February 1962, with a note describing it as the builders' coat of arms

Right. André Malraux's annotated typescript of his funeral eulogy for Le Corbusier. He writes, "After him, architecture changed – but so did architects."

Excellences, Mesdames, Messieurs,

Au moment où le gouvernement décidait de rendre à Le Corbusier l'hommage solennel de la France, il recevait le télégramme suivant :

" Les architectes grecs, avec une profonde tristesse, décident de déléguer leur président aux obsèques de Le Corbusier, pour déposer sur sa tombe, de la terre de l'Acropole ".

Et, hier : " L'Inde, où se trouvent plusieurs des chefs-d'oeuvre de Le Corbusier, et la capitale qu'il a construite : Chandigarh, viendra verser sur ces cendres l'eau du Gange, en suprême hommage ".

Voici donc l'éternelle revanche . Il est beau que la Grèce soit présente dans cette cour illustre qu'ordonnèrent tour à tour Henri II, Richelieu, Louis XIV et Napoléon, et que, ce soir, la déesse pensive incline lentement sa lance sur ce cercueil.

Et c'est bien à un symbole fraternel que s'adressent ces symboles . Le Corbusier a connu de grands rivaux, dont quelques-uns nous font d'ailleurs l'honneur d'être présents ; et les autres sont morts . Mais aucun n'a signifié avec une telle force la révolution de l'architecture, parce qu'aucun n'a été si longtemps, si patiemment, insulté .

à travers l'outrage que la gloire prend son suprême éclat, et cette gloire-là s'adressait à une oeuvre plus qu'à une personne, qui s'y prêtait peu . Après avoir pendant tant d'années pris pour atelier le large couloir d'un couvent désaffecté, l'homme qui avait conçu des capitales est mort dans une cabane solitaire . Les baigneurs qui rapportèrent le corps du vieux nageur ignoraient qu'il s'appelât Le Corbusier . Mais peut-être eût-il été content de savoir que lorsqu'ils le voyaient chaque jour descendre vers la mer, ils l'appelaient l'Ancien.

Dès sa jeunesse, il avait été peintre, sculpteur, et, plus secrètement, poète . Il ne s'était battu ni pour la peinture, ni pour la sculpture, ni pour la poésie : il ne s'est battu que pour l'architecture . Avec une véhémence qu'il n'éprouva pour rien autre, parce que l'architecture seule rejoignait passionné de ce qu'on peut faire pour l'homme .

Sa phrase fameuse : " Une maison est une machine à habiter " ne le peint pas du tout . Ce qui le peint, c'est : " La maison doit être l'écrin de la vie " . La machine à bonheur . Il a toujours rêvé de villes, et les projets de ses " cités radieuses " sont des tours surgies d'immenses jardins . Il avait écrit : " L'axe de l'homme, c'est l'harmonie qui l'accorde à lui-même – à la communauté

3

– à la nature – et probablement à l'univers ". Cet agnostique a construit l'église et le couvent les plus saisissants du siècle . Il disait, à la fin de sa vie : " J'ai travaillé pour ce dont les hommes d'aujourd'hui ont le plus besoin : le silence et la paix ". Et le principal monument de Chandigarh devait être surmonté d'une gigantesque Main de Paix, sur laquelle seraient venus se poser les oiseaux de l'Himalaya. La main de paix n'est pas encore en place ...

Cette noblesse parfois involontaire s'accommodait fort bien de théories souvent prophétiques et presque toujours agressives, d'une logique enragée, qui ont été, pour les architectes, un des ferments du siècle .

Il y avait chez lui un créateur que nous ne pouvons pas séparer du théoricien, mais qui ne se confond pas avec lui . Disons qu'il en est le frère jumeau. Le Corbusier était avant tout l'artiste qui avait dit en 1920 : " L'architecture est le jeu savant, correct et

magnifique des formes assemblées dans la lumière ", et, plus tard : " bétons si rudes révèlent que, sous eux, nos sensibilités sont fines ... " . Il inventait au nom de la logique des formes admirablement arbitraires .

n'oubliait jamais, que ses maisons n'étaient pas seulement des maisons, que ses villes imaginaires n'étaient pas seulement des villes, et que Chandigarh était tout autre chose que la capitale du Pendjab. Il a puissamment expliqué ce qu'il aimait, et c'est pourquoi les architectes grecs envoient la terre de l'Acropole " à l'homme qui sentit et aima la Grèce ". Mais ce ne sont pas ses écrits qui ont révélé la fraternité secrète de la Grèce et de l'Inde : c'est Chandigarh . Ce ne sont pas ses théories qui ont rendu manifeste la grande et profonde parenté des formes de l'architecture millénaire : ce sont ses oeuvres .

de Neutra, celui des architectes américains qui regrettent ce que vous pouviez faire encore .

Voici la voix du Président des Etats-Unis : " Son influence était universelle, et ses travaux sont chargés d'une pérennité qu'ont atteinte peu d'artistes de notre histoire..."

Et voici enfin la France – celle qui vous a si souvent méconnu, celle que vous portiez dans votre coeur lorsque vous avez choisi Français – qui vous dit, par la voix de son plus grand poète :

" Je te salue, au seuil sévère du tombeau !"

Adieu, mon vieux maître et mon vieil ami.

Bonne nuit ...

Voici l'hommage des villes épiques, les fleurs funèbres de New-York et de Brasilia.

Voici l'eau sacrée du Gange, et la terre de l'Acropole...

Le Corbusier, vous que j'ai vu si ému par l'hommage filial du Brésil, voici l'hommage du monde ...

Au Japon, le jour commence, et les six chaînes de télévision projettent votre musée de Tokyo; l'aube point dans l'Inde où les passereaux de Chandigarh secouent leurs ailes sur vos monuments, pendant que nos moineaux s'endorment sur l'église de Ronchamp. De l'autre côté de la terre, le Ministère de Rio, l'épopée de Brasilia, vont s'allumer dans le soir .

Comme le cortège des femmes de l'Inde portant la terre vers avec le geste des porteuses d'amphores,

de l'architecture contemporaine " et voici Costa, qui venu suivre votre cercueil depuis la plage tragique .

Voici sa fille, qui a drapé votre catafalque.

Voici les architectes de la Grèce, et ceux de l'Inde.

Voici le message d'Aalto, qui a transformé la Finlande ; celui de l'Angleterre, qui dit : " Il n'est pas un architecte de moins de soixante ans qui n'ait été influencé par lui " .

Voici celui

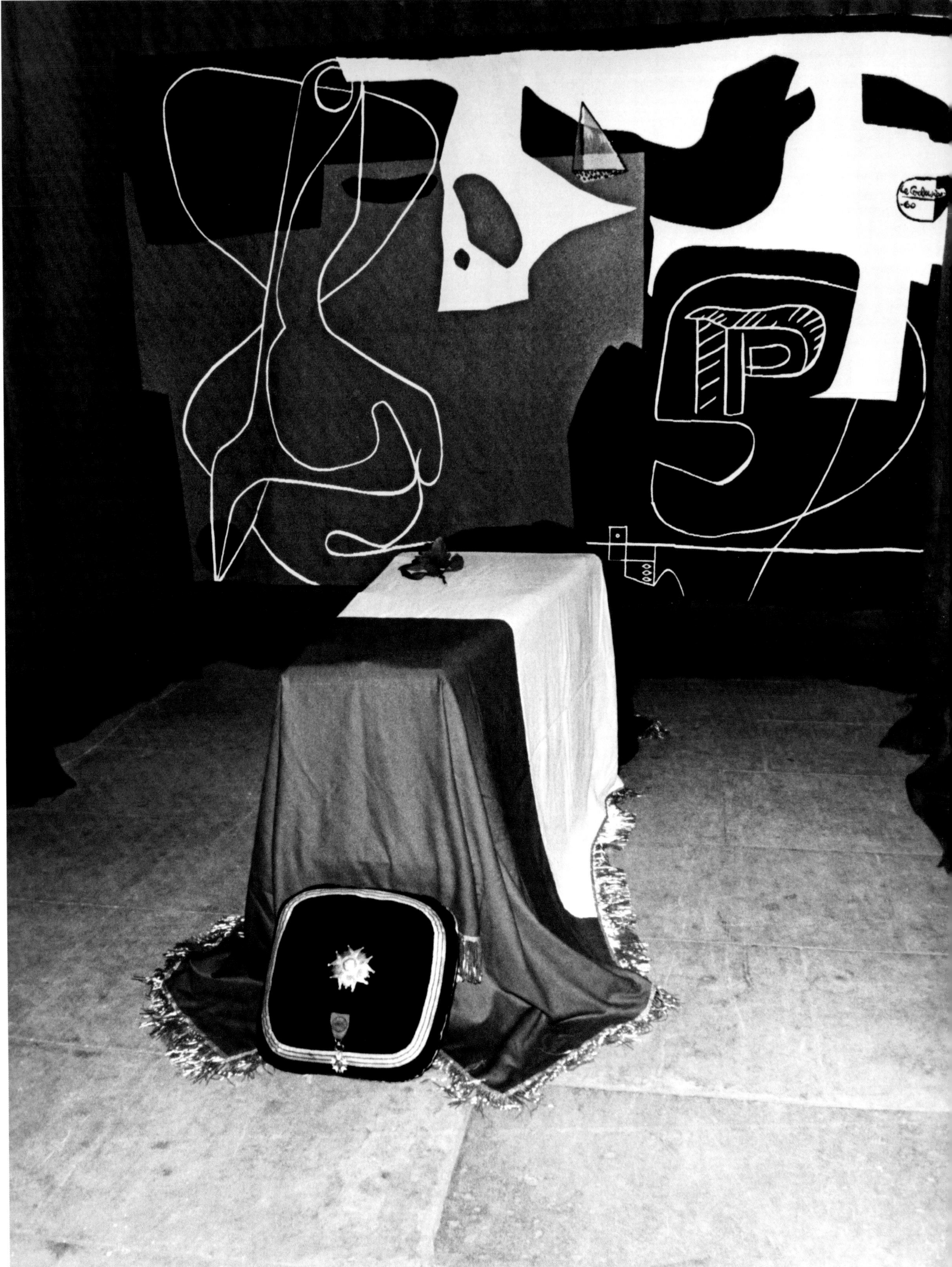

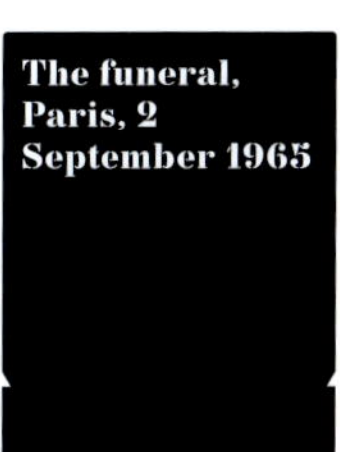

The funeral, Paris, 2 September 1965

An elaborate funeral was staged at the Cour Carré of the Louvre. High government officials gathered with friends, colleagues, and admirers to mourn the monumental figure who was lauded as one of the greatest architects of the twentieth century.

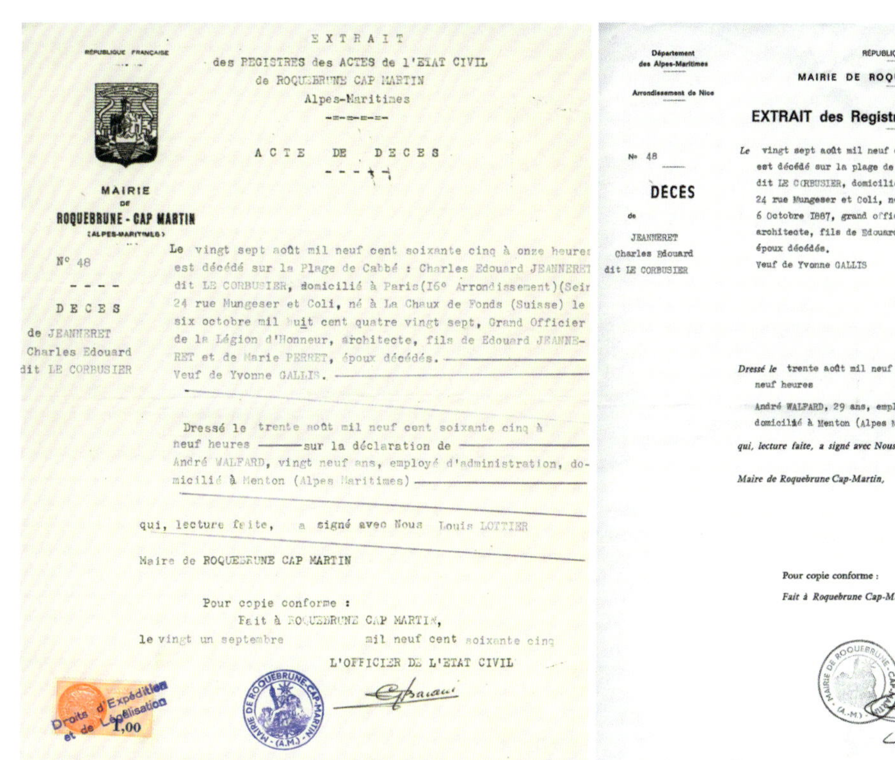

RÉPUBLIQUE FRANÇAISE

MAIRIE DE ROQUEBRUNE - CAP MARTIN (ALPES-MARITIMES)

EXTRAIT
des REGISTRES des ACTES de l'ETAT CIVIL
de ROQUEBRUNE CAP MARTIN
Alpes-Maritimes

ACTE DE DECES

N° 48

DECES
de JEANNERET
Charles Edouard
dit LE CORBUSIER

Le vingt sept août mil neuf cent soixante cinq à onze heures est décédé sur la Plage de Cabbé : Charles Edouard JEANNERET dit LE CORBUSIER, domicilié à Paris (16° Arrondissement) (Seine) 24 rue Mungeser et Coli, né à La Chaux de Fonds (Suisse) le six octobre mil huit cent quatre vingt sept, Grand Officier de la Légion d'Honneur, architecte, fils de Edouard JEANNERET et de Marie PERRET, époux décédés. Veuf de Yvonne GALLIS.

Dressé le trente août mil neuf cent soixante cinq à neuf heures sur la déclaration de André WALFARD, vingt neuf ans, employé d'administration, domicilié à Menton (Alpes Maritimes)

qui, lecture faite, a signé avec Nous Louis LOTTIER

Maire de ROQUEBRUNE CAP MARTIN

Pour copie conforme :
Fait à ROQUEBRUNE CAP MARTIN,
le vingt un septembre mil neuf cent soixante cinq
L'OFFICIER DE L'ETAT CIVIL

Droits d'Expédition et de Légalisation 1.00

MAIRIE DE ROQUEBRUNE-CAP-MARTIN (A.-M.)

Département des Alpes-Maritimes

Arrondissement de Nice

RÉPUBLIQUE FRANÇAISE

MAIRIE DE ROQUEBRUNE CAP-MARTIN

EXTRAIT des Registres des Actes de Décès

N° 48

DECES
de
JEANNERET
Charles Edouard
dit LE CORBUSIER

Le vingt sept août mil neuf cent soixante cinq à onze heures est décédé sur la plage de Cabbé : Charles Edouard JEANNERET dit LE CORBUSIER, domicilié à Paris 16° arondissement (Seine) 24 rue Mungeser et Coli, né à La Chaux de Fonds (Suisse) le 6 Octobre 1887, grand officier de la légion d'honneur, architecte, fils de Edouard JEANNERET et de Marie PERRET époux décédés,
Veuf de Yvonne GALLIS

Dressé le trente août mil neuf cent soixante cinq à neuf heures sur la déclaration de André WALFARD, 29 ans, employé d'administration, domicilié à Menton (Alpes Maritimes)

qui, lecture faite, a signé avec Nous Louis LOTTIER

Maire de Roquebrune Cap-Martin,

Pour copie conforme :
Fait à Roquebrune Cap-Martin, le 27 Octobre 1981

L'Officier de l'Etat Civil,

Opposite. Le Corbusier's coffin, laid in state, Cour Carré, Musée du Louvre, Paris

Above left and right. Le Corbusier's certificates of death, issued by Roquebrune-Cap-Martin, documenting his time and place of death as 11 a.m. on 27 August 1965, at Cabbé beach

Below. Plans and elevations by Le Corbusier, 18 May 1955, for the tomb for himself and his wife, Yvonne

Following pages. The tomb at Roquebrune-Cap-Martin, where Le Corbusier and Yvonne are interred

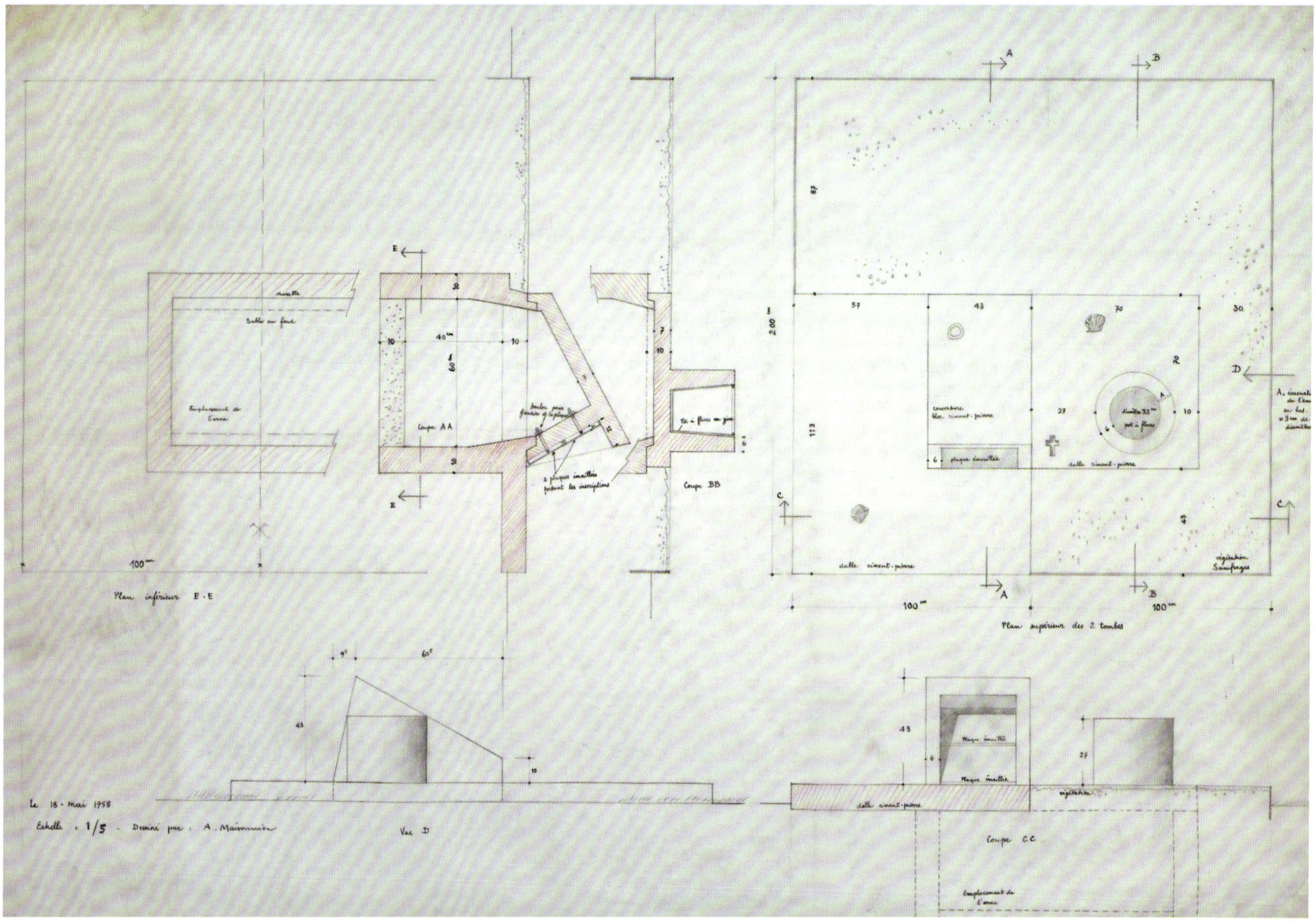

ici repose
Charles Edouard Jeanneret
dit
Le Corbusier
né
le 6 octobre 1887
mort
le 27 août 1965
à Roquebrune Cap-Martin
ici repose
Yvonne Le Corbusier
née
Jeanne Victorine Gallis
le 1er janvier-1892
morte
le 5 octobre-1957
à Paris

Documents: English Translation

Editor's Note

French architectural terms are translated in the glossary (opposite page); correspondence, annotated drawings and plans, and publications are translated in the booklet. Translations of writings by Le Corbusier are by John Tittensor; other translations are by Alexandra Bonfante-Warren (from the French), Abigail Asher (from the Italian), and Teresa Waldes (from the Catalan). The translations of Le Corbusier's writings reflect his idiosyncratic style as faithfully as possible. For clarity, the spelling of proper names has been corrected and standardized.

French/English Glossary of Architectural Terms

A
à conserver – to be kept, retained
à construire – to be built
à démolir – to be demolished
abri – shelter
accès – access
achat – purchase
aéroport – airport
aile – wing
alimentation – food supplies
allée – walkway
amphithéâtre – amphitheater
annexe – annex
appartement – apartment
argile – clay
armoire – closet
arrêt d'autobus – bus stop
arrivée – arrival
artisanat – trades, crafts
ascenceur / asc – elevator
atelier – studio
autel – altar
auto – car
axe – axis

B
baignoire – bathtub
balcon – balcony
baldaquin – canopy, baldaquin
banquette – bench
baquet à lessive – laundry tub
bassin – pool
bâtiment – building
béton – concrete
béton brut – raw concrete
bibliothèque – library
blanc – white
bleu – blue
bois – wood
bonne – maid
bord de mer – seashore
bouche d'arrosage – water-spout, spigot
boulon – bolt
boutique – shop
branche – branch
brevet – patent
brise-soleil – sunshade
brise-vent – windbreak
brosse – brush
brun – brown
buanderie – laundry room
bureau – office

C
cabinet du docteur – doctor's office
caisse – ticket office
canalisation – pipe
canon à ciment – cement gun
cantine – canteen
casier – compartment
cave – cellar
centre paroissial – parish-center
chai – wine cellar
chainette – small chain
chaise – chair
chambre / ch. à coucher – bedroom
chambre d'amis / d'hôte – guest room
chambre d'hôtel – hotel room
chape – screed
charbon – charcoal
château d'eau – water tower
chaudière – boiler
chauffage – heating
chemin – path
chemin de fer – railroad
cheminée de ventilation – ventilation chimney
ciment – cement
clinique – private hospital
cloison – partition wall
cloison coulissante – sliding wall
cloison portante – bearing wall
cloison volante – non-load-bearing wall
clôture – fence
coin de feu – hearth
coin repas – dining nook
colonie (de vacances) – summer camp
commerce – shop
conservateur – curator
construction existante – existing building
construction neuve – new building
contrôle – checkpoint
côté – side
coton – cotton
couleur – color
couloir – corridor
coupe – section
coupe longitudinale – longitudinal section
coupe transversale – transverse section
coupe vent – windbreak
cour / courette – courtyard
couvert – covered
cuisine – kitchen
cuivre – copper
cuivre martelé – hammered copper

D
dalle – tile, slab
débarras – storage room
desserte / dressoir – sideboard
dessiné – drawn
diamètre – diameter
disponible – available
dispositif de couverture – roofing system
dispositif d'ossature – frame system
disposition – layout
doigt – finger
domestique – servant
dortoir – dormitory
douche – shower

E
eaux pluviales – rainwater
échelle – scale
école – school
église – church
électricité – electricity
embarcadère – pier
emplacement – spot
enfant – child
entrée – entrance
entrepôt – warehouse
entresol – mezzanine floor
escalier – stairs
escalier de secours – fire escape
est – east
estrade – podium
étage – floor, story
évier – sink
évacuation – drainage

F
façade – facade
façade latérale – side facade
façade principale – main facade
face antérieure – front facade
face postérieure – back facade
fauteuils – armchairs
femme – woman
fenêtre – window
fenêtre d'angle – corner window
fer – iron
fidèles – congregation
fille – girl
fontaine – fountain
fosse sceptique – septic tank
fourneau – stove
foyer – hearth, household
frigidaire – refrigerator

G
gaine – sheath
galerie – gallery
garçon – boy
garde-manger – pantry
garderie – nursery
gazon – lawn
gérance – management
gradins – stands
grand – large
gravier – gravel
guichet d'entrée – ticket office
gymnase – gymnasium

H
habitation – housing
hall – lobby
hauteur – height
homme – man

I
implantation – site plan
inférieur – lower
inscriptions – inscriptions

J
jardin – garden
jaune – yellow
joint – joint

K
kiosque – kiosk

L
laine – wool
lanterneau – skylight
largeur – width
lattis – lathing
lavabo – washbowl
laverie – laundry room
léger – light
lessiveuse – laundry tub
lieu-dit – locality
lingerie – laundry
lit – bed
local – room
loge – lodge
lourd – heavy

M
machineries – machinery
maison – house
maison des jeunes – youth center
malade – sick
mât – mast
matériel de couchage – bedding
matériel pour bureaux – office supplies
ménage – housekeeping
mer – sea
modelage – modelling
monte-charge – freight elevator
mur de clôture – enclosing wall
mur mitoyen – common wall
muret – low wall
musée – museum
musique – music

N
nettoyage – cleaning
niveau – level
noir – black
nord – north

O
office – servants' hall
ouest – west
ouvert – open
ouverture – opening

P
palier – landing
papier goudronné – tar paper
parking / parquement – parking lot
parloir – parlor
paroi – partition wall
parquet – wooden floor
partie – part
passage – passageway
passerelle – footbridge
pavé de verre – glass brick
pavillon – pavilion
peinture – paint
pelouse – lawn
penderie – wardrobe
personnel – staff, personnel
petit – small
pierre – stone
piéton – pedestrian
pignon – gable
piscine – swimming pool
piste – track
plafond – ceiling
plage – beach
plan – plan
plan de situation – site plan
plancher – wooden floor
plaque émaillée – enameled plaque
plate-forme – platform
plâtre – plaster
plein-air – outdoor
poste d'eau – water supply point
poutraison – wooden roof frame
préau – covered playground
presbytère – presbytery
presse – press
profil – profile
propriété – property
public – audience
puisage – ground water extraction
pupitre – desk

Q
quartier – area

R
radiateur – radiator
rampe d'entrée / rampe d'accès – entrance, access ramp
rangée – row
rangement – storage
récréation – recreation
réfectoire – refectory
renseignements (bureau des) – information desk
revêtement – coating
rez-de-chaussée – ground floor
rideau – curtain
rivière – river
robinet – tap
rocher – rock
rondin – log
rouge – red
route – road
rue – street
rue intérieure – interior street

S
sable – sand
salle – room
salle à manger – dining room
salle commune – common room
salle d'attente – waiting room
salle de bains – bathroom
salle de classe / cours – classroom
salle de conférence – conference room
salle de jeux – playroom
salle de lecture – reading room
salle de sport – gymnasium
salle de télévision – TV room
salle de vente – auction room
salle paroissiale – parish hall
santé – health
scène – stage
sculpture – sculpture
sentier – path
séparé – separated
service santé – medical services
services de ravitaillement – supply services
services sociaux – social services
socle – base
sol – ground
solive – joist
sortie – exit
soupente – attic
sous-sol – basement
stade – stadium
stalle – stall
station-service – gas station
sud – south
supérieur – upper

T
talus – slope
tapis – rug
tapisserie – tapestry
tas de sable – sandpile
terrain artificiel / terre-plein – earthwork
terrain sportif – athletic fields
terrasse – terrace
terre – soil
théâtre – theater
tissu – fabric
toile cirée – oilcloth
toilette – toilet
toit / toiture – roof, roofing
tour d'ascenseur – elevator shaft
transformable – convertible
treille – vine arbor
tribune – podium
trottoir – sidewalk

U
urbanisme – urban planning
urne – funerary urn

V
valise – suitcase
vélo – bicycle
vernis – paint, varnish
vert – green
vestiaire – cloakroom, locker room
vide – empty space
vide-ordures – rubbish chute
visiteurs – visitors
vitrage – glazing
voie – path, route
voie privée – private road
voiture – car
vue d'avion – aerial view
vue intérieure – interior view

Z
zone maritime – waterfront

Childhood and Early Travels (1887–1917)

—P. 25

Furniture designs by Charles L'Eplattenier

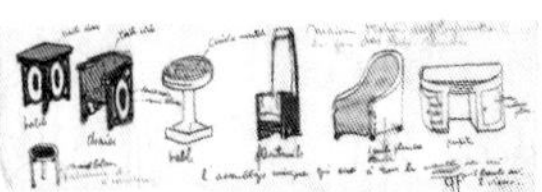

[LEFT TO RIGHT, TOP TO BOTTOM]
oilcloth / oilcloth / hammered copper / Maison Kohn. [Hoflieferant] opposite the Boulevards Museums

black paint
white paint

table / chair / table / armchairs / 1 single panel kiln-dried / desk / same plane

white paint
bedroom stool

the sole assembly system for all these pieces of furniture is this 1 ball with 2 screws

—P. 29

Sketches exploring the pine tree as a decorative architectural element, c. 1907

white trunks / blue gouache
roots sienna black
background ultramarine
leaves sienna green

—P. 34

Sketch of the Piazza del Campo, Siena, 1907

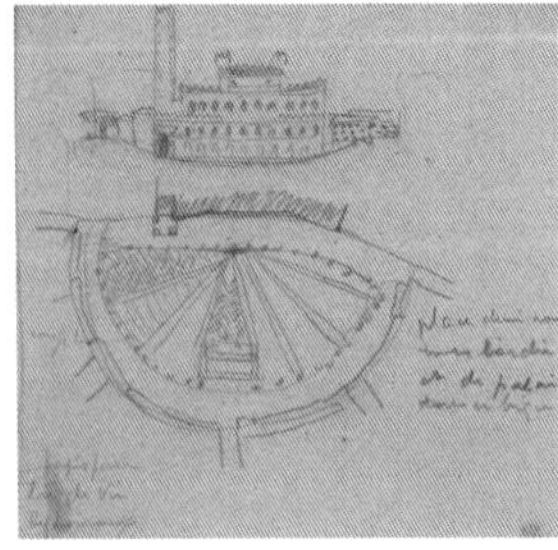

[LEFT]
red brown

wine-colored
persian carpets
belfry [?]

[RIGHT]
half-rou[nd] square with full border and of the palace all made of brick

—P. 34

Sketches of facade and details, Baptistry of St. John, Siena, 1907

[TOP RIGHT]
(1907) Siena

[MIDDLE RIGHT]
marble base white, pink basalt, column, white, pink and brown

[BOTTOM LEFT]
1382 ⅙ weak ⅓ weak ⅓ very strong
The very elaborate base pierced by 3 doors with a handsome cornice; all the sculptures in very low relief, everything very blond; —from the cornice rise the 4 uprights which overlap only slightly onto the large area that includes the colonnettes (very low relief, merging at the edges): this area is pierced by two windows, deep-set but heavily chamfered and pierced in the middle by a frame. [?] pink marble has been used for the lower part, the door columns and the edges of the sculptures. the [?] of the doors [?] richly ornamented with sculptures and inlays.

—P. 35

Sketches of Palazzo Vecchio, Florence, 1907

[TOP LEFT]
these 2 groups of windows are vertically aligned with each other. the vault is attached to the wall and surrounds the window as such with proudly sculpted white marble decorated with coats of arms.
[TOP MIDDLE SKETCH]
7 crenellations / 4 crenellations / weak
10 vaults / 4 vaults / 6 vaults / strong

[TOP RIGHT]
note how well this curved facade works an unbroken line of tie rods under the belfry as many unglazed windows as crenellations but not aligned with them. —the 2 windows under the belfry are smaller, the surrounds are even bigger, plain masonry. The 4 vaults under the belfry are smaller; there are no sculpted heads at the spring of the vaults, which run sloping but without projecting all the way to the big wall

3 groups of vertically aligned windows of which the middle 2 have been blocked up

placed vertically beneath the belfry 2 smaller windows of which the top one is ornamented differently.

plain wall, entry to one side vertically beneath the second-last window—systematically set forward on each side of the door, 2 very ugly statues, Adam and Eve; farther out still on big cubic bases 2 colossal statues, The Victor very ugly and Michelangelo's David (at present the David has been removed with its base) which is a great shame and completely spoils the door by leaving it no raison d'être.

Above the door a charming arrangement of coats of arms with 2 lions in high relief (green stone) the rest in white marble. —In a space under the overhang of the machicolation are handsome coats of arms painted in rich tones (white, black, red, blue, and gold.)

[BOTTOM LEFT]
note the overhang

the corner crenellation with the raised tip is always higher than the crenellations in the middle.

Note that the belfry is rectangular. In the upper part 3 levels on the sides, 4 on the front. etc.

[BOTTOM RIGHT]
4 enormous columns (enormous because the access door to the top is in one of them) support the crown; the capitals are superbly strong and finely done; all the delicacy of the edifice is accumulated in the upper part at a formidable height. —In the lower part the eye sees only the rock of the overhang, oppressive for the soul. In all the upper part the [craftsman] shows himself an artist: he has decorated his crenellations the little square windows are divided by a pretty marble colonnette; the machicolations are tapered, the vaults finely worked with a white fillet (light yellow) At the very top the lion stands out as a black wrought-iron silhouette against the sky. It's magnificent.

at the bottom of the machicolations, coats of arms in colors more subtle than lower down.

—P. 37

Sketches of the plan and cross section of Certosa del Galluzo, the fourteenth-century Carthusian monastery in Val d'Ema, 1907

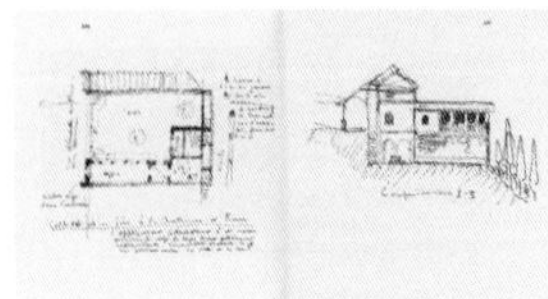

[LEFT]
Splendid view of Florence and the Apennines

2 small seats in the embrasure

[PLAN: TOP TO BOTTOM, LEFT TO RIGHT]
garden / loggia / study / bedroom / M's room / cloister

[RIGHT]
b the pool for water for the garden
a well with chain
c terracotta rim to sit on with flowers against the wall

[BOTTOM]
A brother's cell in the Carthusian monastery of Ema would apply admirably to workers' housing, the buildings of the loggia being entirely independent. amazing tranquility; the high wall could frame the view of the street.

Cross section I – II

—P. 38

Charles-Edouard Jeanneret to his parents, from Italy, 9 October 1907

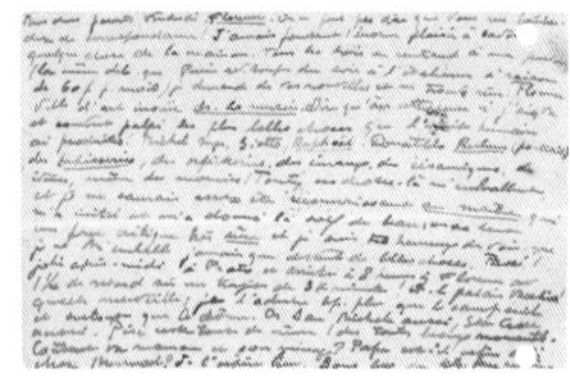

My dear parents, Friday. Florence. You couldn't say you're bombarding me with letters! All the same, it would be an enormous pleasure to know something about home. Every evening when I get back to my boarding house (the same room as Perrin, plus Italian-style evening meal for 60 francs a month) I ask for news of you and find nothing. Florence incredible art City in the museums. To think that as of now I've seen and often handled some of the most beautiful things the human spirit has ever created. Michelangelo, Giotto, Raphael. Donatello Rubens (portraits) tapestries, gold and silver ware, enamels, ceramics, ivory, and even mummies! All these things knock me out, and I could never express my gratitude to the master who introduced me to beauty and gave me a thirst for it; I feel I have a very sure critical sense and am delighted to see that I only ever get excited by beautiful things. Spent a nice afternoon in Prato, and reached Florence at 8, 1¼⁄6 hours late for a trip lasting 34 minutes! Oh, the Palazzo Vecchio! what a marvel;
I admire it very much, more than the Campanile and the Duomo. Then there's San Michele too, and Santa Croce too. Even so, Pisa remains one of the great moments. How's Mom doing with her house cleaning?
Did Dad finally go to Mermod's?
I hope so. Big kisses from the son, and goodbye.

—P. 38

Sketches of the interior of the Basilica of Santa Croce, Florence, 1907

[TOP LEFT SKETCH]
pillars 1.50 dim

these pillars only project 5 cm in the entire church 14 pillars

[BOTTOM LEFT SKETCH]
the entire construction is of brown stone all the infilling is white lime.

[TOP RIGHT SKETCH]
octagonal pillars without capitals admirably strong and simple

The secret of the enormous grandeur St Croce takes on lies in the alignment abcdefgh enormous luminous ogive formed by the plain wall of the brightly lit transept and seen through the interlacing of vaults and pillars.

principle of large areas very very large, held up by enormous arches with very few pillars.

there are only 7 pillars on each side of the nave

[BOTTOM RIGHT SKETCH]
roof structure with a span of at least 20 meters all painted with green, red and white ornamentation, natural color of brown wood.

—P. 40

Detail of interior columns and capitals, Basilica of San Vitale, Ravenna, 15 October 1907

6th century
Ravenna San Vitale
Porphyry columns. Carved and gilded capitals. Modeled stucco vaults. The rest mosaic. oct. 1907.
Ch.E. Jeanneret

—P. 41

Rendering of mosaic depicting, as Jeanneret notes, "procession of 21 virgins," Basilica of Sant'Apollinare Nuovo, Ravenna, 15 October 1907

St Apollinaris-the-New. Ravenna. 1907

Procession of 21 virgins. all making different gestures, but whose finery alternates 1 to 1, the necklaces and belts are made with fragments of mother-of-pearl, which creates a very distinctive effect. Before the decline the guttae must have been very noble. The effect of the palms, very subtle and delicious. In brief, mostly secondary hues, with lots of gold and strong red, green, and blue highlights, mostly green and red.—underscored by a modeled stucco frieze. The interplay of the gold sequins is also obtained by the more or less oblique placing of mosaic fragments.

—P. 43

Sketches of Piazza San Marco, Venice, 1907

[LEFT]
a superb engraving
this size
a big beautiful end-paper
ask for a comparable frame

[MIDDLE]
a seething crowd

Veduta della Piazza di S. Marco nell ultimo giorno di Carnevale
(Domenico Luisa)
(Big double engraving 50 x 38 cm)

[RIGHT]
View of Piazza di S. Marco

—P. 43

Sketches of exterior details, Doge's Palace, Venice, 1907

[BOTTOM LEFT]
The big roll molding a has prevailed and follows every phase of the curve, the overall envelope of the molding is 1 double chamfer; take good note of this and don't think that this molding is hollowed out. In this way it achieves considerable body force and plasticity.

[TOP RIGHT]
All in all the voids of the trefoils don't count in the construction, they don't weaken it at all, on the contrary they prevent chipping of the bonding B always leading, in the long term, to the points c the memory of the solid walls of the Parthenon which have taken on a singular appearance. Remember this procedure when a great weight has to rest on assemblages like this.

[BOTTOM RIGHT]
The windows are set into the facade. A single strip scored to create shades of gray surrounds the window

—P. 44

Charles-Edouard Jeanneret to his parents, from Vienna, 3 November 1907

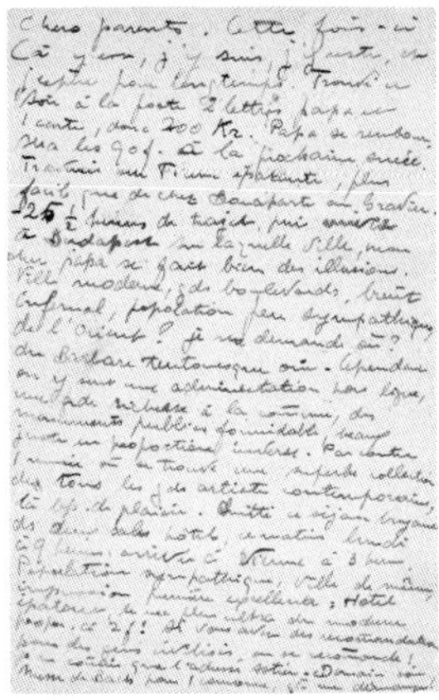

Dear parents. This time it's okay, I'm here, I'm staying and I hope for a long time. At the post office this evening found 2 letters dad and 1 card, so 200 Kr. Dad will be paid back the 90 f. next time round. Amazing crossing of Fiume, easier than from Bonaparte's to Le Gravier.—25½ hours' travel, then arrival in Budapest, a city my dear dad has lots of illusions about. Modern, wide boulevards, infernal noise, people not very nice, from the East? I wonder where? Teutonic barbarism yes. However you sense an excellent administrative system, a very wealthy city, some great public monuments, beautiful in exactly inverse proportion. On the other hand 1 museum with a superb collection of all the great contemporary artists, really enjoyed myself there. Finished the noisy stay in two dirty hotels this Monday morning at 9 o'clock, arrival in Vienna at 3 o'clock. People agreeable, city likewise, first impression excellent: Hotel a knockout, the ne plus ultra of clean modernity, for 2 f. if you have any civilized people to recommend, we recommend ourselves. I know only the Astier address. Tomorrow evening, Bach Mass for 1 crown, I'm so impatient!

—P. 44

Charles-Edouard Jeanneret to his parents, from Vienna, 17 November 1907

My dear parents. Your son's losing his grip, getting bad-tempered. Everything's going wrong, everything's mocking us! But if nothing else my calves are building up. Tuesday chasing people nowhere to be found. Finally Wednesday the Swiss Minister very nice, then running madly all over Vienna for rooms, went on for 2 whole days; finally, miraculously, in the mass of sordid overpriced hovels found 1 pretty room, 4th floor, with Christian people, patriots, looks good to me and for 28 f. The others were 40 to 70 f. Found something similar for Perrin. Today chased madly after the trunk, pointless, couldn't get it; I'm enraged and chomping at the bit; a religious holiday into the bargain, shops closed, forced inactivity.—Got on friendly terms with Blondin from Geneva. The schools aren't looking good. Fees very high, no room. No information to be had. To kill time this afternoon, at the Herbstaustellung ~~exhi~~ less pitiful, disconcerting. Hard going in other words. Poste restante again, will

[RIGHT MARGIN]
soon send happier news, I hope.

—P. 44

Envelope from the Vienna letter, 17 November 1907

[TOP]
we wash at the Germans' as often as we can

[RIGHT]
I receive nothing but compliments on my

[BOTTOM]
exquisite ~~proportion~~ pronunciation! everywhere I'm taken

[LEFT]
for a native of Baden or an Englishman!

—P. 44

Envelope from the Vienna letter, 3 November 1907

[BOTTOM LEFT]
Big kisses to all, I'm waiting for details of Albert and news of you as well. The least details interest me. I realize that I'm a thoroughbred, Mrs. Blum was right, I'm a terrible pessimist.

—P. 45

Notes and facade sketch, c. 1910, Knize department store, Vienna, designed by Adolf Loos in 1909–10

A very handsome store [?] all in cyanite green. The charm comes from the monolithic look. The window panes are mounted in natural maple.

The mount a is this size little curtains of green silk. then a/ little table of ~~sil~~ maple also. The house monogram placed on the corner of the window pane. on the architrave, the awards 1 on the right, 2 on the left of polished brass

—P. 45

Plans and sections, Café Fledermaus, Vienna, 1907

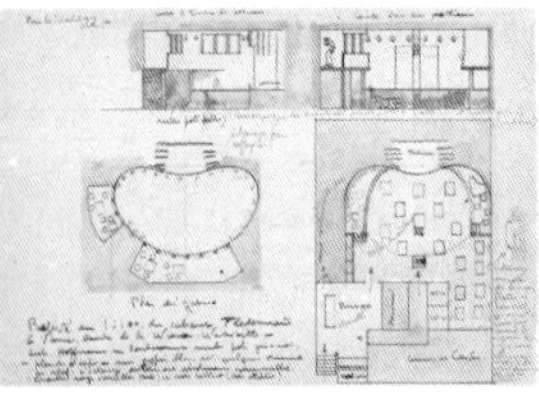

[TOP LEFT]
Paris 16 April 1907
Ch. E. Jt

[TOP LEFT PLAN]
section through the podium

polished marble (slabs)

note that the balustrade comes just up to the height of a seated man (interior)

[TOP RIGHT PLAN]
Section facing the podium

[BOTTOM LEFT PLAN]
lighting by reflection

plan of the galleries
Drawing 1:10 of the Fledermaus Cabaret in Vienna, built by the Wiener Werkstätte — arch. Hoffmann, — Base polished gray-black marble, floor — carpet — wall white gypsum with some relief ornamentation. The surrounding lighting is absolutely remarkable. Furniture vermilion (cloth) and gloss black (kiln-dried wood)

[BOTTOM RIGHT PLAN]
podium / behind the scenes / level 0.60 / soft carpet
bar / ceramic tiles / staff / WC
cloakroom / kitchens and cellars

lighting set in the wall flame so slight that you can't see it when the bulbs of the [?] are lit but shines [astonishingly] once they are turned off

—P. 50

Charles-Edouard Jeanneret to his parents, from Munich, 29 June 1910 (first two pages)

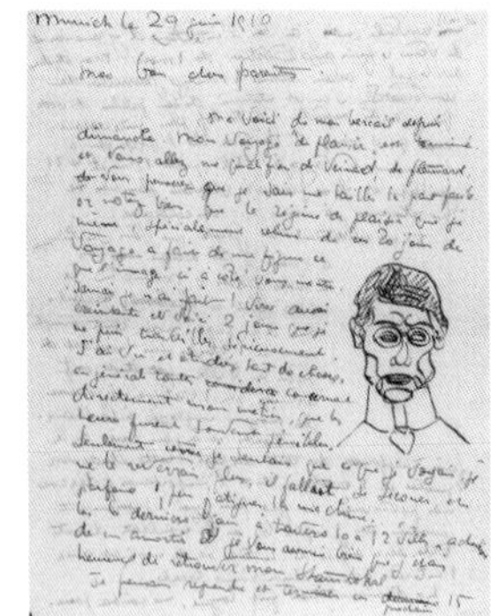

Munich, 29 June 1910

My dearest parents.
Here I am back in the fold since Sunday. My "pleasure" trip is over. and you're going to call me lucky, lazy, and you'll be thinking I know how to take things easy. But note that the pleasurable way of life I've been leading, especially during these 20 days of travel has made my face what the picture on the side shows you. I've never had such an exhausting trip and for the last 2 days I haven't been able to work seriously. I've seen and studied so many things in general all ~~considera~~ concerning my profession directly, that the hours often pass painfully. But since I felt that what I was seeing I would never see again, I had to shake myself up, and sometimes tire the machine out a little. The last 6 days through 10 to 12 cities, really finished me off and I can tell you I was glad to get back to my Stamlokal.

I thought I'd be starting again and getting finished these ~~last~~ next 15

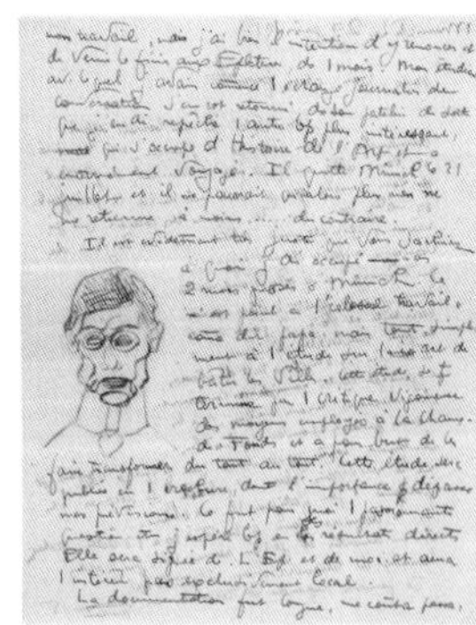

my work, but I mean to drop it and come finish it at Les Eplatures, in 1 month. My student with whom I had begun daily conversation exchanges has gone back to his country town so I picked up another 1 much more interesting, who's doing History of Art and has traveled a lot. He's leaving Munich on 21 July, and maybe then there'll be nothing holding me back, at least… the contrary.

It's obviously quite right that you should know what I've spent ~~my~~ these last 2 months doing in Munich. Not at all a "colossal job" as dad says, but quite simply a study on the art of building cities. This study f ends with a vigorous critique of the methods used at La Chaux-de-Fonds and is aimed at changing them from A to Z. This study will be published as a brochure, which has turned out bigger than I expected. For me this was a passionate issue and I set great store by ~~these~~ its direct results. It will be signed by L'Ep. and me and its interest will not be exclusively local.

The documentation was a lengthy business, and cost me […]

—P. 51

Watercolor of Schloss Sanssouci, Potsdam, 1910

[LEFT]
I was astonished by a strange, utter solitude … all of a sudden the police arrive and throw me out howling like wolves! … I had only just finished my work

[RIGHT]
this watercolor was done on 5 Nov. 1910 at 3 p.m. in Potsdam at the intersection of the Schloss and the Sans-Souci at the moment when Wilhelm II and tsar Nicholas of Russia were about to go by

—P. 51

Sketch of Schloss Sanssouci, c. October 1910

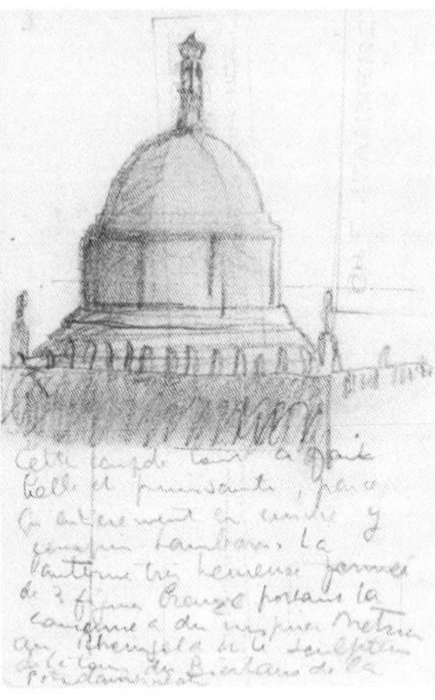

This dome really handsome and commanding, because entirely of copper including drum. The very harmonious lantern formed by 3 figures bronze supporting the lantern must have inspired Metrier for the rheingold and the sculptor of the tower of the Bierhaus on Potsdamerplatz

—P. 58

Sketches of the Parthenon, Athens, 1911

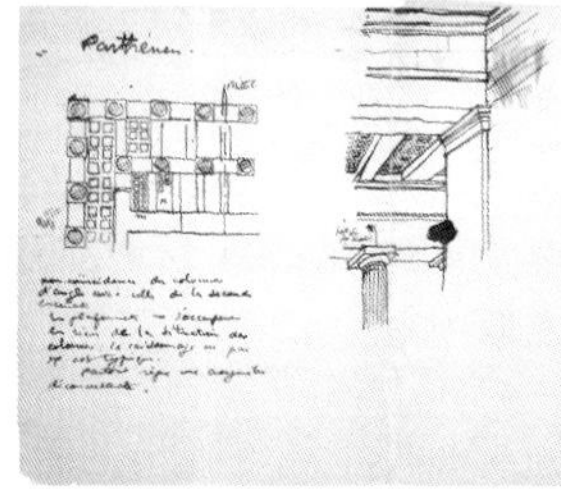

[TOP LEFT]
Parthenon

Mittel

[RIGHT]
must be narrower

[BOTTOM LEFT]
the corner columns not coincident with those of the second precinct.

the ceiling work takes no account of the placing of the columns; e.g., the coffering here is typical.

everywhere a disconcerting asymmetry prevails.

—P. 59

Sketch of the Parthenon, Athens, 1911

The ext wall of the temple of Jupiter is made of fine glazed stucco divided into panels and the effect is beautiful.
The grooves are
14½ / 5½ / 2
what is characteristic is a–b

[RIGHT]
La foule aura [?] de Cézanne et de Claudel

—P. 60

Sketches and plans of House of the Silver Wedding, Pompeii, 13–28 September 1911

[LEFT TO RIGHT, TOP TO BOTTOM]
abacus molding

Villa of Diomedes

garden pillar / terrace / outer wall / section

fountain
pavilion

2 stories the houses overlooking the garden

—P. 61

Plan of the Forum, Pompeii, September 1911

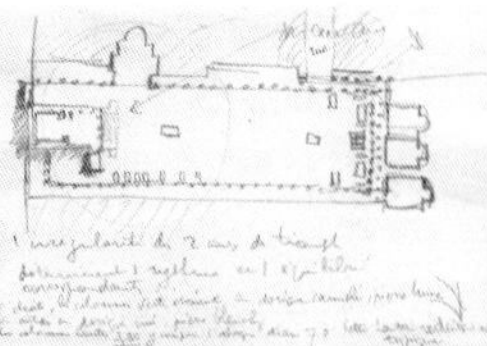

The asymmetry of the two triumphal arches establishes a corresponding rhythm and equilibrium

On the right, the green column were fluted Doric, brown stone

The others round Doric, white stone

The columns tall, 3.85 including the abacus diam 70 This small lantern is characteristic

—P. 64

Charles-Edouard Jeanneret and Léon Perrin to the La Chaux-de-Fonds theater, 26 July 1912

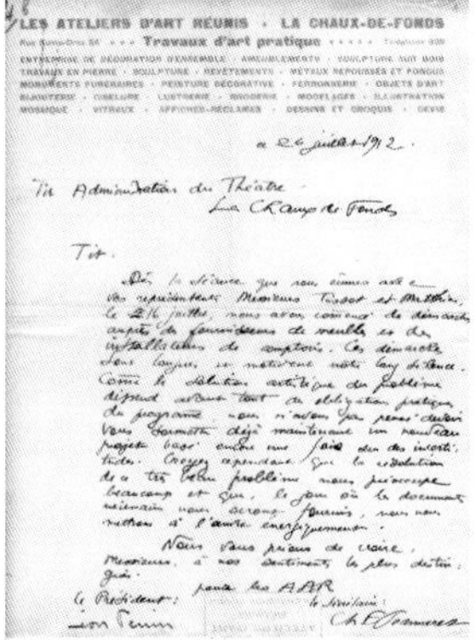
LES ATELIERS D'ART RÉUNIS · LA CHAUX-DE-FONDS
Travaux d'art pratique

This 26 July 1912

Messrs the Administrators, Théâtre La Chaux-de-Fonds

Sirs,

Since our session with your representatives Messrs Tissot and Mathias on 16 July, we have begun canvassing suppliers of furniture and installers of counters. This is a lengthy business and is the reason for our long silence. As the artistic solution to the problem depends above all on the practical obligations contained in the brief, we thought there was no need to submit a new project based yet again on uncertainties. Rest assured that we are giving all our attention to solving this very complex problem and that once we have received the necessary documents we shall go to work energetically.

Yours faithfully,
For the AARs

President:
Léon Perrin

Secretary:
Ch E Jeanneret

—P. 64

Letterhead for Charles-Edouard Jeanneret and his firm, La Chaux-de-Fonds, 1912

CH.-E. JEANNERET · ARCHITECTE

Ch.-E. Jeanneret Architect
Architect of the Ateliers d'Art Réunis (United Art Studios)

Construction of villas, country homes, rental buildings – Industrial constructions – Specializing in reinforced concrete – Renovations and repairs – Shop interiors – Interior design – Landscape design

La Chaux-de-Fonds, 54 rue Numa-Droz *2 August 1912*. Telephone 939

—PP. 80–81

Page from *Oeuvre complète: Volume 1, 1910–29*, reproducing sketches Jeanneret made on his trip to Venice, Rome, and France

[TOP LEFT SKETCH]
To be added to the view of the Piazzetta de Marieschi
A. San Giorgio maggiore B. ?
D. Countless statues
E obelisk at the corner of the cornice
a dome = unity with the others
G Regular flagstones (are there no drawings of the panels available now?)
"Forum minus Dini … etc."

[TOP MIDDLE SKETCH]
to be extended / to be extended
canal
quay / quay

A the bell tower at the end of a long square
B overall unity provided by the steeples
B' in low relief
The dentil in various forms characterizes all the houses
The unity of the paving (cobblestones and flagstones). The porch of each house and church is a neutral point.
E a cross set in the ground.
G (plan) the street // to the canal closes off the view
"Templum et platea F.F. Ord. min. Conventualium etc."
Marchieri

[TOP RIGHT SKETCH]
The diameters or dimensions or areas of the squares resulting from the competitions Boffran, Soufflot, Servandoni etc. took part in, – are fairly constant

80 toises / Place des Vosges (Royale) / realized

80 / end rue de Tournon lined up Luxembourg / project
75 / Bercy crossroads / project

70x80 / Vendôme / realized
ditch

90 / Louis XV Concorde

200 / market / 60/60 / 60/60

70/70 / Vieux Louvre / realized

90/65 / in front of Vieux Louvre (St Germain l'auxerrois)

Stanislas Nancy (royal square XV)

40/36 / royal square in Reims

Madeleine / meeting point with the place de la Concorde, already realized
Later came a bridge and the Palais Bourbon

market

The need to open up the city, to gut it a little, led to using the Seine as a divide, not previously the case (triggered by Henri IV's Pont Neuf attempt)

Seine

[MIDDLE AND BOTTOM LEFT SKETCHES]
CAPITOLII ROMANI VERA IMAGO UT NUNC EST

NB another engraving (exactly the same) is additionally divided by radii on the square (paged as 13)

in Roma per Gio Vascosmo Rossi alla Pace

big etching 50x35. Superb with very big classical lettering in the upper part

Here fragment of a plan at the beginning of the album

[MIDDLE CENTER SKETCH]
President's residence / Statue of the King / city hall

Elevation of the royal square in Rennes
seen from the clocktower side

[MIDDLE RIGHT SKETCH]
Triumphal fountain built in Nancy on Place de l'Intendance / rue Royale / rue St Rémy /

60 toises x 50 / "the statue of the king can be seen from almost everywhere" architect Gabriel

in Nancy the statue of Louis XV was in the middle of Place Stanislas
standing statue / ancient warrior
4 seated women / octagonal

Hotel des fermes du Roy / Hotel de la bourse

Hotel de Dordogne / Garonne fountain

Garonne river

pilasters
columns / statue / columns

Bordeaux royal square

[BOTTOM RIGHT SKETCH]
the belfry
hotel des fermes
it goes underneath

belfry
steeples
sculpted mullions
iron grid
statue visible in this splendid setting
the rest being houses

as ancient warrior
trophies on the ground

here use is made of what already exists

—P. 81

Notes by Jeanneret about various family members and friends, 30 April 1917

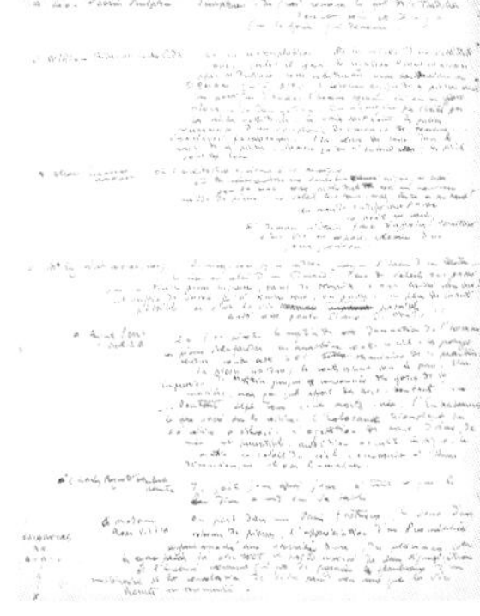

To Léon Perrin
Sculpture: a way of getting back to tradition Everything is folly and there's Only folly

To William Ritter and Janko Cadra
The contemplative life… From the niche of a cathedral … yes. Alas, one must look ahead and fulfill one's destiny. This cathedral is as much a House for the DEVIL as for GOD. The tragic heroism of these stones is worthy of a gateway to hell; here man expresses in a titanic effort his damnation. One can't imagine Chartres by looking at other cathedrals: the foundations are like the successive levels of a symphony of brass and thunders … unfinished, inevitably. Moonlight in the darkness of these stones, a clamor that goes unheard; the centuries are too remote.

To Albert Jeanneret musician
Where architecture is equivalent to music. where you will feel with a sensibility as acute as me In the night this cathedral ~~of~~ is a new world of stone. The sun kills everything, but still leaves so much! an indifferent world goes by the poet is alone if only tomorrow was not all business! Yet it's Life and hope, one day toward being able.
To Mr. Eug Will lawyer (my)
Can you make out whether this dial marks the hour of a destiny …
– mine
or that of an Edmond? – So many sun have crossed its old rough stone, so many storms have left it purposeless! It's enough to know that through everything, we pass. As much beauty as Possible and ~~normal support~~ life is possible And this poor Chaux-de-Fonds too!!

To Auguste Perret architect
Here one penetrates the mystery of man's damnation. these stone raised in anathema against the sky. These fists held out against this wicked LAW of gravity. Stone is hard; the roads cry out beneath our steps. An impression of almost consummate control over the forces of matter, but with what effort from flying buttresses! …
And yet seven towers were stillborn. The blaze, the sacred fire on the hill, the holocaust triumphing over the hill has failed. The turbulence of so many souls, of night is perceptible, listening obscures symbol, in the morning the sun in the sky was restoring these human things to their rightful dimensions.

To Charles Auguste Humbert painter
Day after day I taste everything the Good lord has put on his table.

To Mrs. Rose Vildra
One loses in lavish Paris the sense of a volume for stones, the appreciation of a Prometheus having wrenched flames from hard quarries, and having set them down there, with all the senseless weight of their signification and the senseless torment that made pygmies the burning torches of a millennium and the consolation of living for all those whom life batters and torments.

[LEFT]
CHARTRES 30 APRIL 1917

2 Becoming Le Corbusier
(1917–1926)

—P. 88
Pages from Charles-Edouard Jeanneret's journal, 12 May 1918

[…] of another destiny, mine, the hard and vehement, the solitary and violent and indefatigable. This city is beautiful, and life is becoming good there.

My thoughts on art rise toward ~~bie~~ ever the plastic, ~~all~~ a form, a line more esoteric. My attempts are formless, disappointing. My entire imagination is at work. I want a clarity, a sheen, a sharpness that tolerate only pure pencil, discipline and rhythm, and moderation of color. And I paint filth. My women are bestially lascivious, prurient, in heat. And I stop work on a female nude, for the texture of her back, her breasts, her mouth is so adorable, they're like a sudden dream I would spoil with my coarse fingers. My sensual excesses are almost all outside of ~~the~~ this bed and I get a more intimate painful joy from thrusting my tongue into a great fresh rose, one of those roses now filling my bedrooms, so big, so red, so dense, so depths, and whose fragrance is a saliva oh so much more refreshing!

Just now I'm enjoying the good times too much, and my courage collapses at the idea of beginning an art task. In twenty hurried minutes, to throw one's cry on paper, with violent stains of red ocher and blue, this was the intoxicating promise of a possible talent demanding only the time to express itself. But to envisage maybe every week one whole good day for painting calmly, that's the anguish of an entire vocation to be faced. Paint seriously? Hold on, that means becoming a painter. I shrink from the trap my hand is moving toward.

And inside me, the choice has already been made. Instinctively I make for home to avoid pointless camaraderie. Or if I head for the attractions of the boulevards where the women are, it's to find an expression of the most mathematically ideal form of the dream of beauty that my brushes ~~don't~~ strive to try to create.

Sudden encounters: yesterday a word in a conversation about the tomb of the Medici, and all this Sunday it's been Michelangelo and Leonardo haunting me. The women of Titian and Giorgione. Italy forever! And a style ever more formal, written, an Egyptian clarity. I still have more faith in modern painting, more faith in those many people who dream like me, but who, more gifted, actually achieve.

How alone a man is in the world. I received from Mom a long letter nothing to do with any of this. First this cannon, these bombers, which no longer exist and were never any more of a nuisance than a horsefly that stings you when you're running through the fields. And then above all a […]

—P. 88
Charles-Edouard Jeanneret to officials in La Chaux-de-Fonds, 6 October 1921

Paris, 6 October

Residential Police of the commune of LA Chaux-de-Fonds

Sirs,

Having definitively left La Chaux-de-Fonds to devote myself completely to my Paris office, I would be obliged if you could tell me what I must do to put my residential status in order.

I hold a passport. My birth certificate is held at the State Chancellery.

Regarding payment of my taxes, I shall inform you when I have contacted the Canton finance department.

Sincerely yours,

C. E Jeanneret
Architect
20 rue Jacob, Paris

—P. 89
Charles-Edouard Jeanneret to his parents, 17 February 1918

Paris, this 17 Feb. 1918

My dear ones.

I've been deliberately ignoring you! Since November 1917, you haven't found the time to write to me—three months! It took the bombers and their bombs. I'd decided not to be the first to break this unbelievable silence. Maybe you think of me every day, the way I so frequently think of you, but that remains in the realm of the intangible. It's vital that something be said from time to time, given that our senses are organized to perceive objectively. You'll never see me late with my letters unless you push me to it. So much for that.

In fact the bombers could have annihilated me, along with all those people who drew an unlucky number that night. A bomb fell right by my office and another one right by where I live. I was halfway between the two and spent the alert on the Pont des Arts; the sight was incredible and you could hear everything. But amid the roar of the cannons and the crashing of the bombs, I couldn't make anything out clearly, and I only found out the next day that the bombers had at last reached Paris and dumped their scrap metal. The moon's coming back, and the Boche will be back with it. Right now, on this freezing night, you can hear the drone of the fighter planes. What Parisians are being offered is psychological safety.

This freezing night has more pressing concerns for me. At Alfortville I've more than 1500 francs' worth of merchandise, made over the last three days, and by tomorrow the frost could have wiped it out. The best laid plans of mice and men. Alfortville is taking up a lot of my time. This venture will become interesting and rewarding if the "ifs" remain "ifs" and don't come too nastily true. Since my recent adventures I've opted for a salutary skepticism which in no way limits my spirit and energy. I'm more than ever ready to try anything, and mature enough to cope with life's setbacks. This could have been a triumphal letter. I've been making an enormous effort these last two months. The symphony was on its way to a dazzling tutti… Collapse. Incident … maybe accident! Alas, despite my fighting spirit, my heart is still feeble and suffers.

Out of the embers of my chaux-de-Fonnière adventure—still smoking over there—I'm vain enough to want to blow fanfares like a fart up their nose, like banners to brandish over them As long as I don't get the satisfaction I'm after, what I say will remain obscure, like what I'm writing here. I'm waiting, I'm working on the situation that will allow my self-respect its revenge.

Apart from that, about this life of mine you want details, nothing, or very little. In any case, to have done with the subject, rest assured that Mr. Montparnasse and Mr. Montmartre, whom you were worried about, never see me. My entire life is taken up between the Opera and St. Augustin, where the heart of business beats. And my work is nothing but business, intensely and for as many working hours as there are in the day. This would be sickening if I weren't finding some pleasure in it; if, in the intense life of business, I weren't starting to unearth lots of the secrets of the human mind—its beauties, or at least its grandeur.

[RIGHT MARGIN]
"them" the fools and the jealous

II
And so my dwelling remains empty, and even, some nights when I haven't moved a chair for almost a week, hostile—as if death might manifest itself in these impassive objects: a cup, a curtain, a flowerpot, laid out by the alien hand of a cleaning woman in a pattern no longer my own.

It's true that my office is agreeable, and in a locality I appreciate more every day. My early Paris days, on rue de Belzunce, were bleak.

Some evenings, though, the weather's fine and I paint. Everything goes into an album, each page home to a sensation. I'm increasingly convinced that man works for himself alone, to assuage the strange passions that are born with him and whose slave he is. And yet if he is actually to live—and not simply wear himself out—this effort must be known, discussed, and hated or loved by others; there has to be contact with people.

Ozenfant and I have realized that we are neighbors, him on rue de Penthièvre, me on rue d'Astorg, a hundred meters from each other. We often eat dinner together and his company is crucial to me. He's head and shoulders above me: there's a seriousness about his painting that allows limitless hope for the new trend in ideas, which rejects laxness in favor of harmony with the splendor of science. His spirit is grounded in real philosophy, in an affirmativeness that underpins the sheer boldness of his dream.

He earns his living running one of the most discerning fashion houses, together with Poiret's sister—who's fallen out with her brother. At the same time, in his work Ozenfant is constantly harassed by idiot fate—without letting it get him down, though. Innovators can't escape their destiny, and that destiny is always up to expectations.

Yes, dear dad, your letter was a tad "couldn't give a damn," and that's no compliment. You say, or write, "Has man gone back to being a beast for … ; has he lost his nobility? etc." You know very well it's not so. This is self-deception, a way of skirting the real problem. The man in the trenches is not a beast, he is of the most sublime nobility; and there are millions like him in every country. For on the contrary, the war has exalted mankind. The real question, rather, is to know why and for what we're fighting, in the name of what contemptible false idol, false belief, or criminally false ideal. On the contrary, the problem has to be looked at in terms of its solutions, because solutions there are. And the worst upheavals in attitudes or the conventions will never be anything compared to the horrors of these times. Dear dad, your last letter but one was magnificent in its style and ideas. In your next one, snap out of it! Excuse me, but it's because I know you can do it; it's because I'm so sorry to think that with all your talents, you're not leaving us enough tangible memories. I've told you over and over: you had the best possible remedy for your disgusting profession. And there's still time. You could have written the diary[…]

—P. 95

Letter of agreement from the Société d'Applications du Béton Armé (SABA) to Charles-Edouard Jeanneret, 24 June 1918

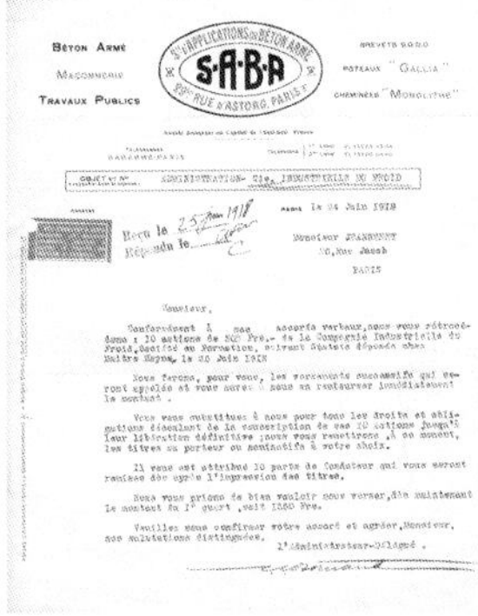

Subject and no. to be identified in the reply Administration. 01. Industrielle du froid

Paris 24 June 1918
Received on *25 June 1918*
Replied on [?]

Monsieur Jeanneret
20 rue Jacob
Paris

Sir,
In accordance with our verbal agreement, we convey: 10 shares for 500 Frs.—of the Compagnie Industrielle du Froid, a Company-in-Formation, pursuant to the Articles filed with Maître Moyne, 25 June 1918.

We will make all subsequent required payments on your behalf, and you will reimburse us that amount immediately.

You will stand in for us for all rights and obligations resulting from the subscription of these 10 Shares until they are entirely paid up; we will deliver the certificates to you at that time, either to bearer or registered as you prefer.

You are assigned 10 founders' shares, which will be delivered to you as soon as the certificates are printed.

Would you be so kind as to pay us now the amount due for the first quarter, that is, 1,250 Frs.

Please confirm your agreement, and believe us to be, Sir, most sincerely yours,

the Managing Director,
[signature]

—P. 96

Front and back of postcard of Paris with doodles by Charles-Edouard Jeanneret, c. 1923

[TOP TO BOTTOM, LEFT TO RIGHT]
TOILET PAPER OR REVOLUTION

regulating line

NO ENTRY
WATCH OUT OZENFANT

The Almanach Salesman.

The dung beetle*

[LEFT TO RIGHT, TOP TO BOTTOM]
What about your prospectuses?? old man!

Long live Louis XV
Go ahead, hey bastard
The dung beetle[*]
foolish simpleton

the bicycle for cleaning glasses

BICYCLE SCAFFOLDING! FOR HORSES

LOOK O'CUNT-O-CLAST-BIDET
like Mr. faux-pas of the same name
don't bawl me out—ok?
Happy New Year! A juicy pay packet
–O august Perret—
–gust'av—
Claude Perret biznizman
Buggered by the Solomite Representative.

[*Play on Le Corbusier's name:
le Corps Bousier
le corps = body
bousier = dung beetle]

—P. 96

Amédée Ozenfant to Charles-Edouard Jeanneret, 14 June 1921

14 June 1921

My dear Jeanneret,

I tried to call you yesterday morning beginning at 9:30, the connection only went through around half past noon and you had gone out.

I put the call through again, and hope to have better luck.

I'm glad of your letter, received yesterday morning; it is proof that you are reflecting on the directions to give your life.

I have, believe me, suffered a great deal in these last months because of the disorder brought into your life by the several circumstances … ; you had reached an extremely overexcited state that caused me to suffer for you, for you seemed very unhappy and very much at sea. At sea to such an extent that I really didn't know what to tell you—knowing very well that there wasn't much you could do at the moment, don't take that as a lack of understanding or selfishness!

I'm very aware—and have commiserated with you about it—that an important cog is missing in your life, that's why sometimes the whole machine "free wheels," unfortunately it's very hard not to install it oneself, the most devoted friendship can't help much.

One must first of all get clear in one's mind that to fulfill its purpose this cog must be
1: in place
2: that its place must be made for it, and that is not only of the senses; basically, it's the mechanism of the heart; the heart or what we agree to call that that's what has to be satisfied when all is said and done. You know what dis-illusionment comes with venal love.

You're going to have to address this; you have gas but no oil; even if it takes time one has to take care of the oil, otherwise it seizes up.

You were seized up; you have to look within yourself; I think you'll find that the casualties of the struggle and of life have somewhat atrophied a certain softness without which one is somewhat steely; sometimes one must put oneself a little in other people's place; the marvelous man of action that you are should sometimes make room for a little less rationalism, I'm expressing myself badly; not always in every case take the shortest path even when it means stepping on the toes of one's fellow creatures; civilized life must sometimes be marveled at, for it is marvelous that because of a social contract people don't slaughter each other in the street.

Above all you must be careful not to present yourself under the sometimes jarring light of the man who considers only the goal without assessing the means he employs; not to show too much one's contempt for the mass of others.

You know as well as I do that only merits count but we mustn't show this too much to the others of both sexes.

Sometimes you're like a tank, I admire that but let's not overdo anything.

You must give up affairs once and for all because they can corrupt you ambitious ones—yes, you.

Morality exists—there are physiological reasons for it, too.
Wartime affairs were corrupting; the people you associated with immoral; my father was not an ambitious man, that's why he's still a decent man. I don't have time to go into this now, but we'll chat about it again.

I don't entirely understand your letter when it talks of the need for us two to remain very close; you express yourself poorly. I created our union, of course it was providential for us. What symptom of a breach do you see? Sometimes I've had to feel sorry to see you with so little free time, regretted not seeing you work at the painting as much as necessary; that'll end; don't let it get you down.
I'm writing this letter in dribs and drabs because I'm interrupted at every line. Don't read any curtness into it old man; I beg you to stay in Cabourg for the week it was frightening to watch you live your life, you must get a little stupid in the sun, you were sick, it's too soon to put on the yoke again.

Your friend,
Ozenfant

—P. 102

Charles-Edouard Jeanneret to Raoul La Roche, 5 April 1921

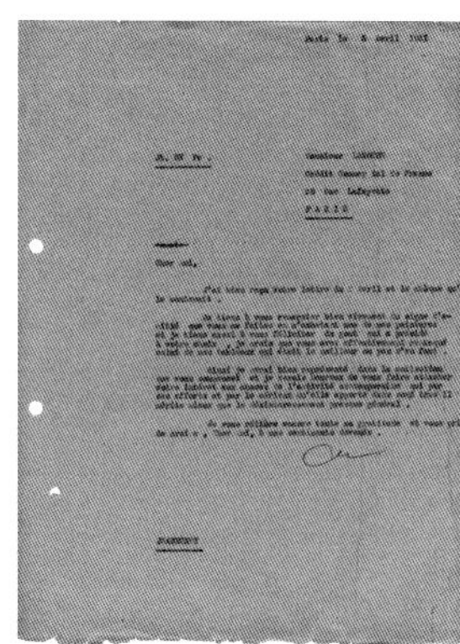

Paris, 5 April 1921

Mr. LAROCHE
Crédit Commercial de France
20 rue Lafayette
PARIS

~~Sir~~
Dear Friend,

Thank you for your letter of 2 April and the check it contained.

I would like to offer my warm thanks for your sign of friendship in buying one of my paintings, and would also like to congratulate you on the taste that governed your choice. I feel that you really have identified the best, or close to the best, from among my paintings.

Thus I shall be represented in the collection you are beginning to build up and would be pleased to guide you toward aspects of a contemporary scene that, in terms of hard work and dedication, deserves something better than near-general disinterest.

Assuring you once again of my deep gratitude. Sincerely yours,

[signature]
JEANNERET

—P. 104

Postcard from Le Corbusier to Yvonne Gallis, 26 December 1925

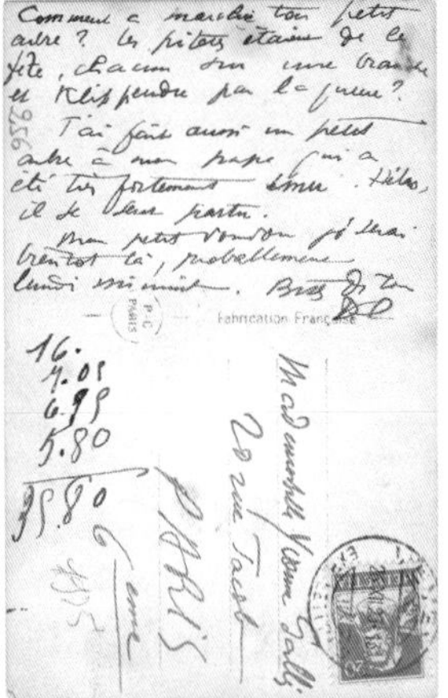

How did your little tree go? The [?] were there, each one on a branch and Klip hanging by his tail?

I also made a little tree for my father who was very touched. Alas, he feels he is leaving us.

My little Vonvon I'll soon be there, probably Monday midnight.

Kisses from your DD

—P. 108

André Bauchant to "Mr. Jeanneret," 10 August 1924

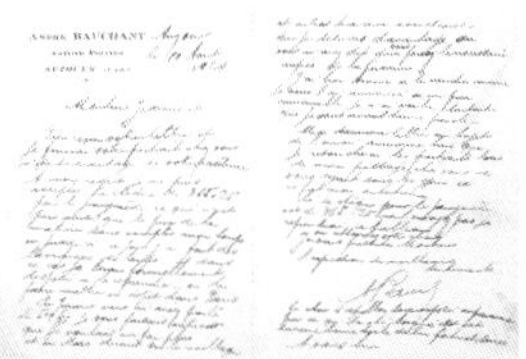

Auzouer
10 August 1924

Mr. Jeanneret,
Received your letter and I will finish your portrait at your place, not having the advantage of your patience.

I regret I cannot accept your check for 365.25 for the Ganymede which is just so to speak the cost of the material without counting my time because up until today I've given up my time—and in that case I shall be absolutely prepared to take it back—or have it put on consignment in Paris.

In January you talked about 500 Frs. I hinted that I wanted a little more and last March given the regluing and other additional jobs—that I wanted more then or you told me you'd take the necessary steps with the person.

In fact, I've found someone to sell it to as I told you I would for a suitable price I didn't want to mostly because I'd given you my word.

My ~~last~~ letter on the subject of the delivery in fact lets you know that I'll retouch the portraits when I come through at your place, because I don't have you in front of me and such was my intention

If the check for the Ganymede is for 365.25 don't send it I'll take the painting back or wait for your client

Best wishes,

[signature]

Apollo's chariot will be exhibited beforehand because it was [?] and is on good linen canvas, strong and tightly woven.

Best

—P. 112

Mimeograph handbill announcing *L'Esprit Nouveau*, c. 1920

L'ESPRIT NOUVEAU [THE NEW SPIRIT]

This is an expression we have been encountering more and more often in recent times. Will this be the name definitively taken by a highly distinctive state of mind we cannot help but notice around us? Is it only the germination of seeds existing in the fortunate early years of this century, or has the new spirit sprung fully armed and helmeted out of this long war? These are questions we are not foolish enough to think we can answer in a few lines.

To present this spirit of our epoch, to explain to all and lead all to understand the new, and at first sight most disconcerting creations of today's artists and writers, a review has been founded which has taken the very name, "L'ESPRIT NOUVEAU"

Its extremely curious program embraces:

EXPERIMENTAL AESTHETICS, PAINTING, SCULPTURE, ARCHITECTURE, LITERATURE, MUSIC, AESTHETICS FOR ENGINEERS, MUSIC HALL, CINEMA, THEATER, DRESS, BOOKS, FURNITURE, SPORTS, AESTHETICS OF MODERN LIFE etc.

Henceforth all those wishing to keep up with the trends of their time—intellectuals, men of action—will easily be able to do so thanks to this Review of a totally new kind and offering each month 130 pages of text and all sorts of other material. It will be of great service to all those who should make up a nation's elite, which is to say artists, academics, writers, industrialists, engineers and retailers, those true creators of the New Spirit.

3 Urban Visions and Purist Villas (1922–1935)

—P. 125

Renderings of the Immeubles-Villas for Paris reproduced in a journal

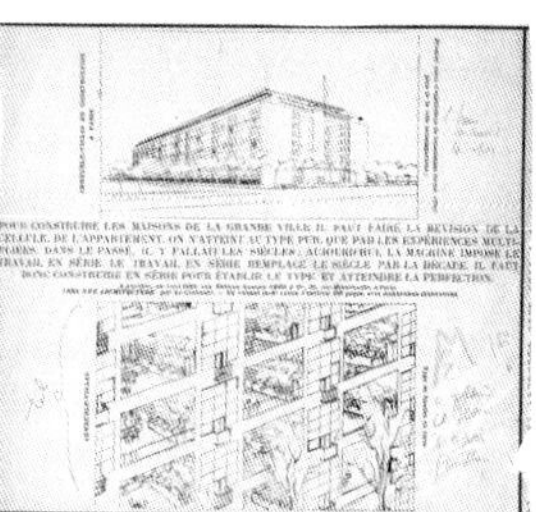

[TOP LEFT]
APARTMENT-VILLAS UNDER CONSTRUCTION IN PARIS.

[TOP RIGHT]
First attempt to apply closed development (See plan of the contemporary city.)

The hour / of work / of rest

[MIDDLE]
TO BUILD HOMES FOR THE GREAT CITIES WE MUST RECONSIDER THE CELL, THE APARTMENT. WE CAN ACHIEVE THE PURE TYPE ONLY THROUGH MULTIPLE EXPERIMENTS. IN THE PAST, IT TOOK CENTURIES; TODAY, MACHINES IMPOSE MASS PRODUCTION. MASS PRODUCTION REPLACES CENTURIES WITH DECADES. THUS WE MUST MASS-BUILD TO ESTABLISH THE TYPE AND ACHIEVE PERFECTION.

Forthcoming in April 1923, from Éditions Georges CRÈS & Cie, 21 rue Hautefeuille, in Paris. VERS UNE ARCHITECTURE, by Le Corbusier. – One volume in octavo of about 300 pages, with many illustrations.

[BOTTOM LEFT]
VILLA-APARTMENTS.

[BOTTOM RIGHT]
Example of the glass facade.

To be redone this drawing according Pavilion

—P. 130

Typescript by Le Corbusier, "Une cité contemporaine" (A contemporary city)

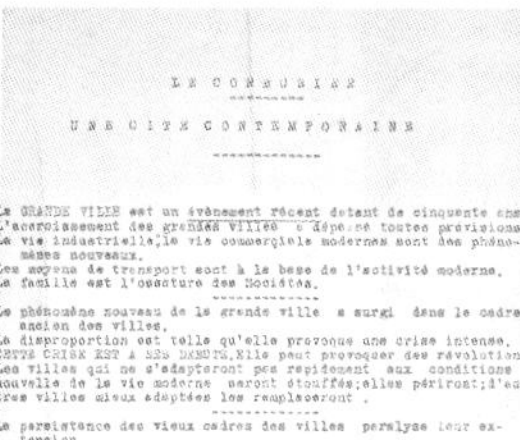

LE CORBUSIER
A CONTEMPORARY CITY

The BIG CITY is a recent event going back fifty years. The growth of big cities has outstripped all predictions.

Modern industrial life and modern trading life are new phenomena.

Means of transport are the basis of modern business.

The family is the framework of Societies.

The new phenomenon of the big city has arisen in the old urban context.

The discrepancy is such that it is causing a grave crisis. THIS CRISIS IS ONLY BEGINNING. It could cause revolutions. Cities that do not adapt rapidly to the new conditions of modern life will suffocate; they will die; other, better-adapted cities will replace them.

The survival of the old city structures paralyzes their expansion.

Industrial and trading life will be wiped out in old-fashioned cities.

The conservative system in the big cities prevents expansion of transport, clogs the cities, weakens the economy, kills progress, discourages innovation.

The breakdown of the old cities and the intensity of modern work lead human beings to irritability and illness. Modern life demands the recovery of expended energy. Hygiene and psychological well-being depend on cities' layout. Without hygiene or psychological well-being the family cannot survive. A country that lets the institution of the family decay dies.

Today's cities cannot cope with the transformations in modern life. They must be transformed.

To transform cities, we must pinpoint the fundamental principles of modern urban planning.
Big cities govern the lives of their countries. If the big city suffocates, the country bogs down.

—P. 133

Plans comparing population density in Paris in previous centuries and Le Corbusier's recommended schemes for two different densities in modern cities

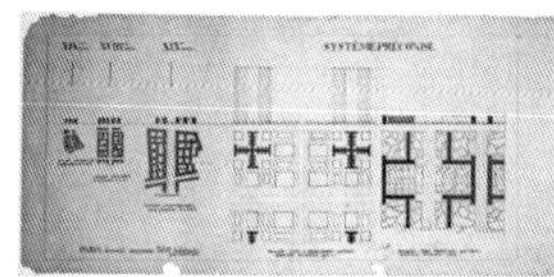

[TOP TO BOTTOM, LEFT TO RIGHT]
14th CENTURY
Density: 200 inhabitants per hectare
Planted area: zero

18th CENTURY
Density: 400–800
Planted area: zero

19th CENTURY
Boulevard Haussmann
Density: 200 inhabitants
Planted area: 5–10%

PARIS average density: 360 inhabitants per hectare

RECOMMENDED SYSTEM
Density: 800–1,200 inhabitants per hectare
PLANTED AREA: 95%

Density: 300 inhabitants per hectare
PLANTED AREA: 85%

—P. 146

Le Corbusier to Amédée Ozenfant, November 1926

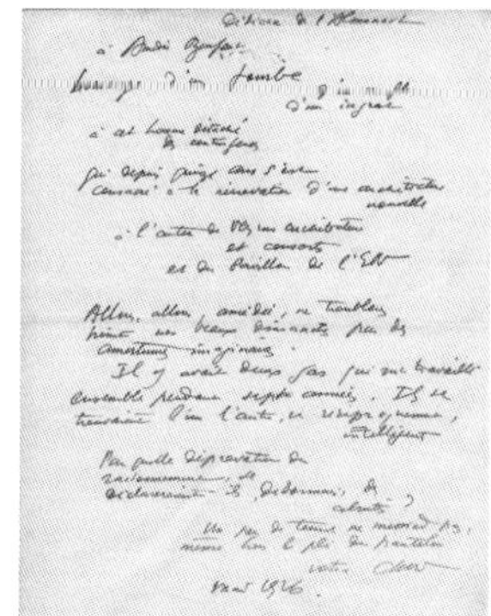

Dedication for the Almanac

to Amédée Ozenfant

this homage from a double-dealer
a boor
an ingrate
to a man indifferent to contingencies
who for fifteen years dedicated himself to the regeneration of a new architecture
to the author of *Vers une architecture* and the rest
the creator of the Pavillon de l'Esprit Nouveau
Come, come, Amédée, let's not ruin our fine Sundays with imaginary bitternesses.

There were two guys who worked together for seven years. They found each other, and reciprocally, intelligent

By what irrational perverseness would they now declare themselves idiots?

A little civility isn't unbecoming even outside the crease of the trousers

Your Ch. E. Jeanneret
Nov. 1926

—P. 146

Le Corbusier to Amédée Ozenfant, 14 December 1928

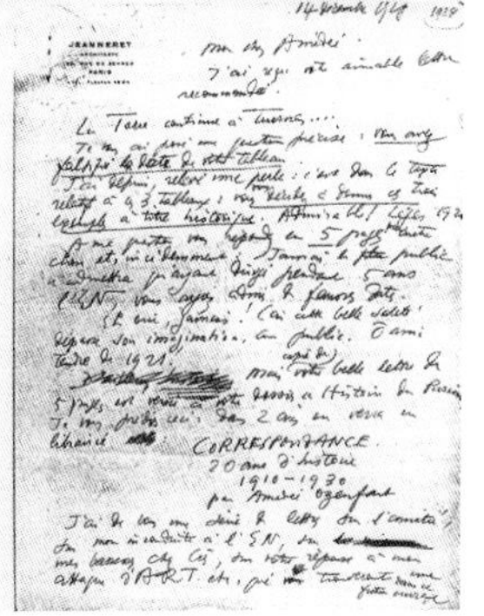

14 December 1928

My dear Amédée.

I received your kind certified-delivery letter.

The World keeps turning…

I asked you a specific question: You falsified the date of your picture.

Since then I've found a gem: it's in the text relating to these 3 pictures: you decide to give these three examples on historical grounds. Admirable! Léger 1926. You reply to my question with 5 pages about something else and, incidentally: Never will the ~~plu~~ public accept that having directed the EN for 5 years, you accepted false dates.

Oh yes, never! Because that lowdown dirty trick defies the public's imagination. Oh loving friend of 1921!

~~For that matter~~ history. But copy of your fine letter of 5 pages has gone into your "history of Purism" file. I predict this to you: in 2 years we'll see in the bookshops :

CORRESPONDENCE
20 years of history
1910–1930
by Amédée Ozenfant

I have a series of letters from you on friendship, on my misconduct at the EN; on ~~the level~~ my despicable behavior at Crès's, on your reply to my attack on ART. etc. which will find a [blank] in this future book

—P. 152

Letter from the commissioner general of the *Exposition des arts décoratifs et industriels modernes* to Le Corbusier, 10 February 1925

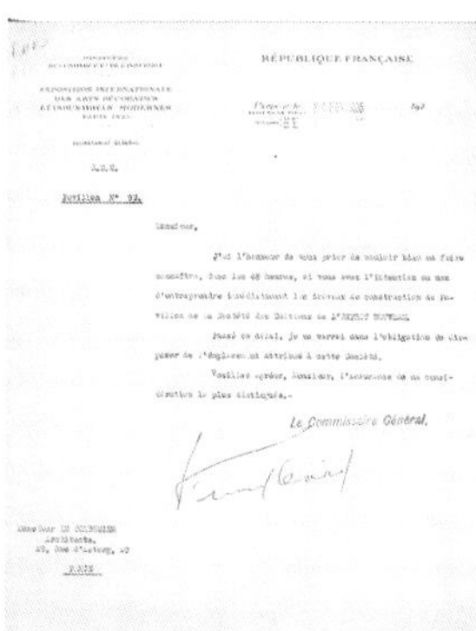

10 February 1925

Sir,

I have the honor to ask you to be so kind as to let me know, within the next 48 hours, if you intend or no to begin work immediately on the construction of the Pavillon de l'Esprit Nouveau publishers.

After that, I shall be obliged to make other arrangements for the space assigned to that Company.

I am, Sir, yours very truly,

The Commissioner General
[signature]

Mr. Le Corbusier
Architect,
29 rue d'Astorg
PARIS

—P. 160

First page of letter from Le Corbusier to William Ritter and Janko Czadra, 18 January 1926

18 January 1926

Dear friends,

Yes, my father is dead. You know how close we were, all four of us; the two sons and their parents loved and respected each other and there were never any problems. On the contrary, when we young ones were able to reverse the roles a little, and give our parents helpful advice and sometimes a helping hand, our relationship became even more affectionate. The house took on the atmosphere of gentleness it had when we were small. Certain specific circumstances made this present house a ~~sit~~ place of well-being and therapy for the heart. And so my dear father died in ~~circum~~ perfect peace. During the two months since his ~~death~~ end had become inevitable, he was in the little house by the lake, which was like a splendid musical link between the proud landscape and the inexorable drama. Maybe you don't know that 4 meters from the lake I built a house like a rail car, with an uninterrupted window 11 meters long looking out over the water and to the mountains in the background.

~~In w~~ At this time of year the site rolls out its changes and a polar majesty fills the soul with content and restfulness. ~~In~~ Were you well enough acquainted with my father to know how day after day he identified with the serenity of this place? The words spoken over his remains were always the same: this was a man of peace. From his silence, and from the meditation always hidden deep inside him, there nonetheless emanated acting on all, (and so powerfully on the humble) a radiant force. Dead, with his hands crossed on his chest, in his white shroud, this was no longer Mr. Jeanneret; it was a Reformer, a man of those great centuries of reckless thought. My father was timid yet bold. Before his judgment, so gently but firmly put, all his countless friends had been arrested […]

[LEFT MARGIN]

Enclosed the autograph for Mr. Czech, regulation format. Most honored!

—P. 160

Le Corbusier to his mother, 3 May 1927

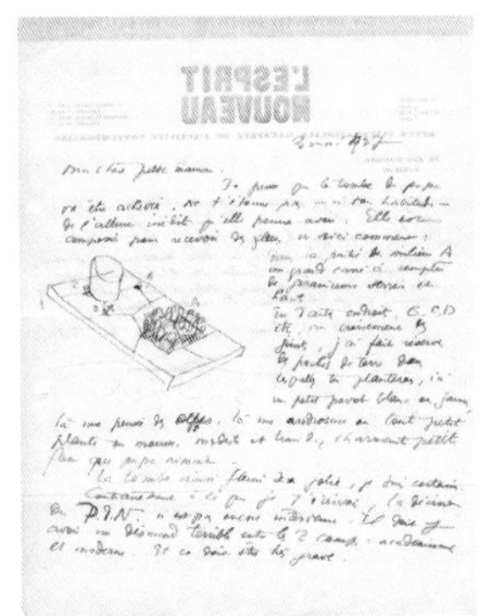

3 May 1927

My dear little mom,

I think dad's grave will soon be finished. Don't be shocked — as you usually are — by its possibly unusual appearance. It's been made to receive flowers, like this: in the middle part A is a big square to be packed tight with tall geraniums.

In other places B, C, D, etc., where the joints meet, I've set aside pockets of earth in which you'll plant here a little yellow or white poppy, there an alpine pansy, there a primula or any little plant or moss, modest and timid, any charming little flower dad liked.

With the flowers on it like that the grave will be pretty, I'm sure.

Contrary to what I wrote you, the Palace of Nations has still not made its decision. There must be a terrible difference of opinion between the two camps: the academic and the modern. And it must be very serious.

—P. 164

Henri Frugès to Le Corbusier, from Bordeaux, 13 November 1923

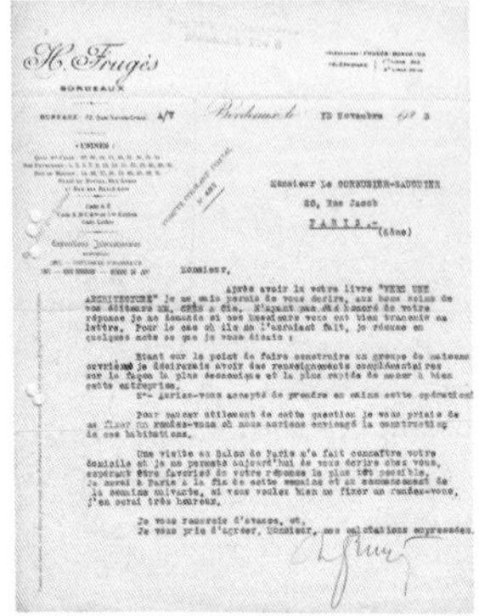

Bordeaux 13 November 1923

Mr. Le CORBUSIER-SAUGNIER
20 rue Jacob
PARIS. (6th)

Sir,

After reading your book "VERS UNE ARCHITECTURE" I permitted myself to write you, in care of your publishers Messrs. CRÈS & Cie. Not having had the honor of a reply from you I wonder if these Gentlemen conveyed my letter to you. In case they have not done so, I will summarize in a few words what I said:

As I am about to have a group of workers' houses built I would like additional information on the most economical and fastest way to complete this undertaking.

2nd — Would you accept to take this business in hand?

In order to chat usefully on the subject I asked you to make an appointment during which we would have planned construction of these houses.

A visit to the Paris Salon introduced me to your house and I permit myself today to write you at your house, in the hopes of being favored with a reply as soon as possible. I will be in Paris at the end of this week and the beginning of next week. If you would like to make an appointment, I will be very pleased.

I thank you in advance, and am most sincerely yours,

[signature]

—P. 164

Undated newspaper article recounting visit by Anatole de Monzie, minister of public works, to the inauguration of the Quartier Moderne Frugès

AUX « QUARTIERS MODERNES » DU MONTEIL

UNE VISITE DE M. DE MONZIE

Ministre des travaux publics

IN MONTEIL'S "MODERN NEIGHBORHOODS"

A VISIT BY Mr. DE MONZIE
Minister of Public Works

We were invited to join, on Sunday, the group accompanying Mr. de Monzie, minister of public works, on his visit to the Quartiers Modernes Frugès, located in Monteil, two kilometers past the borough of Pessac, about two hundred meters from the departmental road.

It was ten o'clock when the minister made his entrance into the "modern neighborhoods." He was accompanied by Messrs. Arnault, prefect of the Gironde; H. Frugès; Le Corbusier and Pierre Jeanneret, architects of the neighborhoods; Masse, the minister's chief of staff; etc.

Mr. de Monzie was greeted by Mr. Cordier, mayor of Pessac; Barrès, president of the Chamber of Commerce; Charles Cazalet, Mongermon, Bourdon, Dubois, Girardet, Caillet, Petitjean, Maurice Raynal, Albert Jeanneret, director of the French School of Rhythmics and Physical Education; Lallier, Victor de La Fortelle, Lenief, Badovici, Zervos, Mrs. Laborderie, lawyer of the Court of Appeals; several deputy mayors and city councilors from Pessac; Brezzi, president of the Pessac Tourist Office; etc.

The minister visited the "modern neighborhoods," as photographers took pictures and camera operators shot films.

On either side of a drive ending at the railroad line stand one- and two-story houses, all built in a uniform style. They suggest an Oriental landscape. In fact, the cube-shaped buildings look like what one finds in Morocco, for example. The roofs have been replaced by terraces, on which gardens have been laid out. The walls are painted white, blue, or burnt sienna, which only seems to emphasize the impression of one of those picturesque tableaux that one sees beneath African skies.

At first, the architect's ideas astonish, surprise, then soon the eye adjusts, and in the end one finds pleasure and charm in buildings that in the beginning had disoriented even the most up-to-date minds. This is, in a word, a neighborhood of Rabat or Fez, seemingly miraculously placed on a corner of our pretty Bordeaux suburb.

Mr. de Monzie and the people of his entourage visited several houses, from basement to terrace. A few have been completed and furnished in the modern taste. One notices that there are air and light in every room.

When the visit was over, the minister of public works went to villa n. 14, on whose terrace short speeches were delivered.

Mr. Frugès thanked the minister for coming and explained how it came about that he, an industrialist, was led to get involved in construction. He was guided, he said, only by the thought of finding some solution to the housing crisis.

After his compliments to Messrs. Le Corbusier and Pierre Jeanneret, the two architects in the group, Mr. Frugès thanked all those who participated in any degree in this experiment, and stressed that the presence of the minister of public works at this event represented for him the most meaningful of encouragements.

Mr. Le Corbusier, speaking next explained his technique. His exposition was followed by everyone with the keenest interest.

The minister of public works said how glad he was to have been able to accept the invitation made to him. Anything having to do with the housing crisis claims his attention. He congratulated all those who, in any capacity whatever, do what they can to resolve this desperate problem.

The gathering, both gracious and intimate, was followed by a champagne reception.

[CAPTION]

The houses of the "modern neighborhoods."
Inset, center: Mr. de Monzie, ministe of public works.

—P. 178

Le Corbusier and Pierre Jeanneret to Mrs. Meyer, October 1925

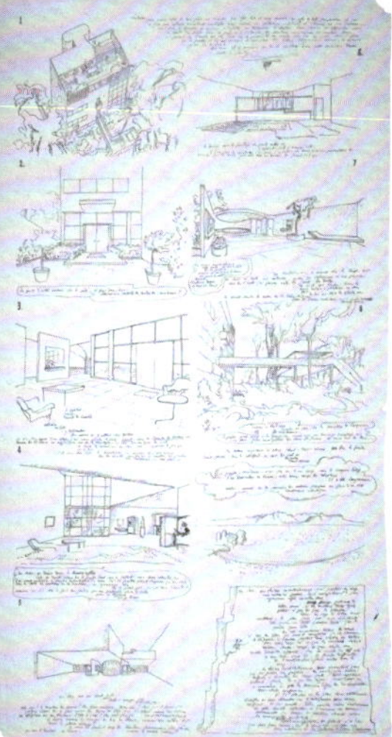

1) Dear Madam,

)ur dream has been to make you a ıouse as smooth and seamless as a vell-proportioned box; one not ıfflicted with countless rough edges hat give an effect of artificial, illu- ory picturesqueness, and are jarring ınder the light, and only add to the urrounding cacophony. We are ›pposed to the craze in this country ınd abroad for complicated, discor- lant houses. We think that the uni- ied is stronger than the scrappy. You nust not think this smoothness is lue to laziness; on the contrary, it is he outcome of long-ripened plan- ıing. Simplicity is not facility. 'rankly, there would be something ıoble about this house in its leafy etting.

(2) … The main entrance would ›e on the side; not set frontally. Vould this bring the wrath of the Academy down on our heads?

(3) … The hall, large and lrenched with light … with closet ınd washroom discreetly out of ight. There is direct access from the ervice core. And upstairs is the ıigh-ceilinged living room, above he shade of the trees and so with a plendid, leafy view. And more sky… f the servants are well housed, the ıouse will be well maintained. No ttic, but instead a garden, solarium ınd swimming pool.

(4) … One has an outlook from he living room, amid a flood of light. nside the double glazing of the pic- ure window is a greenhouse that ıstantly neutralizes the coldness of he glass surface: big, strange plants ıf the kind you see in the glass- ıouses of châteaux and botany ›vers; an aquarium, etc. … Via the ittle door set on the house's main xis you take a footbridge leading lown into the garden, where you can ıat lunch or dinner beneath the rees.

(5) … This floor is a single oom: living room, dining room, etc., library. And of course the cylindrical service core. Right in the middle. Of course! To make it usable. It's made out of cork bricks that insulate it like a telephone box or a thermos. A weird idea! But not so weird as all that… Natural, that's all. The services run through the house from bottom to top, like an artery. Where could it be better placed? … The walls at the far end and those of the core could be ducted. You can see the boudoir—with its built-in furnishings.

(6) … The boudoir gives onto the foliage of the big trees and the "summer dining room." If you want to put on a show, you can dress here, then descend one of the two staircases leading to the stage in front of the big window.

(7) … The service core continues up to the door beside the swimming pool. Behind the pool and the service core you have breakfast (the first drawing shows this clearly). From the boudoir you go out onto the roof, where there are no tiles, no slates, but instead a solarium and a swimming pool, with grass growing between the paving stones. Above is the sky: The walls mean that nobody roundabout can see you. In the evening you see the stars and the dark shape of the Folie St-James. Sliding screens offer total privacy.

(8) … A touch of Robinson Crusoe inventiveness and a little like in Carpaccio's paintings. Fun … This isn't a classical French garden, but a wild copse where, thanks to the woodland of the Parc St-James, you'd think you're miles from Paris.

… The service core takes the sun directly, so much the better. Through the windows, highset beneath the ceiling, you see sky and trees… So much the better.

This project is not something dashed off between phone calls by some studio draftsman. It has been developed slowly, lovingly, in the course of days of perfect tranquility spent contemplating a classical site.

These ideas … these architectural themes shot through with a certain poetry have been subjected to the most rigorous rules of building… Twelve equidistant reinforced concrete posts hold up the floors economically. Inside the concrete cage thus created the plan makes play with a simplicity such that one is tempted (really tempted!) to consider it simpleminded… For years we have been used to seeing plans so complicated you have the impression of people with their internal organs on the outside. We have insisted on keeping the internal organs on the inside, carefully arranged, so that only a limpid form appears. Not so easy as all that! To tell the truth, this is architecture's big problem: making things fit in.

For poetry to come bubbling out, these architectural themes need strict adjacencies that are not easy to resolve. Once the thing is done, everything looks natural and easy. And that is a good sign. But when we began to lay down the initial lines of the composition, it was total confusion.

If the structure and the plan are extremely simple, the builder can be allowed to be less strict. Which counts. Which counts a great deal, in fact, and the painful constraints of economy only become forgivable when the solution … sings the praises of the architects! This last bit of fatuity is only put in as a joke. After all, one has to laugh now and then.

Paris, October 1925
<u>Le Corbusier and Pierre Jeanneret</u>

—P. 181

Albin Peyron, commissioner general of the Salvation Army, to Le Corbusier and Pierre Jeanneret, 20 January 1928

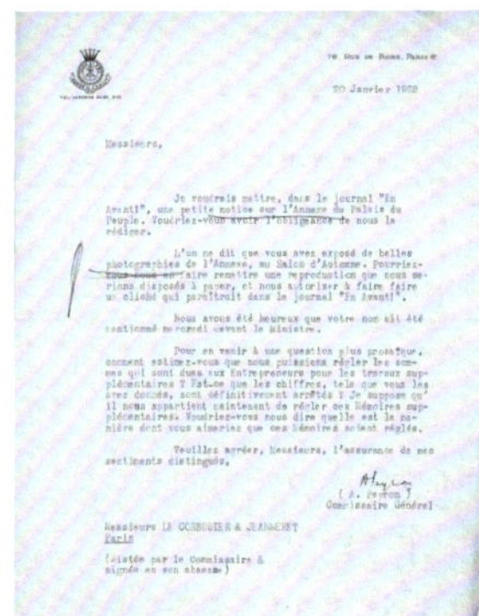

20 Janvier 1928

Messieurs,

Je voudrais mettre, dans le journal "En Avant!", une petite notice sur l'Annexe du Palais du Peuple. Voudriez-vous avoir l'obligeance de nous la rédiger.

L'on me dit que vous avez exposé de belles photographies de l'Annexe, au Salon d'Automne. Pourriez-vous nous en faire remettre une reproduction que nous serions disposés à payer, et nous autoriser à faire faire un cliché qui paraîtrait dans le journal "En Avant!".

Nous avons été heureux que votre nom ait été mentionné mercredi devant le Ministre.

Pour en venir à une question plus prosaïque, comment estimez-vous que nous puissions régler les sommes qui sont dues aux Entrepreneurs pour les travaux supplémentaires ? Est-ce que les chiffres, tels que vous les avez donnés, sont définitivement arrêtés ? Je suppose qu'il nous appartient maintenant de régler ces Mémoires supplémentaires. Voudriez-vous nous dire quelle est la manière dont vous aimeriez que ces Mémoires soient réglés.

Veuillez agréer, Messieurs, l'assurance de mes sentiments distingués,

(A. Peyron)
Commissaire Général

Messieurs LE CORBUSIER & JEANNERET
Paris

(dictée par le Commissaire & signée en son absence)

20 January 1928

Sirs,

I would like to put, in the magazine "En Avant!" a <u>brief account of the Annex</u> of the Palais du Peuple. Would you be kind enough to write it for us.

I'm told that you exhibited beautiful <u>photographs</u> of the Annex at the Salon d'Automne. Could you procure us a reproduction, which we would be prepared to pay for, and authorize us to have a print made, which would appear in the magazine "En Avant!"

We were glad your name was mentioned on Wednesday in the Minister's presence.

To come to a more prosaic matter, how do you consider we might pay the sums due the Contractors for the additional work? Are the figures, as you gave them, definitely final? I suppose it's up to us now to pay these additional Accounts. Would you tell us how you would like these accounts paid.

I am, Sirs, respectfully yours,

[signature]
(A. Peyron)
Commissioner General
Messrs. LE CORBUSIER & JEANNERET

<u>Paris</u>
(Dictated by the Commissioner and signed in his absence)

—P. 186

Page from a description of the Weissenhof-Siedlung housing exhibition, with list of participating architects

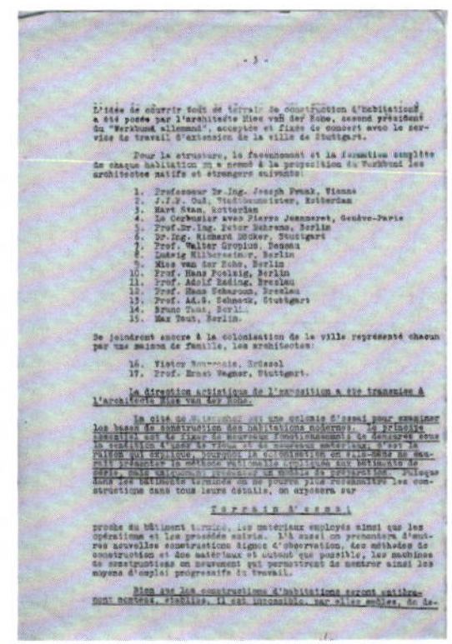

- 3 -

L'idée de couvrir tout le terrain de construction d'habitations a été posée par l'architecte Mies van der Rohe, second président du "Werkbund allemand", acceptée et fixée de concert avec le service de travail d'extension de la ville de Stuttgart.

Pour la structure, le façonnement et la formation complète de chaque habitation on a nommé à la proposition du Werkbund les architectes natifs et étrangers suivants:

1. Professeur Dr.Ing. Joseph Frank, Vienne
2. J.J.P. Oud, Stadtbaumeister, Rotterdam
3. Mart Stam, Rotterdam
4. Le Corbusier avec Pierre Jeanneret, Genève-Paris
5. Prof.Dr.Ing. Peter Behrens, Berlin
6. Dr.Ing. Richard Döcker, Stuttgart
7. Prof. Walter Gropius, Dessau
8. Ludwig Hilberseimer, Berlin
9. Mies van der Rohe, Berlin
10. Prof. Hans Poelzig, Berlin
11. Prof. Adolf Rading, Breslau
12. Prof. Hans Scharoun, Breslau
13. Prof. Ad.G. Schneck, Stuttgart
14. Bruno Taut, Berlin
15. Max Taut, Berlin.

Se joindront encore à la colonisation de la ville représenté chacun par une maison de famille, les architectes:

16. Victor Bourgeois, Brüssel
17. Prof. Ernst Wagner, Stuttgart.

The idea of covering the entire property with residential construction was proposed by the architect Mies van der Rohe, second president of the "German Werkbund," accepted, and decided, in conjunction with the department of works for the expansion of the city of Stuttgart.

For the structure, construction, and complete shaping of each residence the following native and foreign architects were named, following the Werkbund's proposal:

1. Professor Dr. Engineer Joseph Frank, Vienna
2. J. J. P. Oud, Municipal Housing Architect, Rotterdam
3. Mart Stam, Rotterdam
4. Le Corbusier with Pierre Jeanneret, Geneva-Paris
5. Professor Dr. Engineer Peter Behrens, Berlin
6. Dr. Engineer Richard Döcker, Stuttgart
7. Prof. Walter Gropius, Dessau
8. Ludwig Hilberseimer, Berlin
9. Mies van der Rohe, Berlin
10. Prof. Hans Poelzig, Berlin
11. Prof. Adolf Rading, Breslau
12. Prof. Hans Scharoun, Breslau
13. Prof. Ad. G. Schneck, Stuttgart
14. Bruno Taut, Berlin
15. Max Taut, Berlin

The following architects, each one to be represented by a single-family home, will also participate in the colonization of the city:

16. Victor Bourgeois, Brussels
17. Prof. Ernst Wagner, Stuttgart

<u>The exhibition's artistic direction has been assigned to the architect Mies van der Rohe.</u>

<u>The city of Weissenhof is a test colony, to allow the bases of modern residences to be explored. The essential principle is to establish a new functionality for homes with old and new materials; this is why colonization in and of itself cannot display the rational method applied to mass-produced buildings, but only display a preparatory model.</u> Since it will no longer be possible to inspect the constructions in their every detail once the buildings are completed, there will be exhibited on

<u>Experimental site</u>

near the completed building, the materials employed, as well as the operations and processes followed. Other new constructions meriting attention will also be displayed there, as well as building methods and materials, and, to the extent possible, construction machinery in motion, which will thereby make it possible to show the work's progressive applications of it.

<u>Although all the residential buildings will be entirely assembled and put up, it is impossible, based on them alone, to</u> […]

—P. 188

Postcard from Le Corbusier to Pierre Jeanneret, 1927

P.S. As for the library and BLC2 on a terrace, it would be a good idea to add another shelf for books etc. As in BL. C1 same partitions may be without sliding metal plates. What's your thought about it?

[BOTTOM LEFT]
37½
Library

[BOTTOM RIGHT]
Pierre
take a look
pls.

—P. 188

Letter from the Weissenhof construction office to Le Corbusier and Pierre Jeanneret, 7 July 1927

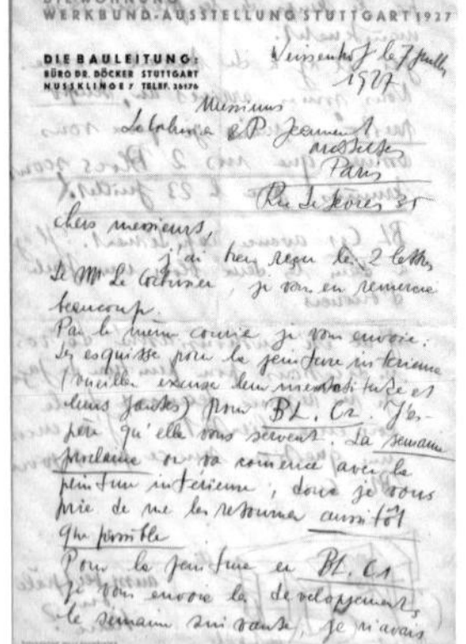
DIE WOHNUNG
WERKBUND-AUSSTELLUNG STUTTGART 1927
DIE BAULEITUNG:
BÜRO DR. DÖCKER STUTTGART

Weissenhof 7 July 1927

Messrs. Le Corbusier and P. Jeanneret
architects
Paris
Rue de Sèvres 35

Dear Sirs,

I did indeed receive Mr. Le Corbusier's 2 letters, thank you very much.

By the same post I'm sending: The sketches for the interior painting (please excuse their inaccuracy and errors) for BL. C2. I hope they will be useful to you. Next week, they'll start painting the interiors, so please send them back as soon as possible.

As for the painting in BL. C1, I'll send you updates next week, I had

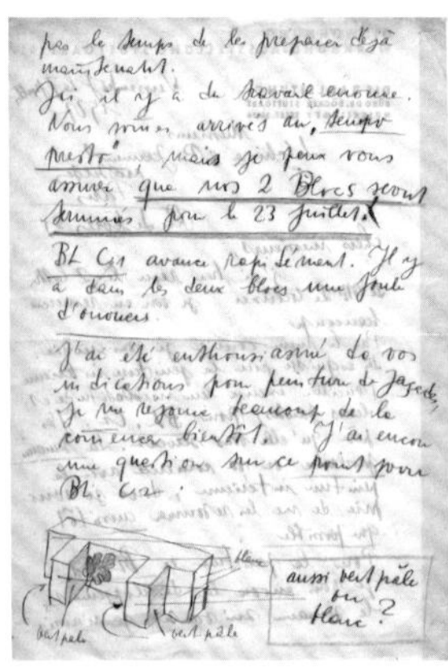

no time to prepare it now.

There's an enormous amount of work here. We've come to the "tempo presto," but I can assure you that our 2 Blocks will be finished for 23 July. BL. C1 is going ahead fast. There's a crowd of workers in both blocks.

I'm enthusiastic about your suggestions for painting the facades, and I'm really delighted to be starting soon. I still have a question on this point for BL. C2.

[SKETCH]
white
pale green / pale green
also pale green or white?

—P. 194

Document by Le Corbusier certifying that Charlotte Perriand has worked as an associate at the rue de Sèvres office on "household equipment," 17 March 1932

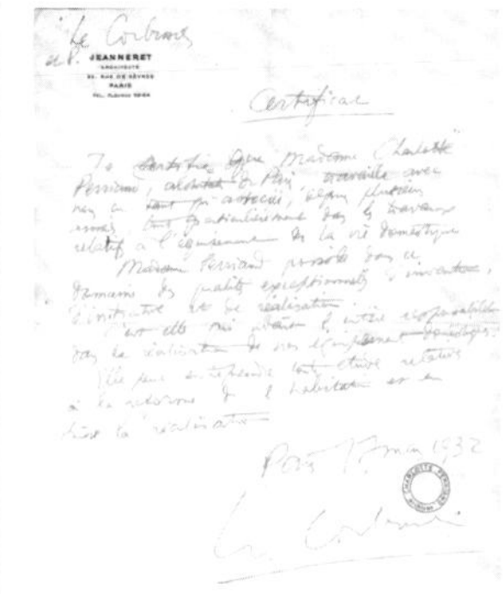
JEANNERET
Certificat

Le Corbusier and P. Jeanneret

Certificate

I certify that Mrs. Charlotte Perriand, Paris architect, has been working with us as an associate for several years, most especially in respect to household equipment.

In this field Mrs. Perriand possesses exceptional abilities in terms of inventiveness, initiative, and realization.

She bore sole responsibility for the creation of our domestic equipment.

She is capable of undertaking any study on housing reform and ensuring its implementation.

Paris 17 March 1932
Le Corbusier

—P. 194

E. Bonifay, secretary general of the Salon d'Automne, to Le Corbusier, 15 June 1931

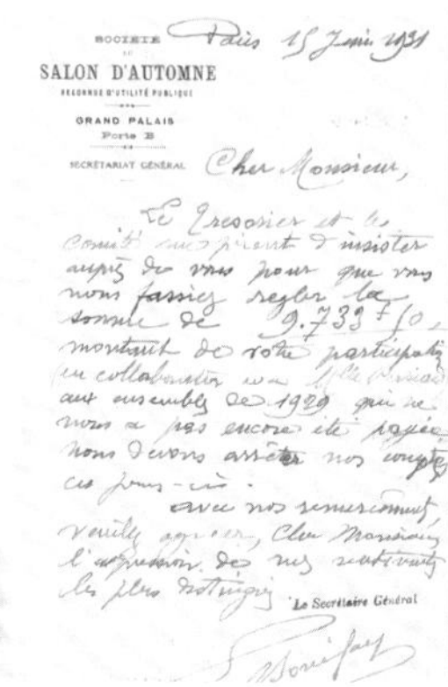
SOCIÉTÉ DU
SALON D'AUTOMNE
GRAND PALAIS
SECRÉTARIAT GÉNÉRAL
Le Secrétaire Général

Paris 15 June 1931

Dear Sir,

The Treasurer and the Committee have asked me to insist that you settle the sum of 9,733 francs 50, the cost of your participation (in collaboration with Miss Perriand) in the 1929 constructions, which has not yet been paid for. We must close our accounts now.

With our thanks, we are, Dear Sir, yours respectfully,

The Secretary General
[signature]

—P. 202

Pages from *Oeuvre complète: Volume 1, 1910–29*

THE FIVE POINTS OF A NEW ARCHITECTURE

1. Pilotis. Detailed, determined research has led to partial constructions that can be considered scientifically sound. These results open up new prospects for architecture, and these prospects are available to urban planning, which can use them to find a solution to the great sickness of today's cities.

The house on *pilotis*! The house was sinking into the ground: dark, often damp premises. Reinforced concrete gives us *pilotis*. The house is in the air, far from the ground; the garden runs under the house, the garden is also on the house, on the roof.

2. Garden roofs. For centuries a traditional roof structure usually gets through winter with its weight of snow, as long as the house is heated with stoves.

As soon as central heating is installed, the traditional roof structure is no longer suitable. The roof must no longer project upward, but must be hollowed downward. It must send rainwater toward the interior, not the exterior.

An indisputable truth: cold climates demand the elimination of the sloping roof structure in favor of flat roofs with water run-off inside the house.

Reinforced concrete is the new means of achieving a uniform roof. Reinforced concrete expands considerably. This expansion causes cracking at times of abrupt contraction. Instead of trying to get rid of rainwater quickly, try to maintain a constant moisture level on the concrete of the roof terrace and thus an even temperature for the reinforced concrete. A special protective measure: sand covered with thick cement tiles with gaps between them and grass growing in the gaps. The sand and roots mean the water only filters through slowly. Terrace-gardens become luxuriant: flowers, shrubs and trees, lawn.

Various reasons, to do with technical considerations, economy, comfort, and personal feelings lead us to opt for the flat roof.

3. The open plan. Until now: load-bearing walls; rising from the basement, they are overlaid on each other, making up the first floor and the stories, up to the roof structure. The plan is the slave of the load-bearing walls. Reinforced concrete in house-building brings the open plan! The stories no longer stack up separately. They are free. Real savings in building terms, with rigorous use of each centimeter. Real savings in money terms. Easy logic of the new plan!

4. Horizontal windows. The window is one of the house's basic goals. Progress has brought liberation. Reinforced concrete has created a revolution in the history of the window. The windows can run from one end of the facade to the other. The window is the house's *classic mechanical element*; for all our townhouses, villas, worker's houses, all our rental buildings…

5. The free facade. Set back from the facade, the posts are inside the house. The floor continues in cantilever. The facade is now no more than a light membrane of insulation or windows.

The facade is free; the windows can run uninterrupted from one end of the facade to the other.

Le Corbusier and Pierre Jeanneret

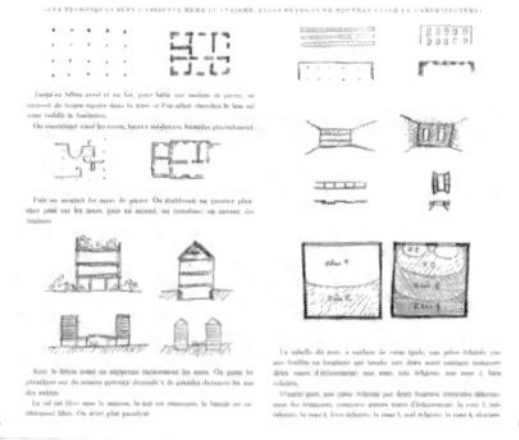

Until the coming of reinforced concrete and steel, to build a stone house you dug wide channels in the soil and went looking for the right ground for the foundations.

This led to the making of cellars: relatively useless areas, generally damp.

Then you built up the stone walls. An initial floor was laid on the walls, then a second, and a third; openings were made for windows.

With reinforced concrete the walls are completely done away with. The floors are supported by thin posts set far apart.

The ground under the house is free, the roof can be used again, the facade is completely free. You're no longer paralyzed.

The diagram says this: a room lit by a horizontal window joining two walls provides two lighting zones: one very bright, and zone 2, bright.

On the other hand, the same area of glass used for two vertical windows with a pier between them, provides four lighting zones: zone 1, very bright; zone 2, bright; zone 3, badly lit; zone 4, dark.

—P. 205

Description of Le Corbusier's "twelve little inventions," from *Le Corbusier lui-même*, 1970

12 little inventions

Le Corbusier as inventor? … Why not? All you have to do is check out the work he's done and his plans for the future… And here's an assortment of twelve little inventions from a list that's much longer…

—ASBESTOS PIPING, 1919: An absolutely new use for fibro-cement (éverit-éternit). Le Corbusier, inventor of the asbestos pipe. Currently in general use.

—TYPOGRAPHY, 1920: Use of the entire page in printing (Arrault Printers in Tours). Now widely used.

—PILOTIS—INDEPENDENT SKELETON—THE FREE PLAN—THE FREE FACADE—THE ROOF GARDEN!

Plus five ideas currently well known to architects.

—FURNITURE, 1927: Compartments as the basis of housing. Using a standard frame, very different facilities can be provided according to the use planned for the compartments.

Now very widely used.

—AUTOMOBILE, 1928: Le Corbusier and Pierre Jeanneret design a "maximum car": rear-engined, aerodynamic, economically sized, all modern conveniences, lots of luggage space, fully reclining seats. The exterior design reflects these necessities, with simple curves (flat, slightly embossed pressed sheet). Convertible: roof slides backward. Now very widely used.

—NEUTRALIZING WALL, 1929: Created as part of the plans for the Centrosoyuz in Moscow, the neutralizing wall comprises two membranes a few centimeters apart, allowing for constant ventilation and a constant temperature. Not yet put into use.

—LIFEBOAT, 1930: A lifeboat integrated into the hull of the mother vessel and automatically ejected in case of shipwreck. Not used.

—SUNSHADE, 1930–65: A system allowing for maximum effect from the sun in winter, with complete cutoff in the hottest periods of summer. Thirty-five years of fine-tuning.

A system now known to architects around the world.

—UNLIMITED GROWTH MUSEUM, 1931: The museum begins at the center and expands over time as a square spiral; the entrance is underneath at the center. A single type of beam, a single type of glazing. Since built by Le Corbusier in Ahmedabad in India, and in Tokyo.

—VENTILATORS, 1945: Vertical slits in a wall, closed off with metal mosquito mesh and fitted with a pivoting shutter. Perfect ventilation guaranteed.

—THE MODULOR, 1942, 1948, 1945: A range of construction sizes for human use. Mathematical system of proportion based on the human body. Used by many architects and creative artists.

—SHEETS OF CORRUGATED GLASS, 1957: A reasonable solution for modern glazing.

The vitreous film of facades independent of the load-bearing structure is stiffened by slim reinforced concrete members. Use of the Modulor allows for considerable variation in the distribution of the members.

This is a far from exhaustive list, but we must not omit an invention Le Corbusier came up with for his own personal use: the rubber band pencil holder. You may know that Le Corbusier made enormous use of color pencils in his notes, studies, and lecture preparation. The use of several rubber bands enables the pencils to be held together in the left hand, in the pocket, in the street, or when traveling. But there's a secret to this! There was a special way of tangling the rubber bands up together… And only Le Corbusier knew it! …

—P. 204

Pierre Savoye to Le Corbusier, 24 March 1930

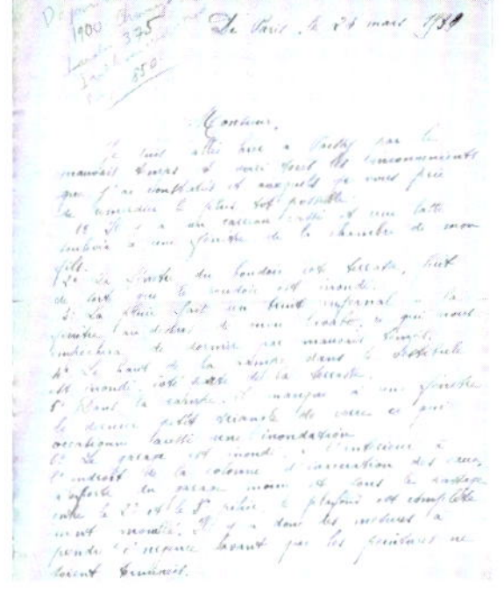

Expenses
1,900 Chrome plating
Washbowl 375
Install water enamel and trad
Waste outlet 850

From Paris, 24 March 193[?]

Sir,

I went to Poissy yesterday in bad weather and here are all the problems I noted and which I would like you to rectify as soon as possible.

1. There is a broken pane and a slat coming off a window in my son's room.

2. The terrace-side window of the boudoir leaks so much that the boudoir is flooded.

3. The rain makes an infernal racket on the window above my washbowl, which will stop us from sleeping in bad weather.

4. The upper part of the ramp in the vestibule is flooded on the terrace-door side.

5. One of the ramp windows is missing the last little glass triangle, which also lets water in.

6. The garage is flooded inside at the waste outlet point, right at the door of the garage, and under the passage between the 2nd and 3rd pillar the ceiling is completely soaked. So steps need to be taken urgently before the painting is finished.

We have given thought to the making of the road. Mr. Cormier has made the following proposition: Dig out to a depth of 0.10 m; 0.15 or 0.20 of clinker and clay, 0.10 m of pebbles; sand, spreading, watering and rolling at a cost of 25 francs per m2. With the new estimate there is about 600 m2.

We are not accepting Mr. Crépin's price of 28 francs per m2, but are inclined to give him [the job] at the same price, i.e. 25 francs per m2. The road works at the same time as the uprooting, on the understanding, of course, that if [?] some stumps appear next year, Mr. Crépin will have to bear the uprooting costs (if he can come down to 25 francs per m2) we shall look for another garden firm.

If Mr. Crépin agrees, I'd like him to send me the details of the roadworks, just as Mr. Cormier did.

Yours faithfully,
E. Savoye

—P. 204

Le Corbusier to Mr. Crépin, landscape contractor, 17 July 1930

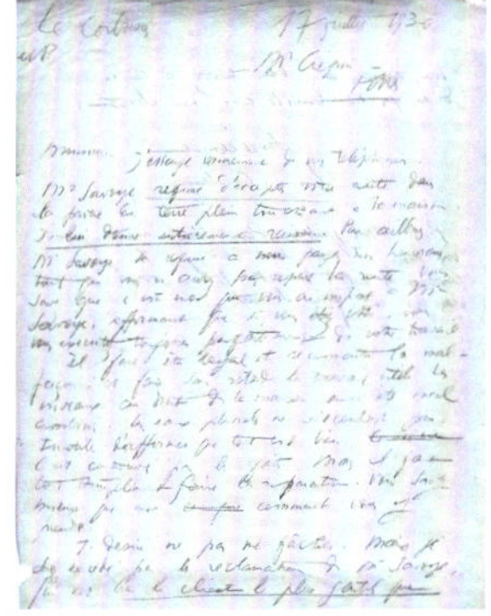

Le Corbusier and P.

17 July 1930

Mr. Crépin
PARIS
Sir.

I have tried in vain to phone you. Mr. Savoye refuses to accept your road in the part of the platform next to the house. I think he is absolutely right. Moreover, Mr. Savoye refuses to pay us our fee as long as you have not repaired the road. You know that it was I who insisted that Mr. Savoye take you on, telling him that you were expensive but always did your work perfectly.

So you must honestly acknowledge the faulty workmanship and do the necessary without delay. The levels to the right of the house have been badly matched. The rainwater doesn't run off. No point telling me everything's fine. ~~It's not~~ It's contradicted by the facts. But it's a simple matter of doing the repairs. You know better than I do ~~what~~ how to go about this.

I don't want to get worked up. But I'm exasperated by the complaints from Mr. Savoye, who is certainly the nicest client

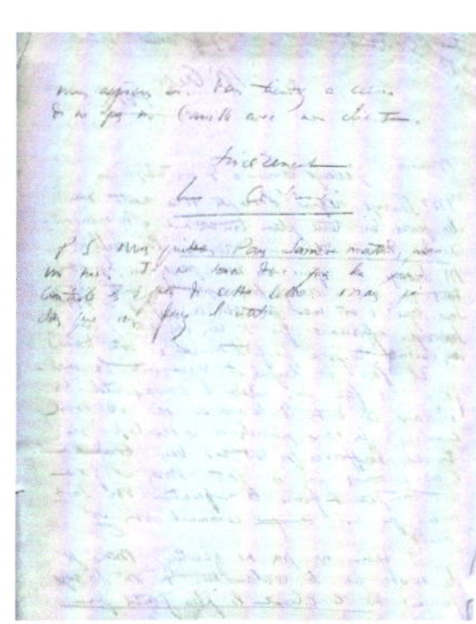

we've ever had. You must make sure not to make me fall out with my client.

Sincerely,
Le Corbusier

P.S. We're leaving Paris Saturday morning for a month. So I won't be around to check the outcome of this letter. But I know you'll do the necessary.

—P. 204

Le Corbusier to Pierre Savoye, 15 October 1930

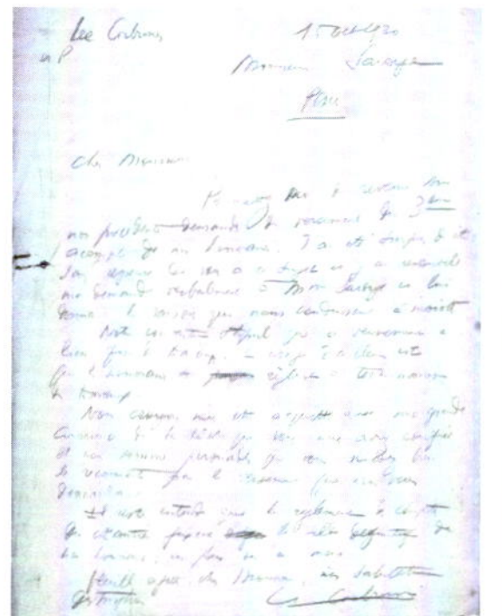

Le Corbusier and P.
15 Oct 1930

Mr. Savoye
Paris

Dear Sir,

Allow me to mention once more our earlier requests for payment of the 3rd installment of our fees. I was surprised not to have had an answer from you in this regard and made a further, verbal request to Mrs. Savoye, giving her our reasons for insisting.

Our contract stipulates that this payment take place at the end of the work. And it is customary that the fees be paid when work has been completed.

We feel that we carried out most conscientiously the task you entrusted us with and are certain that you are ready to acknowledge this via the payment we are requesting from you.

It is understood that payment of the building costs will establish the final balance of our fees, be this more or less.

Yours faithfully,
Le Corbusier

—P. 204

Le Corbusier to Eugénie Savoye, 28 June 1931

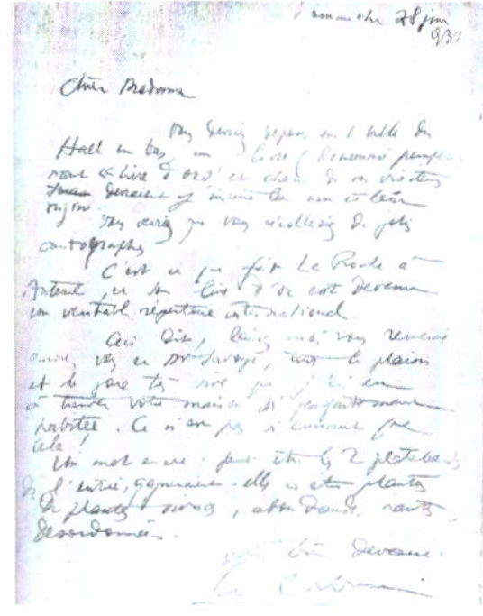

Sunday 28 June 1931

Dear Madam

You should put what's called a visitors' book on the table in the Hall downstairs and each visitor ~~will~~ should write in their name and where they're from.

That way you harvest a healthy crop of excellent autographs.

This is what La Roche does at Auteuil, and his visitors' book has become a veritable international who's who.

Having said this, let me thank you both again, yourself and Mr. Savoye, for all the pleasure and delight it was for me to find your house so perfectly lived in. It's not the case all that often!

One more thing: perhaps the 2 flowerbeds at the entrance would benefit from being planted with perennials that are tall, prolific, and disorderly.

Sincerely yours,
Le Corbusier

—P. 204

Pierre Savoye to Mr. Cormier, contractor, 7 September 1936

Cormier / 12½ Savoye

7 Sept 1936

Sir,

I hope you are back from your holidays and will be able to come to Poissy.

There are leaks in the entrance and the ramp and the garage wall is absolutely soaked.

In addition, there are still leaks in my bathroom, which floods every time it rains; the water comes in through the ceiling window. The gardener's walls are soaked too. I would really like all this to be sorted out

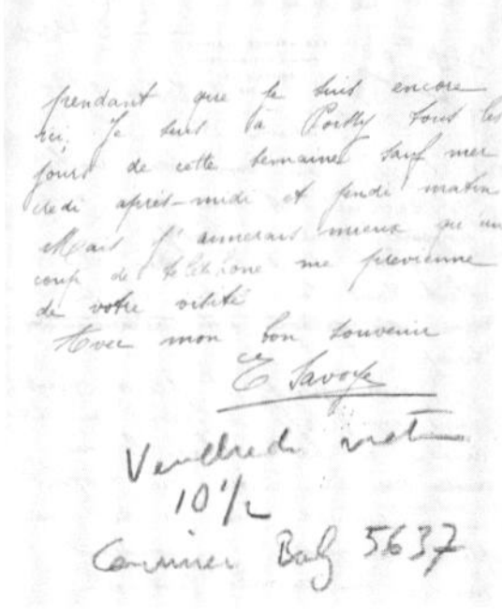

E. Savoye

Vendredi matin

10½

Cormier Balz 5637

while I am still here; I am at Poissy every day this week except Wednesday afternoon and Thursday morning.

But I would prefer that you let me know by phone when you are coming.

Yours ever,
E Savoye

Friday morning
10½
Cormier Balz 5637

—P. 204

Eugénie Savoye to Mr. Goudeau, chairman of the construction firm for the villa, 11 October 1937

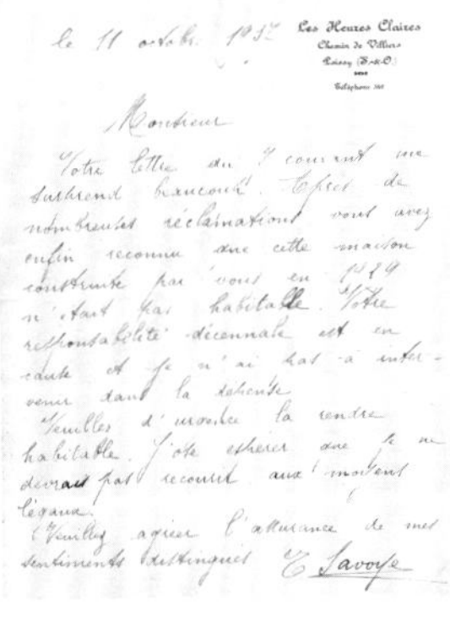

Le 11 octobre 1937

Les Heures Claires

Monsieur

E Savoye

11 October 1937

Sir

Your letter of the 7th of this month astonishes me. After numerous complaints you have finally acknowledged that this house built by you in 1929 was not habitable. Your ten-year guarantee is applicable here and it is not up to me to intervene at my own expense.

Please make it habitable urgently. I trust I shall not have to resort to legal measures.

Yours faithfully,
E. Savoye

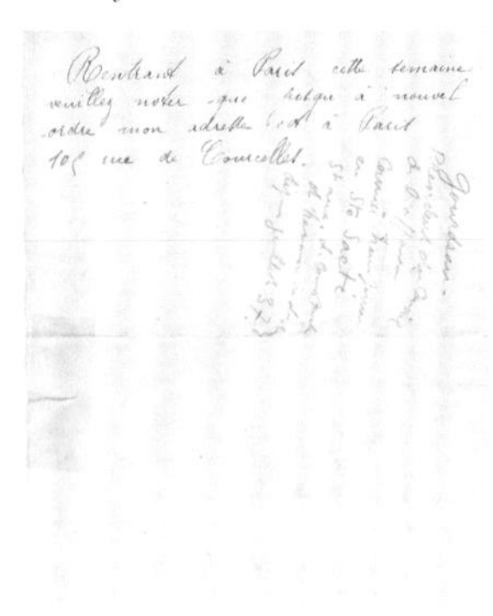

Revenant à Paris cette semaine veuillez noter que jusqu'à nouvel ordre mon adresse est à Paris 109 rue de Courcelles.

Returning to Paris this week please note that until further notice my new address is in Paris 109 rue de Courcelles.

[RIGHT]
Goudeau Chairman of the Board of the Cormier business now called Sacté Building and Industrial Works since July 37.

—P. 214

Salubra to Le Corbusier, 25 April 1931

SALUBRA S.A. / BÂLE

25 Avril 1931.

Cher Monsieur,

Comme convenu nous vous soumettons par ce même courrier – comme papiers d'affaires recommandés – ce qui suit:

1.) Une maquette de la marque Salubra et à votre choix quatre maquettes "Le Corbusier" (dont celle marquée d'une croix nous conviendrait le mieux) ainsi qu'une couverture d'album, sur laquelle veuillez placer les maquettes choisies, les coller et nous retourner la couverture ainsi munie des deux maquettes "Salubra" et "Le Corbusier".

2.) Un jeu complet des harmonies de couleurs ainsi qu'il sera présenté dans les albums. Aucune marge au haut, 4 m/m au bas et du côté libre, marge suffisante pour onglet.

3.) Echantillons d'autres cartons pour les harmonies de couleurs. (NB. Le carton brun du jeu ci-dessus nous semble le meilleur, la couleur brune nous paraît agréable et, la partie visible étant presque nulle, ne peut guère gêner.)

4.) Deux lunettes en carton brun, qui pourraient aussi être exécutées en un des cartons d'autres couleurs selon les échantillons mentionnés ci-dessus.

5.) Un échantillon de la nuance 70: terre de Sienne nature claire qui – probablement par erreur – ne figure sur aucune des harmonies de couleurs. Veuillez s.v.p. nous indiquer où elle doit être placée ou si elle peut être supprimée.

Nous vous serions très obligés si vous vouliez bien nous donner vos instructions au sujet de ces cinq questions aussitôt qu'il vous sera possible.–

Télégrammes: Salubra Bâle. Code: ABC 6th Edition. Téléphone: Safran 5228.
Case postale: 28 Bâle 16. Compte de chèques postaux V 0586.

25 April 1931.

Dear Sir,

As agreed we are submitting to you by this same post – as registered printed paper – the following:

1.) A model of the Salubra logo and, to be selected by you, four "Le Corbusier" models (the ones marked with a cross would suit us best) as well as a catalog cover, upon which please place the selected models, glue them, and return to us the cover thus provided with the two "Salubra" and "Le Corbusier" models.

2.) A complete set of color harmonies as it will be displayed in the catalogs. No margin at the top, 4mm at the bottom, and on the outside, enough margin for a tab.

3.) Samples of other cardboards for the color harmonies. (Note: We think the brown cardboard of the set above is the best, we find the brown attractive, and because almost none of it will show, it can't possibly disturb.)

4.) Two brown cardboard lunettes, which could also be made of one of the cardboards of other colors in keeping with the samples mentioned above.

5.) A sample of shade 70: light burnt sienna, which – probably by mistake – doesn't appear in any of the color harmonies. Please let us know where it should go or whether it can be omitted.

We would be very obliged to you if you would give us your instructions concerning these five questions at your earliest convenience.

—P. 214

Advertisement for Le Corbusier's Salubra wallpaper

Le Corbusier – Salubra wallpapers

In 1932, Le Corbusier created the first collection of Salubra wallpapers, which he christened "The color keyboard." He wrote the text about it himself, describing in it very clearly his concept of the use of colors for wallpapers. Here is an excerpt from what he said:

"Salubra is oil paint in rolls. Salubra wallpapers are light-fast and washable. Instead of putting several coats of paint on the walls and ceilings in an atmosphere of a noisy, dusty construction site, one can now put oil paint on in rolls, leaving it for last and in all serenity.

"To the architect, always more or less at the mercy of a house painter's poor workmanship, Salubra offers great peace of mind, because they guarantee consistent qualities of tone and material with their always-exact proportions of oil and tint.

"The choice of colors is no longer made amid the fracas and discomfort of a work site. Thanks to 'oil paint in rolls,' it takes place safely and calmly, from systematically assembled samples which are actual pieces of the final product."

— So wrote Le Corbusier in 1932.

Le Corbusier has always militated for the purity and aesthetics of materials. The fact is that, sought after though he is in the four corners of the world, he finds the time today to create a new collection for Salubra, proving the importance he gives to wallpaper and evidence of his determinant experience with Salubra.

At your supplier, ask to see the 1959 Le Corbusier–Salubra collection or write directly for complete information to Salubra S.A., Wallpaper Manufacturer, Basel/Switzerland.

—P. 220

Le Corbusier to Yvonne

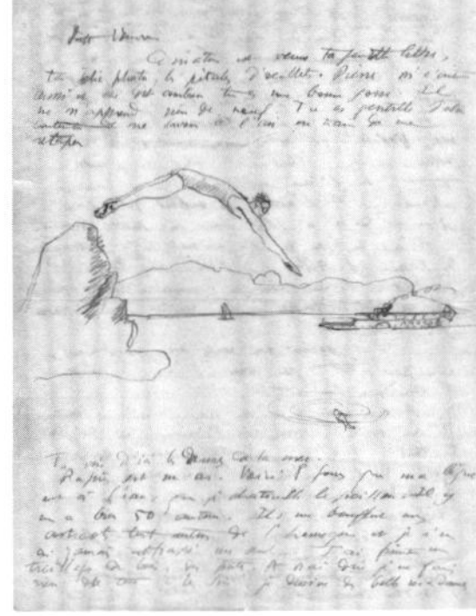

Little Vonvon

This morning came your sweet letter, your pretty photo, the carnation petals. Pierre wrote too and tells me what a good kid you are. As if I didn't know. It's nice of you to be pleased to learn I'm outdoors getting myself back into shape.

From here you can see the dramas of the sea.

[?] is a champ. For a week now my line's been in the water and I've been teasing the fish. There are easily 50 of them around it. They eat my maggots all around the hook and I've never caught a single one. I've painted a wooden trellis and some doors. To tell the truth I'm doing nothing at all. In the evening I draw beautiful ladies

I find in my mother's books. You're going to be insanely jealous. And just what have you come across in a drawer? terrible secrets????????? I hardly dare come home!

And imagine, I traveled 3rd class from Vallorbe and sure as eggs they're back – and I'm scratching! And I'm about to set off to explain things to the pharmacist. From now on I must never forget to travel with my special ointment.

So you didn't get my fat letter with pages for Albert, Pierre and yourself? Or my card? I'm doing my duty, so as not to get a telling-off for not writing when I get home.

I can't come back with my parents. My father's not well. If they can they'll come in late October.

To tell the truth I don't know when I'm coming back. It depends on Pierre, who makes all the decisions. But I don't think it'll be long. And I'm so glad to be seeing you again, and to hear you cooing or shouting, and see the peepee on the floor and Klip taking a bath in a washbasin.

I'm writing this in front of the house. It's very cold; summer's over. Hey my little Vonvon baby, big kisses from your sweetie!

[RIGHT MARGIN]
If this letter arrives in time, tell Pierre that Rivoire can come with us in the car; my parents have dropped the idea. But he should come alone and a day in advance so we can go out in the car and decide on a few things for the house.

[TOP]
Enclosed [?] letter to be given to Blondel: Blondel's address, pavillon de l'Esprit Nouveau, Exposition des Arts Déco – URGENT

4

In Search of the Big Commission (1926–1942)

—P. 224

Letter from the secretary general of the League of Nations, Geneva, to Pierre Jeanneret, 5 May 1927

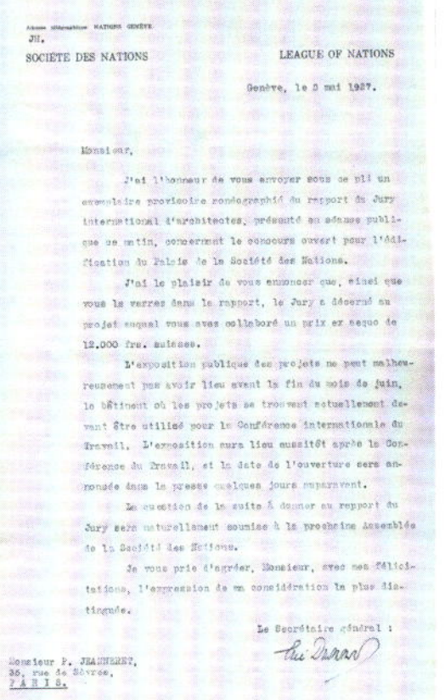

Adresse télégraphique NATIONS GENÈVE
JH.
SOCIÉTÉ DES NATIONS — LEAGUE OF NATIONS

Genève, le 5 mai 1927.

Monsieur,

J'ai l'honneur de vous envoyer sous ce pli un exemplaire provisoire ronéographié du rapport du Jury international d'architectes, présenté en séance publique ce matin, concernant le concours ouvert pour l'édification du Palais de la Société des Nations.

J'ai le plaisir de vous annoncer que, ainsi que vous le verrez dans le rapport, le Jury a décerné au projet auquel vous avez collaboré un prix ex aequo de 12.000 frs. suisses.

L'exposition publique des projets ne peut malheureusement pas avoir lieu avant la fin du mois de juin, le bâtiment où les projets se trouvent actuellement devant être utilisé pour la Conférence internationale du Travail. L'exposition aura lieu aussitôt après la Conférence du Travail, et la date de l'ouverture sera annoncée dans la presse quelques jours auparavant.

La question de la suite à donner au rapport du Jury sera naturellement soumise à la prochaine Assemblée de la Société des Nations.

Je vous prie d'agréer, Monsieur, avec mes félicitations, l'expression de ma considération la plus distinguée.

Le Secrétaire général :

Monsieur P. JEANNERET,
35, rue de Sèvres,
PARIS.

eneva, 5 May 1927

ir,

have the honor to send you here-ith an interim Roneoed copy of the eport of the International Jury of rchitects, presented at a public ıeeting this morning, concerning ıe competition opened for con-ruction of the League of Nations uilding.

It is my pleasure to inform you ıat, as you will see in the report, the ıry awarded the plans on which you ollaborated a shared prize of 12,000 wiss francs.

The public exhibition of the lans, unfortunately, cannot take lace before the end of June, ecause the building where the lans are at present must be used for ıe International Labor Conference. he exhibition will take place imme-iately following the Labor onference, and the date of the pening will be announced in the ress a few days beforehand.

The question of the next steps be taken following the Jury's eport will naturally be submitted at ıe next Assembly of the League of ations.

Sir, with my most sincere con-ratulations, I am yours truly,

he Secretary General:
ignature]

r. P. JEANNERET,
5 rue de Sèvres
ARIS

—P. 227

"What the Public Doesn't Know about the Project for the League of Nations," by Le Corbusier and Pierre Jeanneret, published by Galerie Georges Bernheim, Paris, 1928

From 1 to 21 June 1928

Galerie Georges Bernheim,
109 Faubourg St-Honoré

EXHIBITION OF THE PROJECT OF THE LEAGUE OF NATIONS by Le Corbusier and P. Jeanneret

What the Public Doesn't Know about the Project for the League of Nations by Le Corbusier and P. Jeanneret

May 1927.—By a plurality, the jury of *professionals* awarded this project first prize and selected it for execution (from among 377 projects, representing 14 kilometers of plans).

At the jury's 63rd meeting, Mr. Lemaresquier (a French juror delegated by the Academy) *excludes the plan, claiming it was reproduced by a mechanical process* (instead of being drawn directly in ink).

Thereupon, nine equal prizes are awarded, with each juror naming a winner. Result: an incongruous mix of five academic designs and four modern ones—an exact reflection of the make-up of the jury.

June 1927.—Public exhibition of the designs, in Geneva. The general public's interest focuses on this L.C. and P. J. design, for it represents the modern spirit (countless articles in newspapers and magazines).

September 1927.—General Assembly of the League of Nations. Dramatic turn of events. The Assembly decides, before any selection, to raise the sum to be awarded by 50 percent. Protests from the professional Associations against this *breach of contract. Now the battle lines are drawn between the Academy and the modern spirit.*

Only the L.C. and P. J. design does not exceed the allocated sum of 13 million gold francs (the *sine qua non* condition of the competition).

The four academic designs cost 27 million, 40 million, 45 million, 50 million; their creators declared 13 million, but experts have decried the lie. The new sum (19½), in the end raised to 24 million, will make it possible to approach the academic designs.

Arbitrariness is the order of the day: Six *ambassadors* are charged by the Assembly of Nations with selecting the design to be executed, *with a precise mandate*, cost of construction and functional efficiency.

The technical experts consulted by the ambassadors select the L.C. and P. J. design: the Czechoslovakian expert; the expert from the government of the Swiss Federation; Geneva's municipal expert.

27 December 1927.—The *ambassadors* do not select a *design*, they select an *architect*: Mr. Nénot, a member of the Institute and President of the Salon of French Artists (27 million) and assign him three academic colleagues: Mr. Broggi (Italian) 40 m., Mr. Vago (Italo-Hungarian) 40 m., Mr. Lefebvre (French) 50 m.

Worldwide protest against this second breach of contract: professional associations from Switzerland, Czechoslovakia, Holland, France, Sweden, Denmark, Germany, Austria, etc.; from the most important technical people of France, Germany, America, Scandinavia, Switzerland, etc.; appeal to the world elite by the leaders of the "*French Resurgence*"; countless reprimands to the League of Nations (L.O.N.) from the major newspapers and magazines.

L.C. and P. J. send to the L.O.N. Council a petition drawn up by Mr. Prudhomme, an attorney at the Court of Justice, professor in the Faculties of Law, *requesting the annulment of the Ambassadors' verdict.* This petition limits its arguments to the flagrant, *purely legal errors* committed by the L.O.N. in the matter of the Palace.

5 March 1928.—The *Council of Nations* meets. The petition addressed to it *is not delivered* by Sir Eric Drummond, Secretary General of the L.O.N. (The petition printed on 30 pages was sent registered in 25 copies.)

The Council confirms the Ambassa-dors' decision: *four architecture firms are charged with finalizing the design for the Palace according to a program that has nothing to do with the four firms' designs.* **On the contrary, the new design is inspired directly by the L.C. and P. J. design.** One of the ambassadors stated: "The L.C. and P. J. project will be very useful to us in building the new Palace."

The *Secretary General* did not see fit to acknowledge receipt of the petition to Mr. Prudhomme. So it is sent again to the Council of Nations for the June session.

Nevertheless, a month later, in response to a registered letter from Mr. Prudhomme, the Geneva Secretariat General informs him that the L.O.N. recognizes only matters among nations and not those of individuals (!).

The petition is the first legal proceedings undertaken against the L.O.N. since it was founded. There is no jurisdiction that can judge the L.O.N., *the supreme agency of human justice.* The case fascinates the judicial circles. How to follow up such a petition?

A person of some importance, involved since the beginning with the matter of the competition, has stated: "This competition was fixed from the start; the Academy was chosen to build; the competition was just for show. Furthermore, because of the violent outburst of national ambitions, the compromise of the four architects was settled upon to satisfy political appetites. What were chosen were countries and architects of the Academy, *not a single one of the competition designs* (the farce of the competition cost the 377 entrants more than 20 million!). In important articles, the major world newspapers dubbed the maneuver: "The Palace Scandal."

The designs were never objectively discussed, *except by the jury of professionals* and later by the experts. Because the designs (on average 30 to 40 meters of plans apiece) were in crates.

Behind the curtain of brief public statements, *secret* diplomacy was going on: four academic architects are chosen; four modern architects are turned down. The fifth academic architect (Mr. Labro) could not in all decency be accepted, because of his relationship with Mr. Lemaresquier, the architect of Paris's "Nouveau Cercle Militaire," a juror of the competition, and the stage manager of the incident (the jury's 63rd meeting) that made it possible for the Academy to triumph and defeat the modern spirit.

The exhibition of L.C. and P. J.'s project will allow those interested in the architectural question to study this much-discussed design for the palace, which no one, so to speak, has ever seen.

—P. 228

Program from CIAM I, 25–29 June 1928, La Sarraz, Switzerland

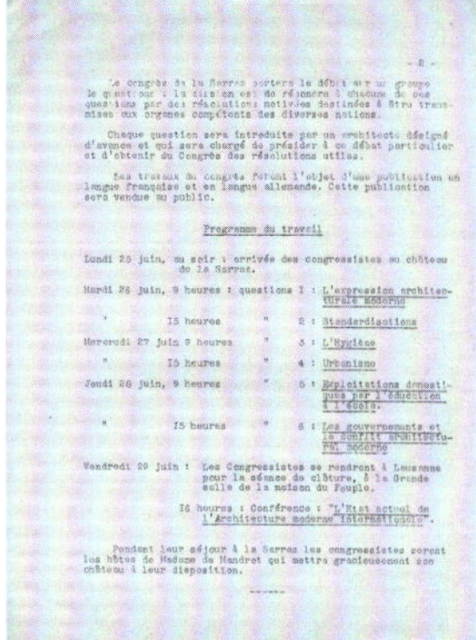

- 2 -

Le Congrès de La Sarraz portera le débat sur un groupe de questions : sa mission est de répondre à chacune de ces questions par des résolutions motivées destinées à être transmises aux organes compétents des diverses nations.

Chaque question sera introduite par un architecte désigné d'avance et qui sera chargé de présider à ce débat particulier et d'obtenir du Congrès des résolutions utiles.

Les travaux du congrès feront l'objet d'une publication en langue française et en langue allemande. Cette publication sera vendue au public.

Programme du travail

Lundi 25 juin, au soir : arrivée des congressistes au château de La Sarraz.

Mardi 26 juin, 9 heures : questions 1 : L'expression architecturale moderne
" 15 heures " 2 : Standardisations
Mercredi 27 juin 9 heures " 3 : L'Hygiène
" 15 heures " 4 : Urbanisme
Jeudi 28 juin, 9 heures " 5 : Exploitations domestiques par l'éducation à l'école.
" 15 heures " 6 : Les gouvernements et le conflit architectural moderne

Vendredi 29 juin : Les Congressistes se rendront à Lausanne pour la séance de clôture, à la Grande salle de la maison du Peuple.

16 heures : Conférence : "L'Etat actuel de l'Architecture moderne internationale".

Pendant leur séjour à La Sarraz les congressistes seront les hôtes de Madame de Mandrot qui mettra gracieusement son château à leur disposition.

The Congress at La Sarraz will discuss a group of questions: its mission is to respond to each of these questions with considered resolutions intended to be communicated to the relevant agencies of the various nations.

Each question will be introduced by an architect named beforehand, who will be charged with chairing that particular discussion and obtaining useful resolutions from the Congress.

The Congress's work will be published in French and German. The publication will be sold to the public.

Work program
Monday 25 June, evening: arrival of the participants at the château of La Sarraz.

Tuesday 26 June, 9:00:
questions 1: The expression of modern architecture
[Tuesday 26 June,] 15:00
2: Standardizations
Wednesday 27 June, 9:00
3: Sanitation
[Wednesday 27 June,] 15:00
4: Urban planning
Thursday 28 June, 9:00
5: Domestic uses by education at school
[Thursday 28 June,] 15:00
6: Governments and the modern architectural struggle
Friday 29 June: The participants will go to Lausanne for the closing session in the Great Hall of the Maison du Peuple.
16:00: Lecture: "The Present State of International Modern Architecture."

During their stay in La Sarraz, the participants will be the guests of Mrs. de Mandrot, who will graciously put her manor at their disposition.

—P. 228

List of the twenty-two nations represented at CIAM I

Les groupes nationaux actuellement reconnus sont organisés partout où l'architecture moderne possède un moyen agissant: en Algérie, Angleterre, Autriche, Brésil, Belgique, Espagne, Finlande, France, Grèce, Hollande, Hongrie, Japon, Indochine, Italie, Norvège, Pologne, Suède, Suisse, Turquie, Tchécoslovaquie, U.S.A., Yougoslavie.

Follows "moral [?] material"

The currently recognized national groups are organized everywhere modern architecture has the means to act: in Algeria, England, Austria, Brazil, Belgium, Spain, Finland, France, Greece, Holland, Hungary, Japan, Indochina, Italy, Norway, Poland, Sweden, Switzerland, Turkey, Czechoslovakia, U.S.A., Yugoslavia.

—P. 232

"Le Corbusier in Barcelona," *La Publicitat* (Barcelona), 18 May 1928

Informacions de «La Publicitat»

Le Corbusier a Barcelona

News from "La Publicitat"

Le Corbusier in Barcelona
The famous architect's comments on the city

Recently some friends and I had the honor of meeting with Le Corbusier during his short stay in our city to give two lectures. I thought it would be interesting to report the great architect's comments as he walked around and took in the sights.

Our discussions were just friendly chats rather than carefully thought out disquisitions. He charmed us with his spontaneous comments. By reporting them, I must acknowledge I am being indiscreet. But it is tempting to transcribe some aspects of his profound vision… and it is also necessary to satisfy the great interest aroused by his visit. These arguments should serve to justify my indiscretion vis-à-vis Le Corbusier, to whom I offer my apologies.

Much has been written and theorized about Le Corbusier's oeuvre, and opinions run the gamut. He sometimes takes on the role of a builder and at other times that of a polemicist. His books, articles, and lectures fascinate intellectuals worldwide. Le Corbusier is strong enough to endure all kinds of criticism. He himself laughingly quoted to us an article published in the Paris newspaper "L'Intransigeant" (this quote is not verbatim as I could not get hold of the paper): "The three people that appeal most to the young nowadays are Josephine Baker, Charlie Chaplin, and Le Corbusier."

Dear reader, since the main reason that persuaded you to read this article was the headline, I should now summarize my conversations with Le Corbusier. I will not add any comments, just some necessary clarifications, and I believe I will thus deserve your thanks. And since Le Corbusier likes a system of classifying compartments, allow me to use it now.

Here's what Le Corbusier says:

WHILE HAVING LUNCH AT "LA FONT DEL LLEO" RESTAURANT.—During the gestation of a building project, the worst thing an architect can do is draw. If when one is thinking about a project one draws it right away, the limitations inherent to the pencil cause the idea to be subject to the image and prevent the intellect from working freely. One should think for a long time before getting down to drawing because by thinking without the influence of any image the brain conceives an idea in all its dimensions and all its elements, inside and outside, above and below a building.

AT BARON GUELL'S HOUSE.—The arcades of your farmhouses are charming. Your regional traditions are an inexhaustible source of inspiration. I have noticed, however, although I am not speaking about this house, that too often you copy traditional ornamentation without grasping your racial view of the past. What a beautiful garden. I don't know any city equal to it in this respect.

MONASTERY OF PEDRALBES.—Such modern simplicity! The austerity of the tracery is breathtaking. This is one of the best things I have seen in your country. I have been really surprised by your Gothic architecture.

STAIRCASE AT THE LLOTJA PALACE.—Imagine these staircase arches built of plaster with the same shape: surely we would not like them. Their charm derives from the stereotomic lines of the stone that stimulate the intellect and give pleasure to the soul.

SANTA MARIA DEL MAR CHURCH.—The interior of this church is among the most beautiful I have ever seen. The decision to make the interior look as large as possible is very good.

THE CATHEDRAL.—The architect who built this had a very sharp sense of how to balance volumes. Your Gothic architecture has totally seduced me and I would go so far as to say I prefer it to ours.

BISBE STREET.—*Note*: It was a pity we were not able to get our guest's opinion about the recently inaugurated Gothic bridge. Although he looked at it for quite a while, his attention was quickly focused on a store window displaying religious statuettes. He was fascinated by it and he kept saying "c'est joli, ça [that's pretty]." Afterward I did not dare ask any further and chose to respect his silence. Le Corbusier keeps talking …

PLAÇA DEL REI (KING'S SQUARE).—This spot has a somewhat Florentine air to it, which makes it charming.

DINING AT THE RITZ.—I believe your country is very suitable to provide a growth medium for the new living architecture. In Germany, a sense of opulent ostentation and Nordic confusion are obstacles, while in Russia we struggle against brainy complications and in France we find a misunderstood traditional refinement.

I advocate an essentially Latin architecture because of its mathematical ratios and conceptual clarity. Do you understand why I believe it is suitable for your country where there are clear and well-reasoned structural solutions?

ON THE WAY TO SITGES.—I very much enjoyed my visit to Madrid and Toledo. The people are very kind! Their world over there is so different from yours! The Castilian plains are very interesting and exude a deeply pathetic feeling. I noticed something remarkable in Madrid: I think they went directly from candles to electricity, bypassing the intermediate steps of oil and gas. (*Note*: This phrase should be interpreted by reference to its aesthetic equivalencies.)

Something that impressed me in Castile are the donkeys. It's fun to look at a peasant astride a donkey!

I found Andalusian dance and flamenco singing very moving. Their songs begin with a deep and sentimental melodic curve. It's like the undulations of their landscape; the persistent and harmonic pulsation made by the feet of the dancer suddenly bursts forth; human individuality struggling and manifesting itself within the span of nature. Harmonic coexistence in the integral reality of our life.

WALKING AROUND SITGES.—Misguided architects are a curse we must endure in every country. See how awful the houses built with artistic conceit look in these admirable streets! Ah! You say the name of this house is "Sea and Sky," a very pretty and appropriate name … you need to be an American to come up with something like this. Look at that house next to the church; that's where archaeology ends and life goes on after being interrupted by such archaeological opulence. It feels good to look at your landscapes; I find them stronger than Italian landscapes.

GAUDI.—This house (La Pedrera) has balanced grandeur.

It is interesting to see that Gaudí uses the same solution I use in reinforced concrete buildings, i.e., a beam working in a "pivoting" system.

If houses like this one filled a whole street, perhaps we would be unable to sleep.

SAGRADA FAMILIA CHURCH.—We should all remove our hats in front of this wonderful building! It is, however, regrettable that decoration overwhelms mathematical reasoning. There is a strange contradiction in the work of this genius. Perhaps due to the influence of his times? Gaudí must have been a exceptional personality. I remember how about fifteen years ago we in Paris were very enthusiastic when we discovered his architecture.

If space allowed, I could go on remembering other discussions on various topics, all of them of great interest coming as they do from such an intelligent celebrity, but I have probably said too much. To conclude, I am pleased to report that Le Corbusier left Barcelona by air and flew to Marseille. He does indeed live by his own principles. He not only theorizes machinism but also practices it.

Marius GIFREDA

—P. 250

Pamphlet commemorating the inauguration of the Cité de Refuge, 7 December 1933

LA CITÉ DE REFUGE

AIMEZ-VOUS LES UNS LES AUTRES.

THE CITE DE REFUGE

Its Mission:
A combination of temporary shelter, triage, and processing center, and an information and referral office in direct and ultrafast contact with charitable organizations providing public and private assistance, employment office, charitable work-aid office, nighttime shelter, and help to men, women, mothers, and children, the **Cité de Refuge** will be the Factory for Good where the gears of the human machine worn down by life will be overhauled.

"The flagless army of the wretched must have a hope, a home where, along with bread and a bed, advice, and work are given; a Cité de Refuge where every affliction will have its confidant, defender, and guide, where everyone will rediscover their joy… And it will be the greatness of this project that it will be built to serve, not as a retreat, but on the contrary, to create new tomorrows." (André LABARTHE).

" … Why another building, why another solicitation in the realm of Charity, which is so fragmented there is danger of diminishing the harvests or seeing them misused if they are disseminated? Because what will be offered here exists nowhere else. And it is essential to create it.

"When misfortune attacks a family, where is the shelter against bad luck, abandonment, lack? What door is there to knock at? How many steps more, on top of steps soon wearied in aimless searching: and discouragement often stops in his effort to pull himself up again the man who was unable to go directly and quickly to those who could address his problem.

"So he stops at the side of the painful, seemingly endless road, and in the ditch he finds the companions always ready to readily take him in: begging, alcoholism, and vice.

"Tomorrow, here, in the vast home, at the slightest fear, the lightest threat, as well as after the burdensome past, anyone who comes will be received in all brotherhood. With affectionate familiarity the causes of their misery will be sorted out, their life's troubles will be cleared up, body and conscience will be deloused, and once the will is reawakened and comforted, once confidence in oneself and others is revived, those who need such help will be directed or led to the appropriate charity or public service. In hospitals, there is something called triage. Victims of street accidents are brought there; they receive a first-aid dressing and after an examination they are sent exactly where they must be treated. The Cité de Refuge will be an emergency room for victims of themselves or of society. In fact, it will achieve with the most modern practical processing methods the highest aspirations of an ideal honored by all. (Justin GODART).

"This staff and its small army in action are one of the clearest manifestations of **the social service that a group can provide, of one man's power to achieve, and of the sublime might of enthusiasm."**

LOVE ONE ANOTHER.

[CAPTIONS]
Photograph of the Model

The Princess de Polignac signs the record of the laying of the 1st stone

Mrs. Commissioner Peyron and the Minister of Public Health
A Room for a Mother and Child

A men's Dormitory

—P. 253

Le Corbusier to his mother, from Buenos Aires, 29 October 1929

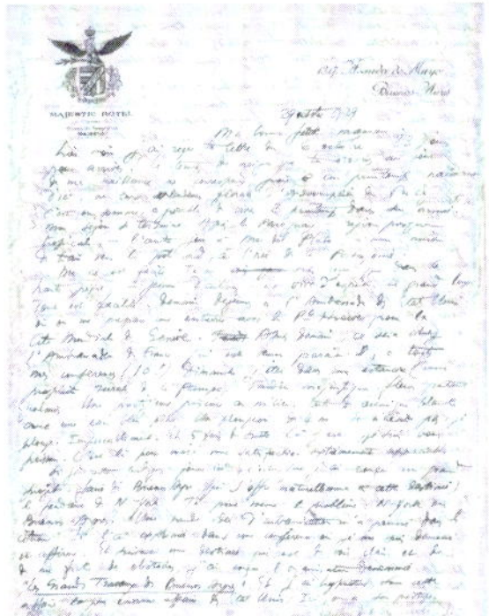

29 October 1929

My sweet little mom.

last night I got your letter of 6 October. 23 days to get here. The snowy weather you mention on the day I was born isn't much like the burgeoning spring here, or the floral splendors of Assumption Day in Paraguay. In short, it's agreeable to have 2 springtimes in your year! My stay is coming to an end. After Paraguay, an almost tropical region—the other day at Mar del Plata, an overnight train ride toward the South Pole, on the fringe of Patagonia.

My life is easy. I ~~see only~~ am welcomed only by the top brass,—young as it happens—and bright. The lap of luxury. Everything's easy. Lunch tomorrow at the United States Embassy where they're setting up an interview for me with President Hoover for the World Civic Center in Geneva. ~~Thurs~~ The day after tomorrow I'll be at the home of the French Ambassador, who's attended, it seems, all my lectures (10!). Sunday I was in an estancia (a country property on the Pampas). Magnificent garden, flowers everywhere, palm trees. A glamorous swimming pool in the middle, all white ceramic with pale blue water. A 4-meter diving board. I don't hesitate: I dive. Impeccably. And five times in a row. So there, I'm a real fish. For me that's something extremely satisfying.

If I'm staying a few days here, it's because I've come up with a big project: to make Buenos Aires (which by its very nature lends itself to the plan) a counterpart to N-York. I even raise the issue: N-York or Buenos Aires? A great idea for urbanization has sprung up in my head. I outlined it in a lecture during which I went to great lengths to make my point. And obeying my destiny, which is to be clear-sighted and not give a damn about obstacles, I thought up an organization called "The Great Redevelopment of Buenos Aires." And with this idea I mesmerized one of the biggest companies in the United States. But if necessary they can go to HELL! You're respected here.

You speak, knowing that. And you're listened to. The North Americans are young and strong, simple and guileless. For them, act. In architecture they are utterly backward. And so they believe me. I think my next trip to the United States will be something big.

Here I'm being told to "tell Loucheur" this or that regarding the pitiful state of France's representation. Argentina worships Paris. They speak perfect French. My friend Gonzales Garrano (descendant of a viceroy) is a man of great, subtle culture, with whom I speak frankly, on equal terms. Yesterday we were visiting the gigantic German liner Cap Arcona together. He meets one of the valets; they embrace like brothers, for Garrano had traveled on the liner this summer. This morning I did his portrait. It wasn't easy. I was absolutely beside myself. Finally it worked, by dint of sheer energy and because I didn't give in. He was thrilled.

They're arranging for me to overfly Buenos Aires. What a business! Minister of Foreign Aff, President of the Rep., Minister of war, not to mention all the aviation departments. Negotiations have been going on for 3 weeks!

I'd been asked to give lectures in Cordoba, in the center of Argentina, then in Santiago de Chile. I refused, since I can't stay forever. Rio de Janeiro telegraphed asking me to stay 10 days.

My program is São Paulo Brazil (my friend Prado, the coffee king). Stay with him, visit the plantations, maybe encounter snakes 12 meters long (Cendrars!) and lectures at 10,000 francs each. Maybe some jobs there.

Little mom, I hope this doesn't sound like a fairy tale to you. I remain a modest little guy, hoping to get back to his 20 rue Jacob, to his oil painting, to the faithful company of VVon; and to see my little mother again soon. If I put up with this wandering life, it's because I think maybe I'll get the money that will mean I can make life easier for those around me, for my family who haven't had the same chance to make "big money."

Bye little mom. I'm sending this letter airmail. It'll arrive quickly. Can you imagine that a French plane carrying 500 kg

[LEFT MARGIN]
of letters from B-Aires to Paris earns a million francs?

[RIGHT MARGIN]
People always make fun of France. I assure you that the Latécoère airline between Toulouse and the whole of South America is splendidly punctual, conscientious, and efficient. Big kisses from your Ed.

—P. 255

Sketches from Le Corbusier's lectures in Buenos Aires, 3–19 October 1929, and Brazil, December 1929

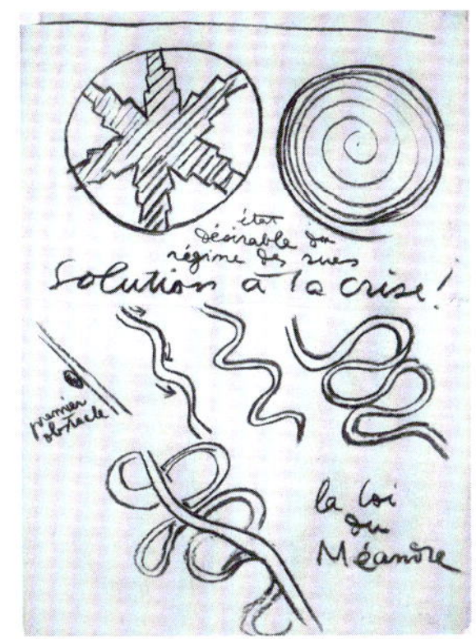

[TOP TO BOTTOM]
desirable system of street layout

the answer to the crisis!

first obstacle

the law of the Meander

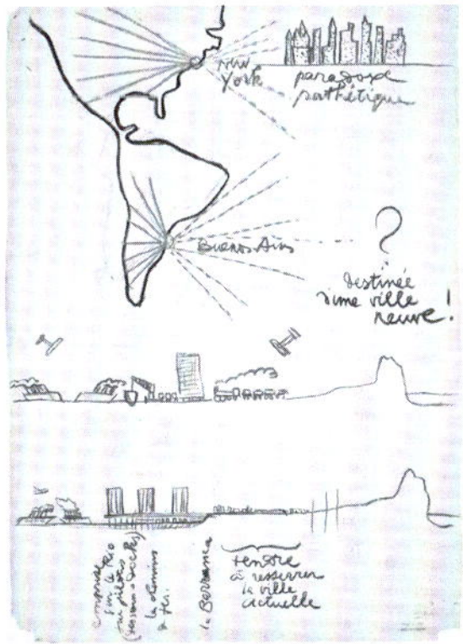

[LEFT TO RIGHT, TOP TO BOTTOM]
New York
pathetic paradox

Buenos Aires ?
destiny of a new city!

area on the Rio on piles (underneath = docks) railroad track

La Barranca

try to condense the present city

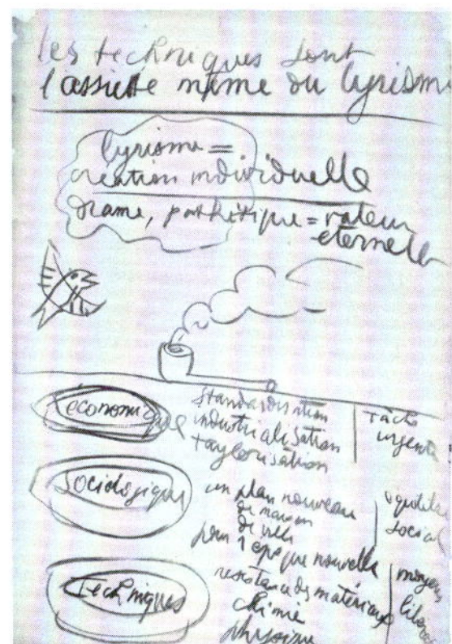

[LEFT TO RIGHT, TOP TO BOTTOM]
Technology is the very basis of lyricism

lyricism =
individual creativity
drama, pathos = eternal value

economic / standardization industrialization taylorization / urgent task

sociological / a new plan for a house for a city for a new era / social equilibrium

techniques / strength of materials chemistry physics / liberating resources

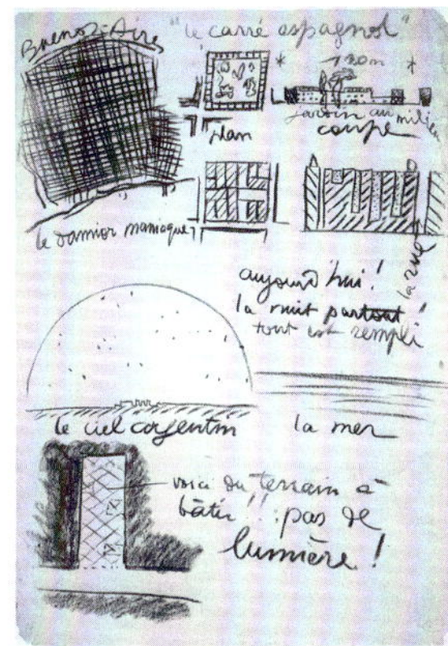

[LEFT TO RIGHT, TOP TO BOTTOM]
Buenos Aires / "The Spanish square" / 120 meters

plan / garden in the middle / section

the obsessive checkerboard / the street

today!
night everywhere
everything is filled in
the argentinean sky / the sea
here's building land!! no light!

[LEFT TO RIGHT, TOP TO BOTTOM]
death to the "corridor street"!

the sky

here's the enemy! / American-style / "old style"

the illusion of plans! / another illusion!

sky / the "steps"

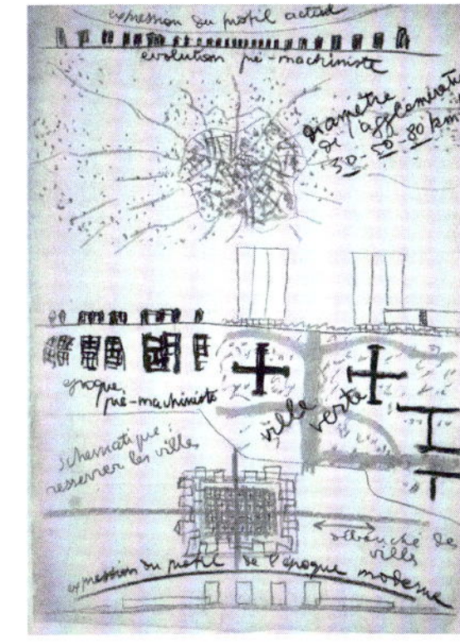

[LEFT TO RIGHT, TOP TO BOTTOM]
outline of the present profile
pre-machine evolution

diameter of the built-up area 30–50 – 80 km!!

pre-machine era / green city

diagram: condense cities

city outlets

outline of the modern era profile

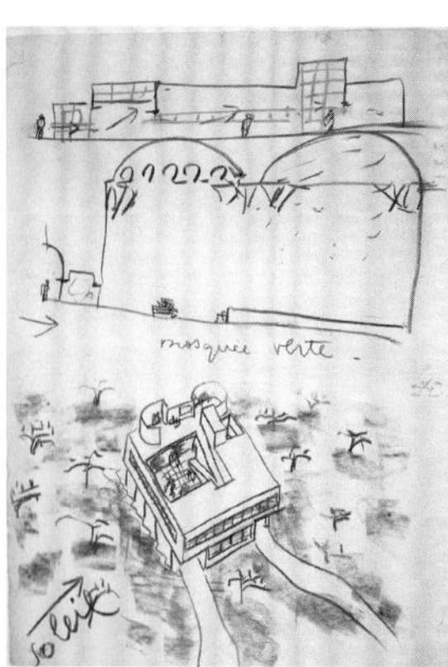

green mosque

sun

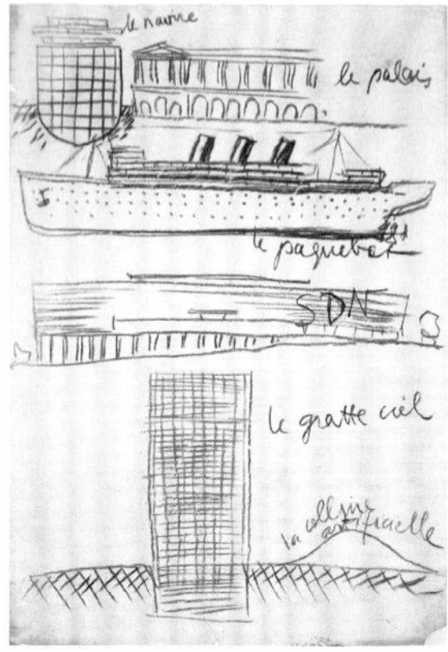

[TOP TO BOTTOM]
the ship

the palace

the liner

League of Nations

the skyscraper

the artificial hill

—P. 260

Diagram of strategy for organizing public works in Buenos Aires, from Le Corbusier's South American lecture tour, 1929

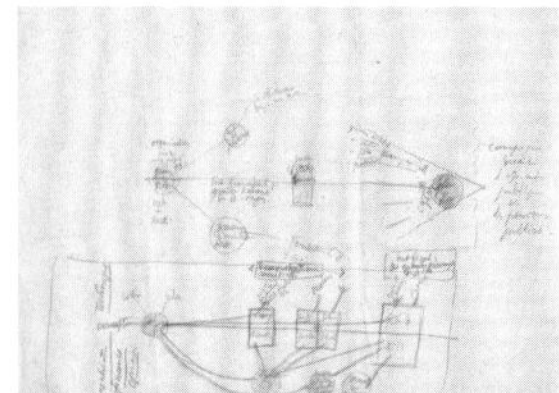

[TOP SKETCH]
[TOP TO BOTTOM, LEFT TO RIGHT]
organization with headquarters at B[uenos] A[ires]
urb[anist] + arch[itect]

La Paolera dagnino Pastore
provincial urb[anist]

main aim: public works in B[uenos]—Aires
architecture works

French state office
Foundations Cy + Steel

will make aviation / metro / port / skyscraper / bank

Planning committee / map B[uenos] A[ires]

Campaign aimed at public opinion and the authorities

[BOTTOM SKETCH]
[TOP TO BOTTOM, LEFT TO RIGHT]
technique
corruption
building / finance / opinion

Corbu / summary

immediate demonstrations
arch[itects] maybe as arbitrators etc.
architecture works
Foundation Cy

Paolera
province urb[anist] + arch[itect] works
finance consultancy
planning committee

final goal: the major works in B[uenos] A[ires]

various architectures
Paolera
Map of B[uenos] A[ires]

—P. 262

Le Corbusier to Josephine Baker, 4 February 1935

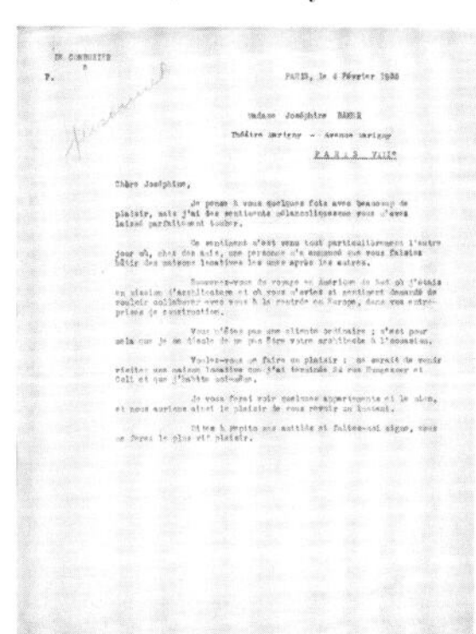

PARIS, 4 February 1935

Mrs. Joséphine BAKER
Théâtre Marigny–Avenue Marigny
PARIS VIII

Dear Joséphine,

I think of you sometimes with a great deal of pleasure; I must tell you of the melancholy feelings I have because you dropped me so resoundingly.

This feeling was particularly acute the other day when, at the house of some friends, someone told me you were building rental accommodation units in quick succession.

Do you recall my trip to South America on architectural business and that you had so kindly asked me to work with you on your building ventures when I got back to Europe.

You are no ordinary client; and this is why it grieves me not to be your architect in this instance.

Will you do me a favor: this would be to come visit a rental building I've completed at 24 rue Nungesser et Coli and which I live in myself.

I'll show you a few apartments and mine and we would have the pleasure of seeing each other for a moment.

Give Pepito my best regards and get in touch, that would give me the greatest pleasure.

—P. 262

Le Corbusier to Josephine Baker, 2 January 1936

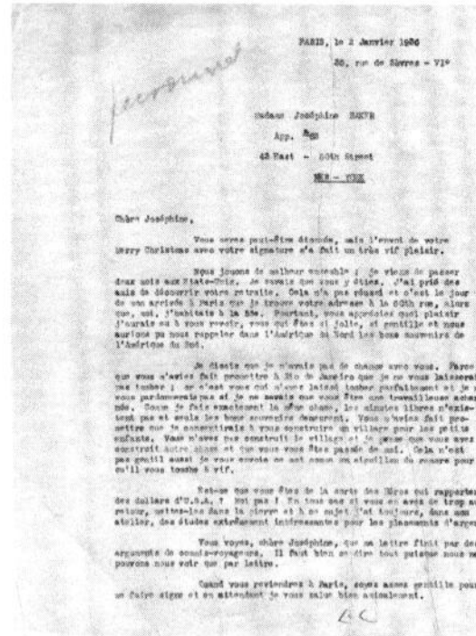

PARIS, 2 January 1936

35 rue de Sèvres–VI

Mrs. Joséphine BAKER
Apt. A62
43 East 60th Street
NEW-YORK

Dear Joséphine,

Maybe you'll be very surprised, but I was delighted by the Merry Christmas you sent with your signature.

We're sharing bad luck: I've just spent two months in the United States. I knew you were there. I begged friends to find your hiding place. This didn't work and it was the day I arrived in Paris that I found your address on 60th Street, while I had been living on 55th. Even so, you're aware of the pleasure it would have been for me to see you again, you who are so pretty and sweet, and in North America we would have been able to recall our fond memories of South America.

As I said, I had no luck with you. Because in Rio de Janeiro you had made me promise I wouldn't drop you; when in fact it was you who dropped me resoundingly and I wouldn't forgive you if I didn't know you to be a compulsive worker. As I'm exactly the same, free time is nonexistent and only the fond memories remain. You had made me promise to agree to build a village for small children for you. You haven't built this village and I think you've built something else and done it without me. That's not very nice so I'm sending this letter as a goad to remorse that will cut you to the quick.

Does this mean you are one of those Heroes who bring dollars from the U.S.A.? I'm not! In any case, if you have too many of them when you come back, put them into bricks and mortar and while we're on the subject I still have, in my studio, some extremely interesting studies for the placing of money.

You see, dear Joséphine, that my letter is ending with a traveling salesman's spiel. We have to tell each other everything since we can see each other only by letter.

When you come back to Paris, be so kind as to get in touch and in the meantime all my best wishes.

L–C

—P. 264

Le Corbusier to the Chief of the French Naturalization Department, 2 May 1930

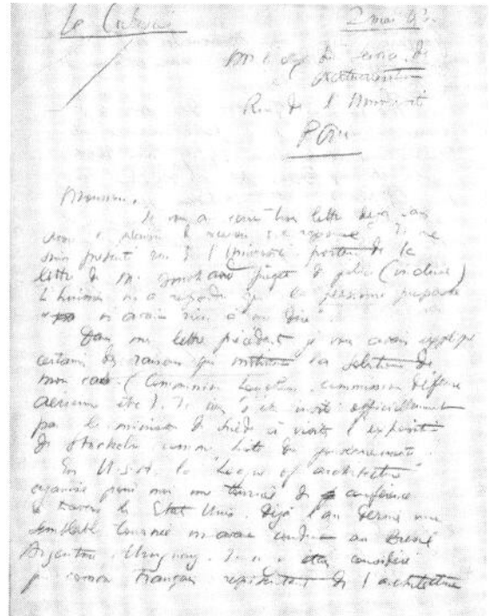

Le Corbusier

2 May 1930
Chief of the Naturalization Department
Rue de l'Université
Paris

Sir,

I have already written you three letters without having the pleasure of receiving your reply. I went to rue de l'Université with the letter from Mr. Guichard prefect of police (enclosed) The attendant told me that the person in charge "had nothing to say to me." In my previous letters I had explained to you some of the reasons making resolution of my case desirable. (Loucheur Commission, aerial defense commission, etc.). I have just been officially invited by the Swedish minister to visit the Stockholm exhibition, as a guest of their government.

In the U.S.A. the "League of architecture" is organizing a lecture tour for me around the United States. Already last year a similar tour had taken me to Brazil, Argentina, and Uruguay. There I was considered totally French, representing

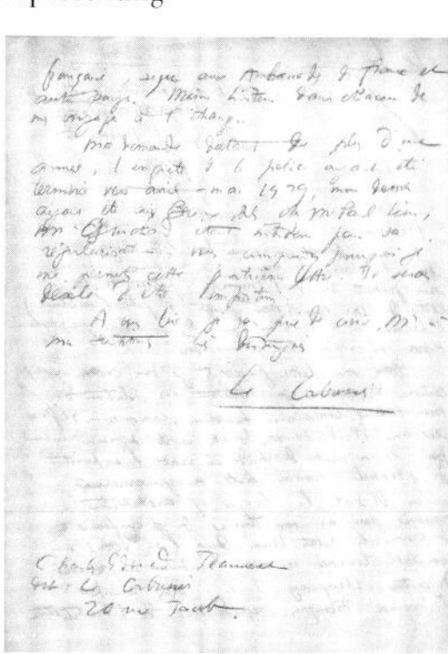

French architecture, and welcomed at the Embassies of France and other countries. The same applies to all my trips abroad.

My request going back more than a year; the police investigation having been completed around March–April 1929, my file having been with Mr. Paul Léon at the Beaux Arts, and Mr. Guichard having requested settlement of this matter, you will understand why I take the liberty of this fourth letter. I have no wish to appear importunate.

Looking forward to hearing from you, I remain, yours faithfully,

Le Corbusier

Charles-Edouard Jeanneret
known as: Le Corbusier
20 rue Jacob

—P. 264

The Director General of Fine Arts of the French Republic to Le Corbusier, 21 May 1935

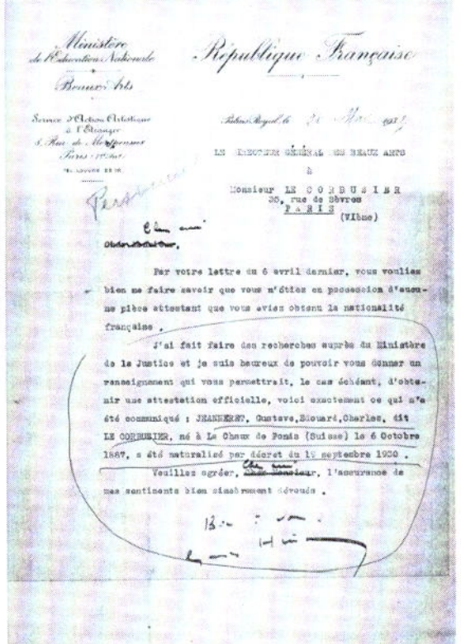

Ministère de l'Education Nationale
Beaux-Arts
Service d'Action Artistique à l'Etranger

République Française

Palais Royal, le 21 Mai 1935

LE DIRECTEUR GÉNÉRAL DES BEAUX ARTS
à
Monsieur LE CORBUSIER
35, rue de Sèvres
PARIS (VIème)

Cher ami
~~Cher Monsieur~~,

Par votre lettre du 6 avril dernier, vous vouliez bien me faire savoir que vous n'étiez en possession d'aucune pièce attestant que vous aviez obtenu la nationalité française.

J'ai fait faire des recherches auprès du Ministère de la Justice et je suis heureux de pouvoir vous donner un renseignement qui vous permettrait, le cas échéant, d'obtenir une attestation officielle, voici exactement ce qui m'a été communiqué : JEANNERET, Gustave, Edouard, Charles, dit LE CORBUSIER, né à La Chaux de Fonds (Suisse) le 6 Octobre 1887, a été naturalisé par décret du 19 septembre 1930.

Veuillez agréer, Cher ami ~~Cher Monsieur~~, l'assurance de mes sentiments bien sincèrement dévoués.

Palais Royal, *21 May* 1935

Personnel
THE DIRECTOR GENERAL OF THE FINE ARTS
to
Mr LE CORBUSIER
35 rue de Sèvres
PARIS (VIème)

Dear friend
~~Dear Sir~~,

By your letter of 6 April last, you informed me that you have in your possession no document proving that you obtained French citizenship.

I had research done at the Ministry of Justice and I am glad I can give you information that would allow you, if necessary, to obtain an official certificate, here's exactly what was communicated to me: JEANNERET, Gustave, Edouard, Charles, known as LE CORBUSIER, born in La Chaux de Fonds (Switzerland) 6 October 1887, was naturalized by a decree of 19 September 1930.

Please believe me to be ~~Dear Sir~~, *Dear friend*, sincerely yours,

Best Regards
[signature]

—P. 278

Giuseppe Bottai to Le Corbusier, 18 January 1934

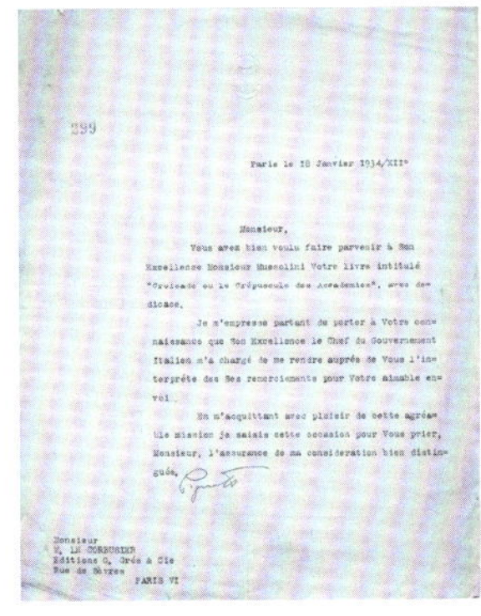

299

Paris le 18 Janvier 1934/XII°

Monsieur,

Vous avez bien voulu faire parvenir à Son Excellence Monsieur Mussolini Votre livre intitulé "Croisade ou le Crépuscule des Académies", avec dédicace.

Je m'empresse partant de porter à Votre connaissance que Son Excellence le Chef du Gouvernement Italien m'a chargé de me rendre auprès de Vous l'interprète des Ses remerciements pour Votre aimable envoi.

En m'acquittant avec plaisir de cette agréable mission je saisis cette occasion pour Vous prier, Monsieur, l'assurance de ma considération bien distinguée.

Monsieur
M. LE CORBUSIER
Editions G. Crès & Cie
Rue de Sèvres
PARIS VI

Paris 18 January 1934/XII

Sir,

You were kind enough to send His Excellency Mr. Mussolini Your book titled "Croisade ou le Crépuscule des Académies," with a dedication.

Hence I hasten to let You know that His Excellency the Head of the Italian Government has charged me to convey to You His thanks for your gracious dispatch.

It is with pleasure that I acquit myself of this agreeable task, and take the opportunity to pray you believe me to be, Sir, most respectfully yours,

[signature]

Sir
Mr LE CORBUSIER
Editions G. Crès & Cie
Rue de Sèvres
PARIS VI

—P. 278

Le Corbusier, *Croisade ou le crépuscule des académies* (Crusade or the Twilight of the Academies), 1933, interior pages

Une autre planche de l'album lui apparut parallèlement à des images concomitantes... « Eupalinos, songeait-il, recherchait la raison des choses. »

Il fut frappé par les analogies qui, dans cette présente époque, lient l'une à l'autre toutes les œuvres entreprises pour obtenir l'efficacité des gestes et atteindre à la glorification de l'esprit.

Et il était persuadé que l'architecture a ce don miraculeux de mettre toutes les choses en harmonie.

Another plate in the album appeared to him along with accompanying images... "Eupalinos, he mused, sought the reason of things."

He was struck by the similarities that, in the present age, connect one to another all the works intended to achieve efficient motion and attain the glorification of the spirit.

And he was convinced that architecture has this miraculous gift, to put all things in harmony.

Toujours appuyé au bastingage de la galère, Le Corbusier se souvint qu'un soir, après qu'il avait harangué une foule de gens venus pour s'informer, il avait eu la sensation que quelqu'un s'était levé. Et, qu'ayant évoqué les leçons de l'histoire, l'interrupteur l'avait désigné du doigt et s'était écrié : « Cet homme ment-il ? Cet homme qui prêche à son tour une croisade ? »

Still leaning on the mason's wheelbarrow, Le Corbusier recalled that one evening, after lecturing to a crowd of people who had come to find out what was going on, he had the feeling someone had stood up. And that, conjuring up the lessons of history, the interrupter pointed a finger at him and cried out: "Is this man lying? This man who is also preaching a crusade?"

—P. 286

Le Corbusier to his mother, 29 April 1934

Sunday evening
29 April 1934

My dear little mom

A tough week.

Moving out the papers all the papers 17 years of papers!

What a plunge into the past! it's breaking my arms!

Remark. Recognized one thing: that everything was remarkably orderly, in my own way. No muddle.

Helped by Schniewindt, Klip's buddy, who lives on the 1st floor of the Boulogne building, really makes me feel better.

Won the psychological battle with Yvonne. The apartment was shown to her, finished, curtains, most of the furniture (new) after a good lunch at Schniewindt's on the 1st floor. She was amazed, happy. But pretended to say nothing. It was the first time she'd made the Boulogne trip.

The apartment's great. It was dangerous for me to go live in a building of my own. Really, it's magnificent. There's a view over the countryside with no sense of being perched up on the 7th or 8th floor, thanks to architectural stratagems. No giddiness that way. The garden a poem. Lawn, lilac, roses, and more, and what a horizon!

A great guest room. For you. But you'll have to wait until we've moved in. The practical side very well organized by cleaning lady, delivery men, concierge.

That's the real way to do it, to be in rental accommodation under conditions like these. All the advantages. No landlord problems. Heating, security, etc.

Pierrefeu is living under me. Delighted.

Duclos (Breuillot from Algiers's daughter) also on the 2nd. Delighted. Winter's going to move in on the 4th. Blumenstein, my dentist, on the 5th.

All these apartments are paradises, and all completely different

I did well to leave it so late. That way I'm pretty sure of having designed something that suits my work.

Bought a dog: a wirehaired griffon (schnauzer), son of champions. For the moment he's still suckling his mother, for another four weeks.

That's a page turned. A cycle finished. 17 years in an old place on Rue Jacob. The Parc des Princes location couldn't be better. Certainly the liveliest area in Paris.

Excuse me, my head's bursting with it. Exhausted and fed up. I'm yawning. It's midnight. We move the bedsheets Wednesday and then beddy-bye's over there.

This note to explain my silence. Your last letter ADMIRABLE. A passage on nature and the spring worthy of your son! (Hmm, the boy's modest!) I read it to Pierrefeu.

[LEFT MARGIN]
Yawning again! All this dredging through the past! A real purge! Love from your Ed.

—P. 286

Le Corbusier and Yvonne to his mother, 28 May 1934

Monday morning 28 May 1934

My dear little mom,

A little note to say hello to you and our friends the Dubois.

The sky is radiant and for two weeks now we've been living in a miraculous new setting: a home that's heavenly, because everything is sky and light, space and simplicity.

After grumbling on principle, Yvonne did what cats do: she went round and round in her new box and now she's purring. That means that broom in hand and polishing endlessly she's running her house with the jubilation of a conqueror. She won't say so, though, because she's as obstinate as a little donkey.

I'm very pleased with her. Finally an end to the grim nightmare of Rue Jacob where we lived all cramped up, me 17 years, she 12 years.

As I've always told you,

Yvonne is the best of kids. But she's got her own ideas and habits. She's a very specific kind of little animal and it's not worth trying to change her nature. And for what, anyway? To turn her into a bourgeoise. A waste of effort! you wouldn't succeed and there's no interest in trying. But what I can say is that her tastes and mine are well matched, and go together while being different. And we practice "The freedom of the sea," i.e., we leave each other in peace. The apartment fits admirably with this form of wisdom.

I was in London for 6 days. Worked a lot. Usefully and with no self-interest. This lack of self-interest, which makes me pass for an idiot among people in a hurry, is gradually bringing its reward.

This reward recently showed up in a miraculous way: the state's going to make me director of the 1937 Exposition annex. An enormous affair that's going to unleash dreadful passions. Everything's been signed and the Chambers have to ratify it. It will cause a bit of a storm. But I think it will go through. After what, 3 years of war with so many enemies!

If I'm not torpedoed (which is not impossible) this will be something great and decisive.

I'll be in Rome between 3 and 13 June. And that's all. If I wanted to tell you everything this letter would need 100 pages.

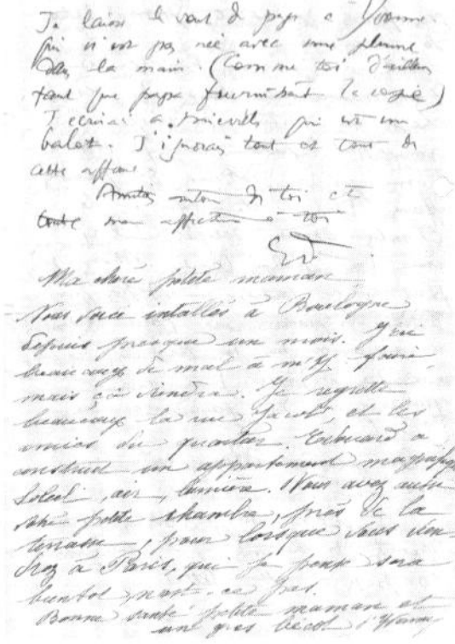

I'm leaving the bottom of the page to Yvonne, who wasn't born with a pen in her hand. (Like you, as long as dad was around) I'll write to Mieville who's a blockhead. I knew strictly nothing about this business.

Best wishes to all those around you and all my love to you

Ed

My dear little mom

So here we are in Boulogne, been here
a month now. I'm finding it hard to get used to, but that will come. I miss Rue Jacob a lot, and my friends in the neighborhood. Edouard has built a magnificent apartment, sun, air, light. You have your little room too, near the terrace, for when you come to Paris, which I think will be soon, no?

Wishing you good health mom and a big kiss from Yvonne

—P. 287

Le Corbusier and Yvonne to his mother, 11 February 1935

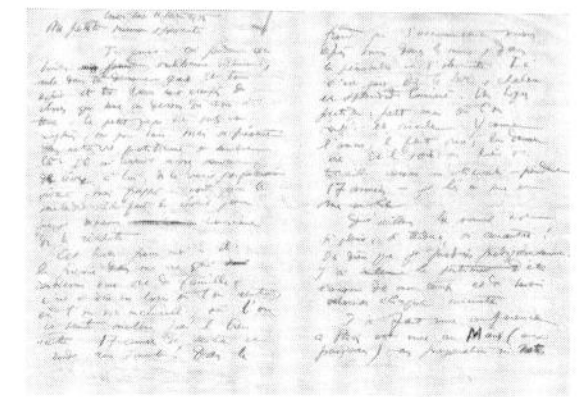

Monday evening 11 February 1935

My spartan little mom.

I've been thinking about you during this suddenly glacial winter, alone in your cheerful home. And your mind and heart are concentrating on things above the down to earth. Little dad is under his Cypress, some distance away, but so present in our daily lives, so often there. Quite often I find myself dreaming of him, believing that he's totally alive but stricken by some mortal illness. It takes the alarm to bring me back to reality.

For me this winter has been the first to ~~be~~ involve a family life, that is to say a home you go into, where you're welcomed and you feel well-being loosen you up. 17 years of harsh, hard Rue Jacob! Amid the cold that built up in the walls month after month, in the half-light and darkness. Here it's pleasure as soon as you get up, warmth and splendid light. A practical home, but one where you can breathe and move about. Yvonne brightens it up, makes it lively, gives it life. And in the evening, instead of working like a dog—during 17 years—I read a little, then go to bed.

And the working day is so full, so taut, so concentrated. They say I have a prodigious output. I only know that I use my time economically and get the most out of every minute. I gave a talk in Paris and one in Le Mans (to the farmers) with no preparation or notes

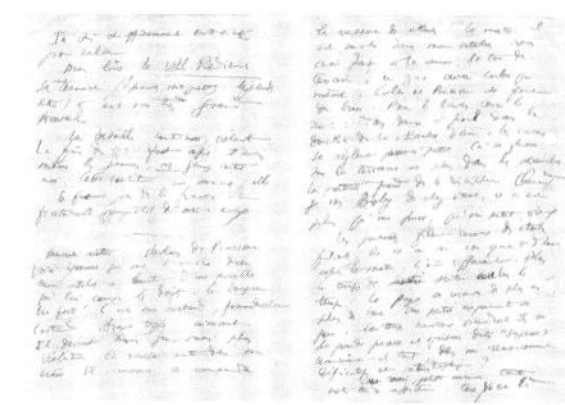

I've had enough training at that. My book *La Ville Radieuse* is being finished (proofs, dummies, captions, etc.) it's really a lot of work.

The battle goes on, violently. The end of 1934 was tough. I even had my young people, my young people against me. That coalition's been overcome, by my frank, fraternal friendship for them.

Wednesday morning. Let's talk about Pinceau. Here's Yvonne leading him into my studio on a string that's cutting her fingers. That guy pulls hard! He's beefy, incredibly beefy. Good-hearted and loving. He's getting less crazy, but more violent. Reason's starting to get into his skull. He's beginning to understand the connections between things. Mornings he lies in my studio after going for a run around the land opposite with Corbu leading him. Corbu and Pinceau are good for each other. Here's how you wash him: Both stripped off in the guest-room shower, the poo problem's gradually being settled. He does it on the terrace and not in the bedrooms any more. Nature is learning discipline. When I see Varet's Boby, he's no more than a flea, a little old man.

The days go by like shooting stars. A quarter of an hour after morning and it's evening. It's unbelievable. No time left for feeling the time pass. The country's more and more covered with mud. A harrowing game's being played: will the new era come or will the enormous laziness and selfishness called "wisdom" smother everything, in a definitive, disastrous renunciation?

Bye, little mom, with all our tender affection,

Your Yv and Ed

—P. 290

F.L. Ganura to Le Corbusier, 19 January 1935

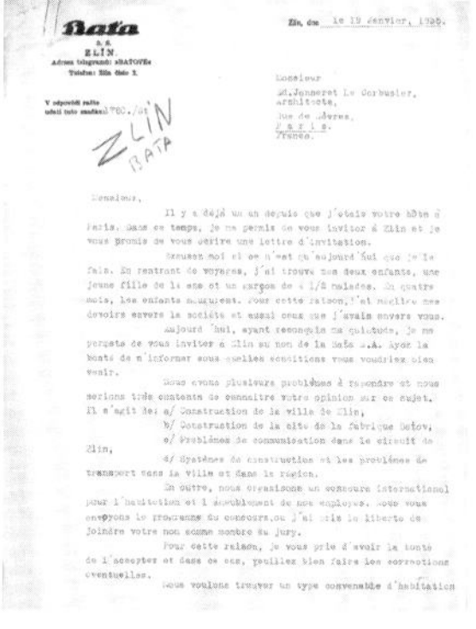

Zlín, 19 January, 1935

Mr.
Ed. Jeanneret Le Corbusier,
Architect,
Rue de Sèvres,
Paris.
France.

Sir,

A year has passed since I was your guest in Paris. During this time, I permitted myself to invite you to Zlín and I promised to write you a letter of invitation.

Forgive me if I have not done so until today. When I returned from my travels, I found my two children, a girl of 14 and a boy of 4½, sick. In four months, the children died. This is why I have neglected my social responsibilities as well as those I had toward you.

Today, having regained my quietude, I permit myself to invite you to Zlín on behalf of Bata, S.A. Be so kind as to let me know under what conditions you would be willing to come.

We have several problems to address and we would be very glad to know your opinion on the subject. It concerns:

a/ Building the city of Zlín;

b/ Building the city of the Batov factory

c/ Communication problems in the area of Zlín

d/ Construction systems and transportation problems in the city and the region.

We are also organizing an international competition for housing and furniture for our employees. We are sending you the program of the competition, to which I took the liberty of adding your name as a member of jury.

Therefore, please be so kind as to accept, and in this case, please make any necessary corrections.

We wish to find a suitable type of housing

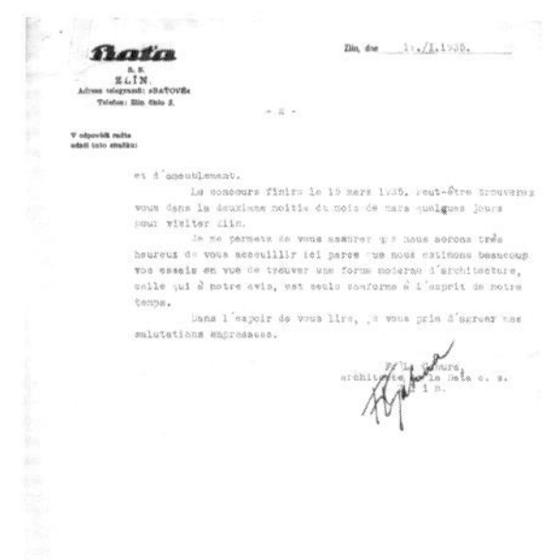

and furniture.

The competition will end on 15 March 1935. Perhaps you will find a few days in the second half of March to visit Zlín.

I permit myself to assure you that we will be very happy to receive you here because we esteem very highly your experiments aimed at discovering a modern form of architecture, the only one, in our opinion, in keeping with the spirit of our time.

Hoping to hear from you, I am yours very sincerely,

[signature]
F.L. Ganura
architect for Bata a. s.
Zlín.

—P. 296

Letter and drawing from Le Corbusier in New York to Jean Labatut at Princeton University, 4 December 1935

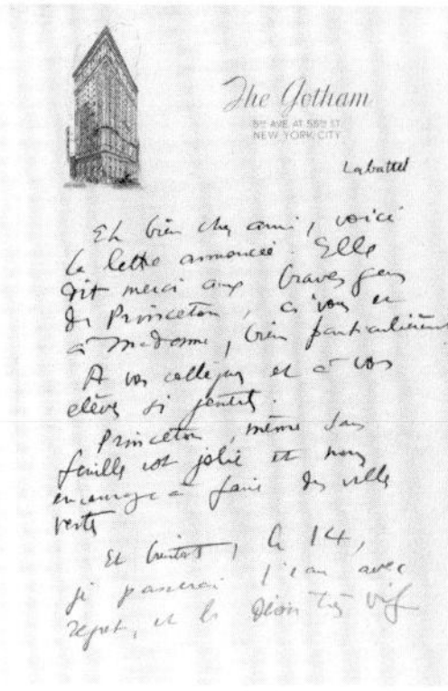

Labatut

Well dear friend, here's the promised letter. It says thank you to the good people of Princeton, most especially to you and your wife.

To your colleagues and your students, who are so nice.

Even without leaves Princeton is pretty and encourages us to make green cities

And soon, the 14th, I'll regretfully cross the water, and would really like

[TOP]
Princeton bowler hat

[BOTTOM RIGHT]
to come back and shake your hand.

Goodbye,
Le Corbusier

4 dec. 1935

—P. 297

Drawing for Princeton University lecture, 14–15 November 1935

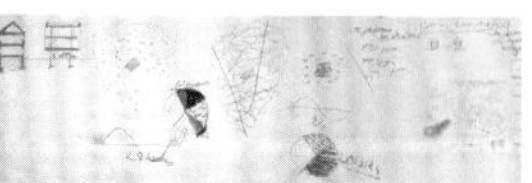

[TOP TO BOTTOM, LEFT TO RIGHT]
24 hours

24 [?] transports

LEISURE ACTIVITIES

spread out garden housing blocks

essential pleasures

elevated garden housing blocks by creation of the artificial terrasses

plots / 220,000 residents / 2,000

sky

sport at the foot of the buildings

separation of cars and pedestrians

—P. 300

Marguerite Tjader Harris to Le Corbusier, 25 April 1932

CHAMP MONTANEY
BLONAY
S/VEVEY
Le 25 avril

Cher Monsieur Le Corbusier :

Il y a une semaine, j'ai reçue cet~~t~~e lettre que j'avais adressée à vous il y a plus qu'un mois. Comme vous voyais, j'avais fait une stupide faute d'adresse, en écrivant Rue de Seine, au lieu de Sevre. Ainsi, j'espère que vous pardonnerez mon silence.

Maintenant j'ai de tres mauvaises nouvelles de l'Amérique. Toute ma famille est dans un état financier très critique, et je ne pourrais avoir que la moitié de la somme nécessaire pour construire la maison. J'ai pas encore abandonné l'espoir de la construire cependant, et je fais des plans pour quitter cette grande maison, pour vivre très simple-

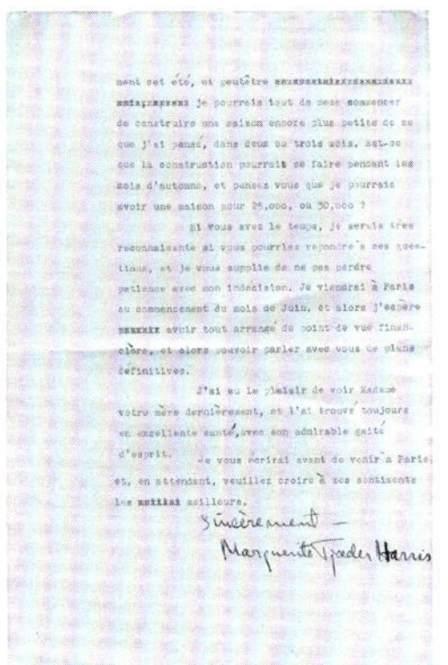
ment cet été, et peutêtre ~~xxxxxxxxxxxxxxxxxxxxxx~~ je pourrais tout de meme commencer de construire une maison encore plus petite de ce que j'ai pensé, dans deux ou trois mois. est-ce que la construction pourrait se faire pendant les mois d'automne, et pensez vous que je pourrais avoir une maison pour 25,000, ou 30,000 ?

Si vous avez le temps, je serais tres reconnaissante si vous pourriez répondre à ces questions, et je vous supplie de ne pas perdre patience avec mon indécision. Je viendrai à Paris au commencement du mois de Juin, et alors j'espère ~~xxxxxx~~ avoir tout arrangé du point de vue financière, et alors pouvoir parler avec vous de plans définitives.

J'ai eu le plaisir de voir Madame votre mère dernièrement, et l'ai trouvé toujours en excellente santé, avec son admirable gaité d'esprit. Je vous écrirai avant de venir à Paris, et, en attendant, veuillez croire à mes sentiments les ~~[illegible]~~ meilleurs.

Sincèrement —
Marguerite Tjader Harris

25 April

Dear Mr. Le Corbusier:

A week ago I received this letter, which I had sent you more than a month ago. As you see, I had made a stupid mistake with the address, writing Rue de Seine, instead of Sèvres. So I hope you will excuse my silence.

Now I have very bad news from America. My whole family is in very critical financial condition, and I will be able to get only half the amount necessary to build the house. I haven't yet given up hope of building it however, and I'm making plans to move out of this big house, to live very simply this summer and maybe I can still start building an even smaller house than I was thinking, in two or three months. Could construction be done in the autumn, and do you think I could have a house for 25,000 or 30,000?

If you have the time, I would be very grateful if you could answer these questions, and please do not lose patience with my wavering. I will be coming to Paris in early June, and then I hope to have everything arranged from the financial point of view, and so be able to talk with you about definite plans.

I had the pleasure of seeing your mother recently, and found her as ever in excellent health, with her wonderfully cheerful spirit.

I'll write you before coming to Paris, and in the meantime please believe me to be,

Sincerely,
Marguerite Tjader Harris

—P. 300

Marguerite Tjader Harris to Le Corbusier, 2 May 1932

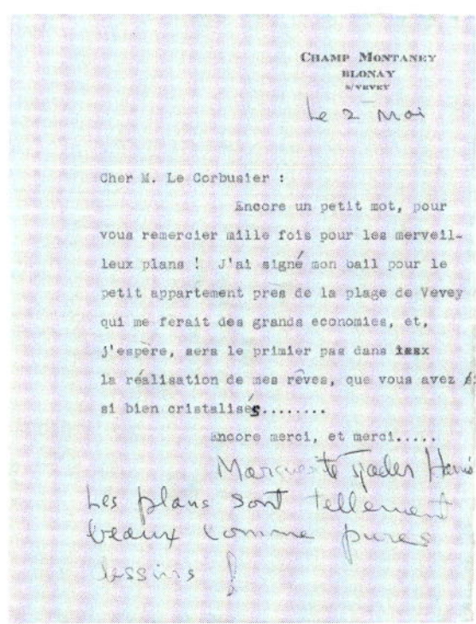
CHAMP MONTANEY
BLONAY
S/VEVEY
Le 2 mai

Cher M. Le Corbusier :

Encore un petit mot, pour vous remercier mille fois pour les merveilleux plans ! J'ai signé mon bail pour le petit appartement pres de la plage de Vevey qui me ferait des grands economies, et, j'espère, sera le primier pas dans ~~[illegible]~~ la réalisation de mes rêves, que vous avez si bien cristalisés.......

Encore merci, et merci.....

Marguerite Tjader Harris

Les plans sont tellement beaux comme pures dessins !

2 May

Dear Mr. Le Corbusier:

Another little note, to thank you a thousand times over for the marvelous plans! I signed the lease for the little apartment near the beach at Vevey, which will save me a great deal, and, I hope, will be the first step in realizing my dreams, which you have so well crystalized…

Again, thanks, and thanks …

Marguerite Tjader Harris

The plans are so beautiful purely as drawings!

—P. 302

Le Corbusier to Marguerite Tjader Harris, 31 October 1935

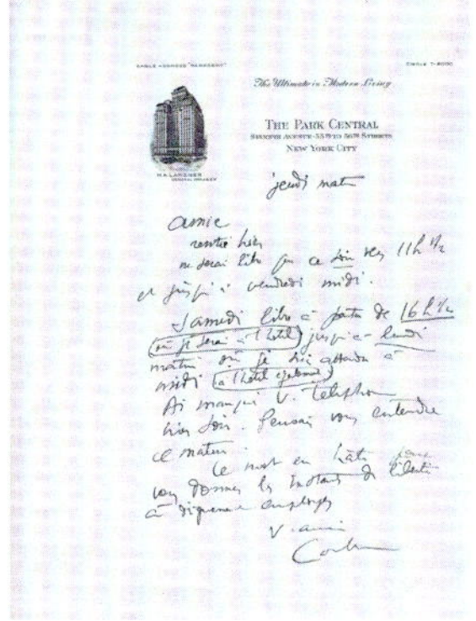

Thursday morning

Dear

Back yesterday

will only be free this <u>evening</u> around 11:30 and until Friday noon

Saturday free from <u>4:30 pm when I shall be at the hotel</u> until <u>Monday</u> noon <u>also at the hotel</u>.

Missed yr phone call last night. Expected to hear from you this morning.

This quick word to give you the moments of freedom to be fittingly used.

yr friend
Corbu

—P. 302

Le Corbusier to Marguerite Tjader Harris, 8 November 1935

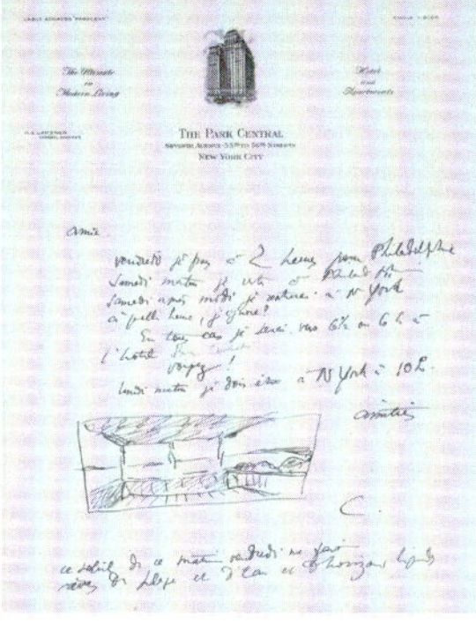

Dear

Friday I leave for Philadelphia at 2 o'clock

Saturday morning I stay in Philadelphia

Saturday afternoon I'll stay in N York

what time, I don't know?

In any case I'll be at the hotel around 6:30 or 6

Come see!

Monday morning I have to be in N York at 10.

Affectionately,
C.

This Friday morning sun makes me dream of beach and water and liquid horizons

—P. 303

Le Corbusier to Marguerite Tjader Harris, 14 December 1935

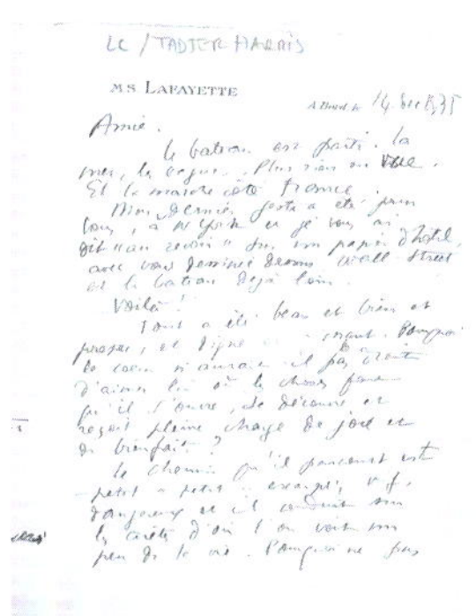

14 Dec 1935

Dear

The ship has left. The sea, the waves. Nothing left in sight. And heading for France.

My last act was for you, in N. York and I said "goodbye" to you on hotel paper with a drawing of you, Wall Street and the ship already far away.

So that's it!

Everything was beautiful and fine and right, and fitting and loving. Why shouldn't the heart have the right to love in places where things cause it to open up, lay itself bare, and receive its full dose of joy and well-being?

The path it follows is – little by little – steep, lively, and dangerous and leads onto the ridges that show you a bit of life. Why not

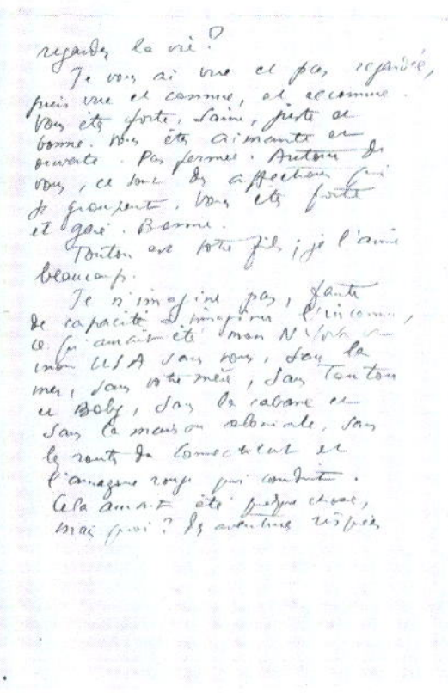

look at life?

I saw you and didn't look at you, then saw and knew you, and recognized you. You're strong, healthy, honest and good. You're loving and receptive. Not closed. Around you affection accumulates. You are strong and joyous. Good.

Toutou is your son; I'm very fond of him.

Lacking the ability to imagine the unknown, I can't imagine what my N. York and my USA would have been without you, without the sea, without your mother, without Toutou and Boby, without the cabin and without the colonial house, without the roads of Connecticut and the red amazon who leads. That would have been something. But what? Risky adventures

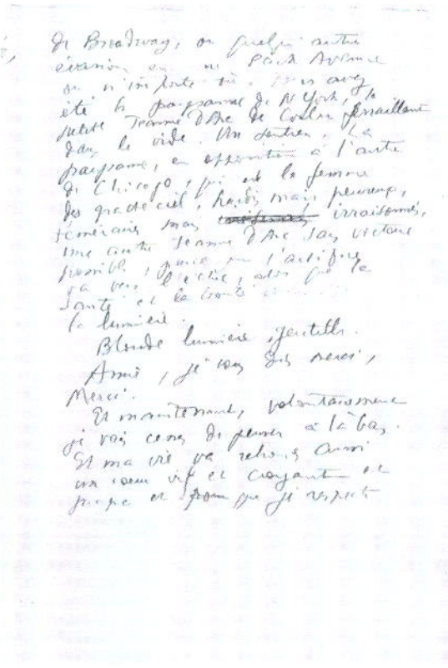

on Broadway, or some other escape into a Park Avenue or anywhere at all. You were the New York native, Corbu's little Joan of Arc working away in the void. A mainstay. The native, unlike the other one in Chicago, who is a woman of the skyscrapers that are bold yet fearful, rash yet ~~unres~~ unreasoned, another

Joan of Arc with no victory possible, because artifice leads to failure, while health and goodness go toward the light.

Blond, gentle light.

Dear, I say thank you, Thank you.

And now, deliberately I'm going to stop thinking of over there. And my life is also going to rediscover a lively, believing, pure heart and one I respect

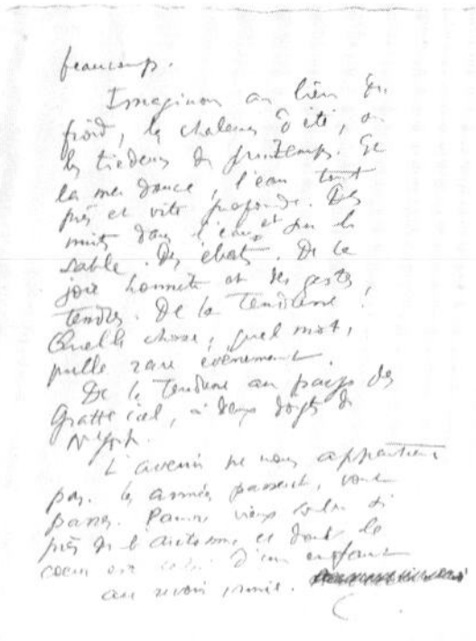

very much.

Let us imagine, instead of the cold, the heat of summer, or the warmth of spring. And the gentle sea, the water so close and quickly deep. Nights in the water and on the sand. Lovemaking. Honest joy and tender gestures.

Tenderness! What a thing, what a word, what a rare event. Tenderness in the land of the Skyscrapers, a stone's throw from N. York.

The future does not belong to us. The years pass, and are going to pass. Poor old Corbu so close to the autumn, and whose heart is that of a child.

Goodbye, darling.
C.

I'm sending with this letter 4 drawings done for you.

2 ~~representing~~ express the budding idea of the picture of the building. I'll ~~make~~ clarify it with under the eyes the seashells whose color is so beautiful.

—P. 304

Le Corbusier and Pierre Jeanneret to Mr. Berger, secretary general of SIA (Society of Automobile Engineers), 31 March 1936

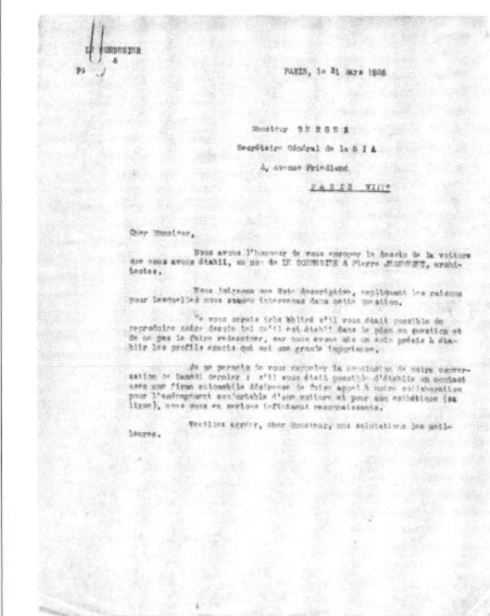

Paris, 31 March 1936

Mr. BERGER
Secretary General of the SIA
3 avenue Friedland
<u>Paris VIIIe</u>

Dear Sir,

We have the honor to send you the drawing of the car that we have designed, on behalf of LE CORBUSIER & Pierre JEANNERET, architects.

We attach a descriptive Note, explaining the reasons why we involved ourselves in this matter.

I would be very obliged to you if you could reproduce our drawing as it appears in the design in question and not have it redrawn, because we have taken precise care to fix the exact profiles, which are very important.

I permit myself to remind you of the end of our conversation last Saturday: if you could possibly establish contact with an automobile company that wishes us to collaborate in the comfortable design of a car and in its aesthetics (its line), we would be infinitely grateful to you.

Dear Sir, please believe me to be yours truly.

—P. 304

Mr. Berger to Le Corbusier, 7 April 1936

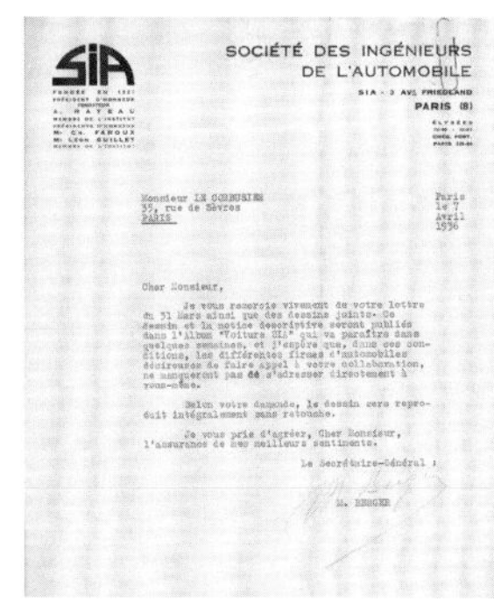

Mr. LE CORBUSIER
35 rue de Sèvres
<u>PARIS</u>

Paris, 7 April 1936

Dear Sir,

I thank you heartily for your letter of 31 March and for the attached drawings.

The drawing and the descriptive leaflet will be published in the "SIA Car" catalog, which will come out in a few weeks, and I hope that, this being the case, the various automobile companies that wish you to collaborate will address themselves to you directly.

As you requested, the drawing will be reproduced in its entirety without retouching.

Please believe me to be, Dear Sir, sincerely.

The Secretary General:
[signature]
Mr. BERGER

—P. 304

Le Corbusier to Giovanni Agnelli, president of FIAT, 6 October 1936

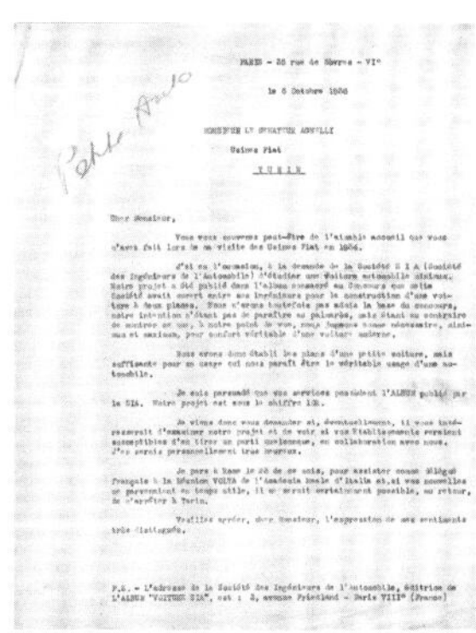

Little Car
PARIS–35 rue de Sèvres–VIe
6 October 1936

SENATOR AGNELLI
Fiat Plant
<u>TURIN</u>

Dear Sir,

You will perhaps recall the friendly welcome you gave me when I visited the Fiat plant in 1934.

At the request of the SIA (Society of Automobile Engineers), I had the opportunity to work on a basic car. Our project was published in the album devoted to the competition the Society organized between its engineers for the construction of a two-seater car. However we did not observe the basic rules of the competition, our intention being not to take the prize but, on the contrary, to show from our point of view what we considered the necessary minima and maxima for true comfort in a modern car.

Thus we drew up the plans for a car that, though small, fit with what seemed to us the true purpose of an automobile.

I am sure that your company has the ALBUM published by the SIA. Our project is number 102.

My purpose in writing is to ask you if you might be interested in looking at our project and to see if your Company would be ready to make use of it, in association with us. Personally this would make me very happy.

I am leaving for Rome on the 23rd of this month as French delegate to the Accademia Reale d'Italia's VOLTA Meeting, and if I hear from you in time, it would certainly be possible for me to stop off in Turin on the way back.

With my best wishes.

P.S. The address of the Society of Automobile Engineers, publishers of the "SIA CAR" ALBUM, is: 3 avenue Friedland—Paris VIIIe (France)

—P. 304

Giovanni Agnelli to Le Corbusier, 9 October 1936

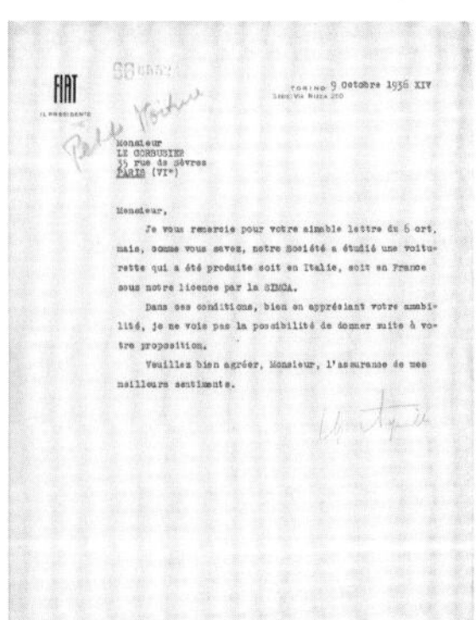

Little Car
9 October 1936 XIV

Mr.
LE CORBUSIER
35 rue de Sèvres
<u>PARIS</u> (VIe)

Sir,

Thank you for your kind letter of 6 Oct., but, as you know, our Firm has designed a minicar that has been manufactured in Italy and, licensed by us, by SIMCA in France.

Under the circumstances, while I appreciate your kindness, I see no possibility of following up on your proposal.

Believe me to be, Sir, yours truly,

[signature]

Paris, Vichy, and the War (1937–1943)

—P. 311

Elevations of display panels for "Agrarian Reform" exhibit, Pavillon des Temps Nouveaux, Paris, 1937

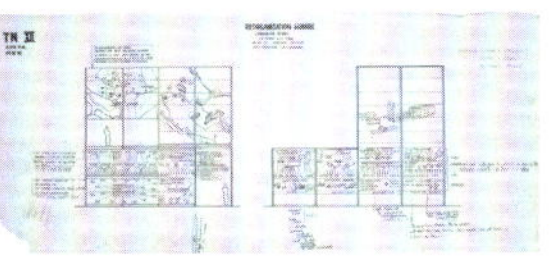

AGRARIAN REORGANIZATION
RURAL PLANNING
THE RETURN TO THE SOIL
NO URBANIZATION OF CITIES WITHOUT DEVELOPING THE COUNTRYSIDE
Industry will provide equipment

[LEFT SKETCH: TOP TO BOTTOM, LEFT TO RIGHT]
IT IS THE LAND (TERRAIN AND SEASONS) THAT DECIDE, NOT PEOPLE
generalizations in farming are a recipe for failure; first individual regions need to be defined

A RURAL MUNICIPALITY MUST COMPRISE:
FAMILY FARMS working the soil
THE VILLAGE AS COMMUNITY
shared services, cooperative ventures

LAND CONSOLIDATION
A PROJECT FOR A CLEARLY DEFINED REGION
THE RETURN TO THE SOIL IS POSSIBLE ONLY VIA FAMILY FARMING BACKED BY COLLECTIVE RESOURCES (METHODS AND EQUIPMENT)

BRITTANY / BEAUCE / NORMANDY / RHONE / PROVENCE / GARONNE / SAONE / CHAMPAGNE / AUVERGNE / BORDELAIS / SAVOY / ALSACE

1st STAGE The local network
THE SILO / THE CLUB
2nd STAGE THE COOPERATIVE
3rd STAGE: CITY HALL
ACCOMMODATION
SCHOOL / POST OFFICE

DIAGRAM: PLAN FOR A REGIONAL AGRICULTURAL ECONOMY
THE WORKSHOP / THE COOPERATIVE
THE RADIANT VILLAGE
THE SILO / SHARED SERVICES

ANIMAL RAISING
SILO / NATIONAL FEDERATION
STOREHOUSE
WATER FORESTS
INTERNATIONAL OR NATIONAL FEDERATION

FAMILY FARMS
THE MUNICIPAL COUNCIL / ADMINISTRATION
FARMING
HYGIENE LEISURE
CANTONS, DISTRICT
REGIONAL FARMING FEDERATION
STATISTICS

CULTURAL OFFICE
FAMILY-BASED OFFICE

industrial
implementation
backbone
modern farm accommodation
view of an interior

[RIGHT SKETCH: TOP TO BOTTOM, LEFT TO RIGHT]
THE FARM (DETAILS AND FUNCTIONING)
EXPLANATORY TEXT

TOOLS THAT SERVE PEOPLE
SLUM FARMS

DOCUMENTS

Merchant
The fair
Social
The fair
Tomorrow
insufficient
Merchant
The silo and the cooperative
Social the club:
Consequence
Van
And new local network

THE VILLAGE (DETAILS AND FUNCTIONING)
EXPLANATORY TEXT

COOPERATIVE WORK

ABANDONED VILLAGES

DOCUMENTS

NEEDS AND MEETING THEM
THE PRODUCERS
COOPERATIVE SILOS
VEHICLE DOCKS / RAILROAD / PORT
DOCKS

COOPERATIVE DISTRIBUTION SERVICES
INDIVIDUALS / THE FAMILIES / GROUPS
THE CONSUMERS

INPUT FROM COLLECTIVE METHODS

THE INTERMEDIARIES
COVERED MARKETS
PROXIES
AGENTS

DOCUMENTS

Reminder 4 points urb[anism]
Urban food provision
(new unité d'habitation)

THE LAND OF France
IS WHERE THE FRENCH SHOULD REALLY BE COLONIZING

RESOURCES
ROADS
THE CAR
BIG INDUSTRY TAKES OVER BUILDING

FAMILY FARMING

HOARDABLE MONEY = THE CURB

HUMAN CURRENCY IS NEEDED

TABLE WITH DOCUMENTS

the Ocean-Danube canal = location for industries
+ The Canal des 2 Mers Bordeaux-Sète = industry (with free port)
+ Rhône to Rhine

Diagram / Map
France / industrial / cultivated land
Badly placed / well placed / abandoned / being worked

TOTAL AREA = 176.40 m²
TOTAL PHOTOS = 125 m²
TOTAL PAINTING = 51.40m²

create photographic link here
total photos
26 May 1937

THESIS
Road civilization replacing railroad civilization
industrial building of farms and villages

OUTLINE

OBSTACLES

Producers
Silos
Transport
General services
Branches
Consumers

—P. 311

Sketch of exhibit circulation scheme, Pavillon des Temps Nouveaux, 1937

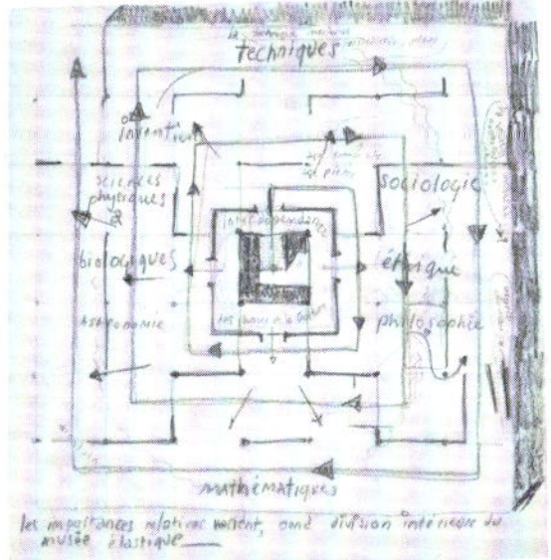

[TOP, IN RED]
techniques

[LEFT, IN RED]
invention
physical & biological sciences
astronomy

[RIGHT, IN RED]
sociology
ethics
philosophy

[BOTTOM, IN RED]
mathematics
the relative importances vary, so internal division of the expandable museum

[TOP, IN BLUE]
modern technology
possibilities = plans

[LEFT, IN BLUE]
einstein

[MIDDLE, IN BLUE]
bronze age, etc.
stone age

[RIGHT, IN BLUE]
modern society internal contradictions
new spirit

[MIDDLE, IN GRAY]
cultural things interdependence

—P. 316

First page of letter from Le Corbusier to his mother, 19 February 1937

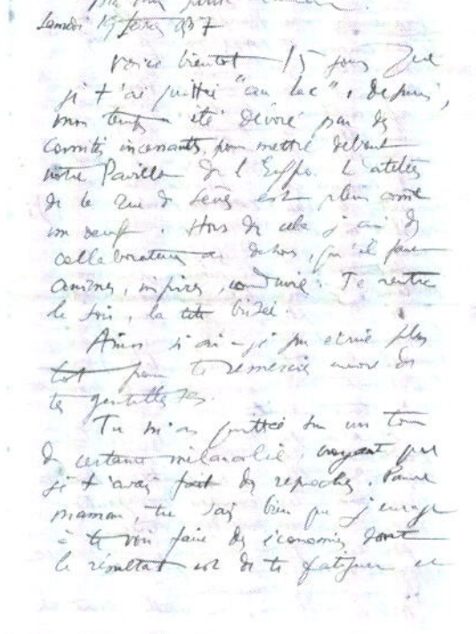

My dear little mom.
Saturday 19 February 1937

It's almost two weeks since I left you "at the Lake," and since then my time has been swallowed up by endless committees for setting up our Pavilion at the Expo. The studio on rue de Sèvres is full to bursting. On top of which I have outside collaborators I have to motivate, inspire, and lead. I come home in the evenings with my head splitting.

That's why I haven't been able to write sooner to thank you for your kindness.

You left me on a slightly melancholy note, thinking I had reproached you. Poor mom, you know very well that it makes me furious to see you economizing and as a result tired and [...]

—P. 316

Two pages of letter from Le Corbusier to his mother, 25 June 1937

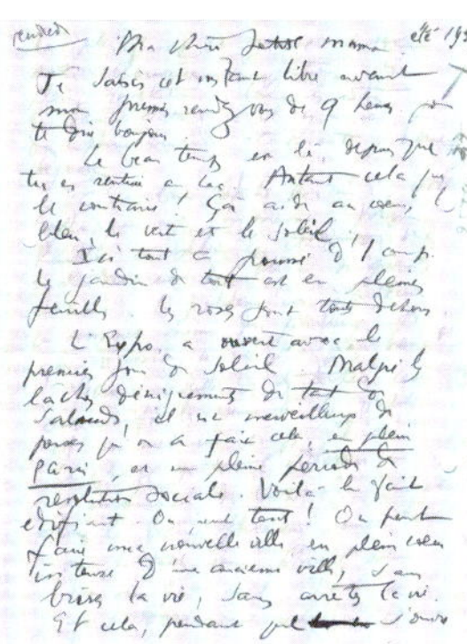

Friday / summer 1937

My dear little mom.

I'm grabbing this free moment to say hello before my first appointment at 9.

The weather's been fine since you went back to the Lake. Better that than the opposite! It makes one feel good inside, the blue, the green, and the sun.

Here everything has grown all at once. The roof garden is in full leaf. The roses are all out.

The Expo opened the first sunny day. Despite the despicable criticisms of all those bastards, it's marvelous to think that we've done this, in the heart of Paris, and in the midst of a social revolution. It's very instructive. Everything's possible! You can create a new city right in the vigorous heart of an ancient one, without wrecking its life, without halting its life. And you can do it while

the biggest, most serious struggle between workers and bosses is starting. In the midst of a revolution. I hope the others do the same. There's amazing worker discipline here. A wisdom.

This Expo is immense, and far from being completed. My pavilion was delayed by my sickness and blunders in big factories. The problem is that it's as risky as you can get. If it works it will really be something.

Pierre has risen out of his Communist torpor and is finally

opening his eyes to reality and pitching in. I'm in charge of the entire interior—town planning in the modern era—and all the big talkers have left us is their big talk and not a single concrete fact. We're the ones making things happen now and [...]

—P. 321

Sketch of a gallery interior, with notes, for *Le Corbusier: Oeuvre plastique, 1917–1937, Tableaux et architecture*, Kunsthaus, Zurich, 1938

[LEFT TO RIGHT, TOP TO BOTTOM]
~~Koenig~~
~~Kunsthaus~~

Orig[inal]

Beginning or do drawing [?]

large painting / small picture / architect's sketch

small room
1 big photo of picture

+ a few interior photos
Pavilion Nungesser
+ Léger studio / studio
+ His Majesty
+ Louis Carré
studio / statue

black paper
black paper / ordinary fabrics / white paper

—P. 322

Le Corbusier to Marguerite Tjader Harris, 8 December 1937

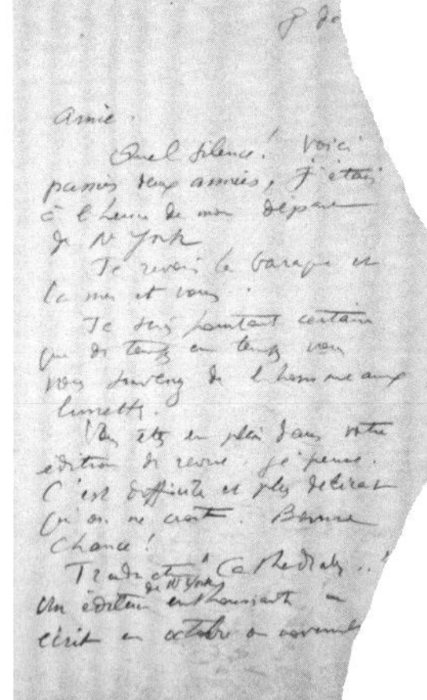

8 Dec.

Dear,

What a silence! Two years ago, I was about to leave N York.

I see the house again and the sea and you.

In spite of everything, I'm sure that from time to time you remember the man with the glasses.

You're taken up with publishing your magazine, I imagine. It's hard and trickier than you think. Good luck!

Translation "Cathedrals ... An enthusiastic N York publisher wrote in October or November.

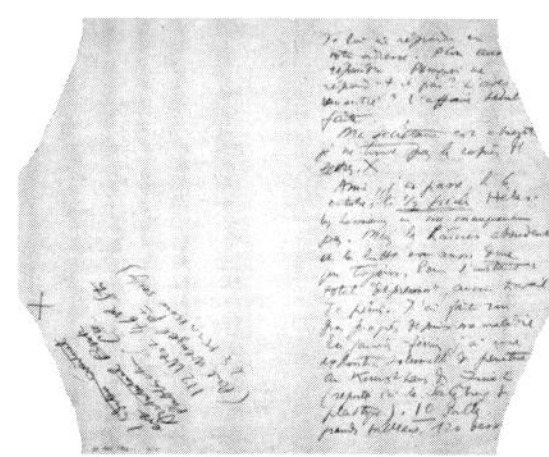

[LEFT PAGE]
The possible publisher is Architectural Book Publishing Co 112 West 46th Street (Paul Wenzel Pt LE Krakow secty)

[RIGHT PAGE]
I answered him [?] your address. Plon also [?] answered. Why doesn't he answer? Have you met him? The matter seems [?] settled.

My secretary is away I can't find the copies of letters.*

Dear, I passed <u>the ½ century mark</u> on 6 October. Alas. I don't miss the honors. But hate is everywhere and the struggle is as hard as ever. For the moment total "depression," no work. I paint. I've made great progress since my sickness. In January–February I'm having a solemn exhibition of painting [?] at the Kunsthaus in Zurich [?] (known here as the Salzburg of [?] plastic). 10 rooms. Big pictures, 120 drawings.

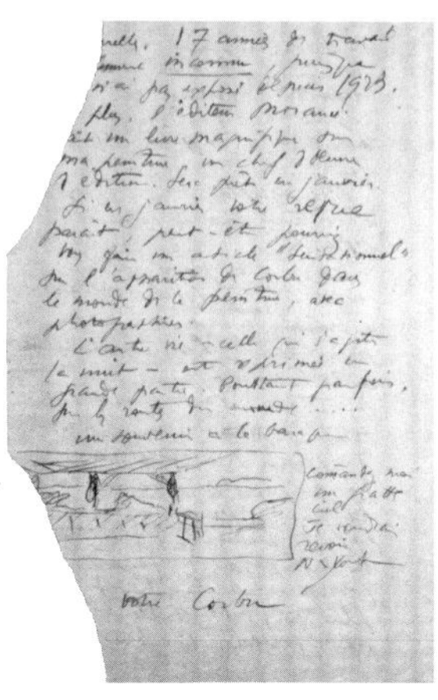

[?] 17 years of work. [?] <u>unknown</u>, because I've not exhibited since 1923. [?] more, Morancé the publisher [?] is printing a magnificent book on my painting, a publishing masterpiece. Will be ready in January.

If your magazine comes out in January, maybe you could print a "sensational" article on Corbu's appearance in the world of painting, with photographs.

The other life—the restless night-time one—is largely suppressed. Yet sometimes, on the roads of the world ...

My best to the house.

Commission a skyscraper I'd like to see N York again.

your Corbu

—P. 325

First page of letter from Le Corbusier to Jean Badovici, 1 January 1950

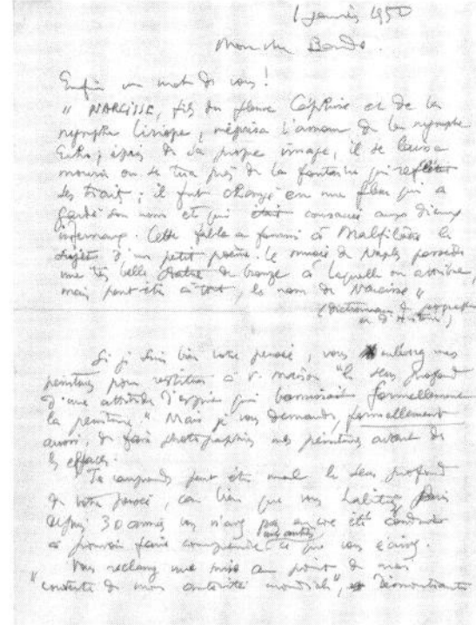

1 January 1950

Dear Bado.

Word from you at last!

"NARCISSUS, son of the river Cephisus and the nymph Liriope, spurned the love of the nymph Echo; enamored of his own image, he let himself die or took his life near the fountain that reflected his features; he was changed into a flower that has kept his name and was consecrated to the gods of the underworld. This fable provided Malfilâtre with the subject of a little poem. The museum in Naples has a very handsome bronze statue named—but perhaps erroneously—Narcissus" (Dictionary of Geography and History)

If I follow your line of thought, you will be removing my paintings to restore to your house "the deep sense of a state of mind that formally banished painting." But I ask you, equally <u>formally</u>, to have my paintings photographed before effacing them.

Maybe I do not fully grasp the deep meaning of your thought, for although you have been living in Paris for 30 years you have not yet succeeded in making others understand what you write.

You ask me for a summary of the situation "validated by my worldwide authority," ~~and~~ demonstrating [...]

—P. 329

Verso of *Dessin prémonitoire* (Premonitory Drawing), 1938

Premonitory drawing: (veritable scene of carnage St. Tropez at Mrs. Pégurin's where we're staying, after dinner I did this watercolor + 2 or 3 others.

at 6 in the morning I go to the beach (where the locals go, port of St. Tropez).

There were waves. I was doing some underwater swimming.

Bang! an impact. It's a motoscaff (??) a motorboat (15 m long) running over the top of me. I get rolled from prow to poop deck. I hold onto my air, telling myself: I'll come to the end of the bottom of the boat. I end up in the propellor! Two meters of stitches (the right thigh chopped off, the calf cut, the arm sliced, the head gashed. It was

(X) from the Telephone Company in

[TOP]
Le Havre. 4 weeks in hospital, sewn up without anesthetic (because of the gash in my skull).

—P. 329

Le Corbusier to his mother, from central hospital, Saint-Tropez, 23 August 1938

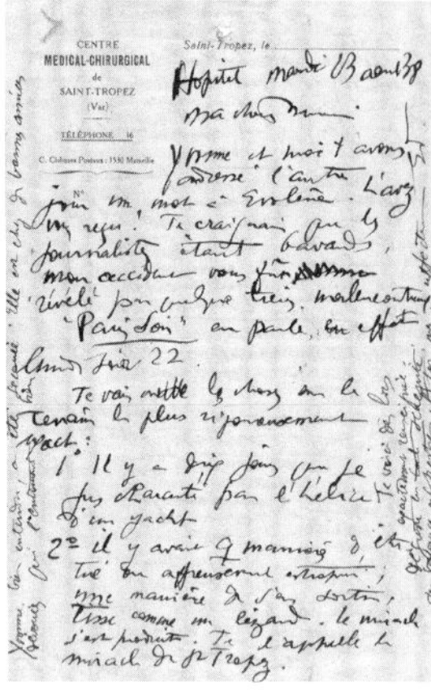

Hospital Tuesday 23 August 38

My dear mom.

The other day Yvonne and I sent you a note at Evolène. Did you get it? I'm worried that the journalists were indiscreet and you unfortunately heard about my accident from a third party.

"<u>Paris Soir</u>" reported it on the evening of Monday 22nd.

I'm going to give you an absolutely exact account:

1. Ten days ago I got chopped up by the propeller of a yacht
2. there were <u>9</u> ways of being killed or hideously crippled; one way of pulling through intact. The miracle happened. I call it the miracle of St. Tropez.

[LEFT MARGIN]
Yvonne was naturally pretty shaken. She's with close friends who are really looking after her.

[RIGHT MARGIN]
So now you know the right version. Enjoy your holidays in the Alps without worrying. Love Ed

—P. 329

First page of letter from Le Corbusier to his mother from Saint Tropez, 21 September 1938

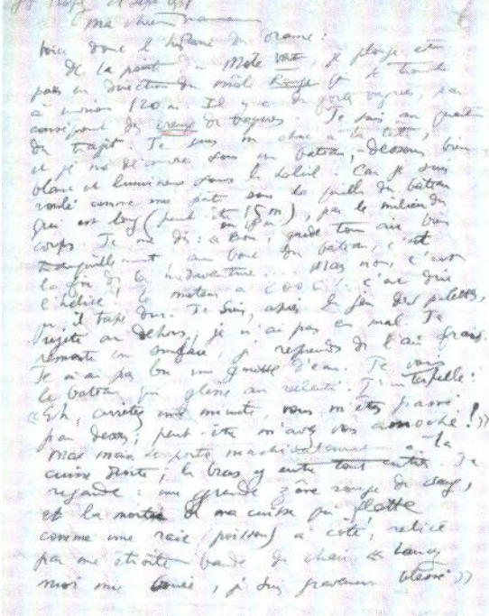

St. Tropez 21 Sept. 1938

My dear mom

Here's the story of my accident: I dive off the end of the green jetty and set off toward the red jetty, about 120 meters away. The waves are big, so there are troughs. I've done a quarter of the distance. I feel a blow to the head, and find myself under a boat—a bright white underside shining in the sun. I'm being rolled horizontally like a stick of spaghetti along the keel, which is maybe 15 or 18 meters. I tell myself, "Right, hold your air in calmly, at the other end of the boat your problems are over." But then comes the propeller, and with a 200 HP motor it hits hard. After getting whirled around by the blades I'm thrown clear, no pain. I surface, breathe in. I haven't swallowed a drop of water. I see the boat sliding slowly away and call out, "Hey, hang on a minute, you went over me; maybe you've injured me!" Automatically my hand goes to my right thigh, sinks in to the thickness of my arm. And I'm looking at an enormous patch of blood, and half my thigh floating like a ray (fish), with just a strip of skin holding it on. "Throw me a life preserver, I'm seriously hurt!"

—P. 329

First page of letter from Le Corbusier to Marguerite Tjader Harris, 22 December 1938

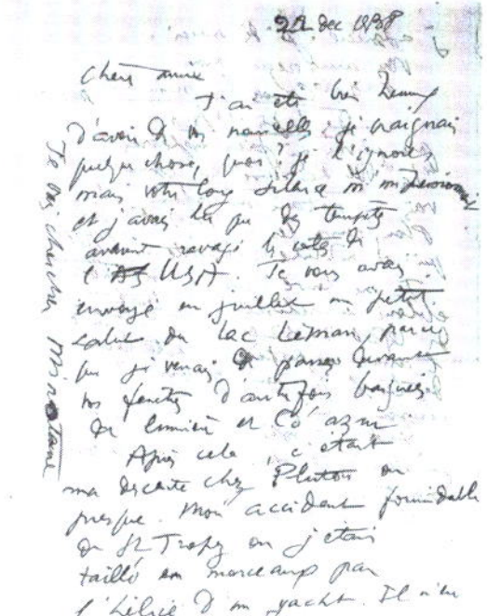

22 Dec. 1938

Dear friend.

I was so pleased to get your news. I feared something, but what? I don't know.

But your long silence had a powerful effect on me and I'd read of storms ravaging the coast of the ~~At~~ USA. In July I'd sent you a little hello from Lake Geneva, having just walked by your windows once drenched in light and sky-blue.

After that came my descent to Pluto or almost. My dreadful accident at St. Tropez where I was carved up by the propeller of a yacht. It [...]

[LEFT MARGIN]
I'm going to pick up Minotaure

—P. 330

Le Corbusier to his mother, 18 November 1938

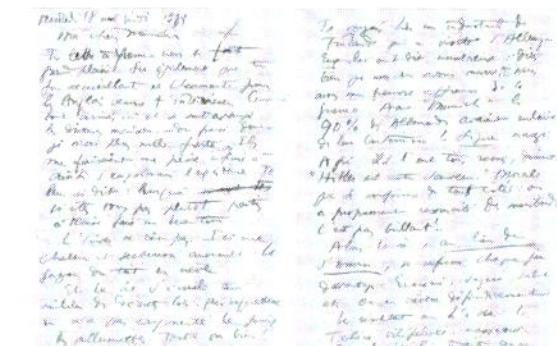

Friday 18 Nov. noon 1938

My dear mom

Your letter to Yvonne was a great pleasure for all of us. Also found out that you were welcoming and charming with the English people who came to interview you. They came here and had to put up with the various houses—from the past that I'm no longer proud of at all. It really upset me to see them having such a lousy time. I said to them: Why didn't you go to Venice and see the sights.

Winter isn't coming. Here abnormal heat and dryness. The roof lawn is dying.

And life goes on in the midst of Orders in Council. To be nice they haven't put up the price of matches. Everything is all right!

Yesterday I saw an industrialist from Finland who had been to Germany.

A lot of them told him, "Tell everybody we're fed up. We're scared to death of War." Before "Munich" 90 percent of the Germans had taken off their Nazi boutonnières. Since then, they've all put it back, saying: "Hitler's our savior." And this is confirmed everywhere you look: the dying really have been brought back to life. It's not great!

And so life, instead of opening up, is closing more each day: Economics, wisdom, salvation, etc. We'll die of it once and for all. We've seen the results: Czechoslovakia reviled and massacred. And the Jews treated in a way you would never have dared imagine. Chamberlain for me is like a very dangerous retrograde black man: the city, money, cash!

That apart, we keep busy. I've got a little government work. Bits and pieces. I'm also helping create youth centers. We try to help out these youngsters shattered by the slump,—wrecks.

Louis Carré is organizing my Paris painting show for 25 Nov.–12 Dec. with meticulous care. And I'll get beaten up; my friends won't like it. But Carré is going to manage my output and as I was saying, painting can sometimes bring you a living, at a time when everything's teetering here.

Even so I'm hoping for work in London. Some young people of good family, talented architects, want to set up the firm "Le Corbusier and Partners."

I have little flames lit all over the world. I'm keeping them burning.

My English visitors were delighted with you. The little lady who's American is nice. It seems that the weather is wonderful.

Don't forget to give Lang my "kindest regards," in other words my warm friendship and best wishes. No more than six children given the present state of affairs.

A word about our health: Yv[onne] tired and irritated by a dirty, disgusting, nasty buzzard. We chucked him out on Monday. I'm in good shape, scars excellent, everything will vanish in time. Something already forgotten, now just a ghostly memory.

Bye little mom. Affectionately,
Y and Ed.

—P. 330

Le Corbusier to his mother and brother, from Paris, 3 September 1939

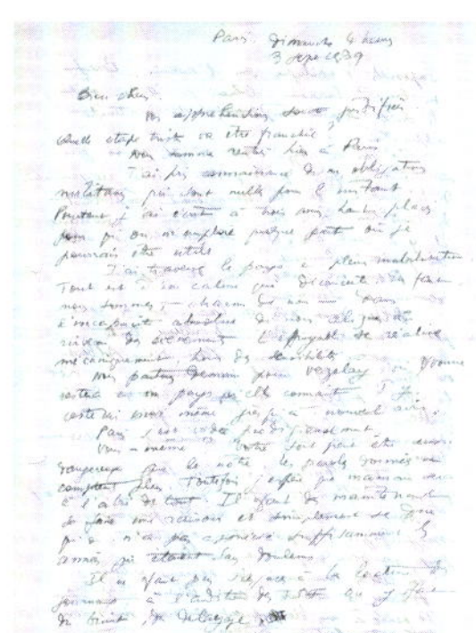

Paris Sunday 4 o'clock
3 Sept. 1939

Dear ones.

Your fears are justified. What will the next sad stage be?

We came back to Paris yesterday.

I was informed of my military obligations which for the moment are non-existent. Even so, I've written to three highly placed friends asking for a job somewhere where I might be useful.

I crossed a country in the throes of mobilizing. Everything so calm it throws you. In fact, we are—each one of us—absolutely incapable of coping with what's happening. Appalling things are taking place mechanically, beyond our capacity to react.

We're leaving tomorrow for Vézelay where Yvonne can stay in a region she knows. I'll be staying there myself until further notice.

Paris has emptied out enormously.

And you? Your future could be as dangerous as ours. Words of honor no longer count. However I hope Mom will be sheltered from everything. Now we must accept things and simply face the fact that we failed to adequately appreciate the painless years.

No point in getting annoyed reading the papers and listening to the radio. It's all noise and puffery.

—P. 330

Le Corbusier to his mother and brother, from Vézelay, 9 September 1939

Vézelay 9 Sept. 1939

Dear ones

Sunday afternoon Vézelay, in a handsome, empty room lent to me by Mrs. Simon, the mother of Simon the house painter from the Pavillon des Temps Nouveaux 37. Yvonne is drowsing in her room in the annex of the Cheval Blanc. Are here since Monday evening. Had been to Paris last Saturday and Sunday. Bado has made available a very pretty old house that he's done up. But for the moment we don't know what we're going to do. I've put my name down at four places including Jean Giraudoux to be useful in some way. If I don't have any news soon I'll go to Paris to see.

I have read a book on the true story of Hitler. You can see that the blind alley was waiting for him: war. And now here it is! His friends are starting to abandon him, beginning with ~~Germ~~ Italy and Spain. I think Italy has surprises in store for us common sense would seem to indicate. As for Spain, she's had a taste of Germany and that was enough. Hitler's backed by an army out for revenge and big industry. But what an explosive substance (later) this Germanic empire will be. By explosive, I mean likely to explode, break up, etc.

What a mechanical adventure modern war is: the gears start meshing and don't stop. And the world's in a state of upheaval. What unique power! When will this power be put at the service of

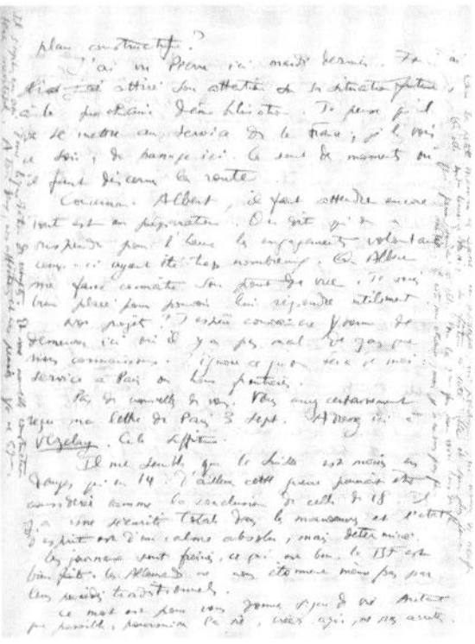

a constructive plan?

I saw Pierre here last Tuesday. I drew his attention to his future situation, when demobilization comes. I think he'll put himself at France's service; I'm seeing him this evening when he comes through. These are moments when you have to work out what your path is.

As for Albert, we'll have to keep waiting. Everything's in preparation. They say that voluntary enlistments are suspended for the moment, there being too many of them. Albert needs to let me know his point of view. I'm well placed to give a useful answer.

Our projects? I hope to convince Yvonne to stay here where there are quite a few people we know. I don't know what they'll do with me: service in Paris, or abroad.

No news from you. You will certainly have received my letter from Paris of 3 Sept. Write here to <u>Vézelay</u>. That's enough.

It seems to me that Switzerland is less in danger than in 14. And this war could be considered the conclusion of the one of 18. There's total security in the maneuvers and the state of mind is one of absolute but determined calm. The newspapers are under control, which is good. The radio is well organized. The Germans don't even surprise us with their traditional methods.

I'm writing to give you a sign of life. As far as possible, we must continue our lives, create, act, and not stop.

[RIGHT MARGIN]
Let my little mother not worry about strategy or politics, or wear out her nerves. Let her be happy to have one son beside her and her younger one thinking of her often. For the second time we're out of the fray. It's a stroke of luck, but I'm not proud of it.

[LEFT MARGIN]
What's really happening is a settling of scores. And a new construction will be inevitable. All our love to both of you, Yv and Ed.

—P. 332

Plan, 21 December 1939, showing wartime and postwar uses of Ecoles Volantes

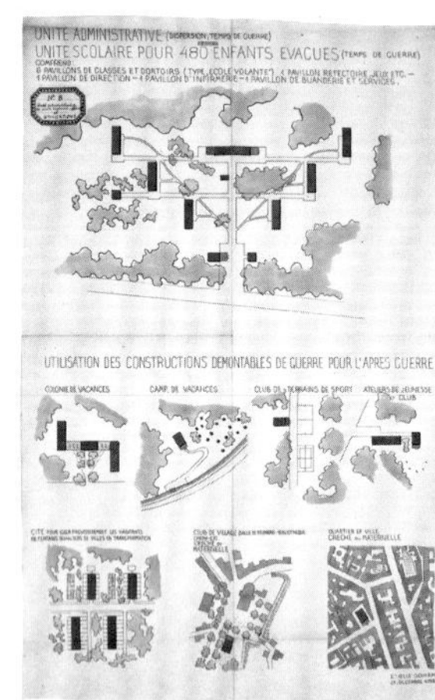

[TOP TO BOTTOM, LEFT TO RIGHT]
ADMINISTRATIVE UNIT (DISPERSION, WARTIME)
SCHOOL UNIT FOR 480 EVACUATED CHILDREN (WARTIME)

INCLUDES:
6 PAVILIONS CLASSROOMS AND DORMITORIES ("TEMPORARY SCHOOL" TYPE)
1 PAVILION DINING HALL, GAMES ETC. —
1 PAVILION ADMINISTRATION – 1 PAVILION INFIRMARY – 1 PAVILION LAUNDRY AND SERVICES.

USE OF WARTIME KNOCKDOWN CONSTRUCTIONS AFTER THE WAR

SUMMER CAMP / SUMMER CAMP / SPORTS CLUB / YOUTH WORKSHOPS AND CLUB

TEMPORARY ACCOMMODATION FOR RESIDENTS OF CERTAIN NEIGHBORHOODS UNDERGOING CONVERSION / VILLAGE CLUB (MEETING ROOM – LIBRARY – CINEMA – ETC. CHILDCARE CENTER OR NURSERY SCHOOL / URBAN NEIGHBORHOOD CHILDCARE CENTER OR NURSERY SCHOOL

SCALE 0.001 PER METER
21 DECEMBER 1939

—P. 336

Le Corbusier to his mother, from Ozon, 18 August 1940

my room

Ozon via Tournay
18 August 1940

1) My dear little mom.

On 10 September you'll be 80, which proves that one is still young at that age. Eighty years and you're still a companion to your sons, unworried by the generations, combating the years, and always smiling and laughing.

You see us now closer to you than ever, trusting you, ensuring that nothing harms you, and that your enthusiasm and your faith in what's good increase each day. Our family is pretty small, but it's close and solid, and the clear memory of dad builds the fourth corner of the wall, and our kind aunt Pauline is the fifth point of the Star.

So there's everything summed up, brief, but dense and positive.

Let me say on the occasion of this wonderful celebration that I think of Albert, whose ties to you are so strong. He's close to you in this

extraordinary year, my god just think that a simple incident of the calendar could have hurled him into some distant place pounded into the ground by all those defenses. Instead he found himself close to you and you spent every day of this tragic year together and talked about it. He supported you when things flagged. Alone, you would have been a source of torment for us. With him things are healthy, and solid. You were able to hold on. And I owe him that, which is a lot for I owe him this quietude that is a true force for action and whose absence might have caused me to take wrong paths during these days we've been through and that necessitated quick, intelligent action.

our courtyard

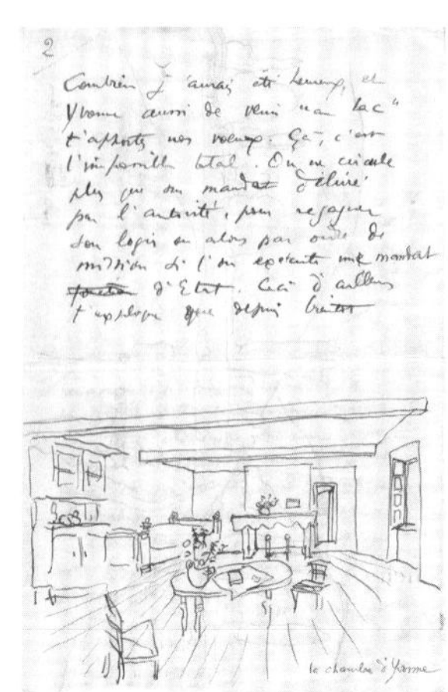

2)
How happy I would have been, and Yvonne too to come "to the Lake" and bring you my best wishes, that's totally impossible. You can only travel with a pass issued by the authorities, to return home or under orders for a state ~~function~~ mission. This is also why for nearly

Yvonne's room

[FAR LEFT]
Pic du Midi

[LEFT]
Our bath at 5:30

[RIGHT]
3) two months, I'm in sandals and without a jacket. I remember as if in a dream my trip to the East in 1910 when I only ever got my passport out once for 2 minutes at Rutschuk on the Bulgarian border.

Let's be happy with what's available: the feelings that fly over the battlefields and can humbly

Pierre

our house

Tarbes-Toulouse road

4) be put down on white paper. My little mom, this letter that your faithful friend Bertha Nuss will give you as the clock strikes your 80 years, asks you to believe in our great filial affection, in our profound gratitude, in our sincere and delighted admiration.

your Yvonne and Edouard
+ Pinceau

—P. 338

French Minister of Munitions to Le Corbusier, 18 November 1939

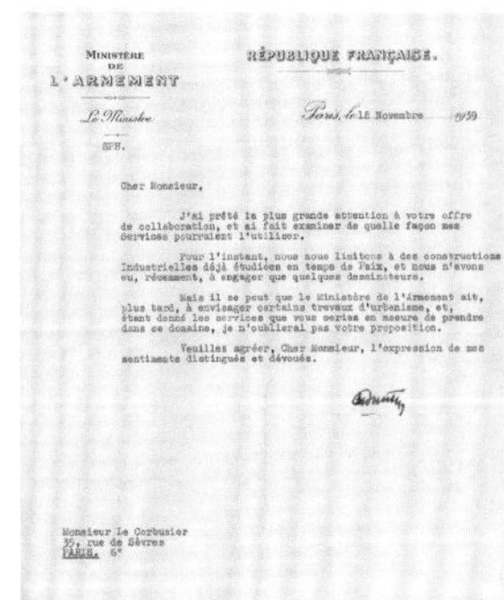

MINISTÈRE DE L'ARMEMENT

Le Ministre

SPE.

RÉPUBLIQUE FRANÇAISE.

Paris, le 18 Novembre 1939

Cher Monsieur,

J'ai prêté la plus grande attention à votre offre de collaboration, et ai fait examiner de quelle façon mes Services pourraient l'utiliser.

Pour l'instant, nous nous limitons à des constructions Industrielles déjà étudiées en temps de Paix, et nous n'avons eu, récemment, à engager que quelques dessinateurs.

Mais il se peut que le Ministère de l'Armement ait, plus tard, à envisager certains travaux d'urbanisme, et, étant donné les services que vous seriez en mesure de prendre dans ce domaine, je n'oublierai pas votre proposition.

Veuillez agréer, Cher Monsieur, l'expression de mes sentiments distingués et dévoués.

Monsieur Le Corbusier
35, rue de Sèvres
<u>PARIS.</u> 6°

Paris, 18 November 1939

Dear Sir,

I gave your offer of collaboration the greatest attention, and had it reviewed to see how my Services might employ it.

At the moment, we are limiting ourselves to Industrial buildings already designed in Peacetime, and have had to hire, recently, only a few draftsmen.

But the Ministry of Munitions might, later on, be considering certain urban planning projects, and, given the services that you would be able to provide in this area, I will not forget your offer.

Please believe me, Dear Sir, to be most sincerely yours,

[signature]
Mr. Le Corbusier
35 rue de Sèvres
PARIS, 6e

—P. 339

Notes for a lecture to a Vichy women's group, December 1940

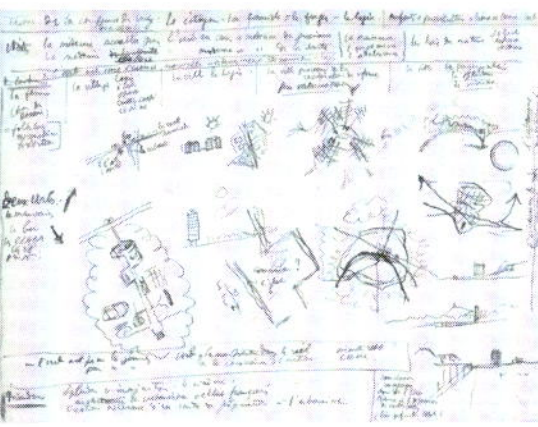

[LEFT TO RIGHT, TOP TO BOTTOM]
Subject of the Vichy lecture Dec. 1940: the citizen—the family—the household—housing / children = childcare = playgrounds and buildings=urb[anism]

Unités / medicine crushed by current urban planning = quack medicine
medicine ~~Health~~ constructed by modern [urban planning] = health [medicine]

Birth / eugenics / adolescence

the laws of nature:
sun / space / greenery

Urban planning is a new science—speeds—and in 3 dimensions—housing

Le Corbusier
the farm (no drawing)
= folklore / regionalism / tradition

the village
housing / school / sport / co-op center / public-spiritedness

the city / housing

the city process of carrying out reforms by enhancement

the city
the urban landscape / splendor / public-spiritedness

the school remains / the nightclub / the homicide road

traditional urbanism [RIGHT MARGIN]

two urb[rbanism]s
the bad
the good / the CIAMs / 1928 / League of Nations

begin ? with block 6

urbanism of the new era

[RIGHT MARGIN]

—the urban planning is for the young / by [the young]

Urban planning = manipulation in real life of the awareness of nature

Urban Planning minister / CEPU

Giraudoux / Splendor and imagination—public-spiritedness / architecture and town planning = French éclat / need to create a center for preparation for urbanism

conclusion: these are glimpses of the Urb[anism] / Science in 3 dimensions of built cubes (read entire definition)

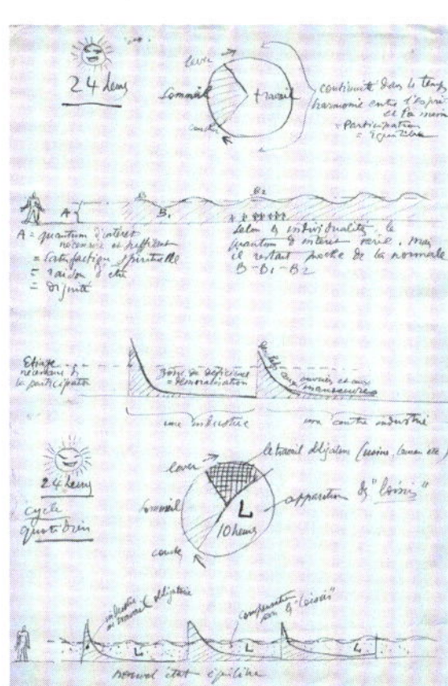

[LEFT TO RIGHT, TOP TO BOTTOM]
24 hours
get up / sleep / go to bed
work
continuity in time / harmony between mind and hand = participation
= equilibrium

A = quantum of necessary interest is sufficient / = spiritual satisfaction / = raison d'être / = dignity
depending on the individual, quantum of interest varies, but it remained close to the normal:
B-B1-B2

Backup needed if
shortfall zone / = demoralization /
one industry
from bosses to workers and laborers / another industry

24 hours daily cycle / get up / sleep / go to bed
compulsory work (factory, office, etc.) / arrival of "leisure" / 10 hours)

industry of work (compulsory) compensation via "leisure"

new state of balance /

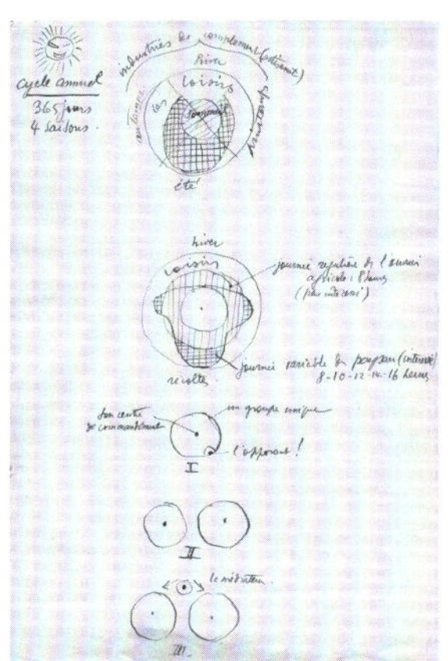

[TOP TO BOTTOM]
annual cycle / 365 days / 4 seasons
secondary industries (trades) / winter / autumn / spring / summer / leisure / sleep

winter / leisure / standard farm worker's day: 8 hours (not interested) / variable farmer's day (interested)
8—10—12—14—16 hours / harvests

I its command center / a single group /the opponent!
II
the mediator
III

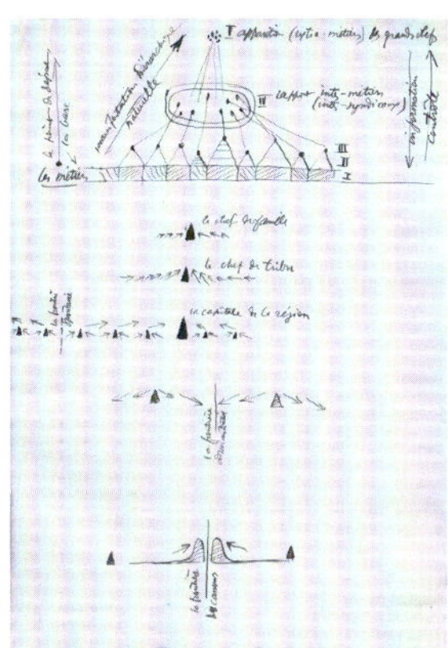

[LEFT TO RIGHT, TOP TO BOTTOM]
The starting point / the base / the professions
natural emergence of a hierarchy
V appearance (outside professions) of the great leaders
IV inter-profession relationship (inter-trade union)
information
control

the head of the family
the chief of the tribe

the spontaneous frontier / the capital of the region

the administrative frontier

the cannon frontier

—P. 340

General Director of Fine Arts to Le Corbusier, Vichy, 16 October 1940

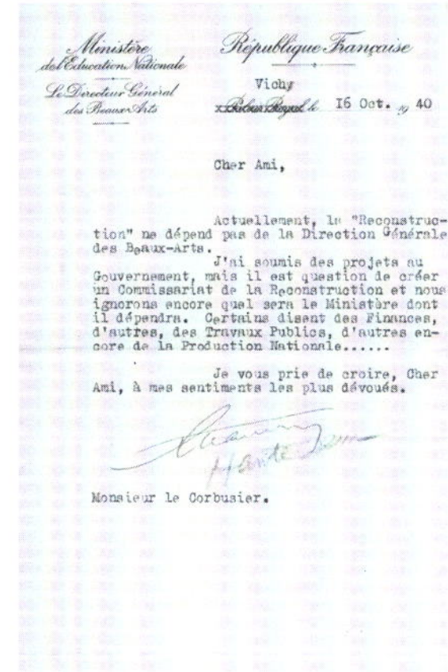

Ministère de l'Education Nationale
Le Directeur Général des Beaux-Arts

République Française

Vichy
~~Palais Royal~~, le 16 Oct. 19 40

Cher Ami,

Actuellement, la "Reconstruction" ne dépend pas de la Direction Générale des Beaux-Arts.

J'ai soumis des projets au Gouvernement, mais il est question de créer un Commissariat de la Reconstruction et nous ignorons encore quel sera le Ministère dont il dépendra. Certains disent des Finances, d'autres, des Travaux Publics, d'autres encore de la Production Nationale......

Je vous prie de croire, Cher Ami, à mes sentiments les plus dévoués.

[signature]

Monsieur Le Corbusier.

Vichy 16 Oct. 1940

Dear Friend,

At present, "Reconstruction" does not fall under the Directorate of the Fine Arts.

I have submitted projects to the Government, but it is a question of creating a Department of Reconstruction and we do not know yet under which Ministry that will fall. Some say Finances, others, Public Works, still others National Product…

I am, Dear Friend, devotedly yours,

[signature]
Mr. le Corbusier.

—P. 340

First page of letter from Le Corbusier to his mother and brother, from Vichy, 17 January 1941

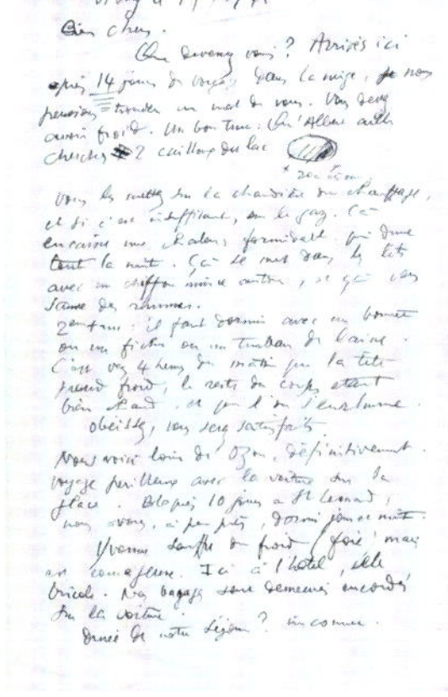

Vichy 17/1/41

Dear ones.

What are you up to? Arriving here after 14 days of traveling through snow, we thought we'd find a word from you. You must be cold. A good tip: Albert has to go get 2 stones from the lake

20 to 25 cm

You put them on the heating furnace, and if that's not good enough, on the gas. They accumulate incredible heat that lasts all night. You put them in the beds wrapped in a thin cloth, and it stops you from catching cold.

2nd tip: you must sleep wearing a bonnet or a woolen scarf or turban. It's around 4 in the morning that your head cools down, while the rest of the body is nice and warm, and then you catch cold.

Do this, you'll be pleased.

Here we are a long way from Ozon, for good. perilous journey in the car on the ice. Held up for 10 days at St. Léonard, we slept practically day and night.

Yvonne is feeling the cold (liver) but is bearing up. Here at the hotel she finds little things to do. Our bags have stayed tied on the car.

Length of our stay? unknown.

—P. 340

First two pages of letter from Le Corbusier to his mother and brother, from Vichy, 31 January 1941

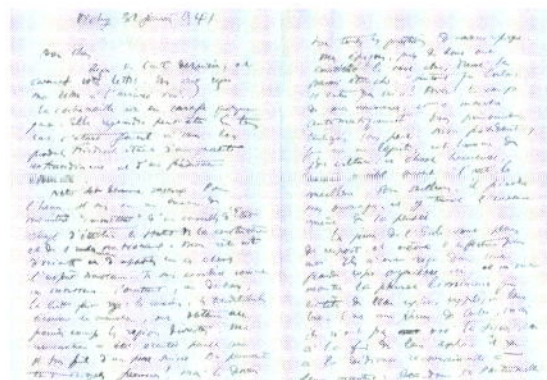

Vichy 31 January 1941

Dear ones.

Received yr last card, and before that your letter. You got my letter on arrival here.

The pigmeat is stranded somewhere. Maybe it'll come through. In any case, it was nice of you. The Friedrich products were of extraordinary quality and amazingly packaged.

Our future remains gloomy. For the moment I'm in the office at the "consultant" ministry of a Council of State in charge of drawing up the statutes for national building and urban planning. My role is to provide guidelines that bring the new spirit to bear. I'm regarded as a real somebody. At the same time, outside, the struggle is ferocious. The graybeards, the traditionalists are in control and got the devastated regions at the very first try. My nomination was rejected because I'm the son of a Swiss. You feel like dropping everything!

But Duty obliges me to hold fast, and ignore all questions of personal pride. My Prix de Rome imitators have set up a closed shop, raised impenetrable walls. "Just make sure Corbu doesn't get in!" Given my birth, that worked automatically. But we're forging on regardless. My President, a jurist, is highly cultured and, a stroke of luck, a sensitive man receptive to the best art. He also dips into my books and comes up with the very essence of their thinking.

The young people at the School are very respectful and even affectionate toward me. They welcomed me into a big exhibition organized here and showed me the sentence used as an epigraph to explain their aims. It's a sentence from Corbu, but they didn't dare put my name to it, because at the end of the exhibition there's a dedication to their masters: Beaudoin, and Pontremoli from the Ecole des Beaux-Arts.

—P. 341

Secretary of State for Labor to Le Corbusier, Vichy, 10 October 1941

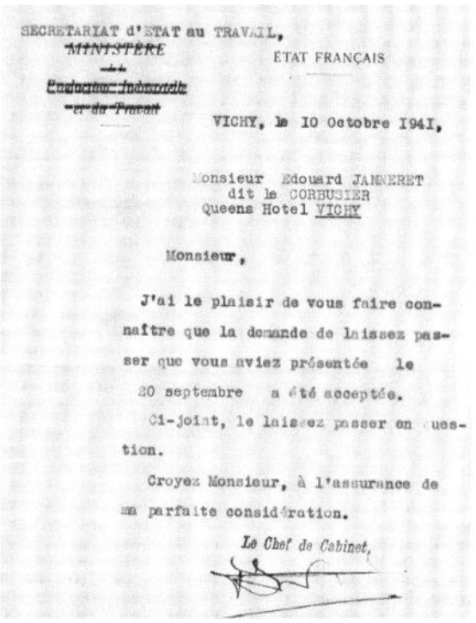

SECRETARIAT d'ETAT au TRAVAIL,
~~MINISTÈRE de l'Production Industrielle et du Travail~~

ÉTAT FRANÇAIS

VICHY, le 10 Octobre 1941,

Monsieur Edouard JANNERET
dit le CORBUSIER
Queens Hotel VICHY

Monsieur,

J'ai le plaisir de vous faire connaître que la demande de laissez passer que vous aviez présentée le 20 septembre a été acceptée.

Ci-joint, le laissez passer en question.

Croyez Monsieur, à l'assurance de ma parfaite considération.

Le Chef de Cabinet,

VICHY, 10 October 1941

Mr. Edouard JEANNERET
Known as le CORBUSIER
Queens Hotel VICHY

Sir,

It is my pleasure to inform you that the request for a laissez-passer that you presented on 20 September has been accepted.

Attached, the laissez-passer in question.

I am, Sir, yours very truly,

First Secretary,
[signature]

—P. 341

Letter from the office of Philippe Pétain to Le Corbusier, 4 November 1942

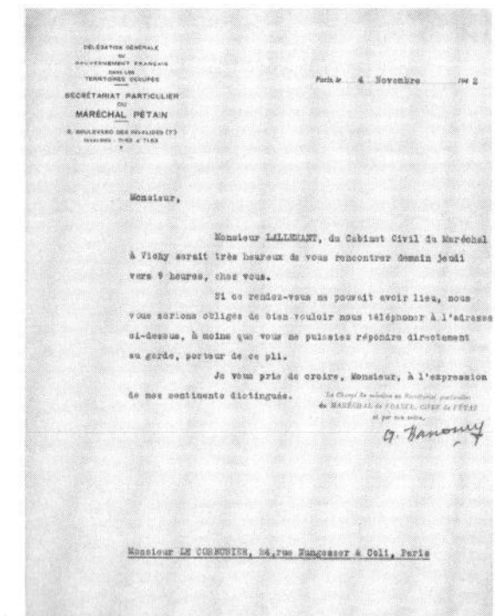

DÉLÉGATION GÉNÉRALE DU GOUVERNEMENT FRANÇAIS DANS LES TERRITOIRES OCCUPÉS
SECRÉTARIAT PARTICULIER DU MARÉCHAL PÉTAIN

Paris, le 4 Novembre 1942

Monsieur,

Monsieur LALLEMANT, du Cabinet Civil du Maréchal à Vichy serait très heureux de vous rencontrer demain jeudi vers 9 heures, chez vous.

Si ce rendez-vous ne pouvait avoir lieu, nous vous serions obligés de bien vouloir nous téléphoner à l'adresse ci-dessus, à moins que vous ne puissiez répondre directement au garde, porteur de ce pli.

Je vous prie de croire, Monsieur, à l'expression de mes sentiments distingués.

Monsieur LE CORBUSIER, 24, rue Nungesser & Coli, Paris

Paris, 4 November 1942

Sir,

Mr. LALLEMANT, of the Marshal's Civilian Cabinet in Vichy would be very glad to meet with you tomorrow Thursday around 9:00 a.m. at your home.

If this appointment cannot take place, we would be obliged if you would telephone us at the address above, unless you can reply directly to the guardsman, bearer of this note.

I am, Dear Sir, respectfully yours,

The Chargé d'affaires in the Private Office of the MARSHAL of FRANCE, HEAD of STATE and by his order,
[signature]

Mr. LE CORBUSIER, 24 rue Nungesser & Coli, Paris

—P. 342

Le Corbusier to his mother, from Ozon, 31 October 1940

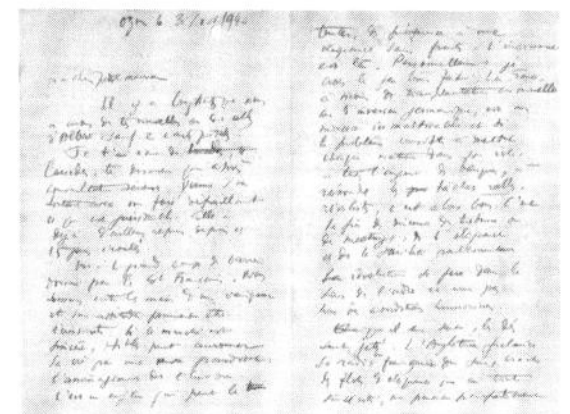

Ozon 31 October 1940

My dear little mom

It's a long time since we've had news of you or Albert, except for 2 postcards.

I wrote you from Lourdes, telling you that after serious consultation, Yvonne turns out to have a liver that is weak but curable. She's already picked up over the last two weeks.

Here's the bet of the French Gov[ernmen]t. We're in the hands of a victor whose attitude could be crushing. If the deal is honest, Hitler can round off his career with something grandiose: the remaking of Europe. This is a gamble that could tempt him, in preference to pointless revenge. That's the unknown factor. Personally I think things are looking good. Unless there's an importing of criminals or a German invasion, France remains a morsel that can't be chewed, and if the problem consists in giving each nation its part to play, killing the banks' money, and getting the real, realistic work done, everything's okay. That will mean the end of speeches in stadiums and meetings, the end of eloquence and parliamentary sterility. The revolution will aim at order, not at inhuman situations.

Whatever the case, the die is cast. England is railing. Its evening broadcasts in French, spitting waves of eloquence that in all sincerity seem to me perfectly meaningless, although dangerous when they fall on ears too susceptible to high-flown rhetoric.

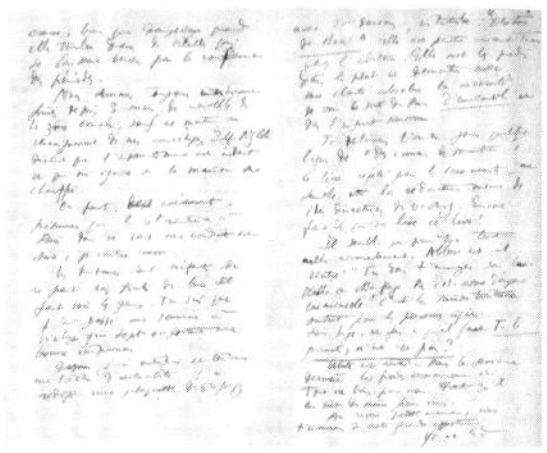

For 3 months now we've had no news whatsoever from the occupied zone, except a message this morning from our concierges saying that the apartment is intact and that they don't know if there will be any heating.

Events seem to indicate that the Gov[ernmen]t will return to Paris. In this case my course is clear: I shall return too.

Distance is pernicious. You can't work from a long way away. You have to see people. You know I spent a week in Vichy in late September and came away with a good impression.

Since then I've worked on and completed a very relevant project: a 50-page booklet with 20 drawings called "Destin de Paris" [Destiny of Paris]. It went off to the publisher yesterday. It really goes to the point by demonstrating perfectly the need to see Paris's fate overall and in the light of the new spirit.

The other day I reread a few lines from "Des canons, des munitions" [Guns, Ammunition]. Rejected by the Communists, the book seems to me the perfect outline of Vichy's main ideas. But we still have to get people to read it!

Everything seems to be going as usual for you. Is Albert back? You must be at loose ends without him. Keep an eye on the heating. No criminal money saving! This is the dangerous time of the year, especially for the aged. Be sensible and do what's necessary. You promise, right?

Winter came back to Paris last week. The cold is beginning here. Everything's fine with us. Make sure it's the same for you.

Goodbye, little mom, we send all our love.

Yv and Ed.

—P. 342

Text for a radio presentation about *Sur les quatre routes (The Four Routes)*, c. 1942, Gallimard, Paris, 1941

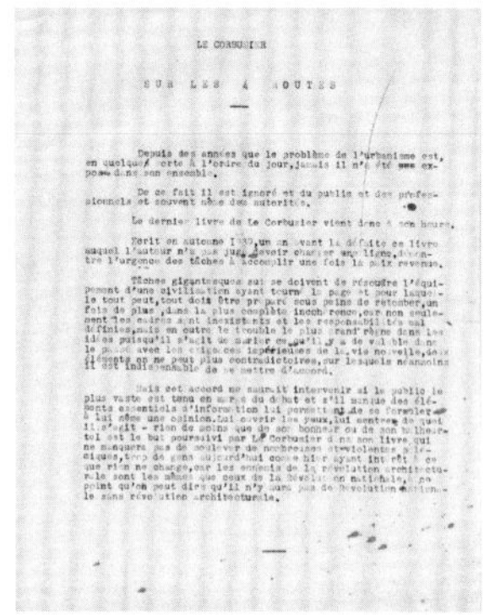

LE CORBUSIER

SUR LES 4 ROUTES

Depuis des années que le problème de l'urbanisme est, en quelque sorte à l'ordre du jour, jamais il n'a été exposé dans son ensemble.

De ce fait il est ignoré et du public et des professionnels et souvent même des autorités.

Le dernier livre de Le Corbusier vient donc à son heure.

Ecrit en automne 1939, un an avant la défaite ce livre auquel l'auteur n'a pas jugé devoir changer une ligne, démontre l'urgence des tâches à accomplir une fois la paix revenue.

Tâches gigantesques qui se doivent de résoudre l'équipement d'une civilisation ayant tourné la page et pour laquelle tout peut, tout doit être préparé sous peine de retomber, une fois de plus, dans la plus complète incohérence, car non seulement les cadres sont inexistants et les responsabilités mal définies, mais en outre le trouble le plus grand règne dans les idées puisqu'il s'agit de marier ce qu'il y a de valable dans le passé avec les exigences impérieuses de la vie nouvelle, deux éléments on ne peut plus contradictoires, sur lesquels néanmoins il est indispensable de se mettre d'accord.

Mais cet accord ne saurait intervenir si le public le plus vaste est tenu en marge du débat et s'il manque des éléments essentiels d'information lui permettant de se former à lui même une opinion. Lui ouvrir les yeux, lui montrer de quoi il s'agit - rien de moins que de son bonheur ou de son malheur - tel est le but poursuivi par Le Corbusier dans son livre qui ne manquera pas de soulever de nombreuses et violentes polémiques, trop de gens aujourd'hui comme hier ayant intérêt à ce que rien ne change, car les ennemis de la révolution architecturale sont les mêmes que ceux de la Révolution nationale, à ce point qu'on peut dire qu'il n'y aura pas de Révolution nationale sans révolution architecturale.

LE CORBUSIER

ON THE 4 ROUTES

For years the urbanism problem has been, so to speak, part of the agenda, but it has never been outlined in its entirety.

As a result it remains unknown both to the public and professionals and often even to the authorities.

Thus Le Corbusier's latest book appears just at the right time.

Written in the fall of 1939, a year before France's defeat, this book, not a single line of which the author has seen fit to change, demonstrates the urgency of the tasks to be accomplished once peace returns.

Gigantic tasks aimed at resolving the question of amenities for a civilization that is making a fresh start and for which everything can and must be made ready if it is not to slide yet again into utter disorganization. Not only are the necessary frameworks nonexistent and the responsibilities ill-defined, there is also the greatest confusion in terms of ideas, as the task is to combine what is worthwhile from the past with the imperatives of the new life—two diametrically opposed notions on which, nonetheless, it is vital that we reach agreement.

But this agreement cannot come about if the general public is excluded from the debate and if it lacks the basic information needed for it to form an opinion of its own. To open the public's eyes, to show it what is at stake—nothing less than its happiness or unhappiness—is Le Corbusier's aim in a book that will certainly stir up much violent controversy: too many people now, as in the past, have a vested interest in ensuring that nothing changes, for the enemies of the architectural revolution are the very same as the enemies of the National Revolution—so much so that it can be said that there will be no National Revolution without architectural revolution.

—P. 343

Postcard from Alexis Carrel, to Le Corbusier, 19 February 1942

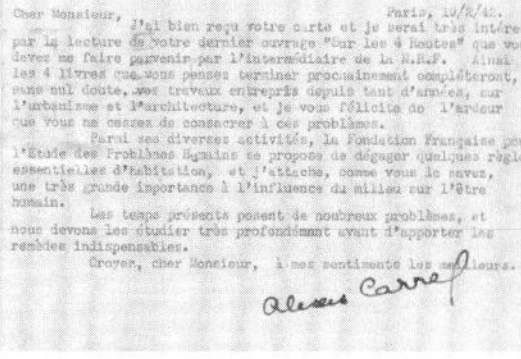

Cher Monsieur,

Paris, 19/2/42.

J'ai bien reçu votre carte et je serai très intéressé par la lecture de votre dernier ouvrage "Sur les 4 Routes" que vous devez me faire parvenir par l'intermédiaire de la N.R.F. Ainsi les 4 livres que vous pensez terminer prochainement compléteront, sans nul doute, vos travaux entrepris depuis tant d'années, sur l'urbanisme et l'architecture, et je vous félicite de l'ardeur que vous ne cessez de consacrer à ces problèmes.

Parmi ses diverses activités, la Fondation Française pour l'Etude des Problèmes Humains se propose de dégager quelques règles essentielles d'habitation, et j'attache, comme vous le savez, une très grande importance à l'influence du milieu sur l'être humain.

Les temps présents posent de nombreux problèmes, et nous devons les étudier très profondément avant d'apporter les remèdes indispensables.

Croyez, cher Monsieur, à mes sentiments les meilleurs.

Paris, 19/2/42.

Dear Sir,

I received your card and I will be very interested to read your latest work "Sur les 4 Routes," which you will have to send me through the N.R.F. So, the 4 books you expect to finish soon will undoubtedly complement the works you undertook so many years ago on urban planning and architecture, and I congratulate you on the ardor that you still devote to these problems.

Among its various activities, the French Foundation for the Study of Human Problems intends to define certain essential rules of housing, and, as you know, I attach a very great importance to the effect of the surroundings upon the human being.

These times present many problems, and we must study them in great depth before applying the necessary remedies.

Believe me, dear Sir, to be yours truly,

[signature]

—P. 347

Le Corbusier's hand-written notes describing plans for a "green factory"

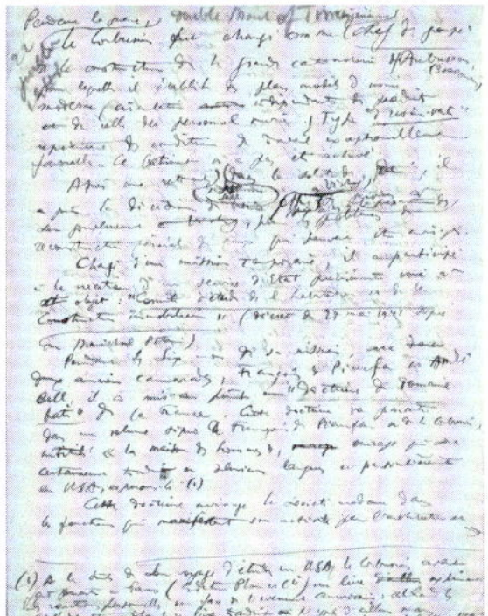

[IN RED]
22 July 1941 / double March of Time

During the war, Le Corbusier was made engineer team leader for the construction of the cartridge factory at Aubusson (3,000 workers) for which he drew up plans for a model modern factory (products circulating independently of the workers). A kind of "green factory" offering exceptional working conditions. This building was not finished.

After withdrawing of ~~seven~~ seven months into solitude, ~~of~~ in Vichy, he decided to come offer his services to ~~prep~~ help with the preparations of his government ~~in Vichy~~, for the anticipated problems associated with overall national reconstruction.

Given a temporary assignment, he took part in the creation of a government body for this purpose: "The Advisory Committee for Housing and Construction" (Decree of 27 May 1941 signed by Marshal Pétain)

During the six months of his assignment with ~~form~~ two former associates, François de Pierrefeu and André Boll, he drew up a "doctrine for built-up areas" in France. This doctrine will appear in a book by François de Pierrefeu and Le Corbusier titled "La maison des hommes" [The Home of Men], which will certainly be translated into several languages and, it is especially to be hoped, in the USA. (1)

This doctrine looks at modern society in terms of the functions expressing its architectural activity and [...]

(1) After his field trip to the USA, Le Corbusier published (with Plon, in Paris) a book expressing his personal reactions to the American phenomenon: "Quand les Cathédrales étaient blanches," translated in N York [When the Cathedrals Were White]. But if no publisher sensed the taste or the courage of the American public.

—P. 347

Le Corbusier's "L'Usine Verte: Workplace Architecture," extracted from *Les trois établissements humains* (*The Three Human Establishments*), Formes et Couleurs, Lausanne, 1944

Workplace architecture
THE GREEN FACTORY
by LE CORBUSIER

The factory is a big establishment whose function it is to turn out products. There raw or secondary materials are transformed into objects. The machines are the driving force, possessing infinitely more power, speed, and precision than human hands. In the factory metals, pastes, fibers, pellets, liquids, and gases undergo manipulation and combination. Combined with the noise, not to say infernal din, the vibrations, dust, and smells, not to say stenches, maintain a sometimes hellish atmosphere heightened by flames, heat, smoke, and fumes.

Light comes in through the roof or enormous windows, bringing with it the heat or cold of the particular season.

The machines amplify all human actions—crushing, chewing, pulping, rolling, stretching, blowing, and hammering—and often in grimacingly distorted ways. All this gesticulating is awe-inspiring: sometimes the slowness of giants—the great drop hammers and presses—and sometimes the swiftness of dangerous creatures, snaking, flashing, galloping, and sliding, with weird, crazed limbs going every which way.

Meanwhile dust and waste settle on them all, and on the floors, walls, and frameworks.

Thus, with one thing leading to another, modern work has generated extra-human conditions that cannot fail to influence the behavior of those sharing the adventure of machines. Psychologically as well as physically. People can only come to terms with some of the effects of these abnormal conditions: the others dominate, enslave, and do violence to them.

So much so that modern work can be seen from one point of view as a terrible penance, the price to pay for some unconsciously committed crime.

A weight pressing on modern society, work is perceived by many as a punishment.

In contrast with this gloomy picture there exists a joyful, enthusiastic, and exciting description of modern work as the outcome of impromptu arrangements that have given rise to dignified working conditions in total harmony with the respect due to human beings. For modern work can give those performing it a sense of its grandeur and a perception of its beauty.

Socially speaking, everything remains to be resolved in terms of the correct interpretation of the rights and duties involved in work, but builders must waste no time in taking charge of workplace planning: productive use of space, conservation of rural areas, industrial estates and their quality, and last but not least zones of exchange: the biology of their traffic and of the assembling of their buildings, and their efficiency.

Notably in respect to industry and the factory of the century of the first machine cycle, the black factory will be open to replacement by the "Green Factory."

[BOTTOM]
Mr. Le Corbusier has given us exclusive publication rights for this study, which is an excerpt from a book soon to be published by Denoël under the title "Les trois établissements humains" [The Three Human Establishments]. The book is appearing under the aegis of CIAM (International Congresses of Modern Architects) and is part of the ASCORAL (Association of Builders for Architectural Regeneration) series.

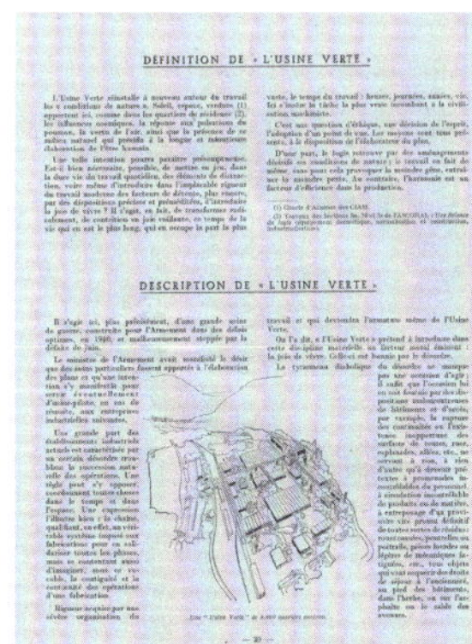

DEFINITION OF THE "GREEN FACTORY"

The Green Factory restores nature's conditions to work. As in residential areas (1) sun, space, and greenery (2) provide the cosmic influences, the response to the pulsation of the lungs, the advantages of air and the presence of the natural setting that governed the long, meticulous shaping of the human being.

This intention may seem presumptuous. Is it really necessary, indeed possible, to feed elements of diversion into the hard life of daily work; and not only to introduce factors for relaxation into the implacable harshness of modern work, but also to inject joie de vivre, deliberately and with premeditation? The issue is the radical transformation, from contrition to courageous joy, of this part of existence that is the longest and the most all-consuming: the hours, the days, the years, the lifetime taken up by work. This is the most vital task facing the civilization of the machine.

The question is an ethical one, involving a decision of the spirit, the deliberate adoption of a point of view. All the necessary means are there at the planner's disposal.

On the one hand living accommodation is returning to nature's conditions via decisive developments; and work is doing the same, but without giving rise to the slightest inconvenience or the slightest loss. On the contrary, harmony is a factor for efficiency in production terms.

(1) See ASCORAL *Une science du logis* sections 3a, 3b, and 3c (domestic equipment, standardization and construction, industrialization).
(2) See the CIAM Athens Charter.

DESCRIPTION OF THE "GREEN FACTORY"

The establishment in question is a large war factory built very quickly for the Ministry of Armaments in 1940, but unfortunately halted by France's defeat in June.

The Minister for Armaments had said that he wanted special care to be given to the plans, so that this project, should it prove successful, might eventually serve as a pilot for later industrial undertakings.

Characteristic of a large proportion of today's industrial establishments is a disorderliness that hampers the natural sequence of operations. This can be countered by a rule calling for overall coordination in time and space. The term that covers it is the production line, which refers to a manufacturing system unifying every phase of the process, but which at the same time sees manufacturing in terms of operations that are contiguous and continuous.

This rigorousness is achieved by strict organization of work and will become the very backbone of the Green Factory. As has been said, the "Green Factory" claims to introduce a conspicuously moral factor into this materialist discipline: the joie de vivre that is ruled out by disorderliness.

The petty despot of disorderliness never misses a chance: all he needs is the opportunity provided by ill-advised siting of buildings and access points—for example, breaks in continuity or the inappropriate presence of roads, streets, esplanades, and paths serving no other purpose than to furnish pretexts for unsupervised wandering by the personnel, unsupervised circulation of products and materials, and the stockpiling, initially temporary but very quickly indefinite, of all sorts of leftovers: broken wheels, posts and beams, bits of worn-out machinery, etc., all of them destined with time to overstay their welcome at the foot of buildings, in the grass, or on the asphalt or sand of the roadways.

[CAPTION]
A "Green Factory" housing some 3,000 workers.

To keep disorderliness at bay, it suffices to deny it access (the question is one of circulation) to areas specified a priori as not to be occupied (the question is one of the reciprocal placing of buildings). These areas will be declared 'not to be occupied' so that nobody may enter them and nothing be put there. Their function will thus be unrelated to the manufacturing process: they will be a combination of architectural and landscaped spaces.

The work, then, is seen as taking place in a setting specially prepared, set aside, or designed, and offering harmonious views of buildings surrounded by lawn, of groves of trees and pleasing areas of sky.

Some further details:

The sequence of the manufacturing operations can be ordered as a continuous line, a one-way transport thoroughfare on which all movement in the opposite direction is avoided. Skillfully planned, it will justify its description as a single transport thoroughfare: this hard, smooth concrete path traversing the entire factory precinct—including the grassed areas—will be used by small carts, powered by electricity or other means, to transport products from the raw materials weighbridge at the entry, the sheds where these materials are stored, and the processing workshops to the storeroom for finished products and the loading bay. This path links one building to another and inside the workshops it branches out to serve each machine.

All operations take place at floor level, on the concrete of the path or the floor of the workshops. This materials and merchandise circuit is strictly off limits to the personnel, whether laborers or clerical staff.

So what route do the personnel follow? And first, where do they come from?

They come from their homes via the road that runs past the factory gate.

And where do they go? To the garage for bikes, motorbikes, and cars; then to the clocking-in area at the factory entrance, without losing a minute to any distractions; then to their work stations, i.e., each in place by his machine after stopping off at the lockers and the washroom.

At the end of the shift they will retrace their steps. In the course of the day some of them will have been summoned to the central offices or will have had to visit the social services department (social workers, doctor, etc.). To do this they will not wander through the factory or the surrounding area.

The itinerary described above is surprisingly similar to the phases of the circulation of the blood or the lymph in the body of an organic being. It takes the form of a tree trunk that branches out where necessary, and represents a highly developed economy of effort, at once sober, concise and rigorously exact. This is a far cry from the traditional grid of streets or avenues that almost always serves in factories as the matrix for traffic involving materials, products, laborers, clerical staff, and management.

In respect to the industrial establishment under consideration here, three diagrams suffice to illustrate the Green Factory theory.

THE RAW MATERIALS CIRCUIT

I shall begin with a brief summary of the basic manufacturing process under consideration here.

Three essential raw materials are used: lead, brass, and steel.

Steel is needed in greater quantities because of tool-making requirements.

In addition, the explosives are kept in a powder store well away from the factory, and are delivered only in small quantities, hour by hour.

Arriving by rail, the steel, lead, and brass are unloaded and weighed at point A. [steel] P. [lead] L. [brass] The concrete path begins here and leads to P1, the lead shed, and to A1 and L1, respectively, the steel and brass depositories; it branches off to P2 and the turning shop, to A2 for chroming and the toolmaking, finishing, and machine shops, and to L2 and the other turning shop. Having served the various machines, it continues to P3 and L3 and the packaging, labeling, and loading shops.

It ends at P4 L4, the warehouse giving onto the railway loading platform.

[DIAGRAM KEY]
LEAD
BRASS
STEEL

[CAPTION]
The materials circuit.

CIRCUIT DU PERSONNEL
(ouvriers et employés)

PLAN DE MASSES DE L'ETABLISSEMENT INDUSTRIEL
CONÇU EN " USINE VERTE "

The traffic on the concrete path is limited to small electric carts and apart from their drivers no other staff members may use the thoroughfare. The path is poured into the grass and its hard, compact surface provides no hold for weeds.

PERSONNEL CIRCUIT

(laborers and clerical personnel)
3,500 laborers and clerical staff—men and women—come to the factory by road in the course of the day.

VM is the parking lot for their bikes, motorbikes and other vehicles.

P is the clocking-in point.

S, the access to the social services department (social workers, doctor and dining hall). The building is opposite P.

At this point the path leaves the ground, remaining fairly horizontal, while the ground slopes toward the river.

Thus the path becomes a raised passageway running level with the sawtooth roofs of the workshops. The passageway is enclosed by walls and a ceiling: it is a square tube.

At V the passageway branches, and stairways lead to the changing rooms of the loading shops. At V1 the turning and machinery shops are served in the same way. At V2 the tool-making shop is served. Last of all is V3, the office building.

It should be pointed out that where there is human traffic there must also be provision for lighting, water, and heating. And so the passageway will also house the pipes for lighting, water, and heating. These will run side by side beneath the ceiling, visible and readily accessible. To optimize their functioning they too follow the most economical route.

From the changing rooms situated at mezzanine level, the personnel will go down to the first-floor washrooms, whose many doors give directly onto the workshops.

The personnel circuit is indicated by a solid black line on the drawing.

The circuit for the electric carts is indicated in red.

Lastly, marked out by hatching, the road for cars, with its parking area, serves the office building directly.

This traffic plan is revolutionary, matching the proposals of modern urbanism for big cities in which pedestrians and cars must be separated.

This traffic system is based on the strictest economy. It moves from indoors to outdoors, embodying an organization the very same as that of life.

SITE PLAN OF THE INDUSTRIAL ESTABLISHMENT DESIGNED AS A "GREEN FACTORY"

The buildings are arranged according to the demands of the terrain and manufacturing requirements: their shape and size is in each case in proportion to their functions. Light is generously and systematically distributed throughout the workshops using appropriate methods.

But at certain points where the sun poses no problem, large vertical windows will provide views of landscapes that have been judiciously retained or designed. The spaces between the buildings and their walls will give rise to harmonious groupings with generous vistas of sky and views into the distance. Grass comes right up to the foot of these glass walls giving onto the countryside: the original trees have been kept and others planted to embellish the site.

One of the walls of the passageway is glazed, offering this rural prospect to the mass of people passing by.

The three floors of the office block provide a view onto the river.

[CAPTION]
Large vertical windows will provide views of the surrounding landscape.

TOUT EST ORDONNÉ ET PROPRE

EVERYTHING IS ORDERLY AND CLEAN

Upkeep is taken care of by nature herself, which is reassuring: this upkeep covers grass, leaves, and branches that change with the seasons.

For the objectors there will remain a single argument: the workshop windows will be dirty and broken, as has been the case in industry for the last hundred years.

Reply: Bata, in Czechoslovakia, has already surrounded the buildings of its factories with greenery, and the windows are scrupulously looked after and as clean as those of any dwelling.

We are aware that the modern world, taking possession of its working tools in the course of today's great shift, has already turned its back on the cruel indifference of the mechanistic nineteenth century and its legacy of sprawling cities, cities black with soot, and the horrors of the machine age.

This instance of a green factory is due entirely to chance, to the exceptional circumstances of wartime and a demonstration intended as exemplary. The debacle of defeat halted the works before their completion.

However, the principle can be considered worthwhile and a landmark in the establishing of linear industrial estates.

[CAPTION]
The Green Factory. New working conditions.

—P. 348

Cost estimates, 7 June 1940, for Murondin housing for forty children

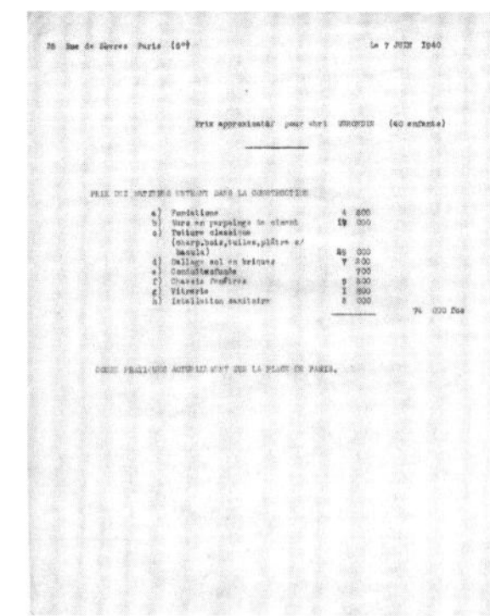
35 Rue de Sèvres Paris (6e) Le 7 JUIN 1940

Prix approximatif pour abri MURONDIN (40 enfants)

PRIX DES MATIÈRES ENTRANT DANS LA CONSTRUCTION

a)	Fondations	4 600
b)	Murs en parpaings de ciment	1[illegible] 000
c)	Toiture classique (charp. bois, tuiles, plâtre s/ bacula)	29 000
d)	Dallage sol en briques	7 200
e)	Conduit fumée	700
f)	Chassis fenêtres	9 500
g)	Vitrerie	1 800
h)	Installation sanitaire	5 000
		74 000 Frs

PRIX PRATIQUÉS ACTUELLEMENT SUR LA PLACE DE PARIS.

35 rue de Sèvres, Paris (6e)

7 June 1940

Approximate cost of MURONDIN shelter (40 children)

COST OF BUILDING MATERIALS
a) Foundations / 4,600
b) Cinder-block walls / 1[?],000
c) Conventional roofing (wood frame, tiles, plaster on lathing) / 29,000
d) Brick floor / 7,200
e) Waste-heat flue / 700
f) Window sashes / 9,500
g) Glass / 1,800
h) Plumbing / 5,000

74,000 Frs

CURRENT RATE IN PARIS.

—P. 348

Architect Raymond Audigier to Le Corbusier, 19 November 1940

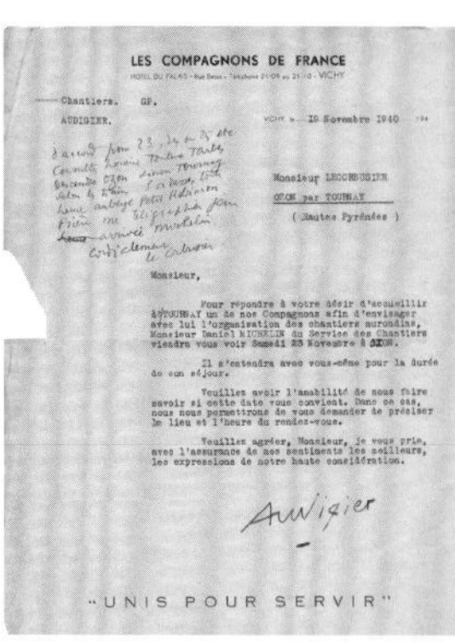
LES COMPAGNONS DE FRANCE
HÔTEL DU PALAIS · VICHY

Chantiers. GP.
AUDIGIER.

VICHY le 19 Novembre 1940

Monsieur LECORBUSIER
OZON par TOURNAY
(Hautes Pyrénées)

Monsieur,

Pour répondre à votre désir d'accueillir à TOURNAY un de nos Compagnons afin d'envisager avec lui l'organisation des chantiers murondins, Monsieur Daniel MICHELIN du Service des Chantiers viendra vous voir Samedi 23 Novembre à OZON.

Il s'entendra avec vous-même pour la durée de son séjour.

Veuillez avoir l'amabilité de nous faire savoir si cette date vous convient. Dans ce cas, nous nous permettrons de vous demander de préciser le lieu et l'heure du rendez-vous.

Veuillez agréer, Monsieur, je vous prie, avec l'assurance de nos sentiments les meilleurs, les expressions de notre haute considération.

Audigier

"UNIS POUR SERVIR"

okay for 23, 24, or 25, etc. Check timetable Toulouse Tarbes get off Ozon otherwise Tournay depending on the trains. Call any time at Petit Robinson inn. Please telegraph me for day arrival Michelin
Best regards,
Le Corbusier

VICHY 19 November 1940

Mr. LE CORBUSIER
OZON via TOURNAY
(Hautes-Pyrénées)

Sir,

In response to your wish to receive one of our Compagnons in TOURNAY, so that together you might see how to organize the Murondin building sites, Mr. Daniel MICHELIN, of the Building Sites Service, will come see you on Saturday 25 November at OZON.

He will work out the length of his stay with you directly.

Would you be so kind as to let us know if the date is convenient for you. If so, please specify the place and time of the meeting.

Please believe me to be, Sir, yours very sincerely,

[signature]

—P. 349

Le Corbusier's article "Les Constructions Murondins," published in *Techniques et architecture*, July 1945

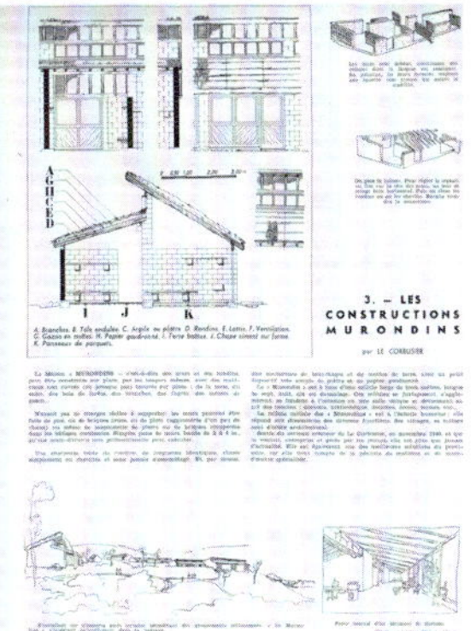

[SECTION KEY]
A. Branches
B. Corrugated iron
C. Clay or plaster
D. Logs
E. Lathwork
F. Ventilation
G. Grass sod
H. Tar paper
I. Dirt
J. Cement screed on bed
K. Wood floor panels

[TOP RIGHT]
The walls are up, forming cells whose width is constant. In theory the walls always form right angles, which ensures stability.

Putting the roof on. To ensure evenness, a piece of exactly horizontal sawn timber is laid on the tops of the walls. Then the logs are nailed or screwed into place. Then comes the covering.

3.—"MURONDIN BUILDINGS"
by LE CORBUSIER

The "MURONDIN" (that is to say, "wall" and "log") House can be built on site, by the occupants, from unworked (or almost) materials available on the site: earth, sand, forest wood, branches, bundles of branches, grass sods, etc.

Not having to bear any great weight, the walls can be made of wattle and daub, adobe bricks, or earth blocks (with a little lime added), or even masonry—stone or bricks recovered from collapsing buildings. Simple wall sections 2 to 4 meters high that non-professionals can put up.

The roof frame is made entirely of logs all of identical length, nailed or pegged, with no assemblage required. The covering is foliage and grass sod plus a very simple plaster and tar paper system.

The "Murondin" is based on a cell three meters wide, and seven, eight, ten, or more meters long. These cells are set side by side, they accumulate, and when necessary they can form a single room for specific needs: dormitory, library, showers, schoolroom, farmhouse, etc.

The initial "Murondin" cell is scaled to the human body; it corresponds to the dimensions required by various functions. Its windows and roof are architect-designed.

Sprung from the creative brain of Le Corbusier in November 1940, and taken up and managed by young people, as he wished, it is now more relevant than ever. It is also one of the best temporary solutions, in that it takes account of the shortage of materials and specialist manpower.

[BOTTOM CAPTION]
Adaptable to any kind of terrain and lending itself to picturesque groupings, the "Murondin" fits naturally into this landscape.

[BOTTOM CAPTION]
Hall of a dormitory building.
(From a brochure published by Chiron)

—P. 350

Postcard from J. Grosperrin to Etienne Chiron, 29 March 1942

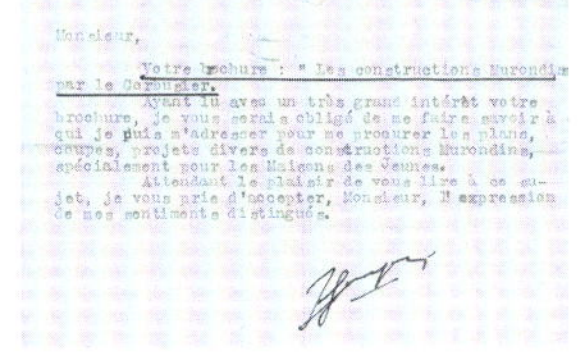

Monsieur,

Votre brochure : " Les constructions Murondins " par le Corbusier.

Ayant lu avec un très grand intérêt votre brochure, je vous serais obligé de me faire savoir à qui je puis m'adresser pour me procurer les plans, coupes, projets divers de constructions Murondins, spécialement pour les Maisons des Jeunes.

Attendant le plaisir de vous lire à ce sujet, je vous prie d'accepter, Monsieur, l'expression de mes sentiments distingués.

Sir,

<u>Your brochure: Les constructions "Murondins" by le Corbusier.</u>

Having read your brochure with very great interest, I would be obliged to you if you would let me know from whom I might procure the plans, sections, various designs for Murondin buildings, especially the Youth Houses.

In anticipation of the pleasure of hearing from you, please believe me,
Sir, most respectfully yours,

[signature]

—P. 350

Sketch for the cover of *Les constructions "Murondins"*

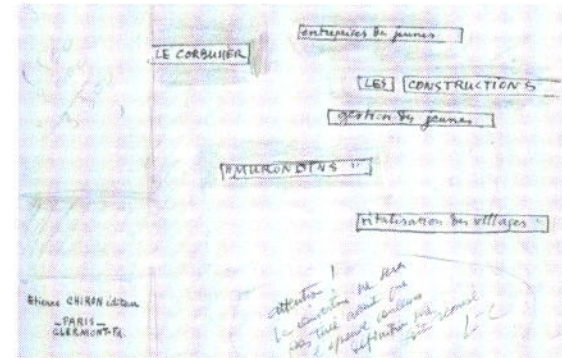

[TOP TO BOTTOM]
young people's businesses
LE CORBUSIER

THE CONSTRUCTIONS

management by young people

"MURONDINS"

injecting life into the villages

Attention! The cover will not be printed before the definitive color proof has been given to me. L-C.

—P. 350

Sketch for one page of *Les constructions "Murondins"*

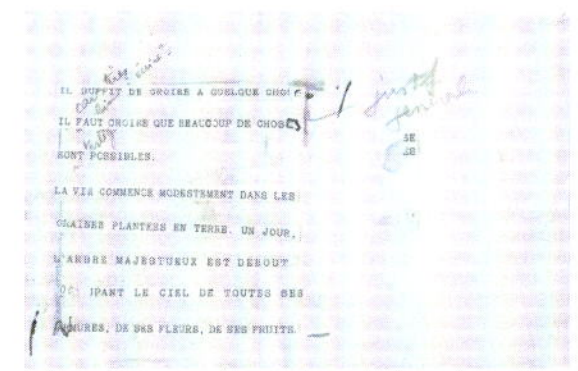

IT IS ENOUGH TO BELIEVE IN SOMETHING.

WE MUST BELIEVE THAT MANY THINGS ARE POSSIBLE.

LIFE BEGINS MODESTLY IN THE SEEDS PLANTED IN THE EARTH. ONE DAY THE MAJESTIC TREE STANDS TALL, FILLING THE SKY WITH ALL ITS BRANCHES, FLOWERS, AND FRUIT.

—P. 350

Deputy Regional Commissioner, Lyon, to Etienne Chiron, 20 March 1942

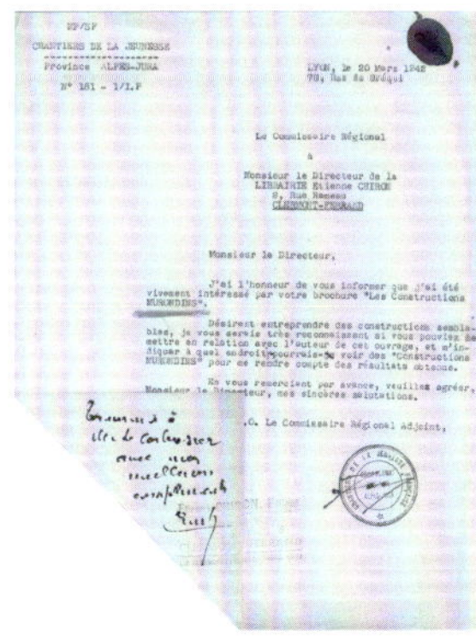

LYON, 20 March 1942
73 rue de Créqui

The Regional Commissioner
to the Director of the
Etienne CHIRON BOOKSTORE
8 rue Rameau
<u>CLERMONT-FERRAND</u>

To the Director,

I have the honor to inform you that I was keenly interested in your brochure Les constructions "Murondins."

Because I wish to undertake similar buildings, I would be very grateful to you if you could put me in touch with the author of this work, and tell me where I might see some "MURONDINS Constructions" to get an idea of the results that have been achieved.

Thanking you in advance, Director, I am most sincerely yours,

The Deputy Regional Commissioner,
[signature]

[BOTTOM LEFT]
sent to Le Corbusier with my best regards
[signature]

—P. 352

Secretary General of Fine Arts to Le Corbusier, from Vichy, 27 February 1942

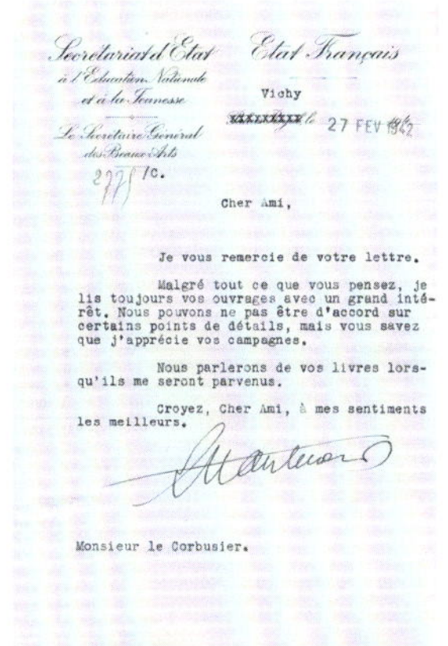

Secrétariat d'État à l'Éducation Nationale et à la Jeunesse
Le Secrétaire Général des Beaux-Arts
2775/C.

État Français
Vichy
le 27 FEV 1942

Cher Ami,

Je vous remercie de votre lettre.

Malgré tout ce que vous pensez, je lis toujours vos ouvrages avec un grand intérêt. Nous pouvons ne pas être d'accord sur certains points de détails, mais vous savez que j'apprécie vos campagnes.

Nous parlerons de vos livres lorsqu'ils me seront parvenus.

Croyez, Cher Ami, à mes sentiments les meilleurs.

Monsieur le Corbusier.

Vichy, 27 February 1942

Dear Friend,

Thank you for your letter.

Whatever you might think, I always read your works with great interest.

We cannot agree on certain points of details, but you know I value your campaigns.

We'll talk about your books after they arrive.

I am, Dear Friend, yours truly,

[signature]
Mr. le Corbusier.

—P. 352

First page of letter from Le Corbusier to Charles Trochu, 7 March 1942

<u>Le Corbusier</u> to Mr. Charles Trochu
President of the Paris City Council

7 March 1942

My dear President.

The tragic bombardments of this week will open sooner than we might have imagined the debate on the very essence of the problem of the urbanization of Paris.

1. large factories have been destroyed
2. suburbs have been wiped out

1° Once again the question arises of <u>transplanting</u> large factories <u>elsewhere</u>. Elsewhere? An exact answer can and must be given: it is to be found in the book "<u>La Maison des hommes</u>," to be published by Plon late in March.

If 20,000 Renaud workers leave Paris, they take 60 to 100,000 people with them. If factories other than Renaud are transplanted, 500,000 or 1 million residents will leave the Paris region.

2° Will the suburbs be rebuilt? No and for a number of reasons: a/ transplanting of worker populations <u>elsewhere</u>. Danger of creating Red zones yet again. Resistance from urbanization theory in [...]

—P. 354

Preparatory sketches for *La maison des hommes*, 1942

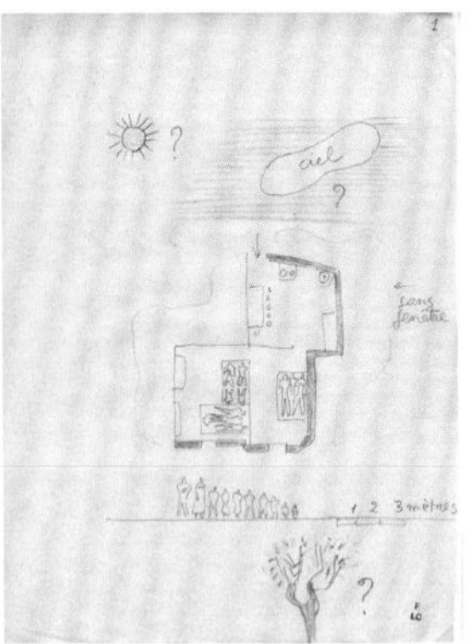

Sky

No window

1 2 3 meters

Lawful

Contemporary disaster

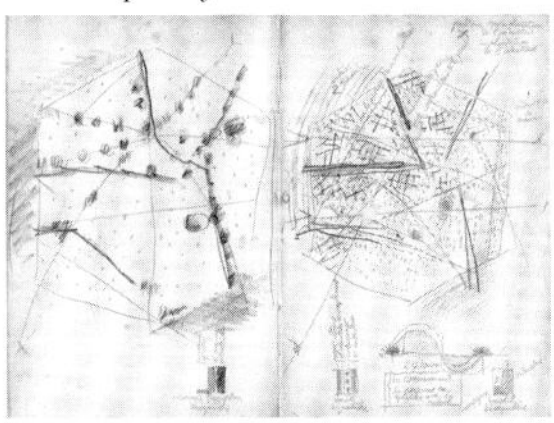

[LEFT PAGE]
agrarian economy / industrial economy
anemia / congestion
imbalance

[RIGHT PAGE: IN RED]
1 basement industry
2 linear industry
3 backup industry

[RIGHT PAGE: LEFT TO RIGHT, TOP TO BOTTOM]
industry on the route of merchandise

inevitable places of differences of opinions
problem: transplantation of industry / —setting up of industry

agriculture and backup industry
trades and industry

unity / balance

24 hours
the community
the person in balance with nature

3 country
7 industry
duality / imbalance

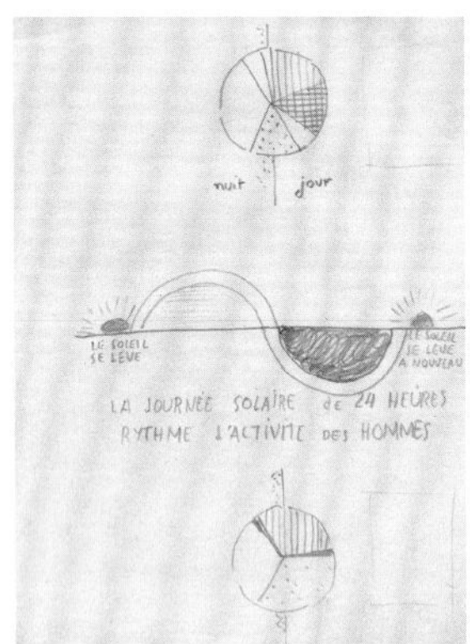

[LEFT TO RIGHT, TOP TO BOTTOM]
night / day

THE SUN RISES / THE SUN RISES AGAIN

THE SOLAR DAY OF 24 HOURS RHYTHM OF HUMAN ACTIVITY

—P. 355

Preparatory sketch for *La maison des hommes*, 1942

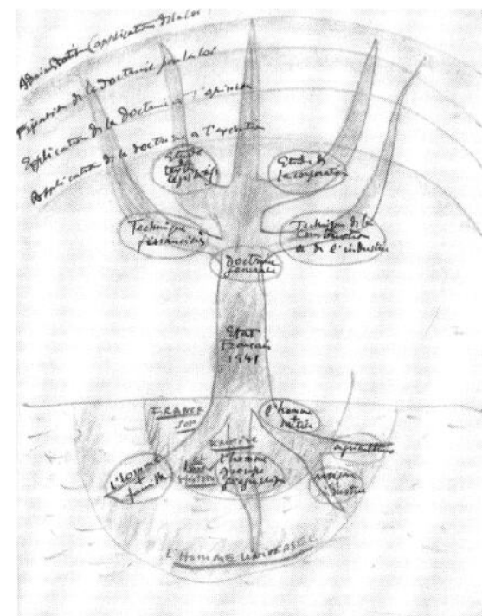

Administration (application of the law)

Establishment of the doctrine by law

Explanation of the doctrine to public opinion

Application of the doctrine to implementation

[CIRCLED IN BLUE, CLOCKWISE FROM TOP LEFT]
Study of the legislation
Study of the corporation
Technique of construction and industry
General doctrine
Financial techniques

French State 1941

[UNDERLINED IN BLUE]
<u>FRANCE ITS EMPIRE AND ITS HISTORY</u>

<u>THE UNIVERSAL MAN</u>

[CIRCLED IN RED, CLOCKWISE FROM TOP]
man + trade
agriculture
tradesman and industry
man geographic group
man + family

—P. 356

Pages from *La maison des hommes*, 1942 [Translation from *The Home of Men*, Architectural Press, London, 1948]

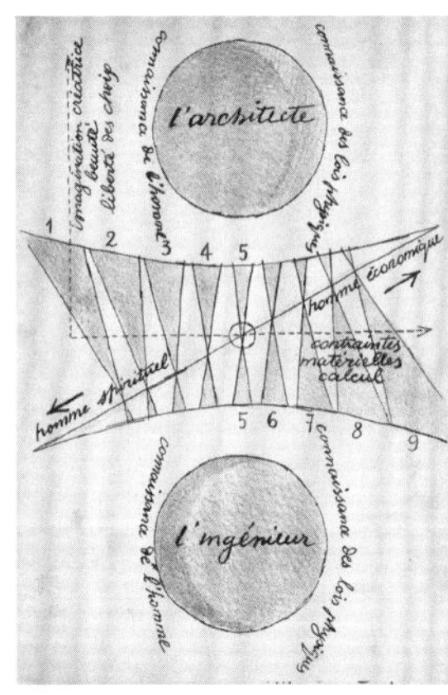

[LEFT TO RIGHT, TOP TO BOTTOM]
creative imagination / beauty / freedom of choice

knowledge of people
the architect
knowledge of the laws of physics

spiritual man
economic man
material constraints calculations

knowledge of people
the engineer
knowledge of the laws of physics

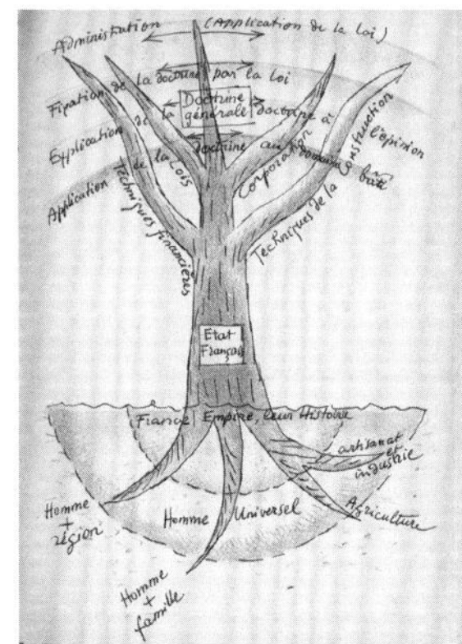

[LEFT TO RIGHT, TOP TO BOTTOM]
Administration (Application of the law)
Establishment of the doctrine by law
Explanation of the doctrine to the public
General doctrine
Application of the doctrine to the built-up area

Laws / Corporation
Financial techniques / Building techniques

French State

France / Empire, their History

Man + region
Man + family
Universal man
Agriculture
Trades and industry

—P. 357

Pages from *La maison des hommes*, 1942

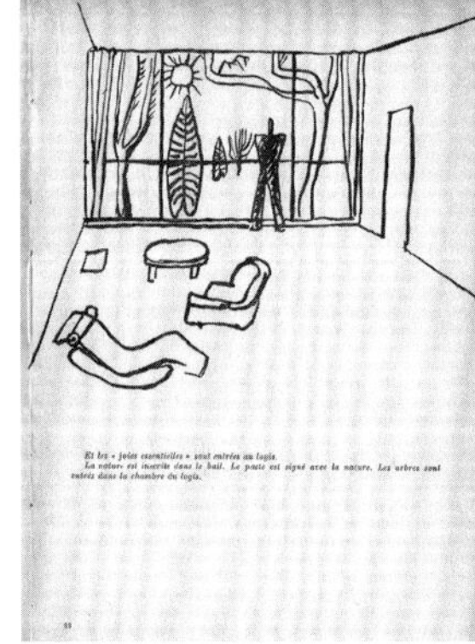

And the "essential joys" have entered the dwellings.

Nature is inscribed in the lease, a pact is signed with nature. Trees are present in the room of the dwelling.

In the heart of the business city where the skyscrapers raise their heads, the town still remains green. The trees are kings; men, under their cover, live in the domain of proportion; the link "nature-man" is re-established.

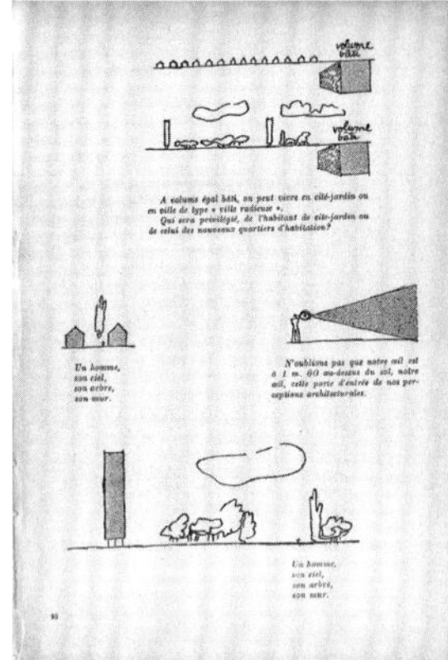

With equivalent built volumes, one can live in a "garden" city, or in a town of the type "radiant" city.

Who will be privileged, the inhabitant of the garden city or that of the new quarters of habitation?

A man,
his sky,
his tree,
his wall.

Let us not forget that our eye is five feet six inches above the ground; our eye, this gate of entry of our architectural perceptions.

A man,
his sky,
his tree,
his wall.

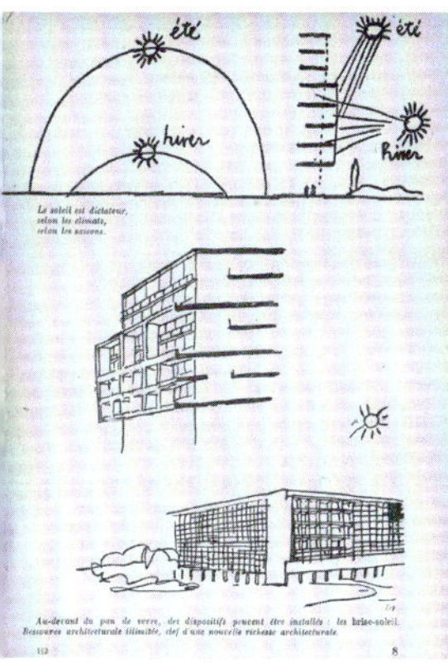

summer
winter
The sun is the dictator; according to climates, according to seasons.

Before the glass skin a further element can be installed, the "sun-breaker", unlimited architectural resource, the key to new architectural riches.

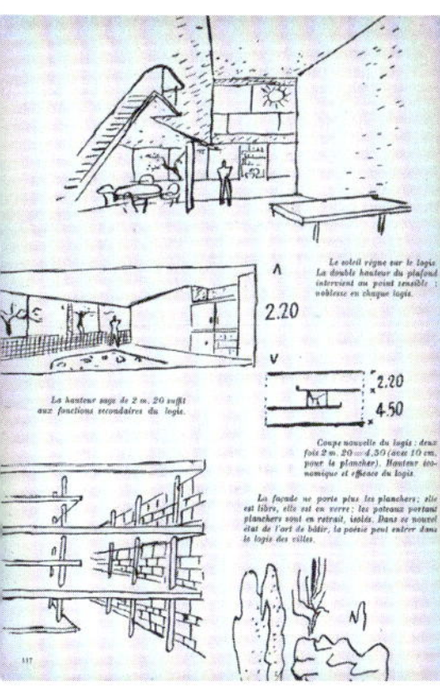

The sun reigns above the dwelling, the double-height of the ceiling introduces a subtle essential: Nobility in each dwelling.

The sensible height of 7 feet 3 inches suffices for the secondary functions of the dwelling.

The new section of the dwelling: twice 7 feet 3 inches plus 6 inches for the floor equals 15 feet. An economic and effective measure for the dwelling.

The facade no longer carries the floors: it is free, it is of glass; the floor carrying columns stand in isolation. In this new stage of the art of building, poetry can enter the dwellings of towns.

The same technical conquests, on another scale, applied to the agricultural workers' dwelling, which is assembled from elements produced in large multiples by big industry, furnishing the same resources to the creative mind.

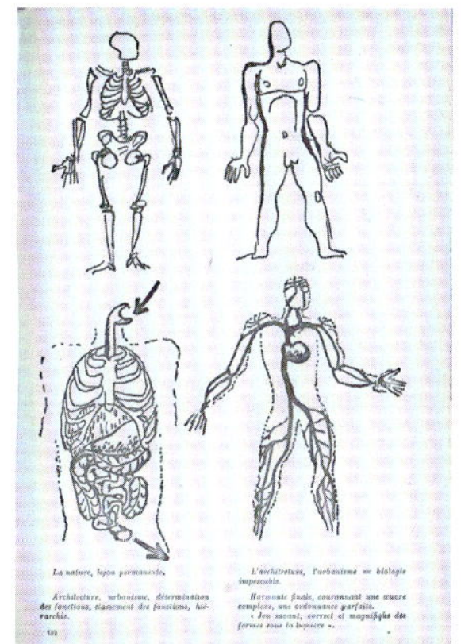

Nature, the eternal lesson.

Architecture, town planning, determination of functions, classification of functions, hierarchy.

Architecture, town planning = impeccable biology.

Final harmony crowning a complex work, an arrangement of perfection.

"The intelligent, correct and magnificent play of forms in light."

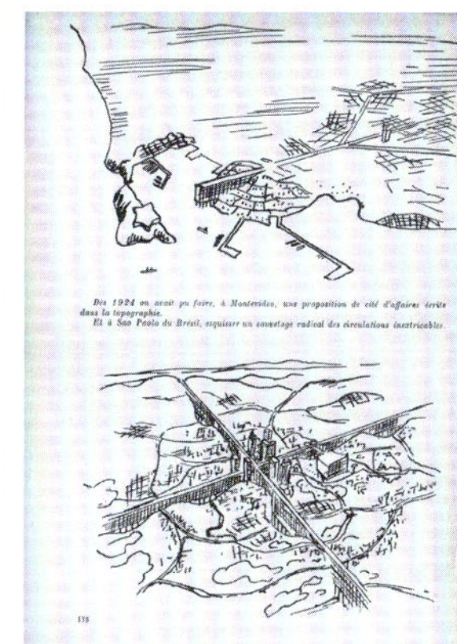

Since 1924 one could have made at Montevideo a proposition for a business city inscribed in the topography.

And at Sao Paolo in Brazil one could have sketched a radical system cutting a way through inextricable circulations.

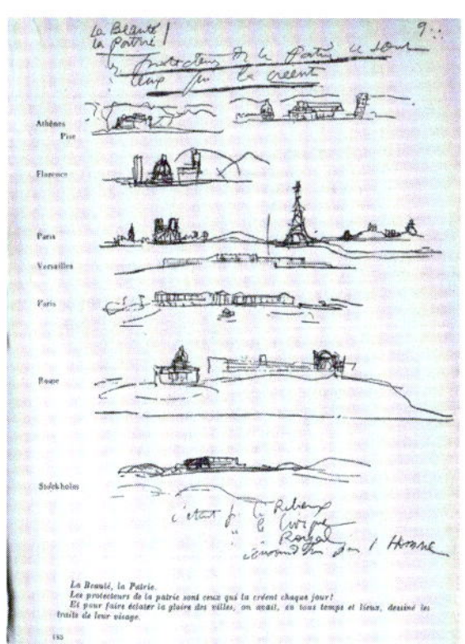

Beauty / The motherland
The protectors of the motherland are those which create her.

It was the religious [?] / civic / royal [?] Man

Beauty and the Motherland.

The protectors of the Motherland and those which create her each day!

And to proclaim the glory of our towns one has, in all times and places, sketched the features of their visages.

—P. 358

Typescript of *La charte d'Athènes*, with Le Corbusier's notes, c. 1941

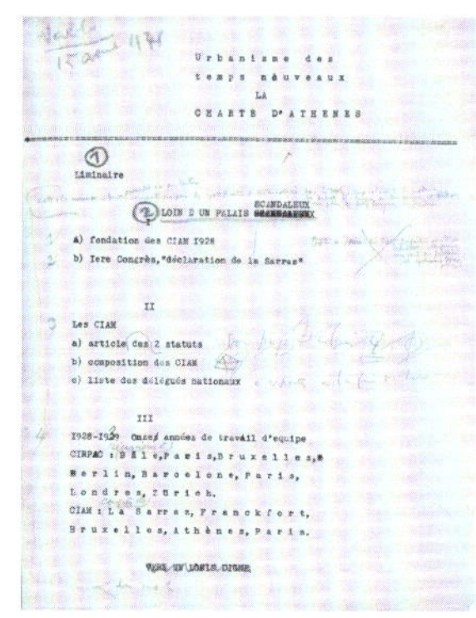

Urbanisme des temps nouveaux
LA
CHARTE D'ATHENES

(1) Liminaire

(2) LOIN D UN PALAIS SCANDALEUX

a) fondation des CIAM 1928
b) Iere Congrès, "déclaration de la Sarraz"

II

Les CIAM
a) article des 2 statuts
b) composition des CIAM
c) liste des délégués nationaux

III

1928-1939 Onze années de travail d'equipe
CIRPAC : Bâle, Paris, Bruxelles, Berlin, Barcelone, Paris, Londres, Zürich.
CIAM : La Sarraz, Franckfort, Bruxelles, Athènes, Paris.

VERS UN LOGIS DIGNE

Table [of contents]
15 August 1941

Urbanism for New Times
THE ATHENS CHARTER

1 Preliminaries

note: the ~~present~~ version presented here to the reader sometimes includes rectifications of terminology in the texts, which were the outcome of bilingual or trilingual debates and ~~dite~~ and of more than ten languages present

2 FAR FROM A SCANDALOUS PALACE

1 a) founding of the CIAMs 1928
2 b) 1st Conference, "declaration of La Sarraz"

Text to be written on League of Nations abuse of authority
result: indifferent to the core of the problem because exclusively political matter

II
3 The CIAMs
a) article of the 2 statutes
b) make-up of the CIAMs *~~see page 5th Congress 4 O~~*
c) list of the national delegates *to be put at the end of the book*

III
4 1928–19239 Eleven years of teamwork
CIRPAC: *meeting at* Basel, Paris, Brussels, Berlin, Barcelona, Paris, London, Zurich
CIAM: *congress of* La Sarraz, Frankfurt, Brussels, Athens, Paris
~~TOWARD A WORTHY HOUSING~~

—P. 358

Le Corbusier to his mother and brother, from Vichy, 6 October 1941

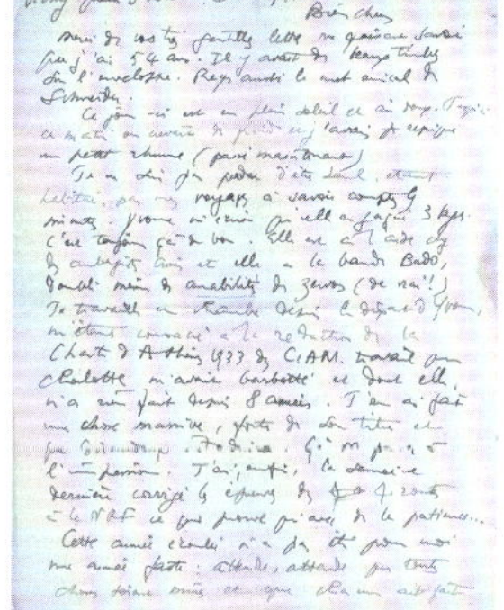

Vichy. queen's hotel. 6 Oct 1941

Dear ones

Thank you for your very kind letters letting me know I'm 54. There were two handsome stamps on the envelope.

Also received the friendly note from Schneider.

Today it's very sunny and mild. Until this morning we were dying of cold and I'd caught another little cold (gone now).

It doesn't bother me being alone, as my travels have got me used to counting the minutes. Yvonne writes that she's put on 3 kg which is a good thing. She's happy with our innkeeper friends and she has the Bado gang, plus even polite remarks from zervos (no kidding!)

I've been working in my room since Yvonne left, devoting myself to writing up the CIAM'S 1933 Athens Charter. A job Charlotte stole from me and which she's done nothing on for 8 years. I've made it into something huge, with its impressive title, and Giraudoux will do the introduction. It's going off to the printer's. Finally, last week, I corrected the proofs of the 4 roads for the NRF which shows that with patience…

This last year hasn't been a great one for me: waiting and waiting for everything to mature and for everyone to put on

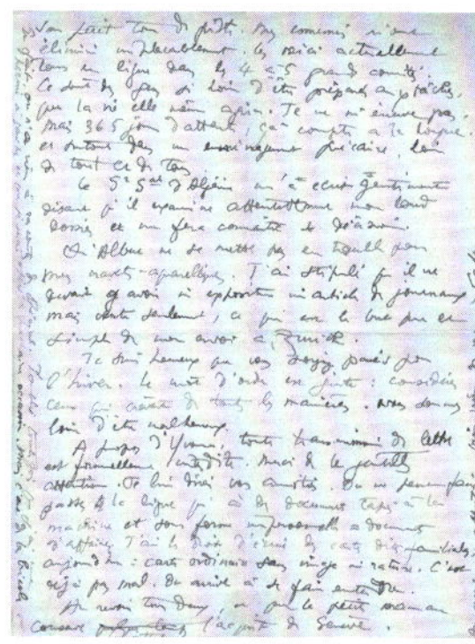

their little performances. My enemies have kept me out implacably. Currently they're lined up in the 4 or 5 big committees. They're people so totally unprepared for the work that life will take its course. I don't get angry. But 365 days' waiting takes its toll. and especially in temporary quarters away from everything and everybody.

The Gov[ernor] Gen[era]l. of Algeria wrote to me, kindly saying he would examine my weighty application attentively and inform me of his decision.

No need for Albert to worry about my watercolor daubs. I've stipulated that there should be no exhibition and no newspaper articles, just a sale, which is the aim, pure and simple, of sending them to Zurich.

I'm pleased that you're prepared for the rigors of winter. The watchword is: think of those who are dying every which way. We're far from being wretched.

Regarding Yvonne, all letters are strictly forbidden. Thank you for the kind thought. I'll pass on your regards. The only things you can get across the line are impersonal typewritten documents = business documents. I have the right to write "family" cards, now = ordinary card with no picture or erasures.

That's not so bad. You manage to make yourself understood.

Goodbye to both of you, and may little mom long retain what she got from Geneva.

[LEFT MARGIN]
Nothing special to tell you in fact. But I forgot to say I have a left-sided hernia and will be operated on soon. But it's nothing.

[RIGHT MARGIN]
Goodbye and love from yr Corbu

—P. 359

Mock-ups of individual pages from *La charte d'Athènes*, 1943

LE PROJET RÉPOND AUX ARTICLES 23 • • • 63 DE LA CHARTE D'ATHÈNES

LA VILLE ET SA RÉGION
ARTICLES 1•3•4•5• CARACTÈRE ÉCONOMIQUE, GÉOGRAPHIQUE ET POLITIQUE DE LA VILLE
POUR ORLÉANS : CARACTÈRES DOMINANTS
1 ORLÉANS VILLE CARREFOUR, CENTRE D'ÉCHANGES
2 LA LOIRE
3 CENTRE ADMINISTRATIF DE LA RÉGION

HABITATION
ARTICLES 23•24•25•26•27•28•29• HYGIÈNE, ENSOLEILLEMENT, SURFACES VERTES, DÉGAGEMENT DES VOIES DE COMMUNICATION, TECHNIQUES MODERNES •

LOISIRS
ARTICLES 35•36•37•38•39•40• AMÉNAGEMENT DES JEUX ET DES SPORTS, AMÉNAGEMENT DE PARCS, TERRAINS DE SPORT STADES, PLAGES ETC....

TRAVAIL
ARTICLES 46•49•50• DISTANCES ENTRE LIEUX DE TRAVAIL ET LIEUX D'HABITATION, ARTISANAT A L'INTÉRIEUR DE LA VILLE LIAISON DE LA CITÉ D'AFFAIRES AVEC LES QUARTIERS D'HABITATION ET L'ARTISANAT

CIRCULATION
ARTICLES 59•60•61•62•63• ANALYSE DE L'ENSEMBLE DE LA CIRCULATION DANS LA VILLE ET DANS SA RÉGION CROISEMENT DES VOIES DE CIRCULATION, PRIORITÉ DU PIÉTON, ETC....

THE PROJECT MEETS THE REQUIREMENTS OF ARTICLES 23 • • • 63 OF THE ATHENS CHARTER

THE CITY AND ITS REGION
ARTICLES 1•3•4•5• ECONOMIC, GEOGRAPHICAL AND POLITICAL CHARACTER OF THE CITY
FOR ORLEANS: PRINCIPAL CHARACTERISTICS
1 ORLEANS CROSSROADS, TRADING CENTER
2 THE RIVER LOIRE
3 ADMINISTRATIVE CENTER OF ITS REGION

HOUSING
ARTICLES 23•24•25•26•27•28•29• HYGIENE, SUNLIGHT, GREEN SPACES, CREATION OF ROADS, MODERN TECHNOLOGY •

LEISURE ACTIVITIES
ARTICLES 35•36•37•38•39•40• LAYOUT FOR GAMES AND SPORTS FACILITIES, LAYOUT OF PARKS, SPORTS AREAS, STADIUMS, BEACHES, ETC...

WORK
ARTICLES 46•49•50• DISTANCES BETWEEN WORKPLACES AND PLACES OF RESIDENCE, TRADES AREAS IN THE CITY, LINK BETWEEN THE BUSINESS DISTRICT WITH RESIDENTIAL AND TRADES NEIGHBORHOODS.

TRAFFIC
ARTICLES 59•60•61•62•63• OVERALL ANALYSIS OF TRAFFIC IN THE CITY AND ITS ENVIRONS, INTERSECTION OF ROADS, PEDESTRIAN PRIORITY, ETC...

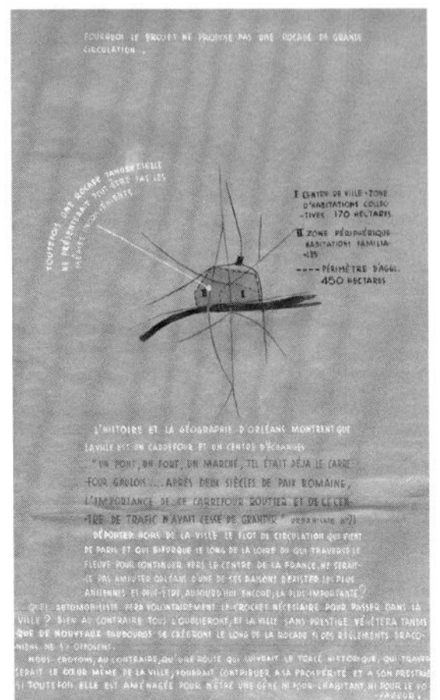

WHY THE PROJECT DOES NOT INCLUDE A MAJOR BYPASS.

EVEN SO, MAYBE A TANGENTIAL BYPASS WOULD NOT POSE THE SAME PROBLEMS

I DOWNTOWN•COLLECTIVE LIVING AREA 170 HECTARES
II PERIPHERAL ZONE FAMILY DWELLINGS
--- OVERALL BUILT-UP AREA 450 HECTARES

THE HISTORY AND GEOGRAPHY OF ORLEANS SHOW THE CITY AS A CROSSROADS AND A TRADING CENTER

"A BRIDGE, A PORT, A MARKET, SUCH WAS THE GAULISH CROSSROADS ... DURING TWO CENTURIES OF PAX ROMANA THE IMPORTANCE OF THIS CROSSROADS AND TRAFFIC CENTER GREW UNINTERRUPTEDLY" URBANISME NO. 71

IF THE TRAFFIC COMING FROM PARIS AND BRANCHING OFF ALONG THE LOIRE OR CROSSING THE RIVER TO CONTINUE TOWARD CENTRAL FRANCE WERE DIVERTED AWAY FROM THE CITY CENTER, WOULD THIS NOT CUT ORLEANS OFF FROM ONE OF ITS OLDEST—AND MAYBE STILL MOST IMPORTANT—REASONS FOR EXISTING?

WHAT DRIVER WOULD WILLINGLY MAKE THE DETOUR NEEDED TO GO INTO THE CITY? IN FACT EVERYBODY WOULD FORGET THE CITY WHICH, STRIPPED OF ITS PRESTIGE, WOULD STAGNATE WHILE NEW SUBURBS SPRANG UP ALONG THE BYPASS UNLESS PREVENTED BY STRINGENT REGULATIONS.

WE BELIEVE, ON THE CONTRARY, THAT A ROAD FOLLOWING THE HISTORIC ROUTE AND RUNNING THROUGH THE HEART OF THE CITY COULD CONTRIBUTE TO ITS PROSPERITY AND PRESTIGE, ON CONDITION THAT THE ROAD IS LAID OUT SO AS NOT TO BE A PROBLEM FOR RESIDENTS OR TRAVELERS.

—P. 361

Structure of work sections and committees of the CIAM group ASCORAL

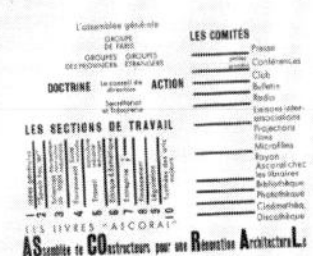

[LEFT]
The general assembly
PARIS GROUP
PROVINCIAL GROUPS / FOREIGN GROUPS

DOCTRINE / The governing council / ACTION
Secretariat and Treasury

THE WORK SECTIONS
1 General ideas
2 "Know how to inhabit"
3 Sciences of housing
equipment / standardizat[ion] / industrializ[ation]
4 Equipment
Health / illness
5 Work
agriculture / industry / trade
6 Ethics & Aesthetics
7 Enterprise
A / B
8 Financing
9 Legislation
10 Synthesis of the major "arts"

"ASCORAL" BOOKS

[RIGHT]
THE COMMITTEES
Press
small / large Lectures
Club
Bulletin
Radio
Relations between associations
Film / Microfilm projections
Ascoral shelf at the Booksellers
Library
Photo library
Film library
Record library

ASsemblée de COnstructeurs pour une Rénovation ArchitecturaLe [Assembly of Builders for an Architectural Renovation]

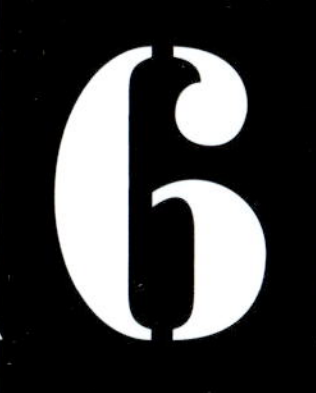

Grand Projects on a Human Scale (1942–1952)

—P. 370

Notes for a lecture at the Théâtre Sarah Bernhardt, Paris, 7 March 1945

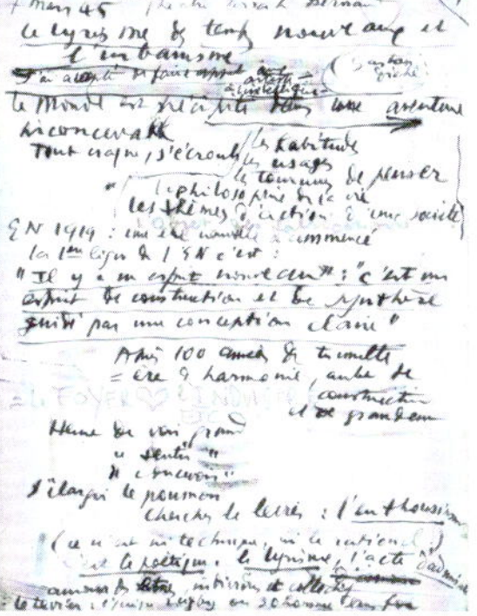

7 March 45 Théâtre Sarah Bernhardt

The lyricism of the new era and urban planning
I've agreed to back the artists and intelligence Gaston Diehl

The world has been hurled into an inconceivable adventure
Everything is cracking, habits are crumbling
customs
ways of thinking
the philosophy of life
society's spheres of action
the things being manufactured

In 1919 a new era began
The 1st line of "L'Esprit Nouveau" is:
There is a new spirit: "it is a spirit of construction and synthesis guided by a clear conception"

After 100 years of tumult
= era of harmony, dawn of construction and grandeur
= THE HOUSEHOLD [LOVES] INDUSTRY, ETC.

Time to think big / "to feel" / "to conceive" / to expand the lung / to seek the lever: enthusiasm
this is neither technology, nor the rational, it is the poetic, lyricism, the act of admiration / love of human beings, individually and collectively the lever: rugby team or 30 fearless men

the impetus, = what changes everything

impetus: FAITH / the cath[edrals] were white

impetus: EAGERNESS ADVENTURE ARROGANCE PRIDE
the pathos of today

Alas Paris end of world war: the years of exhaustion of the [?] in the things of the spirit: substitutes
Taste—Parisian—in the whitest decadence for everything is made of plaster: the little Venetian negro the Marly-style horses—the king's sphinx, the acanthus chandelier cardboard, the unfinished [?], the oak paneling patinated with the Trojan white of disasters

Modern furniture imitates all styles, in elegant interpretations available to a gutless public desperate for reassurance: styles: fake rustic, fake grandeur that

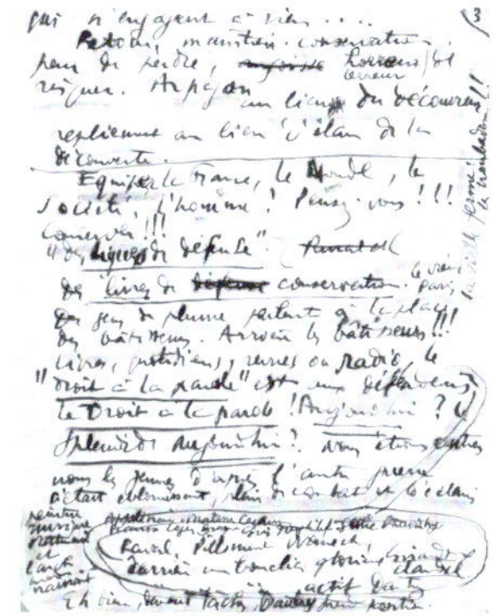

commit you to nothing …
Return, safeguarding. Status quo.
Fear of losing, anguish horror / terror of taking chances. Pinchpenny instead of discoverer.
Withdrawal instead of impetus to discovery.

Equip France, the World, Society, mankind? You're kidding!! Keep the status quo!!!
"defense leagues"
books on keeping the status quo. Old Paris, the old farm! The troubadours!!
Hack writers speak in place of builders. Down with the builders!!!
Books, daily papers, magazines or radio, the "right to speak" belongs to the defenders
The Right to Speak! Today! Our Splendid Today? we were different we the youth of after the other war it was dazzling, full of combat and lightning

painting
music
statuary
and arch[itecture]
mode[rn]
was being born

Apollinaire, Matisse, Cézanne, Picasso, Léger, Braque, Gris, [?], Satie, Stravinsky, Ravel, [?]
behind a glorious shield Giraudoux, Claudel
active Dautry
Well, [?]

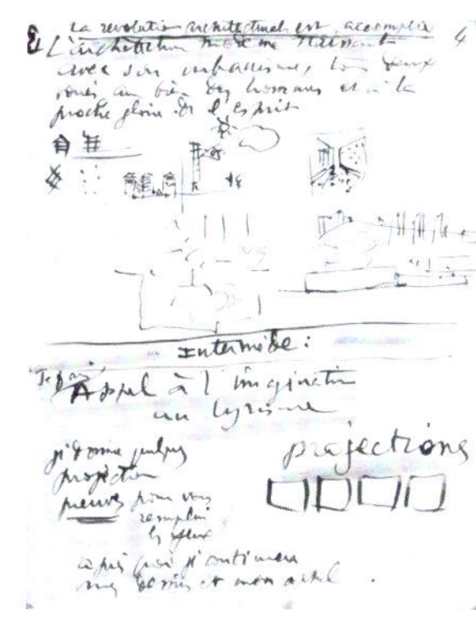

The architectural revolution has been accomplished
And modern Architecture is being born with its urbanism, both dedicated to human well-being and the imminent glory of the spirit

Interlude:
I'm calling on the imagination, on the lyricism
I offer a few projections
proofs to fill your eyes
after which I shall continue my plans and my call.

lyricism of modern times
architecture and urbanism

[?]

all the technologies the biggest programs

The architectural revolution has been accomplished

14,000 spectators

[?]

but!: hope / 480 m high

= lyricism probably as timely

Rio has begun! / joie de vivre

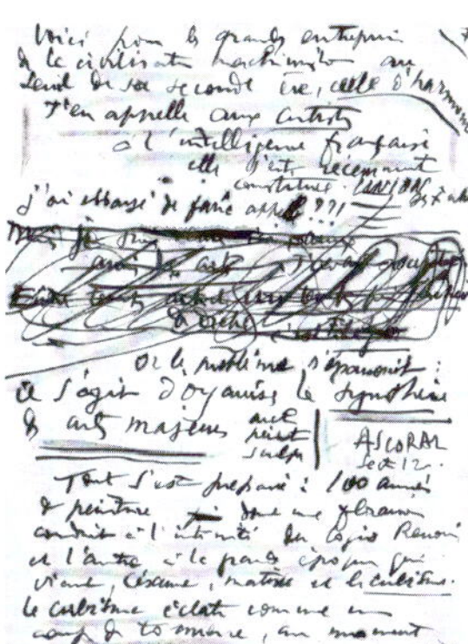

Here for the great enterprises of the machine civilization on the threshold of its second era, that of harmony
I call on artists in the name of French intelligence the UNION of the [?] was recently formed
I tried to put out a call??!

But the problem is growing: the thing is to organize the unification of the major arts
arch[itecture] paint[ing] sculp[ture] / ASCORAL Sect 12

Everything has been prepared: 100 years of painting [?] leads to the intimacy of Renoir's box at the theater and the other to the great epoch that is coming, Cézanne, Matisse, and Cubism. Cubism bursts like a thunderclap when photography,

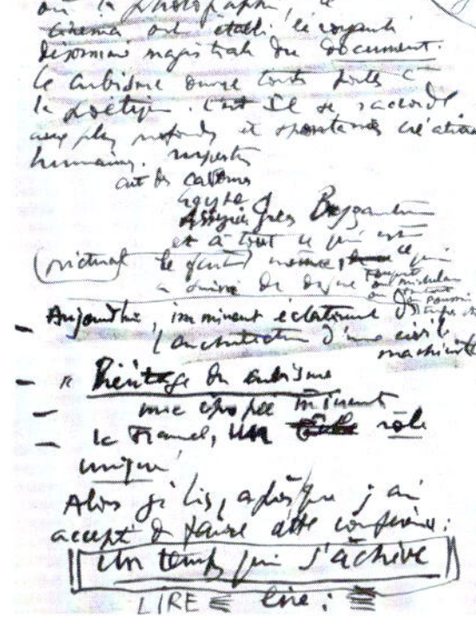

cinema have established the now magisterial royalty of the document. Cubism opens all doors like the poetic. It harmonizes with the deepest, most spontaneous human creations.
Rock paintings
Art of the caves
Egypt
Assyria Greeks Byzantine
And with everything that is the pictorial act, which worthily followed [?] or Michelangelo or Tintoretto or Poussin, Ingres, etc.
Today, imminent explosion in architecture of a machine civilization
heritage of Cubism
An imminent epic
France, a unique role
So I read, after I agreed to give this lecture:

A time is ending
READ read:

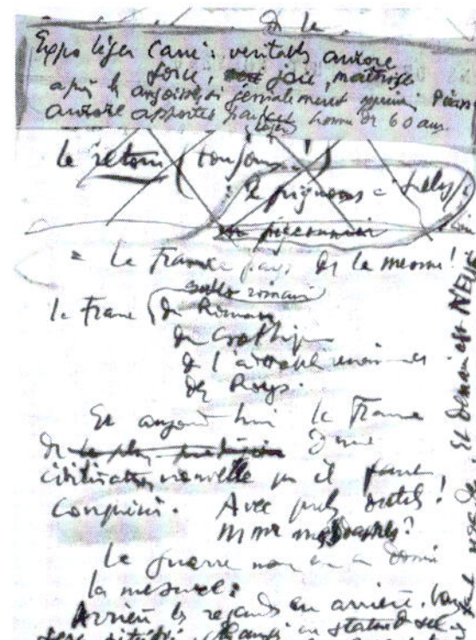

Straightforward Léger show: real luminosity strength, joy, mastery after all that brilliant anguish [?]
Picasso luminosity brought by Léger man of 60.

= France country that sets the standards!
France of the medieval / of the gothic / of the renaissance / of the Kings
And today the France of a new civilization that must be won. With what tools?
Ladies Gentlemen?
The war gave us the measure of the task:
Backward looking backward. You will be petrified, turned into a pillar of salt. You must look forward. And tomorrow is NEW.

—P. 377

Le Corbusier's sketches for his Modulor system, 29 December 1943 to 5 January 1946, on leftover *L'Esprit Nouveau* stationery, showing the evolution of his ideas

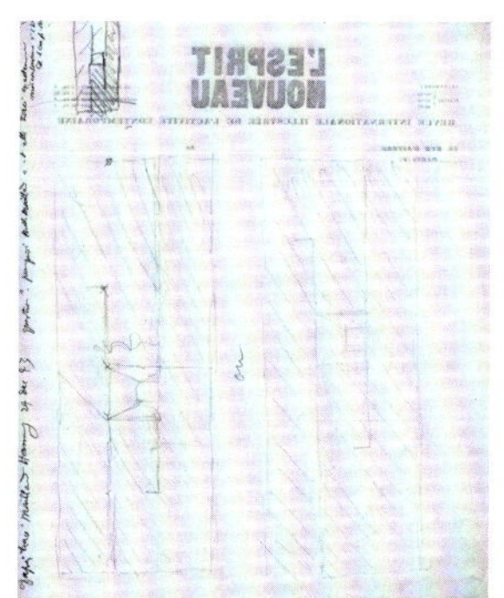

Sheet III / 29 Dec. 43

[LEFT MARGIN]
According to Maillard Hanning line / 29 Dec. 43
Question? Why did Miss Maillard draw exactly miraculously to the scale of 1 cm per meter?

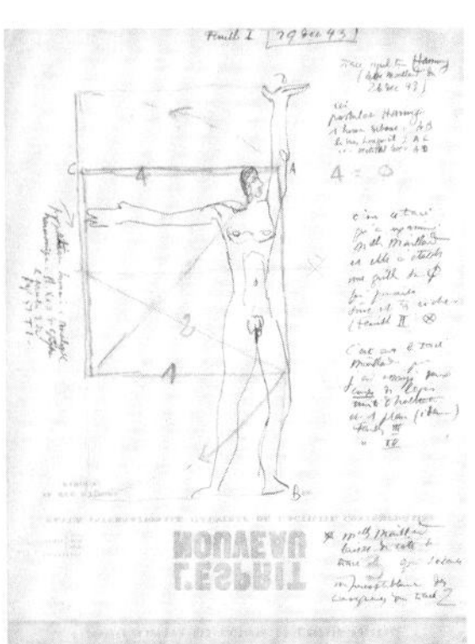

Sheet I / 29 Dec. 43

Hanning regulating line
(letter Miss Maillard of 2 Dec. 43)

here Hanning postulate
1 man upright = AB
the arm horizontal = AC
[the arm] raised vertically = AD
A = Ø

This is the line examined by Miss Maillard and she set up a grid on Ø which appears certain and very rewarding.
(Sheet II *)

using the Maillard line I tried two sections of unité d'habitation accommodation and 1 plan (idem)
Sheet III
[Sheet] IV

* Miss Maillard leaves out line 3 which diverges imperceptibly from the consequences of line 2
[LEFT MARGIN]
human proposition = Analysis
harmonic: Pl. XXII of Ghyka
the golden section
page 51 *TI

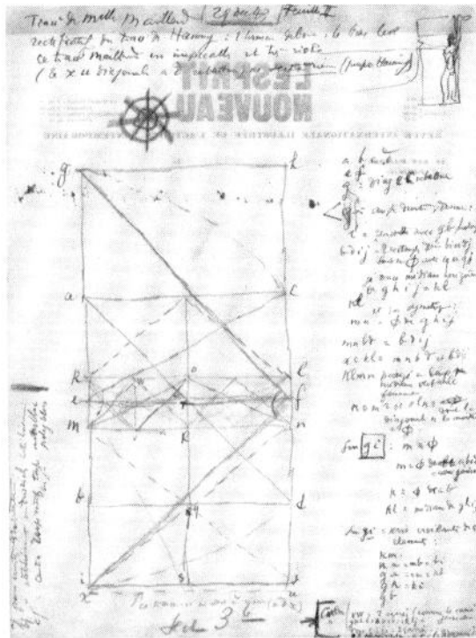

Miss Maillard's line / 29 Dec 43 / Sheet II

correction of Hanning's line: 1 man upright, arm raised
This Maillard line is impeccable and very rewarding
(x u diagonal a d rabatted) serves no purpose (Hanning's idea)

a b c d
e f
g = diagonal e c rabatted
g f = right angle, gives:
i = meeting with g b photocopy
b d i j = 2 rectangle in which bi and d j are in ω with I g and q j
I draw horizontal median
now g h i j = k l
k l and j a symmetrical:
m n b d = b d i j
a c k l = m n b d and b d i f
vertical median
provides
k o m r and o l n r whose diagonal and a half
= Ø

on g i: m = Ø
m = Ø d e a f t = a b c d = generative square
k = Ø d e a b
k l = median of g h i j
On g i = growing series of 5 elements:
k m
k a = m b = b i
g a = a m = k l
g k = k i
g b

this line serves no purpose (a d x)

Sect 3b

Corbu v w = 2 squares (like the square g k h l = a b c d = i k l j = generative)
on which c h j i = 2 squares
c perpendicular to e c (= 1/2 d e g original square)

[LEFT MARGIN]
a/ for housing units
b/ for industrial establishments
linear estate
c/ for cooperative center type monoblock / multiblock

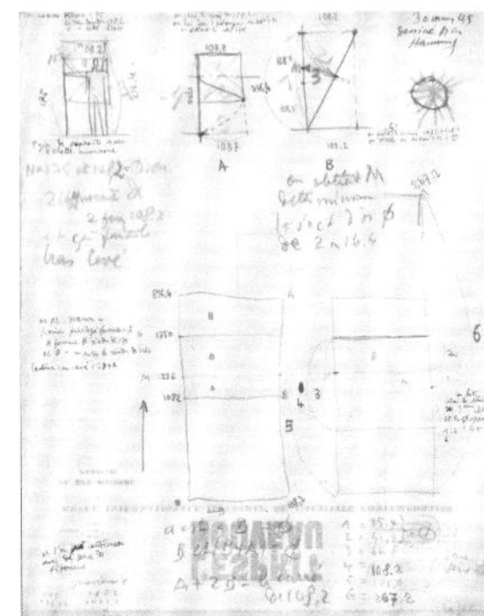

[TOP TO BOTTOM, LEFT TO RIGHT]
man standing 175
arm outstretched 108.2
arm raised 216.4

Contact made with human scale

N = 175 and 108.2 = Ø
216.4 m comes from 2 x 108.2 and that makes the raised arm

now, M determines a special point that gives A
A gives B, residue of 175
and B gives another B, residue of 2164
read on the square = 2B + A

and you can continue with Fibonacci series

you place the square of 108.2
you add a golden section
you get the dimension 175
a is a / B = Ø
B and (B + A) = Ø
A + 2B = the square

30 March 45
drawn by Hanning

you take the 2 squares 108.2 + 108.2
you divide into golden section = M

you obtain M
delta minimum
golden mean Ø of 2 m 16.4

then you read the structure on 3rd square and the Ø apparently 1, 2, 3, 4, 5, 6

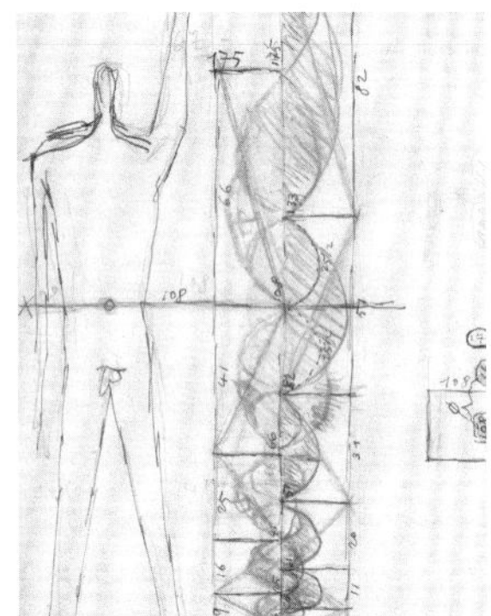

aboard the cargo ship "Vernon S. Hood"
16 January 1946
L–C

the Corbu golden mean for the design of prefabricated structures

—P. 379

Drawing with a "Modulor woman," 1952

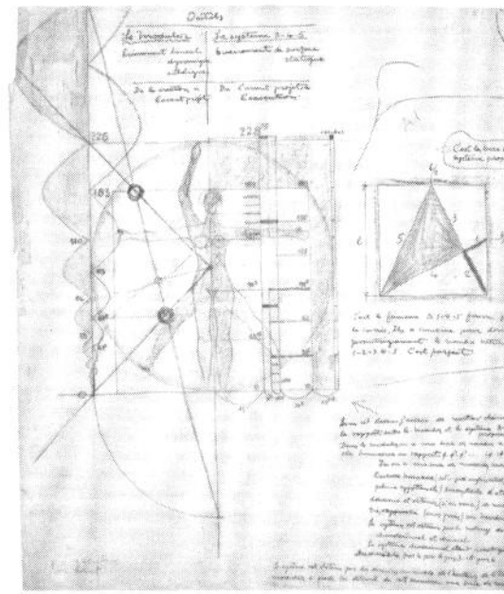

[TOP TO BOTTOM, LEFT TO RIGHT]
Tools
The Modulor
A lineal, dynamic, aesthetic event
From creation to preliminary design

The 3–4–5 system
Static surface event
From preliminary design to creation

This is the basis of the proposed system

This is the wonderful 3–4–5 provided by the square. They combine to give geometrically the natural number 1-2-3-4-5. It's perfect.

With this drawing I'm trying to show clearly the relationship between the Modulor and the proposed 3–4–5 system

In the Modulor we have a series of numbers on a human scale in the relationship Ø–Ø²–Ø³... 2Ø–2Ø²–2Ø³

Here we have a series of modules also on a human scale (30⁵–current English foot, 7,625 Egyptian palms, etc.) able to be added up to obtain (if you like) a measurement system very close (within a cm) to the Modulor.

The system is obtained by mixing the duodecimal and decimal systems.
The duodecimal system has the advantage of being divisible by 2 by 4 by 3 and by 6.

The system is obtained by appropriate divisions of the height of the 6-foot Modulor man. In this way we obtain a series of Modulors.

—P. 382

Postcard from Princeton University Professor Jean Labatut, 10 August 1947

[TOP LEFT]
On my return from Princeton I found this card among my papers. Please excuse me, and thank you again.

10 August 1947

My dear Corbu,

The students came back delighted with their visit to rue de Sèvres and their written impressions of their afternoon with you are the proof—another landmark in the program of practical teaching begun at Fontainebleau this year. I'm pleased that I insisted on their seeing at least one of your works. The color of the trees in the foreground, the woman tennis player, and the pianist in swimming trunks round off the composition perfectly. On our way to see the Gobelins factory we made a short detour to the Cité Refuge. Their written impressions of this work show that they were able to envisage it despite the results of the explosions in 1944. On the way through they also saw the Lurçat school complex at Villejuif. The day before yesterday we were at the building sites in Orléans, Sully, and Gien, as well as Germiny and St. Benoit. on Wednesday we'll be discussing modern architecture in Chartres and on Friday they'll be attending the 15th of August ceremony in Reims cathedral to see it in action. My thanks again to you and Bodiansky.

See you soon in Fontainebleau, Paris, New York, or Princeton.

Labatut

—P. 392

Le Corbusier included this diagram in a letter to Wallace K. Harrison, 28 August 1947

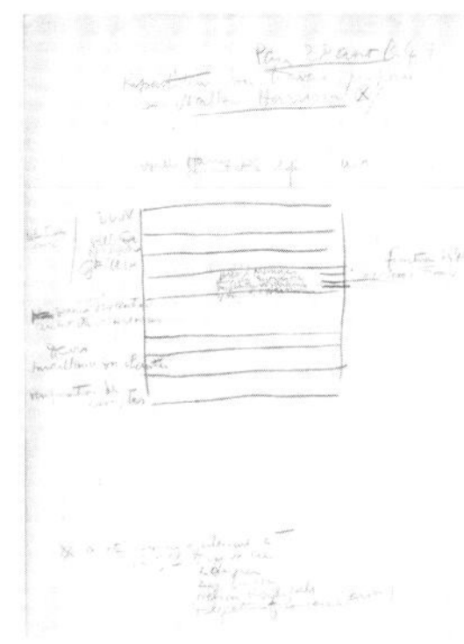

Paris 28 August 1947
Division of work proposed to Wallace Harrison*

Wallace Harrison
Head architect USA

Relations with U.N. / City of New York / USA Government

Working drawing
Architects and engineers

Brazil Niemeyer
United Kingdom Entwistle
Argentina Williams
Yugoslavia Weissmann

Finished drawings
Le Corbusier France

Estimate
Site monitoring

Checking of accounts

* has also been submitted to
Secretary-general
Langier
Ben Cohen
Nelson Rockefeller
French Mission (Parod)

—P. 393

"Outline of the Headquarters' Commission Report," from the Joint Advisory Committee on the Plan of UN Headquarters

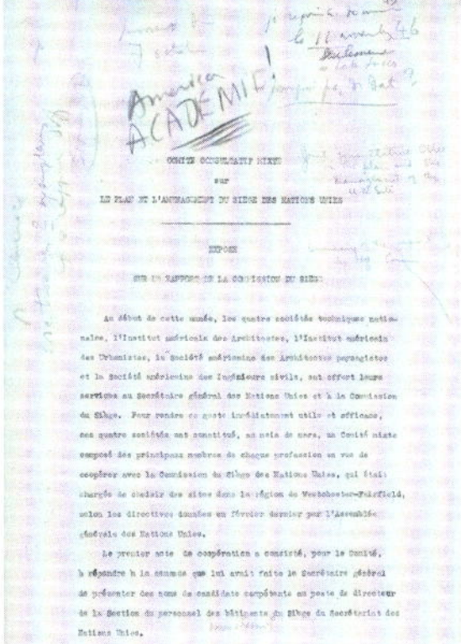

[LEFT MARGIN]
comes from 7 Oct
for Lawrence, find 2 copies of this report
please 31 March 1947

[RIGHT]
I receive this document only on
11 November 1946 at Lake Success
Why no date?

JOINT ADVISORY COMMITTEE on THE PLAN AND LAYOUT OF UNITED NATIONS HEADQUARTERS

OUTLINE OF THE HEADQUARTERS COMMISSION REPORT

Early this year the four national technical bodies—the American Institute of Architects, the American Institute of Urban Planners, the American Society of Landscape Architects, and the American Society of Civil Engineers—offered their services to the secretary general of the United Nations and the Headquarters Commission. To make this gesture useful and effective immediately, in March these four bodies set up a Joint Committee comprising leading members of each profession, with a view to cooperating with the United Nations Headquarters Commission; the Commission had the task of choosing sites in the Westchester-Fairfield area, in line with the directives laid down in February by the United Nations General Assembly.

The Committee's first act of cooperation was a reply to the secretary general's request for the names of candidates competent to fill the post of director of the Building Staff Department of the United Nations Secretariat.

—P. 397

Collage of Le Corbusier's plans, models, and drawings for UN Headquarters, 1947

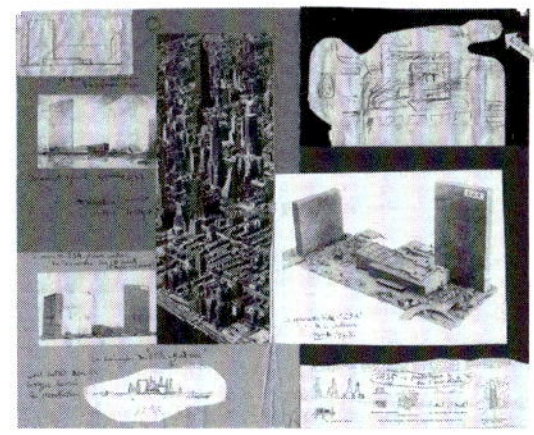

[LEFT PAGE]
Drawing by Le Corbusier 25 May 1947

Official document September 1947

Manhattan! magical disaster

Model 23. A. focal point of the discussions between the 10 experts, 15 March–15 June 47

The principles of the "Radiant City" have entered the spiky biology of Manhattan

[RIGHT PAGE]
26 February 1947 Le Corbusier had created this project

The model known as "23A" by Le Corbusier March 1947

1935 L-C's prediction regarding the East River

The skyscrapers now / Manhattan today... tomorrow maybe? / Enhancing the East River / Manhattan turned into a Green City

(These drawings illustrate "Quand les cathédrales étaient blanches," 1935)

—P. 403

Le Corbusier to Saul Steinberg, 5 January 1956

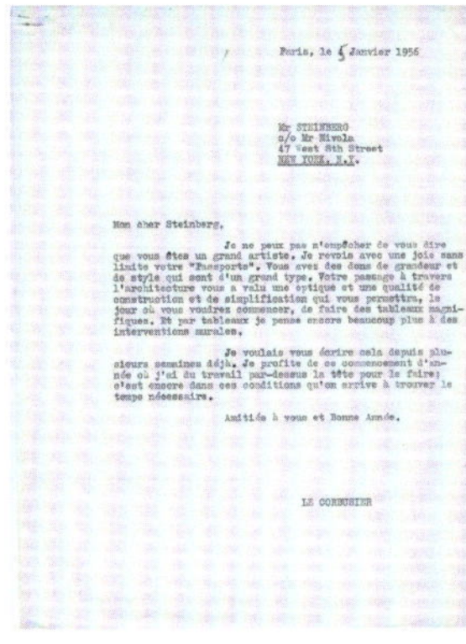

Paris, le 5 Janvier 1956

Mr STEINBERG
c/o Mr Nivola
47 West 8th Street
NEW YORK, N.Y.

Mon cher Steinberg,

Je ne peux pas m'empêcher de vous dire que vous êtes un grand artiste. Je revois avec une joie sans limite votre "Passports". Vous avez des dons de grandeur et de style qui sont d'un grand type. Votre passage à travers l'architecture vous a valu une optique et une qualité de construction et de simplification qui vous permettra, le jour où vous voudrez commencer, de faire des tableaux magnifiques. Et par tableaux je pense encore beaucoup plus à des interventions murales.

Je voulais vous écrire cela depuis plusieurs semaines déjà. Je profite de ce commencement d'année où j'ai du travail par-dessus la tête pour le faire; c'est encore dans ces conditions qu'on arrive à trouver le temps nécessaire.

Amitié à vous et Bonne Année.

LE CORBUSIER

Paris, 5 January 1956

Mr. STEINBERG
c/o Mr. Nivola
47 West 8th Street
NEW YORK, N.Y.

My dear Steinberg,

I simply have to tell you that you are a great artist. I am looking at your "Passports" again with enormous pleasure. You are gifted with immense grandeur and style. The time you spent as an architect has given you a viewpoint and a capacity for construction and simplification that will enable you, once you decide to start, to produce magnificent paintings. And when I say paintings I'm thinking in particular of murals.

I've been wanting to write you for several weeks. And at the beginning of this year, when I'm up to my neck in work, I'm doing it; these are still the only circumstances that let one find the necessary time.

Best regards and a Happy New Year.

LE CORBUSIER

—P. 413

Schematic drawing of the organization of communal services for the Unité d'Habitation, Marseille, 1946

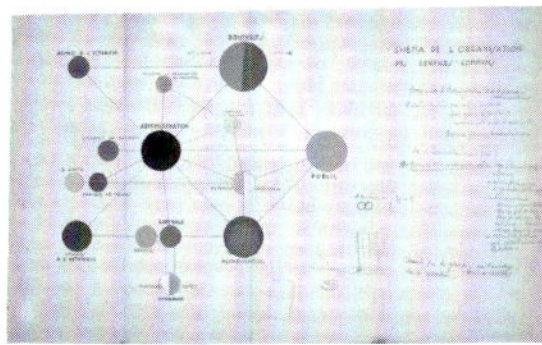

SCHEMATIC DRAWING OF THE ORGANIZATION OF COMMUNAL SERVICES

Administration and management grouping (internal personnel)
Administration not too large like a rental agency (little ingoing and outgoing traffic) group management and administration together

No cooperative (badly managed)

* Private managers—concessionnaire
—fixed rental + discount
—criteria dependent on how the building is organized
—Discount for consumers (deducted from the rent) to encourage residents to buy their provisions in the building
—Ticket system for automatically checking purchases

Checking by the management—no personnel—no reception

[FOR THE TERMS IN THE DIAGRAM, SEE THE GLOSSARY, P. 3]

—P. 413

Le Corbusier to Charlotte Perriand, 2 May 1946

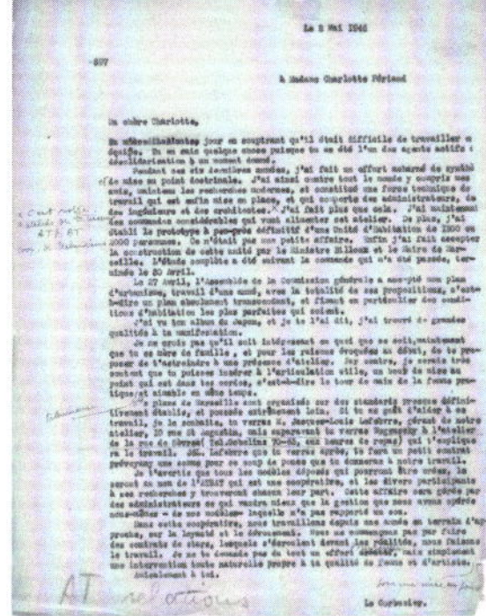

2 May 1946

to Mrs. Charlotte Périand

My dear Charlotte,

You [wrote me the other] day sighing that it was difficult to work in a team. You know what you're talking about as at one point you were one of the active agents in the breakup process.

Over the last six years I've been working relentlessly at summarizing *and* honing the doctrine. And in the face of everyone including my friends, I've kept up-to-date research going and built up a technical workforce that is now functioning, and that includes administrators, engineers, and architects.* I've done more than that. I now have substantial commissions that are going to sustain this studio. What's more, I've established the near- definitive prototype for a Unité d'Habitation for 1,500 or 2,000 people. This was no small matter. Lastly I've had the building of this Unité accepted by Minister Billoux and the Mayor of Marseille. Following the commission I received, the complete design was finished on 30 April.

On 27 April the meeting of the General Commission accepted my urbanism plan, a year's work, with all its proposals, that is to say an absolutely comprehensive plan laying down in particular the most perfect living conditions.

I saw your Japan album, and as I told you, I found your work excellent.

I don't think there's any point at all, now that you're the mother of a family, and for the reasons mentioned at the beginning, in suggesting that you should have to work in the studio. On the other hand, I'd be very pleased if you could contribute to the necessary coordination a little of the fine tuning that is one of your skills, by which I mean the touch of a woman who is practical, *talented,* and amiable.

The plans for Marseille are organized according to near-definitive standards and are at a very advanced stage. If you're interested in helping with this job, and I hope you are, go see Mr. Jacques-Louis Lefebvre, director of our studio at 10 rue St. Augustin, but before that you must see Wogensky at the rue de Sèvres studio (Tel. Gobelins 70-63, at mealtimes), who will explain the job to you. J-L. Lefebvre, whom you will see afterward, will give you a little contract stipulating an amount for the helping hand you'll be providing for our work.

I warn you that all the models that may be created will be registered in the name of ATBAT, which is a cooperative, and the various participants in the research will each get their share. This venture will be managed by administrators, which will be better than the management—of our models—we've practiced ourselves, which hasn't brought in a cent.

In this cooperative we've been working on the preliminaries for a year, in a spirit of loyalty and commitment. We don't start by issuing star-type contracts, which would not stand up to the realities, we do the work. I'm not asking you at all for a ~~creative~~ *inventive* effort, but simply a quite natural contribution in line with your capacity as woman and artist.

Ever yours,

Le Corbusier.

[LEFT MARGIN]
* *It's our "staff of builders" ATBAT cooperative of technicians*

—P. 418

Le Corbusier to Pablo Picasso, 21 May 1952

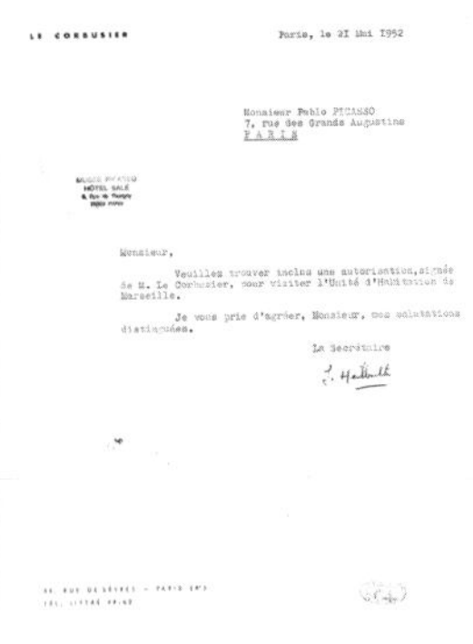

Paris, 21 Mai 1952

Mr. Pablo PICASSO
7 rue des Grands Augustins
PARIS

Monsieur,

Please find enclosed an authorization, signed by Mr. Le Corbusier, to visit the Unité d'Habitation in Marseille.

Please believe me to be, Sir, yours truly,

The Secretary
[signature]

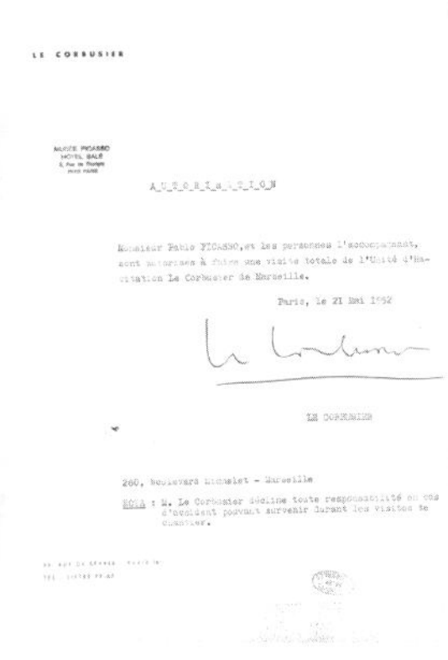

A_U_T_H_O_R_I_Z_A_T_I_O_N

Mr. Pablo PICASSO, and the persons with him, are authorized to visit all of Le Corbusier's Unité d'Habitation in Marseille.

Paris, 21 May 1952

[signature]
LE CORBUSIER

280 boulevard Michelet–Marseille
NOTA: Mr. Le Corbusier declines all responsibility in case of accidents that might occur during visits to the construction site.

—P. 420

Undated newspaper headline about the Unité d'Habitation in Marseille

L'ARCHITECTE LE CORBUSIER CONTRUIT A MARSEILLE LA « CITÉ-JARDIN VERTICALE »

Une ville radieuse!
ANNONCENT LES "BATISSEURS"
Une caserne! PROTESTENT LES "BARBUS"

THE ARCHITECT LE CORBUSIER BUILDS THE "VERTICAL GARDEN CITY" IN MARSEILLE
A radiant city!
DECLARE THE "BUILDERS"
A barracks! PROTEST THE "GRAYBEARDS"

Le Corbusier is an avowed enemy of horizontal garden cities—like those one sees in the Parisian suburbs. He considers them *the greatest waste of modern times* […]

—P. 420

Telegram from André Wogenscky to Le Corbusier

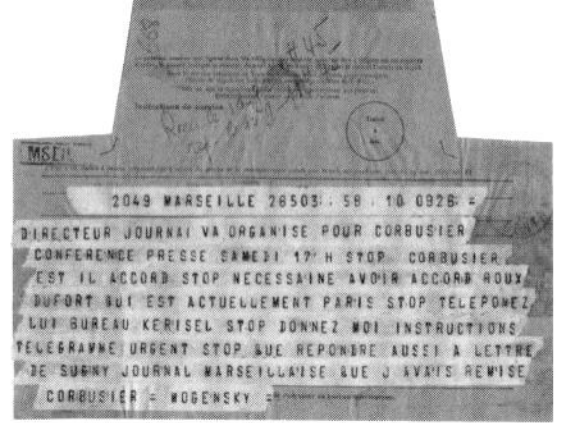

NEWSPAPER EDITOR-IN-CHIEF WILL ORGANIZE FOR CORBUSIER PRESS CONFERENCE SATURDAY 17:00 STOP DOES CORBUSIER AGREE STOP NEED AGREEMENT ROUX DUFORT WHO IS CURRENTLY PARIS STOP TELEPHONE HIM KERISEL OFFICE STOP GIVE ME INSTRUCTIONS TELEGRAM URGENT STOP ALSO WHAT REPLY TO SUGNY LETTER NEWSPAPER MARSEILLAISE THAT I HAD GIVEN CORBUSIER = WOGENSCKY

—P. 420

Le Corbusier to André Wogenscky, 14 October 1948

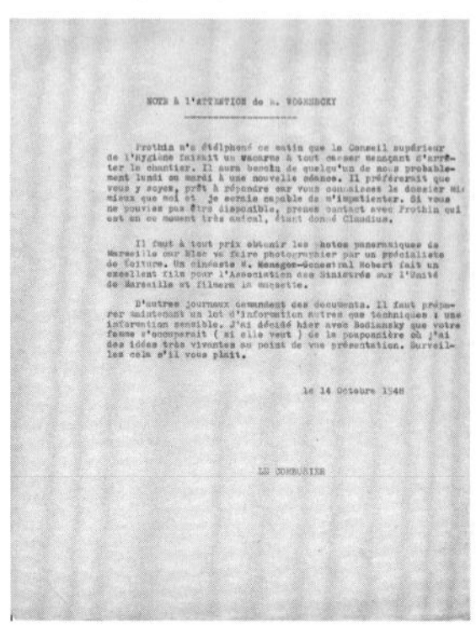

NOTE FOR THE ATTENTION OF MR. WOGENSCKY

Prothin phoned me this morning saying that the Hygiene Committee was kicking up a terrible fuss and threatening to halt the project. One of us will need to be there probably Monday or Tuesday for a further meeting. It would be better that you go with the answers ready since you know the project better than I do and I'd be likely to lose my patience. If you can't make yourself available, contact Prothin, who's very amiable at present, given Claudius.

We have to obtain at all costs the panoramic photos of Marseille as Bloc wants to get photographs taken by a roof specialist. A filmmaker, Mr. Robert Menegoz-Genestral, is making an excellent film on the Marseille Unité for the Victims' Association, and will film the model.

Other newspapers are asking for material. Right now we have to prepare a batch of relevant non-technical information. Yesterday I decided with Bodiansky that your wife (if she's willing) would take care of the nursery, for which I have some very dynamic ideas. Please keep an eye on that.

14 October 1948

LE CORBUSIER

—P. 434

Le Corbusier to Helena Simkhovitch, from Bogotá, 24 February 1950

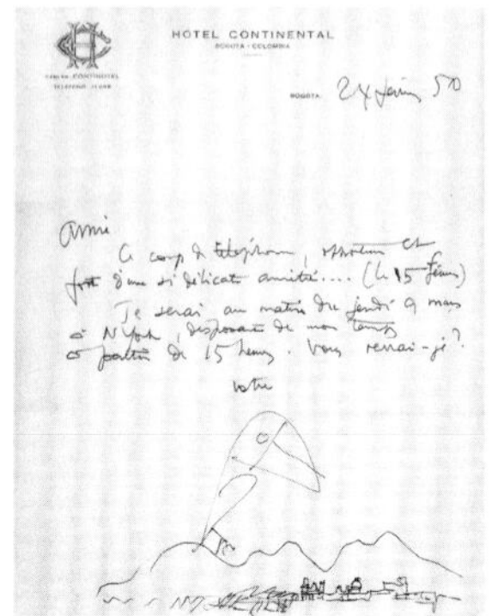

24 February 1950

Dear

That telephone call, timely and full of such exquisite friendship … (15 February)

I'll be in N York the morning of Thursday 9 March, and free from 3 in the afternoon. Will I see you?

Your,

[drawing]

—P. 434

Le Corbusier to Helena Simkhovitch, 11 July 1950

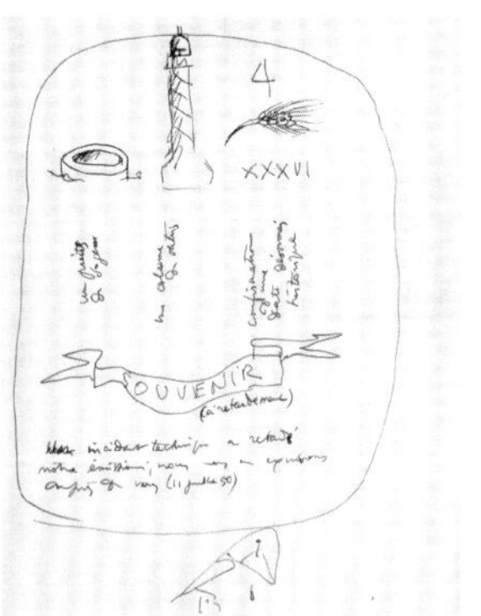

[LEFT TO RIGHT, TOP TO BOTTOM]
a well of wisdom

a column of virtues

Confirmation of a henceforth historic date

MEMORY (delayed-action)

Technical incident delayed our broadcast; please accept our apologies (11 July 50)

7 Passage to India (1950–1962)

—P. 438

Le Corbusier to fellow CIAM member José Luis Sert, 30 November 1950

LE CORBUSIER Paris, le 30 Novembre 1950

Monsieur José Luis SERT
33 West 42nd Street
NEW YORK 18 N.Y.

Mon cher Sert,

Le Secrétaire Général du Gouvernement du Punjab vient d'avoir de longues discussions avec moi, *j'ici à Paris*, me demandant conseil pour la construction de la nouvelle capitale du Punjab aux Indes.

Ce mandataire du Gouvernement hindou est allé à Londres, en Suisse, en Belgique et son enquête bien orientée a fini par le conduire à des décisions intéressantes pour notre politique des C.I.A.M. Cette décision est celle-ci :

1º) Le Corbusier sera nommé "Architectural Advisor to the Government of Punjab – Capital Project.
2º) Maxwell Fry et Pierre Jeanneret seront nommés "Senior Architects" sur place pour diriger l'Office du Plan qui sera formé d'un collège de jeunes architectes hindous diplômés en U.S.A., en Angleterre ou ailleurs.
3º) Un certain circuit s'établira entre les dessinateurs de l'Office du Plan et l'Atelier Le Corbusier à Paris afin qu'il en résulte une certaine "instruction".
4º) D'autres membres des C.I.A.M., par exemple Alfred Roth de Zurich, un ou deux Milanais, un ou deux Français etc.. pourront compléter au fur et à mesure ce premier équipe. Jane Drew rejoindra Maxwell Fry dès qu'elle le pourra.

Cet arrangement de principe a satisfait pleinement le mandataire hindou accompagné de l'ingénieur en chef de l'entreprise.

J'ai eu deux conversations téléphoniques avec Londres avec Maxwell Fry et Jane Drew hier et aujourd'hui. Hier Maxwell Fry avait compris que son collègue serait Emery et il n'était pas d'accord. Aujourd'hui j'ai rectifié en disant qu'il s'agissait de Pierre Jeanneret.

…/…

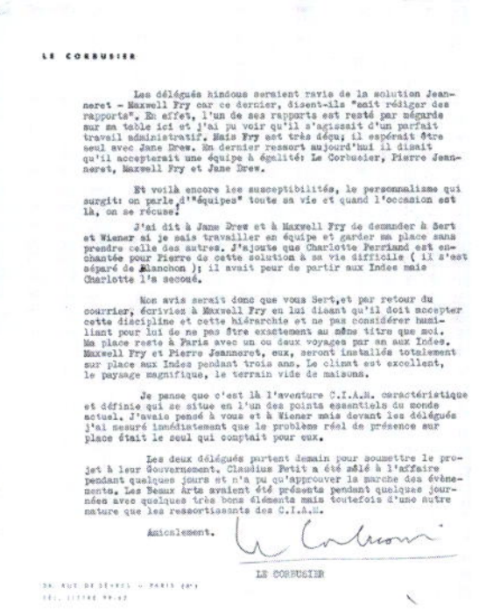

LE CORBUSIER

Les délégués hindous seraient ravis de la solution Jeanneret – Maxwell Fry car ce dernier, disent-ils "sait rédiger des rapports". En effet, l'un de ses rapports est resté par mégarde sur ma table ici et j'ai pu voir qu'il s'agissait d'un parfait travail administratif. Mais Fry est très déçu; il espérait être seul avec Jane Drew. En dernier ressort aujourd'hui il disait qu'il accepterait une équipe à égalité: Le Corbusier, Pierre Jeanneret, Maxwell Fry et Jane Drew.

Et voilà encore les susceptibilités, le personnalisme qui surgit: on parle d'"équipes" toute sa vie et quand l'occasion est là, on se récuse!

J'ai dit à Jane Drew et à Maxwell Fry de demander à Sert et Wiener si je sais travailler en équipe et garder ma place sans prendre celle des autres. J'ajoute que Charlotte Perriand est enchantée pour Pierre de cette solution à sa vie difficile (il s'est séparé de Blanchon); il avait peur de partir aux Indes mais Charlotte l'a secoué.

Mon avis serait donc que vous Sert, et par retour du courrier, écriviez à Maxwell Fry en lui disant qu'il doit accepter cette discipline et cette hiérarchie et ne pas considérer humiliant pour lui de ne pas être exactement au même titre que moi. Ma place reste à Paris avec un ou deux voyages par an aux Indes. Maxwell Fry et Pierre Jeanneret, eux, seront installés totalement sur place aux Indes pendant trois ans. Le climat est excellent, le paysage magnifique, le terrain vide de maisons.

Je pense que c'est là l'aventure C.I.A.M. caractéristique et définie qui se situe en l'un des points essentiels du monde actuel. J'avais pensé à vous et à Wiener mais devant les délégués j'ai mesuré immédiatement que le problème réel de présence sur place était le seul qui comptait pour eux.

Les deux délégués partent demain pour soumettre le projet à leur Gouvernement. Claudius Petit a été mêlé à l'affaire pendant quelques jours et n'a pu qu'approuver la marche des évènements. Les Beaux Arts avaient été présents pendant quelques journées avec quelques très bons éléments mais toutefois d'une autre nature que les ressortissants des C.I.A.M.

Amicalement.

LE CORBUSIER

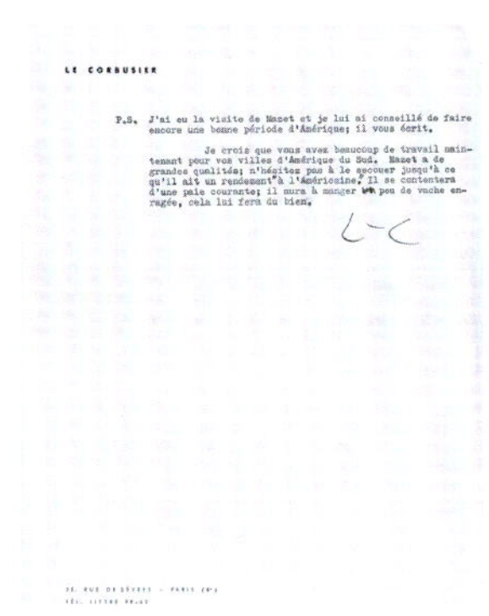

LE CORBUSIER

P.S. J'ai eu la visite de Mazet et je lui ai conseillé de faire encore une bonne période d'Amérique; il vous écrit.

Je crois que vous avez beaucoup de travail maintenant pour vos villes d'Amérique du Sud. Mazet a de grandes qualités; n'hésitez pas à le secouer jusqu'à ce qu'il ait un rendement "à l'Américaine." Il se contentera d'une paie courante; il aura à manger un peu de vache enragée, cela lui fera du bien.

L–C

Paris, 30 November 1950

Mr. José Luis SERT
33 West 42nd Street
NEW YORK 18 N.Y.

My dear Sert,

The Secretary General of the Government of Punjab has just had lengthy discussions with me *here in Paris*, asking my advice about the construction of the new capital of Punjab in India.

This representative of the Hindu Government has visited London, Switzerland, and Belgium and his carefully targeted investigation has ultimately led him to decisions interesting for CIAM and its policy. This decision is:

1. Le Corbusier will be appointed "Architectural Advisor to the Govern-ment of Punjab–Capital Project."

2. Maxwell Fry and Pierre Jeanneret will be appointed "Senior Architects" on site for running the Planning Office, which will comprise a group of young Hindu architects certificated in the USA, in England, or elsewhere.

3. A certain circuit will be set up between the Planning Office draftsmen and the Le Corbusier Studio in Paris so as to produce a certain "instruction."

4. Other CIAM members, for example Alfred Roth from Zurich, one or two from Milan, one or two Frenchmen, etc., may be added to this initial crew as we go along. Jane Drew will be rejoining Maxwell Fry as soon as she can.

This arrangement in principle was to the complete satisfaction of the representative, who was accompanied by the head of the venture.

I had two telephone conversations with London with Maxwell Fry and Jane Drew yesterday and today. Yesterday Maxwell Fry had understood that his colleague would be Emery and he wasn't in agreement. Today I set things right telling him it was Pierre Jeanneret.

The Hindu delegates say they're delighted with the Jeanneret–Maxwell Fry solution, for Fry, according to them, "knows how to write reports." As it happens, by an oversight one of his reports was left on a table here and I noticed that it was a perfect bit of administrative work. But Fry is very disappointed; he was hoping to be alone with Jane Drew. As a last resort yesterday he said he would accept an even team: Le Corbusier, Pierre Jeanneret, Maxwell Fry, and Jane Drew.

So touchiness and personal considerations are cropping up yet again; people talk about "teams" all their lives, and when the chance comes along they change their minds!

I told Jane Drew and Maxwell Fry to ask Sert and Wiener if I know how to work as part of a team and hold down my own place without stealing other people's. I should add that Charlotte Perriand is delighted that Pierre has found this solution to his difficult existence (he's left Blanchon); he was scared about going to India, but Charlotte gave him a good shakeup.

My opinion is that you Sert should write straightaway to Maxwell Fry telling him he has to accept this discipline and hierarchy and not see it as humiliating for him to not have exactly the same status as me. My place is still in Paris, with one or two trips per year to India. Maxwell Fry and Pierre Jeanneret will be in India full time for three years. The climate is excellent, the countryside magnificent, and the land has no houses on it.

I think that the real, clearly defined CIAM adventure is there, in what's currently one of the world's vital places. I had thought of you and Wiener but when I was with the delegates I saw at once that the very real problem of being there on site was the only one that counted for them.

The two delegates are leaving tomorrow to submit the project to their Government. Claudius Petit was involved in the affair for a few days and could only approve of the way things were going. The Beaux-Arts were also present for a few days, with some very fine people, but of a different kind from the CIAM representatives.

Best regards,

[signature]
LE CORBUSIER

P.S. Mazet called in and I advised him to spend plenty of time in America; he's writing to you.

I think you have lots of work now with your cities in South America. Mazet has lots to recommend him and don't hesitate to shake him up until he starts delivering the goods "American style." He'll be happy with the going pay rate; he'll have to live through some hard times and it'll do him good.

L–C

—P. 438

Le Corbusier to Yvonne while flying to Bombay

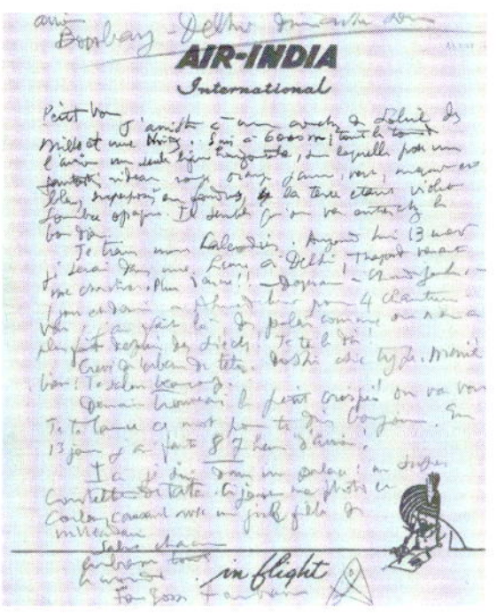

AIR-INDIA International

in flight

in flight
Bombay—Delhi Sunday evening

Little Von,

I'm watching an Arabian nights sunset. Am at 6,000 meters; all round the plane is a single horizontal line, overlaid with a fantastic curtain of red orange yellow, mauve, and blue, all merging into each other, and the earth a dark opaque violet. It's as if we were about to drop in on God.

I'm sticking to my schedule. Today 13 Nov. I'll be in Delhi in an hour. With Thapar coming to meet me. Out of ink!! —Tomorrow in Chandigarh, —1 day and a half in Ahmedabad for four jobs. Von, there I've made palaces like no one has for centuries, I swear!

Exhausted by all the brainwork. Doshi a great guy. Menié's fine. Sends a big hello.

Tomorrow I'll see little Crispin! We'll see what happens! This is just a note to say hello. In 13 days I've flown 87 hours.

Right now I'm in a palace: a Super-Constellation. Here's a color photo of me chatting with a millionaire's daughter.

Hi to all.
Love to everybody
Big kisses from your kid.

—P. 438

Le Corbusier to his mother, en route to India, 15 December 1956

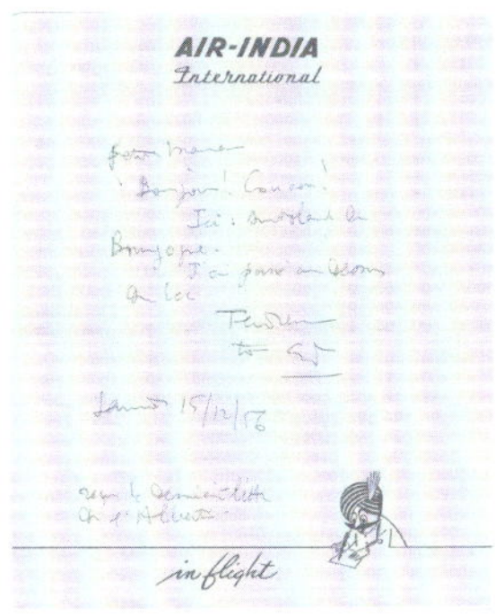

AIR-INDIA International

in flight

little Mom

Hello! Hi!
Here: flying over Burgundy.
I went over the lake

Love,
your Ed

Saturday 15/12/56

got Albert's last letter

—P. 439

Article from *Le Franc Tireur*, 8 May 1950

Sur les plans de Le Corbusier

CHANDIGARH

capitale ultra-moderne de 500.000 habitants va surgir au pied de l'Himalaya

Revenant de la nouvelle République du Punjab, l'architecte Le Corbusier a tenu hier une conférence de presse pour expliquer ce que sera la capitale de cette République : Chandigarh.

C'est une ville prévue pour 500.000 habitants, qui va s'élever sur un magnifique plateau campagnard, à proximité du chemin de fer et des routes. Delhi-Simla, Simla-Lahore et Carral-Latiala. Le plateau est légèrement incliné. Il monte doucement, face aux grandioses montagnes de l'Himalaya.

Déjà depuis un an les approvisionnements en canalisations, les stocks de matériaux de constructions, briques, ciment, etc., s'accumulent sur le vaste terrain.

C'est dans le sens de la compréhension des traditions et de l'éthique indiennes que Le Corbusier a préparé les plans de Chandigarh.

Tout est prévu pour apporter aux futurs habitants les « joies essentielles », c'est-à-dire le soleil, l'espace, la verdure. Il y aura une séparation très nette entre le piéton et l'automobiliste.

Si la construction de quelques buildings a été prévue, en revanche la grande majorité des maisons ne comportera qu'un seul étage. Et les indiens qui ont, paraît-il, l'habitude de coucher à la belle étoile, pourront, tout à leur aise, transporter leur lit sur les terrasses — recouvertes d'une toiture — qui domineront les maisons.

Enfin, Chandigarh, grâce à des dispositions d'urbanisme et d'architecture, sera mis à l'abri des bassesses de la spéculation et de ses corollaires désastreux : la banlieue. Il n'y aura pas de banlieue dans la cité ultra-moderne de la nouvelle République du Punjab.

From Le Corbusier's design

CHANDIGARH

the ultra-modern capital of 500,000 inhabitants will spring up at the foot of the Himalayas

On his return from the new Republic of Punjab, the architect Le Corbusier held a press conference yesterday to describe in detail what the Republic's capital, Chandigarh, will be.

It is a city planned for 500,000 inhabitants, which will rise on a magnificent plateau in the countryside, near the railroad line and the Delhi–Simla, Simla–Lahore, and Karal–Latiala highways. The plateau is on a slight incline. It rises gently, facing the grandeur of the Himalaya mountains.

For a year now, the supplies of drainpipes, stocks of building materials, bricks, cement, etc., have been piling up on the vast site.

Le Corbusier based his designs for Chandigarh on an understanding of Indian traditions and moral philosophy.

Everything is planned to bring the future residents the "essential joys," that is, sun, space, and greenery. There will be a very clear separation between pedestrians and drivers.

While the plan calls for some multistory buildings, the great majority of the houses will be on only one floor. The Indians, who apparently customarily sleep outside, will be able to easily take their beds onto the—roofed—terraces atop their homes.

Finally, thanks to its urban planning and architecture, Chandigarh will be protected from the tawdriness of speculation and its disastrous corollary: the suburb. There will be no suburbs in the ultramodern city of the new Republic of Punjab.

—P. 442

Le Corbusier to Yvonne, from Simla, India, 9 or 10 March 1951

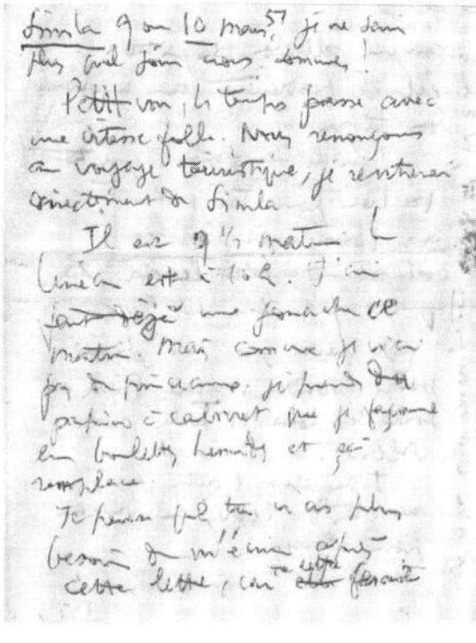

Simla 9 or 10 March 51, I don't know what day it is anymore!

Little Von, time's passing at a crazy speed. We're giving up the tourist trip, I'll come back directly from Simla.

It's 9½ in the morning. The office is at 10. I've already done a gouache this morning. But as I don't have any brushes, I roll toilet paper into damp balls and that takes their place.

I think you don't need to write to me any more after this letter, for ~~it~~ your letter would

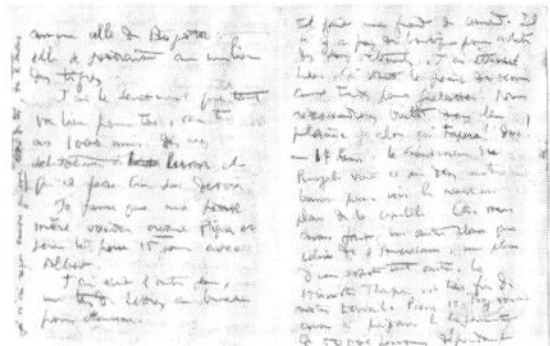

[LEFT MARGIN]
I've still received only one letter from you, dated 2 March

go the same way as the Bogotá one: it would get lost among the tigers.

I have the feeling everything's going well for you, as you have 1,000 friends. Say hello to ~~luan~~ Luan for me and tell him to do his duty.

I think my little mom will come before Easter and will be there for 2 weeks with Albert.

The other day at the office I wrote a stack of letters to everybody.

It's icy cold. There's no store to buy underwear. I was sneezing yesterday. A great idea to come to India to shiver. We're soon going down to the plain and there it'll be baking! really!

—2 p.m.: the Governor of Punjab is coming to our office this evening to see the new plan of the capital. Because we've made a different plan from the American's, in quite a different spirit.
Thapar, the Minister, is very proud of our work. Pierre and Fry are going to have to prepare housing for 50,000 people depending on

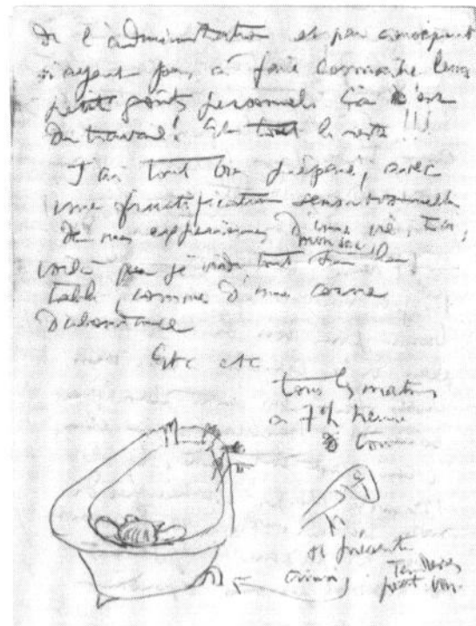

the government and so not entitled to make their little personal tastes known. That's a lot of work! And there's all the rest!!!

I've prepared everything carefully, with sensational benefits from my experiences of a lifetime. Here I'm pouring everything out onto the work table, as if from a horn of plenty.

Etc. etc.

every morning at 7½ a.m. your, [drawing] presents himself like this.

Much love little Von.

—P. 442

Le Corbusier to his mother, from Simla, India, 9 November 1951

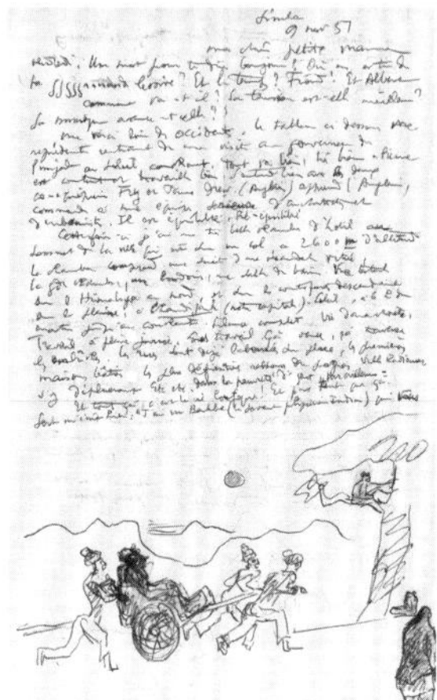

Simla
9 Nov. 51

My dear little Mom,

Friday. A note to say hello. How are you making out with the biiiiiiiiig load of washing? And the weather? Cold!

And how's Albert going? is his blood pressure better? Is his music making progress?

Here I'm a long way from the west. The picture below shows me on my way back from visiting the governor of Punjab at sunset. Everything's fine, just fine. Pierre's happy and working well. getting along well with his two teammates Fry and Jane Drew (English) learning English, running a serious team of architects and urbanists. He's stable. Again

This time I have a lovely hotel room at the top of the town which is on a pass 2,600 meters up. The room has a suite, a glassed-in veranda, The big bedroom, a dressing room, a bathroom. Sweeping view of the Himalayas to the north and the foothills descending to the plain, at Chandigarh (our capital). Sun, at 6 in the morning until sunset. Absolute silence. Life of a recluse. Work all day, a lot of work. It's going ahead, cutting through the obstacles. The streets are already ploughed, the first houses built. The most definitive resources of the Radiant City progress will be put into action there Etc. etc. But amidst a shortage of money.

And all this is the crazy life. And not as crazy as all that. Yesterday Sert wrote to me: "I saw Bahbe (the scholarly Indian physicist) who has put you

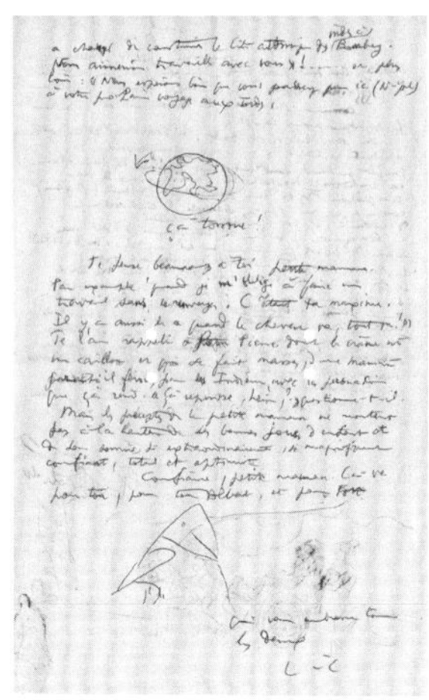

in charge of building India's Atomic City in Bombay. We would like to work with you"! … and further on: "We really hope you'll stop by here (N York) on your next trip to India."

things are going ahead!

I think of you a lot little mom. For example when I force myself to do a job without putting it off. That was your saying. There was also "when the hair's okay, everything's okay!" I mentioned it to ~~Per~~ Pierre whose skull is like a stone and who gets himself massaged ferociously it seems, by the Indians convinced that it helps "it's growing back, hey?" he asks.

But little Mom's precepts don't reach as high as his chubby kid's cheeks and his smile, so extraordinarily, so magnificently confident, total, and optimistic.

Don't worry, little mom. Things are going well for you, for your Albert, and for Your,
[drawing]

who sends love to you both

L-C

—P. 443

Sketches of site plan of Chandigarh, with note to Marguerite Tjader Harris, 4 March 1952

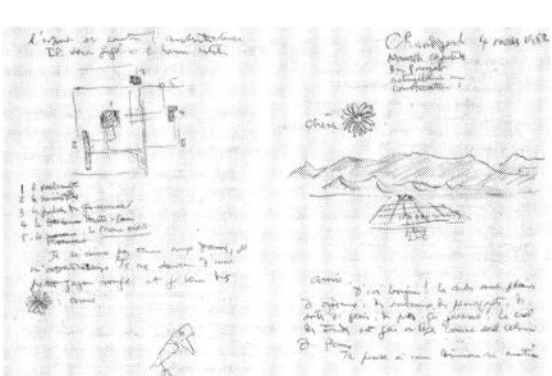

[LEFT PAGE]
The spirit is against architecture
It will be judged when the time is right

1 the parliament
2 the ministers
3 the governor's residence
4 the High Court
5 the Monument: the Open Hand

I don't like writing to ladies, I get emotional. I remember a little red lawn and I say to you: dear

[RIGHT PAGE]
Chandigarh 4 March 1952
New capital of the Punjab currently being built

Dear [Marguerite]

150,000 inhabitants
plans L-C

Dear.

Hello from here! The trees are full o- birds: crows, parrots, sorts of jays, magpies. Such chattering! The sky o India is gay and light like that of Paris.

I'm thinking of you on Sunday morning.

—P. 445

Pages from Le Corbusier's sketchbook "Punjab, Simla, Chandigarh, March 1951"

ALBUM
PUNJAB
SIMLA
CHANDIGARH
MARCH 1951

Its place = 24 NC sliding door left lower shelf = with the series of albums and Sketchbooks

27 Dec. 64 at Cap-Martin decided to consult this album for "La défense" (jullian)

the horde everywhere
2 cows
1 man

addressed to God the ultimate reality the hindus' morning prayer seeing in harmony with all men animals and inanimate things

at the brickworks they make bricks with a hand mold like the Egyptians

great vintage PCI Punjab Capital

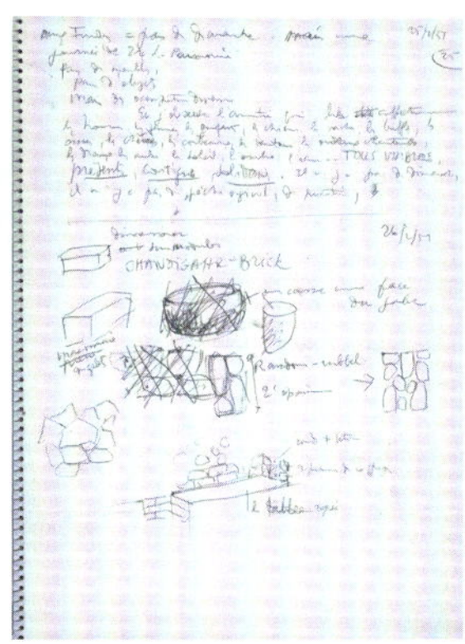

25/2/51

in India = no Sunday but a day of 24 h[ours] of harmony

No furniture, no objects but different activities

And I observe the other affectionately linking men, women, children, dogs, cows, buffalo, donkeys, goats, crows, vultures, songbirds, God's trees sun, shade, water. . . . ALL VISIBLE, present, close, united. There's no Sunday, there's no original sin, no punishment

26/2/51

Design on Modulor
CHANDIGARH-BRICK

you break one side of the pebble

masonry stone pebbles

Random-rubble
2nd thickness

round pebbles + concrete
2 formwork stones

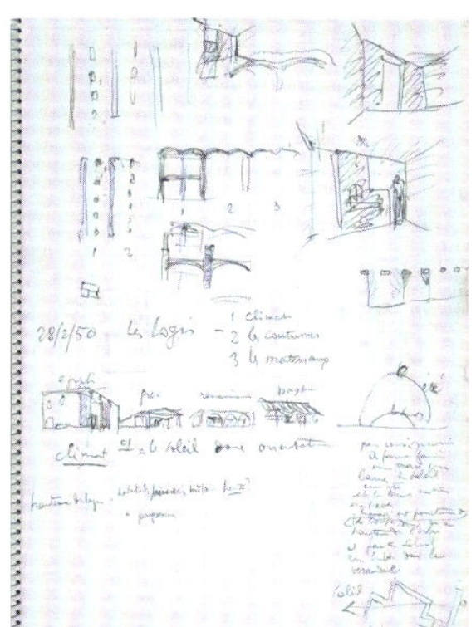

28/2/50

The housing
1 climate
2 the customs
3 the materials

egypt / greek / renaissance / peasant / summer / winter

Climate c/ = the sun and thus aspect

height of the houses-princely habits high?
peasant [habits]

consequently we have to make a layout that stops the sun in summer and lets it in in winter

the layout depends on the section: and so on the height of the shelter
there must be sun in winter inside the veranda

Sun
for the housing

—P. 448

Sketches for Chandigarh, from Le Corbusier's notebook, 1950–52

Chandigarh 1 March 51
Completion of the creation of the plan of the Capital on the report 7 to 7

Chandigarh
Birth of a capital
3 March 51

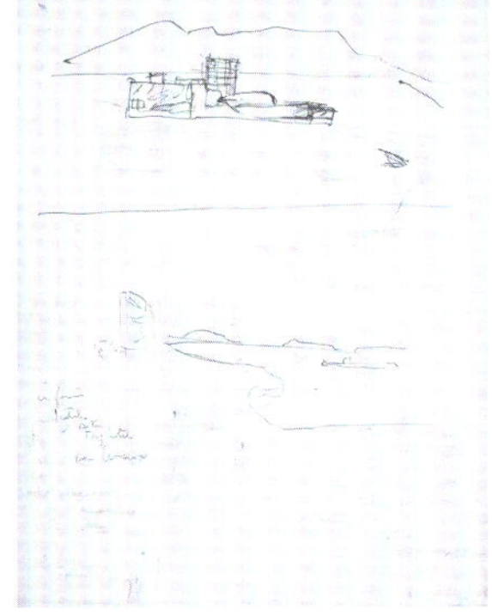

to do hotel
next door
Taj hotel
for offices

the dog

the water
the [river]

the bed

Gira Sarabhai

—P. 449

Sketches for Chandigarh, from Le Corbusier's notebook, 1950–52

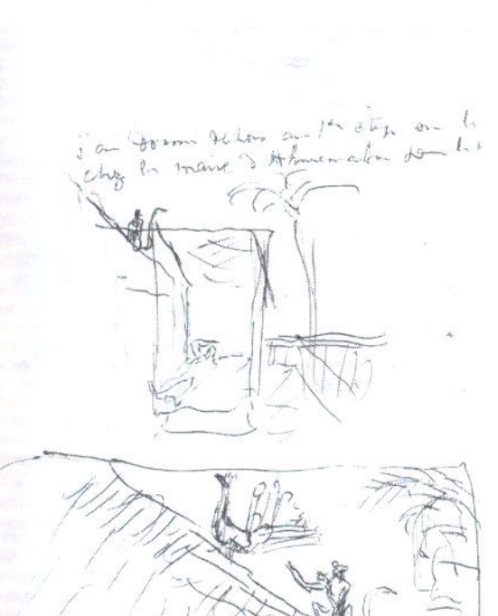

I slept outside on the 1st floor on the open terrace at the mayor of Ahmedabad's under the mosquito net

at dawn a wild monkey + a wild peacock came and got together on the cornice

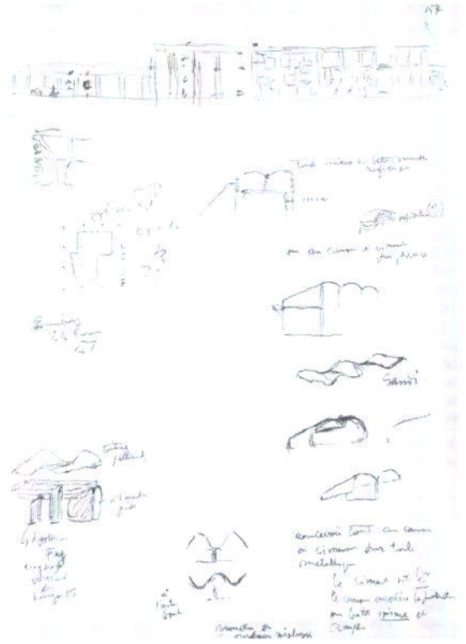

[LEFT TO RIGHT, TOP TO BOTTOM]
thin tile of foam concrete
prefabricated wall

the water
the bed

expedition (?)
due to the cement gun on site

Bombay 24 March 51

Gaudí

roofing film
in the shade / wattle and daub

System Fry used vertical and horizontal

design with the cement gun on metal netting
the cement is there
the gun speeds up production
we're building thin and spacious
at the other end
geometry and distributed areas

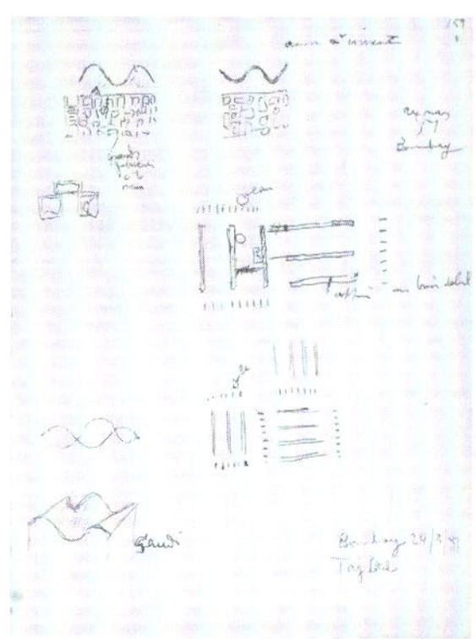

[LEFT TO RIGHT, TOP TO BOTTOM]
cement gun

big structures built by hand

24 March 51
Bombay

water

support / a sunshade

bed

Gaudí

Bombay 24/3/51
Taj Hotel

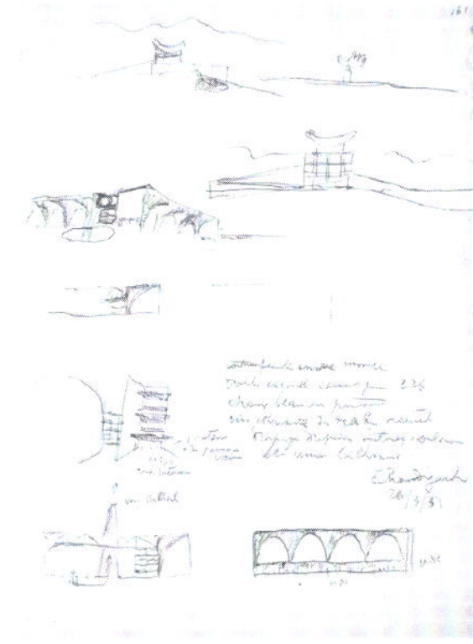

[LEFT]
1 motor + Wanner panels
indoor street
see Balbah

[RIGHT]
roofing sheet reverse thin
double shell cement gun 226
whitewash all over
solid wood natural teak
coverings hangings plain saturated Kashmir colors

Chandigarh 26/3/51

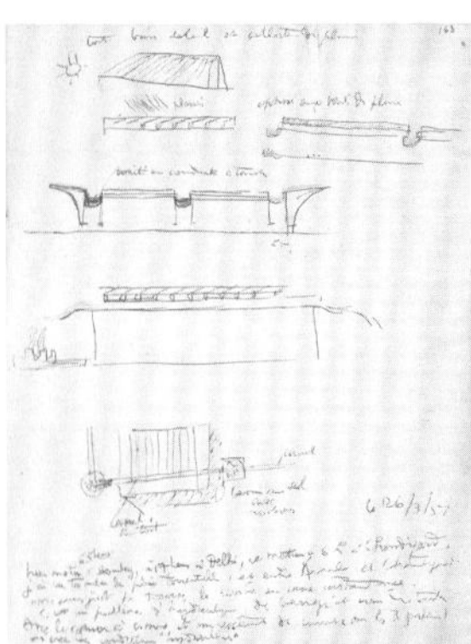

sunbathing and rainwater collector roof

rain / as opposed to storm winds

treated as pipe and trench

5 m

Canal to the roof
pool on the ground with rocks

26/3/51

yesterday morning at 5 o'clock in Bombay, at 5 p.m. in Delhi, this morning at 6 in Chandigarh I saw torrential rain falling and between Kovral and Chandigarh we just managed to cross the river a matter of seconds
It's a hydraulics problem, a dam problem and not [?]
with the cement gun and a coating of cement (on the 3 palaces) we create "hydraulic" conditions.

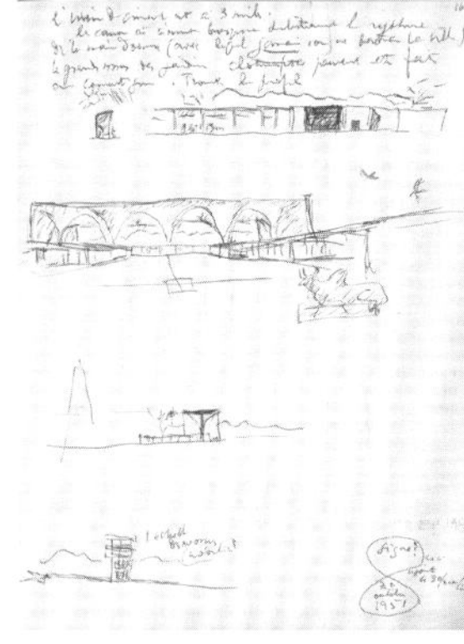

the cement factory is 3 miles away
the cement gun abruptly speeds up the rhythm of the workforce (with which we'll never build the city)
the high walls of the enclosed gardens etc. can be done with the cement gun. Find the profile

The scale of the measurements (Modulor)

sign?
this added 30/Oct./51
30 October 1951

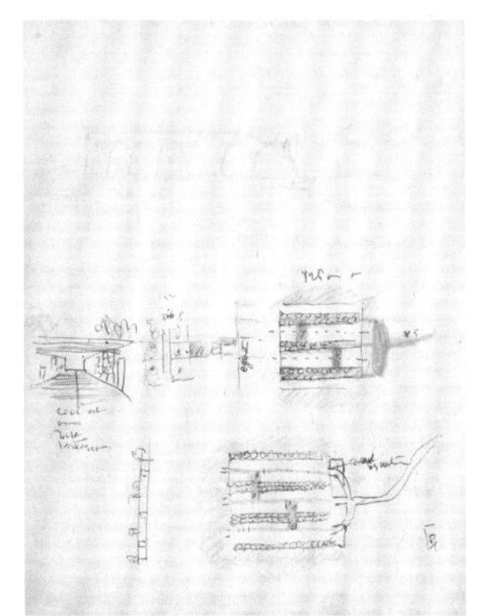

Sewer

This is an indoor street

Awning for the cars

—P. 466

Notes by Le Corbusier, 22 November 1951

22 Nov. 51 / South Block / Pandit Nehru
appointment 11 a.m.

I'm there at 10 a.m. Stroll to the end of the Palaces and the (Indian) stone bull. At 10:45 sprint toward N[ehru]'s office. One minute's wait: I have the time to see the newspaper headlines plane CRASH last night in Calcutta Death of one of the executive leaders of the liberation [?]

This is my big opportunity!

Nehru welcomes me at the door, ushers me in gravely, indicates I can speak French with him: I express my regrets. I present my respects, tell him that I am bringing and will continue to bring all my intelligence as well as all my sensibility and my heart to this task that delights me ~~in fact~~ pinnacle of career in humility not to say complaint. To get architecture out of its dead crust express it and give it grandeur and subtlety.

I tell him that Thapar and Varma hold their posts down well and have earned the devoted respect of the architects. Tell him I'm happy to be working for India, now a strong country, in beneficial ferment. I pronounce Varma's "Chandigarh, symbol of the freedom of India unfettered by the tradition of the past."

Nehru remains very grave. I add that since 1948 I have been obsessed and pursued by the symbol of the Open Hand. I wanted to set it at the end of the Capitol, set against the Himalayas. They wanted to involve me in the sterile battle of extremes. I rejected it. And I thought that with the modern world so full of intellectual and material riches, it was time to open one's hand to receive and to give.

Nehru smiled and nodded approvingly. I became very moved at this point by our conversation and the tragic events of the morning. I stopped short and Nehru left his office with me saying sadly, And now I'm going to the funeral.

—P. 466

Le Corbusier to his mother, from India, April 1952, enclosing French translations of two letters

Translation

The Administrator of the Capital
to Mr. Le Corbusier
Architectural adviser for
The Capital at Chandigarh

Simla 5 April 52

Dear Mr. Le Corbusier

I enclose a copy of the note Mr. Nehru wrote to the Indian Planning Commission.

He has asked me to say that he is very interested by what you told him and would be pleased if you could provide an outline (which could be in French) about your ideas regarding the building project in India. He would like you to come to Delhi for a day or two to discuss your ideas with the Planning Commission. He would like you to send him a note before you come to Delhi, and once he has received it he will set a date.

Mr. Nehru writes that he was delighted to visit Chandigarh* and wishes all of us success with this handsome project. A large part of the good impression made on Mr. Nehru is due to your efforts and I would like to express here my appreciation of and gratitude for your contribution.

Sincerely,
Thapar

Translation

Secretariat of the Prime Minister
Camp "La Retraite"
Masholra

HOUSING
Two days ago I had the chance to visit the works for Chandigarh, the new capital of Punjab. This was my first visit. The site seems to me ideal from many points of view. I have seen the plans and the "master plan" for the city. This latter was originally due to Mr. Albert Mayer, an American. But those plans have been changed, although the basic principles

* our capital, under construction

remain the same. I think that the underlying concept is very sound and that when it has been implemented the result will be an attractive city combining modern conceptions of urban planning with the needs of the community, given our own habits and customs and the demands of the climate.

2 The Punjab Government has appointed as chief adviser Mr. Corbusier, known as perhaps the world's leading architectural authority. He has in addition hired a number of other foreign experts. Mr. Corbusier is most enthusiastic about the project and I am pleased that he is able to be of such help to us.

3 I am of course extremely interested in the accommodation to be provided for our civil servants. Broadly speaking, they seem good and not too expensive. During a conversation Mr. Corbusier told me he was surprised and a little disappointed that in our buildings and houses we copy foreign practice without taking account of our own climate and other factors. We have formed the habit of approaching problems in the Anglo-Saxon way, that is to say, one largely dictated by foreign engineers or by local engineers who have been trained abroad, and we have a tendency to forget that India is different from Western countries. I feel that Mr. Corbusier was making an important point and that we should commit ourselves to the modifications needed to make our buildings better suited to Indian conditions while at the same time giving them artistic value. In the past we have given little attention to architecture and related aesthetic matters. This does not necessarily involve great expense.

5 What people want above all is not a small area of enclosed space, but the necessary sanitation, lighting and water facilities. The rest is secondary, granted of course that it remains important and should match the climate, whether cold or hot, rainy or relatively dry.

4 What is most important, however, is that our housing design be rethought, especially low-cost housing. Nothing is more horrible than the "peasant" or "servants" quarters that were standard during the English era and continue to be built with a few variations. This accommodation was seen in terms of a single small, cramped, dark room. Our worker housing has more or less stuck to this model. When the issue of improvement came up, we did not think of two rooms instead of one. Sometimes we went further by adding a shower, toilet, or kitchen, but the basic concept remained unchanged. I think this concept needs to be re-evaluated.

6 I am increasingly convinced that a fundamental requirement should be to provide sanitation, lighting, and water. The main part of the cost has to do with the actual building and we have generally lost out because of this basic expense. A dwelling is supposed to provide privacy, but the fact is that a room 3m x 4 or 3.6m lived in by a dozen people, or even only four or five, offers no privacy. An open space is more private!

7 I am writing to draw attention to two points: first that we should think about what Mr. Corbusier has suggested, i.e. that our buildings, whether big or small, should be designed to meet Indian conditions; and second that our low-cost housing must embody above all the basic principle of sanitation, light, and water. To this we should also add whatever else circumstances allow.

Whatever the case, simple huts provided with these facilities would be infinitely preferable to non-temporary constructions.

Note that the Public Works Department regulations, most

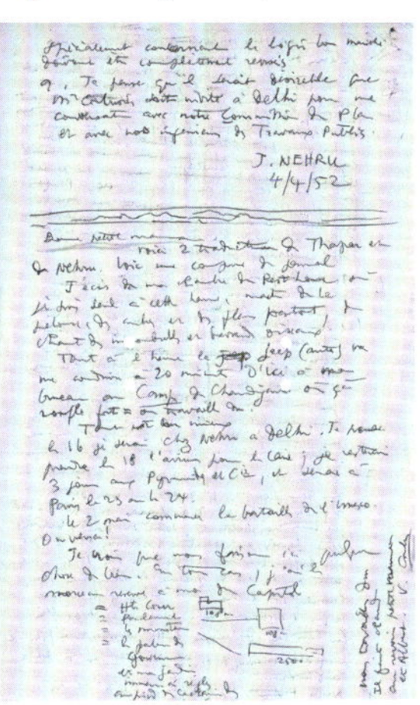

especially with regard to low-cost housing, must be completely revised.

I think it desirable that Mr. Corbusier be invited to Delhi for discussions with our Planning Commission and our Public Works engineers.

J. NEHRU
4/4/52

My darling little mom,

Here are 2 translations from Thapar and Nehru. Together with a newspaper cutting.

I'm writing from my room in the Rest House, where I'm alone at this time of day, master of the lawn, with trees and flowers everywhere and the song of countless noisy birds.

Soon the jeep (car) is going to take me 20 minutes from here to my office at Camp Chandigarh, where snoozing = working hard.

Everything's for the best. On the 16th I'll be at Nehru's in Delhi. I think I'll be taking the plane to Cairo on the 18th. I'll stay three days in the Land of the Pyramids, and will be in Paris the 23rd or 24th.

On 2 May the Battle of Unesco begins. We shall see!

I think we're doing something good here. In any case, I have my own part of the Capitol to work on:

= High Court
= Parliament House
= the ministries
= the governor's residence and a vast garden to be laid out at the foot of the mountain chain

[RIGHT MARGIN]
We are working hard. The weather is hot

Bye little mom and Albert
Yr. Corbu

—P. 470

First page of article from unidentified French journal regarding Chandigarh

[CAPTION]
The city rises before a mountainous horizon.

The famous French architect Le Corbusier and his collaborator, Pierre Jeanneret, are building the new capital of the Punjab, Chandigarh, the "radiant city" of India, located 150 miles north of Delhi, capital of the Republic of India. The friendly Franco-Indian relations have a long history, especially with the Punjab. Some of Napoleon's generals—Ventura, Court, Avitabile, Allard—helped the Maharajah Ranjit Singh, king of the Northwest Indies, train the best Indian army of the nineteenth century. Today, French architects are helping the Punjab build a capital that will be, we hope, the best city in India.

The need for a new capital for the divided state of the Punjab arose from the partition of India in 1947, which left Lahore, its former capital, in Pakistan. Simla, a resort town in the Himalayas and temporary capital of the eastern Punjab, does not lend itself to being an administrative center, because its climate is extreme and it is very far from the plains. The government decided to build a new city. Very few world capitals have been built from the ground up: Saint Petersburg was built by Peter the Great on uninhabited marshland; Washington, on the Potomac swamps; while Canberra, in Australia, turned a sheep station into a flourishing city. In India, New Delhi was merely an addition to the ancient city of Delhi.

One of the most important considerations in planning a new capital is the choice of building site. After studying a number of locations, it was decided to build the new city in the region located at the foot of the Himalaya Mountains, near the road from Ambala to Simla. The site has many natural advantages: a central situation, a mild climate, accessibility, an abundance of materials, natural drainage, and hard soil (for building on), and it is fertile. It is bordered on both sides by rivers that have water only in the rainy season, and that are intended to be turned into verdant carpets. Furthermore, the site has the advantage of a splendid panorama, with the snow-crowned peaks of the Himalayas in the background. It offers Le Corbusier a magnificent opportunity to apply his philosophy of architecture—a philosophy that insists upon "sun, space, greenery, and the possibility of silence" for all citizens.

CHANDIGARH—CITY
A CAPITAL BUILT BY FRENCH ARCHITECTS

The city was planned for half a million inhabitants. The original plan was made by an American urbanist, Albert Mayer. This plan was then discussed and modified by a team of architects that included, besides Le Corbusier and Pierre Jeanneret, Maxwell Fry and his associate, Jane Drew. Ably assisted by Indian engineers, headed by Mr. Varma, these technicians put the finishing touches on the design.

The layouts of cities exercise a powerful influence on the organization of contemporary life. In planning how to construct or group buildings, an architect also directs the citizens' way of life. And conversely, he must observe closely how the people actually live, and put his plans together in such a way that they can be happy there. Perhaps Chandigarh will be the first city in India where these two opposing points of view will be respected. As paradoxical as it may seem, it is foreign architects who have guaranteed that Chandigarh will be a city that is realized in "the Indian spirit."

The plan of the new capital has been described as "the architect's dream." The city is divided into sectors, each of these sectors ½ x ¾ miles. Enclosed by a system of roads, these sectors would be quasi-independent entities, were they not connected to one another by strips of greenery going southwest to northeast, and by commercial streets running southeast to northeast. Each sector provides housing for 5,000 people in the areas of low density and 20,000 people in the more populous areas. Though easily accessible from the city's system of major roads, the sectors will be completely protected from the dangers of traffic, and from dust, noise, and the smell of gasoline, etc. All the sectors will be complete entities, with their own schools, playgrounds, parks, commercial districts, libraries, and clubs, in addition to the homes.

Each sector is further subdivided into a number of communities comprising about 150 houses with six to seven hundred inhabitants—the size of an ordinary Punjabi village. It will be less expensive to build such community centers and they will also retain the communal life and healthy surroundings, with open spaces planted with trees, which is one of the characteristics of the Punjabi villages.

[CAPTION]
Pandit Nehru and Le Corbusier.

—P. 477

Sketched plan of a courtroom, High Court, Chandigarh, 16 June 1954

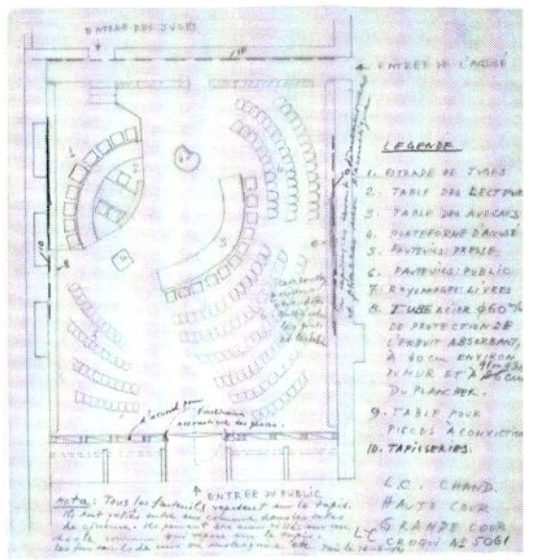

[TOP LEFT]
JUDGES' ENTRANCE

[MIDDLE]
The curves can be different according to taste and requirements

The carpets will be sized and situated according to acoustics

okay for acoustic sloping of the mirrors

[BOTTOM LEFT]
PUBLIC ENTRANCE
Note: All seats rest on the carpet
They are joined as in cinemas.
They can also be screwed onto a common base that rests on the carpet.
The seats are leather, imitation leather, etc. / Paris 16-6-54

[RIGHT, TOP TO BOTTOM]
ENTRANCE OF THE ACCUSED

LEGEND
1. JUDGES' BOXES
2. CLERKS' TABLE
3. LAWYERS' TABLE
4. BOX FOR THE ACCUSED
5. SEATING: PRESS
6. SEATING: PUBLIC
7. SHELVES: BOOKS
8. STEEL TUBE Ø 60 mm TO PROTECT THE ABSORBENT COATING APPROX. 40 cm 91 or 113 cm FROM THE WALL AND 86 cm FROM THE FLOOR
9. TABLE FOR EVIDENCE
10. CARPETS

L.C. CHAND[IGARH]
SUPREME COURT
HIGH COURT
L-C SKETCH No. 5061

—P. 484

First two pages of a letter from Le Corbusier to his mother, 30 November 1952

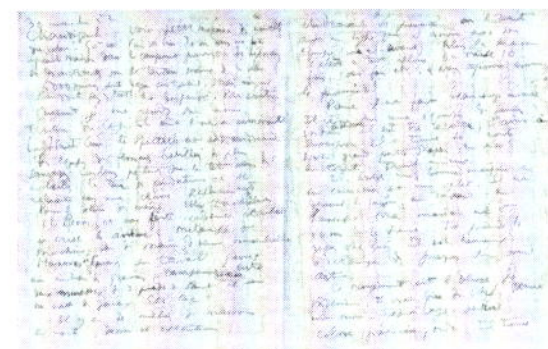

30 November 52

Chandigarh. Little mom, here's news from the colonist! Everything's fine! Really fine. I'm living in a most agreeable house in the temporary engineers' and architects' camp on the very site of the city.

5,000 people are already at work. But you wouldn't know it; everything is dispersed. But when I go to the Capitol to my plot where we've begun the High Court there's the extraordinary spectacle of teams of women wearing the wildest colors, carrying the earth for the foundations in baskets on their heads and taking turns in a mind-boggling human chain. The same goes for the concrete. They work for 12 hours, driven by a powerful sung, shouted rhythm. A multitudinous mix of machines and workers. Men and women working, kids in the midst of the rubble, they camp at night between two walls 3 feet high and under a reed mat. Etc. Etc.

There are thousands of houses underway, design and building. A job crops up: we handle it with a guy who comes along with his team (see earlier). Then the house goes up at top speed. We do this 10 times, 1,000 times etc. "We work like ants"!

Pierre has made himself much loved. He rules a team of young Indian architects. They listen to him closely; he likes to teach. He's found his path in life. Thapar, our big boss, is delighted. So much the better.

He lives in a good house, has a cook and a valet. He's stayed the same, but better, and happy. My house is 10 meters from his. I eat at his house. He's pleased to chat about his art.

This camp is the work of the engineers, in fact of the chief, Varma my friend. Open-minded, smiling, calm, precise, orderly. He finds [...]

—P. 487

Sketch of a Marseille restaurant interior with a tapestry woven from Chandigarh cotton

Marseille restaurant Michelet with piece of tapestry woven Chandigarh cotton 226/113. System of hanging from ceiling = rails under ceiling. From time to time a Picaud or Tabar tapestry. the ceiling = shunting yard or curtain rod.

They say that in the restaurant in the shopping street there's a stock made by firm Chandigarh cotton carpets for sale to the public + the seats Pieur (?)
Thapar in the cement
five-year plan
home weaving
thanks to the Modulor

—P. 498

Sketches of Chandigarh from Le Corbusier's notebooks, 1950–52 and 1952–59

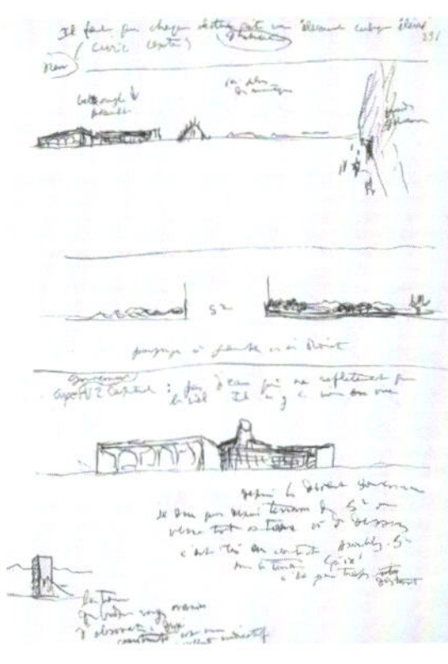

Each housing sector must have a large-volume element (civic Center)
Drew

nice angle assembly / here no more mountains / governor's facade

S2
landscape to left and right
V2 governor Capitol thoroughfare: pools that reflect only the sky. There is nothing to be seen

from in front of the governor's remember that from the Gvnr's land you'll see all around and from above this is very close contact
Assembly–Gvnr
on the spot / Okay!
It's not too far away
the glazed red brick observation tower, already constructed is an excellent indicator

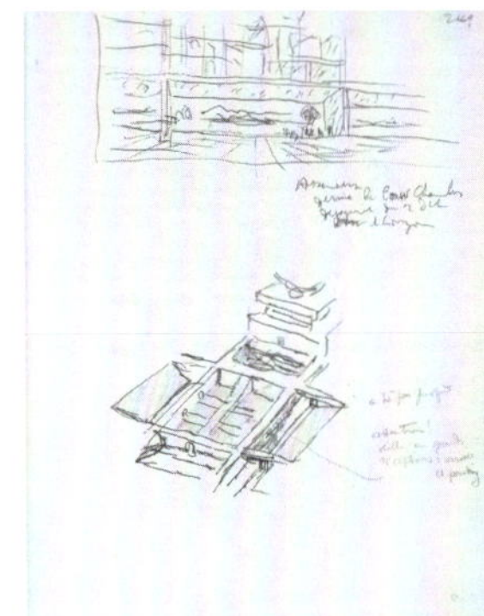

Assembly
behind the low Chambers are set off by [?] the horizon

very shallow

attention!
keep an eye on the big receptions = arrival and parking lot

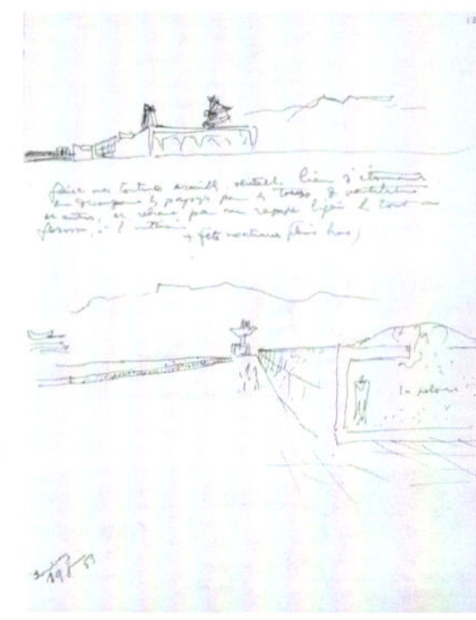

Make an accessible roof, a truly surprising place by cutting out openings for the ventilation stacks etc., and using a lightweight ramp to link the whole thing to the forum, inside + celebrations at night (full moon)

the lawn

Mumbai, 19 June 1953

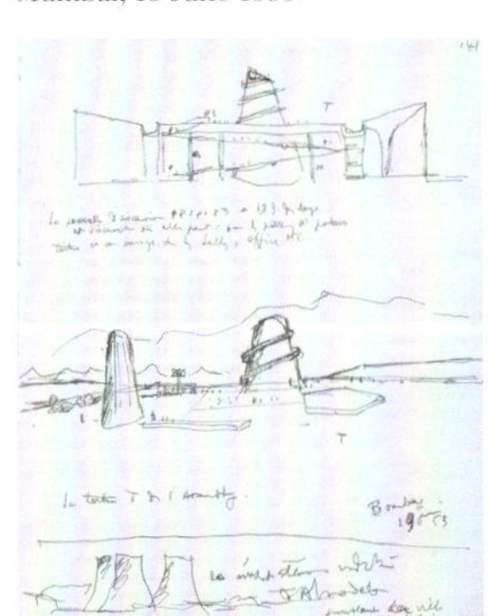

The rising walkway PP1 p2 p3 is 1.83 wide and hooks on where it can: on the posts holding up the roof and as it runs along the rooms, offices, etc.

the roof T of the Assembly / Mumbai 19 June 53

the [?] of Ahmedabad flying over the city before landing

—P. 500

Detail sketches of Assembly chamber, Palace of the Assembly, 12 January 1954

12/2/54

[LEFT]
noon celebration of the Summer solstice

[RIGHT]
flared
reflected
acoustic
closing disk in case of rain
air
no! see B below

sealed off
an inclined plane B
or room in C

Chandigarh Nov. 12/11/54
we could call the red bedroom "red home" and the blue bedroom "blue home" and paint them accordingly

—PP. 512–13

Le Corbusier's sketches showing various architectural responses to climatic conditions, January 1952

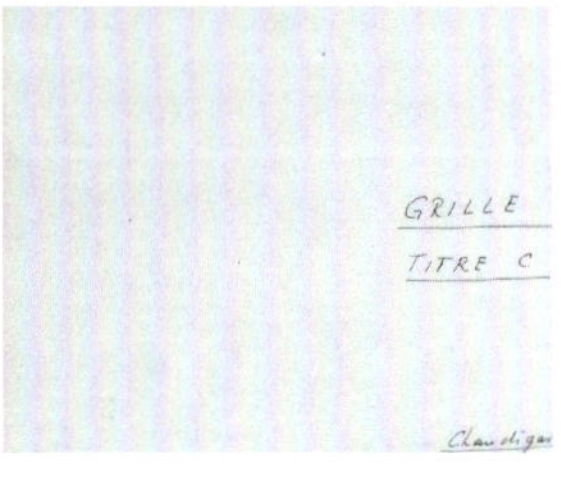

CLIMATE GRID TYPE C

Chandigarh Houses 110 m²

Atelier Le Corbusier
35 rue de Sèvres Paris 6
18 January 1952

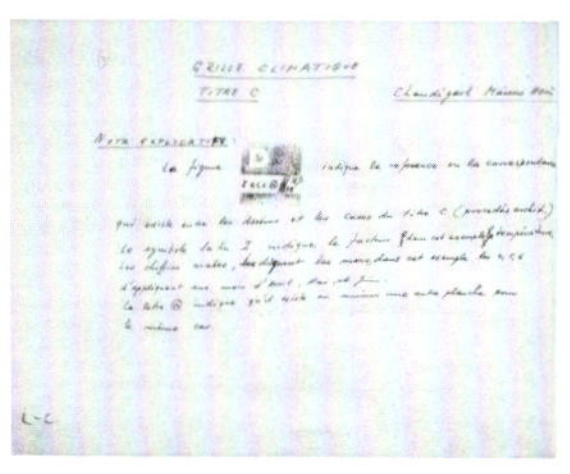

CLIMATE GRID TYPE C / Chandigarh Houses 110 m²

EXPLANATORY NOTE:

The formula [D I 4, 5, 6 a / 18/1/52] indicates the reference or the correspondence existing between the drawings and the type C boxes

The Latin symbol I indicates the factor in this example the temperature
The Arabic numerals indicate the months, in this example 4, 5, 6 apply to the months of April, May, and June.
The letter a indicates that there is at least one more illustration for the same example.

L–C

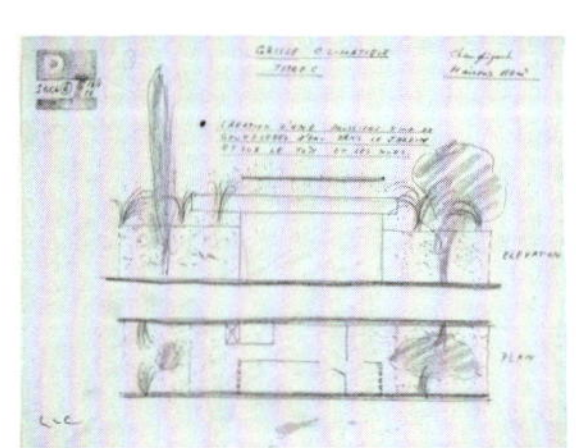

D
I 4, 5, 6 B / 18/1/52

CLIMATE GRID TYPE C / Chandigarh / Houses 110 m²

• CREATION OF A FINE DUST OF WATER DROPLETS IN THE GARDEN AND ON THE ROOF AND WALLS

L–C

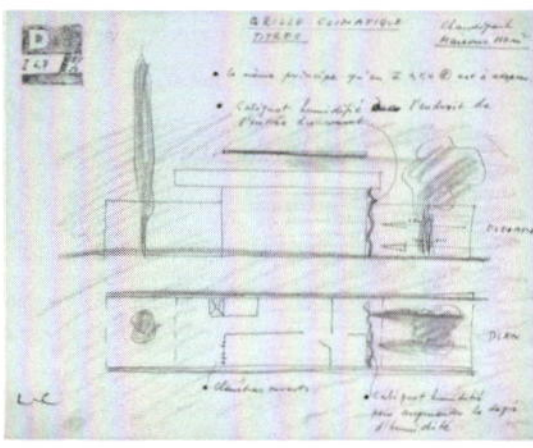

D
II 6, 7 / 18/1/52

CLIMATE GRID TYPE C / Chandigarh / Houses 110 m²

• the same principle is to be adopted as for I 4, 5, 6B

• damp calico at wind entry point

wind / wind / wind /wind

• screen walls open

• damp calico to increase the moisture level

L–C

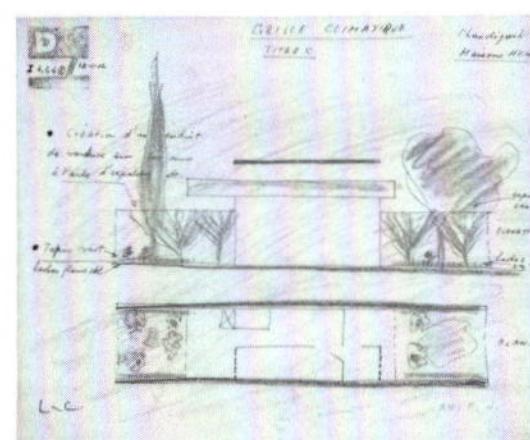

D
I 4, 5, 6 C / 18/1/52

CLIMATE GRID TYPE C / Chandigarh / Houses 110 m²

[LEFT]
• Creation of a coating of greenery on the walls with espaliers, etc.

• Green carpet herbs flowers, etc.

[RIGHT]
espaliers etc.

herbs flowers, etc.

L–C

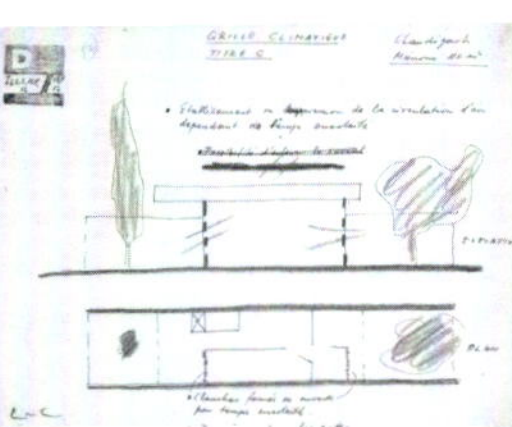

D
II 1, 2, 3, 10, 11, 12 / 18/1/52

CLIMATE GRID TYPE C / Chandigarh / Houses 110 m²

• Activation or deactivation of air circulation depending on sunlight Possibility of removing the sunshade

• Screen walls open or closed in sunny weather

• Same for the doors
L–C

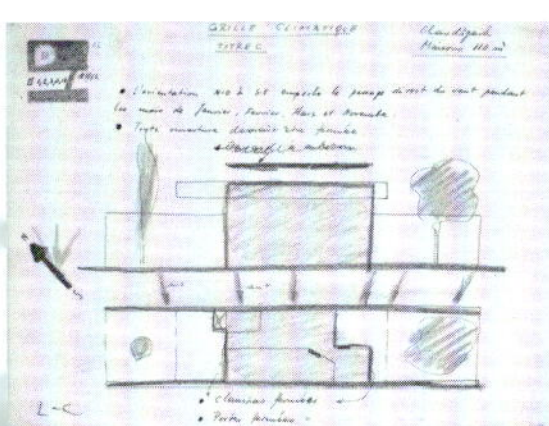

D
III 1, 2, 3, 11, 12 / 18/1/52

CLIMATE GRID TYPE C /
Chandigarh / Houses 110 m^2

• NW-SE aspect stops wind passage during the months of January, February, March, and November

• All openings should be closed
~~Sunshade to be removed~~

wind / wind

• Screen walls closed

• Doors closed

L–C

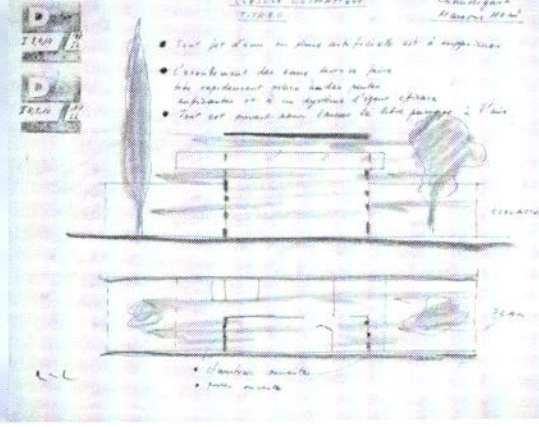

D
I 8, 9, 10 / 18/1/52

D
II 8, 9, 10 / 18/1/52

CLIMATE GRID TYPE C /
Chandigarh / Houses 110 m^2

• All fountains and artificial rain are to be done away with

• Water run-off should happen very quickly via adequate sloping and an efficient drainage system

• Everything is open to allow free air flow

• Screen walls open
• Doors open

L–C

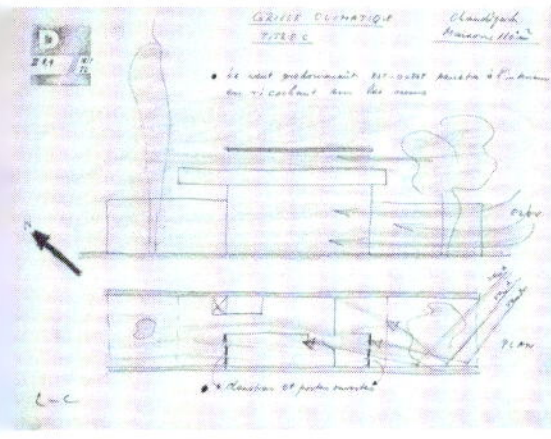

D
III 8, 9 / 18/1/52

CLIMATE GRID TYPE C /
Chandigarh / Houses 110 m^2

• The prevailing EAST-WEST wind reaches the interior by being deflected by the walls

wind / wind / wind

• Screen walls and doors open

L–C

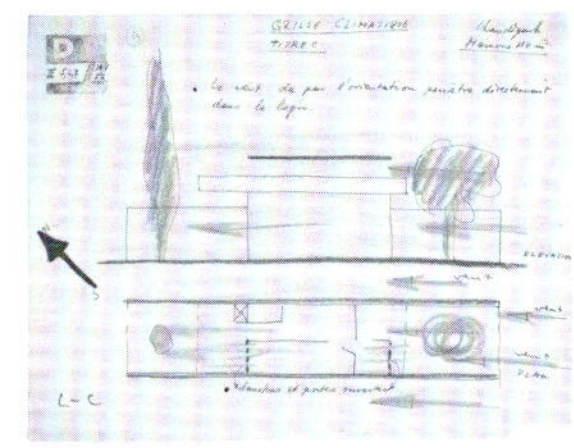

D
III 5, 6, 7 / 18/1/52

CLIMATE GRID TYPE C /
Chandigarh / Houses 110 m^2

• The aspect means the wind enters the building directly

wind / wind / wind

• Screen walls and open doors

L–C

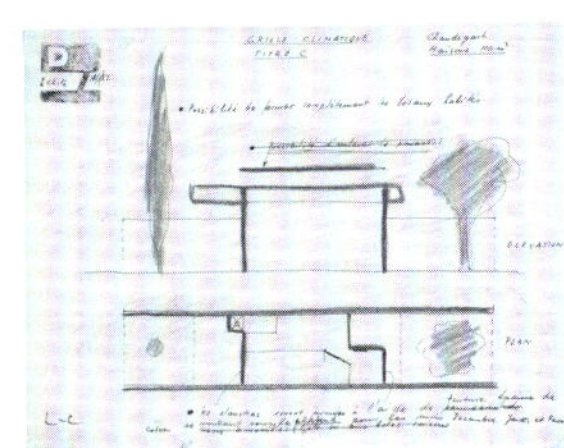

D
I 1, 2, 12 / 18/1/52

CLIMATE GRID TYPE C /
Chandigarh / Houses 110 m^2

• The residential premises can be closed off completely
~~The sunshade can be removed~~

• The screen walls are closed off with thick hanging of cotton fitting closely against the ceiling in December, Jan., and February
~~glass coverings detachable in summer or during good weather~~

L–C

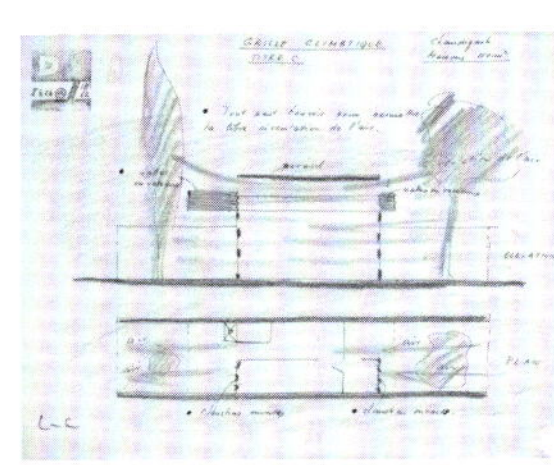

D
I 4, 5, 6a / 18/1/52

CLIMATE GRID TYPE C /
Chandigarh / Houses 110 m^2

• Everything can be opened to allow free air flow

• mats or reeds / sunshade / air flow / mats or reeds

air / air

air / air

• screen walls open
• screen walls open

L–C

D
IV 4, 5, 6, 7, 10 B / 18/1/52

CLIMATE GRID TYPE C /
Chandigarh / Houses 110 m^2

• The sunshade and the awning increase shade areas

sun / sunshade

L–C

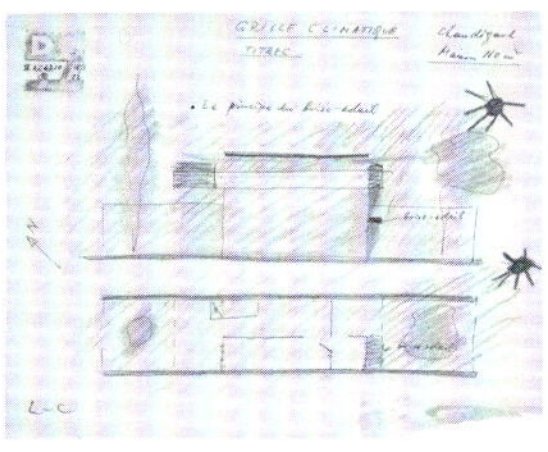

D
IV 4, 5, 6, 7, 10 B / 18/1/52

CLIMATE GRID TYPE C /
Chandigarh / Houses 110 m^2

• The sunshade principle

sunshade
sunshade

L–C

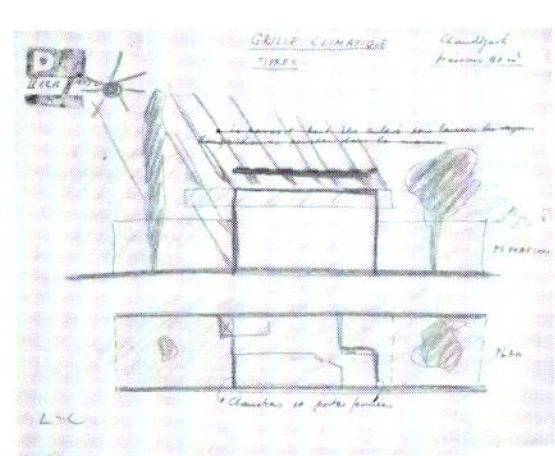

D
IV 1, 2, 12 / 18/1/52

CLIMATE GRID TYPE C /
Chandigarh / Houses 110 m^2

~~The sunshade can be removed to let the warm rays of the sun into the house~~

Screen walls and doors closed

L–C

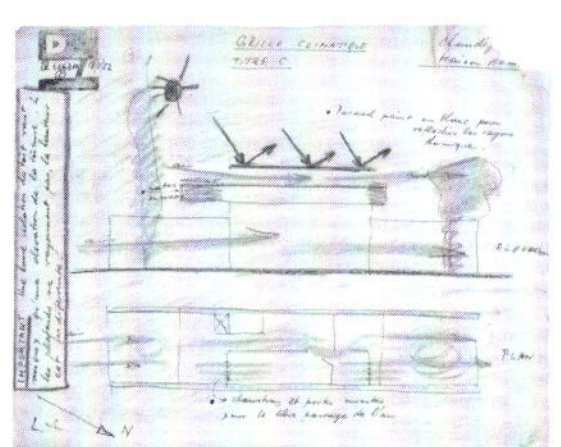

D
IV 4, 5, 6, 7, 10 C / 18/1/52

CLIMATE GRID TYPE C /
Chandigarh / Houses 110 m^2

• Sunshade painted white to reflect the sun's rays

air

• mats or reeds

air
air

• Screen walls and doors open to let air flow freely

L–C

[LEFT MARGIN]
IMPORTANT: Good roof insulation is better than a raised roof. If the ceilings are not radiating heat, their height makes no difference.

—P. 518

Minnette de Silva to Le Corbusier, December 1955

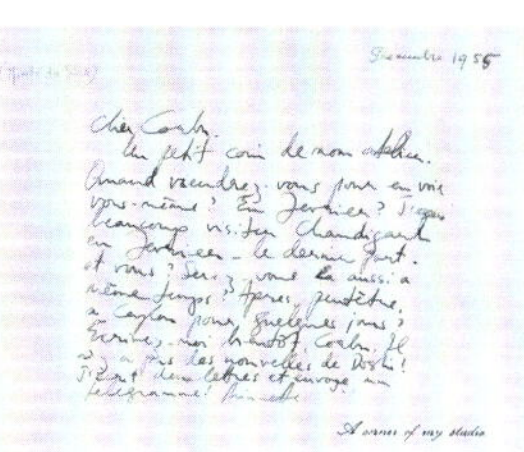

December 1955

Dear Corbu.

A little corner of my studio.

When will you come see it yourself? In February? I very much hope to visit Chandigarh in February—the latter part—and you? Will you be there at the same time? Afterward, maybe, Ceylon for a few days? Write me soon, Corbu. There is no news from Doshi! I wrote two letters and sent a telegram! Minnette

—P. 518

First page of letter from Minnette de Silva to Le Corbusier, 26 November 1956

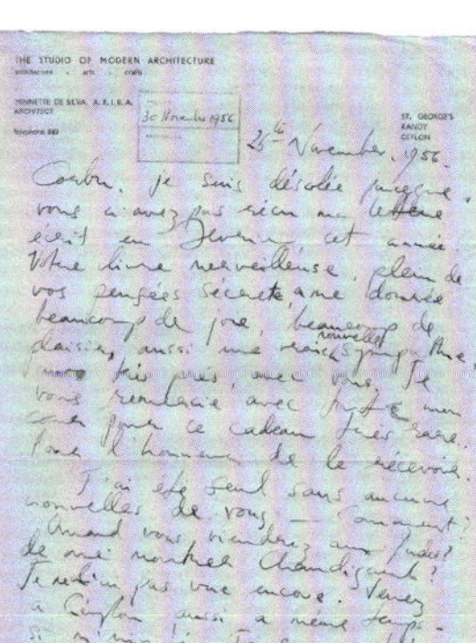

26 November 1956

Corbu, I'm so sorry you didn't get the letter I wrote you in February, this year.
Your marvelous book, full of your private thoughts, gave me much joy, much pleasure, and also a true, new sympathy, very close, with you. I thank you with all my heart for this very rare gift. For the honor of receiving it.

I was alone with no news of you—How? When will you come to India? to show me Chandigarh? I haven't seen it yet. Come to Ceylon, too, at the same time. If you invite me I will be able to very […]

—P. 524

Detail of plan, Villa Sarabhai, Ahmedabad, 2 February 1955

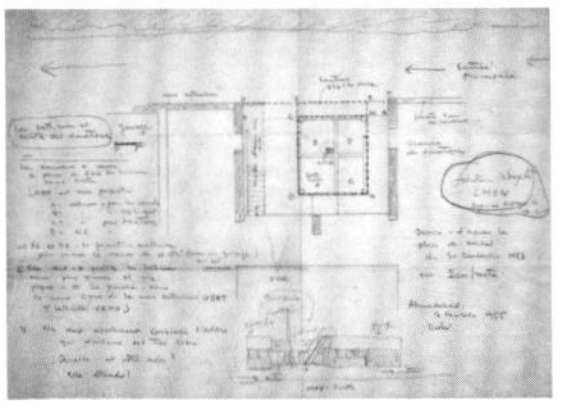

[LEFT]
Servants' bathroom and toilets / garage / ~~garage~~

Mrs. Manorama needs 4 rooms at least 4' x 4' for toilets
LMNO is my proposal
A = bathroom for the dishes
B = [bathroom] for the laundry
C = [bathroom] for servants
D = WC [for servants]
and PL and MR—Proposal for closing off the house on this side (with mesh fence which is necessary)

1) She wants—if possible the bathrooms even bigger and she suggests—including them—in the same line as the outside wall USRT (bathroom—SRNO)

2) She absolutely wants to keep the tree which in fact is very beautiful
What do you think?
She's waiting!

[TOP SKETCH]
outside wall / height 226 + the slab

stairs to the roof

tree / bathroom

[BOTTOM SKETCH]
view

kitchen

servants / kitchen / garage

entry / entry

LMXY—Toilet

[RIGHT]
main entry

window halfway up

servants' bedroom

solution adopted LMON reply sent 14.2.55

Drawing from Michel's plan of 30 December 1953
scale. 2 cm / meter

Ahmedabad
2 February 1955
Doshi

—P. 524

Le Corbusier to Manorama Sarabhai, 1 May 1956

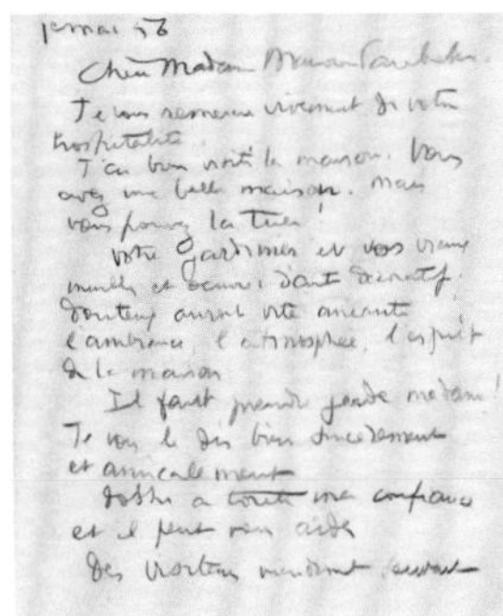

1 May 56

Dear Mrs. Manorama Sarabhai,

Thank you so much for your hospitality.
I have been to see the house. You have a fine house, but you run the risk of killing it.

Your gardener, your old furnishings and dubiously decorative works of art will very quickly destroy its ambience, atmosphere and spirit.

You must take care! I say this as a matter of sincere friendship.

Doshi has all my confidence and he can help you

There will often be visitors [...]

—P. 537

Three-page proposal by Gautam Sarabhai, 23 March 1951, for a municipal museum for Ahmedabad

23 March 1951

Proposal for the Municipal Museum, Ahmedabad by Shri Gautam Sarabhai

The Municipal Council is to be congratulated for finally having been able to draw up the project for a Museum in Ahmedabad and having succeeded in finding 1,500,000 rupees for the building.

In this city it is not enough simply to have a place for housing and looking after objects of interest; also needed is a place that will become the city's cultural center. In this way, although it is the case that Museums can be useful for conserving and classifying artistic, literary, natural history, and scientific specimens, it is no less true that they can serve a purpose that is just as useful and certainly much more practical in people's lives. They can be a potent tool in a visual education program, especially in a place where so many are uneducated.

They can be home to countless subjects of interest and the ideal would be to have a museum for each subject—a museum of Fine Arts, Archaeology, Natural History, Industry—of Science—of Commerce, etc… —but this is not yet feasible owing to lack of funds. Consequently the sole alternative is to take items from all over and try to accumulate them in the modest museum our financial means allow for. However, scraps of information are useless if they are not coordinated. So it is preferable, initially, to restrict the scope of this Museum and begin modestly. It is better to have a few very comprehensive sections than many made of bits and pieces. New sections can then be added as financial capacities allow. For the present, then, the Museum will comprise the following sections:

I. SECTIONS

1. Regional archaeology (archaeology of Upper Gujarat). (Specimens not in danger of being damaged by the weather can be placed in the gardens.)
2. Indian art—Painting and Sculpture.

For the moment, resources being limited, the permanent collection will be gradually built up so as to show the characteristic works of the past. The contemporary arts will be illustrated by works on loan.

We shall perhaps call on Dr. Hermann Goetz for help in drawing up a detailed plan of this section.
3. Art in everyday life.

We shall be able to collect and display everyday objects whose shape, texture, color or design have a characteristic beauty.
4. Natural History

Putting together a large Natural History section is very costly and the idea has had to be shelved for the moment. However, there remains the possibility of organizing a small section for the city's schoolchildren, with stuffed specimens side by side with living animals and birds (such as deer, rabbits, parrots, etc.) and common local snakes. There could also be a small aquarium and terrarium. The intention would not be to set up a real zoo, but to give the public and children the pleasure of seeing live animals. Mr. H. G. Acharya could perhaps be induced to make a plan for this section.
5. Indian Anthropology

This section would illustrate the ways of life, crafts, and customs of the native peoples of India. No such section exists in any other Indian museum.
6. A small section dealing with the history of India and the natural resources of Gujarat, with the help of paintings and engravings.
7. An interesting library would be adjacent to the Museum. It could be home to books, photographs, photographic plates, films, and disks.
II. AUTHORIZED EXPENSES

Rs. 4.12.500 for the building
Rs. 4.12.500 for electricity, fixtures and fittings, windowpanes, etc…
Rs. 50.000 for the library
Rs. 1.00.000 for the permanent collections of the sections mentioned above
Rs. 50.000 for laying out the terrain, including trees, cages for the animals and birds, etc…
Rs. 10.25.000 Total

III. PERSONNEL

The appointment of a Director will cost Rs. 800-50-1200. An advertisement could be placed in the main news- papers in Bombay, Delhi, Calcutta, and Madras. The Director will immediately be required to submit a detailed project, after which the rest of the personnel can be hired. A model for the advertisement to be placed in the main newspapers is attached.

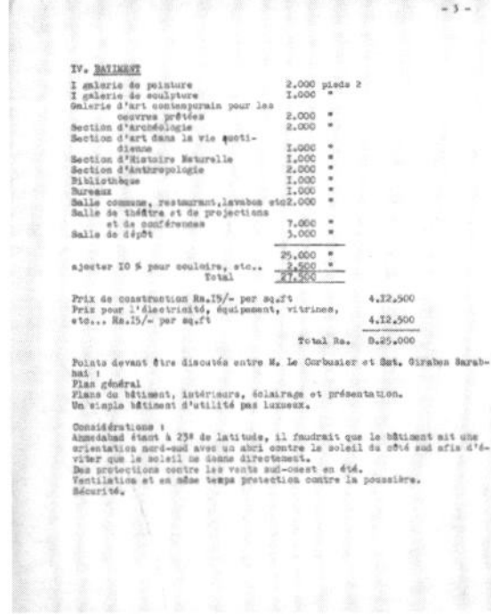

IV. BUILDING

I painting gallery / 2,000 sq. ft.
I sculpture gallery / 1,000 sq. ft.
Gallery of contemporary art for loaned works / 2,000 sq. ft.
Archaeology section / 2,000 sq. ft.
Art in daily life section / 1,000 sq. ft.
Natural History section / 1,000 sq. ft.
Anthropology section / 2,000 sq. ft.
Library / 1,000 sq. ft.
Offices / 1,000 sq. ft.
Public space, restaurant, washrooms, etc. / 2,000 sq. ft.

Theater, cinema, lecture theater / 7,000 sq. ft.
Reserves 3,000 sq. ft.
25,000 sq. ft.
add 10% for corridors, etc…
2,500 sq. ft.
Total 27,500 sq. ft.
Construction cost Rs. 15/- per sq. ft.
4.12.500
Cost of electricity, fittings, windowpanes, etc… / Rs. 15/- per sq. ft. / 4.12.500
Total Rs. / 8.25.000

Points to be discussed by Mr. Le Corbusier and Giraben Sarabhai:
Site plan
Plans of the building, interiors, lighting and presentation.
A simple, utilitarian, no-frills building.

Remarks:
Ahmedabad being at Latitude 23, th building will require a north-south aspect, with a shelter on the south side to avoid the sun striking it directly.
Protection against south and west winds in summer.
Ventilation combined with protection against dust.
Security.

—P. 537

Le Corbusier to Jawaharlal Nehru, 27 December 1954

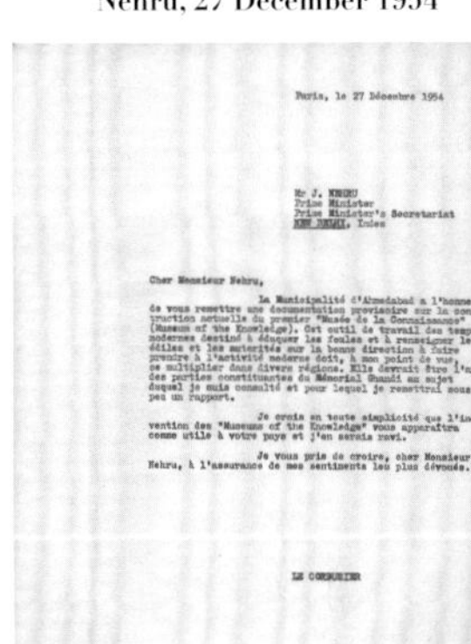

Paris, 27 December 1954

Mr. J. Nehru
Prime Minister
Prime Minister's Secretariat
NEW DELHI, India

Dear Mr. Nehru,

The Municipality of Ahmedabad ha the honor of submitting to you the provisional documentation on the current construction of the "Museu of the Knowledge." Intended to educate the general public and to infor the city fathers and the authorities on how to set modern activity on th right path, this museum is a moderr tool that should, in my view, exist in many different regions. It should be an integral part of the Gandhi

Memorial, for which I am consultant and regarding which I shall soon submit a report.

It is my honest opinion that the invention of the "Museums of the Knowledge" will seem to you useful for your country, and this would please me enormously.

Respectfully yours,

LE CORBUSIER

—P. 546

Sketch of the Bhakra Dam site, Nangal Township, India, 1955–58

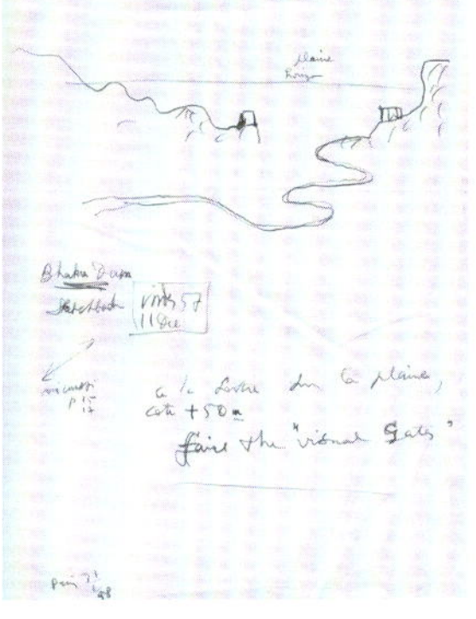

plain
horizon

Bhakra Dam
Sketchbook / India 57 11 Dec.

see also p. 15 p. 17

at the exit onto the plain,
dimension + 50 m
make the "visual Gates"

Paris 31/1/58

—P. 549

Le Corbusier to Talati, 10 December 1957

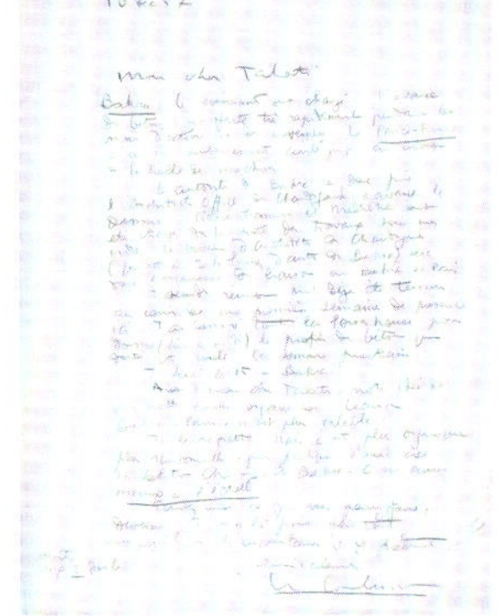

10 Dec. 57

My dear Talati.

Bhakra: Things have changed. The concrete went ahead very fast during October and November. The Powerhouse has had its basement poured up to the level of the machine room.

So the authority in Bhakra asked the Architects Office in Chandigarh to push ahead with the drawings. Pierre Jeanneret and Malhotra have been put in charge of the work to come under my orders. So the Architects Office in Chandigarh (which is 2 hours by car from Bhakra) will be the Bhakra-Paris liaison body.

2 big meetings have already been held during my first week here. I drew the entire Powerhouse so as to provide (at noon yesterday) the profiles for the concrete that is to be poured next week.

I'll be in Bhakra the 15th.

And so, my dear Talati, our idea of making you the Bhakra-Paris liaison body doesn't stand.

I'm sorry about this but it's more organic, more reasonable, and more practical to have set up the Chandigarh Bhakra solution. It's also better in terms of scale.

Write and tell me what you intend to do. I'm here to do all I can if circumstances allow.

Yours,

Le Corbusier

[LEFT]
Best wishes to the 2 Doshis

—P. 551

Article from *Le Journal du Dimanche* (France), 7 December 1958

Avant de quitter ce soir l'Inde pour le Japon

André Malraux a visité Chandighar

(la capitale la plus moderne du monde)

en compagnie de Le Corbusier

(De notre envoyé spécial Serge MAFFERT.)

NEW-DELHI, 7 décembre (par câble).

M. ANDRE MALRAUX quitte ce soir l'Inde pour Tokio. Il dèvait avoir hier soir un dernier entretien avec le président Nehru, au cours d'un dîner offert par l'ambassadeur de France, M. Ostrorog.

Le ministre délégué à la présidence du Conseil avait consacré la fin de la semaine à visiter l'Inde de demain — et même d'après-demain. Il s'est rendu vendredi à 200 kilomètres au nord de Delhi, à Chandigahr, capitale de l'Etat du Pendjab, construite de toutes pièces par le célèbre architecte franco-suisse Le Corbusier.

L'expédition ministérielle était partie la veille au soir par un de ces extraordinaires trains indiens sortis tout droit des livres de Kipling. Locomotive de type Far-West, wagons de bois où chacun est censé apporter son **bedding** (matériel de literie),

Après la matinée consacrée à la visite du barrage géant de Bhakra, symbole de la volonté d'industrialisation de l'Inde, André Malraux et sa suite partirent par la route pour Chandighar.

Une ville entièrcment artificielle

Chandighar est la nouvelle capitale de l'Etat indien du Pendjab (30 millions d'habitants). Commencée il y a huit ans, cette ville entièrement artificielle, irréelle, prodigieuse par son étendue, sera peut-être terminée un jour. Elle constitue l'expérience la plus audacieuse d'urbanisme jamais tentée. En compagnie de Le Corbusier, André Malraux visita le cadre existant de cette capitale, dont les lignes, les formes et la conception générale sont très éloignées de l'Inde traditionnelle et probablement de toute véritable humanité.

Before leaving India for Japan this evening André Malraux visited Chandigarh (the world's most modern capital) with Le Corbusier (By our special correspondent Serge MAFFERT.)
NEW DELHI, 7 December (by wire)

Mr. ANDRE MALRAUX leaves India for Tokyo this evening. Last night he was supposed to have a final meeting with President Nehru, during a dinner offered by the French ambassador, Mr. Ostrorog.

The minister assigned to the presidency of the cabinet dedicated the end of the week to visiting the India of tomorrow—and even the day after tomorrow. On Friday, he traveled 200 kilometers north of Delhi, to Chandigarh, capital of Punjab State, built from the ground up by the famous Franco-Swiss architect Le Corbusier.

The ministerial expedition had left the evening before, on one of those extraordinary Indian trains straight out of the books of Kipling. Far West–type locomotives and wooden cars where everyone is supposed to bring their own bedding.

After spending the morning visiting the giant Bhakra Dam, a symbol of India's drive to industrialization, André Malraux and his entourage took the road for Chandigarh.

An entirely artificial city

Chandigarh is the new capital of the Indian state of Punjab (30 million inhabitants). Begun eight years ago, this entirely artificial, unreal, spectacularly vast city will perhaps someday be finished. It constitutes the boldest experiment in urban planning ever attempted. With Le Corbusier, André Malraux visited the existing skeleton of this capital, whose lines, shapes, and overall conception are very far from those of traditional India and probably from all genuine humanity.

The Sacred and the Sublime (1950–1959)

—P. 558

Cost estimates for contruction of Notre-Dame-du-Haut, November 1950

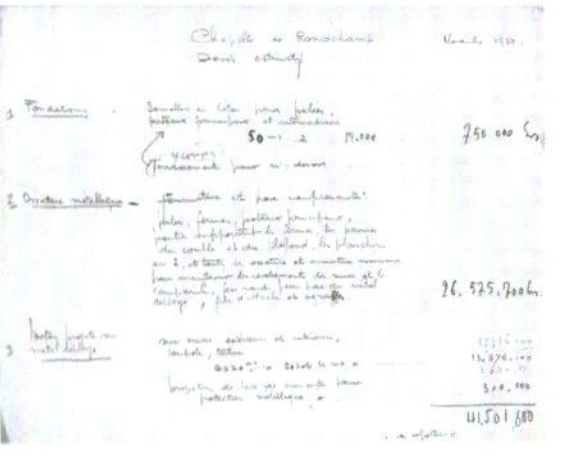

Chapel at Ronchamp / November 1950
Estimate

1 Foundations
Concrete footings for landings main and intermediate posts including Earthmoving for above
50 m³ at 19,000 / 750,000 frs

2 Metal frame / Supply and installation including: landings, iron components, main posts, beams supporting the iron components, the vaults of the roof space and ceiling, the floor panels, and all the frames and armatures needed for fixing the wall coverings and the bell tower, round rods for fixing the expanded metal, fixing wire, and staples / 26,575,700 frs.

3 Concrete sprayed on expanded metal on exterior and interior walls, domes, roof / 15,216,100
6,020 m² at 2,305 per m² / 13,876,100
milk of cement sprayed for metal protection / 1,640,000 / 300,000
carried over = 41,501,800

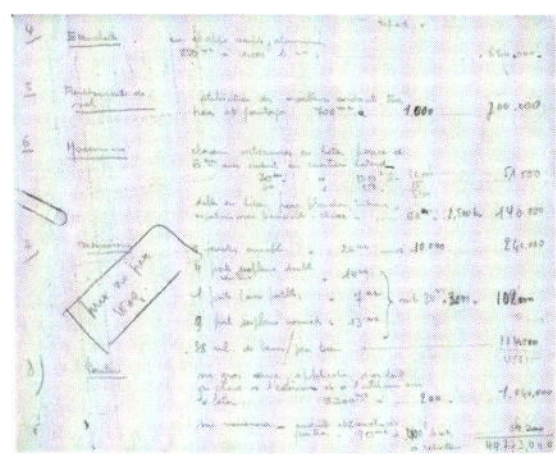

4 Waterproofing
flexible screed, aluminum
850 m² at 1,000 per m² / 850,000

5 Flooring
use of existing rubble stone, sorted laid and pointed / 700 m² at 1,000 / 700,000

6 Masonry
6 cm sanded concrete interior walls with lime-and-cement mortar
30 m² at 1,200 per 36,000 / 51,000
60 m² at 250 / 15
concrete slabs for gallery floors, stairs with gangways, pulpits
56 m² at 2,500 frs. / 140,000

7 Woodwork
price checked by Wog.
5 opening windows = 24 m² / 10,000 / 24,000
4 double leaf isoplane doors = 14 m²
1 door (stable-type) = 7 m²
9 normal isoplane doors = 13 m²
total 34 m² at 3,000 = 102,000
38 linear meters of benches / good price / 114,000

8 Painting
on framework, application of lime wash on the concrete indoors and outdoors / 5,200 m² at 200 / 1,040,000

on woodwork—and 2 layers for windows—90 m at 400 per m² / 34,200
carried over 44,773,000

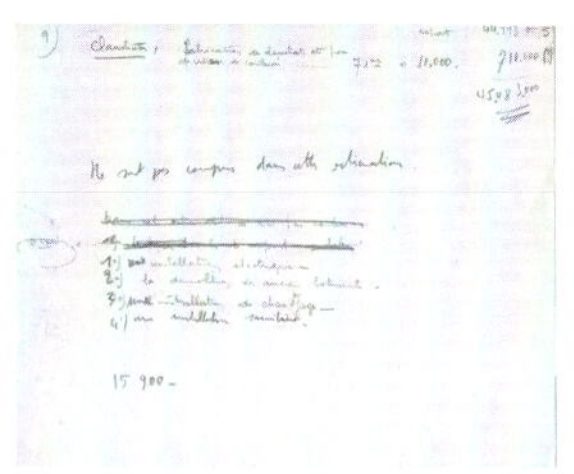

9 Screen walls
Making of screen walls and fitting of colored windows / 71 m² at 10,000 / 710,000 (?)
45,483,000

Not included in this estimate

~~in this estimate are not included~~
remaining ~~1°)~~ ~~windows all the~~

1°) electrical system
2°) demolition of old buildings
3°) heating system
4°) toilets

15,900

—P. 558

Agreement between Le Corbusier and the development corporation for Notre-Dame-du-Haut, Ronchamp

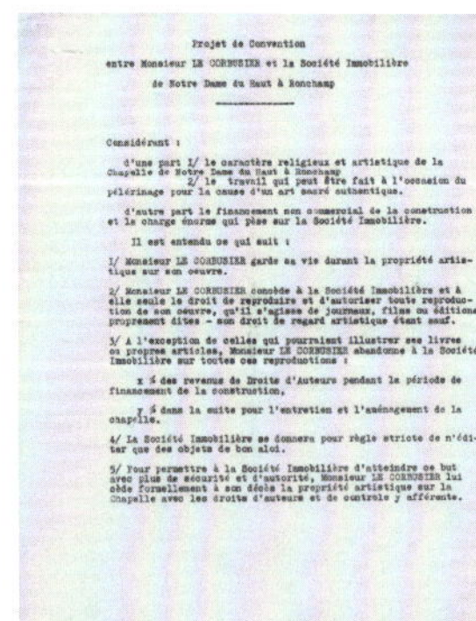

Agreement between Mr. LE CORBUSIER and the development corporation of Notre-Dame-du-Haut in Ronchamp
Considering:

on the one hand
1/ the religious and artistic character of the Chapel of Notre-Dame-du-Haut in Ronchamp

2/ the work that can be done on the occasion of the pilgrimage in the cause of an authentically religious art.

on the other hand the non-commercial financing of the construction and the enormous expense that is burdening the Development Corporation.

The following is agreed:
1/ Mr. LE CORBUSIER retains the artistic copyright to his work during his lifetime.
2/ Mr. LE CORBUSIER grants the Development Corporation and it alone the right to reproduce and to authorize any reproduction of his work, whether in the press, films, or actual publications—without compromising his artistic control.
3/ With the exception of those that could illustrate his books or his own articles, Mr. LE CORBUSIER relinquishes to the Development Corporation on all such reproductions:

x% of revenues from royalties during the financing period of construction,

y% afterward to maintain and decorate the chapel
4/ The Development Corporation will bind itself strictly to publishing only high-quality objects.
5/ So that the Development Corporation may achieve this goal more securely and with more authority, Mr. LE CORBUSIER expressly cedes, at his death, the artistic copyright to the Chapel with the royalties and control pertaining thereto.

—P. 560

Le Corbusier to Father Bourdin, parish priest of Notre-Dame- du-Haut, Ronchamp, 17 October 1951

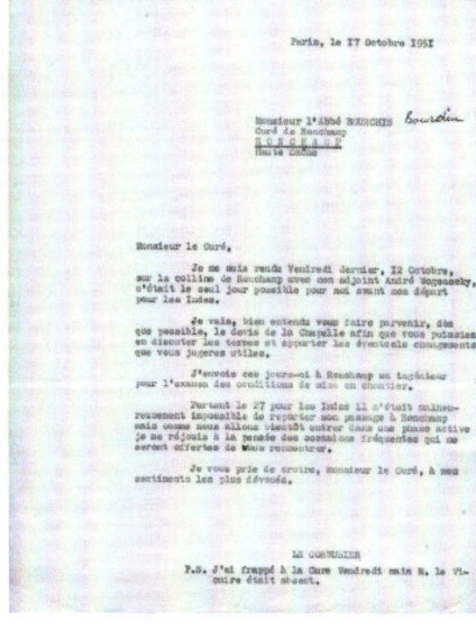

Paris, 17 October 1951

Father BOURCHIS *Bourdin*
Parish priest of Ronchamp
RONCHAMP
Haute Saône

Father,

On last Friday, 12 October, I went to the hill at Ronchamp with my assistant André Wogensky; this was the only day possible for me before leaving for India.

Naturally I will make sure you receive, as soon as possible, the estimate for the Chapel, so that you can discuss the content and make any changes you find necessary.

In the next few days I shall be sending an engineer to Ronchamp to look into the business of getting the building work under way.

As I am leaving for India on the 27th, it was unfortunately impossible for me to change the date of my visit to Ronchamp, but as we will soon be moving into an active phase, I am delighted at the thought of the many opportunities we will have to meet each other.

Respectfully yours,

LE CORBUSIER

P.S. I knocked at the Father's door on Friday, but he was out.

—P. 560

Front and back of an unsigned note, 23 January 1952

Ronchamp ce 21 Janvier 1952
Monsieur l'Architecte 23/1/52
Vous voudrez bien excuser cette simple carte (je suis seul en ce moment) destinée à vous accuser réception de votre bonne lettre du 17 Oct.
Je vous avertis que la démolition de la chapelle actuelle se fera par nos soins et nous pourrons, d'après vos prescriptions, faire le pavage en pierre de récupération.

Ronchamp this 21 January 1952
23/1/52

Mr. Architect

Please excuse this simple card (I am alone at the moment) intended to acknowledge receipt of your nice letter of the 17th Oct.

I am advising you that we will be seeing to the demolition of the present chapel, and we will be able to, according to your instructions, do the paving with salvaged stones.

Je vous demande de prévoir le permis de construire, démarche qui est de votre ressort s'il vous plaît.
Il faut aussi descendre le prix total de votre chapelle à 40 000 000 ou à peu près en réduisant les proportions sans nuire à l'harmonie de l'édifice. 250 places suffiront largement. Prévoir également une protection parfaitement étanche pour la statue en hiver.
Quelle somme nous sera demandée en acompte?
Enfin je voudrais avoir une dizaine de grandes photos et une centaine de cartes postales de notre future chapelle.

I am requesting that you anticipate the construction permit, a step that is within your purview, please.

Also, the total cost of your heating apparatus must come down to 40,000,000 or thereabouts, by reducing the proportions without harming the building's harmony. 250 seats are more than enough. In addition, include water- tight protection for the statue in winter.

How much will they ask us for on account?

Finally, I'd like ten or so large photos and a hundred or so postcards of our future chapel.

[LEFT MARGIN]
I remain, Mr. Architect, yours sincerely.

—P. 560

Le Corbusier to Father Bourdin, 17 January 1952

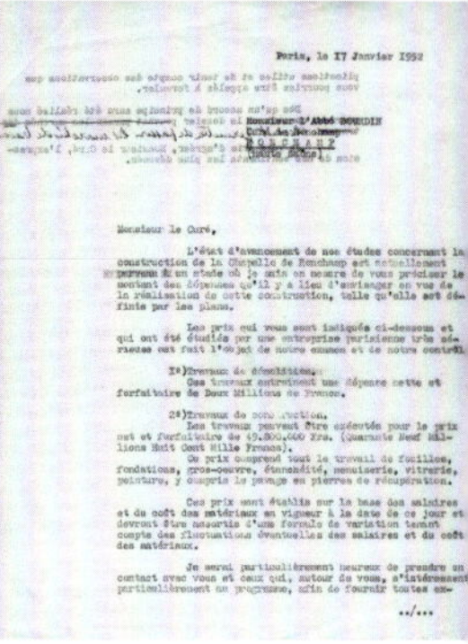

Paris, 17 January 1952

Father BOURDIN
Parish priest of Ronchamp
RONCHAMP
(Haute Saône)

Father,

Our studies regarding the building of the Ronchamp Chapel have now reached the stage where I can give you the anticipated cost of carrying out construction as laid down in the plans.

The prices indicated below have been calculated by a highly competent Paris company and we have examined and checked them.

1. Demolition works
These works will entail a lump sum of two million francs.

2. Construction works
The works can be carried out for a lump sum of 49,800,000 Francs (forty-nine million eight hundred thousand francs).

This includes all excavation, foundations, framework, waterproofing, carpentry, glazing, painting, and paving with salvaged stone.

The prices are based on the current cost of labor and materials and will be accompanied by a variation provision making allowance for any fluctuations that may occur in wages and the cost of materials.

I will be especially pleased to meet with you and the other people taking a close interest in this project so as to provide all necessary explanations and take account of any observations you may wish to make.

As soon as an agreement in principle has been reached, we shall be able to draw up the documents allowing us to call for bids:

Respectfully yours,

LE CORBUSIER

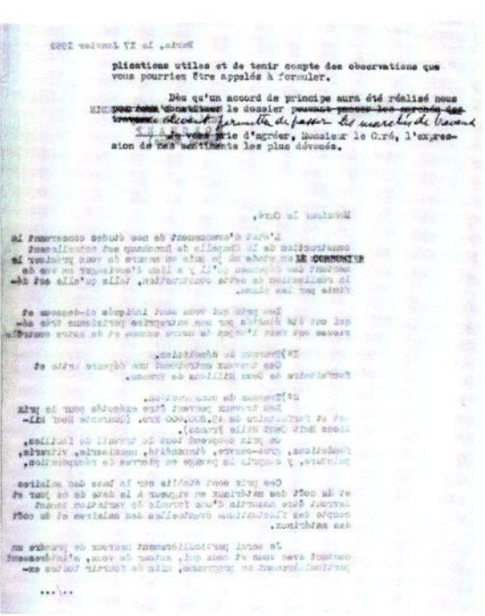

—P. 561

Le Corbusier to Father Bourdin, 31 July 1952

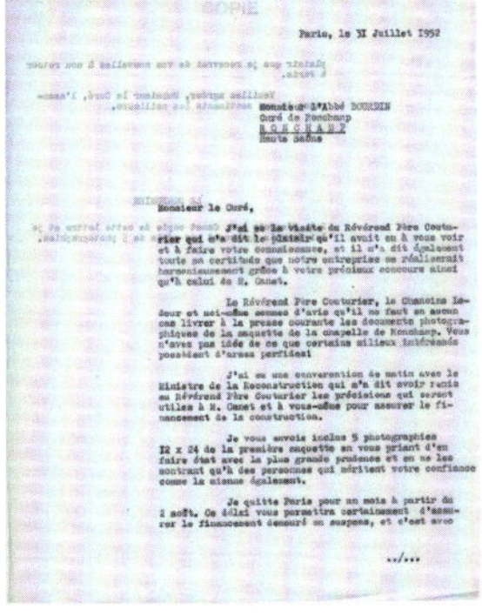

Paris, 31 July 1952

Father BOURDIN
Parish priest of Ronchamp
RONCHAMP
(Haute Saône)

Father,

I had a visit from Reverend Father Couturier who told me how pleased he was to see you and get to know you, and he also said he was certain that our venture would be carried through with no dissension thanks to your invaluable help and that of Mr. Canet.

Reverend Father Couturier, Canon Ledeur and myself agree that under no circumstances should the press be given photographs of the model of the Ronchamp Chapel. You have no idea of how treacherous and dangerous certain self-interested circles can be!

I spoke this morning with the Minister for Reconstruction, who said he had received from Reverend Father Couturier the information Mr. Canet and yourself need to ensure the financing of the construction.

I include with this letter five 12x24 photographs of the first model, requesting that you mention them in the most prudent terms and show them only to people worthy of your trust and mine.

I am leaving Paris for a month on 2 August. This will certainly leave you time to obtain the remaining finance and I

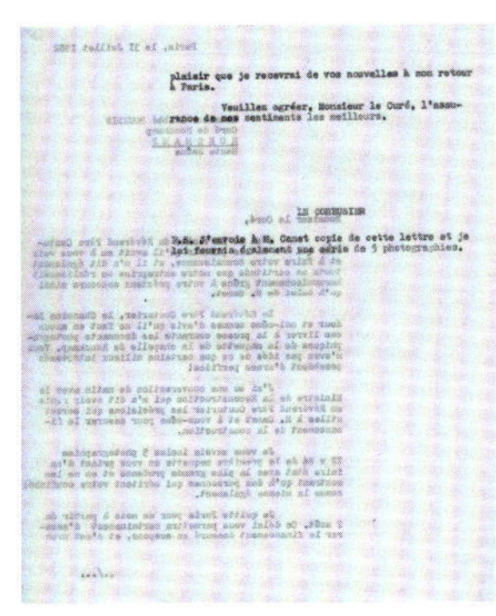

look forward with pleasure to hearing from you on my return to Paris.

Respectfully yours,

LE CORBUSIER

P. S. I am sending Mr. Canet a copy of this letter and also providing him with a set of 5 photographs.

—P. 566

Transverse sections of Notre-Dame-du-Haut, Ronchamp, 20 October 1953

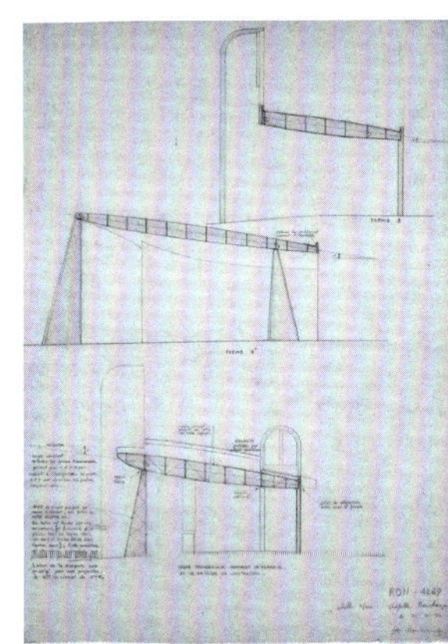

[TOP DRAWING]
TRUSS 3

scale drawing of the coating cement + waterproofing

TRUSS 4'
[BOTTOM LEFT]
horizontal

constant angle for all transversal trusses, going through x and y and in relation to the horizontal—points x and y are in the middle of the longitudinal beams

4 cm 5 of cement sprayed with cementgunonexpandedmetallaths0,4—

The battening is stretched on an armature [round rods Ø set every 120 cm in one direction and every 120 cm in the other]—This armature is itself attached to posts and metal trusses

The steel of the frame will be protected by a sprayed layer of milk of cement 0.5 cm

[BOTTOM DRAWING]
perpendicular support

shell, cement sprayed onto expanded metal battening

waterproofing protected by aluminum film

hinged support

[to be decided according to spans]

TRANSVERSE SECTION
SHOWING TRUSS C AND THE PRINCIPLE OF CONSTRUCTION

[BOTTOM RIGHT]
RON 4269
scale 1/100
Ronchamp Chapel
20—10—53
A. Maisonnier

—P. 582

Notebook studies for the window openings in the south wall of Notre-Dame-du-Haut, Ronchamp

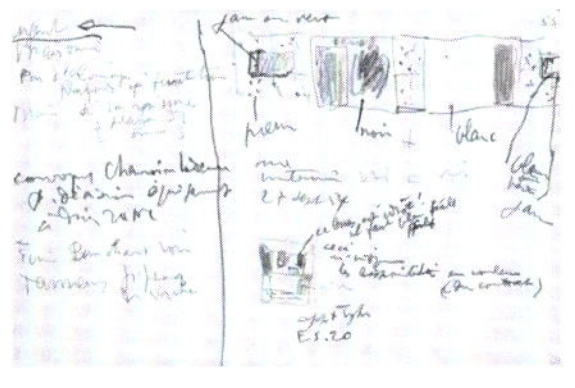

[LEFT]
Urgent

Maisonnier
No lighting ceiling that'd make hole
But at the groove ceiling wall
Call in Canon Ledeur for fittings decisions
to dinner 24 NC

Write Bauchant see Tanners for cowhides

[RIGHT]
yellow or green
stone / black / white
blue or green yellow
[?]

[LEFT]
copper A
cement A
cement A'
and mastic strip stars

[RIGHT]
painted blue oxide
clear ice with black (cooking)

clear

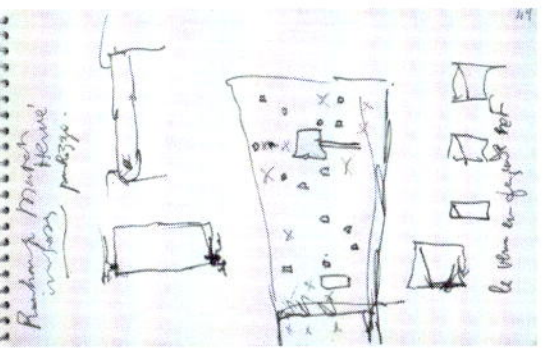

Ronchamp Match insist on Hervé for Rizzo

glass on ext[erior] facade

—P. 582

Interior elevation of the south wall of Notre-Dame-du-Haut, Ronchamp

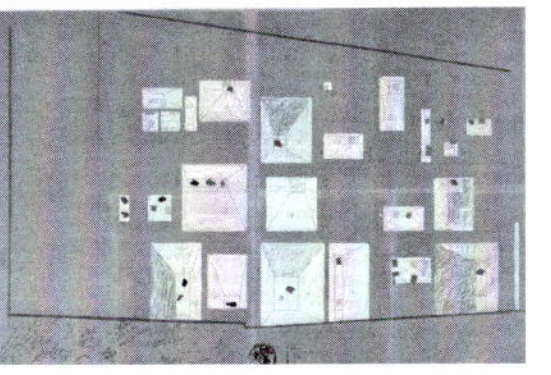

[TOP RIGHT]
INTERIOR
ELEVATION
SOUTH FAÇADE
RON[champ] Chapel

[BOTTOM]
Father Ledeur order a friend of Jean Prouvé-Luc Perrot who has melted glass from the glass works at St Just s/Loire (= St Gobain)
they are very keen to help

can pour shaped slabs

Document for Modulor 2
16 April 54

Christ Symbol

beautiful as the moon

Star of the sea

Morning star

song of songs, book of wisdom

shining like the sun

mystical rose

ivory tower

house of gold

blue / white / yellow

—P. 587

Sigfried Giedion to the president of the chapel's building association, 29 June 1955

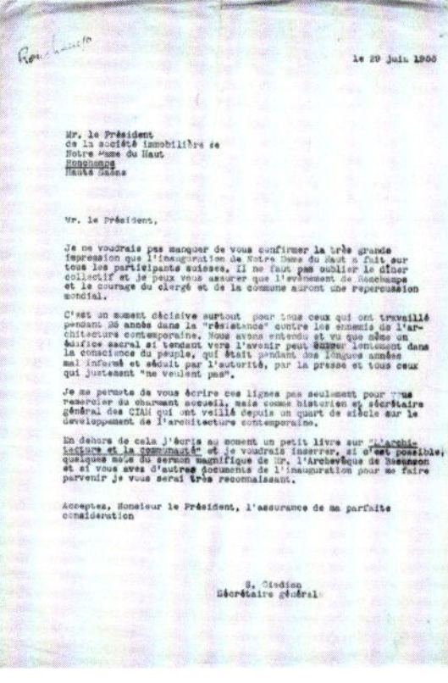

Ronchamp
29 June 1955

The President
of the building association of
Notre Dame du Haut
Ronchamp
Haute-Saône

Mr. President,

I wish to reaffirm the very great impression the inauguration of Notre Dame du Haut made upon all the Swiss participants. This includes the group dinner and I can assure you that the Ronchamp event and the courage of the clergy and the parish will have a worldwide impact.

This is a decisive moment especially for all those who have worked for 25 years in the "resistance" against the enemies of contemporary architecture. We have heard and seen that even a sacred building that is so future- oriented can slowly enter the consciousness of the people, who had for long years been misinformed and led astray by the authorities, the press, and all those who just "don't want."

I take the liberty of writing these lines not only to thank you for the delightful reception, but as the historian and secretary general of the CIAMs, which for a quarter century have shepherded the development of modern architecture.

In addition I am at the moment writing a small book on "Architecture and Community" and would like to insert, if possible, a few words from the magnificent sermon by Msgr. the Archbishop of Besançon and if you have other documents from the inauguration to send me I would be very grateful.

Mr. President, please believe me to be your most sincerely,

S. Giedion
Secretary General

—P. 588

Front and back of card for "pilgrims," to Notre-Dame-du-Haut, Ronchamp

Thank you

Thanks to you the financing of this world-renowned Chapel will soon be completed.

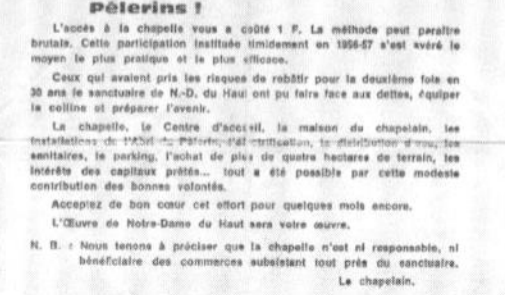
Pèlerins !

Pilgrims!

Admission to the chapel costs you 1 F[ranc]. This approach may seem churlish. This fee, timidly established in 1956–57, has proved to be the most practical and efficient method.

Those who took the risks to rebuild the sanctuary of N.-D. du Haut for the second time in 30 years were able to settle their debts, build on the hill, and prepare the future.

The chapel, Visitors' Center, chaplain's house, fittings for the Pilgrims' Shelter, electrification, water supply, plumbing, the parking lot, purchase of more than four hectares of land, interest on the loans … everything has been made possible by this modest goodwill contribution.

Accept this effort with an open heart for a few more months.

The Achievement of Notre-Dame du Haut will be your achievement.

N.B.: We wish to make it clear that the chapel is neither responsible for nor profits from the businesses around the sanctuary.

The chaplain.

—P. 588

Clipping from *Ouest France* (Rennes), 4 December 1956

Les conférences des « Amis de l'Art »
L'APPORT DE LE CORBUSIER DANS L'ART SACRÉ
par le R. P. COCAGNAC
directeur de la revue de l'« Art Sacré »

Le Corbusier vu par Len.

The "Friends of Art" Lectures
THE CONTRIBUTION OF LE CORBUSIER TO SACRED ART
by the Rev[erend] F[ather] COCAGNAC
editor of "Art Sacré" magazine

It is a friendly conversation more than a lecture, says the R[everend] F[ather] Cocagnac, who specifies, my job being to concern myself with the religious art that interests me, I leave to others the task of talking about his contribution to architecture.

But speaking of religious art means emphasizing the decadence that, beginning in the last century, particularly affected this category of expression: the pernicious influence of an exhausted academicism, false intellectualism, the invasion of the temple by the merchants and finally of all those who brought a gimcrack that satisfied the clergy and the faithful. And to top it all off, "the dismal farce called Saint-Sulpice."

Architecture called upon all the stylish minds: false [text missing] pilgrimage in the church at Ronchamp, Le Corbusier's bold endeavor.

To revive religious art, the R[everend] F[ather] Cocagnac concluded, we need men of "good will," who, along with genuine talent, have the humility that is the complement of competence.

To judge by the public buildings raised since the war, we are not, alas, there yet.
LEN

[CAPTION]
Le Corbusier seen by Len

—P. 588

Ministry of Mail and Telecommunications to Le Corbusier, 17 December 1963

RÉPUBLIQUE FRANÇAISE
MINISTÈRE DES POSTES ET TÉLÉCOMMUNICATIONS
DIRECTION GÉNÉRALE DES POSTES

Paris, 17 DEC 1963

Mr. LE CORBUSIER
Architect
35 rue de Sèvres
PARIS 6th

Master,

Mr. MARETTE, Minister of Mail and Telecommunications, was taken by a request to dedicate a postal stamp to the Chapel of Notre-Dame du Haut at Ronchamp, designed and built by your efforts.

Mr. MARETTE is thinking of responding favorably to the request that was presented to him, but wishes first to obtain your agreement since it is understood that your name would appear on the stamp.

If this plan, as I hope, meets with your assent, I would therefore be very obliged if you would sign and return the attached authorization to me.

Please believe me to be, Dear Master, most sincerely yours,

For the Minister of Mail,
/The Director General of Mail,
Manager of Issues,

[signature]
VANET

—P. 588

Proprietor of the store Maison R. André to Le Corbusier, 9 June 1958

AU BON MARCHÉ
MAISON R. ANDRÉ
RONCHAMP (HTE-SAÔNE)

Mr. LE CORBUSIER
35 RUE DE SEVRES
PARIS

Sir,

I apologize for bothering you, but your Chapel attracts an enormous number of people, and, because we have no souvenirs to offer when visitors ask me for them, I permit myself to come ask if it would be agreeable to you to authorize me to have reproduced on little napkins, cloths, scarves a few printed images of your Chapel, to be chosen by you of course.

I dare hope that you will give me the chance to revive business in Ronchamp a little bit, which is dying more and more, and I thank you for it in advance.

In hopes of a favorable reply, I am, Sir, yours very truly,

[signature]

—P. 591

Layouts for Le Corbusier's book *Ronchamp*

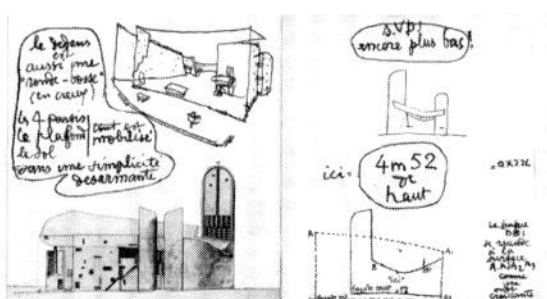

[LEFT PAGE]
the inside is also a "sculpture in the round" (in reverse)
the 4 walls / the ceiling / the floor / everything is brought together in disarming simplicity

[RIGHT PAGE]
PLEASE!
lower down still!

here = 4m 52 high = 2x226
Surface BB1 joins up with surface A.A1.A2.A3 like a growing wave

[LEFT PAGE]
Observe the play of the shadows
play the game …
Shade,—clear or blurred
Cast shadows: sharp
Cast shadows,—rigorous outline
but arabesque or cut-out so

[RIGHT]
spellbinding! Counterpoint and figure / Music
Great music!
Try to look at the images upside down, or give them a ¼ turn.
You'll discover the game!

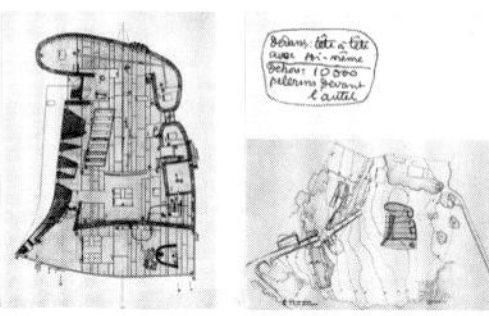

inside: alone
<u>with oneself</u>
Outside: 10,000
pilgrims before the altar

—P. 595

Le Corbusier to Pierre Matisse, 6 April 1957

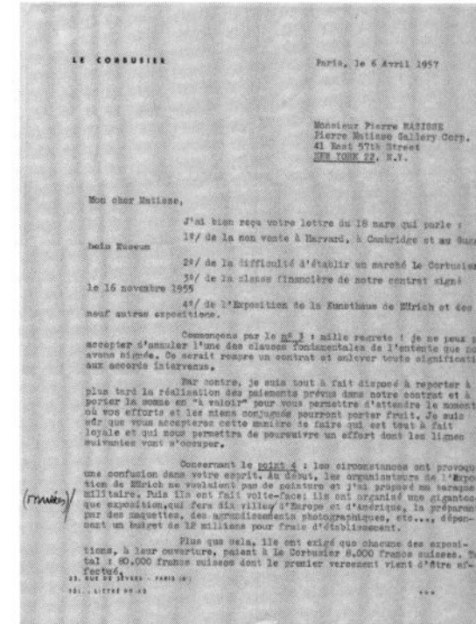
LE CORBUSIER
Paris, le 6 Avril 1957

Paris, 6 April 1957

Mr. Pierre MATISSE
Pierre Matisse Gallery Corp.
41 East 57th Street
<u>NEW YORK 22</u>, N.Y.

My dear Matisse,

Thank you for your letter of 18 March, which mentions:

1/ the non-sale at Harvard, Cambridge and the Guggenheim Museum

2/ the difficulty of setting up a Le Corbusier market

3/ the financial clause of our contract signed 16 November 1955

4/ the Exhibition at the Zurich Kunsthaus and the other nine exhibitions.

Let's begin with no. 3: I'm really sorry, but I cannot agree to the canceling of one of the basic clauses of the agreement we signed. This would be breach of contract and would make our subsequent agreements meaningless.

On the other hand, I am more than ready to postpone the payments provided for in our contract and to put them on hold against the time when your efforts and mine combined can bear fruit. I'm sure you'll accept this way of doing things which is completely fair and will allow us to continue with the effort the following lines will be devoted to.

Concerning point 4: the circumstances have gotten you confused. At the start the organizers of the Zurich Exhibition wanted no paintings and I suggested an army barracks. Then they changed their mind; they organized a gigantic exhibition, which will travel to ten cities/*museums* in Europe and America, and prepared it with models, blow-ups of photographs, etc… , spending 12 million in setting-up expenses.

On top of that, they demanded that each exhibition, when it opened, should pay Le Corbusier 8,000 Swiss francs. Total: 80,000 Swiss francs, of which the first payment has just been made.

And on top of that again, once the "setting-up expenses" for the ten exhibitions have been recovered, the profits from each exhibition will be paid to Le Corbusier.

So you can see that I no longer put up with always being considered as honored by those who want to work with me. There comes a time when he who shows his work honors he who puts it on show.

These ten exhibitions will take two to three years. The contract with the promoters stipulates that the pictures, tapestries, and sculptures can be replaced during the tour at the initiative of L-C. The agreement further stipulates that Le Corbusier has the right to check the accounting of the Swiss Banks Union in respect of the exhibitions.

So you see that a firm attitude has broken down the barriers and obstacles long raised against me.

This morning I had a letter from the organizers of the Zurich exhibition telling me that the committee was very disappointed by the quantity of pictures I had planned to show, which is to say those listed below:

6 Bulls / Matisse
1 Bull / 24 N.C.
1 Icon 3 / 24 N.C.
1 Icon 1 / Matisse
1 Embrazza / Cassou
1 Big Ubu / Cassou
1 Under a Shed / Cassou
1 T 20 Fig. Plates 1919 / Cassou
1 T 20 Fig. 1920 / Cassou
making 14 in all.

These gentlemen go on to say: "In our conversations in Paris it was always a question of some thirty pictures (taking the different periods into account). 14 would seem to be absolutely too low a number for an exhibition that ought to give an all-round impression of your work. So I ask that you look into the matter again and inform me of your decision. In addition, the number of sculptures is also very limited. In your 1955 program you included original drawings, sketches, and sketchbooks. It is planned that this material will be exhibited in closed vitrines.

Then there is the other matter, that of anti-Corbu obstructionism. This comes in two forms. There is the obstructionism of the architects, which has now been quashed.

And there is the second one, that of the Montparnasse artists, which went into action at the time of the Corbu exhibition at the Musée National d'Art Moderne in 1953. Here is the explanation: I went thirty years without exhibiting, 1923–53, with the exception of an exhibition at the Louis Carré gallery in 1938. The Occupation changed everything with regard to Carré. Almost all my paintings were in his gallery. When I returned to Paris in 1942, I learned that my pictures had migrated to my packer Robinot's premises. What had happened exactly? The threat from the Occupation at that time.

But when ten years later, in 1953, Cassou asked me to agree to an exhibition in his museum; there were signs of all-round displeasure among the artists. My own friends showed their ill-humor. The thirty years' silence had created a vacuum and Corbu's sudden appearance at the Musée d'Art Moderne then the creation of the permanent exhibition (strictly on Cassou's initiative and without my knowledge) caused what you can well imagine: terrible jealousy!

Another factor came into play: artists have always kept their distance from architecture and taken no interest in the vital phenomenon that gripped the modern world after the 1918 war. No one gave a damn about architects (and they thoroughly deserved it). But one day and unmistakably, in the case of Gropius for example, people realized that the architect was someone capable of understanding the arts, and being intimately involved in them. But in Montparnasse they remained cut off from architecture; they were against planned layout; they started demanding walls to paint on, but indulged in no contact with actual building and expected architects to turn out projects not paintings. The period before the storm is, for example, well illustrated by the purchase by the Museum of Modern Art in New York (Barr) of my seventh picture painted in 1920. When I arrived in New York for the first time in January 1946, I found the room with the Cézannes, Rousseaus, Bauchants, Braques, Gris, etc… then through a doorway to the "Demoiselles d'Avignon," the 1920 Corbu picture, Fernand Léger's "Le Grand Déjeuner" and, on the other side of the wall, Mondrian, Van Doesburg…

But around 1950 a Japanese magazine showed the waiting room of Zeckendorf's office on Madison Avenue where, in pride of place and very well positioned by Zeckendorf's Chinese architect, was the Corbu picture from the Museum of Modern Art in New York.

And little by little, in Paris, Montparnasse, and New York, where they followed the trend, a thorough-going vendetta started against Corbu the painter.

In 1954 there was a magnificent exhibition at the Kunsthalle

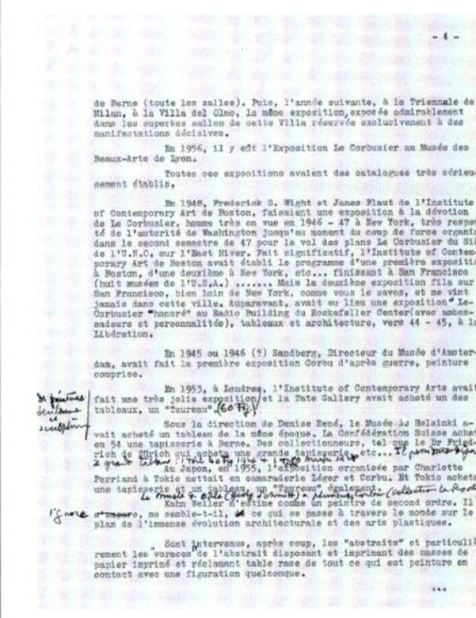

\- 4 -

de Berne (toute les salles). Puis, l'année suivante, à la Triennale de Milan, à la Villa del Olmo, la même exposition, exposée admirablement dans les superbes salles de cette Villa réservée exclusivement à des manifestations décisives.

En 1956, il y eût l'Exposition Le Corbusier au Musée des Beaux-Arts de Lyon.

Toutes ces expositions avaient des catalogues très sérieusement établis.

En 1948, Frederick S. Wight et James Plaut de l'Institute of Contemporary Art de Boston, faisaient une exposition à la dévotion de Le Corbusier, homme très en vue en 1946 - 47 à New York, très respecté de l'autorité de Washington jusqu'au moment du coup de force organisé dans le second semestre de 47 pour le vol des plans Le Corbusier du Siège de l'U.N.O. sur l'East River. Fait significatif, l'Institute of Contemporary Art de Boston avait établi le programme d'une première exposition à Boston, d'une deuxième à New York, etc… finissant à San Francisco (huit musées de l'U.S.A.) ……. Mais la deuxième exposition fila sur San Francisco, bien loin de New York, comme vous le savez, et ne vint jamais dans cette ville. Auparavant, avait eu lieu une exposition "Le Corbusier "honoré" au Radio Building du Rockefeller Center (avec ambassadeurs et personnalités), tableaux et architecture, vers 44 - 45, à la Libération.

En 1945 ou 1946 (?) Sandberg, Directeur du Musée d'Amsterdam, avait fait la première exposition Corbu d'après guerre, peinture comprise.

En 1953, à Londres, l'Institute of Contemporary Arts avait fait une très jolie exposition et la Tate Gallery avait acheté un des tableaux, un "Taureau".

Sous la direction de Denise René, le Musée de Helsinki avait acheté un tableau de la même époque. La Confédération Suisse acheta en 54 une tapisserie à Berne. Des collectionneurs, tel que le Dr Friedrich de Zürich qui acheta une grande tapisserie, etc…

Au Japon, en 1955, l'exposition organisée par Charlotte Perriand à Tokio mettait en camaraderie Léger et Corbu. Et Tokio acheta une tapisserie et un tableau, un "Taureau" également.

Kahn Weiller m'estime comme un peintre de second ordre. Il ~~s'empare~~ l'ignore, me semble-t-il, de ce qui se passe à travers le monde sur le plan de l'immense évolution architecturale et des arts plastiques.

Sont intervenus, après coup, les "abstraits" et particulièrement les "voraces" de l'abstrait disposant et imprimant des masses de papier imprimé et réclamant table rase de tout ce qui est peinture en contact avec une figuration quelconque.

…

in Bern (every room). Then the following year, at the Milan Triennale at the Villa del Olmo, the same exhibition, admirably displayed in the superb rooms of this Villa exclusively reserved for major events.

In 1956 there was the Le Corbusier exhibition in the Musée des Beaux- Arts in Lyon.

All these exhibitions had meticulously prepared catalogs.

In 1948 Frederick S. Wight and James Plaut of the Institute of Contemporary Art in Boston devoted an exhibition to Le Corbusier, a prominent figure in New York in 1946–47, highly respected by the authorities in Washington until the power play in the second half of 1947 with the theft of the Le Corbusier plans for the UN headquarters on the East River. Significantly, the Institute of Contemporary Art in Boston had drawn up the program for an initial exhibition in Boston, a second in New York, etc… finishing in San Francisco (eight American museums)… But the second exhibition took off for San Francisco, a long way from New York, as you know, and never reached that city. Beforehand there had been a "Tribute to Le Corbusier" exhibition at the Radio Building in the Rockefeller Center (with ambassadors and celebrities), paintings and architecture, around 1944–45, at the time of the Liberation.

In 1945 or 1946 (?) Sandberg, Director of the Amsterdam Museum, had organized the first postwar Corbu exhibition, including painting.

In 1953, in London, the Institute of Contemporary Arts had put on a very handsome exhibition (*only painting and sculpture*) and the Tate Gallery had bought one of the pictures, a "Bull."

Under the direction of Denise René, the Helsinki Museum had bought a painting from the same period. In 1954 the Swiss Confederation ~~bought~~ *buys* a tapestry in Bern. Collectors like Dr. Friedrich of Zurich who bought a big tapestry, etc… *He already has two big pictures: 1 canvas size F40 1926 + 1 size F80 seascape 1928*

In Japan in 1955, the exhibition organized by Charlotte Perriand in Tokyo put Léger and Corbu side by side. And Tokyo bought a tapestry and a painting, also a "Bull."

The museum in Basel (Georg Schmitt) has several Corbus (La Roche collection)

Kahnweiler considers me a second-rate painter. He ~~grabs~~ *is ignorant* of, it seems to me, what is happening around the world in terms of the enormous changes in architecture and the plastic arts.

Later on came the "abstracts" and in particular the "insatiables" of abstract art, who had masses of paper to print their demands for a clean slate regarding everything to do with any kind of figuration in painting.

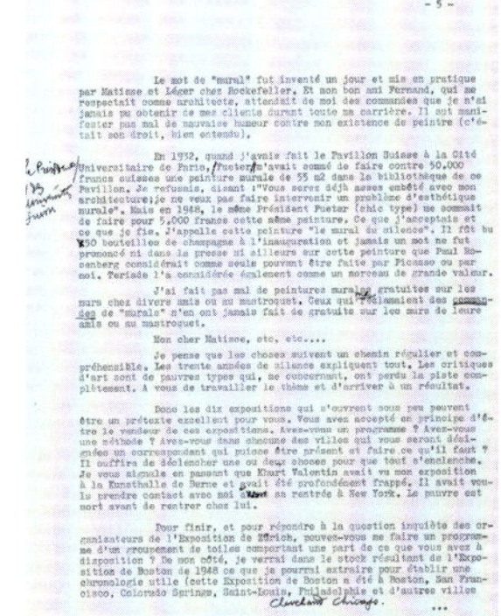

\- 5 -

Le mot de "mural" fut inventé un jour et mis en pratique par Matisse et Léger chez Rockefeller. Et mon bon ami Fernand, qui me respectait comme architecte, attendait de moi des commandes que je n'ai jamais pu obtenir de mes clients durant toute ma carrière. Il sut manifester pas mal de mauvaise humeur contre mon existence de peintre (c'était son droit, bien entendu).

En 1932, quand j'avais fait le Pavillon Suisse à la Cité Universitaire de Paris, Fueter m'avait sommé de faire contre 50.000 francs suisses une peinture murale de 55 m2 dans la bibliothèque de ce Pavillon. Je refusais, disant :"Vous serez déjà assez embêté avec mon architecture;je ne veux pas faire intervenir un problème d'esthétique murale". Mais en 1948, le même Président Fueter (chic type) me sommait de faire pour 5.000 francs cette même peinture. Ce que j'acceptais et ce que je fis. J'appelle cette peinture "le mural du silence". Il fût bu 50 bouteilles de champagne à l'inauguration et jamais un mot ne fut prononcé ni dans la presse ni ailleurs sur cette peinture que Paul Rosenberg considérait comme seule pouvant être faite par Picasso ou par moi. Teriade l'a considérée également comme un morceau de grande valeur.

J'ai fait pas mal de peintures murales gratuites sur les murs chez divers amis ou au mastroquet. Ceux qui réclamaient des commandes de "murals" n'en ont jamais fait de gratuits sur les murs de leurs amis ou au mastroquet.

Mon cher Matisse, etc, etc….

Je pense que les choses suivent un chemin régulier et compréhensible. Les trente années de silence expliquent tout. Les critiques d'art sont de pauvres types qui, me concernant, ont perdu la piste complètement. A vous de travailler le thème et d'arriver à un résultat.

Donc les dix expositions qui s'ouvrent sous peu peuvent être un prétexte excellent pour vous. Vous avez accepté en principe d'être le vendeur de ces expositions. Avez-vous un programme ? Avez-vous une méthode ? Avez-vous dans chacune des villes qui vous seront désignées un correspondant qui puisse être présent et faire ce qu'il faut ? Il suffira de déclencher une ou deux choses pour que tout s'enclenche. Je vous signale en passant que Khurt Valentin avait vu mon exposition à la Kunsthalle de Berne et avait été profondément frappé. Il avait voulu prendre contact avec moi à sa rentrée à New York. Le pauvre est mort avant de rentrer chez lui.

Pour finir, et pour répondre à la question inquiète des organisateurs de l'Exposition de Zürich, pouvez-vous me faire un programme d'un groupement de toiles comportant une part de ce que vous avez à disposition ? De mon côté, je verrai dans le stock résultant de l'Exposition de Boston de 1948 ce que je pourrai extraire pour établir une chronologie utile (cette Exposition de Boston a été à Boston, San Francisco, Colorado Springs, Saint-Louis, Philadelphie et d'autres villes

…

The word "mural" was invented one day and put into practice by Matisse and Léger at the Rockefeller. And my good friend Fernand, who respected me as an architect, was counting on me for commissions I never managed to get from my clients throughout my career. He displayed quite a lot of ill will toward my existence as a painter (as he was entitled to, naturally).

In 1932, when I had done the Pavillon Suisse at the Cité Universitaire in Paris, Fueter, *the President of the Swiss Universities*, had called on me, for a fee of 50,000 Swiss francs, to do a 55 m² mural for the Pavillion library. I refused, saying: "You're already going to have enough problems with my architecture; I don't want to add in a mural aesthetics problem." But in 1948 the same President Fueter (a nice guy) asked me to do the same painting for 5,000 francs. Which I accepted and which I did. I call this painting "the mural of silence." 50 bottles of champagne got drunk at the opening and not a single word was said in the press or elsewhere about this painting, which Paul Rosenberg thought could have been done by only Picasso or me. Tériade also considered it a work of great value.

I've done quite a few murals for free in the homes of various friends and in bars. The people who were asking *me* for commissioned murals have never done them for free on their friends' walls or in bars.

My dear Matisse, etc., etc…

I think things are taking their normal, understandable course. The thirty years of silence explain everything. Art critics are sad cases who have lost track of the situation completely where I'm concerned. It's up to you to work on the subject and get some results.

So the ten exhibitions that are opening shortly could be an excellent pretext for you. In principle you've agreed to be the seller for these exhibitions. Do you have a program? Do you have a method? Do you have, in each of the cities whose names I'll give you, an agent who can be on the spot and do the necessary? It will be enough to set one or two things in motion and the rest will follow automatically. I mention in passing that Kurt Valentin had seen my exhibition at the Kunsthalle in Bern and was really struck by it. He wanted to get in touch with me ~~before~~ *on* his return to New York. The poor guy died before he got back home.

In closing, and to answer the anxious question of the organizers of the Zurich exhibition, could you put together for me a program of a set of canvases including part of what you have available? For my part, I'll look into the stock from the 1948 Boston Exhibition and see what I can take out with a view to establishing a useful chronology (this Boston Exhibition was in Boston, San Francisco, Colorado Springs, St. Louis, *Cleveland, Chicago*, Philadelphia and other cities

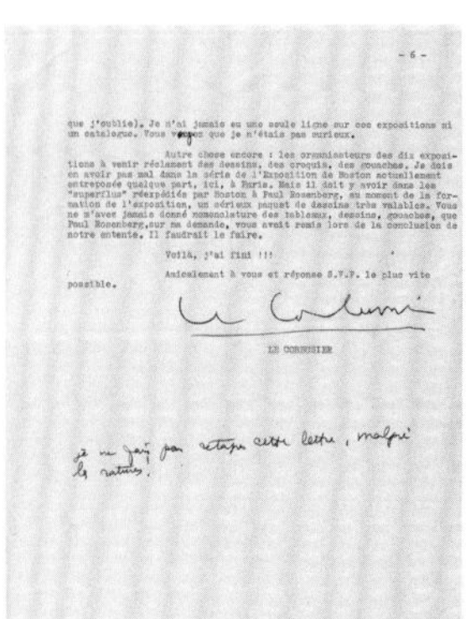

- 6 -

que j'oublie). Je n'ai jamais eu une seule ligne sur ces expositions ni un catalogue. Vous voyez que je n'étais pas curieux.

Autre chose encore : les organisateurs des dix expositions à venir réclament des dessins, des croquis, des gouaches. Je dois en avoir pas mal dans la série de l'Exposition de Boston actuellement entreposée quelque part, ici, à Paris. Mais il doit y avoir dans les "superflus" réexpédiés par Boston à Paul Rosenberg, au moment de la formation de l'exposition, un sérieux paquet de dessins très valables. Vous ne m'avez jamais donné nomenclature des tableaux, dessins, gouaches, que Paul Rosenberg, sur ma demande, vous avait remis lors de la conclusion de notre entente. Il faudrait le faire.

Voilà, j'ai fini !!!

Amicalement à vous et réponse S.V.P. le plus vite possible.

[signature]

LE CORBUSIER

je ne fais pas retaper cette lettre, malgré les ratures!

I've forgotten). I never had a single line about these exhibitions or a catalog. You can see that I wasn't curious.

Still another thing: the organizers of the upcoming ten exhibitions are asking for drawings, sketches, and gouaches. I must have quite a few in the Boston Exhibition series, currently in storage somewhere here in Paris. But among the "surplus" sent back to Paul Rosenberg by Boston there must be quite a number of very worthwhile drawings. You never gave me the list of the paintings, drawings, and gouaches that Paul Rosenberg, at my request, handed over to you when our agreement was signed. This should be done.

So there, I've finished!!!

Yours, and answer please as quickly as possible,

[signature]
LE CORBUSIER

I'm not going to retype this letter, in spite of the crossings-out!

—P. 598

Article from *Combat*, 18 November 1953

Le Corbusier, créateur célèbre
— et encore maudit ? —
expose ses œuvres plastiques

POUR le Français moyen, Le Corbusier est l'homme de « l'urbanisme » qui fit à l'époque — 1925 — quelques bruit ; celui des plans de la SDN, du pavillon des Temps nouveaux et, plus récemment, de la Cité Radieuse.

Pourtant l'architecte écrit lui-même qu'une partie de son temps va à la peinture « tremplin essentiel de l'œuvre créatrice qu'il a réalisée dans les domaines de l'organisation bâtie de la société. »

Et il s'élève avec vigueur contre l'opposition arbitraire que l'on fait de ces deux formes d'art :

« La spécialisation, nous déclare-t-il en parcourant la vaste salle du musée d'art moderne où il expose depuis hier ses œuvres plastiques, la spécialisation tue notre temps. Comme si tout ne se tenait pas... Mais d'architecture, toute œuvre d'art en est pleine : un poème, un dessin, une jolie femme... Les mots qui isolent chacune d'elles sont faux — ou peut-être n'ont-ils plus de sens parce que nous ne savons plus nous en servir... Qu'est-ce qu'un architecte ? A coup sûr autre chose qu'un monsieur qui manie le double mètre et le devis. Et la peinture ? On me l'a interdite trente ans durant, et l'on continue... mais le vocabulaire n'est plus en cause ; c'est que je ne manie pas le pinceau, la pipe à la bouche et assis dans un fauteuil. »

Rêveur : « J'avais trente et un ans lorsque je fis ma première toile. Je travaillais à heures perdues, la nuit... ». Et rapprochant ces heures précieuses mais dures, de cette autre, si autre qu'il vit actuellement, Le Corbusier ajoute : « Aucune des quatre personnalités officielles que j'attendais ce matin n'est venue... »

« La raison de ma vie, dit-il abruptement, c'est la vision des choses... »

Une quarantaine de toiles, trois sculptures, des plans et des photographies de vastes peintures murales en témoignent. Ils prouvent également, par delà une perception attentive, une puissance créatrice à coup sûr pas assouvie. Et dans ce jaillissement, qui soulèvera encore maints commentaires, il n'y a pas place à la facilité. On y retrouve la rigueur de l'homme habitué à tabler sur le matériau. « Quel que soit le thème choisi, commente-t-il lui-même, il n'y a ici rien d'arbitraire. La spéculation m'est interdite ». C'est évident : le souci des volumes qui cerne la couleur comme les masses.

Mais dans cette production linéaire l'humain dans sa forme la plus brutale, les viscères, prend pourtant forme d'obsession. On le note avec curiosité.

Mais c'est sur un mot positif que se termine cette visite. Face au décor mural du Cap-Martin, il dit :

« J'aime le mur... »

France RAVENEL.

Le Corbusier, famous—and still accursed?—creative personality, exhibits his works of art.

For the average Frenchman Le Corbusier is the "urbanism" man who caused something of a stir back in 1925, with his design for the League of Nations headquarters and the Pavillion des Temps Nouveaux, and more recently with his Radiant City.

Nonetheless the architect himself has written that he devotes part of his time to painting as "the vital launchpad for his creative work in the architectural organization of society."

And he vigorously contests the arbitrary distinction made between these two art forms:

"Specialization," he told us in the enormous room in the Musée d'Art Moderne where his painting and sculpture exhibition opened yesterday, "is destroying our age. As if everything were not part of a whole... But every work of art is shot through with architecture: a poem, a drawing, a pretty woman... The words that separate them are misleading—or maybe they no longer have any meaning because we don't know how to use them. What is an architect? You can bet your life he's not just someone with a folding rule who can do you an estimate. And painting? I was banned from it for thirty years, and still am ... but the vocabulary's accepted now: and I don't wield my brush sitting in an armchair with a pipe in my mouth."

The tone becomes dreamy: "I was thirty-one when I did my first painting. I worked at night, during my spare time." And comparing that precious—but tough—period with the very different one he is living through now, Le Corbusier adds, "Not one of the four official figures I expected this morning showed up." Then, abruptly, "The whole rationale of my life is a vision of things."

The evidence is forty pictures, three sculptures, plans, and photographs of enormous murals. And in addition to an acute perceptiveness, they point to a creative power that is certainly not exhausted. And in this creative outpouring, which will still generate considerable commentary, there is no place for facility. Here we find the exigency of a man accustomed to counting on his materials. "Whatever the subject," he observes, "there's nothing arbitrary here. I can't allow myself to speculate." This is clear in that concern with volume that determines both color and shape.

But everywhere in this use of line the human, in its most brutal, visceral form, takes on the form of an obsession. This piques one's curiosity.

But the visit ends on a positive note: Looking at the mural from Cap-Martin he says, "I love walls, ..."

France Ravenel

—P. 598

Article from *L'Aurore*, 10 November 1953

ARGUS de la PRESSE
37, Rue Bergère, PARIS (9e)

N° de débit

L'AURORE

10 NOVEMBRE 1953

Voici "la femme" vue par Le Corbusier...

... d'Art moderne, ses anciennes réalisations ... tableaux et sculptures...

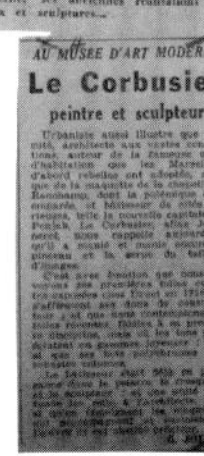

AU MUSÉE D'ART MODERNE

Le Corbusier

peintre et sculpteur

Here's "the woman" as seen by Le Corbusier...

... who since yesterday has been showing his early artistic creations (1913–1932)—paintings and sculptures ...

AT THE MUSEE D'ART MODERNE

Le Corbusier
painter and sculptor

An urban planner as famous as he is hotly debated; an architect on a grand scale, creator of the Unité d'Habitation—which the people of Marseille first rejected, then adopted—and of the controversial chapel at Ronchamp; builder of such radiant cities as the new capital of Punjab: today Le Corbusier, alias Jeanneret, reminds us that he has wielded, and continues to wield, the image-maker's brush and blade.

It is a moving experience to see again his early cubist canvases, exhibited by D[?] in 1929, with their assertion of his gifts as a constructor; and to contemplate his recent paintings, still faithful to that initial school, but with the pure colors now bursting out into joyous nuances; and with them his robust, colored sculptures.

The builder was already potentially present in the painter, fresco maker, and sculptor; and a deep unity links these works to the architect, as do the models that accompany and comment on the oeuvre of this steadfast creator.

—P. 598

Article from *France Soir*, 21 November 1953

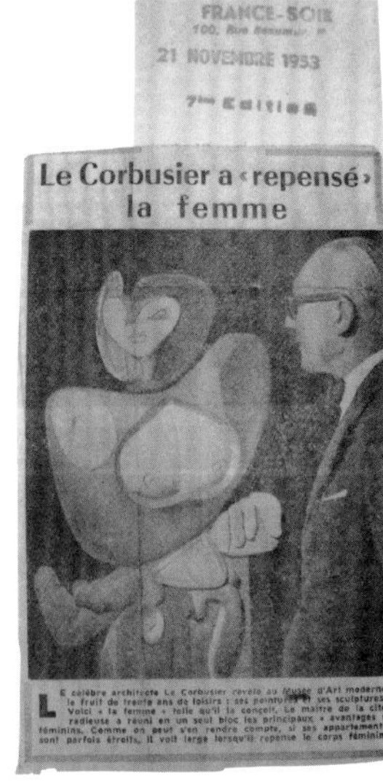

FRANCE-SOIR

21 NOVEMBRE 1953

7me Edition

Le Corbusier a «repensé» la femme

LE célèbre architecte Le Corbusier révèle au Musée d'Art moderne le fruit de trente ans de loisirs : ses peintures et ses sculptures. Voici « la femme » telle qu'il la conçoit. Le maître de la cité radieuse a réuni en un seul bloc les principaux « avantages » féminins. Comme on peut s'en rendre compte, si ses appartements sont parfois étroits, il voit large lorsqu'il repense le corps féminin.

Le Corbusier has "rethought" the woman.

At the Musée d'Art Moderne the famous architect Le Corbusier has revealed the fruit of thirty years' leisure time: his paintings and sculptures. Here is "woman" as he imagines her. The master of the radiant city has brought together the main female "charms" in a single entity. As one can see here, although his apartments might sometimes be cramped, he doesn't stint when he rethinks the female body.

—P. 598

Le Corbusier to Joseph Savina, 28 June 1951

28 juin 51

Mon cher Savina

Totem

Votre grande sculpture est arrivée, celle d'après le dessin Vézelay 1926-42. C'est bien, Savina, fort, nourri ; il y a du coeur et de l'estomac là-dedans ; je parle de la présence du sculpteur. C'est rude, comme je vous l'avais écrit d'après les photos, mais c'est corrigeable. Le Musée d'Art Moderne de N.York, fait en ce moment une expo Corbu (préliminaire) (avant la grande de 1952.) La photo agrandie de la sculpture sert d'affiche. J'ai donné votre nom bien entendu.

Je serai au 8e congrès CIAM du 7 au 14 juillet à Londres. Je partirai le 25 juillet pour la côte d'Azur (un mois) - serai à St Dié le 22 juillet.

Il faudrait vous arranger à venir dans un des intervalles, pour travailler la statue. Prendre des outils. J'ai ici Andréou (un des miens du bureau) qui est sculpteur-menuisier, mouleur, d'une habileté de singe. Il pourra nous aider. Programme : il y a un bout de bois à ajouter (vous apporterez un morceau de bois) vous passeriez quelques jours 24 N-C dans la chambre d'amis - lit et boustifaille.

Organisez cela, avertissez moi à temps. J'ai préparé deux nouveaux dessins de sculpture polychrome. Et je vous entretiendrai des sculptures sur sable à marée descendante de mon ami Nivola de N York (j'en ai fait moi même aussi).

A l'Atelier 35 Sèvres, boulot gigantesque. Au revoir Savina. Amitiés à Rose à la fifille et à vous, d'Yvonne et de moi.

Voir croquis au dos -----

28 June 51

My dear Savina

Your big sculpture has arrived, *Totem*, the one made from the Vézelay drawing of 1926–42. It's good, Savina, it's strong, rich; it's got heart and guts. It's rough, as I wrote you after seeing the photos, but that can be fixed. The New York Museum of Modern Art is putting on just now a Corbu exhibition (preliminary) (before the big one in 1952). The poster is a blown-up photo of the sculpture. I gave your name, of course.

I'll be at the 8th CIAM congress in London from 7–14 July. I'm leaving on 25 July for the côte d'Azur (a month)—will be at St. Dié on 22 July.

You'll have to arrange to come during one of the intervals to work on the statue. Bring tools. I have Andréou here (one of my studio guys) who's a sculptor-carpenter, mold-maker, and deft as a monkey. He'll be able to help us. Program: there's a bit of wood to add (you'll bring a piece of wood) you'll spend a few days at 24 N-C in the guest room—bed and grub.

Get this organized and let me know in time. I've prepared two new drawings for a multicolored sculpture. And I'll tell you about the sand sculptures made at low tide by my New York friend Nivola (I've made some too).

Masses of work at the 35 Sèvres studio. Goodbye Savina. Best wishes to Rose, the little girl and you, from Yvonne and from me.

[drawing]

See the sketch on the back

—P. 598

Le Corbusier to Joseph Savina, 1 September 1953

Cap-Martin Roquebrune
Etoile de mer. 1 Sept. 53

My dear Savina

I had brought here vol. 1 of 17 July.

There was the CIAM-AIX congress (19–26 July). Here first 10 days of total sleep (24 hours). I got back from India exhausted.

Pleased that you're happy with Vol. 5 complete works. Obviously it would be ideal if we could work in the same city. Alas.

The Corbu show in November 53 is going to be very big. I'd like to show
1 the colored statue of 1946–47 (which is in my living room) with
2 the nails, monochrome. (It was in my solo show in London at the Institute of Contemporary Art – fine show). I think this second one is still needed (can be dismantled, need to bring state 2 to Paris (I have photos of it) and state 3 (to be colored by me) or not?!) If you could send it to Paris as quickly as possible (end Sept. or early October, you could retouch it with me.

Something paradoxical happened in Nantes that highlights the cruel reality of the relationships Building + major art, get this:

Back from India 2 July (exhausted) I had a week of meetings with the UNESCO Committee starting the 5th. I had to look over the plans of the various jobs in France + some demanding fine tuning for Chandigarh (2 palaces currently under construction). One day I'm told, "Boss, this evening we have to have life-size drawings of the 'Modulors' of the Reinforced Concrete in Nantes, they have to be in the formwork for the week of the 29th." I did it in an hour on the blackboard. We did the tracings. They went to Ajaccio by plane, to Barberis, the carpenter working on Nantes. They also told me: with the Studio closed the 17th, and the CIAM congress the 19–26 in Aix, Barberis will get the chamfered wood to Aix and you'll sculpt there during the congress. Then they changed their minds: so I'm not driven mad by the 300 congress participants, the wood will go to Marseille, to the "Unité." Three mornings a car took me to Marseille and there, in the "retail street" on the 7th floor, currently being set up, I carved the wood with the most adorable of Barberis's carpenters, who did his work admirably. Having left Marseille on the 27th, I heard no more about this, except that the making of the iron reinforcing is going ahead full steam at Rezé. And that's how circumstances and implacable deadlines mean that the wooden forms for Nantes in Brittany come from Corsica and weren't carved by Savina. I felt like weeping. But I'm experienced in the spirit of sacrifice that is the lot of the real workers in the building business and not that of Messrs the painters and sculptors of montparnasse Côte d'Azur.

– Drawings pages 229 + 242
Girsberger Volume 5
bottom of page middle
on the right top

1 page 238, Volume 5 Zurich
2 p. 245

P. 229. Drawing done in the plane February 1951 before arriving in Cairo, in Album I. I'll send you a photo blow-up. An Aubusson tapestry on this same subject is being finished right now. I must have several studies of the subject. I'll see. I think you see it in the round.

P. 242. The subject on the right is beautiful. Made of several movable Colored pieces. The base is meant to express a landscape (as for example, also, on page 242, project on the left (top). I'll have to take the volume study further (the presence of the rectangular frame) the pivoting of various pieces, etc.)

Two projects will that would win me over one day = p. 242 , a) top left, b) in the middle. But there's also a question of size. Maybe 140 high for a) (See p. 84, third image, used as a surface for a desk)

b) and also a) could be 2.26 meters (See page 84, first image). But for that there would have to be a commission for building a house (when)?

Best wishes from Y and me to you / Rose / + little girl

Corbu

—P. 603

Le Corbusier to André Wogenscky, 9 February 1953

NOTE for Mr. WOGENSCKY dictated by L–C on 9/2/53

Father Couturier, who has obtained the commission from the Monastery near Lyon, wants to have me visit Thoronet (?) Abbey, situated behind Toulon. He would join me in Marseille when I get there and a car would have to be hired for the trip from Marseille to Thoronet and back.

Conclusion: Plan a discussion-lecture meeting with the tenants and prepare a mock-up of the monthly bulletin in advance with someone in charge. Choose someone young from the Studio capable of handling it. I'll let you get on with this.

P.S. Prepare the members' cards with divisions like those on the Ascoral card and point out that the bulletin correspondent will be at 35 rue de Sèvres, but as a Member of the Ascoral.

—P. 603

André Wogenscky to Father Couturier, 11 May 1953

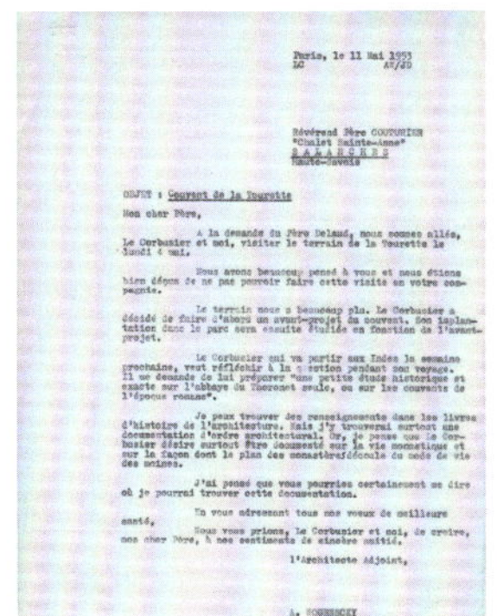

Paris, le 11 Mai 1953
LC [illegible]

Révérend Père COUTURIER
"Chalet Sainte-Anne"
SALANCHES
Haute-Savoie

OBJET : Couvent de la Tourette

Mon cher Père,

A la demande du Père Delaud, nous sommes allés, Le Corbusier et moi, visiter le terrain de la Tourette le lundi 4 mai.

Nous avons beaucoup pensé à vous et nous étions bien déçus de ne pas pouvoir faire cette visite en votre compagnie.

Le terrain nous a beaucoup plu. Le Corbusier a décidé de faire d'abord un avant-projet du couvent. Son implantation dans le parc sera ensuite étudiée en fonction de l'avant-projet.

Le Corbusier qui va partir aux Indes la semaine prochaine, veut réfléchir à la question pendant son voyage. Il me demande de lui préparer "une petite étude historique et exacte sur l'abbaye du Thoronet seule, ou sur les couvents de l'époque romane".

Je peux trouver des renseignements dans les livres d'histoire de l'architecture. Mais j'y trouverai surtout une documentation d'ordre architectural. Or, je pense que Le Corbusier désire surtout être documenté sur la vie monastique et sur la façon dont le plan des monastères découle du mode de vie des moines.

J'ai pensé que vous pourriez certainement me dire où je pourrai trouver cette documentation.

En vous adressant tous nos voeux de meilleure santé,

Nous vous prions, Le Corbusier et moi, de croire, mon cher Père, à nos sentiments de sincère amitié.

l'Architecte Adjoint,

A. WOGENSCKY

Paris, 11 May 1953

Reverend Father COUTURIER
"Chalet Sainte-Anne"
SALANCHES
Haute-Savoie

SUBJECT: Monastery at La Tourette

My dear Father,

At Father Delaud's request, we went, Le Corbusier and I, to visit the site at La Tourette on Monday 4 May.

We thought of you a great deal and were very disappointed that we couldn't make this visit in your company.

We liked the site very much. Le Corbusier decided to make a rough draft of the convent first. Its siting in the park will then be designed on the basis of the rough draft.

Le Corbusier, who is leaving for India next week, wants to think about it during his trip. He asks me to prepare for him "a brief study, historical and precise, of just Thoronet Abbey, or of the convents of the Roman era."

I can find information in books on the history of architecture. But I would find mainly architectural material there. However, I think Le Corbusier mainly wants material on monastic life and on how the layouts of the monasteries derive from the monks' way of life.

I thought you would certainly be able to tell me where I could find this material.

We send you our best wishes for your health, and Le Corbusier and I are, my dear Father, most sincerely yours,

Assistant Architect,
A. WOGENSCKY

—P. 603

Father Couturier to Le Corbusier, 8 December 1953

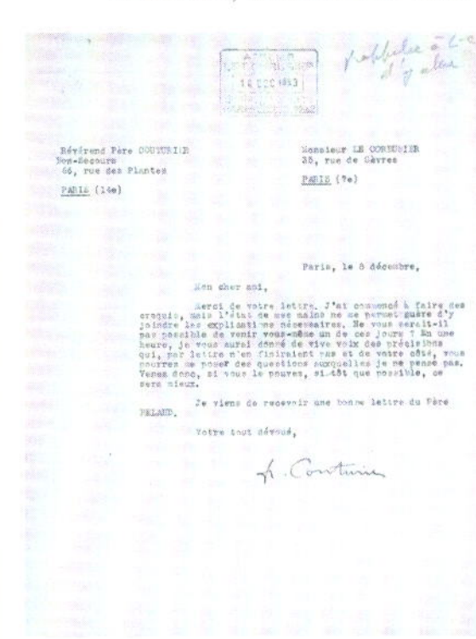

Révérend Père COUTURIER
Bon-Secours
66, rue des Plantes
PARIS (14e)

Monsieur LE CORBUSIER
35, rue de Sèvres
PARIS (7e)

Paris, le 8 décembre,

Mon cher ami,

Merci de votre lettre. J'ai commencé à faire des croquis, mais l'état de mes mains ne me permet guère d'y joindre les explications nécessaires. Ne vous serait-il pas possible de venir vous-même un de ces jours ? En une heure, je vous aurai donné de vive voix des précisions qui, par lettre n'en finiraient pas et de votre côté, vous pourrez me poser des questions auxquelles je ne pense pas. Venez donc, si vous le pouvez, si-tôt que possible, ce sera mieux.

Je viens de recevoir une bonne lettre du Père BELAUD.

Votre tout dévoué,

Reverend Father COUTURIER
Bon-Secours
66 rue des Plantes
PARIS (14th)

Mr. LE CORBUSIER
35 rue de Sèvres
PARIS (7th)

Paris, 8 December

My dear friend,

Thank you for your letter. I've started making some sketches, but because of the condition of my hands I can't attach the necessary explanations. Couldn't you come yourself one of these days? In an hour face to face, I could give you details that would be interminable in a letter, and for your part you could ask me questions that I haven't thought of. So please do come, if you can, as soon as possible, it would be better.

I just received a good letter from Father BELAUD

Sincerely yours,

[signature]

—P. 620

Sketch of Le Corbusier's hand drawing his symbol for the word *right* in *Le poème de l'angle droit*.

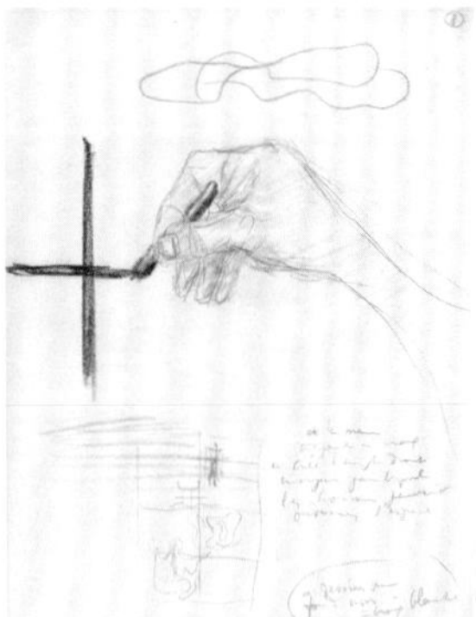

and the hand tracing a cross created the medium right angle with which men can orchestrate space

to be drawn on black background = white cross

—P. 620

Two schemes for the layout of images in *Le poème de l'angle droit*, 22 December 1951

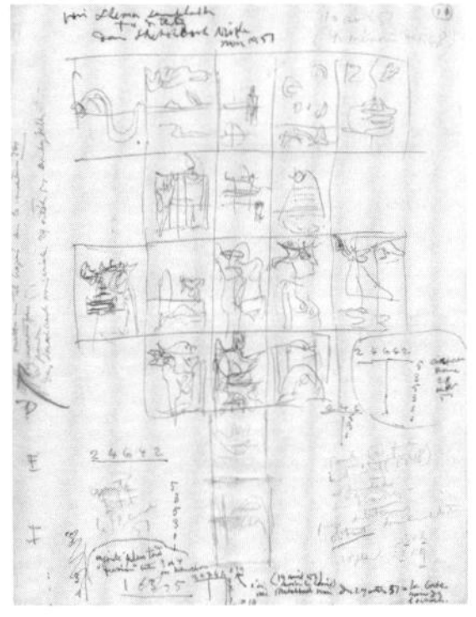

[TOP LEFT]
see similar diagram + texts in black Nivola sketchbook 1951

[TOP RIGHT]
10 August 51
(from memory of 1948)

[LEFT MARGIN]
put a sketch like this on the back cover
The front cover to be taken from black Nivola sketchbook 29 October 51

[BOTTOM LEFT]
added 12 August 51

added later
"fusion" between 3 and 4
then you read 2 4 7 4 2 = 19
(19 April 51)
[BOTTOM RIGHT]
airport Rome
28 Nov 51

Everything here was intuitive (1948) spontaneous disordered then suddenly got its architecture = 3 x 6
18 plates = 2 x 9

here airplane Cairo
see black sketchbook of 29 October 51 = the black box of the scale

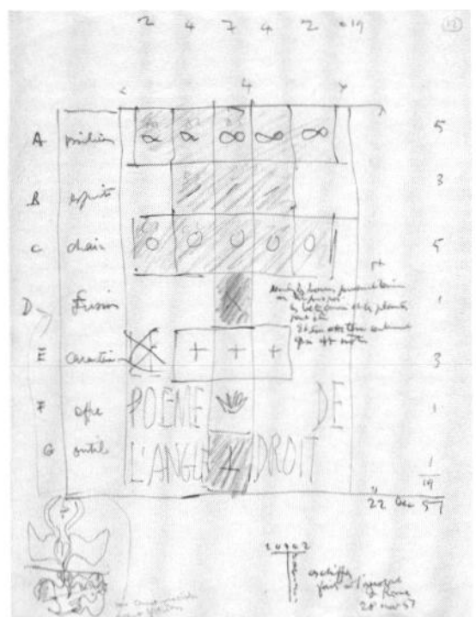

[LEFT]
A environment
B spirit
C flesh
D fusion
E nature
F offer
G tool

[RIGHT]
Only people can say things like this.
Animals and plants too maybe
And only on this earth of ours

POEM OF THE RIGHT ANGLE

22 Dec. 51

[BOTTOM LEFT]
see Nivola's black notebook before Yverdon

[BOTTOM RIGHT]
these calculations done at the airport in Rome
28 Nov. 51

—P. 626

Le Corbusier to L.C. Kalff, "general art director" of Philips, 14 September 1956

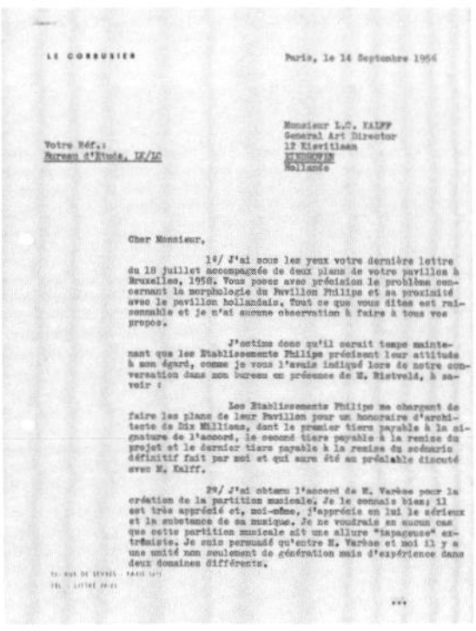

LE CORBUSIER

Paris, le 14 Septembre 1956

Votre Réf.:
Bureau d'Etude, LK/LC

Monsieur L.C. KALFF
General Art Director
12 Kievitlaan
EINDHOVEN
Hollande

Cher Monsieur,

1°/ J'ai sous les yeux votre dernière lettre du 18 juillet accompagnée de deux plans de votre pavillon à Bruxelles, 1958. Vous posez avec précision le problème concernant la morphologie du Pavillon Philips et sa proximité avec le pavillon hollandais. Tout ce que vous dites est raisonnable et je n'ai aucune observation à faire à tous vos propos.

J'estime donc qu'il serait temps maintenant que les Etablissements Philips précisent leur attitude à mon égard, comme je vous l'avais indiqué lors de notre conversation dans mon bureau en présence de M. Rietveld, à savoir :

Les Etablissements Philips me chargent de faire les plans de leur Pavillon pour un honoraire d'architecte de Dix Millions, dont le premier tiers payable à la signature de l'accord, le second tiers payable à la remise du projet et le dernier tiers payable à la remise du scénario définitif fait par moi et qui aura été au préalable discuté avec M. Kalff.

2°/ J'ai obtenu l'accord de M. Varèse pour la création de la partition musicale. Je le connais bien; il est très apprécié et, moi-même, j'apprécie en lui le sérieux et la substance de sa musique. Je ne voudrais en aucun cas que cette partition musicale ait une allure "tapageuse" extrémiste. Je suis persuadé qu'entre M. Varèse et moi il y a une unité non seulement de génération mais d'expérience dans deux domaines différents.

...

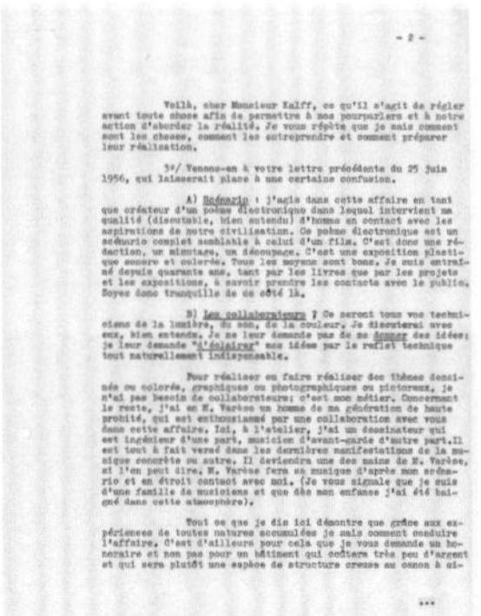

- 2 -

Voilà, cher Monsieur Kalff, ce qu'il s'agit de régler avant toute chose afin de permettre à nos pourparlers et à notre action d'aborder la réalité. Je vous répète que je sais comment sont les choses, comment les entreprendre et comment préparer leur réalisation.

3°/ Venons-en à votre lettre précédente du 25 juin 1956, qui laisserait place à une certaine confusion.

A) Scénario : j'agis dans cette affaire en tant que créateur d'un poème électronique dans lequel intervient ma qualité (discutable, bien entendu) d'homme en contact avec les aspirations de notre civilisation. Ce poème électronique est un scénario complet semblable à celui d'un film. C'est donc une rédaction, un minutage, un découpage. C'est une exposition plastique sonore et colorée. Tous les moyens sont bons. Je suis entraîné depuis quarante ans, tant par les livres que par les projets et les expositions, à savoir prendre les contacts avec le public. Soyez donc tranquille de ce côté là.

B) Les collaborateurs ? Ce seront tous vos techniciens de la lumière, du son, de la couleur. Je discuterai avec eux, bien entendu. Je ne leur demande pas de me donner des idées; je leur demande "d'éclairer" mes idées par le reflet technique tout naturellement indispensable.

Pour réaliser ou faire réaliser des thèmes dessinés ou colorés, graphiques ou photographiques ou picturaux, je n'ai pas besoin de collaborateurs; c'est mon métier. Concernant le reste, j'ai en M. Varèse un homme de ma génération de haute probité, qui est enthousiasmé par une collaboration avec vous dans cette affaire. Ici, à l'atelier, j'ai un dessinateur qui est ingénieur d'une part, musicien d'avant-garde d'autre part. Il est tout à fait versé dans les dernières manifestations de la musique concrète ou autre. Il deviendra une des mains de M. Varèse, si l'on peut dire. M. Varèse fera sa musique d'après mon scénario et en étroit contact avec moi. (Je vous signale que je suis d'une famille de musiciens et que dès mon enfance j'ai été baigné dans cette atmosphère).

Tout ce que je dis ici démontre que grâce aux expériences de toutes natures accumulées je sais comment conduire l'affaire. C'est d'ailleurs pour cela que je vous demande un honoraire et non pas pour un bâtiment qui coûtera très peu d'argent et qui sera plutôt une espèce de structure creuse au canon à ci-

...

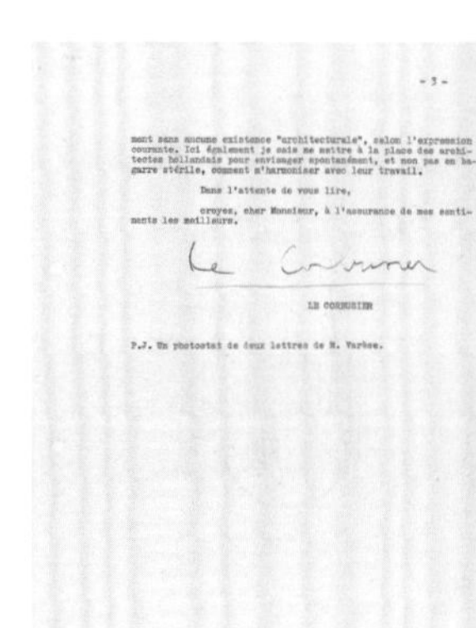

- 3 -

ment sans aucune existence "architecturale", selon l'expression courante. Ici également je sais me mettre à la place des architectes hollandais pour envisager spontanément, et non pas en bagarre stérile, comment m'harmoniser avec leur travail.

Dans l'attente de vous lire,

croyez, cher Monsieur, à l'assurance de mes sentiments les meilleurs.

LE CORBUSIER

P.J. Un photostat de deux lettres de M. Varèse.

Paris, 14 September 1956

Mr. L. C. Kalff
General Art Director
12 Kievitlaan
EINDHOVEN
Holland

Dear Sir,

1/ I have before me your last letter of 18 July, accompanied by two plans for your pavilion in Brussels, 1958. You home in exactly on the problem of the form of the Philips Pavilion and its proximity to the Dutch pavilion. Everything you say is reasonable and I have no comments to make in any respect.

Thus I feel it is now time for the Philips Company to spell out their attitude toward me, as I indicated to you during our conversation in my office, in the presence of Mr. Rietveld. Specifically:

The Philips Company is commissioning me to draw up the plans of their Pavilion for an architect's fee of Ten Million, of which the first third is payable on signature of the contract, the second on delivery of the project, and the third on delivery of the definitive scenario as prepared by me after prior discussion with Mr. Kalff.

2/ I have obtained Mr. Varèse's consent for the creation of the musical score. I know him well; he is much respected and I myself respect the commitment and meaningfulness of his music. In no case do I want this score to be "flashy" and extreme. I am convinced that there exists between Mr. Varèse and myself a unity not only of generation but also of experience in two different fields.

These, then, dear Mr. Kalff, are the matters to be settled before all others so that our negotiations and our project become a reality. I repeat that I know how things are, how to approach them and how to go about their realization.

3/ To come to your preceding letter of 25 June 1956, which leaves room for a degree of confusion.

A) Scenario: my role here is that of the creator of an electronic poem shaped by my capacities (open to discussion, of course) as a man in contact with the aspirations of our civilization. This electronic poem is a complete scenario similar to that of a film. Thus it contains text, timing, and breakdown. It is an exhibition using visuals, sound, and colors. No methods are excluded. I have forty years' experience, via books, projects, and exhibitions, in learning how to make contact with the public. In that respect you may rest easy.

B) The collaborators? They will be your light, sound, and color technicians. I shall discuss things with them, of course. I do not ask them to give me ideas; I ask them to "clarify" my ideas with the naturally indispensable technical input.

To create or organize the creation of subjects that are drawn or colored, graphic or photographic or pictorial, I need no collaborators; this is my profession. As for the rest, I have in Mr. Varèse an upright man of my generation who is very keen to work with you on this project. Here at the studio I have a draftsman who is both engineer and avant-garde musician. He is well acquainted with the latest aspects of concrete and other music. He will become, so to speak, one of Mr. Varèse's helpers. Mr. Varèse will compose his music according to my scenario and in close contact with me. (I should like to point out that I come from a family of musicians and have been drenched in music since childhood.)

Everything I say here demonstrates that thanks to my accumulation of all kinds of experience I know how to run this project. This is why, I should add, I am asking a fee, and not for a building that will cost very little money and will be, rather, a kind of hollow cement- gun structure with no "architectural" existence, to use the current expression. Here too I know how to put myself in the place of the Dutch architects, so as to imagine things spontaneously, and without pointless squabbling, and thus how to function in harmony with their work.

Looking forward to hearing from you,

Sincerely yours,

[signature]
LE CORBUSIER

Enclosed a photostat of two letters from Mr. Varèse.

—P. 626

Le Corbusier to L.C. Kalff, 29 January 1957

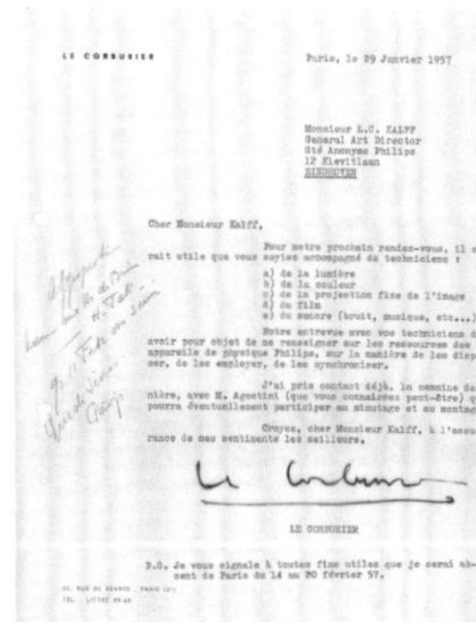

LE CORBUSIER

Paris, le 29 Janvier 1957

Monsieur L.C. KALFF
General Art Director
Sté Anonyme Philips
12 Kievitlaan
EINDHOVEN

Cher Monsieur Kalff,

Pour notre prochain rendez-vous, il serait utile que vous soyiez accompagné de techniciens :

a) de la lumière
b) de la couleur
c) de la projection fixe de l'image
d) du film
e) du sonore (bruit, musique, etc...)

Notre entrevue avec vos techniciens doit avoir pour objet de me renseigner sur les ressources des appareils de physique Philips, sur la manière de les disposer, de les employer, de les synchroniser.

J'ai pris contact déjà, la semaine dernière, avec M. Agostini (que vous connaissez peut-être) qui pourra éventuellement participer au minutage et au montage.

Croyez, cher Monsieur Kalff, à l'assurance de mes sentiments les meilleurs.

LE CORBUSIER

P.S. Je vous signale à toutes fins utiles que je serai absent de Paris du 14 au 20 février 57.

Paris, 29 January 1957

Mr. L.C. Kalff
General Art Director
Philips Inc.
12 Kievitlaan
EINDHOVEN

Dear Mr. Kalff,

For our next meeting it would be helpful if you came accompanied by technicians for:

a) lighting
b) color
c) stills projection
d) film
e) sound (effects, music, etc...)

The aim of our meeting with your technicians should be to provide me with information on the capacities of Philips apparatuses, and on how to set them up, use them, and synchronize them.

Last week I contacted Mr. Agostini (whom you know, perhaps), who may be able to help with the timing and editing.

Yours faithfully,

[signature]
LE CORBUSIER

P.S. Just in case, I should mention that I shall not be in Paris between 14–20 February 1957.

—P. 626

Le Corbusier to L.C. Kalff, 22 July 1958

Paris, 22 July 1958

Mr. L.C. Kalff
General Art Director
Philips
12 Kievitlaan
EINDHOVEN

Dear Mr. Kalff,

Here is the letter I received from the Musée de l'Homme, where they were so nice to me during my long period of research in their photo library. It is a shame to see real service badly rewarded. I'm sure you will be willing to sort this out at the Musée de l'Homme.

Like me, you agree that it would be overdoing things to expect me to pay Philips's bills.

I should like to mention, among other things, that I have never had a word of thanks from your Steering Committee for the enormous effort I put into your Pavilion. That is purely and simply called human ingratitude.

When an architect has constructed a building, the client invites him for meal at the conclusion of the works and gives him a little smile, even if it's a bit forced. The publicity Philips got out of the Electronic Poem is enormous and nobody there has any idea of the immense difficulties that had to be overcome to make this work.

With my very best wishes.

LE CORBUSIER

—P. 626

L.C. Kalff to Le Corbusier, 28 July 1958

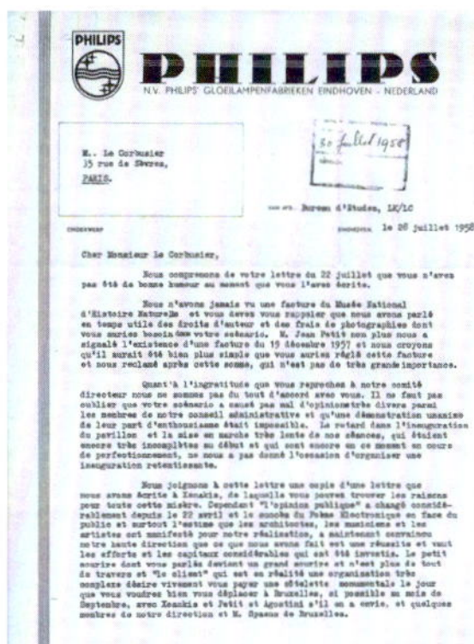

Mr. Le Corbusier
35 rue de Sèvres
PARIS.

EINDHOVEN, 28 July 1958

Dear Mr. Le Corbusier,

We understand from your letter of 22 July that you were not in a good mood when you wrote it.

We never saw an invoice from the National Museum of Natural History and you must remember that we spoke in a timely way about the royalties and the fees for the photographs you would need in your scenario. Nor did Mr. Jean Petit alert us to the existence of an invoice of 19 December 1957 and we think it would have been much simpler for you to have paid this invoice and asked us later for the amount, which is not very great.

As for the ingratitude of which you accuse our board of directors we disagree entirely with you. It must be recalled that your scenario evoked many very different opinions among our executive committee, and that any unanimous demonstration of enthusiasm on their part was impossible. The delay in the inauguration of the pavilion and the very slow start of our meetings, which were still very incomplete at the beginning, and which are still now being improved, gave us no opportunity to organize a resounding inauguration.

We attach to this letter a copy of a letter that we wrote Xenakis, where you may find the reasons for all this trouble. And yet "public opinion" has changed considerably since 22 April and the success of the Electronic Poem in the public's eyes and especially the esteem that the architects, musicians, and artists have expressed for our production, have now convinced our upper management that what we have done is a success and worth the considerable efforts and money that were invested. The little smile you speak of becomes a big smile, and is no longer a scowl at all, and "the client," which is in reality a very complex organization, would heartily love to treat you to a monumental chop anytime you decide to come to Brussels, if possible in September, with Xenakis and Petit and Agostini if he feels like it, and a few members of our board and Mr. Spaens from Brussels.

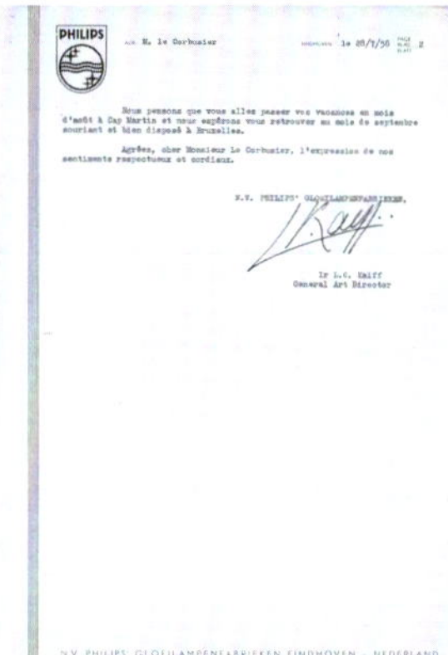

We think you'll be spending your August holidays at Cap-Martin and in September we hope to see you smiling and in good humor in Brussels.

Yours faithfully,

[signature]
L.C. Kalff
General Art Director

—P. 626

Le Corbusier to L.C. Kalff, 20 June 1957

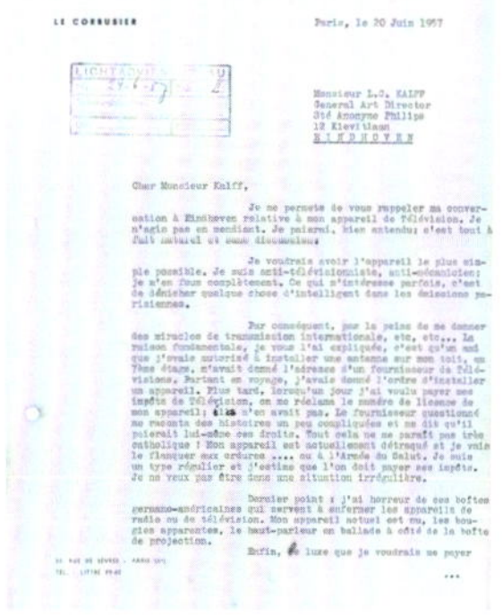

Paris, 20 June 1957

Mr. L.C. Kalff
General Art Director
Philips Inc.
12 Kievitlaan
EINDHOVEN

Dear Mr. Kalff,

I am taking the liberty of reminding you of my conversation in Eindhoven concerning my Television set. I am not coming to beg. I shall pay, of course; that is quite natural and requires no discussion.

I should like to have the simplest set possible. I am anti-television and anti-mechanical; I don't give a damn. What interests me sometimes is to unearth something intelligent in the broadcasts in Paris. And so there's no point giving me miracles of international transmission, etc, etc…The basic reason, as I explained to you, is that a friend I had permitted to install an antenna on my roof, on the 7th floor, had given me the address of a supplier of Television sets. As I was leaving on a trip, I gave instructions for a set to be installed. Later, wanting to pay my Television license fee, I was asked for the number of my set; it did not have one. When I questioned the supplier he started telling me all sorts of complicated tales and how he would pay the license fee himself. All this seems a little shady to me. My set is currently playing up and I'm going to throw it out … or give it to the Salvation Army. I'm a straightforward guy and feel that one ought to pay one's taxes. I don't want to find myself in a legally tricky situation.

One last point: I can't stand these German-American boxes that are used to shut radios and TV sets away in. My present set has no frills: you can see the valves and the loudspeaker is sitting beside the projection box.

Lastly, the luxury I'd like to offer myself

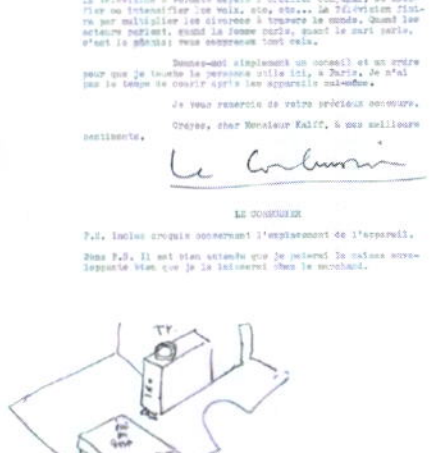

is that my wife or I should be able to shut the television up, or modify or intensify the voices, etc, etc…whenever we want, from the nuptial bed. Television is going to push up the divorce rate around the world. When the actors are talking, and the wife is talking, and the husband is talking, it's chaos; you understand all that.

Just give me some advice and an order form so that I can contact the right person here, in Paris. I don't have the time to go chasing after sets myself.

Thanking you for your valuable help,

Sincerely yours,

[signature]
LE CORBUSIER

P.S. Enclosed is a sketch of the layout of the set.
2nd P.S. I shall of course pay for the cabinet, even though I shall leave it at the store.

—P. 626

L.C. Kalff to Mr. Meyerstein, 25 June 1957

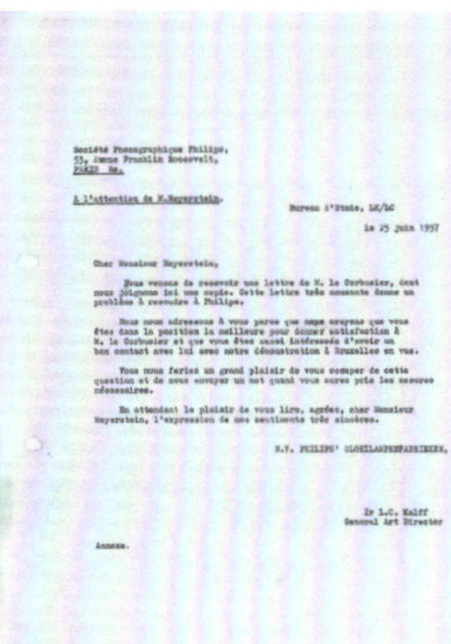

Société Phonographique Philips
53 avenue Franklin Roosevelt
PARIS 8th.

Attention: Mr. Meyerstein.

25 June 1957

Dear Mr. Meyerstein,

We have just received a letter from Mr. Le Corbusier, a copy of which we attach here. This very amusing letter poses a problem that Philips must solve.

We are turning to you because we believe that you are in the best position to give Mr. Le Corbusier satisfaction, and that you, too, are interested in having a good exchange with him, in view of our demonstration in Brussels.

You would be doing us a great favor if you were to take care of this matter and drop us a line when you have taken the necessary steps.

Awaiting the pleasure of your reply, we are, Mr. Meyerstein, sincerely yours,

L.C. Kalff
General Art Director

—P. 626

L.C. Kalff to Le Corbusier, 25 June 1957

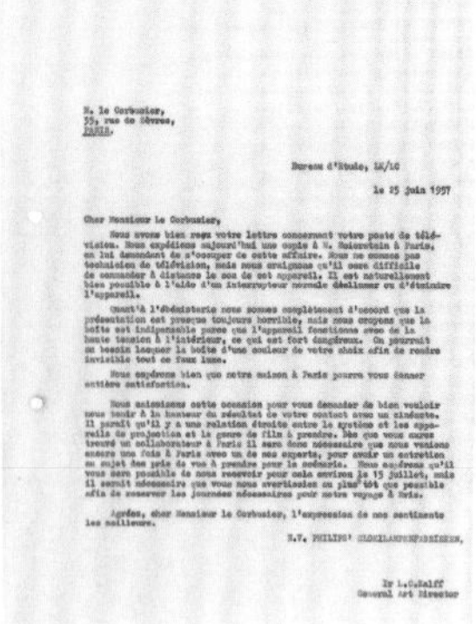

Mr. Le Corbusier,
35 rue de Sèvres
PARIS.

25 June 1957

Dear Mr. Le Corbusier,

We received your letter about your television set. We will send a copy today to Mr. Meyerstein in Paris, asking him to take care of this matter. We are not television technicians, but we fear it will be difficult to operate the set's sound long distance. It is naturally quite possible to turn the set on or off with an ordinary switch.

As for the cabinetry, we entirely agree that its appearance is almost always horrible, but we think the box is necessary because the mechanism works with high voltage inside, which is very dangerous. If absolutely necessary, the box could be painted in a color of your choice so as to hide all that shabby ostentation.

We sincerely hope that our Paris office will be able to give you entire satisfaction.

We avail ourselves of this opportunity to ask you to please keep us informed about the upshot of your contact with a filmmaker. There seems to be a close relationship between the system and machinery of projection and the kind of film to be shot. As soon as you have found a collaborator in Paris it will therefore be necessary for us to come to Paris again with one of our experts, to meet on the subject of what to shoot for the script. We hope you will be able to receive us to that end around 15 July, but it would be necessary for you to let us know as soon as possible so that we might set aside the days necessary for our trip to Paris.

We are, dear Mr. Le Corbusier, yours truly,

L.C. Kalff
General Art Director

—P. 632

Le Corbusier to L.C. Kalff, 3 July 1956

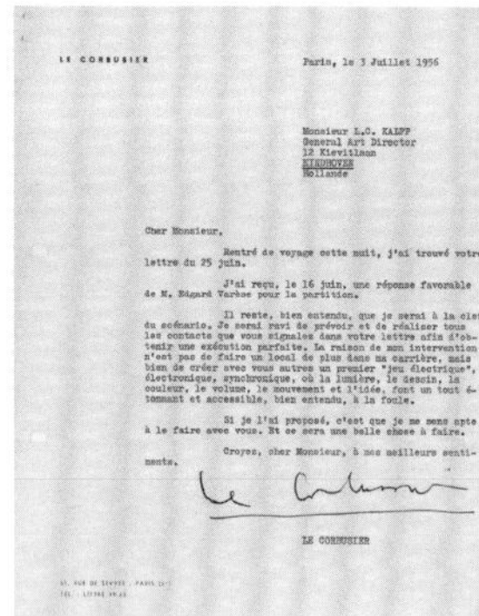

Paris, 3 July 1956

Mr. L.C. Kalff
General Art Director
Philips Inc.
12 Kievitlaan
EINDHOVEN
Holland

Dear Sir,

On my return from a trip this evening I found your letter of 25 June.

On 16 June I received a favorable reply from Mr. Edgard Varèse regarding the score.

It remains, of course, understood that I shall be responsible for the scenario. I shall be delighted to look into and organize all the contacts mentioned in your letter so as to obtain a perfect performance. The aim of my initiative is not to add another building to my career, but to create, with the rest of you, the first "electric game"—electronic and synchronic—in which light, drawing, color, volume, movement, and ideas add up to something both astonishing and, naturally, available to all.

If I have made this suggestion, it is because I feel myself the right person to undertake it with you. And this will be a fine thing to do.

Respectfully yours,

LE CORBUSIER

—P. 632

Edgard Varèse to Le Corbusier, 16 June and 30 July 1956

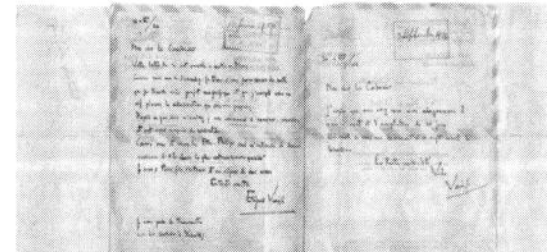

[LEFT PAGE]
16–VI/56

My dear Le Corbusier,

Your letter of the 12th arrived this morning—Thanks.

Since you asked, I want to tell you right away that I think your project is magnificent and that I accept with the greatest pleasure the collaboration that you propose.

On the basis of what you wrote I will start pondering, imagining, and anticipating ways to make it happen.

Like you and the Philips Company I'm interested only in creating "the most extraordinary thing possible."

I'll be in Paris in late autumn and am delighted that I'll see you again.

With kind regards,
Edgard Varèse

Please remember me warmly to Xenakis.

[RIGHT PAGE]
30–VII/56

My dear Le Corbusier,

I hope you received my aerogram of thanks and acceptance of 30 June.

A word from you reassuring me on the subject would be welcome.

With kind regards,
Your Varèse

—P. 632

Le Corbusier to Edgard Varèse, 3 November 1956

Paris, 3 November 1956

Mr. Edgard VARESE
168 Sullivan Street
NEW YORK 12, N.Y.

My dear Varèse,

I'm leaving for India around 12 November; I shall be back only around 18 or 20 December. The Nasser affair is behind all this confusion. So we could see each other at the end of the year and if you prefer to spend Christmas in New York, just come in January.

I've seen Mr. Kalff, General Art Director of Philips in Eindhoven, since the letter I sent you on 24 October 1956. He completely and honestly agrees that the necessary arrangements regarding author's rights should be governed by common sense. He will certainly come to Paris when you're here.

I told you I had reached a "gentleman's agreement" *with Philips* by letter (you received the relevant excerpts on 24 October 1956). My work is well advanced: the plans have been drawn up and accepted, and the engineers are doing their calculations. Construction can't wait (this is a Universal Exposition and labor and materials are very hard to find). The whole thing can work only if I can hand in the scenario, as agreed, in early January. And this scenario has to be prepared with you.

I'm sending a copy of this letter to Mr. Kalff who will contact you directly should it be necessary.

Yours,

LE CORBUSIER

—P. 632

Le Corbusier to Edgard Varèse, 1 February 1957

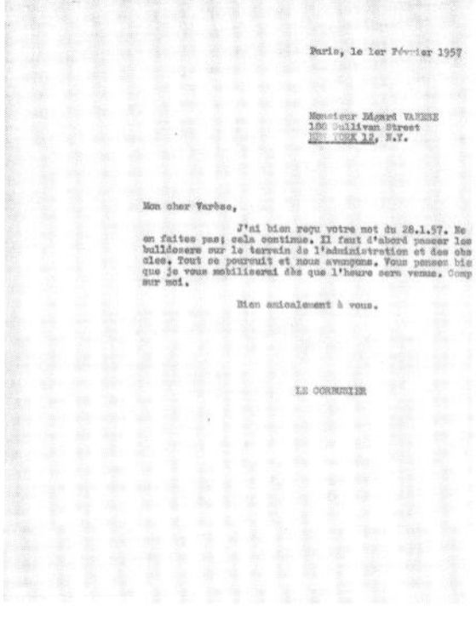

Paris, 1 February 1957

Mr. Edgard VARESE
188 Sullivan Street
NEW YORK 12, N.Y.

My dear Varèse,

I got your letter of 28.1.57. Don't worry; things are going ahead. First of all we have to bulldoze the authorities and the obstacles out of the way. Everything's on the move and we're making progress. Rest assured that I'll call on you when the time is ripe. You can count on me.

Ever yours,

LE CORBUSIER

—P. 632

Le Corbusier to Edgard Varèse, 22 June 1957

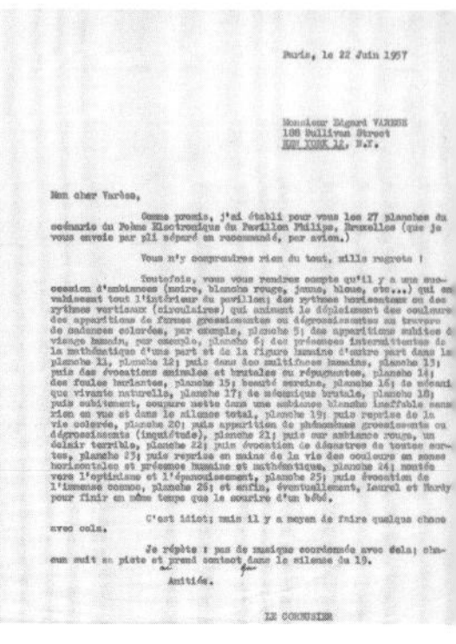

Paris, 22 June 1957

Mr. Edgard VARESE
188 Sullivan Street
NEW YORK 12, N.Y.

My dear Varèse,

As promised, I've prepared for you the 27 plates for the Electronic Poem scenario for the Philips Pavilion in Brussels (I'm sending them separately by certified delivery air mail.)

I'm terribly sorry, but you're going to find them completely incomprehensible.

Even so, you'll realize that there's a series of ambiences (black, white red, yellow, blue, etc....) that take over the entire interior of the pavilion; horizontal rhythms or vertical (circular) rhythms that liven up the display of colors; the appearance of swelling and shrinking shapes via color modulations, as in plate 5; sudden appearances of the human face, as in plate 6; the intermittent presence of mathematics on the one hand and the human face on the other, as in plate 11, plate 12; multiple human faces, plate 13; then brutish or repugnant suggestions of animals, plate 14; howling crowds, plate 15; serene beauty, plate 16; natural, living mechanisms, plate 17; brutal mechanisms, plate 18; then suddenly, an abrupt shift to an ineffable white ambience with nothing in sight and total silence, plate 19; then a return to the life of color, plate 20; then appearance of swelling and shrinking phenomena (anxiety), plate 21; then a terrible flash of lightning in a red ambience, plate 22; then an evocation of disasters of all kinds, plate 23; then a return to the life of colors in horizontal areas, and presence of the human and the mathematical, plate 24; an upswing toward optimism and fulfillment, plate 25; then an evocation of the immense cosmos, plate 26; and lastly, maybe, a conclusion with Laurel and Hardy at the same time as the smile of a baby.

It's idiotic; but there's a way of doing something with this.

I repeat: no music coordinated with this; each person follows his own path and makes contact *only* in the silence of plate 19.

Yours,

LE CORBUSIER

—P. 632

Le Corbusier to Edgard Varèse, 18 February 1958

Paris, le 18 Février 1958

Monsieur Edgard VARESE
c/o Mrs Sliaker
38 Gragelstraat
EINDHOVEN

Mon cher Varèse,

Inclus vous allez trouver copie des décisions que j'ai prises à Cap Martin la semaine dernière dans mon lit pris par la grippe. Ces décisions sont définitives.

J'ai répondu à tous vos désirs, c'est à dire en vous laissant la primauté des terminaisons musicales (entr 384 et 480). Vous êtes maître chez vous à ce moment là. J'ai supprimé le film Kast. Votre musique se déploiera dans l'ombr la lumière, la couleur et sans aucune distraction.

Par contre, je me suis replié personnellement à la seconde 241. Malgré ma bonne volonté, je ne peux pas dim nuer la période des 40 secondes de silence absolu où seront entendues les paroles nécessaires, soit de 241 à 280 secondes Donc de 241 à 280 on coupe la musique purement et simplement. Puisqu'il y avait un zéro à 240 (silence) on le prolongera jusqu'à 280. Là, vous pourrez faire un raccord. C'est l'effor que je vous demande ayant fait, de mon côté, l'effort le plus grand.

Pour bien mettre les choses au point, je vous donne copie de ma récapitulation du 15 février 1958 écrite dans mon lit et qui a valeur de décision définitive.

Je prépare pour Mr Jansen, Illuminating Engineer, le nécessaire pour le convoquer à Paris afin de fixer le minutage définitif des ambiances colorées.

Bien amicalement à vous.

P.S. Le livre "Ronchamp" vous est expédié aujourd'hui

LE CORBUSIER

Paris, 18 February 1958

Mr. Edgard VARESE
c/o Mrs. Sliaker
38 Gragelstraat
EINDHOVEN

My dear Varèse,

You will find attached a copy of the decisions I made last week in Cap Martin while in bed with the flu. These decisions are definitive.

I have met your every wish, i. e., by giving you absolute control over the musical terminations (between 384 and 480). You're completely in charge at that point. I have eliminated the film Kast. Your music will flow forth in light, shade, and color, and with no distractions.

On the other hand, I've personally gone back to second 241. With the best will in the world, I cannot reduce the period of 40 seconds of absolute silence during which the necessary words will be heard, i.e., from 241 to 280 seconds. So from 241 to 280 the music purely and simply stops. Since there was a zero at 240 (silence), it will be extended to 280. At that point you can create a link. I ask you for this effort, having made a great effort on my side.

To bring everything thoroughly up to date, I'm giving you a copy of my recap of 15 February 1958, written in bed and representing a definitive decision.

For Mr. Jansen, the Illuminating Engineer, I'm making the necessary preparations to have him come to Paris to set up the definitive timing of the colored ambiences.

Ever yours,

LE CORBUSIER
P.S. The book "Ronchamp" is being sent to you today.

—PP. 636-37

Le Corbusier's schematic renderings, May 1957, of images for the *Poème électronique* at the Philips Pavilion, Brussels

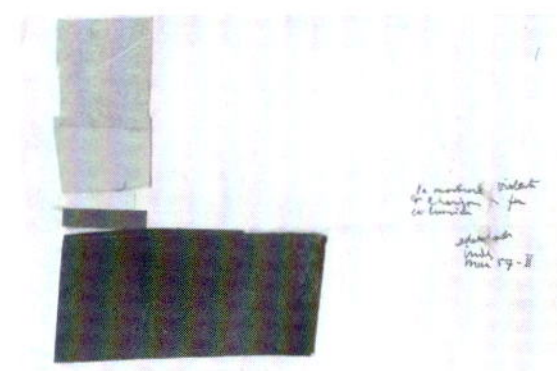

The violent bite
of the iron horizon
and light

Sketchbook India May 57–II

objects
in cinema
in projection
put them in
the windows
alternately

continuous movement of the colored verticals and also alternately of expanding spheres of images

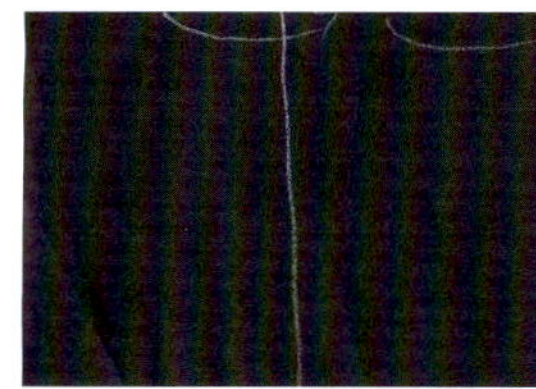

cinema
a face
awakes
and smiles
then
stunned

all yellow

with a great spotlight

the moon
an interesting
spotlight

lapping water
black with zipaton

the snow

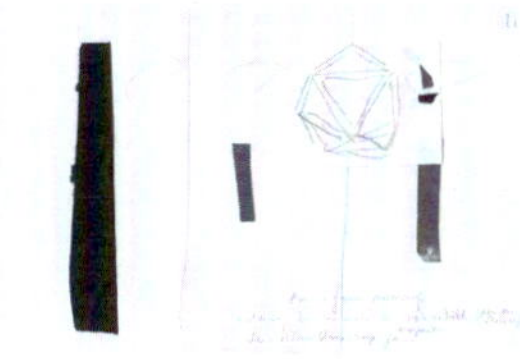

on 3 successive backgrounds
blacklight lighting of dodecahedron
(special paint)
single lightning flash white, red, yellow

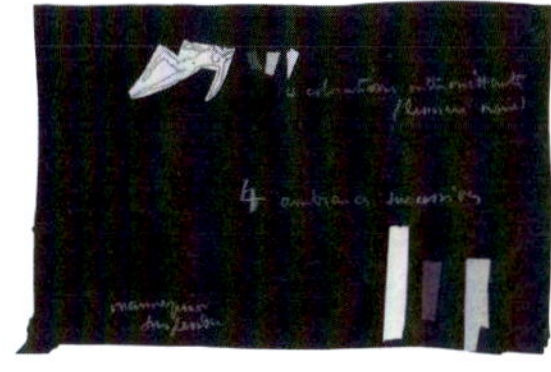

4 intermittent colorations (black light)

4 successive ambiences

hanging figure

[LEFT]
choose various faces

here: first, cave holes on B black background

on A and B simple dynamic interplay of colors at different speeds

then
introduction
of faces
including Laurel and Hardy

Sketchbook India
May 57 II p14

[RIGHT]
alternating black and white
slow rhythms + 3 chords
+ internals
the colored movement sweeps through the room

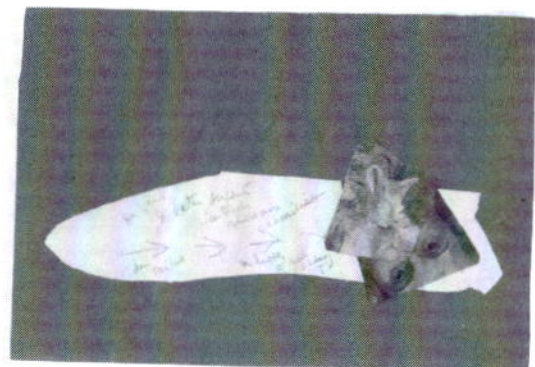

worms
foolish snakes
grasshoppers
rhinoceros
chameleon

Jean Painlevé struggles to the death
cinema TV

howling crowds

beautiful men women gods
by Fragonard

the storks
admirable
television TV
movements of hands
TV

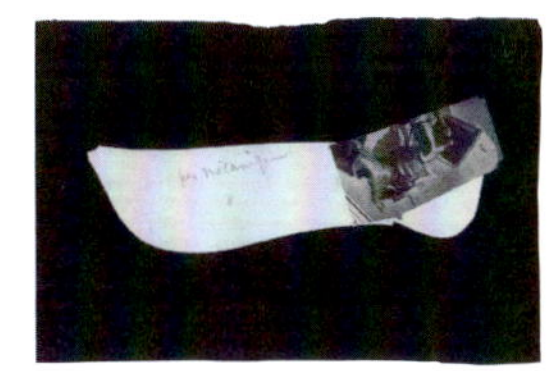

mechanisms

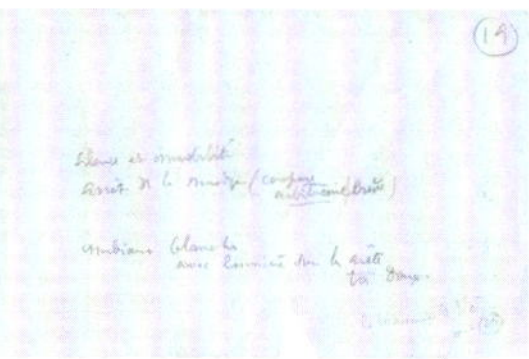

silence and immobility
the music stops (cut arbitrarily/brief)

white ambience with light on the edges very soft

the braveness of the soul or at 25

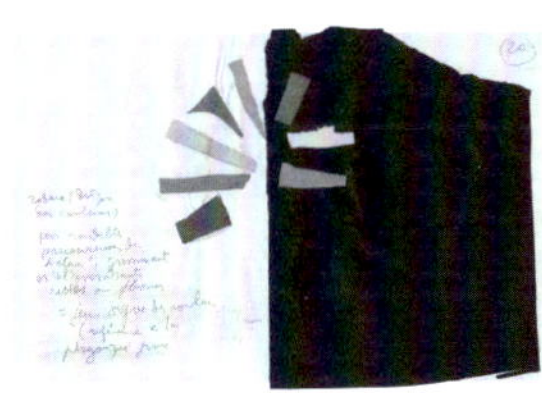

rose window (disk of colors) in slices crossing surfaces, expanding and contracting sharp or blurred = original set of colors (reference to pure physics)

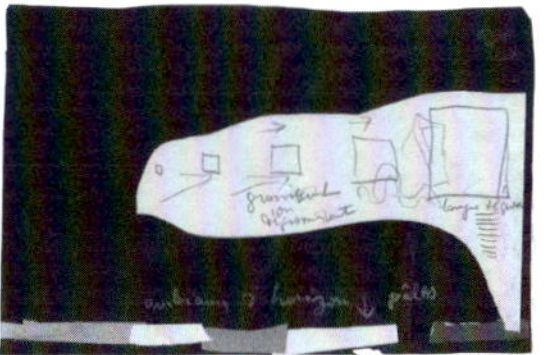

enlarging or reducing

long sequence

ambience of pale horizon

silent
in H1 / H2 / H alternatively
always mass
film, silent

lightning flash
atomic explosion
shipwreck
war
concentration
Donald Duck in B and Hirth in H
Simultaneous "horse of the apocalypse" on white ambience

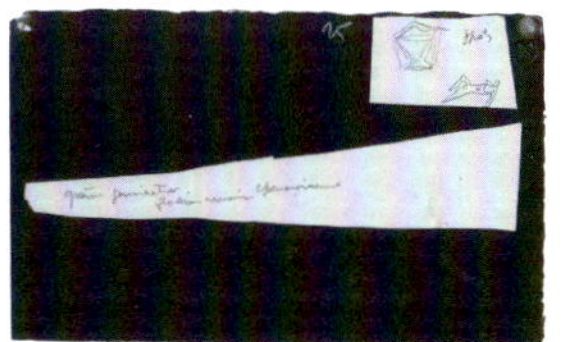

spotlights

seed germination
blooming flowering of chestnut tree

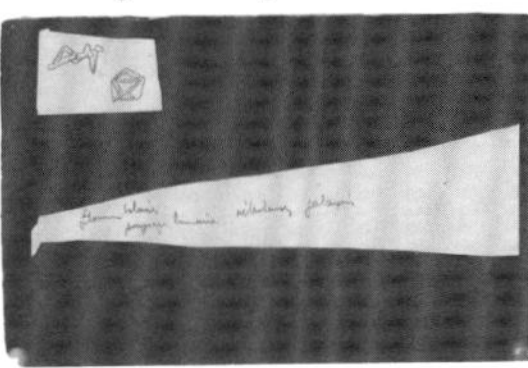

solar flames
lunar landscape
nebulae galaxies

white

a wide black equator

smile baby

Laurel and Hardy

—P. 640

Magazine article, "Philips," *Edilizia Moderna* (Italy), August 1958

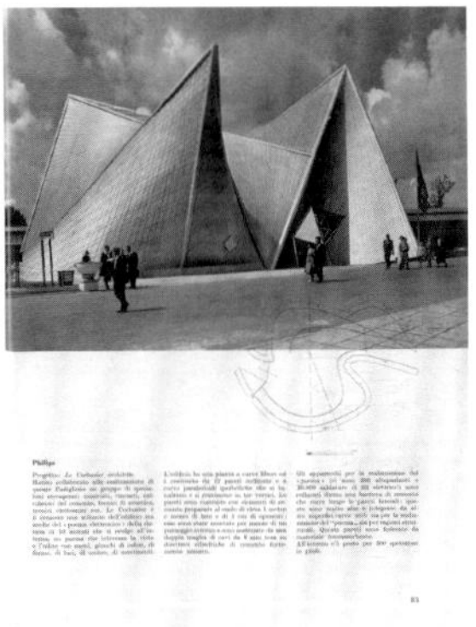

Philips

Design: Le Corbusier, Architect
A varied group of specialists collaborated to produce this Pavilion: musicians, filmmakers, cement technicians, acoustic technicians, electronics technicians, etc. Le Corbusier was the creator of not only the building but also the 10-minute-long "electronic poem" that unfolds in the interior, a poem that is both seen and heard, with sounds and shifting colors, shapes, light, shadow, and movement.

The building has a curving floor plan and is composed of 12 tilted walls, each one a hyperbolic-paraboloid curve, rising to meet in three peaks. The walls are built of panels of concrete cast on the ground, each one approximately 1.5 meters wide and 5 cm thick; they were mounted using an internal scaffolding and held in place by a double webbing of 8 mm cables affixed to cylindrical posts of strongly reinforced concrete.

The devices for producing the "poem" (there are 300 loudspeakers and 30,000 spot-welds on the electrical wires!) are set behind a concrete barrier that runs along the lateral walls: these very high walls have other superficial curves built in, which serve a structural purpose and serve in the production of the "poem." These walls are lined with sound-absorbent material.

Inside the pavilion is room for 500 standing spectators.

9 Mediterranean Days (1950–1959)

—P. 651

Le Corbusier to Marguerite Tjader Harris, 4 October 1954

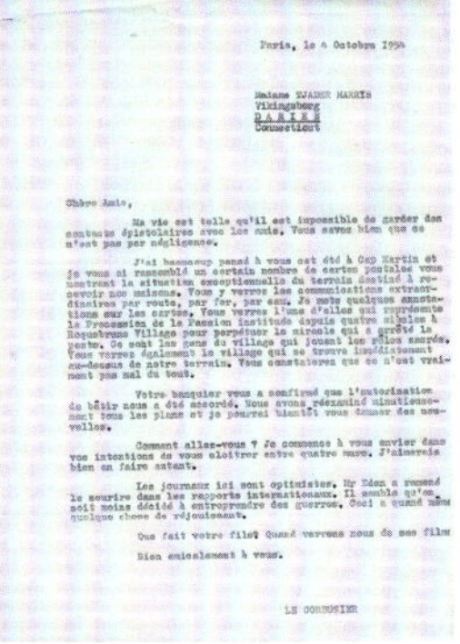

aris, 4 October 1954

rs. TJADER HARRIS
ikingsborg
ARIEN
onnecticut

ear friend,

ith the life I lead I just can't keep touch with my friends by letter. ou know very well it's not a question of neglecting them.

I thought of you a great deal is summer at Cap-Martin and I put gether for you a set of postcards owing you the remarkable siting of e land our houses are to be built n. There you'll see the extraordiary road, rail, and water transport etworks. You'll see one of the cards owing the Passion Procession ating back four hundred years in oquebrune village and celebrating e miracle that halted the plague. he people of the village play the cred roles. You'll also see the village, which is situated immediately ove our land. You'll note that it's ally not bad at all.

Your banker has given you conmation that the building permit is been granted. We've gone back rupulously over all the plans and ll soon have some news for you.

The newspapers here are optiistic. Mr. Eden has brought a smile ck into international relationships. seems that people will be less ady to go to war. That at least is use for rejoicing.

What's your son doing? When e we going to see his films?

Ever yours,

E CORBUSIER

—P. 651

Three postcards of the Côte d'Azur, enclosed with letter to Marguerite Tjader Harris, 4 October 1954

1 the terrain
2 our neighbor Badovici
3 the land belonging to me
4 the beach
A the railroad
B National Highway 7
Paris Rome
D the grand corniche [road]
[E] the station

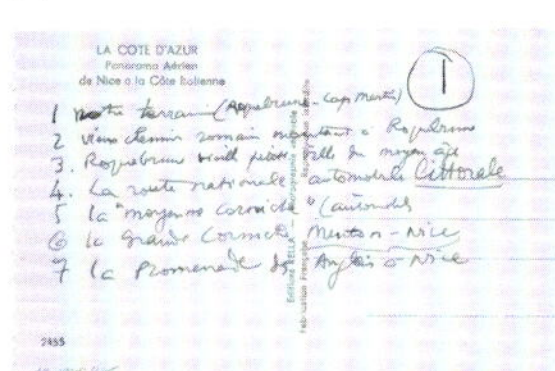

1 our plot [Roquebrune-Cap-Martin]
2 old Roman road going up to Roquebrune
3 Roquebrune little old medieval town
4 National highway along the coast
5 the "mid-corniche" [automobiles]
6 the grand corniche Menton–Nice
7 the Promenade des Anglais in Nice

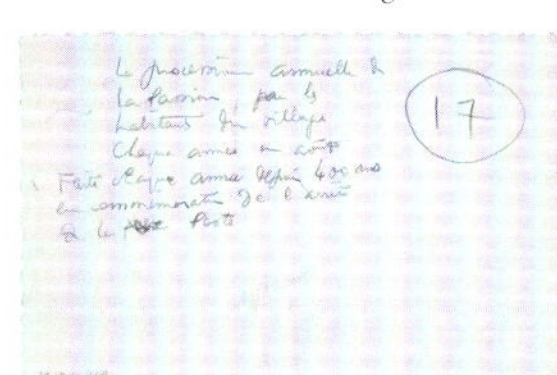

The annual Passion procession, by the people of the village
Each year in August
Held every year for 400 years in commemoration of the year of the Plague

—P. 653

Le Corbusier's sketch for his mother, 26 December 1952, showing the location of his property

Here Prince of Monaco

A = railroad
B = sea road
C = mid-corniche [road]
D = grand corniche [road]

here my cabin [the terrain]

—P. 653

Le Corbusier to his mother and brother, 31 August 1955

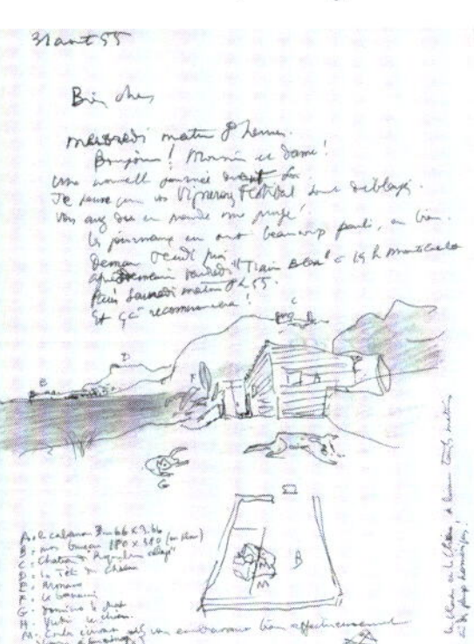

31 August 1955

Dear ones,
Wednesday morning 8 o'clock.

Good morning! Sir and madam!
A new day before you.
I imagine your Wine Festival's over.
It must really have worn you out!

The papers said lots of nice things about it.

Tomorrow Thursday then day after tomorrow Friday "Blue Train" at 7 p.m. at Monte Carlo

Paris Saturday morning 8:55
And it'll start all over again!

A = the cabin 3.66 x 3.66 m
B = my office 180 x 380 [plan]
C = "Roquebrune village" Château
D = the Dog's Head
E = Monaco
F = the banana tree
G = Domino the cat
H = Yuki the dog
M = Corbu writing and Yvonne doing her housework sending you all their love,

[drawing]
[RIGHT MARGIN]
Every morning the dog and the cat indulge in Homeric games!

—P. 661

Le Corbusier to the mayor of Roquebrune-Cap-Martin, 9 August 1958

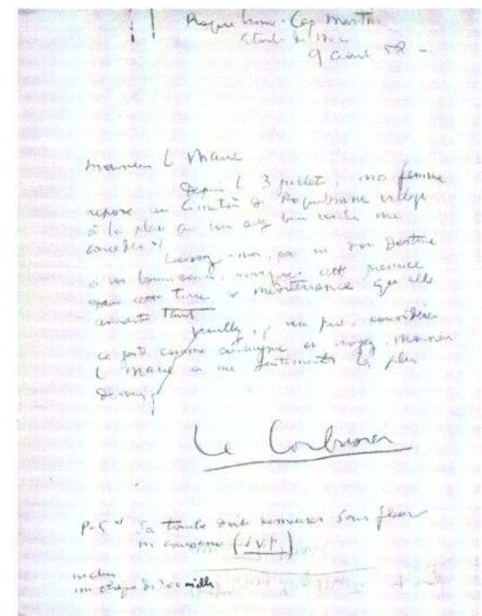

Roquebrune-Cap-Martin
Etoile de Mer
9 August 58

Mr. Mayor

Since 3 July my wife has been at rest in the Roquebrune village cemetery in the allotment you so kindly gave me.*

With this gift to be used for works of charity, I should like to signal her presence in this Mediterranean countryside she loved so much.

I request that this gesture remain anonymous. With best regards,

Le Corbusier

P-S *There should be no wreaths or flowers on her grave at any time. (please)

enclosed a check for 200 thousand

—P. 661

Le Corbusier's sketch of Roquebrune-Cap-Martin, 17 June 1958

17 June 58

Dear ones both of you!

Came back Sunday morning from a week at Roquebrune cemetery building Yvonne's tomb with Bertocchi (the mason whose son was Yvonne's godson).

Nest perched 300m higher than our cabin. To transport the loads you need a mule, then the shoulders of men.

From Monday morning to noon Saturday Bertocchi did the digging, foundations and exposed cement. It's great!

[LEFT MARGIN]
Listened to your record. There were other people. I wasn't able to listen a second time. I'll do it. Careful, your musicians don't seem up to the task. You have to demand better or

[RIGHT MARGIN]
let the recording professionals do their job?!

[TOP MARGIN]
Big kisses to the little mom. I'm stressed out and overwhelmed with work.

[BOTTOM]
the tomb

—P. 662

Sketch of a bedroom and the Corbusian *corbeau* (crow), from Simla, India, 14 March 1951

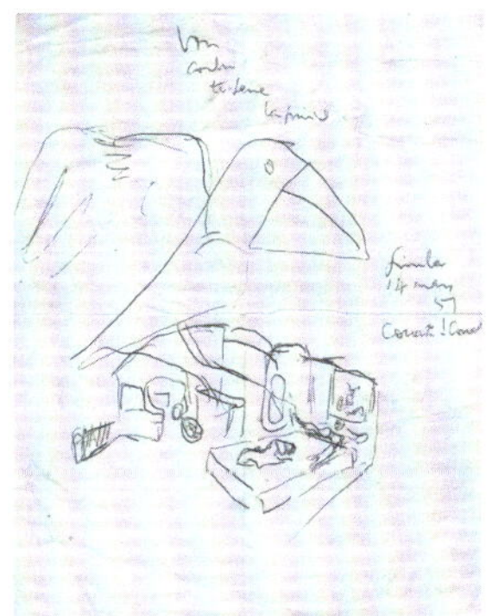

Von

Corbu shakes your hand

Simla
14 March
51
Caw! caw

—P. 662
Le Corbusier's sketch of his hand drawing a scene of Venice, December 1951

the bridge of sighs

IS THERE a crisis in Arts?

on account 27,000 francs
L-C
Dec. 51

paid to the order of Yv
L-C
Victorine
Jeanne

—P. 662
Sketch, 9 December 1953, depicting the coming New Year

sister Anne / 1953 / 1954

here is 9 Dec. 53

Corbu joyfully salutes this anniversary of the illustrious birth and puts his faith in 54 to get you back on your feet again.

—P. 663
Sketch of the *corbeau* (crow) dropping a gift to Yvonne for the New Year, 1954

[LEFT]
With all the love that comes from 31 years of perfect happiness

[RIGHT]
Dear Von my beloved

Here's a little very big present for 1954 to make you happy and make you promise your Corbu, who follows your worries hour by hour, that you will put on the white shoes, that you will eat soup, that you will come every day after ~~dinner~~ lunch

[RIGHT MARGIN]
and walk 200 paces to the wood, to get you used to walking again

—P. 663
Postcard from Le Corbusier to Yvonne, from Italy, 15 March 1955

15 March 55

Little Von. We're flying over Dijon. I want to tell you of all my love and deep tenderness for you. And I'm unhappy thinking of you alone and ill. I turned my big picture around this morning, because it's not finished. Keep telling yourself that you have a [E]dou[ard] out of the ordinary who is watching over you every minute, although you don't know it. Big kisses. Your [E]dou[ard].

—P. 666
Selected pages of Le Corbusier's book *Poésie sur Alger*, Falaize, Paris, 1950

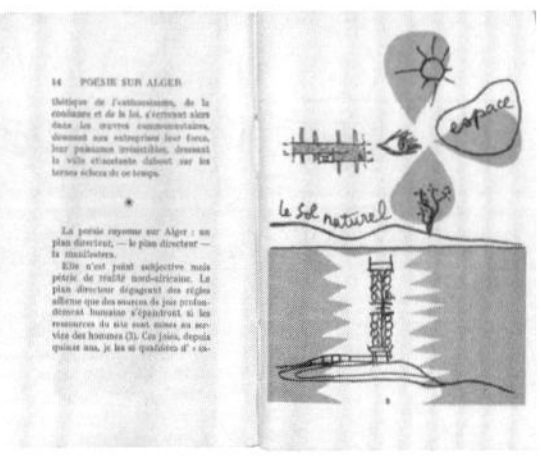

[… aes]thetics of enthusiasm, confidence and faith, taking their place in community works, giving companies their irresistible strength and power, raising the gleaming city upright on the dreary failures of these times.

Poetry shines on Algiers: a master plan—the master plan—will make it known.

This poetry is not subjective, but shot through with North African reality. Laying down rules, the master plan asserts that sources of profoundly human joy will spread if the site's resources are deployed in the interests of people (3). For fifteen years I have been describing these joys as "space" […]

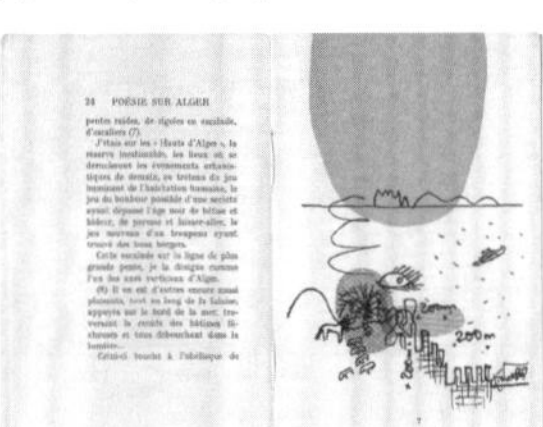

[…] steep slopes, precipitous channels, staircases (7).

I was on the "Heights of Algiers," that invaluable reserve, the place where the urban planning events of tomorrow will happen, this plinth for the imminent interplay of human habitation, the interplay of the happiness possible for a society that has transcended the dark age of stupidity and ugliness, laziness and carelessness, the new interplay of a flock that has found good shepherds.

I dub this climb up the steepest line one of Algiers's vertical axes.

(8) There are others, too, just as agreeable, all along the cliff, right on the seashore, running through the layer of sorry buildings and all leading to the light…

This axis grazes the obelisk of […]

[At the] time of this conversation the plan was to build *a métro, under ground*, to take these people away quickly, far out into housing developments—out in the sticks! Another project was built-for-rental boxes at the foot of the Casbah on the "Navy" land reclaimed by slum demolition. Yes, rental boxes in the heart of French Africa and on the very face of Algiers, right smack on the nose of the face! On this superlative piece of African soil!!! Misfortune! Irresponsibility! Vacuity! Annihilation of poetic values! Assassination of poets!

In this lower part of the town where the waves roll in, in all this port built up out of landfill and stones infiltrated by salt water, palms would be very much at home, the tall palms of the oases […]

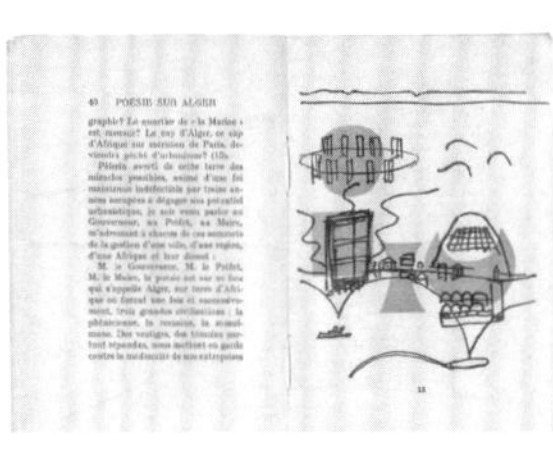

[…] The "Navy" district is in danger? Will the cape of Algiers, this African cape on the same meridian as Paris, become an urban planning disgrace? (15)

As a well-informed pilgrim to this land of possible miracles, driven by a faith rendered constant and unshakeable by thirteen years spent identifying its planning potential, I came to speak to the Governor, the Prefect, and the Mayor, addressing these leading lights about the running of a city, a region, an Africa, and saying to them:

Messrs Governor, Prefect, and Mayor, poetry lies on the place called Algiers, on that soil of Africa where three great civilizations once succeeded each other: Phoenician, Roman, and Muslim. Everywhere vestiges standing as testimony warn us of the mediocrity of our venal undertakings;

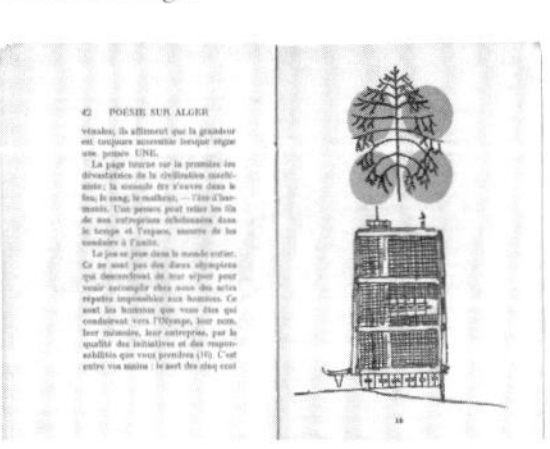

they assert that grandeur is always attainable when a SINGLE system of thought rules.

The page is turning on the first, devastating era of the machine civilization; the second—the era of harmony—is beginning with fire, the sword and distress. A system of thought can bring together the threads of our undertakings spread over time and space, in the certainty of leading them to unity.

The issue is being played out all over the world. It is not gods descending from their sojourn on Olympus who will carry out feats considered impossible for men, but the men you yourselves are who will bear their own names, memory, and undertakings toward Olympus thanks to the character of the initiatives taken and the responsibilities assumed (16). It is in your hands; the fate of the five hundred […]

—P. 669
Page from a study prepared by Le Corbusier and others for the CIAM conference planned for Algiers in 1955

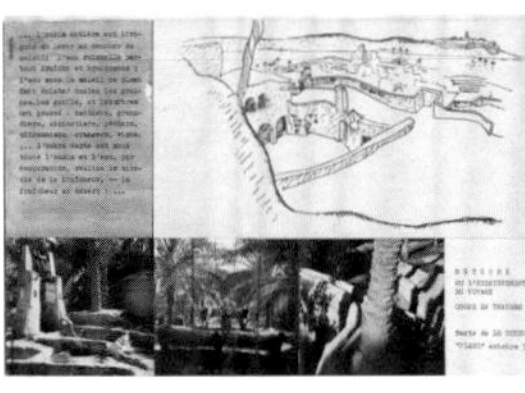

… The whole oasis is watered from sunrise to sunset; water streams everywhere, cool and murmuring; under the blazing sun the water makes all the seeds swell and burst, and the trees have shot up: date palms, pomegranates, apricots, peaches, lemons, oranges, and vines. … Green shade covers the whole oasis and through evaporation the water works the miracle of coolness,—coolness in the desert! …

—P. 674
Site plan, 22 December 1953 Rob vacation villas, Roquebrune-Cap-Martin

[RIGHT, TOP TO BOTTOM]
22 December 1953

red line
descent from the last wave

Note! 30 Dec. 1953
with red and black I've scribbled back in the blue crosses (erased) on the rocks, marking the houses. But I might be wrong on the seafront alignment of the axes (here) A on the crescent on axis B on the sea front on axis F

—P. 676

Le Corbusier's associate André Wogenscky to the builder, Roger Bertrand, 26 May 1952

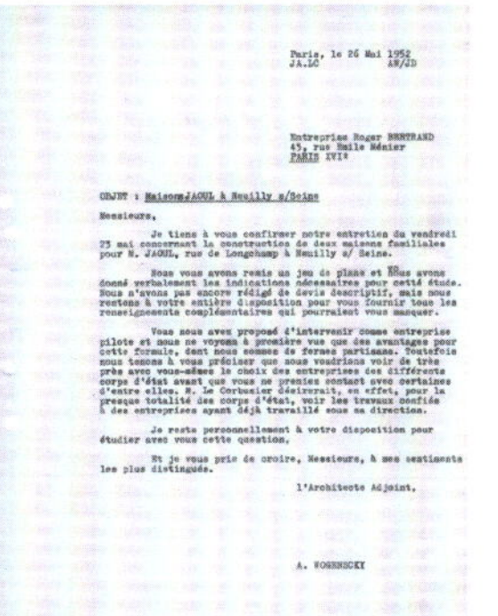

Paris, le 26 Mai 1952
JA.LC AW/JD

Entreprise Roger BERTRAND
43, rue Emile Ménier
PARIS XVI°

OBJET : Maisons JAOUL à Neuilly s/Seine

Messieurs,

Je tiens à vous confirmer notre entretien du vendredi 23 mai concernant la construction de deux maisons familiales pour M. JAOUL, rue de Longchamp à Neuilly s/ Seine.

Nous vous avons remis un jeu de plans et nous avons donné verbalement les indications nécessaires pour cette étude. Nous n'avons pas encore rédigé de devis descriptif, mais nous restons à votre entière disposition pour vous fournir tous les renseignements complémentaires qui pourraient vous manquer.

Vous nous avez proposé d'intervenir comme entreprise pilote et nous ne voyons à première vue que des avantages pour cette formule, dont nous sommes de fermes partisans. Toutefois nous tenons à vous préciser que nous voudrions voir de très près avec vous-mêmes le choix des entreprises des différents corps d'état avant que vous ne preniez contact avec certaines d'entre elles. M. Le Corbusier désirerait, en effet, pour la presque totalité des corps d'état, voir les travaux confiés à des entreprises ayant déjà travaillé sous sa direction.

Je reste personnellement à votre disposition pour étudier avec vous cette question.

Et je vous prie de croire, Messieurs, à mes sentiments les plus distingués.

l'Architecte Adjoint,

A. WOGENSCKY

Paris, 26 May 1952

Company Roger BERTRAND
43 rue Emile Ménier
PARIS XVI

SUBJECT: The JAOUL Houses in Neuilly s/Seine

Sirs,

I wish to confirm our conversation of Friday 23 May concerning the construction of two family homes for Mr. JAOUL, rue de Longchamp in Neuilly s/Seine.

We delivered to you a set of plans and gave you verbally the details necessary for the design. We have not yet drawn up an estimate with specifications, but we remain entirely at your disposal to supply you with all the additional information you might be missing.

You proposed that we act as overall contractor and at first glance we see only advantages in this structure, in which we firmly believe. Nevertheless, we wish to clarify that we would want to consider carefully, with you, the choice of the contractors of the various trades before you contact some of them. In fact, Mr. Le Corbusier would wish, in the case of nearly all the trades, to see the building work entrusted to contractors who have already worked under his direction.

I remain personally at your disposal to go over this matter with you.

I am, Sirs, yours truly,

Associate Architect,
A. WOGENSCKY

—P. 676

André Wogenscky to André Jaoul, 23 July 1952

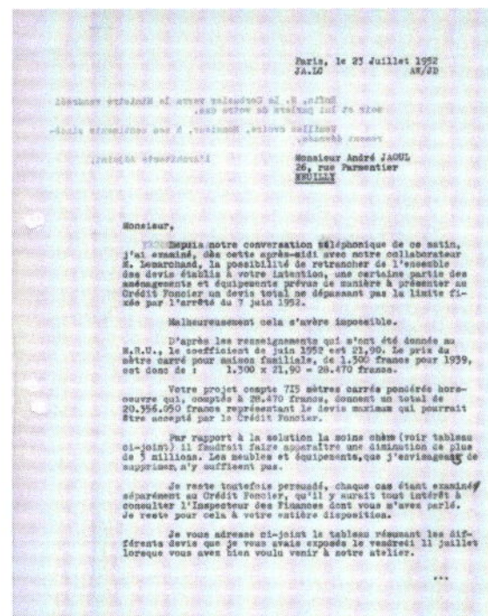

Paris, le 23 Juillet 1952
JA.LC AW/JD

Monsieur André JAOUL
26, rue Parmentier
NEUILLY

Monsieur,

Depuis notre conversation téléphonique de ce matin, j'ai examiné, dès cette après-midi avec notre collaborateur M. Lemarchand, la possibilité de retrancher de l'ensemble des devis établis à votre intention, une certaine partie des aménagements et équipements prévus de manière à présenter au Crédit Foncier un devis total ne dépassant pas la limite fixée par l'arrêté du 7 juin 1952.

Malheureusement cela s'avère impossible.

D'après les renseignements qui m'ont été donnés au M.R.U., le coefficient de juin 1952 est 21,90. Le prix du mètre carré pour maison familiale, de 1.300 francs pour 1939, est donc de : 1.300 x 21,90 = 28.470 francs.

Votre projet compte 715 mètres carrés pondérés hors-oeuvre qui, comptés à 28.470 francs, donnent un total de 20.356.050 francs représentant le devis maximum qui pourrait être accepté par le Crédit Foncier.

Par rapport à la solution la moins chère (voir tableau ci-joint) il faudrait faire apparaître une diminution de plus de 3 millions. Les meubles et équipements, que j'envisageais de supprimer, n'y suffisent pas.

Je reste toutefois persuadé, chaque cas étant examiné séparément au Crédit Foncier, qu'il y aurait tout intérêt à consulter l'Inspecteur des Finances dont vous m'avez parlé. Je reste pour cela à votre entière disposition.

Je vous adresse ci-joint le tableau résumant les différents devis que je vous avais exposés le vendredi 11 juillet lorsque vous avez bien voulu venir à notre atelier.

...

Paris, 23 July 1952

Mr. André JAOUL
26 rue Parmentier
NEUILLY

Sir,

After our telephone conversation of this morning, I have already explored, this afternoon with our collaborator Mr. Lemarchand, the possibility of subtracting from the overall estimates we drew up for you, a certain portion of the planned design and fittings so as to show the Crédit Foncier a total estimate that does not exceed the limit established by the decree of 7 June 1952.

Unfortunately that proved impossible.

According to the information given me at the M[inistry of] R[econstruction and] U[rbanism], the coefficient for June 1952 is 21.90. The price per square meter for a family home, 1,300 francs for 1939, thus comes to: 1,300 x 21.90 = 28,470 francs.

Your design is for 715 square meters weighted for the external dimensions, which at 28,470 francs give a total of 20,356,050 francs, which represents the maximum estimate acceptable to the Crédit Foncier.

As for the less expensive solution (see the attached table) we would have to show a figure more than 3 million lower. The furniture and appliances, which I was thinking of eliminating, aren't enough.

I still believe since each case is examined individually at the Crédit Foncier that it would greatly behoove us to consult the Treasury Officer you spoke of. I remain at your complete disposal for that.

I am attaching for you the table summarizing the different estimates I went over with you on Friday 11 July when you were so kind as to come to our studio

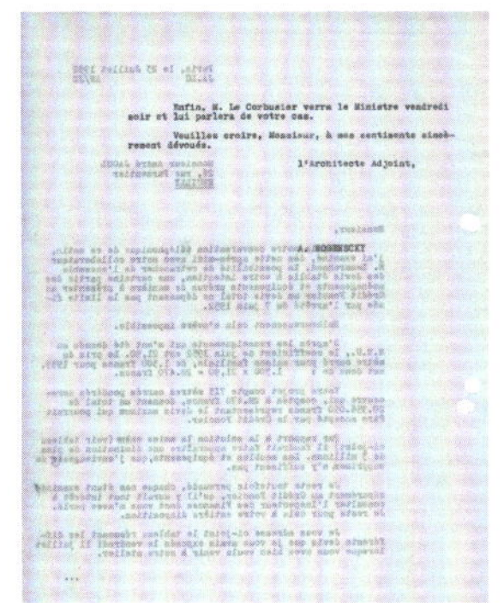

Enfin, M. Le Corbusier verra le Ministre vendredi soir et lui parlera de votre cas.

Veuillez croire, Monsieur, à mes sentiments sincèrement dévoués.

l'Architecte Adjoint,

A. WOGENSCKY

Finally, Mr. Le Corbusier will see the Minister Friday evening and will speak to him about your case.

I am, Sir, sincerely yours,

Associate Architect
A. WOGENSCKY

—P. 676

André Wogenscky to André Jaoul, 20 May 1953

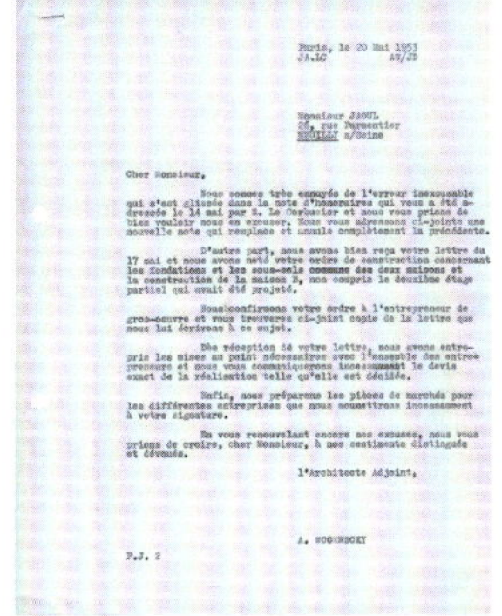

Paris, le 20 Mai 1953
JA.LC AW/JD

Monsieur JAOUL
26, rue Parmentier
NEUILLY s/Seine

Cher Monsieur,

Nous sommes très ennuyés de l'erreur inexcusable qui s'est glissée dans la note d'honoraires qui vous a été adressée le 14 mai par M. Le Corbusier et nous vous prions de bien vouloir nous en excuser. Nous vous adressons ci-jointe une nouvelle note qui remplace et annule complètement la précédente.

D'autre part, nous avons bien reçu votre lettre du 17 mai et nous avons noté votre ordre de construction concernant les fondations et les sous-sols communs des deux maisons et la construction de la maison B, non compris le deuxième étage partiel qui avait été projeté.

Nous confirmons votre ordre à l'entrepreneur de gros-oeuvre et vous trouverez ci-joint copie de la lettre que nous lui écrivons à ce sujet.

Dès réception de votre lettre, nous avons entrepris les mises au point nécessaires avec l'ensemble des entrepreneurs et nous vous communiquerons incessamment le devis exact de la réalisation telle qu'elle est décidée.

Enfin, nous préparons les pièces de marchés pour les différentes entreprises que nous soumettrons incessamment à votre signature.

En vous renouvelant encore nos excuses, nous vous prions de croire, cher Monsieur, à nos sentiments distingués et dévoués.

l'Architecte Adjoint,

A. WOGENSCKY

P.J. 2

Paris, 20 May 1953

Mr. JAOUL
26 rue Parmentier
NEUILLY s/Seine

Dear Sir,

We are very vexed about the inexcusable error that slipped into the fee memorandum that was sent to you on 14 May by Mr. Le Corbusier and we beg you to please excuse us. We are sending you attached a new memorandum that replaces and completely supersedes the previous one.

On another front, we received your letter of 17 May and have noted your construction order concerning the two buildings' common foundations and basements and construction of house B, not including the projected partial second story.

We are confirming your order with the structural contractor and you will find herewith a copy of the letter we wrote him on the subject.

As soon as we received your letter, we began finalizing details with all the contractors and we will immediately inform you of the exact estimate of the construction as it is determined.

Finally, we are preparing the contracts for the various contractors, which we will immediately submit for your signature.

We apologize again, and remain most respectfully yours,

Associate Architect,
A. WOGENSCKY

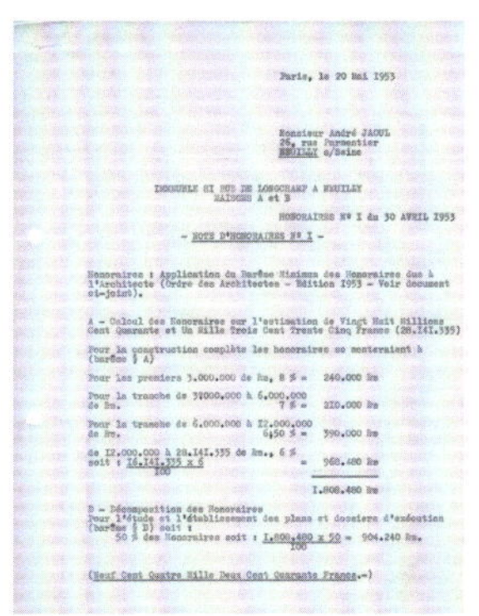

Paris, le 20 Mai 1953

Monsieur André JAOUL
26, rue Parmentier
NEUILLY s/Seine

IMMEUBLE 81 RUE DE LONGCHAMP A NEUILLY
MAISONS A et B

HONORAIRES N° I du 30 AVRIL 1953

- NOTE D'HONORAIRES N° I -

Honoraires : Application du Barême Minimum des Honoraires dus à l'Architecte (Ordre des Architectes - Edition 1953 - Voir document ci-joint).

A - Calcul des Honoraires sur l'estimation de Vingt Huit Millions Cent Quarante et Un Mille Trois Cent Trente Cinq Francs (28.141.335)

Pour la construction complète les honoraires se monteraient à (barême § A)

Pour les premiers 3.000.000 de Frs, 8 % = 240.000 Frs

Pour la tranche de 3.000.000 à 6.000.000 de Frs. 7 % = 210.000 Frs

Pour la tranche de 6.000.000 à 12.000.000 de Frs. 6,50 % = 390.000 Frs

de 12.000.000 à 28.141.335 de Frs., 6 % soit : 16.141.335 x 6 / 100 = 968.480 Frs

1.808.480 Frs

B - Décomposition des Honoraires
Pour l'étude et l'établissement des plans et dossiers d'exécution (barême § B) soit :
50 % des Honoraires soit : 1.808.480 x 50 / 100 = 904.240 Frs.

(Neuf Cent Quatre Mille Deux Cent Quarante Francs.-)

Paris, 20 May 1953

Mr. André JAOUL
26 rue Parmentier
NEUILLY s/Seine

BUILDING 81 RUE DE LONGCHAMP IN NEUILLY
HOUSES A and B
FEES No. 1 of 30 APRIL 1953
STATEMENT OF FEES No. 1

Fees: Application of the Minimum Scale of Fees due the Architect (Architects' Association –Edition 1953– See attached document).

A—Calculation of the fees on the value of Twenty-Eight Million One Hundred Forty-One Thousand Three Hundred Thirty-Five Francs (28,141,335)

For the entire construction the fees would total (scale § A)

For the first 3,000,000 Frs. 8% = 240,000 Frs.

For amounts from 3,000,000 to 6,000,000 Frs. 7% = 210,000 Frs.

For amounts from 6,000,000 to 12,000,000 Frs. 6.5% = 390,000 Frs.

from 12,000,000 to 28,141,335 Frs., 6%, that is, 16,141,335 x 6 divided by 100 = 968,480 Frs.
1,808,480 Frs.

D—Breakdown of the Fees
For designing and preparing the plans and files of execution (scale § D), or, 50% of the fees, or: 1,808,480 x 50 divided by 100 = 904,240 Frs.

(Nine Hundred Four Thousand Two Hundred Forty Francs.—)

—P. 683

Le Corbusier's sketch of his mother at age ninety-one, 10 September 1951

at age 91 Marie Charlotte Amélie Jeanneret Perret [?] beneath the sun, the moon, the mountains, the lake, and home surrounded by the affectionate admiration of her children. 10 September 1957

10 Retrospection (1954–1965)

—P. 698

Sketches for the Church of Saint-Pierre, Firminy-Vert, 1960

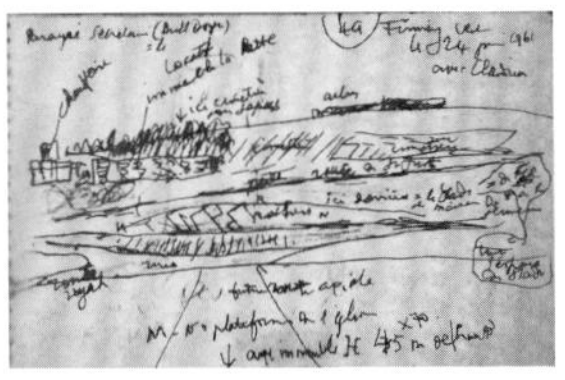

[LEFT TO RIGHT, TOP TO BOTTOM]
Brayré Secretary (Bulldozer)
= rental accommodation

Firminy Vert
24 June 1961
with Claudius

boiler house / La Patte apartment block / here cemetery under fir trees / trees

cemetery / cemetery
old St Just road

rocks / here behind = the FIR[miny] stadium / the youth center

royal road / streets / the whole stadium space

future expressway
M–N = church platform
axis apartment block H 45x70m high

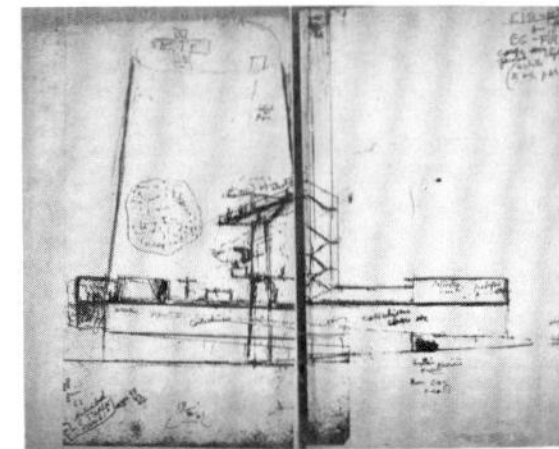

[TOP TO BOTTOM, LEFT TO RIGHT]
FIR[miny] CH[urch]
generalized section

Easter sun

singer / electro[nic] organ

catechism / catechism classes etc.

back entrance open

Nice spot

18 June 61
see Sketchbook
LC TURIN
May 61
L–C

—P. 702

Le Corbusier to his associate Fernand Gardien, 7 July 1959

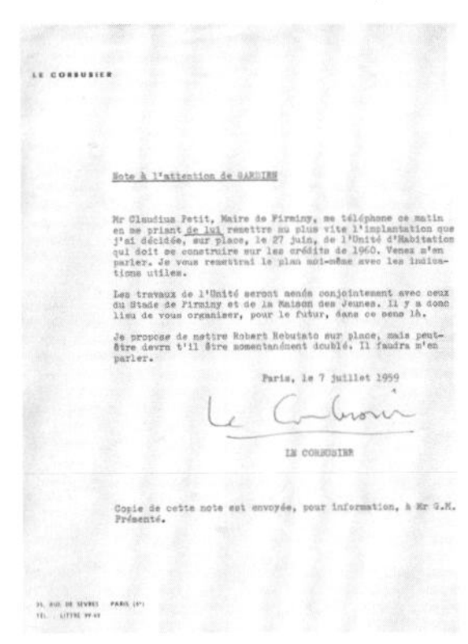

LE CORBUSIER

Note à l'attention de GARDIEN

Mr Claudius Petit, Maire de Firminy, me téléphone ce matin en me priant de lui remettre au plus vite l'implantation que j'ai décidée, sur place, le 27 juin, de l'Unité d'Habitation qui doit se construire sur les crédits de 1960. Venez m'en parler. Je vous remettrai le plan moi-même avec les indications utiles.

Les travaux de l'Unité seront menés conjointement avec ceux du Stade de Firminy et de la Maison des Jeunes. Il y a donc lieu de vous organiser, pour le futur, dans ce sens là.

Je propose de mettre Robert Rebutato sur place, mais peut-être devra t'il être momentanément doublé. Il faudra m'en parler.

Paris, le 7 juillet 1959

LE CORBUSIER

Copie de cette note est envoyée, pour information, à Mr G.M. Présenté.

35, RUE DE SEVRES PARIS (6e)
TEL. : LITTRE 99-62

<u>Note for the attention of GARDIEN</u>

Mr. Claudius Petit, Mayor of Firminy, phoned this morning asking me to provide <u>him</u> as soon as possible with the location I chose on site, on 27 June, for the Unité d'Habitation, which is to be built with funds available in 1960. Come and see me about it. I shall give you the plan myself, with the necessary indications.

Work on the Unité will be carried out in tandem with that on the Firminy Stadium and the Youth Center. So you should organize things for the future with that in mind.

I intend to put Robert Rebutato on the site, but maybe someone will have to take his place for the moment. You'll need to speak with me about this.

Paris, 7 July 1959.

[signature]
LE CORBUSIER

A copy of this note has been sent for information to Mr. G.M. Presented.

—P. 702

Le Corbusier to his associate André Maisonnier, 8 July 1959

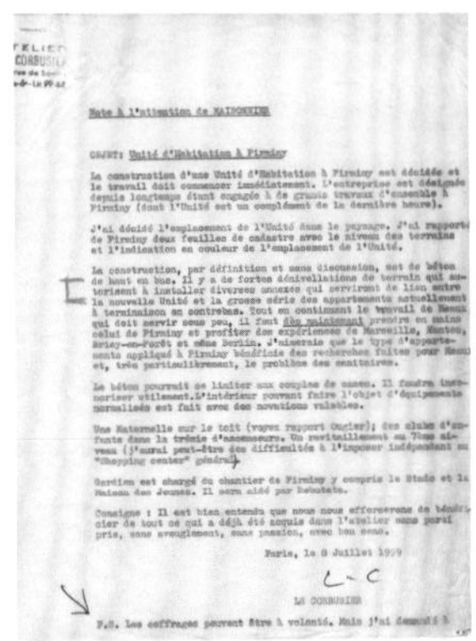

Note à l'attention de MAISONNIER

OBJET: Unité d'Habitation à Firminy

La construction d'une Unité d'Habitation à Firminy est décidée et le travail doit commencer immédiatement. L'entreprise est désignée depuis longtemps étant engagée à de grands travaux d'ensemble à Firminy (dont l'Unité est un complément de la dernière heure).

J'ai décidé l'emplacement de l'Unité dans le paysage. J'ai rapporté de Firminy deux feuilles de cadastre avec le niveau des terrains et l'indication en couleur de l'emplacement de l'Unité.

La construction, par définition et sans discussion, est de béton de haut en bas. Il y a de fortes dénivellations de terrain qui autorisent à installer diverses annexes qui serviront de lien entre la nouvelle Unité et la grosse série des appartements actuellement à terminaison en contrebas. Tout en continuant le travail de Meaux qui doit servir sous peu, il faut dès maintenant prendre en mains celui de Firminy et profiter des expériences de Marseille, Nantes, Briey-en-Forêt et même Berlin. J'aimerais que le type d'appartements appliqué à Firminy bénéficie des recherches faites pour Meaux et, très particulièrement, le problème des sanitaires.

Le béton pourrait se limiter aux couples de cases. Il faudra insonoriser utilement. L'intérieur pouvant faire l'objet d'équipements normalisés est fait avec des novations valables.

Une Maternelle sur le toit (voyez rapport Ougier); des clubs d'enfants dans la trémie d'ascenseurs. Un ravitaillement au 7ème niveau (j'aurai peut-être des difficultés à l'imposer indépendant au "Shopping center" général).

Gardien est chargé du chantier de Firminy y compris le Stade et la Maison des Jeunes. Il sera aidé par Rebutato.

Consigne : Il est bien entendu que nous nous efforcerons de bénéficier de tout ce qui a déjà été acquis dans l'atelier sans parti pris, sans aveuglement, sans passion, avec bon sens.

Paris, le 8 Juillet 1959

L–C

LE CORBUSIER

P.S. Les coffrages peuvent être à volonté. Mais j'ai demandé à

<u>Note for the attention of MAISONNIER</u>

Re: <u>Unité d'Habitation, Firminy</u>

It has been decided to build a Unité d'Habitation at Firminy and work is to begin at once. The undertaking dates back a considerable time, being part of major housing estate works in Firminy (with the Unité as a last-minute addition).

I have chosen the location of the Unité in the local landscape. I have brought back from Firminy two cadastral sheets giving the levels and indicating the location of the Unité in color.

By definition and without being open to discussion, the construction will be concrete from top to bottom. Marked differences of level mean that various annexes can be built to serve as links between the new Unité and the extensive series of apartment blocks being built lower down. While continuing the works at Meaux, which should soon be usable, we must <u>immediately</u> start on the Firminy project and take advantage of our experiences in Marseille, Nantes, Briey-en-Forêt, and even Berlin. I would like the type of apartment used for Firminy to benefit from the research done for Meaux, most especially in respect to the bathroom and toilet problems.

The concrete could be limited to the pairs of compartments. Adequate soundproofing will be needed. The interior, which can make use of standardized items, will incorporate appropriate innovations.

A nursery school on the roof (see the Ougier report); children's clubs in the elevator shaft. A food store on the 7th level (I may have some problems getting this accepted separately from the "Shopping Center.")

Gardien is in charge of the Firminy job, including the Stadium and the Youth Center. He will be helped by Rebutato.

Note: It is to be understood that we will take maximum advantage of everything already achieved in the studio, without preconceptions, blinders, or overzealousness, and applying common sense.

Paris, 8 July 1959.

L–C
LE CORBUSIER

P.S. The formwork can be random. But this time I asked

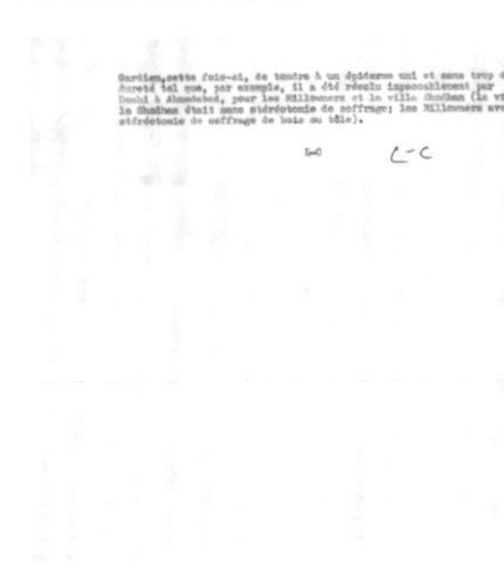

Gardien, cette fois-ci, de tendre à un épiderme uni et sans trop de dureté tel que, par exemple, il a été résolu impeccablement par Doshi à Ahmedabad, pour les Millowners et la villa Shodhan (la villa Shodhan était sans stéréotomie de coffrage; les Millowners avec stéréotomie de coffrage de bois ou tôle).

L–C L–C

Gardien to stretch a simple, not too rigid membrane just as, for example, Doshi had done impeccably for the Millowners and the Shodhan Villa at Ahmedabad – the Shodhan Villa with smooth formwork, the Millowners with relief formwork of wood or sheet metal.

L–C

—P. 704

Selected pages from Le Corbusier's sketchbook number 50, from his trip to Baghdad, 8–13 November 1957

[TOP]
Tigris N–6 to –7

wall

[LEFT]
here the palm groves and orange trees
N5

[RIGHT]
alluvium
N–5 / new aligned palm grove
= alluvium loop
N

If house in N–5

[BOTTOM]
N + 5m

access road
access to city

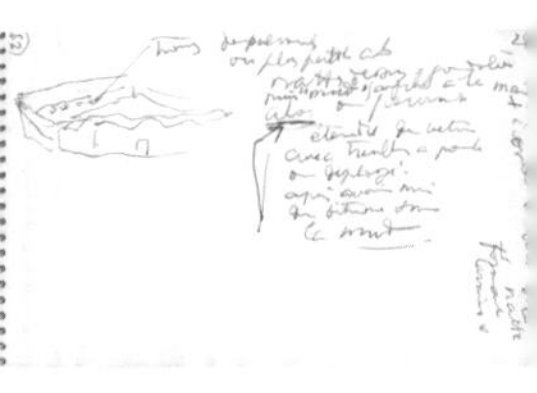

holes for palm trees or smaller trees
mats on top = warped then hand-made clay mud

[RIGHT MARGIN]
+ flow off the end of the mat forming gutter

then we could lay concrete with chicken wire or expanded metal afte laying bitumen on the <u>mud</u>

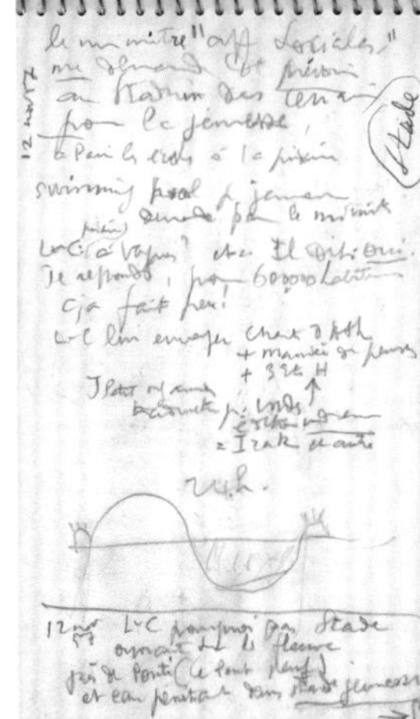

the minister "Social Aff[air]s" asks <u>me</u> to <u>plan</u> for the Stadium, areas <u>fo</u> young people

in Paris schools at the swimming pool
swimming pool for young people requested by the minister
L–C: swimming pool with waves? et
He says: <u>yes</u>. I answer, for 600,000 inhabitants that's not much!
L–C to send him Athens charter
+ Way of thinking?
+ 3 Et[ablissement]s H[umains]

J. Petit to organize translation for India
<u>Indian</u> edition
= Iraq and others

24 h[ours]

12 Nov. 57
L–C why not stadium opening onto the river near Ponti (the Pont Neuf) and water entering the <u>youth stadium</u>

[LEFT MARGIN]
12 Nov. 57

[RIGHT MARGIN]
Stadium

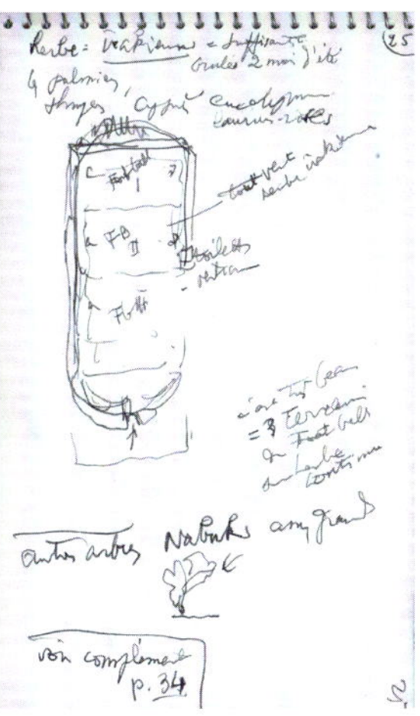

grass = Iraqi = sufficient
burned 2 months summer

the palms
thujas / cypresses / eucalyptuses
oleanders

C Football 1 / all green / Iraqi grass

FB II / toilets / dressing rooms

FB III

it's very beautiful
= 3 football pitches on continuous grass

other trees Nabuks quite tall

see additions p.34

—P. 708

Postcard from Ernest Weismann, Kunio Maekawa, and Junzo Sakakura to Le Corbusier, from Mt. Fuji, Japan, 17 August 1958

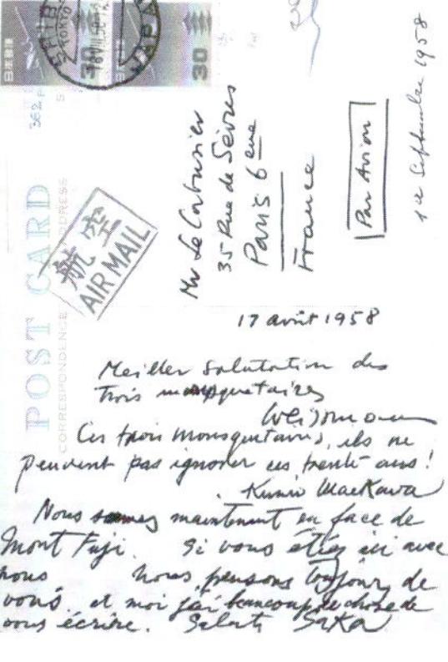

17 August 1958

Best wishes from the three musketeers

Weismann

These three musketeers can't ignore these last thirty years!

Kuni Maekawa

We are now facing Mount Fuji. If only you were here with us. We think of you always and I have a lot to write to you about.

Best wishes, Saka

—P. 711

Le Corbusier to Junzo Sakakura, 7 September 1959

Paris, 7 September 1959

Mr. Junzo Sakakura
6 Akasaka Hinoki-Cho
Minato-Ky
TOKYO

My dear Sakakura,

I received the Japanese review Sinkentiku with good photographs of the Museum.

I've had no news of the opening or of you, either from Maekawa or Taka. I've had no photographic material, no press stuff! The only thing that worries me is that the invitation to the opening made for me by Foreign Affairs, and sent to me as well, omits any mention that the building was made according to my plans.

I have the impression that you did a very good job on the building. I'd like to have some photo documentation, because the reproductions in the magazines are not good enough; you can't recognize the materials.

Thanking you in advance and best wishes to you all

LE CORBUSIER

P.S. Going by the few photographs I've received, the execution of the Museum seems to be perfect and is a real tribute to your professional skills (the three of you) as well as to uncompromising Japanese integrity. This is one of the essential aspects of the Japanese soul, which I discovered as a youthful admirer of prints, netsuke, etc. I'm delighted to have been able to carry this work through with you all.

If I could find the time I'd also be delighted to do the photographic mural for the 19th-century Great Hall, which should represent a thorough rehabilitation of that astonishing century.

If you get the chance, could one of you send me a translation of the article by Kenchiku Bunke that contains photos of work by Auguste Perret and of Ronchamp.

L-C

—P. 712

Drawing for tapestry, 18 August 1956, included with the letter of 22 August, 1956

[BOTTOM LEFT]
the line mn + the line mp designating the visible part of the curtain

[BOTTOM RIGHT]
Cap-Martin
18 / 8 / 56

BULL XIV
Yesterday I got the order from Tokyo to make sure that the woven tapestries for the theater were delivered there on 28 August

This morning I designed this second project with 2 pictures: a Bull Abduction of Europa + Bull XI

The Modulor immediately provided the basis for my composition, but I had to settle for a degree of inexactitude, not having the necessary time [...]

—P. 713

Le Corbusier's secretary to Junzo Sakakura, 30 May 1956

Paris, 30 May 1956

Mr. Junzo Sakakura
8 Akasaka-hinokicho
Minatoku
Tokyo
Sir,

Mr. Le Corbusier has asked me to inform you that on 12.4.56 he received from you a big envelope containing wool samples, but with no accompanying letter.

He would like you to let him have as soon as possible:

1/ The exact measurements of the theater curtain

2/ A drawing of "front stage" (what the stage curtain and its surrounds look like)

Thanking you in advance,
With all best wishes,

The Secretary

—P. 713

Le Corbusier to Junzo Sakakura, 17 July 1956

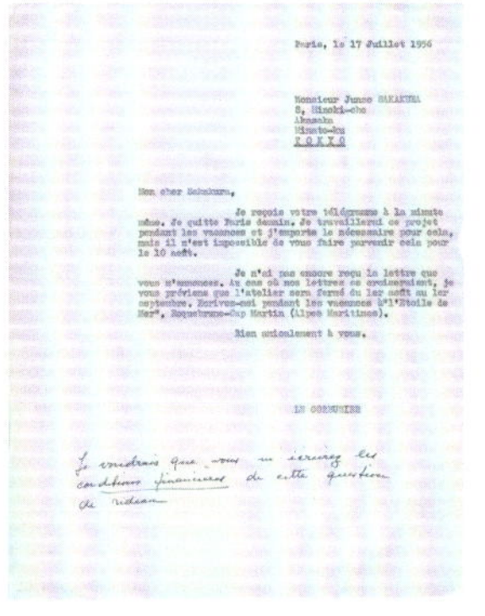

Paris, 17 July 1956

Mr. Junzo Sakakura
8 Hinoki-cho
Minato-ku
Tokyo

My dear Sakakura,

I received your telegram this very minute. I'm leaving Paris tomorrow. I shall work on the project during my vacation and will be taking the necessary with me, but there is no way I can get it to you for 10 August.

I haven't yet received the letter you mention. In case our letters cross, I should warn you that the studio will be closed from 1 August to 1 September. During the holidays, write to me at "L'Etoile de Mer," Roquebrune-Cap-Martin (Alpes-Maritimes).

With all best wishes,

LE CORBUSIER

I'd like you to send me in writing the financial terms of this curtain business

—P. 713

Junzo Sakakura to Le Corbusier, 13 August 1956

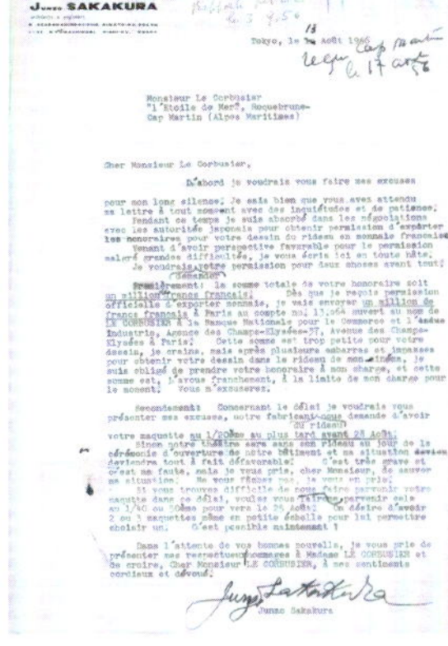

Tokyo, 13 August 1956
Received Cap-Martin 17 August 56

Mr. Le Corbusier
"L'Etoile de Mer," Roquebrune
Cap-Martin (Alpes-Maritimes)

Dear Mr. Le Corbusier,

Let me begin by excusing myself for my long silence. I know that you were awaiting my letter from one moment to the next, anxiously and patiently.

During all this time I've been busy with negotiations with the Japanese authorities to get permission to send you your fee for the curtain design in French currency.

Despite considerable difficulty I have just had a seemingly favorable decision on the matter, and I am now writing to you as quickly as possible.

I should mainly like to ask your permission for two matters:

First: your total fee, which is one million French francs. As soon as I receive official permission to send the money out of the country, I shall send one million French francs to Paris, marked for account no. 13,064, in the name of Le Corbusier, at the Banque Nationale pour le Commerce et l'Industrie, Champs-Elysées–37 Agency, Avenue des Champs-Elysées, Paris. I fear that this sum is too small for your design, but after a number of awkward situations and stalemates in the course of obtaining your design for the curtain of my cinema, I find myself forced to pay your fee myself, and frankly, this sum is the best I can do at present. Please excuse me.

Second: regarding the deadline, please excuse me, but our curtain manufacturer is asking for your 1:20 model by 28 August at the latest.

If not, our theater will be without its curtain on the day of the opening ceremony for our building and this will put me in a very difficult situation. This is very serious, and the fault is mine, but I beg you, dear Sir, save the day for me. Please do not be angry with me.

If you have difficulty in getting your model to us by this date, could you send the 1:40 or 1:50 model by around 25 August. We would like to have 2 or 3 models, even on a small scale, for the manufacturer to be able to choose one. Is that possible now?

Hoping for a favorable reply, I should like to pass on my best regards to Mrs. LE CORBUSIER, together with my best wishes to you, Dear Mr. LE CORBUSIER.

[signature]
Junzo Sakakura

—P. 713

Note from Le Corbusier regarding color palette for curtain, 21 August 1956

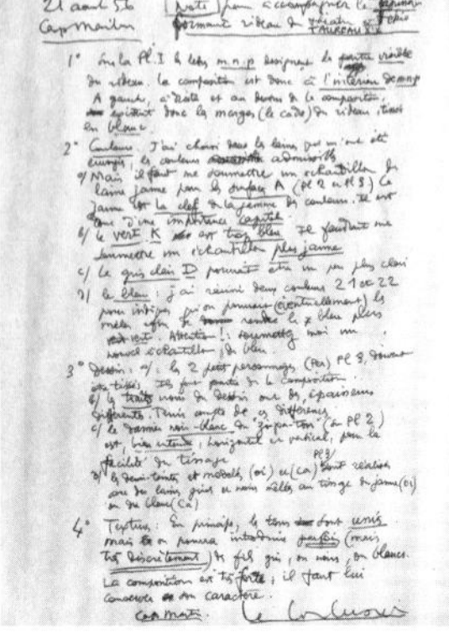

21 August 56
Cap-Martin

Note to accompany the Tapestry for the theater curtain in Tokyo
BULL XIV

1. On Plate 1 the letters m.n.p designate the visible part of the curtain. So the composition is inside m.n.p.

Thus to the left and right and above the composition, there are the margins (the frame) of the curtain, woven in white.

2. Colors. I have chosen acceptable colors from among the wools sent to me.

a/ But I need to be given a yellow wool sample for the areas A (plates 2 and 3). This yellow is the key to the color range. So it is vitally important.

b/ The green K is too blue. You need to send me a more yellow sample.

c/ The light gray D could be a little lighter.

d/ The blue: I have brought together two colors, 21 and 22, to indicate the possibility of mixing them to get a greener blue. N.B. send me a new sample of blue.

3. Drawing: a/: the 2 little figures (Per) Pl 3, must be woven. They are part of the composition.

b/ The black lines in the drawing are of different thicknesses. Take note of these differences.

c/ The black-white checkerboard of the "zi-pa-ton" (Pl 2) is, of course, horizontal and vertical, to facilitate the weaving.

d/ the half-tones and models (oi) and (ca) (Pl 3) are done with gray and black wools mixed during weaving with yellow (oi) or white (ca)

4. Textures: In theory, the tones are uniform, but we could slip in ~~sometimes~~ (but ~~very discreetly~~) some gray, black, or white thread.

The composition is very powerful; its character has to be retained.

Cap-Martin
Le Corbusier

—P. 713

Le Corbusier to Junzo Sakakura, 22 August 1956

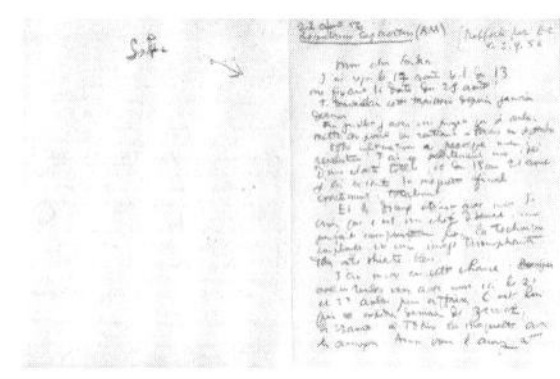

[LEFT PAGE]
Saka

[RIGHT PAGE]
22 August 56
Roquebrune-Cap-Martin (A.M.)

My dear Saka.

On 17 August I got your letter of the 13th giving me 28 August as a deadline!
I've been working on this tapestry since last January.

Late July I had a project I wanted to hone when back in Paris in September.
Your ultimatum triggered a revolution! I suddenly had a crystal-clear idea and between August 18–21 I did the final model, exactly and completely.

And the gods were with me. I think it's a masterpiece, a perfect composition for the medium and a triumphal image for your blue theater.

And another stroke of luck: Boesiger and I had a business appointment on August 21–22. So tomorrow, August 23, he's going to send the model from Zurich to Tokyo, together with

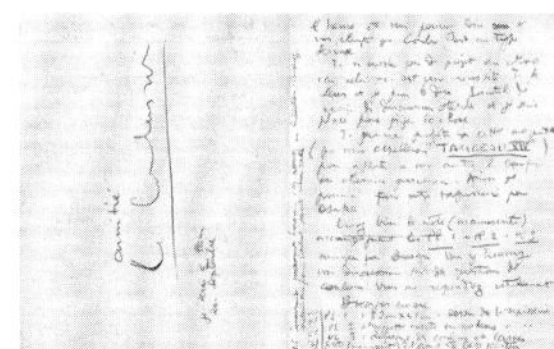

the associated stuff. That means you'll have it on time and you'll be able to tell your clients that Corbu is someone they can count on.

I'm not sending a choice of projects, because this one is a real success. I feel it and can say so. No point getting involved in sterile discussions, and I'm well placed to make a judgment.

I'll be able to bring the experience gained from this model (which we'll call "BULL XIV") to bear on another one. Which means I can do your tapestry for Osaka.

Read closely the note (hand-written) accompanying Pl. 1 and Pl. 2 + Pl. 3 sent by Boesiger. It contains a discussion of color matters. I hope to have a positive reply.

Boesiger is sending
a/ PL. 1 = 32 cm x 48 cm = drawing of the tapestry
b/ PL. 2 = Exact model in color of the tapestry
c/ PL. 3 = References for the colors and wools
d/ Note (handwritten) 21 August 56 Cap-Martin

[LEFT MARGIN]
P.S. Regarding payment fees / M. await my instructions. Keep authorization for possible second curtain Osaka

[LEFT PAGE]
Best wishes,

Le Corbusier
I'll be in Paris in September

—P. 713

An explanation of the hand-weaving process used to make the curtain

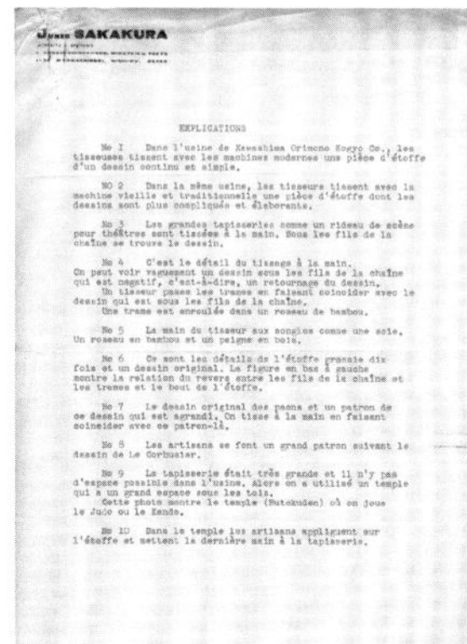

Junzo SAKAKURA

EXPLICATIONS

No I Dans l'usine de Kawashima Orimono Kogyo Co., les tisseuses tissent avec les machines modernes une pièce d'étoffe d'un dessin continu et simple.

NO 2 Dans la même usine, les tisseurs tissent avec la machine vieille et traditionnelle une pièce d'étoffe dont les dessins sont plus compliqués et élaborants.

No 3 Les grandes tapisseries comme un rideau de scène pour théâtres sont tissées à la main. Sous les fils de la chaîne se trouve le dessin.

No 4 C'est le détail du tissage à la main.
On peut voir vaguement un dessin sous les fils de la chaîne qui est negatif, c'est-à-dire, un retournage du dessin.
Un tisseur passe les trames en faisant coincider avec le dessin qui est sous les fils de la chaîne.
Une trame est enroulée dans un roseau de bambou.

No 5 La main du tisseur aux ongles comme une scie. Un roseau en bambou et un peigne en bois.

No 6 Ce sont les détails de l'étoffe grossie dix fois et un dessin original. La figure en bas à gauche montre la relation du revers entre les fils de la chaîne et les trames et le bout de l'étoffe.

No 7 Le dessin original des paons et un patron de ce dessin qui est agrandi. On tisse à la main en faisant coincider avec ce patron-là.

No 8 Les artisans se font un grand patron suivant le dessin de Le Corbusier.

No 9 La tapisserie était très grande et il n'y pas d'espace possible dans l'usine. Alors on a utilisé un temple qui a un grand espace sous les toits.
Cette photo montre le temple (Butokuden) où on joue le Judo ou le Kendo.

No 10 Dans le temple les artisans appliquent sur l'étoffe et mettent la dernière main à la tapisserie.

EXPLANATIONS

No. 1 In the Kawashima Orimono Kogyo Co. factory, the women use modern machines to weave lengths of cloth with a continuous, simple design.

No. 2 In the same factory, the men use the old, traditional machines to weave lengths of cloth with more complicated, more elaborate designs.

No. 3 Large tapestries such as stage curtains for theaters are woven by hand. The design is placed under the threads for the warp.

No. 4 Here are the details of the hand-weaving process. One can make out a design under the threads of the warp. This is negative, i.e., a reversal of the design.

A weaver runs the weft through, following the design set under the threads of the warp.

The weft is rolled around a bamboo shuttle.

No. 5 The weaver's hand, with nails like a saw. A bamboo shuttle and a wooden comb.

No. 6 These are details of the fabric enlarged ten times and an original design. The figure at the bottom shows the relationship between the threads of the warp and the weft and the end of the fabric.

No. 7 The original peacock design and an enlarged pattern for this design. Weaving is by hand, working to this pattern.

No. 8 The craftsmen make a big pattern according to Le Corbusier's design.

No. 9 The tapestry was very big and there was not enough room in the factory. So a temple was used, which offered a large covered area.

This photo shows the temple (Butokuden) where Judo and Kendo are practiced.

No. 10 In the temple the craftsmen press the fabric and put the finishing touches to the tapestry.

—P. 719

José Luis Sert, dean of the Harvard University Graduate School of Design, to Le Corbusier, 16 October 1958

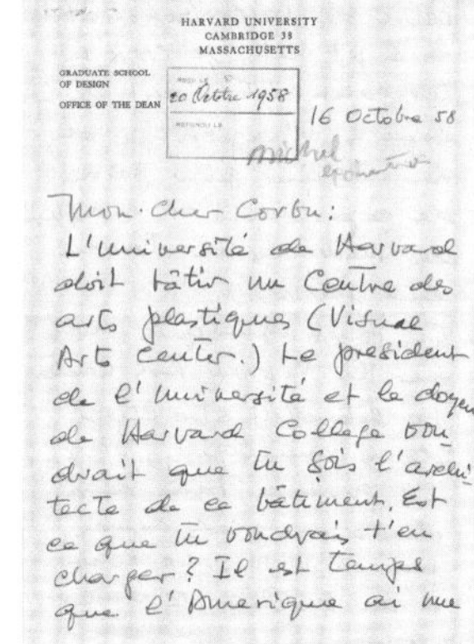

HARVARD UNIVERSITY
CAMBRIDGE 38
MASSACHUSETTS

GRADUATE SCHOOL OF DESIGN
OFFICE OF THE DEAN

20 Octobre 1958

16 Octobre 58

Mon cher Corbu:
L'université de Harvard doit bâtir un Centre des arts plastiques (Visual Arts Center.) Le président de l'université et le doyen de Harvard College voudrait que tu sois l'architecte de ce bâtiment. Est ce que tu voudrais t'en charger? Il est temps que l'Amérique ai une

Received 20 October 1958
16 October 58
Michel [?]

My Dear Corbu:

Harvard University will be building a center for the plastic arts (Visual Arts Center). The president of the University and the dean of Harvard College would like you to be the architect for this building. Would you be willing to take this on? It's about time America had a

oeuvre de Le Corbusier et le sujet est, je crois, interesant. Il s'agit des espaces d'exposition et des ateliers pour faire des experiments et enseigner des méthodes de travail aux jeunes.
Ci-joint quelques notes sur le Visual Arts Center. Le site doit être choisi dans quelques jours. La surface bâtie sera de 50.000 pieds carrées plus ou moins. Le cout d'un million de dollars.

work by Le Corbusier and the subject is, I think, interesting. It involve exhibition spaces and studios for experiments and for teaching working methods to young people.

Herewith, a few notes on the Visual Arts Center. The site will be selected in a few days. The built surface will be 50,000 square feet, more or less. The cost of one million dollars.

HARVARD UNIVERSITY
CAMBRIDGE 38
MASSACHUSETTS

GRADUATE SCHOOL OF DESIGN
OFFICE OF THE DEAN

2

Le plan peut être assez libre, et je crois que tu pourrais faire quelque chose vraiment bien.
Tes amis ici, seraient bien contents d'avoir une oeuvre de Corbu a Harvard.
Veux-tu me dire si cela t'interesse? Si c'est oui, j'espère te voir bientôt a Cambridge. Tu recevras dans ce cas

The design can be fairly free and I think you could do something really good.

Your friends here would be very glad to have a work by Corbu at Harvard.

Would you let me know if this interests you? If so, I hope to see you soon in Cambridge. In which case, you'll receive

une communication officielle.

Amitiés

an official letter.

Regards,
José Luis

—P. 719

Le Corbusier to José Luis Sert, 27 October 1958

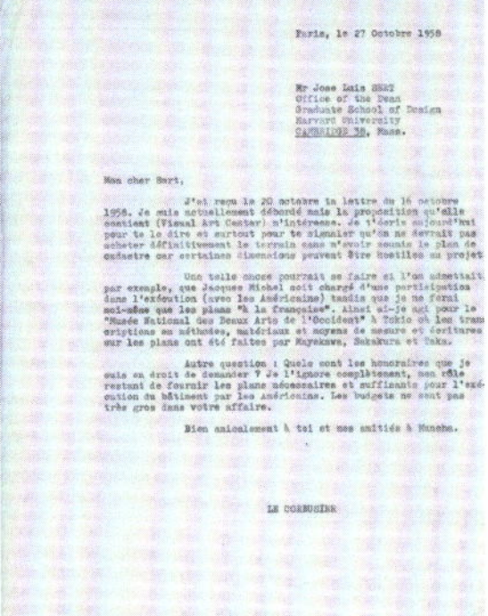

Paris, 27 October 1958
Mr. José Luis SERT
Office of the Dean
Graduate School of Design
Harvard University
<u>CAMBRIDGE 38</u>, Mass.

My dear Sert,

I got your letter of 16 October 1958 on 20 October. Right now I'm snowed under, but the proposal in the letter (Visual Arts Center) interests me. I'm writing to tell you this and to point out that you should not definitively acquire the land before showing me the land register, since some of the measurements could go counter to the project.

A project like this is feasible if it is agreed, for example, that Jacques Michel should take part in the realization (with the Americans), while I myself would only do the "French-style" plans. This is the way I worked for the "National Museum of Western Art" in Tokyo, with the rendering of methods, materials, means of measurement, and the notations being done by Maekawa, Sakakura, and Taka.

Another question: What fee am I entitled to ask? I have no idea, my role being restricted to providing plans sufficient for the Americans to construct the building. The budgets for your project are not very large.

Ever yours and best wishes to Muncha.

LE CORBUSIER

—P. 719

Le Corbusier to Edward Reynolds, 19 October 1959

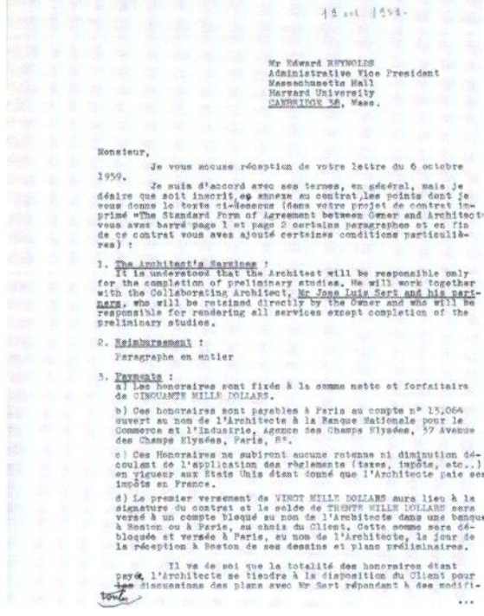

19 Oct. 1959

Mr. Edward REYNOLDS
Administrative Vice President
Massachusetts Hall
Harvard University
<u>CAMBRIDGE 38</u>, Mass.

Sir,

Thank you for your letter of 6 October 1959.

I agree in general with the terms proposed, but would like to see added, as a rider to the contract, the points outlined below (in your printed draft contract "The Standard Form of Agreement between Owner and Architect," you have struck out certain paragraphs on page 1 and page 2 and at the end of the contract you have added certain specific conditions):

1. <u>The Architect's Services</u>:
It is understood that the Architect will be responsible only for the completion of preliminary studies. He will work together with the Collaborating Architect, <u>Mr. Jose Luis Sert and his partners</u>, who will be retained directly by the Owner and who will be responsible for rendering all services except completion of the preliminary studies.

2. <u>Reimbursement</u>:
The entire paragraph

3. <u>Payments</u>:
a) The fee is set at the lump sum of FIFTY THOUSAND DOLLARS.

b) This fee is payable in Paris into account no. 13,064 opened in the name of the Architect at the Banque Nationale pour le Commerce et l'Industrie, Agence Champs Elysées, 37 Avenue des Champs Elysées, Paris 8.

c) This fee will be subject to no withholdings or deductions resulting from the application of regulations (duties, income tax, etc...) in force in the United States, given that the Architect pays income tax in France.

d) The first installment of TWENTY THOUSAND DOLLARS will be made once the contract has been signed and the balance of THIRTY THOUSAND DOLLARS paid into an escrow account in the Architect's name in a bank in either Boston or Paris, as the Client chooses. This sum will be unfrozen and paid in Paris, in the Architect's name, on the day his drawings and preliminary plans are received in Boston.

It goes without saying that once the fee has been paid in full, the Architect will remain at the Client's disposal for discussions of the plans with Mr. Sert bearing on any

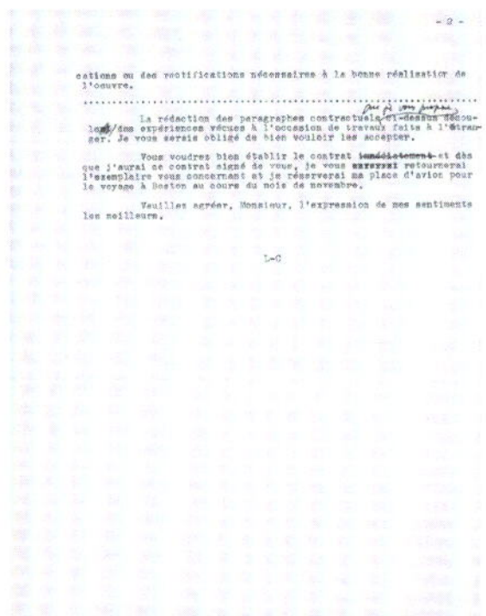

modifications or rectifications necessary to the sound execution of the project.

The clauses *I suggest* above for the contract result from my direct experience of work undertaken abroad. I would be obliged if you agreed to accept them.

Please draw up the contract ~~immediately~~ and as soon as I have received it, with your signature, I shall return your copy and book my plane ticket for the trip to Boston in November.

Yours faithfully,

L-C

—P. 728

First page of a letter from president of the Association of Municipal Hospitals to Le Corbusier, 18 November 1963

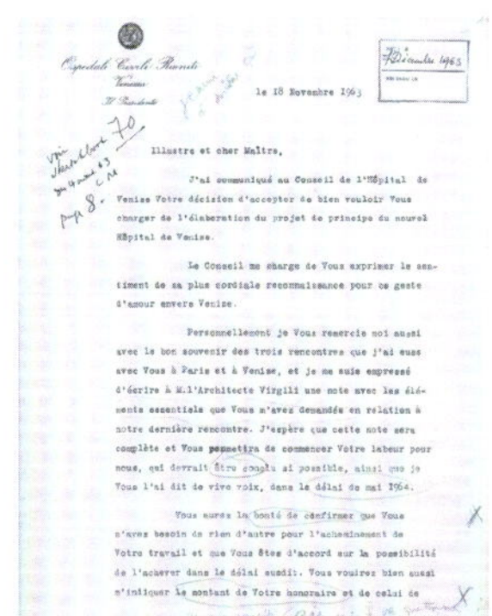

Jeanne follow up

See Sketchbook <u>70</u>, 4 August 63 page 8
Received 7 December 1963

18 November 1963
Illustrious and dear Master,

I have communicated to the Board of the Venice Hospital Your decision accepting to undertake the provisional design of the new Venice Hospital.

The Board instructs me to express to You its heartfelt gratitude for this gesture of love for Venice.

Personally I too thank You with the enjoyable memory of the three meetings I had with You in Paris and Venice, and I hastened to write Mr. Architect Virgili a note with the essential elements You requested at our last meeting. I hope this note will be complete and will allow You to begin your labor for us, which should be completed if possible, as I told You when we spoke, by May 1964.

Please be so kind as to confirm that there is nothing else You require to get Your work underway and that You agree with the possibility of finishing in the aforementioned time frame. Please tell me also the amount of Your fee and that of [...]

Ask Virgili / Answer: he will ask Venice

—P. 728

President of the Association of Municipal Hospitals to Le Corbusier, 31 July 1964

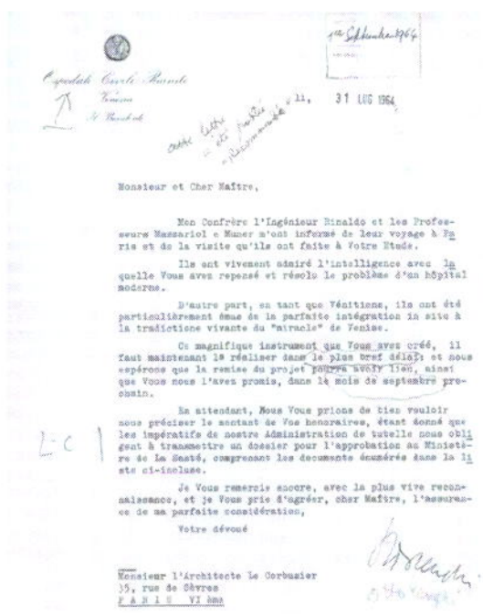

Received 1st September 1964
31 July 1964

Sir and dear Master,

My colleague Engineer Rinaldo and Professors Mazzariol and Muner told me of their trip to Paris and the visit they made to Your Studio.

They very much admired the intelligence with which You rethought and resolved the problem of a modern hospital.

But also, as Venetians, they were particularly moved by the perfect integration in situ into the living tradition of the "miracle" of Venice.

The magnificent instrument that You have created must now be realized in the shortest time possible, and we hope that the design can be delivered, as You promised us, this September.

In the meantime, please let us know exactly what Your fees will come to, since our Trustees require us to submit a file to be approved by the Ministry of Health, to include the documents itemized in the attached list.

I thank You again, with the keenest gratitude, and I remain, dear Master, most respectfully yours,

[signature]

Mr. Architect Le Corbusier
35 rue de Sèvres
<u>PARIS VI</u>

—P. 728

Contract for the Venice Hospital project, 29 March 1965

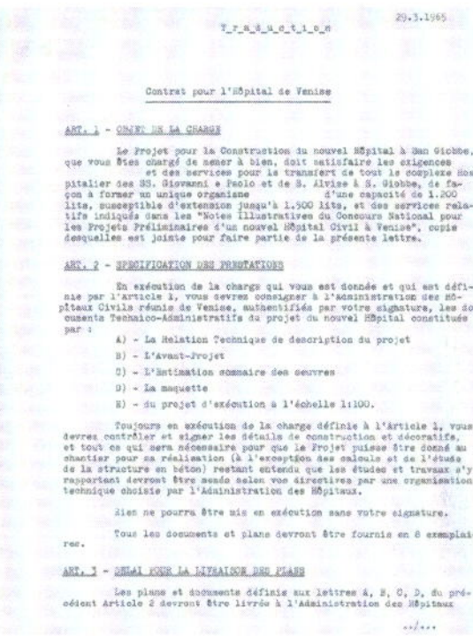

29.3.1965
Translation

<u>Contract for the Venice Hospital</u>

<u>ART. 1 – PURPOSE OF THE COMMISSION</u>
The Design for the Construction of the new Hospital in San Giobbe, which you are commissioned to carry out, must satisfy the needs [blank] and of the services for the transfer of the entire complexes of the Hospitals of SS. Giovanni e Paolo and S. Alvise to S. Giobbe, so as to comprise a single entity [blank] with a capacity of 1,200 beds, extensible to 1,500 beds, and with the relative services, indicated in the "Annotations to the National Competition for Preliminary Designs for a new Municipal Hospital in Venice," a copy of which is attached as part of the present letter.

<u>ART. 2 – SPECIFICATION OF RESPONSIBILITIES</u>
In fulfillment of the commission given to you, and defined in Article 1, you must deliver to the Administration of the Association of Municipal Hospitals of Venice, certified by your signature, the Technical/Administrative documents of the design for the new Hospital, to comprise:

A) – The Technical Account of the description of the project
B) – The Preliminary Plan
C) – A Summary Estimate of the works
D) – The model
E) – of the execution design at a scale of 1:100.

Also in fulfillment of the commission described in Article 1, you must oversee and sign off on the details of construction and decoration, and of everything necessary for the Design to be given to the work site and be carried out (with the exception of the calculations and design for the concrete structure), with the understanding that the designs and works pertaining to them must be carried out following your guidelines by a technical organization chosen by the Hospitals Administration.

Nothing may be executed without your signature.

All documents and plans must be supplied in 8 copies.

ART. 3—TIMETABLE FOR THE DELIVERY OF THE PLANS
The plans and documents described in letters A, B, C, D, of the preceding Article 2 must be delivered to the Administration of the Association of Municipal Hospitals of Venice

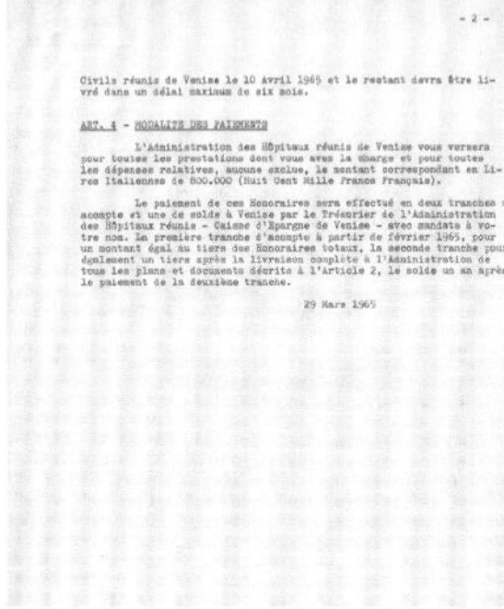

on 10 April 1965 and the balance must be delivered within a time frame of no more than six months.

ART. 4—METHOD OF PAYMENTS
The Administration of the Association of Venice Hospitals will pay you for the performance of all tasks assigned you and for all relative expenses, bar none, a sum in Italian Lire corresponding to 800,000 (Eight Hundred Thousand French Francs).

The payment of these Fees will be effected in two installments on account and one of the balance in Venice by the Treasurer of the Administration of the Association of Hospitals—the Venice Savings Bank—in money orders in your name. The first installment on account on or after February 1965, in an amount equal to one third the total Fees, the second installment also for one third after complete delivery to the Administration of all plans and documents itemized in Article 2, the balance one year after payment of the second installment.

29 March 1965

—P. 734

Le Corbusier's notes on his copy of Homer's *Iliad*

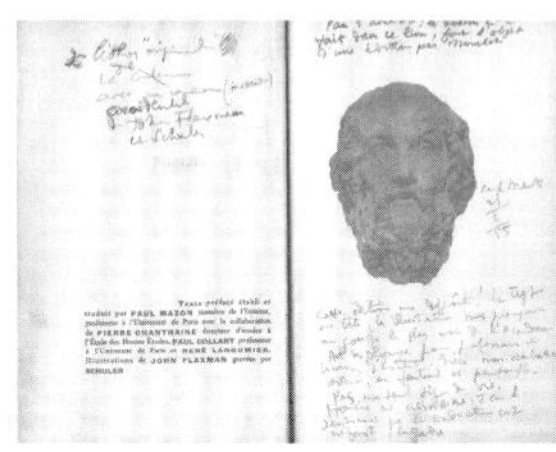

[LEFT]
"original" lithographs by Le Corbusier with the accidental (unexpected) support of John Flaxman and Schuler

[RIGHT]
Paris 5 April 64: the L–C drawings in this book have been published by Mourlot.

This edition is sickening! The typeface is stupid. The illustrations plunge you into the darkest abyss of the Olympian academicism of teachers and illustrious artists. Greece in the flabby, verbose, pipe and slippers vein. Not a single sign of life. Homer assassinated. My feeling is that the translation is toxic and lugubrious.

—P. 738

Cover by Le Corbusier for his brother Albert's album *Sonate pour violon seul* (Sonata for Solo Violin)

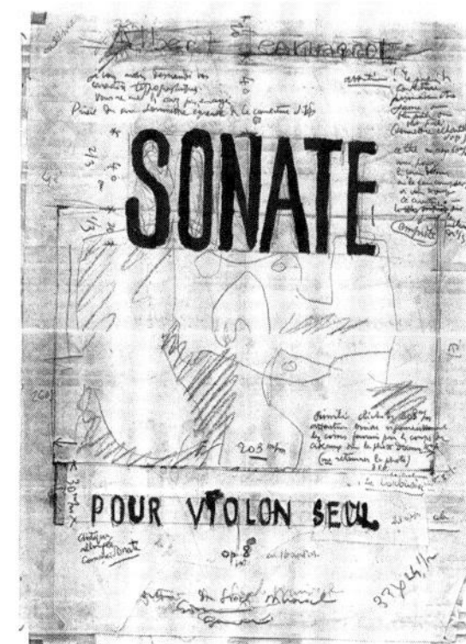

[TOP LEFT]
I had asked you for your typography fonts
You have not sent them to me
Please let me see the proof of the cover

[TOP RIGHT]
N.B.! the cover paper could be yellow on pale blue or pale green
(let me see a sample please)
this title at most 60 m/m
you can have it drawn or typeset, if you can find this font.—
The title ~~encroaches~~ encroaches on the picture by ⅓

[MIDDLE RIGHT]
halftone block 203 m/m
N.B. keep strictly to the corners made by the scissor cuts on photo document n.A (do not reverse the photo) please
Le Corbusier
Le Corbusier

[BOTTOM LEFT]
antique
elongated
like Sonata

[BOTTOM MIDDLE]
Editions du Siècle Musical
Geneva

—P. 740

Le Corbusier to his brother, Albert, 18 February 1960

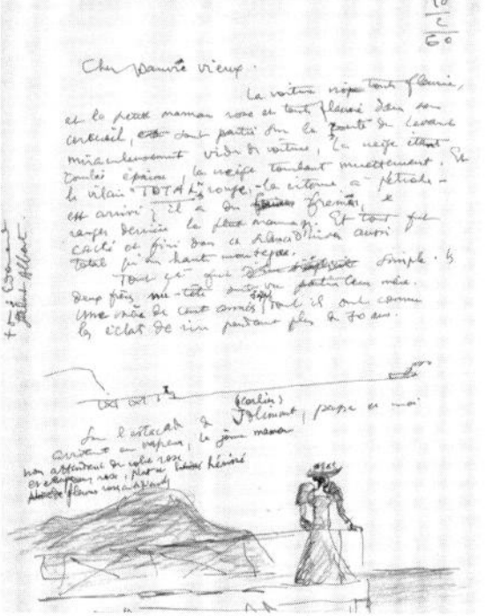

18
2
60

Dear poor old chap.

The black car filled with flowers and little pink mom all covered with flowers in her coffin set off down a Route du Levant miraculously bare of traffic; the snow had fallen heavily, snow falling mutely. Then the ugly red "TOTAL" tanker came along, must have braked, and pulled in behind little mom. And everything was hidden and over in a winter silence as total as in the mountains.

All this was ~~simplicity~~ simple. Bareheaded, the two brothers watched their mother go.

A mother a hundred years old whose peals of laughter they knew for more than 70 years.

(Corbu)
On the pier at Jolimont, dad and I arriving by steamer, young mom waiting for us in a pink dress and a flat pink hat ~~covered~~ covered with artificial roses.

[LEFT MARGIN]
your Edouard
All the best Albert

—P. 740

Carola Giedion-Welcker, art historian and wife of Sigfried Giedion, to Le Corbusier, 26 February 1960

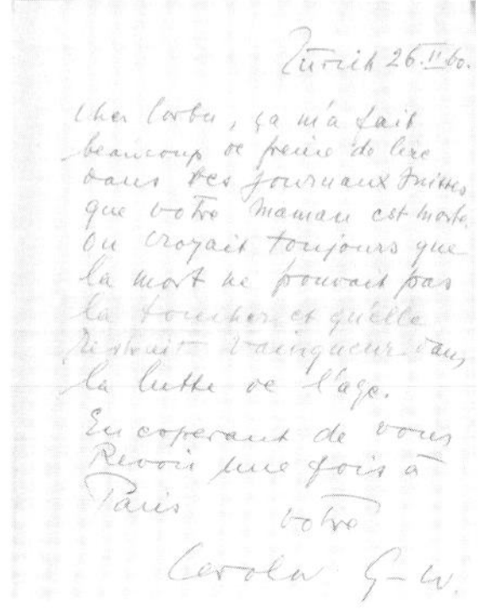

Zurich 26 II 60

Dear Corbu, I was so sorry to read in the Swiss newspapers that your Mom died. We always thought death couldn't touch her and that she would emerge the victor in the fight against age.

Hoping to see you again in Paris.

Yours,

Carola G–W

—P. 741

Yvonne and Le Corbusier to his mother, 29 August 1952

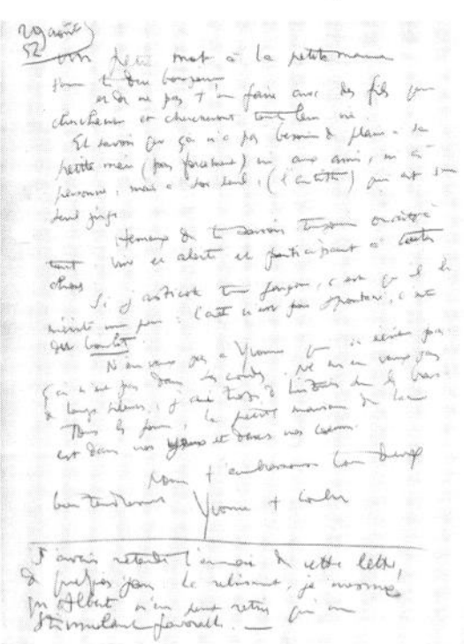

29 August 52

A little note to the little mom to say hello and tell you not to worry about sons who are on a quest and will be all their lives. And to let you know that the important thing here is not to please one's little mother (not necessarily), nor one's friends, nor anybody at all, but just oneself (the artist), who is one's sole judge.

Pleased to know you're still observant, lively, and alert and taking part in everything.

If I harass your son, it's because he deserves it a little: Art isn't spontaneous, it's work.

Don't be angry with Yvonne for not writing. It's not her thing. And don't hold my long silences against me, I've too much to worry about.

Every day the little Lake house is in our eyes and our hearts.

With much love,

Yvonne + Corbu

I held off sending this letter for a few days. Rereading it, I realize that it can only do Albert good.

—P. 741

Le Corbusier to his mother on her birthday, 7 September 1964

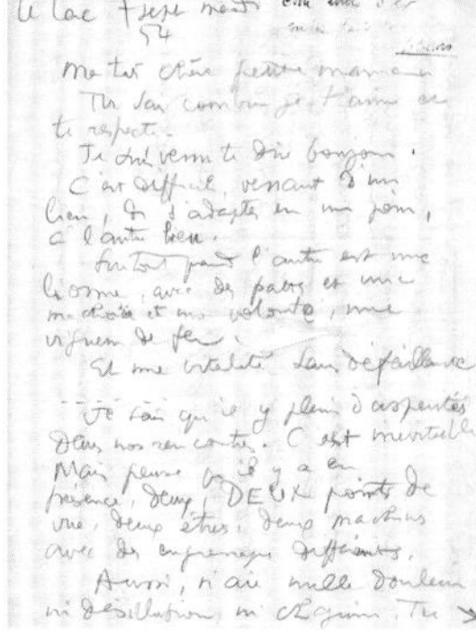

This letter from Ed really made me cry
The Lake 7 Sept 54 Tuesday

My dearest little mom,

You know how much I love and respect you.

I'm writing to say hello.

It's not easy leaving one place and adapting to another overnight. Especially when the other place is a lioness, with claws and jaws and will power and the strength of steel.

And inexhaustible vitality.

I know there are lots of conflicts between us. That's inevitable. But remember that it's a matter of two, TWO points of view, two beings, two machines with different gearings.

So don't feel pain, or disillusion or sorrow. You

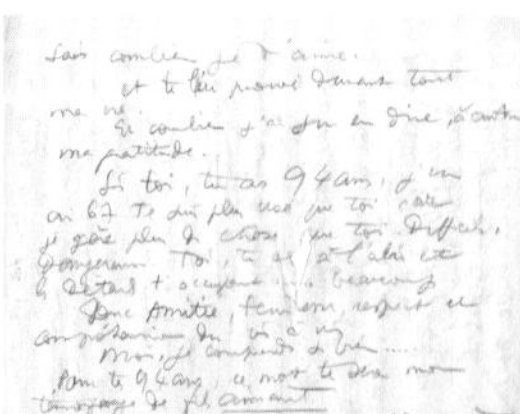

know how much I love you.

And I've proved it to you all my life.

And how often I've told others of my gratitude towards you.

You're now 94, and I'm 67. I'm more worn out than you because I have more to worry about. Difficult things. Dangerous things. You're protected and very taken up with little details.

So Friendship, love, respect and understanding towards the other person

I understand all this so well...

For your 94th birthday, this note is testimony from a loving son.

Your Edouard

—P. 741

Le Corbusier to his mother and brother, Albert, from Chandigarh, 19 December 1957

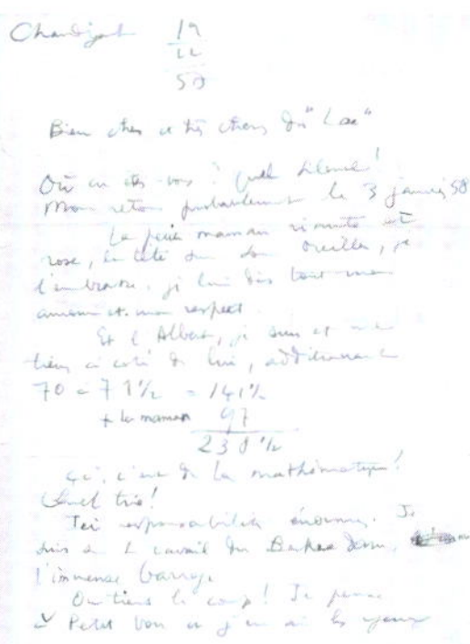

:handigarh 19
12
57

)ear and dearest ones at the "-lake,"

What's happening? What a ong silence!

Back probably 3 January 58.

For little mom laughing and ›ink, with her head on the pillow, all ny love and respect. As for Albert, 'm with him and sticking with him, ıdding up

70 to 71½ = 141½ + mom 97 = 238½

hat's what I call math!

What a trio.

Enormous responsibilities here. 'm working on the ~~mmm~~ immense 3hakra Dam.

I'm hanging on! I think of Little /on and it brings tears to my eyes.

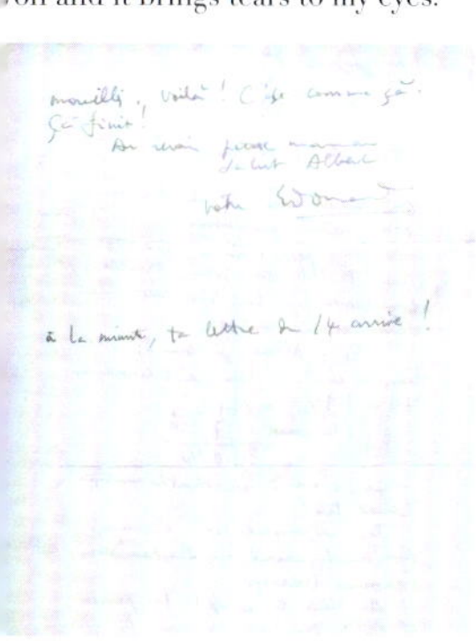

nd that's the way it is. he end is in sight!

Bye little mom,

All the best Albert

'our Edouard

your letter of the 14th has arrived this very minute!

—P. 741

Le Corbusier to his mother, 18 August 1959

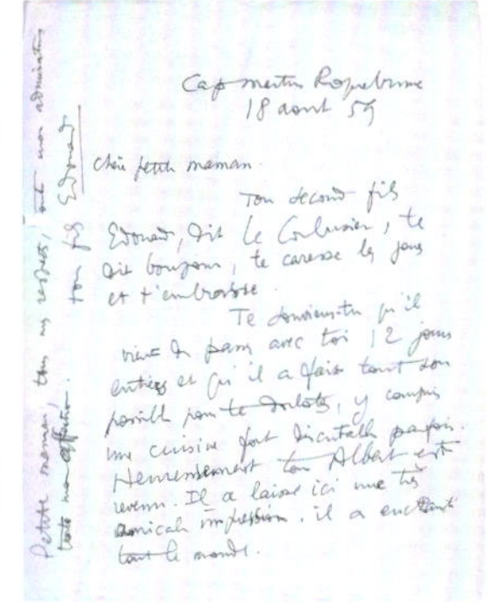

Cap-Martin Roquebrune
18 August 59

Dear little mom.

Your second son Edouard, aka Le Corbusier, says hello, strokes your cheeks and gives you a big kiss.

Do you remember that he's just spent 12 whole days with you and did everything he could to pamper you, even if the cooking was sometimes pretty terrible. Luckily your Albert's back. People here found him a really nice guy. Absolutely charming.

[LEFT MARGIN]

Little mom, all my best wishes, all my admiration, all my affection, your son Edouard

—P. 748

Press clippings reporting Le Corbusier's death

LE CORBUSIER SE NOIE

LA MORT DU CÉLÈBRE ARCHITECTE LE CORBUSIER

L'architecture des « Cités radieuses »

Il était une fois, un petit horloger...

LE CORBUSIER DROWNS AT ROQUEBRUNE-CAP-MARTIN

Aged 78, the famous architect has a heart attack while swimming

Menton: The famous architect Charles Jeanneret-Gris, better known as Le Corbusier, died of a heart attack yesterday morning at Roquebrune-Cap Martin, where he was on holidays. Charles Le Corbusier, who was 78, suffered a heart attack while taking his habitual morning swim off Le Buze Beach, near the Villa Casa Del Mare, which belongs to actress Silvana Mangano and her film producer husband Dino de Laurentiis.

From the beach a tourist, Mr. Simon Auzieblo, saw him suddenly in difficulty. He rushed into the water and brought out the architect who, it seems, was already dead.

Even so, Mr. Auzieblo tried the impossible, using mouth-to-mouth resuscitation.

Local ambulancemen were quickly on the scene and gave him oxygen, but in vain.

Menton medical examiner Dr. Bernard was called in and administered a heart stimulant that proved no more effective than the previous measures.

Finally, after an hour of unsuccessful efforts, the body of Charles Le Corbusier was taken to the chapel of repose at Menton hospital.

A regular at Roquebrune-Cap-Martin, where he had been coming on vacation for the last 15 years, the architect had arrived on the coast two weeks ago. Living in a primitive cabin, he ate every day at "L'Etoile de Mer," a modest family pension.

[caption]

A recent photo of Le Corbusier with the faithful caretaker of the tiny 4 x 3 meter cabin where one of the world's greatest architects liked to retreat to in summer. The cabin had only one door and one window. The interior has all modern conveniences. The bed and the table both fold into the walls. The sanitary facilities are set in a miniature toilet block.

Bernard Zehrfuss: "One of the greatest of this century"

"The whole of the current generation of architects works according to what Le Corbusier did," said Bernhard Zehrfuss, winner of the Rome Prize and architectural adviser to the Ministry of Construction, on learning of Le Corbusier's death.

"The impetus he gave modern architecture and his influence on architects are enormous," he added. "His death is a loss not only to France but to the world. He was indisputably one the greatest of this century."

"Le Corbusier could still have brought many new ideas," he concluded.

The architecture of the "Cités radieuses"

Le Corbusier, whose real name was Charles-Edouard Jeanneret-Gris, was born at La Chaux-de-Fonds, Switzerland, on 6 October 1887.

Beginning as an engraver and watchmaker, he very soon turned to architecture. After visits to Italy, Austria, and Germany, he settled in Paris in 1916 and took out French nationality.

Working with the Perret brothers, he constantly advocated a new concept of housing with open terraces, horizontally lit from wall to wall and supported by concrete posts.

He built many detached houses in this spirit in the Paris suburbs and all over France, before being called on by heads of state elsewhere to carry out large-scale planning ventures that included the university dormitory in Rio de Janeiro, the Bogotá Urbanization Plan (1950), and the designing and building of the new capital of Punjab in India (1951–56). In France this period also saw the creation of a number of "Cités radieuses," notably in Marseille and Nantes (1945–56).

One of the five members of the international advisory committee for the UNESCO headquarters in Paris and the United Nations building in New York, he also drew up the plans for the Museum of the 20th Century to be built at the La Défense traffic circle in Paris.

His revolutionary ideas about architecture found expression in a host of articles and books.

"He is the greatest architect in the world," said Minister for Culture André Malraux when the French government made him a Grand Officer of the Legion of Honor on 18 December 1963.

Le Corbusier held an honorary doctorate from the University of Zurich and was an associate member of the Royal Institute of British Architects. On 27 April 1965, in his studio, he received from the president of the Boston Society of Architects a Harvard University decoration for the buildings he made at the Harvard Carpenter Center.

There was once a little watchmaker

"In India I succeeded in achieving absolute control over the sun." An astonishing declaration that only the man described by André Malraux as "the greatest architect in the world" could have dared make without fear of ridicule.

Control of the sun, control of color and light and stone—all of this is Le Corbusier.

At a very early age Charles-Edouard Jeanneret-Gris, the little watchmaker from La Chaux-de-Fonds, realized that he was made to revolutionize architecture; and he would do so in the face of all obstacles and despite the hostility, not to say the hatred, generated by his conception of a different world—a "livable" world where humanity would find happiness.

Moving to Paris, he became the disciple of Auguste Perret, the "pope of reinforced concrete." And whether in the form of *pilotis* or sunshades, reinforced concrete would become one of the keys to Le Corbusier's world.

Characteristically, one of his first buildings was "L'Esprit Nouveau" pavilion at the Arts and Crafts Exhibition in Paris in 1927. But after beginning in Paris, he very quickly became someone foreign countries were competing for, while his own country—he had taken out French nationality in 1916—heaped criticism on him. Before the opening of his famous "Cité Radieuse" in Marseille in 1952, he already had to his credit the Centro Soyuz in Moscow (1931), the university dormitory in Rio de Janeiro, and the urbanization plan for Bogotá. He would also create, in the near-desert of India's Punjab, a brand new capital: Chandigarh.

Finally, in Marseille, French people began to "live Le Corbusier." A truly revolutionary apartment block, the "unité d'habitation" took off toward the sun from its thirty-six steel and concrete *pilotis*; its shopping street was halfway up a building whose facade was divided into a host of small areas marked by violent contrasts of color.

"It is now a proven fact," wrote Le Corbusier, "that a wall finds its own impetus when line and color take over."

This truly was a builder who wrote, and wrote a lot, and even came out with books of theory early in his career, before he had realized any large-scale projects: once the great American architect Frank Lloyd Wright refused to receive him on the grounds that he "didn't talk to journalists."

The titles of the books indicated an impressive agenda: *Toward an Architecture*, *When the Cathedrals Were White*, *The Home of Men*, and *Poem of the Right Angle*.

For Le Corbusier was a poet too, as well as a painter and sculptor. He would say of his pictures, "I have made my painting a coherent process of invention, seeking above all proportion, true geometrical and mathematical proportion."

To bring proportion and people together in architecture he invented the "Modulor"—"A range of harmonic dimensions on a human scale, applicable to both architecture and mechanics."

Over the last twenty years Le Corbusier has built everywhere—Brazil, Japan, the USSR, and the United States—but very little in France. The famous housing block in Marseille, which the locals irreverently refer to as "the Crackpot's House," drew harsh criticism: the Society for General Aesthetics in France actually went as far as taking out a lawsuit against him—and lost.

Tetchy, obstinate, Gide-like behind his heavy glasses, and always working like crazy, Le Corbusier did not really let it worry him. And soon there came resounding revenge

Profonde émotion dans le monde

Constructeur du « grand navire » du Bd Michelet

Deep regret around the world

PARIS—Deep regret around the world after the tragic death of Le Corbusier

"In Old Europe, changing Latin America, timeless India, and all over the world, he triggered fountains of hope." Thus did UNESCO director general René Maheu speak of the achievements of the deceased. "Le Corbusier was a great mind. This is what made him a great artist. UNESCO will never forget what it owes him."

As Jean Cassou, chief curator at the Musée d'Art Moderne in Paris, put it, "No one deserves more than Le Corbusier the fine title of humanist. He will go down as one of the founders of the humanism of our times."

"There is no architect under sixty who has not been influenced by him," said Richard Sheppard, whose own realizations include Churchill College, Cambridge. "His book *Toward an Architecture*, published in 1922, was a revelation for us. Everything he has done since then has had worldwide significance."

In Rome architect Francesco Vacchini, director of the Fabbrica of St. Peter's, said, "Le Corbusier's style had a marked influence on the religious architecture revival. This is a great loss for modern architecture."

In Stockholm, leading Swedish town planner Sven Backstrom commented, "Le Corbusier was indisputably a genius. His work has been of vital importance all over the world because of the power of his ideas and his breadth of vision. He has left a deep mark on his time."

Celebrated Finnish architect Alvar Aalto said in Helsinki, "For me Le Corbusier's death means the loss of a dear friend and a world-renowned architect." Aarne Ervi, representing the younger generation of major Finnish architects, added, "Thanks to Le Corbusier and his 'functionalism' the world has inherited a new conception of everything architecture has to offer humanity."

Learning of the death, the director of the architecture department at MoMA in New York announced that he would lose no time in putting on a commemorative exhibition.

Builder of the "big ship" on Boulevard Michelet
Le Corbusier is dead: a painter and architect, but also a philosopher who challenged the fundamentals of town planning has died suddenly, and the people of Marseille will feel this loss more keenly than others.

For them Le Corbusier is not only a great man, but also the creator of a local monument: that "Cité radieuse" that raises its sixteen stories like a powerful ship. Tourists buy postcards of it, and every year architecture students flock to study this work by a pioneer. The "Cité radieuse" is no longer avant-garde and Le Corbusier's disciples have done better since then, but this concrete block remains a testimonial: an image of great striving and great hope.

There was a time when "the Crackpot's House" was good for a laugh; but it is not the kind of thing you can ignore, and even now it is hard to resist the sheer grandeur of a building whose rugged beauty is founded on such a delicate balance.

Great creators are lucky: they live on in their works. Le Corbusier will live on around the world for many years to come, and as long as his big ship remains at anchor on Boulevard Michelet, Edouard Jeanneret-Gris will keep his place in the memory of the people of Marseille.

Oscar Niemeyer
"The real genius of contemporary architecture"
Oscar Niemeyer, the designer of Brasilia, is currently in Paris, and made the following statement on learning of the death of Le Corbusier:
"It is with deep sadness that I speak to you of Le Corbusier. He was the greatest genius, the real genius of contemporary architecture.

I have been turning to Le Corbusier since architecture school, reading his books, studying his works, drawn to his talent and his role as a fighter so often misunderstood."

[caption]
With the pennant at half-mast, Le Corbusier's dog waits in vain for his master on the roof of the cabin.

Emotion et consternation dans le monde
LE CORBUSIER EST MORT
HIER A ROQUEBRUNE CAP MARTIN
• Le célèbre architecte a péri noyé dans la petite crique où il passait ses vacances depuis de nombreuses années

Emotion and distress around the world.

LE CORBUSIER DIED YESTERDAY AT ROQUEBRUNE-CAP-MARTIN.

The famous architect drowned in the little cove where he had spent his vacation for many years
MENTON.—French architecture, the world's architecture, is in mourning. A mourning shared by the entire world. Le Corbusier is gone. He who was considered one of the world's great architects died of a heart attack while bathing in a little cove on the Côte d'Azur, the "Plage du Grabet" at Roquebrune-Cap-Martin, in the Alpes-Maritimes.

Every year since 1957, the cove had welcomed the elderly builder, who was 78 years old. He spent his vacations there like a hermit, in a tiny bungalow 4 meters by 3. Built of concrete, the white-painted shack had only one door and one window with green shutters. Around there, they called it: **"The lonely beach house."** The interior, however, displayed every modern comfort and convenience. The bed can fold into a wall, like the table. The plumbing fixtures occupied small chambers within a miniature bathroom.

It was in this setting that Le Corbusier came to rest. He came sometimes for short visits, but every summer he spent several weeks here. (Continues on last page)

[CAPTION]
Le Corbusier, the little Swiss watchmaker who became the world's greatest architect.

—P. 749

UN GRAND URBANISTE DISPARAIT
LE CORBUSIER EST MORT
Le célèbre architecte s'est noyé
– crise cardiaque –
en se baignant à Roquebrune Cap-Martin
Il était âgé de 78 ans
En page 12 : Nos informations — En page 3 : Le Corbusier et Marseille

A GREAT CITY PLANNER PASSES AWAY.

LE CORBUSIER HAS DIED.

The famous architect drowned—heart attack—while bathing at Roquebrune-Cap-Martin. He was 78 years old

On page 12: Our report—On page 3: Le Corbusier and Marseille

[RIGHT MARGIN]
Le Corbusier's revolutionary experience: the world-renowned "Radiant City" of boulevard Michelet.

LE CORBUSIER (78 ans) SE NOIE
A ROQUEBRUNE-CAP-MARTIN
LE CHIEN-LOUP DE LE CORBUSIER

LE CORBUSIER (78) DROWNS AT ROQUEBRUNE-CAP-MARTIN.

[CAPTION]
Le Corbusier showing the model for the block of apartments he designed for the city of Nantes in Rezé.

The "architect of the year 2000" had built among others a block of apartments in Marseille (called by some "the crazy man's house") and the city of Chandigarh, in India (See last page)

LE CORBUSIER'S GERMAN SHEPHERD awaits his master in vain on the roof of the little beach house

[CAPTION]
This is the faithful dog of the deceased; when he was away, the animal always waited for his master on the roof of the little beach house at Roquebrune-Cap-Martin; victim of a heart attack during his daily bathing—he was an excellent swimmer—Le Corbusier, 78, was married, with no children.

Les cendres de LE CORBUSIER ont été inhumées dans le petit cimetière de Roquebrune

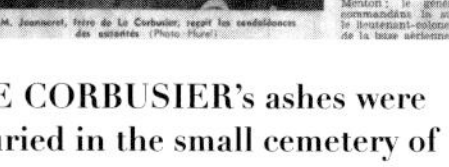

LE CORBUSIER's ashes were buried in the small cemetery of Roquebrune

[TOP CAPTION]
A simple plaque shows that there lies one of the greatest architects of our time ...
The burial of Le Corbusier's ashes took place yesterday afternoon, in the tiny cemetery of Roquebrune-Cap-Martin, where he will lie beside his wife, beneath a very simple tombstone.

Many people, friends Le Corbusier knew and didn't know, people from Roquebrune and Menton, surrounded national and local figures to pay a final tribute to the famous architect.

Among the latter, we noted: Mr. Anthonioz, representing Mr. André Malraux; Mr. René Cassin, vice-president of the State Council; Mr. Fourneret, director of the departmental staff of the prefect; Mr. Lottier, mayor of Roquebrune-Cap-Martin; and the entire city council; Mr. Lucien Rhein, first assistant deputy mayor, representing Mr. Francis Palmero, deputy mayor of Menton; General Morel, commanding the subdivision; Wing Commander Mangeot, from air force base 943.

[LEFT CAPTION]
Mr. Jeanneret, Le Corbusier's brother, receives the authorities' condolences

—P. 751

André Malraux's annotated typescript of his funeral eulogy for Le Corbusier

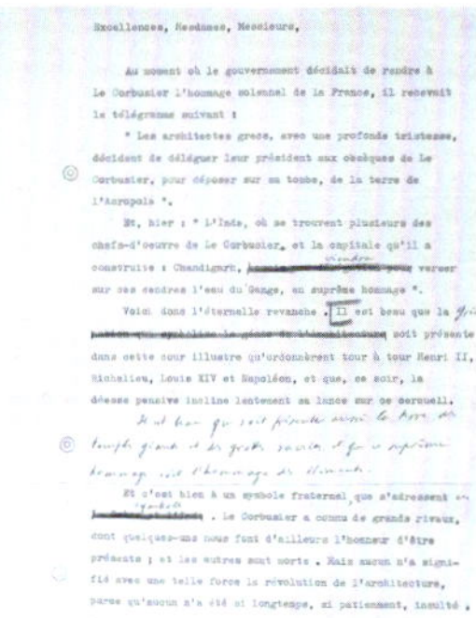

Excellences, Mesdames, Messieurs,

Au moment où le gouvernement décidait de rendre à Le Corbusier l'hommage solennel de la France, il recevait le télégramme suivant :

" Les architectes grecs, avec une profonde tristesse, décident de déléguer leur président aux obsèques de Le Corbusier, pour déposer sur sa tombe, de la terre de l'Acropole ".

Et, hier : " L'Inde, où se trouvent plusieurs des chefs-d'oeuvre de Le Corbusier, et la capitale qu'il a construite : Chandigarh, viendra verser sur ses cendres l'eau du Gange, en suprême hommage ".

Voici donc l'éternelle revanche . Il est beau que la Grèce soit présente dans cette cour illustre qu'ordonnèrent tour à tour Henri II, Richelieu, Louis XIV et Napoléon, et que, ce soir, la déesse pensive incline lentement sa lance sur ce cercueil.

Et c'est bien à un symbole fraternel que s'adressent ces symboles . Le Corbusier a connu de grands rivaux, dont quelques-uns nous font d'ailleurs l'honneur d'être présents ; et les autres sont morts . Mais aucun n'a signifié avec une telle force la révolution de l'architecture, parce qu'aucun n'a été si longtemps, si patiemment, insulté .

Excellencies, Ladies, Gentlemen, Just when the government had decided to give Le Corbusier France's state tribute, it received the following telegram:

"The Greek architects, with profound sorrow, have decided to send their president to Le Corbusier's funeral to place soil from the Acropolis on his tomb."

And, yesterday: "India, where there are several of Le Corbusier's masterpieces and the capital he built: Chandigarh, *will come* pour water from the Ganges over his ashes, as a supreme tribute."

Here, then, the inevitable vindication. It is a fine thing that Greece is present in this illustrious court, which was commanded in turn by Henri II, Richelieu, Louis XIV, and Napoleon, and that, this evening, the pensive goddess slowly lowers her lance over this coffin.

It is a fine thing that there also be present the land of giant temples and sacred caves, and that this supreme tribute be the tribute of the elements.

And indeed it is to a symbol of brotherhood that these *symbols* are addressed. Le Corbusier had great rivals, some of whom in fact honor him with their presence; and the others have died. But none of them signified so powerfully architecture's revolution, because none were so long and so patiently insulted.

His glory *reached* its supreme brilliance through gross offense, and that kind of glory covered the work more than the person, who was little disposed to it. After using the broad hallway of a deconsecrated convent as a studio for so many years, the man who had designed capitals died in an isolated little bungalow. The bathers who brought back the old swimmer's body did not know his name was Le Corbusier. But he might have enjoyed knowing that every day when they watched him go down to the sea, they called him The Ancient.

From his youth, he had been a painter, a sculptor, and, more secretly, a poet. He fought for neither painting, nor sculpture, nor poetry: He only fought for architecture. With a vehemence he felt for nothing else, because architecture alone answered *his* passionate *hope* for what can be done for man.

His famous phrase: "A house is a machine for living" does not portray him at all. What portrays him is: "The house must be life's jewel case." The machine for happiness. He always dreamed of cities, and the designs for his "radiant cities" are towers emerging from immense gardens. He once wrote: "Man's axis is the harmony that puts him in tune with himself—with his community—with nature—and probably with the universe." This agnostic built the most striking church and monastery of the century. He would say, at the end of his life: "I have worked for what the men of today need most: silence and peace." And his chief monument, Chandigarh, was supposed to be surmounted by a gigantic Hand of Peace, on which the birds of the Himalayas would have come to rest. The hand of peace is not yet in place . . .

This sometimes unwilling nobility went hand-in-hand with often prophetic, nearly always provocative theories, with a wild logic, that have been, for architects, one of the leavenings of the century. *All theories are condemned to be masterpieces or to oblivion. But he brought architects the awe-inspiring responsibility they bear today, to create the agreement between the suggestions of earth and those of spirit. After him, architecture changed—but so did architects.*

There was in *him* a creator that we cannot separate from—*but that* did not merge with—the theoretician. Let us say it was its twin brother. Le Corbusier was, above all, the artist who said in 1920: "Architecture is the skillful, correct, and

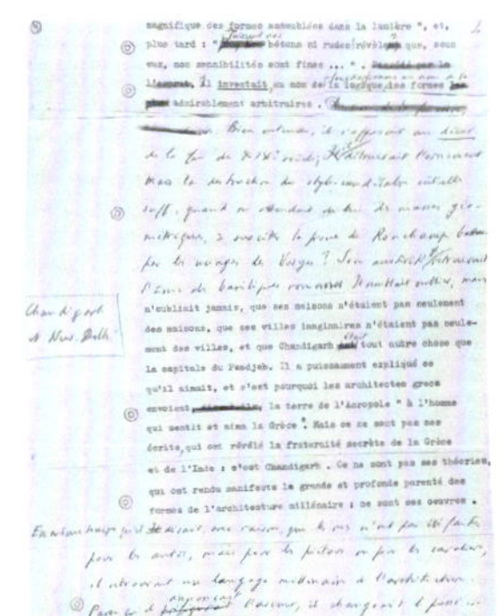

magnifique des formes assemblées dans la lumière ", et, plus tard : " bétons si rudes révèlent que, sous eux, nos sensibilités sont fines ... " . Il investait, au nom de la logique, les formes admirablement arbitraires .

n'oubliait jamais, que ses maisons n'étaient pas seulement des maisons, que ses villes imaginaires n'étaient pas seulement des villes, et que Chandigarh était tout autre chose que la capitale du Pendjab. Il a puissamment expliqué ce qu'il aimait, et c'est pourquoi les architectes grecs envoient la terre de l'Acropole " à l'homme qui sentit et aima la Grèce ". Mais ce ne sont pas ses écrits, qui ont révélé la fraternité secrète de la Grèce et de l'Inde : c'est Chandigarh . Ce ne sont pas ses théories, qui ont rendu manifeste la grande et profonde parenté des formes de l'architecture millénaire : ce sont ses oeuvres .

magnificent play of forms assembled inside light," and, later: "*Let our* so-rough concretes reveal that, beneath them, our sensibilities are delicate . . ." He invented, under the *aegis of function* and that of logic, wonderfully arbitrary shapes. *Of course, he stood against late nineteenth-century decoration; he destroyed ornamentation, but would destroying the "candelabra style" have been enough when what awaited us from him were geometric masses, the raising of the Ronchamp prow, whipped by the clouds of the Vosges? His austerity rediscovered in it the soul of the Romanesque basilicas. He appeared to forget*, but never forgot, that his houses were not just houses, that his imaginary cities were not just cities, and that Chandigarh was anything but the capital of the Punjab. He powerfully unfolded what he loved, and that is why the Greek architects are sending the earth of the Acropolis "to the man who felt and loved Greece." But it is not his writings that revealed the hidden brotherhood of Greece and India: it is Chandigarh. It is not his theories that made manifest the great and profound relationships among the forms of millennial architecture: it is his works.

At the same time that he was saying, rightly, that streets were not made for cars, but for pedestrians and horseback riders, he was rediscovering a millennial language of architecture. Because he was heralding the future, he was changing the past . . .

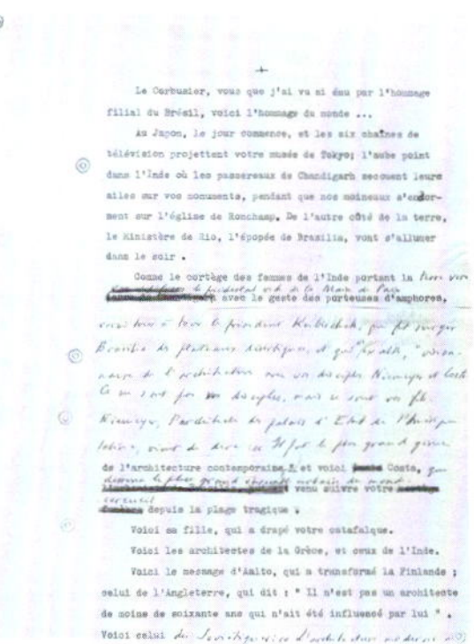

Le Corbusier, vous que j'ai vu si ému par l'hommage filial du Brésil, voici l'hommage du monde ...

Au Japon, le jour commence, et les six chaînes de télévision projettent votre musée de Tokyo; l'aube point dans l'Inde où les passereaux de Chandigarh secouent leurs ailes sur vos monuments, pendant que nos moineaux s'endorment sur l'église de Ronchamp. De l'autre côté de la terre, le Ministère de Rio, l'épopée de Brasilia, vont s'allumer dans le soir .

Comme le cortège des femmes de l'Inde portant la terre vers le piédestal vide de la Main de Paix avec le geste des porteuses d'amphores,

de l'architecture contemporaine " et voici Costa, venu suivre votre cercueil depuis la plage tragique .

Voici sa fille, qui a drapé votre catafalque.

Voici les architectes de la Grèce, et ceux de l'Inde.

Voici le message d'Aalto, qui a transformé la Finlande ; celui de l'Angleterre, qui dit : " Il n'est pas un architecte de moins de soixante ans qui n'ait été influencé par lui " .

Voici celui

Le Corbusier, you whom I have seen so moved by Brazil's filial homage, here is the homage of the world...

In Japan, the day begins, and the six television channels broadcast your Tokyo museum; dawn comes up in India, where the sparrows of Chandigarh shake their wings on your monuments, while our house sparrows go to sleep on the church at Ronchamp. On the other side of the world, the Ministry in Rio, the epic of Brasilia, is about to light up in the evening.

Like the procession of Indian women bearing the *earth toward the empty pedestal of the Hand of Peace* with the movement of amphora-bearers, *here now is President Kubitschek, who caused Brasilia to rise from the desert plateaus, and who exalted you, "visionary of architecture, with your disciples Niemeyer and Costa." They are not your disciples, but they are your sons. Niemeyer, the architect of government buildings in Latin America, just now said: "He was* contemporary architecture's greatest genius," and here is Costa, *who designed the world's largest urban complex*, come to follow your coffin from the tragic shore.

Here is his daughter, who draped your catafalque in black.

Here are the architects of Greece, and those of India.

Here is the message from Aalto, who transformed Finland; the one from England that says: "Not one architect under sixty has not been influenced by him." Here is the one *from the Soviets: "Modern architecture has lost its greatest master." Here is* Neutra's, and the one from the American architects, who miss what you could still have done.

Here is the voice of the president of the United States: "His influence was universal and his works are invested with a permanent quality possessed by those of very few artists in our history..."

And finally, here is France—which so often failed to appreciate you, which you carried in your heart when you chose to *become* French *once more after two hundred years*—which says to you, through the voice of its greatest poet:

"I bow to you, at the tomb's harsh threshold!"

Farewell, my old master, and my old friend.

Good night...

Here is the tribute of the epic cities, funeral flowers from New York and Brasilia.

Here is the sacred water of the Ganges, and the earth of the Acropolis...

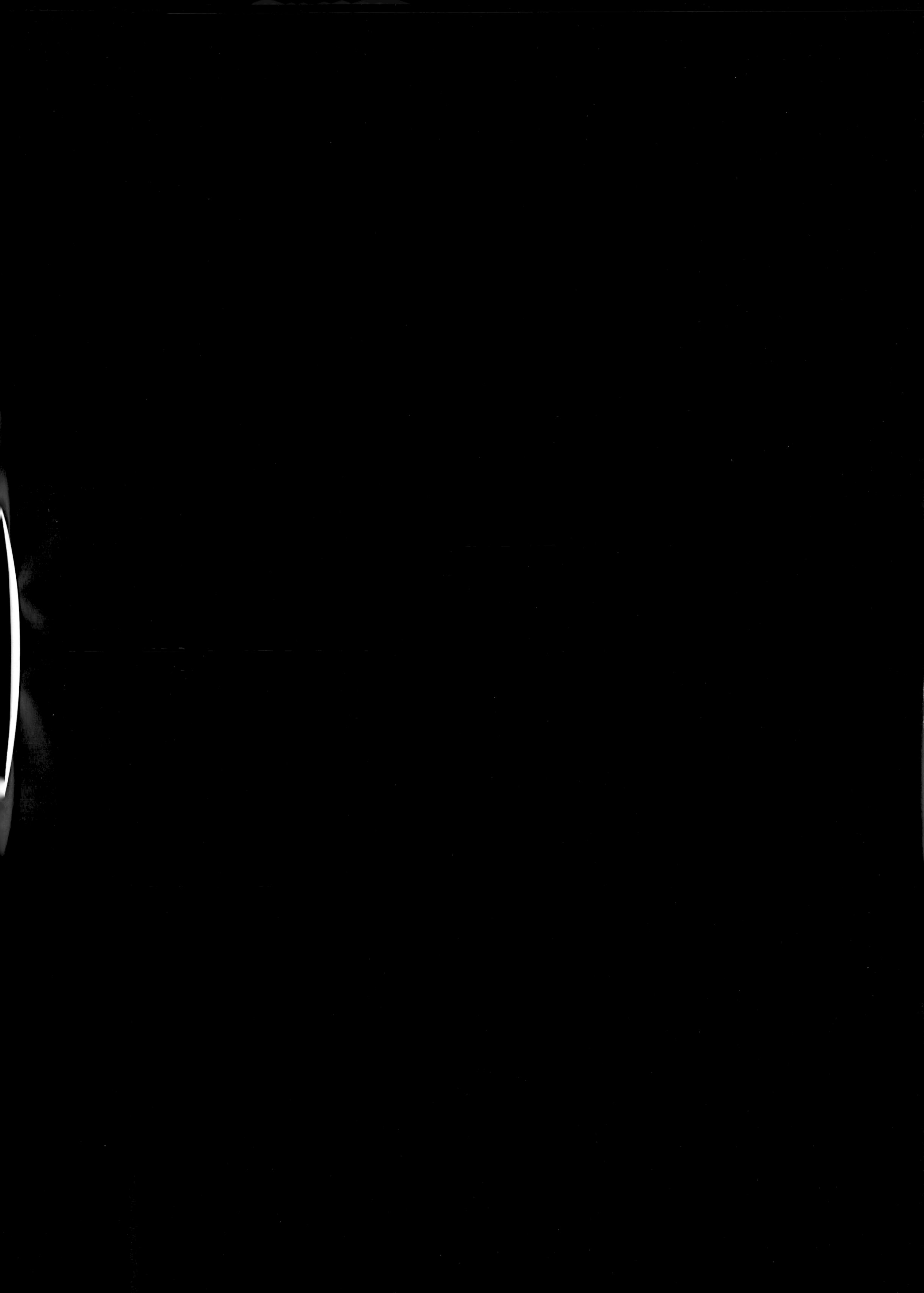

Notes
Chronology
Selected Bibliography
Index

Notes

"The Man with a Hundred Faces"
Jean-Louis Cohen

1. Fernand Léger on his first encounter with Le Corbusier, in 1920, in Jean Petit, *Le Corbusier lui-même* (Geneva: Editions Rousseau, 1970), p. 54.

2. Le Corbusier to Josef Červ, 18 January 1926, Bibliothèque de la Ville, La Chaux-de-Fonds, Switzerland.

3. Business card of Charles-Edouard Jeanneret, in Petit, *Le Corbusier lui-même*, p. 45.

4. Le Corbusier, "eyes that do not see . . ." in *Toward an Architecture* (Los Angeles: Getty Research Institute, 2007), p. 145; originally published as *Vers une architecture* (Paris: G. Crès & Cie, 1923).

5. Le Corbusier, *Les constructions "Murondins"* (Paris and Clermont-Ferrand, France: Etienne Chiron, 1942).

6. Le Corbusier, "Regulating lines," in *Toward an Architecture*, p. 131.

7. Le Corbusier, *The Modulor: A Harmonious Measure to the Human Scale, Universally Applicable to Architecture and Mechanics* (London: Faber and Faber, 1961); originally published as *Le Modulor* (Boulogne, France: Editions de l'Architecture d'Aujourd'hui, 1950).

8. Le Corbusier, *L'ONU et l'honnêteté fondamentale, histoire documentée de la naissance d'une cité du siège des Nations-Unies*, December 1947, Fondation Le Corbusier, Paris (hereafter FLC), I3-9-201–233.

9. Le Corbusier to James Johnson Sweeney, 3 August 1957, FLC, R3(4)483.

10. Le Corbusier, quoted in Cäsar Menz, Naïma Jornod, and Isabelle Payot Wunderli, ed., *Le Corbusier ou la synthèse des arts* (Geneva: Musée Rath, 2006), back cover.

11. Le Corbusier's copy of Friedrich Nietzsche, *Ainsi parlait Zarathoustra*, trans. Henri Albert (Paris: Mercure de France, 1908), 15th ed., is at the Fondation Le Corbusier, Paris. The English translation cited here is by Graham Parkes from *Thus Spoke Zarathustra* (Oxford: Oxford University Press, 2005), p. 21.

12. Le Corbusier to Junzo Sakakura, 7 September 1959, FLC, R3(2)101.

13. Le Corbusier, "The Lesson of Rome," in *Toward an Architecture*, p. 193.

14. Le Corbusier, quoted in Pierre Mazars, "Il avait su devenir un architecte vénitien," *Le Figaro Littéraire* (2–8 September 1965).

15. Le Corbusier to his mother, n.d. (June 1926), FLC, R1(6)145.

16. Le Corbusier to his mother, 15 December 1931, FLC, R2(1)138.

17. Willy Boesiger, ed., *Le Corbusier et son atelier rue de Sèvres 35, Oeuvre complète 1957–1965* (Zurich: Les Editions d'Architecture, 1965), p. 182.

18. *New York Herald Tribune*, 22 October 1935, p. 21.

19. Maximilien Gauthier, *Le Corbusier ou l'architecture au service de l'homme* (Paris: Denoël, 1944), p. 257.

20. Charles-Edouard Jeanneret to William Ritter, 26 September 1914, FLC, R3(18)386.

21. Hélène Parmelin, "L'homme qui veut construire des cités radieuses," *L'Humanité*, 19 May 1948.

22. Moisei Ginzburg, "Mezhdunarodny front sovremennoi arkhitektury," in *Sovremennaia Arkhitektura* 1, no. 2 (1926): 42.

Chapter Introductions
Tim Benton

Excerpts are cited in quotation marks, followed by their source or attribution.

1. Childhood and Early Travels (page 19)

"heaven on earth": Charles-Edouard Jeanneret to Charles L'Eplattenier, 19 September 1907, Fondation Le Corbusier, Paris (hereafter FLC), E2(12)6.

"unjust degree": Charles-Edouard Jeanneret to his parents, 2 December 1910, FLC, R1(5)50.

2. Becoming Le Corbusier (page 85)

"world of ideas": Charles-Edouard Jeanneret to his parents, 10 November 1920, FLC, R1(6)93.

"teach others": Charles-Edouard Jeanneret to his parents, 17 March 1924, FLC, R1(6)195.

4. In Search of the Big Commission (page 223)

"(up to you)": Le Corbusier to Marguerite Tjader Harris, 23 February 1949, Centre for Canadian Architecture, Montreal, CCA b 45.

"(or hardly)!!!": Le Corbusier, Sketchbook 2, D16, p. 240, FLC.

6. Grand Projects on a Human Scale (page 363)

"your honorable city": Le Corbusier to Helena Simkhovitch, 28 February 1948, Getty Research Institute, Los Angeles, 850980 f4.

7. Passage to India (page 437)

"long experience": Le Corbusier to Mr. Bajpay, secretary to Prime Minister Jawaharlal Nehru, 20 June 1952, recalling a meeting with Nehru on 17 April, FLC, P3(5)90.

"rough simplicity": Le Corbusier, Sketchbook 3, J36, p. 313, FLC.

"head of civilization": Le Corbusier, Sketchbook 2, E18, p. 362, FLC.

"living without fear": Le Corbusier, Sketchbook 3, J36, p. 275, c. 17 March 1955, FLC.

"great leap forward": Le Corbusier, Sketchbook 2, F27, p. 895, FLC.

"no fear": Le Corbusier, quoted in Jean-Louis Cohen, *Le Corbusier: La planète comme chantier* (Paris: Editions Textuel; Carouge-Geneva, Switzerland: Editions Zoé, 2005), p. 146.

"the housing solution": Le Corbusier, Sketchbook 3, K41, p. 574, FLC.

"an intelligent prince": Le Corbusier, Sketchbook 3, J39, p. 451, 13 November 1955, FLC.

8. The Sacred and the Sublime (page 555)

"lovers of the mythic": Le Corbusier, Sketchbook 3, H33, p. 128, FLC.

"learning its lessons": Le Corbusier, radio interview with Max Favalelli and Pierre Gillon, "Ce soir on cambriole," 21 July 1960 (partial transcription made 8 August 1975), FLC.

"silence and peace": Le Corbusier, quoted in François Biot, *Le Corbusier et l'architecture sacrée: Sainte-Marie-de-la-Tourette-Eveux* (Lyon, France: La Manufacture, 1985), p. 9.

"reached the ground": Father Bonnet, ibid.

"trying to achieve": Father Bonnet, ibid.

9. Mediterranean Days (page 643)

"happier than a prince": Le Corbusier to Marguerite Tjader Harris, 15 February 1955, Centre for Canadian Architecture, 79, 1.

"worth having": Le Corbusier to Professor Fueter, 17 March 1950, FLC, 12(7)89.

10. Retrospection (page 685)

"for a long time": Guillermo Jullian de la Fuente, quoted in Pablo Allard, "Bridge over Venice: Speculations on Cross-Fertilization of Ideas between Team 10 and Le Corbusier," in *Case: Le Corbusier's Venice Hospital and the Mat Building Revival*, ed. Hashim Sarkis (Cambridge, Mass.: Harvard Design School; Munich and New York: Prestel, 2001), p. 30.

"reassuring to die": Le Corbusier, 12 November 1952, Sketchbook 2, F26, pp. 850–51, FLC.

"machine for emotion": André Malraux, funeral eulogy, 2 September 1965, transcribed from a recording at the FLC.

"Good night": Ibid.

Chronology

Please note:

For a complete list of publications by Charles-Edouard Jeanneret/Le Corbusier, see the Selected Bibliography.

1887 6 October—born Charles-Edouard Jeanneret-Gris, at 38 rue de Serre, La Chaux-de-Fonds, Switzerland. Parents: Georges-Edouard Jeanneret-Gris (1855–1926) and Marie Jeanneret-Perret (née Marie-Charlotte-Amélie Perret, 1860–1960); married 11 May 1883. Brother: Jacques-Henri Albert Jeanneret (1886–1973).

1891 Attends Miss Colin's Froebel School, La Chaux-de-Fonds.

1900 Enrolls in watch-engraving studies at the Ecole d'Art, La Chaux-de-Fonds.

1902 Formally admitted to the Ecole d'Art; comes under the influence of artist and professor Charles L'Eplattenier.

1904–5 Starts having vision problems.

1905 L'Eplattenier establishes a new Cours Spécial et Supérieur de Composition Décorative (Special and Superior Class of Decorative Composition), with Jeanneret among the first students. With L'Eplattenier's encouragement, he shifts course of study from engraving to architecture.

First known architectural design: Beau-Site, building for the Union Chrétienne de Jeunes Gens, La Chaux-de-Fonds.

1905–7 First building: Villa Fallet, 1 chemin de Pouillerel, La Chaux-de-Fonds, collaboration with students of the Ecole d'Art and René Chapallaz (commission: 1905; construction: 1906–7).

1906 Music room, Villa Matthey-Doret, La Chaux-de-Fonds, with students of the Cours Spécial (demolished 1963).

1906 Students of the Cours Spécial redecorate the Chapelle Indépendante, a Protestant chapel, Cernier-Fontainemelon, Val-de-Ruz, Switzerland (interior demolished).

1907 Travels to Italy with friend Léon Perrin: Tuscany (visits the Certosa del Galluzzo, a Carthusian monastery in Val d'Ema), Florence, Siena, Bologna, Padua, Ferrara, Gargano, Pisa, Ravenna, Milan; Budapest and Vienna; meets architect Josef Hoffmann, designer Koloman Moser, and artist Gustav Klimt.

1907–8 Villa Jacquemet, 8 chemin de Pouillerel, La Chaux-de-Fonds.

1907–8 Villa Stotzer, 6 chemin de Pouillerel, La Chaux-de-Fonds.

1908 First trip to Paris; also visits Rouen and Le Havre, France.

Travel drawings exhibited at the Pie IX Nazionale Kunst Ausstellung der Schweiz, Kunsthalle und Stadtkasino, Basel.

1908–9 Works for the Perret Frères studio, Paris, for fifteen months; learns about reinforced-concrete construction.

1909 Returns to La Chaux-de-Fonds to work on various building projects.

Second trip to Paris, via Nuremberg, Munich, Strasbourg, and Nancy. Takes a number of courses at the Ecole des Beaux-Arts, Paris; meets architects Frantz Jourdain, Henri Sauvage.

Project:
- "Maison Bouteille" for Perret Frères.

c. 1909 Meets painter and art critic William Ritter, who lives in Neuchâtel, Switzerland.

1909–10 Cofounder of Les Ateliers d'Art Réunis (United Art Studios), an association of colleagues from the Ecole d'Art.

1910 Spends January–April in a traditional Jura farmhouse, on the slopes of Mont-Cornu, Switzerland.

Travels to Berlin; attends a Deutscher Werkbund Congress and the exhibitions *Ton-Kalk-Zement* and *Allgemeine Städtebau-Ausstellung*. Commissioned by Les Ateliers d'Art Réunis to study German design and teaching methods. Meets architects Ludwig Mies van der Rohe and Walter Gropius, as well as industrialist Wolf Dohrn, one of the founders of the garden city at Hellerau (located just outside Dresden).

Projects:
- Designs artists' workshops, gardens, communal space, office, and salesroom for Les Ateliers d'Art Réunis, La Chaux-de-Fonds.
- Study for the redesign of the Place de Gare, La Chaux-de-Fonds.

1910–11 October/November–March—works for five months in Peter Behrens's studio, Berlin. Travels to Dresden-Hellerau, Germany; meets Heinrich Tessenow, architect of the garden city at Hellerau.

1910–15 Writes "La Construction des villes" (The Construction of Cities), an unpublished manuscript.

1911 The "Voyage d'Orient": Travels for five months with friend August Klipstein to cities including Dresden; Prague; Vienna; Budapest; Belgrade; Bucharest; Turnovo, Gabrovo, and Kazanluk, Bulgaria; Istanbul, Turkey; Greece (spends three weeks on Mount Athos, Athens); and Italy: Naples, Pompeii, Rome, Florence, Pisa.

Publishes impressions of his Voyage d'Orient in a series of articles in *La feuille d'avis de La Chaux-de-Fonds*.

Returns to La Chaux-de-Fonds; lives in the Ferme du Couvent. Establishes, under L'Eplattenier, the Nouvelle Section de l'Ecole d'Art (New Section of the Art School), with Georges Aubert and Léon Perrin, and is appointed to the faculty. Opens an office at 54 rue Numa Droz.

1912 Projects:
- Maison du Diable, Le Locle, Switzerland.
- Town Hall, Le Locle, competition.

1912 Villa Favre-Jacot, 6 côte des Billodes, Le Locle, with sculptural reliefs by Léon Perrin.

1912 Villa Jeanneret-Perret ("La Maison Blanche"), for his parents, 12 chemin de Pouillerel, La Chaux-de-Fonds.

1912 Publication of his first book, *Etude sur le mouvement d'art décoratif en Allemagne*.

1913 Travels to Germany; visits the Internationale Baufach-Ausstellung, Leipzig.

Project:
- Paul Ditisheim Department Store and Warehouse, La Chaux-de-Fonds.

1913 Interior of Jules Ditisheim apartment, La Chaux-de-Fonds (demolished).

1913 Anatole and Solomon Schwob apartments, La Chaux-de-Fonds (demolished).

1913 Exhibits *Langage de pierres* (1907–13), suite of watercolors from the Voyage d'Orient, at the Salon d'Automne, Paris.

1914 Travels to France and Germany: Colmar, Strasbourg, Nancy, Cologne (for *Werkbund-Kongress und Ausstellung*), and Lyon (for *Exposition internationale urbaine: "La Cité Moderne"*).

Opposition from some of the Ecole's faculty, supported by the local press, results in closing the Nouvelle Section de l'Ecole d'Art; L'Eplattenier resigns.

Projects:
- Banque Cantonale de Neuchâtel, Neuchâtel, Switzerland, competition.
- Cité-Jardin aux Crêtets, a garden city estate in La Chaux-de-Fonds.
- Villa Klipstein, Laubach, Germany.

1914–15 Invents "Dom-ino" system using low-cost, modular, concrete structures, in collaboration with Max Du Bois and Juste Schneider (patent application 1916).

1914–17 Interior of Marcel Levaillant studio, La Chaux-de-Fonds (demolished).

1915 Projects:
- Pont Butin, over the Rhône, Geneva, with Max Du Bois.
- Villa Zbinden, Erlach, Switzerland.

1915 Interior of Hermann and Ernest-Albert Ditisheim apartment, La Chaux-de-Fonds (demolished).

1916 Project: Villa Paul Poiret, Bormes les Mimosas, France.

1916 Cinéma La Scala, 52 rue de la Serre, La Chaux-de-Fonds (partially demolished; rebuilt 1971).

1916–17 Villa Schwob ("Maison Turque"), 167 rue de Doubs, La Chaux-de-Fonds (with sculptural reliefs by Léon Perrin).

1917 January—moves to Paris; October—moves to an apartment at 20 rue Jacob, where he will spend th next seventeen years. Sets up first office, at 20 rue de Belzunce; mov to 29 rue d'Astorg a few months later.

Becomes architectural consultant to Max Du Bois's civil engineerin firm SABA (Société d'Applicatio du Béton Armé); continues until 1919. Du Bois also makes him administrator of SEIE (Société d'Entreprises Industrielles et d'Etudes), for which he designs industrial buildings and housing projects in concrete.

Invests in and runs brick factory, Briqueterie d'Alfortville; business later goes bankrupt.

May—meets painter and critic Amédée Ozenfant at a function organized by the group Art et Liberté. Meets artists Georges Braqu Juan Gris, Jacques Lipchitz, and Pablo Picasso.

Project:
- Centrale Thermique and housin estates, Saintes (Charente-Maritime), France.

1917 Château d'Eau Podensac, rue Pierre-Vincent, Podensac (Gironde), France.

1917 Usine Hydroélectrique, L'Isle-Jourdain (Vienne), France.

1917–18 Projects:
- Abattoirs Frigorifiques, Challuy and Garchizy (Nièvre), France.

1917–19 Cité Ouvrière (workers' cottages rue Raphaël-Hennion and route d'Envermeu, St.-Nicholas-d'Aliemont (Seine-Maritime), France (commission: May 1917; design: 1918–19).

1918 Sues Anatole Schwob over fees f Villa Schwob.

Becomes manager of the Société des Applications l'Everite (Everit is a prefabricated construction system using asbestos fiber and concrete panels).

November—loses vision in his left eye, due to a detached retina, while painting *La cheminée* (The Mantelpiece); this is the work tha he claims to be his first painting, though others predate it.

With Ozenfant, organizes exhibition of paintings at Galerie Thomas, Paris. The accompanying publication, *Après le cubisme*, is a founding document of the art movement Purism.

1919 With poet Paul Dermée and Ozenfant, founds the magazine *L'Esprit Nouveau: Revue Internationale d'Esthétique*; editorial office at rue du Cherche-Midi, Paris. The first issue (of twenty-eight) is published 15 October 1920; publication stops in 1925.

Projects:
- Maison Monol housing—row houses that employ the Everite-Eternit system.
- Monol workers' housing project, Vouldy, Troyes (Aube), France.

1919–20 Project:
- Cité Ouvrière Saint-Gobain, workers' housing, Thourotte (Oise), France.

1920 Adopts pseudonym "Le Corbusier-Saugnier" for articles on architecture in *L'Esprit Nouveau* (continues to sign his paintings Charles-Edouard Jeanneret until 1930). "Trois rappels à MM. les architectes," in *L'Esprit Nouveau*, no. 2, November 1920, is the first article he signs "Le Corbusier." Starts to use a drawing of a crow (*corbeau*) as a signature on some correspondence.

Meets artist Fernand Léger.

Projects:
- Cité du Pont-Vert, workers' settlement, Thourotte (Oise), France.
- Maison Citrohan I—development of housing cells in poured concrete.
- Workers' housing, Grand-Couronne (Seine-Maritime), France.

1921 Travels to Rome with Ozenfant and Mme. Bongard, owner of Galerie Thomas.

Société des Applications l'Everite goes bankrupt.

Project:
- Villa Montmorency, Paris.

Second Purist exhibition, Galerie Druet, Paris, with Ozenfant; businessman Raoul La Roche buys his first painting by Jeanneret.

1921–22 Villa Berque—décor, salon-music room extension, terrace enlargement, for Jean Berque—10 rue Poissin, Auteuil, Paris.

1922 Pierre Jeanneret, his younger cousin, becomes a partner in the Le Corbusier-Jeanneret architectural practice.

Meets Yvonne Gallis, a thirty-year-old dressmaker and model, who soon moves in with him at rue Jacob.

Travels to Venice and Vicenza, Italy, with Raoul La Roche.

Gives first lecture at the Sorbonne, Paris.

Projects:
- Maison Citrohan II.
- Immeubles-Villas, apartment block that is an elaboration on Maison Citrohan II.

Presentation of Ville Contemporaine ("City for Three Million Inhabitants"), including a model of Maison Citrohan, at the Salon d'Automne, Paris.

1922–23 Villa Vaucresson, for Georges Besnus, 85 boulevard de la République and rue Garrel, Vaucresson (Hauts-de-Seine), France (commission: 1922; design: January–May 1923; construction: 1923).

1922–24 Villa Amédée Ozenfant, 53 avenue Reille, Paris (commission: 1922; design: 1923; construction: 1923–24).

1923 Opens studio at 35 rue des Sèvres, Paris, with Pierre Jeanneret supervising day-to-day operations.

Pierre-André Emery joins the office.

Project:
- Maison Ribot, workers' housing named for author of 1908 housing law in France, which provide loans for privately developed workers' housing that comply with low-cost standards.

Exhibits models of Maison Ribot and Villa Vaucresson at the Salon d'Automne.

Publication of *Vers une architecture* (collection of articles from *L'Esprit Nouveau*).

Exhibits paintings at Salon des Indépendants, Paris.

Exhibits paintings with Ozenfant at Léonce Rosenberg's Galerie L'Effort Moderne, Paris.

1923–24 Project:
- Peugeot housing estate, Audincourt (Doubs), France (commission: 1923; design: 1924).

1923–24 Maison de Weekend, Rambouillet (Yvelines), France—"theoretical project" for the Salon d'Automne of 1924.

1923–24 La Petite Maison, for his parents, 21 route de Lavaux, Corseaux, Switzerland.

1923–25 Projects:
- Maison Mongermon, square du Docteur Blanche, Auteuil, Paris.
- Villa Sigismund Marcel, square du Docteur Blanche, Auteuil, Paris.

1923–25 Cité de Lège workers' housing, route de Porge, Lège (Gironde), France (commission: November 1923; design: 1923–24; construction: 1924–25).

1923–25 Villa Albert Jeanneret–Lotti Raaf, 8 square du Docteur Blanche, Auteuil, Paris (commission: 1923; design: 1924; construction: 1924–25).

1923–25 Villa Raoul La Roche, 10 square du Docteur Blanche, Auteuil, Paris (commission: 1923; design: 1923–24; construction: 1925). The two adjoining villas are known as Villa La Roche–Jeanneret.

1923–25 Villa Jacques Lipchitz, 9 allée des Pins, Boulogne-sur-Seine (now Boulogne-Billancourt, Hauts-de-Seine), France (commission: 1923; design: 1923–24; construction: 1924–25).

1923–26 Project:
- Villa Victore Canale, 3 rue des Arts, Boulogne-sur-Seine (now Boulogne-Billancourt, Hauts-de-Seine), France (commission: 1923; design: 1923–26; construction: 1924–26; not completed to Le Corbusier's design).

1923–26 Villa Miestchaninoff, 7 rue des Arts and allée des Pins, Boulogne-sur-Seine (now Boulogne-Billancourt, Hauts-de-Seine), France (commission: 1923; design: 1923–26; construction: 1924–26).

1923–27 Villa Paul Ternisien, 5 allée des Pins and rue Denfert-Rochereau, Boulogne-sur-Seine (now Boulogne-Billancourt, Hauts-de-Seine), France.

1923–28 Project:
- Ecole de Rythmique et d'Education Corporelle on the roof of the existing Salle Pleyel, Paris.

1924 Projects:
- Esplanade du Grand Palais, Paris.
- Housing estate, Bois Colombes (Hauts-de-Seine), France.

1924 Maison du Tonkin (for Henri Frugès), rue Jean Descas, Bordeaux (Gironde), France (demolished).

1924–25 Project:
- Maison Casa Fuerte, square du Docteur Blanche, Auteuil, Paris.

1924–25 Pavillon de l'Esprit Nouveau, Exposition des arts décoratifs et industriels modernes, Paris (commission: 1924; design: 1924–25; construction and exhibition: 1925; demolished 1926; replica constructed in Bologna, 1977).

1924–26 Project:
- Apartment-Gallery Paul Guillaume, Paris.

1924–26 Quartier Moderne Frugès, avenue Henri Frugès and rue Le Corbusier, quartier Monteil, Pessac (Gironde), France (commission: July 1924; design: July 1924–26; construction: 1925–26).

1924–28 Villa Antonin Planeix, 24 bis boulevard Masséna, Paris (commission: 1924; design: 1924–27; construction: 1927–28).

1925 Partnership with Ozenfant ends. *L'Esprit Nouveau* ceases publication (with issue number 28).

Alfred Roth joins the office.

Plan Voisin, Paris (project); exhibited at the Pavillon de l'Esprit Nouveau, *Exposition internationale des arts décoratifs et industriels modernes*, Paris. Gertrude Stein introduces him to Minister of Construction Anatole de Monzie at the exhibition.

Project:
- Villa, Bordeaux (Gironde), France.

1925–26 Projects:
- Immeubles-Villas, Boulogne-sur-Seine (now Boulogne-Billancourt, Hauts-de-Seine), France.
- Villa Berque garage and dwelling units, Paris.
- Villa Meyer, Neuilly-sur-Seine (Hauts-de-Seine), France (commission: 1925; design, first scheme: 1925; design, second scheme: 1926).

1925–26 Garage Sensaud de Lavaud, 50 rue de Maillot, Neuilly-sur-Seine (Hauts-de-Seine), France (demolished).

1926 11 April—Father dies.

Projects:
- Atelier Dampt, Paris.
- Atelier Dutheil, Paris.
- Galerie Pellegrini, Paris.
- Garage Raspail for Compagnie Générale des Voitures (CGV), Paris.
- Housing estate, Quincy-sous-Sénart (Essonne), France.
- Maison Mmes. Joseph and Hanau, Vaucresson (Hauts-de-Seine), France.
- Manufacture de Tapis Frugès, carpet factory, Bordeaux (Gironde), France.
- Rooftop stadium addition, CGV, rue Cardinet, Paris.
- Villa Polignac-Singer, Neuilly-sur-Seine (Hauts-de-Seine), France

Exhibits six canvases, Künstlerhaus, Vienna.

1926–27 Annex of the Palais du Peuple, Salvation Army dormitory extension, 29 rue des Cordelières, Paris (commission: 1926; design: 1926; construction: 1926–27).

1926–27 Maison Guiette, 32 Populierenlaan, Antwerp, Belgium.

1926–27 Villa Cook, 6 rue Denfert-Rochereau, Boulogne-sur-Seine (now Boulogne-Billancourt, Hauts-de-Seine), France (commission: April 1926; design: May–September 1926; construction July 1926–March 1927).

1926–27 Villas Weissenhof, for the Weissenhof-Siedlung housing exhibition, sponsored by the Deutscher Werkbund and coordinated by Ludwig Mies van der Rohe, Am Weissenhoff 30, Stuttgart, Germany.

1926–28 Competition for Palais des Nations, headquarters of the League of Nations, Geneva. Le Corbusier's design is among the 9 (out of 377 entries) that tie for first prize. After losing the commission to a team of academic architects, he and Sigfried Giedion orchestrate a protest campaign.

1926–28 Villa Stein-de Monzie, 17 rue du Professeur Victor-Pauchet, Garches (Hauts-de-Seine), France (commission: 1926; design: 1926–27; construction: 1927–28).

1926–36 Centrosoyuz Building (Central Union of Consumer Cooperatives, later Ministryof Light Industry), Myasnitskaya N 35/41, Ulitsa Kirova 39, Moscow (invitation to preliminary, limited competition: 1926).

1927 Meets Charlotte Perriand and hires her as furniture designer.

Lectures in Frankfurt and Brussels.

1927–28 Pavillon Nestlé, Foire de Paris, Paris (commission: 1927; design: 1927–28; construction: 1928; demolished 1928).

1927–28 Turns away from Purist iconography in his painting and moves toward the female nude, organic form, and Surrealist imagery.

1927–29 Villas Church, 1 avenue Halphen, Ville d'Avray (Hauts-de-Seine), France (Villa A: 1927–28; Villa B: 1927–29; Villa C: 1928–29; demolished: 1965).

1927–29 In collaboration with Perriand and Pierre Jeanneret, creates "machines for sitting in": *le siège tournant*, *le fauteuil à dossier basculant*, *le grand confort*, *la chaise longue*, and *la table tube d'avion*. Thonet produces and markets a limited run.

1928 First trip to Moscow; lectures in Moscow and Prague.

First trip to Spain; lectures in Madrid and Barcelona; discovers work by Antonio Gaudí.

June – cofounds Congrès Internationaux d'Architecture Moderne (CIAM), with Sigfried Giedion as the first secretary general; the first meeting is in La Sarraz, Switzerland.

Projects:
- Villa Ocampo, Buenos Aires.
- Wanner Apartments, Geneva.

Swiss critic Alexander von Senger publishes his book *Krisis der Architektur* (Zurich: Rascher, 1928), which includes the essay "Le cheval de Troie du bolchévisme" (The Trojan Horse of Bolshevism), attacking Le Corbusier.

Begins to draw "objets à réaction poétique" (poetic objects).

Louis Loucheur produces legislation in France to make government funds available for housing construction.

1928–29 Villa Baizeau (Bézeult), Sainte Monique, Carthage, Tunisia.

1929 Makes first trip to South America, at the invitation of Argentine intellectual Victoria Ocampo; lectures in Buenos Aires, Rio de Janeiro, and São Paulo. Meets Josephine Baker on board the *Giulio Cesare*, from Buenos Aires to Rio de Janeiro; they sail back to Paris on the *SS Lutétia*.

First trip to Algiers.

Second trip to Moscow.

Attends CIAM II, Frankfurt am Main, Germany.

Kunio Maekawa, José Luis Sert, and Ernest Weismann join the office.

Projects:
- Church, Tremblay-les-Gonesse (Seine-Saint-Denis), France.
- Imprimerie Draeger et Frères, Montrouge (Hauts-de-Seine), France, printing works, modernization of an earlier building by Paul Lebret.
- Maison Canneel, Brussels.
- Maisons Loucheur.
- Mundanéum, "Center of Centers," and World Museum, "Center of All Knowledge," Geneva.
- Quartier Montéclin, Bièvres (Essone), France.
- Urban planning studies of Rio de Janeiro, Montevideo, São Paulo, and Buenos Aires.
- Villa Albert Jacquin, Bois-Colombes (Hauts-de-Seine), France, based on Maisons Loucheur, 1928.

"Ma maison," sketch of a house employing industrial shell vaults, the basis of later design of 24 rue Nungesser-et-Coli.

Exhibits furniture designs in an installation entitled "L'Equipement intérieur d'une habitation," at Salon d'Automne, Paris.

1929–30 Asile Flottant, barge adapted to a dormitory for the French Salvation Army, quai d'Austerlitz, Paris.

1929–31 Villa de Mandrot, 503 route de l'Artaude, le Pradet, Toulon (Var), France (commission: 1929; design: 1929–30; construction: 1931).

1929–32 Beistegui apartment, 13 avenue des Champs-Elysées, Paris (commission: 1929; design: 1929–30; construction: 1930–32; demolished).

1929–33 Cité de Refuge, headquarters for the French Salvation Army, 12 rue Cantagrel and 37 rue du Chevalaret, Paris (commission: 1929; design: 1929–1930; construction: 1930–33).

1929–33 Pavillon Suisse, Cité Universitaire, 7 boulevard Jourdan, Paris (commission: 1929; design: 1930–31; construction: 1931–33).

1930 Final visit to Moscow; meets theater directors Vsevolod Meyerhold and Alexandr (A.Y.) Tairov and filmmaker Sergei Eisenstein.

Attends CIAM III, Brussels.

Travels to Spain with Fernand Léger, Pierre Jeanneret, and Albert Jeanneret.

19 September – becomes a French citizen.

18 December – marries Yvonne Gallis.

Projects:
- Redesign of the Carrefour Raspail – the intersection of boulevard Raspail, rue de Sèvres, and rue de Babylone, Paris.
- Villa M. Goldenberg, Paris.
- Villa Errazuris, Chile (built in Japan by Antonin Raymond, 1933).

1930 Pavillon d'Aviation STAR, Le Bourget (Seine-Saint-Denis), Paris (commission: April 1930; construction: June–October 1930; demolished).

1930 Paints *La main et le silex* (Hand and Flint), which includes an early appearance of the Open Hand motif.

c. 1930 Adopts pseudonym "Le Corbusier" for painting.

1930–31 Projects:
- Concours Rosenthal, "Ville Verte," competition for the development of the Porte-Maillot, Paris.
- Palais des Soviets, invitational competition, Moscow.

1930–35 Develops concept of the Ville Radieuse.

1931 Travels to Spain with Pierre Jeanneret, then Morocco and Algeria. Lectures on urbanism in Algiers, at the invitation of the Amis d'Alger.

Junzo Sakakura joins the office.

Projects:
- Cinéma La Coupole, Montparnasse, Paris.
- Musée d'Art Contemporain, Paris.
- Musée des Artistes Vivants, Nesles-la-Vallée (Val-d'Oise), France.

Exhibits competition scheme for Porte Maillot at Salon d'Automne, Paris.

Sues the League of Nations committee, alleging plagiarism by winning architects.

Alexander von Senger publishes *Le cheval de Troie du bolchévisme*, extracted from his book *Krisis der Architektur*, in which he attacks Le Corbusier; it becomes a basic text for the Nazi campaign against modernism.

1931–32 Contributes essays to *Plans*, a right-wing magazine devoted to art and politics.

1931–33 Immeuble Clarté condominium block, 2 rue St. Laurent, Geneva.

1931–34 Immeuble Molitor, apartment block Parc de Princes, 24 rue Nungesser-et-Coli and 23 rue de la Touelle, Porte Molitor, Boulogne-sur-Seine (now Boulogne-Billancourt, Hauts-de-Seine), Paris (commission: 1931; design: 1931–33; construction: 1932–34). He and Yvonne will live in a duplex apartment on the seventh and eighth floors for the rest of their lives.

1932 Attends meeting of Comité International pour la Résolution des Problèmes de l'Architecture Contemporaine (CIRPAC), the executive body of CIAM, in Barcelona.

Lectures in Amsterdam, Rotterdam, Delft, and Zurich.

Projects:
- Apartment block, Lafon, Algiers.
- Apartment building, Algiers.
- Cité d'Hébergement, Salvation Army, dormitory, Paris.
- Domain Durand, houses, Oued Ouchaia, Algeria.
- Plan Obus A ("Fort-L'Empereur"), first urban planning studies, Algiers.
- Project A, city plan of Vincennes for the 1937 *Exposition internationale des arts et des techniques*, Paris.
- Zürichhorn building, Zurich.

1932 Exhibits model of Palais des Soviets at Union des Artistes Modernes, Paris.

1932–35 Project:
- Immeubles Invalides, apartment block, Esplanade des Invalides, Paris (commission: 1932; design: 1932–35).

1933 Lectures in Stockholm, Göteborg, Oslo, Antwerp, and Algiers.

Attends CIAM IV, Athens, where he helps formulate the Athens Charter.

Projects:
- Macià plan, city plan for Barcelona.
- Plan Obus B, urban planning studies for Algiers.
- Ponsik apartments, Algiers.
- Rentenanstalt building, Zurich.
- Urban planning studies for Geneva, Stockholm, and Antwerp.

Collaborates on magazine *Préludes*, with editors Hubert Lagardelle and Pierre Winter.

Conservative critic Camille Mauclair publishes a series of attacks on Le Corbusier, "L'architecture va-t-elle mourir?" in *Le Figaro*.

1933–34 Project:
- Immeuble GB, Boulogne-sur-Seine (now Boulogne-Billancourt, Hauts-de-Seine), France.

1934 Lectures in Rome, Milan, Barcelona, and Athens.

Projects:
- "Ferme Radieuse" (Radiant Farm), semi-industrialized agricultural collective.
- Plan Obus C, urban planning studies for Algiers and Nemours, Algeria.
- Workers' apartments, Zurich.

1934–35 Projects:
- Concours pour le Musée d'Art Moderne, Paris, competition.
- Expansion of Maison M. Heng, Paris.
- Plan B, Unité, Bastion Kellerman, Paris, for the 1937 *Exposition internationale des arts et des techniques*.

1934–35 Petite Maison de Weekend ("Villa Henfel," "Villa Félix") 49 avenue de Chesnay, La Celle-Saint-Cloud (Yvelines), France (commission: 1934; design: 1934–35; construction: 1935).

1934–36 Project:
- Apartment building, rue Saint-Amand, Paris, Société de Constructions Métalliques Dubois et Lepeu.

1935 First trip to United States. At the invitation of Nelson Rockefeller and the Museum of Modern Art, New York, he gives a lecture at the museum and the museum presents an exhibition of his work. Spends two months on a lecture tour across the U.S., speaking at twenty different venues in ten states.

Meets Albert Camus in Algiers.

Meets Breton cabinetmaker Joseph Savina in Brittany.

Projects:
-Apartment building, Montmartre, Paris.
- Apartment building, rue Fabert, Paris.
- Apartment building, Nemours, Algeria.
- Centre d'Esthétique Contemporaine, based on Musée à Croissance Illimitée (1931).
- House for a college president, Chicago.
- Maison Dr. Rameaux, Romainville (Seine-Saint-Denis), France.
- Musée de la Ville et de l'Etat, Paris.
- Office for Société FACOM (a toolmaking company), Gentilly (Val-de-Marne), France.
- Urban planning study, New York City.
- Urban planning study of Zlín, Czechoslovakia, for Bat'a.
- Urban plan, Hellocourt, Lorraine, France, for Bat'a.

1935 Villa Le Sextant, for Mme. Peyron, 17 avenue de l'Océan, La Palmyre–Les Mathes (Charente-Maritime), France.

1935 At the invitation of his friend the publisher Jean Badovici, paints a mural at Maison Badovici, Vézelay, France.

Les Arts dits primitifs, exhibition organized by Louis Carré and installed in Le Corbusier's apartment, 24 rue Nungesser-et-Coli.

1935–37 Project:
- "Boutique standard pour Bat'a," standardized design for Bat'a shoestores, Strasbourg (Bas-Rhin), France.

1935–38 Project:
- Planning studies for Boulogne-sur-Seine (now Boulogne-Billancourt, Hauts-de-Seine), France.

1936 Second trip to South America, for a conference in Rio de Janeiro; flies there on the *Graf Zeppelin*.

Projects:
- Cité Universitaire, Rio de Janeiro.
- Ilôt Insalubre No. 6, Paris.
- Study for a stadium seating 100,000 ("Centre de Réjouissance pour 100,000 Personnes"), Paris.

Designs tapestries for Marie Cuttoli.

1936–37 Pavillon des Temps Nouveaux, *Exposition internationale des arts et des techniques*, Porte Maillot, boulevard de l'Amiral-Bruix, Paris (demolished).

1936–43 Consultant to architects Carlos de Azevado Leão, Lucio Costa, Jorge Moreira, Oscar Niemeyer, Alfonso Reidy, and Ernani Vasconcelos on the Brazilian Ministry of Education and Public Health (Ministry of Education and Culture), Rua da Imprensa 16, Rio de Janeiro.

1937 Attends CIAM V at the Pavillon des Temps Nouveaux, Paris.

Charlotte Perriand leaves the office.

Projects:
- Cartesian Skyscraper, apartment block.
- Maison de Weekend Jaoul.
- Pavilion for Bat'a, *Exposition internationale des arts et des techniques*, Paris.
- Pavilion for the *Exposition de l'Eau*, Liège, Belgium.
- Plan de Paris, city plan for Paris.

1937–39 Project:
- Monument for Paul Vaillant-Couturier, competition, Villejuif (Val-de-Marne), France.

Paints eight or nine murals, Villa E.1027 ("Maison Badovici"), Roquebrune-Cap-Martin, France.

1938 August—injured by a motorboat while swimming off the coast of Saint-Tropez, France; undergoes two operations at the Hôpital Saint-Tropez.

Projects:
- City plan, Buenos Aires.
- Cooperative village.
- French pavilion for an international exposition, San Francisco.
- Plan Obus D, urban planning studies for Algiers.
- Skyscraper, Palais de Justice, and Cité des Affaires, Algiers.

Exhibition of paintings, Galerie Roland Balayet–Louis Carré, Paris.

Exhibition, *Le Corbusier, Oeuvre plastique, 1919–37, Architecture et tableaux*, Kunsthaus, Zurich.

1938–39 PROJECTS: Biological Station, Roscoff (Finistère), France. Refurbishment of place de la Mairie, the public esplanade surrounding the city hall designed by Tony Garnier (1934), Boulogne-sur-Seine (now Boulogne-Billancourt, Hauts-de-Seine), France.

1938–39 Expansion of the Centre Scientifique de la Main-d'Oeuvre (CSMO), 9–11 rue Le Bua, Paris (commission: 1938; design: 1938; construction: 1938–39; demolished).

1938–40 Centre d'Etude du Travail ("Centre de Réadaptation et des Gymnastiques des Jeunes Chômeurs"), 9–11 rue Le Bua, Paris (commission: 1938; design: 1938–39; construction: 1940; demolished).

1939 Meets Jean Giraudoux at the initial meeting of Comité d'Etudes Préparatoires d'Urbanisme (CEPU; Committee for Preparatory Studies in Urban Planning).

André Wogenscky joins the office.

Projects:
- Arundell Clarke and Entwistle House, London.
- Ecoles Volantes et Constructions Démontables, temporary wartime housing, with Jean Prouvé.
- Maisons Montées à Sec.
- Plan Obus E, urban planning studies for Algiers.
- Stadium Vallé de Var, France.

Ideal Home exhibition featuring Le Corbusier's work, London.

1940 June 11 (just before the Germans occupy Paris on June 14)—Le Corbusier closes his office in Paris and moves to Ozon (Hautes-Pyrénées) with Yvonne and Pierre Jeanneret. In November, Pierre and Charlotte Perriand move to Grenoble, Switzerland, and join the Resistance.

Vichy law permits only Auguste Perret, Eugène Freyssinet, and Le Corbusier to practice architecture in France without diplomas.

Projects:
- Maison S.P.A. Lannemezan (Hautes-Pyrénées), France.
- Pavillon pour Quarante Hommes, with Jean Prouvé.

1940 "L'Usine Verte," Moutiers-Rozeille, near Aubusson (Creuse), France (commission: 1940; design: 1940; construction: 1940; halted in June 1940; demolished).

1940 Completes mural for Centre de Réadaptation et des Gymnastiques des Jeunes Chômeurs (demolished).

1940–44 Project:
- Constructions Murondins.

1941 January—moves to Vichy with Yvonne.

Appointed to Comité d'Etude pour la Reconstruction et l'Urbanisme (Study Committee for Reconstruction and Urban Planning) by Prime Minister Philippe Pétain.

Visits Algiers.

Project:
- Reconstruction, Vallée de la Cure, Vézelay, Asquins, and Saint-Père (Yonne), France.

Exhibition of gouaches, Galerie W. Boesinger, Zurich.

1942 With Yvonne, moves from Vichy to occupied Paris.

Sent to Algiers by Vichy regime to develop plans for the city.

Projects:
- "Plan Directeur," city plan for Algiers.
- Residence ("Domaine Agricole"), Peyrissac, Cherchell, Algeria.

1943 Reopens office on the rue de Sèvres as "atelier des recherches esthétiques" (studio for aesthetic research).

Establishes the research collective Assemblée de Constructeurs pour une Rénovation Architecturale (ASCORAL; Assembly of Builders for an Architectural Renovation).

Development of *Le Modulor*, with Gerald Hanning and Elisa Maillard, begins at a meeting of ASCORAL.

Project:
- La Cité Linéaire Industrielle.

1943–44 Project:
- L'Usine Verte, continuing development of this scheme of 1940.

1943–46 Project:
- City plan for reconstruction of Saint-Gaudens, Miramont, and Valentine (Haute-Garonne) (commission: 1943; design: 1945–46).

1944 *The New Spirit: Le Corbusier—Architect, Writer, Painter*, retrospective exhibition, organized by the Walker Art Center, Minneapolis.

1944–64 Makes sculptures in collaboration with Joseph Savina.

1945 Meets Eugène Claudius-Petit, Minister of Reconstruction and Urbanization.

André Wogensky becomes responsible for the day-to-day management of the office.

1945–46 Project:
- City plan for reconstruction of Saint-Dié (Vosges), France (commission: 1945; design: 1945–46).

1945–47 Project:
- City plan for reconstruction of La Rochelle–La Pallice (Charente-Maritime), France (commission: May 1945; design: May 1945–November 1947).

1945–48 Project:
- Usine SCAN (Société des Constructions Aéronavales), La Rochelle–La Pallice (Charente-Maritime), France.

1945–51 Project:
- Basilica and housing estate, Plan d'Aups-Sainte-Baume (Var), France.

1945–52 Unité d'Habitation ("Cité Radieuse," 280 boulevard Michelet, Marseille (Bouche-du-Rhône) (commission: July 1945; design: July 1945–March 1947; construction: October 1947–October 1952).

1946 Travels to the United States as a goodwill ambassador for the French Ministry of Foreign Affairs; meets Albert Einstein, Princeton, New Jersey.

Vladimir Bodiansky joins the office.

1946–47 Participates in designing the United Nations headquarters, New York; final design (which Le Corbusier always claimed as partly his) is credited to American architect Wallace K. Harrison.

1946–50 Usine Claude et Duval, 1 avenue de Robache, Saint-Dié (Vosges), France (commission: 1946; design: 1946–48; construction: 1948–50).

1947 Lectures in Bogotá, Colombia.

Attends CIAM VI at Bridgwater, England.

Atelier de Bâtisseurs (ATBAT; Studio of Builders) set up, under leadership of Vladimir Bodiansky, to prepare engineering drawings for the Unité d'Habitation.

Project:
- Office Public d'Habitations à Loyer Modéré (office for social housing), plan and construction of garden city competition, Antony (Hauts-de-Seine), France.

Paints mural in his office.

Exhibitions of paintings and watercolors, Kunsthaus, Vienna, and painting at Stedelijk, Amsterdam.

After the independence of India and its partition into India and Pakistan, plans are made to build a new town, Chandigarh, as capital of the Indian Punjab.

1947–48 Albert Mayer, of the New York firm Mayer Whittlesey and Glass, is commissioned to prepare a master plan for the new capitol complex at Chandigarh, India, in consultation with American landscape designer and theorist Clarence Stein; Polish-born American architect Matthew Nowicki is retained to develop the architectural design.

1948 Attends CIAM VII, Bergamo, Italy.

Projects:
- Renovations of Magasin Bally (shoe store), Paris.
"Roq and Rob" vacation housing, Roquebrune-Cap-Martin (Alpes-Maritimes), France.

Restoration of Cité de Refuge, Salvation Army, Paris.

Paints large mural at the Pavillon Suisse, Cité Universitaire, Paris.

1948–55 Unité d'Habitation, boulevard Le Corbusier, Rezé-Nantes (Loire-Atlantique), France (commission: 1948; design: 1949–53; construction: 1953–55).

1948–65 Collaborates with Pierre Baudouin on tapestries at Aubusson, France; they complete some twenty tapestries together.

1949 Iannis Xenakis joins the office.

Project:
- Marseille-Veyre city plan, Marseille-Veyre (Bouches-du-Rhône), France.

1949–50 Maison Curutchet, 320 boulevard 53, Barrio del Bosque, La Plata, Argentina.

1949–50 Founds the Association pour la Synthèse des Arts (Society for the Synthesis of the Arts) with André Bloc, founder and editor of *L'Architecture d'Aujourd'hui*; they plan an exhibition on the theme (unrealized).

1950 31 August—Matthew Nowicki killed in plane crash in Egypt, during preparation of preliminary drawings for Chandigarh city center.

Punjab state engineer P. L. Varma and administrator P. N. Thapar consult with Bruno Zevi and others to replace Nowicki; they recruit E. Maxwell Fry and Jane Drew (members of CIAM), with Le Corbusier (initially only as consultant) and Pierre Jeanneret.
Project:
- "Plan pilote," city plan, Bogotá, Colombia.

For the Paris Mint, designs medal bearing his own likeness and featuring the Open Hand motif.

1950–55 Chapelle Notre-Dame-du-Haut, Ronchamp (Haute-Saône), France (commission: 1950; design: 1950–51; construction: 1953–55; inauguration: June 1955).

1951 18 February—begins first of twenty-three trips to India; visits Chandigarh, Simla, andAhmedabad. During four days at work in Simla, makes master plan of Chandigarh, partially based on the Mayer plan.

Appointed Government Architectural Advisor—consulting architect for the design of Chandigarh—by the government of Punjab.

In Ahmedabad (Gujarat), meets future clients in Sarabhai family (Gira [artist] and Gautam [architect] Sarabhai); Mayor Chinubhai Chimanbhai; Manorama Sarabhai (the mayor's sister); and Surottam Hutheesing, secretary of the Millowners' Association.

Selection board for UNESCO Headquarters, Paris, rejects Le Corbusier for commission for UNESCO building.

Lectures in Bogotá, Colombia.

Attends CIAM VIII, Hoddesdon, England.

Balkrishna V. Doshi joins the office.

Projects:
- Concours du quartier de Rotterdam, competition, Strasbourg (Bas-Rhin), France.
- Museum of Knowledge, Chandigarh.
- Dam, Le Chastang (Corrèze), France.

Makes mural and sand sculpture at home of Costantino Nivola, Long Island, New York.

1951–52 The "Petit Cabanon," Promenade Le Corbusier, Roquebrune-Cap-Martin (Alpes-Maritimes), France.

1951–52 Millowners' Association Building, Ashram Road, Ranchhodlal Marg, Navarangpura, Ahmedabad (construction 1952–54).

1951–55 High Court, Palace of Justice, Chandigarh (construction: 1952–55; inauguration: 19 March 1955).

1951–55 Maisons Jaoul, 81 bis rue de Longchamp, Neuilly-sur-Seine (Hauts-de-Seine), France (commission: June 1951; design: June 1951–March 1952; construction: summer 1953–late 1955).

1951–56 Villa Sarabhai, 4 Shahibag, Ahmedabad (construction 1954–56).

1951–56 Villa Shodhan, Kharawala Road, Ellis Bridge (construction 1954–56).

1951–58 Cultural Center and Museum, partially realized as the "Museum of the City," Bhagtacharya Road, Paldi, Ahmedabad.

1951–58 Secretariat, Chandigarh (design: starts 1951; construction: 1954–58; inauguration: 1958).

1951–62 Palace of the Assembly, Chandigarh (construction: 1951–62; inauguration: 15 April 1964).

1952 Visits Egypt (Giza) on return to Paris from third trip to India.

Projects:
- Marseille "sud" city plan, Marseille (Bouches-du-Rhône), France.
- Proposal for Monument of the Open Hand, based on opening pages of *Thus Spoke Zarathustra*, by Friedrich Wilhelm Nietzsche.
- Proposal for workers' housing, Chandigarh.

Le Corbusier, exhibition of painting and sculpture, Musée National d'Art Moderne, Paris.

1952–53 Project:
- Quartier expérimental ("HEM Roubaix"), Roubaix (Nord), France.

1952–54 Project:
- Governor's Palace (Raj Bhavan), Chandigarh.

1952–57 Aéro-Club de Doncourt, Aéroport de Doncourt-lès-Conflans, Doncourt-lès-Conflans (Meurthe-et-Moselle), France, with Jacques and Bernard Ogé and Jean Prouvé.

1952–59 Maison du Brésil, Cité Universitaire, 4 avenue Brésil and boulevard Jourdan, Paris, with Lucio Costa (commission: 1952; design: 1953–56; construction: 1956–59).

1952–68 Museum, Chandigarh.

1952–85 Monument of the Open Hand and Pit of Consideration, Chandigarh (design: 1952–64; construction: 1985).

1952–90 Art Gallery, Chandigarh.

1953 Receives Gold Medal from the Royal Institute of British Architects (RIBA).

Attends CIAM IX, Aix-en-Provence.

Project:
- Maisons Loucheur, type "La Rochelle," La Rochelle (Charente-Maritime), France.

Exhibition of tapestries, Musée des Beaux-Arts, La Chaux-de-Fonds.

1953–60 Sainte-Marie-de-La-Tourette, Eveux-sur-l'Arbresle (Rhône), France (commission: March 1953; design: May 1953–58; construction: August 1956–September 1960; inauguration: 19 October 1960).

1953–64 Yacht Club on Sukhna Lake, Chandigarh.

1954 Exhibition of tapestries, Galerie Denise René, Paris.

Exhibition of paintings and tapestries, Kunsthalle Bern.

1954–57 Unités de camping, Roquebrune-Cap-Martin (Alpes-Maritimes), France (five units built by Thomas Rebutato based on the "Roq and Rob" project).

1955 November—travels to Japan to investigate the site of the National Museum of Western Art, Tokyo, which he has been commissioned to design.

Lectures in Berlin.

1955 Wooden model of Monument of the Open Hand executed in situ, Chandigarh (demolished).

1955–56 Project:
- Maisons Rurales, Chessy (Seine-et-Marne), France.

1955–57 Project:
- Maison Montées à Sec, Lagny (Seine-et-Marne), France, with Jea
Prouvé.

1955–57 Tomb of Le Corbusier and Yvonne Gallis, cemetery, Roquebrune-Cap-Martin (Alpes-Maritimes), France (design: 1955–57; construction: 1957).

1955–58 Construction of Bhakra Dam, Nangal Township (Himachal Pradesh), India.

**1955–60 Project:
- Unité d'Habitation et Quartier Nouveau, Meaux (Seine-et-Marne) France.**

1955–63 Unité d'Habitation, 1 avenue du Docteur P. Giry, Briey-en-Fôret (Meurthe-et-Moselle), France (commission: 1955; design: 1956–57; construction: 1958–63).

1955–65 Maison des Jeunes et de la Culture ("Espace Le Corbusier"), route de Saint-Just-Malmont "Le Razes," Firminy-Vert (Loire), France (commission: 1955; design 1955–61; construction: 1961–65).

1955–67 Unité d'Habitation, "Les Bruneaux," Firminy-Vert (Loire), France (commission: 1955; design 1959–64; construction: 1965–67).

1955–68 Stade-Firminy, 1 route de Noyers, Firminy-Vert (Loire), France (com mission: 1955; design: 1956–66; construction: 1966–68).

1956 Lectures in Baghdad.

Project:
- Hospital, Flers (Orne), France.

Le Corbusier, exhibition of paintings, enamels, tapestries, and sculptures, Musée de Lyons, Lyon, France.

1956–58 Unité d'Habitation, Berlin-Charlottenburg ("Le Corbusier Hochhaus"), Flatowallee 16, Berlin-Charlottenburg.

1956–59 National Museum of Western Art, 7-7 Ueno-koen, Taito-ku, Ueno, Tokyo.

1956–64 Project:
- Olympic sports complex, Baghdad.

1957 5 October—Death of Yvonne.

Retrospective exhibition, *Capitales*, Kunsthaus, Zurich.

Le Corbusier: Les Taureaux (The Bulls), exhibition of paintings, Pierre Matisse Gallery, New York.

1957–58 Philips Pavilion ("Poème électronique"), Brussels world's fair, with Edgard Varèse and Iannis Xenakis (demolished).

1957–60 The Tower of Shadows, The Geometrical Hill, and The Monument to the Martyr (all monuments), Chandigarh.

1958 Project:
- Reconstruction of West Berlin, Germany.

1958–63 Carpenter Center for the Visual Arts, Harvard University, 24 Quincy Street, Cambridge, Massachusetts [commission: 1958; design: 1958–61; construction: 1961–63; inauguration: May 1963].

1959 Reorganizes office; releases Iannis Xenakis.

1959–65 College of Architecture, Chandigarh.

1959–65 College of Art, Chandigarh.

1960 15 February—mother dies.

1960–61 Projects:
- Unité d'Habitation, Brétigny-sur-Orge (Essonne), France.
- Unité d'Habitation, Tours (Indre-et-Loire), France.
- Unité d'Habitation, Villacoublay (Yvelines), France.

1960–62 Kembs-Niffer lock/floodgate, Neuf-Brisach canal, junction Huningue-Rhin, Kembs-Niffer (Haut-Rhin), France [commission: 1960; design: 1960–61; construction: 1961–62].

1960–63 Project:
- Unité d'Habitation, Roussillon (Isère), France [commission: 1960; design: 1960–63].

1960–2006 Saint-Pierre de Firminy, place du Mail, "Firminy-Vert," Firminy-Vert (Loire), France [commission: 1960; design: 1961–74; construction: 1970–2006].

1961 Receives Gold Medal from American Institute of Architects.

Project:
- Hôtel et Palais d'Orsay, hotel and cultural center, Paris.

Designs six tapestries for High Court, Palace of Justice, and three for Palace of the Assembly, Chandigarh.

1962 Travels to Brazil to prepare studies for new cultural buildings in Brasilia.

1962 Building site sales office ("Espace Le Corbusier"), Plan d'Aups-Sainte-Baume, route D-80 to Saint-Zacharie, Plan d'Aups-Sainte-Baume (Var), France (incomplete).

1962 Completes enameled doors for Palace of the Assembly, Chandigarh (gift of French government); inaugurated 15 April 1964.

1962–65 Project:
- Palais des Congrès, Palace of Congress, Strasbourg (Bas-Rhin), France [commission: April 1962; design: July 1962–July 1965].

1962–68 Centre Le Corbusier ("Heidi Weber Haus," "La Maison d'Homme"), Höschgasse 8, Zürichhorn Park, Zurich.

1963 Made Grand Officier, Légion d'Honneur.

Projects:
- Museum of the Twentieth Century scheme, Erlenbach, Switzerland.
- "Sector 7," town center, Chandigarh.

1963–65 Project:
- Museum of the Twentieth Century, Nanterre (Hauts-de-Seine), France [commission: 1963; design: 1964–65].

1963–66 Project:
- Hospital, Venice.

1964 April–May, final trip to India, for inauguration of Palace of the Assembly, Chandigarh.

Final design and working drawings of Monument of the Open Hand, Chandigarh.

1965 27 August—dies while swimming off the coast of Roquebrune-Cap-Martin, France.

2 September—official funeral rites, Cour Carré, Musée du Louvre, Paris; internment, cemetery Roquebrune-Cap-Martin.

1968 Fondation Le Corbusier established in the Villa La Roche–Jeanneret, Paris.

1973–80 Sports center/gymnasium, based on Olympic sports complex of 1956–64, Baghdad.

1977 Replica of Pavillon de l'Esprit Nouveau, piazza Costituzione 11, Bologna, Italy.

Selected Bibliography

Books by Charles-Edouard Jeanneret, 1912–25

Etude sur le mouvement d'art décoratif en Allemagne [Study of the Decorative Art Movement in Germany]. La Chaux-de-Fonds, Switzerland: Haefeli et Cie, 1912.

Jeanneret and Amedée Ozenfant. *Après le cubisme*. Paris: Edition des Commentaires, 1918. Translated by John Goodman as *After Cubism* in Carol S. Eliel, *L'Esprit nouveau: Purism in Paris* (Los Angeles: Los Angeles County Museum of Art; New York: Harry N. Abrams, 2001).

Jeanneret and Amedée Ozenfant. *La peinture moderne* [Modern Painting]. Paris: Crès, 1925.

Books by Le Corbusier, 1923–68

Le Corbusier-Saugnier [Jeanneret's initial pseudonym in *L'Esprit Nouveau*, where the essays in the book first appeared]. *Vers une architecture*. Paris: Crès, 1923. Translated by John Goodman as *Toward an Architecture* (Los Angeles: Getty Research Institute, 2007).

Almanach d'architecture moderne [Almanac of Modern Architecture]. Paris: Crès, 1925.

L'art décoratif d'aujourd'hui [The Decorative Art of Today]. Paris: Crès, 1925.

Urbanisme. Paris: Crès, 1925. Translated by Frederick Etchells as *The City of To-morrow and Its Planning* (London: J. Rodker, 1929).

Architecture d'époque machiniste [Architecture of the Machine Age]. Paris: Librairie Félix Alcan, 1926.

Le Corbusier and Pierre Jeanneret. *Requête adressée à la Société des Nations* [Request Addressed to the League of Nations]. Paris: Imprimerie Union, 1928.

Une maison, un palais [A House, A Palace]. Paris: Crès, 1928.

Le Corbusier and Pierre Jeanneret. *Ihr gesamtes Werk von 1910–1929* [Their Complete Works 1910–1929]. Zurich: Verlag Dr. H. Girsberger, 1930. Translated into French as *Oeuvre complète 1910–1929* (Zurich: Girsberger, 1937).

Précisions sur un état présent de l'architecture et de l'urbanisme [Precisions on the Present State of Architecture and Urban Planning]. Paris: Crès, 1930.

Le Corbusier and Pierre Jeanneret. *Requête à Monsieur le Président du Conseil de la Société des Nations* [Request to Mr. President of the Council of the League of Nations]. Paris: Imprimerie Union, 1931.

Croisade ou le crépuscule des académies [Crusade or the Twilight of the Academies]. Paris: Crès, 1933.

Le Corbusier and Pierre Jeanneret. *Ihr gesamtes Werk von 1929–1934* [Their Complete Works 1929–1934]. Zurich: Girsberger, 1934. Translated into French as *Oeuvre complète 1929–1934* (Zurich: Girsberger, 1935).

Aircraft: The New Vision. London and New York: The Studio, 1935.

La ville radieuse. Boulogne, France: Architecture d'Aujourd'hui, 1935. Translated by Pamela Knight as *The Radiant City: Elements of a Doctrine of Urbanism to Be Used as the Basis of Our Machine-Age Civilization* (New York: Orion Press, 1967).

Quand les cathédrales étaient blanches: Voyage au pays des timides. Paris: Plon, 1937. Translated by Francis E. Hyslop, Jr., as *When the Cathedrals Were White: A Journey to the Country of Timid People* (New York: Reynal and Hitchcock, 1947).

Les tendances de l'architecture rationaliste en rapport avec la peinture et la sculpture [Tendencies of Rationalist Architecture in Connection with Painting and Sculpture]. Rome: Reale Accademia d'Italia, 1937.

Des canons, des munitions? Merci! Des Logis . . . S.V.P. [Guns, Ammunition? Thanks! Housing . . . Please]. Boulogne, France: Architecture d'Aujourd'hui, 1938.

Le Corbusier and Pierre Jeanneret. *L'îlot insalubre n°6* [Squalid Block No. 6]. Paris: Imprimerie Tournon, 1938.

———. *Oeuvre complète 1934–1938* [Complete Works 1934–1938]. Zurich: Editions Dr. H. Girsberger, 1938.

Destin de Paris [Destiny of Paris]. Paris and Clermont-Ferrand, France: F. Sorlot, 1941.

Sur les quatre routes. Paris: Gallimard, 1941. Translated by Dorothy Todd as *The Four Routes* (London: D. Dobson, 1947).

Les constructions "Murondins" [Constructions "Murondins"]. Paris and Clermont-Ferrand, France: Etienne Chiron, 1942.

Le Corbusier and François de Pierrefeu. *La maison des hommes*. Paris: Plon, 1942. Translated by Clive Entwistle and Gordon Holt as *The Home of Men* (London: Architectural Press, 1948).

La charte d'Athènes. Paris: Plon, 1943. Translated by Anthony Eardley as *The Athens Charter* (New York: Grossman Publishers, 1973).

Entretien avec les étudiants des écoles d'architecture. Paris: Denoël, 1943. Translated by Pierre Chase as *Talks with Students from the Schools of Architecture* (New York: Princeton Architectural Press, 1999).

Les trois établissements humains. Paris: Denoël, 1945. Translated by Eulie Chowdhury as *The Three Human Establishments* (Chandigarh, India: Punjab Government, Department of Town and Country Planning, 1979).

Manière de penser l'urbanisme. Boulogne, France: Architecture d'Aujourd'hui, 1946. Translated by Eleanor Levieux as *Looking at City Planning* (New York: Grossman Publishers, 1971).

Oeuvre complète 1938–1946 [Complete Works 1938–1946]. Zurich: Girsberger, 1946.

Propos d'urbanisme. Paris: Bourellier, 1946. Translated by Clive Entwistle as *Concerning Town Planning* (London: Architectural Press, 1947).

UN Headquarters: Practical Application of a Philosophy of the Domain of Building. New York: Reinhold, 1947.

Grille C.I.A.M. d'urbanisme: Mise en application de la Charte d'Athènes [C.I.A.M. Grid of Urban Planning: Implementation of the Athens Charter]. Boulogne, France: Architecture d'Aujourd'hui, 1948.

New World of Space. New York: Reynal and Hitchcock; Boston: Institute of Contemporary Art, 1948.

Le Modulor: Essai sur une mesure harmonique à l'échelle humaine applicable universellement à l'architecture et à la mécanique. Boulogne, France: Architecture d'Aujourd'hui, 1950. Translated by Peter de Francia and Anna Bostock as *The Modulor: A Harmonious Measure to the Human Scale Universally Applicable to Architecture and Mechanics* (London: Faber and Faber, 1954).

Poésie sur Alger [Poetry on Algiers]. Paris: Falaize, 1950.

L'unité d'habitation de Marseille [Unité d'Habitation, Marseille]. Paris: Le Point, 1950.

Oeuvre complète 1946–1952 [Complete Works 1946–1952]. Zurich: Girsberger, 1953.

Une petite maison [A Small House].Zurich: Girsberger, 1954.

Architecture du bonheur: L'urbanisme est une clef [Architecture of Happiness: Urban Planning Is Key]. Paris: Presses de l'Ile de France, 1955.

Le Modulor II: La parole est aux usagers. Boulogne, France: Architecture d'Aujourd'hui, 1955. Translated by Peter de Francia and Anna Bostock as *Modulor 2, 1955: Let the User Speak Next* (London: Faber and Faber, 1958).

Poème de l'angle droit [Poem of the Right Angle]. Paris: Tériade, 1955.

Les plans de Paris: 1956–1922 [Plans of Paris: 1956–1922]. Paris: Editions de Minuit, 1956.

Oeuvre complète 1952–1957 [Complete Works 1952–1957]. Zurich: Girsberger, 1957.

Von der Poesie des Bauens [Regarding the Poetry of Building]. Zurich: Im Verlag der Arche, 1957.

Ronchamp: Les carnets de la recherche patiente [Ronchamp: The Notebooks of Patient Research]. Zurich: Girsberger, 1957.

L'atelier de la recherche patiente [Workshop of Patient Research]. Paris: Vincent Fréal, 1960.

Orsay, Paris 1961. Paris: Forces Vives, 1961.

Oeuvre complète 1957–1965 [Complete Works 1957–1965]. Zurich: Editions d'Architecture, 1965. *Oeuvre complète: Les dernières oeuvres* was published in 1970 by Birkhäuser in Basel, which published the complete eight-volume set in 1995.

Mise au point [Clarification]. Paris: Forces Vives, 1966.

Le voyage d'Orient. Paris: Forces Vives, 1966. Translated by Ivan Žaknić as *Journey to the East* (Cambridge, Mass.: MIT Press, 1987; rev. ed. 2007).

Les maternelles vous parlent [The Nursery Schools Talk to You]. Paris: Gonthier, 1968.

Books about Le Corbusier

Bacon, Mardges. *Le Corbusier in America: Travels in the Land of the Timid*. Cambridge, Mass.: MIT Press, 2001.

Baltanás, José. *Walking through Le Corbusier: A Tour of His Masterworks*. London: Thames and Hudson, 2005.

Benton, Tim. *The Villas of Le Corbusier and Pierre Jeanneret 1920–1930*. Rev. and expanded ed. Basel: Birkhäuser, 2007.

Boesiger, Willy, and Hans Girsberger, eds. *Le Corbusier 1910–65*. 1967. Reprint. Basel: Birkhäuser, 1999.

Brooks, H. Allen. *Le Corbusier's Formative Years: Charles-Edouard Jeanneret at La Chaux-de-Fonds*. Chicago: University of Chicago Press, 1997.

———, ed. *Le Corbusier*. Princeton, N.J.: Princeton University Press, 1987.

Burri, René. *Le Corbusier: Moments in the Life of a Great Architect*. Edited and with texts by Arthur Rüegg. 2nd ed. Basel: Birkhäuser, 1999.

Cohen, Jean-Louis. *Le Corbusier and the Mystique of the USSR: Theories and Projects for Moscow, 1928–1936*. Translated by Kenneth Hylton. Princeton, N.J.: Princeton University Press, 1992.

———. *Le Corbusier: La planète comme chantier*. Paris: Editions Textuel; Geneva: Editions Zoé, 2005.

Curtis, William J. R. *Le Corbusier: Ideas and Forms*. London: Phaidon Press, 1986.

Eliel, Carol S. *L'Esprit nouveau: Purism in Paris*. With essays by Françoise Ducros and Tag Gronberg. Los Angeles: Los Angeles County Museum of Art; New York: Harry N. Abrams, 2001.

Frampton, Kenneth. *Le Corbusier: Architect of the Twentieth Century*. New York: Harry N. Abrams, 2002.

Gans, Deborah. *The Le Corbusier Guide*. 3rd ed. New York: Princeton Architectural Press, 2006.

Jencks, Charles. *Le Corbusier and the Continual Revolution in Architecture*. New York: Monacelli Press, 2000.

Jenger, Jean, ed. *Le Corbusier: Choix de lettres*. Basel: Birkhäuser, 2002.

Joly, Pierre. *Le Corbusier à Paris: Essai sur une esthétique de l'architecture*. Paris: Délégation à l'Action Artistique de la Ville de Paris, 1987.

Le Corbusier: Early Works by Charles-Edouard Jeanneret-Gris. With contributions by Geoffrey Baker and Jacques Gubler. London: Academy Editions; New York: St. Martin's Press, 1987.

Le Corbusier et le livre. Barcelona: Collegi Oficial d'Arquitectes de Catalunya; Paris: Fondation Le Corbusier, 2005.

Lyon, Dominique. *Le Corbusier vivant*. Paris: Telleri, 1999.

Maniaque, Caroline. *Le Corbusier et les Maisons Jaoul: Projets et fabrique*. Paris: Picard, 2005.

Moos, Stanislaus von. *Le Corbusier: Elements of a Synthesis*. Cambridge, Mass.: MIT Press, 1979.

———, and Arthur Rüegg, eds. *Le Corbusier before Le Corbusier: Applied Arts, Architecture, Painting, Photography, 1907–1922*. New Haven, Conn.: Yale University Press, 2002.

Petit, Jean. *Le Corbusier lui-même*. Geneva: Editions Rousseau, 1970.

———. *Un couvent de Le Corbusier* [A Monastery by Le Corbusier]. Paris: Forces Vives, 1961.

Raeburn, Michael, and Victoria Wilson, eds. *Le Corbusier: Architect of the Century*. London: Arts Council of Great Britain, 1987.

Sekler, Eduard F., and William Curtis. *Le Corbusier at Work: The Genesis of the Carpenter Center for the Visual Arts*. Cambridge, Mass.: Harvard University Press, 1978.

Smet, Catherine de. *Le Corbusier: Un architecte et ses livres*. Baden, Switzerland: Lars Müller Publishers, 2005.

Turner, Paul Venable. *The Education of Le Corbusier*. New York: Garland, 1977.

Index

Please note:

"LC" refers to Le Corbusier.
Italicized numbers refer to illustrations.

50 aquarelles de Music-Hall, *118–19*

Aalto, Alvar, 751
Abramovitz, Max, 363, *398*
Acropolis, 19, *56–57*, 685
Addis Ababa, 15
AEG Turbine Factory Assembly Hall, Berlin, *53*
Agadir, Morocco, 15
Agnelli, Giovanni, 304
Agostini, Philippe, *639*
Ahmedabad, India, 437, 498, 521, *522–23*, 523
  Millowners' Association Building, 437, 523, 540, *540–45*
  Museum and Cultural Center, 523, 534, *534–39*, 709
  Villa Sarabhai, 437, 523, 524, *524–29*, 676
  Villa Shodhan, 437, 523, 530, *530–33*
Aircraft: The New Vision, *279*
airplanes, 8, 129, *129*, *131*, *279*, 310
Alfortville, France, brick factory in, 13, 14, 85, *92*
Algeria and North Africa, 48, 266, *266–67*
Algiers
  LC's book of poetry for, 11, *666*, 667
  Plan Obus, 10, 11, 15, 223, 266, *268*, 269, *269–71*, 272, 342, 361
  proposed CIAM conference in, 668, *668–69*
  skyscraper designs for, *269*, *270–71*, 274, *274–75*, 490
Almanach d'architecture moderne, *116*
Amigos de la Ciudad, 257
Amigos del Arte, 252, 254, *254*
apartment of LC, rue Jacob, Paris, *84*, 85, *86–87*, 87, *122*, *200–201*
apartment of LC, rue Nungesser-et-Coli, Paris, *6*, 14, 280, *280–87*, *308*, *337*, 364
  roof garden, 280, 282, *284*, *285*
  studio, 280, *280*, *365*, *706–7*, *732–33*
Après le cubisme, 85, 100, *100*, 136
Architectural Design (journal), *587*
Architectural Forum (journal), *472*
architectural office of LC, 121, 134, 361, 382, 406
  black book (ledger) of, *135*, *744*
  filming of, *736–37*
  LC at work in, *364*, *406*, *686–91*, *745*
  mural in, 406, *406–7*, *736*
  staff/students in, 134, *194*, 195, 364, 372, *406*, *520–21*, 521, 626, *627*, 647
  See also Jeanneret, Pierre; Perriand, Charlotte
Architectural Record (journal), *727*
Architectures d'aujourd'hui (film), 16
L'Architecture Vivante (journal), 14
Argentina, 15, 252, *252*, 253, *255*, 257, *260*, 432, *432–33*, 530
L'art décoratif d'aujourd'hui, 11, 14, 67, *116*
Art et Liberté, 96
L'Art Sacré (journal), 555, *603*
ASCORAL (architect-engineer collective), 309, *360–61*, 361, 363
Asile Flottant, Paris, 180, *246*, 247, *247*, 249
ATBAT (Atelier des Bâtisseurs), 9, 363
Ateliers d'Art Réunis, 50, 64
Athens, 8, 19, 56, *56–57*, 58, *58–59*, 70, 228, 230
Athens Charter, 10, 358, *358–59*
Audigier, Raymond, *348*, 349
automobiles, 8, 124, 129, *129*, 203
  designs for, 304, *304–5*

Badovici, Jean, 14, *230*, 325, *326*, 330
  villa of, 14, *324*, 325, *325–28*, *642*, 643
Baghdad Sports Center, 704, *704–5*
Baker, Josephine, 14, 262, *262–63*
Balkans. *See* Eastern Europe
Barberine dam, Swiss Alps, 546
Barbéris, Charles, 643
Barcelona, 232, *232–33*, 643
Bat'a, projects for, 15, 290, *290–91*
Les bâtisseurs (film), 16
Bauchant, André, 12, *108–9*
Bauhaus, *186–87*
Behrens, Peter, 19, 50, 52, 53, 68, 186
Beistegui, Charles de, 14
  penthouse of, 212, *212–13*
Berlin, 8, 15, 164, 701
  LC's work with Behrens, 50, 52, 53
Bertocchi, Salvatore, 643
Besnus, Georges, and villa of, 128, *128*
béton brut, 17, 363, 372, 409, 540, *543*, 602
Bhakra Dam, Nangal Township, India, 546, *546–49*, 551
Blum, Léon, 16, 310
Bodiansky, Vladimir, 9, *387*, *391*, *392*, 395, *395*
Boesiger, Willy, *717*
Bogotá, 15, 434, *434–35*
Bombay, 437, *522*
Bottai, Giuseppe, 15, 278
Boulogne-sur-Seine, France, 12, 148, *148–49*, 168, *168–69*
Bourdin, Father, correspondence with LC, *560–61*, 564
La bouteille de vin rouge (painting), *99*
Braque, Georges, 9
Brazil, 15, 48, 223, 253, *253*, 257, *257–61*, *263*, 393
Breuer, Marcel, 194
brise-soleil, 203
  Algiers skyscraper, 274, *274–75*, 490
  Carpenter Center, 718, *726*
  Chandigarh capitol, 474, *483*, 490, *490*, *491–92*
  Millowners' Association Building, 540
  Saint-Dié factory, 372, *374*
  Unité d'Habitation, 409, *424*, 490
  Villa Shodhan, 530
Brunel, Charles, 15
Brussels world's fair, 11, 626, 640, *640*.
  See also Philips Pavilion
Budapest, 34, 45
Buenos Aires, 15, 252, 253, *255*, 257, *260*
bulls, 12, *441*, 444, 496, *496*, 498, 600, 696
  paintings of, *592*, 593
Burnham, Daniel H., 15
Burov, Andrei, *234–35*

cabanon of LC, Roquebrune-Cap-Martin, 9, 13, 14, 643, 650, *650–59*
  LC's death near, 685, 747, *748–49*, *753*
  LC's life and work in, *656–59*, *664–65*, *746–47*
  location of, 643, 644, *644–45*, *651–53*
  sketches/plans of, 650, *654–55*
Café Fledermaus, Vienna, *45*
Des canons, des munitions? Merci! Des logis . . . S.V.P., 11, *318–19*, 319
Caravansary, Edirne, Turkey, 54, *55*
Carpenter Center for the Visual Arts, Harvard University, Cambridge, Mass., 685, 718, *718–27*
  brise-soleil, 718, *726*
  press coverage of, *719*, *727*
  sketches/plans of, *720–21*
Carrel, Alexis, 343, *343*
Cartesian skyscraper (unbuilt), 272, *272–73*, 274, *274–75*
catalan vault, 9, *529*, 643, *677–81*
Centre Le Corbusier, Zurich. *See* Weber, Heidi, pavilion for
Centrosoyuz Building, Moscow, 12, 13, 223, 234, *234–43*
Certosa del Galluzzo, Val d'Ema, Italy, 19, 36, *37*, 62, 124, 126, 424, 602
CHAND (bulletin), 519
Chandigarh, India, projects in, 10, 13, 14, 15, 309, 436–517, 524, *552*, 558, 709
  and Bhakra Dam, 546, *546–49*, 551
  capitol complex, 437, 438, *454*, *464–65*, *473*
  construction of, *456–57*
  Governor's Palace, 437, 438, *454*, 496, *496–97*, 600
  Grille Climatique for, *512–13*, 513
  High Court, 288, 437, 438, *454*, 460, 474, *474–89*, *498*
  Malraux's visit to, *550–51*, 551
  master plan, *450–53*
  Monument of the Open Hand, 438, *454*, 460, *460–63*, *498*, 551, *552*
  Nehru's sponsorship of, 10, 437, *462*, *465*, 466, *466–71*, 496, 516, 541, 546
  Palace of the Assembly, 437, 438, *454*, 460, 496, 498, *498–511*, 699
  press coverage of, *439*, *454*, *470–72*, 516, *516*, *551*, *552*
  Secretariat, 437, 438, *454*, 490, *490–95*
  workers' housing, *512–13*, 513, *514–15*
Chapallaz, René, 47
Charbonnier, Georges, 16
Chareau, Pierre, 228
Charensol, Georges, 16
La charte d'Athènes, 10, 358, *358–59*
La Cheminée (painting), *98*
Chenal, Pierre, 16
Church, Henry, and villa of, 121, 176, *176–77*
CIAM (Congrès Internationaux d'Architecture Moderne), 10, 15, 17, *122*, 438, *518*, 587, 718
  and ASCORAL, 309, *360–61*, 361
  and Athens Charter, 10, 358, *358–59*
  CIAM IV (Athens), 228, *230–31*
  CIAM VI (Bridgewater, England), 621
  CIAM IX (Dubrovnik,Yugoslavia), 668
  disbanding of, 228, 668
  executive of (CIRPAC), *232*
  founding of, 216, 223, 228, *228–29*
  proposed Algiers conference, 668, *668–69*
Cité de Refuge, Paris, 36, 180, 223, *248*, 249, *249–51*
Cité Universitaire, Paris, Pavillon Suisse, 223, 265, *265*
Clarté apartment block, Geneva, 8
Claudius-Petit, Eugène, 14, 438, 685, *697*, 699, 701
Coates, Wells, 621
Cocteau, Jean, 112
Colombia, 15, 434, *434–35*
Composition à la lanterne et à la guitare (painting), *99*
concrete, 8, 82, 121, 137, 234
  béton brut, 17, 363, 372, 409, 540, *543*, 602
  reinforced, 47, 48, 202, 564
Congrès Internationaux d'Architecture Moderne.
  See CIAM
"La construction des villes" (unpublished work), 10
"Les Constructions Murondins" (article), *349*, 351
Les Constructions "Murondins" (pamphlet), *350–51*
Constructions Murondins, Paris, 8–9, 309, 348, *348–51*
Cook, William, and villa of, 121, 168, *168–69*
Corbett, Harvey Wiley, 10
Corseaux, Switzerland. *See* Petite Maison, Lac Léman
Côte d'Azur. *See* Roquebrune-Cap-Martin
Couturier, Father Marie-Alain, 555, 560, *603*
Cranbrook Academy, Michigan, *298–99*
Croisade, ou le crepuscule des académies, 213, *278*
Csadra, Janko, 81, 160
Cubism, 11, 12
Cuttoli, Marie, and tapestries by, 288, *288*
Czechoslovakia, 15, 290, *290–91*

de Gaulle, Charles, 17, 409
Dermée, Paul, 85
De Silva, Minnette, 518, *518–19*
Dessin prémonitoire (painting), 329, *329*
Destin de Paris, 342, *342*
Diogenes, 14
Ditisheim, Hermann, interiors for, 76, *77*
Ditisheim, Paul, store/warehouse project for (unbuilt), *75*
Doesburg, Theo van, 112
Doge's Palace, Venice, *42–43*
"Dom-ino" system, 8, *78–79*, 82, 203, 269, 530, 718
Doshi, Balkrishna V., 513, *520–21*, 521, *545*
Drew, Jane, 437, 438, *444*, *471*, 513
Du Bois, Max, 8, 74, 87, 102
Dubreuil, Hyacinthe, 14
Duval, Jean-Jacques, *373*, *375*

Eastern Europe, LC's tour of, 8, 10, 19, 54, *54–59*, 75
  book based on, 10, 17, 55, 58
Ecole d'Art, La Chaux-de-Fonds, 19, *24–27*, 64
Ecole des Beaux-Arts, Paris, 12, 364
Ecoles Volantes, *332–33*, 333, *335*
Einstein, Albert, 382–*83*
Eisenstein, Sergei, *235*
Epstein, Jean, 16
L'équipe: "La victorieuse" (painting), *185*
L'Esprit Nouveau (journal), 14, 16, 85, 112, 112–15, 129, 146
  books based on, 11, 115, 116
  See also *Vers une architecture*
Ethiopia, 15
Etoile de Mer (Rebutato restaurant), 643, *646–47*, 647, *648–49*, 650
Etude sur le mouvement d'art décoratif en Allemagne, 10, *50*, 51
Eveux-sur-l'Arbresle, France. *See* Sainte-Marie-de-la-Tourette
exhibitions by LC
  Galerie Thomas, 11, *100–101*
  Kunsthaus, Zurich, 320, *320–23*
  Musée d'Art Moderne, 593, *598*
  Museum of Modern Art, *294–95*, 295
  Pierre Matisse Gallery, 12, 593, *594–95*
  Walker Art Center, *366*, 367, *367–69*
Exposition internationale des arts décoratifs et industriels modernes (1925), 15, *152*
  Pavillon de l'Esprit Nouveau, 121, 152, *152–57*, 158, 164

Faisal II (King of Iraq), 704
Fallet, Louis, 28–29, 47
  villa of, 7, 28, *28–31*, 34
The Fall of Barcelona (painting), 16
family of LC, 7, 9, 13, 14, 16, 19
  first house for parents, 13, 19, *70–73*, 150
  second house for parents, 13, 150, *150–51*, 301, *682–83*, *739*
  See also under Jeanneret; Gallis, Yvonne
Fascism, 15, 16, 278, 309
Favre-Jacot, Georges, and villa of, 19, 68, *68–69*
Félix, Henry, and house of, 217, *217*, 558
La femme au guéridon et au fer à cheval (painting), *323*
Femme, cordage, bateau et porte ouverte (painting), *289*
Femme et coquillage (painting), *405*
Ferme Radieuse concept, 309
FIAT company, 304
Firminy-Vert, France, municipal projects in, 10, 685, 692, *692–703*
  church, 685, *698–99*, 699
  cultural center, 694, *694–97*
  cultural/youth center (design), 8, 685, *692–93*
  stadium, 685, *692*
  Unité d'Habitation, 685, *700*, 701, *701–3*
"The Five Points of a New Architecture," 79, 170, *202–3*, 203, 224, *234*
  and Villa Cook, 168, *168–69*
  and Villa Savoye, 204, *204–11*
  and Villa Stein–de Monzie, 16, 170, *170–75*, 204
Flaxman, John, illustrations of *Iliad* by, *734*, 735
Flegenheimer, Julien, 226
Florence, 8, 19, 34, *35–39*, *63*
  See also Certosa del Galluzzo
Fondation Le Corbusier, 17, 102, 141, 743
Forestier, Jean Claude Nicolas, 15
France, 8–17
  during German Occupation, 8–9, 14, 16, 309, *330–31*, 336
  postwar reconstruction of, 309, 35
  354, *354–57*, *360–61*, 361, 372, *372–7*
  See also Paris
"France ou Allemagne?" (unpublished work), 10, 12
French Resistance, 14, 16, 336
Froebel, Friedrich Wilhelm, 9

Frugès, Henri, 15, 121, 164
housing development of, 13, 121, 164, *164–67*, 186
Fry, Maxwell, 437, 438, 513
furniture design, 74, *75–77*, 121, 156, 194, *194*, *195–99*, *425*

Galerie "L'Effort Moderne," showing at, *100*
Galerie Thomas exhibition, 11, *100–101*
Gallis, Yvonne, 104, *104–5*, 107, *108–9*, *122*, 160, *162–63*, 163, *167*, *218–21*, 266, 325, *326*, 329, *337*, 340, *647*, *662*
death of, 660, *661–62*
LC's marriage to, 13–14, 218, *218–19*, 223
and Paris apartment, 14, 280, 281, 286–87, *337*, 364
tomb of, *661*, *753–55*
See also under letters by LC
Garches, France. *See* Villa Stein–de Monzie
Garden City concept, 164, *297*, 424
Garnier, Tony, 164
Gaudí, Antonio, 232, 233
Gauthier, Maximilien, 16
The Gay Science (Nietzsche), 12
Geneva, 8, 9, 12, 121, 125, 223
geometry, importance of, 9, 204.
See also Modulor system
Germany, 8, 9, 10, 12, 16, 19, 50, *50–53*
Giedion, Sigfried, 15, 223, 228, *232*, *587*
Giraudoux, Jean, 358, *358*
Golts, Georgi, *235*
Governor's Palace, Chandigarh (unbuilt), 437, 438, *454*, 496, *496–47*, 600
Graf Zeppelin, 260, *260*
Grasset, Eugène, 48
Gray, Eileen, 14, 325
and Badovici villa, 14, *324*, 325, *325–28*, 643
Greece, 8, 10, 19, 54, 56, *56–59*
Gris, Juan, 145
Gropius, Walter, 15, 52, 186, *187*, *232*, 244, 704
Guggenheim Museum, New York, 12
Gujarat Institute of Civil Engineers and Architects, Ahmedabad, *523*

Harrison, Wallace K., 386, *387*, 392, 394, *395*, *397*
Harvard University, *735*. *See also* Carpenter Center
Heidi Weber Pavilion. *See* Weber, Heidi, pavilion for
Hellocourt, France, 15, 290, *290*
Hénard, Eugène, 10
Hervé, Lucien, 16
High Court, Chandigarh, 437, 438, *454*, 460, 474, *474–85*, 488, *498*
construction of, *478–79*
opening/dedication of, *482–83*
plans/sketches of, *474–77*
tapestries in, 288, 486, *486–87*, *489*
Hitler, Adolf, 330
Hoffmann, Josef, 44, 45, 68
Houriet, Louis, *31*
Humbert, Charles Auguste, 81
Hussein, Saddam, 704
Hutheesing, Surottam, *530*, *532*, *541*
Huxtable, Ada Louise, 727

Iliad (Homer), *734*, 735
Immeubles-Villas (apartment design), 36, 124, *125–27*
India, 436–553
animals/bulls in, *441*, 444, *444*, 496, *496*, 498, 540
LC's letters from, *438*, *442–43*, *466*, *484*
LC's travels in, *440–41*, *444*, *446–47*, *552–53*
See also Ahmedabad; Chandigarh
Iraq, sports center in, 704, *704–5*
Istanbul, 8, 19, 54, *54–55*
Italy, 16
LC's first trip to, 8, 13, 19, *34–43*
LC's second trip to, 54, *60–63*

Jaoul, André, 14, 643, 676
Jaoul, Maisons, Neuilly-sur-Seine, 9, 14, 643, 676, *676–81*
Japan, 12, 15, *708*, 709, *709–13*
Jeanneret, Albert (brother), 13, *21*, *32*, *49*, *52*, *71*, *72*, 81, *112*, *122*, *230*, 232, *682*, *739*
LC's cover designs for music by, 738, *738*
and Villa La Roche–Jeanneret, *140*, 141, *141–45*
See also Villa La Roche–Jeanneret
Jeanneret, Charles-Edouard. *See* Le Corbusier
Jeanneret, Marie-Charlotte-Amélie (mother), 13, *20–21*, *32*, *72–73*, 160, 161, 301, 306, 330, *739*
death of, 740, *740*
hundredth birthday of, 682, *682–83*
See also under letters by LC
Jeanneret, Pierre (cousin), *105*, *107*, *108–9*, *122–23*, *134*, 188, *194*, *219*, 228, *230*, 232, *425*
partnership with LC, 9, 14, 16, 121, 123, 124, 134, *134–35*, 304–5
political differences/breakup with LC, 14, 309, 336
portraits of, *108*, *134*
work in Chandigarh, 14, 309, 437, *454–55*, *483*, *548–49*
Jeanneret-Gris, Georges-Edouard (father), 7, *20–21*, *32*, *72–73*
death of, *160–61*
Jeunes, Les, 309
Johnson, Philip, 294, *294*, 295
Jullian de la Fuente, Guillermo, 685
Junod, Charles-Henri, 9
Jura mountains, Switzerland, region of, 13, 19, *22–23*, 28, 47. *See also* La Chaux-de-Fonds

Kalff, L.C., *626–27*, 627, *631*, *639*
Karachi, *522*
Klee, Paul, 9
Klipstein, August, 14, 54, *54*, 74
Knize department store, Vienna, *45*
Kolli, Nikolai, *235*
Kunsthaus, Zurich, exhibition at, 320, *320–23*

Labatut, Jean, 296, 382
La Chaux-de-Fonds, Switzerland, 7, 8, 10, 13, 19, *22–23*, *29*, 50
and Ecole d'Art, 19, *24–27*, 64
LC's comments on, 23, 67, 74
LC's early projects in, 19, *28–31*, *46–47*, 64, *68–73*, *75*, *82–83*
LC's furniture/interior projects in, 74, *75–77*
LC's house for parents, 13, 19, *70–73*, 150
and pine-tree studies/motifs, *26–27*, 28, *29–30*, 64, *66–67*
rebuilding of, 9, 20
La Plata, Argentina, 432, *432–33*, 530
La Roche, Raoul, 102, 121, 140, 743
album of watercolors for, *102–3*
villa of, 102, 129, 141, *140–41*, *144–45*, 146, 292, 743
See also Villa La Roche–Jeanneret
La Sarraz, Switzerland, first CIAM meeting at, *122*, 216, 228, *228–29*. *See also* CIAM
La Tourette, monastery of. *See* Sainte-Marie-de-la-Tourette
Lac Léman, Switzerland, *103*. *See also* Petite Maison, Lac Léman
League of Nations headquarters, Geneva (design), 11, 223, 224, *224–26*, 363
and LC's protest at loss, 11, 223, *227*
Le Corbusier, 7–17
birth/childhood of, 9, 19, *20–22*
boating accident of, *328*, 329, *329*
and crow image, *662–63*, 663
death of, 685, 747, *748–49*, *753*
as depicted by others, *108*, *146*, *254*, *294*, *384–85*, *402–3*, *588*
early career/travels of, 7–8, 19, *34–46*, *50–63*, 75
and engineer-architect relationship, *750–51*
failed businesses of, 13, 14, 16, 85, *92*
on film, 16, *736–37*
as French citizen, 264, *264*
friends of, 14–15, 19, *31*, *32*, *52*, *54*, *72*
funeral of, 685, 750–51, *751–52*, *753*
and "Grands Projets," 223, 224
as historian, 12–13, 19
as Legion of Honor recipient, 310
marital infidelities of, 14, 223, 301, *302–3*
photographs of, *6*, *18*, *33*, *49*, *53*, *65*, *74*, *84*, *86–87*, *120*, *147*, *200–201*, *222*, *308*, *317*, *321*, *334*, *337*, *352–53*, *362*, *384–85*, *436*, *554*, *684*
and photography, 15, 16
politics of, 14, 16–17, 309
pseudonym of, 7, 85, 112, 113
self-portrait of, *91*
self-publicity by, 15–16
sketchbooks of, 8, *45*, *75*, *233*, *388–89*, *434*, *445*, *448–49*, *496–98*, *556–57*, *582*, 685, *704*
spirituality of, 555
tomb of, *661*, *753–55*
See also under Jeanneret; family of LC; Gallis, Yvonne
Le Corbusier: Oeuvre plastique, 1919–1937, Tableaux et architecture (Kunsthaus exhibition, Zurich), 320, *320–23*
Le Corbusier (Musée d'Art Moderne exhibition), 593, *598*
Le Corbusier, ou l'architecture au service de l'homme (Gauthier), 16
Le Corbusier lui-même, 17, *203*
lectures by LC, 371
in France, 338, *338–39*, *370*, *421*
in Italy, *371*, *381*, *670–71*
in South America, 252, *253–56*, 257, 278
in Spain, 232
in U.S., 292, *292–94*, 296, *296–97*
Léger, Fernand, 7, 12, 14, *106–7*, *156*, *230*, 232, *294*, 325
Le grand Ubu (painting), *593*
Le Locle, Switzerland, 19, 68, *68–69*
Le Piquey, France, LC's vacations in, *123*, *162–63*, 163, 643
L'Eplattenier, Charles, 12, 19, *24*, *25*, 27, 28, 44, 64, 576
Le Pradet, France. *See* Villa de Mandrot
Le Thoronet, France, cloister of, 12, 602
letters by LC, 7, *146*, *160*, *188*, *296*, *325*, *595*
to mother, 13, *253*, *286–87*, *316*, *329–30*, 330, *340*, *342*, *358*, *438*, *442*, *466*, *484*, *653*, *740*
to Nehru, *462*, *465*, *534*, *537*
to parents, *38*, *44*, *50*, *89*
to Tjader Harris, *302–3*, *322*, *329*, *443*, *651*
to Yvonne, *220*, *438*, *442*, *662–63*, 663
Levaillant, Marcel, 118
Lhote, André, poster by, *106*
Lignes de la main (painting), *185*
Lipchitz, Jacques, 12, 121
house/studio of, 12, 148, *148–49*
sculpture by, *155*, *285*
Lissitzky, El, 9, *173*
Loos, Adolf, 44, 45, 112
Louvre, Cour Carré of, and LC's funeral, 685, *752–53*
Lutétia, SS, 14, 257, 262, *262*
Lye, Len, photograms of LC by, 382, *384–85*

Maekawa, Kunio, *708*, 709
La main rouge (painting), *323*
Une maison, un palais, 11, *116*, 223, *227*
Maison Blanche. *See* Villa Jeanneret-Perret
Maison Citrohan (design), 36, 121, 124, *124*, 128, 129, 148, 164, 186, 530
Maison Curutchet, La Plata, 432, *432–33*, 530
Maison de la Culture, Firminy-Vert, 694, *694–97*
facade relief, *694*, *696–97*
La maison des hommes, *347*, *352*, 354, *354–57*
Maison des Jeunes et de la Culture, Firminy-Vert (design), 8, 685, *692–93*
Maison Lipchitz, Boulogne-sur-Seine, 12, 148, *148–49*
Maison Miestchaninoff, Boulogne-sur-Seine, 148, *148–49*
Maison Monol (design), 8, 217, 524, 530, 558
Maisons Jaoul, Neuilly-sur-Seine, 9, 14, 643, 676, *676–81*
Mallet, Robert, 16
Mallorca, Spain, 233, *233*
Malraux, André, 17, *550–51*, 551
eulogy for LC, 685, 750–51, *751*
Mandrot, Hélène de, 216
and founding of CIAM, 216, 228, *228*
villa of, 12, 204, 216, *216*, 217, 228
See also CIAM
Markelius, Sven, *387*
Marseille, 9. *See also* Unité d'Habitation
"Marseille La Grande" project, 410, *411*
Matisse, Henri, 288
Matthey, Octave, *31*
Mayer, Albert, 10, 451
Mazzariol, Giuseppe, *730–31*
Michelangelo, 12, 19, 38, 62
Miestchaninoff, Oscar, 121
house/studio of, 148, *148–49*
Mies van der Rohe, Ludwig, 7, 52, 186, *187*, 194
Milan, 34, 309, *670*
Milan Triennale, *371*, *381*, *670–71*
Millowners' Association Building, Ahmedabad, 437, 523, 540, *540–45*
Ministry of Education building, Rio de Janeiro, 393
Le Modulor, 11, *380*, 382
Modulor 2, *380*
Modulor system, 9, 203, 361, *362*, 363, 372, 376, *376–81*, 382, 409, 490, 620, 643, 650, *670*
Modulor man, *376–78*, *381*, *405*, *431*, *450*, *517*, *552*, *648*
Modulor woman, *378–79*
Mondrian, Piet, 9, *173*
Montevideo, 223
Monument of the Open Hand, Chandigarh, 438, *454*, 460, *460–63*, *498*, 551, *552*
Monzie, Anatole de, *164*, 165
Monzie, Gabrielle de, 170
Villa Stein–de Monzie, 16, 170, *170–75*, 204
Morocco, 15
Moscow, 11, 15, 121, 309
Centrosoyuz Building, 12, 13, 223, 234, *234–43*
Palais des Soviets design, 14, 244, *244–45*
See also Russia
Mundanéum project, Geneva, 9, 12
Munich, *50*, 51
murals by LC
in Badovici villa, 14, *324*, 325, *325–28*, *642*, 643
in Nivola home, 404, *405*
in office, 406, *406–7*, *736*
in Pavillon de l'Esprit Nouveau, *154*
at Rebutato restaurant, *646–49*
in Villa Sarabhai, *529*
See also paintings by LC
Musée d'Art Moderne, Paris, exhibition at, 593, *598*
Musée du XXième Siècle, Paris (unbuilt), 17
Museum and Cultural Center, Ahmedabad, 523, 534, *534–39*, 709
Museum of Modern Art (MoMA), New York, 14, 302, *362*
and exhibition of LC's work, *294–95*, 295
and LC's lecture tour, 292, *294*
Mussolini, Benito, 278, 309
Mythologie figurée de la Grèce, *25*

National Museum of Western Art, Tokyo, 12, 15, *708*, 709, *709–13*
natural objects, as inspiration, 11, 555, *599*, 600, *600–601*
Nature morte à la cruche blanche sur fond bleu (painting), *99*
Nature morte à la pile d'assiettes et au livre (painting), *99*
Nature morte à l'oeuf (painting), *98*
Nehru, Jawaharlal, 10, 437, 466, *466–71*, 496, 516, 541, 546
LC's letters to, *462*, *465*, 534, *537*
See also Chandigarh
Nénot, Henri-Paul, 226
Nestlé exhibition pavilion, Paris, 182, *182–83*
Neuilly-sur-Seine, France. *See* Maisons Jaoul
Neutra, Richard, *640*, 751
The New Spirit: Le Corbusier—Architect, Writer, Painter (Walker Art Center exhibition, Minneapolis), *366*, 367, *367–69*
New World of Space, 326
New York, 11, 12, 14, 16, 17, 245, 272

  - and LC's lecture tour, *292–94*
  - and Tjader Harris, 223, *302–3*
  - and United Nations building, 11, 17, 363
- *New Yorker* (journal), *294*, 402, *402*
- *New York Times*, *294*
- Niemeyer, Oscar, *387*, *391*, 393, *393*, *395*
- Niestlé, Daniel, 14
- Nietzsche, Friedrich, 12
- Nitzchke, Oscar, *387*
- Nivola, Costantino, and family of, 14, 404, *404–5*
- North Africa/Algeria, LC's trip to, 266, *266–67*
- Notre-Dame, Cathedral of, Paris, 9, *48*
- Notre-Dame-du-Haut, Ronchamp, 12, 13, 555, *556–57*, 557, *558–91*
  - construction of, *564–67*
  - correspondence concerning, *558*, *560–61*, 564
  - and "crab's shell" roof, 555, 600
  - enameled door of, *576*, 577, *577–80*
  - inauguration of, *570*, *572*, *574*, *586*
  - interior of, 577, *581–85*
  - LC's book on, *590–91*
  - model of, *561*, *563*, 564
  - original chapel, 555, 557, *558*, 560
  - responses to, 587, *587–88*
  - sketches/plans of, *556–57*, *559*, *562–63*

- Obus project. *See* Plan Obus
- Ocampo, Victoria, and villa of (unbuilt), 252, *253*
- ocean liners, 8, 129, *129*
- *Oeuvre complète*, 11, 14, *80–81*, *202*, 278, 279, 717, *742–43*, 743
- Open Hand motif, *434*, *448*, *458–59*, *466*, 620, *695*
  - and LC's letters to Nehru, *462*, *465*
  - as monument, 438, *454*, 460, *460–63*, *498*, 551, *552*
- Orsanmichele, Florence, *36*, 37
- Oubrerie, José, 685, 699
- Oud, J.J.P., 186
- Ozenfant, Amédée, 11, 14, *72*, 85, 89, *96–97*, *105*, 108, 121, *122*, 145, *146*, 163, 325
  - books cowritten with LC, 85, 100, *100*
  - and *L'Elan* (journal), 85, 98
  - and *L'Esprit Nouveau* (journal), 14, 85, *112*, 112–15, 146
  - and Galerie Thomas exhibition, *100–101*
  - LC's break with, 146
  - LC's house/studio for, 9, *136*, 137, *137–40*, 148
  - and Purism, 11, 14, 85, 98, *99*, 100, *145*, 184
- Ozon, France, LC's wartime residence in, 309, 336, 340

- paintings by LC, 11–12, 14, 16, 85, *98–103*, *156*, *592*, 593, *593–95*
  - La Roche watercolors, *102–3*
  - of late 1920s/early 1930s, *184–85*
  - music-hall watercolors, *118–19*
  - and Purism, 11, 14, 85, 98, *99*, 100, 112, 121, *145*, 184
  - as tapestries, 288, *288–89*
  - *See also* exhibitions by LC; murals by LC
- Pakistan, 438, *522*
- Palace of the Assembly, Chandigarh, 437, 438, *454*, 460, 496, 498, *498–511*
  - conical chamber, 498, *498–502*, 506, *506*, 699
  - interior of, 506, *506–11*
  - portico roof, 498, *503–5*
  - tapestries in, *508–11*
- Palais du Peuple, Paris, 180, *180–81*, 247
- Palais des Soviets, Moscow, design for, 14, 244, *244–45*
- Palazzo Vecchio, Florence, *35*
- Palma de Mallorca, cathedral in, 233, *233*
- Pantheon, Rome, *62*
- *parasol* (overhanging roof), 474, *481*, 534
- Paris, 8–9, 10, 11–12, 14, 16, 17, 19, *48*, 81, 85, *86–89*, *133*, 213
  - and LC's failed business, 13, 14, 16, 85, *92*
  - and LC's industrial projects, 92, *93–95*
  - nightlife of, 8, *90*, *118–19*
  - and Plan Voisin project, 10, 15, 16, *131*, 152, 158, *158–59*
  - Salvation Army projects in, 36, 180, *180–81*, 223, *246–51*
  - *See also individual Paris projects*; *see also* apartment of LC (both entries)
- Parthenon, 19, *56*, *58–59*, 70
- *Patris II*, *SS*, CIAM IV conference aboard, 228, *230–31*
- Pavillon de l'Esprit Nouveau, Paris, 121, 152, *152–57*, 158, 164
- Pavillon de Temps Nouveaux, Paris, 223, 309, 310, *310–16*, 319, 714
- Pavillon Nestlé, Paris, 182, *182–83*
- Pavillon Suisse, Cité Universitaire, Paris, 223, 265, *265*
- *Pêcheuse d'Arcachon* (painting), *185*
- *La peinture moderne*, 85, *116*
- Perret, Auguste, 8, 14, 16, 19, 48, 81, 85, 96, 121, 244
- Perret brothers, firm of, 8, 48, 121
- Perriand, Charlotte, 14, 16, 121, 194, *194*, *230*, 309, 358, 363
  - furniture designs by, *195–99*, *425*
  - and Unité d'Habitation, 412, *413*, *414*, *425*
- Perrin, Léon, 14, *32*, 34, 41, 49, 64, 81
- Pessac, France, housing development in, 13, 121, 164, *164–67*, 186
- Pétain, Philippe, 340, *341*, 361
- Petit, Jean, 11, 17
- Petite Maison, Lac Léman, 13, 150, *150–51*, 301, *682–83*, *739*
- Petite Maison de Weekend, La Celle, France, 217, *217*, 558
- Peyron, Albin, 181
- Philips Electronics, 626, 627, 641
- Philips Pavilion, Brussels, 8, 11, 12, 626, *626–41*
  - correspondence concerning, *626*, *632*, 634, 639
  - models of, 626, *628–29*
  - and *Poème électronique*, 11, 626, 627, 632, 633, *634–37*, *639–40*
- Piazzo del Campo, Siena, *34*
- Piazzo San Marco, Venice, *42–43*
- Picasso, Pablo, 12, 288, *418*, *425*
- Pierrefeu, François de, 354. See also *La maison des hommes*
- Pierre Matisse Gallery, exhibition at, 12, 593, *594–95*
- *pilotis*, 10, 202, 203, 204, 276, 474, 534, 602, *726*
  - Centrosoyuz building, 234, *242*
  - Pavillon Suisse, 265, *265*
  - Unité d'Habitation, *423*, 474
  - Villa Savoye, 204, *204–8*, *295*, *367*
  - Villa Tjader Harris, *301*
- Pinceau (LC's dog), *284*, *287*, *336*, *353*
- Pisa, Italy, *34*, *63*
- Plan Obus, Algiers, 10, 11, 15, 223, 266, *268*, 269, *269–71*, 272, 342, 361
- *Plans* (journal), 11, 16, 309
- *Plans de Paris*, 11
- Plan Voisin project, Paris, 10, 15, 16, *131*, 152, 158, *158–59*
- Podensac, France, water tower in, 92, *94–95*
- *Le poème de l'angle droit*, 12, 620, *620–25*
- *Poème électronique*, 11, 626, 627, 632, 633, *634–37*, *639–40*
- *Poésie sur Alger*, 11, *666*, 667
- Poissy, France. *See* Villa Savoye
- Pompeii, Italy, 19, *60–61*, 61
- Ponti, Gio, 704
- Popular Front, 14, 16
- *Précisions sur un état present de l'architecture et de l'urbanisme*, 197, 253, 255, 278, *279*
- *Préludes* (journal), 309
- Princeton, N.J.
  - LC's lecture at Princeton University, 296, *296–97*
  - and LC's meeting with Einstein, 382–*83*
  - student visit to LC's office, 382
- *promenade architecturale*, 82, 141, 168, 176, 506, *506*, 540, 718
- Prouvé, Jean, 333, *425*
- Punjab, India, 10, 14, 438. *See also* Chandigarh
- Purism, 11, 14, 85, 98, *99*, 100, 112, 121, *145*, 184
  - and villa architecture, 121, 437, 643

- *Quand les cathédrales étaient blanches*, 11, 297, 306, *306–7*, 382, *382*, 397
- Quartier de la Marine, Algiers, 274, *274–75*
- Quartier Moderne Frugès, Pessac, 13, 121, 164, *164–67*, 186

- Raaf, Lotti, *122*
- radiant city. *See* Ville Radieuse
- Ravenna, Italy, 34, *40–41*, 41
- Rebutato, Robert, 647
- Rebutato, Thomas, 643, *646–47*, 647, 650, 672, 747
  - restaurant of, 643, *646–47*, 647, *648–49*, 650
- Redressement Français, 16, 309
- Régamey, Pierre, 555
- "Réponse à Moscou" (unpublished work), 11
- *Revue Marg* (journal), *552*
- Rio de Janeiro, 15, 48, 223, 253, *253*, 257, *257–61*, *263*, 393
- Ritter, William, 14, 16, 19, 23, 74, 81, 160, *160*, 184
- Rockefeller, John D., Jr., 397
- Rockefeller, Nelson, 295, 397, *397*
- Romania, 54
- Rome, 19, 62, *62*, *80–81*, *97*, 309
- Ronchamp, France, chapel of. *See* Notre-Dame-du-Haut
- *Ronchamp: Les carnets de la recherche patiente*, *590–91*
- roof garden/terrace, 178, 202, 203
  - Beistegui apartment, *212–13*
  - LC's apartment, 280, 282, *284*, *285*
  - Saint-Dié factory, *375*
  - Secretariat, Chandigarh, *493*
  - Unité d'Habitation, *414*, *426–29*
  - Villa La Roche–Jeanneret, *143*
  - Villa Sarabhai, 524, *527*
  - Villa Savoye, *205–6*
- Roq and Rob vacation villas, Roquebrune-Cap-Martin (unbuilt), 643, 672, *672–75*
- Roquebrune-Cap-Martin, France, 14, 643, 644, *644–45*, *651*, *661*
  - LC's death in, 685, 747, *748–49*, *753*
  - LC's tomb in, *661*, *753–55*
  - vacation villas, 643, 672, *672–75*
  - See also Badovici, Jean; *cabanon* of LC; Rebutato, Thomas
- Rosenberg, Léonce, 100
- Roth, Alfred, 228, 409
- rue de Sèvres, Paris, LC's office on. *See* architectural office of LC
- rue Jacob, Paris, LC's apartment on. *See* apartment of LC, rue Jacob
- rue Nungesser-et-Coli, Paris, LC's apartment on. *See* apartment of LC, rue Nungesser-et-Coli
- Russia, 12, 16, 17. *See also* Moscow; Soviet Union

- Saarinen, Eliel, *299*
- Saint-Dié, France, reconstruction project and factory in, 10, 17, 372, *372–75*
- Saint-Pierre, Church of, Firminy-Vert, 685, *698–99*, 699
- Saint-Tropez, LC's boating accident in, *328*, 329, *329*
- Sainte-Marie-de-la-Tourette, Eveux-sur-l'Arbresle, 12, 13, 17, 555, 602, *602–19*
  - altars of, *616*
  - construction of, *611*
  - Dominican monks of, *602*, *606–13*
  - interiors of, *616–19*
  - light cannons of, *615–17*
  - sketches/plans of, *602*, *605*, *608*, *610*
- Sakakura, Junzo, *708–9*, 709, *711–13*
- Salmona, Rogelio, 15
- Salon d'Automne, 148
  - of 1922, 121, 124, 128, 130, 223
  - of 1927, *194*
  - of 1929, 14, 194, *195*, *196*, *199*
- Salubra, wallpaper/color keys for, 214, *214–15*, *681*
- Salvation Army, projects for, Paris, 180
  - Asile Flottant, 180, *246*, 247, *247*, 249
  - Cité de Refuge, 36, 180, 223, *248*, 249, *249–51*
  - Palais du Peuple, 180, *180–81*, 247
- Samper, Germán, 15
- San Marco, Basilica of, Venice, *42*
- Sant'Apollinaire Nuovo, Basilica of, Ravenna, *41*, 41
- Santa Croce, Basilica of, Florence, *38*
- Santa Maria Novella, Church of, Florence, *39*
- San Vitale, Basilica of, Ravenna, *40*, 41
- São Paulo, 257
- Sarabhai, Gautam, 537, *537*
- Sarabhai, Gira, 524, *524*, 525
  - villa of, 437, 523, 524, *524–29*, 676
- Savina, Joseph, 12, *596–98*
- Savoye, Pierre and Eugénie, and villa of, 17, 129, 203, 204, *204–11*, 292, *295*, *367*
- Schloss Sanssouci, Potsdam, *51*
- Schwob villa, La Chaux-de-Fonds, 19, 36, 82, *82–83*, 128
- sculpture by LC, 11, 12, *404*, *446–47*
  - and collaboration with Savina, 12, *596–98*
- Secretariat, Chandigarh, 437, 438, *454*, 490, *490–95*
  - *brise-soleil* in, *491–92*
  - construction of, *490–91*
  - roof garden of, *493*
- Senger, Alexander von, 309
- Seraglio, Istanbul, *55*
- Sert, José Luis, 15, *122*, *232*, 310, 325, 404, *435*, *438*
  - and Carpenter Center, 685, 718, *718*
- Siena, Italy, *34*
- Simkhovitch, Helena, 223, 363, 434
- Simla, India, office in, 442, *463*. *See also* Chandigarh
- skyscrapers, 16, *295*, 306, *307*
  - Cartesian, 272, *272–73*, 274, *274–7*
  - and Plan Voisin, 158, *158–59*
  - as proposed for Algiers, *269*, *270–71*, 274, *274–75*, 490
  - and Ville Contemporaine, 130, *130–33*, 257
- Smithson, Peter and Alison, *577*
- Sobolev, Nikolai, *235*
- Société Immobilière, 281, *281*
- Society of Automobile Engineers, French (SIA), 304
- South America, LC's tour of, 8, 15, 121, 249, 252, 253, *253–61*, 278. *See also individual countries and cities*
- Soviet Union, 11, 12, 13. *See also* Moscow; Russia
- Spain, 16, 232, *232–33*, 643
- St. John, Baptistry of, Siena, *34*
- St. Peter's Basilica, Rome, 19, 62
- Stalin, Joseph, 12
- Stein, Gertrude, 168, 170
- Stein, Michael and Sarah, 121, 170
  - Villa Stein–de Monzie, 16, 170, *170–75*, 204
- Steinberg, Saul, 402, *402–3*
- Strassova, Helena, 446
- Stuttgart, Weissenhof-Siedlung housing exhibition in, 121, 129, 186, *186–93*, 194, *367*
- Süleyman Mosque, Istanbul, *54–55*
- *Sur les quatre routes*, 342, *342–43*
- Sweeney, James, 12
- Switzerland. *See* Geneva; La Chaux-de-Fonds; La Sarraz; Le Locle; Petite Maison, Lac Léman; Vevey

- tapestries
  - in High Court, Chandigarh, 288, 486, *486–87*, *489*
  - and LC's paintings, 288, *288–89*
  - in Palace of the Assembly, Chanc garh, *508–11*
- *Taureau II* (painting), *592*
- *Taureau V* (painting), *592*
- Taylorism, 8, 16
- Teige, Karel, 9, 309
- Thonet (furniture manufacturer), 156, 197
- *Thus Spake Zarathustra* (Nietzsche), 12

Tjader Harris, Marguerite, *300*, 301, *301–3*, 518, 643
LC's letters to, *302–3*, *322*, *329*, *443*, *651*
LC's relationship with, 14, 223, 301, *302–3*
LC's villa design for, 300, *301*
Tokyo, 12, 15, *708*, 709, *709–13*
transportation, LC's interest in, 8, 129, *129*, 260, *260*, *279*, 304, *304–5*
Les trois établissements humains, 10, 11, 309, *347*, *361*
Trouin, Léon, 410
Turkey, 8, 13, 19, 54, *54–55*
Tuscany, Italy, 13, 62, *62–63*

UN Headquarters: Practical Application of a Philosophy of the Domain of Building, *398*
Union Sacrée, 16
Unité d'Habitation, Firminy-Vert, 685, *700*, 701, *701–3*
Unité d'Habitation, Marseille, 14–15, 36, 363, *378*, *403*, *408*, 409, *409–31*, 474, 672, 685, 701
brise-soleil in, 409, *424*, 490
construction of, *416–18*
criticism of, *420*
inauguration of, *429*
kitchen plan, *414–15*, 415, *425*
LC's artwork for, *430–31*
life in, *422–28*
roof terrace, *414*, *426–29*
Unité d'Habitation projects, in other cities, 701
United Nations building, New York, 386, *386–401*
and credit for design of, 397–98
design 23A (LC), 363, *395*, *397*, *401*
design 23/32, *391*
design 32 (Niemeyer), *391*, *395*
LC's bitterness over, 11, 17, 363, 386, 401
LC's book on, *398*
United States, LC's tour of, 14, 223, 272, 292, *292–99*, *302–3*, *306*, 306–7
Unwin, Raymond, 15
Urbanisme, 10, 11, 85, *116*
urban planning, 9–10, 15, 16
Garden City concept, 164, *297*, 424
Plan Voisin, Paris, 10, 15, 16, *131*, 152, 158, *158–59*
postwar reconstruction, 309, 352, 354–61
Ville Contemporaine, 121, 124, 130, *130–33*, 223, 257, 276
Ville Radieuse, 15, 223, 265, 276, *276–77*, 280, 292, *397*, 457
See also CIAM; Vichy regime; *see also specific cities*
Usine Verte project (unbuilt), 344, *344–47*
"L'Usine Verte: Workplace Architecture," *346–47*

Val d'Ema, Italy, monastery at, 19, 36, *37*, 62, 124, 126, 424, 602
Valencia, Reinaldo, 15
Varèse, Edgard, 11, 12, *631–33*, 633, 641
Varma, P.L., *454–55*
vault, catalan, 9, *529*, 643, *677–81*
Venice, 309, *729*
hospital of (unbuilt), 13, 685, 728, *728–31*
LC's trip to, 42, *42–43*, *80–81*
vernacular architecture, 8–9
in La Chaux-de-Fonds, *28–31*, *46–47*
primitivist, 216–17, *216–17*
See also Maisons Jaoul; Notre-Dame-du-Haut; Villa Sarabhai; Villa Shodhan
Vers une architecture, 9, 11, 12, 15, 17, 58, 85, *116–17*, 129, 148, 165, 175, 193, *254*
Vesnin, Alexander, *234*
Vevey, Switzerland, 300, *301*. *See also* Petite Maison, Lac Léman; Tjader Harris, Marguerite
Vézelay, France, 14, 330, 333, 336, 643
Vichy regime, LC's involvement with, 16, 309, 336, *340–41*, *352*, 361, 364, 466
and breakup with cousin, 14, 309
and Constructions Murondins, 8–9, 309, 348, *348–51*
and reconstruction proposals, 309, *341*, *352*, 354, *354–57*
and residence in Vichy, 340, *340–41*, 361
and urban planning lecture, 338, *338–39*
and urban planning writings, 342, *342–43*, *347*, *352*, 354, *354–57*
See also France
Vienna, 34, 44, *44–45*, 47, 48, 50
Vilamajo, Julio, *387*
Vildra, Rose, 81

Villa Berque, Paris-Auteuil, 110, *110*
Villa Church, Paris, 176, *176–77*
Villa Cook, Boulogne-sur-Seine, 168, *168–69*
Villa de Mandrot, Le Pradet, 12, 204, 216, *216*, 217, 228
Villa E.1027 (Badovici villa), Roquebrune-Cap-Martin, 14, *324*, 325, *325–28*, *642*, 643
Villa Fallet, La Chaux-de-Fonds, 7, 28, *28–31*, 34
Villa Favre-Jacot, Le Locle, 19, 68, *68–69*
Villa Jacquemet, La Chaux-de-Fonds, 47, *47*
Villa Jeanneret-Perret, La Chaux-de-Fonds, 13, 19, *70–73*, 150
Villa La Roche, 102, 129, 141, *140–41*, *144–45*, 146, 292, 743
Villa La Roche–Jeanneret, Paris, 9, *140*, 141, *141–45*, 204
Villa le Sextant, France, 297, *297*
Villa Meyer, Paris (unbuilt), 178, *178–79*
Villa Sarabhai, Ahmedabad, 437, 523, 524, *524–29*, 676
Villa Savoye, Poissy, 17, 129, 203, 204, *204–11*, 292, *295*, *367*
and *pilotis*, 204, *204–8*, *295*, *367*
Villa Schwob, La Chaux-de-Fonds, 19, 36, 82, *82–83*, 128
Villa Shodhan, Ahmedabad, 437, 523, 530, *530–33*
Villa Stein–de Monzie, Garches, 16, 170, *170–75*, 204
Villa Stotzer, La Chaux-de-Fonds, *46*, 47
Villa Tjader Harris, Vevey (unbuilt), 300, *301*
Villa Vaucresson, Vaucresson, France, 128, *128*
Ville Contemporaine, 121, 124, 130, *130–33*, 223, 257, 276
Ville Radieuse, 15, 223, 265, 276, *276–77*, 280, 292, *397*, 457
La ville radieuse, 10, 11, *196*, *203*, 272, *276–77*
Voisin (automobile), 16, *129*, 158
Voitures Minimum and Maximum, 304, *304–5*
Le voyage d'Orient, 10, 17, 55, 58
Vue sur les toits de Paris (painting), *98*

Wagner, Otto, 44
Walker Art Center exhibition, Minneapolis, *366*, 367, *367–69*
Wanner, Edmond, 125
Weber, Heidi, pavilion for, Zurich, 714, *714–17*
Weismann, Ernest, *232*, *391*, *708*, 709
Weissenhof-Siedlung housing exhibition, Stuttgart, 121, 129, 186, *186–93*, 194, *367*
Wiener, Paul Lester, 15, *435*
World War II, LC's life and work during, 8–9, 14, 16, 309, 330–61
Wright, Frank Lloyd, 7, 9, 10, 704
writings and publications by LC, 10–11, 12, 15, 17, 278, *278–79*. See also *L'Esprit Nouveau*; *see also individual books and articles*

Xenakis, Iannis, 626, *627*

Zervos, Christian and Yvonne, 14
Zlín, Czechoslovakia, 15, 290, *290–91*
Zurich
Heidi Weber Pavilion, 714, *714–17*
Kunsthaus exhibition, 320, *320–23*

Text Credits

The following were sources for English-language quotations by Charles-Edouard Jeanneret/Le Corbusier:

Charles-Edouard Jeanneret and Amedée Ozenfant, Après le cubisme, 1918. Translated by John Goodman as After Cubism in Carol S. Eliel, L'Esprit nouveau: Purism in Paris (Los Angeles: Los Angeles County Museum of Art; New York: Harry N. Abrams, 2001).

Le Corbusier, Entretien avec les étudiants des écoles d'architecture, 1943. Translated by Pierre Chase as Talks with Students from the Schools of Architecture (New York: Princeton Architectural Press, 1999).

———, New World of Space. New York: Reynal and Hitchcock; Boston: Institute of Contemporary Art, 1948.

———, Quand les cathédrales étaient blanches: Voyage au pays des timides, 1937. Translated by Francis E. Hyslop, Jr., as When the Cathedrals Were White: A *Journey to the Country of Timid People* (New York: Reynal and Hitchcock, 1947).

———, *Vers une architecture*, 1923. Translated by John Goodman as *Toward an Architecture* (Los Angeles: Getty Research Institute, 2007).

———, *La ville radieuse*, 1935. Translated by Pamela Knight as *The Radiant City: Elements of a Doctrine of Urbanism to Be Used as the Basis of Our Machine-Age Civilization* (New York: Orion Press, 1967).

———, *Le voyage d'Orient*, 1966. Translated by Ivan Žaknić as *Journey to the East* (Cambridge, Mass.: MIT Press, 2007).

"Le Corbusier." In John Peter, *The Oral History of Architecture: Interviews with the Greatest Architects of the Twentieth Century*. New York: Harry N. Abrams, 1994.

Illustration Credits

Unless otherwise indicated below, all images are credited to the Fondation Le Corbusier, Paris. All reasonable efforts have been made to contact and credit the copyright holders for images used in this publication. If there are any inadvertent omissions, the publisher will remedy this in future editions if informed.

Numbers indicate page number: t=top, b=bottom, l=left, c=center, r=right.

Cover. Le Corbusier in his private office at 35 rue de Sèvres, 1959
Agenzia Fotografica Industrial, 728 b, 730 b, 731
Air India, 519 t
Album Ahrenberg, 718
Alinari Archives, Florence, 37 t
Paul Almassy / AKG Images, 184
APIS/KEYSTONE Press, 736, 737, 752
Artemis Verlag, Zurich, 97 bl: Reproduced from *Le Corbusier and the Continual Revolution in Architecture* by Charles Jencks (New York: Monacelli Press, 2000): p. 121
Associated Press/Marty Lederhandler, 399
ATP Bilderdienst, 683 t
Avery Architectural and Fine Arts Library, Columbia University in the city of New York, 386 bl, 387 t, 397 b, 398 t
Geoffrey H. Baker, 29 br
Marius Bar, 216 t
Y. Bellenand, 698
Courtesy Tim Benton, 681 b
Merrill C. Berman Collection, 106
Bettmann/Corbis, 206 t
Bodé, 317
Bodo Rasch Archives/Private Collection, 187 tr: Reproduced from *Le Corbusier, Vivant*, by Dominique Lyon (Paris: Telleri Press, 1999): p. 42
W. Boesiger, 647, 656 t + bl, 658 t, 659 t
Borlui, 729 bl
Private Collection, Mario Botta, Switzerland, 329 t + c; 460 t (photographer Enrico Cano)
Courtesy Bowdoin College Archives, 293 tr
Estate Brassaï / GrandPalaisRmn, 200–201
Charles Bueb, 567 b, 568 tc + tr + b
René Burri/Magnum Photos, cover, 281 tr, 283 t, 284 bl, 285 tr, 407 t, 422 b, 423 tl + tr, 424 tr + b, 426, 427, 430 t, 529 tl, 554, 570 b, 574 b, 579, 583, 584–85, 586, 589, 604, 605 b, 606–7, 608 bl + br, 609, 610, 611 tl + bl + br, 612 t, 613, 614, 615 bl, 617, 619 t, 686, 687, 688, 689, 690, 691, 706–7, 715 t, 717, 721 t, 732, 733, 742
J. Caps, 616 tl
Claude Caroly, 211 b
J. Cellard, 422 tl
Collection Centre Canadien d' Architecture/ Canadian Centre of Architecture, 302 tr, 303 b, 443, 651 tr + c +b, 652
Chevojon, 217 t
Courtesy Jean-Louis Cohen, 30 b, 95 r, 234, 235 t, 300 br
Compagnie Aerienne Française, 274 bl
Horacio Coppola, 433 t + bl
© Cranbrook Archives, Richard G. Askew, photographer, 187, 298–99
William J R Curtis, 68 t, 83 cr: Reproduced from *Le Corbusier: Ideas and Forms* by William J R Curtis (London: Phaidon Press, 1986): pp. 40, 45; 210 br: Reproduced from *Le Corbusier, Architect of the Century* by William J R Curtis (Balding + Mansell UK Limited, 1987): fig. 30
Yves Debrain, 682
Robert Doisneau, 275, 331, 337, 353, 406 br, 409 bl, 425 tr
Balkrishna Doshi–Vastu-Shilpa Foundation, 463, 484, 520 tl + tr, 529 tr + b, 530, 542 t, 545
Bibliothèque Littéraire Jacques Doucet, Paris, 750, 751
Editec, 533
Richard Einzig/Suisse, 600 t
Sergei Eisenstein Archive, 235 t: Reproduced from *Le Corbusier and the Mystique of the USSR* by Jean-Louis Cohen (New Jersey: Princeton University Press, 1992): p. 48
Reproduced from *L'Esprit Nouveau: Purism in Paris, 1918–1925* by Françoise Ducros and Carol S. Eliel (New York: Harry N. Abrams, 2001), 99 tl
Fonds Le Corbusier, BVCF, 18, 20 t, 22 t, 24, 28 t, 30 t, 31, 53 t, 64 tl, 70 bl + br, 76 b
Foto Liter, 553
Foto Marburg/Art Resource, NY, 53 b
Y. Futagawa, 711 bl
Gasser, 716
Getty Images/Hulton Archive, 187 tl
Getty Images/Nina Leen, 308, 365, 408
Getty Images/Three Lions, 428 bl
Getty Images/Joan Woolicombe Collection, 190 b
Research Library, The Getty Research Institute, Los Angeles, California (850833), 730 tl
Research Library, The Getty Research Institute, Los Angeles, California (850980), 370, 434 tl + tr
Research Library, The Getty Research Institute, Los Angeles, California (870438), 626 t + cl + b, 632 tl + cl
Research Library, The Getty Research Institute, Los Angeles, California (920083), 96 bl + br, 108 br, 112 tr,
Research Library, The Getty Research Institute, Los Angeles, California (950064), 197, 227 tl + r, 281 c + b
Ludwig Glaeser, 703 b
Emile Gos (Musée de l'Elysée, Lausanne), 122 br, 229 t
Marius Gravot, 156 b, 208 t, 209 t, 211 t, 213 bl, 249 tl + tr, 265 cl
Rene Groebli, 566 t + bl, 574 t
Hanssler, 714 cr
© Harvard University Loeb Library, 230 b, 302 tl + b, 438 t, 723, 727
Lucien Hervé / Getty Images, 154 t, 166 tl, 169 tl, 196 t + bl, 213 tr + br, 245 b, 271 tl + tr, 312 tl, 374, 375, 416 t + br, 428 bc + br, 431, 440, 441, 456 t, 485, 488, 490 b, 491, 501 t, 532 b, 542 b, 543, 544, 561 tl + tr + cl + cr, 565 b, 567 t, 569 b, 581 tr, 596 bl, 616 br, 618 tl, 628 bl, 649 tr, 661 b, 664–65, 679–80, 701 b, 746, 747
InterPresse/KEYSTONE Press, 739 t
Ivanoff, 277
Pierre Jeanneret, 444 tr, 450–51, 479 b, 499 t + br, 503 b, 505 b
Vauthier Jeanneret, 480
Pierre Joly et Véra Cardot, 504, 506 b, 510, 612 b, 615 tl + tr + br, 616 tr, 648 b, 694 b, 695
Kandinsky Archive, 598 tl + tr + c
KEYSTONE Press, 601 b, 671, 684, 745
Georges H. Le Bihan, 432 cl + cr
Marcel Lombard, 571
DR Lossen, 192 b
Courtesy of the Len Lye Foundation, Govett-Brewster Art Gallery, 384, 385
Clara MacKenzie, 724, 725
Philippe Maestri, 646 bl
Jeet Malhotra, 444 tl, 490 t, 493, 499 bl, 502 b, 548, 549 br
Félix H. Man, 649 b
Sd. H.S. Mathur, 478, 549 l
The Pierre Matisse Gallery Archives, The Pierpont Morgan Library, New York. MA, 5020, photos by Joseph Zehavi, 2008, 594, 595
Richard H. Mercer, 386 t
Album Mione, 6
Bernhard Moosbrugger, 569 t
Musée Picasso, Paris, 418 tr + cr
The Museum of Modern Art/ Licensed by SCALA/ Art Resource, NY, 293 tl, 294, 295 b
Courtesy of the Archives of Costantino Nivola, 404, 405 t + c
Lennart Olson, 481 bl, 492
Le Parisien Libéré, 432 b
Rondal Partridge, 506 t
Prantal K. Patel, 534, 535, 547 cr
© Archives Charlotte Perriand–ADAGP 2008, 194 tl + tr + bl, 195 b, 414 br, 425 cr
Claudius Petit, 507
Philips Company Archives, 627, 629, 630, 631 t, 633, 638, 639
Photographie Industrielle du Sud Ouest, 417 t + bl, 425 b
Photopress, 739 b
Jacques de Potier, 550
S. Presser, 419, 421 b
Princeton University Library, 296
Publifoto, 371
Folco Quilici © Fratelli Alinari, 37 b
Marcel de Renzis, 417 br, 650
Marc Riboud, 483 tl + tr, 514, 515
J. Richard, 422 tr
Willy Rizzo, 520 b
Sagarra y Torrents, 232 tr + br
Albin Salaün, 274 t, 276 cl, 312 b, 313 t +b, 314 t + b + cr
A. Scarnati, 381
Sciarli, 424 tl, 428 t, 429 b
Photo Suresh Sharma/Eric Touchaleaume archives, 483 bl, 517
© Hans Silvester/Rapho, 572 t , 573, 575, 580, 581 tl
Comité Michel Sima / Bridgeman Images, 364, 376, 563 b, 593 b, 621
Kidder Smith, 423 bl
Starink, 631 b
Christian Staub, 526 br, 539 b
© The Saul Steinberg Foundation, 402
Andre Steiner, 284 br, 599
Richard Stern, 362
Léon Stynen, 503 t
Studio Guy, 694 tr, 696 t
Studio Jasz, 251 t
Studio Vidal, 416 bl
Arvind J. Talati, 526 tl + bl, 527, 528, 539 t + c, 541 t
Collection Tallandier/ Rue des Archives, 107 b; Reproduced from *Le Corbusier: La planète comme chantier*, by Jean-Louis Cohen (Paris: Les Editions Textuel, 2005): p. 64
G. Thiriet, 177 bc
Time & Life Pictures/Getty Images, 453 b, 670
Time & Life Pictures/Getty Images/James Burke, 457, 481 tl, 482, 483 br, 489
Time & Life Pictures/Getty Images/Frank Scherschel, 387 b
UNESCO, 647 br
Courtesy Walker Art Center, Minneapolis, 366, 367, 368, 369
Peter Willi, 142 b, 145 bl, 286 b, 282, 285 b
Robert Winkler, 581 cl; Reproduced from *Le Corbusier 1910–65* by Willy Boesiger and Hans Girsberger (Basel: Birkhäuser, 1999): p. 261w

Note

Unless otherwise indicated, all works illustrated in this volume are by or attributed to Charles-Edouard Jeanneret/Le Corbusier or his studio.

References to building levels in photographs and architectural drawings follow European practice: the bottom floor of a building is the ground floor; the floor above it is the first floor.

For a French/English glossary of architectural terms and for translations of the foreign-language documents reproduced here, see the booklet accompanying this volume.

Contributors

Jean-Louis Cohen was a scholar, curator, critic and teacher. Cohen served as the Sheldon H. Solow Professor in the History of Architecture at the Institute of Fine Arts, New York University for nearly three decades. He was considered to be one of the world's foremost experts on Le Corbusier, Mies van der Rohe, Frank Lloyd Wright, Robert Venturi, and Frank Gehry, among others.

Tim Benton is Professor Emeritus of Art History, Open University, Milton Keynes, England.

Acknowledgments

The publisher would like to offer special thanks to the Fondation Le Corbusier, Paris, particularly director Michel Richard and archivists Isabelle Godineau and Delphine Studer. Historian Arnaud Dercelles and architect Julia Gartner provided essential assistance with scholarly research at the Fondation. Olivia Bastien and Olivier Broncard, of Transparence, offered tireless help in scanning myriad original documents at the Fondation. Tim Benton, Jean-Louis Cohen, and Kurt Forster were invaluable sources of information and advice.
The publisher is also grateful to writer Ron Broadhurst; translators John Tittensor, Elizabeth Clegg, and Alexandra Bonfante-Warren (from the French), Abigail Asher (from the Italian), and Teresa Waldes (from the Catalan); Casie Kesterson for her assistance at the Getty Research Institute; and Ruth Nivola and family for their help in locating archival materials.

Phaidon Press Limited
2 Cooperage Yard
London E15 2QR

Phaidon Press Inc.
111 Broadway
New York, NY 10006

Phaidon SARL
55, rue Traversière
75012 Paris

phaidon.com

First published in 2008
Second edition published 2014
Reprinted in paperback 2019
Reprinted in hardback 2025

ISBN 978 1 83729 101 4

A CIP catalogue record of this book is available from the British Library and the Library of Congress.

Designed by Julia Hasting
Printed in China